CONTENT OVERVIEW

Teacher's Manual, Volume 1

The New Look of Results T4
Proven Results T6
Unique Program Structure T8
- Lesson Structure
- Daily Problem Solving
- Ongoing Assessment

Support for All Students T18
- Universal Access
- Adaptations for Saxon Math

Components T22
Professional Development T24
Table of Contents T25
California Mathematics Standards Coverage T37

Problem Solving Overview 1A
Section 1: **Lessons 1–10, Investigation 1** 7A
Section 2: **Lessons 11–20, Investigation 2** 63A
Section 3: **Lessons 21–30, Investigation 3** 135A
Section 4: **Lessons 31–40, Investigation 4** 205A
Section 5: **Lessons 41–50, Investigation 5** 275A
Section 6: **Lessons 51–60, Investigation 6** 343A
English/Spanish Math Glossary T753
Index T765

Teacher's Manual, Volume 2

Table of Contents T5
California Mathematics Standards Coverage T17

Section 7: **Lessons 61–70, Investigation 7** 409A
Section 8: **Lessons 71–80, Investigation 8** 473A
Section 9: **Lessons 81–90, Investigation 9** 541A
Section 10: **Lessons 91–100, Investigation 10** 603A
Section 11: **Lessons 101–110, Investigation 11** 669A
Section 12: **Lessons 111–114** 732A
English/Spanish Math Glossary T753
Index T765

ABOUT THE AUTHOR

Stephen Hake has authored six books in the **Saxon Math** series. He writes from 17 years of classroom experience as a teacher in grades 5 through 12 and as a math specialist in El Monte, California. As a math coach, his students won honors and recognition in local, regional, and statewide competitions.

Stephen has been writing math curriculum since 1975 and for Saxon since 1985. He has also authored several math contests including Los Angeles County's first Math Field Day contest. Stephen contributed to the 1999 National Academy of Science publication on the Nature and Teaching of Algebra in the Middle Grades.

Stephen is a member of the National Council of Teachers of Mathematics and the California Mathematics Council. He earned his BA from United States International University and his MA from Chapman College.

Table of Contents

Integrated and Distributed Units of Instruction

Section 1 *Lessons 1–10, Investigation 1*

		Page	California Strands Focus
	Lesson Preparation • **Problem Solving Overview**	1A **1**	NS, MR
Overview	*Lessons 1–10, Investigation 1*	7A	
Lesson 1	*Lesson Preparation* • **Sequences**	7G **7**	AF, MR
Lesson 2	*Lesson Preparation* • **Place Value**	13A **13**	NS, MR
Lesson 3	*Lesson Preparation* • **Writing Numbers Through 999**	17A **17**	NS, SDAP, MR
Lesson 4	*Lesson Preparation* • **Missing Addends**	23A **23**	AF, SDAP
Lesson 5	*Lesson Preparation* • **Expanded Form**	27A **27**	NS, AF
Lesson 6	*Lesson Preparation* • **Adding Three-Digit Numbers**	31A **31**	NS, MR
Focus on Concepts A	• **Why the Addition Algorithm Works**	**36**	NS, MR
Lesson 7	*Lesson Preparation* • **Missing Numbers in Subtraction**	37A **37**	AF, MR
Lesson 8	*Lesson Preparation* • **Inverse Operations: Adding and Subtracting**	41A **41**	AF, MR
Lesson 9	*Lesson Preparation* • **Order of Operations, Part 1**	46A **46**	AF, MR
Lesson 10	*Lesson Preparation* • **Subtracting Three-Digit Numbers with Regrouping**	53A **53**	NS, MR
Focus on Concepts B	• **Why the Subtraction Algorithm Works**	**58**	NS, MR
Investigation 1	*Lesson Preparation* • **Writing Word Problems**	59B **59**	NS, AF, MR
Cumulative Assessment	Power-Up Test 1, Cumulative Test 1, Performance Task 1	Standards Benchmark Check Point	

California Strands Key:
NS = Number Sense
AF = Algebra and Functions
MG = Measurement and Geometry
SDAP = Statistics, Data Analysis, and Probability
MR = Mathematical Reasoning

TABLE OF CONTENTS

Section 2 Lessons 11–20, Investigation 2

		Page	California Strands Focus
Overview	*Lessons 11–20, Investigation 2*	63A	
Lesson 11	*Lesson Preparation* • **Adding Columns of Numbers with Regrouping**	63G **63**	NS, MR
Lesson 12	*Lesson Preparation* • **Word Problems About Combining**	67A **67**	NS, MR
Lesson 13	*Lesson Preparation* • **Elapsed Time Problems** Activity Finding Time	73A **73**	NS
Lesson 14	*Lesson Preparation* • **Subtraction Across Zeros**	81A **81**	NS, MR
Focus on Concepts C	• **Subtracting Across Zeros — Why It Works**	**87**	NS, MR
Lesson 15	*Lesson Preparation* • **Word Problems About Separating**	89A **89**	NS, AF, MR
Cumulative Assessment	Power-Up Test 2, Cumulative Test 2, Test-Day Activity 1		
Lesson 16	*Lesson Preparation* • **Word Problems About Comparing**	95A **95**	NS, MR
Lesson 17	*Lesson Preparation* • **Lines, Segments, Rays, and Angles** Activity Real-World Segments and Angles	101A **101**	MG, MR
Lesson 18	*Lesson Preparation* • **Triangles, Rectangles, Squares, and Circles** Activity Drawing a Circle	109A **109**	MG, MR
Lesson 19	*Lesson Preparation* • **Representing Fractions**	115A **115**	NS
Focus on Concepts D	• **Why Does a Fraction Represent Division?**	**120**	NS, MR
Lesson 20	*Lesson Preparation* • **Perimeter** Activity Different Perimeters	121A **121**	MG, MR
Investigation 2	*Lesson Preparation* • **Number Lines** Activity Drawing Number Lines	128B **128**	NS, MR
Cumulative Assessment	Power-Up Test 3, Cumulative Test 3, Performance Task 2, Benchmark Test 1		Standards Benchmark Check Point

California Strands Key:
NS = Number Sense
AF = Algebra and Functions
MG = Measurement and Geometry
SDAP = Statistics, Data Analysis, and Probability
MR = Mathematical Reasoning

Section 3 Lessons 21–30, Investigation 3

		Page	California Strands Focus
Overview	*Lessons 21–30, Investigation 3*	135A	
Lesson 21	*Lesson Preparation* • **Temperature** Activity Measuring Temperature	135G **135**	NS, MR
Lesson 22	*Lesson Preparation* • **Rounding to the Nearest Ten or Hundred**	141A **141**	NS, MR
Lesson 23	*Lesson Preparation* • **Multiplication**	149A **149**	AF, MR
Lesson 24	*Lesson Preparation* • **Multiplication Facts (0's, 1's, 2's, 5's)**	156A **156**	NS, MR
Lesson 25	*Lesson Preparation* • **Multiplication Facts (9's and Squares)**	161A **161**	NS, MR
Cumulative Assessment	Power-Up Test 4, Cumulative Test 4, Test-Day Activity 2		
Lesson 26	*Lesson Preparation* • **Parentheses and the Associative Property**	167A **167**	AF
Lesson 27	*Lesson Preparation* • **Writing Numbers Through Hundred Thousands**	173A **173**	NS
Lesson 28	*Lesson Preparation* • **Dollars and Cents**	180A **180**	NS, AF
Lesson 29	*Lesson Preparation* • **Fractions of a Dollar**	187A **187**	NS
Lesson 30	*Lesson Preparation* • **Multiplication Facts (Memory Group)**	193A **193**	AF, MR
Investigation 3	*Lesson Preparation* • **Area Models** Activity 1 Finding Perimeter and Area Activity 2 Estimating Perimeter and Area	198B **198**	MG
Cumulative Assessment	Power-Up Test 5, Cumulative Test 5, Performance Task 3	Standards Benchmark Check Point	

California Strands Key:
NS = Number Sense
AF = Algebra and Functions
MG = Measurement and Geometry
SDAP = Statistics, Data Analysis, and Probability
MR = Mathematical Reasoning

Section 4 Lessons 31–40, Investigation 4

		Page	California Strands Focus
Overview	*Lessons 31–40, Investigations 4A and 4B*	205A	
Lesson 31	*Lesson Preparation* • **Exploring Perimeter and Area** Activity Different Areas	205G **205**	NS, MG
Lesson 32	*Lesson Preparation* • **Fractions and Mixed Numbers**	213A **213**	NS, MR
Lesson 33	*Lesson Preparation* • **Naming Lines and Line Segments**	219A **219**	MG
Lesson 34	*Lesson Preparation* • **Relating Multiplication and Division** Activity Using a Multiplication Table to Divide	225A **225**	AF, MR
Focus On Concepts E	• **Why Can't We Divide by Zero?**	**232**	NS, MR
Lesson 35	*Lesson Preparation* • **Inverse Operations: Multiplying and Dividing**	233A **233**	NS, AF
Cumulative Assessment	Power-Up Test 6, Cumulative Test 6, Test-Day Activity 3		
Lesson 36	*Lesson Preparation* • **Order of Operations, Part 2**	239A **239**	AF, SDAP, MR
Lesson 37	*Lesson Preparation* • **Multiplying Multiples of 10 and 100, Part 1**	247A **247**	NS, MR
Lesson 38	*Lesson Preparation* • **Multiplying Two-Digit Numbers**	253A **253**	NS, MR
Focus On Concepts F	• **Different Ways to Think About Multiplication**	**258**	NS, MR
Lesson 39	*Lesson Preparation* • **Word Problems About Multiplication**	259A **259**	NS, AF, MR
Lesson 40	*Lesson Preparation* • **Rounding to the Nearest Thousand**	265A **265**	NS, MR
Investigation 4	*Lesson Preparation* • **Relating Fractions and Decimals**	271B **271**	NS
Cumulative Assessment	Power-Up Test 7, Cumulative Test 7, Performance Task 4, Benchmark Test 2	Standards Benchmark Check Point	

California Strands Key:
NS = Number Sense
AF = Algebra and Functions
MG = Measurement and Geometry
SDAP = Statistics, Data Analysis, and Probability
MR = Mathematical Reasoning

Section 5 Lessons 41–50, Investigation 5

		Page	California Strands Focus
Overview	*Lessons 41–50, Investigation 5*	275A	
Lesson 41	*Lesson Preparation* • **Decimal Place Value**	275G **275**	NS, MR
Lesson 42	*Lesson Preparation* • **Units of Length**	281A **281**	AF, MG
Lesson 43	*Lesson Preparation* • **Tenths and Hundredths on a Number Line**	287A **287**	NS, MR
Lesson 44	*Lesson Preparation* • **Equivalent Decimals**	293A **293**	NS, MR
Lesson 45	*Lesson Preparation* • **Adding and Subtracting Decimal Numbers**	299A **299**	NS, MR
Cumulative Assessment	Power-Up Test 8, Cumulative Test 8, Test-Day Activity 4		
Lesson 46	*Lesson Preparation* • **Rounding to the Nearest Whole Number**	305A **305**	NS
Lesson 47	*Lesson Preparation* • **Reading and Writing Numbers in Millions**	311A **311**	NS, MR
Focus On Concepts G	• **Why Do We Round Large Numbers?**	**317**	NS, MR
Lesson 48	*Lesson Preparation* • **Rounding Large Numbers**	318A **318**	NS, MR
Lesson 49	*Lesson Preparation* • **Reading and Writing Numbers Through Hundred Millions**	323A **323**	NS, MR
Lesson 50	*Lesson Preparation* • **Polygons**	329A **329**	MG
Investigation 5	*Lesson Preparation* • **Displaying Data Using Graphs** Activity Displaying Information on Graphs	335B **335**	SDAP, MR
Cumulative Assessment	Power-Up Test 9, Cumulative Test 9, Performance Task 5		Standards Benchmark Check Point

California Strands Key:
NS = Number Sense
AF = Algebra and Functions
MG = Measurement and Geometry
SDAP = Statistics, Data Analysis, and Probability
MR = Mathematical Reasoning

Section 6 *Lessons 51–60, Investigation 6*

		Page	California Strands Focus
Overview	*Lessons 51–60, Investigation 6*	343A	
51	*Lesson Preparation* • **Adding Large Numbers**	343G **343**	NS
52	*Lesson Preparation* • **Subtracting Large Numbers**	349A **349**	NS, MR
53	*Lesson Preparation* • **Word Problems About Division**	355A **355**	AF, MR
54	*Lesson Preparation* • **Remainders**	361A **361**	AF, MR
55	*Lesson Preparation* • **Factors and Multiples** Activity Using Arrays to Find Factors	369A **369**	NS, MG
Cumulative Assessment	Power-Up Test 10, Cumulative Test 10, Test-Day Activity 5		
56	*Lesson Preparation* • **Prime and Composite Numbers**	376A **376**	NS, MR
57	*Lesson Preparation* • **Comparing and Ordering Fractions** Activity Comparing Fractions	381A **381**	NS
58	*Lesson Preparation* • **Rate Word Problems**	387A **387**	AF, MR
59	*Lesson Preparation* • **Multiplying Large Numbers**	393A **393**	NS, MR
60	*Lesson Preparation* • **Rate Word Problems with a Given Total**	399A **399**	AF, MR
Investigation 6	*Lesson Preparation* • **Collecting Data with Surveys** Activity Class Survey	404B **404**	SDAP, MR
Cumulative Assessment	Power-Up Test 11, Cumulative Test 11, Performance Task 6, Benchmark Test 3	Standards Benchmark Check Point	

California Strands Key:
NS = Number Sense
AF = Algebra and Functions
MG = Measurement and Geometry
SDAP = Statistics, Data Analysis, and Probability
MR = Mathematical Reasoning

Section 7 Lessons 61–70, Investigation 7

		Page	California Strands Focus
Overview	*Lessons 61–70, Investigation 7*	409A	
Lesson 61	*Lesson Preparation* • **Estimating Arithmetic Answers**	409G **409**	NS, MR
Lesson 62	*Lesson Preparation* • **Rounding to the Nearest Tenth**	417A **417**	NS, MR
Lesson 63	*Lesson Preparation* • **Order of Operations, Part 3**	423A **423**	AF
Focus on Concepts H	• **How Do We Write Expressions?**	**429**	AF, MR
Lesson 64	*Lesson Preparation* • **Two-Step Equations**	431A **431**	AF
Lesson 65	*Lesson Preparation* • **Exponents**	436A **436**	NS, MR
Cumulative Assessment	Power-Up Test 12, Cumulative Test 12, Test-Day Activity 6		
Lesson 66	*Lesson Preparation* • **Area of a Rectangle**	441A **441**	NS, MG
Lesson 67	*Lesson Preparation* • **Remaining Fractions**	447A **447**	NS
Lesson 68	*Lesson Preparation* • **Division with Two-Digit Answers, Part 1**	451A **451**	NS, AF, MR
Lesson 69	*Lesson Preparation* • **Division with Two-Digit Answers, Part 2**	457A **457**	NS, AF
Lesson 70	*Lesson Preparation* • **Similar and Congruent Figures** Activity Determining Similarity and Congruence	463A **463**	MG, MR
Investigation 7	*Lesson Preparation* • **Coordinate Graphing**	468B **468**	AF, MG
Cumulative Assessment	Power-Up Test 13, Cumulative Test 13, Performance Task 7		Standards Benchmark Check Point

California Strands Key:
NS = Number Sense
AF = Algebra and Functions
MG = Measurement and Geometry
SDAP = Statistics, Data Analysis, and Probability
MR = Mathematical Reasoning

Section 8 Lessons 71–80, Investigation 8

		Page	California Strands Focus
Overview	*Lessons 71–80, Investigation 8*	473A	
Lesson 71	*Lesson Preparation* • **Multiplying by Multiples of 10**	473G **473**	NS, MR
Lesson 72	*Lesson Preparation* • **Division with Two-Digit Answers and a Remainder**	479A **479**	NS, MR
Focus on Concepts I	• **How the Division Algorithm Works**	**485**	NS, MR
Lesson 73	*Lesson Preparation* • **Capacity**	487A **487**	NS, AF
Lesson 74	*Lesson Preparation* • **Word Problems About a Fraction of a Group**	493A **493**	NS, MR
Lesson 75	*Lesson Preparation* • **Division Answers Ending with Zero**	499A **499**	NS
Cumulative Assessment	Power-Up Test 14, Cumulative Test 14, Test-Day Activity 7		
Lesson 76	*Lesson Preparation* • **Finding Information to Solve Problems**	505A **505**	NS, SDAP, MR
Lesson 77	*Lesson Preparation* • **Fraction of a Set**	513A **513**	NS, MR
Lesson 78	*Lesson Preparation* • **Measuring Turns** Activity 1 Rotations and Degrees Activity 2 Rotations and Congruence	517A **517**	MG, MR
Lesson 79	*Lesson Preparation* • **Division with Three-Digit Answers**	525A **525**	NS
Lesson 80	*Lesson Preparation* • **Mass and Weight**	531A **531**	NS, AF
Investigation 8	*Lesson Preparation* • **Investigating Equivalent Fractions with Manipulatives** Activity 1 Using Fraction Manipulatives Activity 2 Understanding How Fractions and Decimals are Related	537B **537**	NS, MR
Cumulative Assessment	Power-Up Test 15, Cumulative Test 15, Performance Task 8, Benchmark Test 4		Standards Benchmark Check Point

California Strands Key:
NS = Number Sense
AF = Algebra and Functions
MG = Measurement and Geometry
SDAP = Statistics, Data Analysis, and Probability
MR = Mathematical Reasoning

Section 9	Lessons 81–90, Investigation 9	Page	California Strands Focus
Overview	***Lessons 81–90, Investigation 9***	541A	
Lesson 81	*Lesson Preparation* • **Classifying Triangles**	541G **541**	MG, MR
Lesson 82	*Lesson Preparation* • **Symmetry** Activity Reflections and Lines of Symmetry	547A **547**	MG, MR
Lesson 83	*Lesson Preparation* • **Division with Zeros in Three-Digit Answers**	555A **555**	NS, AF
Lesson 84	*Lesson Preparation* • **Multiplying by 10, 100, and 1000**	561A **561**	NS, AF
Lesson 85	*Lesson Preparation* • **Multiplying Multiples of 10 and 100, Part 2**	567A **567**	NS, MR
Cumulative Assessment	Power-Up Test 16, Cumulative Test 16, Test-Day Activity 8		
Lesson 86	*Lesson Preparation* • **Multiplying Two Two-Digit Numbers, Part 1**	572A **572**	SDAP, MR
Lesson 87	*Lesson Preparation* • **Remainders in Word Problems**	577A **577**	NS, MR
Lesson 88	*Lesson Preparation* • **Multiplying Two Two-Digit Numbers, Part 2**	581A **581**	NS, MR
Lesson 89	*Lesson Preparation* • **Mixed Numbers and Improper Fractions** Activity Modeling Mixed Numbers and Improper Fractions	586A **586**	NS
Lesson 90	*Lesson Preparation* • **Classifying Quadrilaterals** Activity 1 Quadrilaterals in the Classroom Activity 2 Symmetry and Quadrilaterals	593A **593**	MG
Investigation 9	*Lesson Preparation* • **Analyzing Relationships**	600B **600**	MG, MR
Cumulative Assessment	Power-Up Test 17, Cumulative Test 17, Performance Task 9	Standards Benchmark Check Point	

California Strands Key:
NS = Number Sense
AF = Algebra and Functions
MG = Measurement and Geometry
SDAP = Statistics, Data Analysis, and Probability
MR = Mathematical Reasoning

Section 10 Lessons 91–100, Investigation 10

		Page	California Strands Focus
Overview	*Lessons 91–100, Investigation 10*	603A	
Lesson 91	*Lesson Preparation* • **Estimating Multiplication and Division Answers**	603G **603**	NS, MR
Lesson 92	*Lesson Preparation* • **Comparing and Ordering Fractions and Decimals**	609A **609**	NS
Lesson 93	*Lesson Preparation* • **Two-Step Problems**	615A **615**	NS
Lesson 94	*Lesson Preparation* • **Two-Step Problems About a Fraction of a Group**	622A **622**	NS, MR
Lesson 95	*Lesson Preparation* • **Describing Data** Activity Collecting Data	627A **627**	AF, SDAP, MR
Cumulative Assessment	Power-Up Test 18, Cumulative Test 18, Test-Day Activity 9		
Lesson 96	*Lesson Preparation* • **Geometric Solids** Activity Geometric Solids in the Real World	633A **633**	MG
Lesson 97	*Lesson Preparation* • **Constructing Prisms** Activity Constructing Prisms	639A **639**	MG, MR
Lesson 98	*Lesson Preparation* • **Fractions Equal to 1 and Fractions Equal to $\frac{1}{2}$**	646A **646**	NS
Lesson 99	*Lesson Preparation* • **Changing Improper Fractions to Whole Numbers or Mixed Numbers**	653A **653**	NS
Lesson 100	*Lesson Preparation* • **Adding and Subtracting Fractions with Common Denominators**	659A **659**	NS, MR
Investigation 10	*Lesson Preparation* • **Graphing Relationships**	665B **665**	AF
Cumulative Assessment	Power-Up Test 19, Cumulative Test 19, Performance Task 10, Benchmark Test 5		Standards Benchmark Check Point

California Strands Key:
NS = Number Sense
AF = Algebra and Functions
MG = Measurement and Geometry
SDAP = Statistics, Data Analysis, and Probability
MR = Mathematical Reasoning

Section 11 Lessons 101–110, Investigation 11

		Page	California Strands Focus
Overview	*Lessons 101–110, Investigation 11*	669A	
Lesson 101	*Lesson Preparation* • **Formulas**	669G **669**	NS, AF
Lesson 102	*Lesson Preparation* • **The Distributive Property**	674A **674**	NS, AF
Focus on Concepts J	• **Thinking About Multiplying Two-Digit Numbers**	**680**	NS
Lesson 103	*Lesson Preparation* • **Equivalent Fractions**	681A **681**	NS
Focus on Concepts K	• **Use Equivalent Fractions to Find Common Denominators**	**688**	NS, MR
Lesson 104	*Lesson Preparation* • **Rounding Whole Numbers Through Hundred Millions**	689A **689**	NS, MR
Lesson 105	*Lesson Preparation* • **Factoring Whole Numbers**	695A **695**	NS
Cumulative Assessment	Power-Up Test 20, Cumulative Test 20, Test-Day Activity 10		
Lesson 106	*Lesson Preparation* • **Reducing Fractions**	700A **700**	NS
Lesson 107	*Lesson Preparation* • **Multiplying a Three-Digit Number by a Two-Digit Number**	705A **705**	NS, MR
Lesson 108	*Lesson Preparation* • **Analyzing Prisms**	710A **710**	MG
Lesson 109	*Lesson Preparation* • **Constructing Pyramids** Activity Constructing Models of Pyramids	715A **715**	MG
Lesson 110	*Lesson Preparation* • **Simple Probability**	721A **721**	SDAP
Investigation 11	*Lesson Preparation* • **Probability** Activity Probability Experiments	727B **727**	SDAP
Cumulative Assessment	Power-Up Test 21, Cumulative Test 21, Performance Task 11	Standards Benchmark Check Point	

California Strands Key:
NS = Number Sense
AF = Algebra and Functions
MG = Measurement and Geometry
SDAP = Statistics, Data Analysis, and Probability
MR = Mathematical Reasoning

Section 12 Lessons 111–114

		Page	California Strands Focus
Overview	*Lessons 111–114*	732A	
Lesson 111	*Lesson Preparation* • **Multiplying Three-Digit Numbers**	732G **732**	NS, MR
Lesson 112	*Lesson Preparation* • **Simplifying Fraction Answers**	737A **737**	NS
Lesson 113	*Lesson Preparation* • **Renaming Fractions and Common Denominators**	742A **742**	NS, MR
Lesson 114	*Lesson Preparation* • **Perimeter and Area of Complex Figures**	747A **747**	AF, MG
Cumulative Assessment	Power-Up Test 22, Cumulative Test 22, Test-Day Activity 11	Standards Benchmark Check Point	

California Strands Key:
NS = Number Sense
AF = Algebra and Functions
MG = Measurement and Geometry
SDAP = Statistics, Data Analysis, and Probability
MR = Mathematical Reasoning

California Mathematics Standards Coverage

California Standards		LESSON AND PAGE NUMBER
Number Sense		
NS 1.0	Students understand the place value of whole numbers and decimals to two decimal places and how whole numbers and decimals relate to simple fractions. Students use the concepts of negative numbers:	**2** (pp. 13–16), **3** (pp. 17–22), **13** (pp. 73–80), **16** (pp. 95–100), **19** (pp. 115–119), **FOC D** (p. 120), **Inv. 2** (pp. 128–134), **21** (pp. 135–140), **22** (pp. 141–148), **26** (pp. 167–172), **27** (pp. 173–179), **28** (pp. 180–186), **29** (pp. 187–192), **Inv. 3** (pp. 198–204), **32** (pp. 213–218), **35** (pp. 233–238), **37** (pp. 247–252), **38** (pp. 253–257), **39** (pp. 259–264), **40** (pp. 265–270), **Inv. 4** (pp. 271–274), **41** (pp. 275–280), **42** (pp. 281–286), **43** (pp. 287–292), **44** (pp. 293–298), **45** (pp. 299–304), **46** (pp. 305–310), **47** (pp. 311–316), **FOC G** (p. 317), **48** (pp. 318–322), **49** (pp. 323–328), **51** (pp. 343–348), **52** (pp. 349–354), **57** (pp. 381–386), **58** (pp. 387–392), **59** (pp. 393–398), **61** (pp. 409–416), **62** (pp. 417–422), **67** (pp. 447–450), **68** (pp. 451–456), **72** (pp. 479–484), **74** (pp. 493–498), **75** (pp. 499–504), **76** (pp. 505–512), **77** (pp. 513–516), **Inv. 8** (pp. 537–540), **85** (pp. 567–571), **88** (pp. 581–585), **89** (pp. 586–592), **91** (pp. 603–608), **92** (pp. 609–614), **94** (pp. 622–626), **98** (pp. 646–652), **99** (pp. 653–658), **100** (pp. 659–664), **101** (pp. 669–673), **103** (pp. 681–687), **104** (pp. 689–694), **106** (pp. 700–704), **112** (pp. 737–741), **113** (pp. 742–746), **114** (pp. 747–752)
NS 1.1	Read and write whole numbers in the millions.	**38** (pp. 253–257), **47** (pp. 311–316), **48** (pp. 318–322), **49** (pp. 323–328), **104** (pp. 689–694)
NS 1.2	Order and compare whole numbers and decimals to two decimal places.	**2** (pp. 13–16), **3** (pp. 17–22), **16** (pp. 95–100), **Inv. 2** (pp. 128–134), **21** (pp. 135–140), **22** (pp. 141–148), **26** (pp. 167–172), **27** (pp. 173–179), **38** (pp. 253–257), **Inv. 4** (pp. 271–274), **41** (pp. 275–280), **42** (pp. 281–286), **43** (pp. 287–292), **44** (pp. 293–298), **45** (pp. 299–304), **47** (pp. 311–316), **49** (pp. 323–328), **57** (pp. 381–386), **62** (pp. 417–422), **Inv. 8** (pp. 537–540), **85** (pp. 567–571)
NS 1.3	Round whole numbers through the millions to the nearest ten, hundred, thousand, ten thousand, or hundred thousand.	**22** (pp. 141–148), **Inv. 3** (pp. 198–204), **38** (pp. 253–257), **40** (pp. 265–270), **42** (pp. 281–286), **FOC G** (p. 317), **48** (pp. 318–322), **51** (pp. 343–348), **52** (pp. 349–354), **59** (pp. 393–398), **61** (pp. 409–416), **68** (pp. 451–456), **75** (pp. 499–504), **88** (pp. 581–585), **91** (pp. 603–608), **104** (pp. 689–694)
NS 1.4	Decide when a rounded solution is called for and explain why such a solution may be appropriate.	**22** (pp. 141–148), **38** (pp. 253–257), **39** (pp. 259–264), **46** (pp. 305–310), **61** (pp. 409–416), **62** (pp. 417–422), **72** (pp. 479–484), **75** (pp. 499–504), **98** (pp. 646–652), **114** (pp. 747–752)
NS 1.5	Explain different interpretations of fractions, for example, parts of a whole, parts of a set, and division of whole numbers by whole numbers; explain equivalence of fractions (see Standard 4.0).	**13** (pp. 73–80), **19** (pp. 115–119), **FOC D** (p. 120), **29** (pp. 187–192), **32** (pp. 213–218), **35** (pp. 233–238), **57** (pp. 381–386), **67** (pp. 447–450), **74** (pp. 493–498), **77** (pp. 513–516), **Inv. 8** (pp. 537–540), **89** (pp. 586–592), **94** (pp. 622–626), **98** (pp. 646–652), **99** (pp. 653–658), **100** (pp. 659–664), **103** (pp. 681–687), **106** (pp. 700–704), **112** (pp. 737–741), **113** (pp. 742–746)
NS 1.6	Write tenths and hundredths in decimal and fraction notations and know the fraction and decimal equivalents for halves and fourths (e.g., $\frac{1}{2}$ = 0.5 or .50; $\frac{7}{4} = 1\frac{3}{4}$ = 1.75).	**28** (pp. 180–186), **29** (pp. 187–192), **Inv. 4** (pp. 271–274), **42** (pp. 281–286), **43** (pp. 287–292), **44** (pp. 293–298), **Inv. 8** (pp. 537–540), **92** (pp. 609–614), **99** (pp. 653–658)
NS 1.7	Write the fraction represented by a drawing of parts of a figure; represent a given fraction by using drawings; and relate a fraction to a simple decimal on a number line.	**13** (pp. 73–80), **19** (pp. 115–119), **32** (pp. 213–218), **37** (pp. 247–252), **Inv. 4** (pp. 271–274), **42** (pp. 281–286), **57** (pp. 381–386), **67** (pp. 447–450), **74** (pp. 493–498), **77** (pp. 513–516), **Inv. 8** (pp. 537–540), **89** (pp. 586–592), **92** (pp. 609–614), **94** (pp. 622–626), **98** (pp. 646–652), **99** (pp. 653–658), **100** (pp. 659–664), **103** (pp. 681–687), **106** (pp. 700–704), **112** (pp. 737–741)
NS 1.8	Use concepts of negative numbers (e.g., on a number line, in counting, in temperature, in "owing").	**Inv. 2** (pp. 128–134), **21** (pp. 135–140), **58** (pp. 387–392), **76** (pp. 505–512), **101** (pp. 669–673)

California Mathematics Standards Coverage

California Standards		LESSON AND PAGE NUMBER
NS 1.9	Identify on a number line the relative position of positive fractions, positive mixed numbers, and positive decimals to two decimal places.	**32** (pp. 213–218), **42** (pp. 281–286), **43** (pp. 287–292), **44** (pp. 293–298), **46** (pp. 305–310), **47** (pp. 311–316), **62** (pp. 417–422), **92** (pp. 609–614), **98** (pp. 646–652)
NS 2.0	Students extend their use and understanding of whole numbers to the addition and subtraction of simple decimals:	**22** (pp. 141–148), **45** (pp. 299–304), **46** (pp. 305–310), **51** (pp. 343–348), **52** (pp. 349–354), **61** (pp. 409–416), **62** (pp. 417–422), **66** (pp. 441–446), **73** (pp. 487–492), **80** (pp. 531–536)
NS 2.1	Estimate and compute the sum or difference of whole numbers and positive decimals to two places.	**22** (pp. 141–148), **45** (pp. 299–304), **46** (pp. 305–310), **51** (pp. 343–348), **52** (pp. 349–354), **61** (pp. 409–416), **62** (pp. 417–422), **73** (pp. 487–492), **80** (pp. 531–536)
NS 2.2	Round two-place decimals to one decimal or the nearest whole number and judge the reasonableness of the rounded answer.	**46** (pp. 305–310), **62** (pp. 417–422), **66** (pp. 441–446), **73** (pp. 487–492), **80** (pp. 531–536)
NS 3.0	Students solve problems involving addition, subtraction, multiplication, and division of whole numbers and understand the relationships among the operations:	**5** (pp. 27–30), **6** (pp. 31–35), **FOC A** (p. 36), **10** (pp. 53–57), **FOC B** (p. 58), **Inv. 1** (pp. 59–62), **11** (pp. 63–66), **12** (pp. 67–72), **14** (pp. 81–86), **FOC C** (pp. 87–88), **15** (pp. 89–94), **16** (pp. 95–100), **22** (pp. 141–148), **27** (pp. 173–179), **FOC E** (p. 232), **37** (pp. 247–252), **FOC F** (p. 258), **51** (pp. 343–348), **52** (pp. 349–354), **57** (pp. 381–386), **65** (pp. 436–440), **68** (pp. 451–456), **69** (pp. 457–462), **71** (pp. 473–478), **72** (pp. 479–484), **FOC I** (pp. 485–486), **73** (pp. 487–492), **74** (pp. 493–498), **75** (pp. 499–504), **78** (pp. 517–524), **79** (pp. 525–530), **83** (pp. 555–560), **84** (pp. 561–566), **85** (pp. 567–571), **87** (pp. 577–580), **91** (pp. 603–608), **93** (pp. 615–621), **95** (pp. 627–632), **101** (pp. 669–673), **102** (pp. 674–679), **FOC K** (p. 688), **107** (pp. 705–709), **111** (pp. 732–736), **114** (pp. 747–752)
NS 3.1	Demonstrate an understanding of, and the ability to use, standard algorithms for the addition and subtraction of multidigit numbers.	**5** (pp. 27–30), **6** (pp. 31–35), **FOC A** (p. 36), **10** (pp. 53–57), **FOC B** (p. 58), **Inv. 1** (pp. 59–62), **11** (pp. 63–66), **12** (pp. 67–72), **14** (pp. 81–86), **FOC C** (pp. 87–88), **15** (pp. 89–94), **16** (pp. 95–100), **22** (pp. 141–148), **27** (pp. 173–179), **37** (pp. 247–252), **51** (pp. 343–348), **52** (pp. 349–354), **57** (pp. 381–386), **65** (pp. 436–440), **68** (pp. 451–456), **69** (pp. 457–462), **71** (pp. 473–478), **73** (pp. 487–492), **74** (pp. 493–498), **78** (pp. 517–524), **87** (pp. 577–580), **101** (pp. 669–673), **102** (pp. 674–679)
NS 3.2	Demonstrate an understanding of, and the ability to use, standard algorithms for multiplying a multidigit number by a two-digit number and for dividing a multidigit number by a one-digit number; use relationships between them to simplify computations and to check results.	**FOC E** (p. 232), **FOC F** (p. 258), **69** (pp. 457–462), **72** (pp. 479–484), **FOC I** (pp. 485–486), **75** (pp. 499–504), **79** (pp. 525–530), **83** (pp. 555–560), **84** (pp. 561–566), **102** (pp. 674–679), **FOC K** (p. 688)
NS 3.3	Solve problems involving multiplication of multidigit numbers by two-digit numbers.	**71** (pp. 473–478), **84** (pp. 561–566), **85** (pp. 567–571), **95** (pp. 627–632), **107** (pp. 705–709), **111** (pp. 732–736)
NS 3.4	Solve problems involving division of multidigit numbers by one-digit numbers.	**51** (pp. 343–348), **69** (pp. 457–462), **72** (pp. 479–484), **75** (pp. 499–504), **79** (pp. 525–530), **83** (pp. 555–560), **87** (pp. 577–580), **91** (pp. 603–608), **93** (pp. 615–621), **114** (pp. 747–752)
NS 4.0	Students know how to factor small whole numbers:	**24** (pp. 156–160), **25** (pp. 161–166), **31** (pp. 205–212), **55** (pp. 369–375), **56** (pp. 376–380), **65** (pp. 436–440), **71** (pp. 473–478), **105** (pp. 695–699), **106** (pp. 700–704)
NS 4.1	Understand that many whole numbers break down in different ways (e.g., $12 = 4 \times 3 = 2 \times 6 = 2 \times 2 \times 3$).	**24** (pp. 156–160), **25** (pp. 161–166), **31** (pp. 205–212), **55** (pp. 369–375), **56** (pp. 376–380), **65** (pp. 436–440), **71** (pp. 473–478), **105** (pp. 695–699)
NS 4.2	Know that numbers such as 2, 3, 5, 7, and 11 do not have any factors except 1 and themselves and that such numbers are called prime numbers.	**55** (pp. 369–375), **56** (pp. 376–380), **105** (pp. 695–699), **106** (pp. 700–704)

California Mathematics Standards Coverage

California Standards		LESSON AND PAGE NUMBER
Algebra and Functions		
AF 1.0	Students use and interpret variables, mathematical symbols, and properties to write and simplify expressions and sentences:	**1** (pp. 7–12), **4** (pp. 23–26), **5** (pp. 27–30), **7** (pp. 37–40), **8** (pp. 41–45), **9** (pp. 46–52), **Inv. 1** (pp. 59–62), **12** (pp. 67–72), **15** (pp. 89–94), **16** (pp. 95–100), **20** (pp. 121–127), **23** (pp. 149–155), **26** (pp. 167–172), **28** (pp. 180–186), **30** (pp. 193–197), **Inv. 3** (pp. 198–204), **31** (pp. 205–212), **34** (pp. 225–231), **35** (pp. 233–238), **36** (pp. 239–246), **39** (pp. 259–264), **42** (pp. 281–286), **45** (pp. 299–304), **53** (pp. 355–360), **54** (pp. 361–368), **58** (pp. 387–392), **60** (pp. 399–403), **63** (pp. 423–428), **FOC H** (pp. 429–430), **64** (pp. 431–435), **66** (pp. 441–446), **68** (pp. 451–456), **69** (pp. 457–462), **Inv. 7** (pp. 468–472), **73** (pp. 487–492), **76** (pp. 505–512), **80** (pp. 531–536), **83** (pp. 555–560), **84** (pp. 561–566), **Inv. 9** (pp. 600–602), **93** (pp. 615–621), **95** (pp. 627–632), **Inv. 10** (pp. 665–668), **101** (pp. 669–673), **102** (pp. 674–679), **114** (pp. 747–752)
AF 1.1	Use letters, boxes, or other symbols to stand for any number in simple expressions or equations (e.g., demonstrate an understanding and the use of the concept of a variable).	**1** (pp. 7–12), **4** (pp. 23–26), **5** (pp. 27–30), **7** (pp. 37–40), **8** (pp. 41–45), **9** (pp. 46–52), **Inv. 1** (pp. 59–62), **12** (pp. 67–72), **15** (pp. 89–94), **16** (pp. 95–100), **20** (pp. 121–127), **23** (pp. 149–155), **26** (pp. 167–172), **28** (pp. 180–186), **30** (pp. 193–197), **Inv. 3** (pp. 198–204), **34** (pp. 225–231), **35** (pp. 233–238), **36** (pp. 239–246), **39** (pp. 259–264), **42** (pp. 281–286), **45** (pp. 299–304), **53** (pp. 355–360), **58** (pp. 387–392), **60** (pp. 399–403), **63** (pp. 423–428), **64** (pp. 431–435), **66** (pp. 441–446), **68** (pp. 451–456), **69** (pp. 457–462), **Inv. 7** (pp. 468–472), **73** (pp. 487–492), **76** (pp. 505–512), **80** (pp. 531–536), **83** (pp. 555–560), **84** (pp. 561–566), **Inv. 9** (pp. 600–602), **Inv. 10** (pp. 665–668), **101** (pp. 669–673)
AF 1.2	Interpret and evaluate mathematical expressions that now use parentheses.	**9** (pp. 46–52), **26** (pp. 167–172), **36** (pp. 239–246), **42** (pp. 281–286), **54** (pp. 361–368), **63** (pp. 423–428), **64** (pp. 431–435), **66** (pp. 441–446), **102** (pp. 674–679)
AF 1.3	Use parentheses to indicate which operation to perform first when writing expressions containing more than two terms and different operations.	**9** (pp. 46–52), **26** (pp. 167–172), **36** (pp. 239–246), **54** (pp. 361–368), **63** (pp. 423–428), **FOC H** (pp. 429–430), **64** (pp. 431–435), **Inv. 7** (pp. 468–472), **Inv. 9** (pp. 600–602), **93** (pp. 615–621), **95** (pp. 627–632), **102** (pp. 674–679)
AF 1.4	Use and interpret formulas (e.g., area = length × width or $A = lw$) to answer questions about quantities and their relationships.	**31** (pp. 205–212), **42** (pp. 281–286), **66** (pp. 441–446), **Inv. 7** (pp. 468–472), **73** (pp. 487–492), **80** (pp. 531–536), **84** (pp. 561–566), **Inv. 9** (pp. 600–602), **Inv. 10** (pp. 665–668), **101** (pp. 669–673), **114** (pp. 747–752)
AF 1.5	Understand that an equation such as $y = 3x + 5$ is a prescription for determining a second number when a first number is given.	**64** (pp. 431–435), **Inv. 7** (pp. 468–472), **73** (pp. 487–492), **80** (pp. 531–536), **84** (pp. 561–566), **Inv. 9** (pp. 600–602), **93** (pp. 615–621), **Inv. 10** (pp. 665–668)
AF 2.0	Students know how to manipulate equations:	**9** (pp. 46–52), **26** (pp. 167–172), **36** (pp. 239–246), **63** (pp. 423–428)
AF 2.1	Know and understand that equals added to equals are equal.	**9** (pp. 46–52), **26** (pp. 167–172), **36** (pp. 239–246), **63** (pp. 423–428)
AF 2.2	Know and understand that equals multiplied by equals are equal.	**26** (pp. 167–172), **36** (pp. 239–246), **63** (pp. 423–428)
Measurement and Geometry		
MG 1.0	Students understand perimeter and area:	**20** (pp. 121–127), **Inv. 3** (pp. 198–204), **31** (pp. 205–212), **42** (pp. 281–286), **55** (pp. 369–375), **66** (pp. 441–446), **93** (pp. 615–621), **98** (pp. 646–652), **114** (pp. 747–752)
MG 1.1	Measure the area of rectangular shapes by using appropriate units, such as square centimeter (cm^2), square meter (m^2), square kilometer (km^2), square inch (in^2), square yard (yd^2), or square mile (mi^2).	**Inv. 3** (pp. 198–204), **31** (pp. 205–212), **42** (pp. 281–286), **66** (pp. 441–446), **93** (pp. 615–621), **98** (pp. 646–652), **114** (pp. 747–752)

California Mathematics Standards Coverage

California Standards		LESSON AND PAGE NUMBER
MG 1.2	Recognize that rectangles that have the same area can have different perimeters.	**Inv. 3** (pp. 198–204), **31** (pp. 205–212), **55** (pp. 369–375)
MG 1.3	Understand that rectangles that have the same perimeter can have different areas.	**Inv. 3** (pp. 198–204), **31** (pp. 205–212), **42** (pp. 281–286)
MG 1.4	Understand and use formulas to solve problems involving perimeters and areas of rectangles and squares. Use those formulas to find the areas of more complex figures by dividing the figures into basic shapes.	**20** (pp. 121–127), **Inv. 3** (pp. 198–204), **31** (pp. 205–212), **42** (pp. 281–286), **66** (pp. 441–446), **114** (pp. 747–752)
MG 2.0	Students use two-dimensional coordinate grids to represent points and graph lines and simple figures:	**Inv. 7** (pp. 468–472), **Inv. 9** (pp. 600–602), **Inv. 10** (pp. 665–668)
MG 2.1	Draw the points corresponding to linear relationships on graph paper (e.g., draw 10 points on the graph of the equation $y = 3x$ and connect them by using a straight line).	**Inv. 7** (pp. 468–472), **Inv. 9** (pp. 600–602), **Inv. 10** (pp. 665–668)
MG 2.2	Understand that the length of a horizontal line segment equals the difference of the x-coordinates.	**Inv. 7** (pp. 468–472), **Inv. 9** (pp. 600–602), **Inv. 10** (pp. 665–668)
MG 2.3	Understand that the length of a vertical line segment equals the difference of the y-coordinates.	**Inv. 7** (pp. 468–472), **Inv. 9** (pp. 600–602), **Inv. 10** (pp. 665–668)
MG 3.0	Students demonstrate an understanding of plane and solid geometric objects and use this knowledge to show relationships and solve problems:	**17** (pp. 101–108), **18** (pp. 109–114), **20** (pp. 121–127), **33** (pp. 219–224), **50** (pp. 329–334), **55** (pp. 369–375), **70** (pp. 463–467), **78** (pp. 517–524), **81** (pp. 541–546), **82** (pp. 547–554), **90** (pp. 593–599), **96** (pp. 633–638), **97** (pp. 639–645), **103** (pp. 681–687), **108** (pp. 710–714), **109** (pp. 715–720)
MG 3.1	Identify lines that are parallel and perpendicular.	**17** (pp. 101–108), **33** (pp. 219–224), **50** (pp. 329–334), **90** (pp. 593–599), **97** (pp. 639–645), **108** (pp. 710–714), **109** (pp. 715–720)
MG 3.2	Identify the radius and diameter of a circle.	**18** (pp. 109–114), **33** (pp. 219–224), **82** (pp. 547–554)
MG 3.3	Identify congruent figures.	**55** (pp. 369–375), **70** (pp. 463–467), **78** (pp. 517–524), **97** (pp. 639–645), **108** (pp. 710–714)
MG 3.4	Identify figures that have bilateral and rotational symmetry.	**82** (pp. 547–554), **90** (pp. 593–599), **103** (pp. 681–687)
MG 3.5	Know the definitions of a right angle, an acute angle, and an obtuse angle. Understand that 90°, 180°, 270°, and 360° are associated, respectively, with $\frac{1}{4}$, $\frac{1}{2}$, $\frac{3}{4}$, and full turns.	**17** (pp. 101–108), **50** (pp. 329–334), **78** (pp. 517–524), **81** (pp. 541–546), **82** (pp. 547–554), **90** (pp. 593–599), **97** (pp. 639–645), **109** (pp. 715–720)
MG 3.6	Visualize, describe, and make models of geometric solids (e.g., prisms, pyramids) in terms of the number and shape of faces, edges, and vertices; interpret two-dimensional representations of three-dimensional objects; and draw patterns (of faces) for a solid that, when cut and folded, will make a model of the solid.	**50** (pp. 329–334), **96** (pp. 633–638), **97** (pp. 639–645), **108** (pp. 710–714), **109** (pp. 715–720)
MG 3.7	Know the definitions of different triangles (e.g., equilateral, isosceles, scalene) and identify their attributes.	**18** (pp. 109–114), **20** (pp. 121–127), **81** (pp. 541–546)

California Mathematics Standards Coverage

California Standards		LESSON AND PAGE NUMBER
MG 3.8	Know the definition of different quadrilaterals (e.g., rhombus, square, rectangle, parallelogram, trapezoid).	**18** (pp. 109–114), **50** (pp. 329–334), **90** (pp. 593–599)
Statistics, Data Analysis, and Probability		
SDAP 1.0	Students organize, represent, and interpret numerical and categorical data and clearly communicate their findings:	**Inv. 5** (pp. 335–342), **Inv. 6** (pp. 404–408), **76** (pp. 505–512), **79** (pp. 525–530), **80** (pp. 531–536), **95** (pp. 627–632), **Inv. 10** (pp. 665–668), **Inv. 11** (pp. 727–731)
SDAP 1.1	Formulate survey questions; systematically collect and represent data on a number line; and coordinate graphs, tables, and charts.	**Inv. 5** (pp. 335–342), **Inv. 6** (pp. 404–408), **80** (pp. 531–536), **95** (pp. 627–632), **Inv. 11** (pp. 727–731)
SDAP 1.2	Identify the mode(s) for sets of categorical data and the mode(s), median, and any apparent outliers for numerical data sets.	**95** (pp. 627–632), **Inv. 10** (pp. 665–668), **Inv. 11** (pp. 727–731)
SDAP 1.3	Interpret one- and two-variable data graphs to answer questions about a situation.	**Inv. 5** (pp. 335–342), **76** (pp. 505–512), **79** (pp. 525–530), **Inv. 10** (pp. 665–668), **Inv. 11** (pp. 727–731)
SDAP 2.0	Students make predictions for simple probability situations:	**3** (pp. 17–22), **4** (pp. 23–26), **5** (pp. 27–30), **36** (pp. 239–246), **72** (pp. 479–484), **82** (pp. 547–554), **86** (pp. 572–576), **110** (pp. 721–726), **Inv. 11** (pp. 727–731), **114** (pp. 747–752)
SDAP 2.1	Represent all possible outcomes for a simple probability situation in an organized way (e.g., tables, grids, tree diagrams).	**3** (pp. 17–22), **4** (pp. 23–26), **5** (pp. 27–30), **36** (pp. 239–246), **72** (pp. 479–484), **82** (pp. 547–554), **86** (pp. 572–576), **110** (pp. 721–726), **Inv. 11** (pp. 727–731)
SDAP 2.2	Express outcomes of experimental probability situations verbally and numerically (e.g., 3 out of 4; $\frac{3}{4}$).	**110** (pp. 721–726), **Inv. 11** (pp. 727–731), **114** (pp. 747–752)
Mathematical Reasoning		
MR 1.0	Students make decisions about how to approach problems:	**1** (pp. 7–12), **4** (pp. 23–26), **5** (pp. 27–30), **7** (pp. 37–40), **8** (pp. 41–45), **9** (pp. 46–52), **10** (pp. 53–57), **FOC B** (p. 58), **Inv.** 1 (pp. 59–62), **11** (pp. 63–66), **12** (pp. 67–72), **13** (pp. 73–80), **14** (pp. 81–86), **FOC C** (pp. 87–88), **15** (pp. 89–94), **17** (pp. 101–108), **18** (pp. 109–114), **Inv. 2** (pp. 128–134), **21** (pp. 135–140), **22** (pp. 141–148), **23** (pp. 149–155), **24** (pp. 156–160), **25** (pp. 161–166), **28** (pp. 180–186), **30** (pp. 193–197), **Inv. 3** (pp. 198–204), **31** (pp. 205–212), **FOC E** (p. 232), **35** (pp. 233–238), **36** (pp. 239–246), **38** (pp. 253–257), **FOC F** (p. 258), **45** (pp. 299–304), **46** (pp. 305–310), **Inv. 5** (pp. 335–342), **53** (pp. 355–360), **54** (pp. 361–368), **58** (pp. 387–392), **59** (pp. 393–398), **Inv. 6** (pp. 404–408), **62** (pp. 417–422), **63** (pp. 423–428), **68** (pp. 451–456), **76** (pp. 505–512), **87** (pp. 577–580), **Inv. 9** (pp. 600–602), **92** (pp. 609–614), **93** (pp. 615–621), **94** (pp. 622–626), **97** (pp. 639–645), **105** (pp. 695–699), **108** (pp. 710–714), **Inv. 11** (pp. 727–731), **112** (pp. 737–741), **113** (pp. 742–746)
MR 1.1	Analyze problems by identifying relationships, distinguishing relevant from irrelevant information, sequencing and prioritizing information, and observing patterns.	**1** (pp. 7–12), **4** (pp. 23–26), **5** (pp. 27–30), **7** (pp. 37–40), **8** (pp. 41–45), **9** (pp. 46–52), **10** (pp. 53–57), **Inv. 1** (pp. 59–62), **11** (pp. 63–66), **12** (pp. 67–72), **13** (pp. 73–80), **14** (pp. 81–86), **15** (pp. 89–94), **17** (pp. 101–108), **18** (pp. 109–114), **Inv. 2** (pp. 128–134), **21** (pp. 135–140), **22** (pp. 141–148), **23** (pp. 149–155), **24** (pp. 156–160), **25** (pp. 161–166), **28** (pp. 180–186), **30** (pp. 193–197), **Inv. 3** (pp. 198–204), **31** (pp. 205–212), **FOC E** (p. 232), **35** (pp. 233–238), **36** (pp. 239–246), **38** (pp. 253–257), **45** (pp. 299–304), **46** (pp. 305–310), **Inv. 5** (pp. 335–342), **53** (pp. 355–360), **54** (pp. 361–368), **58** (pp. 387–392), **59** (pp. 393–398), **Inv. 6** (pp. 404–408), **62** (pp. 417–422), **63** (pp. 423–428), **68** (pp. 451–456), **76** (pp. 505–512), **87** (pp. 577–580), **Inv. 9** (pp. 600–602), **92** (pp. 609–614), **93** (pp. 615–621), **94** (pp. 622–626), **97** (pp. 639–645), **105** (pp. 695–699), **108** (pp. 710–714), **Inv. 11** (pp. 727–731), **112** (pp. 737–741), **113** (pp. 742–746)

California Mathematics Standards Coverage

California Standards		LESSON AND PAGE NUMBER
MR 1.2	Determine when and how to break a problem into simpler parts.	**FOC B** (p. 58), **FOC C** (pp. 87–88), **31** (pp. 205–212), **FOC F** (p. 258), **68** (pp. 451–456), **76** (pp. 505–512), **93** (pp. 615–621), **94** (pp. 622–626)
MR 2.0	Students use strategies, skills, and concepts in finding solutions:	**2** (pp. 13–16), **3** (pp. 17–22), **4** (pp. 23–26), **5** (pp. 27–30), **6** (pp. 31–35), **7** (pp. 37–40), **8** (pp. 41–45), **9** (pp. 46–52), **10** (pp. 53–57), **FOC B** (p. 58), **11** (pp. 63–66), **12** (pp. 67–72), **13** (pp. 73–80), **14** (pp. 81–86), **15** (pp. 89–94), **16** (pp. 95–100), **17** (pp. 101–108), **18** (pp. 109–114), **19** (pp. 115–119), **20** (pp. 121–127), **Inv. 2** (pp. 128–134), **22** (pp. 141–148), **24** (pp. 156–160), **25** (pp. 161–166), **26** (pp. 167–172), **28** (pp. 180–186), **Inv. 3** (pp. 198–204), **31** (pp. 205–212), **32** (pp. 213–218), **36** (pp. 239–246), **37** (pp. 247–252), **38** (pp. 253–257), **FOC F** (p. 258), **39** (pp. 259–264), **40** (pp. 265–270), **42** (pp. 281–286), **43** (pp. 287–292), **44** (pp. 293–298), **45** (pp. 299–304), **46** (pp. 305–310), **47** (pp. 311–316), **FOC G** (p. 317), **48** (pp. 318–322), **49** (pp. 323–328), **Inv. 5** (pp. 335–342), **51** (pp. 343–348), **52** (pp. 349–354), **53** (pp. 355–360), **54** (pp. 361–368), **55** (pp. 369–375), **56** (pp. 376–380), **57** (pp. 381–386), **58** (pp. 387–392), **59** (pp. 393–398), **60** (pp. 399–403), **Inv. 6** (pp. 404–408), **61** (pp. 409–416), **62** (pp. 417–422), **63** (pp. 423–428), **64** (pp. 431–435), **67** (pp. 447–450), **68** (pp. 451–456), **69** (pp. 457–462), **Inv. 7** (pp. 468–472), **71** (pp. 473–478), **73** (pp. 487–492), **74** (pp. 493–498), **75** (pp. 499–504), **76** (pp. 505–512), **77** (pp. 513–516), **80** (pp. 531–536), **Inv. 8** (pp. 537–540), **81** (pp. 541–546), **82** (pp. 547–554), **83** (pp. 555–560), **84** (pp. 561–566), **85** (pp. 567–571), **88** (pp. 581–585), **89** (pp. 586–592), **90** (pp. 593–599), **Inv. 9** (pp. 600–602), **91** (pp. 603–608), **92** (pp. 609–614), **93** (pp. 615–621), **94** (pp. 622–626), **95** (pp. 627–632), **97** (pp. 639–645), **98** (pp. 646–652), **99** (pp. 653–658), **100** (pp. 659–664), **101** (pp. 669–673), **102** (pp. 674–679), **104** (pp. 689–694), **106** (pp. 700–704), **107** (pp. 705–709), **108** (pp. 710–714), **109** (pp. 715–720), **Inv. 11** (pp. 727–731), **112** (pp. 737–741), **113** (pp. 742–746)
MR 2.1	Use estimation to verify the reasonableness of calculated results.	**46** (pp. 305–310), **52** (pp. 349–354), **59** (pp. 393–398), **62** (pp. 417–422), **91** (pp. 603–608)
MR 2.2	Apply strategies and results from simpler problems to more complex problems.	**Inv. 7** (pp. 468–472), **76** (pp. 505–512), **Inv. 9** (pp. 600–602), **101** (pp. 669–673)
MR 2.3	Use a variety of methods, such as words, numbers, symbols, charts, graphs, tables, diagrams, and models, to explain mathematical reasoning.	**2** (pp. 13–16), **3** (pp. 17–22), **4** (pp. 23–26), **5** (pp. 27–30), **6** (pp. 31–35), **7** (pp. 37–40), **8** (pp. 41–45), **9** (pp. 46–52), **10** (pp. 53–57), **11** (pp. 63–66), **12** (pp. 67–72), **13** (pp. 73–80), **14** (pp. 81–86), **15** (pp. 89–94), **16** (pp. 95–100), **17** (pp. 101–108), **18** (pp. 109–114), **19** (pp. 115–119), **20** (pp. 121–127), **Inv. 2** (pp. 128–134), **22** (pp. 141–148), **24** (pp. 156–160), **25** (pp. 161–166), **26** (pp. 167–172), **28** (pp. 180–186), **Inv. 3** (pp. 198–204), **31** (pp. 205–212), **32** (pp. 213–218), **36** (pp. 239–246), **37** (pp. 247–252), **38** (pp. 253–257), **FOC F** (p. 258), **39** (pp. 259–264), **40** (pp. 265–270), **42** (pp. 281–286), **43** (pp. 287–292), **44** (pp. 293–298), **45** (pp. 299–304), **46** (pp. 305–310), **47** (pp. 311–316), **48** (pp. 318–322), **49** (pp. 323–328), **Inv. 5** (pp. 335–342), **51** (pp. 343–348), **52** (pp. 349–354), **53** (pp. 355–360), **54** (pp. 361–368), **55** (pp. 369–375), **56** (pp. 376–380), **57** (pp. 381–386), **58** (pp. 387–392), **59** (pp. 393–398), **60** (pp. 399–403), **Inv. 6** (pp. 404–408), **61** (pp. 409–416), **62** (pp. 417–422), **63** (pp. 423–428), **64** (pp. 431–435), **68** (pp. 451–456), **Inv. 7** (pp. 468–472), *continued*

California Mathematics Standards Coverage

California Standards		LESSON AND PAGE NUMBER
MR 2.3, *continued*	Use a variety of methods, such as words, numbers, symbols, charts, graphs, tables, diagrams, and models, to explain mathematical reasoning.	**71** (pp. 473–478), **73** (pp. 487–492), **74** (pp. 493–498), **75** (pp. 499–504), **80** (pp. 531–536), **Inv. 8** (pp. 537–540), **81** (pp. 541–546), **82** (pp. 547–554), **85** (pp. 567–571), **88** (pp. 581–585), **89** (pp. 586–592), **90** (pp. 593–599), **Inv. 9** (pp. 600–602), **92** (pp. 609–614), **93** (pp. 615–621), **94** (pp. 622–626), **95** (pp. 627–632), **97** (pp. 639–645), **98** (pp. 646–652), **99** (pp. 653–658), **101** (pp. 669–673), **102** (pp. 674–679), **104** (pp. 689–694), **106** (pp. 700–704), **107** (pp. 705–709), **108** (pp. 710–714), **109** (pp. 715–720), **Inv. 11** (pp. 727–731), **112** (pp. 737–741)
MR 2.4	Express the solution clearly and logically by using the appropriate mathematical notation and terms and clear language; support solutions with evidence in both verbal and symbolic work.	**FOC B** (p. 58), **13** (pp. 73–80), **Inv. 2** (pp. 128–134), **31** (pp. 205–212), **42** (pp. 281–286), **45** (pp. 299–304), **64** (pp. 431–435), **67** (pp. 447–450), **81** (pp. 541–546), **83** (pp. 555–560), **84** (pp. 561–566), **Inv. 11** (pp. 727–731), **113** (pp. 742–746)
MR 2.5	Indicate the relative advantages of exact and approximate solutions to problems and give answers to a specified degree of accuracy.	**39** (pp. 259–264), **FOC G** (p. 317), **61** (pp. 409–416), **93** (pp. 615–621)
MR 2.6	Make precise calculations and check the validity of the results from the context of the problem.	**12** (pp. 67–72), **15** (pp. 89–94), **16** (pp. 95–100), **28** (pp. 180–186), **51** (pp. 343–348), **52** (pp. 349–354), **68** (pp. 451–456), **69** (pp. 457–462), **71** (pp. 473–478), **74** (pp. 493–498), **77** (pp. 513–516), **88** (pp. 581–585), **Inv. 9** (pp. 600–602), **91** (pp. 603–608), **100** (pp. 659–664)
MR 3.0	Students move beyond a particular problem by generalizing to other situations:	**1** (pp. 7–12), **3** (pp. 17–22), **FOC A** (p. 36), **8** (pp. 41–45), **9** (pp. 46–52), **Inv. 1** (pp. 59–62), **12** (pp. 67–72), **13** (pp. 73–80), **15** (pp. 89–94), **16** (pp. 95–100), **Inv. 2** (pp. 128–134), **FOC D** (p. 120), **20** (pp. 121–127), **22** (pp. 141–148), **24** (pp. 156–160), **25** (pp. 161–166), **28** (pp. 180–186), **31** (pp. 205–212), **FOC E** (p. 232), **36** (pp. 239–246), **37** (pp. 247–252), **40** (pp. 265–270), **41** (pp. 275–280), **42** (pp. 281–286), **44** (pp. 293–298), **46** (pp. 305–310), **47** (pp. 311–316), **Inv. 5** (pp. 335–342), **51** (pp. 343–348), **52** (pp. 349–354), **54** (pp. 361–368), **59** (pp. 393–398), **FOC H** (pp. 429–430), **66** (pp. 441–446), **68** (pp. 451–456), **69** (pp. 457–462), **72** (pp. 479–484), **FOC I** (pp. 485–486), **73** (pp. 487–492), **78** (pp. 517–524), **81** (pp. 541–546), **82** (pp. 547–554), **85** (pp. 567–571), **88** (pp. 581–585), **93** (pp. 615–621), **100** (pp. 659–664), **FOC K** (p. 688), **Inv. 11** (pp. 727–731), **111** (pp. 732–736)
MR 3.1	Evaluate the reasonableness of the solution in the context of the original situation.	**1** (pp. 7–12), **3** (pp. 17–22), **8** (pp. 41–45), **9** (pp. 46–52), **Inv. 1** (pp. 59–62), **12** (pp. 67–72), **13** (pp. 73–80), **15** (pp. 89–94), **22** (pp. 141–148), **31** (pp. 205–212), **36** (pp. 239–246), **40** (pp. 265–270), **46** (pp. 305–310), **Inv. 5** (pp. 335–342), **51** (pp. 343–348), **52** (pp. 349–354), **72** (pp. 479–484), **88** (pp. 581–585), **100** (pp. 659–664)
MR 3.2	Note the method of deriving the solution and demonstrate a conceptual understanding of the derivation by solving similar problems.	**12** (pp. 67–72), **16** (pp. 95–100), **28** (pp. 180–186), **41** (pp. 275–280), **FOC H** (pp. 429–430), **66** (pp. 441–446), **FOC I** (pp. 485–486), **78** (pp. 517–524), **93** (pp. 615–621), **FOC K** (p. 688), **111** (pp. 732–736)
MR 3.3	Develop generalizations of the results obtained and apply them in other circumstances.	**FOC A** (p. 36), **Inv. 2** (pp. 128–134), **FOC D** (p. 120), **20** (pp. 121–127), **24** (pp. 156–160), **25** (pp. 161–166), **FOC E** (p. 232), **36** (pp. 239–246), **37** (pp. 247–252), **42** (pp. 281–286), **44** (pp. 293–298), **47** (pp. 311–316), **51** (pp. 343–348), **54** (pp. 361–368), **59** (pp. 393–398), **68** (pp. 451–456), **69** (pp. 457–462), **73** (pp. 487–492), **81** (pp. 541–546), **82** (pp. 547–554), **85** (pp. 567–571), **Inv. 11** (pp. 727–731), **111** (pp. 732–736)

Lesson Planner

Lesson	New Concepts	Materials	Resources
61	• Estimating Arithmetic Answers		• Power Up I Worksheet
62	• Rounding to the Nearest Tenth	• Manipulative Kit: rulers	• Power Up I Worksheet
63	• Order of Operations, Part 3		• Power Up J Worksheet
64	• Two-Step Equations		• Power Up J Worksheet
65	• Exponents	• Manipulative Kit: rulers	• Power Up J Worksheet
Cumulative Assessment			• Cumulative Test 12 • Test-Day Activity 6
66	• Area of a Rectangle		• Power Up J Worksheet
67	• Remaining Fractions		• Power Up I Worksheet
68	• Division with Two-Digit Answers, Part 1		• Power Up I Worksheet
69	• Division with Two-Digit Answers, Part 2		• Power Up I Worksheet
70	• Similar and Congruent Figures		• Power Up I Worksheet • Lesson Activity 22
Cumulative Assessment			• Cumulative Test 13 • Performance Task 7
Inv. 7	• Coordinate Graphing	• Grid paper	• Lesson Activity 8

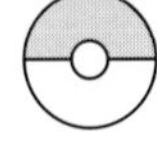
All resources are also available on the Resources and Planner CD.

Additional Resources

- Instructional Masters
- Reteaching Masters
- Refresher Lessons for California Standards
- Calculator Activities
- Resources and Planner CD
- Assessment Guide
- Performance Tasks
- Instructional Transparencies
- Answer Key CD
- Power Up Workbook
- Written Practice Workbook

Math Highlights

Enduring Understandings — The "Big Picture"

After completing Section 7, students will understand that:

- There is an order of operations when simplifying equations.
- A power is called an exponent.
- A formula can be used to find the area of a rectangle.
- There are rules to determine if a number is divisible by 3 or 9.

Essential Questions

- Why are parentheses used in equations?
- How are exponents related to multiplication?
- How do I find the area of a rectangle?
- How do I know if a number is divisible by 3 or 9?

Math Content Highlights	Math Processes Highlights
Number Sense • **Estimating Arithmetic Answers** *Lesson 61* • **Rounding to the Nearest Tenth** *Lesson 62* • **Order of Operations** *Lesson 63* • **Exponents** *Lesson 65* • **Remaining Fractions** *Lesson 67* • **Division with Two-Digit Answers** *Lessons 68, 69* **Algebraic Thinking** • **Two-Step Equations** *Lesson 64* • **Word Problems Using Division** *Lessons 68, 69* **Geometry and Measurement** • **Area of a Rectangle** *Lesson 66* • **Similar and Congruent Figures** *Lesson 70* • **Coordinate Graphing** *Investigation 7*	**Problem Solving** • **Strategies** – **Draw a Picture or Diagram** *Lesson 64* – **Find or Extend a Pattern** *Lesson 62* – **Make or Use a Table, Chart, or Graph** *Lesson 70* – **Make an Organized List** *Lessons 61, 66* – **Make It Simpler** *Lessons 64, 67* – **Use Logical Reasoning** *Lessons 63, 65, 68, 70* – **Work Backwards** *Lesson 68* – **Write a Number Sentence or Equation** *Lessons 62, 69* • **Real-World Applications** *Lessons 61, 63, 64, 65, 66, 67, 69* **Communication** • **Discuss** *Lessons 61, 63, 66, 68, 69, 70, Investigation 7* • **Explain** *Lessons 61, 62, 63, 64, 65, 66, 68, 69, 70, Investigation 7* • **Formulate** *Lesson 69* **Connections** • **Math to Math** – **Order of Operations and Algebra** *Lessons 63, 64* – **Division and Number Sense** *Lessons 67, 68, 69* – **Geometry and Problem Solving** *Lessons 66, 70* • **Math and Other Subjects** – **Math and Geography** *Lessons 62, 67, 68* – **Math and Sports** *Lessons 62, 64, 66, 67, 69* **Representation** • **Model** *Lessons 62, 65, 70, Investigation 7* • **Represent** *Lessons 61, 62, 63, 64, 65, 66, 67, 69, 70* • **Formulate an Equation** *Lessons 63, 64* • **Using Manipulative/Hands On** *Lessons 61, 62, 63, 64, 65, 66, 67, 68, 69, 70*

Universal Access

Support for universal access is included with each lesson. Specific resources and features are listed on each lesson planning page. Features in the Teacher's Manual to customize instruction include the following:

Teacher's Manual Support

Alternative Approach	Provides a different path to concept development. *Lessons 61–63, 66, 68–70*
Manipulative Use	Provides alternate concept development through the use of manipulatives. *Lesson 64*
Flexible Grouping	Provides suggestions for various grouping strategies tied to specific lesson examples. *TM page 466A*
Inclusion	Provides ideas for including all students by accommodating special needs. *Lessons 61–70, Inv. 7*
Developing Academic Language	Provides a list of new and maintained vocabulary words along with words that might be difficult for English learners. *Lessons 61–70, Inv. 7*
English Learners	Provides strategies for teaching specific vocabulary that may be difficult for English learners. *Lessons 61–70, Inv. 7*
Errors and Misconceptions	Provides information about common misconceptions students encounter with concepts. *Lessons 61–70*
Extend the Example	Provides additional concept development for advanced learners. *Lessons 61–70*
Extend the Problem	Provides an opportunity for advanced learners to broaden concept development by expanding on a particular problem approach or context. *Lessons 61–70, Inv. 7*
Early Finishers	Provides additional math concept extensions for advanced learners at the end of the Written Practice. *Lessons 61, 70*
Investigate Further	Provides further depth to concept development by providing additional activities for an investigation. *Investigation 7*

Additional Resources

The following resources are also available to support universal access:

- Adaptations for Saxon Math
- English Learner Handbook
- Online Activities
- Performance Tasks
- Refresher Lessons for CA Standards
- Reteaching Masters

Technology

Student Resources

- Student Edition eBook
- Calculator Activities
- Online Resources at **www.SaxonMath.com/Int4ActivitiesCA**

Teacher Resources

- Resources and Planner CD
- Test and Practice Generator CD
- Monitoring Student Progress: eGradebook CD
- Teacher's Manual eBook CD
- Answer Key CD
- Adaptations for Saxon Math CD
- Online Resources at **www.SaxonMath.com**

Cumulative Assessment

The assessments in Saxon Math are frequent and consistently placed to offer a regular method of ongoing testing.

Power-Up Test: Allow no more than ten minutes for this test of basic facts and skills.

Cumulative Test: Next, administer this test, which checks mastery of concepts in previous lessons.

Test-Day Activity and Performance Task: The remaining class time can be spent on these activities. Students can finish the Test-Day Activity for homework. Advanced learners can complete the extended Performance Task in another class period.

After Lesson 65

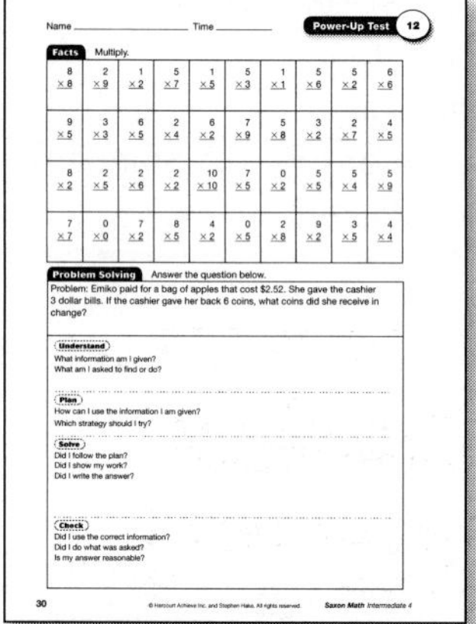
Power-Up Test 12

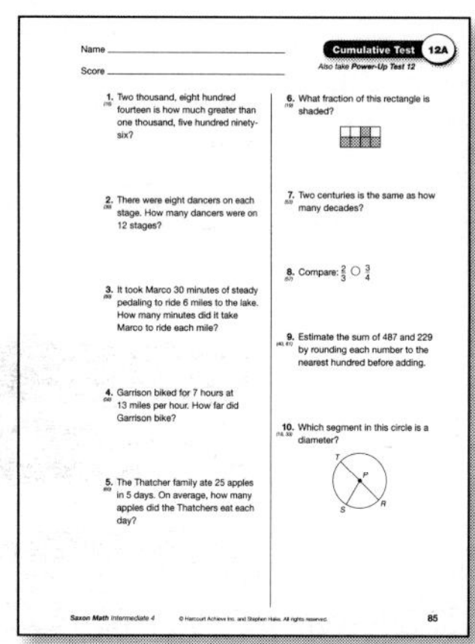
Cumulative Test 12

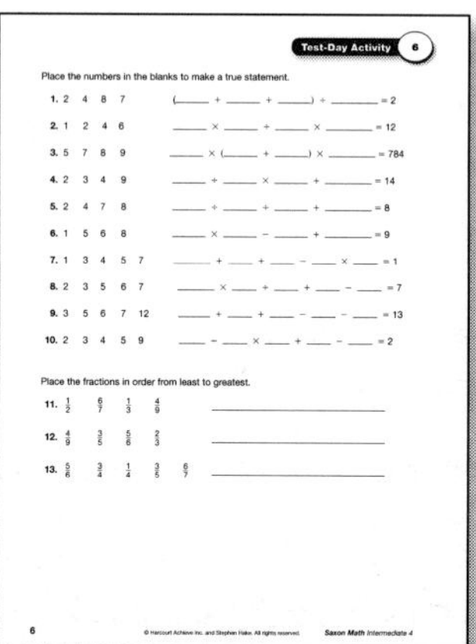
Test-Day Activity 6

After Lesson 70

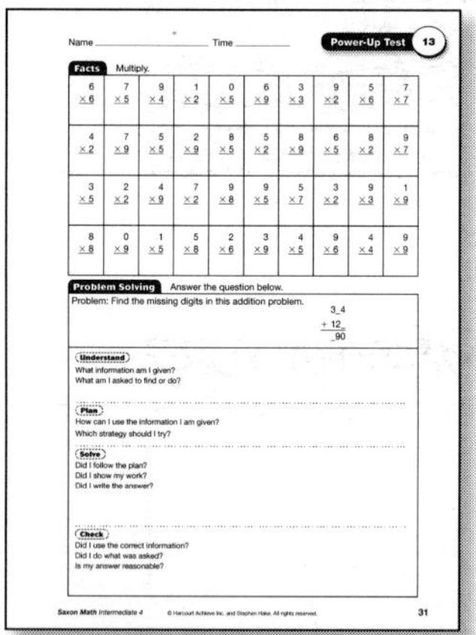
Power-Up Test 13

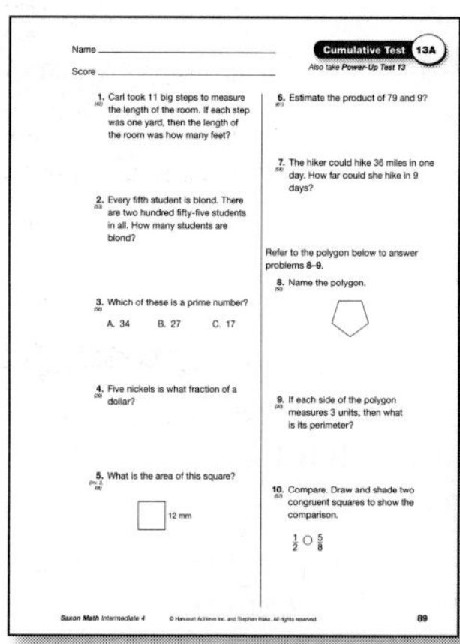
Cumulative Test 13

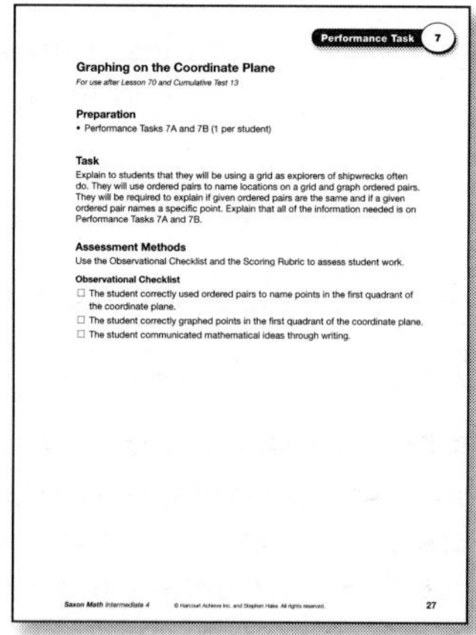
Performance Task 7

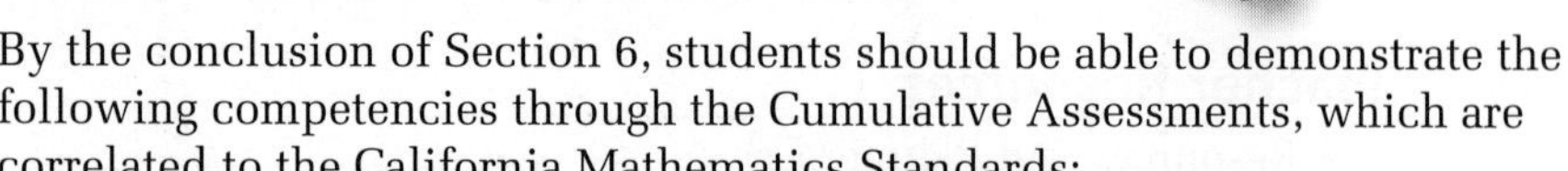

Evidence of Learning — What Students Should Know

By the conclusion of Section 6, students should be able to demonstrate the following competencies through the Cumulative Assessments, which are correlated to the California Mathematics Standards:

- Use estimation and rounding when working with integers and decimal numbers. **NS 1.3, MR 2.1, MR 2.3, MR 3.1**
- Identify numbers as prime or composite. **NS 4.1, NS 4.2, MR 2.3**
- Use the order of operations to evaluate expressions. **AF 1.1, AF 1.2, AF 1.3, AF 2.1, AF 2.2, MR 2.3**

Reteaching

Students who score below 80% on assessments may be in need of reteaching. Refer to the Reteaching Masters for reteaching opportunities for every lesson.

Benchmarking and Tracking the California Mathematics Standards

Benchmark Tests

Benchmark Tests correlated to lesson concepts allow you to assess student progress after every 20 lessons. An End-of-Course Test is a final benchmark test of the complete textbook. The Benchmark Tests are available in the Assessment Guide.

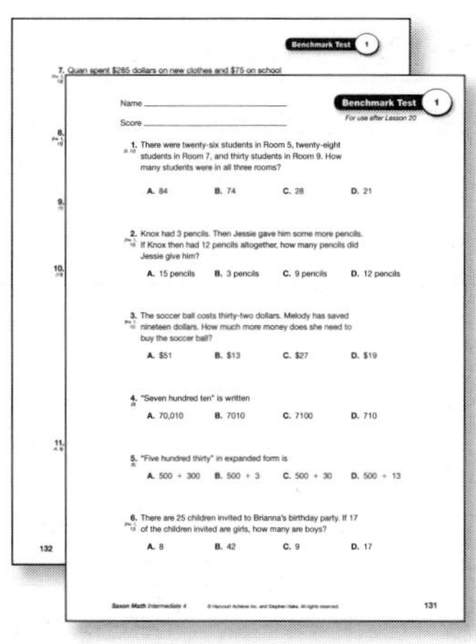
Benchmark Test 1

7. Quan spent $285 dollars on new clothes and $75 on school

Name ______________________

Score ______________________

Benchmark Test 1
For use after Lesson 20

1. There were twenty-six students in Room 5, twenty-eight students in Room 7, and thirty students in Room 9. How many students were in all three rooms?

   A. 84 **B.** 74 **C.** 28 **D.** 21

2. Knox had 3 pencils. Then Jessie gave him some more pencils. If Knox then had 12 pencils altogether, how many pencils did Jessie give him?

   A. 15 pencils **B.** 3 pencils **C.** 9 pencils **D.** 12 pencils

3. The soccer ball costs thirty-two dollars. Melody has saved nineteen dollars. How much more money does she need to buy the soccer ball?

   A. $51 **B.** $13 **C.** $27 **D.** $19

4. "Seven hundred ten" is written

   A. 70,010 **B.** 7010 **C.** 7100 **D.** 710

5. "Five hundred thirty" in expanded form is

   A. 500 + 300 **B.** 500 + 3 **C.** 500 + 30 **D.** 500 + 13

6. There are 25 children invited to Brianna's birthday party. If 17 of the children invited are girls, how many are boys?

   A. 8 **B.** 42 **C.** 9 **D.** 17

132

Saxon Math Intermediate 4 131

Monitoring Student Progress: eGradebook CD

To track California Standards mastery, enter students' scores on Cumulative Tests and Benchmark Tests into the Monitoring Student Progress: eGradebook CD. Use the report titled *Benchmark Standards Report* to determine which California Standards were assessed and the level of mastery for each student. Generate a variety of other reports for class tracking and more.

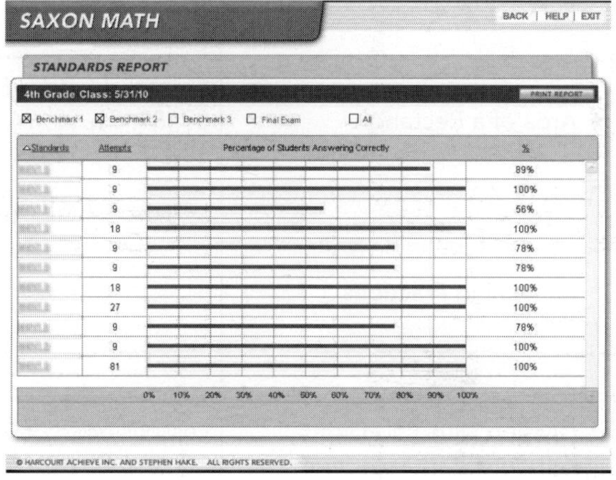
SAXON MATH BACK | HELP | EXIT

STANDARDS REPORT

4th Grade Class: 5/31/10 PRINT REPORT

☒ Benchmark 1 ☒ Benchmark 2 ☐ Benchmark 3 ☐ Final Exam ☐ All

Standards	Attempts	Percentage of Students Answering Correctly	%
[illegible]	9		89%
[illegible]	9		100%
[illegible]	9		56%
[illegible]	18		100%
[illegible]	9		78%
[illegible]	9		78%
[illegible]	18		100%
[illegible]	27		100%
[illegible]	9		78%
[illegible]	9		100%
[illegible]	81		100%

0% 10% 20% 30% 40% 50% 60% 70% 80% 90% 100%

© HARCOURT ACHIEVE INC. AND STEPHEN HAKE. ALL RIGHTS RESERVED.

Test and Practice Generator CD

Test items also available in Spanish.

The Test and Practice Generator is an easy-to-manage benchmarking and assessment tool that creates unlimited practice and tests in multiple formats and allows you to customize questions or create new ones. A variety of reports are available to track student progress toward mastery of the California Standards throughout the year.

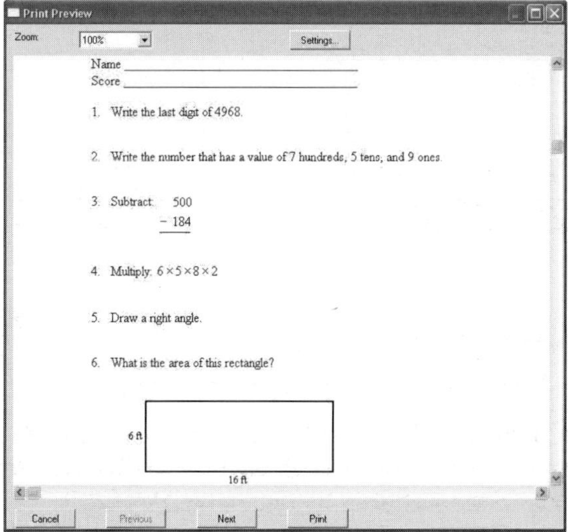
Print Preview

Zoom 100% Settings...

Name ______________________

Score ______________________

1. Write the last digit of 4968.

2. Write the number that has a value of 7 hundreds, 5 tens, and 9 ones.

3. Subtract: 500 − 184

4. Multiply: $6 \times 5 \times 8 \times 2$

5. Draw a right angle.

6. What is the area of this rectangle?

Cancel Previous Next Print

Content Trace

Lesson	New Concepts	Practiced	Assessed	Looking Forward
61	• Estimating Arithmetic Answers	Lessons 61, 62, 63, 65, 66, 67, 68, 69, 70, 71, 72, 73, 76, 81, 86, 90, 93, 99, 102, 104	Tests 12, 13, 14, 16, 18, 22	Lessons 62, 65, 71, 79, 84, 85, 86, 88, 91, 92, 102, 104, 107
62	• Rounding to the Nearest Tenth	Lessons 62, 63, 64, 65, 66, 67, 69, 70, 72, 83, 86, 92, 99, 100	Test 13	Lessons 79, 91, 104, 107
63	• Order of Operations, Part 3	Lessons 63, 64, 65, 66, 67, 68, 69, 70, 73, 75, 76, 77, 82, 84, 85, 91, 92, 96, 100, 102, 103, 104, 109, 112, 114	Tests 15, 16, 17, 20, 21	Lessons 64, 65, 102
64	• Two-Step Equations	Lessons 64, 65, 66, 67, 68, 69, 70, 71, 73, 74, 76, 77, 78, 81, 82, 83, 87, 88, 90, 91, 92, 93, 95, 98, 103, 104, 106, 110, 112	Tests 13, 14, 21	Lessons 65, 102
65	• Exponents	Lessons 65, 66, 67, 68, 69, 70, 71, 72, 73, 74, 75, 76, 77, 78, 79, 80, 82, 85, 87, 88, 91, 92, 93, 94, 95, 96, 97, 98, 99, 100, 102, 104, 105, 108, 109	Tests 13, 14, 15, 18, 20, 21, 22	Lessons 71, 84, 85, 86, 88, 91, 102, 104, 105
66	• Area of a Rectangle	Lessons 66, 67, 68, 69, 70, 71, 72, 75, 78, 79, 80, 81, 82, 87, 89, 91, 93, 94, 95, 96, 97, 98, 100, 102, 104, 106, 107, 111, 112, 114	Tests 13, 17, 18, 19, 20	Lessons 70, 78, 81, 82, 90, 96, 97, 108, 109, 114
67	• Remaining Fractions	Lessons 67, 68, 69, 70, 71, 72, 74, 76, 95, 105, 110	Tests 14, 16, 18	Lesson 74, Investigation 8, Lessons 87, 89, 92, 94, 98, 99, 100, 103, 106, 111, 112, 113
68	• Division with Two-Digit Answers, Part 1	Lessons 68, 69, 72, 75, 88, 94, 97, 106	Test 14, 22	Lessons 69, 72, 75, 79, 83, 87, 91
69	• Division with Two-Digit Answers, Part 2	Lessons 69, 70, 71, 72, 73, 74, 75, 78, 79, 81, 86, 88, 90, 92, 96, 97, 98, 99, 100, 102, 109	Tests 14, 22	Lessons 72, 75, 79, 83, 87, 91
70	• Similar and Congruent Figures	Lessons 70, 71, 72, 73, 74, 75, 76, 82, 89, 91, 94	Tests 14, 17	Lessons 78, 81, 82, 90, 96, 97, 101, 108, 109, 114
Inv. 7	• Coordinate Graphing	Lessons 71, 72, 73, 74, 75, 76, 77, 78, 79, 81, 84, 87, 88, 89, 90, 92, 93, 111	Test 14	Investigations 9, 10

Planning & Preparation

• Estimating Arithmetic Answers

Objectives

- Use rounding to estimate arithmetic answers.
- Determine if an estimated answer is more than, equal to, or less than the actual answer.
- Decide when an estimate is needed to solve a problem.
- Use rounding to estimate solutions to problems involving money amounts.

Prerequisite Skills

- Rounding numbers to the nearest ten, hundred and thousand using a number line.
- Estimating solutions to multiplication word problems using rounding.

Materials

Instructional Masters

- Power Up I Worksheet
- Lesson Activity 8*
- Lesson Activity 14*

Manipulative Kit

- Rulers*

Teacher-provided materials

- Number line, index cards, grid paper*

**optional*

California Mathematics Content Standards

NS 1.0, 1.3 Round whole numbers through the millions to the nearest ten, hundred, thousand, ten thousand, or hundred thousand.

NS 1.0, 1.4 Decide when a rounded solution is called for and explain why such a solution may be appropriate.

NS 2.0, 2.1 Estimate and compute the sum or difference of whole numbers and positive decimals to two places.

MR 2.0, 2.3 Use a variety of methods, such as words, numbers, symbols, charts, graphs, tables, diagrams, and models, to explain mathematical reasoning.

MR 2.0, 2.5 Indicate the relative advantages of exact and approximate solutions to problems and give answers to a specified degree of accuracy.

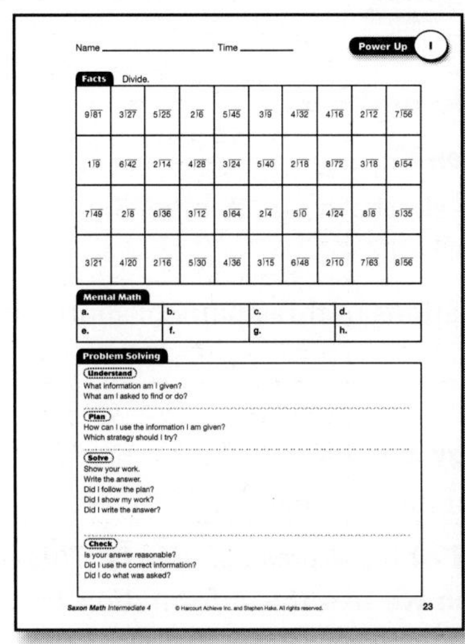

Name ______________ Time ________ **Power Up I**

Facts Divide.

9)81	3)27	5)25	2)6	5)45	3)9	4)32	4)16	2)12	7)56
1)9	6)42	2)14	4)28	3)24	5)40	2)18	8)72	3)18	6)54
7)49	2)8	6)36	3)12	8)64	2)4	5)0	4)24	8)8	5)35
3)21	4)20	2)16	5)30	4)36	3)15	6)48	2)10	7)63	8)56

Mental Math

a.	b.	c.	d.
e.	f.	g.	h.

Problem Solving

Understand
What information am I given?
What am I asked to find or do?

Plan
How can I use the information I am given?
Which strategy should I try?

Solve
Show your work.
Write the answer.
Did I follow the plan?
Did I show my work?
Did I write the answer?

Check
Is your answer reasonable?
Did I use the correct information?
Did I do what was asked?

Saxon Math Intermediate 4 © Harcourt Achieve Inc. and Stephen Hake. All rights reserved. 23

Power Up I Worksheet

Universal Access

Reaching All Special Needs Students

Special Education Students	At-Risk Students	English Learners	Advanced Learners
• Inclusion (TM) • Adaptations for Saxon Math	• Alternative Approach (TM) • Error Alert (TM) • Reteaching Masters • Refresher Lessons for California Standards	• English Learners (TM) • Developing Academic Language (TM) • English Learner Handbook	• Extend the Example (TM) • Extend the Problem (TM) • Early Finisher (SE) • Online Activities

TM=Teacher's Manual
SE=Student Edition

Developing Academic Language

Maintained	**English Learner**
arithmetic	reasonable
estimate	
number line	
product	
sum	

Problem Solving Discussion

Problem

Garcia is packing his clothes for summer camp. He wants to take three pairs of shorts. He has four different pairs of shorts from which to choose—tan, blue, white, and black. What are the different combinations of three pairs of shorts that Garcia can pack?

Focus Strategy  **Make an Organized List**

Understand *Understand the problem.*

"What information are we given?"

Garcia has four different pairs of shorts: **1.** tan, **2.** blue, **3.** white, and **4.** black.

"What are we asked to do?"

We are asked to find the combinations of three pairs of shorts that Garcia can pack.

Plan *Make a plan.*

"What problem-solving strategy can we use?"

We can *make an organized list* of the combinations.

"Notice that Garcia will pack 3 of his 4 pairs of shorts. This means that he will leave 1 pair at home. How can we use this information to organize our list?"

Each possible combination *does not include* one of the pairs. Thus, we can first find the combination that does not include tan, then the combination that does not include blue, then the combination that does not include white, and finally, the combination that does not include black.

Solve *Carry out the plan.*

"What is the combination of three pairs that does not include tan?"

blue, white, black

"What is the combination of three pairs that does not include blue?"

tan, white, black

"What is the combination of three pairs that does not include white?"

tan, blue, black

"What is the combination of three pairs that does not include black?"

tan, blue, white

Check *Look back.*

"What are the combinations of shorts Garcia can pack?"

1. blue, white, black; **2.** tan, white, black; **3.** tan, blue, black; **4.** tan, blue, white

"Are our answers reasonable?"

Our answers are reasonable, because each combination we found is a combination of three pairs of shorts from the given list of four pairs.

"How did we organize our list, and how did this help us find all the combinations?"

Each possible combination does not include one of the pairs. Thus, we organized our list by thinking of the color that could be excluded and then listing the other three colors. We found a possible combination for each color of shorts that were excluded, and this means that we found all the combinations.

LESSON 61

• Estimating Arithmetic Answers

California Mathematics Content Standards

NS 1.0, 1.3 Round whole numbers through the millions to the nearest ten, hundred, thousand, ten thousand, or hundred thousand.

NS 1.0, 1.4 Decide when a rounded solution is called for and explain why such a solution may be appropriate.

NS 2.0, 2.1 Estimate and compute the sum or difference of whole numbers and positive decimals to two places.

MR 2.0, 2.5 Indicate the relative advantages of exact and approximate solutions to problems and give answers to a specified degree of accuracy.

Power Up

facts Power Up I

count aloud Count by halves from $\frac{1}{2}$ to 6 and back down to $\frac{1}{2}$.

mental math Multiply a number by 10 in problems **a–c.**

a. **Number Sense:** 12×10 120

b. **Number Sense:** 120×10 1200

c. **Number Sense:** 10×10 100

d. **Money:** Jill paid for a pencil that cost 36¢ with a $1 bill. How much change should she receive? 64¢

e. **Money:** One container of motor oil costs $3.75. How much do 2 containers cost? $7.50

f. **Fractional Part:** The whole circle has been divided into quarters. What fraction of the circle is shaded? What fraction is not shaded? $\frac{1}{4}$; $\frac{3}{4}$

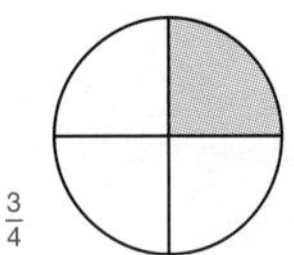

g. **Estimation:** Phil plans to buy lasagna for $5.29 and a drink for $1.79. Round each price to the nearest 25 cents and then add to estimate the total cost. $7.00

h. **Calculation:** $48 + 250 + 6 + 6$ 310

problem solving Choose an appropriate problem-solving strategy to solve this problem. Garcia is packing his clothes for summer camp. He wants to take three pairs of shorts. He has four different pairs of shorts from which to choose—tan, blue, white, and black. What are the different combinations of three pairs of shorts that Garcia can pack? Tan, blue, white; tan, blue, black; tan, white, black; blue, white, black

Facts Divide.

9 9)81	9 3)27	5 5)25	3 2)6	9 5)45	3 3)9	8 4)32	4 4)16	6 2)12	8 7)56
9 1)9	7 6)42	7 2)14	7 4)28	8 3)24	8 5)40	9 2)18	9 8)72	6 3)18	9 6)54
7 7)49	4 2)8	6 6)36	4 3)12	8 8)64	2 2)4	0 5)0	6 4)24	1 8)8	7 5)35
7 3)21	5 4)20	8 2)16	6 5)30	9 4)36	5 3)15	8 6)48	5 2)10	9 7)63	7 8)56

Power Up

Facts

Distribute **Power Up I** to students. See answers below.

Count Aloud

Before students begin the Mental Math exercise, do these counting exercises as a class.

Mental Math

Encourage students to share different ways to mentally compute these exercises. Strategies for exercises are listed below.

d. Count Up with Pennies and Dimes

36¢ + 4 pennies = 40¢;
40¢ + 6 dimes = $1;
6 dimes + 4 pennies = 64¢

Subtract Dimes, then Pennies

$1 − 60¢ = 40¢; 40¢ − 4¢ = 36¢;
60¢ + 4¢ = 64¢

e. Double $3 and Double 75¢

double $3 = $6 and double 75¢ = $1.50;
$6.00 + $1.50 = $7.50

Add $4, then Subtract 25¢

$3.75 + $4.00 = $7.75;
$7.75 − $0.25 = $7.50

Problem Solving

Refer to **Problem-Solving Discussion,** p. 409H.

New Concept

Discussion

Introduce the lesson by writing the following problem on the board or overhead:

$396 + 512 = n$ and $300 + 500 = 800$

Then ask the question below and invite a variety of explanations.

"Is the answer reasonable? Give a reason to support your answer." No; sample: 396 is about 400 and 512 is about 500, so the sum of 396 and 512 should be about $400 + 500$ or 900.

Error Alert

Remind students of the importance of checking their work, and then point out that an estimate is a practical and efficient way to check a sum, difference, product, or quotient for reasonableness.

Example 1

Ask students to describe the advantages and disadvantages of rounding the addends to the nearest ten instead of to the nearest hundred. Encourage a variety of responses, and then point out that whenever possible, mental math should be used to make an estimate, and although rounding to the nearest ten will provide an estimate that is closer to the exact sum, rounding to the nearest ten and then finding the sum of the rounded numbers is more difficult to perform mentally than rounding to the nearest hundred. For this reason, lead students to generalize that whenever a rounding place is not specified, rounding to the greatest place of one or more of the numbers will produce a reasonable estimate of the answer.

Example 2

Active Learning

After you discuss the solution, ask:

"The solution shows that the product of 70 and 5 is 350. Explain how we can find the product using only mental math." When one factor is a multiple of 10, we write the same number of zeros that are in the factors to the right of the product of the nonzero digits; $7 \times 5 = 35$, $70 \times 5 = 350$

(continued)

New Concept

We can estimate arithmetic answers by rounding numbers. Estimating does not give us the exact answer, but it can give us an answer that is close to the exact answer. For some problems, an estimate is all that is necessary to solve the problem. When an exact answer is needed, estimating is a way to decide whether our exact answer is reasonable. Estimating is useful for many purposes, such as mentally adding price totals when shopping.

Example 1

Estimate the sum of 396 and 512.

> **Thinking Skills**
> **Discuss**
> Which place is used to round a 3-digit number to the nearest hundred?
>
> tens place

To estimate, we first round the number to the nearest hundred. We round 396 to 400 and 512 to 500. Then we find the estimated sum by adding 400 and 500.

$$\begin{array}{r} 400 \\ +\ 500 \\ \hline 900 \end{array}$$

The estimated sum of 396 and 512 is **900.** The exact sum of 396 and 512 is 908. The estimated answer is not equal to the exact answer, but it is close.

Example 2

Estimate the product of 72 and 5.

> **Thinking Skills**
> **Connect**
> Which place is used to round a 2-digit number to the nearest ten?
>
> ones place

$$\begin{array}{r} 70 \\ \times\ 5 \\ \hline 350 \end{array}$$

We round the two-digit number, but we generally do not round a one-digit number when estimating. The estimated product of 72 and 5 is **350.**

The exact product of 72 and 5 is 360. The estimated product is a little less than the exact answer, 360, because 72 was rounded down to 70 for the estimate.

Example 3

To estimate 7 × 365, Towanda multiplied 7 by 400. Was Towanda's estimate more than, equal to, or less than the actual product of 7 and 365?

Towanda's estimate was **more than the actual product** of 7 and 365 because she rounded 365 up to 400 before multiplying.

English Learners

Tell students that **reasonable** means acceptable, sensible, logical, sound, understandable. So when checking whether an answer is **reasonable,** students are checking if it is sensible. Ask:

"What are some reasonable estimates of the product of 72 × 5? Show how you estimated the product." 350; $70 \times 5 = 350$

Example 4

Estimate the answer to 43 ÷ 8.

To estimate division answers, we want to use numbers that divide easily, so we change the problem slightly. We keep the number we are dividing by, which is 8, and we change the number that is being divided, which is 43, to a compatible number. We change 43 to a nearby number that can be divided easily by 8, such as 40 or 48. Using 40, the estimated answer is **5.** Using 48, the estimated answer is **6.** Since 43 is between 40 and 48, the actual answer is more than 5 but less than 6. That is, the exact answer is 5 plus a remainder.

Example 5

Nicola wants to buy a box of cereal for $5.89, a gallon of milk for $3.80, and a half gallon of juice for $2.20. Nicola has $13.00. Does she have enough to pay for the groceries?

Thinking Skills

Verify

How do we round $3.80 to the nearest dollar? Explain your thinking.

Sample: 80¢ is greater than 50¢, so I rounded up to the next dollar.

Since we don't need an exact answer we can round the prices of each item to the nearest dollar.

The cereal cost $5.89, which is closer to $6 than to $5.

The milk cost $3.80, which is closer to $4 than to $3.

The juice cost $2.20, which is closer to $2 than to $3.

Item	Price	Rounded to the Nearest Dollar
cereal	$5.89	$6
milk	$3.80	$4
juice	$2.20	$2

To estimate the total, we add the rounded numbers.

$6 + $4 + $2 = $12

Nicola's estimated grocery bill was **about $12.**

Explain Suppose that Nicola wanted to be sure she had enough money to purchase all of the items *before* she reached the checkout line. How should she round the prices? Explain your reasoning.

Sample: She should round all of the prices up to the next dollar so that she knows she has enough.

Inclusion

Use this strategy if the student displays:

- Difficulty with Abstract Concept Processing.
- Difficulty with Logical Reasoning.

Estimating Arithmetic Answers
(Individual)

Materials: number line

- Write 56 × 7 on the board. Have students use a number line to round 56 to the nearest ten. Ask:

"What multiplication problem will we use to estimate the product?" 60 × 7

Have students find the estimate and the actual product and compare them.

Math Background

There are other estimation methods that are useful in certain situations. For example, *clustering* is useful for estimating the sum of several numbers that are close to the same value. For example, consider this sum:

$$\begin{array}{r} 378 \\ 412 \\ 423 \\ 390 \\ +\ 409 \\ \hline \end{array}$$

There are 5 addends, and all 5 are fairly close to 400, so we can estimate their sum by multiplying 400 by 5.

$$\begin{array}{r} 400 \\ \times\ \ 5 \\ \hline 2000 \end{array}$$

New Concept *(Continued)*

Example 3

Active Learning

Ask students to describe three different generalizations that can be used to decide if an estimate will be more than, less than, or approximately equal to an actual product. Sample: If both factors are rounded up, the estimate will be greater than the product; If both factors are rounded down, the estimate will be less than the product; If one factor is rounded up and the other factor is rounded down, the estimate will be close to the product.

Example 4

Connection

As you discuss the solution, remind students that compatible numbers are numbers that are easy to divide mentally because they are related division facts.

Extend the Example

Challenge your advanced learners to name a compatible dividend they would use to estimate each of these quotients.

75 ÷ 9 55 ÷ 6 25 ÷ 4

Point out that changing 75 ÷ 9 to 72 ÷ 9, changing 55 ÷ 6 to 54 ÷ 6, and changing 25 ÷ 4 to 24 ÷ 4 is different than rounding because 75 rounds to 80, 55 rounds to 60, and 25 rounds to 30. Then remind students again that compatible numbers are numbers that are easy to divide mentally because they are related division facts.

Example 5

After students talk about possible answers for the **Explain** question, lead them to generalize that it is always a good idea to round amounts up when deciding if there is enough money to make a purchase. Point out that rounding up increases the certainty of knowing if there is enough money, and given that many purchases also involve sales tax (which can be difficult to compute), rounding up also helps compensate for possible taxes.

(continued)

New Concept (Continued)

Lesson Practice

Guided Practice

Use these problems as guided practice to check the students' understanding of today's concept.

Problem i (Explain)

Make sure students understand that because 5000 is less than 5280, the product of 5000 × 5 will be less than the product of 5280 × 5.

Then ask them to explain how to find the product of 5 and 5000 using only mental math. Write three zeros to the right of the product of 5 × 5; 5 × 5000 = 25,000

Problems a–h

Error Alert

Because the rounding places are not indicated, explain that students should round to the greatest place. Point out that in problem **a,** for example, the greatest place is the tens place.

After students find the exact answers, remind them to decide the reasonableness of those answers by comparing them to the estimates.

Closure The questions below help assess the concepts taught in this lesson.

"Explain how to use compatible numbers to estimate the quotient of 65 ÷ 8." Sample: Rounding 65 to 70 would make it difficult to find the quotient using only mental math, so we change 65 to 64, then divide; A reasonable estimate of 65 ÷ 8 is 64 ÷ 8 or 8.

"How can we know if an estimated sum or product will be greater than or less than the exact answer?" Sample: When adding or multiplying, if the numbers are rounded up, the estimate will be greater than the exact answer; If the numbers are rounded down, the estimate will be less than the exact answer.

"Why is estimating an important skill?" Sample: It is a fast way to check an exact answer for reasonableness.

Lesson Practice

Estimate the answer to each arithmetic problem. Then find the exact answer.

a. 59 + 68 + 81 210; 208 **b.** 607 + 891 1500; 1498

c. 585 − 294 300; 291 **d.** 82 − 39 40; 43

e. 59 × 6 360; 354 **f.** 397 × 4 1600; 1588

g. 42 ÷ 5 8; 8 R 2 **h.** 29 ÷ 7 4; 4 R 1

i. (Explain) Dixie estimated the product of 5 and 5280 by multiplying 5 by 5000. Was Dixie's estimate more than, equal to, or less than the actual product? Why?

i. Dixie's estimate was less than the actual product because she rounded 5280 down to 5000 before multiplying.

j. Mariano would like to purchase a notebook computer, a wireless mouse, and an accessory carrying bag. The cost of each item is shown in the table.

Item	Cost
Notebook computer	$845
Wireless mouse	$27.50
Accessory bag	$39.95

What is a reasonable estimate of Mariano's total cost? Explain your thinking. Sample: Sales tax will increase the cost of each item, so I rounded the cost of each item up before adding; A reasonable estimate of the total cost is $900 + $30 + $40, or $970.

Written Practice

Distributed and Integrated

▸ ***1.** (58) A comfortable walking pace is about 3 miles per hour. How far would a person walk in 4 hours at a pace of 3 miles per hour? Make a table to solve the problem. 12 miles

Hours	Miles
1	3
2	6
3	9
4	12

2. (60) The Johnson Family drank 33 glasses of milk in 3 days. How many glasses of milk is that each day? 11 glasses

Alternative Approach: Using Manipulatives

To help students understand the concept of estimating products, have them write the multiples of 100 from 100 to 1,000 on separate index cards. Ask students to estimate the product for 275 × 5. First have students find the number on a card that is closest to 275. Explain that 275 is closest to 300. Explain to students that they can use basic facts and patterns to estimate the product of 300 × 5. Have students estimate the product of additional multiplication problems with 3-digits. The same process can be followed to estimate the product of problems with 4-digits.

▸ *3. (Inv. 3, 31) a. **Analyze** Find the perimeter and area of this rectangle. Remember to label your answer with "units" or "square units". 22 units; 24 square units

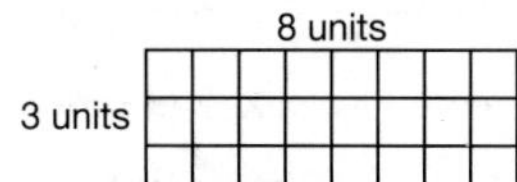

b. **Represent** Sketch a rectangle that is four units wide with the same area as the rectangle in part **a.** What is the perimeter of this new rectangle?

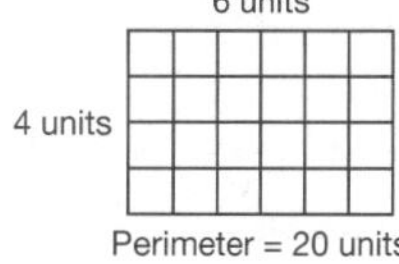

▸ 4. (55) **Multiple Choice** Which of these numbers is *not* a factor of 12? B

A 6 **B** 5 **C** 4 **D** 3

5. (13) The starting time was before sunrise. The stopping time was in the afternoon. What was the difference between the two times? 12 hours 5 minutes

6. (47) **Represent** One square mile is 3,097,600 square yards. Use words to write that number of square yards. three million, ninety-seven thousand, six hundred square yards

7. (57) a. What fraction of this pentagon is not shaded? $\frac{3}{5}$

b. Is the shaded part of this pentagon more than $\frac{1}{2}$ or less than $\frac{1}{2}$ of the pentagon? less than $\frac{1}{2}$

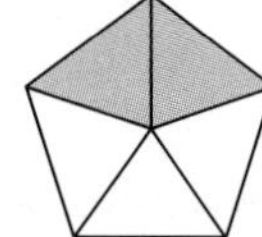

8. (RF12) According to this calendar, what is the date of the last Saturday in July 2019? July 27, 2019

JULY 2019

S	M	T	W	T	F	S
	1	2	3	4	5	6
7	8	9	10	11	12	13
14	15	16	17	18	19	20
21	22	23	24	25	26	27
28	29	30	31			

Written Practice

Math Conversations

Independent Practice and Discussions to Increase Understanding

Problem 1

Extend the Problem

Challenge advanced learners to write an equation that can be used to find the distance walked in miles (m) for any number of hours (h). Sample: $m = 3h$ or $m = 3 \cdot h$

Ask them to write an equation that can be used to find the number of hours walked (h) for any number of miles walked (m). Sample: $h = m/3$ or $h = m \div 3$

Problem 3a **Analyze**

Extend the Problem

"What other rectangles will have an area of 24 square units? Find the perimeter of each rectangle you name." Possible rectangles: 1 row of 24 squares, $P = 50$ units; 2 rows of 12 squares, $P = 28$ units; 4 rows of 6 squares, $P = 20$ units; 6 rows of 4 squares, $P = 20$ units; 8 rows of 3 squares, $P = 22$ units; 12 rows of 2 squares, $P = 28$ units; 24 rows of 1 square, $P = 50$ units

Problem 4 **Multiple Choice**

Test-Taking Strategy

Before students solve the problem, ask:

"What is the remainder when a number is divided by a factor of itself? Give an example to support your answer." Zero; sample: 2 is a factor of 6 and $6 \div 2 = 3$ R 0

"How can we use this fact to help find the correct answer to problem 4?" Divide 12 by each choice; A division that produces a remainder is the correct choice.

Extend the Problem

"Write a digit after 12 to change it to a three-digit number that has all four choices as factors." 120

(continued)

Written Practice *(Continued)*

Math Conversations *(cont.)*

Problem 9 **Estimate**

Invite volunteers to share their examples with the class.

Problem 11 **Justify**

Lead students to generalize from the problem and its solution that whenever a rounding place is not indicated, one or more numbers should be rounded to the greatest place. In this example, the greatest place is tens.

Problem 22

Prior to completing the arithmetic, ask students to decide if 600 × 3 is a reasonable estimate of the exact answer, explain why or why not, and then name the product.

600 × 3 is a reasonable estimate because 600 is close to 603; 600 × 3 = 1800

After completing the arithmetic, remind students to use the estimate to help decide the reasonableness of the exact answer.

Problems 23–25

Ask students to use compatible numbers and make an estimate of each quotient before completing the arithmetic, and then use the estimate to help decide the reasonableness of the exact answer.

(continued)

▶ ***9.** (61) **Estimate** To estimate the product of two factors, a student rounded one factor down and left the other factor unchanged. Was the estimate greater than the exact product or less than the exact product? Give an example to support your answer. Less than; sample: The exact product of 5 × 12 is 60, but rounding 12 to the nearest ten produces a product of 5 × 10, or 50.

10. (32) **Represent** To what mixed number is the arrow pointing? $7\frac{5}{8}$

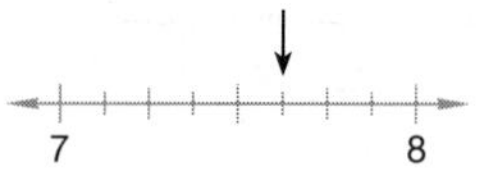

▶ ***11.** (61) **Justify** Sofia estimated that the exact product of 4 × 68 is close to 400 because 68 rounded to the nearest hundred is 100, and 4 × 100 = 400. Was Sofia's estimate reasonable? Explain why or why not. No; sample: A better estimate would be to round 68 to the nearest ten instead of to the nearest hundred; 4 × 70 = 280

***12.** (47) **Represent** Which of the following is the number 3,003,016? B

A three million, three hundred sixteen
B three million, three thousand, sixteen
C three hundred million, sixteen
D three hundred million, three thousand, sixteen

13. (28) \$6.25 + \$4 + \$12.78 \$23.03

14. (45) 3.6 + 12.4 + 0.84 16.84

15. (8, 28, 52) \$30.25 − b = \$13.06 \$17.19

16. (52) 149,384 − 98,765 = 50,619

***17.** (59) 409 × 7 = 2863

18. (59) 5 × \$3.46 \$17.30

19. (59) \$0.79 × 6 \$4.74

20. (51) 155,340 + 32,688 = 188,028

21. (37) 600 × 6 = 3600

▶ ***22.** (59) 607 × 3 = 1821

▶ ***23.** (54) 45 ÷ 6 7 R 3

▶ ***24.** (54) $\frac{83}{9}$ 9 R 2

▶ ***25.** (54) $7\overline{)60}$ 8 R 4

*26. (Inv. 6) This line plot shows the number of times some students visit the city zoo each year. Use this line plot to answer parts **a–c.**

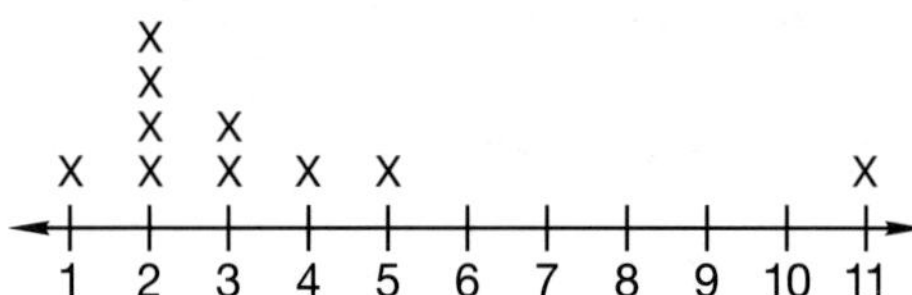

a. How many students were surveyed? 10 students

b. What is the mode? 2 visits

c. Is there an outlier? If yes, what is it? 11 visits

▸ **27.** (Inv. 4) Name the shaded part of this rectangle as a fraction and as a decimal. $\frac{3}{10}$; 0.3

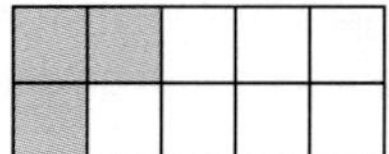

28. (29) How much money is $\frac{1}{4}$ of a dollar? 25¢

▸*29. (50) **Represent** Draw a hexagon. A hexagon has how many vertices? See student work; 6 vertices

Written Practice *(Continued)*

Math Conversations *(cont.)*

Problem 27

Extend the Problem

Ask students to name the unshaded part of the rectangle as a fraction and as a decimal. $\frac{7}{10}$, 0.7

Problem 29 **Represent**

Have volunteers draw their different hexagons on the board or overhead. Point out to the class that the question did not ask for a regular hexagon. Any 6-sided closed figure would have been correct.

Problem 30 **Interpret**

Extend the Problem

To provide additional practice collecting and choosing an appropriate graph for displaying data, encourage interested students to choose a topic for which they can collect weekly data, display that data in an appropriate graph, and then share their findings with their classmates. Data suggestions include recording daily precipitation amounts or time of local sunrises and sunsets.

(continued)

Written Practice (Continued)

Errors and Misconceptions

Problem 17

Students can make a wide variety of errors when a number with an internal zero (such as 409) is multiplied by another number. Make sure students understand that in this problem:

- the product of the ones place is 63 ones, and we write 3 ones and regroup 60 ones as 6 tens by writing 6 in the tens column;
- the product of the tens place is 0, and we write 6 in the tens place because the sum of 0 and the 6 regrouped tens is 6;
- the product of the hundreds place is 28 hundreds, and we write 8 in the hundreds column and write 2 in the thousands column to show the regrouping of 20 hundreds as 2 thousands.

After students solve the problems, engage students in a discussion about the practical uses of polygons in everyday life. Pose the following question:

"Why do you suppose traffic signs, like stop signs and speed limit signs, use shapes like octagons and rectangles instead of tridecagons and pentadecagons?" See student work.

***30.** (Inv. 5) **Interpret** The line graph shows the temperature at different times on a winter morning at Hayden's school. Use the graph to answer the questions that follow.

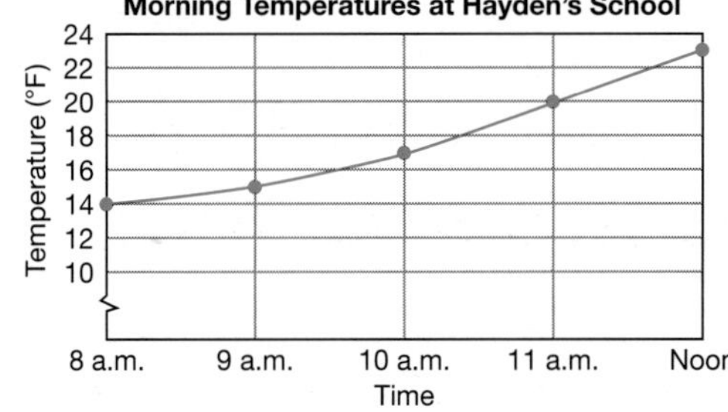

a. At what time was the first temperature of the morning recorded? What was that temperature? 8 a.m.; 14°F

b. Was the noon temperature warmer or colder than the 10 a.m. temperature? How many degrees warmer or colder? Warmer; 6°F

Real-World Connection

How many line segments make up a pentagon? That's easy, right? The answer is 5. How many line segments make up a pentacontagon? Not so easy. The answer is 50. A pentacontagon is not commonly known, but it is indeed a polygon. Refer to the table to learn the names and attributes of less commonly known polygons.

Name of Polygon	Number of Sides
heptagon	7
nonagon	9
hendecagon	11
tridecagon	13
pentadecagon	15

a. Name a polygon that has 8 less sides than a tridecagon. pentagon

b. Name a polygon that has more sides than a heptagon but fewer sides than a nonagon. octagon

c. Name a polygon that has 12 more sides than a triangle. pentadecagon

d. Choose two polygons from the table above and draw models of them. See student work.

Looking Forward

Estimating arithmetic answers prepares students for:

- **Lesson 62,** rounding to the nearest tenth.
- **Lesson 65,** evaluating an exponential expression for a given value.
- **Lesson 71,** multiplying by multiples of 10.
- **Lesson 79,** division with three-digit quotients.
- **Lesson 84,** multiplying whole numbers and money amounts by 10, 100, and 1000.
- **Lesson 85,** multiplying two or more multiples of 10 and 100.
- **Lessons 86 and 88,** multiplying two-digit numbers.
- **Lesson 91,** estimating multiplication and division answers.
- **Lesson 92,** comparing and ordering fractions and decimals using a number line.
- **Lesson 104,** rounding whole numbers through hundred millions.
- **Lesson 107,** multiplying a three-digit number by a two-digit number.

Planning & Preparation

• Rounding to the Nearest Tenth

Objectives

- Use a number line to round two-place decimal numbers to the nearest tenth.
- Round money amounts to the nearest dime.
- Estimate the sum or difference to a word problem involving decimals.

Prerequisite Skills

- Identifying place value of a digit in a decimal through hundredths.
- Locating and naming tenths and hundredths on a number line.
- Estimating the sum or difference for a word problem.

Materials

Instructional Masters

- Power Up I Worksheet
- Lesson Activity 14*

Manipulative Kit

- Rulers

Teacher-provided materials

- Number line, place-value chart*

**optional*

California Mathematics Content Standards

NS 1.0, 1.2 Order and compare whole numbers and decimals to two decimal places.

NS 1.0, 1.4 Decide when a rounded solution is called for and explain why such a solution may be appropriate.

NS 1.0, 1.9 Identify on a number line the relative position of positive fractions, positive mixed numbers, and positive decimals to two decimal places.

NS 2.0, 2.1 Estimate and compute the sum or difference of whole numbers and positive decimals to two places.

NS 2.0, 2.2 Round two-place decimals to one decimal or the nearest whole number and judge the reasonableness of the rounded answer.

MR 2.0, 2.1 Use estimation to verify the reasonableness of calculated results.

MR 2.0, 2.3 Use a variety of methods, such as words, numbers, symbols, charts, graphs, tables, diagrams, and models, to explain mathematical reasoning.

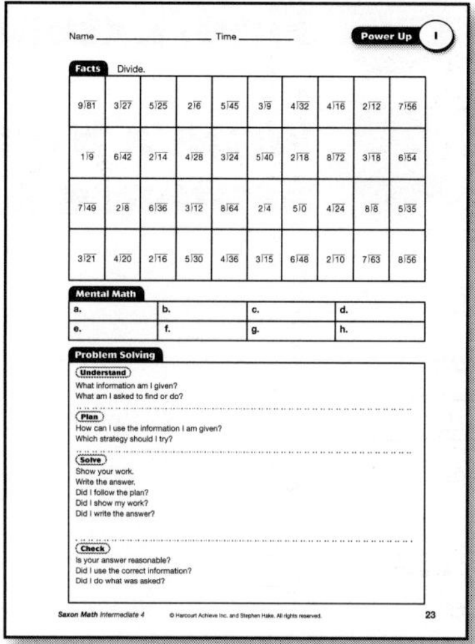

Name ____________ Time ________ **Power Up I**

Facts Divide.

$9\overline{)81}$	$3\overline{)27}$	$5\overline{)25}$	$2\overline{)6}$	$5\overline{)45}$	$3\overline{)9}$	$4\overline{)32}$	$4\overline{)16}$	$2\overline{)12}$	$7\overline{)56}$
$1\overline{)9}$	$6\overline{)42}$	$2\overline{)14}$	$4\overline{)28}$	$3\overline{)24}$	$5\overline{)40}$	$2\overline{)18}$	$8\overline{)72}$	$3\overline{)18}$	$6\overline{)54}$
$7\overline{)49}$	$2\overline{)8}$	$6\overline{)36}$	$3\overline{)12}$	$8\overline{)64}$	$2\overline{)4}$	$5\overline{)0}$	$4\overline{)24}$	$8\overline{)8}$	$5\overline{)35}$
$3\overline{)21}$	$4\overline{)20}$	$2\overline{)16}$	$5\overline{)30}$	$4\overline{)36}$	$3\overline{)15}$	$6\overline{)48}$	$2\overline{)10}$	$7\overline{)63}$	$8\overline{)56}$

Mental Math

a.	b.	c.	d.
e.	f.	g.	h.

Problem Solving

Understand
What information am I given?
What am I asked to find or do?

Plan
How can I use the information I am given?
Which strategy should I try?

Solve
Show your work.
Write the answer.
Did I follow the plan?
Did I show my work?
Did I write the answer?

Check
Is your answer reasonable?
Did I use the correct information?
Did I do what was asked?

Saxon Math Intermediate 4 23

Power Up I Worksheet

Universal Access

Reaching All Special Needs Students

Special Education Students	At-Risk Students	English Learners	Advanced Learners
• Inclusion (TM) • Adaptations for Saxon Math	• Alternative Approach (TM) • Error Alert (TM) • Reteaching Masters • Refresher Lessons for California Standards	• English Learners (TM) • Developing Academic Language (TM) • English Learner Handbook	• Extend the Example (TM) • Extend the Problem (TM) • Early Finisher (SE) • Online Activities

TM=Teacher's Manual

Developing Academic Language

New	**Maintained**	**English Learner**
equivalent decimals	tenth	freestyle

Problem Solving Discussion

Problem

The following page shows a sequence of triangular numbers. The third term in the sequence, 6, is the number of dots in a triangular arrangement of dots with three rows. Notice that in this sequence the count from one number to the next increases. Find the number of dots in a triangular arrangement with 8 rows. Explain how you arrived at your answer and how you can verify your answer.

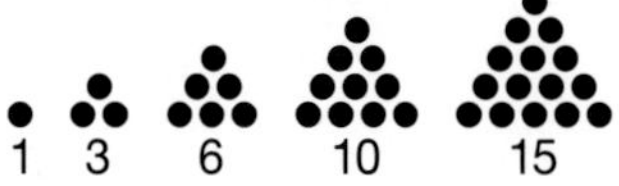

Focus Strategies

Find/Extend a Pattern

2+3=5 **Write a Number Sentence or Equation**

Understand *Understand the problem.*

"What information are we given?"

We are shown a sequence of triangular numbers (1, 3, 6, 10, and 15) and their pictorial representations.

"What are we asked to do?"

We are asked to find the number of dots in a triangular pattern with 8 rows of dots.

Plan *Make a plan.*

"What problem-solving strategy can we use?"

We can *find and extend a pattern* that describes the number of dots.

Solve *Carry out the plan.*

"At the top of each triangle is 1 dot. Below the top dot are 2 dots. Thus, in the first two rows of each triangular arrangement, there are 1 + 2 = 3 dots. What number sentence describes the number of dots in the top three rows?"

There are $1 + 2 + 3 = 6$ dots in the top three rows.

"What number sentence can we write to find the number of dots in a triangular arrangement with 4 rows? ... 5 rows? ... 6 rows? ... 7 rows? ... 8 rows?"

$$1 + 2 + 3 + 4 = 10$$
$$1 + 2 + 3 + 4 + 5 = 15$$
$$1 + 2 + 3 + 4 + 5 + 6 = 21$$
$$1 + 2 + 3 + 4 + 5 + 6 + 7 = 28$$
$$1 + 2 + 3 + 4 + 5 + 6 + 7 + 8 = 36$$

Check *Look back.*

"How many dots are in a triangular arrangement with 8 rows?"

36 dots

"Is our answer reasonable?"

We know that our answer is reasonable, because the numbers of dots follow a pattern. We see that the increase from one triangular number to the next is a sequence of counting numbers:

+2 +3 +4 +5 +6 +7 +8
1 3 6 10 15 21 28 36

"What problem-solving strategies did we use, and how did they help us?"

We *found a pattern* that helped us *write a number sentence* to find the number of dots in a triangular pattern with 8 rows.

Alternate Strategy
Draw a Picture or Diagram; Act It Out or Make a Model

To help students check their answer, have them draw a diagram of an arrangement with 8 rows. Students can also *make a model* by using counters to build a triangular arrangement with 8 rows.

LESSON 62

• Rounding to the Nearest Tenth

California Mathematics Content Standards

NS 1.0, 1.9 Identify on a number line the relative position of positive fractions, positive mixed numbers, and positive decimals to two decimal places.
NS 2.0, 2.1 Estimate and compute the sum or difference of whole numbers and positive decimals to two places.
NS 2.0, 2.2 Round two-place decimals to one decimal or the nearest whole number and judge the reasonableness of the rounded answer.
MR 2.0, 2.1 Use estimation to verify the reasonableness of calculated results.

Power Up

facts Power Up I

count aloud Count by fourths from $5\frac{1}{4}$ to 10.

mental math

a. **Number Sense:** 14 × 10 140

b. **Money:** Sean bought a ream of paper for $6.47 and a box of staples for $1.85. What was the total cost? $8.32

c. **Fractional Parts:** Compare: $\frac{1}{4} < \frac{1}{2}$

d. **Geometry:** What is the perimeter of a square that is 6 inches on each side? 24 in. or 2 ft

e. **Time:** Crystal phoned her friend at 4:05 p.m. They talked for 22 minutes. What time did Crystal's phone call end? 4:27 p.m.

f. **Measurement:** Ray cut a 1-foot length of string from a larger piece that was 22 inches long. How many inches of string remained? 10 in.

g. **Estimation:** Washington School has 258 students. Lincoln School has 241 students. Round each number to the nearest ten and then add to estimate the total number of students. 500 students

h. **Calculation:** 400 + 37 + 210 − 17 630

problem solving Choose an appropriate problem-solving strategy to solve this problem. The following page shows a sequence of triangular numbers. The third term in the sequence, 6, is the number of dots in a triangular arrangement of dots with three rows. Notice that in this sequence the count from one number to the next increases. Find the number of dots in a triangular arrangement with 8 rows. Explain how you arrived at your answer and how you can verify your answer.

Facts Divide.

9 9)81	9 3)27	5 5)25	3 2)6	9 5)45	3 3)9	8 4)32	4 4)16	6 2)12	8 7)56
9 1)9	7 6)42	7 2)14	7 4)28	8 3)24	8 5)40	9 2)18	9 8)72	6 3)18	9 6)54
7 7)49	4 2)8	6 6)36	4 3)12	8 8)64	2 2)4	0 5)0	6 4)24	1 8)8	7 5)35
7 3)21	5 4)20	8 2)16	6 5)30	9 4)36	5 3)15	8 6)48	5 2)10	9 7)63	7 8)56

Power Up

Facts
Distribute **Power Up I** to students. See answers below.

Count Aloud
Before students begin the Mental Math exercise, do these counting exercises as a class.

Mental Math
Encourage students to share different ways to mentally compute these exercises. Strategies for exercises are listed below.

b. Subtract 15¢ and Add 15¢
$6.47 − 15¢ = $6.32; $1.85 + 15¢ = $2;
$6.32 + $2.00 = $8.32

Add $2, then Subtract 15¢
$6.47 + $2.00 = $8.47;
$8.47 − $0.15 = $8.32

h. Compute from Left to Right
400 + 37 = 437; 437 + 210 = 647;
647 − 17 = 630

Decompose 17
400 + 37 + 210 − 10 − 7; 437 + 200 − 7;
637 − 7 = 630

Problem Solving
Refer to **Problem-Solving Discussion,** p. 417B.

New Concept

Discussion

Introduce the lesson by asking volunteers to describe various methods that can be used to round numbers, and give an example of each method.

Active Learning

As you discuss the explanation of how to round 1.26 to the nearest tenth, ask:

"On this number line, what number in tenths is less than 1.26?" 1.2

"What number in tenths is greater than 1.26?" 1.3

"What number is halfway between 1.2 and 1.3?" 1.25

"When rounding to the nearest tenth, 1.26 rounds to 1.3. Explain why." Sample: On the number line, 1.26 is to the right of 1.25, and since 1.26 is greater than 1.25, 1.26 rounds to 1.3.

Example 1

Active Learning

Before discussing the solution, ask:

"Does this number line show numbers in tenths or in hundredths? Explain your answer. " Both tenths and hundredths; 7.5 and 7.6 are numbers in tenths, and the numbers from 7.50 to 7.60 are numbers in hundredths.

"What number is halfway between 7.50 and 7.60?" 7.55

Example 2

Error Alert

Make sure students understand that because we are rounding each amount to the nearest ten cents, the rounded amounts must be multiples of a dime, and $42.43 must be rounded to either $42.40 or to $42.50, and $40.68 must be rounded to either $40.60 or to $40.70.

Also make sure students understand that because the **Analyze** question is asking them to round to the nearest quarter, the rounded amounts must be multiples of 25¢. Therefore, $42.43 must be rounded to either $42.25 or to $42.50 (the nearest multiples of 25¢), and $40.68 must be rounded to either $40.50 or to $40.75 (the nearest multiples of 25¢).

Extend the Example

Challenge your advanced learners to find the total amount paid for gasoline for the two months rounded to the nearest ten cents.

(continued)

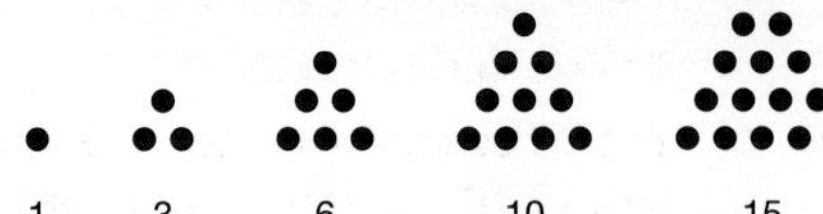

36 dots; sample: I found the answer by continuing the sequence and verified by drawing triangular patterns.

New Concept

We learned to use a number line to round a two place decimal to the nearest whole number. We can also use a number line to round a two place decimal to the nearest tenth. This number line is divided into ten equal segments. In Lesson 44 we learned that 1.2 and 1.20 are **equivalent decimals,** which is shown in the art below.

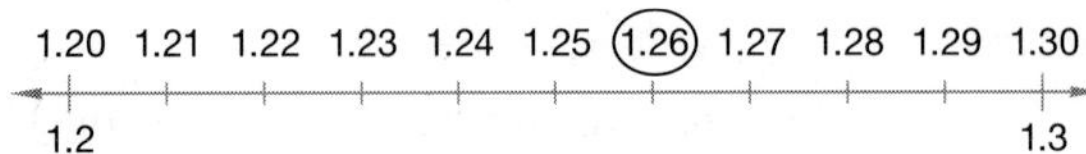

The decimal number 1.26 is between 1.2 and 1.3. We can see that 1.26 is closer to 1.3 than it is to 1.2. So, 1.26 rounded to the nearest tenth is 1.3.

Explain What is 1.25 rounded to the nearest tenth? Explain why. 1.3; 1.25 is halfway between 1.2 and 1.3, so we round up.

Example 1

Round 7.52 to the nearest tenth.

Rounding 7.52 to the nearest tenth is the same as rounding $7.52 to the nearest ten cents. Just as $7.52 is between $7.50 and $7.60, 7.52 is between 7.5 and 7.6, as shown on the number line below.

7.50 7.51 (7.52) 7.53 7.54 7.55 7.56 7.57 7.58 7.59 7.60
7.5 7.6

We can see that 7.52 is closer to 7.5 than 7.6, so, 7.52 rounded to the nearest tenth is **7.50 or 7.5.**

Example 2

Last month, Mr. Garcia paid $40.68 for a tank of gasoline. This month he paid $42.43 for a tank of gas. To the nearest ten cents, how much more did he pay this month?

Since we are asked to find the amount to the nearest ten cents, we will round both numbers to the nearest dime. Then we can subtract.

Math Background

Rounding is not to be confused with **truncation,** which refers to reducing the number of digits to the right of a decimal point by discarding them. For example:

2.1946883 truncated to 4 decimals is 2.1946

32.00012 truncated to 4 decimals is 32.0001

In some cases, rounding and truncating will produce the same results. When this occurs, it is merely coincidence. Truncation does not round up or down; it merely shortens a number to a particular number of digits.

Alternative Approach: Using Manipulatives

To assist students in rounding to different place-value positions, display a number in a place-value chart. Ask students to round the number to the nearest tenth. Ask:

"Why do you look at the digit to the right of the tenth's place?" The digit to the right determines whether the digit in the tenth's place will increase by 1 or stay the same.

$42.43 rounds to $42.40

$40.68 rounds to $40.70

$$\begin{array}{r} \$42.40 \\ -\ \$40.70 \\ \hline \$1.70 \end{array}$$

To the nearest ten cents Mr. Garcia paid **$1.70** more for a tank of gas this month.

Analyze How much more did Mr. Garcia pay to the nearest quarter? $42.50 − $40.75 = $1.75

Example 3

Mrs. Jensen bought 1.33 pounds of cheddar cheese and 1.86 pounds of Swiss cheese. To the nearest tenth of a pound, how much cheese did she buy altogether?

Since we are asked to find the amount to the nearest tenth of a pound, we need to round both numbers to the nearest tenth. Then we can add.

1.33 rounds to 1.30

1.86 rounds to 1.90

$$\begin{array}{r} 1.30 \\ +1.90 \\ \hline 3.20 \end{array}$$

To the nearest tenth of a pound, Mrs. Jensen bought **3.2 pounds** of cheese.

Analyze How can you check that the estimate is reasonable? Sample: Round to the nearest whole number, 1 + 2 = 3.

Lesson Practice Round each number to the nearest ten cents:

a. $4.79 $4.80 **b.** $3.25 $3.30 **c.** $0.33 $0.30

Round each number to the nearest tenth:

d. 5.43 5.40 or 5.4 **e.** 0.47 0.50 or 0.5 **f.** 3.62 3.60 or 3.6

Round each number to the nearest quarter:

g. $0.89 $1 **h.** $1.46 $1.50 **i.** $1.10 $1

j. Beth and Tamarra competed in a 100-meter freestyle swim race. Beth finished in 51.9 seconds. Tamarra finished in 50.39 seconds. To the nearest tenth of a second, how much faster was Tamarra? 1.5 seconds

English Learners

Explain to students that swimming **freestyle** is a competition in which any stroke may be used, according to the swimmer's choice. Say:

"Swimmers can choose many different ways of swimming in a freestyle competition."

"What are some strokes you might see in a freestyle swimming race?" Samples: the crawl, the butterfly, the backstroke

New Concept *(Continued)*

Example 3

Active Learning

Prior to discussing the solution, ask:

"What are the only two possible answers when rounding 1.33 to the nearest tenth?" 1.3 or 1.4

"What are the only two possible answers when rounding 1.86 to the nearest tenth?" 1.8 or 1.9

Lesson Practice

Guided Practice

Use these problems as guided practice to check the students' understanding of today's concept.

Problem j

Challenge advanced learners to name the exact number of seconds using only mental math. 1.51 sec

Problems a–f
Error Alert

Prior to rounding each number, ask students to name the digit that is in the rounding place, and name the two possible amounts or numbers that each amount or number can be rounded to.

a: 7; $4.70 or $4.80

b: 2; $3.20 or $3.30

c: 3; $0.30 or $0.40

d: 4; 5.4 or 5.5

e: 4; 0.4 or 0.5

f: 6; 3.6 or 3.7

Problems g–i
Error Alert

Prior to rounding each number, ask students to name the two multiples of 25¢ that represent the possible amounts that each amount can be rounded to.

g: $0.75 or $1.00

h: $1.25 or $1.50

i: $1.00 or $1.25

Closure **The questions below help assess the concepts taught in this lesson.**

"What is 2.74 rounded to the nearest tenth? Explain why you named that number." 2.7; sample: 2.74 is between 2.7 and 2.8; 2.74 rounds to 2.7 because 2.74 is closer to 2.7 than to 2.8.

"Explain how to round an amount of money to the nearest dime and to the nearest quarter." Sample: To round an amount to the nearest dime, choose the multiple of 10¢ that the amount is nearest; To round an amount to the nearest quarter, choose the multiple of 25¢ that the amount is nearest.

Written Practice

Math Conversations

Independent Practice and Discussions to Increase Understanding

Problem 1 (Analyze)

Extend the Problem

Challenge advanced learners to write an equation that can be used to find the distance walked in miles (m) for any number of hours (h). Sample: $m = 6h$ or $m = 6 \cdot h$

Then have them write an equation that can be used to find the number of hours walked (h) for any number of miles walked (m). Sample: $h = m/6$ or $h = m \div 6$

Problems 5–7

Ask students to make an estimate of each product before completing the arithmetic, and then use the estimate to help decide the reasonableness of the exact answer. (Remind students that whenever possible, they should use mental math to make estimates.) Sample:

problem **5:** A reasonable estimate is 1500 because 470 rounds to 500 and 500 × 3 is 1500.

problem **6:** A reasonable estimate is 2400 because 394 rounds to 400 and 6 × 400 is 2400.

problem **7:** A reasonable estimate is 3600 because 856 rounds to 900 and 900 × 4 is 3600.

Problem 8a (Interpret)

"Before we name the median, how must we arrange these numbers?" From least to greatest or from greatest to least

Problem 10 (Model)

"What denominator is present in each of the mixed numbers?" 3 or thirds

"Into how many equal parts should we divide the distance between the consecutive whole numbers on our number line? Explain why you named that number." Three; sample: Dividing the number line into thirds will allow us to show the locations of $1\frac{2}{3}$ and $2\frac{1}{3}$.

(continued)

Written Practice

Distributed and Integrated

▶ *1. (58) (Analyze) Alphonso ran 6 miles per hour. At that rate, how far could he run in 3 hours? Make a table to solve this problem. 18 miles

Hours	Miles
1	6
2	12
3	18

2. (20) Find the perimeter and area of this rectangle: 22 units; 30 square units

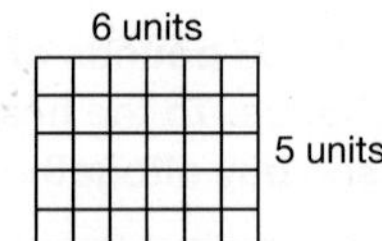

3. (Inv. 4) (Represent) Aletta ran 100 meters in twelve and fourteen hundredths seconds. Use digits to write her time. 12.14 seconds

4. (50) Taydren drew an octagon and a pentagon. How many sides did the two polygons have altogether? 13 sides

▶ *5. (59) 470 × 3 1410 ▶ *6. (59) 6 × 394 2364 ▶ *7. (59) 856 × 4 3424

*8. (Inv. 6) (Interpret) Use this set of data to answer parts **a** and **b**.

5, 3, 6, 5, 9, 1, 5, 4, 3

▶ **a.** What is the median? 5 should be 9?

b. What is the mode? 5

9. (32) (Represent) To what mixed number is the arrow pointing? $7\frac{2}{5}$

▶ *10. (32) (Model) Draw a number line and show the locations of 0, 1, 2, $1\frac{2}{3}$, and $2\frac{1}{3}$. Sample: 0, 1, $1\frac{2}{3}$, 2, $2\frac{1}{3}$, 3

11. (27) (Represent) Mount Rainier stands four thousand, three hundred ninety-two meters above sea level. Use digits to write that number. 4392 meters

Inclusion

Use this strategy if the student displays:

- Difficulty with Abstract Concept Processing.
- Difficulty with Large Group Instruction.

Rounding to the Nearest Tenth (Whole Group)

Materials: number line; place-value chart

- Draw the number line below on the board.

1.0 1.1 1.2 1.3 1.4 1.5 1.6 1.7 1.8 1.9 2.0

- Write 1.32 on the board, and show students where it would fall on the number line. Ask, ***"What number to the nearest tenth is 1.32 closest to?"*** 1.3
- Have students create their own number lines to round to the nearest tenth and round these numbers.

2.58 2.98 2.21

- Write this word problem on the board: ***"Johnny owed Cecilia two dollars and 54 cents. Rounded to the nearest tenth, how much did Johnny owe Cecilia?"*** \$2.5 or \$2.50
- Instruct students to use their number lines if they struggle in rounding the number.

12. Mo'Nique could make 35 knots in 7 minutes. How many knots could she make in 1 minute? 5 knots
(60)

13. Estimate the sum of 6810 and 9030 by rounding each number to the nearest thousand before adding. 16,000
(61)

▶ *14. Estimate the sum of $12.15 and $5.95. Then find the exact sum.
(61) $18.00; $18.10

15. $20 − ($8.95 + 75¢) $10.30
(9, 28)

16. 23.64 − 5.45 18.19
(45)

17. 43¢ × 8 = $3.44
(38)

18. $3.05 × 5 = $15.25
(59)

19. $2.63 × 7 = $18.41
(59)

20. **Connect** Rewrite this addition problem as a multiplication problem and find the answer: 5 × 64 = 320
(23)

64 + 64 + 64 + 64 + 64

▶ *21. $5\overline{)47}$ 9 R 2
(54)

▶ *22. $7\overline{)65}$ 9 R 2
(54)

▶ *23. $3\overline{)26}$ 8 R 2
(54)

*24. $\frac{39}{6}$ 6 R 3
(54)

*25. $4r = 48$ 12
(54)

*26. 46 ÷ 8 5 R 6
(54)

▶ 27. **Model** Use an inch ruler to find the lengths of segments *AB*, *BC*, and *AC*. $\overline{AB} = 1\frac{1}{4}$ in.; $\overline{BC} = 1\frac{1}{2}$ in.; $\overline{AC} = 2\frac{3}{4}$ in.
(33, 42)

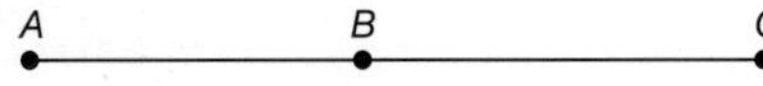

▶ *28. **Multiple Choice** Which of the following is 6.25 rounded to the nearest tenth? D
(62)

A 6.0 **B** 6.10 **C** 6.20 **D** 6.30

*29. **Represent** How many yards are equal to 5280 ft? 1760 yd
(42)

Written Practice *(Continued)*

Math Conversations *(cont.)*

Problem 14

Extend the Problem

Remind students that an estimate and an exact answer are compared to help decide the reasonableness of that answer. Then ask students to suggest different strategies they might follow if an estimate is not close to an exact answer.

Problems 21–23

Ask students to use compatible numbers and make an estimate of each quotient before completing the arithmetic, and then use the estimate to help decide the reasonableness of the exact answer.

Problem 27 Model

Ask students to also measure the segments in centimeters. Segment *AB*: 3.2 cm; segment *BC*: 3.8 cm; segment *AC*: 7 cm

Problem 28 Multiple Choice

Test-Taking Strategy

Prior to having students solve the problem, ask,

"Which place in a decimal number is the tenths place?" The first place to the right of the decimal point

(continued)

Written Practice *(Continued)*

Math Conversations *(cont.)*

Problem 30c Interpret

Ask students to justify their answers. 1 mile = 5280 feet, and 4600 feet is less than 5280 feet.

Errors and Misconceptions

Problem 15

An answer of $11.80 indicates that the student worked from left to right instead of completing the operation in parentheses first. Review the order of operations with these students.

Problem 25

Make sure students recognize the expression $4r$ as the product of two factors; one factor is 4, and the other factor is unknown.

If students have difficulty finding the value of r, say:

"The equation 4r = 48 is read as 'Four times what number is 48?'"

***30.** (27, 42, Inv. 5) **Interpret** The lengths of three land tunnels in the United States are shown in the graph. Use the graph to answer parts **a–c.**

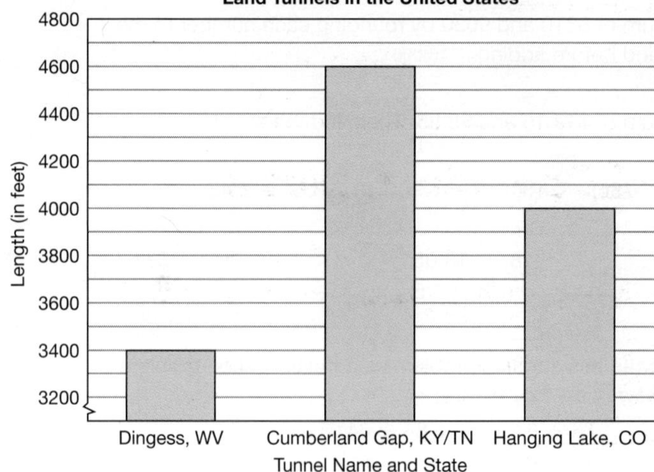

a. Write the names of the tunnels in order from shortest to longest.
Dingess, Hanging Lake, Cumberland Gap

b. How many feet longer is the Hanging Lake Tunnel than the Dingess Tunnel? 600 feet longer

▶ **c.** Is the Cumberland Gap tunnel greater or less than one mile long?
Less than one mile

422 **Saxon Math** *Intermediate 4*

Teacher Tip

Make a supply of place-value charts available for students to use as they work with decimal numbers and rounding.

Encourage students to use these aids in working with larger numbers and any time that calls for rounding.

Looking Forward

Rounding two-place decimal numbers to the nearest tenth prepares students for:

- **Lesson 79,** division with three-digit quotients.
- **Lesson 91,** estimating the answers to multiplication and division problems.
- **Lesson 104,** rounding whole numbers through hundred millions.
- **Lesson 107,** multiplying a three-digit number by a two-digit number.

Planning & Preparation

• Order of Operations, Part 3

Objectives

- Use the order of operations to simplify expressions and equations.
- Write and simplify expressions with more than two terms and different operations.
- Use parentheses to indicate which operation to perform first.
- Demonstrate equals added to equals are equal.
- Demonstrate equals multiplied by equals are equal.
- Substitute a value for a variable.

Prerequisite Skills

- Adding and subtracting from left to right to simplify an expression.
- Simplifying and comparing expressions that contain parentheses.
- Writing an expression with more than two terms.
- Multiplying and dividing from left to right to simplify an expression.

Materials

Instructional Masters

- Power Up J Worksheet

Manipulative Kit

- Two-color counters, color tiles, money manipulatives*

**optional*

California Mathematics Content Standards

AF 1.0, 1.1 Use letters, boxes, or other symbols to stand for any number in simple expressions or equations (e.g., demonstrate an understanding and the use of the concept of a variable).

AF 1.0, 1.2 Interpret and evaluate mathematical expressions that now use parentheses.

AF 1.0, 1.3 Use parentheses to indicate which operation to perform first when writing expressions containing more than two terms and different operations.

AF 2.0, 2.1 Know and understand that equals added to equals are equal.

AF 2.0, 2.2 Know and understand that equals multiplied by equals are equal.

MR 2.0, 2.3 Use a variety of methods, such as words, numbers, symbols, charts, graphs, tables, diagrams, and models, to explain mathematical reasoning.

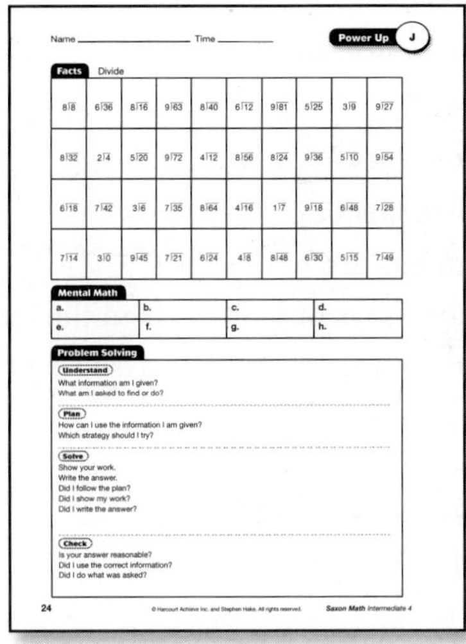

Name ____________ Time ________ **Power Up J**

Facts Divide

$8\overline{)8}$	$6\overline{)36}$	$8\overline{)16}$	$9\overline{)63}$	$8\overline{)40}$	$6\overline{)12}$	$9\overline{)81}$	$5\overline{)25}$	$3\overline{)9}$	$9\overline{)27}$
$8\overline{)32}$	$2\overline{)4}$	$5\overline{)20}$	$9\overline{)72}$	$4\overline{)12}$	$8\overline{)56}$	$8\overline{)24}$	$9\overline{)36}$	$5\overline{)10}$	$9\overline{)54}$
$6\overline{)18}$	$7\overline{)42}$	$3\overline{)6}$	$7\overline{)35}$	$8\overline{)64}$	$4\overline{)16}$	$1\overline{)7}$	$9\overline{)18}$	$6\overline{)48}$	$7\overline{)28}$
$7\overline{)14}$	$3\overline{)0}$	$9\overline{)45}$	$7\overline{)21}$	$6\overline{)24}$	$4\overline{)8}$	$8\overline{)48}$	$6\overline{)30}$	$5\overline{)15}$	$7\overline{)49}$

Mental Math

a.	b.	c.	d.
e.	f.	g.	h.

Problem Solving

Understand
What information am I given?
What am I asked to find or do?

Plan
How can I use the information I am given?
Which strategy should I try?

Solve
Show your work.
Write the answer.
Did I follow the plan?
Did I show my work?
Did I write the answer?

Check
Is your answer reasonable?
Did I use the correct information?
Did I do what was asked?

24 © Harcourt Achieve Inc. and Stephen Hake. All rights reserved. *Saxon Math Intermediate 4*

Power Up J Worksheet

Universal Access

Reaching All Special Needs Students

Special Education Students	At-Risk Students	English Learners	Advanced Learners
• Inclusion (TM) • Adaptations for Saxon Math	• Alternative Approach (TM) • Error Alert (TM) • Reteaching Masters • Refresher Lessons for California Standards	• English Learners (TM) • Developing Academic Language (TM) • English Learner Handbook	• Extend the Problem (TM) • Online Activities

TM=Teacher's Manual

Developing Academic Language

Maintained
expression
order of operations
parentheses
simplify
substitute

English Learner
substitute

Problem Solving Discussion

Problem

Half of the students in Gabriel's class are girls. Do we know how many students are in this class? Do we know whether there are more boys or more girls in the class? Do we know whether the number of students in the class is even or odd?

Focus Strategy

Use Logical Reasoning

Understand *Understand the problem.*

"What information are we given?"

Fifty percent of the students in the class are girls.

"What questions are we asked to answer?"

Can we determine how many students are in the class?

Can we find whether there are more boys or more girls in the class?

Can we find whether the number of students in the class is even or odd?

Plan *Make a plan.*

"What problem-solving strategy can we use?"

We can *use logical reasoning* and number sense.

Solve *Carry out the plan.*

"Are there more boys or more girls in the class?"

Neither. If 50% of the students are girls, then the other 50% of the students are boys. This means the number of girls and boys in the class is equal.

"Is the sum of two equal numbers even or odd?"

Whether the numbers are even or odd, the sum of two equal whole numbers is always even. For example, $1 + 1 = 2$; $2 + 2 = 4$; $3 + 3 = 6$; $4 + 4 = 8$.

"Is there an even or an odd number of students in the class?"

There is an even number of students.

"Can we know how many students are in the class?"

No. We would need more information to find the total number of students.

Check *Look back.*

"Did we find the answers to the questions that were asked?"

Yes. We don't know how many students are in the class, but we do know that there is an equal number of boys and girls and an even number of students.

LESSON

63

• Order of Operations, Part 3

California Mathematics Content Standards

AF 1.0, 1.2 Interpret and evaluate mathematical expressions that now use parentheses.

AF 1.0, 1.3 Use parentheses to indicate which operation to perform first when writing expressions containing more than two terms and different operations.

AF 2.0, 2.1 Know and understand that equals added to equals are equal.

AF 2.0, 2.2 Know and understand that equals multiplied by equals are equal.

Power Up

facts Power Up J

count aloud Count down by thousands from 20,000 to 1000.

mental math Multiply three numbers in problems **a–c.**

a. **Number Sense:** $6 \times 7 \times 10$ 420

b. **Number Sense:** $5 \times 8 \times 10$ 400

c. **Number Sense:** $12 \times 10 \times 10$ 1200

d. **Money:** \$7.59 + \$0.95 \$8.54

e. **Money:** Sydney had \$5.00. Then she spent \$3.25 on photocopies. How much money does she have left? \$1.75

f. **Geometry:** Compare: $4\frac{1}{2}$ in. ⊙< radius of a circle with a 10 in. diameter

g. **Estimation:** Henry estimated that his full drinking glass contained 400 mL of water. Is this a reasonable estimate? Yes

h. **Calculation:** $470 - 30 + 62 + 29$ 531

problem solving Choose an appropriate problem-solving strategy to solve this problem. Half of the students in Gabriel's class are girls. Do we know how many students are in this class? Do we know whether there are more boys or more girls in the class? Do we know whether the number of students in the class is even or odd? No; yes, same number; yes, even

Facts Divide

1 8)8	6 6)36	2 8)16	7 9)63	5 8)40	2 6)12	9 9)81	5 5)25	3 3)9	3 9)27
4 8)32	2 2)4	4 5)20	8 9)72	3 4)12	7 8)56	3 8)24	4 9)36	2 5)10	6 9)54
3 6)18	6 7)42	2 3)6	5 7)35	8 8)64	4 4)16	7 1)7	2 9)18	8 6)48	4 7)28
2 7)14	0 3)0	5 9)45	3 7)21	4 6)24	2 4)8	6 8)48	5 6)30	3 5)15	7 7)49

Power Up

Facts

Distribute **Power Up J** to students. See answers below.

Count Aloud

Before students begin the Mental Math exercise, do these counting exercises as a class.

Mental Math

Encourage students to share different ways to mentally compute these exercises. Strategies for exercises are listed below.

c. Multiply from Left to Right

$12 \times 10 = 120$; $120 \times 10 = 1200$

Use the Associative Property

$12 \times 10 \times 10 = 12 \times 100 = 1200$

d. Add \$1, then Subtract 5¢

\$7.59 + \$1 = \$8.59;

\$8.59 − \$0.05 = \$8.54

Subtract 5¢, Add 5¢

\$7.59 − \$0.05 + \$0.95 + \$0.05;

\$7.54 + \$1.00 = \$8.54

Problem Solving

Refer to **Problem-Solving Strategy Discussion,** p. 423B.

New Concept

Explanation

Previously, students learned to simplify expressions and solve equations that contained two related operations—addition and subtraction, or multiplication and division. In this lesson, students will find any of the four operations present, and follow the familiar order of operations to simplify the expressions and solve the equations.

Instruction

Prior to discussing how to simplify the expression 24 ÷ 2 – 2, make sure students can recall the order of operations from memory. Ask those students who cannot recall the steps to record them on an index card and use it as a reference throughout the lesson.

As you discuss how to simplify 24 ÷ 2 – 2, remind students that before the order of operations can be followed, they must first identify the operations that are present in the expression or equation.

After you have discussed how to simplify 24 ÷ 2 – 2 and 24 ÷ (2 – 2), point out that students should apply the order of operations correctly and carefully because there is no easy way for them to check their work, except for solving the problem a second time.

Example 1

Active Learning

Before discussing the solution, ask:

"What operations are present in this expression?"

"Which of those operations do we perform first? Explain why."

After you have discussed the solutions, ask:

"Whenever we simplify an expression, why is it important for us to use the order of operations correctly and carefully?" Sample: There is no simple method for checking our work.

Extend the Example

Challenge your advanced learners to work in pairs or in small groups and explore if reversing the order of operations and using inverse operations can be used to check the answers.

(continued)

We have learned some rules about the order of operations.

Order of Operations

- Complete operations inside parentheses first.
- Multiply and divide from left to right.
- Add and subtract from left to right.

We follow the order of operations whenever we simplify expressions or solve equations. Notice that the order of operations indicates that we multiply and divide from left to right before we add and subtract. Today, we are going to simplify expressions using all four operations.

When an expression includes both division and subtraction, we divide before we subtract.

In this expression, first we divide 24 by 4. Then we subtract 2.

24 ÷ 4 – 2 (Step 1: 24 ÷ 4; Step 2: – 2)

Step 1: 24 ÷ 4 = 6
Step 2: 6 – 2 = **4**

If we want the steps done in a different order, we use parentheses to show which operation should be completed first.

In the expression below, the parentheses tell us to subtract first and then divide.

24 ÷ (4 – 2) (Step 2: 24 ÷; Step 1: (4 – 2))

Step 1: 4 – 2 = 2
Step 2: 24 ÷ 2 = **12**

Example 1

Simplify each expression:

a. 35 + 7 × 3 **b. 56 ÷ (4 + 3)** **c. 35 – 5 × 2**

We can use the order of operations to simplify each expression.

a. We multiply before we add.

35 + 7 × 3	First multiply 7 by 3.
35 + 21	Then add 35 and 21.
56	The answer is 56.

b. We complete the operation inside the parentheses first.

$56 \div (4 + 3)$	First add 4 and 3.
$56 \div 7$	Then divide 56 by 7.
8	The answer is 8.

c. We multiply before we subtract.

$35 - 5 \times 2$	First multiply 5 by 2.
$35 - 10$	Then subtract 10 from 35.
25	The answer is 25.

Discuss Where would we place parentheses in the expression $35 - 5 \times 2$ so it will simplify to an answer of 60? Place parentheses around $35 - 5$; $(35 - 5) \times 2 = 60$

Example 2

Evaluate $(20 \div 5) + (2 \times 3) - m$ when $m = 7$.

$(20 \div 5) + (2 \times 3) - m$	Substitute 7 for *m*.
$(20 \div 5) + (2 \times 3) - 7$	Divide 20 by 5.
$4 + (2 \times 3) - 7$	Multiply 2 by 3.
$4 + 6 - 7$	Add and subtract from left to right.
3	The answer is 3.

Example 3

Solve each equation.

a. If $5 \times 2 + 10 = 100 \div 10 + r$, what does *r* equal?

b. If $(15 - 8) \times 9 = (49 \div 7) \times d$, what does *d* equal?

a. The equals sign shows us that the quantities on both sides of the equation are equal.

$5 \times 2 + 10 = 100 \div 10 + r$	Multiply and divide from left to right.
$10 + 10 = 10 + r$	For both sides of the equation to be equal, *r* must equal 10.
$10 + 10 = 10 + 10$	Substitute 10 for *r*.
$20 = 20$	Check.

We can see that **$r = 10$** because we added the same number to equal amounts.

New Concept *(Continued)*

Example 2

Error Alert

Point out that it is a good idea to substitute for m ($m = 7$) as the first step in simplifying the expression. Although the operations in this expression do not require the substitution to be completed immediately, students will find in other examples that the substitutions must be completed before the order of operations can be applied. Encourage students to reduce the potential complication of simplifying expressions by always completing the substitution(s) first.

Example 3

Extend the Example

Challenge your advanced learners to demonstrate how each equation can be solved using an inverse operation. Sample for problem **a:**

Step 1: Multiply and divide from left to right.

$$5 \times 2 + 10 = 100 \div 10 + r$$
$$10 + 10 = 10 + r$$

Step 2: Subtract 10 from both sides.

$$10 + 10 = 10 + r$$
$$10 + 10 - 10 = 10 + r - 10$$

Step 3: Simplify.

$$10 + 10 - 10 = 10 + r - 10$$
$$10 = r$$

(continued)

Math Background

A common mnemonic device to remember the correct order of operations is PEMDAS. Some people remember it by the sentence *"Please excuse my dear Aunt Sally."*

PEMDAS stands for:

1. **P**arentheses
2. **E**xponents
3. **M**ultiplication and **D**ivision
4. **A**ddition and **S**ubtraction

First work within parentheses, then exponents, then multiplication and division (left to right), and then addition and subtraction (left to right). If parentheses are enclosed within other parentheses, work from the inside out.

English Learners

Explain that **substitute** is a verb that means to exchange or replace. In example 2, the phrase "substituting 7 for *m*" means to replace *m* with the number 7. Say:

"Substitute can also be an adjective, such as substitute teacher. What does a substitute teacher do?" Sample: Replaces the regular teacher

Have students share their own sentences that use the word **substitute.**

New Concept *(Continued)*

Lesson Practice

Guided Practice

Use these problems as guided practice to check the students' understanding of today's concept.

Problems a–f

Work through the first problem with the whole class as a review.

Problems a–f
Error Alert

Before students complete any arithmetic for each problem, ask them to identify the operations that are present, and then name the order in which those operations will be performed.

Closure The questions below help assess the concepts taught in this lesson.

"Explain how the order of operations is used to simplify an expression that contains addition, subtraction, multiplication, division, and parentheses." Complete the operations in parentheses first. Then, multiply and divide from left to right. Finally, add and subtract from left to right.

Write the expression shown below on the board or overhead and ask students to simplify the expression when $b = 4$. 10

$$6 + 12 \div (10 - b) \times 2$$

Written Practice

Math Conversations

Independent Practice and Discussions to Increase Understanding

Problem 3

"Which is a smaller unit of measure, centimeters or millimeters?" millimeters

"Describe the relationship shared by centimeters and millimeters." 1 cm = 10 mm

Encourage students to look at the rulers in problem **6** to check their answers.

(continued)

b. $(15 - 8) \times 9 = (49 \div 7) \times d$	Simplify inside the parentheses first.
$7 \times 9 = 7 \times d$	For both sides of the equation to be equal, d must equal 9.
$7 \times 9 = 7 \times 9$	Substitute 9 for d.
$63 = 63$	Check.

We can see that $\boldsymbol{d = 9}$ because we multiplied equal amounts by the same number.

Lesson Practice

Connect Simplify each expression. Remember to use the order of operations.

a. $4 \times 2 + 16 \div 8$ 10 **b.** $27 \div 3 - 2 + 7$ 14

c. $6 + (10 - 4) \times 3$ 24 **d.** $9 \times (12 - 3) - 5$ 76

Evaluate Simplify each expression when $k = 5$.

e. $20 - 10 \div k$ 18 **f.** $6 \times (2 + k) - 5$ 37

g. **Explain** If $s + 50 = t + 50$, is the equation below true? Why or why not?

$$s \times 10 = t \times 10$$

Yes; $s = t$ because equals added to equals are equal; Therefore $s \times 10 = t \times 10$ because equals multiplied by equals are equal.

Written Practice *Distributed and Integrated*

Formulate Write and solve equations for problems **1** and **2.**

1. (15) Celeste has three hundred eighty-four baseball cards. Nathan has two hundred sixty baseball cards. Celeste has how many more cards than Nathan? $384 - 260 = d$; 124 cards

2. (39) Forty-two students could ride in one bus. There were 3 buses. How many students could ride in all the buses? 3 buses × 42 students in one bus = n students, or $3 \times 42 = n$; 126 students

▶ ***3.** (42) Jazmyn's house key is 4 cm long. How many millimeters long is her house key? 40 mm

▶ ***4.** (43) **Represent** Write a decimal and a fraction (or a mixed number) to represent each point. Point *A:* 0.4 and $\frac{4}{10}$ or $\frac{2}{5}$; Point *B:* 1.1 and $1\frac{1}{10}$; Point *C:* 1.5 and $1\frac{5}{10}$ or $1\frac{1}{2}$

A B C
0 1 2

Inclusion

Use this strategy if the student displays:

- Slow Learning Rate.
- Difficulty with Directionality.

Order of Operations (Individual)

Materials: two-color counters

- Have students model this equation using counters: $4 + 3 = 5 + 2$

  Then have students model this equation:

  $$(4 + 3) \times 2 = (5 + 2) \times 2$$

- Remind them that we simplify the portion of the equation within parentheses first. Ask, ***"Is the first equation true?"*** Yes ***"How do you know?"*** Both sides of the equation are equal. ***"By what number did you multiply each side of the first equation to make the second equation?"*** 2 ***"Is the second equation true? Explain."*** Yes; Both sides of the second equation are equal because we multiplied both sides of the first equation by the same number, and equals multiplied by equals are equal.

5. (19) **Represent** Copy this hexagon and shade one sixth of it.  

***6. a.** (42) This toothpick is how many centimeters long? 5 cm

b. This toothpick is how many millimeters long? 50 mm

▶ ***7.** (Inv. 6) **Interpret** Use this set of data to answer parts **a–c.**

16, 32, 24, 60, 24, 16, 31, 19, 20

a. What is the mode? 16, 24

b. What is the median? 24

c. Is there an outlier? Name it. Yes; 60

8. (20, 42) **Analyze** If each side of a square is 1 yard long, then what is the perimeter of the square in feet? 12 feet

▶ ***9.** (61) **Explain** The number of students enrolled at each of three elementary schools is shown in the table below.

Elementary School Enrollment

School	Number of Students
Van Buren	412
Carter	495
Eisenhower	379

Use rounding to make a reasonable estimate of the total number of students enrolled at the three schools. Explain your answer. About 1,300 students; sample: Round each enrollment to the nearest hundred, and then add; A reasonable estimate is 400 + 500 + 400, or 1300 students.

***10.** (33, 45) Segment *AB* is 3.5 cm long. Segment *AC* is 11.6 cm long. How long is segment *BC*? Write a decimal subtraction equation and find the answer. $11.6 - 3.5 = c$; 8.1 cm

A B C

Alternative Approach: Using Manipulatives

Have students use two-color counters to model simple equations that contain addition. You can use equations similar to those shown below.

$7 + 3 = 10$

$12 + 5 + 1 = 18$

Then have students choose one of the equations and add the same number to both sides of the equation. Have students model the new equation. Ask:

"What number did you add to both sides of the equation?" See student work.

"Are both sides of the equation still equal? Explain." Yes; Equals added to equals are equal.

Teacher Tip

Provide access to two-color counters, colored tiles, and money manipulatives for students to use to model equations and solve for a missing number.

Written Practice (Continued)

Math Conversations *(cont.)*

Problem 4 Represent

"On this number line, the distance from 0 to 1 and from 1 to 2 is divided into how many equal parts?" Ten equal parts

"What number does each tick mark on the number line represent? Explain your answer." Sample: A number of tenths; Each tick mark represents one more tenth than the tick mark to its left, and one fewer tenth than the tick mark to its right.

Problem 7 Interpret

"Can a data set have more than one median, mode, or outlier? Explain your answer." A data set will have only one median, but may have more than one mode or outlier, or no mode or outlier whatsoever.

Problem 9 Explain

Extend the Problem

Challenge advanced learners to use only mental math and explain why the estimate will be greater or less than the exact answer. Sample: The decrease of 412 to 400 (which is 12) is less than the sum of the increases of 495 to 500 and 379 to 400 (which is 5 + 21 or 26). Since the numbers were increased more than they were decreased, the estimate will be greater than the exact answer.

(continued)

Written Practice *(Continued)*

Math Conversations *(cont.)*

Problem 13 **Estimate**

Extend the Problem

Encourage all of your students to find the exact cost of the meal using only mental math by subtracting 5¢ from \$8.95 and adding 5¢ to \$7.95. \$8.00 + \$8.90 = \$16.90

Problems 14 and 15

Ask students to use compatible numbers and make an estimate of each quotient before completing the arithmetic, and then use the estimate to help decide the reasonableness of the exact answer.

Problems 24–28

Extend the Problem

Before students complete any arithmetic for each problem, ask them to identify the operations that are present, and then name the order in which those operations will be performed.

Errors and Misconceptions

Problem 5

Some students may find it helpful if you point out that drawing a line segment from each vertex to the opposite vertex, or drawing a line segment from the midpoint of each side to the midpoint of the opposite side, are two ways to divide a regular hexagon into 6 equal parts.

11. (58, 60) **a.** Hugo rode 60 miles in 5 hours. His average speed was how many miles per hour? 12 miles per hour

b. Hugo could ride 21 miles in 1 hour. At that rate, how many miles could Hugo ride in 7 hours? 147 mi

***12.** (56) The first three prime numbers are 2, 3, and 5. What are the next three prime numbers? 7, 11, 13

▸ ***13.** (61, 62) **Estimate** Claudia's meal cost \$7.95. Timo's meal cost \$8.95. Estimate the total price for both meals by rounding each amount to the nearest dime before adding. \$17

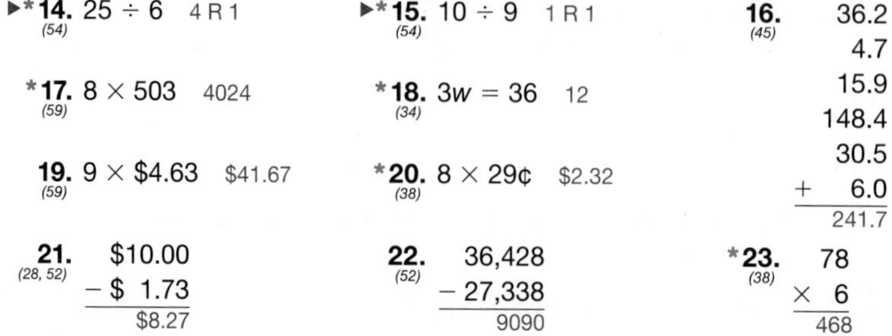

▸ ***14.** (54) $25 \div 6$ 4 R 1

▸ ***15.** (54) $10 \div 9$ 1 R 1

16. (45)

$$\begin{array}{r} 36.2 \\ 4.7 \\ 15.9 \\ 148.4 \\ 30.5 \\ + \quad 6.0 \\ \hline 241.7 \end{array}$$

***17.** (59) 8×503 4024

***18.** (34) $3w = 36$ 12

19. (59) $9 \times \$4.63$ \$41.67

***20.** (38) $8 \times 29¢$ \$2.32

21. (28, 52)

$$\begin{array}{r} \$10.00 \\ - \$\ 1.73 \\ \hline \$8.27 \end{array}$$

22. (52)

$$\begin{array}{r} 36{,}428 \\ - 27{,}338 \\ \hline 9090 \end{array}$$

***23.** (38)

$$\begin{array}{r} 78 \\ \times \ 6 \\ \hline 468 \end{array}$$

▸ ***24.** (9) $6 + 5 = 5 + t$ 6

▸ ***25.** (63) $(2 + 3) \times 8 = 5 \times f$ 8

▸ ***26.** (9) $a + 5 = 25 + 5$ 25

▸ **27.** (63) $(25 \div 5) + (3 \times 7) - 1$ 25

▸ ***28.** (9, 45) **Explain** Solve the equation below and describe the steps in the order you completed them.

$$4.7 - (3.6 - 1.7)$$

2.8; sample: First subtract 1.7 from 3.6, which is 1.9. Then subtract 1.9 from 4.7, which equals 2.8.

29. (20, 42) **a.** Find the perimeter of this rectangle in millimeters. 100 mm

b. Find the area of this rectangle in square centimeters. 6 sq. cm

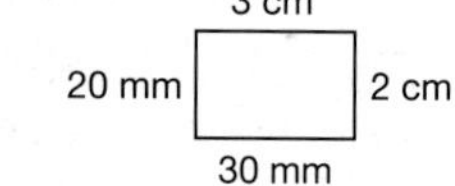

30. (17) **Multiple Choice** Each angle of this triangle is ____. A

A acute **B** right

C obtuse **D** straight

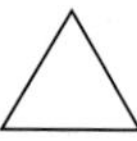

Using the order of operations to simplify expressions and equations prepares students for:

- **Lesson 64,** solving two-step equations.
- **Lesson 65,** evaluating an exponential expression for a given value.
- **Lesson 102,** using the Distributive Property to solve multiplication problems.

California Mathematics Content Standards
AF 1.0, 1.3 Use parentheses to indicate which operation to perform first when writing expressions containing more than two terms and different operations.
MR 3.0, 3.2 Note the method of deriving the solution and demonstrate a conceptual understanding of the derivation by solving similar problems.

• How Do We Write Expressions?

When we write a math expression, we must write it so that the steps to simplify it are clear. Without clear steps an expression can be simplified incorrectly, which is why we use the order of operations.

Example 1

$$5 \times 4 + 6 \div 2 - 4$$

Unless we know the order of operations, it is not clear which operation should be done first. This expression will be easier to simplify if parentheses are added.

$$(5 \times 4) + (6 \div 2) - 4$$

Now we can see exactly how to simplify this expression.

$$20 + 3 - 4 = 23 - 4 = 19$$

Mathematicians have agreed on an order of operations. Here are some rules arranged in order:

- Do operations in parentheses first.
- Multiply and divide from left to right.
- Add and subtract from left to right.

Evaluate Simplify each expression using the order of operations.

a. $6 + 3 \times (2 - 1) + 9 \div 3$ 12 **b.** $(7 - 3) + 5 \times 8 - (4 \times 2)$ 36

Example 2

$$(2 \times 3) + ((6 \times 2) \div (3 \times 2)) - 3$$

Sometimes too many parentheses are confusing. Include only those parentheses that are needed or find another way to write the expression.

Using a fraction bar to show the division helps make the order of operations clear.

$$(2 \times 3) + \frac{6 \times 2}{3 \times 2} - 3 = 6 + \frac{12}{6} - 3 = 6 + 2 - 3 = 5$$

Explain Why is it important to be clear when writing math expressions?

Sample: Depending on the order that the operations are done, the answers will be different. The clearer the expression is, the less chance for error.

FOCUS ON CONCEPTS H

How Do We Write Expressions?

Use this page to enhance conceptual understanding of key mathematical concepts.

Guided Instruction

Emphasize the need for clarity when writing expressions. Point out that it is important both to avoid excessive use of parentheses and to include necessary parentheses. Remind students that parentheses are used in pairs.

Discuss other ways of making expressions clearer, such as using a division bar when appropriate instead of a division sign, and using a dot instead of the multiplication sign. If students have begun work with variables they may also drop multiplication symbols between a number and a letter ($7a$ instead of writing $7 \times a$ or $7 \cdot a$).

Extending the Concept

Write the numbers 10, 8, 6, 4, and 2, on the board. Challenge advanced learners to keep these numbers in order and insert operation symbols and parentheses between them to make expressions equal to 0, 1, 2, 3, 4, 5, and 6.

Samples: $(10 + 8) \times (6 - (4 + 2)) = 0$;
$(10 - 8 + 6) \div (4 \times 2) = 1$;
$(10 + (8 - 6)) \div (4 + 2) = 2$;
$(10 - 8) + (6 \div (4 + 2)) = 3$;
$(10 + 8 + 6) \div (4 + 2) = 4$;
$((10 + 8) \div 6) + (4 \div 2) = 5$;
$(10 + (8 - 6)) \div (4 - 2) = 6$

Using order of operations to yield a given number from a set of numbers, will give students a better understanding of order of operations than simply following them to evaluate expressions. You may also make the task easier by allowing students to use the numbers in any order.

(continued)

Closure

The question below helps assess the concepts taught in this lesson.

"Why is it important that an expression be written as clearly as possible?" Sample: If it is clear, then everyone will find the same value for the expression.

Apply Add parentheses two ways to this expression. Then simplify.

10 + 6 − (2 × 4) − 4 ÷ 2

Sample: (10 + 6) − 2 × (4 − 4) ÷ 2 = 16; 10 + 6 − (2 × 4) − 4 ÷ 2 = 6

Evaluate Simplify each expression using the order of operations.

c. (5 × 1) − ((8 − 3) × 2 ÷ (6 + 4)) + 7 11

d. 4 × ((8 + 5) − 6 + (7 × 0)) − 9 19

Planning & Preparation

• Two-Step Equations

Objectives

- Solve two-step equations.

Prerequisite Skills

- Solving an addition word problem in which the total is given and an addend is missing.
- Using the addition algorithm to find the missing number in a subtraction problem.
- Finding the missing factor of a multiplication problem.

Materials

Instructional Masters

- Power Up J Worksheet

Manipulative Kit

- Rulers, balance scales, color tiles*

**optional*

California Mathematics Content Standards

AF 1.0, 1.1 Use letters, boxes, or other symbols to stand for any number in simple expressions or equations (e.g., demonstrate an understanding and the use of the concept of a variable).

AF 1.0, 1.2 Interpret and evaluate mathematical expressions that now use parentheses.

AF 1.0, 1.3 Use parentheses to indicate which operation to perform first when writing expressions containing more than two terms and different operations.

AF 1.0, 1.5 Understand that an equation such as $y = 3x + 5$ is a prescription for determining a second number when a first number is given.

MR 2.0, 2.3 Use a variety of methods, such as words, numbers, symbols, charts, graphs, tables, diagrams, and models, to explain mathematical reasoning.

MR 2.0, 2.4 Express the solution clearly and logically by using the appropriate mathematical notation and terms and clear language; support solutions with evidence in both verbal and symbolic work.

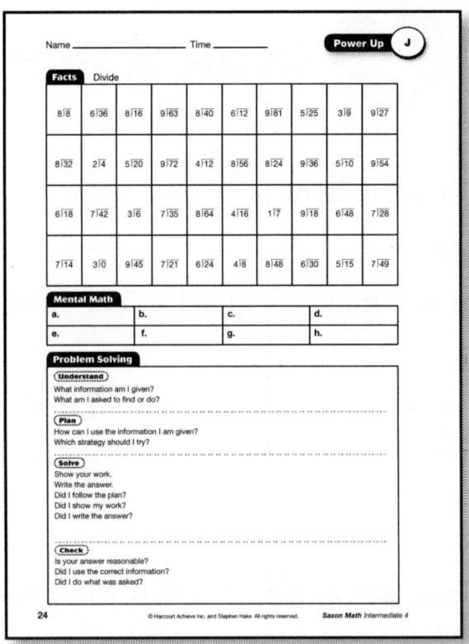

Name ________ Time ________ Power Up J

Facts Divide

$8\overline{)8}$	$6\overline{)36}$	$8\overline{)16}$	$9\overline{)63}$	$8\overline{)40}$	$6\overline{)12}$	$9\overline{)81}$	$5\overline{)25}$	$3\overline{)9}$	$9\overline{)27}$
$8\overline{)32}$	$2\overline{)4}$	$5\overline{)20}$	$9\overline{)72}$	$4\overline{)12}$	$8\overline{)56}$	$8\overline{)24}$	$9\overline{)36}$	$5\overline{)10}$	$9\overline{)54}$
$6\overline{)18}$	$7\overline{)42}$	$3\overline{)6}$	$7\overline{)35}$	$8\overline{)64}$	$4\overline{)16}$	$1\overline{)7}$	$9\overline{)18}$	$6\overline{)48}$	$7\overline{)28}$
$7\overline{)14}$	$3\overline{)0}$	$9\overline{)45}$	$7\overline{)21}$	$6\overline{)24}$	$4\overline{)8}$	$8\overline{)48}$	$6\overline{)30}$	$5\overline{)15}$	$7\overline{)49}$

Mental Math

a.	b.	c.	d.
e.	f.	g.	h.

Problem Solving

Understand
What information am I given?
What am I asked to find or do?

Plan
How can I use the information I am given?
Which strategy should I try?

Solve
Show your work.
Write the answer.
Did I follow the plan?
Did I show my work?
Did I write the answer?

Check
Is your answer reasonable?
Did I use the correct information?
Did I do what was asked?

24 © Harcourt Achieve Inc. and Stephen Hake. All rights reserved. *Saxon Math Intermediate 4*

Power Up J Worksheet

Universal Access

Reaching All Special Needs Students

Special Education Students	At-Risk Students	English Learners	Advanced Learners
• Inclusion (TM) • Adaptations for Saxon Math	• Error Alert (TM) • Reteaching Masters • Refresher Lessons for California Standards	• English Learners (TM) • Developing Academic Language (TM) • English Learner Handbook	• Extend the Example (TM) • Extend the Problem (TM) • Online Activities

TM=Teacher's Manual

Developing Academic Language

Maintained	English Learner
Commutative Property of Multiplication	survey
equation	
multiplication	
parentheses	
product	

Problem Solving Discussion

Problem

Shamel is making lemonade for her lemonade stand. The package of powdered lemonade says that each package makes 1 quart of lemonade. If Shamel wants to make $1\frac{1}{2}$ gallons of lemonade, how many packages of powdered lemonade will she need? Explain how you found your answer.

Focus Strategies

Make It Simpler

Draw a Picture or Diagram

Understand *Understand the problem.*

"What information are we given?"

Each package of powdered lemonade makes 1 quart of lemonade.

"What are we asked to do?"

We are asked to find the number of packages of powdered lemonade needed for $1\frac{1}{2}$ gallons. We are also asked to explain how we found our answer.

Plan *Make a plan.*

"How can we use the information we know to solve the problem?"

We know how many packages of lemonade are needed for each quart, so we will find how many quarts are in $1\frac{1}{2}$ gallons. We can draw this diagram to show the relationship among units of liquid measurement.

Solve *Carry out the plan.*

"How many quarts are in 1 gallon?"

In our diagram, Q stands for "quart" and G stands for "gallon." There are four Q's inside the G, so there are 4 quarts in a gallon.

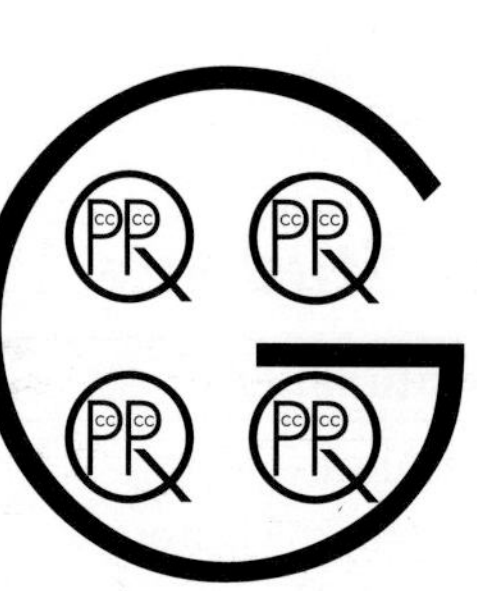

"How many quarts are in a half gallon?"

A half gallon is one half of 4 quarts, which is 2 quarts.

"How many quarts are in $1\frac{1}{2}$ gallons?"

There are 4 qt + 2 qt = 6 qt in $1\frac{1}{2}$ gallons. We can show this with a diagram.

"How many packages of powdered lemonade are needed to make $1\frac{1}{2}$ gallons?"

Shamel needs 1 package for each quart. She wants to make 6 quarts, so she needs 6 packages of powdered lemonade.

Check *Look back.*

"Is our answer reasonable?"

We know that our answer is reasonable, because there are 4 quarts in a gallon and 2 quarts in a half-gallon. Thus, there are 4 qt + 2 qt = 6 qt in $1\frac{1}{2}$ gallons.

"Explain how we solved the problem."

We found how many quarts are in $1\frac{1}{2}$ gallons. We *drew a diagram* to help us solve the problem. We can also say that we *made the problem simpler* by changing the amount of $1\frac{1}{2}$ gallons into quarts.

LESSON

64

California Mathematics Content Standards

AF 1.0, 1.2 Interpret and evaluate mathematical expressions that now use parentheses.

AF 1.0, 1.3 Use parentheses to indicate which operation to perform first when writing expressions containing more than two terms and different operations.

AF 1.0, 1.5 Understand that an equation such as y = 3x + 5 is a prescription for determining a second number when a first number is given.

• Two-Step Equations

facts Power Up J

count aloud When we count by fives from 1, we say the numbers 1, 6, 11, 16, and so on. Count by fives from 1 to 51.

mental math Multiply four numbers in problems **a–c.**

a. Number Sense: $6 \times 4 \times 10 \times 10$ 2400

b. Number Sense: $3 \times 4 \times 10 \times 10$ 1200

c. Number Sense: $4 \times 5 \times 10 \times 10$ 2000

d. Money: Alex had $10.00. Then he bought a cap for $6.87. How much money does Alex have left? $3.13

e. Time: J'Narra must finish the test by 2:30 p.m. If it is 2:13 p.m., how many minutes does she have left to finish? 17 min

f. Measurement: Five feet is 60 inches. How many inches tall is a person whose height is 5 feet 4 inches? 64 in.

g. Estimation: Choose the more reasonable estimate for the width of a computer keyboard: 11 inches or 11 feet. 11 in.

h. Calculation: $\sqrt{49} + 6 + 37 + 99$ 149

problem solving Choose an appropriate problem-solving strategy to solve this problem. Shamel is making lemonade for her lemonade stand. The package of powdered lemonade says that each package makes 1 quart of lemonade. If Shamel wants to make $1\frac{1}{2}$ gallons of lemonade, how many packages of powdered lemonade will she need? Explain how you found your answer. 6 packages; See student work.

Facts Divide

8)8 = 1	6)36 = 6	8)16 = 2	9)63 = 7	8)40 = 5	6)12 = 2	9)81 = 9	5)25 = 5	3)9 = 3	9)27 = 3
8)32 = 4	2)4 = 2	5)20 = 4	9)72 = 8	4)12 = 3	8)56 = 7	8)24 = 3	9)36 = 4	5)10 = 2	9)54 = 6
6)18 = 3	7)42 = 6	3)6 = 2	7)35 = 5	8)64 = 8	4)16 = 4	1)7 = 7	9)18 = 2	6)48 = 8	7)28 = 4
7)14 = 2	3)0 = 0	9)45 = 5	7)21 = 3	6)24 = 4	4)8 = 2	8)48 = 6	6)30 = 5	5)15 = 3	7)49 = 7

Facts

Distribute **Power Up J** to students. See answers below.

Count Aloud

Before students begin the Mental Math exercise, do these counting exercises as a class.

Mental Math

Encourage students to share different ways to mentally compute these exercises. Strategies for exercises are listed below.

a. Multiply 10's

$6 \times 4 \times 100$; $24 \times 100 = 2400$

Multiply from Left to Right

$24 \times 10 \times 10$; $240 \times 10 = 2400$

d. Count On from $6.87 to $10

$6.87 + 13¢ = $7; $7 + $3 = $10; $3 + 13¢ = $3.13

Subtract $7, then Add 13¢

$10 − $7 = $3; $3 + 13¢ = $3.13

Problem Solving

Refer to **Problem-Solving Strategy Discussion,** p. 431B.

New Concept

Instruction

If more than one step is needed to solve an equation, the order in which the steps are performed is often important. In this lesson, students will practice a common first step in solving equations which is to perform the arithmetic that does not involve the missing number.

Active Learning

As students discuss answers to the **Verify** question, identify those answers that describe substitution in some way, and point out that substitution is the most effective way to check an answer that represents a missing number in an equation. Then invite a volunteer to write the equation $2n = 7 + 5$ on the board or overhead and demonstrate a check of the answer by substituting 6 for n. Sample:

$$2n = 7 + 5$$
$$2(6) = 7 + 5$$
$$12 = 12$$

Point out that because the equation $12 = 12$ is a true statement, the solution checks.

Example 1

Error Alert

Make sure all of your students understand that a multiplication dot is different from a decimal point by asking them to describe the characteristics of each. Sample: A multiplication dot is raised and has space on both sides. A decimal point is aligned with the bottoms of digits and usually has a digit on both sides.

Extend the Example

Challenge your advanced learners to write and solve a different multiplication equation that includes 3, 4, 6, and m, and then share their work with their classmates. Sample: $6m = 4 \cdot 3$; $m = 2$

Example 2

Instruction

Have students note that for this equation, two operations are present (multiplication and addition), and neither operation can be performed until the substitution has been made.

Connection

In upcoming lessons, students will learn that an equation such as $y = 3x + 4$ represents the equation of a line.

(continued)

New Concept

The equation below means "2 times what number equals 7 plus 5?"

$$2n = 7 + 5$$

It takes two steps to solve this equation. The first step is to add 7 and 5 ($7 + 5 = 12$), which gives us this equation:

$$2n = 12$$

The second step is to find n. Since $2 \times 6 = 12$, we know that n is 6.

$$n = \mathbf{6}$$

Verify How can we check the answer? Substitute 6 for n in the original equation, then simplify; $2 \times 6 = 7 + 5$, so $12 = 12$

Example 1

Reading Math

We read this equation as "3 times what number equals 4 times 6?"

Find m in the following equation: $3m = 4 \cdot 6$

A dot is sometimes used between two numbers to indicate multiplication. So $4 \cdot 6$ means "4 times 6." The product of 4 and 6 is 24.

$$3m = 4 \cdot 6$$
$$3m = 24$$

Now we find m. Three times 8 equals 24, so m equals 8.

$$3m = 24$$
$$m = \mathbf{8}$$

Verify How can we check the answer? Substitute 8 for m in the original equation and then simplify; $3 \cdot 8 = 4 \cdot 6$, so $24 = 24$

Example 2

Math Symbols

We can show 3 times x in different ways.

$3 \times x$
$3 \cdot x$
$3x$

If $y = 3x + 4$, then what is y when $x = 2$?

The equation $y = 3x + 4$ shows us how to find the number that y equals when we know the number x equals.

This equation means, "To find y, multiply x by 3 and then add 4."

In this equation, x is 2, so we multiply 3 times 2 and then add 4.

$y = 3x + 4$	Substitute 2 for x.
$y = (3 \cdot 2) + 4$	Work inside the parentheses first.
$y = 6 + 4$	Add.
$y = 10$	The answer is 10.

When x is 2, $\mathbf{y = 10}$.

Analyze What is y when $x = 3$? 13

Math Background

The aim in solving equations is to isolate the unknown on one side of the equation. Starting with the equation $3x + 5 = 10$, we want to get this equation into the form $x = ...$ or $...... = x$. This may involve several steps.

Two-step equations are solved like one-step equations. In two-step equations, the order in which we do the calculations makes a difference. In Example 2, we start with the equation $y = 3x + 4$ and are asked to find y when $x = 2$. To find the value of y when $x = 2$, the multiplication inside the parentheses was worked before the addition was done. This enabled us to rewrite the equation as $y = 6 + 4$ and find that when $x = 2$ then $y = 10$.

Lesson Practice

Find each missing number:

a. $2n = 2 + 8$ 5 **b.** $2 + n = 2 \cdot 8$ 14

c. **Explain** If $y = 2x + 5$, then what is y when $x = 3$? Explain your thinking. 11; $(2 \cdot 3) + 5 = 6 + 5$ or 11

Written Practice

Distributed and Integrated

Formulate Write and solve equations for problems **1** and **2.**

▶ **1.** (12) There were 150 seats in the cafeteria. If 128 seats were filled, how many seats were empty? $128 + p = 150$; 22 seats

▶ **2.** (16, 45) Anaya ran 100 meters in 12.14 seconds. Marion ran 100 meters in 11.98 seconds. Marion ran 100 meters how many seconds faster than Anaya? $12.14 - 11.98 = d$; 0.16 sec

3. (27, 52) Forty-two thousand is how much greater than twenty-four thousand? 18,000

4. (39, 59) Keenan bought his lunch Monday through Friday. If each lunch cost $1.25, how much did he spend on lunch for the week? $6.25

5. (20, Inv. 3) Find the perimeter and area of this rectangle: 18 units; 20 square units

5 units

4 units

6. (11, 12, 22) **Explain** Re'Bekka read 30 pages a day on Monday, Tuesday, and Wednesday. She read 45 pages on Thursday and 26 pages on Friday. How many pages did she read in all? Explain why your answer is reasonable. 161 pages; sample: Round the number of pages read each day to the nearest ten, and then find the sum; $30 + 30 + 30 + 50 + 30 = 170$

▶ ***7.** (64) **Evaluate** If $y = 4x + 1$, then what is y when $x = 3$? 13

Inclusion

Use this strategy if the student displays:

- Difficulty with Written Symbols.
- Hearing Impairment.

Two Step Equations (Whole Group)

Materials: balance scale, colored tiles

- Write $3n = 12$ and draw a scale on the board. Place $3n$ on one side of the scale and 12 on the other side of the scale. Ask, ***"What does 3n mean?"*** 3 times *n* ***"What number must n be so that 3 times n equals 12?"*** 4
- Model the equation using the balance scale and colored tiles. Show that 3 and 12 are not balanced, but 3 groups of 4 and 12 are balanced.
- Write $3n = 12 + 3$ on the board and draw a scale so that $3n$ is on one side and $12 + 3$ is on the other side. Ask, ***"What is 12 + 3?"*** 15 ***"What must n be so that 3 times n equals 15?"*** 5
- Model the solution using the balance scale. Show that 3 and 15 are not balanced, but 3 groups of 5 and 15 are balanced.

New Concept *(Continued)*

Lesson Practice

Guided Practice

Use these problems as guided practice to check the students' understanding of today's concept.

Problems a and b

Before completing any arithmetic for each problem, ask:

"What operation can we perform to help make it easier to find the missing number?" problem **a:** add 2 and 8; problem **b:** multiply 2 and 8

"How should we rewrite the equation after performing that operation?" problem **a:** $2n = 10$; problem **b:** $2 + n = 16$

Problem c

Extend the Problem

"For this equation, the value of y is 11 when x = 3. It is possible, however, for y to have a different value. Explain how this is possible, and give an example to support your explanation." Substitute a different value for *x;* sample: If $x = 0$, then $y = 5$.

Problems a and b

Error Alert

Some students may need help remembering to first solve the side of the equation without the variable.

Closure

The questions below help assess the concepts taught in this lesson.

Write the equation $5n = 8 + 7$ on the board or overhead. Then ask:

"To find the missing number that n represents, what step should we complete first?" Add $8 + 7$

"How should we rewrite the equation after completing that step?" $5n = 15$

"How do we read the equation that remains?" Five times what number is fifteen?

"What is the value of n?" $n = 3$

Write the equation $2n = 10 - 6$ on the board or overhead and ask students to solve for the missing number. $n = 2$

Written Practice

Math Conversations

Independent Practice and Discussions to Increase Understanding

Problems 1 and 2 (Formulate)

Extend the Problem

Remind students of the importance of checking their work, and ask them to check their work for these problems by writing and solving a different equation, and then comparing answers.

Problem 7 (Evaluate)

Extend the Problem

Challenge advanced learners with this question:

"What is the value of x when y = 1?" $x = 0$

Problem 8 (Interpret)

Invite a volunteer to explain how to find the median of the data using only mental math. Sample: Point to the "X" representing the least number and point to the "X" representing the greatest number. Continue pointing to least and greatest pairs of "X's" until only one number remains in the middle. The median is 12.

Problem 9 (Estimate)

Make sure students recognize that because they are being asked to estimate the weight, they should not find the exact sum of the weights and then round that sum to the nearest tenth. Instead, they should round the addends.

Problem 10 (Analyze)

Extend the Problem

Offer this challenge to your advanced learners:

"Without extending the table, describe three different ways you can use the information in the table to find how far the truck could travel in 6 hours." Sample: Add the distances shown for 1, 2, and 3 hours; Double the distance shown for 3 hours; Triple the distance shown for 2 hours.

Problem 13

Manipulative Use

After students have calculated the length of segment *AC*, have them use a ruler to measure the segment to check their answer. Make sure they align the tick mark representing zero on their rulers with point *A* on the segment.

(continued)

▸ *8. (Inv. 6) **Interpret** This line plot shows the number of times some students ride their bikes in a month. Use this line plot to answer parts **a–c**.

Number of Times Riding a Bike

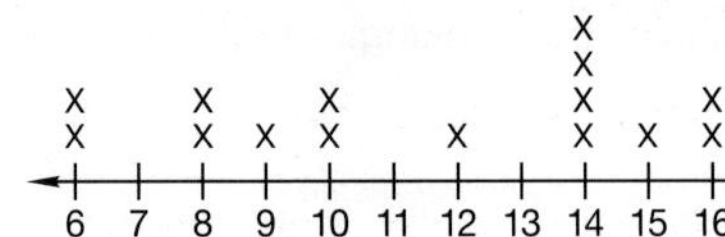

a. How many students were surveyed? 15 students

b. What is the mode? 14 times

c. Is there an outlier? If yes, what is it? No

▸ *9. (62) **Estimate** Mr. Anderson bought three packages of chicken. They weighed 2.36 pounds, 3.75 pounds, and 1.71 pounds. To the nearest tenth of a pound, how much chicken did Mr. Anderson buy?
$2.4 + 3.8 + 1.7 = 7.9$ pounds

▸ 10. (58) **Analyze** Driving at a highway speed limit of 65 miles per hour, how far can a truck travel in 3 hours? Make a table to solve this problem.
195 miles

Hours	Miles
1	65
2	130
3	195

*11. (60) **Formulate** If a biker traveled 24 miles in 4 hours, then the biker traveled an average of how many miles each hour? Write an equation to solve this problem. $24 \div 4 = m$; 6 miles

*12. (18, 42) **a.** What is the diameter of this shirt button in centimeters? 1 cm

b. What is the radius of this shirt button in millimeters?
5 mm

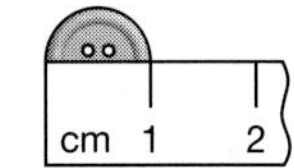

▸*13. (33, 45) Segment *AB* is 2.7 cm long. Segment *BC* is 4.8 cm long. How long is segment *AC*? Write a decimal addition equation and find the answer.
$2.7 + 4.8 = 7.5$; 7.5 cm

14. (28) \$8 + \$9.48 + 79¢ \$18.27

15. (45) 5.36 + 2.1 + 0.43 7.89

16. (28, 51)
$$\begin{array}{r} \$165.45 \\ +\ \$\ 59.47 \\ \hline \$224.92 \end{array}$$

17. (52)
$$\begin{array}{r} 37{,}102 \\ -\ 18{,}590 \\ \hline 18{,}512 \end{array}$$

18. (63) $(9 - 5) \times 6 \div 8$ 3

*19. (59) \$1.63 × 4 \$6.52

*20. (59) 6 × 391 2346

21. (59) 7 × \$2.56 \$17.92

English Learners

To **survey** is to gather information from or about a population. Explain that when a group of people have been asked questions to gather information from them, it is said they have been surveyed. Ask:

"Give examples of why people might be surveyed."

Sample: To find out what foods they like, to find out whether they prefer to drink orange juice or lemonade, to find out whether they live in the city or the country

*22. (54) $3\overline{)19}$ 6 R 1

*23. (54) $9\overline{)40}$ 4 R 4

24. (54) $\frac{59}{6}$ 9 R 5

▶*25. (62) **Represent** Round each number to the given place:

a. Round 2.56 to the nearest tenth. 2.6

b. Round \$4.35 to the nearest ten cents. \$4.40

c. Round \$4.35 to the nearest twenty-five cents. \$4.25

▶*26. (63) **Analyze** Simplify each expression. Remember to use the order of operations.

a. $3 \times 5 + 40 \div 8$ 20 **b.** $64 \div 8 - 6 + 12$ 14

▶*27. (63) **Formulate** Assume $a = b$. Then use the letters a, b and the number 5 to write an equation that shows "when the same number is added to equal amounts the sums are equal." Sample: $a + 5 = b + 5$ when $a = b$

28. (Inv. 4, 43) **Represent** Write twelve and three tenths as a mixed number and as a decimal number. $12\frac{3}{10}$; 12.3

*29. (55) **Multiple Choice** Which of these numbers is a factor of both 12 and 20? B

A 3 **B** 4 **C** 5 **D** 6

▶ 30. (17) **Represent** Draw a triangle that has one right angle. Sample: [right triangle]

Looking Forward

Solving two-step equations prepares students for:

- **Lesson 65,** evaluating an exponential expression for a given value.
- **Lesson 102,** using the Distributive Property to solve multiplication problems.

Written Practice *(Continued)*

Math Conversations *(cont.)*

Problem 25 Represent

Ask students to identify the digit that is in each rounding place before they complete the arithmetic.

Problem 26 Analyze

Before they simplify each expression, ask students to name the operations that are present, and describe the order in which those operations will be performed.

Problem 27 Formulate

Invite volunteers to share their equations with the class by writing them on the board or overhead.

Problem 30 Represent

Extend the Problem

"One angle of a right triangle is a right angle. Can one of the other angles of a right triangle be an obtuse angle? Explain why or why not." No

Invite volunteers to make a sketch on the board or overhead to support their answers.

Errors and Misconceptions

Problem 3

More than one answer is possible. For example, some students may write the standard form of eighteen thousand and others may write the word form of 18,000.

Problems 22 and 23

Ask students to use compatible numbers and make an estimate of each quotient before completing the arithmetic, and then use the estimate to help decide the reasonableness of the exact answer.

Planning & Preparation

• Exponents

Objectives

- Read exponents.
- Write a power as a whole number and an exponent.
- Evaluate an exponential expression for a given value.
- Write an expression using exponents.

Prerequisite Skills

- Identifying and memorizing the memory group of multiplication facts.
- Using the multiplication algorithm to multiply a two-digit number by a one-digit number.

Materials

Instructional Masters

- Power Up J Worksheet

Manipulative Kit

- Rulers

Teacher-provided materials

- Number cubes*

**optional*

California Mathematics Content Standards

NS 4.0, 4.1 Understand that many whole numbers break down in different ways (e.g. 12 = 4 × 3 = 2 × 6 = 2 × 2 × 3.)

MR 1.0, 1.2 Determine when and how to break a problem into simpler parts.

MR 2.0, 2.3 Use a variety of methods, such as words, numbers, symbols, charts, graphs, tables, diagrams, and models, to explain mathematical reasoning.

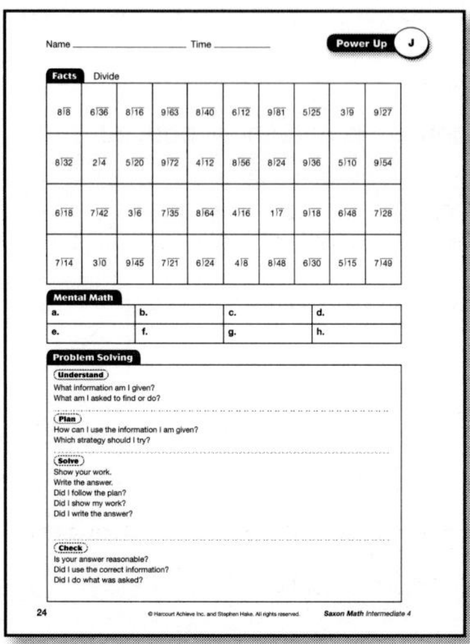

Power Up J Worksheet

Reaching All Special Needs Students

Special Education Students	At-Risk Students	English Learners	Advanced Learners
• Inclusion (TM) • Adaptations for Saxon Math	• Error Alert (TM) • Reteaching Masters • Refresher Lessons for California Standards	• English Learners (TM) • Developing Academic Language (TM) • English Learner Handbook	• Extend the Example (TM) • Extend the Problem (TM) • Online Activities

TM=Teacher's Manual

Developing Academic Language

New	Maintained	English Learner
base	expression	customer service
exponent	multiple	
	simplify	

Problem Solving Discussion

Problem

Jamisha paid a dollar for an item that cost 44¢. If she got back four coins in change, what should the four coins have been?

Focus Strategy  **Use Logical Reasoning**

Understand *Understand the problem.*

"What information are we given?"

Jamisha paid $1.00 for a $0.44 item.

"What are we asked to do?"

We are asked to find which coins Jamisha received in change if she got back four coins.

Plan *Make a plan.*

"How can a cashier 'count up' to make change for a purchase?"

Cashiers can count up from the purchase price to the amount the customer paid.

"What problem-solving strategies can we use to solve the problem?"

We can *use logical reasoning* by counting up.

Solve *Carry out the plan.*

"How many pennies does the cashier need to count up from 44¢ to 45¢?"

The cashier needs one penny to count up from the purchase price of 44¢ to 45¢.

"How many nickels does the cashier need to count up from 45¢ to 50¢?"

The cashier needs one nickel to count up from 45¢ to 50¢.

"One penny and one nickel is two coins. According to the problem, how many more coins does the cashier use?"

The cashier uses four coins, so we need to look for two more coins that would raise the total from 50¢ to $1.00.

"What two coins does the cashier need to count up from 50¢ to $1.00?"

The cashier can count up from 50¢ to $1.00 with two quarters.

"What four coins should Jamisha have received in change?"

Two quarters, one nickel, and one penny

Check *Look back.*

"Is our answer reasonable?"

We know that paying $1.00 for a 44¢ item results in 56¢ of change. Our answer is reasonable because two quarters, one nickel, and one penny have a total value of 25¢ + 25¢ + 5¢ + 1¢ = 56¢.

"What is another way we could have solved this problem?"

The amount of change Jamisha should receive is 56¢. We could have asked ourselves, "What are four coins that total 56¢?" We might think, "2 quarters is 50¢, so Jamisha would receive 2 other coins worth 6¢." We know that a nickel and a penny total 6¢.

"How could we extend this problem?"

We can find options for the change Jamisha would have received if the cashier was out of quarters. However, we would not find another combination that uses exactly four coins.

Power Up

Facts
Distribute **Power Up J** to students. See answers below.

Count Aloud
Before students begin the Mental Math exercise, do these counting exercises as a class.

Mental Math
Encourage students to share different ways to mentally compute these exercises. Strategies for exercises are listed below.

d. Decompose and Rearrange Factors
$4 \times 10 \times 5 \times 10$; $4 \times 5 \times 10 \times 10$; $20 \times 100 = 2000$

Multiply Nonzero Digits, Write 0's
Think $4 \times 5 = 20$, and write 2 zeros after 20; $40 \times 50 = 2000$.

f. Add Place Values
$6 + $2 = $8; 40¢ + 30¢ = 70¢; 8¢ + 9¢ = 17¢; $8 + 70¢ + 17¢ = $8.87

Add 1¢, then Subtract 1¢
$6.48 + $2.40 = $8.88; $8.88 − $0.01 = $8.87

Problem Solving
Refer to **Problem-Solving Strategy Discussion,** p. 436B.

New Concept

Active Learning
Invite students to explain how the Commutative and Associative Properties apply to multiplication. Sample: We can change the order of two factors (commutative property); We can multiply three factors in any order (associative property).

(continued)

LESSON 65

• Exponents

California Mathematics Content Standards

NS 4.0, 4.1 Understand that many whole numbers break down in different ways (e.g. $12 = 4 \times 3 = 2 \times 6 = 2 \times 2 \times 3$.)
MR 1.0, 1.2 Determine when and how to break a problem into simpler parts.
MR 2.0, 2.3 Use a variety of methods, such as words, numbers, symbols, charts, graphs, tables, diagrams, and models, to explain mathematical reasoning.

Power Up

facts Power Up J

count aloud Count by fives from 1 to 51.

mental math Multiply two numbers ending in zero in problems **a–d.** (Example: 30×40 equals 3×10 times 4×10. We rearrange the factors to get $3 \times 4 \times 10 \times 10$, which is 1200.)

a. **Number Sense:** 40×40 1600
b. **Number Sense:** 30×50 1500
c. **Number Sense:** 60×70 4200
d. **Number Sense:** 40×50 2000
e. **Powers/Roots:** $2^2 + 2$ 6
f. **Money:** $6.48 + $2.39 $8.87
g. **Estimation:** Each bottled water costs 99¢. If Ms. Hathcoat buys 1 bottle for each of her 24 students, about how much money will she spend? $23.76
h. **Calculation:** $\sqrt{64} - 6 + 37 + 61$ 100

problem solving Choose an appropriate problem-solving strategy to solve this problem. Jamisha paid a dollar for an item that cost 44¢. If she got back four coins in change, what should the four coins have been? 2 quarters, 1 nickel, and 1 penny

New Concept

To find the product of three numbers, we first multiply two of the numbers. Then we multiply the answer we get by the third number. To multiply four numbers, we must multiply once more. In any multiplication we continue the process until no factors remain.

Facts Divide

1 8)8	6 6)36	2 8)16	7 9)63	5 8)40	2 6)12	9 9)81	5 5)25	3 3)9	3 9)27
4 8)32	2 2)4	4 5)20	8 9)72	3 4)12	7 8)56	3 8)24	4 9)36	2 5)10	6 9)54
3 6)18	6 7)42	2 3)6	5 7)35	8 8)64	4 4)16	7 1)7	2 9)18	8 6)48	4 7)28
2 7)14	0 3)0	5 9)45	3 7)21	4 6)24	2 4)8	6 8)48	5 6)30	3 5)15	7 7)49

Example 1

Multiply: 3 × 4 × 5

First we multiply two of the numbers to get a product. Then we multiply that product by the third number. If we multiply 3 by 4 first, we get 12. Then we multiply 12 by 5 and get 60.

Step 1	Step 2
$3 \times 4 = 12$	$12 \times 5 = \mathbf{60}$

It does not matter which two numbers we multiply first. If we multiply 5 by 4 first, we get 20. Then we multiply 20 by 3 and again get 60.

Step 1	Step 2
$5 \times 4 = 20$	$20 \times 3 = \mathbf{60}$ ← same answer

The order of the multiplications does not matter because of the Commutative Property of Multiplication, which we studied in Lesson 23.

Example 2

Multiply: 4 × 5 × 10 × 10

We may perform this multiplication mentally. If we first multiply 4 by 5, we get 20. Then we multiply 20 by 10 to get 200. Finally we multiply 200 by 10 and find that the product is **2000.**

Formulate What is another combination of factors that has a product of 2000? Sample: 2 × 10 × 100

Sometimes when we simplify an expression that includes exponents, we will multiply more than two factors.

An **exponent** is a number that shows how many times another number (the **base**) is to be used as a factor. An exponent is written above and to the right of the base.

base ⟶ 5^2 ⟵ exponent

5^2 means 5 × 5.

5^2 equals 25.

If the exponent is 2, we say "squared" for the exponent. So 5^2 is read as "five squared." If the exponent is 3, we say "cubed" for the exponent. So the **exponential expression** 2^3 is read as "two cubed."

Inclusion

Use this strategy if the student displays:

- Difficulty with Abstract Concept Processing.
- Difficulty with Large Group Instruction.

Exponents (Pairs)

Material: none

- Write 3 + 3 + 3 + 3 + 3 on the board. Ask, ***"Is there a shorter way to write this addition problem?"*** 3 × 5

  Remind students that multiplication can be used to find the sum of repeated addition.
- Write 3 × 3 × 3 × 3 × 3 on the board and tell students that there is a shorter way to write repeated multiplication. Place an equal sign next to the repeated multiplication and ask, ***"What is the number, or base, being multiplied?"*** 3 ***"How many times is 3 being multiplied?"*** 5
- Write 3^5 on the board and explain that the exponent means the number is being repeated 5 times in a multiplication problem.
- Write 4^3 on the board and ask students to write it as a repeated multiplication problem.

New Concept *(Continued)*

Example 1

Instruction

Point out that the two factors students choose to multiply first can affect the ease of the calculation. As you discuss the solution, make sure students understand that both methods of finding the product are correct, and generalize from the example that when we multiply, the order in which the factors are multiplied does not matter.

Example 2

Extend the Example

Challenge advanced learners to describe a variety of ways to find the product using only mental math. Sample: First multiply 10 × 10 to get 100, then multiply 4 × 5 to get 20, and finally multiply 20 × 100 to get 2000.

Lead students to generalize from their answers that whenever we multiply by 10 (or by a multiple of 10), we can write the number of zeros in the factors to the right of the product of the nonzero digits. (For the factors 4 × 5 × 10 × 10, we would write two zeros to the right of the product of 4 × 5 × 1 × 1.)

Reading Math

After you discuss how to read an exponent of 2 as "squared" and 3 as "cubed", explain that exponents greater than 3 are read "to the '*n*th' power." For example, 3^4 is read "three to the fourth power" and 10^7 is read "ten to the seventh power."

(continued)

New Concept (Continued)

Example 3

Error Alert

It is important for students to understand that two steps are needed to simplify expressions involving exponents such as 5^2 or 2^3. The first step involves deciding how many times the base is used as a factor. The second step involves naming the product of those factors.

It is also important for students to recognize that although two operations are present, the multiplications (5 × 5) and (2 × 2 × 2) are completed before the addition because the order of operations states that if multiplication and addition are both present, multiplication is completed before addition.

Example 4

Extend the Example

Invite volunteers to write a variety of factors on the board or overhead such as 2 × 2 × 2 × 2 and 8 × 8 × 8 × 8 × 8, and then challenge volunteers to rewrite each expression using an exponent.

Challenge advanced learners to use variables such as $a \cdot a \cdot a$ (a^3) and $n \cdot n \cdot n \cdot n$ (n^4).

Lesson Practice

Guided Practice

Use these problems as guided practice to check the students' understanding of today's concept.

Problems a and b

Before naming each product, invite volunteers to describe the different ways the factors can be arranged. Sample: (problem **a**) multiply 2 × 3 first or multiply 3 × 4 first.

Problems c and d

Error Alert

Before naming each product, invite volunteers to state the base, and state the number of times the base is used as a factor. Sample: (problem **c**) 8 is the base, and 8 is used as a factor two times; 8 × 8

Problems e and f

Error Alert

Remind students that two different operations are present, and the order of operations states we must multiply before we subtract.

(continued)

Example 3

Simplify: $5^2 + 2^3$

We will add five squared and two cubed. We find the values of 5^2 and 2^3 before adding.

5^2 means 5 × 5, which is 25.

2^3 means 2 × 2 × 2, which is 8.

Now we add 25 and 8.

25 + 8 = **33**

Example 4

Rewrite this expression using exponents:

5 × 5 × 5

Five is used as a factor three times, so the exponent is 3.

$\mathbf{5^3}$

Evaluate Why do we write 5 × 5 × 5 as 5^3 instead of 5 × 3?

5 × 5 × 5 = 125; If we write this as 5 × 3 our product is 15, not 125, because 5 × 3 = 5 + 5 + 5.

Lesson Practice

Simplify:

a. 2 × 3 × 4 24

b. 3 × 4 × 10 120

c. 8^2 64

d. 3^3 27

e. $10^2 - 6^2$ 64

f. $3^2 - 2^3$ 1

g. Rewrite this expression using exponents: 4^3

4 × 4 × 4

Written Practice

Distributed and Integrated

▸ ***1.** (Inv. 3) A rectangular wall is covered with square tiles. The wall is 4 tiles long and 3 tiles wide. In all, how many tiles are on the wall? 12 tiles

2. (12) There were two hundred sixty seats in the movie theater. All but forty-three seats were occupied. How many seats were occupied? 217 seats

3. (39, 59) At the grand opening of a specialty food store, five coupons were given to each customer. One hundred fifteen customers attended the grand opening. How many coupons were given to those customers altogether? 575 coupons

4. (28) **Analyze** What is the value of 5 pennies, 3 dimes, 2 quarters, and 3 nickels? $1.00

Math Background

An expression of the form a^n is read "a to the nth power." For example, 6^4 is read "6 to the fourth power."

When n is 2, we can say "a to the second power" or "a squared." The terms "a squared" come from the fact that a^2 is the area of a square with side length a. Example 5 of the lesson shows that the area of a square with side length 5 inches is (5 inches)^2, or 25 square inches.

When n is 3, we can say "a to the third power" or "a cubed." The terms "a cubed" come from the fact that a^3 is the volume of a cube with edges of a. For example, the volume of a cube with edge length 2 centimeters is (2 centimeters)^3, or 8 cubic centimeters.

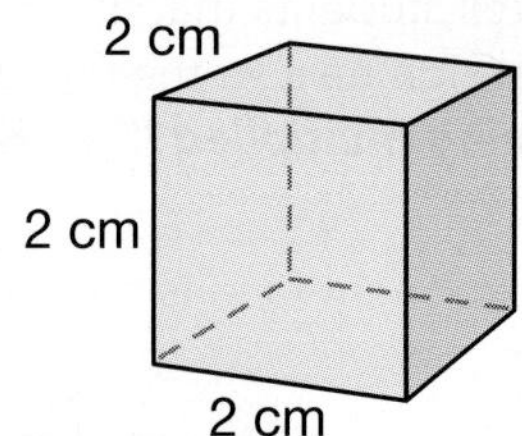

▶ *5. (64) **Evaluate** If $y = 2x + 3$, then what is y when $x = 4$? 11

*6. (Inv. 6) **Interpret** Use this data to answer parts **a** and **b.**

20, 30, 50, 80, 40, 10, 90

a. What is the mode? There is no mode.

b. What is the median? 40

▶ *7. (62) **Represent** Round each number to the given place.

a. Round 3.12 to the nearest tenth. 3.1

b. Round $7.55 to the nearest ten cents. $7.60

*8. (42) **a.** The line segment shown below is how many centimeters long? 3 cm

b. The segment is how many millimeters long? 30 mm

mm 10 20 30 40 50 60

cm 1 2 3 4 5 6

▶ 9. (55) The first four multiples of 9 are 9, 18, 27, and 36. What are the first four multiples of 90? 90, 180, 270, 360

▶ 10. (57) **Represent** Compare: $\frac{2}{3} \bigcirc \frac{2}{5}$. Draw and shade two equal rectangles to show the comparison. $>$

11. (58) Badu can ride her bike an average of 12 miles per hour. At that rate, how many miles could she ride in 4 hours? Make a table to solve this problem. 48 miles

Hours	Miles
1	12
2	24
3	36
4	48

12. (28, 51) $375.48 + $536.70 = $912.18

13. (51) 367,419 + 90,852 = 458,271

14. (45) 42.3 + 57.1 + 28.9 + 96.4 + 38.0 = 262.7

15. (28, 52) $20.00 − $19.39 = $0.61

16. (52) 310,419 − 250,527 = 59,892

English Learners

Explain to students that **customer service** is assistance and other resources that a company provides to the people who buy or use its products. Say:

"When you need to return an item to a store you go to customer service."

"Why else might you go to customer service?" See student work.

New Concept *(Continued)*

Closure

The questions below help assess the concepts taught in this lesson.

"What properties of multiplication allow us to multiply two or three factors in any order?" The commutative and associative properties

"What is an exponent, and what does an exponent represent? Give an example to support your answer." Sample: An exponent represents the number of times a base is to be used as a factor; $2^5 = 2 \times 2 \times 2 \times 2 \times 2 = 32$

Write "$2^2 + 2^3$" on the board or overhead and ask students to simplify the expression. $2^2 + 2^3 = 4 + 8 = 12$

Written Practice

Math Conversations

Independent Practice and Discussions to Increase Understanding

Problem 1

"To solve this problem, should we use a perimeter formula or an area formula? Explain how you know." An area formula; sample: Area is a measure of a surface, and distance is a measure of the length of the border of a surface.

Problem 5 **Evaluate**

Extend the Problem

Have students work in small groups to develop an organized or systematic way to find all of the possible ways to make $1 using only coins. Upon completion of the activity, have the groups compare their findings.

Problem 7 **Represent**

Ask students to identify the digit that is in each rounding place before they complete the arithmetic.

Problem 9

Extend the Problem

Have students compare the two lists of multiples and describe their similarities and differences.

(continued)

Written Practice *(Continued)*

Math Conversations *(cont.)*

Problem 10 Represent

Extend the Problem

Challenge students to state a generalization about comparing fractions that have the same numerator. Sample: If the numerators of two or more fractions are the same, the fraction with the greatest denominator is the least fraction and the fraction with the least denominator is the greatest fraction.

Problems 20–22

Ask students to use compatible numbers and make an estimate of each quotient before completing the arithmetic, and then use the estimate to help decide the reasonableness of the exact answer.

Problems 23–26

Before students complete any arithmetic for each problem, ask them to identify the operations that are present, and then name the order in which those operations will be performed.

Problem 27 Explain

Invite volunteers to write examples on the board or overhead to support their answers.

Problem 29

"Describe two relationships shared by the radius and the diameter of a circle." Sample: The length of a diameter is twice the length of a radius and the length of a radius is one-half the length of a diameter.

Problem 30 Estimate

Extend the Problem

Challenge your students to state a generalization that explains why the quotient of $50 \div 5$ is greater than the quotient of $47 \div 5$. Sample: Increasing a dividend without changing its divisor increases the quotient.

Errors and Misconceptions

Problem 10

Make sure students recall that whenever two shapes are drawn and then divided to compare two fractions, the shapes must be exactly the same size and shape (e. g. congruent).

Problem 24

Watch for students who simplify 4^2 as 4×2 or 8, and/or simplify 10^2 as 10×2 or 20.

Problem 30

Make sure students recognize that solving the problem first involves finding the elapsed time from 7 a.m. to noon (5 hours).

17. (59) $\$6.08 \times 7$ — \$42.56

18. (38) 86×4 — 344

19. (38) $59¢ \times 8$ — \$4.72

▶* **20.** (54) $3\overline{)23}$ 7 R 2

▶* **21.** (54) $8\overline{)30}$ 3 R 6

▶* **22.** (54) $5\overline{)33}$ 6 R 3

▶* **23.** (63) $(8 \times 2) \div (2 \cdot 2)$ 4

▶* **24.** (Inv. 3, 65) $\sqrt{36} + 4^2 + 10^2$ 122

▶ **25.** (64) $9 + m = 27 + 72$ 90

▶ **26.** (64) $6n = 4 \cdot 12$ 8

▶* **27.** (63) Explain If $p = r$ is the equation below true? How do you know? Equals multiplied by equals are equal.

$$p \cdot 100 = r \cdot 100$$

28. (33, 42) Model Use an inch ruler to find the lengths of segments *AB, BC,* and *AC.* $\overline{AB} = 1\frac{3}{4}$ in.; $\overline{BC} = 1\frac{1}{2}$ in.; $\overline{AC} = 3\frac{1}{4}$ in.

A ———— B ———— C

▶* **29.** (18, 42) If the diameter of a coin is 2 centimeters, then its radius is how many millimeters? 10 mm

▶* **30.** (61) Estimate From 7 a.m. until noon, the employees in a customer service department received 47 phone calls. What is a reasonable estimate of the number of calls that were received each hour? Explain how you found your answer. Sample: about 10 calls; Round 47 to the nearest ten and then divide by 5 hours; $50 \div 5 = 10$

Looking Forward

Evaluating an exponential expression for a given value prepares students for:

- **Lesson 71,** multiplying by multiples of 10.
- **Lesson 85,** multiplying two or more multiples of 10 and 100.
- **Lessons 86 and 88,** multiplying two two-digit numbers.
- **Lesson 91,** estimating the answers to multiplication and division problems.
- **Lesson 102,** using the Distributive Property to solve multiplication problems.
- **Lesson 105,** factoring whole numbers.

Cumulative Assessments and Test-Day Activity

Assessment

Distribute **Power-Up Test 12** and **Cumulative Test 12** to each student. Have students complete the Power-Up Test first. Allow 10 minutes. Then have students work on the **Cumulative Test.**

Test-Day Activity

The remaining class time can be spent on **Test-Day Activity 6.** Students can begin the activity in class and complete it as homework.

Planning & Preparation

• Area of a Rectangle

Objectives

- Use the formula $A = lw$ to find the area of a rectangle.
- Estimate the area of a rectangle by rounding to the nearest whole number.
- Choose the appropriate unit of measure for a given situation.

Prerequisite Skills

- Identifying the length and width of a rectangle.
- Classifying quadrilaterals by parallel sides.
- Using a formula to determine the perimeter of any rectangle.

Materials

Instructional Masters

- Power Up J Worksheet
- Lesson Activity 8*

Manipulative Kit

- Color tiles*

Teacher-provided materials

- Grid paper*

**optional*

California Mathematics Content Standards

NS 2.0, 2.2 Round two-place decimals to one decimal or the nearest whole number and judge the reasonableness of the rounded answer.

AF 1.0, 1.1 Use letters, boxes, or other symbols to stand for any number in simple expressions or equations (e.g., demonstrate an understanding and the use of the concept of a variable).

AF 1.0, 1.2 Interpret and evaluate mathematical expressions that now use parentheses.

AF 1.0, 1.4 Use and interpret formulas (e.g., area = length × width or $A = lw$) to answer questions about quantities and their relationships.

MG 1.0, 1.1 Measure the area of rectangular shapes by using appropriate units, such as square centimeter (cm^2), square meter (m^2), square kilometer (km^2), square inch (in^2), square yard (yd^2), or square mile (mi^2).

MG 1.0, 1.4 Understand and use formulas to solve problems involving perimeters and areas of rectangles and squares. Use those formulas to find the areas of more complex figures by dividing the figures into basic shapes.

MR 3.0, 3.2 Note the method of deriving the solution and demonstrate a conceptual understanding of the derivation by solving similar problems.

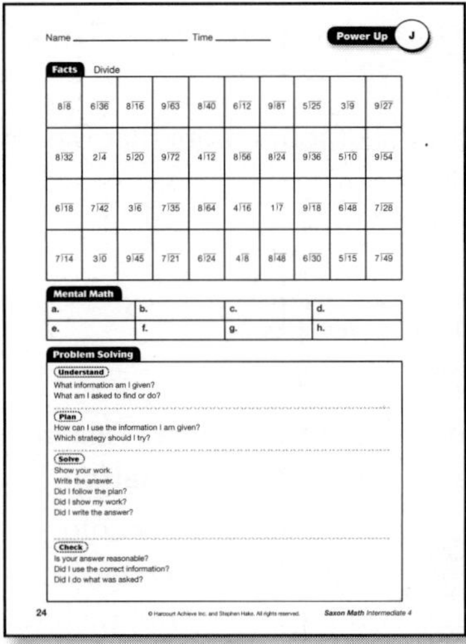

Name ____________ Time ________ **Power Up J**

Facts Divide

$8\overline{)8}$	$6\overline{)36}$	$8\overline{)16}$	$9\overline{)63}$	$8\overline{)40}$	$6\overline{)12}$	$9\overline{)81}$	$5\overline{)25}$	$3\overline{)9}$	$9\overline{)27}$
$8\overline{)32}$	$2\overline{)4}$	$5\overline{)20}$	$9\overline{)72}$	$4\overline{)12}$	$8\overline{)56}$	$8\overline{)24}$	$9\overline{)36}$	$5\overline{)10}$	$9\overline{)54}$
$6\overline{)18}$	$7\overline{)42}$	$3\overline{)6}$	$7\overline{)35}$	$8\overline{)64}$	$4\overline{)16}$	$1\overline{)7}$	$9\overline{)18}$	$6\overline{)48}$	$7\overline{)28}$
$7\overline{)14}$	$3\overline{)0}$	$9\overline{)45}$	$7\overline{)21}$	$6\overline{)24}$	$4\overline{)8}$	$8\overline{)48}$	$6\overline{)30}$	$5\overline{)15}$	$7\overline{)49}$

Mental Math

a.	b.	c.	d.
e.	f.	g.	h.

Problem Solving

Understand
What information am I given?
What am I asked to find or do?

Plan
How can I use the information I am given?
Which strategy should I try?

Solve
Show your work.
Write the answer.
Did I follow the plan?
Did I show my work?
Did I write the answer?

Check
Is your answer reasonable?
Did I use the correct information?
Did I do what was asked?

24 Saxon Math Intermediate 4

Power Up J Worksheet

Universal Access

Reaching All Special Needs Students

Special Education Students	At-Risk Students	English Learners	Advanced Learners
• Inclusion (TM) • Adaptations for Saxon Math	• Alternative Approach (TM) • Error Alert (TM) • Reteaching Masters • Refresher Lessons for California Standards	• English Learners (TM) • Developing Academic Language (TM) • English Learner Handbook	• Extend the Example (TM) • Extend the Problem (TM) • Online Activities

TM=Teacher's Manual

Developing Academic Language

Maintained	**English Learner**
area	driveway
formula	
length	
perimeter	
squared	
width	

Problem Solving Discussion

Problem

Dasha plans to use only four different colored pencils to color the states on a United States map. She has five different colored pencils from which to choose—red, orange, yellow, green, and blue. What are the combinations of four colors Dasha can choose? (There are five combinations.)

Focus Strategy  **Make an Organized List**

Understand *Understand the problem.*

"What information are we given?"

Dasha has five pencil colors: **1.** red, **2.** orange, **3.** yellow, **4.** green, and **5.** blue.

"What are we asked to do?"

We are asked to find the combinations of four colors that Dasha could use to color her United States map.

Plan *Make a plan.*

"What problem-solving strategy can we use?"

We can *make an organized list* of the combinations.

"Notice that Dasha will pick four of her five colors. This means that she will not use one of the colors. How can we use this information to organize our list?"

Each possible combination *does not include* one of the colors. Thus, we can find the combination that does not include red, then the combination that does not include orange, then the combination that does not include yellow, then the combination that does not include green, and finally, the combination that does not include blue.

Solve *Carry out the plan.*

"What is a combination of four colors that does not include red?"

orange, yellow, green, blue

"What is a combination of four colors that does not include orange?"

red, yellow, green, blue

"What is a combination of four colors that does not include yellow?"

red, orange, green, blue

"What is a combination of four colors that does not include green?"

red, orange, yellow, blue

"What is a combination of four colors that does not include blue?"

red, orange, yellow, green

Check *Look back.*

"How many combinations did we find?"

We found five combinations of four colors that Dasha could use to color her map.

"Is our answer reasonable?"

We know that our answer is reasonable, because each possible combination excludes exactly one of the colors. We cannot find any other combinations, because there are no other colors from Dasha's set that can be excluded from a combination.

LESSON 66

• Area of a Rectangle

California Mathematics Content Standards

NS 2.0, 2.2 Round two-place decimals to one decimal or the nearest whole number and judge the reasonableness of the rounded answer.

MG 1.0, 1.1 Measure the area of rectangular shapes by using appropriate units, such as square centimeter (cm^2), square meter (m^2), square kilometer (km^2), square inch (in^2), square yard (yd^2), or square mile (mi^2).

MG 1.0, 1.4 Understand and use formulas to solve problems involving perimeters and areas of rectangles and squares. Use those formulas to find the areas of more complex figures by dividing the figures into basic shapes.

Power Up

facts Power Up J

count aloud Count down by fives from 51 to 1.

mental math Multiply three numbers, including numbers ending in zero, in problems **a–c.**

a. Number Sense: $3 \times 10 \times 20$ 600

b. Number Sense: $4 \times 20 \times 30$ 2400

c. Number Sense: $3 \times 40 \times 10$ 1200

d. Powers/Roots: $2^2 + 5^2$ 29

e. Geometry: Altogether, how many sides do 3 hexagons have? 18 sides

f. Money: Logan owes $10.00 for his club dues. He has $9.24. How much more money does Logan need? $0.76

g. Estimation: Liev wants to buy 6 stickers that each cost 21¢. Liev has $1.15. Does he have enough money to buy 6 stickers? No

h. Calculation[1]**:** $\sqrt{16}$, × 2, × 2, + 4, × 2 40

problem solving Choose an appropriate problem-solving strategy to solve this problem. Dasha plans to use only four different colored pencils to color the states on a United States map. She has five different colored pencils from which to choose—red, orange, yellow, green, and blue. What are the combinations of four colors Dasha can choose? (There are five combinations.) Red, orange, yellow, green; red, orange, yellow, blue; red, orange, green, blue; red, yellow, green, blue; orange, yellow, green, blue

[1] As a shorthand, we will use commas to separate operations to be performed sequentially from left to right. In this case, $\sqrt{16} = 4$, then $4 \times 2 = 8$, then $8 \times 2 = 16$, then $16 + 4 = 20$, then $20 \times 2 = 40$. The answer is 40.

Power Up

Facts

Distribute **Power Up J** to students. See answers below.

Count Aloud

Before students begin the Mental Math exercise, do these counting exercises as a class.

Mental Math

Encourage students to share different ways to mentally compute these exercises. Strategies for exercises are listed below.

b. Multiply Nonzero Digits, Write Zeros

$4 \times 2 \times 3 = 24$; $4 \times 20 \times 30 = 2400$

f. Count Up from $9.24, then Add

$9.24 + 6¢ = $9.30; $9.30 + 70¢ = $10; 6¢ + 70¢ = 76¢

Count Back from $10, then Add

$10 − 70¢ = $9.30; $9.30 − 6¢ = $9.24; 70¢ + 6¢ = 76¢

g. Round, Multiply, Compare

21¢ rounds to 20¢; 6 × 20¢ = 120¢; $1.20 > $1.15; not enough money

Problem Solving

Refer to **Problem-Solving Strategy Discussion,** p. 441B.

Facts Divide

1 8)8	6 6)36	2 8)16	7 9)63	5 8)40	2 6)12	9 9)81	5 5)25	3 3)9	3 9)27
4 8)32	2 2)4	4 5)20	8 9)72	3 4)12	7 8)56	3 8)24	4 9)36	2 5)10	6 9)54
3 6)18	6 7)42	2 3)6	5 7)35	8 8)64	4 4)16	7 1)7	2 9)18	8 6)48	4 7)28
2 7)14	0 3)0	5 9)45	3 7)21	4 6)24	2 4)8	6 8)48	5 6)30	3 5)15	7 7)49

New Concept

Active Learning

As you discuss the formula $A = l \times w$, ask:

"In the formula A = l × w, what does each letter represent?" *A* represents the area of the rectangle, *l* represents the length, and *w* represents the width.

"Each time we use the formula 'area equals length times width,' will we always use the same number for l and for w? Explain why or why not." No; sample: Different rectangles have different lengths and widths.

Error Alert

When students multiply a length and a width to find the area of a rectangle, some students may conclude that the longest dimension of the rectangle is its length. While other students, because of how the rectangle is drawn, will conclude that the longest dimension is its width. Explain that both conclusions are acceptable because we simply multiply the two measures, and the Commutative Property of Multiplication enables us to multiply two numbers in any order.

Example 1

As you discuss part **a** of the solution, make sure students understand that the perimeter formula is used because we are finding the distance around the box.

As you discuss part **b** of the solution, make sure students understand that the area formula is used because we are finding a measure of an entire surface (or face) of the rectangle.

Extend the Example

Extend the part **a** solution by reminding students of the importance of checking their work, and inviting advanced learners to describe an addition equation that could be used to check the answer. Sample: 10 in. + 10 in. + 8 in. + 8 in.

(continued)

We have learned to find the perimeter and area of rectangles. We know that the distance around a figure is its perimeter and the number of square units that cover a figure is its area.

Today we are going to learn a formula to find the area of a rectangle. We know that we can multiply 3 by 6 to find the total number of square centimeters that cover this figure.

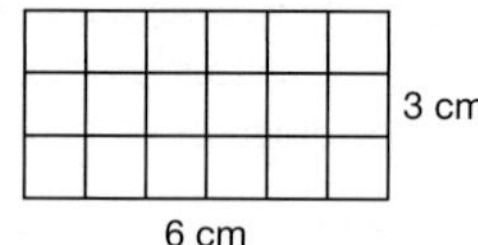

$6 \times 3 = 18$ square cm

We multiplied the length times the width to find the area. So, the formula for finding the area is Area = length × width or $A = l \times w$.

$$\begin{aligned} A &= l \times w \\ &= 6 \text{ cm} \times 3 \text{ cm} \\ &= (6 \times 3) \times (\text{cm} \times \text{cm}) \\ &= 18 \text{ sq. cm or } 18 \text{ cm}^2 \end{aligned}$$

We read 18 cm^2 as 18 square centimeters.

Example 1

Robin has a box that is 8 in. wide and 10 in. long.

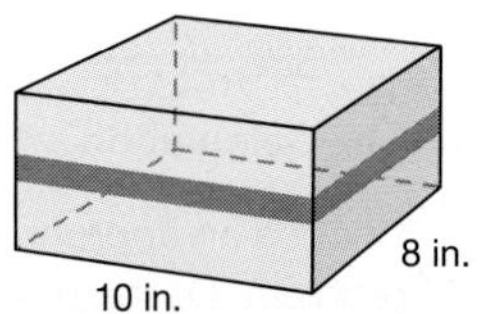

a. She wants to paint a stripe all around the box. How long will the stripe be?

b. She wants to use fabric inside the box to cover bottom. How much fabric does she need?

Math Background

"If I know the perimeter of a rectangle, can I figure out its area?"

No. For example, all three rectangles below have a perimeter of 12 units, but their areas are all different.

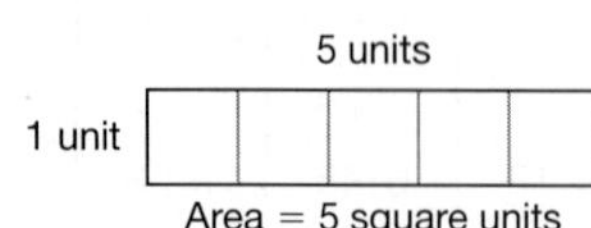

Area = 5 square units

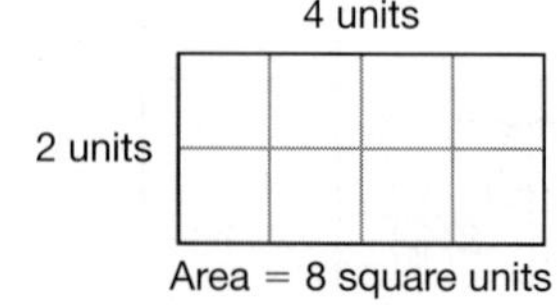

Area = 8 square units

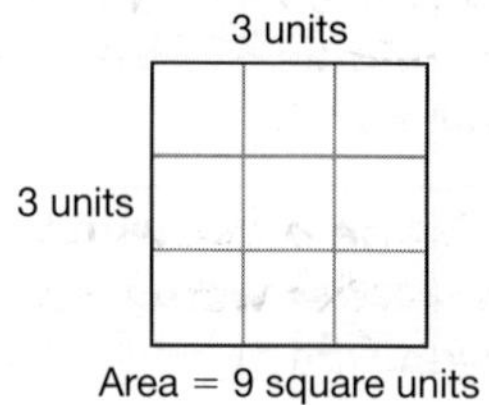

Area = 9 square units

a. The stripe will be painted around the box. We can use the perimeter formula to find the distance around the box.

$$\begin{aligned} P &= 2l + 2w \\ &= (2 \times 10) + (2 \times 8) \\ &= 20 + 16 \\ &= 36 \text{ in.} \end{aligned}$$

The stripe will be **36 in.** long.

b. The fabric liner will cover the bottom of the box. We can use the area formula to find the area of the bottom of the box.

$$\begin{aligned} A &= l \times w \\ &= 10 \times 8 \\ &= 80 \\ &= 80 \text{ in}^2 \end{aligned}$$

Robin needs **80 in^2** of fabric.

Reading Math

We read 80 in^2 as 80 square inches.

Discuss Why did we write the amount of fabric as 80 in^2 and not 80 in.? Area is measured in square units, perimeter is measured in linear units.

Example 2

Reading Math

We read s^2 as "s squared," which means $s \times s$.

Use the formula for the area of a square to find the area of this square.

5 in.

The formula for the area of a square is $A = s^2$. The length of each side is 5 in. Replace the "s" in the formula with 5 in.

$$A = (5 \text{ in.})^2$$

Multiplying 5 in. × 5 in., we find the area of the square is 25 sq. in. We can write the answer **25 in^2** or **25 sq. in.**

Example 3

Michelle wants to have her driveway repaved. The driveway is 8.25 ft by 42.75 ft. Estimate the area of the driveway.

To estimate, we will first we round each measurement to the nearest whole number.

8.25 ft rounds to 8 ft

42.75 ft rounds to 43 ft

English Learners

Say, ***"The word driveway is made up of two smaller words—drive and way—which tell the meaning of the single word, driveway. Driveway is a compound word. It is made up of two smaller words."***

Say, ***"Name other words that are made up of smaller words and tell their meaning."*** Samples: backpack, sunrise, etc

New Concept *(Continued)*

Example 2

Reading Math

Point out that although s^2 is read "s squared," both "in^2" and "sq. in." are read as "square inches."

Example 3

Error Alert

Have students note that this problem asks them to estimate the area of the driveway, but does not specifically tell them to round the dimensions of the driveway to make the estimate, or use the given dimensions and round the answer. Explain that unless a problem involving estimation specifically asks us to round an answer to a given place, we always round the numbers that are used to find the answer. Point out that using the given dimensions and rounding the answer is the same as finding an exact answer, which is very different than finding an estimate.

(continued)

New Concept (Continued)

Lesson Practice

Guided Practice

Use these problems as guided practice to check the students' understanding of today's concept.

Problems a and b

Before students begin any arithmetic, write the formulas $P = 2l + 2w$ and $A = l \times w$ on the board or overhead and invite volunteers describe the substitutions that need to be made in order to solve each problem.

Problem b
Error Alert

Remind students that they must first round each dimension to the nearest whole number before multiplying.

Closure

The questions below help assess the concepts taught in this lesson.

"Explain how finding the perimeter of a shape is different than finding its area." Sample: Perimeter is a measure of the distance around the outside of the shape; Area is a measure of the amount of surface the shape covers.

"Explain how to use the formulas $P = 2l + 2w$ and $A = l \times w$ to find the perimeter and area of a rectangle." Substitute the length of the rectangle for l, substitute the width of the rectangle for w, and then follow the order of operations to simplify the equation.

Written Practice

Math Conversations

Independent Practice and Discussions to Increase Understanding

Problem 2 (Analyze)

Extend the Problem

"If Alejandro's mower was 18 inches wide instead of 24 inches wide, would he have to push the mower more times or fewer times along the length of his yard? Explain why." More times; sample: Less of the yard is being mowed.

Problem 3

Remind students of the importance of checking their work, and then ask them to use a multiplication fact to check their answers.

(continued)

Now we can use the area formula.

$$A = l \times w$$
$$= 43 \text{ ft} \times 8 \text{ ft}$$
$$= 344 \text{ ft}^2$$

The area of the driveway is **344 ft²**.

Lesson Practice

a. Matthew's kitchen is 9 ft wide and 15 ft long. What is the perimeter and area of the room? $P = 48$ ft, $A = 135$ ft²

b. What is the area of this rectangle rounded to the nearest whole number? 240 m²

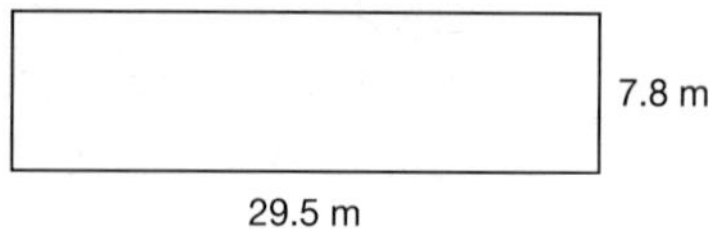

(rectangle: 29.5 m by 7.8 m)

Written Practice

Distributed and Integrated

1. (58) Christie's car travels 18 miles on each gallon of gas. How many miles can it travel on 10 gallons of gas? 180 miles

▶ ***2.** (20, 42, 53) (Analyze) Alejandro mowed a yard that was 50 feet wide. Each time he pushed the mower along the length of the yard, he mowed a path 24 inches wide. To mow the entire yard, how many times did Alejandro need to push the mower along the length of the yard? 25 times

▶ ***3.** (53) A gift of $60 is to be divided equally among 6 children. What amount of money will each child receive? $10

4. (13) Soccer practice lasts for an hour and a half. If practice starts at 3:15 p.m., at what time does it end? 4:45 p.m.

▶ ***5.** (46, 62) **a.** Round 4.37 to the nearest tenth. 4.4

b. Round 4.37 to the nearest whole number. 4

c. Round $8.34 to the nearest ten cents. $8.30

d. Round $8.34 to the nearest dollar. $8.00

Inclusion

Use this strategy if the student displays:

- Difficulty with Abstract Concept Processing.
- Difficulty with Large Group Instruction.

Area of a Rectangle (Individual)

Material: grid paper

- Have students draw a 4 × 3 rectangle on their grid paper. Ask them to label the sides and find the rectangle's perimeter by adding up all four sides. Ask, ***"What is perimeter of the rectangle?"*** 14 units
- Tell students to shade the inside squares of the rectangle and count up how many there are. Ask, ***"How many squares are inside of the rectangle?"*** 12 squares
- Tell students that this is called the area of the rectangle and it can always be found using the formula $A = l \times w$.
- Have students draw 3 rectangles on their grid paper and label their side lengths. Have students find the area of each rectangle and have a partner check it.

6. Find the perimeter and area of the rectangle at right.
(66)
14 m, 12 m^2

4 m
3 m

▸ ***7.** **Estimate** This key is 60 mm long. The key is how many centimeters long? 6 cm
(42)

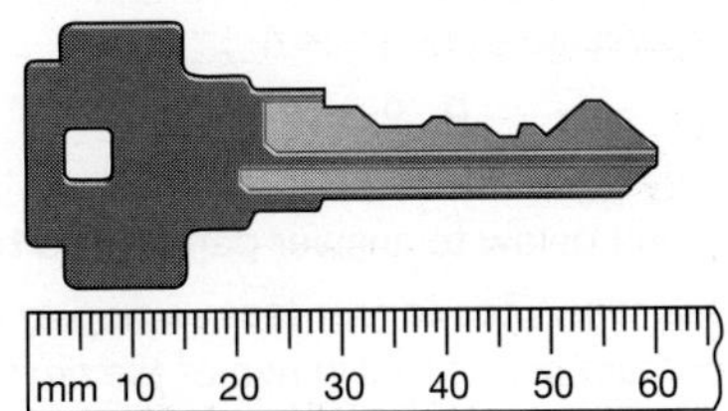

8. According to this calendar, the year 1902 began on what day of the week? Wednesday
(RF12)

DECEMBER 1901						
S	M	T	W	T	F	S
1	2	3	4	5	6	7
8	9	10	11	12	13	14
15	16	17	18	19	20	21
22	23	24	25	26	27	28
29	30	31				

***9.** **Estimate** A sheet of paper is 8.5 in. wide and 11 in. long. Estimate the area of the paper. Explain your thinking. 99 in^2; Round 8.5 in. to the nearest whole number and multiply: 9×11
(Inv. 3, 61)

10. A meter equals 100 centimeters. If each side of a square is 1 meter long, then what is the perimeter of the square in centimeters? 400 cm
(20, 42)

11. List the first four multiples of 70. 70, 140, 210, 280
(55)

12. $1.68 + 32¢ + $6.37 + $5 $13.37
(28)

13. $4.3 + 2.4 + 0.8 + 6.7$ 14.2
(45)

14. **Explain** Find $10 − ($6.46 + $2.17). Describe the steps you used.
(9, 28, 52)
$1.37; sample: First add ($6.46 + $2.17 = $8.63), and then subtract ($10.00 − $8.63 = $1.37).

15. $5 \times 4 \times 5$ 100
(65)

16. 359×7 2513
(59)

17. 5×74 370
(38)

18. $4\overline{)30}$ 7 R 2
(54)

19. $5\overline{)43}$ 8 R 3
(54)

20. $8\overline{)76}$ 9 R 4
(54)

Written Practice *(Continued)*

Math Conversations *(cont.)*

Problem 5

Before students round each number, ask them to name the rounding place, and then name the two possible numbers that the given number could be rounded to.

problem **a:** tenths; 4.3 or 4.4

problem **b:** ones; 4 or 5

problem **c:** dimes or tenths of a dollar; $8.30 or $8.40

problem **d:** dollars; $8 or $9

Problem 7 **Estimate**

"Describe the relationship shared by centimeters and millimeters."

1 cm = 10 mm

(continued)

Alternative Approach: Using Manipulatives

To model the area of a 2-by-3-inch rectangle using colored tiles, distribute at least six tiles to each group of students. Instruct students to arrange the tiles to form a 2-by-3 rectangle. (Remind them that each tile is one square inch and that each side has a measure of one inch.) Then have students count the tiles to find the area of a 2-by-3-inch rectangle in square inches.

Written Practice *(Continued)*

Math Conversations *(cont.)*

Problems 24–26

Before students complete any arithmetic for each problem, ask them to identify the operations that are present, and then name the order in which those operations will be performed.

Problem 27 Analyze

Make sure students recognize that extra information is present in the problem.

Problem 29 Multiple Choice

Test-Taking Strategy

Remind students that a sensible way to identify the figure that is *not* a hexagon is to first identify those figures that are hexagons.

Problem 30  Represent

Extend the Problem

Have advanced learners write their own word problems for others to solve using the information in this table. Sample: What animal has the same weight as the sum of the weights of the ringtail monkey and the chicken? (the otter)

Errors and Misconceptions

Problem 3

Students whose answer is \$1 did not complete the division. Demonstrate for these students how the four steps of the division algorithm are repeated as often as needed to divide \$60 by 6, and then offer the divisions below for additional practice.

\$50 ÷ 5 \$10   \$80 ÷ 8 \$10   \$30 ÷ 3 \$10

Also remind these students of the importance of checking their work.

Problem 11

A common error when naming multiples of a number is to not name the number itself. Remind students that a multiple of a number is the product of that number and a counting number, and point out that since the counting numbers are 1, 2, 3, and so on, the first multiple of every number is that number times 1. The second multiple of every number is that number times 2. The third multiple of every number is that number times 3. And so on.

***21.** (64) $6n = 30 + 18$ 8

***22.** (65) $3^3 + 2^3$ 35

***23.** (64) If $y = 2x + 8$, then what is y when $x = 6$? 20

Connect Simplify each expression. Remember to use the order of operations.

▸*24. (63) $8 \times 5 + 45 \div 9$ 45

▸*25. (63) $49 \div 7 - 5 + 9$ 11

▸*26. (63) **Evaluate** Simplify each expression when $v = 4$.

a. $36 - 12 \div v$ 33

b. $6 + (8 - v) \times 10$ 46

▸*27. (12) **Analyze** Use the information below to answer parts **a** and **b.**

Kamili scored two goals when her soccer team won 5 to 4 on November 3. To make the playoffs, her team needs to win two of the next three games.

a. How many goals were scored by Kamili's teammates? 3 goals

b. Kamili's team has won four games and lost three games. Altogether, how many games does Kamili's team need to win to make the playoffs? 6 games

28. (17) **a.** **Classify** Angles C and D of this polygon are right angles. Which angle appears to be an obtuse angle? Angle B

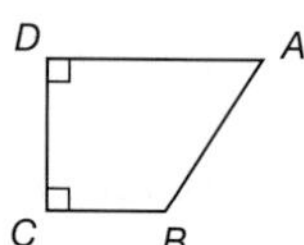

b. **Classify** Which segments are perpendicular? $\overline{DC}$ and $\overline{CB}$, $\overline{DC}$ and $\overline{DA}$

c. **Classify** Which segments are parallel? $\overline{DA}$ and $\overline{CB}$

▸*29. (50) **Multiple Choice** Which of the following is *not* a hexagon? C

A 
B 
C 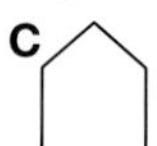
D 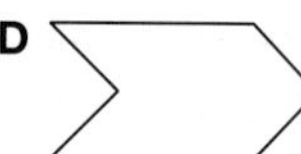

▸*30. (Inv. 5) **Represent** The average weights of some animals are shown in the table. Make a bar graph to display the data. See student work.

Average Weights of Animals

Animal	Weight (in pounds)
Domestic Rabbit	8
Otter	13
Ringtail Monkey	6
Chicken	7

446 *Saxon Math* Intermediate 4

Looking Forward

Estimating and calculating the area of a rectangle prepares students for:

- **Lesson 70,** identifying similar and congruent figures.
- **Lesson 78,** measuring turns.
- **Lesson 81,** classifying triangles by angle measures and the length of its sides.
- **Lesson 82,** identifying and drawing lines of symmetry.
- **Lesson 90,** classifying quadrilaterals.
- **Lesson 96,** classifying geometric solids by their vertices, edges, and faces.
- **Lesson 97,** making three-dimensional models of rectangular and triangular prisms.
- **Lesson 108,** identifying the attributes of geometric solids.
- **Lesson 109,** describing the attributes of pyramids.
- **Lesson 114,** determining the perimeter and area of complex figures.

Planning & Preparation

• Remaining Fractions

Objectives

- Find the size of a portion of a whole when the size of the other portion is given.

Prerequisite Skills

- Solving an addition word problem in which the total is given and an addend is missing.
- Using the addition algorithm to find the missing number in a subtraction problem.

Materials

Instructional Masters

- Power Up I Worksheet
- Lesson Activity 8*

Manipulative Kit

- Fraction circles*

Teacher-provided materials

- Grid paper*

*optional

California Mathematics Content Standards

NS 1.0, 1.5 Explain different interpretations of fractions, for example, parts of a whole, parts of a set, and division of whole numbers by whole numbers; explain equivalents of fractions (see Standard 4.0).

NS 1.0, 1.7 Write the fraction represented by a drawing of parts of a figure; represent a given fraction by using drawings; and relate a fraction to a simple decimal on a number line.

MR 2.0, 2.4 Express the solution clearly and logically by using the appropriate mathematical notation and terms and clear language; support solutions with evidence in both verbal and symbolic work.

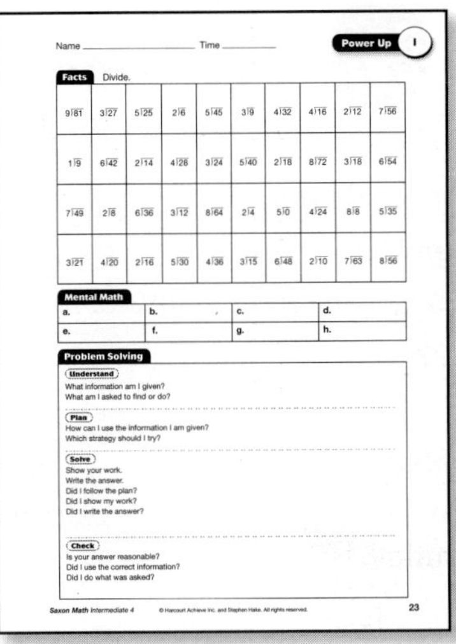

Power Up I Worksheet

Universal Access

Reaching All Special Needs Students

Special Education Students	At-Risk Students	English Learners	Advanced Learners
• Inclusion (TM) • Adaptations for Saxon Math	• Error Alert (TM) • Reteaching Masters • Refresher Lessons for California Standards	• English Learners (TM) • Developing Academic Language (TM) • English Learner Handbook	• Extend the Example (TM) • Extend the Problem (TM) • Online Activities

TM=Teacher's Manual

Developing Academic Language

Maintained	English Learner
compare	cheer
fraction	

Problem Solving Discussion

Problem

Mathea exercised for half of an hour. For half of her exercise time, she was running. For how many minutes was Mathea exercising? For how many minutes was she running?

Focus Strategies

Make It Simpler

Use Logical Reasoning

Understand *Understand the problem.*

"What information are we given?"

Mathea exercised for 50% of an hour. She ran for 50% of her exercise time.

"What fraction is equal to 50%?"

The fraction $\frac{1}{2}$ is equal to 50%.

"What are we asked to determine?"

We are asked to find **1.** how many minutes Mathea was exercising and **2.** how many of those minutes Mathea was running.

Plan *Make a plan.*

"How can we use the information we know to solve the problem?"

We need to find the number of minutes in 50% of an hour. Then we need to find 50% of that number of minutes.

Solve *Carry out the plan.*

"Mathea exercised for 50% of an hour. How many minutes did Mathea exercise?"

One hour is 60 minutes. Half of 60 is 30, so *"Mathea exercised for 30 minutes."*

"Mathea ran for 50% of her exercise time. How many minutes did Mathea run?"

Half of 30 minutes is 15 minutes, so *"Mathea ran for 15 minutes."*

Check *Look back.*

"Are our answers reasonable?"

We know that our answers are reasonable, because half of 60 is 30, and half of 30 is 15.

"What problem-solving strategies did we use, and how did they help us?"

We *made the problem simpler* by changing one hour into 60 minutes. Then we *used logical reasoning* to find the portion of the 60 minutes that Mathea exercised and the portion of the exercise time that she ran.

"How can we represent this problem using a diagram?"

Our diagram might look like this:

50% 30 min | 50% 30 min
1 hour

50% 15 min
15 min 50%
$\frac{1}{2}$ hour

"Why is 50% in the whole circle bigger than 50% in the half circle?"

Fifty percent of one hour is greater than 50% of 30 minutes. In the half circle, we are considering 30 minutes (instead of 60 minutes) as the whole 100%. This diagram helps us see that 50% of 50% is one fourth, and one fourth of an hour is 15 minutes.

Alternate Strategy

Draw a Picture or Diagram

To help the students visualize the problem, have them draw a diagram showing the portion of time that Mathea was exercising and the portion of time that she was running.

LESSON

• Remaining Fractions

California Mathematics Content Standards

NS 1.0, 1.5 Explain different interpretations of fractions, for example, parts of a whole, parts of a set, and division of whole numbers by whole numbers; explain equivalents of fractions (see Standard 4.0).

NS 1.0, 1.7 Write the fraction represented by a drawing of parts of a figure; represent a given fraction by using drawings; and relate a fraction to a simple decimal on a number line.

Power Up

facts Power Up I

count aloud When we count by fives from 2, we say the numbers 2, 7, 12, 17, and so on. Count by fives from 2 to 52.

mental math Multiply numbers ending in two zeros by numbers ending in one zero in problems **a–c.**

a. Number Sense: 200×10 2000

b. Number Sense: 300×20 6000

c. Number Sense: 400×50 20000

d. Fractional Part: $\frac{1}{2}$ of \$10 \$5.00

e. Fractional Part: $\frac{1}{4}$ of \$10 \$2.50

f. Fractional Part: $\frac{1}{10}$ of \$10 \$1.00

g. Estimation: Estimate the total cost of two items priced at \$3.88 each and one item priced at \$5.98. \$14

h. Calculation: 4^2, + 34, + 72, − 24 98

problem solving Choose an appropriate problem-solving strategy to solve this problem. Mathea exercised for half of an hour. For half of her exercise time, she was running. For how many minutes was Mathea exercising? For how many minutes was she running? 30 min; 15 min

New Concept

The whole circle in Example 1 on the following page has a shaded portion and an unshaded portion. If we know the size of one portion of a whole, then we can figure out the size of the other portion.

Power Up

Facts

Distribute **Power Up I** to students. See answers below.

Count Aloud

Before students begin the Mental Math exercise, do these counting exercises as a class.

Mental Math

Encourage students to share different ways to mentally compute these exercises. Strategies for exercises are listed below.

a. Multiply Nonzero Digits, Write Zeros
Write 3 zeros after the product 2×1; $200 \times 10 = 2000$.

b. Multiply Nonzero Digits, Write Zeros
Write 3 zeros after the product 3×2; $300 \times 20 = 6000$.

c. Multiply Nonzero Digits, Write Zeros
Write 3 zeros after the product 4×5; $400 \times 50 = 20,000$.

f. Divide by 10
$\$10 \div 10$; $\$10 \div 10 = \$1$

Problem Solving

Refer to **Problem-Solving Strategy Discussion,** p. 447B.

Facts Divide.

9 9)81	9 3)27	5 5)25	3 2)6	9 5)45	3 3)9	8 4)32	4 4)16	6 2)12	8 7)56
9 1)9	7 6)42	7 2)14	7 4)28	8 3)24	8 5)40	9 2)18	9 8)72	6 3)18	9 6)54
7 7)49	4 2)8	6 6)36	4 3)12	8 8)64	2 2)4	0 5)0	6 4)24	1 8)8	7 5)35
7 3)21	5 4)20	8 2)16	6 5)30	9 4)36	5 3)15	8 6)48	5 2)10	9 7)63	7 8)56

New Concept

Example 1

As you discuss the solution, make sure students understand that when a fraction is used to describe the shaded part of a whole, the numerator of the fraction represents the number of shaded parts, and the denominator represents the number of equal parts into which the whole has been divided.

Active Learning

"What fraction describes any one of the eight equal parts of the circle?" $\frac{1}{8}$

"What fraction describes the whole circle?" $\frac{8}{8}$

Extend the Example

Challenge your advanced learners by asking:

"How do we change the circle so that the equal sign can be used to compare the shaded and unshaded parts of the circle?" Shade one more part.

Example 2

Ask students to explain if the circle in Example 1 can be used to represent the situation in Example 2. Yes; sample: The shaded parts of the circle represent the quesadilla slices taken by Willis, Hunter, and Svelita. The unshaded parts of the circle represent the slices that were not taken.

Example 3

Point out that the fraction $\frac{5}{5}$ represents the unstated information in this example, and make sure students understand that in order to find the fraction of the crowd who did not cheer, we must subtract the fraction of the crowd who did cheer $\left(\frac{2}{5}\right)$ from the whole crowd $\left(\text{which is unstated, and } \frac{5}{5}\right)$.

Error Alert

Some students may need to draw a sketch to help them solve the problem.

(continued)

Example 1

a. What fraction of the circle is shaded?

b. What fraction of the circle is not shaded?

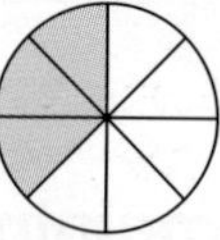

We see that the whole circle has been divided into eight equal parts. Three of the parts are shaded, so five of the parts are not shaded.

a. The fraction that is shaded is $\frac{3}{8}$.

b. The fraction that is not shaded is $\frac{5}{8}$.

Represent Compare the shaded part to the part not shaded using >, <, or =. $\frac{3}{8} < \frac{5}{8}$ or $\frac{5}{8} > \frac{3}{8}$

Example 2

The quesadilla was cut into eight equal slices. After Willis, Hunter, and Svelita each took a slice, what fraction was left?

The whole quesadilla was cut into eight equal parts. Since three of the eight parts were taken, five of the eight parts remained. The fraction that was left was $\frac{5}{8}$.

Example 3

Two fifths of the crowd cheered. What fraction of the crowd did not cheer?

We think of the crowd as though it were divided into five equal parts. We are told that two of the five parts cheered. So there were three parts that did not cheer. The fraction of the crowd that did not cheer was $\frac{3}{5}$.

Lesson Practice

a. What fraction of this rectangle is not shaded? $\frac{5}{6}$

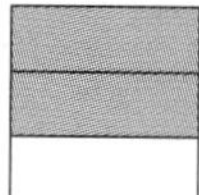

b. Three fifths of the race was over. What fraction of the race was left? $\frac{2}{5}$

Written Practice *Distributed and Integrated*

*1. (67) Two thirds of the pencils are sharpened. What fraction of the pencils are *not* sharpened? Draw a picture to solve the problem. one third

English Learners

A **cheer** is a shout of praise or encouragement. Explain that it is something people do to motivate other people. Cheerleaders, for example, **cheer** during a football game to encourage the football team and audience.

Ask:

"During what other performances might people cheer?" Samples: soccer game, wrestling match, etc.

▶ *2. If $y = 5x + 10$, then what is y when $x = 5$? 35
(64)

*3. Use this information to answer parts **a–c:**
(28, 39, 53)

Thirty students are going on a field trip. Each car can hold five students. The field trip will cost each student $5.

a. How many cars are needed for the field trip? 6 cars

b. Altogether, how much money will be needed? $150

c. Don has saved $3.25. How much more does he need to go on the field trip? $1.75

4. **Analyze** During the summer the swim team practiced $3\frac{1}{2}$ hours a day. If practice started at 6:30 a.m., at what time did it end if there were no breaks? 10:00 a.m.
(13)

▶ *5. **a.** Round 5.26 to the nearest tenth. 5.3
(46, 62)

b. Round 5.26 to the nearest whole number. 5

c. Round $10.65 to the nearest ten cents. $10.70

d. Round $10.65 to the nearest dollar. $11.00

6. A mile is five thousand, two hundred eighty feet. The Golden Gate Bridge is four thousand, two hundred feet long. The Golden Gate Bridge is how many feet less than 1 mile long? 1080 ft
(16, 42, 52)

▶ **7.** **Multiple Choice** Which of these numbers is *not* a multiple of 90? A
(55)

A 45 **B** 180 **C** 270 **D** 360

8. What number is halfway between 300 and 400? 350
(Inv. 2)

9. 37.56 − 4.2 33.36
(45)

10. 4.2 + 3.5 + 0.25 + 4.0
(45) 11.95

11. Each side of a regular polygon has the same length. A regular hexagon is shown to the right. How many millimeters is the perimeter of this hexagon? 60 mm
(20, 42)

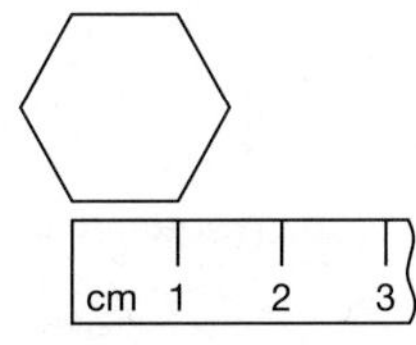

12. $\sqrt{25} \times m = 45$
(Inv. 3, 64) 9

13. $z - 476 = 325$
(6, 8) 801

14. $6a = 12 + 6$ 3
(64)

New Concept *(Continued)*

Lesson Practice

Guided Practice

Use these problems as guided practice to check the students' understanding of today's concept.

Problem a

Before students solve the problem, ask:

"When we write a fraction to represent the shaded part of a whole, what does the numerator of the fraction represent?" The number of shaded parts

"What does the denominator of the fraction represent?" The number of equal parts in the whole

Problem b

Error Alert

Students must recognize that because $\frac{3}{5}$ of the race was completed, the entire race is divided into 5 equal parts.

Closure

The questions below help assess the concepts taught in this lesson.

Sketch a square on the board or overhead, divide the square into 4 equal parts, and shade 3 of those parts. Then ask:

"What fraction of this square is shaded?" $\frac{3}{4}$

"What fraction of this square is not shaded?" $\frac{1}{4}$

"The whole square is made up of shaded parts and unshaded parts. What fraction represents the whole square?" $\frac{4}{4}$

Written Practice

Math Conversations

Independent Practice and Discussions to Increase Understanding

Problem 1

"When we write a fraction to represent the shaded part of a whole, what part of the fraction represents the number of equal parts in the whole?" The denominator

"What part of the fraction represents the number of shaded parts?" The numerator

(continued)

Inclusion

Use this strategy if the student displays:

- Difficulty with Reading.
- Difficulty with Large Group Instruction.

Remaining Fractions (Pair)

Materials: fraction circles

- Have students display fraction circles for $\frac{10}{10}$'s. Read this problem aloud to students:

  "Jonas and Alexis were eating pizza. They finished $\frac{3}{10}$ of their pizza. How much was left?"

- Have students remove $\frac{3}{10}$ of the fraction circle. Ask, ***"How much of the fraction circle remains?"*** $\frac{7}{10}$
- If students struggle to find the amount have them separate the circle into individual fraction parts and count up how many parts.
- Read, ***"The repairman has $\frac{4}{5}$ of a box of nails. He used $\frac{3}{5}$ of the box. How much was left?"*** $\frac{1}{5}$

Lesson 67 449

Written Practice *(Continued)*

Math Conversations *(cont.)*

Problem 2

Extend the Problem

"For this equation, the value of y is 35 when x = 5. It is possible, however, for y to have a different value. Explain how this is possible, and give an example to support your explanation." Substitute a different value for x; sample: If $x = 0$, then $y = 10$.

Problem 5

Before students round each number, ask them to name the rounding place, and then name the two possible numbers that the given number could be rounded to.

problem **a:** tenths; 5.2 or 5.3

problem **b:** ones; 5 or 6

problem **c:** dimes or tenths of a dollar; $10.60 or $10.70

problem **d:** dollars; $10 or $11

Problem 7 Multiple Choice

Test-Taking Strategy

Remind students that paper and pencil arithmetic is not always needed to find a correct answer. Then ask:

"What number is the first multiple of every number?" The number itself

"What is the first multiple of 90?" 90

"Which of the answer choices cannot be a multiple of 90? Explain why." Choice **A**; sample: A multiple of a number is greater than or equal to that number.

Point out that 45 is a *factor* of 90.

Problems 15–20

Before completing any arithmetic for these problems, remind students of the importance of checking their work, and then ask them to make and record an estimate of each answer.

After the arithmetic has been completed, ask students to use their estimates to help decide the reasonableness of the exact answer.

Problem 28

If students are unsure of their answer, encourage them to draw a 6 by 8 rectangle on grid paper to check their work.

Errors and Misconceptions

Problem 18

Students who give 2422 as the answer have forgotten to include the decimal point and dollar sign in the answer. Remind them that problems involving amounts of money often have answers that represent amounts of money. Also point out that asking, "Does my answer make sense?" can often be used to identify incorrect answers.

▸ **15.** (28, 52) $100.00 − $ 31.53 = $68.47

▸ **16.** (52) 251,546 − 37,156 = 214,390

▸ **17.** (8, 10) n + 423 = 618   195

▸ **18.** (59) $3.46 × 7 = $24.22

▸ **19.** (38) 96 × 3 = 288

▸ **20.** (59) $0.59 × 8 = $4.72

***21.** (54) $7\overline{)65}$ 9 R 2

***22.** (54) $5\overline{)38}$ 7 R 3

***23.** (54) $3\overline{)17}$ 5 R 2

Analyze Simplify. Use the order of operations.

***24.** (63) $30 + 10 \times 5$ 80

***25.** (63) $64 - 8 \div 4$ 62

***26.** (65) $56 \div 7 \times 5$ 40

***27.** (33, 42, 45) **Connect** Segment AB is 2.3 cm long. Segment BC is 3.5 cm long. How long is segment AC? Write a decimal addition problem and find the answer.   2.3 + 3.5 = 5.8; 5.8 cm

A   B   C

▸ ***28.** (66) Jennie wants to tile the top of a box that is 6 in. wide and 8 in. long. How many one-inch square tiles does she need?   48 tiles

29. (61) **Estimate** Using rounding, which numbers would you choose to estimate the product of 2 × 65? Explain your reasoning.   Sample: Round 65 to 70 and then multiply, 2 × 70 = 140.

***30.** (Inv. 5, 61) **Interpret** This pictograph shows the maximum speeds that animals can run for a short distance. Use the pictograph to answer the questions that follow.

Animal	Maximum Speed (in miles per hour)
Wart hog	
Wild turkey	
Lion	
Elephant	
Zebra	

Key: = 10 miles per hour

a. Which animals can run at a speed of at least 30 miles per hour? A wart hog, a zebra, and a lion

b. A squirrel can run at a maximum speed of 12 miles per hour. About how many times greater is the maximum speed of a lion? Explain. About 4 times greater; sample: Since 50 is close to 48 and 48 ÷ 12 = 4, the maximum speed of a lion is about 4 times greater than the maximum speed of a squirrel.

Looking Forward

Finding the portion of a whole when the other portion is given prepares students for:

- **Lesson 74,** word problems about a fraction of a group.
- **Investigation 8,** investigating equivalent fractions.
- **Lesson 87,** interpreting the remainder in a division word problem.
- **Lesson 92,** comparing and ordering fractions and decimals.
- **Lesson 94,** two-step problems about fractions of a group.
- **Lesson 98,** Fractions equal to 1 and to $\frac{1}{2}$.
- **Lesson 99,** changing improper fractions to whole or mixed numbers.
- **Lesson 100,** adding and subtracting fractions with common denominators.
- **Lesson 106,** reducing fractions.
- **Lesson 111,** simplifying fractions.
- **Lesson 113,** finding a common denominator and renaming fractions.

Planning & Preparation

• Division with Two-Digit Answers, Part 1

Objectives

- Divide a two-digit number by a one-digit number with a two-digit quotient.
- Check a division problem using multiplication.
- Solve word problems involving multi-digit division.
- Use compatible numbers to estimate a quotient.
- Determine whether a number is divisible by 3.

Prerequisite Skills

- Using multiplication to divide.
- Identifying division facts using a multiplication table.

Materials

Instructional Masters

- Power Up I Worksheet

Manipulative Kit

- Two-color counters, base ten blocks*

**optional*

California Mathematics Content Standards

NS 1.0, 1.3 Round whole numbers through the millions to the nearest ten, hundred, thousand, ten thousand, or hundred thousand.

AF 1.0, 1.1 Use letters, boxes, or other symbols to stand for any number in simple expressions or equations (e.g., demonstrate an understanding and the use of the concept of a variable).

MR 1.0, 1.1 Analyze problems by identifying relationships, distinguishing relevant from irrelevant information, sequencing and prioritizing information, and observing patterns.

MR 1.0, 1.2 Determine when and how to break a problem into simpler parts.

MR 2.0, 2.3 Use a variety of methods, such as words, numbers, symbols, charts, graphs, tables, diagrams, and models, to explain mathematical reasoning.

MR 2.0, 2.6 Make precise calculations and check the validity of the results from the context of the problem.

MR 3.0, 3.3 Develop generalizations of the results obtained and apply them in other circumstances.

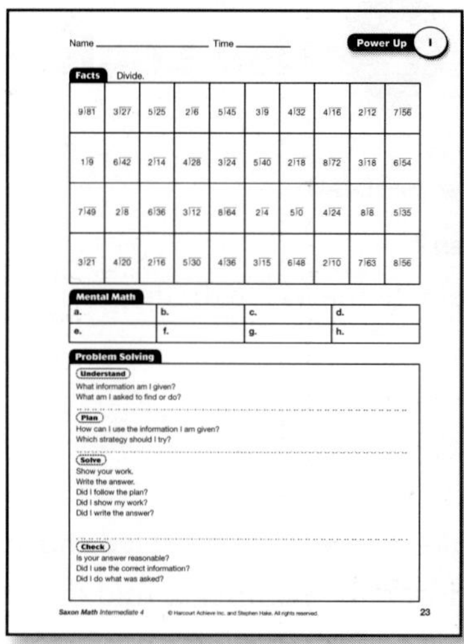

Power Up I Worksheet

Reaching All Special Needs Students

Special Education Students	At-Risk Students	English Learners	Advanced Learners
• Inclusion (TM) • Adaptations for Saxon Math	• Alternative Approach (TM) • Error Alert (TM) • Reteaching Masters • Refresher Lessons for California Standards	• English Learners (TM) • Developing Academic Language (TM) • English Learner Handbook	• Extend the Example (TM) • Extend the Problem (TM) • Online Activities

TM=Teacher's Manual

Developing Academic Language

Maintained	**English Learner**
equal groups	crop
equation	
formula	
multiply	
remainder	

Problem Solving Discussion

Problem

Stephanie solved an addition problem and then erased some of the digits from the problem. She gave it to Ian as a problem-solving exercise. Copy Stephanie's problem on your paper, and find the missing digits for Ian.

```
  7 _ 6
+ _ 4 _
  _ 4 5
```

Focus Strategies

Work Backwards

Use Logical Reasoning

Understand *Understand the problem.*

"What information are we given?"

We are shown an addition problem. Some of the digits are missing.

"What are we asked to do?"

We are asked to find the missing digits.

Plan *Make a plan.*

"What problem-solving strategies can we use to solve this problem?"

We can *use logical reasoning* and *work backwards* to find the missing digits.

Solve *Carry out the plan.*

"Let's start in the ones column, just as if we were adding numbers. What is the missing digit in the column?"

We think, "6 plus what number equals a number that ends in 5?" We know that $6 + 9 = 15$, so the missing digit is 9. We remember to regroup to the tens column.

"What is the missing digit in the tens column?"

We think, "1 (from regrouping) plus what number plus 4 equals a number that ends in 4?" We know that $1 + 9 + 4 = 14$, so the missing digit must be 9. We remember to regroup to the hundreds column.

"What are the two missing digits in the hundreds column?"

We think, "1 (from regrouping) plus 7 plus a number equals the missing digit in the sum." The only possibility is 1 for the bottom addend and 9 for the sum. If we used a digit greater than 1 in the bottom addend, the sum would be greater than 1000, which is a four-digit number.

Check *Look back.*

"Is our answer reasonable?"

We know that our answer is reasonable, because the sum of 796 and 149 is 945, which is the number that we have below the line.

```
  796
+ 149
  945
```

"What problem-solving strategies did we use to solve the problem?"

We *worked backwards* and *used logical reasoning* and number sense to find the missing digits.

"What other problem-solving strategy could we have used to solve the problem?"

We could have used *guess and check.*

Alternate Strategy
Guess and Check

Students can also use number sense to help them guess the digits that could go in the blanks and then check to see if their guess is correct.

LESSON 68

• Division with Two-Digit Answers, Part 1

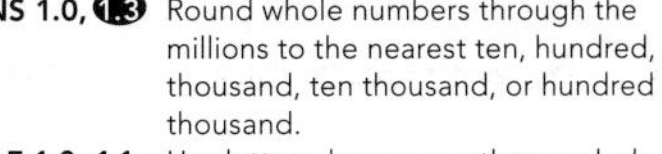

California Mathematics Content Standards

NS 1.0, 1.3 Round whole numbers through the millions to the nearest ten, hundred, thousand, ten thousand, or hundred thousand.

AF 1.0, 1.1 Use letters, boxes, or other symbols to stand for any number in simple expressions or equations (e.g., demonstrate an understanding and the use of the concept of a variable).

MR 1.0, 1.1 Analyze problems by identifying relationships, distinguishing relevant from irrelevant information, sequencing and prioritizing information, and observing patterns.

Power Up

facts Power Up I

count aloud Count down by fives from 52 to 2.

mental math

a. **Number Sense:** $10 \times 20 \times 30$ 6000

b. **Number Sense:** 250×10 2500

c. **Money:** Shatavia had \$5.00. Then she spent \$3.79. How much did she have left? \$1.21

d. **Money:** Tan bought a scorebook for \$6.48 and a whistle for \$2.84. How much did he spend? \$9.32

e. **Geometry:** What is the perimeter of a square with 9-inch sides? Express your answer in feet. 3 ft

f. **Time:** How many years is 1 century plus 4 decades? 140 yr

g. **Estimation:** Estimate 193×5 by rounding 193 to the nearest hundred and then multiplying. 1000

h. **Calculation:** $18 \div 9$, $\times 6$, $\times 6$ 72

problem solving

Choose an appropriate problem-solving strategy to solve this problem. Stephanie solved an addition problem and then erased some of the digits from the problem. She gave it to Ian as a problem-solving exercise. Copy Stephanie's problem on your paper, and find the missing digits for Ian.

$$\begin{array}{r} 7\_6 \\ +\ \_4\_ \\ \hline \_45 \end{array} \qquad \begin{array}{r} 796 \\ +\ 149 \\ \hline 945 \end{array}$$

New Concept

In this lesson we will learn a pencil-and-paper method for dividing a two-digit number by a one-digit number. We will demonstrate the method as we solve the problem on the next page.

Facts Divide.

$9\overline{)81}$ = 9	$3\overline{)27}$ = 9	$5\overline{)25}$ = 5	$2\overline{)6}$ = 3	$5\overline{)45}$ = 9	$3\overline{)9}$ = 3	$4\overline{)32}$ = 8	$4\overline{)16}$ = 4	$2\overline{)12}$ = 6	$7\overline{)56}$ = 8
$1\overline{)9}$ = 9	$6\overline{)42}$ = 7	$2\overline{)14}$ = 7	$4\overline{)28}$ = 7	$3\overline{)24}$ = 8	$5\overline{)40}$ = 8	$2\overline{)18}$ = 9	$8\overline{)72}$ = 9	$3\overline{)18}$ = 6	$6\overline{)54}$ = 9
$7\overline{)49}$ = 7	$2\overline{)8}$ = 4	$6\overline{)36}$ = 6	$3\overline{)12}$ = 4	$8\overline{)64}$ = 8	$2\overline{)4}$ = 2	$5\overline{)0}$ = 0	$4\overline{)24}$ = 6	$8\overline{)8}$ = 1	$5\overline{)35}$ = 7
$3\overline{)21}$ = 7	$4\overline{)20}$ = 5	$2\overline{)16}$ = 8	$5\overline{)30}$ = 6	$4\overline{)36}$ = 9	$3\overline{)15}$ = 5	$6\overline{)48}$ = 8	$2\overline{)10}$ = 5	$7\overline{)63}$ = 9	$8\overline{)56}$ = 7

Power Up

Facts

Distribute **Power Up I** to students. See answers below.

Count Aloud

Before students begin the Mental Math exercise, do these counting exercises as a class.

Mental Math

Encourage students to share different ways to mentally compute these exercises. Strategies for exercises are listed below.

c. Subtract \$3, then 70¢, then 9¢

\$5 − \$3 = \$2; \$2 − 70¢ = \$1.30;
\$1.30 − 9¢ = \$1.21

Count On from \$3.79

\$3.79 + 21¢ = \$4; \$4 + \$1 = \$5;
\$1 + 21¢ = \$1.21

d. Add 16¢, Subtract 16¢

\$2.84 + 16¢ = \$3; \$6.48 − 16¢ = \$6.32;
\$3.00 + \$6.32 = \$9.32

Add by Value, then Combine

Dollars: 2 + 6 = \$8;
Dimes: 8 + 4 = \$1.20;
Pennies: 4 + 8 = 12¢;
Total: \$8.00 + \$1.20 + \$0.12 = \$9.32

Problem Solving

Refer to **Problem-Solving Strategy Discussion,** p. 451B.

New Concept

Active Learning

As you discuss the equal-groups formula that can be used to represent the problem, ask:

"Which two numbers in the equal-groups formula are given in this problem?" The number of groups (3) and the total (78)

"What number are we being asked to find?" The number in each group

Lead students to understand that whenever we use an equal-groups formula, multiplication is used to find the total, and division is used to find the number of groups or the number in each group.

(continued)

New Concept *(Continued)*

Instruction

Before discussing the different steps that are needed to divide 78 by 3, remind students of the importance of checking their work, and then invite them to discuss how multiplication can be used to estimate the exact answer. Sample: Since $3 \times 20 = 60$ and $3 \times 30 = 90$, we know that the answer will be greater than 20 but less than 30. Record the estimate on the board.

Active Learning

Demonstrate the division of 78 by 3 on the board or overhead. As you work, emphasize the concept of place value by asking questions such as:

"When we write a 2 above the 7, what does the 2 represent?" 2 tens

"When we write a 6 below the 7, what does the 6 represent?" 6 tens

"Why do the 2 and the 6 each represent tens?" We multiplied 2 tens by 3; 2 tens × 3 = 6 tens

After students understand that the digit 8 is brought down from the dividend to continue the division, point out that the four steps shown below were just completed to divide tens, and the steps will be repeated again to divide ones:

Divide Multiply Subtract Bring down

Math Language

As you discuss how multiplication can be used to check the answer, say:

"Explain how to check the answer. Use the words 'dividend,' 'divisor,' and 'quotient' in your explanation." Multiply the quotient by the divisor and compare the result to the dividend.

Then remind students of the estimate that was made and recorded earlier in the lesson, and invite a volunteer to explain how it can be used to check the reasonableness of the quotient.

(continued)

The seventy-eight fifth-graders at Washington School will be divided equally among three classrooms. How many students will be in each room?

There are three numbers in this "equal groups" problem: the total number of students, the number of classrooms, and the number of students in each classroom.

Formula:
Number **of** groups × Number **in each** group = Total

Problem:
3 classrooms × n students in each classroom = 78 students

Reading Math
We can write the related equation $78 \div 3 = n$ to represent this problem.

To find the number of students in each classroom, we divide 78 by 3.

$$3\overline{)78}$$

Thinking Skills
Discuss
Why do we write the first digit of the quotient in the tens place?
We are dividing 7 tens.

For the first step we ignore the 8 and divide 7 tens by 3. We write "2" above the 7. Then we multiply 2 by 3 and write "6" below the 7 tens. Then we subtract and write "1."

$$\begin{array}{r} 2 \\ 3\overline{)78} \\ \underline{6} \\ 1 \end{array}$$

Next we "bring down" the 8, as shown here. Together, the 1 ten and 8 form 18 ones.

$$\begin{array}{r} 2 \\ 3\overline{)78} \\ \underline{6}\downarrow \\ 18 \end{array}$$

Thinking Skills
Verify
Why do we write the second digit of the quotient in the ones place?
We are dividing 18 ones.

Now we divide 18 by 3 and get 6. We write the 6 above the 8 in 78. Then we multiply 6 by 3 and write "18" below the 18.

$$\begin{array}{r} 26 \\ 3\overline{)78} \\ \underline{6} \\ 18 \\ \underline{18} \\ 0 \end{array}$$

We subtract and find that the remainder is zero. This means that if the students are divided equally among the classrooms, there will be 26 students in each classroom.

$$78 \div 3 = 26$$

Math Background

We can model $3\overline{)78}$ by using money. We model 78 with 7 tens and 8 ones. First divide the tens into 3 groups. There are 2 tens in each group, with 1 ten left over.

$$\begin{array}{r} 2 \\ 3\overline{)78} \\ \underline{6} \\ 1 \end{array}$$

Trade the leftover ten for 10 ones. There are now 18 ones. Divide the ones into three groups. There are 6 ones in each group and no ones are left over.

$$\begin{array}{r} 26 \\ 3\overline{)78} \\ \underline{6} \\ 18 \\ \underline{18} \\ 0 \end{array}$$

Since multiplication and division are inverse operations, we may arrange these three numbers to form a related multiplication equation.

$$3 \times 26 = 78$$

We can multiply 26 by 3 to check our work.

$$\begin{array}{r} \overset{1}{2}6 \\ \times\ 3 \\ \hline 78 \end{array} \quad \text{check}$$

Example 1

An 87-acre field is divided into 3 equal parts. A different crop will be planted in each part. How many acres is one part of the field?

For the first step we ignore the 7. We divide 8 tens by 3, multiply, and then subtract. Next we bring down the 7 to form 27 ones. Now we divide 27 by 3, multiply, and subtract again.

$$\begin{array}{r} 29 \\ 3\overline{)87} \\ \underline{6}\downarrow \\ 27 \\ \underline{27} \\ 0 \end{array}$$

The remainder is zero, so we see that one part of the field is **29 acres.**

Now we multiply 29 by 3 to check our work. If the product is 87, we can be confident that our division was correct.

$$\begin{array}{r} \overset{2}{2}9 \\ \times\ 3 \\ \hline 87 \end{array} \quad \text{check}$$

Notice that there is no remainder when 87 is divided by 3. That is because 87 is a multiple of 3. We cannot identify the multiples of 3 by looking at the last digit, because the multiples of 3 can end with any digit. However, adding the digits of a number can tell us whether a number is a multiple of 3. If the sum is a multiple of 3, then so is the number. For example, adding the digits in 87 gives us 15 ($8 + 7 = 15$). Since 15 is a multiple of 3, we know that 87 is a multiple of 3.

New Concept *(Continued)*

Example 1

If you sense the need to reinforce understanding of place value during division, ask questions similar to those shown to you earlier in this lesson as you discuss (or demonstrate) the division of 87 by 3.

Math Language

Explain that if there is no remainder when one number is divided by another number, we say that the first number is *divisible* by the second number. Point out, for example, that 8 is divisible by 4 because the division $8 \div 4$ does not produce a remainder.

To provide additional practice in deciding if numbers are divisible by 3, ask students to name a variety of two-digit numbers. After each number is named, write it on the board and invite volunteers to explain why the number is divisible by 3, or explain why it is not. Sample: 74 is not divisible by 3 because 11 is the sum of its digits, and $11 \div 3$ produces a remainder.

(continued)

English Learners

Say, ***"In the first example, the word crop refers to plants– such as fruits, vegetables, or grains–that are grown by farmers or gardeners."***

Ask, ***"What plants might be part of a crop of grain?"*** Samples: wheat, barley, oats

Encourage students to discuss the kinds of plants found in their own family's or a neighbor's garden.

New Concept (Continued)

Example 2

Extend the Example

Challenge advanced learners to name a different division that can be used to estimate the answer, and explain why that division can be used. Sample: The division 36 ÷ 4 can be used because 36 is close to 38 and the quotient can be found using only mental math.

Example 3

Error Alert

Make sure students recognize that the divisibility rule for 3 can be used in place of a paper and pencil division, and understand that both methods will produce the same result.

Lesson Practice

Guided Practice

Use these problems as guided practice to check the students' understanding of today's concept.

Problems a–f

Remind students of the importance of checking their work, and before they begin each division, ask them to work cooperatively to determine a range of estimates for the quotient. Sample for problem **a:** The quotient will range from 10 to 20 because 3 × 10 is 30, 3 × 20 is 60, and the dividend (51) is between 30 and 60.

Problem h

Error Alert

Remind students that a divisibility rule can be used in place of paper and pencil arithmetic to identify the correct answer.

Closure

The questions below help assess the concepts taught in this lesson.

Write 84 ÷ 3 on the board or overhead. Then say:

"Explain how we can decide, using only mental math, if the division 84 ÷ 3 will produce a remainder." Use the divisibility rule for 3; Since the sum of the digits is 12 and 12 is divisible by 3, the division 84 ÷ 3 will not produce a remainder.

Ask students to complete the division and name the quotient (28). Then ask:

"Explain how we can check the answer. Use the words 'dividend,' 'divisor,' and 'quotient' in your explanation." Multiply the quotient by the divisor and compare the result to the dividend.

Example 2

Four students can sit in each row of seats in a school bus. Thirty-eight students are getting on the bus. If each student sits in the first available seat, what is a reasonable estimate of the number of rows of seats that will be filled?

We are asked for a reasonable estimate, so we don't need to find an exact answer. We can round 38 to 40 and divide by 4. We find that a reasonable estimate of the number of rows that will be filled is **10.**

Example 3

Which of these numbers can be divided by 3 with no remainder?

A 56 **B** 64 **C** 45 **D** 73

We add the digits of each number:

A 5 + 6 = 11 **B** 6 + 4 = 10 **C** 4 + 5 = 9 **D** 7 + 3 = 10

Of the numbers 11, 10, and 9, only 9 is a multiple of 3. So the only choice that can be divided by 3 with no remainder is **45.**

Lesson Practice Divide:

a. $3\overline{)51}$ 17 **b.** $4\overline{)52}$ 13 **c.** $5\overline{)75}$ 15

d. $3\overline{)72}$ 24 **e.** $4\overline{)96}$ 24 **f.** $2\overline{)74}$ 37

g. **Connect** Find the missing factor in this equation: $3n = 45$

g. 15

h. **Multiple Choice** Which of these numbers can be divided by 3 with no remainder? How do you know?

A 75 **B** 76
C 77 **D** 79

h. **A**; The sum of 7 and 5 is 12, which is a multiple of 3.

i. Each row of desks in a classroom can seat six students. Twenty-nine students are entering the classroom. If each student sits in the first available seat, what is a reasonable estimate of the number of rows of seats that will be filled? Explain your answer. 5 rows; sample: Round 29 to 30 and 30 ÷ 6 = 5.

Written Practice *Distributed and Integrated*

1. (11, 12) Michael volunteered for sixty-two hours last semester. Milagro volunteered for seven hours. Mitsu and Michelle each volunteered for twelve hours. Altogether, how many hours did they volunteer? 93 hours

Inclusion

Use this strategy if the student displays:

- Difficulty with Directionality.
- Transposing Numbers and Sequences.

Division with Two-Digit Answers, Part 1 (Pairs)

Materials: two-color counters

- Write $3\overline{)84}$ on the board. Tell students to concentrate on the first step of division: 8 tens divided by 3. Instruct students to show 8 counters and divide them into groups of 3. Ask, ***"How many groups of 3 can we make?"*** 2 ***"How many do we have left over?"*** 2 ***"We have 2 groups of 3 tens and 2 tens left over."***
- Have students trade the 2 remaining tens for 20 counters, and add 4 counters from the second step of division. Have students divide 24 into groups of 3. Ask, ***"How many equal groups of 3 can we make?"*** 8
- Show students how to solve the problem on the board. Explain how each step relates to their modeling.
- Write $5\overline{)35}$ on the board. Tell students to use 3 counters and ask, ***"How many groups of 5 can we make?"*** 0
- Have students trade the 3 counters for 30 counters and add 5 and repeat this process. ***"How many groups of 5 can we make?"*** 7

▶ *2. (16, 52) The Matterhorn is fourteen thousand, six hundred ninety-one feet high. Mont Blanc is fifteen thousand, seven hundred seventy-one feet high. How much taller is Mont Blanc than the Matterhorn? 1080 feet

3. (38, 39) There are 25 squares on a bingo card. How many squares are on 4 bingo cards? 100 squares

▶ *4. (53, 68) **Analyze** Ninety-six books were placed on 4 shelves so that the same number of books were on each shelf. How many books were on each shelf? 24 books

5. (RF12, 37) How many years is ten centuries? (*Hint:* A century is 100 years) 1000 years

6. (61) **Estimate** A package of Jose's favorite trading cards costs $1.75. What is a reasonable estimate of the number of packages Jose could purchase with $10.00? Explain your answer. 5 packages; sample: $1.75 is close to $2 and $10 ÷ $2 = 5.

▶ *7. (67) Two fifths of the bottle is empty. What fraction of the bottle is *not* empty? Draw a picture to solve the problem. Three fifths

*8. (64) If $y = 3x + 8$, then what is y when $x = 1$? 11

*9. (63) **Connect** Simplify each expression. Use the order of operations.

a. $32 + 32 \div 4 \times 7$ 88 b. $27 - 12 \times 2 + 7$ 10

▶ c. How could we place parentheses in the expressions for **a** and **b** so it clear how to perform the order of operations? $32 + (32 \div 4) \times 7$; $27 - (12 \times 2) + 7$

10. (20, Inv. 3) a. What is the perimeter of the rectangle shown at right? 18 in.

6 in.

3 in.

b. How many 1-inch squares would be needed to cover this rectangle? 18 squares

11. (25, 42) **Predict** How many millimeters are equal to 10 centimeters? Use the table to decide. 100

Millimeters	10	20	30	40	50
Centimeters	1	2	3	4	5

*12. (31, 66) **Analyze** Mrs. Noh has an herb garden that is 4 ft wide and 9 ft long.

a. What is the area of her garden? 36 ft^2

Alternative Approach: Using Manipulatives

To help students understand the concept of division with two digits, have them model the division with base ten blocks as they divide using the paper-and-pencil method.

Have students show 78 as 7 tens and 8 ones. Have students draw three circles on their paper to make 3 equal groups. Have them place an equal number of tens into each group. Explain to students that they will need to regroup 1 ten, 8 ones as 18 ones. Then have them place an equal number of ones into each group.

Written Practice

Math Conversations

Independent Practice and Discussions to Increase Understanding

Problem 2

Before students use paper and pencil arithmetic to find the exact answer, ask them to use rounding and make an estimate, and then use the estimate to help decide the reasonableness of the exact answer after the paper and pencil arithmetic has been completed.

Problem 4 Analyze

Extend the Problem

Challenge your advanced learners with this problem:

"How can the ninety-six books be arranged on the three shelves so that each shelf has two more books than the shelf below it?" Place 30 books on the bottom shelf, 32 books on the middle shelf, and 34 books on the top shelf.

Problem 7

"When we write a fraction to represent the shaded part of a whole, what does the numerator of the fraction represent?" The number of shaded parts

"What does the denominator of the fraction represent?" The number of equal parts in the whole

Problem 9c

Extend the Problem

Challenge students to place parentheses in each expression to indicate the operation that is to be performed first, and then place brackets in each expression to indicate the operation that is to be performed second. $32 + [(32 \div 4) \times 7]$; $[27 - (12 \times 2)] + 7$

(continued)

Written Practice *(Continued)*

Math Conversations *(cont.)*

Problem 15

Extend the Problem

"How can we write 8 × 8 × 8 using an exponent? Explain your answer." 8^3; Sample: 8 is the base and it is used 3 times, so 3 is the exponent.

Problem 18

Extend the Problem

Students may be interested to learn that the answer is a palindrome. A palindrome is a number that reads the same from left to right as it reads from right to left.

Explain that addition can be used to change a number that is not a palindrome to a number that is by writing the sum of the number and its reversed digits. For example, have students write 51, reverse the digits by writing 15, and then add the numbers. The result (51 + 15 = 66) is a number that is a palindrome.

Point out that for some numbers, the process may need to be repeated more than one time. For example, if we begin with 48, the sum of 48 and 84 is not a palindrome (48 + 84 = 132). So we repeat the process using the number 132 and the result is a palindrome (132 + 231 = 363).

Invite interested students to identify the number of steps it requires to change a variety of 2-digit and 3-digit numbers to palindromes. For some numbers such as 11 or 25, the process is used only once. For many other numbers, it is used two or three times. However, some numbers require many more repetitions. For example, the process is repeated 5 times to change 176 to a palindrome, and 24 times to change 98 to a palindrome.

Errors and Misconceptions

Problem 9c

Students should place parentheses in each expression to indicate the operation that is to be performed first.

Problem 22

Work with students who named an incorrect quotient to complete the division a second time. As you work together, point out that the four steps of the division algorithm—divide, multiply, subtract, bring down—are repeated a second time to find the quotient.

Also remind these students of the importance of using multiplication to check a division quotient.

b. If she doubled the area of her garden, what could the new dimensions be? Sample: 8 ft by 9 ft, 6 ft by 12 ft, or 4 ft by 18 ft

13. (28) \$6.15 − (\$0.57 + \$1.20) \$4.38

14. (52) 43,160 − 8459 34,701

▸ **15.** (65) 8 × 8 × 8 512

16. (59) \$3.54 × 6 \$21.24

17. (38) 8 × 57 456

▸ **18.** (59) 704 × 9 6336

19. (54) $9\overline{)87}$ 9 R 6

20. (54) $7\overline{)32}$ 4 R 4

21. (54) $5\overline{)48}$ 9 R 3

***22.** (68) 96 ÷ 3 32

***23.** (68) $\frac{85}{5}$ 17

24. (68) 96 ÷ 8 12

***25.** (Inv. 3, 65) $\sqrt{36} + n = 6^2$ 30

26. (8, 10) $462 - y = 205$ 257

27. (34) $50 = 5r$ 10

28. (37, 55) **Conclude** Find the next number in this counting sequence:

..., 60, 120, 180, 240, ...

***29.** (18) **Explain** Sierra's arm is 20 inches long. If Sierra swings her arm in a circle, what will be the diameter of the circle? Explain your answer. 40 in.; sample: Her arm is the radius of the circle. Since her arm is 20 inches long, the diameter will be double the length of her arm, or 40 inches.

30. (56) **Multiple Choice** Which of these numbers is a prime number? B

A 1 **B** 2 **C** 4 **D** 9

Looking Forward

Dividing a two-digit number by a one-digit number with a two-digit quotient prepares students for:

- **Lesson 69,** dividing a three-digit number by a one-digit number.
- **Lesson 72,** division with two-digit quotients and a remainder.
- **Lesson 75,** dividing numbers to find a quotient that ends in zero.
- **Lesson 79,** division with three-digit quotients.
- **Lesson 83,** division with zeros in three-digit quotients.
- **Lesson 87,** solving division word problems that involve remainders.
- **Lesson 91,** estimating multiplication and division answers.

Planning & Preparation

• Division with Two-Digit Answers, Part 2

Objectives
- Divide a three-digit number by a one-digit number.
- Check a division problem using multiplication.
- Determine whether a number is divisible by 9.
- Solve word problems involving multi-digit division.

Prerequisite Skills
- Determining whether a number is divisible by 3.
- Using multiplication to divide.
- Identifying division facts using a multiplication table.

Materials

Instructional Masters
- Power Up I Worksheet

Manipulative Kit
- Two-color counters*

Teacher-provided materials
- Place-value workmat*

**optional*

California Mathematics Content Standards

NS 3.0, 3.2 Demonstrate an understanding of, and the ability to use, standard algorithms for multiplying a multidigit number by a two-digit number and for dividing a multidigit number by a one-digit number; use relationships between them to simplify computations and to check results.

NS 3.0, 3.4 Solve problems involving division of multidigit numbers by one-digit numbers.

AF 1.0, 1.1 Use letters, boxes, or other symbols to stand for any number in simple expressions or equations (e.g., demonstrate an understanding and the use of the concept of a variable).

MR 2.0, 2.6 Make precise calculations and check the validity of the results from the context of the problem.

MR 3.0, 3.3 Develop generalizations of the results obtained and apply them in other circumstances.

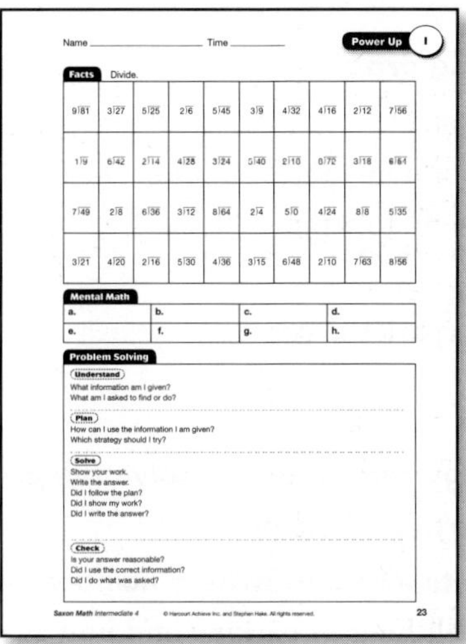
Name Time Power Up I
Facts Divide.
Mental Math
Problem Solving
Understand
Plan
Solve
Check

Power Up I Worksheet

Reaching All Special Needs Students

Special Education Students	At-Risk Students	English Learners	Advanced Learners
• Inclusion (TM) • Adaptations for Saxon Math	• Alternative Approach (TM) • Error Alert (TM) • Reteaching Masters • Refresher Lessons for California Standards	• English Learners (TM) • Developing Academic Language (TM) • English Learner Handbook	• Extend the Example (TM) • Extend the Problem (TM) • Online Activities

TM=Teacher's Manual

Developing Academic Language

Maintained	English Learner
dividend	companion
divisor	
multiple	
quotient	
remainder	

Problem Solving Discussion

Problem

The parking lot charged $1.50 for the first hour and 75¢ for each additional hour. Harold parked the car in the lot from 11 a.m. to 3 p.m. How much money did he have to pay? Explain how you found your answer.

Focus Strategy  **Write a Number Sentence or Equation**

Understand *Understand the problem.*

"What information are we given?"

1. Parking costs $1.50 for the first hour, and 75¢ for each additional hour.
2. Harold parked a car from 11 a.m. to 3 p.m.

"What are we asked to do?"

We are asked to find the price to park the car.

Plan *Make a plan.*

"What problem-solving strategy can we use to solve the problem?"

We can *write a number sentence* to find the price.

"What quantities do we need to know to write a number sentence?"

We need to know the cost for each hour of parking and how many hours the car was parked. We already know the cost for each hour. We need to find how many hours the car was parked.

Solve *Carry out the plan.*

"The car was parked from 11 a.m. to 3 p.m. How many hours is that?"

Four hours

"How much did the first hour cost?"

$1.50

"What was the cost of the additional hours the car was parked?"

The car was parked for four hours total, so it was parked for three additional hours. Each additional hour was $0.75, so the cost after the first hour was $0.75 + $0.75 + $0.75 = $2.25.

"What is a number sentence that describes the total cost to park the car?"

$1.50 + $2.25 = $3.75

Check *Look back.*

"Is our answer reasonable?"

We know that our answer is reasonable, because $1.50 + 75¢ + 75¢ + 75¢ = $3.75.

Alternate Strategy

Make or Use a Table, Chart, or Graph

To help students organize the information and show the cost of parking at the end of each hour, have them make a table. Remind students that the cost of parking is $1.50 for the first hour and then 75¢ for each additional hour.

Hours	1	2	3	4
Cost	$1.50	$2.25	$3.00	$3.75

LESSON 69

• Division with Two-Digit Answers, Part 2

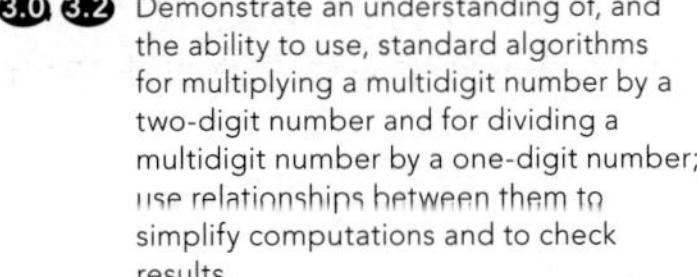

California Mathematics Content Standards

NS 3.0, 3.2 Demonstrate an understanding of, and the ability to use, standard algorithms for multiplying a multidigit number by a two-digit number and for dividing a multidigit number by a one-digit number; use relationships between them to simplify computations and to check results.

NS 3.0, 3.4 Solve problems involving division of multidigit numbers by one-digit numbers.

AF 1.0, 1.1 Use letters, boxes, or other symbols to stand for any number in simple expressions or equations (e.g., demonstrate an understanding and the use of the concept of a variable).

Power Up

facts Power Up I

count aloud Count down by threes from 60 to 3.

mental math

a. **Number Sense:** $12 \times 2 \times 10$ 240

b. **Number Sense:** $20 \times 20 \times 20$ 8000

c. **Number Sense:** $56 + 9 + 120$ 185

d. **Fractional Parts:** What is $\frac{1}{2}$ of $60? $30

e. **Measurement:** Six feet is 72 inches. How many inches tall is a person whose height is 5 feet 11 inches? 71 in.

f. **Measurement:** The airplane is 5500 feet above the ground. Is that height greater than or less than 1 mile? Greater than

g. **Estimation:** Xavier can read about 30 pages in one hour. If Xavier must read 58 pages, about how long will it take him? (Round your answer to the nearest hour.) 2 hr

h. **Calculation:** 6^2, − 18, ÷ 9, × 50 100

problem solving Choose an appropriate problem-solving strategy to solve this problem. The parking lot charged $1.50 for the first hour and 75¢ for each additional hour. Harold parked the car in the lot from 11:00 a.m. to 3 p.m. How much money did he have to pay? Explain how you found your answer. $3.75; See student work.

New Concept

We solve the following problem by dividing:

On a three day bike trip Hans rode 234 kilometers. Hans rode an average of how many kilometers each day?

We find the answer by dividing 234 by 3.

$$3\overline{)234}$$

Facts Divide.

$\begin{array}{r}9\\9\overline{)81}\end{array}$	$\begin{array}{r}9\\3\overline{)27}\end{array}$	$\begin{array}{r}5\\5\overline{)25}\end{array}$	$\begin{array}{r}3\\2\overline{)6}\end{array}$	$\begin{array}{r}9\\5\overline{)45}\end{array}$	$\begin{array}{r}3\\3\overline{)9}\end{array}$	$\begin{array}{r}8\\4\overline{)32}\end{array}$	$\begin{array}{r}4\\4\overline{)16}\end{array}$	$\begin{array}{r}6\\2\overline{)12}\end{array}$	$\begin{array}{r}8\\7\overline{)56}\end{array}$
$\begin{array}{r}9\\1\overline{)9}\end{array}$	$\begin{array}{r}7\\6\overline{)42}\end{array}$	$\begin{array}{r}7\\2\overline{)14}\end{array}$	$\begin{array}{r}7\\4\overline{)28}\end{array}$	$\begin{array}{r}8\\3\overline{)24}\end{array}$	$\begin{array}{r}8\\5\overline{)40}\end{array}$	$\begin{array}{r}9\\2\overline{)18}\end{array}$	$\begin{array}{r}9\\8\overline{)72}\end{array}$	$\begin{array}{r}6\\3\overline{)18}\end{array}$	$\begin{array}{r}9\\6\overline{)54}\end{array}$
$\begin{array}{r}7\\7\overline{)49}\end{array}$	$\begin{array}{r}4\\2\overline{)8}\end{array}$	$\begin{array}{r}6\\6\overline{)36}\end{array}$	$\begin{array}{r}4\\3\overline{)12}\end{array}$	$\begin{array}{r}8\\8\overline{)64}\end{array}$	$\begin{array}{r}2\\2\overline{)4}\end{array}$	$\begin{array}{r}0\\5\overline{)0}\end{array}$	$\begin{array}{r}6\\4\overline{)24}\end{array}$	$\begin{array}{r}1\\8\overline{)8}\end{array}$	$\begin{array}{r}7\\5\overline{)35}\end{array}$
$\begin{array}{r}7\\3\overline{)21}\end{array}$	$\begin{array}{r}5\\4\overline{)20}\end{array}$	$\begin{array}{r}8\\2\overline{)16}\end{array}$	$\begin{array}{r}6\\5\overline{)30}\end{array}$	$\begin{array}{r}9\\4\overline{)36}\end{array}$	$\begin{array}{r}5\\3\overline{)15}\end{array}$	$\begin{array}{r}8\\6\overline{)48}\end{array}$	$\begin{array}{r}5\\2\overline{)10}\end{array}$	$\begin{array}{r}9\\7\overline{)63}\end{array}$	$\begin{array}{r}7\\8\overline{)56}\end{array}$

Power Up

Facts

Distribute **Power Up I** to students. See answers below.

Count Aloud

Before students begin the Mental Math exercise, do these counting exercises as a class.

Mental Math

Encourage students to share different ways to mentally compute these exercises. Strategies for exercises are listed below.

b. Multiply Nonzero Digits, Write Zeros

Write 3 zeros after $2 \times 2 \times 2$;
$20 \times 20 \times 20 = 8000$.

c. Add by Places

$50 + 20 = 70$; $6 + 9 = 15$;
$100 + 70 + 15 = 185$

Change 120 to 100, then Add 20

$56 + 9 = 65$; $65 + 100 = 165$;
$165 + 20 = 185$

e. Subtract 1 Inch from 6 Feet

6 ft − 1 in. = 72 in. − 1 in. = 71 in.

Problem Solving

Refer to **Problem-Solving Strategy Discussion**, p. 457B.

New Concept

Instruction

An essential skill when using the long division algorithm is correctly placing the first digit in the quotient. As you discuss the division of 234 by 3, make sure students understand that the first digit in the quotient is written in the tens place because the digit 2 in the dividend is less than the digit 3 in the divisor. The result of this comparison is that we cannot divide 2 hundreds by 3, so we incorporate the next digit in the dividend and try again. Because the first two digits of the dividend (which represent 23 tens) are greater than the divisor 3, the division can begin and we write the first digit of the quotient in the tens place.

(continued)

New Concept *(Continued)*

As you discuss the solution of dividing 234 by 3, emphasize the four steps of the division algorithm, shown below.

Divide Multiply Subtract Bring down

Make sure students understand that in order to complete this division, we perform the four steps, and then we must perform the four steps a second time.

Error Alert

Use the **Thinking Skills** questions to help students understand the importance of placing the digits correctly in the quotient. Point out that if the first digit in the quotient was incorrectly written in the hundreds place, the quotient is likely to be 780 or 708, which are not sensible answers in the context of the problem because each represents riding a distance each day that is greater than the entire distance ridden.

Remind students of the importance of checking their work, then ask them to discuss different ways to estimate the quotient of 234 ÷ 3. Sample: The quotient of 234 ÷ 3 will be close to 80 because 3 × 80 is 240, and 240 is close to 234.

Example 1

Remind students of the importance of comparing the first digit in the dividend with the divisor to help decide where to place the first digit in the quotient.

As you discuss the solution, make sure students understand that the four steps of the division algorithm (shown below) are used twice to find the quotient.

Divide Multiply Subtract Bring down

Active Learning

After you review how multiplication can be used to check the answer, ask students to suggest different ways that estimation can also be used. Sample: Since 45 can be divided by 9, 450 can also be divided by 9, and a reasonable estimate is 450 ÷ 9 or 50. Since 9 × 5 = 45, 9 × 50 = 450, and 50 is a reasonable estimate because 450 is close to 468.

Connection

After you discuss how to decide if the quotient 468 will produce a remainder when divided by 9, lead students to conclude that if a number is divisible by 9, it also is a multiple of 9 because multiplication and division are inverse operations.

(continued)

To perform the division, we begin by dividing 3)23. We write "7 tens" above the 3 tens of 23. Then we multiply and subtract.

Thinking Skills

Discuss

Why do we write the first digit of the quotient in the tens place?

We are dividing 23 tens.

```
   7
3)234
  21
   2
```

Next we bring down the 4.

```
   7
3)234
  21↓
   24
```

Now we divide 24 by 3. We write "8" above the 4 ones. Then we multiply and finish by subtracting.

Thinking Skills

Verify

Why do we write the second digit of the quotient in the ones place?

We are dividing 24 ones.

```
   78
3)234
  21
   24
   24
    0
```

We find that Hans rode an average of 78 kilometers each day.

We can check our work by multiplying the quotient, 78, by the divisor, 3. If the product is 234, then our division answer is correct.

```
  78
×  3
 234  check
```

Example 1

On a 9-day bike trip through the Rocky Mountains, Vera and her companions rode 468 miles. They rode an average of how many miles per day?

Vera and her companions probably rode different distances each day. By dividing 468 miles by 9, we find how far they traveled if they rode the same distance each day. This is called the *average distance*. We begin by finding 9)46. We write "5" above the 6 in 46. Then we multiply and subtract.

```
   5
9)468
  45
   1
```

English Learners

A **companion** is a person that often accompanies another. For example, people do not particularly like attending the movie theater by themselves, so they take a companion.

Ask:

"Does a companion need to be someone you like? Do you have a companion when you travel to and from school?"

Next we bring down the 8. Now we divide 18 by 9.

$$\begin{array}{r} 52 \\ 9\overline{)468} \\ \underline{45\downarrow} \\ 18 \\ \underline{18} \\ 0 \end{array}$$

We find that they rode an average of **52 miles** per day.

We check the division by multiplying 52 by 9, and we look for 468 as the answer.

$$\begin{array}{r} \overset{1}{5}2 \\ \times\ 9 \\ \hline 468 \end{array} \text{ check}$$

Sample: Multiplication and division are inverse operations; one operation undoes the other operation.

Connect Why can we use multiplication to check a division problem?

Notice in Example 2 that there is no remainder when 468 is divided by 9. That is because 468 is a multiple of 9. Just as we identified multiples of 3 by adding the digits of a number, we can identify multiples of 9 by adding the digits of a number. For the number 468, we have

$$4 + 6 + 8 = 18$$

The sum 18 is a multiple of 9, so 468 is a multiple of 9.

Example 2

Which of these numbers is a multiple of 9?

A 123 **B** 234 **C** 345 **D** 456

We add the digits of each number:

A $1 + 2 + 3 = 6$ **B** $2 + 3 + 4 = 9$

C $3 + 4 + 5 = 12$ **D** $4 + 5 + 6 = 15$

The sums 6, 9, and 12 are all multiples of 3, but only 9 is a multiple of 9. Therefore, only **234** is a multiple of 9 and can be divided by 9 without a remainder.

Lesson Practice

In the division fact $32 \div 8 = 4$,

a. what number is the divisor? 8

b. what number is the dividend? 32

c. what number is the quotient? 4

Math Background

A number that is a multiple of 9 is *divisible* by 9. This means that 9 divides into the number evenly without a remainder. For example, 63 is divisible by 9 because $63 \div 9 = 7$.

Below are several *divisibility* rules:

- **A whole number is divisible by 2 if its ones digit is 0, 2, 4, 6, or 8.**
- **A whole number is divisible by 3 if the sum of its digits is divisible by 3.**
- **A whole number is divisible by 4 if the number formed by its last two digits is divisible by 4.**
- **A whole number is divisible by 5 if its ones digit is 0 or 5.**
- **A whole number is divisible by 6 if it is divisible by both 2 and 3.**
- **A whole number is divisible by 9 if the sum of its digits is divisible by 9.**
- **A whole number is divisible by 10 if its ones digit is 0.**

New Concept *(Continued)*

Example 2

Extend the Example

Challenge advanced learners to explain how mental math can be used to decide if each number is divisible by 2, and then explain how mental math can be used to decide if each number is divisible by 3. The numbers 234 and 456 are divisible by 2 because they are even numbers. All of the numbers are divisible by 3 because the sum of the digits in each number is divisible by 3.

Lesson Practice

Guided Practice

Use these problems as guided practice to check the students' understanding of today's concept.

Problems a–c

Some students may find it helpful to rewrite each division with a division box before identifying the various parts.

After students complete these problems, write "dividend ÷ divisor = quotient" on the board and invite volunteers to record the statement for future use.

Problem j Multiple Choice

Make sure students use the divisibility rule for 9 instead of paper and pencil arithmetic to make each decision. If necessary, remind them that a number is divisible by 9 if the sum of its digits is a multiple of 9.

Problems d–i

Error Alert

To help students correctly place the first digit in the quotient, write one or more of the divisions on the board or overhead and demonstrate how to place that digit.

Remind students of the importance of checking their work by making an estimate prior to beginning the division, or by using multiplication after the division has been completed.

(continued)

New Concept (Continued)

Closure The questions below help assess the concepts taught in this lesson.

"How are the dividend, the divisor, and the quotient of a division problem related?" Sample: The dividend divided by the divisor equals the quotient.

"For any division, explain how to place the first digit in the quotient." Sample: Compare the divisor to the first digit in the dividend. If the divisor is less than or equal to that digit, the first digit of the quotient is placed above the first digit in the dividend. If the divisor is greater than the first digit in the dividend, the first digit in the quotient is placed above the second digit in the dividend.

Write the division $168 \div 6$ on the board or overhead and ask students to find the quotient. $168 \div 6 = 28$

Written Practice

Math Conversations

Independent Practice and Discussions to Increase Understanding

Problem 3 Connect

Encourage students to name the answers using only mental math. If students choose to use paper and pencil arithmetic to solve part a, make sure they recall that finding half of a number is the same as dividing that number by 2.

Problem 4

Extend the Problem

"For this equation, the value of y is 25 when x = 9. It is possible, however, for y to have a different value. Explain how this is possible, and give an example to support your explanation." Substitute a different value for x; sample: If $x = 1$, then $y = 9$.

Problem 5 Represent

"On this number line, the distance from 2 to 3 is divided into 10 equal parts. What does each tick mark of the number line represent? Explain your answer." Tenths; sample: Each tick mark is $\frac{1}{10}$ or 0.1 more than the tick mark to its left, and $\frac{1}{10}$ or 0.1 less than the tick mark to its right.

(continued)

Divide:

d. $3\overline{)144}$ 48 **e.** $4\overline{)144}$ 36 **f.** $6\overline{)144}$ 24

g. $225 \div 5$ 45 **h.** $455 \div 7$ 65 **i.** $200 \div 8$ 25

j. **Multiple Choice** Which of these numbers can be divided by 9 without a remainder? How do you know?

A 288 **B** 377 **C** 466 **D** 555

j. A; The sum of the digits 2, 8, and 8 is 18, which is a multiple of 9. So 288 is a multiple of 9.

k. Find the missing factor in this equation:

$5m = 125$ $m = 25$

Written Practice

Distributed and Integrated

1. (39) Pears cost 59¢ per pound. How much would 4 pounds of pears cost? $2.36

2. (66) Find the perimeter and area of this rectangle: 20 yards; 21 square yards

7 yards

3 yards

▸ ***3.** (69) **Connect** There were three hundred sixty books on the floor. Frankie put half of the books on a table.

a. How many books did Frankie put on the table? 180 books

b. How many books were still on the floor? 180 books

▸ ***4.** (64) If $y = 2x + 7$, then what is y when $x = 9$? 25

▸ ***5.** (43) **Represent** To what decimal number is the arrow pointing? What mixed number is this? 2.7; $2\frac{7}{10}$

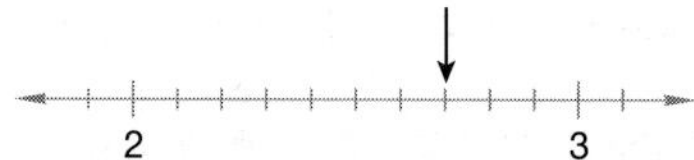

6. (61) **Estimate** Two hundred seventy-two students attend one elementary school in a city. Three hundred nineteen students attend another elementary school. Estimate the total number of students attending those schools by rounding the number of students attending each school to the nearest hundred before adding. 300 + 300 = 600 students

Inclusion

Use this strategy if the student displays:

- Difficulty with Multiple Steps.
- Difficulty with Large Group Instruction.

Division with Two-Digit Answers, Part 2 (Individual)

Materials: paper

- Write $3\overline{)945}$ on the board. Instruct students to divide the 9 by 3 and place the answer above the 9. Then have students cross out the 9 and divide the 4 by 3. Ask, ***"How many equal groups of 3 are there?"*** 1
- Instruct students to place the 1 above the 4, cross out the 4 and then place the remainder of 1 next to the 5 to make 15.
- Have students divide 15 by 3 and write the answer above the 5 (15). Ask, ***"What is the quotient, or answer?"*** 315
- Read aloud ***"Allison had 342 marbles in a jar. She wanted to divide them into groups of 6. How many groups can she make?"*** Have students set up the problem and work it in steps with a partner.

*7. Five sixths of the rolls have been sold. What fraction of the rolls have *not* been sold? Draw a picture to solve the problem. One sixth
(67)

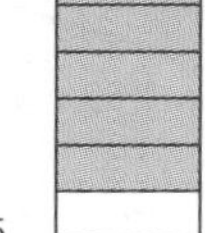

▶ *8. 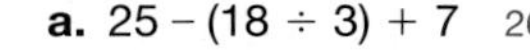 Connect Simplify each expression. Use for the order of operations.
(63)

a. 25 − (18 ÷ 3) + 7 26

b. 30 + (40 ÷ 2) − 5 45

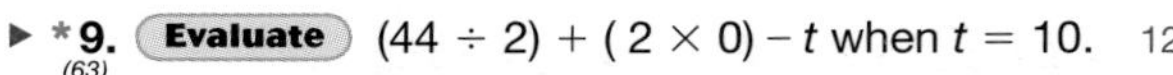

▶ *9. Evaluate (44 ÷ 2) + (2 × 0) − t when t = 10. 12
(63)

▶* 10. Interpret Use the survey information in the bar graph below to answer parts **a–c.**
(Inv. 5, Inv. 6)

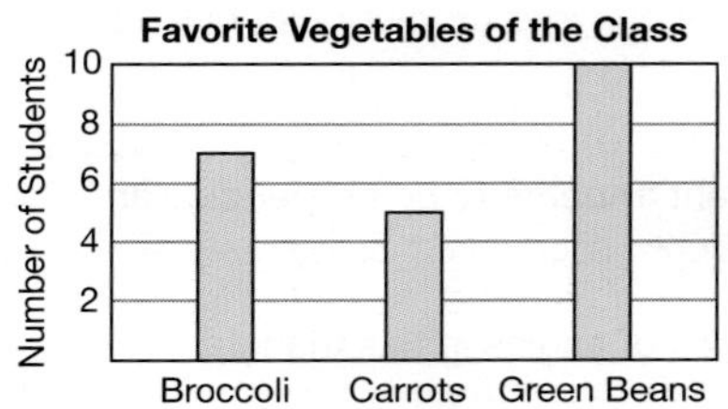

a. How many students were surveyed? 22 students

b. Carrots are the favorite vegetable of how many students? 5 students

c. Is it correct to say that most of the students chose green beans as their favorite vegetable? Why or why not? No; 10 students chose green beans; 12 students chose a different vegetable.

11. Represent The 8 a.m. temperature was −5 degrees Fahrenheit. By 3 p.m., the temperature had increased 10 degrees. What was the 3 p.m. temperature? 5°F
(21)

*12. Represent Round each number to the given place:
(62)

a. Round 10.37 to the nearest tenth. 10.4

b. Round $25.25 to the nearest ten cents. $25.30

13. (51)
$$\begin{array}{r} \$86.47 \\ +\ \$47.98 \\ \hline \$134.45 \end{array}$$

14. (45)
$$\begin{array}{r} 36.7 \\ -\ 18.5 \\ \hline 18.2 \end{array}$$

15. (51)
$$\begin{array}{r} 2358 \\ 4715 \\ 317 \\ 2103 \\ +\ \ 62 \\ \hline 9555 \end{array}$$

▶* 16. $3\overline{)93}$ 31
(68)

▶* 17. $2\overline{)56}$ 28
(68)

Alternative Approach: Using Manipulatives

To help students understand the concept of division with two-digit answers, have students use two-color counters and a place-value workmat to model division as they perform the division using paper and pencil.

Have students make a place-value workmat by dividing a piece of plain paper vertically into 3 equal parts and labeling the parts "hundreds," "tens," and "ones." Then have them use the counters to show the number 123 on the workmat, with each place value separated into groups of 3.

Explain to students that since the hundreds cannot be separated into 3 equal groups, they will need to trade 1 hundred and 2 tens for 12 tens, and then have them separate the 12 tens into groups of 3. Remind them that they will also need to divide the 3 ones into 3 groups of ones.

Have students count the groups in each place value and record the quotient. 0 hundreds, 4 tens, 1 ones, or 41

Written Practice *(Continued)*

Math Conversations *(cont.)*

Problem 8 Connect

For each expression, ask:

"Name the operations that are present, name the operation that will be performed first, and explain why you named that operation."

Problem 9 Evaluate

Extend the Problem

"Would this expression simplify to 12 if the parentheses were removed? Explain why or why not." Yes; Without the parentheses, the order of operations states that multiplication and division are to be completed from left to right before adding or subtracting.

Problem 10 Interpret

Extend the Problem

Invite students to write other word problems that can be solved using the information in the graph, and then challenge other students to solve the problems. Sample: How many more students choose green beans as their favorite vegetable than chose carrots? (5)

(continued)

Written Practice (Continued)

Math Conversations (cont.)

Problems 16–21

Some students may find it helpful if you lead a discussion of how to place the first digit in each quotient. Compare the divisor to the first digit in the dividend. If the divisor is less than or equal to that digit, the first digit of the quotient is placed above the first digit in the dividend. If the divisor is greater than the first digit in the dividend, the first digit in the quotient is placed above the second digit in the dividend.

Problem 28 Formulate

Invite volunteers to share the problems they wrote with the class.

Errors and Misconceptions

Problem 3

Students who name 153 as the answer translated the phrase "three hundred sixty" as 306. Remind these students that "three hundred sixty" represents 300 + 60 or 360.

Problem 7

Although the shapes drawn by students may vary, make sure they understand that the shape is to be divided into 6 equal parts.

Problem 11

One way to remediate incorrect answers is to sketch a number line on the board or overhead and demonstrate how it can be used to solve the problem.

Problem 27

Check students' work to be sure that they simplified each power before subtracting, as the correct answer can be found simply by subtracting the bases.

▶ **18.** (69) $7\overline{)434}$ 62

▶* **19.** (69) 516 ÷ 6 86

▶* **20.** (69) $\frac{279}{9}$ 31

▶ **21.** (69) $\frac{267}{3}$ 89

22. (8, 45) $n - 7.5 = 21.4$ 28.9

23. (59) $6.95 × 8 = $55.60

24. (38) 46 × 7 = 322

25. (59) 460 × 9 = 4140

26. (64) $3a = 30 + 30$ 20

27. (65) $3^2 - 2^3$ 1

▶* **28.** (Inv. 1) **Formulate** Write a multiplication word problem that has a product of 60. See student work.

29. (17) **Conclude** **a.** Which segment appears to be perpendicular to segment *BC*? Segment *AC* (or segment *CA*)

b. Name the types of angles in this triangle. Right, acute

A C B

30. (16, 52)  **Explain** During their professional baseball careers, pitcher Nolan Ryan struck out 5714 batters. Pitcher Steve Carlton struck out 4136 batters. How many more batters did Nolan Ryan strike out? Explain why your answer is reasonable. 1578 batters; sample: Since 5714 rounds to 5700 and 4136 rounds to 4100, the actual difference should be close to 5700 − 4100 or 1600.

Looking Forward

Dividing a three-digit number by a one-digit number prepares students for:

- **Lesson 72,** division with twp-digit quotients and a remainder.
- **Lesson 75,** dividing numbers to find a quotient that ends in zero.
- **Lesson 79,** division with three-digit quotients.
- **Lesson 83,** division with zeros in three-digit quotients.
- **Lesson 87,** solving division word problems that involve remainders.
- **Lesson 91,** estimating multiplication and division answers.

California Mathematics Content Standards

MG 3.0, 3.3 Identify congruent figures.

MR 2.0, 2.3 Use a variety of methods, such as words, numbers, symbols, charts, graphs, tables, diagrams, and models, to explain mathematical reasoning.

Planning & Preparation

• Similar and Congruent Figures

Objectives

- Identify similar figures.
- Identity congruent figures.
- Investigate congruence and area.

Prerequisite Skills

- Classifying polygons by the number of their sides.
- Drawing different kinds of polygons.
- Identifying parallel and perpendicular segments in two- and three-dimensional figures.

Materials

Instructional Masters

- Power Up I Worksheet
- Lesson Activity 22
- Lesson Activity 8*

Teacher-provided materials

- Dot paper, grid paper, scissors*

  **optional*

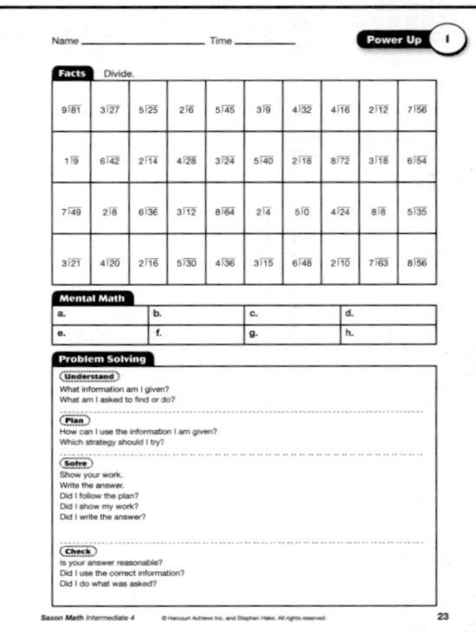
Name ______ Time ______ **Power Up I**

Facts Divide.

9)81	3)27	5)25	2)6	5)45	3)9	4)32	4)16	2)12	7)56
1)9	6)42	2)14	4)28	3)24	5)40	2)18	8)72	3)18	6)54
7)49	2)8	6)36	3)12	8)64	2)4	5)0	4)24	8)8	5)35
3)21	4)20	2)16	5)30	4)36	3)15	6)48	2)10	7)63	8)56

Mental Math

a.	b.	c.	d.
e.	f.	g.	h.

Problem Solving

Understand
What information am I given?
What am I asked to find or do?

Plan
How can I use the information I am given?
Which strategy should I try?

Solve
Show your work.
Write the answer.
Did I follow the plan?
Did I show my work?
Did I write the answer?

Check
Is your answer reasonable?
Did I use the correct information?
Did I do what was asked?

Saxon Math Intermediate 4 © Harcourt Achieve Inc. and Stephen Hake. All rights reserved. 23

Power Up I Worksheet

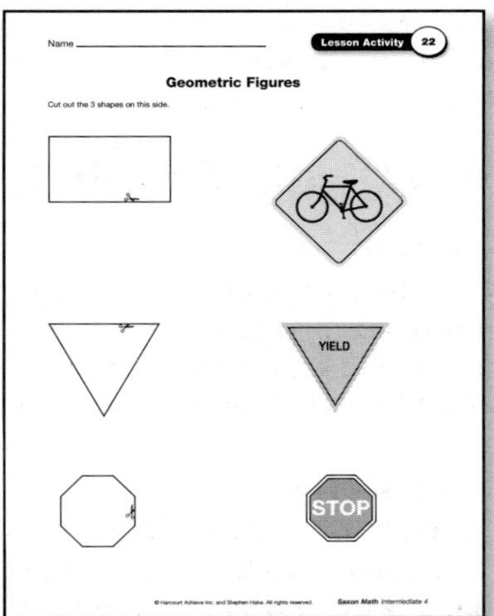
Name ______ **Lesson Activity 22**

Geometric Figures

Cut out the 3 shapes on this side.

© Harcourt Achieve Inc. and Stephen Hake. All rights reserved. *Saxon Math Intermediate 4*

Lesson Activity 22

Reaching All Special Needs Students

Special Education Students	At-Risk Students	English Learners	Advanced Learners
• Inclusion (TM) • Adaptations for Saxon Math	• Alternative Approach (TM) • Error Alert (TM) • Reteaching Masters • Refresher Lessons for California Standards	• English Learners (TM) • Developing Academic Language (TM) • English Learner Handbook	• Extend the Example (TM) • Extend the Problem (TM) • Early Finisher (SE) • Online Activities

TM=Teacher's Manual
SE=Student Edition

Developing Academic Language

New	Maintained	English Learner
similar	congruent octagon rectangle triangle	enlarge

Problem Solving Discussion

Problem

Tazara has ten coins that total one dollar, but only one of the coins is a dime. What are the other nine coins? (There are two possibilities.)

Focus Strategies

Use Logical Reasoning

Make or Use a Table, Chart, or Graph

Understand *Understand the problem.*

"What information are we given?"

Tazara has ten coins that total $1.00. Only one of the coins is a dime.

"What are we asked to do?"

We are asked to find the other nine coins.

Plan *Make a plan.*

"What problem-solving strategy can we use?"

We can *use logical reasoning* to guess combinations of coins and then check the combinations. We can also *make a table* and record the combinations that we find.

"We know that only one of the coins is a dime. How much of the dollar remains to be made up by the rest of the coins?"

We are looking for nine coins that total 90¢.

Solve *Carry out the plan.*

"Suppose Tazara has a half-dollar in addition to the dime. What would be the total value of the other eight coins?"

If Tazara has a half-dollar and a dime (50¢ + 10¢ = 60¢), then she has eight other coins that total 40¢.

"Can we make 40¢ with eight coins?"

Yes. We can use eight nickels, since 8 × 5¢ = 40¢. We found that in addition to the dime, Tazara can have 1 half-dollar and 8 nickels. We can record the entire combination (including the dime) in a table.

"Suppose that Tazara has 1 half-dollar and 1 quarter in addition to the dime. What would be the total value of the other seven coins?"

A half-dollar, quarter, and dime is a total of 50¢ + 25¢ + 10¢ = 85¢, so we need to find seven other coins that total 15¢. If five of the coins are pennies, then the other two coins could be nickels ([1¢ + 1¢ + 1¢ + 1¢ + 1¢] + [5¢ + 5¢] = 15¢). We found that in addition to the dime, Tazara can have 1 half-dollar, 1 quarter, 2 nickels, and 5 pennies. We can record the entire combination (including the dime) in a table.

Combination 1

Coin	#	Value
HD	1	50¢
Q	0	
D	1	10¢
N	8	40¢
P	0	
Total	10	100¢

Combination 2

Coin	#	Value
HD	1	50¢
Q	1	25¢
D	1	10¢
N	2	10¢
P	5	5¢
Total	10	100¢

Check *Look back.*

"Are our answers reasonable?"

Each combination we found includes only one dime and is made up of ten coins that total $1.00.

California Mathematics Content Standards

MG 3.0, 3.3 Identify congruent figures.
MR 2.0, 2.3 Use a variety of methods, such as words, numbers, symbols, charts, graphs, tables, diagrams, and models, to explain mathematical reasoning.

• Similar and Congruent Figures

facts Power Up I

count aloud Count by fives from 1 to 51.

mental math

a. **Number Sense:** $21 \times 2 \times 10$ 420

b. **Number Sense:** $25 \times 2 \times 10$ 500

c. **Number Sense:** $12 \times 4 \times 10$ 480

d. **Money:** $5.36 + $1.98 $7.34

e. **Measurement:** Ten feet is how many inches? 120 in.

f. **Estimation:** Round the prices $2.58 and $6.54 to the nearest dollar and then add to estimate the total. $10

g. **Estimation:** Round the prices $2.58 and $6.54 to the nearest 25 cents and then add to estimate the total. $9

h. **Calculation:** $9^2 + 125 + 37$ 243

problem solving Choose an appropriate problem-solving strategy to solve this problem. Tazara has ten coins that total one dollar, but only one of the coins is a dime. What are the other nine coins? (There are two possibilities.) 1 half-dollar, 1 quarter, 2 nickels, and 5 pennies; or 1 half-dollar and 8 nickels

Look at these four triangles:

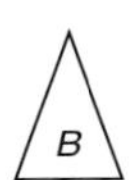

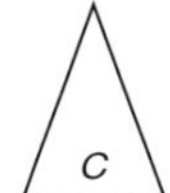

Figures that are the same shape are similar. Figures that are the same shape and the same size are congruent.

Facts Divide.

9 9)81	9 3)27	5 5)25	3 2)6	9 5)45	3 3)9	8 4)32	4 4)16	6 2)12	8 7)56
9 1)9	7 6)42	7 2)14	7 4)28	8 3)24	8 5)40	9 2)18	9 8)72	6 3)18	9 6)54
7 7)49	4 2)8	6 6)36	4 3)12	8 8)64	2 2)4	0 5)0	6 4)24	1 8)8	7 5)35
7 3)21	5 4)20	8 2)16	6 5)30	9 4)36	5 3)15	8 6)48	5 2)10	9 7)63	7 8)56

Power Up

Facts

Distribute **Power Up I** to students. See answers below.

Count Aloud

Before students begin the Mental Math exercise, do these counting exercises as a class.

Mental Math

Encourage students to share different ways to mentally compute these exercises. Strategies for exercises are listed below.

b. Multiply Nonzero Digits, Write Zeros
Write 1 zero after $25 \times 2 \times 1$;
$25 \times 2 \times 10 = 500$.

d. Add $2, then Subtract 2¢
$5.36 + $2 = $7.36; $7.36 − 2¢ = $7.34

Subtract 2¢, Add 2¢
$5.36 − 2¢ = $5.34; $1.98 + 2¢ = $2.00;
$5.34 + $2.00 = $7.34

e. Multiply Nonzero Digits, Write Zeros
Write 1 zero after 1×12;
10×12 in. = 120 in.

Problem Solving

Refer to **Problem-Solving Strategy Discussion**, p. 463B.

New Concept

Discussion

Introduce the lesson by asking students to recall what they know about triangles. Sample: 3 sides; 3 angles; 3 vertices; One angle may be a right angle; One angle may be an obtuse angle; Two or three angles are acute angles

Connection

As you discuss triangles *A*, *B*, *C*, and *D*, lead students to understand that because we can "magnify" triangle *A* or triangle *B* to look exactly like triangle *C*, we know that each angle in triangle *C* is the same measure as each of the corresponding angles in triangles *A* and *B*.

(continued)

New Concept *(Continued)*

Error Alert

Explain that shapes such as triangles do not need to be oriented the same way for them to be similar, congruent, or both similar and congruent. Point out that if triangle *A* was turned upside down, for example, it would still be congruent to triangle *B*. Students will explore this concept in greater detail as they complete the activity in this lesson.

Example 1

Error Alert

Make sure students understand that although all rectangles have four right angles, not all rectangles are similar because the ratios of lengths to widths are not the same in different rectangles. In other words, some rectangles are both long and wide, while others are short and narrow.

Active Learning

You might choose to have students make sketches on the board or overhead to support their answers to the following questions.

"If two figures are similar, are they also congruent? Explain your answer." Not necessarily; Two figures that are similar may be the same size, but their sizes may also be different.

"If two figures are congruent, are they also similar? Explain your answer." Yes; Two figures that are congruent are also similar because their shapes are identical and the ratio of the sides is the same.

Extend the Example

Have advanced learners draw their own shapes that are similar, and both similar and congruent.

Activity

As students complete the first task in the activity, some may place the cut-out shapes on the signs in the same orientation as shown in **Lesson Activity Master 22**. Encourage these students to turn the shapes, in addition to flipping them over, until they recognize that the shapes are not the same.

As they complete the second task, some students may turn the triangle and conclude that the two shapes do not match. Guide these students to turn the triangle, and flip it over if necessary, until the corresponding sides are aligned.

(continued)

Triangles *A* and *B* are both similar and congruent.

Triangles *B* and *C* are not congruent because they are not the same size. However, they are similar because they are the same shape. We could look at triangle *B* through a magnifying glass to make triangle *B* appear to be the same size as triangle *C*.

Triangle *A* and triangle *D* are not congruent and they are not similar. Neither one is an enlarged version of the other. Looking at either triangle through a magnifying glass cannot make it look like the other, because their sides and angles do not match.

Example 1

a. Which of these rectangles are similar?

b. Which of these rectangles are congruent?

A *B* *C* *D*

a. Rectangles *B, C,* and ***D*** are similar. Rectangle *A* is not similar to the other three rectangles because it is not a "magnified" version of any of the other rectangles.

b. Rectangle *B* and **rectangle *D*** are congruent because they have the same shape and size.

Determining Similarity and Congruence

Material needed:
- **Lesson Activity 22**

Model Look at the shapes on the left side of **Lesson Activity 22.** Compare each shape to the figure next to it on the right, and answer each question below.

1. Is the first shape similar to the bike sign? Is the shape congruent to the bike sign? Check your answers by cutting out the shape on the left and placing it on top of the bike sign. Describe the result.

1. No (the shape is a rectangle); no; sample: When I placed the shape on top of the sign I could see that it didn't match. The shape is longer/wider than the stop sign.

2. Yes, the triangle and yield sign are similar and congruent; sample: When I place the triangle on top of the yield sign I can see that they are the same shape and size.

English Learners

Explain that to **enlarge** an object is to increase its size or make it larger. Say:

"When two shapes are similar, one can be an enlarged version of the other."

Ask:

"If we enlarge one dimension of a rectangle but not the other, will the new rectangle be similar to the orginal?" No

Math Background

If two polygons are similar, then the following two statements are true:

- The angles in the two polygons are the same size.
- All the side lengths of one polygon are the same fixed number times the corresponding side lengths in the other polygon. For example, in the similar triangles below, each side length of the larger triangle is 3 times the corresponding side length of the smaller triangle. (Inversely, each side length of the smaller triangle is $\frac{1}{3}$ the size of the corresponding side length of the larger triangle.)

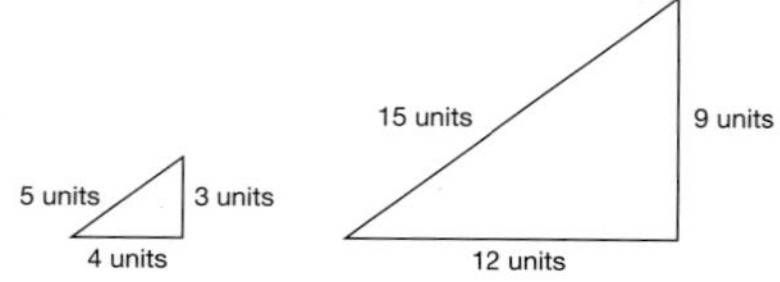

3. Sample: I can fold the paper so that the octagon lays on top of the stop sign and then look through the paper to see if they are the same shape and size; The shapes are similar.

2. Is the triangle similar to the yield sign? Is the triangle congruent to the yield sign? Check your answers by cutting out the triangle and placing it on top of the yield sign. Describe the result.

3. **Discuss** How do you know the octagon on the left is congruent to the stop sign? Are these shapes similar?

Lesson Practice

Refer to the figures below to answer problems **a** and **b**.

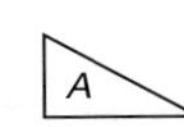

a. Which of these triangles appear to be similar? Triangles *A*, *C*, and *D*

b. Which of these triangles appear to be congruent? Triangles *A* and *C*

Written Practice

Distributed and Integrated

▶ *1. **Analyze** Brett can type at a rate of 25 words per minute. At that rate, how many words can he type in 5 minutes? Make a table to solve this problem. 125 words (58, 59)

1.

Minutes	Words
1	25
2	50
3	75
4	100
5	125

▶ *2. Shakia has five days to read a 275-page book. If she wants to read the same number of pages each day, how many pages should she read each day? 55 pages (53, 69)

▶ 3. **Estimate** Umar ordered a book for \$6.99, a dictionary for \$8.99, and a set of maps for \$5.99. Estimate the price for all three items. Then find the actual price. \$22.00; \$21.97 (28, 46, 51)

4. Patrick practiced the harmonica for 7 weeks before his recital. How many days are equal to 7 weeks? 49 days (39)

5. One third of the books was placed on the first shelf. What fraction of the books was not placed on the first shelf ? $\frac{2}{3}$ (67)

▶ *6. **Represent** To what decimal number is the arrow pointing? What mixed number is this? 1.53; $1\frac{53}{100}$ (43)

Alternative Approach: Using Manipulatives

To help students understand the concept of similar and congruent figures, have them use dot paper to model congruent and similar figures.

Demonstrate how to make two congruent triangles. Ask, ***"How do you know that the two figures are congruent?"*** They have the same size and shape.

Then have the students make two larger similar figures. Ask, ***"How do you know that the two figures are similar?"*** They have the same shape but a different size.

Have students work in pairs to show other examples of congruent and similar figures. Have them record and label each example on dot paper.

New Concept *(Continued)*

Lesson Practice

Guided Practice

Use these problems as guided practice to check the students' understanding of today's concept.

Problems a and b

Work cooperatively with students to complete these problems as a class.

Problems a and b
Error Alert

Make sure students can recognize that three triangles appear to be similar, and point out that students sometimes stop looking after they find two answers that meet the requirements of a question.

Have students use drawing software to show the difference between similar and congruent figures.

Closure The questions below help assess the concepts taught in this lesson.

"When are two figures similar?" When they have the same shape

"When are two figures congruent?" When they have the same shape and the same size

"If two figures are similar, are they also congruent? Explain your answer." Possibly; Two figures that are similar may be the same size, but their sizes may also be different.

"If two figures are congruent, are they also similar?" Yes

Written Practice

Math Conversations

Independent Practice and Discussions to Increase Understanding

Problem 1 **Analyze**

Extend the Problem

Challenge your advanced learners to write an equation that can be used to find the number of words (w) Brett can type for any number of minutes (m). $w = 25m$ or $w = 25 \cdot m$

(continued)

Written Practice *(Continued)*

Math Conversations *(cont.)*

Problem 2

Before students complete any arithmetic, remind them of the importance of checking their work. Then ask them to estimate a range for the exact answer, and use that range after the arithmetic has been completed to help decide if the exact answer is reasonable. Sample: The quotient of $275 \div 5$ will be a between 50 and 60 because $5 \times 50 = 250$ and $5 \times 60 = 300$.

Problem 3 **Estimate**

Extend the Problem

Have volunteers explain how to find the total cost of all three items using only mental math. Sample: Add one cent to each amount to make each a whole-dollar amount, and then subtract three cents from the sum of those amounts.

Problem 6 **Represent**

"Do the smaller tick marks on this number line represent tenths or hundredths? Explain how you know." Hundredths; sample: The distance between two consecutive tenths is divided into ten equal parts.

Problem 8 Multiple Choice

Test-Taking Strategy

Challenge students to give a reason why Choice **A** can immediately be eliminated as a possible answer. Sample: When a larger unit is changed to a smaller unit, the number of smaller units will be greater than the number of larger units.

Problem 11 **Connect**

Make sure students use paper and pencil arithmetic (instead of a ruler) to solve the problem.

Problems 19–21

Some students may find it helpful if you lead a discussion of how to place the first digit in one or more of the quotients.

Problems 24–27

Ask these questions for each problem:

"What operations are present in this expression?"

"In what order should those operations be performed? Explain why."

(continued)

*7. (70) a. **Multiple Choice** Which two triangles appear to be congruent? A and D

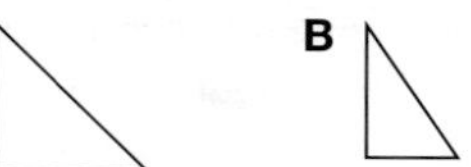

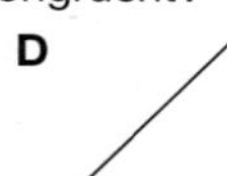

b. **Explain** Explain your answer to part **a.** Sample: Triangles *A* and *D* are congruent because they have the same size and shape.

▸ 8. (42) **Multiple Choice** Cyrus ran a 5-kilometer race. Five kilometers is how many meters? D

A 5 m **B** 50 m **C** 500 m **D** 5000 m

9. (20) What is the perimeter of this triangle? 60 mm

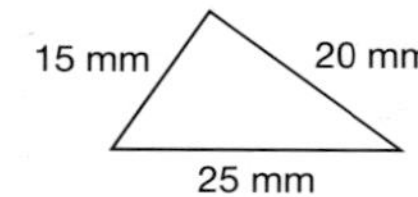

*10. (61, 69) **Estimate** Altogether, 117 students attend 6 different grades of a small elementary school. About the same number of students attend each grade. What is a reasonable estimate of the number of students in each grade? Explain your answer. Sample: about 20 students; 117 rounds to 120 and $120 \div 6 = 20$ students.

▸ *11. (33, 45) **Connect** The length of segment *AB* is 3.6 cm. The length of segment *AC* is 11.8 cm. What is the length of segment *BC*? Write and solve a decimal addition equation and a decimal subtraction equation. $3.6 + c = 11.8$; $11.8 - 3.6 = c$; 8.2 cm

12. (9, 28, 52) $25 − ($19.71 + 98¢) $4.31

13. (64) $12 + 13 + 5 + n = 9 \times 8$ 42

14. (28) $5.00 − $2.92 $2.08

15. (45) $36.21 - 5.7$ 30.51

16. (37) $5 \times 6 \times 9$ 270

17. (38) 5×63 315

18. (59) 478×6 2868

▸ *19. (69) $3\overline{)147}$ 49

▸ *20. (69) $7\overline{)637}$ 91

▸ *21. (69) $4\overline{)136}$ 34

22. (8, 10) $n + 6 = 120$ 114

23. (34, 69) $4w = 132$ 33

▸ *24. (65) $4^2 + 55$ 71

▸ *25. (63) $14 + 7 \times 6$ 56

▸ *26. (64) $3n = 15 + 12$ 9

▸ *27. (63) $40 - 64 \div 8$ 32

Inclusion

Use this strategy if the student displays:

- Weak Conceptualization.
- Difficulty with Large Group Instruction.

Similar and Congruent Figures (Individual)

Materials: Lesson Activity Master 8 (grid paper), scissors

- Pass out one piece of grid paper and instruct students to draw two rectangles with a length of 3 and a width of 2. Next, have students cut out their rectangles and lay them side by side. Have students compare the rectangles to each other and ask, ***"Are the rectangles the same size and shape?"*** Yes
- Tell students if two shapes are the same size and shape they are *congruent*.
- Then have students draw and cut out a rectangle that is 6 units long and 4 units wide. Have students compare the large rectangle to the smaller rectangles. Ask, ***"Are all three rectangles the same size?"*** No ***"Are all three rectangles the same shape?"*** Yes
- Tell students that figures that have the same shape are *similar*.

*28. (66) **Explain** Use a formula to find the area of a square that has a side length of 4 cm. Show your work. 16 cm^2; $A = s^2$, $4 \times 4 = 16$

*29. (45, 62) **Estimate** Round 6.32 and 3.29 to the nearest tenth, then find their sum. $6.3 + 3.3 = 9.6$

30. (18, 42) If the diameter of a playground ball is one foot, then its radius is how many inches? 6 in.

Real-World Connection

Constance, an international businesswoman, lives in New York, New York. She flies to distant cities all over the world. She was curious to know how far she traveled on some of her trips. She did some research on the Internet and wrote down her findings in a table.

Distance from New York (kilometers)	
Beijing, China	10,975
Paris, France	5,828
Jakarta, Indonesia	16,154
Rome, Italy	6,895

a. If Constance flies from New York to Beijing, and back again, how far will she have traveled? 21,950 km

b. If she flies from New York to Jakarta, and back again, how far will she have traveled? 32,308 km

c. On one business trip, Constance flew from New York to Rome. Then she flew from Rome to Paris, and then back to New York. If the distance from Rome to Paris is 1,120 kilometers, how far did Constance fly altogether on the business trip? 13,843 km

Written Practice *(Continued)*

Errors and Misconceptions

Problem 22

Students who give the answer 20 may have translated the expression $6 + n$ as $6n$. Help these students recognize the expression $6 + n$ as the sum of two terms.

Problem 29

Make sure students recall that in a decimal number, the tenths place is the first place to the right of the decimal point.

After solving the problem, challenge advanced learners to solve the following:

"Lima, Peru and Bangkok, Thailand are antipodal cities. This means they lie exactly opposite each other on the globe. If you travel from Lima to Bangkok, you will travel a distance of 12,227 miles. But a scientist might tell you Lima is less than 8,000 miles away from Bangkok. Can you explain why a scientist might say this?" There is a difference between a traveling distance and a straight line distance; If a hole were dug through the Earth from Lima to Bangkok the distance would be slightly less than 8,000 miles (the approximate diameter of the Earth)

Looking Forward

Identifying similar and congruent figures prepares students for:

- **Lesson 78,** measuring turns.
- **Lesson 81,** classifying triangles by angle measures and the length of its sides.
- **Lesson 82,** identifying and drawing lines of symmetry.
- **Lesson 90,** classifying quadrilaterals.
- **Lesson 96,** classifying geometric solids by their vertices, edges, and faces.
- **Lesson 97,** making three-dimensional models of rectangular and triangular prisms.
- **Lesson 101,** using formulas to find area and perimeter.
- **Lesson 108,** identifying the attributes of geometric solids.
- **Lesson 109,** describing the attributes of pyramids.

Cumulative Assessments and Performance Task

Assessments

Distribute **Power-Up Test 13** and **Cumulative Test 13** to each student. Have students complete the **Power-Up Test** first. Allow 10 minutes. Then have students work on the **Cumulative Test.**

Performance Task

The remaining class time can be spent on **Performance Task 7.** Students can begin the task in class or complete it during another class period.

Flexible Grouping

Flexible grouping gives students an opportunity to work with other students in an interactive and encouraging way. The choice for how students are grouped depends on the goals for instruction, the needs of the students, and the specific learning activity.

Assigning Groups

Group members can be randomly assigned, or can be assigned based on some criteria such as grouping students who may need help with a certain skill or grouping students to play specific roles in a group (such as recorder or reporter).

Types of Groups

Students can be paired or placed in larger groups. For pairing, students can be assigned partners on a weekly or monthly basis. Pairing activities are the easiest to manage in a classroom and are more likely to be useful on a daily basis.

Flexible Grouping Ideas

Lesson 63, Example 1 ***Materials: paper***	Divide students into groups of 4 to practice simplifying expressions. Assign each student a number: 1, 2, 3, or 4. Give each group a different expression that can be simplified using the order of operations. • Have each group first simplify the expression without using the order of operations. Then have them simplify using the order of operations. • Groups should discuss the two answers and why the order of operations is important. • Call out a student number, and each student assigned that number must present his or her group's work.
Lesson 68, Example 1 ***Materials: paper***	After guiding the students through Example 1, write three similar division problems on the board. Divide the students into groups of 4. • Have the groups work together to solve the first problem. • Have the groups divide into pairs to solve the second problem. • Direct students to work on the last problem independently and then check their solutions with the group.
Lesson 70, Example 1 ***Materials: none***	Have students form pairs to discuss the difference between similar and congruent figures. • Direct the students to look at the figures in the example without reading the answers below. Then instruct students to think about how the figures differ from one another. • Have students work in pairs to form definitions for *similar* and *congruent*. Have volunteers share their definitions with the class.

Planning & Preparation

• Coordinate Graphing

Objectives

- Locate and plots points in Quadrant I.
- Graph points that will form a polygon.
- Name the coordinates for a point on a given line.
- Subtract the x-coordinates to determine the length of a horizontal line segment.
- Subtract the y-coordinates to determine the length of a vertical line segment.

Prerequisite Skills

- Naming points on a number line.
- Placing positive and negative numbers on a number line.
- Naming line segments using two points on the line.
- Drawing different types of polygons.

Materials

Instructional Masters

- Lesson Activity 8
- Instructional Transparency 27*

Teacher-provided materials

- Grid paper

**optional*

California Mathematics Content Standards

AF 1.0, 1.3 Use parentheses to indicate which operation to perform first when writing expressions containing more than two terms and different operations.

AF 1.0, 1.4 Use and interpret formulas (e.g., area = length × width or $A = lw$) to answer questions about quantities and their relationships.

AF 1.0, 1.5 Understand that an equation such as $y = 3x + 5$ is a prescription for determining a second number when a first number is given.

MG 2.0, 2.1 Draw the points corresponding to linear relationships on graph paper (e.g., draw 10 points on the graph of the equation $y = 3x$ and connect them by using a straight line).

MG 2.0, 2.2 Understand that the length of a horizontal line segment equals the difference of the x–coordinates.

MG 2.0, 2.3 Understand that the length of a vertical line segment equals the difference of the y–coordinates.

MR 2.0, 2.2 Apply strategies and results from simpler problems to more complex problems.

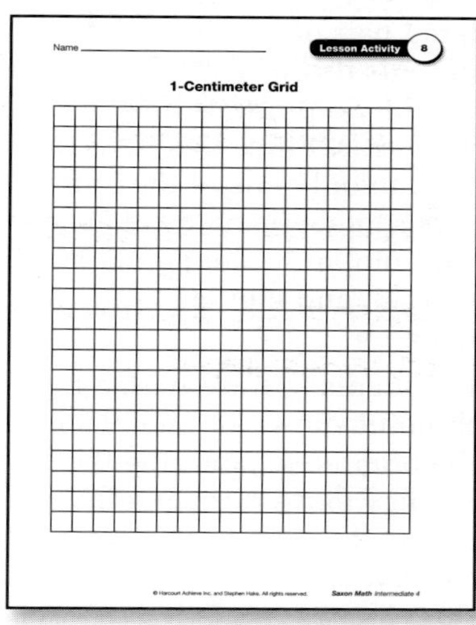

Lesson Activity 8

Universal Access

Reaching All Special Needs Students

Special Education Students	At-Risk Students	English Learners	Advanced Learners
• Inclusion (TM) • Adaptations for Saxon Math	• Error Alert (TM) • Reteaching Masters • Refresher Lessons for California Standards	• English Learners (TM) • Developing Academic Language (TM) • English Learner Handbook	• Extend the Problem (TM) • Investigate Further (SE) • Online Activities

TM=Teacher's Manual
SE=Student Edition

Developing Academic Language

New	Maintained	English Learner
coordinate plane	graph	origin
coordinates	number line	
horizontal	intersect	
ordered pairs	perpendicular	
origin	point	
vertical		
x-axis		
y-axis		

Coordinate Graphing

In this investigation, students will plot and locate points in Quadrant I of the coordinate plane, graph the equation of a line, and use the coordinates of endpoints to determine the length of a line segment.

Instruction

As you discuss the coordinate plane with students, identify the x-and y-axes of the plane as perpendicular number lines, and the origin as the point of intersection of the axes.

Make sure students understand that coordinates on the plane are given in an ordered pair of the form (x, y), where x represents distance along the horizontal axis, and y represents distance along the vertical axis. Since this investigation is limited to only one of the four quadrants of the coordinate plane, explain that students should plot or locate points by starting at the origin, and moving to the right, and then moving up.

Ask students to trace with a finger a path to each point shown on the plane by beginning at the origin and counting the number of units they move horizontally, and then counting the number of units they move vertically, to arrive at each point.
(2, 7) = right 2, up 7; (7, 2) = right 7, up 2; (7, 7) = right 7, up 7

California Mathematics Content Standards

AF 1.0, 1.5 Understand that an equation such as $y = 3x + 5$ is a prescription for determining a second number when a first number is given.

MG 2.0, 2.1 Draw the points corresponding to linear relationships on graph paper (e.g., draw 10 points on the graph of the equation $y = 3x$ and connect them by using a straight line).

MG 2.0, 2.2 Understand that the length of a horizontal line segment equals the difference of the x-coordinates.

MG 2.0, 2.3 Understand that the length of a vertical line segment equals the difference of the y-coordinates.

Focus on

Coordinate Graphing

If we draw two perpendicular number lines so that they intersect at their zero points, we create an area called a **coordinate plane.** Any point within this area can be named with two numbers, one from each number line. Here we show some examples:

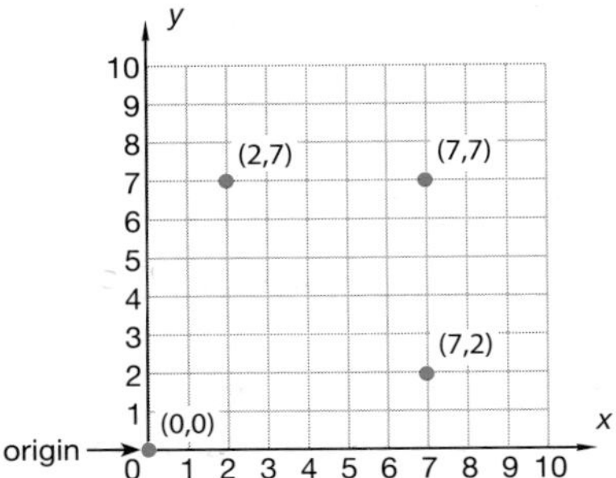

The **horizontal** number line, the line going from left to right, is called the **x-axis.** The **vertical** number line, the line going from top to bottom, is called the **y-axis.** The point where the x-axis and the y-axis intersect is called the **origin.**

The numbers in parentheses are called **coordinates,** which give a point's "address."

All coordinates are **ordered pairs** using the form (x, y).

x-coordinate, y-coordinate

(7, 2)

The first number in parentheses describes a point's horizontal distance from the origin, or the point at (0, 0). The second number in parentheses describes a point's vertical distance from the origin.

If we want to graph a point, such as (7, 2), we start at the origin. We move 7 units to the right, and then we move 2 units up. At that location we make a dot to represent the point and label it (7, 2).

English Learners

Explain to students that the word **origin** means something from which anything begins or starts.

"The origin of a graph is the point (0,0). This is where the axes intersect. We begin graphing a point by starting at the origin."

"The origin of pineapple is South America. They were brought to the United States from Brazil and Paraguay."

"Can anyone tell me the origins of other types of food?"

▸ 1. **Model** Use **Lesson Activity 8** to practice graphing these points. Label each point with its coordinates. See student work.

a. (5, 3) **b.** (6, 2) **c.** (0, 5) **d.** (5, 0)

▸ 2. Is the point at (0, 4) on the *x*-axis or on the *y*-axis? *y*-axis

3. Name the coordinates of a point on the *x*-axis. Sample: (1, 0)

We can use letters to label points on the coordinate plane.

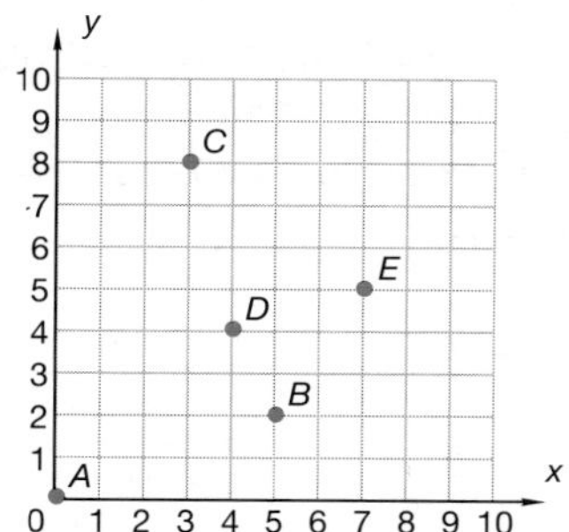

4. The coordinates of point *A* are (0, 0). What is the name for this point? The origin

▸ 5. **Connect** Write the coordinates of each of these points.

a. point *B* (5, 2) **b.** point *C* (3, 8) **c.** point *D* (4, 4) **d.** point *E* (7, 5)

Look at points *L, M, N, and O.* Each point is a vertex (corner) of rectangle *LMNO.*

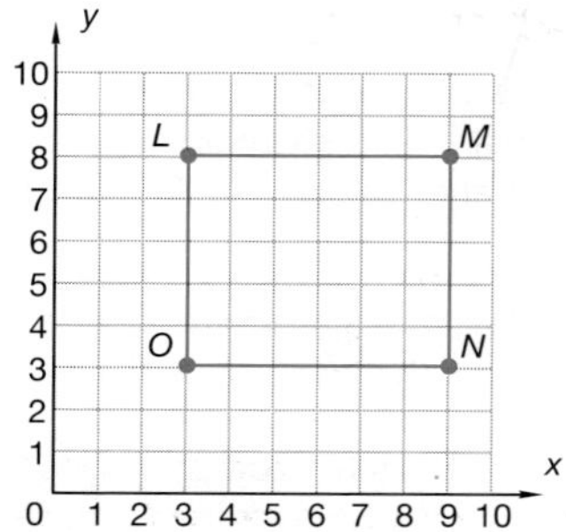

Notice that segment *LM* is one side of the rectangle. We can count the number of units between point *L* and point *M* to find the length of the rectangle. The rectangle is 6 units long.

Inclusion

Use this strategy if the student displays:

- Poor Retention.
- Slow Learning Rate.

Using Coordinate to Graph Points (Pairs)

Materials: Lesson Activity Master 8

- Distribute graph paper to each pair. Have them trace a 10 × 10 square on their paper as you model on the board or overhead.
- Ask, ***"Which letter comes first in the alphabet, x or y?"*** *x*

Explain that when we find points on a coordinate plane, like the one on their grid paper, we start on the bottom, or *x*-axis, and move right or left. Have students label the *x*-axis. Next, explain that we can now move up or down using the numbers on the *y*-axis. Have students label the *y*-axis and the increments along each axis as 0–10.

- ***"Let's graph the point (2, 3). Start at the left corner, called the origin, and move 2 units to the right. Then we move 3 units up. Now we can put a dot at this point. Which coordinate, or number in the pair, did we use first?"*** 2 ***"Which axis was it on?"*** *x*-axis ***"Which coordinate did we use next?"*** 3 ***"Which axis does this number represent?"*** *y*-axis
- Have students graph the points: (4, 6) (1, 9) (0, 4) as you model each step.

Math Conversations

Independent Practice and Discussions to Increase Understanding

Problem 1 Model

To help familiarize students with plotting points on the coordinate plane, place a coordinate grid on the overhead projector, and demonstrate how to plot the first point at (5, 3). Emphasize that whenever we plot points on the coordinate plane, we begin at the origin and move to the right, and then up. Make sure students understand that to plot a point at (5, 3), we move to the right 5 units, we move up 3 units, and then we draw a point.

Active Learning

Invite volunteers to each plot one of the remaining points.

Problem 2

Error Alert

Have students note that either coordinate of an ordered pair can be zero. (For the origin, both the *x*- and the *y*-coordinates are zero.)

Problem 5 Connect

Ask the following questions for each point:

"To identify the location of this point, where must we begin?" The origin or the point at (0, 0)

"Which direction do we move first?" To the right

"How many units must we move to the right to be exactly underneath the point?" point *B:* 5 units; point *C:* 3 units; point *D:* 4 units; point *E:* 7 units

"How many units must we move up to arrive at the point?" point *B:* 2 units; point *C:* 8 units; point *D:* 4 units; point *E:* 5 units

"What ordered pair describes the location of the point?" point *B:* (5, 2); point *C:* (3, 8); point *D:* (4, 4); point *E:* (7, 5)

Instruction

To find the length of a horizontal line segment, the *x*-coordinates of the endpoints must be subtracted. Some students may find it helpful to label the coordinates as shown below.

(9, 8) (2, 8)
x, y x, y

(continued)

Math Conversations *(cont.)*

Problem 6 **Conclude**

"The ordered pairs we have been working with are made up of two numbers. Which number represents the x-coordinate? Which number represents the y-coordinate? Explain how you know." The first number represents the x-coordinate and the second number represents the y-coordinate. All ordered pairs are of the form (x, y).

Problem 8 **Explain**

Error Alert

Watch for opportunities to point out that students need to find only one side length of $ABDC$ because $ABDC$ is a square. ($P = 4s$)

Discussion

As you discuss how to make a table of ordered pairs for the line $y = 2x + 1$, point out that the ordered pairs that are produced in the table represent points on the line. Emphasize the fact that we substitute a variety of numbers for x, then solve for y to produce the pairs.

Active Learning

Remind students that we must follow the order of operations after each substitution. Then ask:

"What operations are present in the equation y = 2x + 1?" Multiplication and addition

"When multiplication and addition are both present in an expression or equation, which operation must we complete first? Explain why." Multiplication is completed first because the order of operations states that we multiply before we add.

Error Alert

When graphing a line, explain that it is a good idea to plot at least 3 points before drawing the line. Explain that if only two points are plotted, it is not possible to know if one point is not correct. However, if 3 or more points are plotted, and one point is not correct, the graph of the line will not be straight, which signals a mistake.

(continued)

Since the coordinates of a point are of the form (x, y), another way to find the length of segment LM is to subtract the x-coordinates of each endpoint.

Coordinates	(x, y)
point M	(9, 8)
point L	(3, 8)

$9 - 3 = 6$ Segment LM is 6 units long.

▸ 6. **Conclude** Which coordinates can we subtract to find the length of segment MN? Write the coordinates and the length. *y*-coordinates; point M (9, 8), point N (9, 3), $8 - 3 = 5$ units

7. **Analyze** What is the perimeter of rectangle $LMNO$? 22 units

▸ 8. **Explain** Find the perimeter of square $ABCD$ without counting units. Explain your thinking. 24 units

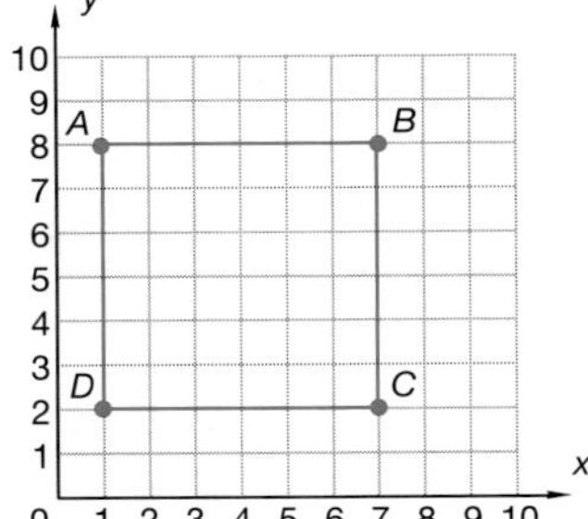

Sample: Subtract the *y*-coordinates of points A and D to find the length of one side of the square. Since $8 - 2 = 6$, and each side of a square has the same length, the perimeter of the square is $6 + 6 + 6 + 6$ or 24 units.

In Lesson 64, we learned how to solve an equation such as $y = 2x + 1$ when we were given the value of x. In this equation, the value of y depends on the value of x, and we can substitute different values for x to make a set of ordered (x, y) pairs. Ordered pairs are coordinates of points on the line $y = 2x + 1$ and we can use the points to graph the line.

For example, to graph the line $y = 2x + 1$, first make a table of ordered pairs by substituting different numbers for x, such as 1, 2, 3, and 4.

$2x + 1 = y$

x	y
1	
2	
3	
4	

The rule for this table is "multiply x by 2 and add 1."

When x is 1, y is 3.

$2x + 1 = y$

x	y
1	3
2	5
3	7
4	9

The result is a table of ordered pairs. The pairs are (1, 3), (2, 5), (3, 7), and (4, 9).

Math Background

René Descartes was a French mathematician and philosopher. His system of Cartesian coordinates, or the coordinate grid, helped mathematicians locate and describe objects and made it possible to plot courses with greater precision. The Cartesian coordinate system is not only used in mathematics, but also in cartography and astronomy.

Now we plot the ordered pairs and connect the points. The result is a graph of the equation $y = 2x + 1$.

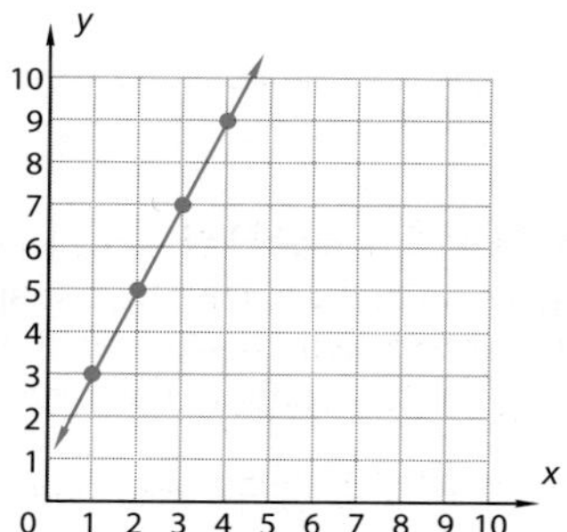

9. **Connect** Write the coordinates of another point that is on this line. Sample: (5, 11)

▸ 10. **Discuss** Do the coordinates (4, 8) represent a point on this line? Explain why or why not. No; sample: They do not satisfy the equation $y = 2x + 1$.

▸ 11. **Model** Use **Lesson Activity 8** to graph five points for the equation $y = 2x + 2$. See student work.

Another type of line is a horizontal line.

This line is the graph of $y = 5$.

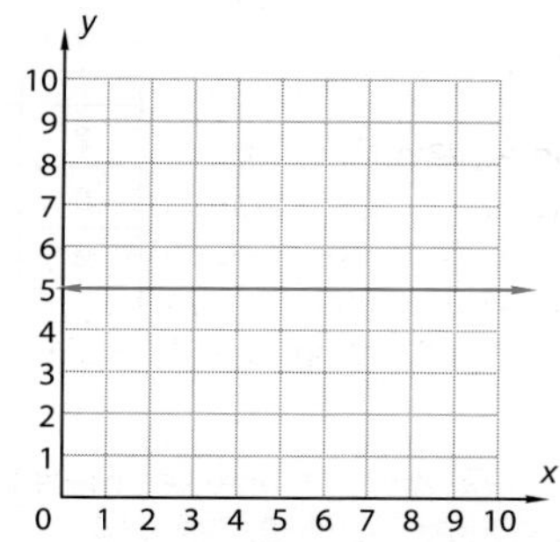

For every value of x, the value of y will always be 5. We can make a list of ordered pairs for this line.

$y = (0 \cdot x) + 5$

x	y
1	5
2	5
3	5

The table tells us that the points (1, 5), (2, 5), and (3, 5) are points on the line $y = 5$.

Math Conversations *(cont.)*

Problem 10 Discuss

Demonstrate how substitution can be used to show that the coordinates do not satisfy the equation.

$$y = 2x + 1$$
$$8 = 2(4) + 1$$
$$8 = 8 + 1$$
$$8 \neq 9$$

Problem 11 Model

Make sure students recall that they should substitute five different numbers for x, and after each substitution, follow the order of operations and solve for y.

Instruction

As you discuss the graph of $y = 5$, substitute 1, 2, and 3 for x in the equation $y = (0 \cdot x) + 5$ to demonstrate that for every value of x, the value of y is 5.

(continued)

Math Conversations *(cont.)*

Problem 12 **Connect**

"If we are given the equation of a line, how can we use substitution to find the coordinates of a point on the line?" Substitute a number for x, then follow the order of operations and solve the equation for y.

Problem 13 **Discuss**

Extend the Problem

Challenge your advanced learners to offer two different reasons why (3, 6) is not on the line $y = 5$. Sample: The y-coordinate of every point on the line $y = 5$ is 5; (3, 6) does not satisfy the equation $y = (0 \cdot x) + 5$.

$$y = (0 \cdot x) + 5$$
$$6 = (0 \cdot 3) + 5$$
$$6 = 0 + 5$$
$$6 \neq 5$$

Problem 14 **Model**

Error Alert

The graph should intercept the y-axis at 3 and pass through (1, 3), (2, 3), (3, 3), and so on.

Closure

The questions below help assess the concepts taught in this lesson.

"When graphing a point where on the graph do we begin?" The origin (0,0)

"Which axis do we move along first?" The x-axis

"Which direction is the y-axis?" vertical

"When we want to graph an equation of a line, what is our first step?" Make a list or table of points along the line

"How do we find points on a line?" We substitute values for one x-coordinate to find the value of y-coordinate.

▸ **12.** **Connect** Write the coordinates of another point that is on this line. Sample: (4, 5)

▸ **13.** **Discuss** Do the coordinates (3, 6) represent a point on this line? Explain why or why not. No; sample: The y-coordinate of every point on the line is 5.

▸ **14.** **Model** Draw a graph for $y = 3$. Name the coordinates for three points on the line. See student work.

a. Since a square has all four sides the same length, we know that the length of each side of the square below is 1 cm. A formula that can be used for finding the perimeter of the square is $P = 4s$ where s equals the length of one side. The perimeter of the square is 4×1 or 4 cm.

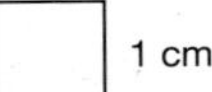

If we use the formula $P = 4s$ to make a table of ordered pairs, then we can graph the relationship between the side length of any square and its perimeter.

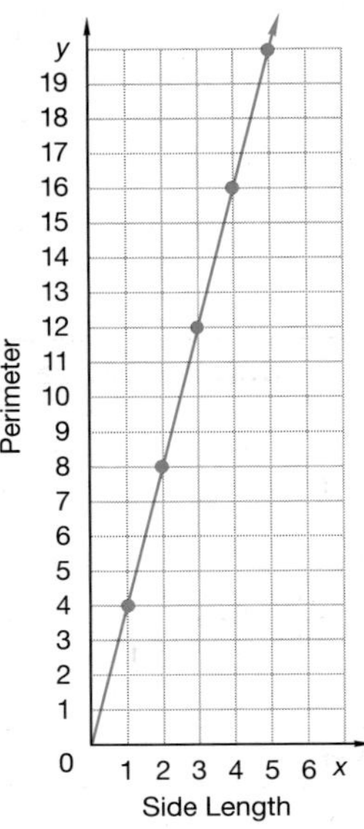

Substitute numbers for s and solve for P.

4s = P

s	P
1	4
2	8
3	12
4	16
5	20

Predict What point on the line represents a square that has a side length of 8 cm? (8, 32)

b. Use **Lesson Activity 8** to graph the equation $y = 4x$. How does the graph of the equation $y = 4x$ compare to the graph of the equation $P = 4s$? Sample: The equations are different ways to represent the same line.

Looking Forward

Locating points on a graph and determining the length of a line segment prepares students for:

Investigations 9 and 10, writing a set of ordered pairs for and graphing an equation such as $y = 3x + 2$.

Lesson Planner

Lesson	New Concepts	Materials	Resources
71	• Multiplying by Multiples of 10		• Power Up H Worksheet
72	• Division with Two-Digit Answers and a Remainder	• Manipulative Kit: rulers	• Power Up H Worksheet
73	• Capacity	• Manipulative Kit: rulers	• Power Up H Worksheet
74	• Word Problems About a Fraction of a Group		• Power Up H Worksheet
75	• Division Answers Ending with Zero		• Power Up H Worksheet
Cumulative Assessment			• Cumulative Test 14 • Test-Day Activity 7
76	• Finding Information to Solve Problems		• Power Up G Worksheet
77	• Fraction of a Set	• Manipulative Kit: rulers • Grid paper	• Power Up G Worksheet • Lesson Activity 8
78	• Measuring Turns	• Scissors, unlined paper	• Power Up G Worksheet
79	• Division with Three-Digit Answers		• Power Up G Worksheet
80	• Mass and Weight		• Power Up G Worksheet
Cumulative Assessment			• Cumulative Test 15 • Performance Task 8
Inv. 8	• Investigating Equivalent Fractions with Manipulatives	• Scissors	• Lesson Activities 11–13

All resources are also available on the Resources and Planner CD.

Additional Resources

- Instructional Masters
- Reteaching Masters
- Refresher Lessons for California Standards
- Calculator Activities
- Resources and Planner CD
- Assessment Guide
- Performance Tasks
- Instructional Transparencies
- Answer Key CD
- Power Up Workbook
- Written Practice Workbook

Math Highlights

Enduring Understandings — The "Big Picture"

After completing Section 8, students will understand that:

- To divide large numbers the division algorithm is useful.
- It is necessary to identify important information in a word problem.
- There is a difference between the mass of an object and the weight of an object.
- Some fractions are equivalent.

Essential Questions

- What is the division algorithm?
- How can I determine if information in a word problem is necessary?
- What is the difference between mass and weight?
- How do I determine if two fractions are equivalent?

Math Content Highlights	Math Processes Highlights
Number Sense • **Multiplying Multiples of 10** *Lesson 71* • **Division Answers Ending with Zero** *Lesson 75* • **Finding Information to Solve Problems** *Lesson 76* • **Fraction of a Set** *Lesson 77* • **Division with Three-Digit Answers** *Lesson 79* • **Equivalent Fractions** *Investigation 8* **Algebraic Thinking** • **Solving Word Problems Involving Multi-Digit Multiplication and Division** *Lessons 71, 72, 75, 79* • **Word Problems About a Fraction of a Group** *Lesson 74* **Geometry and Measurement** • **Capacity** *Lesson 73* • **Measuring Turns** *Lesson 78* • **Mass and Weight** *Lesson 80* **Data Analysis, Statistics, and Probability** • **Double Bar Graphs** *Lesson 76*	**Problem Solving** • **Strategies** – **Act It Out or Make a Model** *Lesson 75* – **Draw a Picture or Diagram** *Lessons 72, 76, 77* – **Guess and Check** *Lesson 80* – **Make or Use a Table, Chart, or Graph** *Lessons 73, 79* – **Make It Simpler** *Lesson 75* – **Use Logical Reasoning** *Lessons 74, 78, 80* – **Work Backwards** *Lessons 71, 74* – **Write a Number Sentence or Equation** *Lessons 71, 73, 77, 78* • **Real-World Applications** *Lessons 73, 75, 77, 78, 80* **Communication** • **Discuss** *Lessons 74, 76, 78, 79, 80* • **Explain** *Lessons 72, 73, 74, 76, 77, 78, 80* • **Formulate** *Lesson 73* **Connections** • **Math to Math** – **Fractions and Problem Solving** *Lessons 74, 77, Investigation 8* – **Division and Number Sense** *Lessons 72, 75, 79* – **Measurement and Mathematical Reasoning** *Lessons 73, 78, 80* • **Math and Other Subjects** – **Math and Geography** *Lessons 73, 76, 79* – **Math and Science** *Lessons 72, 75* – **Math and Sports** *Lessons 72, 74, 75, 77, 79, 80* **Representation** • **Model** *Lessons 77, 78, 79, Investigation 8* • **Represent** *Lessons 71, 72, 75, 76, 77, 78, 79, 80* • **Formulate an Equation** *Lessons 76, 78* • **Using Manipulative/Hands On** *Lessons 71, 72, 73, 74, 75, 76, 77, 78, 79, 80, Investigation 8*

Universal Access

Support for universal access is included with each lesson. Specific resources and features are listed on each lesson planning page. Features in the Teacher's Manual to customize instruction include the following:

Teacher's Manual Support

Alternative Approach	Provides a different path to concept development. *Lessons 71, 73–77, Inv. 8*
Flexible Grouping	Provides suggestions for various grouping strategies tied to specific lesson examples. *TM page 535A*
Inclusion	Provides ideas for including all students by accommodating special needs. *Lessons 71–80, Inv. 8*
Developing Academic Language	Provides a list of new and maintained vocabulary words along with words that might be difficult for English learners. *Lessons 71–80, Inv. 8*
English Learners	Provides strategies for teaching specific vocabulary that may be difficult for English learners. *Lessons 71–80, Inv. 8*
Errors and Misconceptions	Provides information about common misconceptions students encounter with concepts. *Lessons 71–80*
Extend the Example	Provides additional concept development for advanced learners. *Lessons 71, 73–77, 79, 80*
Extend the Problem	Provides an opportunity for advanced learners to broaden concept development by expanding on a particular problem approach or context. *Lessons 71–80*
Early Finishers	Provides additional math concept extensions for advanced learners at the end of the Written Practice. *Lessons 71, 74, 76, 78*
Investigate Further	Provides further depth to concept development by providing additional activities for an investigation. *Investigation 8*

Additional Resources

The following resources are also available to support universal access:

- Adaptations for Saxon Math
- English Learner Handbook
- Online Activities
- Performance Tasks
- Refresher Lessons for CA Standards
- Reteaching Masters

Technology

Student Resources

- Student Edition eBook
- Calculator Activities
- Online Resources at **www.SaxonMath.com/Int4ActivitiesCA**

Teacher Resources

- Resources and Planner CD
- Test and Practice Generator CD
- Monitoring Student Progress: eGradebook CD
- Teacher's Manual eBook CD
- Answer Key CD
- Adaptations for Saxon Math CD
- Online Resources at **www.SaxonMath.com**

Cumulative Assessment

The assessments in Saxon Math are frequent and consistently placed to offer a regular method of ongoing testing.

Power-Up Test: Allow no more than ten minutes for this test of basic facts and skills.

Cumulative Test: Next, administer this test, which checks mastery of concepts in previous lessons.

Test-Day Activity and Performance Task: The remaining class time can be spent on these activities. Students can finish the Test-Day Activity for homework. Advanced learners can complete the extended Performance Task in another class period.

After Lesson 75

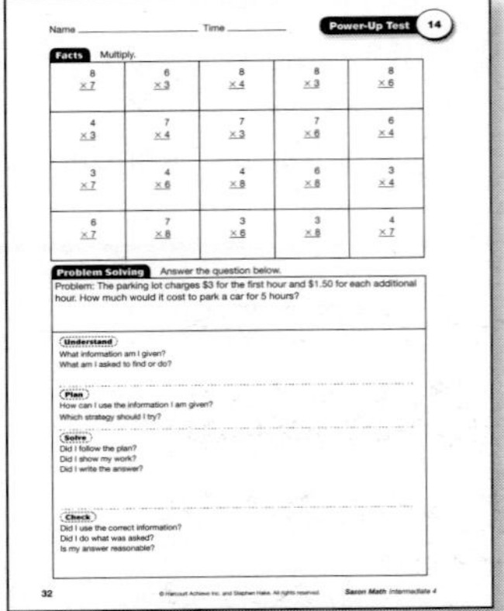

Power-Up Test 14

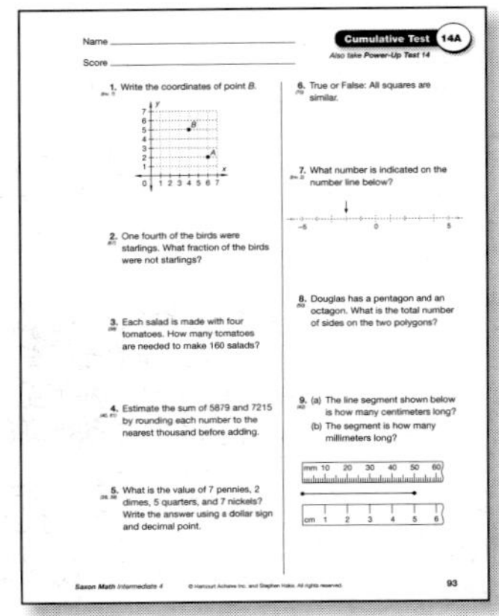

Cumulative Test 14

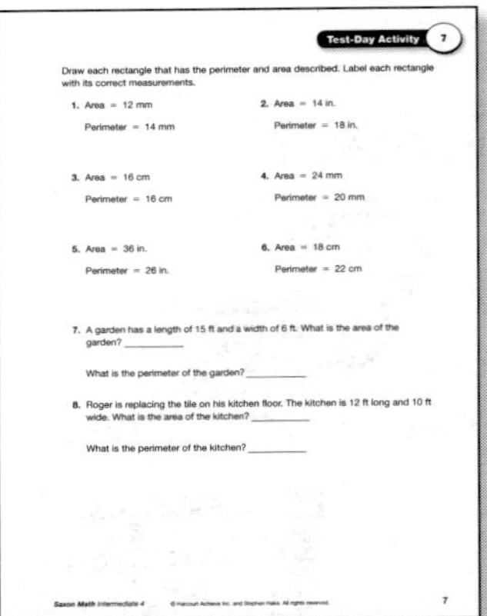

Test-Day Activity 7

After Lesson 80

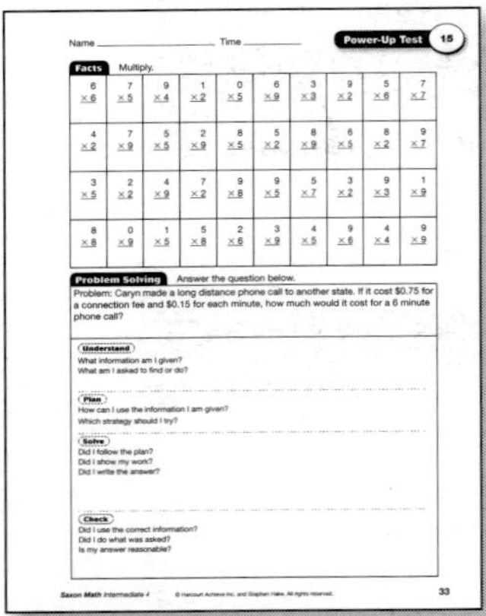

Power-Up Test 15

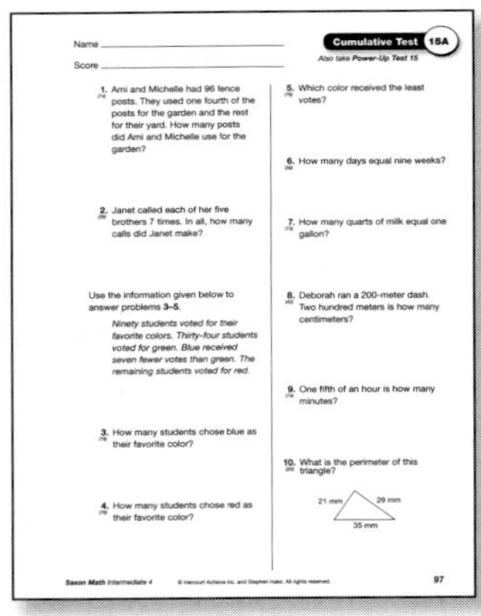

Cumulative Test 15

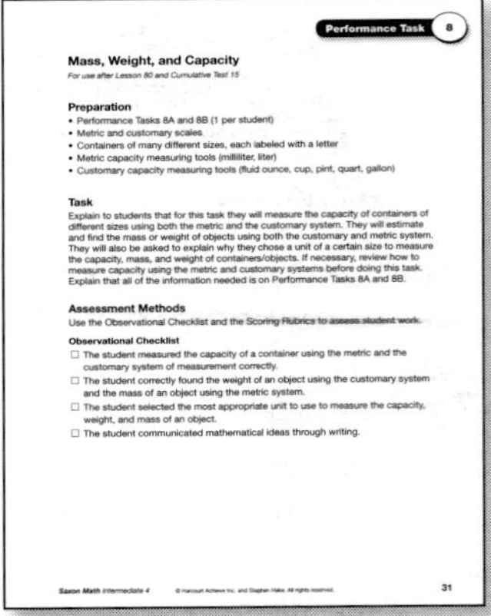

Performance Task 8

Evidence of Learning — What Students Should Know

By the conclusion of Section 8, students should be able to demonstrate the following competencies through the Cumulative Assessments, which are correlated to the California Mathematics Standards:

- Convert between units of liquid measure, weight, and mass. **MR 2.3**
- Solve word problems involving fractions of a group. **NS 1.5, MR 2.3, MR 2.6**

Reteaching

Students who score below 80% on assessments may be in need of reteaching. Refer to the Reteaching Masters for reteaching opportunities for every lesson.

Benchmarking and Tracking the California Mathematics Standards

Benchmark Tests

Benchmark Tests correlated to lesson concepts allow you to assess student progress after every 20 lessons. An End-of-Course Test is a final benchmark test of the complete textbook. The Benchmark Tests are available in the Assessment Guide.

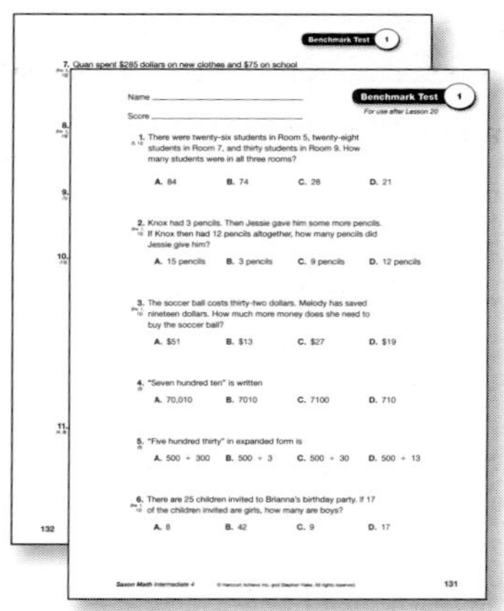

Benchmark Test 1

7. Quan spent $285 dollars on new clothes and $75 on school

Name ____________

Score ____________

Benchmark Test 1

For use after Lesson 20

1. There were twenty-six students in Room 5, twenty-eight students in Room 7, and thirty students in Room 9. How many students were in all three rooms?

A. 84 B. 74 C. 28 D. 21

2. Knox had 3 pencils. Then Jessie gave him some more pencils. If Knox then had 12 pencils altogether, how many pencils did Jessie give him?

A. 15 pencils B. 3 pencils C. 9 pencils D. 12 pencils

3. The soccer ball costs thirty-two dollars. Melody has saved nineteen dollars. How much more money does she need to buy the soccer ball?

A. $51 B. $13 C. $27 D. $19

4. "Seven hundred ten" is written

A. 70,010 B. 7010 C. 7100 D. 710

5. "Five hundred thirty" in expanded form is

A. 500 + 300 B. 500 + 3 C. 500 + 30 D. 500 + 13

6. There are 25 children invited to Brianna's birthday party. If 17 of the children invited are girls, how many are boys?

A. 8 B. 42 C. 9 D. 17

132

Saxon Math Intermediate 4 131

Monitoring Student Progress: eGradebook CD

To track California Standards mastery, enter students' scores on Cumulative Tests and Benchmark Tests into the Monitoring Student Progress: eGradebook CD. Use the report titled *Benchmark Standards Report* to determine which California Standards were assessed and the level of mastery for each student. Generate a variety of other reports for class tracking and more.

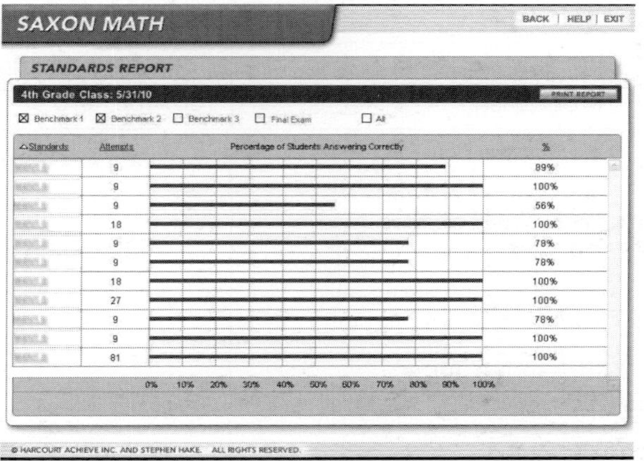

SAXON MATH

BACK | HELP | EXIT

STANDARDS REPORT

4th Grade Class: 5/31/10

PRINT REPORT

☒ Benchmark 1 ☒ Benchmark 2 ☐ Benchmark 3 ☐ Final Exam ☐ All

Standards	Attempts	Percentage of Students Answering Correctly	%
[illegible]	9		89%
[illegible]	9		100%
[illegible]	9		56%
[illegible]	18		100%
[illegible]	9		78%
[illegible]	9		78%
[illegible]	18		100%
[illegible]	27		100%
[illegible]	9		78%
[illegible]	9		100%
[illegible]	81		100%

0% 10% 20% 30% 40% 50% 60% 70% 80% 90% 100%

Test and Practice Generator CD

Test items also available in Spanish.

The Test and Practice Generator is an easy-to-manage benchmarking and assessment tool that creates unlimited practice and tests in multiple formats and allows you to customize questions or create new ones. A variety of reports are available to track student progress toward mastery of the California Standards throughout the year.

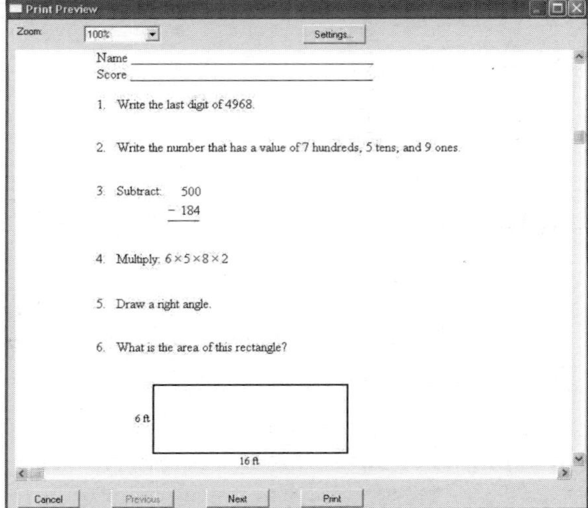

Print Preview

Zoom: 100% Settings...

Name ____________

Score ____________

1. Write the last digit of 4968.

2. Write the number that has a value of 7 hundreds, 5 tens, and 9 ones.

3. Subtract: $500 - 184$

4. Multiply: $6 \times 5 \times 8 \times 2$

5. Draw a right angle.

6. What is the area of this rectangle?

Cancel Previous Next Print

Content Trace

Lesson	New Concepts	Practiced	Assessed	Looking Forward
71	• Multiplying by Multiples of 10	Lessons 71, 72, 73, 74, 75, 76, 77, 78, 79, 80, 81, 82, 83, 84, 85, 86, 87, 89, 91, 92, 94, 95, 96, 98, 103, 104, 105	Tests 14, 17, 22	Lessons 84, 85, 86, 88, 91, 104, 105
72	• Division with Two-Digit Answers and a Remainder	Lessons 73, 74, 75, 76, 77, 78, 80, 82, 84, 85, 87, 95, 98, 99, 100, 101, 105, 111, 112, 113	Test 15	Lessons 75, 79, 83, 87, 91
73	• Capacity	Lessons 73, 74, 75, 76, 77, 78, 79, 83, 85, 88, 90, 93, 114	Test 15	Lesson 80
74	• Word Problems About a Fraction of a Group	Lessons 74, 76, 77, 78, 79, 80, 81, 82, 83, 84, 85, 86, 87, 88, 93, 112	Tests 15, 16, 17, 19	Investigation 8, Lessons 87, 89, 92, 94, 99, 100, 103, 106, 111, 112, 113
75	• Division Answers Ending with Zero	Lessons 75, 76, 77, 78, 79, 80, 81, 82, 94, 97, 105, 113, 114	Test 15	Lessons 79, 83, 87, 91
76	• Finding Information to Solve Problems	Lessons 76, 77, 79, 80, 81, 85, 86, 94, 99, 100, 101, 103, 106, 108, 110	Tests 15, 16	Lesson 93
77	• Fraction of a Set	Lessons 77, 78, 79, 80, 81, 88, 89, 93	Tests 16, 17	Investigation 8, Lessons 89, 92, 94, 98, 99, 100, 106, 111, 112, 113
78	• Measuring Turns	Lessons 78, 79, 80, 81, 82, 84, 85, 87, 92, 93, 107	Test 16	Lessons 81, 82, 90, 96, 97, 108, 109, 114
79	• Division with Three-Digit Answers	Lessons 79, 80, 81, 82, 83, 84, 85, 86, 87, 88, 89, 90, 91, 92, 94, 95, 96, 97, 98, 99, 100, 101, 102, 103, 105, 106, 107, 108, 109, 110, 111, 112, 113, 114	Tests 16, 17, 19, 20	Lessons 83, 87, 91, 104, 107
80	• Mass and Weight	Lessons 80, 81, 82, 83, 84, 85, 87, 88, 100	Tests 16, 17	***Saxon Math*** Intermediate 5
Inv. 8	• Investigating Equivalent Fractions with Manipulatives	Lessons 81, 82, 84, 105, 106, 107, 112	Test 21	Lessons 87, 89, 92, 94, 98, 99, 100, 103, 106, 111, 112, 113

Planning & Preparation

• Multiplying by Multiples of 10

Objectives

- Multiply by multiples of 10.
- Multiply dollars and cents by a two-digit number.
- Solve word problems involving multi-digit multiplication.

Prerequisite Skills

- Identifying and memorizing the memory group of multiplication facts.
- Using the multiplication algorithm to multiply a two-digit number by a one-digit number.

Materials

Instructional Masters

- Power Up H Worksheet

Manipulative Kit

- Base ten blocks*

**optional*

California Mathematics Content Standards

NS 3.0, 3.3 Solve problems involving multiplication of multidigit numbers by two-digit numbers.

NS 4.0, 4.1 Understand that many whole numbers break down in different ways (e.g., $12 = 4 \times 3 = 2 \times 6 = 2 \times 2 \times 3$).

MR 2.0, 2.3 Use a variety of methods, such as words, numbers, symbols, charts, graphs, tables, diagrams, and models, to explain mathematical reasoning.

MR 2.0, 2.6 Make precise calculations and check the validity of the results from the context of the problem.

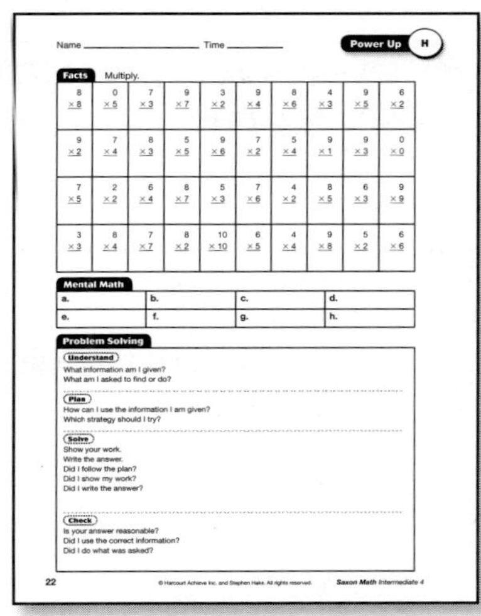

Name ____________ Time ________ **Power Up H**

Facts Multiply.

8 × 8	0 × 5	7 × 3	9 × 7	3 × 2	9 × 4	8 × 6	4 × 3	9 × 5	6 × 2
9 × 2	7 × 4	8 × 3	5 × 5	9 × 6	7 × 2	5 × 4	9 × 1	9 × 3	0 × 0
7 × 5	2 × 2	6 × 4	8 × 7	5 × 3	7 × 6	4 × 2	8 × 5	6 × 3	9 × 9
3 × 3	8 × 4	7 × 7	8 × 2	10 × 10	6 × 5	4 × 4	9 × 8	5 × 2	6 × 6

Mental Math

a.	b.	c.	d.
e.	f.	g.	h.

Problem Solving

Understand
What information am I given?
What am I asked to find or do?

Plan
How can I use the information I am given?
Which strategy should I try?

Solve
Show your work.
Write the answer.
Did I follow the plan?
Did I show my work?
Did I write the answer?

Check
Is your answer reasonable?
Did I use the correct information?
Did I do what was asked?

22 © Harcourt Achieve Inc. and Stephen Hake. All rights reserved. *Saxon Math Intermediate 4*

Power Up H Worksheet

Reaching All Special Needs Students

Special Education Students	At-Risk Students	English Learners	Advanced Learners
• Inclusion (TM) • Adaptations for Saxon Math	• Alternative Approach (TM) • Error Alert (TM) • Reteaching Masters • Refresher Lessons for California Standards	• English Learners (TM) • Developing Academic Language (TM) • English Learner Handbook	• Extend the Example (TM) • Extend the Problem (TM) • Early Finisher (SE) • Online Activities

TM=Teacher's Manual
SE=Student Edition

Developing Academic Language

Maintained
factors
multiple
product

English Learner
bookstore

Problem Solving Discussion

Problem

Cuintan finished his 150-page book on Friday. The day before, he had put the book down after reading page 120. If Cuintan read the same number of pages each day, on what day did Cuintan begin reading his book? Explain how you found your answer.

Focus Strategies

Work Backwards

Write a Number Sentence or Equation

Understand *Understand the problem.*

"What information are we given?"

1. Cuintan finished a 150-page book on Friday.
2. On the day before (Thursday), Cuintan had finished through page 120.
3. Cuintan reads the same number of pages each day.

"What are we asked to do?"

We are asked to find the day that Cuintan began reading the book.

Plan *Make a plan.*

"How can we use the information we know to solve the problem?"

We need to find how many pages Cuintan reads each day. Then we can *work backwards* to find the pages Cuintan read each day.

Solve *Carry out the plan.*

"We are told that Cuintan had read through page 120 on the day before Friday. How can we use this information to find how many pages he read on Friday?"

The book was 150 pages long, so we subtract: 150 pages − 120 pages = 30 pages.

"If Cuintan read 30 pages each day, then how can we count backwards to find the day he started reading the book?"

We can count backwards like this:

Friday	finished through page 150
Thursday	finished through page 120
Wednesday	finished through page 90
Tuesday	finished through page 60
Monday	finished through page 30

We find that Cuintan began reading his book on Monday.

"How can we solve this problem using an equal-groups multiplication pattern?"

We found that Cuintan read 30 pages each day. So we can think, "What number of days times 30 pages equals 150 pages?" (5 days, since 5×30 pages = 150 pages).

Once we know that it took Cuintan 5 days to read the book, we can find the day he started the book. Monday through Friday is 5 days, so Cuintan started the book on Monday.

Check *Look back.*

"Is our answer reasonable?"

We know that our answer is reasonable, because Monday through Friday is 5 days, and Cuintan read 30 pages each day. That is a total of 5×30 pages = 150 pages, which is the length of the book.

LESSON 71

California Mathematics Content Standards

NS 3.0, 3.3 Solve problems involving multiplication of multidigit numbers by two-digit numbers.

NS 4.0, 4.1 Understand that many whole numbers break down in different ways (e.g., $12 = 4 \times 3 = 2 \times 6 = 2 \times 2 \times 3$).

MR 2.0, 2.6 Make precise calculations and check the validity of the results from the context of the problem.

• Multiplying by Multiples of 10

Power Up

facts Power Up H

count aloud Count by fives from 2 to 52.

mental math

a. **Number Sense:** 300×30 9000

b. **Number Sense:** 240×10 2400

c. **Number Sense:** Counting by 5's from 5, every number Cailey says ends in 0 or 5. If she counts by 5's from 6, then every number she says ends in what digits? 1 or 6

d. **Fractional Parts:** $\frac{1}{2}$ of 120 60

e. **Powers/Roots:** $\sqrt{64} \div 4$ 2

f. **Money:** Cantrice bought peanuts for $3.75 and a drink for $2.95. What was the total cost? $6.70

g. **Estimation:** Estimate the cost of 8 action figures that are each priced at $4.95. $40

h. **Calculation:** 9^2, $-$ 60, $\div$ 7, $\times$ 20 60

problem solving Choose an appropriate problem-solving strategy to solve this problem. Cuintan finished his 150-page book on Friday. The day before he had put the book down after reading page 120. If Cuintan read the same number of pages each day, on what day did Cuintan begin reading his book? Explain how you found your answer. Monday; See student work.

New Concept

We remember that the multiples of 10 are the numbers we say when we count by tens starting from 10. The last digit in every multiple of 10 is a zero. The first five multiples of 10 are 10, 20, 30, 40, and 50.

Facts Multiply.

8 × 8 64	0 × 5 0	7 × 3 21	9 × 7 63	3 × 2 6	9 × 4 36	8 × 6 48	4 × 3 12	9 × 5 45	6 × 2 12
9 × 2 18	7 × 4 28	8 × 3 24	5 × 5 25	9 × 6 54	7 × 2 14	5 × 4 20	9 × 1 9	9 × 3 27	0 × 0 0
7 × 5 35	2 × 2 4	6 × 4 24	8 × 7 56	5 × 3 15	7 × 6 42	4 × 2 8	8 × 5 40	6 × 3 18	9 × 9 81
3 × 3 9	8 × 4 32	7 × 7 49	8 × 2 16	10 × 10 100	6 × 5 30	4 × 4 16	9 × 8 72	5 × 2 10	6 × 6 36

Power Up

Facts

Distribute **Power Up H** to students. See answers below.

Count Aloud

Before students begin the Mental Math exercise, do these counting exercises as a class.

Mental Math

Encourage students to share different ways to mentally compute these exercises. Strategies for exercises are listed below.

a. Multiply Nonzero Digits, Write Zeros
Write 3 zeros after 3×3;
$300 \times 30 = 9000$.

d. Divide by 2
$\frac{1}{2}$ of $120 = 120 \div 2 = 60$

f. Change $3.75 to $4, then Subtract 25¢
$4.00 + $2.95 = $6.95;
$6.95 − $0.25 = $6.70

Subtract 5¢, Add 5¢
$3.75 − 5¢ = $3.70; $2.95 + 5¢ = $3;
$3.70 + $3.00 = $6.70

Problem Solving

Refer to **Problem-Solving Strategy Discussion,** p. 473H.

New Concept

Instruction

Begin the lesson by having students count by tens from 10 to 100.

As you discuss how the product of the factors 34×20 is the same as the product of the factors $34 \times 2 \times 10$, remind students that the Associative Property of Multiplication states that the three factors can be multiplied in any order. Point out that the property enables them to group numbers in such a way that it may be possible to multiply the numbers using only mental math.

(continued)

New Concept *(Continued)*

Example 1

Active Learning

Invite students to write 25 × 30 in ways that are different than 25 × 3 × 10 (such as 25 × 15 × 2 and 25 × 6 × 5), and then ask them to compare the difficulty of finding each product using only mental math compared to the ease of finding the product of 25 × 3 × 10.

Lead students to generalize from this example that when one or more factors are multiples of 10, we often can name the product of the factors using only mental math.

Extend the Example

Challenge your advanced learners to rewrite the multiplication 25 × 10 × 10 × 10 to include an exponent. Sample: 25×10^3

Connection

Demonstrate on the board or overhead how the traditional multiplication algorithm for multiplying 34 by 20 will also produce the same product (680) as multiplying the factors by "hanging" a zero to the right. Then encourage students to use the method that is most comfortable whenever they multiply a factor by a multiple of 10.

Example 2

Alternate Method

Invite a volunteer to demonstrate on the board or overhead how the traditional multiplication algorithm (shown below) can also be used to find the product of 34 and 30.

$$\begin{array}{r} 34 \\ \times\ 30 \\ \hline 00 \\ +\ 1020 \\ \hline 1020 \end{array}$$

(continued)

We may think of 20 as 2 × 10. So to find 34 × 20, we may look at the problem this way:

34 × 2 × 10

We multiply 34 by 2 and get 68. Then we multiply 68 by 10 and get 680.

Example 1

Write 25 × 30 as a product of 10 and two other factors. Then multiply.

Since 30 equals 3 × 10, we may write 25 × 30 as

25 × 3 × 10

Three times 25 is 75, and 75 times 10 is **750.**

Analyze Is 25 × (3 × 10) the same as 25 × (10 × 10 × 10)? Why or why not? No; sample: 3 × 10 is not equal to 10 × 10 × 10 because 3 × 10 = 30 and 10 × 10 × 10 = 1000; 3×10 is equal to 10+10+10

To multiply a whole number or a decimal number by a multiple of 10, we may write the multiple of 10 so that the zero "hangs out" to the right. Below we use this method to find 34 × 20.

$$\begin{array}{r} 34 \\ \times\ 20 \end{array} \longleftarrow \text{zero "hangs out" to the right}$$

We first write a zero in the answer directly below the "hanging" zero.

$$\begin{array}{r} 34 \\ \times\ 20 \\ \hline 0 \end{array}$$

Then we multiply by the 2 in 20.

$$\begin{array}{r} 34 \\ \times\ 20 \\ \hline 680 \end{array}$$

Verify Is 20 the same as 10 × 10? Why or why not? No; sample: 2 × 10 = 20; 10 × 10 = 100; 2 × 10 = 10 + 10

Example 2

To complete a spelling test, 30 students each wrote 34 different words. How many spelling words will the teacher check altogether?

We write the multiple of 10 as the bottom number and let the zero "hang out."

$$\begin{array}{r} 34 \\ \times\ 30 \end{array}$$

Next we write a zero in the answer directly below the zero in 30. Then we multiply by the 3. The teacher will check **1020 words.**

$$\begin{array}{r} {}^{1} \\ 34 \\ \times\ 30 \\ \hline 1020 \end{array}$$

Justify How could you check the answer? Sample: 34 × 10 = 340; 340 + 340 + 340 = 1020

474 *Saxon Math* *Intermediate 4*

Math Background

Once we know the basic multiplication facts, it is easier to multiply two or more multiples of 10, 100, 1000, and so on. The key is to break each factor into a product of a one-digit whole number and a power of 10. Here are some examples:

40 × 30 = 4 × 10 × 3 × 10 = 4 × 3 × 10 × 10 = 12 × 100 = 1200

50 × 500 = 5 × 10 × 5 × 100 = 5 × 5 × 10 × 100 = 25 × 1000 = 25,000

7000 × 200 = 7 × 1000 × 2 × 100 = 7 × 2 × 1000 × 100 = 14 × 100,000 = 1,400,000

The pattern in these answers suggests a shortcut: Multiply the nonzero digits of the factors and then affix the total number of 0's in the two factors. For example, to multiply 60 × 400, multiply 6 × 4 to get 24. There is one zero in 60 and two zeros in 400, so affix 3 zeros. The answer is 24,000.

Example 3

A member of a school support staff ordered 20 three-ring binders for the school bookstore. If the cost of each binder was $1.43, what was the total cost of the order?

We write the multiple of 10 so that the zero "hangs out." We write a zero below the zero in 20, and then we multiply by the 2. We place the decimal point so that there are two digits after it. Finally, we write a dollar sign in front. The cost of the order was **$28.60**.

$$\begin{array}{r} \$1.43 \\ \times \quad 20 \\ \hline \$28.60 \end{array}$$

Lesson Practice Multiply the factors in problems **a–f**.

a. 75 × 10 750 **b.** 10 × 32 320 **c.** 10 × 53¢ $5.30

d. $\begin{array}{r} 26 \\ \times\ 20 \\ \hline 520 \end{array}$ **e.** $\begin{array}{r} \$1.64 \\ \times\ 30 \\ \hline \$49.20 \end{array}$ **f.** $\begin{array}{r} 45 \\ \times\ 50 \\ \hline 2250 \end{array}$

g. Write 12 × 30 as a product of 10 and two other factors. Then multiply. 12 × 3 × 10; 360

Written Practice

▸ *** 1.** (Inv. 5) Use the information in the pictograph below to answer parts **a–c**.

Consumed by Matt in One Day	
Water	🥤🥤🥤🥤🥤🥤
Tea	🥤
Milk	🥤🥤🥤🥤
Juice	🥤🥤🥤

Key: 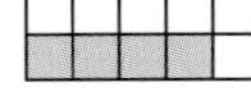 = 1 cup

a. How many pints of liquid did Matt drink in 1 day? 7 pints

b. Matt drank twice as much water as he did what other beverage? juice

c. About how many cups of water does Matt drink in 1 week? 42 cups

2. (67) **a.** What fraction of this rectangle is shaded? $\frac{4}{10}$

b. What fraction of this rectangle is not shaded? $\frac{6}{10}$

English Learners

Say, ***"The word bookstore is made up of two smaller words—book and store—which show the meaning of the single word, bookstore. Bookstore is called a compound word because it is made up of other words."***

Say, ***"Name other words that are made up of smaller words which show their meaning."*** Samples: paperclip, daytime, bookbag, bluebird

New Concept *(Continued)*

Example 3

Error Alert

It is important for students to understand that since the factors contain a total of two decimal places, the product must contain two decimal places.

Lead students to generalize from this example that the number of decimal places in a product is equal to the sum of the number of decimal places in the factors.

Also make sure students understand that we begin counting from the right to place a decimal point in a product.

Lesson Practice

Guided Practice

Use these problems as guided practice to check the students' understanding of today's concept.

Problems a–c

Encourage students to find each product using only mental math.

Remind those students who use paper and pencil computation that the Commutative Property of Multiplication enables them to write the factors in any order.

Problem c

Error Alert

Make sure students understand that although the product can be found without changing 53¢ to dollars and cents, a product of 530¢ of cents must be rewritten as dollars and cents.

Lead students to generalize from this fact that any number of cents greater than 99¢ must be written as dollars and cents.

Problem g

Error Alert

Make sure students rewrite 30 (and not 12) as the product of two factors. Although students may then use paper and pencil to find the product, explain that the goal of rewriting the multiplication is to create an opportunity to name the product using only mental math.

Closure The questions below help assess the concepts taught in this lesson.

"Name the first five multiples of 10." 10, 20, 30, 40, 50

"Explain how we can find the product of two factors, using only mental math, if one factor is a multiple of 10 less than 100." Sample: Write one zero to the right of the product of the nonzero digits.

Write 15 × 40 on the board or overhead and ask students to name the product. 15 × 40 = 600

Written Practice

Math Conversations

Independent Practice and Discussions to Increase Understanding

Problem 1

Make sure students recognize that each symbol represents two equivalent amounts—1 cup and 8 ounces.

To help students complete part **a,** point out that 1 pint and 2 cups are equivalent amounts.

Problem 5 Evaluate

To produce an ordered pair, students should substitute 1 for x, and then follow the order of operations to simplify the right side of the equation. The result will be a value for y, and both x- and y-values should be written as an ordered pair of the form (x, y). The process is then repeated four more times by substituting 2, 3, 4, and then 5 for x.

Extend the Problem

Challenge students to decide if the point (6, 20) is a point on the line, and explain why or why not. Yes; sample: The substitution of 6 for x and 20 for y in the equation $y = 3x + 2$ produces the true statement $20 = 20$.

Problem 6 Analyze

"Name a one-digit prime number and explain why it is a prime number."

Sample: 7 is a prime number because it has only two factors—itself and 1.

(continued)

3. (Inv. 2) **Estimate** Which of these arrows could be pointing to 2500? *B*

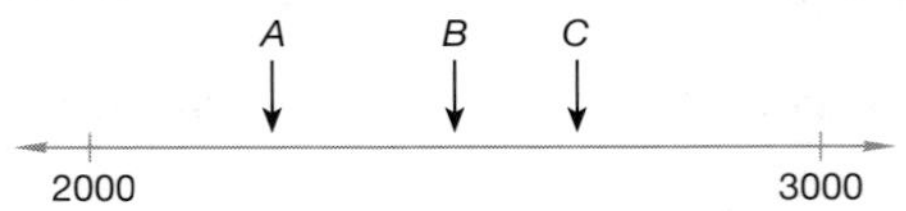

4. (61) **Estimate** Zoe estimated the sum of 682 + 437 + 396 by first rounding each addend to the nearest hundred. What was Zoe's estimate of the actual sum? 700 + 400 + 400 = 1500

▶ *5. (64, Inv. 7) **Evaluate** Write ordered pairs for the equation $y = 3x + 2$ when x is 1, 2, 3, 4, and 5. (1, 5), (2, 8), (3, 11), (4, 14), (5, 17)

▶ *6. (56) **Analyze** Write a two-digit prime number that has a 3 in the ones place. Sample: 23

7. (42) a. **Estimate** The segment below is how many centimeters long? 4 cm

b. The segment is how many millimeters long? 40 mm

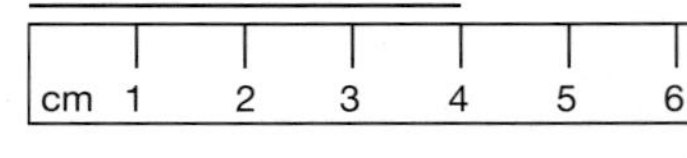

8. (47) **Represent** A company was sold for $7,450,000. Use words to write that amount of money. seven million, four hundred fifty thousand dollars

9. (20, 50) If each side of a hexagon is 1 foot long, then how many inches is its perimeter? 72 in.

10. (51) $93{,}417 + 8{,}915$ — 102,332

11. (8, 52) $42{,}718 - k = 26{,}054$ — 16,664

12. (51) $1307 + 638 + 5219 + 138 + 16$ — 7318

13. (28, 52) $\$100.00 - \$86.32$ — $13.68

14. (52) $405{,}158 - 396{,}370$ — 8,788

Inclusion

Use this strategy if the student displays:

- Difficulty with Abstract Processing.
- Difficulty with Large Group Instruction.

Multiplying by Multiples of 10 (Individual)

Materials: paper

- Pass out paper and have students write 45 × 30 on their paper. Tell students that they are going to turn this into a two-part multiplication problem. Write 45 × 3 on the board. Ask, ***"What number is 3 being multiplied by to get 30?"*** 10
- Add × 10 to the problem on the board. Instruct students to multiply the problem 45 × 3. Ask, ***"What is the product?"*** 135 ***"What does this product need to be multiplied by?"*** 10
- Remind students that when mutliplying by 10 all they do is add a zero to the end of the number. Ask, ***"What is the final product of 45 × 30?"*** 1350
- Write 34 × 40 on the board. Have students work in pairs to breakdown the problem into a two-step multiplication problem and solve the problem.

15. (59) 567 × 8 4536

16. (71) 30 × 84¢ $25.20

17. (59) $2.08 × 4 $8.32

▶*18. (71) 40 × 23 920

▶*19. (71) 20 × 45 900

▶*20. (71) 50 × 36 1800

▶*21. (69) 344 ÷ 4 86

▶*22. (69) $\frac{438}{6}$ 73

▶*23. (69) $5\overline{)355}$ 71

24. (Inv. 3, 34, 69) $\sqrt{16} \times n = 100$ 25

25. (34, 65, 69) $5b = 10^2$ 20

▶*26. (43) **Represent** To what decimal number is the arrow pointing? What mixed number is this? −1.5; $-1\frac{1}{2}$

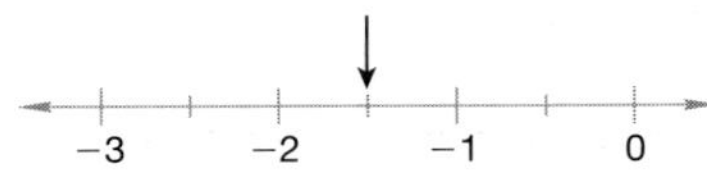

*27. (70) a. **Multiple Choice** Which two rectangles appear to be congruent? **A** and **C**

A

B 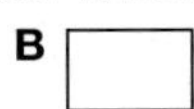

C 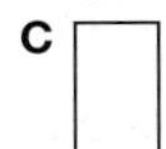

D 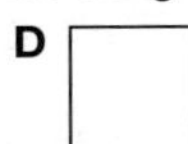

28. (66) Find the perimeter and area of the rectangle shown at right. 16 units; 15 units^2

5 units

3 units

29. (1, 42) The relationship between feet and inches is shown in the table below:

Inches	12	24	36	48	60
Feet	1	2	3	4	5

a. **Generalize** Write a rule that describes the relationship.
Sample: The number of inches is 12 times the number of feet.

b. **Predict** How many inches are equal to 12 feet? 144 inches

Written Practice *(Continued)*

Math Conversations *(cont.)*

Problems 18–23

Before students use paper and pencil arithmetic to find each exact answer, ask them to use rounding and make an estimate. Then use the estimate to help decide the reasonableness of the exact answer after the paper and pencil arithmetic has been completed.

Problem 26 Represent

"On a number line, are negative numbers found to the right of zero or to the left of zero?" To the left of zero

Extend the Problem

"This number line is a horizontal number line. On a vertical number line, where are negative numbers found when compared to zero?" below zero

(continued)

Alternative Approach: Using Manipulatives

To help students understand the concept of multiplying by multiples of 10, have them use base ten blocks to model the same multiplication they show using paper and pencil.

Have students model 11 × 20 using base ten blocks. Explain to students that 11 × 0 = 0 ones and 11 × 2 tens = 22 tens. Regrouping gives 2 hundreds and 2 tens. Have students add the ones, tens, and hundreds to get 2 hundreds, 2 tens, and 0 ones, or 220.

Have students model other examples. Ask:

"When you multiply by a multiple of 10, the product will always have how many ones?" 0

Written Practice *(Continued)*

Math Conversations *(cont.)*

Problem 30 Analyze

Extend the Problem

"Suppose we were asked to place Point D on this coordinate plane so that figure ABDC forms a parallelogram. Where should Point D be placed?" (8, 1)

Errors and Misconceptions

Problem 3

If students have difficulty identifying the correct answer, explain that the number 2500 is located halfway between 2000 and 3000 regardless of the number of tick marks (or lack of tick marks) that divide the distance between those numbers.

Problem 9

Make sure students recognize that they are being asked to find the perimeter in inches when the measure of each side is given in feet.

Problem 25

Students who name 4 as the answer simplified 10^2 as 10×2 or 20.

Engage students in a discussion about using estimation in stores. Identify some advantages and disadvantages of estimating.

▸*30. (50, Inv. 7) Analyze Use the coordinate graph to answer parts **a** and **b**.

a. Write the coordinates for each point. *A*: (2, 8), *B*: (2, 2), *C*: (8, 7)

b. If you drew a segment to connect each point, which polygon would be formed? triangle

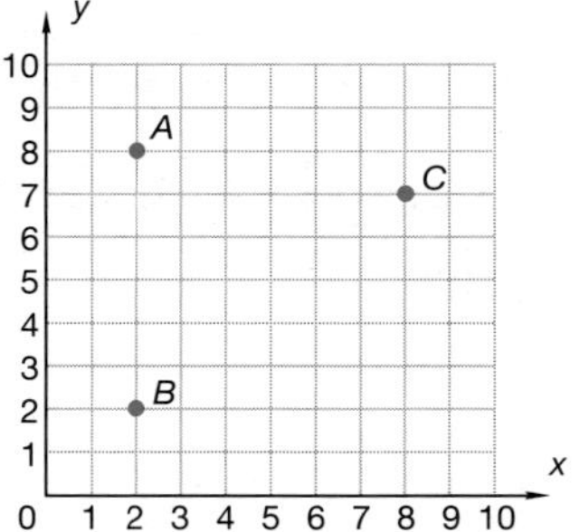

Real-World Connection

Erica and Selena recently entered *The DVD Warehouse* to buy some gifts for their friends and family. *The DVD Warehouse* includes sales tax in its prices. Refer to the tables.

Item	Cost
Comedy DVDs	$17
Action DVDs	$23
Family DVDs	$14
Anime DVDs	$11

Item	Cost
Drama DVDs	$18
History DVDs	$29
Cartoon DVDs	$12
Self-Help DVDs	$27

Erica entered the store with $40. She selected an anime DVD, a cartoon DVD, and an action DVD. Before taking them to the check-out counter she rounded the prices to the nearest 10 dollars. She estimated the cost of the 3 DVDs to be $40.

Selena entered the store with $70. She selected a drama DVD, a history DVD, and a comedy DVD. She also rounded the prices to the nearest 10 dollars before taking them to the check-out counter. She estimated the cost of the 3 DVDs to be $70.

a. When Erica brought her items to the check-out counter, the store clerk told her the total price was $46. Why was Erica's estimated price of $40 too low? She rounded all the prices down.

b. Selena estimated the total cost of her items to be $70. Why was $70 a safe estimate to make? She rounded all the prices up.

Teacher Tip

Be sure to keep plenty of grid paper or copies of **Lesson Activity Master 8** on hand for students who need the extra structure for keeping digits in line.

Looking Forward

Multiplying by multiples of 10 prepares students for:

- **Lesson 84,** multiplying whole numbers and money amounts by 10, 100, and 1000.
- **Lesson 85,** multiplying two or more multiples of 10 and 100.
- **Lessons 86 and 88,** multiplying two two-digit numbers.
- **Lesson 91,** estimating the answers to multiplication and division problems.
- **Lesson 104,** rounding whole numbers to the nearest hundred thousand and the nearest million.
- **Lesson 105,** factoring whole numbers.

Planning & Preparation

• Division with Two-Digit Answers and a Remainder

Objectives

- Find a two-digit answer with a remainder when dividing.
- Use compatible numbers to find a quotient.
- Decide when an estimate is needed to solve a problem.
- Check a division problem using multiplication.
- Solve word problems involving multi-digit division.

Prerequisite Skills

- Solving division problems with a remainder.
- Solving division problems using manipulatives.

Materials

Instructional Masters

- Power Up H Worksheet
- Lesson Activity 8*

Manipulative Kit

- Rulers
- Two-color counters*

Teacher-provided materials

- Index cards, place-value workmat, grid paper*

**optional*

California Mathematics Content Standards

NS 1.0, 1.4 Decide when a rounded solution is called for and explain why such a solution may be appropriate.

NS 3.0, 3.2 Demonstrate an understanding of, and the ability to use, standard algorithms for multiplying a multidigit number by a two-digit number and for dividing a multidigit number by a one-digit number; use relationships between them to simplify computations and to check results.

NS 3.0, 3.4 Solve problems involving division of multidigit numbers by one-digit numbers.

MR 3.0, 3.1 Evaluate the reasonableness of the solution in the context of the original situation.

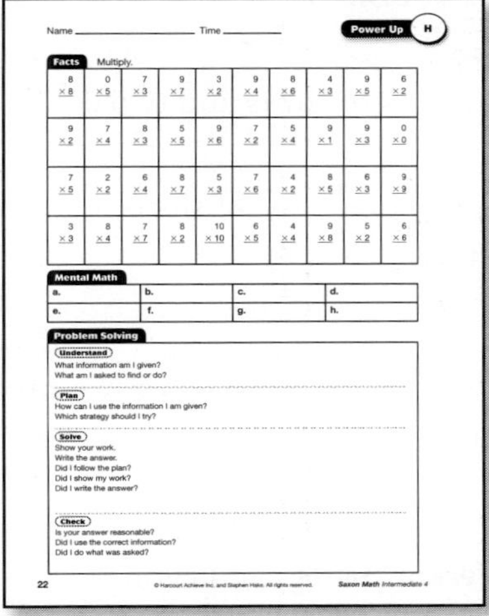

Name ______ Time ______ Power Up H

Facts Multiply.

Mental Math

Problem Solving

Understand

Plan

Solve

Check

Power Up H Worksheet

Universal Access

Reaching All Special Needs Students

Special Education Students	At-Risk Students	English Learners	Advanced Learners
• Inclusion (TM) • Adaptations for Saxon Math	• Error Alert (TM) • Reteaching Masters • Refresher Lessons for California Standards	• English Learners (TM) • Developing Academic Language (TM) • English Learner Handbook	• Extend the Problem (TM) • Online Activities

TM=Teacher's Manual

Developing Academic Language

New	**Maintained**	**English Learner**
tree diagram	combination	complete

Problem Solving Discussion

Problem

Levon has three colors of shirts—red, white, and blue. He has two colors of pants–black and tan. What combinations of one shirt and one pair of pants can Levon make?

Focus Strategy

Draw a Picture or Diagram

Understand ***Understand the problem.***

"What information are we given?"

We are told that Levon has three colors of shirts and two colors of pants.

"What are we asked to do?"

We are asked to find the possible combinations of shirts and pants that Levon can wear.

Plan ***Make a plan.***

"How can we use the information we know to solve the problem?"

We can *make a diagram* to find all the combinations of shirt and pant colors.

Solve ***Carry out the plan.***

"For each shirt, how many different pants can Levon wear? How can we show this in a diagram?"

For each shirt, there are two colors of pants Levon can wear. We can list each shirt color and then draw two branches from each color. At the ends of the branches, we can write the pants colors.

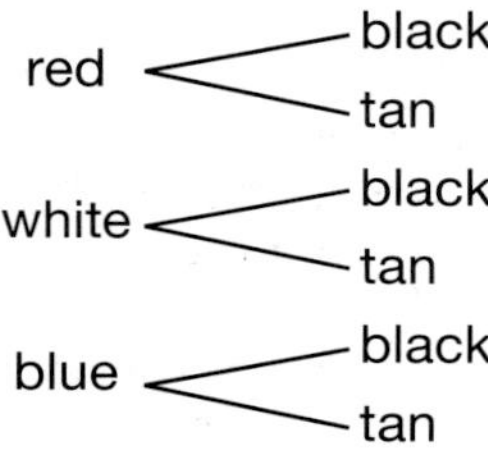

"What combinations are shown by the diagram?"

We have a total of six branches in the diagram, so we find that Levon can make six different combinations of shirt and pant colors:

red, black
red, tan
white, black
white, tan
blue, black
blue, tan

Check ***Look back.***

"How many combinations did we find?"

We found six combinations that Levon can make with three different shirt colors and two different pants colors.

"Is our answer reasonable?"

We know that our answer is reasonable, because there are two possible combinations for each shirt color. There are $2 + 2 + 2 = 6$ combinations for three different shirt colors.

"What kind of diagram did we make to solve this problem?"

We call the diagram we made in this problem a *tree diagram*, because each line we drew to connect a shirt color with a pants color is like a branch of a tree.

LESSON 72

• Division with Two-Digit Answer and a Remainder

California Mathematics Content Standards

NS 1.0, 1.4 Decide when a rounded solution is called for and explain why such a solution may be appropriate.

NS 3.0, 3.2 Demonstrate an understanding of, and the ability to use, standard algorithms for multiplying a multidigit number by a two-digit number and for dividing a multidigit number by a one-digit number; use relationships between them to simplify computations and to check results.

NS 3.0, 3.4 Solve problems involving division of multidigit numbers by one-digit numbers.

MR 3.0, 3.1 Evaluate the reasonableness of the solution in the context of the original situation.

facts Power Up H

count aloud When we count by fives from 3, we say the numbers 3, 8, 13, 18, and so on. Count by fives from 3 to 53.

mental math

a. **Number Sense:** 12 × 20 240

b. **Number Sense:** 12 × 30 360

c. **Number Sense:** 12 × 40 480

d. **Number Sense:** 36 + 29 + 230 295

e. **Money:** Lucas bought a roll of film for $4.87 and batteries for $3.98. What was the total cost? $8.85

f. **Time:** The baseball game started at 7:05 p.m. and lasted 1 hour 56 minutes. What time did the game end? 9:01 p.m.

g. **Estimation:** One mile is about 1609 meters. Round this length to the nearest hundred meters. 1600 m

h. **Calculation:** $\frac{1}{2}$ of 6, × 2, × 5, − 16 14

problem solving Levon has three colors of shirts—red, white, and blue. He has two colors of pants—black and tan. What combinations of one shirt and one pair of pants can Levon make?

Focus Strategy: **Make a Diagram**

Understand We are told that Levon has three colors of shirts and two colors of pants. We are asked to find the possible combinations of shirts and pants that Levon can wear.

Plan We can *make a diagram* to find all the combinations of shirt and pant colors.

Facts Multiply.

8 × 8 64	0 × 5 0	7 × 3 21	9 × 7 63	3 × 2 6	9 × 4 36	8 × 6 48	4 × 3 12	9 × 5 45	6 × 2 12
9 × 2 18	7 × 4 28	8 × 3 24	5 × 5 25	9 × 6 54	7 × 2 14	5 × 4 20	9 × 1 9	9 × 3 27	0 × 0 0
7 × 5 35	2 × 2 4	6 × 4 24	8 × 7 56	5 × 3 15	7 × 6 42	4 × 2 8	8 × 5 40	6 × 3 18	9 × 9 81
3 × 3 9	8 × 4 32	7 × 7 49	8 × 2 16	10 × 10 100	6 × 5 30	4 × 4 16	9 × 8 72	5 × 2 10	6 × 6 36

Power Up

Facts

Distribute **Power Up H** to students. See answers below.

Count Aloud

Before students begin the Mental Math exercises, do these counting exercises as a class.

Mental Math

Encourage students to share different ways to mentally compute these exercises. Strategies for exercises are listed below.

b. Decompose 30

12 × 30 = 12 × 3 × 10; 12 × 3 = 36;
36 × 10 = 360

d. Change 29 to 30, then Subtract 1

36 + 30 + 230 = 66 + 230 = 296;
296 − 1 = 295

e. Add $4, Subtract 2¢

$4.87 + $4 = $8.87;
$8.87 − $0.02 = $8.85

Add $5, Subtract 13¢

$3.98 + $5 = $8.98;
$8.98 − $0.13 = $8.85

Problem Solving

Refer to **Problem-Solving Strategy Discussion,** p. 479B.

New Concept

Alternate Method

You might choose to introduce the lesson by writing the four steps of the division algorithm on the board or overhead, and asking students to stand in a variety of lines with an odd number of students in each line. Then ask the first student in each line to say the first step of the algorithm (divide), ask the second student to say the second step (multiply), and so on, until the sequence of steps has been repeated several times by the students in each line.

(continued)

Solve For each shirt, there are two colors of pants Levon can wear. We can list each shirt color and then draw two branches from each color. At the ends of the branches, we can write the color of the pants, like this:

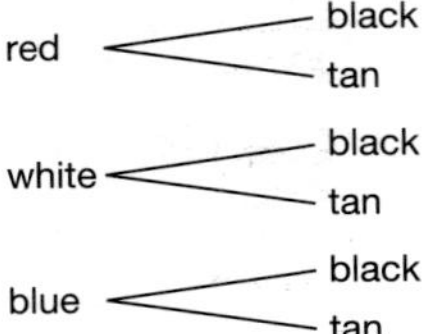

Now we list the combinations formed by the diagram. We have a total of six branches, so we find that Levon can make six different combinations of shirt and pant colors:

red, black; red, tan; white, black; white, tan; blue, black; blue, tan

Check We found six combinations that Levon can make with three different shirt colors and two different pants colors. We know our answer is reasonable because there are two combinations possible for each shirt color. There are 2 + 2 + 2, or 6 combinations for three different shirt colors.

We call the diagram we made in this problem a **tree diagram,** because each line we drew to connect a shirt color with a pants color is like a branch of a tree.

New Concept

The pencil-and-paper method we use for dividing has four steps: divide, multiply, subtract, and bring down. These steps are repeated until the division is complete.

Step 1: Divide.

Step 2: Multiply.

Step 3: Subtract.

Step 4: Bring down.

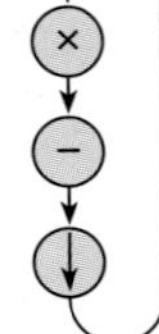

English Learners

Explain that the word **complete** means done, finished, or ended.

Ask, ***"When will you complete the homework that is due Monday?"*** before Monday

Students discuss other things they have done or could do until they were **complete.**

For each step we write a number. When we finish Step 4, we go back to Step 1 and repeat the steps until there are no more digits to bring down. The number left after the last subtraction is the remainder. We show the remainder in the division answer by writing it with an uppercase "R" in front.

Example 1

Divide: 5)137

Step 1: Divide 13 by 5 and write "2."

Step 2: Multiply 2 by 5 and write "10."

Step 3: Subtract 10 from 13 and write "3."

Step 4: Bring down 7 to make 37.

```
   2
5)137
  10↓
   37
```

Now we repeat the same four steps:

Step 1: Divide 37 by 5 and write "7."

Step 2: Multiply 7 by 5 and write "35."

Step 3: Subtract 35 from 37 and write "2."

Step 4: There are no more digits to bring down, so we will not repeat the steps. The remainder is 2. Our answer is **27 R 2.**

```
  27
5)137
  10
   37
   35
    2
```

Thinking Skills

Verify

Why do we write the first digit of the quotient in the tens place?

We are dividing 13 tens.

If we divide 137 into 5 equal groups, there will be 27 in each group with 2 extra.

To check a division answer that has a remainder, we multiply the quotient (without the remainder) by the divisor and then add the remainder. For this example, we multiply 27 by 5 and then add 2.

```
  27     135
×  5   +   2
 135     137  check
```

Example 2

Three hundred seventy-five fans chartered eight buses to travel to a playoff basketball game. About how many fans were on each bus if the group was divided as evenly as possible among the eight buses?

Since we are asked to find "about how many people," we can estimate the answer. We round 375 to the nearest hundred. Instead of dividing 375 by 8, we will divide 400 by 8.

$$400 \div 8 = 50$$

There will be **about 50 people** on each bus.

Math Background

There is a shorthand method of doing long division that requires some mental computation.

We use the method below to find the quotient using pencil and paper.

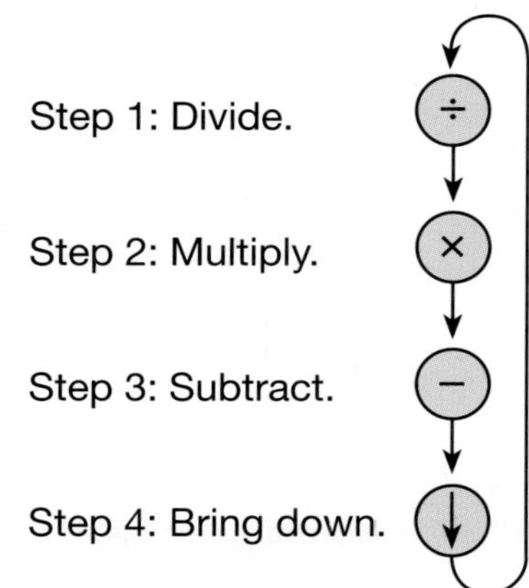

New Concept *(Continued)*

Example 1

Active Learning

As you discuss each step of the solution, ask students to name the step of the division algorithm that each step represents.

As you discuss how to check the answer, have students note that because the quotient includes a remainder, two operations are needed to complete the check. Contrast this fact with the checks of quotients that were completed in earlier lessons—because those quotients consisted only of whole numbers, only one operation was needed to complete the checks.

Error Alert

Continue to stress the importance of correctly placing the first digit in the quotient by comparing the divisor to the first digit in the dividend.

Also stress the importance of comparing the subtraction result in Step 3 of the algorithm to the divisor. Remind students that if the result of the subtraction is greater than or equal to the dividend, the digit in that place of the quotient must be increased.

Example 2

Active Learning

After discussing the solution, ask:

"Is the estimate of about 50 people on each bus greater or less than the actual number of people who will be on each bus? Explain your thinking." Greater; sample: 375 was increased to 400 before dividing; Increasing a dividend increases the quotient.

Extend the Example

Challenge your advanced learners to name the exact number of people who will be on each bus, and explain their answer. Since $375 \div 8 = 46$ R 7, there will be 46 people on one bus and 47 people on each of seven buses.

(continued)

New Concept *(Continued)*

Lesson Practice

Guided Practice

Use these problems as guided practice to check the students' understanding of today's concept.

Problem h

Because there are a number of different ways to estimate, invite volunteers to share their estimates with the class and explain how those estimates were made.

Problems a–f

Error Alert

To help students correctly place the first digit in the quotient, write one or more of the divisions on the board or overhead and demonstrate how to place that digit.

Remind students of the importance of checking their work by making an estimate prior to beginning the division, or by using multiplication (or multiplication and addition if the quotient includes a remainder) after the division has been completed.

Closure The questions below help assess the concepts taught in this lesson.

"What are the four steps we follow whenever we use paper and pencil to divide two numbers?" Divide, multiply, subtract, bring down

"How many times are these steps repeated?" As often as necessary until all of the digits in the dividend have been brought down

"Explain how to check a quotient that includes a remainder." Sample: Multiply the whole number portion of the quotient and the divisor, and add the remainder. Then compare the result to the dividend.

Written Practice

Math Conversations

Independent Practice and Discussions to Increase Understanding

Problem 2 **Estimate**

Accept reasonable estimates.

(continued)

Lesson Practice

Divide:

a. $3\overline{)134}$ 44 R 2 **b.** $7\overline{)240}$ 34 R 2 **c.** $5\overline{)88}$ 17 R 3

d. $259 \div 8$ 32 R 3 **e.** $95 \div 4$ 23 R 3 **f.** $325 \div 6$ 54 R 1

g. Shou divided 235 by 4 and got 58 R 3 for her answer. Describe how to check Shou's calculation. Multiply 58 by 4. Then add 3 to the product.

h. A wildlife biologist estimates that 175 birds live in the 9-acre marsh. What is a reasonable estimate of the number of birds in each acre of the marsh? Explain why your estimate is reasonable. Sample: 175 rounds to 180, and since 9 is a factor of 18, 9 is also a factor of 180; A reasonable estimate is 180 ÷ 9, or 20 birds per acre.

Written Practice

Distributed and Integrated

1. (37) There are 734 students who plan to write letters to the President. The school has 37 boxes of envelopes. Each box contains 20 envelopes. Are there enough envelopes for everyone? How many envelopes are there together? Yes; 740

▸ **2.** (28, 62) **Estimate** Clanatia went to the store with \$9.12. She spent \$3.92. About how much money did Clanatia have left? About \$5.00

3. (55, 56) **a.** Write the product of 63 using two factors. Sample: 7×9

b. Is 63 a prime number? Why or why not? No; sample: It has more than two factors.

4. (67) One fourth of the guests gathered in the living room. What fraction of the guests did not gather in the living room? $\frac{3}{4}$

▸ ***5.** (20, 42, 50) If one side of a regular triangle is 3 centimeters long, then what is its perimeter in

a. centimeters? 9 cm **b.** millimeters? 90 mm

▸ ***6.** (Inv. 2, 43) **Represent** To what decimal number is the arrow pointing? What mixed number is this? −8.89; $-8\frac{89}{100}$

▸ ***7.** (39, 71) **Analyze** Moe read 30 pages a day for 14 days to finish his book. How many pages does the book have? 420 pages

Inclusion

Use this strategy if the student displays:

- Difficulty with Multiple Steps.
- Slow Learning Rate

Division with Two-Digit Answers with a Remainder (Individual)

Materials: index card

- Have students copy the steps for long division on their index card.
- Write $6\overline{)215}$ on the board. Ask, ***"How many times will 6 go into 2?"*** 0

  Instruct students to place a 0 as a place holder over the 2 and ask, ***"How many times will 6 go into 21?"*** 3
- Have students use the steps to work through this division step. Ask, ***"How much is left over?"*** 3

  Remind students to bring down the 5 to the 3 to make 35 and start over on the steps. Ask, ***"What is the quotient?"*** 35 ***"How many remain?"*** 5
- Write $7\overline{)186}$ on the board and have students use their steps to solve for the quotient and remainder.

*8. **Multiple Choice** **a.** Which two triangles appear to be congruent? C and D
(70)

A  B C 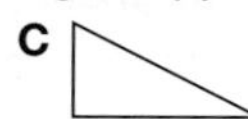 D

b. **Conclude** Explain how you know. Sample: I traced over Triangle **C** and flipped it over onto Triangle **D.** They are the same size and shape.

▸ *9. **Explain** Isabella estimated the product of 389 × 7 to be 2800. Explain how Isabella used rounding to make her estimate. Isabella rounded 389 to the nearest hundred; 400 × 7 = 2800
(61)

▸*10. **Multiple Choice** It is late afternoon. What time will it be in one hour? D
(13)

A 11:25 a.m. B 5:56 a.m.
C 4:56 p.m. D 5:56 p.m.

11. **Represent** Compare: $\frac{3}{4} \bigcirc \frac{4}{5}$. Draw and shade two congruent rectangles to show the comparison. [shaded rectangle] < [shaded rectangle]
(57)

12. 4.325 − 2.5 1.825
(45)

13. 3.65 + 5.2 + 0.18 9.03
(45)

14. $50.00 − $42.60 $7.40
(28, 52)

15. $17.54 + 49¢ + $15 $33.03
(28, 51)

*16. $5\overline{)75}$ 15
(68)

▸*17. $4\overline{)92}$ 23
(68)

*18. $3\overline{)84}$ 28
(68)

19. 398 × 6 2388
(59)

20. 47 × 60 2820
(71)

21. 8 × $6.25 $50.00
(59)

▸*22. $4\overline{)136}$ 34
(69)

▸*23. $\frac{132}{2}$ 66
(69)

24. $6\overline{)192}$ 32
(69)

25. $8n = 120$ 15
(34, 69)

26. $f \times 3^2 = 108$ 12
(34, 65, 69)

27. $7 + 8 + 5 + 4 + n + 2 + 7 + 3 = 54$ 18
(4)

▸*28. Find the perimeter and area of this rectangle: 24 m; 32 m²
(66)

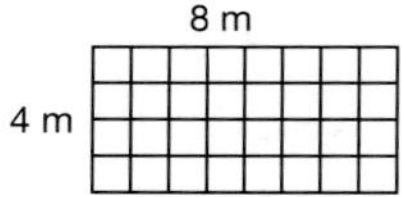

Written Practice *(Continued)*

Math Conversations *(cont.)*

Problem 5

Before students solve part **b,** ask:

"Describe the relationship shared by centimeters and millimeters." 1 cm = 10 mm

Problem 6 Represent

"Do the smaller tick marks on this number line represent tenths or hundredths? Explain how you know." Hundredths; sample: The distance between two consecutive tenths is divided into ten equal parts.

Extend the Problem

To offer a challenge to students, ask:

"Is −8.9 greater or less than −8.8? Explain how you know." Less; sample: −8.9 is farther from zero than −8.8.

Problem 7 Analyze

Discuss the scenario with students, and after they conclude that multiplication is used to find the answer, invite volunteers to suggest ways to rewrite 30 × 14 so that it is possible that the product can be found using only mental math. Sample: 3 × 14 × 10; 3 × 14 = 42, and 42 × 10 = 420

Problem 9 Explain

Extend the Problem

"Is the exact product of 389 × 7 greater or less than Isabella's estimate? Explain how you know." Less; sample: Because 389 is less than 400, 389 × 7 is less than 400 × 7.

Problem 10 Multiple Choice

Test-Taking Strategy

Ask students to explain how the units "a.m." and "p.m." in the answer choices can be used to eliminate one or more choices as possible answers. Sample: Since the given time is 4:56 p.m., a time one hour later will still be a "p.m." time. Answer choices **A** and **B** cannot be correct answers because each time is an "a.m." time.

(continued)

Written Practice *(Continued)*

Math Conversations *(cont.)*

Problem 17

Before students begin each division, ask:

"Compare the divisor to the first digit in the dividend. How do the digits compare?" The divisor is less than the first digit in the dividend.

"Where will the first digit in the quotient be placed? Explain how you know." The first digit in the quotient will be placed above the first digit in the dividend (e.g. the tens place) because 9 tens can be divided into 4 groups; there will be 2 tens in each group and 1 ten left over.

Ask similar questions for problem **18.**

Problems 22 and 23

Before students begin the arithmetic for each problem, invite a volunteer to describe where the first digit in the quotient will be placed, and explain why. In each division, the first digit in the quotient will be placed above the second digit in the dividend (e.g. the tens place) because each divisor is greater than the first digit in the dividend.

Problem 28

Extend the Problem

"What other rectangles have an area of 32 square meters?" Sample: 1 m by 32 m, 2 m by 16 m, 4 m by 8 m, 8 m by 4 m, 16 m by 2 m, 32 m by 1 m

"Which of the rectangles that were named have the smallest perimeter?" Sample: 4 m by 8 m and 8 m by 4 m; Each rectangle has a perimeter of 24 meters.

Errors and Misconceptions

Problem 6

Ask students who name –8.91 as the answer to sketch the number line and write the equivalent decimal –8.90 for –8.9 and –8.80 for –8.8. Then work with the students to label each tick mark between those numbers with the decimal number in hundredths.

*29. (Inv. 7) **Explain** What is the length of segment *AB*? Explain your reasoning. 7 units; Subtract *x*-coordinates; 9 – 2 = 7

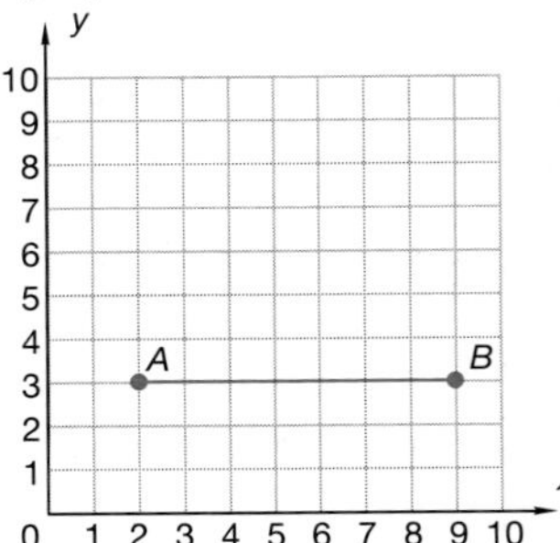

*30. (55) The first four multiples of 18 are 18, 36, 54, and 72. What are the first four multiples of 180? 180, 360, 540, 720

484 **Saxon Math** *Intermediate 4*

Teacher Tip

Some students benefit from using grid paper when solving long-division problems. Provide them with copies of grid paper or **Lesson Activity Master 8** Remind them that each digit should be written in its own square.

Looking Forward

Division with two-digit quotients and a remainder prepares students for:

- **Lesson 75,** dividing numbers to find a quotient that ends in zero.
- **Lesson 79,** division with three-digit quotients.
- **Lesson 83,** division with zeros in three-digit quotients.
- **Lesson 87,** solving division word problems that involve remainders.
- **Lesson 91,** estimating multiplication and division answers.

California Mathematics Content Standards

NS 3.0, 3.2 Demonstrate an understanding of, and the ability to use, standard algorithms for multiplying a multidigit number by a two-digit number and for dividing a multidigit number by a one-digit number; use relationships between them to simplify computations and to check results.

MR 3.0, 3.2 Note the method of deriving the solution and demonstrate a conceptual understanding of the derivation by solving similar problems.

• How the Division Algorithm Works

Look at this rectangle. It represents both $8 \times 4 = 32$ and $32 \div 4 = 8$.

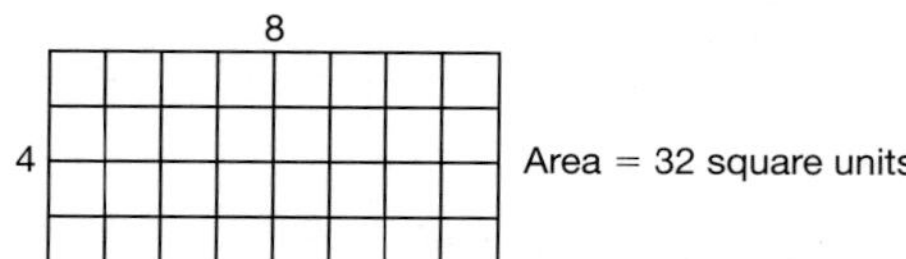

You can think of division as finding the length of a rectangle (the quotient) when you know its area (the dividend) and its width (the divisor).

Example 1

Divide: 408 ÷ 6

We can represent the steps of division by dividing a rectangle into parts. The area of the rectangle is 408 and its width is 6. The first division finds the length of a rectangle with an area of 360.

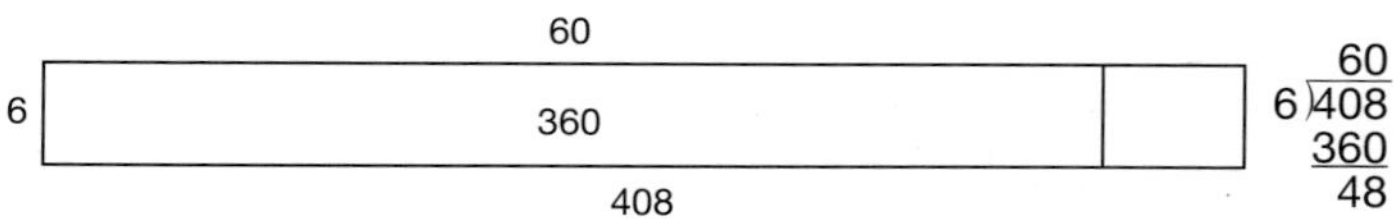

The second division finds the length of a rectangle with an area of 48.

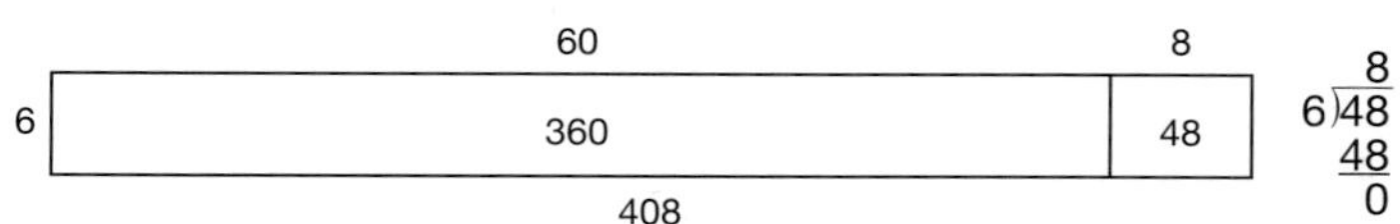

The quotient is 60 + 8, which equals **68.**

Since multiplication and division are related operations, we may check a division answer by multiplying. $68 \times 6 = 408$

How the Division Algorithm Works

Use this page to enhance conceptual understanding of key mathematical concepts.

Guided Instruction

Since multiplication and division are inverse operations, finding the quotient in a division problem is equivalent to finding an unknown factor in a multiplication problem. The division process is actually a way to find an unknown factor when a product and one factor are known.

Because a rectangle (area) model can represent both multiplication and division, it is useful for providing a visual approach to understanding division. In this method, repeated use of a new rectangle for each remainder helps to reinforce understanding of the divide-multiply-subtract-bring down process that students have learned in earlier lessons.

Work through this process step by step with the class.

Extending the Concept

The area of the rectangle in the example was decomposed to match the division algorithm. However, the area could be composed in other ways to find the quotient, as we show below:

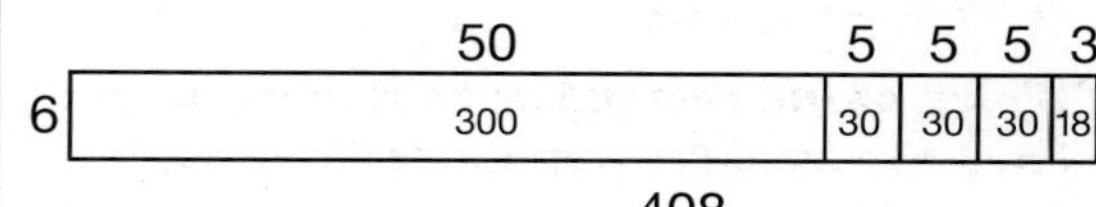

$50 + 5 + 5 + 5 + 3$

Students can suggest other ways to decompose 408 into multiples of 6.

(continued)

Closure

The question below helps assess the concepts taught in this lesson.

"How is the relationship between multiplication and division used in the long division process?" Sample: We can think of the division process as a way to find an unknown factor.

Explain Find each quotient, illustrate how to divide a rectangle representing the division, and show how to check your answer.

a. 210 ÷ 5
42; See student work; 5 × 42

b. 225 ÷ 3
75; See student work; 3 × 75

c. 595 ÷ 7
85; See student work; 7 × 85

Planning & Preparation

• Capacity

Objectives

- Convert between units of liquid measure in the U.S. Customary System.
- Convert between units of liquid measure in the metric system.
- Compare units of liquid measure.
- Describe and graph a relationship between liquid units of measure.

Prerequisite Skills

- Measuring liquids using U.S. Customary System measuring cups.
- Measuring liquids using metric system measuring cups.

Materials

Instructional Masters

- Power Up H Worksheet

Manipulative Kit

- Rulers
- Measuring jars*

Teacher-provided materials

- Beans, marbles, index cards*

*optional

California Mathematics Content Standards

NS 2.0, 2.1 Estimate and compute the sum or difference of whole numbers and positive decimals to two places.

NS 2.0, 2.2 Round two-place decimals to one decimal or the nearest whole number and judge the reasonableness of the rounded answer.

AF 1.0, 1.1 Use letters, boxes, or other symbols to stand for any number in simple expressions or equations (e.g., demonstrate an understanding and the use of the concept of a variable).

AF 1.0, 1.4 Use and interpret formulas (e.g., area = length × width or $A = lw$) to answer questions about quantities and their relationships.

AF 1.0, 1.5 Understand that an equation such as $y = 3x + 5$ is a prescription for determining a second number when a first number is given.

MR 2.0, 2.3 Use a variety of methods, such as words, numbers, symbols, charts, graphs, tables, diagrams, and models, to explain mathematical reasoning.

MR 3.0, 3.3 Develop generalizations of the results obtained and apply them in other circumstances.

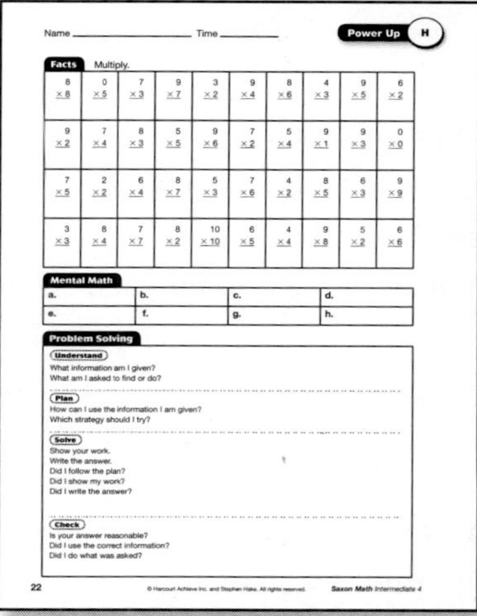

Power Up H Worksheet

Universal Access

Reaching All Special Needs Students

Special Education Students	At-Risk Students	English Learners	Advanced Learners
• Inclusion (TM) • Adaptations for Saxon Math	• Alternative Approach (TM) • Error Alert (TM) • Reteaching Masters • Refresher Lessons for California Standards	• English Learners (TM) • Developing Academic Language (TM) • English Learner Handbook	• Extend the Example (TM) • Extend the Problem (TM) • Online Activities

TM=Teacher's Manual

Developing Academic Language

New	Maintained	English Learner
capacity	cup	abbreviation
fluid ounces	gallon	
	metric system	
	pint	
	quart	
	U.S. Customary System	

Problem Solving Discussion

Problem

The charge for the taxi ride was $2.50 for the first mile and $1.50 for each additional mile. What was the charge for an 8-mile taxi ride? Explain how you solved the problem.

Focus Strategies

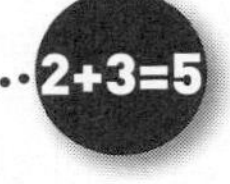

Write a Number Sentence or Equation

Make or Use a Table, Chart, or Graph

Understand *Understand the problem.*

Teacher Note: A similar problem was solved in Lesson 69.

"What information are we given?"

A taxi ride cost $2.50 for the first mile, and $1.50 for each additional mile.

What are we asked to do?"

We are asked to find the charge for an 8-mile taxi ride and to explain our solution.

Plan *Make a plan.*

"What problem-solving strategy can we use to solve the problem?"

We can *write a number sentence* to find the charge.

Solve *Carry out the plan.*

"How much did the first mile of the taxi ride cost?"

The first mile cost $2.50.

"How many more miles was the taxi ride after the first mile?"

The taxi ride was 8 miles, so there were 7 miles after the first mile.

"How much did each of the additional 7 miles cost?"

Each additional mile cost $1.50.

"What is a number sentence that describes the total charge for the taxi ride?"

$\$2.50 + (7 \times \$1.50)$

$= \$2.50 + \$10.50$

$= \$13.00$

Check *Look back.*

"What was the total charge for an 8-mile taxi ride?"

The total charge was $13.00.

"Is our answer reasonable?"

We know that our answer is reasonable, because $2.50 for the first mile plus $10.50 for the additional miles is $13.00 total.

"What is another problem-solving strategy we could have used?"

We could have set up a table to show the charge at the end of each mile driven. Our table might look like this:

Mile	1	2	3	4	5	6	7	8
Cost	$2.50	$4.00	$5.50	$7.00	$8.50	$10.00	$11.50	$13.00

Alternate Strategy

Make or Use a Table, Chart, or Graph

To help students organize the information given and to show the charge at the end of each mile driven, have them display the information in a table. Remind students that a taxi ride costs $2.50 for the first mile, and $1.50 for each additional mile.

LESSON 73

• Capacity

California Mathematics Content Standards

NS 2.0, 2.1 Estimate and compute the sum or difference of whole numbers and positive decimals to two places.

NS 2.0, 2.2 Round two-place decimals to one decimal or the nearest whole number and judge the reasonableness of the rounded answer.

AF 1.0, 1.5 Understand that an equation such as $y = 3x + 5$ is a prescription for determining a second number when a first number is given.

Power Up

facts Power Up H

count aloud Count down by fives from 53 to 3.

mental math

a. **Number Sense:** 21×20 420

b. **Number Sense:** 25×30 750

c. **Number Sense:** 25×20 500

d. **Number Sense:** $48 + 19 + 310$ 377

e. **Money:** Julia has a gift card that is worth $50. She has used the card for $24.97 in purchases. How much value is left on the card? $25.03

f. **Time:** The track meet started at 9:00 a.m. and lasted 4 hours 30 minutes. What time did the track meet end? 1:30 p.m.

g. **Estimation:** At sea level, sound travels about 1116 feet in one second. Round this distance to the nearest hundred feet. 1100 ft

h. **Calculation:** $\sqrt{25}$, $\times 7$, $+ 5$, $+ 10$, $\div 10$ 5

problem solving Choose an appropriate problem-solving strategy to solve this problem. The charge for the taxi ride was $2.50 for the first mile and $1.50 for each additional mile. What was the charge for an 8-mile taxi ride? Explain how you solved the problem. $13.00; See student work.

New Concept

Liquids such as milk, juice, paint, and gasoline are measured in the **U.S. Customary System** in **fluid ounces,** cups, pints, quarts, or gallons. The table on the next page shows the abbreviations for each of these units:

Facts Multiply.

8 × 8 = 64	0 × 5 = 0	7 × 3 = 21	9 × 7 = 63	3 × 2 = 6	9 × 4 = 36	8 × 6 = 48	4 × 3 = 12	9 × 5 = 45	6 × 2 = 12
9 × 2 = 18	7 × 4 = 28	8 × 3 = 24	5 × 5 = 25	9 × 6 = 54	7 × 2 = 14	5 × 4 = 20	9 × 1 = 9	9 × 3 = 27	0 × 0 = 0
7 × 5 = 35	2 × 2 = 4	6 × 4 = 24	8 × 7 = 56	5 × 3 = 15	7 × 6 = 42	4 × 2 = 8	8 × 5 = 40	6 × 3 = 18	9 × 9 = 81
3 × 3 = 9	8 × 4 = 32	7 × 7 = 49	8 × 2 = 16	10 × 10 = 100	6 × 5 = 30	4 × 4 = 16	9 × 8 = 72	5 × 2 = 10	6 × 6 = 36

Power Up

Facts

Distribute **Power Up H** to students. See answers below.

Count Aloud

Before students begin the Mental Math exercises, do these counting exercises as a class.

Mental Math

Encourage students to share different ways to mentally compute these exercises. Strategies for exercises are listed below.

c. Multiply Nonzero Digits, Write Zeros
Write 1 zero after 25×2; $25 \times 20 = 500$.

d. Change 19 to 20, then Subtract 1
$48 + 20 = 68$; $68 + 310 = 378$; $378 - 1 = 377$

Change 48 to 50, then Subtract 2
$50 + 19 = 69$; $69 + 310 = 379$; $379 - 2 = 377$

e. Count On from $24.97
$24.97 + 3¢ = $25; $25 + $25 = $50; $0.03 + $25.00 = $25.03

Problem Solving

Refer to **Problem-Solving Strategy Discussion**, p. 487B.

New Concept

Math Language

Have students note the abbreviations that are used to represent the various units of liquid measure.

Error Alert

Make sure students understand that a *fluid ounce* is a different unit of measure than an *ounce.* (A fluid ounce is a liquid measure; An ounce is a measure of weight.)

(continued)

New Concept *(Continued)*

Observation

If possible, display washed containers for liquids that have labels which indicate a customary measure. Encourage students to discuss how the capacities of the containers appear to compare, and name familiar products that can be purchased in those capacities.

Instruction

Explain that the tree diagram shows Customary units of capacity, and point out that the largest unit of capacity is shown at the top of the diagram, and the smallest unit is shown at the bottom.

Work with students to understand how the diagram can be used to name equivalent measures. For example, to find an equivalent measure for 1 pint, have students find a pint anywhere in the diagram. Explain that moving down from that place shows us that 1 pint is equal to 2 cups, and moving up from that place shows us that 1 pint is equal to $\frac{1}{2}$ quart.

Active Learning

Challenge students to use the diagram and name:

- the number of cups that are equal to 1 quart. 4
- the number of pints that are equal to 1 gallon. 8
- the number of cups that are equal to 1 gallon. 16

Invite volunteers to explain how they found their answers.

Explanation

As you discuss the equivalence table, point out that the columns of the table show exact relationships, and have students note that the relationship shown in the bottom row of the table is an approximation, not an exact relationship.

Example 1

Confirm the solution by having students look at the tree diagram and the equivalence table. (Both show that 1 pint is equal to 2 cups.) Explain that once this relationship is established, arithmetic is used to find the answer.

(continued)

Math Language

Teaspoons and tablespoons are U.S. Customary units of measure for smaller amounts.

1 tablespoon = $\frac{1}{2}$ fluid ounce

1 teaspoon = $\frac{1}{6}$ fluid ounce

Abbreviations for U.S. Liquid Measures

fluid ounce	fl oz
cup	c
pint	pt
quart	qt
gallon	gal

The quantity of liquid a container can hold is the capacity of the container.

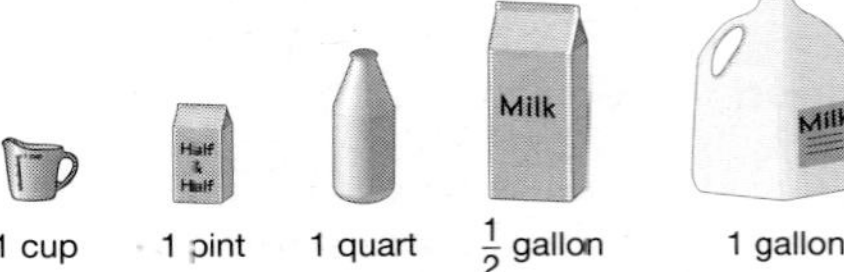

1 cup 1 pint 1 quart $\frac{1}{2}$ gallon 1 gallon

We can see the relationships of cups, pints, quarts, and gallons in the following diagram:

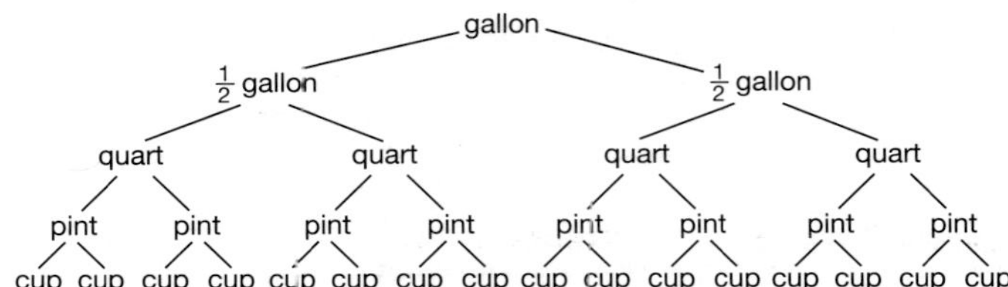

This table also shows equivalence between the units:

Equvalence Table of Units of Liquid Measures

U.S. Customary System	Metric System
8 fl oz = 1 c 2 c = 1 pt 2 pt = 1 qt 4 qt = 1 gal	1000 mL = 1 L
A liter is about 2 ounces more than a quart.	

Example 1

How many fluid ounces are equal to 1 pint ?

A cup is 8 fl oz and 2 cups equal 1 pint. So, a pint is equal to 2 × 8 or **16 fl oz.**

English Learners

Explain that the word **abbreviation** refers to a shortened form of a word. Say and write on the board:

"I can write 2 quarts = $\frac{1}{2}$ gallon, or I can write 2 qt = $\frac{1}{2}$ gal."

Ask students to share other **abbreviations** they know as well as the word they stand for. Sample: ft = feet, in = inches

Example 2

How many pints are equal to 5 quarts?

We can find the answer by setting up a table.

Quarts	1	2	3	4	5
Pints	2	4	6	8	10

5 quarts = **10 pints**

Reading Math

We read $p = 2q$ as "the number of pints is equal to 2 times the number of quarts."

We can write a formula for converting quarts to pints. We use p for pints and q for quarts and write $p = 2q$ or $2q = p$. We can use this formula to convert any number of quarts to pints.

Generalize How could we rewrite the formula $p = 2q$ using x and y?

$y = 2x$ where x = the number of quarts and y = the number of pints.

Example 3

Mrs. McGrath is using 4.78 L of orange juice to make punch. She poured 2.29 L of pineapple juice into the punch. To the nearest tenth of a liter, how much punch did she make?

Before adding we round each number to the nearest tenth.

4.78 L rounds to 4.8 L

2.29 L rounds to 2.3 L

Now we can add. 4.8 L + 2.3 L = **7.1 L**

Lesson Practice

a. Copy and complete this table relating gallons and quarts:

Gallons	1	2	3	4	5	6	7	8
Quarts	4	8						

a.

Gallons	1	2	3	4	5	6	7	8
Quarts	4	8	12	16	20	24	28	32

b. **Predict** How many quarts is 12 gallons? Write a formula to show your answer. Use q for quarts and g for gallons. 48 qt; $4g = q$; $4 \times 12 = 48$

c. One pint is 2 cups and one cup is 8 ounces. How many ounces is one pint? 16 ounces

d. Compare: 100 milliliters ⓧ 1 liter

Math Background

Below are some metric units of capacity, listed in order from smallest to largest:

milliliter, centiliter, deciliter, and liter

Each unit is 10 times the unit to its left (or, equivalently, $\frac{1}{10}$ the unit to its right). To convert from one unit to another, multiply by 10 for each unit we move to the left, or divide by 10 for each unit we move to the right.

For example, suppose we want to convert 450 milliliters to deciliters. This requires moving two units to the right, so we divide by 10 twice: $450 \div 10 = 45$, $45 \div 10 = 4.5$. So 450 milliliters = 4.5 deciliters.

Now suppose we want to convert 23 liters to centiliters. This requires moving two units to the left, so we multiply by 10 twice: $23 \times 10 \times 10 = 2300$ centiliters.

New Concept *(Continued)*

Example 2

After you discuss the **Generalize** question and answer, remind students that using letters such as p to represent pints and q to represent quarts makes the relationship easier to understand and represent. Point out, however, any letter of the alphabet can be used to represent an unknown number.

Extend the Example

Challenge your advanced learners to write a formula that can be used to find the number of quarts (q) for any number of pints (p). $q = p \div 2$ or $q = \frac{p}{2}$

Example 3

Make sure students understand that a liter is a common metric unit of capacity. Point out that another common (but much smaller) metric unit of capacity is the milliliter. If possible, bring a clean medicine dropper to class and display it along with a liter container to help students better understand these units.

Lesson Practice

Guided Practice

Use these problems as guided practice to check the students' understanding of today's concept.

Problem a

Before students complete the table, ask:

"This table compares gallons to quarts. One gallon is equal to what number of quarts?" 1 gal = 4 quarts

Problem b **Predict**

Encourage students to describe one or more ways that the completed table from problem **a** can be used to find the number of quarts that 12 gallons represents. Sample: The table shows that 8 gal = 32 qt and 4 gal = 16 qt. So 8 gallons + 4 gallons or 12 gallons is a measure that is equivalent to 32 quarts + 16 quarts or 48 quarts.

Problem a
Error Alert

Point out that because gallons are numbered consecutively in the table, students need only write multiples of four to find the missing numbers.

(continued)

New Concept (Continued)

Closure The questions below help assess the concepts taught in this lesson.

"Name our customary units of capacity in order from smallest to largest." Fluid ounces, cups, pints, quarts, gallons

"Explain how the units are related." 8 fl oz = 1 c; 2 c = 1 pt; 2 pt = 1 qt; 4 qt = 1 gal

"What customary unit of capacity is about the same as 1 liter?" 1 quart

Written Practice

Math Conversations

Independent Practice and Discussions to Increase Understanding

Problem 1d Multiple Choice

Test-Taking Strategy

Point out that it is sometimes possible to find the answer to a test question using only mental math, and then ask students to explain how they can find this answer simply by looking at the graph. Sample: Find two parts of the circle that represent more than half of the circle.

Problem 3 Estimate

Before making the estimate, remind students that each amount is to be rounded to the nearest dollar, and then ask them to name the two possible amounts each amount could be rounded to. \$4.27: \$4 or \$5; \$5.33: \$5 or \$6; \$7.64: \$7 or \$8

Problem 4

Extend the Problem

Challenge advanced learners to write a formula that can be used to find the number of kilometers (k) for any number of hours (h). $k = 90h$

Then challenge them to write a formula that can be used to find the number of hours (h) for any number of kilometers (k). $h = k \div 90$ or $h = \frac{k}{90}$

(continued)

Written Practice

Distributed and Integrated

*1. (13, 19, Inv. 5) **Interpret** Use this circle graph to answer parts **a–d.**

How Franz Spent His Day

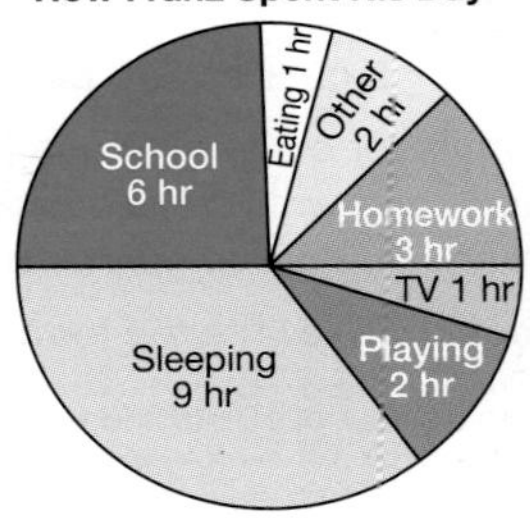

a. What is the total number of hours shown in the graph? 24 hours

b. What fraction of Franz's day was spent watching TV? $\frac{1}{24}$

c. If Franz's school day starts at 8:30 a.m., at what time does it end? 2:30 p.m.

▸ **d. Multiple Choice** Which two activities together take more than half of Franz's day? C

A sleeping and playing **B** school and homework
C school and sleeping **D** school and playing

2. (Inv. 2) **Estimate** Which of these arrows could be pointing to 2250? *A*

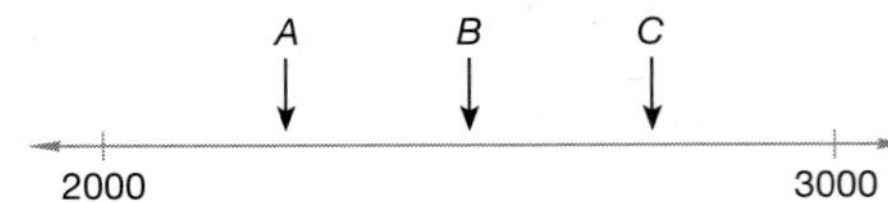

▸ *3. (46, 61) **Estimate** To find a reasonable estimate of \$4.27, \$5.33, and \$7.64 by rounding each amount to the nearest dollar before adding. \$17.00

▸ *4. (58) Kurt drove across the state at 90 kilometers per hour. At that rate, how far will Kurt drive in 4 hours? Make a table to solve the problem. 360 kilometers

Hours	Kilometers
1	90
2	180
3	270
4	360

5. (56) **Verify** Is the product of 3 and 7 a prime number? How do you know? No; sample: The product of 3 and 7 is 21. A prime number has only two factors, and 21 has four factors.

Inclusion

Use this strategy if the student displays:

- Poor Retention.
- Slow Learning Rate.

Capacity (Small Group)

Materials: measuring jars, beans or marbles, index cards

- Pass out materials and tell students they are going to learn about capacity. Have each group write the following on their index cards:

Gallon	________ Quarts
Quarts	________ Pints
Pints	________ Cups
Quarts	________ Cups
Gallon	________ Pints

- Have students fill their gallon jar using quarts. Ask, ***"How many quarts did it take to fill the gallon?"*** 4 ***"How many pints did it take to fill the quart?"*** 2 ***"How many cups did it take to fill the pint?"*** 2 ***"How many cups did it take to fill the quart?"*** 4 ***"How many pints did it take to fill the gallon?"*** 8
- Have students fill in the answers to the blanks on their index cards. Allow students to keep these cards for future reference.

▸ *6. a. What is the perimeter of this square? 20 in.
(20, Inv. 3)

5 inches

b. If the square were to be covered with 1-inch squares, how many squares would be needed? 25 squares

7. **Evaluate** If 5 × 10 ÷ 10 = 50 ÷ *t*, what does *t* equal? How do you know? 10; Equals divided by equals are equal.
(36, 63)

8. **Explain** If (16 + 8) − *f* = (3 × 8) − 7, what does *f* equal? How do you know? 7; Equals subtracted from equals are equal.
(9, 63)

*9. **Evaluate** If *y* = 4*x* + 3, then what is *y* when *x* = 9? 39
(64, Inv. 7)

10. (21, 52) $20.10 − $16.45 = $3.65

11. (28, 51) $98.54 + $ 9.85 = $108.39

12. (59) 380 × 4 1520

13. (71) 97 × 80 7760

▸ *14. (69) 4)328 82

15. (59) $8.63 × 7 $60.41

16. (45) 4.25 − 2.4 1.85

*17. (72) 7)375 53 R 4

*18. (72) 5)324 64 R 4

19. (34, 69) 9*r* = 234 26

*20. (Inv. 3) $\frac{\sqrt{64}}{\sqrt{16}}$ 2

21. (69) $\frac{287}{7}$ 41

*22. (37, 65) 10 × ($6^2 + 2^3$) 440

23. **Analyze** Find the perimeter of this rectangle
(20, 42)

1.5 cm
0.8 cm

a. in centimeters. 4.6 cm

b. in millimeters. 46 mm

24. The thermometer shows the outside temperature on a cold, winter day in Cedar Rapids, Iowa. What temperature does the thermometer show? −3°F
(21)

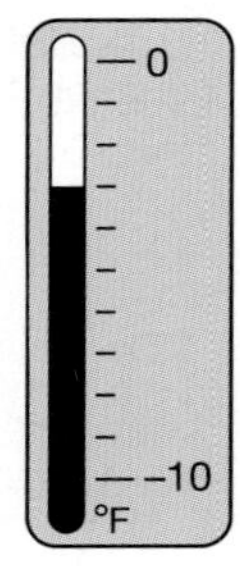

Written Practice (Continued)

Math Conversations (cont.)

Problem 6a

"Name a formula that uses addition to find the perimeter of a square." Sample: $P = s + s + s + s$

"Name a formula that uses multiplication to find the perimeter of a square." Sample: $P = 4s$

Problem 14

"The divisor is 4. Compare the divisor to 3, the first digit in the dividend. Where will the first digit in the quotient be placed?"

Make sure students can conclude that the first digit will be in the tens place because the divisor is greater than the digit in the hundreds place of the dividend.

(continued)

Alternative Approach: Using Manipulatives

Have students use measuring cups to discover the relationship among equivalent measures. Ask students:

"How many cups make a quart?" There are 2 cups to a pint and 2 pints to a quart, so one quart = 4 cups.

"How many cups of water will weigh the same as one pint of water?" 2 cups

Have students find other examples of equivalent measures.

Written Practice (Continued)

Math Conversations (cont.)

Problem 25

Some students may find it helpful to complete the drawings on grid paper.

Problem 28 Explain

It is possible to simply count unit segments to determine the length of segment *BC*. To help students recognize that arithmetic should be used to solve the problem, ask them to begin by naming the coordinates of each endpoint. (5, 3) and (5, 8)

If students have difficulty understanding the next step to complete, point out that subtraction is used to find the length, and lead them to conclude that it is not sensible to subtract the *x*-values of the coordinates because the length of segment *BC* would be 0.

Errors and Misconceptions

Problem 9

Make sure students notice that the substitution must be made before the order of operations can be applied.

Problem 22

Students must recognize that simplifying the powers ($6^2 = 36$ and $2^3 = 8$) represents the first operations that must be completed.

As students work, watch for the common error of simplifying 6^2 as 6×2 or 12 and 2^3 as 2×3 or 6.

*25. (70) Draw two congruent triangles and two similar rectangles. See student work.

*26. (73) Explain How many fl oz are equal to one gallon? Explain how you found your answer. 128 fl oz; 8 oz = 1 c; 4 c = 1 qt, 4 × 8 or 32 oz = 1 qt, 4 qt = 1 gal, 4 × 32 = 128 fl oz

*27. (Inv. 6) Interpret Ten students were asked to name their favorite month. Use the results of this survey to answer questions **a** and **b.**

Five students chose July.

Four students chose August.

One student chose March.

a. What is the mode of this data? July

b. What conclusion could you make based on this survey? Sample: Summer months are more favored than other months.

*28. (Inv. 7) Explain What is the length of segment *BC?* Explain your reasoning. 5 units; Subtract *y*-coordinates; 8 − 3 = 5

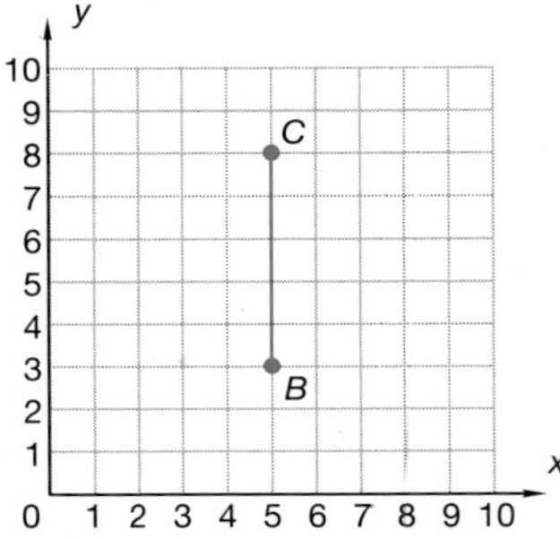

*29. (61, 69) Estimate Cora estimated the quotient of 261 ÷ 5 to be 50. Explain how Cora used a compatible number to make her estimate. Cora changed 261 to 250; 250 ÷ 5 = 50

30. (Inv. 1, 15) Formulate Write and solve a subtraction word problem for the equation $175 - t = 84$. See student work; $t = 91$

Measuring liquids using the customary and the metric systems prepares students for:

- **Lesson 80,** using the customary and the metric systems to determine mass and weight.

Planning & Preparation

• Word Problems About a Fraction of a Group

Objectives

- Draw a diagram to solve problems about a fraction of a group.

Prerequisite Skills

- Drawing and shading pictures of fractions representing halves, thirds, and fourths.
- Writing an equation to solve equal groups word problems where the total is known.

Materials

Instructional Masters

- Power Up H Worksheet
- Lesson Activity 21*
- Lesson Activity 8*

Manipulative Kit

- Two-color counters*

Teacher-provided materials

- Grid paper (centimeter and inch)*

**optional*

California Mathematics Content Standards

NS 1.0, 1.7 Write the fraction represented by a drawing of parts of a figure; represent a given fraction by using drawings; and relate a fraction to a simple decimal on a number line.

MR 2.0, 2.3 Use a variety of methods, such as words, numbers, symbols, charts, graphs, tables, diagrams, and models, to explain mathematical reasoning.

MR 2.0, 2.6 Make precise calculations and check the validity of the results from the context of the problem.

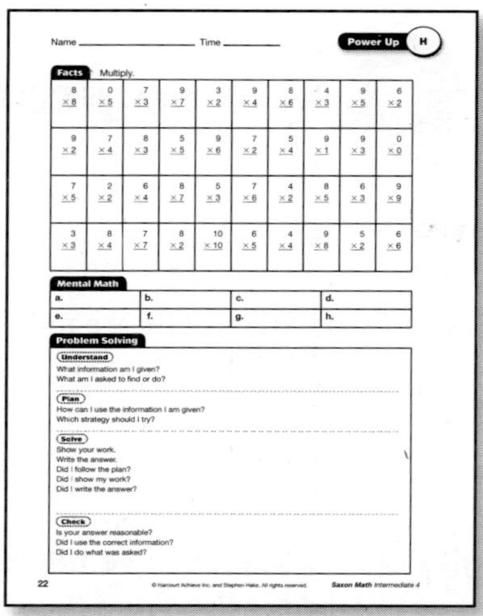

Name ____________ Time ________ **Power Up H**

Facts Multiply.

8 × 8	0 × 5	7 × 3	9 × 7	3 × 2	9 × 4	8 × 6	4 × 3	9 × 5	6 × 2
9 × 2	7 × 4	8 × 3	5 × 5	9 × 6	7 × 2	5 × 4	9 × 1	9 × 3	0 × 0
7 × 5	2 × 2	6 × 4	8 × 7	5 × 3	7 × 6	4 × 2	8 × 5	6 × 3	9 × 9
3 × 3	8 × 4	7 × 7	8 × 2	10 × 10	6 × 5	4 × 4	9 × 8	5 × 2	6 × 6

Mental Math

a.	b.	c.	d.
e.	f.	g.	h.

Problem Solving

Understand
What information am I given?
What am I asked to find or do?

Plan
How can I use the information I am given?
Which strategy should I try?

Solve
Show your work.
Write the answer.
Did I follow the plan?
Did I show my work?
Did I write the answer?

Check
Is your answer reasonable?
Did I use the correct information?
Did I do what was asked?

22 © Harcourt Achieve Inc. and Stephen Hake. All rights reserved. *Saxon Math Intermediate 4*

Power Up H Worksheet

Reaching All Special Needs Students

Special Education Students	At-Risk Students	English Learners	Advanced Learners
• Inclusion (TM) • Adaptations for Saxon Math	• Alternative Approach (TM) • Error Alert (TM) • Reteaching Masters • Refresher Lessons for California Standards	• English Learners (TM) • Developing Academic Language (TM) • English Learner Handbook	• Extend the Example (TM) • Extend the Problem (TM) • Early Finisher (SE) • Online Activities

TM=Teacher's Manual
SE=Student Edition

Developing Academic Language

Maintained	English Learner
divide	sprouted
fraction	

Problem Solving Discussion

Problem

M'Keisha solved a subtraction problem and then erased two of the digits from the problem. She gave the problem to Mae as a problem-solving exercise. Copy M'Keisha's problem on your paper, and fill in the missing digits for Mae.

$$\begin{array}{r} 123 \\ -\ 4\_ \\ \hline \_4 \end{array}$$

Focus Strategies

Work Backwards

Use Logical Reasoning

Understand *Understand the problem.*

"What information are we given?"

We are shown a subtraction problem. Two of the digits are missing.

"What are we asked to do?"

We are asked to find the missing digits.

Plan *Make a plan.*

"What problem-solving strategies can we use to solve this problem?"

We can *use logical reasoning* and *work backwards* to find the missing digits.

Solve *Carry out the plan.*

"Let's start in the ones column, just as if we were subtracting. What is the missing digit in the ones column?"

We think, "3 (or 13) minus what number equals 4?" We know that 13 minus 9 is 4, so we write a 9 in the ones column, which makes the subtrahend 49.

"What is the missing digit in the difference?"

We can simply subtract 49 from 123 to find the difference: $123 - 49 = 74$. The missing digit in the difference is 7.

Check *Look back.*

"Is our answer reasonable?"

We know that our answer is reasonable, because the difference of 123 and 49 is 74, which is the number that we have written below the line.

$$\begin{array}{r} 123 \\ -\ 4\underline{9} \\ \hline \underline{7}4 \end{array}$$

"What problem-solving strategies did we use to solve the problem?"

We *worked backwards* and *used logical reasoning* and number sense to find the missing digits.

LESSON

74

• Word Problems About a Fraction of a Group

California Mathematics Content Standards

NS 1.0, 1.7 Write the fraction represented by a drawing of parts of a figure; represent a given fraction by using drawings; and relate a fraction to a simple decimal on a number line.

MR 2.0, 2.3 Use a variety of methods, such as words, numbers, symbols, charts, graphs, tables, diagrams, and models, to explain mathematical reasoning.

MR 2.0, 2.6 Make precise calculations and check the validity of the results from the context of the problem.

facts Power Up H

count aloud When we count by fives from 4, we say the numbers 4, 9, 14, 19, and so on. Count by fives from 4 to 54.

mental math

a. Number Sense: 25×100 2500

b. Number Sense: 100×40 4000

c. Number Sense: $12 \times 3 \times 100$ 3600

d. Number Sense: Counting by 5's from 5, every number Raven says ends in 0 or 5. If she counts by 5's from 7, then every number she says ends in which digit? 2 or 7

e. Powers/Roots: $\sqrt{4} + 3^2 + 1^2$ 12

f. Measurement: Abdul needs 6 quarts of water to make enough lemonade for the team. How many cups is 6 quarts? 24 cups

g. Estimation: Raoul has $28. Does he have enough money to buy three T-shirts that cost $8.95 each? yes

h. Calculation: $\frac{1}{2}$ of 44, + 6, ÷ 7, − 4 0

problem solving Choose an appropriate problem-solving strategy to solve this problem. M'Keisha solved a subtraction problem and then erased two of the digits from the problem. She gave the problem to Mae as a problem-solving exercise. Copy M'Keisha's problem on your paper, and fill in the missing digits for Mae.

$$\begin{array}{r} 123 \\ -\ 4\_ \\ \hline \_4 \end{array} \qquad \begin{array}{r} 123 \\ -\ 49 \\ \hline 74 \end{array}$$

Facts Multiply.

8 × 8 64	0 × 5 0	7 × 3 21	9 × 7 63	3 × 2 6	9 × 4 36	8 × 6 48	4 × 3 12	9 × 5 45	6 × 2 12
9 × 2 18	7 × 4 28	8 × 3 24	5 × 5 25	9 × 6 54	7 × 2 14	5 × 4 20	9 × 1 9	9 × 3 27	0 × 0 0
7 × 5 35	2 × 2 4	6 × 4 24	8 × 7 56	5 × 3 15	7 × 6 42	4 × 2 8	8 × 5 40	6 × 3 18	9 × 9 81
3 × 3 9	8 × 4 32	7 × 7 49	8 × 2 16	10 × 10 100	6 × 5 30	4 × 4 16	9 × 8 72	5 × 2 10	6 × 6 36

Power Up

Facts

Distribute **Power Up H** to students. See answers below.

Count Aloud

Before students begin the Mental Math exercises, do these counting exercises as a class.

Mental Math

Encourage students to share different ways to mentally compute these exercises. Strategies for exercises are listed below.

a. Multiply Nonzero Digits, Write Zeros
Write 2 zeros after 25×1;
$25 \times 100 = 2500$.

b. Multiply Nonzero Digits, Write Zeros
Write 3 zeros after 1×4;
$100 \times 40 = 4000$.

e. Simplify and Add from Left to Right
$2 + 9 = 11$; $11 + 1 = 12$

g. Round up, then Compare
$\$9 \times 3 = \$27$; $\$28 > \$27$; yes

Problem Solving

Refer to **Problem-Solving Strategy Discussion**, p. 493B.

New Concept

Explanation

In this lesson, students will learn two ways to find a fraction of a group. The fraction will be a unit fraction such as $\frac{1}{2}$, $\frac{1}{3}$, $\frac{1}{4}$, and so on.

Example 1

As you discuss each of the examples in this lesson, remind students that whenever we draw a picture to represent a fraction of a whole, the denominator of the fraction represents the number of equal parts into which the whole is divided, and the denominator is used as a divisor of the whole to find the number that each equal part represents. For example, the fraction $\frac{1}{2}$ in Example 1 indicates that the whole (84 seeds) is divided into 2 equal parts, and each of those parts is 84 seeds ÷ 2 or 42 seeds.

Example 2

Active Learning

"How many students does the rectangle represent?" 27 students

"Why is the rectangle divided into 3 equal parts?" The denominator of the fraction $\frac{1}{3}$ describes the number of equal parts the whole is divided into.

Error Alert

Make sure students understand that to find the number of seeds in each equal part, we divide the total number of seeds by the number of equal parts (in other words, by the denominator of the fraction $\frac{1}{3}$).

(continued)

Reading Math

We can use fractions to name part of a whole, part of a group or number, and part of a distance.

We know that the fraction $\frac{1}{2}$ means that a whole has been divided into 2 parts. To find the number in $\frac{1}{2}$ of a group, we divide the total number in the group by 2. To find the number in $\frac{1}{3}$ of a group, we divide the total number in the group by 3. To find the number in $\frac{1}{4}$ of a group, we divide the total number in the group by 4, and so on.

Example 1

One half of the carrot seeds sprouted. If 84 seeds were planted, how many seeds sprouted?

We will begin by drawing a picture. The large rectangle stands for all the seeds. We are told that $\frac{1}{2}$ of the seeds sprouted, so we divide the large rectangle into 2 equal parts (into halves). Then we divide 84 by 2 and find that **42 seeds** sprouted.

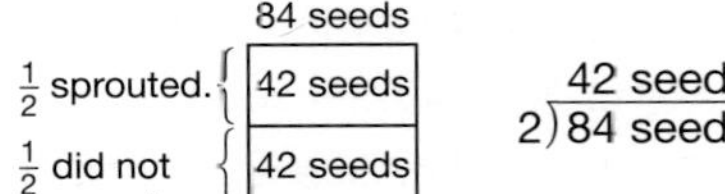

$$2\overline{)84 \text{ seeds}} = 42 \text{ seeds}$$

Discuss How can we use addition to check the answer?

Sample: Compare the sum of $\frac{1}{2}$ and $\frac{1}{2}$ to 1, and compare the sum of 42 and 42 to 84.

Example 2

On Friday, one third of the 27 students purchased lunch in the school cafeteria. How many students purchased lunch on Friday?

We start with a picture. The whole rectangle stands for all the students. Since $\frac{1}{3}$ of the students purchased lunch, we divide the rectangle into 3 equal parts. To find how many students are in each part, we divide 27 by 3 and find that **9 students** purchased a lunch on Friday.

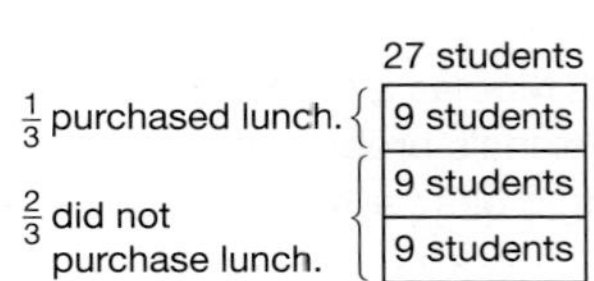

$$3\overline{)27 \text{ students}} = 9 \text{ students}$$

Justify Explain why the answer is correct.

Sample: The sum of $\frac{1}{3}$ and $\frac{2}{3}$ is 1, and the product of 9 and 3 is 27.

Explain that the word **sprouted** means began to grow.

Say, ***"After you plant a seed, it takes a number of days before you will see the plant begin to sprout."***

Ask, ***"Have you ever planted anything from seeds? What are some signs that a plant has begun to sprout?"***

Students may discuss fruits or vegetables that they have seen growing in a garden or a container.

Example 3

One fourth of the team's 32 points were scored by Thi. How many points did Thi score?

We draw a rectangle. The whole rectangle stands for all 32 points. Thi scored $\frac{1}{4}$ of the points, so we divide the rectangle into 4 equal parts. We divide 32 by 4 and find that each part is 8 points. Thi scored **8 points.**

32 points

$\frac{1}{4}$ scored by Thi: 8 points

$\frac{3}{4}$ not scored by Thi: 8 points, 8 points, 8 points

$4\overline{)32 \text{ points}}$ = 8 points

Justify Explain why the answer is correct.

Sample: The sum of $\frac{1}{4}$ and $\frac{3}{4}$ is 1, and the product of 8 and 4 is 32.

Example 4

What is $\frac{1}{5}$ of 40?

We draw a rectangle to stand for 40. We divide the rectangle into five equal parts, and we divide 40 by 5. Each part is 8, so $\frac{1}{5}$ of 40 is **8.**

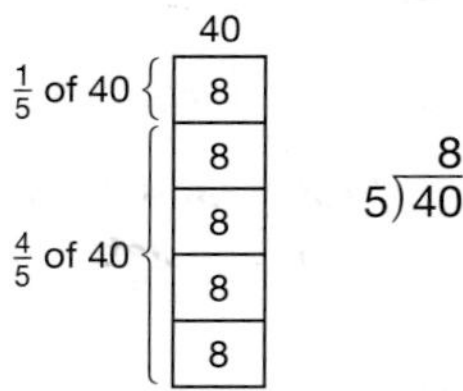

$5\overline{)40}$ = 8

Lesson Practice

Draw a picture to solve each problem:

a. What is $\frac{1}{3}$ of 60? 20

b. What is $\frac{1}{2}$ of 60? 30

c. What is $\frac{1}{4}$ of 60? 15

d. What is $\frac{1}{5}$ of 60? 12

e. One half of the 32 children were boys. How many boys were there? See student work. 16 boys

f. One third of the 24 coins were quarters. How many quarters were there? See student work; 8 quarters

a. 60: $\frac{1}{3}$ of 60: 20; $\frac{2}{3}$ of 60: 20, 20

b. 60: $\frac{1}{2}$ of 60: 30; $\frac{1}{2}$ of 60: 30

c. 60: $\frac{1}{4}$ of 60: 15; $\frac{3}{4}$ of 60: 15, 15, 15

d.

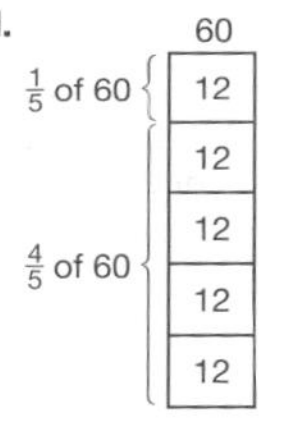

Math Background

We can think of a fraction of a number problem as having an equal groups formula. For example, consider the problem in Example 2:

One fourth of the team's 32 points were scored by Thi. Thi scored how many points?

In this case the groups are the fourths. Here is the formula:

Number of fourths × Number of points in each fourth = Total points

We know that there are 4 fourths in all and that the total in all 4 fourths is 32. Substitute this information into the equation.

$$4 \times n = 32$$

This means $n = 32 \div 4 = 8$. In this solution and the solution in the student lesson, we divide 32 by 4.

New Concept (Continued)

Example 3

Extend the Example

Challenge your advanced learners by saying:

"Describe two different ways to find the number of points that were not scored by Thi." Sample: Add the number of points that $\frac{1}{4}$ represents three times ($8 + 8 + 8 = 24$); multiply the number of points that $\frac{1}{4}$ represents by 3 ($8 \times 3 = 24$).

Invite volunteers to share the different ways with the class.

Example 4

Extend the Example

Challenge your advanced learners to explain how multiplication and division can be used to find $\frac{4}{5}$ of 40. Divide 40 by 5 to find $\frac{1}{5}$ of 40, and then multiply the result by 4; Since $(40 \div 5) \times 4 = 32$, $\frac{4}{5}$ of 40 is 32.

Lesson Practice

Guided Practice

Use these problems as guided practice to check the students' understanding of today's concept.

Problems a–d

Before students draw each picture, ask:

"What number will the entire picture represent?"

"Into how many equal parts will the picture be divided? Explain how you know."

"Explain how division can be used to find the number that each equal part represents."

Problem f

Error Alert

Make sure students understand that the "quarters" in this problem represent coins, and not fractions having a denominator of 4.

Closure

The questions below help assess the concepts taught in this lesson.

"Explain how to draw a diagram that can be used to find $\frac{1}{4}$ of a group of 40." Sample: Draw a rectangle and divide it into 4 equal parts. Divide 40 by 4 find that each equal part is 10, and label each equal part with a 10.

"Suppose that in a fourth grade class of 30 students, one-sixth of the students earned extra credit on a math assignment. How many students earned extra credit? Explain how you know." 5 students; sample: To find $\frac{1}{6}$ of a number, divide the number by 6.

Written Practice

Math Conversations

Independent Practice and Discussions to Increase Understanding

Problem 4 **Analyze**

Extend the Problem

Write "1 mile = 5280 feet" on the board or overhead. Then say:

"Suppose we placed a great number of these 6-inch-long sticks end-to-end. Using only mental math, how many sticks would we need to span a distance of 1 mile? Explain your answer." 10,560; Sample: Two sticks are needed for every foot, so 2 × 5280 is the number of sticks that are needed altogether. Double 5000, double 200, double 80, and then add; 10,000 + 400 + 160 = 10,560

Problem 5 **Multiple Choice**

Test-Taking Strategy

Ask students to explain why choice **D** can immediately be eliminated as a possible answer. $\frac{5}{5}$ represents all of the leaves, or the whole; We are being asked to find only a fraction of the leaves, or part of the whole.

(continued)

Written Practice

Distributed and Integrated

1. (37, 71) There are 77 students who plan to visit a small history museum for their class. The museum allows groups of 5 students to enter the museum every 10 minutes. How many minutes would it take for all 77 students to enter the museum? How many groups would be let in altogether? 160 minutes; 16 groups

2. (16) **Analyze** Monty ran the race 12 seconds faster than Ivan. Monty ran the race in 58 seconds. Ivan ran the race in how many seconds? 70 seconds

3. (74) **Analyze** There were 4 rooms. One fourth of the 56 guests were gathered in each room. How many guests were in each room? 14 guests

▸ **4.** (53) **Analyze** How many 6-inch-long sticks can be cut from a 72-inch-long stick? 12 sticks

▸ **5.** (67) **Multiple Choice** One fifth of the leaves had fallen. What fraction of the leaves had *not* fallen? C

A $\frac{2}{5}$ **B** $\frac{3}{5}$ **C** $\frac{4}{5}$ **D** $\frac{5}{5}$

6. (Inv. 2) **Estimate** Which of these arrows could be pointing to 5263? *A*

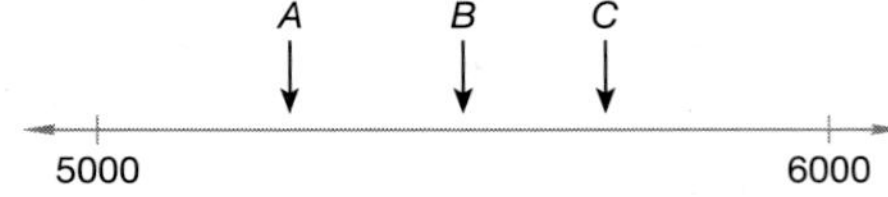

***7.** (64) **Explain** If $y = 5x + 2$, then what is y when $x = 20$? Explain your thinking. 102; Find the product of 5 and 20, first. Then find the sum of 100 and 2, which is 102.

***8.** (50, 70) **Conclude** Which word makes the following sentence false? D

All squares are ______________

A polygons **B** rectangles **C** similar **D** congruent

***9.** (22) **Explain** Cleon would like to estimate the difference between \$579 and \$85. Explain how Cleon could use rounding to make an estimate. Sample: Round to the nearest ten and subtract; \$580 − \$90 = \$490

Alternative Approach: Using Manipulatives

To help students solve word problems about a fraction of a group, have the students act out the problem using counters. For Example 1, have students show the number 32 using counters. Ask:

"How can we find $\frac{1}{2}$ of 32?" We can divide the 32 counters into two equal groups and count to see how many counters are in one group.

Have students use the counters to model other examples in the lesson.

Teacher Tip

Provide copies of **Lesson Activity Master 8** (grid paper) to help students who have difficulty drawing the diagrams. The larger squares on this grid provide more room for labeling the diagrams.

►*10. The triangle at right is equilateral. (20, 42, 50)

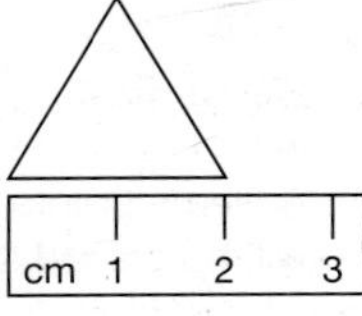

a. How many millimeters is the perimeter of the triangle? 60 mm

b. **Classify** Describe the angles.
All 3 angles are acute.

11. Three liters equals how many milliliters? 3000 mL (73)

►*12. Wilma runs 5 miles in 1 hour. At that rate, how long would it take her to run 40 miles? Make a table to solve the problem. (58)
8 hours

Hours	1	2	3	4	5	6	7	8
Miles	5	10	15	20	25	30	35	40

13. $2n = 150$ 75 (34, 69)

14. $24.25 - (6.2 + 4.8)$ 13.25 (9, 45)

15. (51) $103{,}279 + 97{,}814$ = 201,093

16. (28, 50) $\$36.14 + \$27.95$ = $64.09

17. (52) $39{,}420 - 29{,}516$ = 9,904

18. (8, 28, 52) $\$60.50 - n = \$43.20$ $17.30

19. (59) 604×9 = 5436

20. (71) 87×60 = 5220

21. (59) $\$6.75 \times 4$ = $27.00

►*22. (72) $7\overline{)243}$ 34 R 5

►*23. (72) $5\overline{)323}$ 64 R 3

*24. (8, 52) $n + 1467 = 2459$ 992

►*25. (72) $7\overline{)429}$ 61 R 2

► 26. (72) $189 \div 6$ 31 R 3

► 27. (69) $472 \div 8$ 59

28. (34, 64, 65) $9w = 9^2 + (9 \times 2)$ 11

►*29. (69) $3\overline{)288}$ 96

Inclusion

Use this strategy if the student displays:

- Difficulty with Large Group Instruction.
- Difficulty with Abstract Processing.

Word Problems about a Fraction of a Group (Individual)

Materials: Lesson Activity Master 8 (grid paper)

- Read the following problem aloud, ***"One third of the students eat sandwiches for lunch. If there are 24 students, how many eat sandwiches?"***
- Ask, ***"How many groups will the students be divided into?"*** 3
- Have students outline 24 boxes to make a 3 by 8 (or 4 by 6) rectangle on their grid paper and divide it into 3 equal parts. Ask, ***"What is 24 divided by 3?"*** 8 ***"How many of the groups eat sandwiches?"*** 1
- Have students shade one of the three groups and ask, ***"How many students eat sandwiches for lunch?"*** 8
- Read the following problem aloud, ***"What is $\frac{1}{8}$ of 48?"***

  Have students work in pairs using the grid paper to answer the problem. Suggest students outline 6 by 8 (or 4 by 12) rectangles.

Written Practice *(Continued)*

Math Conversations *(cont.)*

Problem 10

Make sure students understand that if a triangle is equilateral, all of its sides are the same length.

Extend the Problem

Ask students to write a multiplication formula that can be used to find the perimeter (*P*) of any equilateral triangle given (*s*), a side length of the triangle. $P = 3s$

Problem 12

Extend the Problem

Challenge advanced learners to use the rate shown in the table and name the number of minutes it takes Wilma to run $\frac{1}{2}$ mile.
6 minutes

Problems 22, 23, 25–27, 29

Remind students of the importance of checking their work by making an estimate prior to beginning the division, or by using multiplication (or multiplication and addition if the quotient includes a remainder) after the division has been completed.

Before students begin problem **22**, ask:

"Compare the divisor to the first digit in the dividend. How do the digits compare?" The divisor is greater than the first digit in the dividend.

"Where will the first digit in the quotient be placed? Explain how you know." The first digit in the quotient will be placed above the second digit in the dividend (e.g. the tens place) because 24 tens can be divided into 7 groups; There will be 3 tens in each group and 3 tens left over.

Ask similar questions for problems **23**, **25–27**, and **29**.

(continued)

Written Practice *(Continued)*

Math Conversations *(cont.)*

Problem 30 Conclude

Before students name the coordinates of each point, remind them that all coordinates are of the form (x, y), where the x-coordinate represents horizontal distance and the y-coordinate represents vertical distance. In other words, to name the location of the points in this problem, students should begin at the origin and count the number of units they move to the right, then count the number of units they move up.

Errors and Misconceptions

Problem 4

An answer of 11 sticks is a reasonable answer if it is accompanied by an explanation that states only 11 sticks are possible because the saw blade will remove a portion of the stick each time a cut is made.

Provide students with a one-page advertisement from a supermarket or retail store. Challenge students to determine if rounding the prices to the nearest dime would result in an overall savings for the store's customers.

▸*30. (Inv. 7) Conclude Use the coordinate graph to answer parts **a** and **b**.

a. Name the coordinates of each point. *D*: (3, 7), *E*: (3, 1), *F*: (10, 1)

b. Assume points *D*, *E*, and *F* are each a vertex of a square. Point *G* will be placed at the fourth vertex. Name the coordinates of point *G*. *G*: (10, 7)

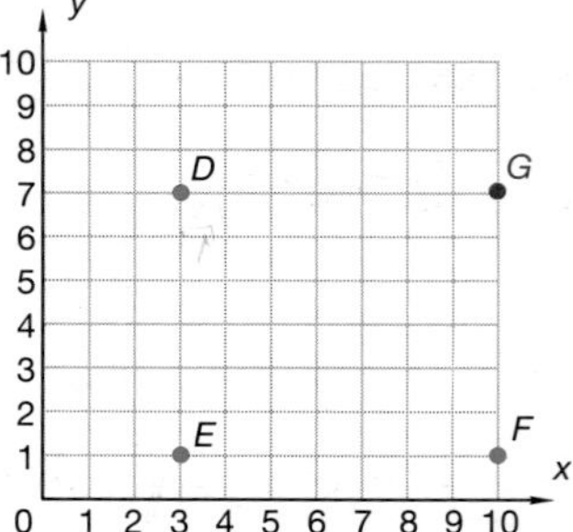

Real-World Connection

Every Saturday morning, Mahina stops by Ms. Hsiao's fruit stand and buys 1 pummelo and 1 carambola. Ms. Hsiao charges her \$1.36 for a pummelo and \$0.72 for a carambola, not including tax. Next week, Ms. Hsiao is going to round the prices of her fruit to the nearest dime. She believes this will make giving change easier for her customers.

a. If Ms. Hsiao rounds the prices of her fruit to the nearest dime, how much will Mahina pay for a pummelo and a carambola? \$2.10

b. By rounding her prices to the nearest dime, how much more money will Mahina have to pay? 2 cents more

c. By rounding the prices, the cost of a pummelo increased but the price of a carambola decreased. Explain why Mahina still had to pay more money. The cost of a pummelo increased by 4 cents while cost of the carambola only decreased by 2 cents.

Looking Forward

Solving word problems about a fraction of a group given prepares students for:

- **Investigation 8,** investigating equivalent fractions.
- **Lesson 87,** interpreting the remainder in a division word problem.
- **Lesson 89,** mixed numbers and improper fractions.
- **Lesson 92,** comparing and ordering fractions and decimals.
- **Lesson 94,** two-step problems about fractions of a group.
- **Lesson 98,** fractions equal to 1 and to $\frac{1}{2}$
- **Lesson 99,** changing improper fractions to whole or mixed numbers.
- **Lesson 100,** adding and subtracting fractions with common denominators.
- **Lesson 103,** finding equivalent fractions.
- **Lesson 106,** reducing fractions.
- **Lesson 111,** simplifying fractions.
- **Lesson 112,** renaming fractions.
- **Lesson 113,** finding a common denominator and renaming fractions.

Planning & Preparation

• Division Answers Ending with Zero

Objectives
- Divide two numbers to find a quotient that ends in zero.
- Solve word problems involving multi-digit division.

Prerequisite Skills
- Solving division problems with two-digit answers and a remainder.
- Finding reasonable estimates of a quotient.

Materials
Instructional Masters
- Power Up H Worksheet

Manipulative Kit
- Two-color counters, base ten blocks*

Teacher-provided materials
- Place-value workmat*

**optional*

California Mathematics Content Standards

NS 1.0, 1.3 Round whole numbers through the millions to the nearest ten, hundred, thousand, ten thousand, or hundred thousand.

NS 1.0, 1.4 Decide when a rounded solution is called for and explain why such a solution may be appropriate.

NS 3.0, 3.2 Demonstrate an understanding of, and the ability to use, standard algorithms for multiplying a multidigit number by a two-digit number and for dividing a multidigit number by a one-digit number; use relationships between them to simplify computations and to check results.

NS 3.0, 3.4 Solve problems involving division of multidigit numbers by one-digit numbers.

MR 2.0, 2.3 Use a variety of methods, such as words, numbers, symbols, charts, graphs, tables, diagrams, and models, to explain mathematical reasoning.

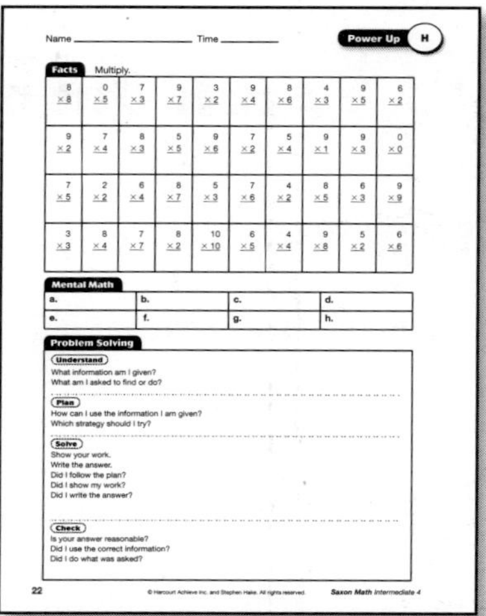

Power Up H Worksheet

Reaching All Special Needs Students

Special Education Students	At-Risk Students	English Learners	Advanced Learners
• Inclusion (TM) • Adaptations for Saxon Math	• Alternative Approach (TM) • Error Alert (TM) • Reteaching Masters • Refresher Lessons for California Standards	• English Learners (TM) • Developing Academic Language (TM) • English Learner Handbook	• Extend the Example (TM) • Extend the Problem (TM) • Online Activities

TM=Teacher's Manual

Developing Academic Language

Maintained	English Learner
digits	employees
division	
multiply	
quotient	
remainder	

Problem Solving Discussion

Problem

Sid wants to know the distance around the trunk of the big oak tree at the park. He knows the distance around the trunk is more than one yard. Sid has some string and a yardstick. How can he measure the distance around the trunk of the tree in inches?

Focus Strategies

Make It Simpler

Act It Out or Make a Model

Understand *Understand the problem.*

"What are we asked to do?"

We are asked to explain how the circumference of a tree trunk can be measured with string and a yardstick.

"Is the circumference of a tree a straight line or a curve?"

The circumference of a tree forms a curve. We cannot use a yardstick to measure a curve; however, we can wrap a string around a curve and then measure the string.

Plan *Make a plan.*

"What problem-solving strategy can we use to solve the problem?"

We can *make the problem simpler* by finding a way to measure a curve with a yardstick, which has a straight edge. We will describe how to *act out the problem.*

Solve *Carry out the plan.*

"How can Sid use a piece of string and a yardstick to measure the distance around a tree?"

Sid could wrap the string around the trunk. Then he could mark the place where the string goes once around (or cut the string at that place). Then Sid could place the string along the straight edge of the yardstick and count out full yard lengths and any fraction of a yard.

"Will the measurement of the string equal the distance around the tree?"

Yes. The length of string that Sid marks off would be equal to the distance around the tree.

Check *Look back.*

"Is our answer reasonable?"

We know that our answer is reasonable, because if we were to wrap a string once around a tree, that length of string would equal the circumference of the tree.

"What problem-solving strategies would we use if we actually carried out this measurement process?"

We would say that we were *acting out the problem.* Also, we might *write a number sentence* to add the whole-yard portions of the circumference to any remaining amount that is less than 1 yard.

LESSON 75

California Mathematics Content Standards

NS 1.0, 1.4 Decide when a rounded solution is called for and explain why such a solution may be appropriate.

NS 3.0, 3.2 Demonstrate an understanding of, and the ability to use, standard algorithms for multiplying a multidigit number by a two-digit number and for dividing a multidigit number by a one-digit number; use relationships between them to simplify computations and to check results.

NS 3.0, 3.4 Solve problems involving division of multidigit numbers by one-digit numbers.

• Division Answers Ending with Zeros

facts Power Up H

count aloud Count down by fives from 54 to 4.

mental math The sum of 38 and 17 is 55. If we make 38 larger by 2 and 17 smaller by 2, then the addition is 40 + 15. The sum is still 55, but the mental addition is easier. Before finding the following sums, make one number larger and the other smaller so that one of the numbers ends in zero.

a. **Number Sense:** 38 + 27 65

b. **Number Sense:** 48 + 24 72

c. **Number Sense:** 59 + 32 91

d. **Number Sense:** 57 + 26 83

e. **Money:** \$6.49 + \$2.99 \$9.48

f. **Measurement:** How many cups is one pint? 2 cups

g. **Estimation:** Choose the more reasonable estimate for the temperature inside a refrigerator: 3°C or 30°C. 3°C

h. **Calculation:** 2 × 9, + 29, + 53, ÷ 10 10

problem solving Choose an appropriate problem-solving strategy to solve this problem. Sid wants to know the distance around the trunk of the big oak tree at the park. He knows the distance around the trunk is more than one yard. Sid has some string and a yardstick. How can he measure the distance around the trunk of the tree in inches? Sample: Sid can wrap the string around the trunk and mark the place where the string goes once around (or cut the string at that place). Then Sid can use the yardstick to count out full yard lengths and any fraction of a yard. The total measurement will be equal to the distance around the trunk.

Facts Multiply.

8 × 8 64	0 × 5 0	7 × 3 21	9 × 7 63	3 × 2 6	9 × 4 36	8 × 6 48	4 × 3 12	9 × 5 45	6 × 2 12
9 × 2 18	7 × 4 28	8 × 3 24	5 × 5 25	9 × 6 54	7 × 2 14	5 × 4 20	9 × 1 9	9 × 3 27	0 × 0 0
7 × 5 35	2 × 2 4	6 × 4 24	8 × 7 56	5 × 3 15	7 × 6 42	4 × 2 8	8 × 5 40	6 × 3 18	9 × 9 81
3 × 3 9	8 × 4 32	7 × 7 49	8 × 2 16	10 × 10 100	6 × 5 30	4 × 4 16	9 × 8 72	5 × 2 10	6 × 6 36

Power Up

Facts

Distribute **Power Up H** to students. See answers below.

Count Aloud

Before students begin the Mental Math exercises, do these counting exercises as a class.

Mental Math

Encourage students to share different ways to mentally compute these exercises. Strategies for exercises are listed below.

a. Add 30, then Subtract 3
38 + 30 = 68; 68 − 3 = 65

Add 20, then Add 7
38 + 20 = 58; 58 + 7 = 65

c. Add 30, then Add 2
59 + 30 = 89; 89 + 2 = 91

e. Add \$3, then Subtract 1¢
\$6.49 + \$3 = \$9.49; \$9.49 − 1¢ = \$9.48

Problem Solving

Refer to **Problem-Solving Strategy Discussion**, p. 499B.

New Concept

Active Learning

Introduce the lesson by asking students to recite the four steps of division (shown below). Then invite a volunteer to explain how often those steps are repeated to divide two numbers. The steps are repeated as often as needed until all of the numbers in the dividend have been brought down.

Divide, Multiply, Subtract, Bring down

Instruction

As you discuss the solution that explains how to divide 200 by 4, make sure students understand that the first digit in the quotient is written in the tens place because the divisor (4) is greater than the first digit in the dividend (2). To begin the division, we must regroup 2 hundreds in the dividend as 20 tens.

Error Alert

Students may not compare the result of the subtraction to the dividend after the "subtract" step or continue the division until all of the digits have been brought down from the dividend (especially when dividing multiples of 10).

Point out the potential for these errors as you discuss the examples in this lesson.

Example 1

As you discuss the solution, emphasize the importance of completing the division. Have students note that after the digit 1 is brought down from the dividend, we again repeat the four steps of division. However, because the divisor (3) is greater than the (1), and there are no other digits to bring down, the division cannot continue. It is essential for students to understand that when division cannot continue, one or more zeros must be written in the quotient to complete the division.

Lead students to generalize from the example that each time a digit is brought down from the dividend, a digit must be written in the quotient.

(continued)

Sometimes division answers end with a zero. It is important to continue the division until all the digits inside the division box have been used. Look at this problem:

Two hundred pennies are separated into 4 equal piles. How many pennies are in each pile?

This problem can be answered by dividing 200 by 4. First we divide 20 by 4. We write a 5 in the quotient. Then we multiply and subtract.

```
    5
 4)200
   20
    0
```

Thinking Skills

Verify

Why do we write the first digit of the quotient in the tens place?

We are dividing 20 tens.

The division might look complete, but it is not. The answer is not "five pennies in each pile." That would total only 20 pennies. There is another zero inside the division box to bring down. So we bring down the zero and divide again. Zero divided by 4 is 0. We write 0 in the quotient, multiply, and then subtract. The quotient is **50.**

```
    50     Check:
 4)200
   20↓        50
    00     ×   4
     0       200
     0
```

We check our work by multiplying the quotient, 50, by the divisor, 4. The product should equal the dividend, 200. The answer checks. We find that there are 50 pennies in each pile.

Sometimes there will be a remainder with a division answer that ends in zero. We show this in the following example.

Example 1

Divide: 3)121

We begin by finding 3)12. Since 12 divided by 3 is 4, we write "4" above the 2. We multiply and subtract, getting 0, but we are not finished. We bring down the last digit of the dividend, which is 1.

```
    4
 3)121
   12
    0
```

Thinking Skills

Verify

Why do we write the first digit of the quotient in the tens place?

We are dividing 12 tens.

Alternative Approach: Using Manipulatives

To help students understand the concept of division answers ending in zero, have students use counters and a place-value workmat to model division as they perform the division using paper and pencil.

Show students how to make a place-value workmat by dividing a piece of plain paper vertically into 3 equal parts. Have them label the parts "hundreds," "tens," and "ones." Then have students use the counters to show the number 200 on the workmat and have them separate each place value into groups of 4. Explain that since the hundreds cannot be separated into groups of 4, they will need to trade 2 hundreds for 20 tens and then separate the 20 tens into equal groups of 4. Explain to students that since the ones have 0 counters, they can make 0 groups of 4.

Have students count the groups in each place value and record the quotient. 0 hundreds, 5 tens, 0 ones, or 50

Now we divide 01 (which means 1) by 3. Since we cannot make an equal group of 3 if we have only 1, we write "0" in the ones place of the quotient. We then multiply zero by 3 and subtract. The remainder is 1.

$$\begin{array}{r} 40 \text{ R } 1 \\ 3\overline{)121} \\ \underline{12} \\ 01 \\ \underline{0} \\ 1 \end{array}$$

Example 2

Mr. Griffith drove 254 miles in 5 hours. About how many miles did he drive each hour?

To find "about how many miles" Mr. Griffith drove each hour, we can use compatible numbers to estimate. Since 250 is close to 254 and is divisible by 5, we divide 250 by 5 to estimate.

250 miles ÷ 5 hours = 50 miles each hour

Mr. Griffith drove **about 50 miles** each hour.

Lesson Practice Divide:

a. $3\overline{)120}$ 40 **b.** $4\overline{)240}$ 60 **c.** $5\overline{)152}$ 30 R 2

d. $4\overline{)121}$ 30 R 1 **e.** $3\overline{)91}$ 30 R 1 **f.** $2\overline{)41}$ 20 R 1

g. **Estimate** The employees in the shipping department of a company loaded 538 boxes into a total of 6 railcars. They put about the same number of boxes into each railcar. About how many boxes are in each railcar? Explain how you found your answer. Sample: about 90 boxes; I rounded 538 to the nearest ten, and then divided; 540 ÷ 6 = 90

Written Practice

Distributed and Integrated

1. (RF1, RF5) Cecilia skated 27 times around the rink forward and 33 times around the rink backwards. In all, how many times did she skate around the rink? 60 times

2. (39) Nectarines cost 68¢ per pound. What is the price for 3 pounds of nectarines? $2.04

▸ ***3.** (12, 14) **Analyze** In bowling, the sum of Amber's score and Bianca's score was equal to Consuela's score. If Consuela's score was 113 and Bianca's score was 55, what was Amber's score? Write an equation to show your work. 58; Amber + Bianca = Consuela; $a + 55 = 113$

New Concept *(Continued)*

Example 2

Demonstrate the division of 250 by 5, or invite a volunteer to demonstrate it, to remind students that one or more zeros sometimes need to be written in a quotient to complete a division.

Extend the Example

Have advanced learners find the exact answer. 50.8 or $50\frac{4}{5}$ miles.

Lesson Practice

Guided Practice

Use these problems as guided practice to check the students' understanding of today's concept.

Problems a–f

Before students begin the arithmetic, remind them of the importance of checking their work. Then say:

"Explain how to check a division answer that includes a remainder. Include the words 'dividend,' 'divisor,' 'quotient,' and 'remainder' in your answer." Sample: Add the remainder to the product of the divisor and the whole number portion of the quotient, and then compare the result to the dividend.

Problems a–f
Error Alert

As students complete each division, remind them that a digit must be written in the quotient each time a digit is brought down from the dividend.

Closure **The questions below help assess the concepts taught in this lesson.**

"Suppose you are dividing two numbers and the divisor is 3. Each time you subtract, what numbers should you see? What numbers should you not see? Explain your answer." We should see any number that is less than 3, and we should not see any numbers that are greater than or equal to 3. If the numbers we see are greater than or equal to 3, the quotient must be increased.

"What must you do in the quotient each time you bring down a digit from the dividend?" Write a digit in the quotient.

Write the division 361 ÷ 6 on the board or overhead and ask students to find the quotient. 361 ÷ 6 = 60 R 1

English Learners

Explain that the word **employees** refers to the people who work for a company. Say:

"I am an employee of this school. What other school employees can you name?"

Discuss with students that some companies are very large and have hundreds or even thousands of **employees.** Some companies have only a few.

Written Practice

Math Conversations

Independent Practice and Discussions to Increase Understanding

Problem 3 **Analyze**

"What operation should we use to solve this problem? Explain why you named that operation." Sample: subtraction; Amber's score is a missing addend, and subtraction is used to find a missing addend.

Problem 4

"Explain how division can be used to check our answer." Finding $\frac{1}{3}$ of a number is the same as dividing the number by 3; Divide 84 by 3 and then compare answers.

Problem 10

Extend the Problem

"Is the year 2019 a leap year? Explain why or why not." No; In a leap year, the month of February has 29 days.

(continued)

► *4. (68) One third of the 84 students were assigned to each room. How many students were assigned to each room? Draw a picture to explain how you found your answer. 28 students

84 students
$\frac{1}{3}$ 28 students
$\frac{2}{3}$ 28 students
28 students

5. (40) Round 2250 to the nearest thousand. 2000

6. (47, 48) **Represent** Use digits to write the number five million, three hundred sixty-five thousand in standard form. Then round it to the nearest hundred thousand. 5,365,000; 5,400,000

*7. (50, 70) **Classify** Write the name of each polygon:

a. five sides pentagon

b. ten sides decagon

c. six sides hexagon

d. eight sides octagon

8. (42) **Estimate** The tip of this shoelace is how many millimeters long?
15 mm

mm 10 20 30 40 50

*9. (73) **Conclude** Choose the more reasonable measure for **a** and **b**.

a. milk for a bowl of cereal: 2 pt or 4 oz 4 oz

b. a full pail of water: 1 pt or 1 gal 1 gal

► 10. (RF12) According to this calendar, what is the date of the last Tuesday in February 2019? February 26, 2019

FEBRUARY 2019

S	M	T	W	T	F	S
					1	2
3	4	5	6	7	8	9
10	11	12	13	14	15	16
17	18	19	20	21	22	23
24	25	26	27	28		

11. (27, 52) **Represent** Forty-two thousand, seven hundred is how much greater than thirty-four thousand, nine hundred? 7800

Teacher Tip

Keep a good supply of centimeter and inch grid paper handy for students who need help aligning digits or making diagrams for division. You can make copies with **Lesson Activity Master 8** (1-centimeter grid paper) and **Lesson Activity Master 23** (1-inch grid paper).

12. (66) Find the perimeter and area of this rectangle: 30 km; 50 km^2

10 km

5 km

* **13.** (Inv. 7) **Conclude** Use the coordinate graph to answer parts **a** and **b.**

► **a.** Name the coordinates for point *P* and point *Q*. *P* (10, 10), *Q* (10, 0)

b. What is the length of segment *PQ*? 10 units

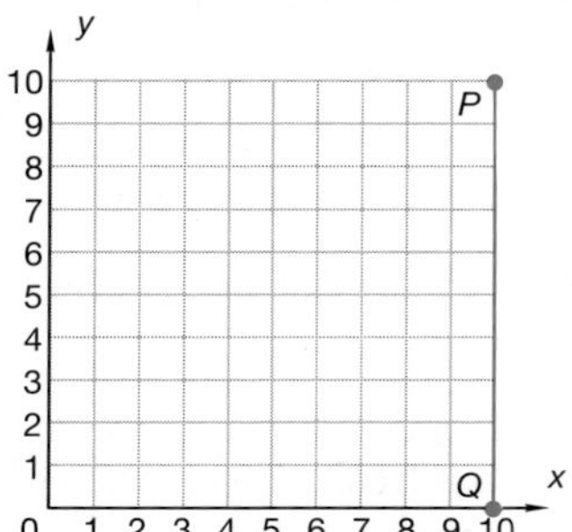

14. (52, 59, 63) 6743 − (507 × 6) 3701

15. (28, 52) \$70.00 − \$63.17 \$6.83

16. (24) 3 × 7 × 0 0

17. (59) \$8.15 × 6 \$48.90

18. (71) 67¢ × 20 \$13.40

19. (45) 4.5 + 0.52 + 1.39 6.41

►* **20.** (72) $5\overline{)323}$ 64 R 3

►* **21.** (72) $4\overline{)159}$ 39 R 3

►* **22.** (72) 329 ÷ 6 54 R 5

* **23.** (75) $\frac{180}{3}$ 60

►* **24.** (65, 68) $5^3 \div 5$ 25

* **25.** (75) 241 ÷ 8 30 R 1

26. (34, 75) 4*n* = 200 50

27. (34, 69) 7*d* = 105 15

28. (8, 10, 11)

$$\begin{array}{r} 473 \\ 286 \\ +\ n \\ \hline 943 \end{array}$$

184

29. (11) 1 + 12 + 3 + 14 + 5 + 26 61

Written Practice (Continued)

Math Conversations (cont.)

Problem 13a **Conclude**

To help students identify the location of point *P* and point *Q*, ask:

"How far to the right of the origin is point (P or Q)?" 10

"How far up from the x-axis is it?" (10 for *P*; 0 for *Q*)

Problem 20–22

Before students complete any arithmetic, remind them of the importance of checking their work. Then ask:

"How can we check a division answer that includes a remainder? Include the words 'dividend,' 'divisor,' 'quotient,' and 'remainder' in your answer." Sample: Add the remainder to the product of the divisor and the whole number portion of the quotient, and then compare the result to the dividend.

Problem 24

"The first term in this expression is read 'five cubed.' Explain how we can find the cube of a number." Sample: Write the factor that the exponent represents three times, then write the product of those factors; 5 × 5 × 5 = 125

(continued)

Inclusion

Use this strategy if the student displays:

- Slow Learning Rate.
- Difficulty with Multiple Steps.

Division Answers Ending with Zero (Individual)

Materials: base ten blocks, paper

- Write $4\overline{)122}$ on the board. Ask, ***"What is the first step in solving this problem?"*** Divide 12 tens by 4. The answer is 3 tens.

  Have student write 3 above the 2 in the tens place. Then ask, ***"What is left to divide?"*** 2 ones. ***"Can we divide 2 by 4?"*** No
- Have students model the problem using their base ten blocks and then using pencil and paper. Tell students to place a 0 above the 2 in the ones place and finish the division steps. Ask, ***"What is the remainder in this problem?"*** 2
- Read aloud:
  "Mrs. Turner read 253 pages in 5 hours. How many pages did she read on average per hour?" Help students set up the division problem and work through the steps.

Written Practice *(Continued)*

Math Conversations *(cont.)*

Problem 30

Extend the Problem

Have students formulate a subtraction question that can be answered by interpreting data from the graph. Then ask volunteers to share their questions with the class and challenge the class to provide the answers.

Errors and Misconceptions

Problem 8

Make sure students recognize that they are to give the measure of only the tip of the shoelace.

Problem 13b

To find the length of a vertical line segment, the *y*-coordinates of the endpoints must be subtracted. Some students may find it helpful to label the coordinates as shown below.

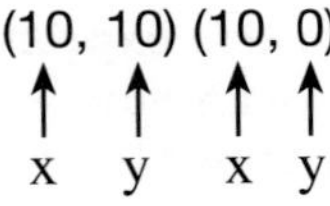

▸* **30.** *(19, Inv. 5)* The bar graph shows the average lifespan in years of several animals. Use the graph to solve the problems that follow.

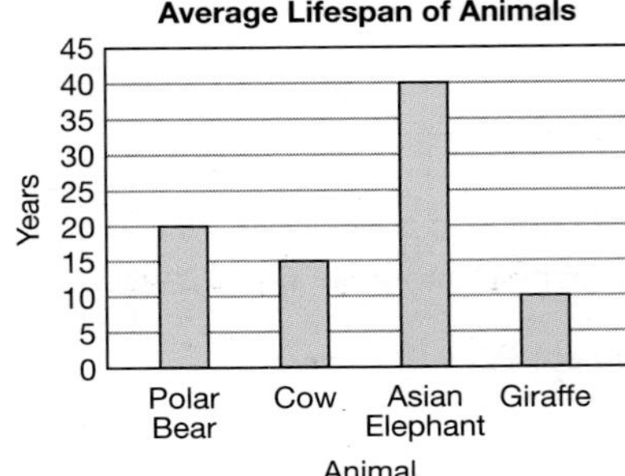

a. Write the names of the animals in order from longest to shortest average lifespan. Asian elephant, polar bear, cow, giraffe

b. What fraction of the average lifespan of an Asian elephant is the average lifespan of a polar bear? $\frac{1}{2}$ or $\frac{20}{40}$

c. When compared to the average lifespan of a giraffe, how many times greater is the average lifespan of an Asian elephant? Four times greater

504 ***Saxon Math*** *Intermediate 4*

Looking Forward

Dividing numbers to find a quotient that ends in zero prepares students for:

- **Lesson 79,** division with three-digit quotients.
- **Lesson 83,** division with zeros in three-digit quotients.
- **Lesson 87,** solving division word problems that involve remainders.
- **Lesson 91,** estimating multiplication and division answers.

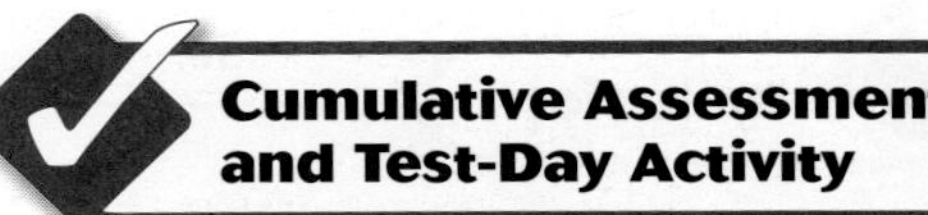

Cumulative Assessments and Test-Day Activity

Assessments

Distribute **Power-Up Test 14** and **Cumulative Test 14** to each student. Have students complete the **Power-Up Test** first. Allow 10 minutes. Then have students work on the **Cumulative Test.**

Test-Day Activity

The remaining class time can be spent on the **Test-Day Activity 7.** Students can begin the activity in class and complete it as homework.

Planning & Preparation

• Finding Information to Solve Problems

Objectives

- Analyze a problem and choose the information needed to solve a problem.
- Solve word problems that have too much information.
- Identify missing information in a problem.
- Solve a problem using a double bar graph.

Prerequisite Skills

- Deciding if the answer to a word problem is reasonable.
- Writing an equation for word problems.

Materials

Instructional Masters

- Power Up G Worksheet
- Lesson Activity 14*

Manipulative Kit

- Money manipulatives*

Teacher-provided materials

- Number line*

**optional*

California Mathematics Content Standards

NS 1.0, 1.8 Use concepts of negative numbers (e.g., on a number line, in counting, in temperature, in "owing").

AF 1.0, 1.1 Use letters, boxes, or other symbols to stand for any number in simple expressions or equations (e.g., demonstrate an understanding and the use of the concept of a variable).

SDAP 1.0, 1.3 Interpret one-and two-variable data graphs to answer questions about a situation.

MR 1.0, 1.1 Analyze problems by identifying relationships, distinguishing relevant from irrelevant information, sequencing and prioritizing information, and observing patterns.

MR 1.0, 1.2 Determine when and how to break a problem into simpler parts.

MR 2.0, 2.2 Apply strategies and results from simpler problems to more complex problems.

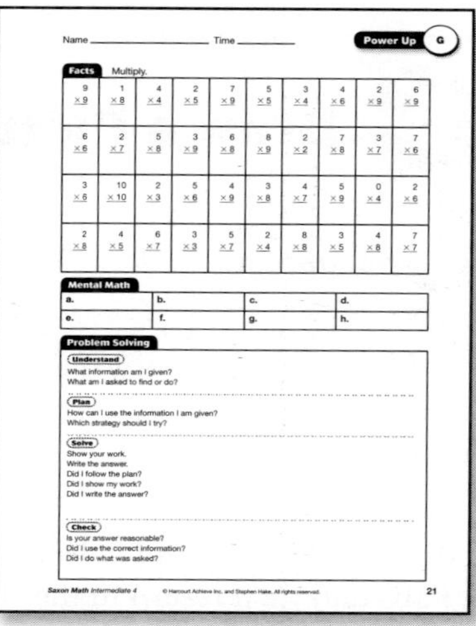

Power Up G Worksheet

Universal Access

Reaching All Special Needs Students

Special Education Students	At-Risk Students	English Learners	Advanced Learners
• Inclusion (TM) • Adaptations for Saxon Math	• Alternative Approach (TM) • Error Alert (TM) • Reteaching Masters • Refresher Lessons for California Standards	• English Learners (TM) • Developing Academic Language (TM) • English Learner Handbook	• Extend the Example (TM) • Extend the Problem (TM) • Early Finisher (SE) • Online Activities

TM=Teacher's Manual
SE=Student Edition

Developing Academic Language

Maintained
bar graph
graphs
number line
tables

English Learner
bank deposit

Problem Solving Discussion

Problem

Phuong and LaDonna are planning a hike in the park. The map of the park's trails is shown at right. Phuong and LaDonna will start at the point labeled Start. They want to visit both Eagle Lookout and Slippery Falls. What is the shortest distance Phuong and LaDonna can hike in order to visit both points and then return to where they started? All distances shown are in kilometers.

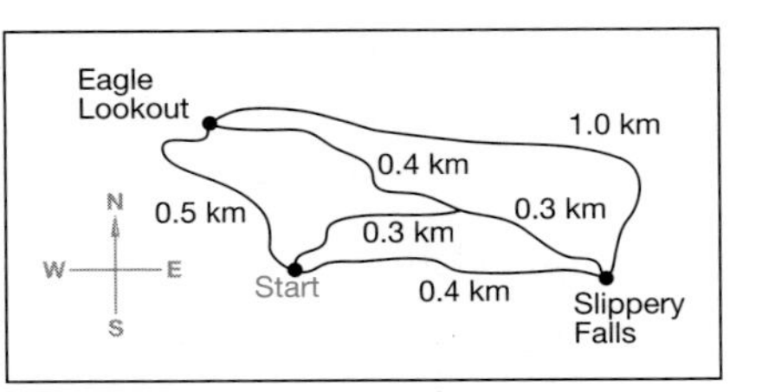

Focus Strategy

Draw a Picture or Diagram

Understand *Understand the problem.*

"What information are we given?"

We are shown a map of park trails. There are three points, and they are labeled Start, Eagle Lookout, and Slippery Falls. The trails between the points are labeled on the map with distances in kilometers.

"What are we asked to do?"

We are asked to find the shortest distance Phuong and LaDonna can hike to visit both Eagle Lookout and Slippery Falls and then return to the starting point.

Plan *Make a plan.*

"How can we use the given information to answer the question?"

We need to *use the diagram* (map) that is provided to find the shortest distance among various possible routes.

Solve *Carry out the plan.*

"There are many ways that Phuong and LaDonna can hike the trails, but they are looking for the shortest route to reach both points of interest. What path can they take?"

Teacher Note: Copy the map onto the board, and have students discuss various paths. For each path, add the distances along the trails to find the total length of the hike.

"What is the shortest distance that Phuong and LaDonna can hike to visit both points and then return to the starting point?"

The shortest distance they can hike is 1.6 kilometers. One of the two possible short routes is shown at right.

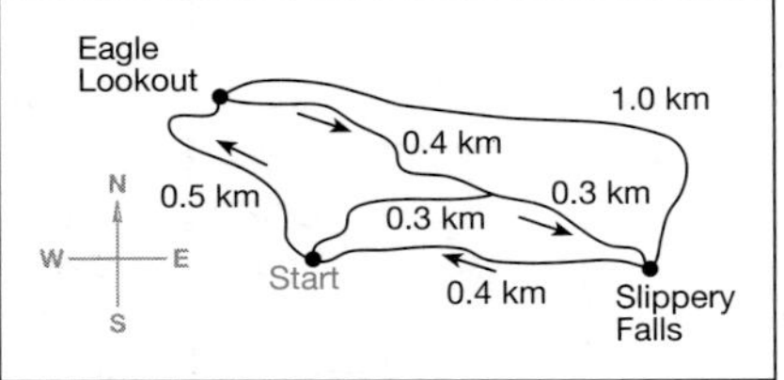

Check *Look back.*

"Is our answer reasonable?"

We know that our answer is reasonable, because 0.5 km + 0.4 km + 0.3 km + 0.4 km = 1.6 km.

LESSON 76

• Finding Information to Solve Problems

California Mathematics Content Standards

NS 1.0, 1.8 Use concepts of negative numbers (e.g., on a number line, in counting, in temperature, in "owing").

SDAP 1.0, 1.3 Interpret one-and two-variable data graphs to answer questions about a situation.

MR 1.0, 1.2 Determine when and how to break a problem into simpler parts.

MR 2.0, 2.2 Apply strategies and results from simpler problems to more complex problems.

Power Up

facts Power Up G

count aloud Count by fives from 1 to 51.

mental math Before adding, make one number larger and the other number smaller.

a. **Number Sense:** 49 + 35 84

b. **Number Sense:** 57 + 35 92

c. **Number Sense:** 28 + 44 72

d. **Number Sense:** 400 × 30 12,000

e. **Money:** KaNiyah owes her brother $10.00. She only has $4.98. How much more money does she need to repay her brother? $5.02

f. **Measurement:** Seven feet is 84 inches. A dolphin that is 7 feet 7 inches long is how many inches long? 91 in.

g. **Estimation:** Each half-gallon of milk costs $2.47. Round this price to the nearest 25 cents and estimate the cost of 3 half-gallon containers of milk. $7.50

h. **Calculation:** $\sqrt{25}$, × 2, ÷ 5, × 15, + 48 78

problem solving Choose an appropriate problem-solving strategy to solve this problem. Phuong and LaDonna are planning a hike in the park. The map of the park's trails is shown at right. Phuong and LaDonna will start at the point labeled "Start."

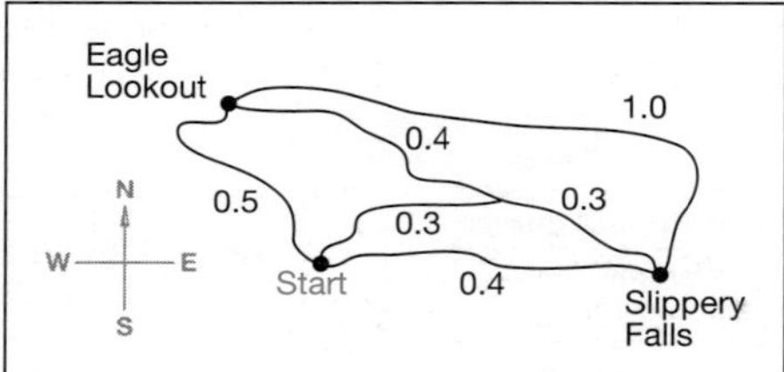

Facts Multiply.

9 × 9 = 81	1 × 8 = 8	4 × 4 = 16	2 × 5 = 10	7 × 9 = 63	5 × 5 = 25	3 × 4 = 12	4 × 6 = 24	2 × 9 = 18	6 × 9 = 54
6 × 6 = 36	2 × 7 = 14	5 × 8 = 40	3 × 9 = 27	6 × 8 = 48	8 × 9 = 72	2 × 2 = 4	7 × 8 = 56	3 × 7 = 21	7 × 6 = 42
3 × 6 = 18	10 × 10 = 100	2 × 3 = 6	5 × 6 = 30	4 × 9 = 36	3 × 8 = 24	4 × 7 = 28	5 × 9 = 45	0 × 4 = 0	2 × 6 = 12
2 × 8 = 16	4 × 5 = 20	6 × 7 = 42	3 × 3 = 9	5 × 7 = 35	2 × 4 = 8	8 × 8 = 64	3 × 5 = 15	4 × 8 = 32	7 × 7 = 49

Facts

Distribute **Power Up G** to students. See answers below.

Count Aloud

Before students begin the Mental Math exercises, do these counting exercises as a class.

Mental Math

Encourage students to share different ways to mentally compute these exercises. Strategies for exercises are listed below.

c. Change 28 to 30, then Subtract 2

30 + 44 = 74; 74 − 2 = 72

Add 50, then Subtract 6

28 + 50 = 78; 78 − 6 = 72

f. Add 7 in. to 84 in.

84 in. + 7 in. = 91 in.

Add 10 in, then Subtract 3 in.

84 in. + 10 in. = 94 in.

94 in. − 3 in. = 91 in.

Problem Solving

Refer to **Problem-Solving Strategy Discussion**, p. 505B.

New Concept

Instruction

Begin the lesson by reminding students that the first step in the problem-solving process involves reading the problem carefully, and reading it a second or third time if necessary, to help understand the relationship of the information it contains, and how that information relates to the question being asked.

Example 1

Begin the example by inviting a volunteer to read the problem aloud. Then ask students to identify the information that each sentence in the problem contains.

Active Learning

Before you discuss each of the three solutions, ask students to identify the sentence or the sentences in the problem that contain the information that is needed to find the answer, and then explain why that information is needed.

Error Alert

Some students may find it difficult to understand the solution to part **c** without the benefit of a calendar. Draw the calendar shown below (or invite a volunteer to draw a calendar of their own design) on the board or overhead that can be used to help solve the problem.

S	M	T	W	Th	F	S
		30	31	1	2	
January				February		

Example 2

As you discuss the solution, have students note that whenever we use a number line to add or subtract two numbers, we begin at zero. We then move or count to the right to represent positive numbers, and move or count to the left to represent negative numbers.

(continued)

They want to visit both Eagle Lookout and Slippery Falls. What is the shortest distance Phuong and LaDonna can hike in order to visit both points and then return to where they started? All distances shown are in kilometers. 1.6 km

New Concept

Part of the problem-solving process is finding the information needed to solve a problem. Sometimes we need to find information in graphs, tables, pictures, or other places. In some cases, we might be given more information than we need to solve a problem. In this lesson we will be finding the information we need to solve a problem.

Example 1

Reading Math

Sometimes problems contain too much information. We need to look for the information that is necessary to solve a problem.

Read this information. Then answer the questions that follow.

The school elections were held on Friday, February 2. Tejana, Lily, and Taariq ran for president. Lily received 146 votes, and Tejana received 117 votes. Taariq received 35 more votes than Tejana.

a. How many votes did Taariq receive?

b. Who received the most votes?

c. Speeches were given on the Tuesday before the elections. What was the date on which the speeches were given?

a. Taariq received 35 more votes than Tejana, and Tejana received 117 votes. So we add 35 to 117 and find that Taariq received **152 votes.**

b. Taariq received the most votes.

c. The elections were on Friday, February 2. The Tuesday when the speeches were presented was 3 days before that. We count back 3 days: February 1, January 31, January 30. The speeches were given on Tuesday, **January 30.**

Example 2

Math Language

Overdraft protection uses bank credit to cover checks that overdraw a checking account.

The balance in Emily's bank account is $50. If she writes a check for $70, what number represents the balance in her account?

The amount of money in a bank account is called a balance. When Emily writes a check, the balance decreases. When she makes a deposit, the balance increases.

English Learners

Explain that making a bank **deposit** means that you're adding money to your bank account. This makes your balance increase.

Say, ***"On the other hand, a withdrawal refers to taking money out of your bank account."***

Ask, ***"What happens to your bank balance when you make a withdrawal?"*** it decreases

Discuss with students the common ways to **deposit** or withdraw money from a back account. Samples: checks, ATM deposits or withdrawals, cash requests made at the bank

We can use a number line to illustrate the balance of Emily's account. We start at zero and move to the right from 0 to 50 to represent $50.

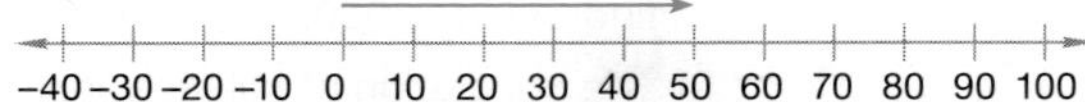

Writing a check is the same as taking dollars away. We can represent writing a check of $70 by moving to the left. We start at 50 and count by tens to 70. We can see that we end at –20.

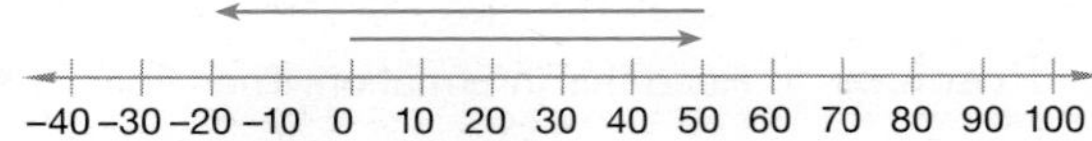

We can represent the balance in Emily's account with a negative number, **–$20.** This means that Emily owes the bank $20.

Discuss How can we write an equation to represent this problem? Sample: $50 – $70 = –$20

Example 3

Use the double bar graph to solve these problems.

a. Did the population of Fairview increase or decrease from 1990 to 2004? Write an equation to show the population change.

b. Which two cities had the same population change from 1990 to 2004?

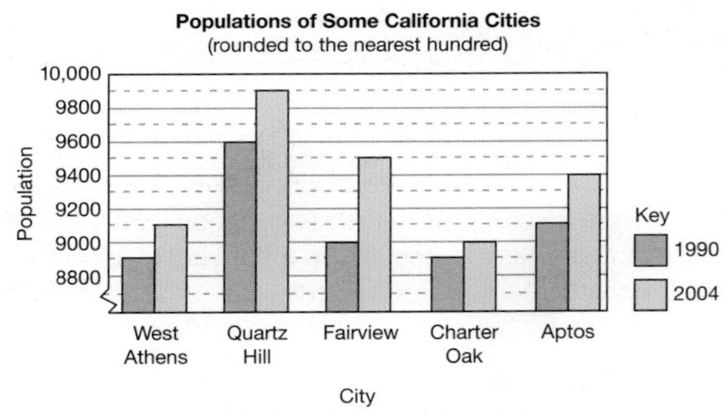

When we need to solve a problem using information in a graph, it is the same as a problem with too much information. We need to look at the graph and find the information we need.

Alternative Approach: Using Manipulatives

Encourage students to draw pictures or make charts to help them organize the information provided in a problem. Restating the information in their own words will help students determine which information is needed, which is missing, and which is important to the problem-solving process.

New Concept *(Continued)*

Extend the Example

Explain that in real-life, writing a check for an amount greater than the balance in an account is not as simple as writing a negative number to represent the new balance. Explain to your advanced learners that banks charge a fee each time this occurs, and then challenge them to write a negative number to represent the amount Emily owes the bank if the bank charges her $40 for her actions. –$20 + –$40 = –$60

Example 3

Error Alert

Remind students of the importance of knowing what each bar of a double graph represents before the graph is used to solve problems.

Also remind students of the importance of identifying what the unlabeled axis divisions of a graph represent by asking:

"The vertical axis of this graph identifies the numbers that some of the horizontal lines represent. However, the broken horizontal lines of this graph have no numbers. How can we decide what number each of those broken lines represents?"

Lead students to generalize that because each broken line appears to be halfway between two solid lines, the broken lines represent the number that is halfway between the given numbers. For example, the first broken line of the graph represents 8700; the second represents 8900 and so on

Extend the Example

"Are the populations shown on the graph exact populations? Explain why or why not." No; The title of the graph states that the data are rounded to the nearest hundred.

"About how many times greater was the population change in the city that changed the most than in the city that changed the least? Explain your answer." Five times greater; sample: The least change was Charter Oak (100), the greatest change was Fairview (500).

(continued)

New Concept *(Continued)*

Lesson Practice

Guided Practice

Use these problems as guided practice to check the students' understanding of today's concept.

Problem a

Before students answer the question from part **a**, ask:

"What information in the problem do we need to find the number of hours Terell worked in all?" The number of hours he worked in the morning and the number of hours he worked in the afternoon

"What information in the problem don't we need to know?" The day Terrell worked and the amount that he earned for each hour he worked

Ask similar questions before students solve parts **b** and **c.**

Problem d
Error Alert

Some students might benefit from using a number line to solve this problem. Remind them to start at 30 and move to the left.

Closure

The questions below help assess the concepts taught in this lesson.

Invite students to share their answers to these questions with the class.

"Describe the first step we should complete whenever we solve a problem." Sample: Read the problem carefully to help understand the relationship of the information it contains and how that information relates to the question being asked.

"Whenever we solve a problem, why is it important to understand the question that is being asked?" Sample: The question identifies the information that is needed to solve the problem.

a. We can see that Fairview had a population of 9000 in 1990. It increased to 9500 by 2004. We can show this with the equation $9000 + n = 9500$. We count on or subtract to find that $n = 500$.

The population of Fairview increased by **500** people between 1990 and 2004.

b. We compare each pair of bars to find an increase that is the same. We can see that **Quartz Hill and Aptos** each increased by 300 people between 1990 and 2004.

Lesson Practice

Read this information. Then solve the problems that follow.

Terell did yard work on Saturday. He worked for 3 hours in the morning and 4 hours in the afternoon. He was paid $6 for every hour he worked.

▸ **a.** How many hours did Terell work in all? 7 hours

b. How much money did Terell earn in the morning? $18

c. How much money did Terell earn in all? $42

▸ **d.** **Analyze** Daniel had $30 in the bank. He wrote a check for $45. What number represents the balance of his account? −$15

e. **Interpret** Use the double bar graph in Example 3 to answer this question. Which city increased by 100 people between 1990 and 2004? Charter Oak

Written Practice

Distributed and Integrated

Formulate Write and solve equations for problems **1–4.**

1. (16) There were 35 students in the class but only 28 math books. How many more math books are needed so that every student in the class has a math book? $35 - 28 = b$; 7 math books

2. (39) Each of the 7 children slid down the water slide 11 times. How many times did they slide in all? $7 \times 11 = t$; 77 times

▸ ***3.** (42, 53) A bowling lane is 60 feet long. How many yards is 60 feet? $60 \div 3 = y$; 20 yd

Inclusion

Use this strategy if the student displays:

- Slow Learning Rate.
- Difficulty with Abstract Processing.

Finding Information to Solve Problems (Small Group)

Materials: money manipulatives, number line

- Read aloud, ***"Andrew owes his mom $10 for a toy she bought him. He only has $4 in his piggy bank. How much more money does Andrew need?"***
- Ask, ***"How much money does Andrew need to give his mom?"*** $10

  Tell students to display ten dollars. Ask, ***"How much of that money can Andrew give his mom now?"*** $4
- Have students take four dollars away from their money. Ask, ***"How much money does Andrew still need to pay his mom?"*** $6
- Have partners work together using a number line to solve the following:

  "Kallie wants to buy a CD that costs $12. She has $2 of her own and her dad will give her $5. How much more money does Kallie need?"

▶ **4.** Wei carried the baton four hundred forty yards. Eric carried it eight hundred eighty yards. Joe carried it one thousand, three hundred twenty yards, and Bernardo carried it one thousand, seven hundred sixty yards. In all, how many yards was the baton carried?
(3, 27, 51)
$440 + 880 + 1320 + 1760 = y$; 4400 yd

5. One third of the members voted "no." What fraction of the members did not vote "no"? $\frac{2}{3}$
(67)

▶ ***6.** **Explain** Marissa would like to estimate the sum of 6821 + 4963. Explain how Marissa could use rounding to make an estimate. Sample: Marissa could round 6821 to 7000 and 4963 to 5000; Then she could add 7000 and 5000 to make an estimate of 12,000.
(40, 61)

***7.** **Generalize** Use this table to write a formula that can be used to convert any number of pints to ounces. Use *o* for ounces and *p* for pints. $16p = o$ or $o = 16p$
(73)

Pints	1	2	3	4	5
Ounces	16	32	48	64	80

8. **Represent** Write the number that is 500,000 greater than 4,250,000. 4,750,000
(47, 51)

▶ ***9.** **Interpret** Use the line graph below to answer parts **a–c.**
(Inv. 5)

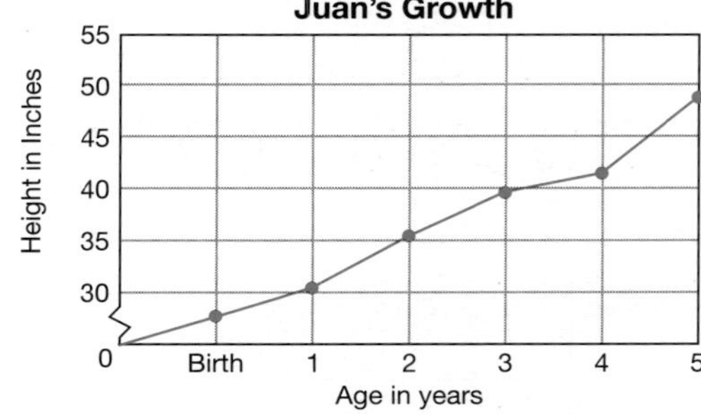

a. About how many inches tall was Juan on his second birthday? About 35 inches

Written Practice

Math Conversations

Independent Practice and Discussions to Increase Understanding

Problem 3 **Formulate**

"One yard is the same as what number of feet?" 3 feet

"If we know the number of yards that 3 feet represents, what operation can we use to find the number of yards that 60 feet represents?" division

Problem 4 **Formulate**

Some students may find it helpful if you explain that in a relay race, a baton is a lightweight, hollow, short length of pipe that is carried by each member of a relay team. A baton is typically made from aluminum, and each team member must pass the baton to the next team member as his or her portion of the race is completed. The members of a competitive relay team are able to pass the baton while running at nearly top speed.

Problem 6 **Explain**

Extend the Problem

"Explain how Marissa could make an estimate that is closer to the exact sum." Sample: Round to a lesser place value, such as hundreds. For example, round 6821 to 6800 and round 4963 to 5000, then add; 6800 + 5000 = 11,800

Work with the students to help them generalize that the accuracy of an estimate depends on the rounding place that is chosen:

- Rounding to a greater place value produces an estimate that is farther away from the exact answer.
- Rounding to a lesser place value produces an estimate that is closer to the exact answer.

(continued)

Written Practice *(Continued)*

Math Conversations *(cont.)*

Problem 9 (Interpret)

Invite interested students to formulate an additional question that can be answered by interpreting data from the graph. Then ask volunteers to share their questions and challenge the class to provide the answers.

Problem 12a (Generalize)

Extend the Problem

The word sentences students write will include an operation. Challenge your students to write a word problem that describes the relationship of the data but includes the opposite operation. Sample: Divide the number of days worked by 30 to find the number of vacation days earned.

(continued)

b. About how many inches did Juan grow between his third and fifth birthdays? About 10 inches

c. Copy and complete this table using information from the line graph:

Juan's Growth

Age	Height
At birth	25 inches
1 year	about 30 inches
2 years	about 35 inches
3 years	about 40 inches
4 years	about 40 inches
5 years	about 50 inches

***10.** (74) (Represent) On the last Friday in May, one fourth of the 280 students in a school were away on a field trip. How many students were on the field trip? Draw a picture to solve the problem. 70 students

280 students
$\frac{1}{4}$ On a field trip: 70 students
$\frac{3}{4}$ Not on a field trip: 70 students, 70 students, 70 students

***11.** (63) (Analyze) Simplify each expression. Remember to use the order of operations.

a. $5 \times 3 + 35 \div 7$ 20

b. $81 \div 9 \times 2 + 7$ 25

c. $100 - (8 + 3) \times 6$ 34

d. $5 \times (10 - 6) \div 5$ 4

***12.** (Inv. 7, 76) The table shows the number of vacation days Carson earns at work:

Days Worked	Vacation Days Earned
30	1
60	2
90	3
120	4
150	5
180	6

▶ **a.** (Generalize) Write a word sentence that describes the relationship of the data. Sample: The number of vacation days multiplied by 30 equals the number of days worked.

b. (Predict) Use the word sentence you wrote to predict the number of days Carson needs to work to earn 10 vacation days. 300 days

510 ***Saxon Math*** *Intermediate 4*

13. (28, 51) $\$60.75 + \$95.75$ $156.50

14. (28, 52) $\$16.00 - \$15.43$ $0.57

15. (45) $3.15 - 3.12$ 0.03

16. (71) 32×30 960

17. (59) 465×7 3255

18. (59) $\$0.98 \times 6$ $5.88

19. (75) $425 \div 6$ 70 R 5

***20.** (72) $462 \div 9$ 51 R 3

***21.** (72) $159 \div 4$ 39 R 3

22. (34, 75) $3r = 150$ 50

23. (63, 65) $10^2 + t = 150$ 50

24. (4) $1 + 7 + 2 + 6 + 9 + 4 + n = 37$ 8

25. (Inv. 3) **a.** If the 3-inch square is covered with 1-inch squares, how many of the 1-inch squares are needed? Nine 1-inch squares

b. What is the area of the 3-inch square? 9 in²

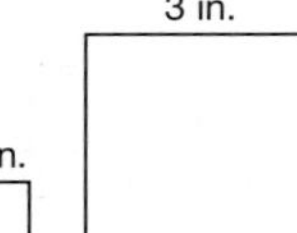

26. (17, 20, 45) **a.** What is the perimeter of this triangle? 4.8 cm

b. Describe the angles of the triangle. Right angle, acute angle

1.2 cm
2.0 cm
1.6 cm

***27.** (64, Inv. 7) **Evaluate** If $y = 3x + 7$, then what is y when $x = 4$? 19

▸***28.** (17) **Conclude** Is $\overline{AB} \perp \overline{BC}$? Why or why not? Yes; They form a right angle.

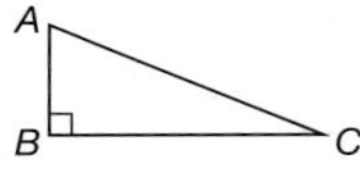

▸ **29.** (70) **Multiple Choice** Three of these triangles are congruent. Which triangle is *not* one of the three congruent triangles? D

A  **B**  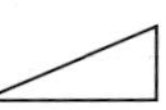 **C**  **D** 

Written Practice *(Continued)*

Math Conversations *(cont.)*

Problem 28 Conclude

You may need to remind some students that the symbol ⊥ means "is perpendicular to."

Problem 29 Multiple Choice

Test-Taking Strategy

If necessary, encourage students to use tracing to help decide that answer choice **D** represents the correct answer.

(continued)

Written Practice (Continued)

Math Conversations (cont.)

Problem 30

"What relationship is shared by the radius and the diameter of a circle? Describe that relationship two different ways." Sample: The length of a radius is one half the length of a diameter; The length of a diameter is twice the length of a radius.

Errors and Misconceptions

Problems 13, 14, and 18

Watch for opportunities to remind students that dollar signs and decimal points are placed in answers that are found by adding, subtracting, multiplying, or dividing amounts of money.

Problems 19–21

Make sure students recognize that because the divisor is greater than the first digit in the dividend, the first digit in the quotient is written in the tens place.

The beach house problem is a precursor to multiplying a fraction times a whole. In later grades, students will learn to solve part **b** by multiplying 5/9 by 783. After students solve the beach house problem, engage them in a conversation about splitting costs fairly between two groups of different sizes. For example:

"Season tickets to the opera are sold in groups of 5. Two members of the Shelton family and three members of the Vazquez family bought season tickets together. The total cost of the tickets was $300. If the families split the cost fairly, how much should the Shelton family have to pay?" $120

▸ ***30.** (18, 45) The radius of this circle is 1.2 cm. What is the diameter of the circle? 2.4 cm

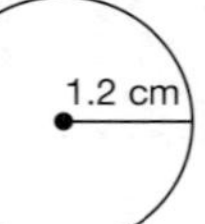

Real-World Connection

There are four people in the Escobar family and five in the Greene family.

The Escobar family and the Greene family went on a vacation together. They rented a beach house for 3 days. The cost of renting the beach house for 3 days was $783.

a. What was the cost per person of renting the beach house? $87

b. If the two families split the cost, how much should the Escobars pay given that they have 4 members in their family? $348; $\left(\frac{783}{9}\right) \times 4$

c. How much should the Greenes pay given that they have 5 people in their family? $435; $\left(\frac{783}{9}\right) \times 5$

512 *Saxon Math* Intermediate 4

Finding information to solve problems prepares students for:

- **Lesson 93,** translating and solving two-step word problems.

Planning & Preparation

• Fraction of a Set

Objectives
- Find a fraction of a set.

Prerequisite Skills
- Using pictures to name fractions.
- Comparing fractions with different denominators using pictorial models and manipulatives.
- Using fraction manipulatives to compare fractions with different denominators.

Materials
Instructional Masters
- Power Up G Worksheet
- Lesson Activity 8
- Lesson Activity 23*

Manipulative Kit
- Rulers
- Two-color counters*

Teacher-provided materials
- Grid paper

**optional*

California Mathematics Content Standards

NS 1.0, 1.5 Explain different interpretations of fractions, for example, parts of a whole, parts of a set, and division of whole numbers by whole numbers; explain equivalents of fractions (see Standard 4.0).

NS 1.0, 1.7 Write the fraction represented by a drawing of parts of a figure; represent a given fraction by using drawings; and relate a fraction to a simple decimal on a number line.

MR 2.0, 2.6 Make precise calculations and check the validity of the results from the context of the problem.

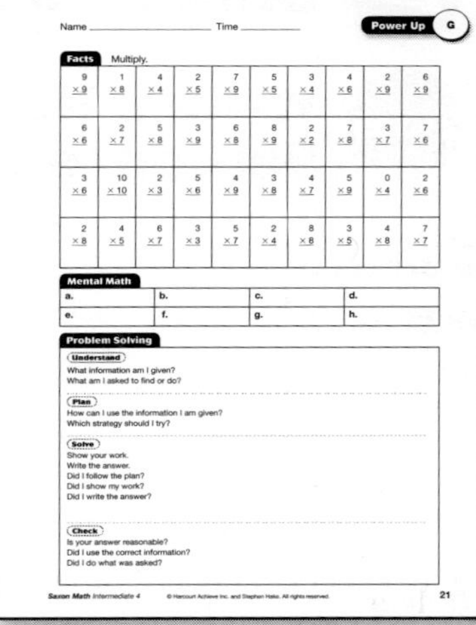
Power Up G Worksheet

Lesson Activity 8

Universal Access

Reaching All Special Needs Students

Special Education Students	At-Risk Students	English Learners	Advanced Learners
• Inclusion (TM) • Adaptations for Saxon Math	• Alternative Approach (TM) • Error Alert (TM) • Reteaching Masters • Refresher Lessons for California Standards	• English Learners (TM) • Developing Academic Language (TM) • English Learner Handbook	• Extend the Example (TM) • Extend the Problem (TM) • Online Activities

TM=Teacher's Manual

Developing Academic Language

Maintained	**English Learner**
fraction	set

Problem Solving Discussion

Problem

Colby wants to cover his bulletin board with square sheets of paper that are 1 foot on each side. His bulletin board is 5 feet wide and 3 feet tall. If Colby has already cut 12 squares of paper, how many more squares does he need to cut? Explain how you found your answer.

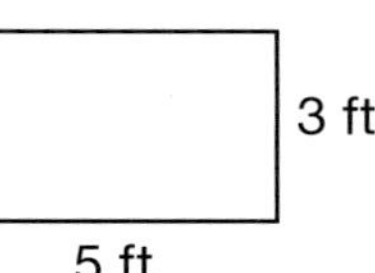

Focus Strategies

Draw a Picture or Diagram

2+3=5 **Write a Number Sentence or Equation**

Understand ***Understand the problem.***

"What information are we given?"

1. Colby has a bulletin board that is 5 feet by 3 feet.
2. He is covering the board with 1-foot square sheets of paper.
3. He has already cut 12 squares of paper.

"What are we asked to do?"

We are asked to find how many more sheets of paper Colby needs to cover the bulletin board.

Plan ***Make a plan.***

"How can we use the information we know to solve the problem?"

We can *draw a diagram* to find how many rows and columns of squares fit on the bulletin board.

Solve ***Carry out the plan.***

"How many 1-foot square sheets of paper are needed to make a row of squares along the horizontal edge of the board?"

Five squares of paper can make a row along the length of the board.

"How many 1-foot square sheets of paper are needed to make a column of squares along the vertical edge of the board?"

Three squares of paper can make a column along the width (height) of the board.

"Let's draw a diagram of the square sheets of paper. We see that Colby can make three rows with five squares in each row. How many squares is this altogether?"

Three rows of five squares each is 3×5 squares $= 15$ squares. We show this in the diagram at right.

3 ft

5 ft

"If Colby has already cut 12 square sheets, how many more sheets does he need to cover the board?"

Colby needs to cut 3 more squares to cover the board (15 sheets − 12 sheets = 3 sheets).

Check ***Look back.***

"Is our answer reasonable?"

We know that our answer is reasonable, because 3 rows of 5 squares is $5 + 5 + 5 = 15$ squares altogether. Colby has cut 12 squares already, so he needs 3 more for a total of 15 squares.

• Fraction of a Set

California Mathematics Content Standards

NS 1.0, 1.5 Explain different interpretations of fractions, for example, parts of a whole, parts of a set, and division of whole numbers by whole numbers; explain equivalents of fractions (see Standard 4.0).

NS 1.0, 1.7 Write the fraction represented by a drawing of parts of a figure; represent a given fraction by using drawings; and relate a fraction to a simple decimal on a number line.

MR 2.0, 2.6 Make precise calculations and check the validity of the results from the context of the problem.

facts Power Up G

count aloud Count by fives from 2 to 52.

mental math Before adding, make one number larger and the other number smaller in problems **a–c.**

a. Number Sense: 55 + 47 102

b. Number Sense: 24 + 48 72

c. Number Sense: 458 + 33 491

d. Number Sense: 15 × 30 450

e. Money: Renee bought a pair of gloves for $14.50 and a hat for $8.99. What was the total cost of the items? $23.49

f. Measurement: Compare: 2 miles (>) 10,000 feet

g. Estimation: An *acre* is a measurement of land. A square plot of land that is 209 feet on each side is about 1 acre. Round 209 feet to the nearest hundred feet. 200 ft

h. Calculation: 7^2, − 1, ÷ 8, + 4, − 4, ÷ 6 1

problem solving Choose an appropriate problem-solving strategy to solve this problem. Colby wants to cover his bulletin board with square sheets of paper that are 1 foot on each side. His bulletin board is 5 feet wide and 3 feet tall. If Colby has already cut 12 squares of paper, how many more squares does he need to cut? Explain how you found your answer. 3 squares; See student work.

3 ft

5 ft

Facts Multiply.

9 × 9 81	1 × 8 8	4 × 4 16	2 × 5 10	7 × 9 63	5 × 5 25	3 × 4 12	4 × 6 24	2 × 9 18	6 × 9 54
6 × 6 36	2 × 7 14	5 × 8 40	3 × 9 27	6 × 8 48	8 × 9 72	2 × 2 4	7 × 8 56	3 × 7 21	7 × 6 42
3 × 6 18	10 × 10 100	2 × 3 6	5 × 6 30	4 × 9 36	3 × 8 24	4 × 7 28	5 × 9 45	0 × 4 0	2 × 6 12
2 × 8 16	4 × 5 20	6 × 7 42	3 × 3 9	5 × 7 35	2 × 4 8	8 × 8 64	3 × 5 15	4 × 8 32	7 × 7 49

Power Up

Facts

Distribute **Power Up G** to students. See answers below.

Count Aloud

Before students begin the Mental Math exercises, do these counting exercises as a class.

Mental Math

Encourage students to share different ways to mentally compute these exercises. Strategies for exercises are listed below.

c. Add 2, Subtract 2

458 + 2 = 460; 33 − 2 = 31;
460 + 31 = 491

Add 30, then Add 3

458 + 30 = 488; 488 + 3 = 491

e. Add $9, then Subtract 1¢

$14.50 + $9.00 = $23.50
$23.50 − $0.01 = $23.49

f. Recall 1 Mile = 5280 Feet

Since 1 mi > 5000 ft, 2 mi > 10,000 ft.

Problem Solving

Refer to **Problem-Solving Strategy Discussion**, p. 513B.

New Concept

Active Learning

A way to introduce today's lesson (in which students will learn to name a fraction of a set) is choose a small group of volunteers to stand in front of the class. Point out that the volunteers represent a set of students, and then ask the seated students questions such as:

"Students with black shoes represent what fraction of the set? What fraction represents the number of students who are wearing sneakers? What fraction of the set has a first name that begins with a vowel?"

Example 1

Error Alert

Be sure to emphasize that whenever we write a fraction to represent a part of a set, the denominator represents the total number of members in the set, and the numerator represents the number of members that are being named. In this example, the numerator names the number of triangles that are not shaded.

Example 2

Extend The Example

Ask your advanced learners to name the fraction of the class that the boys represent. Then ask what fraction represents the entire class. $\frac{13}{25}$, $\frac{25}{25}$

Lesson Practice

Guided Practice

Use these problems as guided practice to check the students' understanding of today's concept.

Problems a and b

Before students solve each problem, ask:

"How many members altogether are in this set?"

"What part of the set are we being asked to name?"

Problem c

"What number should we write for the denominator of the fraction? Explain why you named that number." 27; The denominator represents the total number of students in the set.

Problems a–d

Error Alert

Remind students that the denominator is the bottom number of a fraction.

(continued)

New Concept

Thinking Skills

Discuss

How can we check the answer?

Sample: Subtract the fraction of the set that is not shaded $\left(\frac{4}{7}\right)$ from a fraction representing the whole set $\left(\frac{7}{7}\right)$ and compare.

There are seven circles in the set below. Three of the circles are shaded. The fraction of the set that is shaded is $\frac{3}{7}$.

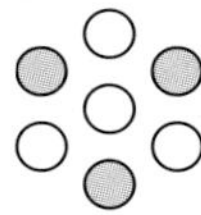

$\frac{3}{7}$ Three circles are shaded. There are seven circles in all.

The total number of members in the set is the denominator (bottom number) of the fraction. The number of members named is the numerator (top number) of the fraction.

Example 1

What fraction of the triangles is not shaded?

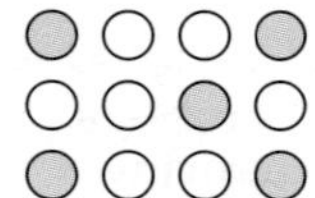

The denominator of the fraction is 9, because there are 9 triangles in all.
The numerator is 5, because 5 of the 9 triangles are not shaded.
So the fraction of triangles that are not shaded is $\frac{5}{9}$.

Thinking Skills

Verify

How can we check the answer?

Sample: Subtract the fraction of the set that is shaded $\left(\frac{4}{9}\right)$ from a fraction representing the whole set $\left(\frac{9}{9}\right)$ and compare.

Example 2

In a class of 25 students, there are 12 girls and 13 boys. What fraction of the class is girls?

Twelve of the 25 students in the class are girls. So the fraction of the class that is girls is $\frac{12}{25}$.

Lesson Practice

a. What fraction of the set is shaded? $\frac{5}{12}$

b. What fraction of the set is not shaded? $\frac{6}{7}$

c. In a class of 27 students, there are 14 girls and 13 boys. What fraction of the class is boys? $\frac{13}{27}$

d. In the word ALABAMA, what fraction of the letters are A's? $\frac{4}{7}$

English Learners

Say, ***"The word set has many meanings and uses, such as a set of dishes. In mathematics, set refers to a group of things that are thought of or grouped together."***

Explain that some examples of **sets** are collections, clusters, and series.

Ask students for examples of things that come in or are thought of as **sets.** Samples: a set of china, a set of ideas, a checkers set

Inclusion

Use this strategy if the student displays:

- Difficulty with Large Group Instruction.
- Difficulty with Abstract Processing

Fraction of a Set (Individual)

Materials: paper

- Tell students to draw 5 equal triangles on their paper. Ask, ***"How many shapes are in your set?"*** 5
- Tell students to shade 3 of the triangles. Ask, ***"How many triangles in the set are shaded?"*** 3

  Tell students that the fraction of triangles shaded is $\frac{3}{5}$.
- Have students draw 7 small circles on their paper and shade 3. Ask, ***"What fraction of circles in the set are shaded?"*** $\frac{3}{7}$

Written Practice

Distributed and Integrated

▸ **1.** (71) **Multiple Choice** To prepare for a move to a new building, the employees of a library spent an entire week packing books in boxes. On Monday, the employees packed 30 books in each of 32 boxes. How many books did those boxes contain? B

A 9600 books **B** 960 books **C** 320 books **D** 350 books

2. (13) The movie was 3 hours long. If it started at 11:10 a.m., at what time did it end? 2:10 p.m.

3. (15, 22) **Explain** Jonathan is reading a 212-page book. If he has finished 135 pages, how many pages does he still have to read? Explain why your answer is reasonable. 77 pages; sample: I used rounding; Round 212 and 135 to 140 and 210 − 140 = 70, which is close to 77.

4. (74) Khalil, Julian, and Elijah each scored one third of the team's 42 points. They each scored how many points? 14 points

5. (40) **Estimate** A family has $4182 in a savings account. Round the number of dollars in the account to the nearest thousand. $4000

▸ ***6.** (28, 51, 52) **Explain** The shirt was priced at $16.98. The tax was $1.02. Sam paid the clerk $20. How much money should Sam get back? Explain your thinking. $2.00; sample: I found the total cost of the shirt. Then I subtracted the total cost from the amount paid.

***7.** (77) What fraction of the letters in the following word are I's? $\frac{7}{34}$

S U P E R C A L I F R A G I L I S T I C E X P I A L I D O C I O U S

▸ ***8.** (76) **Analyze** Use the information below to answer parts **a–c.**

In the first 8 games of this season, the Rio Hondo football team won 6 games and lost 2 games. They won their next game by a score of 24 to 20. The team will play 12 games in all.

a. In the first nine games of the season, how many games did Rio Hondo win? 7 games

b. Rio Hondo won its ninth game by how many points? 4 points

c. What is the greatest number of games Rio Hondo could win this season? 10 games

Math Background

There can be more than one fraction name for a part of a set. For example, three out of nine squares are shaded, so $\frac{3}{9}$ of the squares are shaded. Six of the nine squares are not shaded so $\frac{6}{9}$ of the nine squares are not shaded.

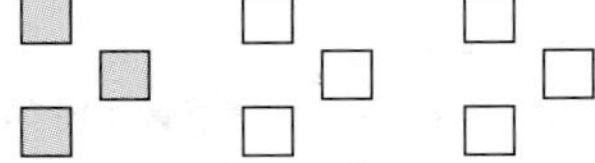

We can divide the set into three equal groups. The squares in one of those groups are shaded, so $\frac{1}{3}$ of the squares are shaded. The squares in two of the groups are not shaded, so $\frac{2}{3}$ of the squares are not shaded.

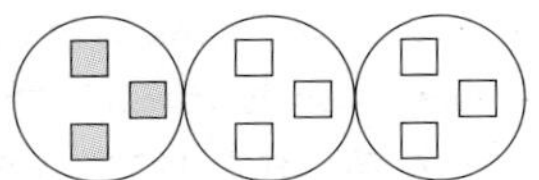

Alternative Approach: Using Manipulatives

To help students understand the concept of fraction of a set, have them use two-color counters to model problems. Have students show that $\frac{5}{8}$ of a set is shaded by counting out a total of 8 counters and using the red side of the counter to show that 5 of the set are shaded. Ask:

"What fraction of the set is not shaded?" $\frac{3}{8}$ is not red.

Have students model other examples of finding a fraction of a set.

New Concept (Continued)

Closure

The questions below help assess the concepts taught in this lesson.

"When we write a fraction to represent part of a set, what does the denominator of the fraction represent?" The total number of members in the set

"What does the numerator of the fraction represent?" The number of members that are being named

"In a set of 8 circles, 5 circles are red and 3 circles are green. What fraction of the set is red?" $\frac{5}{8}$

"What fraction of the letters in your name are vowels?" See student work.

Written Practice

Math Conversations

Independent Practice and Discussions to Increase Understanding

Problem 1 Multiple Choice

Test-Taking Strategy

Point out that an estimate can sometimes be used in place of an exact answer to solve a problem. After students understand that multiplication is used to find the number of books that were packed on Monday, ask them to estimate the number by rounding 32 to 30 and naming the product of 30 × 30 using only mental math. (We write two zeros to the right of the product of 3 × 3.) Then have the students compare the estimate to the various answer choices to see that choice **B** only reasonable answer.

Problem 6 Explain

Before solving the problem, ask:

"What is the amount of tax?" $1.02

"How will the amount of tax affect the cost of the shirt?" The amount of tax will increase the cost of the shirt.

"What is a reasonable estimate of the cost of the shirt, including tax?" $17 + $1, or $18

"What is a reasonable estimate of the amount of change Sam should receive?" $20 − $18, or $2

(continued)

Written Practice *(Continued)*

Math Conversations *(cont.)*

Problem 8 (Analyze)

Before students answer the question from part **a**, ask:

"What information in the problem will we use to find the number of games the team won?" the results of the first eight games and the result of the next game

Ask a similar question before students solve part **b** and part **c**.

Problems 17 and 19

Before students complete any arithmetic, ask them to name the place that the first digit in the quotient will be in, and to explain how they know. The first digit will be in the tens place because the divisor is greater than the digit in the hundreds place.

Problem 25b (Analyze)

Extend the Problem

Ask your students:

"What does it mean when one rectangle is similar to another?" The lengths and widths of the similar rectangle are proportional to the given rectangle.

Problem 30 (Analyze)

Extend the Problem

Challenge all of your students with this question:

"Is Point B closer to one-half or to one whole? Explain how you know." Closer to one whole; sample: The number halfway between $\frac{1}{2}$ and 1 is 0.75; Since $0.76 > 0.75$, 0.76 is closer to 1 than to 0.5.

Errors and Misconceptions

Problem 8b

Students must infer that the phrase "their next game" in the second sentence represents the ninth game played because the first sentence describes the first eight games that were played.

Problem 25b

Make sure students recognize that all of the sides of the rectangle are to be twice as long as the rectangle in part **a**.

Problem 28

Watch for opportunities to remind students that we can produce ordered pairs by substituting numbers for x and solving for y.

9. (23, 26) Compare: $3 \times 4 \times 5 \; (=) \; 5 \times 4 \times 3$

10. (6, 8) $m - 137 = 257$ 394

11. (8) $n + 137 = 257$ 120

12. (45) $1.45 + 2.4 + 0.56 + 7.6$ 12.01

13. (9, 45) $5.75 - (3.12 + 0.5)$ 2.13

14. (71) 38×50 = 1900

15. (59) 472×9 = 4248

16. (59) $\$6.09 \times 6$ = \$36.54

▸ ***17.** (72) $9\overline{)892}$ 99 R 1

***18.** (72) $4\overline{)286}$ 71 R 2

▸ ***19.** (72) $3\overline{)109}$ 36 R 1

20. (75) $121 \div 3$ 40 R 1

21. (75) $122 \div 4$ 30 R 2

***22.** (75) $7\overline{)566}$ 80 R 6

23. (34, 65) $9^2 = 9n$ 9

24. (34, 64, 65) $5w = 5 \times 10^2$ 100

***25.** (20, 42) **a.** (Model) Use a ruler to find the perimeter of the rectangle at right in millimeters. 60 mm

▸ **b.** (Analyze) Draw a rectangle that is similar to the rectangle in part **a** and whose sides are twice as long. What is the perimeter in centimeters of the rectangle you drew? 12 centimeters

***26.** (37, 63) (Evaluate) Simplify each expression when $n = 8$.

a. $82 - 88 \div n$ 71

b. $6 \times (22 + n) - 5$ 175

***27.** (64, Inv. 7) (Evaluate) If $y = 2x + 9$, then what is y when $x = 1, 2,$ and 3? 11, 13, 15

***28.** (Inv. 7) (Represent) Write three ordered pairs for the equation in problem **27.** Then use **Lesson Activity 8** to graph the ordered pairs. See student work

***29.** (73) (Generalize) Use this table to write a formula that can be used to convert any number of quarts to cups. Use q for quarts and c for cups. $4q = c$ or $c = 4q$

Quarts	1	2	3	4	5
Cups	4	8	12	16	20

▸ ***30.** (43) (Analyze) What decimal number names the point marked B on this number line? 0.76

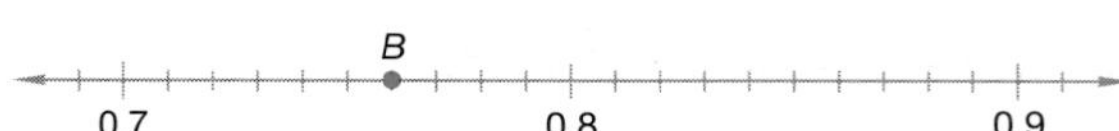

Looking Forward

Finding a fraction of a set prepares students for:

- **Investigation 8,** investigating equivalent fractions.
- **Lesson 89,** renaming and modeling mixed numbers and improper fractions.
- **Lesson 92,** comparing and ordering fractions and decimals.
- **Lesson 94,** solving two-step problems that involve a fraction of a group.
- **Lesson 98,** identifying and writing fractions equal to 1 and to $\frac{1}{2}$.
- **Lesson 99,** changing improper fractions to whole or mixed numbers.
- **Lesson 100,** adding and subtracting fractions with common denominators.
- **Lesson 106,** writing the reduced form of a fraction.
- **Lessons 111–113,** simplifying and renaming fractions, and finding a common denominator.

Planning & Preparation

• Measuring Turns

Objectives

- Describe the amount and the direction of a turn.
- Demonstrate a turn for specific number of degrees.

Prerequisite Skills

- Describing transformations of a figure.
- Using translations, reflections, and rotations to change the position of a figure in quadrant I of the coordinate plane.

Materials

Instructional Masters

- Power Up G Worksheet

Manipulative Kit

- Protractors, clock*

Teacher-provided materials

- Scissors, unlined paper

**optional*

California Mathematics Content Standards

MG 3.0, 3.3 Identify congruent figures.

MG 3.0, 3.5 Know the definitions of a right angle, an acute angle, and an obtuse angle. Understand that 90°, 180°, 270°, and 360° are associated, respectively, with $\frac{1}{4}$, $\frac{1}{2}$, $\frac{3}{4}$, and full turns.

MR 3.0, 3.2 Note the method of deriving the solution and demonstrate a conceptual understanding of the derivation by solving similar problems.

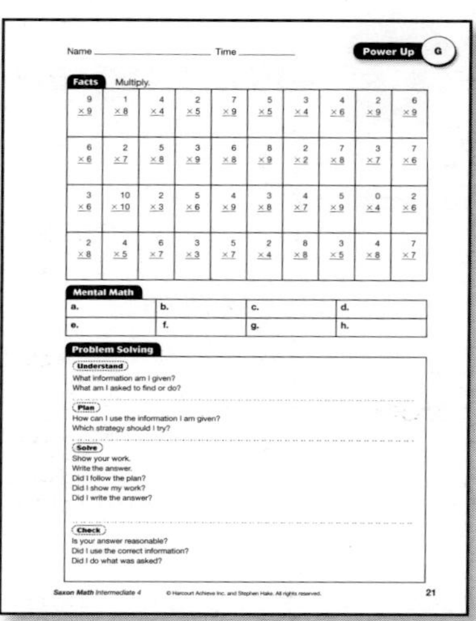
Name ______________ Time ________ **Power Up G**

Facts Multiply.

9 × 9	1 × 8	4 × 4	2 × 5	7 × 9	5 × 5	3 × 4	4 × 6	2 × 9	6 × 9
6 × 6	2 × 7	5 × 8	3 × 9	6 × 8	8 × 9	2 × 2	7 × 8	3 × 7	7 × 6
3 × 6	10 × 10	2 × 3	5 × 6	4 × 9	3 × 8	4 × 7	5 × 9	0 × 4	2 × 6
2 × 8	4 × 5	6 × 7	3 × 3	5 × 7	2 × 4	8 × 8	3 × 5	4 × 8	7 × 7

Mental Math

a.	b.	c.	d.
e.	f.	g.	h.

Problem Solving

Understand
What information am I given?
What am I asked to find or do?

Plan
How can I use the information I am given?
Which strategy should I try?

Solve
Show your work.
Write the answer.
Did I follow the plan?
Did I show my work?
Did I write the answer?

Check
Is your answer reasonable?
Did I use the correct information?
Did I do what was asked?

Saxon Math Intermediate 4 © Harcourt Achieve Inc. and Stephen Hake. All rights reserved. 21

Power Up G Worksheet

Reaching All Special Needs Students

Special Education Students	At-Risk Students	English Learners	Advanced Learners
• Inclusion (TM) • Adaptations for Saxon Math	• Error Alert (TM) • Reteaching Masters • Refresher Lessons for California Standards	• English Learners (TM) • Developing Academic Language (TM) • English Learner Handbook	• Extend the Problem (TM) • Online Activities

TM=Teacher's Manual

Developing Academic Language

New	**Maintained**	**English Learner**
clockwise	congruent	counterclockwise
counterclockwise		
full turn		
half turn		
quarter turn		

Problem Solving Discussion

Problem

Robby is mailing an envelope that weighs 6 ounces. The postage rates are 39¢ for the first ounce and 24¢ for each additional ounce. If Robby pays the postal clerk $2.00 for postage, how much money should he get back?

Focus Strategies

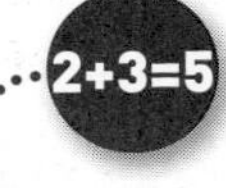

Write a Number Sentence or Equation

Use Logical Reasoning

Understand *Understand the problem.*

"What information are we given?"

1. Robby is mailing an envelope that weighs 6 ounces.
2. Postage rates are 39¢ for the first ounce, and 24¢ for each additional ounce.
3. Robby pays the postal clerk $2.00 for postage.

"What are we asked to do?"

We are asked to find the amount of change Robby should receive.

Plan *Make a plan.*

"How can we use the information we know to solve the problem?"

First, we need to find the total postage. Then we will subtract the total postage from $2.00 to find the change Robby should receive.

Solve *Carry out the plan.*

"How much does the first ounce of postage cost?"

39¢

"How many ounces more than 1 ounce does Robby's envelope weigh?"

Robby's envelope weighs 6 ounces total, so there are 5 ounces of additional postage to pay.

"How much does each additional ounce of postage cost?"

24¢

"What is a number sentence that describes the total postage?"

39¢ + (5 × 24¢) = 159¢ or $1.59

"How much change should Robby receive if he gives the clerk $2?"

The change should be $2.00 − $1.59, which equals $0.41 or 41¢.

Check *Look back.*

"Is our answer reasonable?"

We know that our answer is reasonable because 39¢ is the cost for the first ounce, and $1.20 is the cost for the additional 5 ounces. This is a total of $1.59, which is 41¢ less than $2.00.

"What problem-solving strategies did we use, and how did they help us?"

We *used logical reasoning* to figure how we could find the total postage for the envelope. Then we *wrote number sentences* to calculate the postage and the amount of change Robby should receive from $2.00.

Alternate Strategy
Make or Use a Table, Chart, or Graph

Have students make a table to help them find the postage for the envelope that is being mailed. The table can show the total postage for items with weights of 1 oz through 6 oz. Students can use information from the table to write a number sentence to find the amount of change that Robby should receive (41¢).

LESSON 78

• Measuring Turns

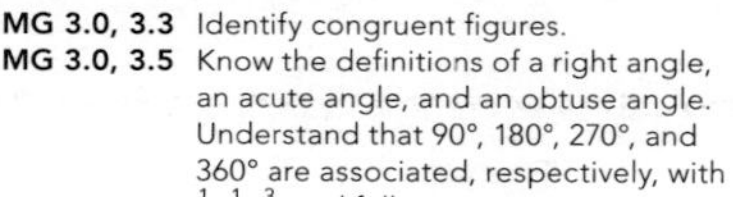

California Mathematics Content Standards

MG 3.0, 3.3 Identify congruent figures.
MG 3.0, 3.5 Know the definitions of a right angle, an acute angle, and an obtuse angle. Understand that 90°, 180°, 270°, and 360° are associated, respectively, with $\frac{1}{4}$, $\frac{1}{2}$, $\frac{3}{4}$, and full turns.
MR 3.0, 3.2 Note the method of deriving the solution and demonstrate a conceptual understanding of the derivation by solving similar problems.

Power Up

facts Power Up G

count aloud Count by fives from 3 to 53.

mental math

a. **Number Sense:** 35 × 100 3500

b. **Number Sense:** Counting by 5's from 5, every number Ramon says ends in 0 or 5. If he counts by 5's from 8, then every number he says ends in which digit? 3 or 8

c. **Fractional Parts:** $\frac{1}{2}$ of $31.00 $15.50

d. **Measurement:** Jenna jogged 3 kilometers. How many meters is that? 3000 m

e. **Money:** The box of cereal cost $4.36. Tiana paid with a $5 bill. How much change should she receive? 64¢

f. **Time:** Rodrigo's school day lasts 7 hours. If Rodrigo attends school Monday through Friday, how many hours is he at school each week? 35 hr

g. **Estimation:** Each CD costs $11.97. Estimate the cost of 4 CDs. $48

h. **Calculation:** $\frac{1}{2}$ of 88, + 11, ÷ 11 5

problem solving Choose an appropriate problem-solving strategy to solve this problem. Robby is mailing an envelope that weighs 6 ounces. The postage rates are 39¢ for the first ounce and 24¢ for each additional ounce. If Robby pays the postal clerk $2.00 for postage, how much money should he get back? 41¢

Facts Multiply.

9 × 9 = 81	1 × 8 = 8	4 × 4 = 16	2 × 5 = 10	7 × 9 = 63	5 × 5 = 25	3 × 4 = 12	4 × 6 = 24	2 × 9 = 18	6 × 9 = 54
6 × 6 = 36	2 × 7 = 14	5 × 8 = 40	3 × 9 = 27	6 × 8 = 48	8 × 9 = 72	2 × 2 = 4	7 × 8 = 56	3 × 7 = 21	7 × 6 = 42
3 × 6 = 18	10 × 10 = 100	2 × 3 = 6	5 × 6 = 30	4 × 9 = 36	3 × 8 = 24	4 × 7 = 28	5 × 9 = 45	0 × 4 = 0	2 × 6 = 12
2 × 8 = 16	4 × 5 = 20	6 × 7 = 42	3 × 3 = 9	5 × 7 = 35	2 × 4 = 8	8 × 8 = 64	3 × 5 = 15	4 × 8 = 32	7 × 7 = 49

Power Up

Facts
Distribute **Power Up G** to students. See answers below.

Count Aloud
Before students begin the Mental Math exercises, do these counting exercises as a class.

Mental Math
Encourage students to share different ways to mentally compute these exercises. Strategies for exercises are listed below.

a. **Multiply Nonzero Digits, Write Zeros**
Write 2 zeros after 35 × 1;
35 × 100 = 3500

c. **Find Half Twice, then Add**
$\frac{1}{2}$ of $30 = $15; $\frac{1}{2}$ of $1 = 50¢;
$15 + 50¢ = $15.50

e. **Subtract $4, then 30¢, then 6¢**
$5 − $4 = $1; $1 − 30¢ = 70¢;
70¢ − 6¢ = 64¢

Count Up from $4.36
$4.36 + 4¢ = $4.40; $4.40 + 60¢ = $5;
4¢ + 60¢ = 64¢

Problem Solving
Refer to **Problem-Solving Strategy Discussion**, p. 517B.

New Concept

Real-World Connection

One way to introduce the lesson is to point out that the word degree (with its symbol °) represents a number of different units in mathematics and science. Two such units that fourth graders learn about are degrees of temperature and degrees of turns. If students find it unusual that the same word is used to represent different units, point out that other languages also use the same word to represent different units. For example, "Grad" in German, "do" in Japanese, "aste" in Finnish, and "stepen" in Bosnian.

Active Learning

As you discuss full, half, and quarter turns, have the students close their textbooks and orient them on their desktops to model clockwise and counterclockwise 360°, 180°, and 90° turns. To complete the turns, some students may find it helpful to imagine their desktop as a clock face.

Activity 1

Perform this activity as a class. To model each turn, have your students begin by facing the same direction.

After the various turns have been completed, make sure students understand the direction of each turn and the number of degrees it represents.

(continued)

As Micah rides a skateboard, we can measure his movements. We might use feet or meters to measure the distance Micah travels. To measure Micah's turns, we may use **degrees.** Just as for temperature measurements, we use the degree symbol (°) to stand for degrees.

If Micah makes a **full turn,** then he has turned 360°. If Micah makes a **half turn,** he has turned 180°. A **quarter turn** is 90°.

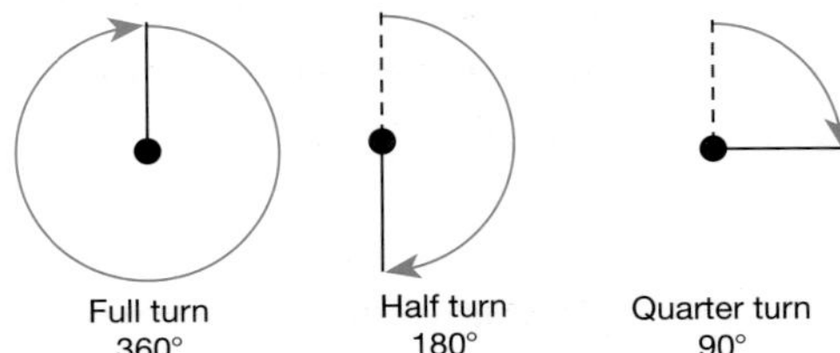

Full turn 360° Half turn 180° Quarter turn 90°

Besides measuring the amount of turn, we may also describe the direction of a turn as **clockwise** or **counterclockwise.**

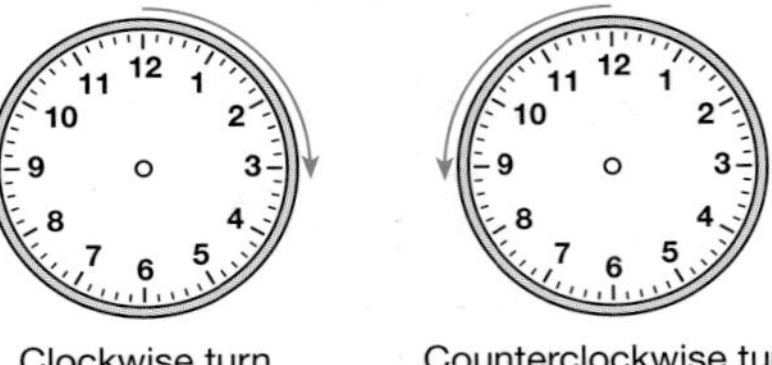

Clockwise turn Counterclockwise turn

For instance, we tighten a screw by turning it clockwise, and we loosen a screw by turning it counterclockwise.

Activity 1

Rotations and Degrees

Stand and perform these activities as a class.

Model Face the front of the room and make a quarter turn to the right.

English Learners

Say, ***"The word counterclockwise means in the direction opposite of clockwise, or the opposite of the way that a clock's hands move. The prefix counter– means against or opposite."***

Ask students to define countermarch. To march against or in the opposite direction of another group of marchers

Math Background

For every counterclockwise rotation, there is an equivalent clockwise rotation and vice-versa. For example, if a figure is rotated 90° counterclockwise, the result is the same as if it had been rotated 270° clockwise. In general, a counterclockwise rotation of n degrees is equivalent to a clockwise rotation of $(360 - n)$ degrees.

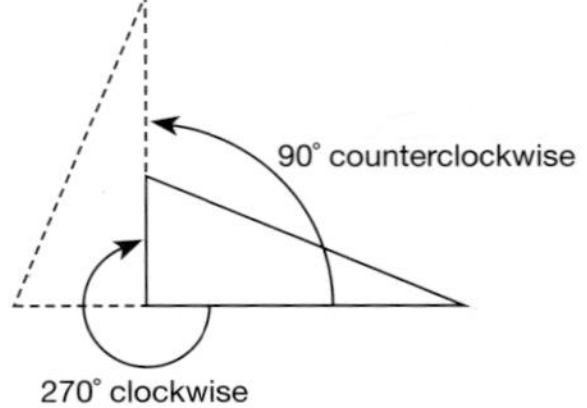

Discuss How many degrees did you turn? Did you turn clockwise or counterclockwise? 90°; clockwise

Return to your original position by turning a quarter turn to the left.

a. How many degrees did you turn? Did you turn clockwise or counterclockwise? 90°; counterclockwise

Face the front of the room and make a half turn either to the right or to the left.

b. How many degrees did you turn? Is everyone facing the same direction? 180°; yes

Start by facing the front. Then make a three quarter turn clockwise.

c. How many degrees did you turn? How many more degrees do you need to turn clockwise in order to face the front? 270°; 90°

Example 1

Mariya and Irina were both facing north. Mariya turned 90° clockwise and Irina turned 270° counterclockwise. After turning, in which directions were the girls facing?

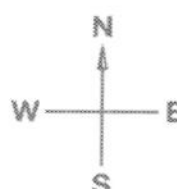

Below we show the turns Mariya and Irina made.

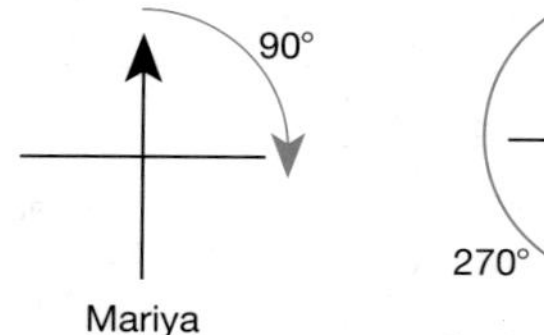

Mariya Irina

After turning 90° clockwise, Mariya was facing east. After turning 270° counterclockwise, Irina was also facing east. (Each quarter turn is 90°, so 270° is three quarters of a full turn.) Both girls were facing **east** after their turns.

New Concept *(Continued)*

Example 1

Active Learning

Invite volunteers to stand and model the turns made by Mariya and Irina. To help students identify the direction of the turns, point out the directions in your classroom that represent north, south, east, and west.

Extend the Example

Invite advanced learners to describe the movements that would be required to move from your classroom to destinations elsewhere on the school grounds. For example, to go outside for recess, students must walk west, and then make a counterclockwise quarter turn (or turn 90° toward the south) and then go out the door.

(continued)

New Concept *(Continued)*

Example 2

Error Alert

Make sure students understand that triangle II will be rotated so that it is on top of triangle I.

Some students may benefit from cutting two congruent triangles from paper, labeling the triangles I and II, and modeling the movement.

(continued)

Example 2

Describe the amount and the direction of a turn about point *A* that would position △II on △I.

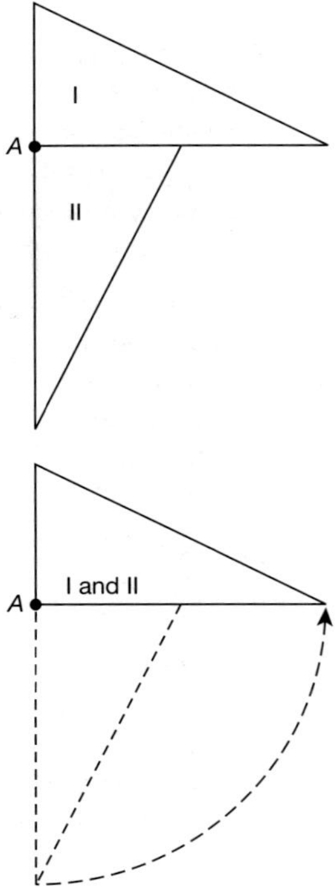

Point A does not move, but the rest of △II is turned to align with △I. One solution is to rotate △II **90° counterclockwise.** The fact that the triangles perfectly match after the rotation shows that they are congruent.

Conclude Describe an alternate way to rotate △II to the position of △I. Sample: Rotate △II 270° clockwise.

Inclusion

Use this strategy if the student displays:

- Difficulty with Large Group Instruction.
- Difficulty with Abstract Processing.

Measuring Turns (Pairs)

Materials: demonstration clock

- Display the clock so that both hands are at 12:00. Tell students they are going to learn about turns using the clock. Move both hands to the 15 minute marker and tell students that this is a 90° turn or quarter turn.
- Move hands back to 12:00 and then show students a half turn or 180° by moving them to the 30 minute marker.
- Finally reposition the clocks at 12:00 and make a full turn or 360° turn by moving the clocks all the way around back to 12:00.
- Have students stand up and face the board. Play a game asking students to turn different amounts: 90°, 180°, 360°, quarter turn, half turn, full turn.

Activity 2

Rotations and Congruence

Materials needed:

- scissors
- unlined paper

One way to show that two figures are congruent is to move one figure to the position of the other figure to see if the two figures perfectly match.

a. Model Fold a sheet of paper in half and cut a shape from the doubled sheet of paper so that two congruent shapes are cut out at the same time. Then position the two figures on your desk so that a rotation is the only movement necessary to move one shape onto the other shape. Perform the rotation to show that the shapes are congruent.

b. Represent On another sheet of paper, draw or trace the two shapes you cut out. Draw the shapes in such a position that a 90° rotation of one shape would move it to the position of the other shape.

Lesson Practice

a. Predict Wakeisha skated east, turned 180° clockwise, and then continued skating. In what direction was Wakeisha skating after the turn? west

Describe each rotation in degrees clockwise or counterclockwise:

b. a quarter turn to the left 90° counterclockwise

c. a full turn to the right 360° clockwise

d. a three quarter turn to the left 270° counterclockwise

e. a half turn to the right 180° clockwise

f. Describe the rotation about point *A* that would position triangle 1 on triangle 2. 180° clockwise or counterclockwise

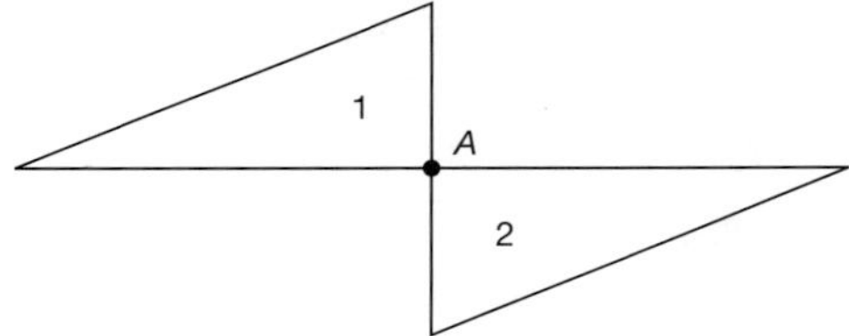

Teacher Tip

You can help your students be successful by teaching all lessons. Do not skip or combine any lessons. The lesson sequence has been carefully planned with the appropriate practice provided in each problem set.

New Concept (Continued)

Activity 2

You might choose to have students work in pairs to complete the activity.

During part **a** of the activity, point out that before one figure is rotated, both figures must be positioned so that they touch in some way. If the figures are positioned so that they do not touch, a movement in addition to a rotation will be needed to position one figure on top of the other.

Extend the Activity

Invite advanced learners to design other rotational activities for their classmates to complete.

Lesson Practice

Guided Practice

Use these problems as guided practice to check the students' understanding of today's concept.

Problem a Predict

Ask your students to stand facing east, and model Wakeisha's movement by turning 180° clockwise.

Problems b–e

Some students may find it helpful to stand and model the turns.

Problem f

Error Alert

Make sure that the answers include both the degree and the direction of the turn.

Invite interested students to trace and cut out the figures to help solve the problem or to check their answers.

Closure

The questions below help assess the concepts taught in this lesson.

"What unit is used to measure turns or rotations?" a degree

"Name three different turns, and name the number of degrees each turn represents." Sample: full turn: 360°; half turn: 180°; quarter turn: 90°

"To turn clockwise, do you move to your right or your left?" To your right

Written Practice

Math Conversations

Independent Practice and Discussions to Increase Understanding

Problem 3

A chin-up is performed by grasping a bar placed above the head, bending the arms, and pulling the body up off the ground until the chin is slightly above the bar.

Problem 5

Before students complete the arithmetic, remind them of the importance of checking their work. Then ask:

"What is a reasonable estimate of the amount of change Melinda should receive? Explain why your estimate is reasonable." Sample: \$10.50; The cost of the book is about \$9 and the tax is about 50¢, so a reasonable estimate is \$20 − \$9.50 or \$10.50.

Extend the Problem

"Using the fewest number of bills and coins possible, which bills and coins would be used to give Melinda her change?" One \$10 bill, one half dollar, and one penny (or one \$10 bill, two quarters, and one penny)

Problem 6a

"What is a factor of a number?" A factor is a number that divides another number evenly (the remainder is zero).

"How is a prime number different than a composite number?" A prime number has exactly two factors, itself and 1; A composite number has more than two factors.

Problem 6b Explain

Extend the Problem

Ask students to name all of the factors of 15. 1, 3, 5, 15

Problem 10 Explain

Point out that 364 rounded to the nearest hundred is 400, 364 rounded to the nearest ten is 360, and both 400 and 360 are not multiples of 7. Then ask:

"Explain how we can make an estimate of the exact answer that does not involve rounding." Sample: Since 7 is a factor of 35, change 364 to 350, then divide; A reasonable estimate of the exact answer is 350 ÷ 7 or 50.

After students find the exact answer, ask them to decide its reasonableness by comparing it to the estimate.

(continued)

Written Practice

Distributed and Integrated

*1. *(RF12)* If it is not a leap year, what is the total number of days in January, February, and March? 90 days

2. *(39)* A tailor made each of 12 children a pair of pants and 2 shirts. How many pieces of clothing did the tailor make? 36 pieces of clothing

► 3. *(16)* Burke did seven more chin-ups than Ariel did. If Burke did eighteen chin-ups, how many chin-ups did Ariel do? 11 chin-ups

4. *(60)* Kadeeja drove 200 miles on 8 gallons of gas. Her car averaged how many miles on each gallon of gas? 25 miles

► *5. *(28, 52)* Melinda paid the clerk \$20.00 for a book that was priced at \$8.95. The tax was 54¢. How much money should she get back? \$10.51

► *6. *(56)* **a.** Which two prime numbers are factors of 15? 3 and 5

► **b.** **Explain** Is 15 a prime number? Why or why not? No; sample: Fifteen has two factors other than 1 and 15.

7. *(20, 42, 50)* If each side of an octagon is 1 centimeter long, what is the octagon's perimeter in millimeters? 80 mm

8. *(74)* **Represent** One third of the 18 marbles were blue. How many of the marbles were blue? Draw a picture to solve the problem. 6 marbles

8. 18 marbles

$\frac{1}{3}$ were blue.	6 marbles
$\frac{2}{3}$ were not blue.	6 marbles
	6 marbles

*9. *(58, Inv. 7)* **a.** **Analyze** The Mendez family hiked 15 miles in 1 day. At that rate, how many miles would they hike in 5 days? Make a table to solve the problem. 75 miles

b. **Formulate** Write an equation to represent the data in the table. number of days × 15 = miles, or $15d$ = miles

9.

Day	Miles
1	15
2	30
3	45
4	60
5	75

►*10. *(53, 69)* **Explain** Mylah picked 364 peaches in 7 days. She picked an average of how many peaches each day? Explain why your answer is reasonable. 52; sample: 7 × 52 = 364

***11. a.** (Inv. 4, 77) **Analyze** Zachary did 100 push-ups last week. He did 59 of those push-ups last Wednesday. What fraction of the 100 push-ups did Zachary do last Wednesday? $\frac{59}{100}$

b. **Represent** Write the answer to part **a** as a decimal number. Then use words to name the number. 0.59; fifty-nine hundredths

***12.** (73) **Generalize** Use this table to write a formula that can be used to convert any number of milliliters to liters. Use *l* for liters and *n* for milliliters. $1000l = n$ or $n = 1000l$

Liters	1	2	3	4	5
Milliliters	1000	2000	3000	4000	5000

13. (9, 45) $4.56 - (2.3 + 1.75)$ 0.51

14. (Inv. 3, 64) $\sqrt{36} + n = 7 \times 8$ 50

15. (65) $3 \times 6 \times 3^2$ 162

16. (Inv. 3, 59) $462 \times \sqrt{9}$ 1386

17. (Inv. 3, 65) $7^2 - \sqrt{49}$ 42

18. (71) 36×50 1800

19. (59) $\$4.76 \times 7$ \$33.32

20. (4) $4 + 3 + 2 + 7 + 6 + 8 + n = 47$ 17

21. (69) $\frac{114}{2}$ 57

▸*22. (72) $5\overline{)182}$ 36 R 2

***23.** (75) $2\overline{)161}$ 80 R 1

24. (34, 75) $2n = \$110$ \$55

25. (75) $5\overline{)400}$ 80

▸*26. (75) $\frac{490}{7}$ 70

▸*27. (Inv. 4) Write 0.32 as a fraction using words. $\frac{32}{100}$; thirty-two hundredths

28. (66) Find the perimeter and area of this square:
12 yd; 9 sq. yd

3 yards

3 yards

Written Practice (Continued)

Math Conversations (cont.)

Problems 22 and 26

Before students begin the arithmetic for each problem, invite a volunteer to explain how multiplication and addition can be used to check a quotient. Add the remainder to the product of the divisor and the whole number

…hen compare

…ecimal number
…t of the decimal
…ths

…number in
…hat number
…nator of that

(continued)

Written Practice (Continued)

Math Conversations *(cont.)*

Problem 29 **Represent**

Extend the Problem

To challenge your students, ask:

"Suppose that the letter E was rotated $\frac{1}{8}$ of a turn instead of a quarter turn. How many degrees would the letter have been rotated? Explain how you know." 45°; sample: A full turn is 360°, and we divide by 8 to find $\frac{1}{8}$; 360° ÷ 8 = 45°

Errors and Misconceptions

Problem 1

It is a misconception for students to assume that every month of February has 28 days. When solving problems of this nature, students should generalize that in a non-leap year, February has 28 days, and in a leap year, February has 29 days. Discuss this generalization with students and lead them to generalize the number of days in a year. Every common year has 365 days; Every leap year has 366 days.

Problem 11

Make sure students do not make an effort to reduce $\frac{59}{100}$; It is a fraction in simplest form.

Challenge advanced learners with the following problem extension:

"When Christina works on a holiday, Mrs. Long pays her double the usual rate. If Christina works on the next holiday, how much will she earn for babysitting 6 hours? How much will she earn for walking Mrs. Long's dog 4 times?" $66; $10

▸ * **29.** (78) **Represent** Draw the capital letter *E* rotated 90° clockwise.

E

30. (17) **Estimate** Which angles in this figure look like right angles? Angle *A*, angle *B*

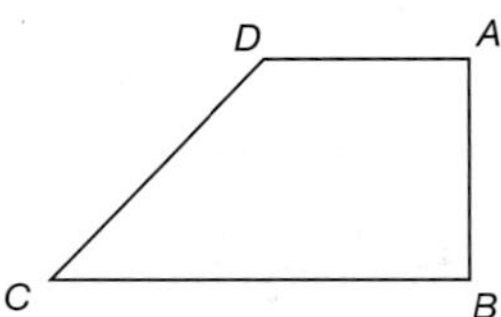

Real-World Connection

Christina earns money by doing different kinds of work for her neighbor, Mrs. Long. Refer to the tables below.

Money Earned by Babysitting

Hours	Dollars
1	5.50
2	11
3	16.50

Money Earned by Dog Walking

Dogs	Dollars
1	1.25
2	2.50
3	3.75

Money Earned by Car Washing

Cars	Dollars
1	7
2	14
3	21

a. If Christina baby sits for Mrs. Long for 4 hours, how much money will she earn? $22

b. Mrs. Long owns 2 cars. If Christina washes Mrs. Long's cars twice this month, how much will she earn? $28

c. Mrs. Long owns 1 dog. If Christina walks Mrs. Long's dog every day, how much will she earn in 1 week? $8.75

524 **Saxon Math** *Intermediate 4*

Looking Forward

Describing the amount and the direction of a turn and demonstrating a turn for specific number of degrees prepares students for:

- **Lesson 81,** classifying triangles by angle measures and the length of its sides.
- **Lesson 82,** identifying and drawing lines of symmetry.
- **Lesson 90,** classifying quadrilaterals.
- **Lesson 96,** classifying geometric solids by their vertices, edges, and faces.
- **Lesson 97,** making three-dimensional models of rectangular and triangular prisms.
- **Lesson 108,** identifying the attributes of geometric solids.
- **Lesson 109,** describing the attributes of pyramids.
- **Lesson 114,** determining the perimeter and area of complex figures.

Planning & Preparation

• Division with Three-Digit Answers

California Mathematics Content Standards

NS 3.0, 3.2 Demonstrate an understanding of, and the ability to use, standard algorithms for multiplying a multidigit number by a two-digit number and for dividing a multidigit number by a one-digit number; use relationships between them to simplify computations and to check results.

NS 3.0, 3.4 Solve problems involving division of multidigit numbers by one-digit numbers.

SDAP 1.0, 1.3 Interpret one- and two-variable data graphs to answer questions about a situation.

Objectives

- Solve division problems with three-digit answers.
- Divide dollars and cents by a one-digit whole number.
- Solve word problems involving multi-digit division.

Prerequisite Skills

- Writing fact families for multiplication and division.
- Showing division three different ways.
- Using multiplication to divide.

Materials

Instructional Masters

- Power Up G Worksheet

Manipulative Kit

- Rulers, two-color counters, base ten blocks*

Teacher-provided materials

- Place-value workmat*

**optional*

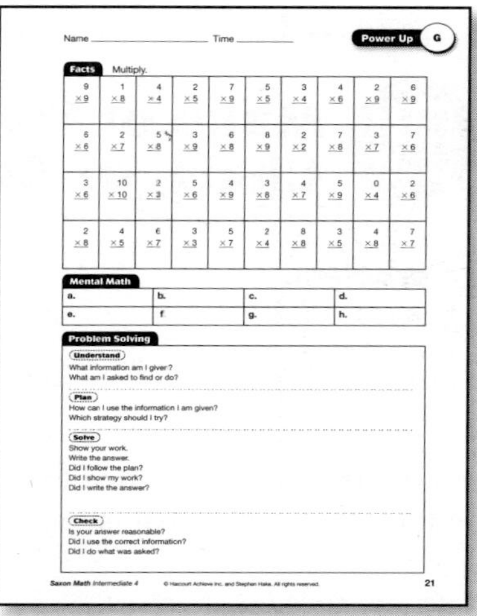
Power Up G
Facts
Multiply.
Mental Math
Problem Solving
Understand
Plan
Solve
Check

Power Up G Worksheet

Universal Access

Reaching All Special Needs Students

Special Education Students	At-Risk Students	English Learners	Advanced Learners
• Inclusion (TM) • Adaptations for Saxon Math	• Error Alert (TM) • Reteaching Masters • Refresher Lessons for California Standards	• English Learners (TM) • Developing Academic Language (TM) • English Learner Handbook	• Extend the Example (TM) • Extend the Problem (TM) • Online Activities

TM=Teacher's Manual

Developing Academic Language

Maintained	English Learner
decimal point	goal
remainder	

Problem Solving Discussion

Problem

The bar graph at right shows the number of students in each of the three fourth-grade classes at Mayfair School. If seven new fourth graders were to start attending the school, how could they be assigned to the classes to make each class equal in size?

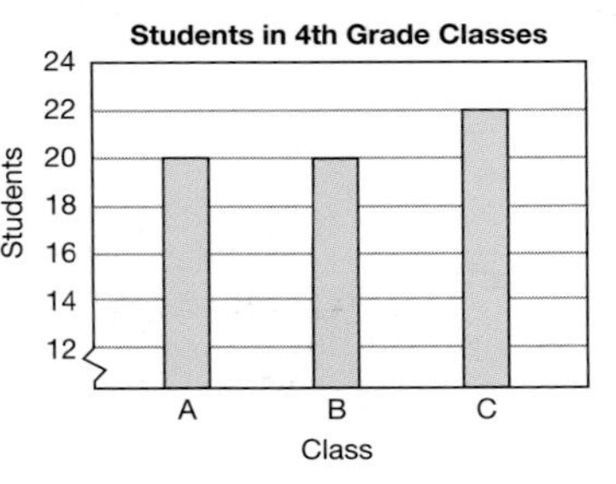

Focus Strategy

Make or Use a Table, Chart, or Graph

Understand *Understand the problem.*

"What information are we given?"

We are shown a bar graph of the number of fourth graders in Classes A, B, and C.

"What are we asked to do?"

We are asked to find how many students should be added to each of the classes if seven new fourth graders came to the school. The goal is to make each class equal in size.

Plan *Make a plan.*

"How can we use the graph to help us solve the problem?"

We need to find how many students are in each class. We do this by reading the tops of the bars against the vertical scale.

"Once we know how many students are in each class, how can we find the number of students that should be added to each class?"

We can try different ways to assign the seven students to the classes until we find a way that makes each class equal in size.

Solve *Carry out the plan.*

"According to the graph, how many students are in each of the three classes?"

Class A has 20 students, Class B has 20 students, and Class C has 22 students.

"How many more students are needed in Classes A and B to make their size equal to Class C?"

If two more students are added to each of Class A and B, those classes would have 22 students (the same number as Class C). Two more students for each of those classes is 4 students altogether.

"If four of the seven new students are added to Classes A and B to make them equal to Class C, there would still be three more new students. How can those three students be assigned to the classes?"

Each class could take one more student, raising each class size to 23 students.

Check *Look back.*

"How many students should be added to each class to make the sizes equal?"

Three students should be added to each of Classes A and B, and one student should be added to Class C.

LESSON 79

• Division with Three-Digit Answers

California Mathematics Content Standards

NS 3.0, 3.2 Demonstrate an understanding of, and the ability to use, standard algorithms for multiplying a multidigit number by a two-digit number and for dividing a multidigit number by a one-digit number; use relationships between them to simplify computations and to check results.

NS 3.0, 3.4 Solve problems involving division of multidigit numbers by one-digit numbers.

facts Power Up G

count aloud Count by fives from 4 to 54.

mental math Before adding, make one number larger and the other number smaller in problems **a–c.**

a. Number Sense: 48 + 37 85

b. Number Sense: 62 + 29 91

c. Number Sense: 135 + 47 182

d. Fractional Part: $\frac{1}{2}$ of \$20 \$10

e. Fractional Part: $\frac{1}{4}$ of \$20 \$5

f. Fractional Part: $\frac{1}{10}$ of \$20 \$2

g. Estimation: Mario earns \$8.95 for each hour he works. About how much does Mario earn for working 6 hours? \$54

h. Calculation: $\sqrt{64}$, × 3, + 1, × 2, + 98 148

problem solving Choose an appropriate problem-solving strategy to solve this problem. The bar graph below shows the number of students in each of the three fourth grade classes at Mayfair School. If seven new fourth graders were to start attending the school, how could they be assigned to the classes to make each class equal in size?

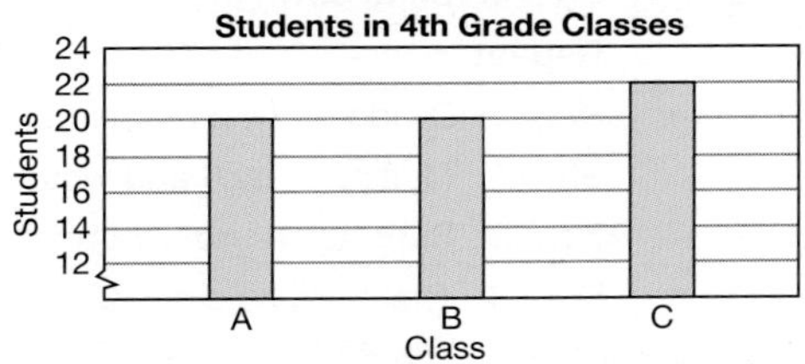

Add 3 students each to Classes A and B, and add 1 student to Class C.

Facts Multiply.

9 × 9 = 81	1 × 8 = 8	4 × 4 = 16	2 × 5 = 10	7 × 9 = 63	5 × 5 = 25	3 × 4 = 12	4 × 6 = 24	2 × 9 = 18	6 × 9 = 54
6 × 6 = 36	2 × 7 = 14	5 × 8 = 40	3 × 9 = 27	6 × 8 = 48	8 × 9 = 72	2 × 2 = 4	7 × 8 = 56	3 × 7 = 21	7 × 6 = 42
3 × 6 = 18	10 × 10 = 100	2 × 3 = 6	5 × 6 = 30	4 × 9 = 36	3 × 8 = 24	4 × 7 = 28	5 × 9 = 45	0 × 4 = 0	2 × 6 = 12
2 × 8 = 16	4 × 5 = 20	6 × 7 = 42	3 × 3 = 9	5 × 7 = 35	2 × 4 = 8	8 × 8 = 64	3 × 5 = 15	4 × 8 = 32	7 × 7 = 49

Power Up

Facts

Distribute **Power Up G** to students. See answers below.

Count Aloud

Before students begin the Mental Math exercises, do these counting exercises as a class.

Mental Math

Encourage students to share different ways to mentally compute these exercises. Strategies for exercises are listed below.

c. Subtract 3, Add 3

135 − 3 = 132; 47 + 3 = 50;
132 + 50 = 182

Add 50, then Subtract 3

135 + 50 = 185; 185 − 3 = 182

e. Divide by 4

$\frac{1}{4}$ of \$20 = \$20 ÷ 4 = \$5

Find $\frac{1}{2}$ of $\frac{1}{2}$ of \$20

$\frac{1}{2}$ of \$20 = \$10; $\frac{1}{2}$ of \$10 = \$5

Problem Solving

Refer to **Problem-Solving Strategy Discussion,** p. 525B.

New Concept

Instruction

List the four steps of the division algorithm on the board or overhead, or display them on a classroom bulletin board. Invite volunteers to describe or explain what happens during each step.

Example 1

As you demonstrate the solution, include the words "divide," "subtract," "compare," and "bring down" in your explanation.

Generalize

Each time you demonstrate the "bring down" step, emphasize the fact that each time a digit is brought down from the dividend, a digit must be written in the quotient.

Extend the Example

After you discuss how multiplication and addition can be used to check the answer, invite one or more advanced learners to explain or demonstrate how estimation can be used. Sample: The divisor is 3; 3 × 200 = 600 and 3 × 300 = 900; Since 794 is between 600 and 900, the quotient will be between 200 and 300.

(continued)

New Concept

We have practiced division problems that have two-digit answers. In this lesson we will practice division problems that have three-digit answers. Remember that the pencil-and-paper method we have used for dividing has four steps.

Step 1: Divide. (÷)

Step 2: Multiply. (×)

Step 3: Subtract. (−)

Step 4: Bring down. (↓)

For each step we write a number. When we finish Step 4, we go back to Step 1 and repeat the steps until no digits remain to bring down.

Example 1

Thinking Skills

Discuss

Why do we write the digit 2 in the hundreds place of the quotient?

We are dividing 7 hundreds.

Divide: $3\overline{)794}$

Step 1: Divide $3\overline{)7}$ and write "2."

Step 2: Multiply 2 by 3 and write "6."

Step 3: Subtract 6 from 7 and write "1."

Step 4: Bring down the 9 to make 19.

Repeat:

Step 1: Divide 19 by 3 and write "6."

Step 2: Multiply 6 by 3 and write "18."

Step 3: Subtract 18 from 19 and write "1."

Step 4: Bring down the 4 to make 14.

Repeat:

Step 1: Divide 14 by 3 and write "4."

Step 2: Multiply 4 by 3 and write "12."

Step 3: Subtract 12 from 14 and write "2."

Step 4: There are no digits to bring down. We are finished dividing. We write "2" as the remainder for a final answer of **264 R 2.**

```
   264 R 2
3)794
  6
  19
  18
   14
   12
    2

Check:
  264
×   3
  792

  792
+   2
  794
```


Math Background

Below is an expanded version of the division algorithm that shows the "partial quotients."

$124 \div 4 = 31$

$100 \div 4 = 25$

$20 \div 4 = 5$

$4 \div 4 = 1$

$25 + 5 + 1 = 31$

To divide dollars and cents by a whole number, we divide the digits just like we divide whole numbers. *The decimal point in the answer is placed directly above the decimal point inside the division box.* We write a dollar sign in front of the answer.

Example 2

Thinking Skills

Justify

How can we check the answer?

Multiply $2.80 by 3 and compare the product to the dividend.

The total cost of three identical items is $8.40. What is the cost of each item?

The decimal point in the quotient is directly above the decimal point in the dividend. We write a dollar sign in front of the quotient.

The cost of each item is **$2.80.**

```
  $2.80
3)$8.40
  6
  2 4
  2 4
    00
    00
     0
```

Example 3

A local company is providing 4245 hats for a town festival. There are 5 different colors of hats and an equal number of each color. How many hats of each color are there?

We divide four-digit numbers the same way we divide three-digit numbers.

First we divide 5)42 Since we are dividing hundreds, we write 8 in the hundreds place of the quotient. Then, we subtract and bring down the 4. We continue to divide, multiply, subtract, and bring down.

There are **849 hats** of each color.

```
   849
5)4245
  40
   24
   20
    45
    45
     0
```

Lesson Practice

a. Copy the diagram at right. Then name the four steps of pencil-and-paper division. See student work; divide, multiply, subtract, bring down

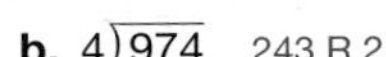

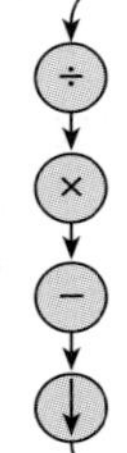

Divide:

b. 4)974 243 R 2

c. $7.95 ÷ 5 $1.59

d. 6)1512 252

e. 8)$50.00 $6.25

Inclusion

Use this strategy if the student displays:

- Difficulty with Multiple Steps.
- Difficulty with Abstract Processing.

Division with Three Digit Answers (Small Group)

Materials: base ten blocks, place-value workmat

- Have students make a place-value workmat by dividing a piece of plain paper vertically into 3 equal parts, with the parts labeled "hundreds," "tens," and "ones." Then have students use counters to show the number 794 on the workmat and have them separate each place value into groups of 3.
- Explain to students that since the hundreds can be separated into 2 groups of 3 with 1 hundred extra, they will need to trade 1 hundred, 9 tens for 19 tens and then separate the 19 tens into groups of 3.
- Have students show that 6 groups of 3 can be made in the tens place with 1 ten extra. They will need to trade 1 ten 4 ones for 14 ones and then divide the 14 ones into groups of 3 and show any extra ones as a remainder.
- Have students count the groups in each place value and record the quotient. 2 hundreds, 6 tens, 4 ones, and 2 extra, or 264 R 2

New Concept (Continued)

Example 2

Error Alert

When dividing a decimal dividend, a common error is to forget to place a decimal point in the quotient. Point out that whenever the divisor is a whole number (such as in Example 2), students can place the decimal point in the quotient *before* starting the arithmetic. (The decimal point is placed directly above the decimal point in the dividend.) Explain that placing the decimal point first will eliminate the error of forgetting to place it after the arithmetic has been completed.

Example 3

This example assumes that the town will receive the same number of each color hat.

Active Learning

As you discuss the solution, emphasize the fact that the first digit in the quotient is written in the hundreds place because the divisor (5) is greater than the first digit in the dividend (4). Then say:

"The first digit in the quotient is in the hundreds place because we cannot divide 4 thousands into 5 equal parts. Describe the regrouping that must be completed in order to place the first digit in the quotient in the hundreds place."

Regroup 4 thousands and 2 hundreds as 42 hundreds. It is possible to divide 42 hundreds into 5 equal groups; There will be 8 hundreds in each group and 2 hundreds left over.

Lesson Practice

Guided Practice

Use these problems as guided practice to check the students' understanding of today's concept.

Problems b–e

Continue to stress the importance of

- correctly placing the first digit in the quotient by comparing the divisor to the first digit in the dividend.
- comparing the subtraction result in Step 3 of the algorithm to the divisor.
- writing a digit in the quotient each time a digit is brought down from the dividend.

Problems b–e

Error Alert

Make sure students use multiplication, multiplication and addition, or an estimate to check their answers.

(continued)

New Concept *(Continued)*

Closure The questions below help assess the concepts taught in this lesson.

"What are the four steps of division?" Divide, multiply, subtract, bring down

"How often should we repeat the steps whenever we divide two numbers?" As often as needed

"When a dividend is an amount of money, where is the decimal point placed in the quotient?" Above the decimal point in the dividend (when the divisor is a whole number)

Write the division $4172 \div 7$ on the board or overhead and ask students to find the quotient. $4172 \div 7 = 596$

Written Practice

Math Conversations

Independent Practice and Discussions to Increase Understanding

Problem 1a Interpret

Ask the following questions to help students solve part **a**:

"How many books has Jay read?" 4 books

"A student read twice as many books as Jay. What number of books represents twice as many?" eight books

"Who read 8 books?" Maria

Problem 1c Interpret

Extend the Problem

Challenge advanced learners to explain how multiplying by 10 and mental math can be used to solve the problem. Sample: Assume Annie read 10 books, and then subtract 160 from the product of 10×160; 10×160 is 1600 because we attach two zeros to the right of the product of 1×16. Then we subtract 100, and then 60, from 1600 to find that Annie read 1440 pages.

Problem 3

Make sure students recognize that this is a multiple-step problem.

(continued)

Written Practice

Distributed and Integrated

*1. (Inv. 5) **Interpret** Use the information in the graph below to answer parts **a–c.**

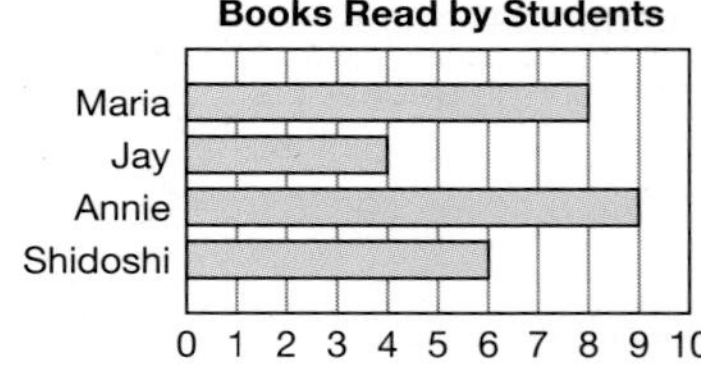

▸ **a.** Which student has read exactly twice as many books as Jay? Maria

b. Shidoshi's goal is to read 10 books. How many more books does he need to read to reach his goal? 4 books

▸ **c.** If the books Annie has read have an average of 160 pages each, about how many pages has she read? 1440 pages

*2. (50, 53) Dala saw some pentagons. The pentagons had a total of 100 sides. How many pentagons did Dala see? 20 pentagons

▸ *3. (Inv. 3) Mariah bought a rectangular piece of land that was 3 miles long and 2 miles wide. She plans to divide the land into two sections of equal area. If she farms one of the sections how many square miles could be farmed? 3 square miles

*4. (28, 37) Max bought 10 pencils for 24¢ each. The tax was 14¢. What was the total cost of the pencils? $2.54

▸ 5. (73) **Multiple Choice** A full pitcher of orange juice contains about how much juice? B

A 2 ounces **B** 2 liters **C** 2 gallons **D** 2 cups

6. (17) **Represent** Draw a triangle that has two perpendicular sides. What type of angles did you draw? Sample: right angle, acute angles

English Learners

A **goal** is a result toward which effort is directed or something to be accomplished or finished. Say:

"If my goal is to read 10 books this summer, it means that I want to finish reading 10 books this summer."

Ask students to share some of their summer **goals** with another student.

7. (74) **Represent** One fourth of the 48 gems were rubies. How many of the gems were rubies? Draw a picture to solve the problem. 12 gems

7.

48 gems

$\frac{1}{4}$ were rubies. { 12 gems

$\frac{3}{4}$ were not rubies. { 12 gems | 12 gems | 12 gems

▶ *8. (Inv. 4, 77) a. **Represent** One hundred fans attended the game, but only 81 fans cheered for the home team. What fraction of the fans who attended the game cheered for the home team? $\frac{81}{100}$

b. Write the answer in part **a** as a decimal number. Then use words to name the number. 0.81; eighty-one hundredths

9. (45) $46.01 - (3.68 + 10.2)$ 32.13

10. (8, 52) $728 + c = 1205$ 477

11. (71) 36×40 1440

12. (71) 20×42 840

13. (71) $\$2.75 \times 10$ $27.50

14. (59) $\$3.17 \times 4$ $12.68

15. (59) 206×5 1030

16. (71) 37×40 1480

17. (79) $3\overline{)492}$ 164

18. (79) $5\overline{)860}$ 172

19. (34, 79) $6m = \$9.30$ $1.55

20. (65, 69) $168 \div 2^3$ 21

▶*21. (75) $240 \div 4$ 60

▶*22. (75) $241 \div 8$ 30 R 1

23. (66) Find the perimeter and area of this rectangle: 32 ft; 60 ft^2

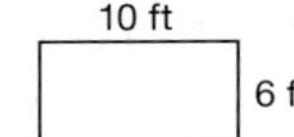

▶*24. (78) **Verify** Which of these letters will look the same if it is turned a half turn? H

H A P P Y

▶*25. (17) **Estimate** Which angle in this figure looks like an obtuse angle? angle *D*

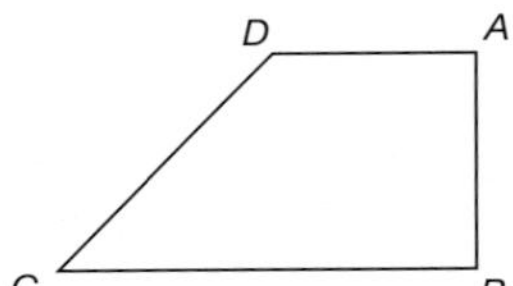

Written Practice *(Continued)*

Math Conversations *(cont.)*

Problem 5 Multiple Choice

Test-Taking Strategy

If students are not able to immediately identify choice **B** as the correct choice, invite them to suggest reasons that will eliminate possible answers. For example, students may be familiar with a 12-ounce can of fruit punch or a 12-ounce bottle of water. Because the capacity of a pitcher is much greater than the capacity of that can or bottle, choice **A** can be eliminated, and choice **D** can be eliminated because 2 cups = 16 ounces.

Problem 8 Represent

Before students complete part **b**, ask:

"What place value does a denominator of 100 represent?" hundredths

"How many digits to the right of the decimal point does a decimal number in hundredths have?" two digits

Problems 21 and 22

Before students complete any arithmetic, remind them of the importance of checking their work. Then ask:

"How can we check a division answer that includes a remainder? Include the words 'dividend,' 'divisor,' 'quotient,' and 'remainder' in your answer." Sample: Add the remainder to the product of the divisor and the whole number portion of the quotient, and then compare the result to the dividend.

"Which operation of the check is not used if the quotient is a whole number?" addition

Problem 24 Verify

Encourage students who have difficulty solving the problem to rotate the page or trace the letters and rotate the tracings.

Problem 25 Estimate

To help students recognize the angle, ask:

"On a new sheet of paper, where can we find an example of a right angle?" Any square corner of the paper is an example of a right angle.

Invite students to use the square corner of a sheet of paper to help solve the problem.

(continued)

Teacher Tip

Some students benefit from using grid paper when solving long-division problems. Provide them with copies of grid paper or **Lesson Activity Master 8**. Remind them that each digit should be written in its own square.

Written Practice (Continued)

Math Conversations (cont.)

Problem 26 Multiple Choice

Test-Taking Strategy

Some students may find it helpful to sketch a number line from −15 to 0 and use it to find the integer that represents Matthew's debt.

Students should begin at zero and move 12 units to the left to represent the number of dollars Matthew borrowed, and then move 4 units to the right to represent the number of dollars he paid back.

Errors and Misconceptions

Problem 2

If students have difficulty recognizing division as the operation that is used to solve this problem, share with them a simpler problem:

"We know a pentagon has 5 sides. Suppose Dala saw only 5 sides. How many pentagons would Dala have seen?" one

"Suppose Dala saw only 10 sides. How many pentagons would Dala have seen?" two

"Explain how you found those answers." I used division and divided the number of sides Dala saw by 5.

Point out that the same method—dividing by 5—should be used to solve problem **2.**

▸*26. (76) **Multiple Choice** Matthew borrowed $12 from his sister, Lisa. He paid her back $4. Lisa kept a record of the money Matthew owes her. Which number represents Matthew's balance with Lisa? C

A $16 **B** −$12 **C** −$8 **D** −$4

*27. (42, Inv. 7) The table shows the relationship between meters and centimeters:

Number of Meters	1	2	3	4	5
Number of Centimeters	100	200	300	400	500

a. **Formulate** Write a formula to represent the relationship. Sample: the number of meters × 100 = the number of centimeters; $m \times 100 = c$

b. **Predict** Use your formula to find the number of centimeters in 10 meters. 1000 centimeters

28. (21) In Dodge City, Kansas, the record high temperature in January, 1989 was 80°F. The record low temperature in January, 1984 was −13°F. How many degrees difference is this? 93 degrees

29. (27) The Peace River is 1210 miles long, and its source is in British Columbia. The Red River is 1290 miles long, and its source is in New Mexico. Which river is longer? The Red River

*30. (43) **Model** Draw a number line from 6 to 7 divided into tenths. On it show the locations of 6.1, $6\frac{3}{10}$, 6.6, and $6\frac{9}{10}$. Sample:

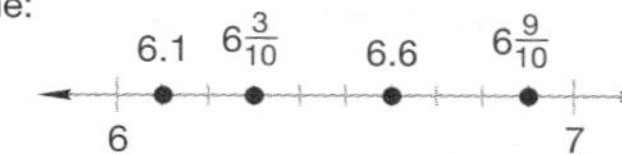

Division with three-digit quotients prepares students for:

- **Lesson 83,** division with zeros in three-digit quotients.
- **Lesson 87,** solving division word problems that involve remainders.
- **Lesson 91,** estimating the answers to multiplication and division problems.
- **Lesson 104,** rounding whole numbers through hundred millions.
- **Lesson 107,** multiplying a three-digit number by a two-digit number.

Planning & Preparation

• Mass and Weight

Objectives

- Identify the units of weight in the customary system and convert between these units.
- Identify the units of mass in the metric system and convert between these units.
- Explain the difference between mass and weight.
- Estimate weight using a balance scale.
- Describe and graph a relationship between units of weight.

Prerequisite Skills

- Comparing measurements in the U.S. Customary and metric systems.
- Converting between units of liquid measure in the U.S. Customary System.
- Converting between units of liquid measure in the metric system.

Materials

Instructional Masters

- Power Up G Worksheet

Manipulative Kit

- Balance scale with weights*

Teacher-provided materials

- Classroom items*

**optional*

California Mathematics Content Standards

NS 2.0, 2.1 Estimate and compute the sum or difference of whole numbers and positive decimals to two places.

NS 2.0, 2.2 Round two-place decimals to one decimal or the nearest whole number and judge the reasonableness of the rounded answer.

AF 1.0, 1.1 Use letters, boxes, or other symbols to stand for any number in simple expressions or equations (e.g., demonstrate an understanding and the use of the concept of a variable).

AF 1.0, 1.5 Understand that an equation such as $y = 3x + 5$ is a prescription for determining a second number when a first number is given.

SDAP 1.0, 1.1 Formulate survey questions; systematically collect and represent data on a number line; and coordinate graphs, tables, and charts.

MR 2.0, 2.3 Use a variety of methods, such as words, numbers, symbols, charts, graphs, tables, diagrams, and models, to explain mathematical reasoning.

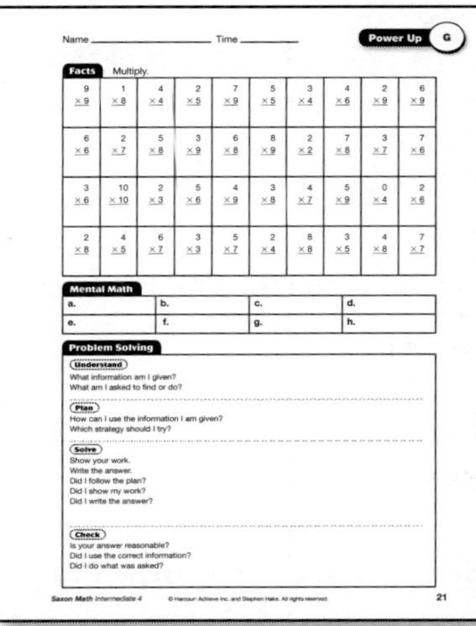

Power Up G Worksheet

Universal Access

Reaching All Special Needs Students

Special Education Students	At-Risk Students	English Learners	Advanced Learners
• Inclusion (TM) • Adaptations for Saxon Math	• Error Alert (TM) • Reteaching Masters • Refresher Lessons for California Standards	• English Learners (TM) • Developing Academic Language (TM) • English Learner Handbook	• Extend the Example (TM) • Extend the Problem (TM) • Online Activities

TM=Teacher's Manual

Developing Academic Language

New	Maintained	English Learner
mass	gram	kilo-
ounce	kilogram	
pound	U.S. Customary System	
ton		
weight		

Problem Solving Discussion

Problem

Tahlia's soccer team, the Falcons, won their match against the Eagles. There were 11 goals scored altogether by both teams. The Falcons scored 3 more goals than the Eagles. How many goals did each team score?

Focus Strategies

Guess and Check

Use Logical Reasoning

Understand *Understand the problem.*

"What information are we given?"

Two teams scored a total of 11 goals in a match. The Falcons scored 3 more goals than the Eagles.

"What are we asked to do?"

We are asked to find the number of goals scored by each team.

Plan *Make a plan.*

"What problem-solving strategy can we use to solve the problem?"

We can use *guess and check.* We can make an educated guess for the number of goals scored by each team and then check whether the guess fits the problem.

Solve *Carry out the plan.*

"We know that 11 goals were scored altogether. What are some number pairs that have a sum of 11?"

6 and 5, 7 and 4, 8 and 3, 9 and 2, 10 and 1

"Which of these number pairs should we use as a guess for the number of goals scored by each team?"

We are looking for a number pair in which one of the numbers is 3 greater than the other number (since the Falcons scored 3 more goals than the Eagles). We can try the number pair 7 and 4.

"How many goals did the Falcons score? How many goals did the Eagles score?"

We guess that the Falcons scored 7 goals and the Eagles scored 4 goals.

Check *Look back.*

"Does our guess fit the problem?"

Yes. If the score was Falcons 7, Eagles 4, then the total number of goals was $7 + 4 = 11$. The difference in the scores is $7 - 4 = 3$.

"Is our answer reasonable?"

We know that our answer is reasonable because 7 goals plus 4 goals is a total of 11 goals, which fits the problem. Also, 7 goals by the Falcons is 3 goals more than the 4 goals by the Eagles.

"What problem-solving strategies did we use?"

We *used logical reasoning* and number sense to find number pairs that have a total of 11. Then we used number sense to *guess and check* the pair that seemed to fit the problem (7 and 4).

• Mass and Weight

California Mathematics Content Standards

NS 2.0, 2.2 Round two-place decimals to one decimal or the nearest whole number and judge the reasonableness of the rounded answer.

AF 1.0, 1.1 Use letters, boxes, or other symbols to stand for any number in simple expressions or equations (e.g., demonstrate an understanding and the use of the concept of a variable).

AF 1.0, 1.5 Understand that an equation such as $y = 3x + 5$ is a prescription for determining a second number when a first number is given.

facts Power Up G

count aloud Count by fourths from $2\frac{1}{2}$ to $7\frac{1}{2}$.

mental math Subtracting two-digit numbers mentally is easier if the second number ends in zero. By increasing both numbers in a subtraction by the same amount, we can sometimes make the subtraction easier while keeping the difference the same. For example, instead of 45 − 28, we can think 47 − 30. We added two to 28 to make it end in zero and then added two to 45 to keep the difference the same. Use this strategy in problems **a–d.**

a. Number Sense: 45 − 39 6

b. Number Sense: 56 − 27 29

c. Number Sense: 63 − 48 15

d. Number Sense: 82 − 35 47

e. Powers/Roots: Compare: $\sqrt{16} - \sqrt{9}$ (=) 1^2

f. Measurement: The high temperature was 84°F. The low temperature was 68°F. The difference between the high and low temperatures was how many degrees? 16 degrees

g. Estimation: Each candle costs $3.05. If Miranda has $12, does she have enough to buy 4 candles? No

h. Calculation: $\frac{1}{4}$ of 24, × 9, − 15, + 51 90

problem solving Choose an appropriate problem-solving strategy to solve this problem. Tahlia's soccer team, the Falcons, won their match against the Eagles. There were 11 goals scored altogether by both teams. The Falcons scored 3 more goals than the Eagles. How many goals did each team score? Falcons 7, Eagles 4

Facts Multiply.

9 × 9 81	1 × 8 8	4 × 4 16	2 × 5 10	7 × 9 63	5 × 5 25	3 × 4 12	4 × 6 24	2 × 9 18	6 × 9 54
6 × 6 36	2 × 7 14	5 × 8 40	3 × 9 27	6 × 8 48	8 × 9 72	2 × 2 4	7 × 8 56	3 × 7 21	7 × 6 42
3 × 6 18	10 × 10 100	2 × 3 6	5 × 6 30	4 × 9 36	3 × 8 24	4 × 7 28	5 × 9 45	0 × 4 0	2 × 6 12
2 × 8 16	4 × 5 20	6 × 7 42	3 × 3 9	5 × 7 35	2 × 4 8	8 × 8 64	3 × 5 15	4 × 8 32	7 × 7 49

Power Up

Facts

Distribute **Power Up G** to students. See answers below.

Count Aloud

Before students begin the Mental Math exercises, do these counting exercises as a class.

Mental Math

Encourage students to share different ways to mentally compute these exercises. Strategies for exercises are listed below.

a. Add 1 to Both Numbers

45 + 1 = 46; 39 + 1 = 40;
46 − 40 = 6

c. Add 2 to Both Numbers

63 + 2 = 65; 48 + 2 = 50;
65 − 50 = 15

Subtract 3 from Both Numbers

63 − 3 = 60; 48 − 3 = 45;
60 − 45 = 15

f. Count Up by Places

68° to 78° = 10°; 78° to 84° = 6°
10 ° + 6° = 16°

Problem Solving

Refer to **Problem-Solving Strategy Discussion,** p. 531B.

New Concept

Explanation

To help students better understand how weight and mass are different, ask them to think about a 12-pound bowling ball. Point out that the weight of the ball is related to the force of gravity, and because the force of gravity on the moon is only about $\frac{1}{6}$ of the force of gravity on Earth, the weight of the bowling ball on the moon is about $\frac{1}{6}$ of 12 pounds, or about 2 pounds. To find $\frac{1}{6}$ of a number we divide the number by 6. The mass of the bowling ball, however, is the same in each place. In other words, the bowling ball does not change if an astronaut carries it to the moon and places it there.

You may choose to have students explore the Internet for examples of objects on different planets.

Instruction

Emphasize the importance of learning the equivalents units of weight that are shown in the table. Encourage those students who do not know the relationships to copy the table and use it for reference whenever necessary.

Example 1

Extend the Example

Challenge advanced learners to answer the following question using only mental math and explain how they found the answer.

"About how many books would there be in a ton of books?" About 1000 books

(continued)

New Concept

There is a difference between *weight* and *mass*. The **mass** of an object is how much matter an object has within itself. **Weight** is the measure of the force of gravity on that object. Though an object's weight depends on the force of gravity, its mass does not. For example, the force of gravity on the moon is less than it is on Earth, so the weight of an object on the moon is less, but its mass remains the same.

The units of weight in the U.S. Customary System are **ounces, pounds,** and **tons.** We can use the word ounce to describe an amount of fluid. However, ounce can also describe an amount of weight. A fluid ounce of water weighs about one ounce.

As we see in the table below, one *pound* is 16 ounces, and one *ton* is 2000 pounds. Ounce is abbreviated oz. Pound is abbreviated lb.

16 oz = 1 lb
2000 lb = 1 ton

A box of cereal might weigh 24 ounces. Some students weigh 98 pounds. Many cars weigh 1 ton or more.

24 ounces

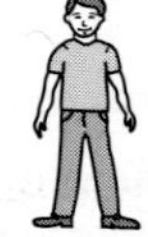

98 pounds

1 ton

Example 1

This book weighs about 2 pounds. Two pounds is how many ounces?

Each pound is 16 ounces. So 2 pounds is 2 × 16 ounces, which is **32 ounces.**

English Learners

Say, ***"The prefix kilo– in the words kilometer and kilogram stands for 1000. Do you know how many meters are in a kilometer? How many grams in a kilogram?"*** 1000; 1000

Ask, ***"What are some other prefixes that stand for a number?"***

If students have difficulty thinking of other examples, write these words on the board and ask students to tell how many sides each figure has.

triangle three

octagon eight

hexagon six

Example 2

The rhinoceros weighed 3 tons. Three tons is how many pounds?

Each ton is 2000 pounds. This means 3 tons is 3×2000 pounds, which is **6000 pounds.**

Grams and *kilograms* are metric units of mass. Recall that the prefix *kilo–* means "thousand." So a kilogram is 1000 grams. Gram is abbreviated g. Kilogram is abbreviated kg.

1000 g = 1 kg

A dollar bill has a mass of about 1 gram. This book has a mass of about 1 kilogram. Since this book has fewer than 1000 pages, each page is more than 1 gram.

Example 3

Choose the more reasonable measure for a–c.

a. pair of shoes: 1 g or 1 kg

b. cat: 4 g or 4 kg

c. quarter: 5 g or 5 kg

a. A pair of shoes is about **1 kg.**

b. A cat is about **4 kg.**

c. A quarter is about **5 g.**

Example 4

How many grams are equal to 5 kilograms?

We can find the answer by setting up a table.

Kilograms	1	2	3	4	5
Grams	1000	2000	3000	4000	5000

5 kilograms = **5000 grams**

Write can write a formula for converting kilograms to grams. We use g for grams and k for kilograms and write $g = 1000k$ or $1000k = g$. We can use this formula to convert any number of kilograms to grams.

Generalize How could we rewrite the formula $g = 1000k$ using x and y?

$y = 1000x$ where x = the number of kilograms and y = the number of grams.

Math Background

"How can a weight in ounces be converted to pounds?"

To convert a weight from ounces to pounds, we divide by 16. To see why, think of the conversion as having equal groups. For example, suppose we want to convert 80 ounces to pounds. Recall the formula for equal groups:

Number of groups × Number of items in each group = Total

In this case, the groups are pounds and the "items" in the groups are ounces. The number of pounds is unknown. The formula becomes:

n pounds × 16 ounces in each pound = 80 ounces

We find n by dividing: $80 \div 16 = 5$. This means 80 ounces is equal to 5 pounds.

New Concept *(Continued)*

Example 2

Active Learning

After discussing the solution, remind students that multiplication is a fast way to find the sum of a repeated addition. Then ask:

"How can repeated addition be used to solve this problem?" 2000 lb + 2000 lb + 2000 lb = 6000 lb

Explanation

Make sure students understand that "gram" and "kilogram" are metric units of mass, and although their use is limited in the United States, their use is widespread elsewhere in the world.

Point out the relationship 1000 grams = 1 kilogram. Then ask:

"How can we find the number of grams if we know the number of kilograms?" Multiply the number of grams by 1000

Example 3

For each part, discuss why the incorrect choice is not appropriate. Sample (for part **a**): The mass of a dollar bill is about 1 gram, and the mass of a pair of shoes is much greater than the mass of a dollar bill.

Example 4

Use this example to lead students to generalize:

- Multiplication is used to change from a larger unit (such as kilograms) to a smaller unit (such as grams).
- Division is used to change from a smaller unit (such as ounces) to a larger unit (such as pounds).

(continued)

New Concept (Continued)

Example 5

Error Alert

Before discussing the solution, remind students that a number rounded to the nearest tenth will have one digit to the right of the decimal point.

Lesson Practice

Guided Practice

Use these problems as guided practice to check the students' understanding of today's concept.

Problems a and b

Remind students that knowing the equivalent relationships shared by ounces, pounds, and tons will enable them complete problems of this nature very quickly.

Problems c–e **Estimate**

Complete these problems as a class and encourage your students to give a variety of reasons for each choice.

Problem f

Error Alert

Make sure students recall that multiplication is used to change a larger unit to a smaller unit.

Closure The questions below help assess the concepts taught in this lesson.

"Name units of weight, units of mass, and explain how the units are related." Weight: ounce, pound, ton; 1 ton = 2000 pounds and 1 pound = 16 ounces; Mass: gram and kilogram; 1 kilogram = 1000 grams

Ask students to name an appropriate unit to measure the:

- weight of a pencil ounce
- weight of a locomotive ton
- weight of a large dog pound
- mass of a refrigerator kilogram
- mass of a coin gram

Example 5

Mr. and Mrs. Gordon purchased two salads at the salad bar. The salads weighed 1.43 lb and 1.37 lb. To the nearest tenth of a pound, how much did the salads weigh?

We are asked to round each number to the nearest tenth.

1.43 lb rounds to 1.4 lb

1.37 lb rounds to 1.4 lb

Now we can add. 1.4 lb + 1.4 lb = **2.8 lb**

Discuss The restaurant charges $2 per pound for a salad. The cashier will round up to the nearest pound. How much did the Gordon's pay for their salads? $6.00

Lesson Practice

a. Dave's pickup truck can haul a half ton of cargo. How many pounds is a half ton? 1000 lb

b. The newborn baby weighed 7 lb 12 oz. The baby's weight was how much less than 8 pounds? 4 oz

Estimate Choose the more reasonable measure in problems **c–e.**

c. tennis ball: 57 g or 57 kg 57 g

d. dog: 6 g or 6 kg 6 kg

e. bowling ball: 7 g or 7 kg 7 kg

f. Seven kilograms is how many grams? 7000 g

g. Which depends on the force of gravity: mass or weight? weight

Written Practice

Distributed and Integrated

1. (13) It takes Tempest 20 minutes to walk to school. At what time should she start for school if she wants to arrive at 8:10 a.m.? 7:50 a.m.

▸ ***2.** (10, 12) A container and its contents weigh 125 pounds. The contents of the container weigh 118 pounds. What is the weight of the container? 7 lb

***3.** (12, 28) Anjelita is shopping for art supplies and plans to purchase a sketchpad for $4.29, a charcoal pencil for $1.59, and an eraser for 69¢. If the amount of sales tax is 43¢ and Anjelita pays for her purchase with a $10 bill, how much change should she receive? $3.00

Inclusion

Use this strategy if the student displays:

- Slow Learning Rate.
- Difficulty with Abstract Processing.

Weight and Mass (Small Group)

Materials: balance scale with gram masses and ounce weights, classroom items

- Have students use the balance scales to determine the mass of various classroom items in grams or kilograms. Ask students to record the name of the item, an estimate of its mass, and its measured mass.
- Next, have students use the balance scales to determine the weight of the same classroom items in ounces or pounds. For each object ask students to record an estimate of the its weight and its measured weight.
- Have students discuss their estimates and measurements with each other. Ask, ***"How accurate were your estimates? What made you choose that estimate?"***

4. According to this calendar, October 30, 1904, was what day of the week? Sunday
(RF12)

OCTOBER 1904						
S	M	T	W	T	F	S
						1
2	3	4	5	6	7	8
9	10	11	12	13	14	15
16	17	18	19	20	21	22
23	24	25	26	27	28	29
30	31					

▶ *5. (78) **Explain** From 3:00 p.m. to 3:45 p.m., the minute hand of a clock turns how many degrees? Explain your thinking. 270°; sample: The minute hand moved 45 minutes, which is a $\frac{3}{4}$ turn around the clock, and $\frac{3}{4}$ is equal to 270° of a full turn.

6. (27, 40) Round three thousand, seven hundred eighty-two to the nearest thousand. 4000

7. (80) The limousine weighed 2 tons. How many pounds is 2 tons? 4000 lb

▶ 8. (74) **Represent** One fifth of the 45 horses were pintos. How many of the horses were pintos? Draw a picture to illustrate the problem. 9 horses

8. 45 horses

$\frac{1}{5}$ pintos: 9 horses

$\frac{4}{5}$ not pintos: 9 horses, 9 horses, 9 horses, 9 horses

*9. (77) **Analyze** What fraction of the set of triangles is shaded? $\frac{3}{10}$

10. (Inv. 2, 27) **Represent** Which point on the number line below could represent 23,650? point *B*

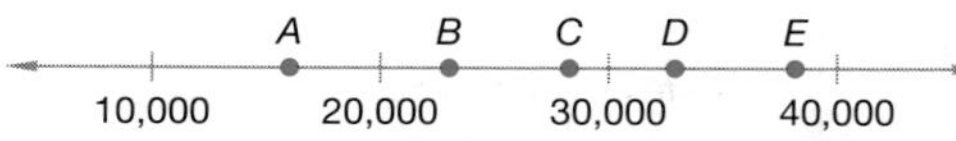

▶ *11. (Inv. 4) **Connect** Write each decimal number as a fraction:

a. 0.1 $\frac{1}{10}$ **b.** 0.01 $\frac{1}{100}$ **c.** 1.11 $1\frac{11}{100}$

12. (28, 51) $\begin{array}{r} \$36.47 \\ +\ \$\ 9.68 \\ \hline \$46.15 \end{array}$

13. (28, 52) $\begin{array}{r} \$30.00 \\ -\ \$13.45 \\ \hline \$16.55 \end{array}$

14. (11) $\begin{array}{r} 6 \\ 8 \\ 17 \\ 23 \\ 110 \\ 25 \\ +\ 104 \\ \hline 293 \end{array}$

15. (59) $\begin{array}{r} 476 \\ \times\ \ 7 \\ \hline 3332 \end{array}$

16. (59) $\begin{array}{r} 804 \\ \times\ \ 5 \\ \hline 4020 \end{array}$

Teacher Tip

Hands-on practice helps students gain experience in estimating weight or mass. To provide practice, set up a Weight/Mass Estimation Center in your classroom. Include a balance scale, a food scale, a bathroom scale, a variety of familiar objects, and record sheets. Students must estimate the weight (mass) of an object, then weigh it, and record the estimate, the weight (mass), and the difference between the estimate and the measure. Students should work toward making better estimates.

Written Practice

Math Conversations

Independent Practice and Discussions to Increase Understanding

Problem 2

Extend the Problem

Challenge students to write an equation to represent the situation, and then name the operation that is used to solve the equation. Sample: $w + 118 = 125$ where w represents the weight of the container in pounds; Subtraction is used to solve a missing addend equation such as $w + 118 = 125$ for w.

Invite volunteers to write different equations on the board or overhead and then to demonstrate how to solve those equations.

Problem 5 Explain

Ask the following questions if students do not recognize a full turn as 360°:

"At 3 o'clock, the hour and minute hands of a clock form a right angle. What is the measure in degrees of a quarter turn?" 90°

"What fraction of a circle does 90° represent?" One quarter or $\frac{1}{4}$

"90° represents $\frac{1}{4}$ of a circle. How many degrees represent $\frac{1}{2}$ of a circle?" 180°

"180° represents $\frac{1}{2}$ of a circle. How many degrees represent a whole circle?" 360°

Problem 8 Represent

Extend the Problem

Challenge advanced learners to name an operation that can be used to check their work, and to explain how that operation is used. Sample: Finding $\frac{1}{5}$ of a number is the same as dividing that number by 5; 5 groups × 9 in each group = 45

Real-World Connection

Students may be interested to learn that "pinto" is a breed of horse. Most pintos are either white with spots of one other color, or colored with spots of white. Although usually associated with early Native Americans, pintos were brought to North America by European explorers, primarily those from Spain.

(continued)

Written Practice (Continued)

Math Conversations (cont.)

Problem 11 Connect

"What place value does a decimal number with one digit to the right of the decimal point represent?" tenths

"When we write a decimal number in tenths as a fraction, what number do we write as the denominator of that fraction?" 10

Ask similar question for two digits (hundredths; 100) to the right of the decimal point.

Problem 20

Encourage students to name the product using only mental math. Make sure they recognize that any number of cents greater than 99¢ must be written as dollars and cents.

Problem 30 Represent

Invite volunteers to share their conclusions with the class.

Errors and Misconceptions

Problem 10

If students have difficulty choosing the point, suggest that they first determine the two numbers on the number line 23,650 is between, and then decide if 23,650 is more than halfway or less than halfway between those numbers.

Problem 18

A common error when simplifying powers is to multiply the base by the exponent. Students who make this error for problem 18 are likely to rewrite 5^2 as 10 and 10^2 as 20, which will produce a value of 0 for n.

Remind these students that an exponent represents the number of times a base is used as a factor, and then ask them to rewrite and simplify the expressions below for additional practice.

4^2 $4 \cdot 4 = 16$ 9^2 $9 \cdot 9 = 81$ 7^2 $7 \cdot 7 = 49$

17. $12.65 - (7.43 - 2.1)$ 7.32 (9, 45)

18. $5^2 + 5^2 + n = 10^2$ 50 (8, 65)

19. Represent Write each of these numbers with words: (Inv. 4)
  a. $2\frac{1}{10}$ two and one tenth
  b. 2.1 two and one tenth

▸*20. $10 \times 23¢$ \$2.30 (71)

*21. 62×30 1860 (71)

*22. $70 \times \$25$ \$1750 (71)

*23. $3\overline{)\$6.27}$ \$2.09 (79)

24. $7\overline{)820}$ 117 R 1 (79)

25. $6\overline{)333}$ 55 R 3 (72)

26. $625 \div \sqrt{25}$ 125 (Inv. 3, 79)

*27. $400 \div 2^3$ 50 (65, 75)

28. $2w = 1370$ 685 (34, 79)

29. Find the perimeter and area of this square. 40 m; 100 m^2 (66)

10 m

▸*30. Represent The table below is based on a survey about favorite flowers. Use the data in the table to make a double bar graph. Write one conclusion based on the graph. (Inv. 6, 76)

Flower	Adults	Children
Rose	6	2
Daisy	4	9
Mum	5	4

See student work; samples: Adults like roses more than children do. Most children liked daisies.

536 ***Saxon Math*** *Intermediate 4*

Looking Forward

Describing items using their mass and weight and determining the difference between them will be further developed in ***Saxon Math*** *Intermediate 5*.

Cumulative Assessments and Performance Task

Assessments

Distribute **Power-Up Test 15** and **Cumulative Test 15** to each student. Have students complete the **Power-Up Test** first. Allow 10 minutes. Then have students work on the **Cumulative Test**.

Performance Task

The remaining class time can be spent on **Performance Task 8**. Students can begin the task in class or complete it during another class period.

Flexible Grouping

Flexible grouping gives students an opportunity to work with other students in an interactive and encouraging way. The choice for how students are grouped depends on the goals for instruction, the needs of the students, and the specific learning activity.

Assigning Groups

Group members can be randomly assigned, or can be assigned based on some criteria such as grouping students who may need help with a certain skill or grouping students to play specific roles in a group (such as recorder or reporter).

Types of Groups

Students can be paired or placed in larger groups. For pairing, students can be assigned partners on a weekly or monthly basis. Pairing activities are the easiest to manage in a classroom and are more likely to be useful on a daily basis.

Flexible Grouping Ideas

Lesson 72, Example 1
Materials: paper

Divide students into groups of 4. The groups should be of varying abilities. Assign each student a number: 1, 2, 3, or 4.

- Assign a division problem with two-digit answers and a remainder to each group. Direct students to work together to solve the problem.
- Any member of the group should be able to present the division problem and explain how they solved it.
- The teacher then calls out a student number, and each student assigned that number must present his or her group's division problem.

Lesson 76, Example 1
Materials: paper

Have students individually answer parts **a–c** for Example 1 without reading the answers. Then divide the students into groups of 4.

- Have students take turns telling the group the strategy they used to solve the problem. All strategies are acceptable.
- One student from the group should be chosen as the Recorder. The group helps the Recorder to write a summary of the strategies that were used.

Lesson 77, Example 2
Materials: counters

Pair students before you teach Lesson 77. Then teach the lesson, stopping before you go over Example 2.

- Have students read the example and discuss strategies to solve it using the counters.
- Have volunteers share their strategies with the class.

Lesson 79, Example 2
Materials: paper

Students will work independently and then in pairs to reinforce division with three-digit answers.

- Write a similar division problem on the board. Have students solve the problem independently.
- Have students form pairs and switch problems to check each other's work.
- The students should ask their partner to explain the steps used to solve the division problem.

Planning & Preparation

• Investigating Equivalent Fractions with Manipulatives

Objectives

- Use fraction manipulatives to model equivalent fractions.
- Use fraction manipulatives to compare fractions.
- Use fraction manipulatives to order fractions.
- Use fraction manipulatives to reduce fractions.
- Use fraction manipulatives to add and subtract fractions.
- Use fraction manipulatives to model mixed numbers.

Prerequisite Skills

- Using pictures to name fractions.
- Drawing and shading pictures of fractions representing halves, thirds, and fourths.
- Using a fraction to find a portion of a group.
- Drawing a picture to represent fractions of a group.

Materials

Instructional Masters

- Lesson Activities 11–13

Teacher-provided materials

- Envelopes or locking plastic bags*

**optional*

California Mathematics Content Standards

NS 1.0, 1.6 Write tenths and hundredths in decimal and fraction notations and know the fraction and decimal equivalents for halves and fourths (e.g., $\frac{1}{2} = 0.5$ or $.50$; $\frac{7}{4} = 1\frac{3}{4} = 1.75$).

NS 1.0, 1.7 Write the fraction represented by a drawing of parts of a figure; represent a given fraction by using drawings; and relate a fraction to a simple decimal on a number line.

MR 2.0, 2.3 Use a variety of methods, such as words, numbers, symbols, charts, graphs, tables, diagrams, and models, to explain mathematical reasoning.

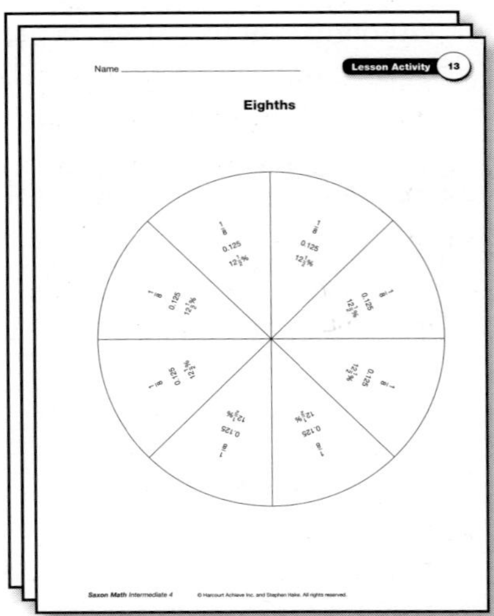

Lesson Activities 11–13

Universal Access

Reaching All Special Needs Students

Special Education Students	At-Risk Students	English Learners	Advanced Learners
• Inclusion (TM) • Adaptations for Saxon Math	• Alternative Approach (TM) • Error Alert (TM) • Reteaching Masters • Refresher Lessons for California Standards	• English Learners (TM) • Developing Academic Language (TM) • English Learner Handbook	• Investigate Further (SE) • Online Activities

TM=Teacher's Manual
SE=Student Edition

Developing Academic Language

New	Maintained	English Learner
reduce	decimal number denominator fractions numerator	reducing

Investigating Equivalent Fractions with Manipulatives

California Mathematics Content Standards

NS 1.0, 1.6 Write tenths and hundredths in decimal and fraction notations and know the fraction and decimal equivalents for halves and fourths (e.g., $\frac{1}{2} = 0.5$ or .50; $\frac{7}{4} = 1\frac{3}{4} = 1.75$).

NS 1.0, 1.7 Write the fraction represented by a drawing of parts of a figure; represent a given fraction by using drawings; and relate a fraction to a simple decimal on a number line.

MR 2.0, 2.3 Use a variety of methods, such as words, numbers, symbols, charts, graphs, tables, diagrams, and models, to explain mathematical reasoning.

Fraction manipulatives can help us better understand fractions. In this investigation we will make and use a set of fraction manipulatives.

Activity 1

Using Fraction Manipulatives

Materials needed:

- **Lesson Activities 11, 12,** and **13**
- scissors
- envelopes or locking plastic bags (optional)

Model Use your fraction manipulatives to complete the following exercises:

1. Another name for $\frac{1}{4}$ is a quarter. How many quarters of a circle does it take to form a whole circle? Show your work.
2. Fit two quarter circles together to form a half circle. That is, show that $\frac{2}{4}$ equals $\frac{1}{2}$. 
3. How many fourths equals $1\frac{1}{4}$? 5 fourths;
4. This number sentence shows how to make a whole circle using half circles:

$$\frac{1}{2} + \frac{1}{2} = 1$$

Write a number sentence that shows how to make a whole circle using only quarter circles. $\frac{1}{4} + \frac{1}{4} + \frac{1}{4} + \frac{1}{4} = 1$

5. How many half circles equals $1\frac{1}{2}$ circles? 3 halves;  
6. Four half circles make how many whole circles? 2 wholes; 

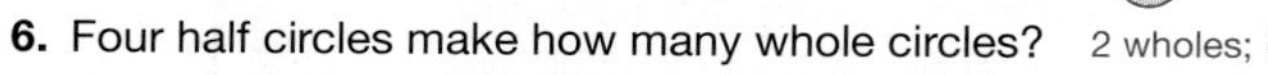

Model Manipulatives can help us compare and order fractions. Use your fraction manipulatives to illustrate and answer each problem:

7. Arrange $\frac{1}{2}$, $\frac{1}{8}$, and $\frac{1}{4}$ in order from least to greatest. $\frac{1}{8}, \frac{1}{4}, \frac{1}{2}$

1. 4 quarters; 

Inclusion

Use this strategy if the student displays:

- Difficulty with Large Group Instruction.
- Slow Learning Rate.

Investigating Equivalent Fractions with Manipulatives (Individual)

Materials: fraction circles, paper

- Write $\frac{1}{2}$ on the board and ask students to model it with fraction circles. Then have students use the fourths circles to make an equal fraction.
- Ask, ***"What fraction is equal to $\frac{1}{2}$?"*** $\frac{2}{4}$ Then have students use the sixths circles to make an equivalent fraction. Ask, ***"What fraction is equivalent to $\frac{1}{2}$?"*** $\frac{3}{6}$
- Write $\frac{3}{5}$ on the board and have students make a model of it on their paper. Tell students to copy the model and then divide it into 10 equal groups.
- Ask, ***"How many parts of the 10 groups are shaded?"*** 6 ***"How many parts would be shaded if there were 20 equal groups?"*** 12

INVESTIGATION 8

Investigating Equivalent Fractions with Manipulatives

In this investigation, students will learn how to use fraction manipulatives to model equivalent fractions, to compare fractions, to reduce fractions, and to add and subtract simple fractions. They will also use fraction manipulatives to explore relationships shared by fractions, decimals, and percents. Each student will make a set of fraction manipulatives to explore and learn about these concepts.

Instruction

Students may work individually, in pairs, or in small groups to complete the activities in this investigation.

Activity 1

Make and distribute one copy per student of **Lesson Activity Masters 11, 12,** and **13.** If possible, copy each **Lesson Activity Master** on a different color of paper—the colors will enable students to easily sort the pieces and quickly distinguish halves from fourths and eighths.

Begin by having students cut out the fraction pieces. Give them some time to examine the pieces and to note that each piece has three labels: a fraction, a percent, and a decimal.

Math Conversations

Independent Practice and Discussions to Increase Understanding

Problems 1–4 Model

As students complete these tasks, establish working rules for this investigation—how much students should interact with each other, how students should show their work, and so on.

(continued)

Math Conversations *(cont.)*

Problem 8 (Model)

Ask students to explain how they ordered the fractions. Sample: I made fractions with eighths for all three fractions and could see that $\frac{3}{4}$ has six $\frac{1}{8}$ pieces, $\frac{1}{2}$ has four $\frac{1}{8}$ pieces, and $\frac{3}{8}$ has three $\frac{1}{8}$ pieces.

Problems 9–10 (Model)

Make sure students position their fraction pieces in the same way that the fractions are positioned in the tasks. It is more difficult to compare the pieces if they are not oriented in the same way.

Problems 11–12 (Generalize)

Error Alert

Students must understand what each of these two questions is asking. Problem **11** is easier to understand because students need only to compare the numerators, but problem **12** is difficult to understand because of the inverse relationship between the numerical value of the denominator and the size of the fraction the denominator represents.

Make sure that students understand that reducing a fraction does not involve shrinking the fraction pieces, but rather, it involves reducing the *number* of equal-size fraction pieces.

Problems 13–16

Have students use their fraction pieces first to represent the given fraction, and then use halves or fourths to represent the same fraction using fewer fraction pieces.

Problems 17–18

Students should begin by using their fraction pieces to represent the first fraction, and then use additional pieces to represent the second fraction.

Problems 19–21

Students should begin by using their fraction pieces to represent the first fraction, and then complete the subtraction by taking away the pieces that represent the second fraction.

Problems 22–28

Explanation

Point out the decimal and percent equivalents that are written on each fraction piece. Make sure students understand that each relationship that is shown is always true for all three forms of the number. For example, it is not true that $\frac{1}{2}$ sometimes equals 0.50; rather, all three forms are *always* equal, and any one form can be substituted for another depending on the form of the number that is needed to solve a problem.

(continued)

▸ **8.** Arrange $\frac{3}{8}$, $\frac{3}{4}$, and $\frac{1}{2}$ in order from greatest to least. $\frac{3}{4}, \frac{1}{2}, \frac{3}{8}$

▸ **9.** $\frac{2}{2}$ ⃝ $\frac{2}{4}$ >   ▸ **10.** $\frac{4}{8}$ ⃝ $\frac{3}{8}$ >

▸ **11.** (Generalize) If the denominators of two fractions are the same, how can we determine which fraction is larger and which is smaller?

▸ **12.** (Generalize) If the numerators of two fractions are the same, how can we determine which fraction is larger and which is smaller?

11. Sample: If the denominators are the same, then the fraction with the greater numerator is the greater fraction.

12. Sample: If the numerators are the same, then the fraction with the greater denominator is the smaller fraction.

Manipulatives can also help us **reduce** fractions. When we reduce a fraction, we do not change the size of the fraction. We just use smaller numbers to name the fraction. (With manipulatives, we use fewer pieces to form the fraction.) For example, we may reduce $\frac{2}{4}$ to $\frac{1}{2}$. Both $\frac{2}{4}$ and $\frac{1}{2}$ name the same portion of a whole, but $\frac{1}{2}$ uses smaller numbers (fewer pieces) to name the fraction.

Use your fraction manipulatives to help you reduce the fractions in problems **13–16.** Show how the two fractions match.

▸ **13.** $\frac{2}{4}$ $\frac{1}{2}$ ▸ **14.** $\frac{2}{8}$ $\frac{1}{4}$

▸ **15.** $\frac{4}{8}$ $\frac{1}{2}$ ▸ **16.** $\frac{6}{8}$ $\frac{3}{4}$

Manipulatives can also help us add and subtract fractions. Illustrate each addition below by combining fraction manipulatives. Record each sum.

▸ **17.** $\frac{1}{4} + \frac{2}{4}$ $\frac{3}{4}$ ▸ **18.** $\frac{2}{8} + \frac{3}{8}$ $\frac{5}{8}$

To illustrate each subtraction in problems **19–21,** form the first fraction; then separate the second fraction from the first fraction. Record what is left of the first fraction as your answer.

▸ **19.** $\frac{3}{4} - \frac{2}{4}$ $\frac{1}{4}$ ▸ **20.** $\frac{4}{8} - \frac{1}{8}$ $\frac{3}{8}$

▸ **21.** $\frac{2}{2} - \frac{1}{2}$ $\frac{1}{2}$

Activity 2

Understanding How Fractions and Decimals are Related

Fraction manipulatives can help us understand how fractions and decimals are related. Use the decimal labels on your manipulatives to answer these problems:

▸ **22.** One half of a circle is what decimal portion of a circle? 0.50 or 0.5

▸ **23.** What decimal portion of a circle is $\frac{1}{4}$ of a circle? 0.25

▸ **24.** What decimal portion of a circle is $\frac{3}{4}$ of a circle? 0.75

English Learners

Explain that **reducing** a fraction does not change the size of the fraction, or its value.

Ask, ***"How many pennies are in $\frac{1}{2}$ dollar? In $\frac{2}{4}$ dollar? In $\frac{5}{10}$ dollar?"*** 50; 50; 50

Say, ***"Reducing a fraction from $\frac{2}{4}$ to $\frac{1}{2}$ does not change the size of the fraction. You reduce $\frac{2}{4}$ to $\frac{1}{2}$ by dividing both the numerator and the denominator by 2."***

Ask students to share other examples of fractions before and after they have been reduced.

Alternative Approach: Using Manipulatives

Use overhead fraction circles that match the students' fraction manipulatives by copying **Lesson Activities 11, 12,** and **13** on transparencies to demonstrate portions of this investigation.

▸ **25.** What decimal number is equivalent to $\frac{1}{3}$? $0.\overline{33}$

▸ **26.** What decimal number is equivalent to $\frac{1}{5}$? 0.20 or 0.2

▸ **27.** What decimal number is equivalent to $\frac{1}{8}$? 0.125

▸ **28.** Compare: $0.125 \; \textcircled{<} \; 0.25$

▸ **29.** Form a half circle using two $\frac{1}{4}$ pieces. Here is a fraction number sentence for the model:

$$\frac{1}{4} + \frac{1}{4} = \frac{1}{2}$$

Write an equivalent number sentence using the decimal numbers on the pieces. 0.25 + 0.25 = 0.50 (or 0.5)

▸ **30.** Form $\frac{3}{4}$ of a circle two ways. First use three $\frac{1}{4}$ pieces. Then use a $\frac{1}{2}$ piece and a $\frac{1}{4}$ piece. Here are the two fraction number sentences for these models:

$$\frac{1}{4} + \frac{1}{4} + \frac{1}{4} = \frac{3}{4} \qquad \frac{1}{2} + \frac{1}{4} = \frac{3}{4}$$

Write equivalent number sentences using the decimal numbers on these pieces. 0.25 + 0.25 + 0.25 = 0.75; 0.5 + 0.25 = 0.75

▸ **31.** Form a whole circle using four $\frac{1}{4}$ pieces. Then take away one of the $\frac{1}{4}$ pieces. Here is a fraction number sentence for this subtraction. Write an equivalent number sentence using the decimal numbers on the pieces. 1 − 0.25 = 0.75

$$1 - \frac{1}{4} = \frac{3}{4}$$

▸ **32.** Form a half circle using four $\frac{1}{8}$ pieces. Then take away one of the pieces. Here is a fraction number sentence for this subtraction. Write an equivalent number sentence using the decimal numbers on the pieces. 0.5 − 0.125 = 0.375

$$\frac{1}{2} - \frac{1}{8} = \frac{3}{8}$$

▸ **33.** Here we show $\frac{3}{4}$ of a circle and $\frac{1}{2}$ of a circle:

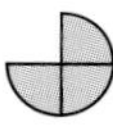 

We see that $\frac{3}{4}$ is greater than $\frac{1}{2}$. In fact, we see that $\frac{3}{4}$ is greater than $\frac{1}{2}$ by a $\frac{1}{4}$ piece. Here we show a larger-smaller-difference number sentence for this comparison:

$$\frac{3}{4} - \frac{1}{2} = \frac{1}{4}$$

Math Conversations *(cont.)*

Problems 29–32

Use overhead fraction circles to demonstrate these problems as students use their fraction manipulatives at their desks.

It is important for students to understand that although some number sentences contain fractions and others contain decimal numbers, each pair of related sentences describes the same relationship of the numbers.

Problem 33

Active Learning

Encourage students to model a variety of fractional parts of a circle using multiple small fraction pieces. Ask them to write addition and subtraction fraction number sentences for their models, and equivalent number sentences using the decimal numbers. Then invite volunteers to use the overhead and share their models and number sentences with the class.

(continued)

Math Background

"How can fractions be reduced without using fraction manipulatives?"

To reduce a fraction, divide the numerator and denominator by a common factor. For example, consider the fraction $\frac{12}{18}$. The number 2 is a common factor of 12 and 18, so divide the numerator and denominator by 2: $\frac{12 \div 2}{18 \div 2} = \frac{6}{9}$. Notice that 3 is a common factor of the 6 and 9, so the fraction $\frac{6}{9}$ can also be reduced: $\frac{6 \div 3}{9 \div 3} = \frac{2}{3}$. Because 2 and 3 do not have a common factor, $\frac{2}{3}$ cannot be reduced. We say that $\frac{2}{3}$ is in *lowest terms.* Notice that we could have reduced $\frac{12}{18}$ to lowest terms in one step by dividing the numerator and denominator by 6.

Teacher Tip

Provide activity mats to prevent fraction pieces from sliding around as students represent the answer to each problem. Mats may be made from fabric or shelf liner that is the same length but twice as wide as a sheet of paper.

Math Conversations *(cont.)*

Closure The questions below help assess the concepts taught in this lesson.

"What other fractions are equal to $\frac{1}{2}$?" Sample: $\frac{2}{4}$ and $\frac{4}{8}$

"Which fraction is reduced, $\frac{6}{8}$ or $\frac{3}{4}$?" $\frac{3}{4}$

"What are three ways to represent the number for 1 of 4 equal parts?" $\frac{1}{4}$, 25%, 0.25

Investigate Further

Problem a

You may need to remind students that $\frac{2}{2}$ is equal to one whole.

Extend the Problem

Challenge your advanced learners by changing each $\frac{1}{2}$ to an equivalent but different fraction like $\frac{2}{4}$, $\frac{3}{6}$, $\frac{4}{8}$, $\frac{5}{10}$, etc. Then ask these students to find the answers.

Investigate Further

a. Parker wanted to make pumpkin bread following the recipe below:

Pumpkin Bread
1 (15 ounce) can pumpkin puree
1 cup vegetable oil
4 eggs
$3\frac{1}{2}$ cups all-purpose flour
3 cups white sugar
$1\frac{2}{4}$ teaspoons baking soda
$1\frac{1}{2}$ teaspoons salt
$1\frac{1}{2}$ teaspoons ground allspice
$1\frac{2}{4}$ teaspoons ground nutmeg
2 teaspoons ground cinnamon
$\frac{1}{2}$ cup chopped walnuts
1 teaspoon baking powder

Use your fraction manipulatives to find each amount.

How many cups will Parker place in a mixing bowl if he combines the oil, flour, sugar, and walnuts first? 8 cups

If Parker combines the baking soda, salt, allspice, nutmeg, and cinnamon in another bowl, how much mixture will be in the bowl? 8 teaspoons

Looking Forward

Investigating equivalent fractions prepares students for:

- **Lesson 87,** interpreting the remainder in a division word problem.
- **Lesson 89,** renaming and modeling mixed numbers and improper fractions.
- **Lesson 92,** comparing and ordering fractions and decimals.
- **Lesson 94,** solving two-step problems that involve a fraction of a group.
- **Lesson 98,** identifying and writing fractions equal to 1 and to $\frac{1}{2}$.
- **Lesson 99,** changing improper fractions to whole or mixed numbers.
- **Lesson 100,** adding and subtracting fractions with common denominators.
- **Lesson 103,** finding equivalent fractions.
- **Lesson 106,** writing the reduced form of a fraction.
- **Lessons 111–113,** simplifying and renaming fractions, and finding a common denominator.

Lesson Planner

Lesson	New Concepts	Materials	Resources
81	• Classifying Triangles	• Manipulative Kit: rulers • Grid paper	• Power Up I Worksheet • Lesson Activity 8
82	• Symmetry	• Manipulative Kit: mirrors, rulers	• Power Up I Worksheet • Lesson Activity 24
83	• Division with Zeros in Three-Digit Answers	• Manipulative Kit: rulers	• Power Up I Worksheet
84	• Multiplying by 10, 100, and 1000		• Power Up I Worksheet
85	• Multiplying Multiples of 10 and 100, Part 2	• Manipulative Kit: rulers	• Power Up G Worksheet
Cumulative Assessment			• Cumulative Test 16 • Test-Day Activity 8
86	• Multiplying Two Two-Digit Numbers, Part 1		• Power Up G Worksheet
87	• Remainders in Word Problems		• Power Up G Worksheet
88	• Multiplying Two Two-Digit Numbers, Part 2	• Grid paper	• Power Up G Worksheet • Lesson Activity 8
89	• Mixed Numbers and Improper Fractions	• Manipulative Kit: rulers • Fraction manipulatives from Investigation 8	• Power Up G Worksheet
90	• Classifying Quadrilaterals	• Manipulative Kit: mirrors	• Power Up I Worksheet • Lesson Activity 25
Cumulative Assessment			• Cumulative Test 17 • Performance Task 9
Inv. 9	• Analyzing Relationships	• Coordinate plane	• Lesson Activity 26

All resources are also available on the Resources and Planner CD.

Additional Resources

- Instructional Masters
- Reteaching Masters
- Refresher Lessons for California Standards
- Calculator Activities
- Resources and Planner CD
- Assessment Guide
- Performance Tasks
- Instructional Transparencies
- Answer Key CD
- Power Up Workbook
- Written Practice Workbook

Math Highlights

Enduring Understandings — The "Big Picture"

After completing Section 9, students will understand that:

- Some figures are symmetrical.
- Multiplying multi-digit numbers requires understanding place value.
- Mixed numbers can be renamed as improper fractions.
- Quadrilaterals can be classified according to their attributes.

Essential Questions

- How do I determine if a figure has a line of symmetry?
- How do I multiply multi-digit numbers?
- What is an improper fraction?
- What makes a quadrilateral a rectangle?

Math Content Highlights	Math Processes Highlights
Number Sense • **Division with Zeros in Three-Digit Answers** *Lesson 83* • **Multiplying by 10, 100, and 1000** *Lesson 84* • **Multiplying Two or More Multiples of 10 and 100** *Lesson 85* • **Multiplying Two Two-Digit Numbers** *Lessons 86, 87* • **Mixed Numbers and Improper Fractions** *Lesson 89* **Algebraic Thinking** • **Solving Word Problems Involving Multi-Digit Division and Multiplication** *Lessons 83, 84* • **Remainders in Word Problems** *Lesson 87* **Geometry and Measurement** • **Classifying Triangles** *Lesson 81* • **Symmetry** *Lesson 82* • **Classifying Quadrilaterals** *Lesson 90* • **Analyzing Relationships** *Investigation 9*	**Problem Solving** • **Strategies** – **Act It Out or Make a Model** *Lesson 88* – **Draw a Picture or Diagram** *Lessons 81, 82, 83, 85, 86, 89* – **Guess and Check** *Lesson 87* – **Make an Organized List** *Lessons 84, 86* – **Make It Simpler** *Lessons 88, 90* – **Write a Number Sentence or Equation** *Lessons 83, 87, 90* • **Real-World Applications** *Lessons 82, 83, 84, 87, 88* **Communication** • **Discuss** *Lessons 82, 83, 84, 89, Investigation 9* • **Explain** *Lessons 81, 82, 84, 85, 88, 89, 90, Investigation 9* • **Formulate** *Lesson 85* **Connections** • **Math to Math** – **Measurement and Geometry** *Lessons 81, 82, 90* – **Multiplication and Number Sense** *Lessons 84, 85, 86, 88* – **Algebra and Geometry** *Investigation 9* • **Math and Other Subjects** – **Math and History** *Lessons 85, 87* – **Math and Geography** *Lessons 82, 84, 89* – **Math and Science** *Lesson 84, 90* – **Math and Sports** *Lessons 81, 83, 84, 85, 88, 89, 90* **Representation** • **Model** *Lessons 81, 88, 90, Investigation 9* • **Represent** *Lessons 81, 82, 83, 84, 85, 86, 87, 88, 89, 90, Investigation 9* • **Formulate an Equation** *Lessons 84, 89* • **Using Manipulative/Hands On** *Lessons 81, 82, 83, 84, 85, 86, 87, 88, 89, 90*

Support for universal access is included with each lesson. Specific resources and features are listed on each lesson planning page. Features in the Teacher's Manual to customize instruction include the following:

Teacher's Manual Support

Alternative Approach	Provides a different path to concept development. *Lessons 81–88, 90*
Manipulative Use	Provides alternate concept development through the use of manipulatives. *Lessons 81, 83, 85*
Flexible Grouping	Provides suggestions for various grouping strategies tied to specific lesson examples. *TM page 598A*
Inclusion	Provides ideas for including all students by accommodating special needs. *Lessons 81–90, Inv. 9*
Developing Academic Language	Provides a list of new and maintained vocabulary words along with words that might be difficult for English learners. *Lessons 81–90, Inv. 9*
English Learners	Provides strategies for teaching specific vocabulary that may be difficult for English learners. *Lessons 81–90, Inv. 9*
Errors and Misconceptions	Provides information about common misconceptions students encounter with concepts. *Lessons 81–90*
Extend the Example	Provides additional concept development for advanced learners. *Lessons 81–90*
Extend the Problem	Provides an opportunity for advanced learners to broaden concept development by expanding on a particular problem approach or context. *Lessons 81–90, Inv. 9*
Early Finishers	Provides additional math concept extensions for advanced learners at the end of the Written Practice. *Lesson 82*
Investigate Further	Provides further depth to concept development by providing additional activities for an investigation. *Investigation 9*

Additional Resources

The following resources are also available to support universal access:

- Adaptations for Saxon Math
- English Learner Handbook
- Online Activities
- Performance Tasks
- Refresher Lessons for CA Standards
- Reteaching Masters

Technology

Student Resources

- Student Edition eBook
- Calculator Activities
- Online Resources at www.SaxonMath.com/Int4ActivitiesCA
  — Real-World Investigation *Lesson 82*

Teacher Resources

- Resources and Planner CD
- Test and Practice Generator CD
- Monitoring Student Progress: eGradebook CD
- Teacher's Manual eBook CD
- Answer Key CD
- Adaptations for Saxon Math CD
- Online Resources at www.SaxonMath.com

Cumulative Assessment

The assessments in Saxon Math are frequent and consistently placed to offer a regular method of ongoing testing.

Power-Up Test: Allow no more than ten minutes for this test of basic facts and skills.

Cumulative Test: Next, administer this test, which checks mastery of concepts in previous lessons.

Test-Day Activity and Performance Task: The remaining class time can be spent on these activities. Students can finish the Test-Day Activity for homework. Advanced learners can complete the extended Performance Task in another class period.

After Lesson 85

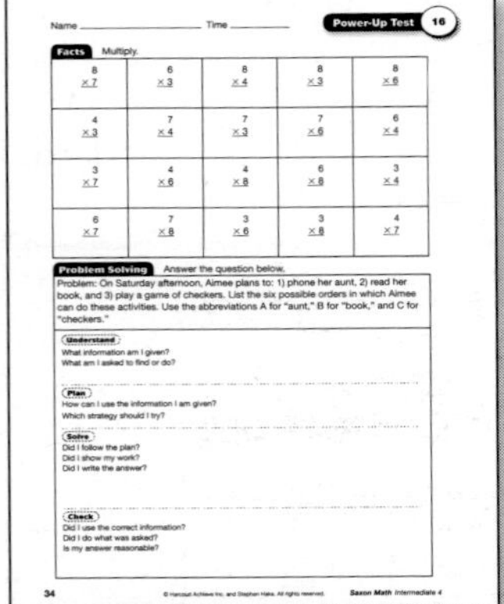

Power-Up Test 16

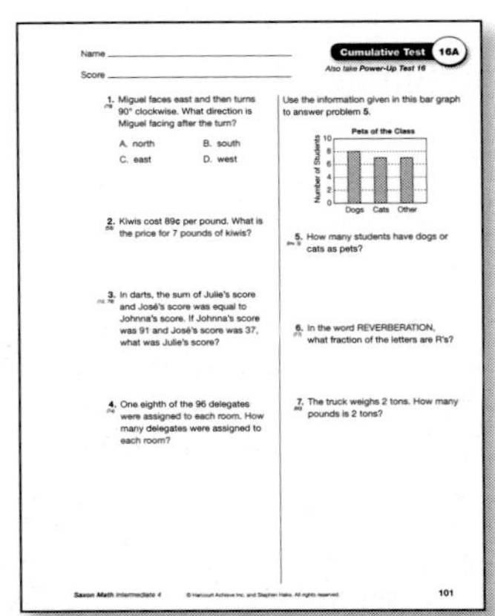

Cumulative Test 16

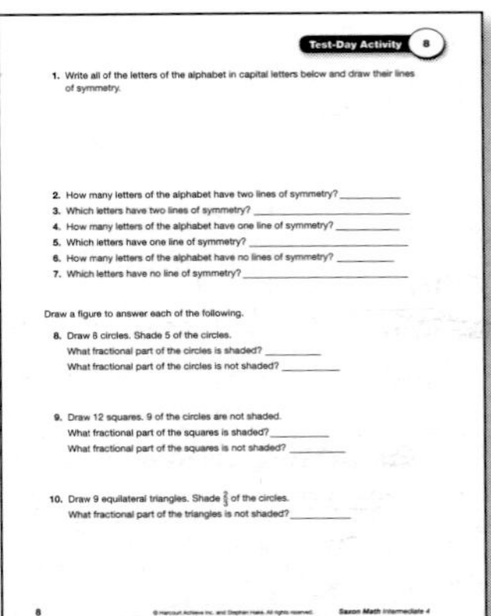

Test-Day Activity 8

After Lesson 90

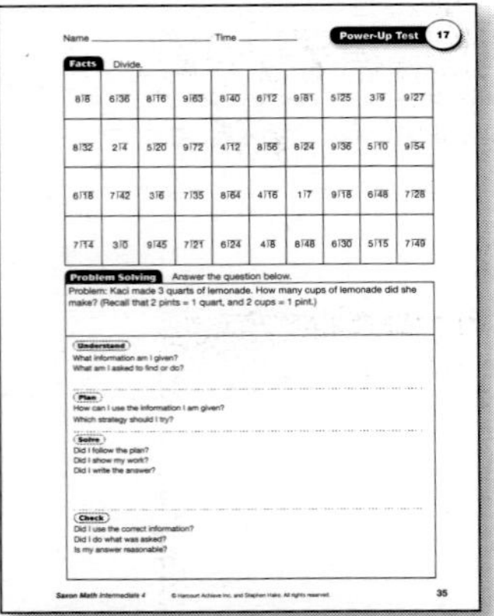

Power-Up Test 17

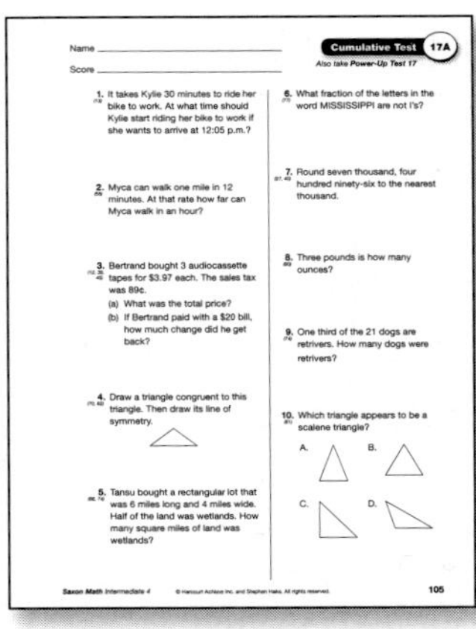

Cumulative Test 17

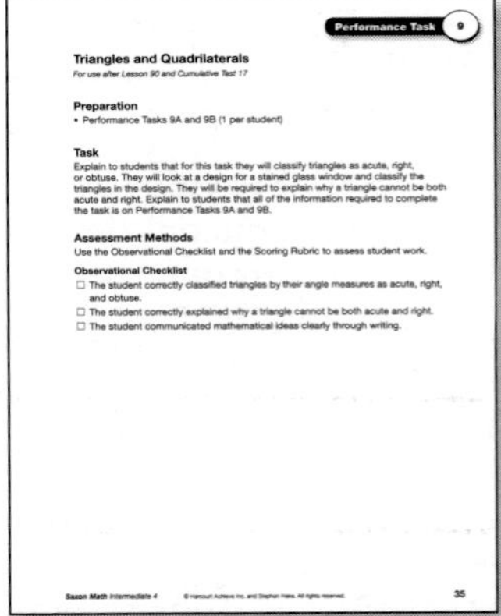

Performance Task 9

Evidence of Learning — What Students Should Know

By the conclusion of Section 9, students should be able to demonstrate the following competencies through the Cumulative Assessments, which are correlated to the California Mathematics Standards:

- Multiply by two-digit numbers. **NS 1.2, NS 1.3, MR 2.6, MR 3.1**
- Classify a triangle by its angles or sides. **MG 3.5, MG 3.7, MR 2.3, MR 2.4, MR 3.3**
- Use the division algorithm to solve word problems involving multi-digit numbers. **NS 3.2, NS 3.4, MR 3.1**

Reteaching

Students who score below 80% on assessments may be in need of reteaching. Refer to the Reteaching Masters for reteaching opportunities for every lesson.

Benchmarking and Tracking the California Mathematics Standards

Benchmark Tests

Benchmark Tests correlated to lesson concepts allow you to assess student progress after every 20 lessons. An End-of-Course Test is a final benchmark test of the complete textbook. The Benchmark Tests are available in the Assessment Guide.

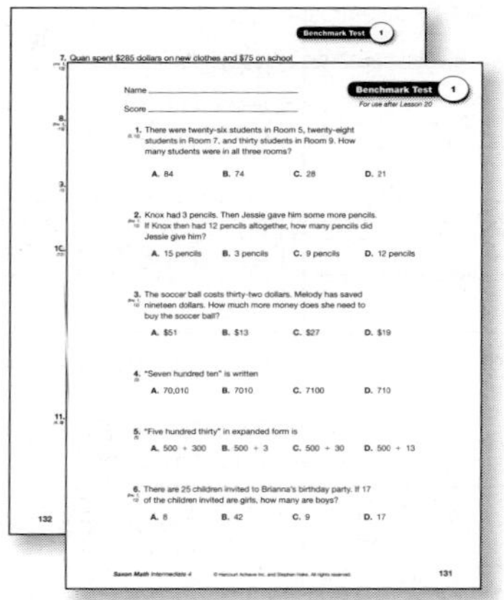

Monitoring Student Progress: eGradebook CD

To track California Standards mastery, enter students' scores on Cumulative Tests and Benchmark Tests into the Monitoring Student Progress: eGradebook CD. Use the report titled *Benchmark Standards Report* to determine which California Standards were assessed and the level of mastery for each student. Generate a variety of other reports for class tracking and more.

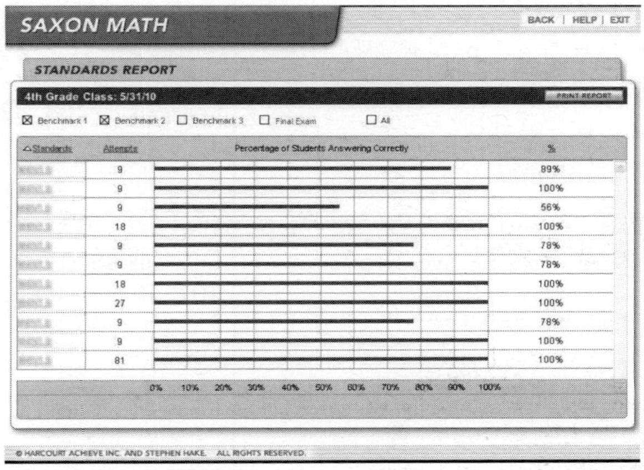

Test and Practice Generator CD

Test items also available in Spanish.

The Test and Practice Generator is an easy-to-manage benchmarking and assessment tool that creates unlimited practice and tests in multiple formats and allows you to customize questions or create new ones. A variety of reports are available to track student progress toward mastery of the California Standards throughout the year.

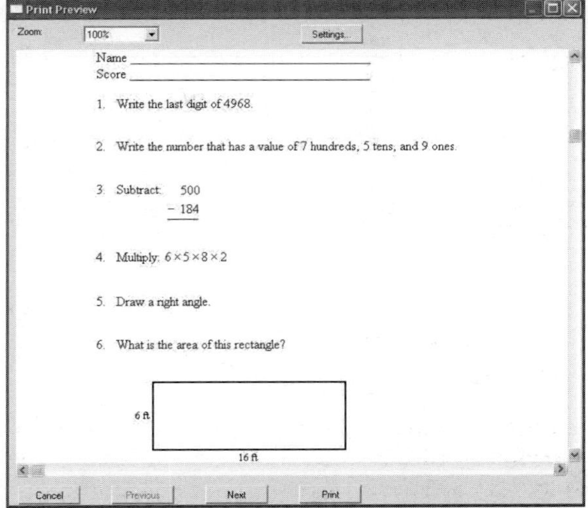

Content Trace

Lesson	New Concepts	Practiced	Assessed	Looking Forward
81	• Classifying Triangles	Lessons 81, 82, 83, 84, 85, 86, 88, 89, 91, 100, 107, 113	Test 17	Lessons 82, 90, 96, 97, 108, 109, 114
82	• Symmetry	Lessons 82, 83, 84, 85, 86 87, 88, 89, 93, 94, 99, 106, 107	Test 17	Lessons 90, 96, 97, 108, 109, 114
83	• Division with Zeros in Three-Digit Answers	Lessons 83, 84, 85, 86, 87, 89, 90, 91, 92, 93, 94, 95, 96, 97, 98, 99, 100, 101, 103, 104, 105, 107, 108, 109, 110, 112, 113, 114	Tests 17, 18, 19, 21	Lessons 87, 91
84	• Multiplying by 10, 100, and 1000	Lessons 84, 85, 86, 87, 88, 89, 92, 94, 96, 98, 100	Tests 17, 18	Lessons 85, 86, 88, 91, 104, 105
85	• Multiplying Multiples of 10 and 100, Part 2	Lessons 85, 86, 87, 88, 89, 90, 92, 93, 95, 96, 97, 98, 99, 100, 101, 102, 103, 104, 105, 114	Tests 18, 19, 20, 21	Lessons 86, 88, 91, 104, 105
86	• Multiplying Two Two-Digit Numbers, Part 1	Lessons 86, 87, 93, 95, 96, 98	Test 19	Lessons 88, 91, 104, 105
87	• Remainders in Word Problems	Lessons 87, 88, 89, 90, 91, 92, 93, 96, 97, 98, 99, 101, 104, 111	Tests 18, 19	Lessons 89, 91, 92, 94, 98, 99, 100, 103, 106, 111, 112, 113
88	• Multiplying Two Two-Digit Numbers, Part 2	Lessons 88, 89, 90, 91, 92, 93, 94, 95, 96, 97, 98, 99, 100, 101, 103, 104, 105, 106, 112, 113	Tests 18, 19, 20	Lessons 91, 104, 105
89	• Mixed Numbers and Improper Fractions	Lessons 89, 90, 91, 92, 93, 94, 95, 96, 97, 98	Tests 18, 20	Lessons 92, 94, 98, 99, 100, 103, 106, 111, 112, 113
90	• Classifying Quadrilaterals	Lessons 90, 91, 92, 93, 94, 99, 103, 106, 111, 112	Tests 18, 19	Lessons 96, 97, 108, 109, 114
Inv. 9	• Analyzing Relationships	Lessons 91, 95, 102, 103, 111	Tests 14, 20	***Saxon Math*** *Intermediate 5*

Planning & Preparation

• Classifying Triangles

Objectives

- Classify a triangle by the measure of its angles.
- Classify a triangle by the length of its sides.
- Draw a triangle by its attributes.

Prerequisite Skills

- Describing and drawing angles as acute, obtuse, right, or straight.
- Drawing different kinds of polygons.
- Identifying a figure's vertices, angles, and edges.

Materials

Instructional Masters

- Power Up I Worksheet
- Lesson Activity 8

Manipulative Kit

- Rulers
- Protractors*

Teacher-provided materials

- Grid paper
- Construction paper, scissors, index cards*

**optional*

California Mathematics Content Standards

MG 3.0, 3.5 Know the definitions of a right angle, an acute angle, and an obtuse angle. Understand that 90°, 180°, 270°, and 360° are associated, respectively, with $\frac{1}{4}$, $\frac{1}{2}$, $\frac{3}{4}$, and full turns.

MG 3.0, 3.7 Know the definitions of different triangles (e.g., equilateral, isosceles, scalene) and identify their attributes.

MR 2.0, 2.3 Use a variety of methods, such as words, numbers, symbols, charts, graphs, tables, diagrams, and models, to explain mathematical reasoning.

MR 2.0, 2.4 Express the solution clearly and logically by using the appropriate mathematical notation and terms and clear language; support solutions with evidence in both verbal and symbolic work.

MR 3.0, 3.3 Develop generalizations of the results obtained and apply them in other circumstances.

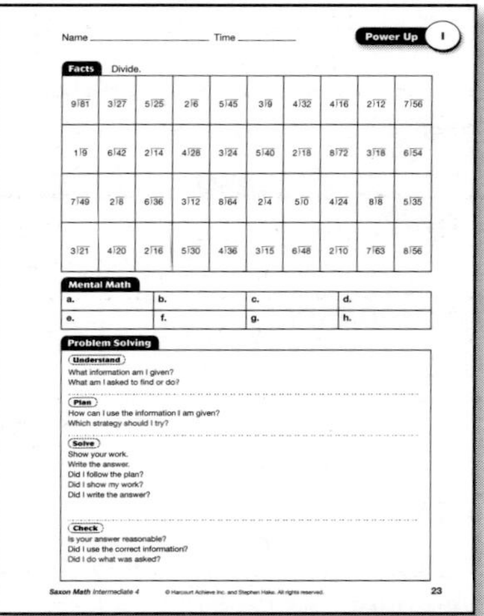

Power Up I Worksheet

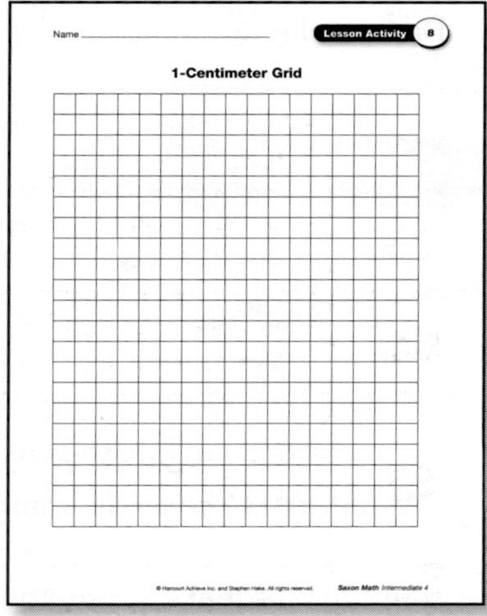

Lesson Activity 8

Universal Access

Reaching All Special Needs Students

Special Education Students	At-Risk Students	English Learners	Advanced Learners
• Inclusion (TM) • Adaptations for Saxon Math	• Alternative Approach (TM) • Error Alert (TM) • Reteaching Masters • Refresher Lessons for California Standards	• English Learners (TM) • Developing Academic Language (TM) • English Learner Handbook	• Extend the Example (TM) • Extend the Problem (TM) • Online Activities

TM=Teacher's Manual

Developing Academic Language

New	Maintained	English Learner
acute triangle	degrees	obtuse
equiangular		
equilateral		
isosceles triangle		
obtuse triangle		
right triangle		
scalene triangle		

Problem Solving Discussion

Problem

In the diagram at right, the circle stands for students who have one or more pets at home. A letter inside the circle stands for a particular student who has a pet. A letter outside the circle stands for a student who does not have any pets.The letter A stands for Adrian, who has a dog. The letter B stands for Brooke, who does not have any pets. Copy the graph on your paper. On the graph, place the letter C for Clarrisa, who keeps a goldfish, and D for David, who does not have pets.

Students with Pets

A

B

Focus Strategy

Draw a Picture or Diagram

Understand ***Understand the problem.***

"What information are we given?"

We are shown a diagram that has two letters. The letter A is inside the circle, and the letter B is outside the circle.

"What does the circle stand for?"

Letters inside the circle stand for students who have pets. Letters outside the circle stand for students who do not have pets.

"What are we asked to do?"

We are asked to place the letters C and D in the diagram. C is for Clarrisa, who has a pet, and D is for David, who does not have a pet.

Plan ***Make a plan.***

"What problem-solving strategy will we use to solve this problem?"

We are asked to *make a diagram* of the situation described in the problem.

Solve ***Carry out the plan.***

"Where do we place letters for Clarrisa and David?"

Clarrisa keeps a pet (goldfish), so the letter C goes inside the circle. David does not have any pets, so the letter D goes outside the circle.

"What should our diagram look like?"

The diagram might look like the diagram at right.

Students with Pets

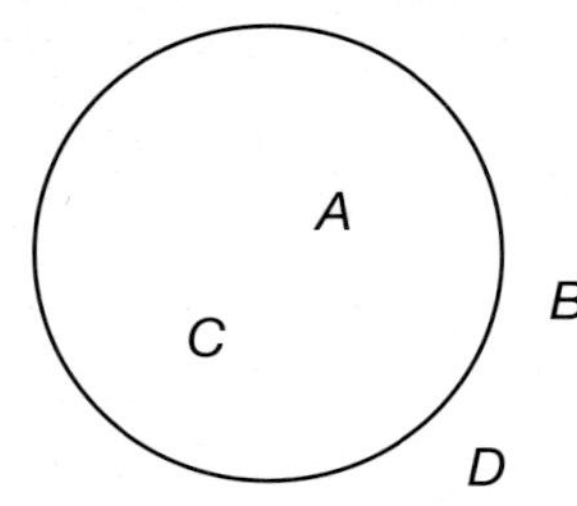

Check ***Look back.***

"Is our answer reasonable?"

We know that our answer is reasonable, because both students who have pets (Adrian and Clarrisa) are represented inside the circle, and both students who do not have pets (Brooke and David) are represented outside the circle.

• Classifying Triangles

California Mathematics Content Standards

- **MG 3.0, 3.5** Know the definitions of a right angle, an acute angle, and an obtuse angle. Understand that 90°, 180°, 270°, and 360° are associated, respectively, with $\frac{1}{4}$, $\frac{1}{2}$, $\frac{3}{4}$, and full turns.
- **MG 3.0, 3.7** Know the definitions of different triangles (e.g., equilateral, isosceles, scalene) and identify their attributes.
- **MR 2.0, 2.4** Express the solution clearly and logically by using the appropriate mathematical notation and terms and clear language; support solutions with evidence in both verbal and symbolic work.

Power Up

facts Power Up I

count aloud Count by fours from 80 to 120.

mental math Find each difference by first increasing both numbers so that the second number ends in zero in problems **a–c.**

a. **Number Sense:** 63 − 28 35

b. **Number Sense:** 45 − 17 28

c. **Number Sense:** 80 − 46 34

d. **Money:** Noah had $10.00. Then he spent $5.85 on lunch. How much money did he have left over? $4.15

e. **Measurement:** How many inches is $\frac{1}{2}$ of a foot? 6 in.

f. **Measurement:** How many inches is $\frac{1}{4}$ of a foot? 3 in.

g. **Estimation:** The total cost for 4 movie rentals was $15.92. Round this amount to the nearest dollar and then divide by 4 to estimate the cost per rental. $4

h. **Calculation:** 5^2, × 2, × 2, × 2, × 2 400

problem solving

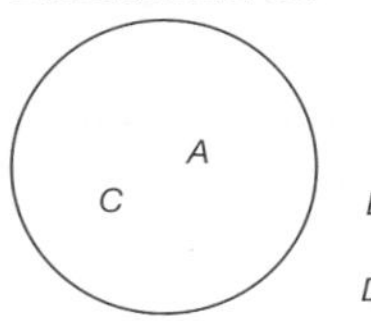

In the diagram at right, the circle stands for students who have one or more pets at home. A letter inside the circle stands for a particular student who has a pet. A letter outside the circle stands for a student who does not have any pets. The letter *A* stands for Adrian, who has a dog. The letter *B* stands for Brooke, who does not have any pets. Copy the graph on your paper. On the graph, place the letter *C* for Clarrisa, who keeps a goldfish, and *D* for David, who does not have pets.

Students with Pets

A

B

Facts Divide.

9 9)81	9 3)27	5 5)25	3 2)6	9 5)45	3 3)9	8 4)32	4 4)16	6 2)12	8 7)56
9 1)9	7 6)42	7 2)14	7 4)28	8 3)24	8 5)40	9 2)18	9 8)72	6 3)18	9 6)54
7 7)49	4 2)8	6 6)36	4 3)12	8 8)64	2 2)4	0 5)0	6 4)24	1 8)8	7 5)35
7 3)21	5 4)20	8 2)16	6 5)30	9 4)36	5 3)15	8 6)48	5 2)10	9 7)63	7 8)56

Power Up

Facts

Distribute **Power Up I** to students. See answers below.

Count Aloud

Before students begin the Mental Math exercises, do these counting exercises as a class.

Mental Math

Encourage students to share different ways to mentally compute these exercises. Strategies for exercises are listed below.

a. Subtract 30, then Add 2

63 − 30 = 33; 33 + 2 = 35

Subtract 3, then Subtract 25

63 − 3 = 60; 60 − 25 = 35

d. Subtract $5, then Subtract 85¢

$10 − $5 = $5; $5 − 85¢ = $4.15

Subtract $6, then Add 15¢

$10 − $6 = $4; $4 + 15¢ = $4.15

Problem Solving

Refer to **Problem-Solving Strategy Discussion,** p. 541H.

New Concept

Active Learning

One way to introduce the lesson is to ask students to stand and use their arms to demonstrate acute, right, and obtuse angles.

Error Alert

As you discuss the different ways to classify triangles, make sure students understand that we classify triangles by their sides and by their angles. Therefore every triangle can be classified two ways. To help reinforce this concept, draw the triangles below on the board or overhead. Ask students to classify each triangle by its sides. Record the responses under each triangle. Then have students classify each triangle by its angles. Record those responses as well.

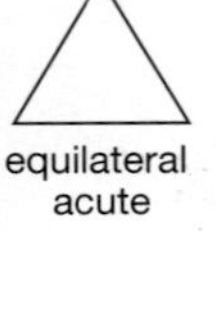
equilateral acute

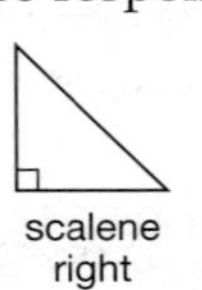
scalene right

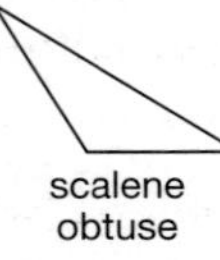
scalene obtuse

scalene acute

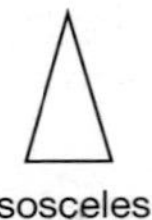
isosceles acute

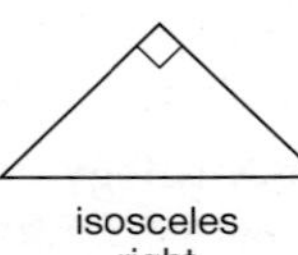
isosceles right

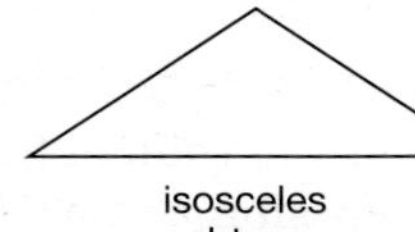
isosceles obtuse

You may have students use drawing software to draw different types of triangles.

Example 1

When drawing right triangles, isosceles triangles, or right isosceles triangles, some students may find it helpful to draw on grid paper.

Alternate Method

Explain that another way to draw a right isosceles triangle is to first draw a right angle with any side lengths. A ruler can then be used to mark off equal lengths for both legs of the right angle. A third line segment can then be drawn to complete the triangle.

Extend the Example

Invite advanced learners to draw an equilateral triangle. After the drawings have been completed, have students describe the method that they used.

(continued)

New Concept

One way to classify (describe) a triangle is by referring to its largest angle as either obtuse, right, or acute. An obtuse angle is larger than a right angle. An acute angle is smaller than a right angle.

Thinking Skills

Conclude

Describe two different characteristics of the angles of an equilateral triangle.

The angles of an equilateral triangle are congruent and acute.

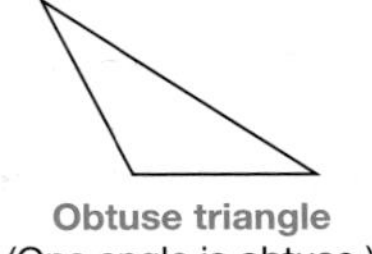
Obtuse triangle
(One angle is obtuse.)

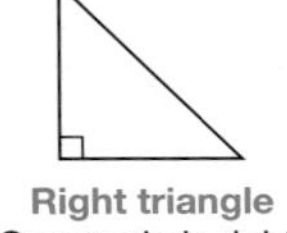
Right triangle
(One angle is right.)

Acute triangle
(All angles are acute.)

Another way to classify a triangle is by comparing the lengths of its sides. If all three sides are equal in length, the triangle is **equilateral.** If at least two sides are equal in length, the triangle is an **isosceles triangle.** If all three sides have different lengths, the triangle is an **scalene triangle.**

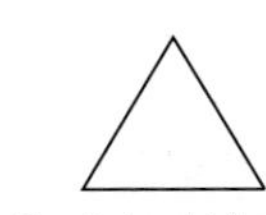
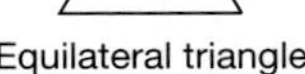
Equilateral triangle

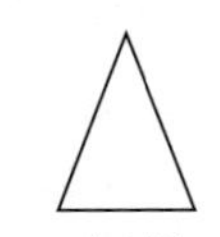
Isosceles triangle

Scalene triangle

Represent Can an isosceles triangle have an obtuse angle? Draw a triangle to support your conclusion. Yes

Sample:

Notice that the three angles of the equilateral triangle are the same size. This means an equilateral triangle is also **equiangular.** Now notice that only two angles of the isosceles triangle are the same size. In a triangle, the number of angles with the same measure equals the number of sides with the same measure.

Example 1

Draw a triangle that is both a right triangle and an isosceles triangle.

A right triangle contains one right angle. An isosceles triangle has two sides of equal length. We begin by drawing a right angle with equal-length sides.

English Learners

Say, ***"The word obtuse means not sharp or pointed."***

Ask, ***"How can you use the definition of obtuse to help you remember whether an obtuse angle is less than or greater than 90°?"*** Sample: An obtuse angle is greater than 90°. It looks like it is not as "sharp" as an acute angle.

Then we draw the third side of the triangle.

Classify Describe the angles of a right triangle. One angle is a right angle and the other two angles are acute angles.

Example 2

Describe this triangle in as many ways as possible.

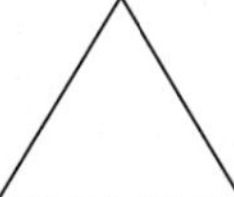

Write can see that this triangle has all sides the same length so it is an **equilateral triangle.** Each angle is acute so it is an **acute triangle.** All three angles are the same number of degrees so it is an **equiangular triangle.** It has two or more sides of the same length, so it is also an **isosceles triangle.**

Conclude Can an isosceles triangle also be a scalene triangle? Why or why not?

No; A scalene triangle has all three sides of different lengths, an isosceles triangle has two sides of the same length.

Lesson Practice

a. **Conclude** Can a right triangle have two right angles? Why or why not?

b. What is the name for a triangle that has at least two sides equal in length? isosceles triangle

c. Draw an acute scalene triangle. Sample:

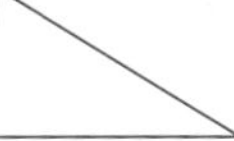

a. No. The sides would not meet to form a triangle; sample:

Written Practice

Distributed and Integrated

*1. (13, 76) **Analyze** Use the following information to answer parts **a–c.**

Freeman rode his bike 2 miles from his house to Didi's house. Together they rode 4 miles to the lake. Didi caught 8 fish. At 3:30 p.m. they rode back to Didi's house. Then Freeman rode home.

a. Altogether, how far did Freeman ride his bike? 12 mi

b. It took Freeman an hour and a half to get home from the lake. At what time did he get home? 5:00 p.m.

Math Background

"Can any three segments form a triangle?"

No. For three segments to form a triangle, the sum of the lengths of the two shortest segments must be greater than the length of the longest segment.

To understand this, we can imagine joining the two shorter segments with a *hinge*. To form a triangle, we need to be able to open the hinge so the unconnected endpoints of the shortest segments meet the endpoints of the longest segment.

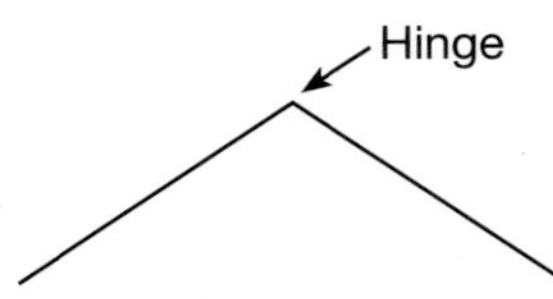

If the combined length of the shortest segments is not as long as the longest segment, the triangle will not be closed no matter how big the angle is.

New Concept *(Continued)*

Example 2

Error Alert

A common error when classifying triangles is to assume that an isosceles triangle always has exactly two sides of equal length. Explain that any triangle is isosceles if it has *at least* two sides of equal length. For this reason, a triangle that is equilateral is also isosceles. However, a triangle that is isosceles is not necessarily equilateral.

Lesson Practice

Guided Practice

Use these problems as guided practice to check the students' understanding of today's concept.

Problem a Conclude

Ask students who answer "yes" to include a sketch that supports their answer.

Problem b Extend the Problem

"Explain why an equilateral triangle is also an isosceles triangle." Sample: If two or more sides of a triangle are equal, the triangle is isosceles; An equilateral triangle is also isosceles because two or more of its sides are equal.

"Is an isosceles triangle also an equilateral triangle? Explain your answer." Not necessarily; If two sides of a triangle are equal, the triangle is isosceles; If all three sides of a triangle are equal, the triangle is both isosceles and equilateral.

Problem c

Error Alert

Ask students to explain why the triangle they drew is an acute scalene triangle.

Closure

The questions below help assess the concepts taught in this lesson.

"How many different ways are triangles classified? Explain your answer." Two ways; Triangles are classified by their sides, and by their angles.

"What are three names we use when we classify the angles of a triangle?" Acute, obtuse, right

"What are three names we use when we classify the sides of a triangle?" Scalene, isosceles, equilateral

Ask students to draw a triangle, and then classify it. See student work.

Written Practice

Math Conversations

Independent Practice and Discussions to Increase Understanding

Problem 1 (Analyze)

Some students may find it helpful to make a sketch or map of the situation.

After each correct answer is identified, invite a volunteer to explain why that answer is correct.

Problem 2 (Conclude)

To help recognize the turn that is necessary, some students may find it helpful to turn their books or trace the letter and vary the orientation of the tracing.

Problem 5 (Estimate)

"Explain how we can decide what each tick mark on the ruler represents." Count the number of equal parts between two consecutive whole inches. Since each inch is divided into four equal parts, each tick mark represents 1 inch ÷ 4, or $\frac{1}{4}$ inch.

Problem 9 (Analyze)

"When we write a fraction to represent part of a set, what does the denominator of the fraction represent?" The total number of members in the set

"What does the numerator of the fraction represent?" The number of members that are being named

Problem 13

Extend the Problem

Challenge advanced learners to decompose one or both factors so that the product can be found using only mental math. Sample: 50 × (10 + 10 + 5) = 500 + 500 + 250 = 1250

Problem 16

Before students complete the arithmetic, ask:

"How many digits should we expect to find in the quotient? Explain why you named that number." Three; Because the divisor is greater than the digit in the thousands place of the dividend, the first digit in the quotient will be in the hundreds place.

"Will the quotient include a remainder? Use a divisibility rule to explain why or why not." No; The divisor is 5, the digit in the ones place of the dividend is 5, and all multiples of 5 have a 5 or a 0 in the ones place.

(continued)

c. Didi caught twice as many fish as Freeman. How many fish did Freeman catch? 4 fish

▶ *2. (78) **Conclude** Describe the number of degrees and the direction of a turn that would move this letter B to an upright position. 90° clockwise or 270° counterclockwise

3. (40, 61) **Estimate** Find a reasonable sum of 4876 and 3149 by rounding each number to the nearest thousand and then adding. 8000

4. (20, 50) **Explain** What is the perimeter of a pentagon if each side is 20 centimeters long? Explain your reasoning. 100 cm; A pentagon has 5 sides, and 5 × 20 = 100.

▶ *5. (42) **Estimate** Find the length of this segment to the nearest quarter inch: $3\frac{1}{2}$ in. or $3\frac{2}{4}$ in.

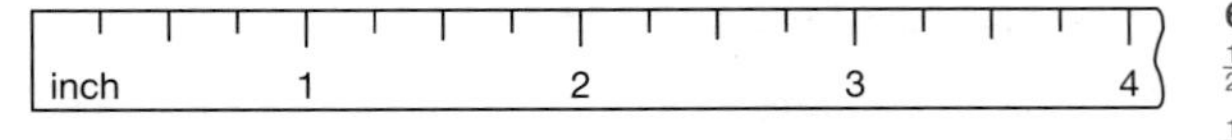

6. 18 players; $\frac{1}{2}$ were on the field. 9 players; $\frac{1}{2}$ were off the field. 9 players

6. (74) **Represent** One half of the 18 players were on the field. How many players were on the field? Draw a picture to illustrate the problem. 9 players

7. (29) A dime is $\frac{1}{10}$ of a dollar. What fraction of a dollar is a penny? $\frac{1}{100}$

*8. (80) **Generalize** Write an equation to show how to convert any number of ounces to pounds. Use o for ounces and p for pounds. $16p = o$ or $o = 16p$

▶ *9. (77) **Analyze** What fraction of the set of triangles is shaded? $\frac{2}{5}$

10. (Inv. 4) **Represent** One millimeter is $\frac{1}{10}$ of a centimeter. Write that number as a decimal number. Then use words to write the number. 0.1; one tenth

*11. (71) 31×20 = 620

12. (71) 51×30 = 1530

▶*13. (71) 25×50 = 1250

14. (79) $7\overline{)1000}$ 142 R 6

15. (79) $3\overline{)477}$ 159

▶ 16. (79) $5\overline{)2585}$ 517

Inclusion

Use this strategy if the student displays:

- Poor Retention.
- Difficulty with Abstract Processing

Classifying Triangles (Individual)

Materials: construction paper, rulers, scissors

- Have students use their ruler and draw a triangle with dimensions: 3 in., 4 in., and 5 in. Students should cut the triangle out and write **Scalene** on it. Then have students create a triangle with dimensions: 4 in., 4 in., and 5 in. and write **Isosceles** on it. Finally have students create a triangle with dimensions of all 5 in. and write **Equilateral** on it.
- Guide students to draw a right angle on the paper. Have students make a triangle around the right angle, cut it out and write **Right** on it. Help student make an obtuse angle, make a triangle out of it, and write **Obtuse** on it. Finally, help students make an acute angle, make a triangle around it, and write **Acute** on it.

17. (79) $\$15.48 \div 9$ $1.72

18. (79) $716 \div 4$ 179

19. (34, 69) $8x = 352$ 44

***20.** (Inv. 8) **Multiple Choice** Which of the following is equivalent to $\frac{1}{2}$? D

A 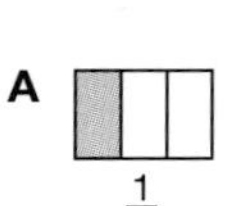 $\frac{1}{3}$

B 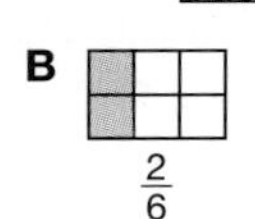 $\frac{2}{6}$

C 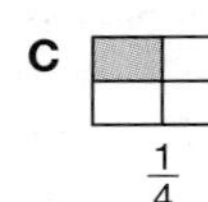 $\frac{1}{4}$

D 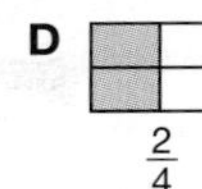 $\frac{2}{4}$

21. (47, 48) **(Represent)** Use digits to write the number three million, eight hundred fifty thousand in standard form. Then round it to the nearest million. 3,850,000; 4,000,000

***22.** (64, Inv. 7) **a.** **(Evaluate)** If $y = 2x + 3$, then what is y when $x = 1, 2$, and 3? 5, 7, 9

▸ **b.** **(Model)** Use **Lesson Activity 8** and graph $y = 2x + 3$ on a coordinate graph. See student work.

23. (RF9, 23, 26) Write the name of the property illustrated by each equation.

a. $a + b = b + a$ Commutative Property of Addition

b. $a(b \cdot c) = (a \cdot b) \cdot c$ Associative Property of Multiplication

c. $a \cdot 0 = 0$ Property of Zero for Multiplication

d. $a + 0 = a$ Identity Property of Addition

▸***24.** (66) Find the perimeter and area of this rectangle: 60 in.; 200 in^2

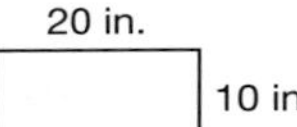

▸ **25.** (81) **(Represent)** Draw an equilateral triangle with sides 2 cm long.

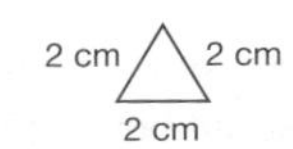

26. (20, 42) What is the perimeter in millimeters of the triangle you drew in problem **25?** 60 mm

Alternative Approach: Using Manipulatives

To help students identify and classify triangles, have them use rulers to measure the sides and a square corner from a piece of paper to compare the angles of triangles to a right angle.

Provide index cards, each with a diagram of a different triangle. Give each pair of students one index card and ask them to measure and label all three sides and all three angles. To compare the angles, instruct students to insert the square corner into each angle of the triangle. If the angle is smaller than the corner, it is an acute angle. If the angle is larger than the square corner, it is an obtuse angle. Ask:

"How do you know if a triangle is equilateral?" Sample: All three sides of the triangle are the same length.

Repeat for isosceles, scalene, right, acute, and obtuse.

Written Practice *(Continued)*

Math Conversations *(cont.)*

Problem 22b (Model)

The line should intercept the y-axis at 3, and pass through the points (1, 5), (2, 7), and (3, 9).

Problem 24

Encourage students to find the perimeter and the area using only mental math.

Problem 25 (Represent)

Manipulative Use

Students will need rulers to draw the triangle that is described in this problem.

Note that the drawing may involve some trial and error because the triangle is an equilateral triangle.

(continued)

Written Practice (Continued)

Math Conversations (cont.)

Problem 27 Conclude

Extend the Problem

"Which sides of the polygon appear to be perpendicular?" Sides AB and AC, and sides AC and CD

Errors and Misconceptions

Problem 24

Remind students who name the perimeter of the rectangle as 30 inches that the perimeter of a rectangle is a measure of its total distance around, and not the sum of its length and its width. Explain that perimeter is a measure of the sum of twice the length and twice the width because a rectangle has two lengths and two widths.

Problem 25

Some students may find it helpful to first draw a 2 cm horizontal line segment to represent the base of the triangle, mark the midpoint of the segment, and then draw a perpendicular vertical line. The upper vertex of the equilateral triangle will be on the perpendicular line.

▶*27. (17) a. Conclude In this polygon, which side appears to be parallel to side *AB*? side *CD* (or side *DC*)

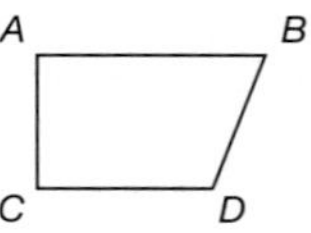

b. Which angle appears to be obtuse? angle *D*

28. (Inv. 5) This graph shows the relationship between Colby's age and Neelam's age. How old was Neelam when Colby was 4 years old? 7 years old

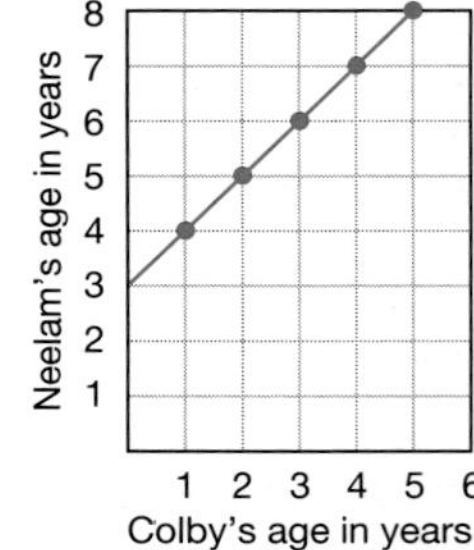

29. (Inv. 4, 45) Represent Each grid represents a decimal number. Write each decimal number. Then write the sum and the difference of those numbers. 0.46; 0.58; 1.04; 0.12

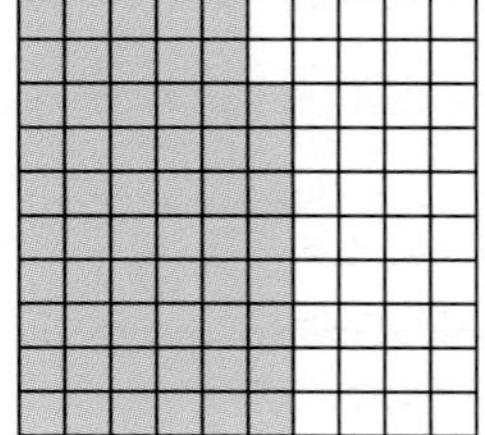

30. (13, 61, 75, 79) Estimate A mail carrier worked from 8 a.m. to noon and from 1 p.m. to 4 p.m. During those times, the carrier delivered mail to 691 homes. About how many deliveries did the carrier make each hour? Explain your answer. Sample: about 100 homes; Change 691 to 700, then divide by 7 hours; $700 \div 7 = 100$

546 *Saxon Math* Intermediate 4

Teacher Tip

Note: Small rectangular mirrors will be needed for the next lesson and Lesson 90.

Looking Forward

Classifying triangles by angle measures and the length of its sides prepares students for:

- **Lesson 82,** identifying and drawing lines of symmetry.
- **Lesson 90,** classifying quadrilaterals.
- **Lesson 96,** classifying geometric solids by their vertices, edges, and faces.
- **Lesson 97,** making three-dimensional models of rectangular and triangular prisms.
- **Lesson 108,** identifying the attributes of geometric solids.
- **Lesson 109,** describing the attributes of pyramids.
- **Lesson 114,** determining the perimeter and area of complex figures.

Planning & Preparation

• Symmetry

Objectives

- Identify and draw lines of symmetry.
- Use reflections to determine if a figure has lines of symmetry.
- Identify figures with rotational symmetry.

Prerequisite Skills

- Describing transformations of a figure.
- Using translations, reflections, and rotations to change the position of a figure in quadrant I of the coordinate plane.

Materials

Instructional Masters

- Power Up I Worksheet
- Lesson Activity 24

Manipulative Kit

- Mirrors, rulers
- Protractors*

Teacher-provided materials

- Construction paper, scissors*

**optional*

California Mathematics Content Standards

MG 3.0, 3.4 Identify figures that have bilateral and rotational symmetry.

MG 3.0, 3.5 Know the definitions of a right angle, an acute angle, and an obtuse angle. Understand that 90°, 180°, 270°, and 360° are associated, respectively, with $\frac{1}{4}$, $\frac{1}{2}$, $\frac{3}{4}$, and full turns.

MR 2.0, 2.3 Use a variety of methods, such as words, numbers, symbols, charts, graphs, tables, diagrams, and models, to explain mathematical reasoning.

MR 3.0, 3.3 Develop generalizations of the results obtained and apply them in other circumstances.

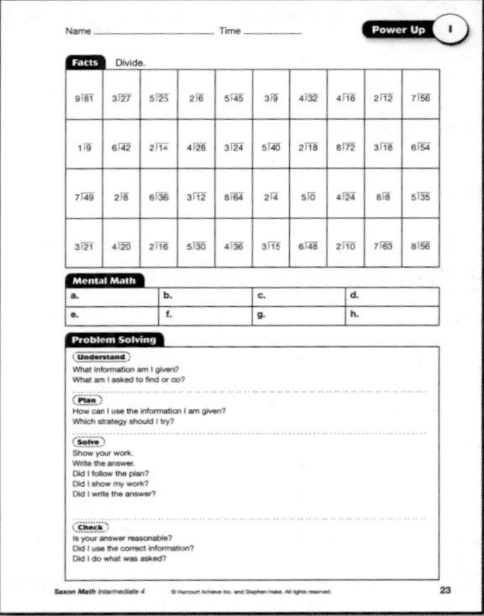

Power Up I Worksheet

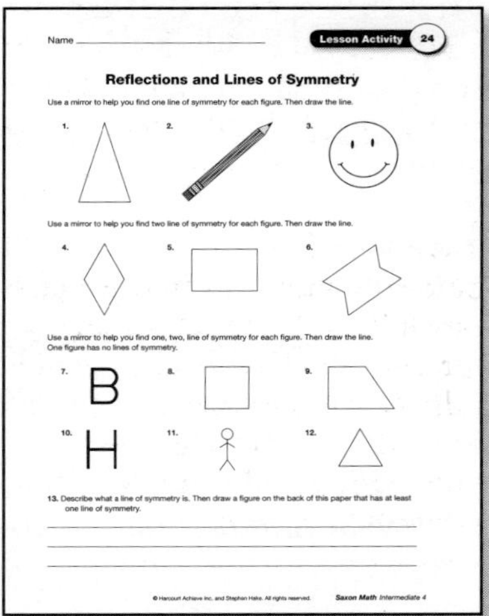

Lesson Activity 24

Universal Access

Reaching All Special Needs Students

Special Education Students	At-Risk Students	English Learners	Advanced Learners
• Inclusion (TM) • Adaptations for Saxon Math	• Alternative Approach (TM) • Error Alert (TM) • Reteaching Masters • Refresher Lessons for California Standards	• English Learners (TM) • Developing Academic Language (TM) • English Learner Handbook	• Extend the Example (TM) • Extend the Problem (TM) • Early Finisher (SE) • Online Activities

TM=Teacher's Manual
SE=Student Edition

Developing Academic Language

New	Maintained	English Learner
line of symmetry	angles	structure
reflective symmetry	diameter	
rotational symmetry	full turn	
symmetry	half turn	
	polygon	
	quarter turn	

Problem Solving Discussion

Problem

Landon is packing a lunch for the park. He will take one bottle of water, a sandwich, and a fruit. He will choose either a ham sandwich or a peanut butter and jelly sandwich. For the fruit, Landon will choose an apple, an orange, or a banana. Make a tree diagram to find the possible combinations of lunches that Landon can pack. Then list each possible combination.

Focus Strategy  **Draw a Picture or Diagram**

Understand *Understand the problem.*

"What information are we given?"

We are told that Landon will take a water, a sandwich, and a fruit to the park. He has two choices of sandwich and three choices of fruit.

"What are we asked to do?"

We are asked to find how many different lunch combinations Landon can pack.

Plan *Make a plan.*

"What problem-solving strategy can we use to solve the problem?"

We can *make a diagram* to find all the combinations of lunches.

Solve *Carry out the plan.*

"What kind of diagram can we make for this type of problem?"

We can make a tree diagram, such as the one we made in Lesson 72.

"We know that Landon will take a water, so we can write 'water' at one end of our tree diagram. How many branches will we extend from 'water' to show the sandwiches Landon can pack?"

There are two types of sandwich that Landon can pack. We can draw two lines from "water" and write "ham" and "PBJ" at the end of the lines, as shown below.

"How many different fruits can Landon pack? How can we show the fruits in our tree diagram?"

For each type of sandwich, there are three different fruits. We can draw three lines that extend from each sandwich and write the different fruits, like this:

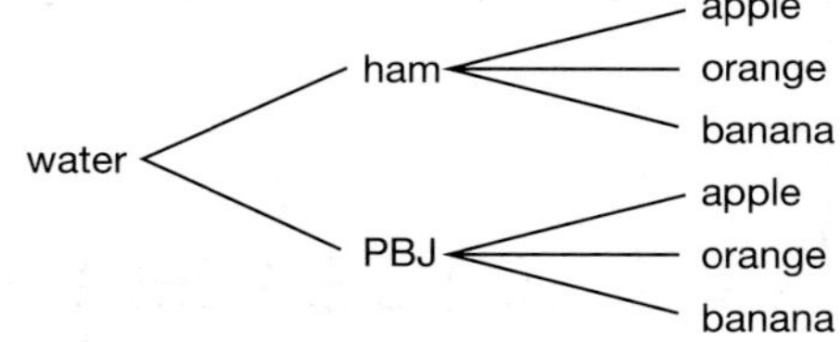

Check *Look back.*

"What combinations of lunch can Landon pack?"

We list the combinations formed by the diagram. We read the items that are placed along each set of branches:

1. water-ham-apple
2. water-ham-orange
3. water-ham-banana
4. water-PBJ-apple
5. water-PBJ-orange
6. water-PBJ-banana

"Are our answers reasonable?"

We know that our answers are reasonable, because each combination we listed is a possible combination of water, a sandwich, and a fruit.

"What kind of diagram did we make, and how did this strategy help us?"

We made a tree diagram to solve the problem. A tree diagram is useful for showing possible combinations when there are several choices.

• Symmetry

California Mathematics Content Standards

MG 3.0, 3.4 Identify figures that have bilateral and rotational symmetry.
MG 3.0, 3.5 Know the definitions of a right angle, an acute angle, and an obtuse angle. Understand that 90°, 180°, 270°, and 360° are associated, respectively, with $\frac{1}{4}$, $\frac{1}{2}$, $\frac{3}{4}$, and full turns.
MR 3.0, 3.3 Develop generalizations of the results obtained and apply them in other circumstances.

Power Up

facts Power Up I

count aloud Count by fives from 3 to 63.

mental math Before adding, make one number larger and the other number smaller in problems **a–c.**

a. Number Sense: 38 + 46 84

b. Number Sense: 67 + 24 91

c. Number Sense: 44 + 28 72

d. Number Sense: 3 × 50 × 10 1500

e. Number Sense: Counting by fives from 5, every number Julio says ends in 0 or 5. If he counts by fives from 9, then every number he says ends in which digit? 4 or 9

f. Geometry: The radius of the truck tire was 15 inches. The diameter of the tire was how many inches? 30 in.

g. Estimation: The total cost for 6 boxes of snack bars was $17.70. Round this amount to the nearest dollar and then divide by 6 to estimate the cost per box. $3

h. Calculation: $\frac{1}{4}$ of 40, × 2, ÷ 10, × 8, + 59 75

problem solving Landon is packing a lunch for the park. He will take one bottle of water, a sandwich, and a fruit. He will choose either a ham sandwich or a peanut butter and jelly sandwich. For the fruit, Landon will choose an apple, an orange, or a banana. Make a tree diagram to find the possible combinations of lunches that Landon can pack. Then list each possible combination. 1. water, ham, apple; 2. water, ham, banana; 3. water, ham, orange; 4. water, PBJ, apple; 5. water, PBJ, banana; 6. water, PBJ, orange

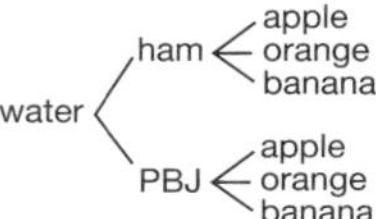

Facts Divide.

9 9)81	9 3)27	5 5)25	3 2)6	9 5)45	3 3)9	8 4)32	4 4)16	6 2)12	8 7)56
9 1)9	7 6)42	7 2)14	7 4)28	8 3)24	8 5)40	9 2)18	9 8)72	6 3)18	9 6)54
7 7)49	4 2)8	6 6)36	4 3)12	8 8)64	2 2)4	0 5)0	6 4)24	1 8)8	7 5)35
7 3)21	5 4)20	8 2)16	6 5)30	9 4)36	5 3)15	8 6)48	5 2)10	9 7)63	7 8)56

Power Up

Facts
Distribute **Power Up I** to students. See answers below.

Count Aloud
Before students begin the Mental Math exercises, do these counting exercises as a class.

Mental Math
Encourage students to share different ways to mentally compute the Mental Math exercises. Sample strategies are listed below.

a. Add 40, then Subtract 2
40 + 46 = 86; 86 − 2 = 84
Add 50, then Subtract 4
38 + 50 = 88; 88 − 4 = 84

d. Attach 2 Zeros to the Product of 3 × 5
3 × 5 = 15; 3 × 50 × 10 = 1500
Use the Associative Property
3 × (50 × 10) = 3 × 500 = 1500

Problem Solving
Refer to **Problem-Solving Strategy Discussion,** p. 547B.

New Concept

Observation

Begin this lesson with a demonstration. Fold a piece of construction paper in half and cut out a free-form shape (begin and end the cut at the folded edge). Unfold the shape to display its symmetry and line of symmetry (the fold line). You might choose to then provide students with construction paper and scissors to make and display symmetric figures of their own design.

Real-World Connection

Give students an opportunity to search for classroom objects that have symmetry, or ask them to name and describe familiar objects that have symmetry.

Alternate Method

Invite students to stand the edge of a mirror upright on the dashed line to verify the symmetry of the butterfly.

Example 1

Students who have difficulty determining a line of symmetry may find it helpful to use a mirror. Have these students stand a small, rectangular mirror on each polygon in different positions until the image in the mirror is exactly the same as the portion of the figure they see in the book.

Error Alert

Watch for students who assume that the diagonal of the rectangle is a line of symmetry. Fold a rectangular (not square) piece of paper along its diagonal to demonstrate that the two halves are not mirror images.

(continued)

New Concept

Thinking Skills

Discuss

Name several real-world examples of line symmetry.

Samples: the design of a cabinet door, the blades of a fan, the lanes of a highway

In nature, we often find balance in the appearance and structure of objects and living things. For example, we see a balance in the wing patterns of moths and butterflies. We call this kind of balance **reflective symmetry,** or just **symmetry.**

The dashes across this drawing of a moth indicate a **line of symmetry.** The portion of the figure on each side of the dashes is the *mirror image* of the other side. If we stood a mirror along the dashes, the reflection in the mirror would appear to complete the figure.

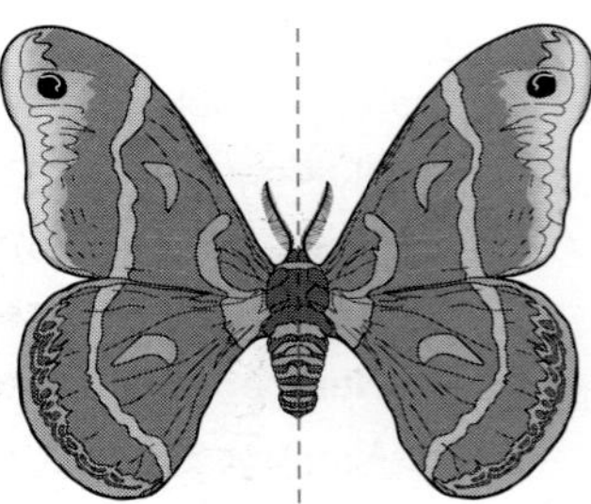

Some polygons and other figures have one or more lines of symmetry.

Example 1

Which of these polygons does *not* have a line of symmetry?

A **B** **C** **D**

The rectangle has two lines of symmetry.

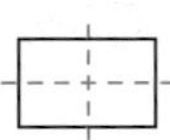

The isosceles triangle has one line of symmetry.

English Learners

Explain that the word **structure** is the way something is arranged or built.

If someone says the structure of a butterfly is balanced, it means the butterfly has symmetrical parts.

Ask:

"Can you think of other things that have a balanced structure?" See student work.

The square has four lines of symmetry.

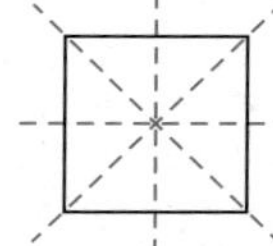

The third polygon has no line of symmetry. The answer is **C.**

Conclude Will every regular polygon always have at least one line of symmetry? Explain why or why not. Yes; sample: All of the angles and all of the sides of a regular polygon are congruent.

About half of the uppercase letters in the alphabet have lines of symmetry.

Example 2

Copy these letters and draw each line of symmetry, if any.

C H A I R

The letters **H** and **I** each have two lines of symmetry. The letters **C** and **A** each have one line of symmetry. The letter **R** has no lines of symmetry.

Represent Print the letters of your first name and describe any lines of symmetry those letters have. See student work.

Reflections and Lines of Symmetry

Materials needed:

- **Lesson Activity 24**
- mirror

Use a mirror to find lines of symmetry in the figures on **Lesson Activity 24.**

Inclusion

Use this strategy if the student displays:

- Difficulty with Large Group Instruction.
- Difficulty with Abstract Processing.

Symmetry (Individual)

Materials: mirrors, ruler, construction paper, scissors

- Have students fold a piece of construction paper in half. Ask them to draw part of a shape (such as half a heart) on the side with the fold. Have them cut out the shape and open it up. Using their pencils, have students trace a line down the crease. Tell students that this is a **line of symmetry** and that the pieces of the shape on either side of the line are congruent to each other.
- Have students use a ruler to draw a square. Show them how to use mirrors to check for symmetry. Have students draw a new shape and check to see if it has symmetry using a mirror.

New Concept *(Continued)*

Example 2

The reason that the uppercase letter I in the textbook has a vertical line of symmetry is because it has width. A vertical line segment has only one line of symmetry because a line segment has no width.

Extend the Example

Challenge advanced learners to draw other letters of the alphabet that have symmetry, and then share and discuss their drawings.

Activity

The number of mirrors you have will help you decide if students can work independently, in pairs, or in small groups.

As students complete the activity, be sure to provide enough time for them to find all of the lines of symmetry in the figures.

After they have finished the activity, invite volunteers to read their definitions of symmetry and display their drawings of a symmetric object.

Instruction

As you discuss rotational symmetry, point out that these figures rotate about a point at their center. (However, these figures can rotate about any point and still display rotational symmetry).

(continued)

New Concept *(Continued)*

Example 3

Active Learning

Ask students to rotate their books as they look for each figure to match its original position. If students work in pairs to model the example, one student can hold a book so that the figures are in the original position, and the other student can turn another book until a figure matches its original position.

Lesson Practice

Guided Practice

Use these problems as guided practice to check the students' understanding of today's concept.

Problems a–f

Some students may not need to copy the figures to identify the lines of symmetry. However, if you choose to have students copy the figures, remind them that if the figures can be folded so that the two halves match exactly, the fold line is a line of symmetry.

(continued)

The symmetry illustrated in Examples 1 and 2 is reflective symmetry. Another type of symmetry is **rotational symmetry.** A figure has rotational symmetry if it matches its original position as it is rotated.

For example, a square has rotational symmetry because it matches itself every quarter turn (90°).

A $\frac{1}{4}$ turn A $\frac{1}{2}$ turn A

Likewise, the uppercase letter H has rotational symmetry because it matches its original position every half turn (180°).

$\frac{1}{2}$ turn

Example 3

Which figures do *not* have rotational symmetry?

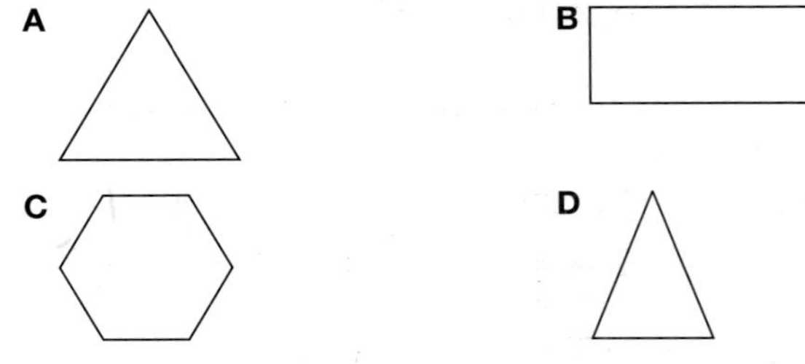

Figure **A** has rotational symmetry because it matches its original position every $\frac{1}{3}$ of a turn (120°).

Figure **B** has rotational symmetry because it matches its original position in one half of a turn (180°).

Figure **C** has rotational symmetry because it matches its original position every $\frac{1}{6}$ of a turn (60°).

Figure **D** does not have rotational symmetry because it requires a full turn (360°) to match its original position.

Discuss Draw a circle with one diameter. Does it have line symmetry? Does it have rotational symmetry? Yes; yes

Alternative Approach: Using Manipulatives

To help students understand the concept of measuring turns, have them use a protractor to model turns. Have students place the protractor on their paper with 0° pointing to the top and 180° pointing to the bottom; ask them to trace around the outside of the protractor beginning at the zero at the top and ending with the 180 at the bottom. Then have students label points showing 0°, 90°, and 180°.

Have students turn the protractor around; finish tracing the circle; label a point to show 270°; and write north, south, east, and west on their paper. Then have them place the protractor on top of the right side of the circle and use the arm of protractor to model clockwise and counterclockwise turns.

550 ***Saxon Math** Intermediate 4*

Lesson Practice Copy each figure and draw the lines of symmetry, if any:

a. 

b. 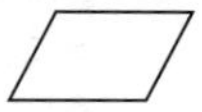 none

c. 

d. W 

e. X 

f. Z none

g. Which figures **a–f** do *not* have rotational symmetry? a and d

h. Which figures in **a–f** have reflective symmetry? a, c, d, and e

i. Which of these polygons have reflective symmetry? A and B

A 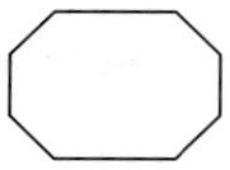

B 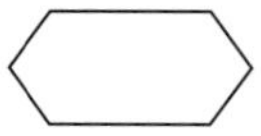

C 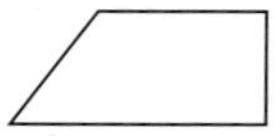

D 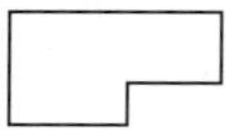

Written Practice

Distributed and Integrated

1. How many kilograms are equal to 3000 grams? 3 kilograms
(80)

▶ ***2.** **Conclude** **a.** Which of these letters does *not* have a line of symmetry? N
(82)

T N V W

b. Which of these letters has rotational symmetry? N

Visit www.SaxonMath.com/Int4/ActivitiesCA for an online activity.

Teacher Tip

You can help your students be successful by teaching all lessons. Do not skip or combine any lessons. The lesson sequence has been carefully planned with the appropriate practice provided in each problem set.

New Concept *(Continued)*

Lesson Practice

Problem f
Error Alert

Some students may state that Z has reflective symmetry, but it does not. However, Z has 180° rotational symmetry about a central point on the letter.

Closure

The questions below help assess the concepts taught in this lesson.

Draw an uppercase X on the board. Then ask:

"How many lines of symmetry does the letter X have? Explain your answer." Two; sample: One line of symmetry is vertical and the other is horizontal. Each line divides the letter into two identical halves.

"Does the letter X have rotational symmetry? Explain your answer." Yes; sample: It matches its original position every half turn (or 180°).

Written Practice

Math Conversations

Independent Practice and Discussions to Increase Understanding

Problem 2 **Conclude**

Before students solve the problems, ask:

"What does it mean if a figure has a line of symmetry?" Sample: The two halves of the figure match exactly if it is folded in half; One half of the figure is a reflection of the other half.

"What does it mean if a figure has rotational symmetry?" Sample: The figure will match its original position in less than a full turn.

Extend the Problem

Challenge advanced learners with this question:

"A square has 90° rotational symmetry because for every 90° it is turned, it matches its original position. A regular pentagon has what degree of rotational symmetry? Explain your answer." 72°; sample: A full turn is 360° and a regular pentagon has 5 sides, so it returns to its original position every 360° ÷ 5 or 72°.

(continued)

Written Practice *(Continued)*

Math Conversations *(cont.)*

Problem 5

"If we know the number of centimeters, how can we find the number of millimeters?" Multiply the number of centimeters by 10.

"If we know the number of millimeters, how can we find the number of centimeters?" Divide the number of millimeters by 10.

Problem 9

Encourage students to trace, cut out, and fold the rectangle to help them decide.

(continued)

***3.** (66) Write the formula for the area of a square. Then find the area of a square with sides 12 inches long. $A = s^2$; 144 sq. in. or 144 in^2

4. (42) Twenty-four inches is how many feet? 2 ft

▸ ***5.** (42) **a.** Segment *YZ* is how many millimeters long? 40 mm

b. Segment *YZ* is how many centimeters long? 4 cm

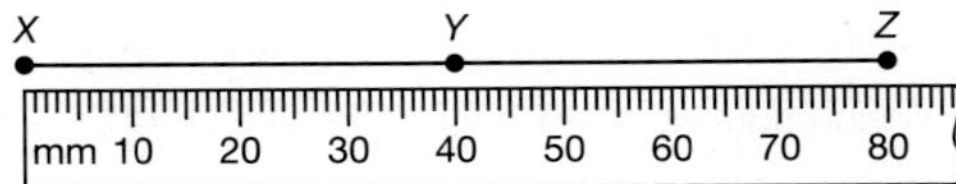

6. (13) Jorge finished eating breakfast at the time shown on the clock. He finished eating lunch 5 hours 20 minutes later. What time did Jorge finish eating lunch? 12:23 p.m.

7. (27) **Represent** Write the number 7528 in expanded form. Then use words to write the number. 7000 + 500 + 20 + 8; seven thousand, five ~~hun~~dred twenty-eight

8. (74) **Represent** One fifth of the 25 band members missed the note. How many band members missed the note? Draw a picture to illustrate the problem. 5 band members

8. 25 members
$\frac{1}{5}$ missed the note. — 5 members
5 members
$\frac{4}{5}$ did not miss the note. — 5 members
5 members
5 members

▸ ***9.** (70, 78) Nikki cut a rectangular piece of paper along a diagonal to make two triangles.

a. How many degrees does Nikki need to turn one triangle so it will lay on top of the other triangle? 180° or a half-turn

b. Are the triangles congruent? Yes

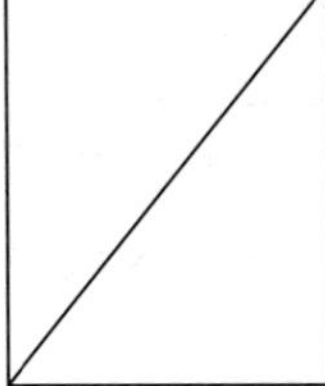

10. (28) \$6.35 + \$14.25 + \$0.97 + \$5 \$26.57

11. (9, 45) 4.60 − (1.4 + 2.75) 0.45

12. (9, 28) \$10.00 − (46¢ + \$1.30) \$8.24

▶*13. **Represent** Draw two rectangles that show that $\frac{1}{5} = \frac{2}{10}$.
(Inv. 8)

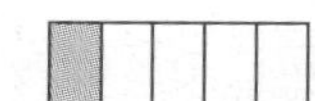
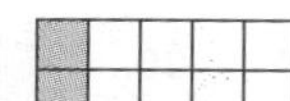

▶*14. **Analyze** Simplify each expression:
(63)

a. $4 + 3 \times 3 - 1$ 12

b. $16 \div 2 \times 4 + 5$ 37

*15. **Verify** Is the product of two prime numbers prime? Why or why not? No; sample: The product of two prime numbers has those numbers as factors, so the product can never be a prime number.
(56)

▶*16. 28×20 560
(71)

▶*17. 13×30 = 390
(71)

18. $\$8.67 \times 9$ = $78.03
(59)

19. $7\overline{)3612}$ 516
(79)

20. $6\overline{)\$33.30}$ $5.55
(79)

21. $8\overline{)4971}$ 621 R 3
(79)

22. $482 \div 5$ 96 R 2
(72)

23. $270 \div 9$ 30
(75)

24. $270 \div \sqrt{9}$ 90
(Inv. 3, 75)

25. $7 + 7 + n = 7^2$ 35
(64, 65)

26. $3n = 6^2$ 12
(34, 65)

▶*27. a. **Represent** Draw an obtuse triangle. Sample:
(17, 81)

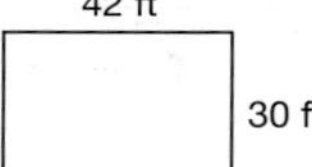

▶ b. **Explain** Describe the segments of the obtuse angle. Explain your thinking. Sample: The segments intersect, but since they do not form a right angle, they are not perpendicular.

28. The classroom was 42 feet long and 30 feet wide. How many 1-foot square floor tiles were needed to cover the floor? 1260 floor tiles
(Inv. 3, 71)

42 ft
30 ft

*29. a. **Classify** In polygon *ABCD*, which side appears to be parallel to side *AD?* side *BC* (or side *CB*)
(17)

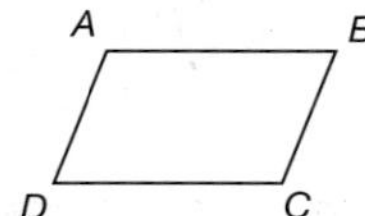

▶ b. Classify the angles. 2 acute angles and 2 obtuse angles

Written Practice *(Continued)*

Math Conversations *(cont.)*

Problem 13 **Represent**

Remind students that whenever they draw two figures to show equivalent fractions or decimals, the figures must be congruent. In other words, they must be exactly the same size and shape.

Problem 14 **Analyze**

Before students complete the arithmetic for each expression, ask:

"What operations are present in this expression?"

"Which of those operations do we perform first? Explain why."

Problems 16 and 17

Encourage students to name the products using only mental math by reminding them that whenever a factor is a multiple of 10, we can write the number of zeros in the factors to the right of the product of the nonzero digits.

Problem 27 a and b

For part **a,** suggest that students use a ruler to draw the triangle, and draw the obtuse angle first. After they draw the triangle, ask them to draw an arrow that points to the obtuse angle.

For part **b,** there are a number of ways that the segments can be described. Invite volunteers to duplicate their drawings on the board or overhead and to describe their segments to the class.

Problem 29b

Suggest that students compare the angles to a benchmark angle, such as a right angle, and ask them to include the terms "acute" and "obtuse" in their answers.

(continued)

Written Practice *(Continued)*

Math Conversations *(cont.)*

Problem 30 (Interpret)

Discuss with students how to choose a sensible interval of the height scale of the graph. For example, point out that an interval of 5 stories may not be sensible because only one building has a height that is a multiple of 5, which means that the heights of three buildings would fall between the lines of the graph.

Errors and Misconceptions

Problem 5b

Students must recognize that because the ruler is a millimeter ruler, the numbers 10, 20, 30, and so on represent the number of millimeters, not the number of centimeters. To identify the number of centimeters, students must know that 10 millimeters is equal to 1 centimeter.

Watch for opportunities to help students convert the numbers 10, 20, 30, and so on to centimeters. (Because each number represents millimeters, and 10 millimeters = 1 centimeter, we change the numbers to represent centimeters by dividing each number by 10; 10 mm = 1 cm, 20 mm = 2 cm, and so on.)

Problems 11 and 12

If students give an answer of 5.95 for problem **11** and/or $10.84 for problem **12**, they simplified the expressions by working from left to right instead of by working in parentheses first.

Challenge advanced learners with the following:

"Eduardo is thinking of a mystery number. He won't tell us what it is, but he will give us two clues. First, the number is greater than 25 but less than 45. And second, the number is a multiple of 3 and a multiple of 4. What is Eduardo's mystery number?" 36

▸* **30.** (Interpret) This table shows the heights of several tall buildings.
(Inv. 5)
Make a bar graph to display the data. See student work.

Tall Buildings in the United States

Building	Location	Height (stories)
The Pinnacle	Chicago, IL	48
Interstate Tower	Charlotte, NC	32
Two Union Square	Seattle, WA	56
28 State Street	Boston, MA	40

Real-World Connection

Eduardo was given a sack of almonds. The label on the sack said it contained 60 almonds. He wanted to make sure, so he opened the sack and spread the almonds on a tabletop to count them. Eduardo recently learned about multiples at school, so he decided to count the almonds using multiples.

a. If Eduardo counts the nuts in groups of 10, what multiples will he name? 10, 20, 30, 40, 50, 60

b. If he counts them in groups of 6, what multiples will he name? 6, 12, 18, 24, 30, 36, 42, 48, 54, 60

c. If he counts the nuts in groups of 7, will Eduardo name 60 as a multiple? No

Identifying and drawing lines of symmetry prepares students for:

- **Lesson 90,** classifying quadrilaterals.
- **Lesson 96,** classifying geometric solids by their vertices, edges, and faces.
- **Lesson 97,** making three-dimensional models of rectangular and triangular prisms.
- **Lesson 108,** identifying the attributes of geometric solids.
- **Lesson 109,** describing the attributes of pyramids.
- **Lesson 114,** determining the perimeter and area of complex figures.

LESSON 83

Planning & Preparation

California Mathematics Content Standards

NS 3.0, 3.4 Solve problems involving division of multidigit numbers by one-digit numbers.

AF 1.0, 1.1 Use letters, boxes, or other symbols to stand for any number in simple expressions or equations (e.g., demonstrate an understanding and the use of the concept of a variable).

• Division with Zeros in Three-Digit Answers

Objectives

- Solve division problems with zeros in three-digit answer.
- Solve word problems involving multi-digit division.

Prerequisite Skills

- Identifying division facts using a multiplication table.
- Solving division problems using manipulatives.
- Dividing a three-digit number by a one-digit number.
- Solving division problems with two-digit answers and a remainder.

Materials

Instructional Masters

- Power Up I Worksheet

Manipulative Kit

- Rulers
- Two-color counters, money manipulatives*

Teacher-provided materials

- Place-value workmat*

*optional

Power Up I Worksheet

Universal Access

Reaching All Special Needs Students

Special Education Students	At-Risk Students	English Learners	Advanced Learners
• Inclusion (TM) • Adaptations for Saxon Math	• Alternative Approach (TM) • Error Alert (TM) • Reteaching Masters • Refresher Lessons for California Standards	• English Learners (TM) • Developing Academic Language (TM) • English Learner Handbook	• Extend the Example (TM) • Extend the Problem (TM) • Online Activities

TM=Teacher's Manual

Developing Academic Language

Maintained	English Learner
digit	pallet
division	
quotient	
remainder	

Problem Solving Discussion

Problem

Twenty-one students went on the field trip to the zoo. Five students rode in the teacher's car. The rest of the students were divided equally among four cars driven by parents. How many students were in each of the cars driven by a parent? Explain how you found your answer.

Focus Strategies

Draw a Picture or Diagram

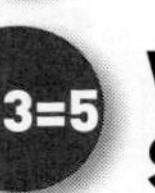

Write a Number Sentence or Equation

Understand ***Understand the problem.***

"What information are we given?"

Twenty-one students rode in cars. Five students rode in the teacher's car, and the remaining students were divided equally among four parents' cars.

"What are we asked to do?"

We are asked to find how many students were in each of the four cars driven by parents and to explain how we found our answer.

Plan ***Make a plan.***

"What problem-solving strategy can we use?"

We can *draw a diagram* to represent the students.

"How can we represent the five cars in the diagram?"

We can draw five circles to represent the cars.

"How can we represent the students in the diagram?"

We can place five dots in the circle that stands for the teacher's car. Then we can place the other dots equally in the other four circles until we have 21 dots altogether.

Solve ***Carry out the plan.***

"What does our diagram look like?"

The diagram might look like this:

Teacher's car	Parents' cars			
5 students	4 students	4 students	4 students	4 students

$5 + 4 + 4 + 4 + 4 = 21$

Check ***Look back.***

"How many students rode in each of the parents' cars?"

Four students rode in each of the four parents' cars.

"Is our answer reasonable?"

We know that our answer is reasonable, because five students in the teacher's car and four students in each of the other four cars is $5 + 4 + 4 + 4 + 4$, or 21 students, which is the number of students in the problem.

"What problem-solving strategies did we use, and how did they help us?"

We drew a diagram to show how the students could divide among the cars. We wrote a number sentence to show that we had considered all 21 students.

"What is another way we could have solved this problem?"

We could have *worked backwards.*

Alternate Strategy

Work Backwards

Students can also solve the problem by first finding how many students did not ride in the teacher's car (21 students − 5 students, which is 16 students). Then they can solve the equal-groups problem, "16 students divided among 4 cars is how many students per car?" The answer is 4 students per car.

LESSON 83

California Mathematics Content Standards

NS 3.0, 3.4 Solve problems involving division of multidigit numbers by one-digit numbers.

AF 1.0, 1.1 Use letters, boxes, or other symbols to stand for any number in simple expressions or equations (e.g., demonstrate an understanding and the use of the concept of a variable).

• Division with Zeros in Three-Digit Answers

Power Up

facts Power Up I

count aloud Count down by halves from 10 to $\frac{1}{2}$.

mental math Before subtracting, make both numbers larger in problems **a–c.**

a. Number Sense: 56 − 29 27

b. Number Sense: 43 − 18 25

c. Number Sense: 63 − 37 26

d. Money: Devin bought a vegetable tray for $7.52 and a bottle of fruit punch for $1.98. What was the total cost? $9.50

e. Time: Compare: 72 hours (>) 2 days

f. Time: About how many days are in 10 years? About 3650 days

g. Estimation: The total cost for 3 boxes of cereal is $11.97. Round this amount to the nearest dollar and then divide by 3 to estimate the cost per box. $4

h. Calculation: $\frac{1}{2}$ of 70, ÷ 7, × 2, + 8, ÷ 9, ÷ 2 1

problem solving Choose an appropriate problem-solving strategy to solve this problem. Twenty-one students went on the field trip to the zoo. Five students rode in the teacher's car. The rest of the students were divided equally among four cars driven by parents. How many students were in each of the cars driven by a parent? Explain how you found your answer. 4 students; See student work.

Facts Divide.

9 9)81	9 3)27	5 5)25	3 2)6	9 5)45	3 3)9	8 4)32	4 4)16	6 2)12	8 7)56
9 1)9	7 6)42	7 2)14	7 4)28	8 3)24	8 5)40	9 2)18	9 8)72	6 3)18	9 6)54
7 7)49	4 2)8	6 6)36	4 3)12	8 8)64	2 2)4	0 5)0	6 4)24	1 8)8	7 5)35
7 3)21	5 4)20	8 2)16	6 5)30	9 4)36	5 3)15	8 6)48	5 2)10	9 7)63	7 8)56

Power Up

Facts

Distribute **Power Up I** to students. See answers below.

Count Aloud

Before students begin the Mental Math exercises, do these counting exercises as a class.

Mental Math

Encourage students to share different ways to mentally compute these exercises. Strategies for exercises are listed below.

c. Subtract 40, then Add 3

63 − 40 = 23; 23 + 3 = 26

Subtract 30, then Subtract 7

63 − 30 = 33; 33 − 7 = 26

d. Add $2, then Subtract 2¢

$7.52 + $2 = $9.52; $9.52 − 2¢ = $9.50

Subtract 2¢ and Add 2¢

$7.52 − 2¢ = $7.50; $1.98 + 2¢ = $2; $7.50 + $2 = $9.50

f. The number of days in 10 years is not exactly 3650 days, because not all years have 365 days.

Problem Solving

Refer to **Problem-Solving Strategy Discussion,** p. 555B.

New Concept

Instruction

Ask the class to recite the steps of division: divide, multiply, subtract, bring down

Example 1

As you demonstrate the solution, include the words "divide," "subtract," "compare," and "bring down" in your explanation.

Instruction

Each time you demonstrate the "subtract" step, emphasize the fact that we must compare the result of the subtraction to the divisor:

- If the result is less than the divisor, the division can continue.
- If the result is greater than or equal to the divisor, we must increase the digit in the quotient before the division can continue.

Generalize

Each time you demonstrate the "bring down" step, emphasize the fact that each time a digit is brought down from the dividend, a digit must be written in the quotient. Students learn in this example that if two digits must be brought down, the digit written in the quotient will be zero.

Error Alert

Remind students that the multiplication 206×3 can be used to check the answer, then invite one or more volunteers to explain or demonstrate how estimation can be used. Sample: Because 6 is divisible by 3, 600 is divisible by 3; Round 618 to 600, then divide; A reasonable estimate is $600 \div 3$ or 200.

(continued)

New Concept

Recall that the pencil-and-paper method we have used for dividing numbers has four steps:

Step 1: Divide. (÷)

Step 2: Multiply. (×)

Step 3: Subtract. (−)

Step 4: Bring down. (↓)

Every time we bring a number down, we return to Step 1. Sometimes the answer to Step 1 is zero, and we will have a zero in the answer.

Example 1

Each weekday afternoon in a small town, 618 newspapers are delivered to customers. The task of delivering the newspapers is divided equally among 3 drivers. How many newspapers does each driver deliver?

Step 1: Divide $3\overline{)6}$ and write "2."

Step 2: Multiply 2 by 3 and write "6."

Step 3: Subtract 6 from 6 and write "0."

Step 4: Bring down the 1 to make 01 (which is 1).

```
    2
3)618
  6
  01
```

Repeat:

Step 1: Divide 3 into 01 and write "0."

Step 2: Multiply 0 by 3 and write "0."

Step 3: Subtract 0 from 1 and write "1."

Step 4: Bring down the 8 to make 18.

Repeat:

Step 1: Divide 3 into 18 and write "6."

Step 2: Multiply 6 by 3 and write "18."

Step 3: Subtract 18 from 18 and write "0."

Step 4: There are no more digits to bring down, so the division is complete. The remainder is zero.

```
  206
3)618
  6
  01
   0
   18
   18
    0
```

Each driver delivers **206 papers.**

Thinking Skills

Verify

Why do we write the digit 2 in the hundreds place of the quotient?

We are dividing 6 hundreds.

Thinking Skills

Discuss

Why do we write the digit 0 in the tens place of the quotient?

There aren't enough tens to divide.

Alternative Approach: Using Manipulatives

To help students understand the concept of division with zeros in three-digit answers, have students use counters and a place-value workmat to model division as they perform the division using pencil and paper.

Have the students make a place-value workmat by dividing a piece of plain paper vertically into 3 equal parts. Have them label the parts "hundreds," "tens," and "ones." Then have students use the counters to show the number 618 on the workmat. Have them separate each place value into groups of 3. Explain that since the tens cannot be separated into groups of 3, there will be no groups of 3 in the tens position. Remind students to trade 1 ten 8 ones for 18 ones before making groups of 3 in the ones position.

Have students count the groups in each place value and record the quotient. 2 hundreds, 0 tens, 6 ones or 206

Example 2

Divide: $4\overline{)1483}$

Step 1: Divide $4\overline{)14}$ and write "3."

Step 2: Multiply 3 by 4 and write "12."

Step 3: Subtract 12 from 14 and write "2."

Step 4: Bring down the 8 to make 28.

Repeat:

Step 1: Divide 4 into 28 and write "7."

Step 2: Multiply 7 by 4 and write "28."

Step 3: Subtract 28 from 28 and write "0."

Step 4: Bring down the 3 to make 03 (which is 3).

Repeat:

Step 1: Divide 4 into 03 and write "0."

Step 2: Multiply 0 by 4 and write "0."

Step 3: Subtract 0 from 3 and write "3."

Step 4: There are no digits to bring down, so the division is complete. We write "3" as the remainder.

```
   370 R 3
4)1483
  12
   28
   28
    03
     0
     3
```

Justify How can we check the answer?

Add the remainder to the product of the quotient and the divisor, and then compare the result to the dividend; $(370 \times 4) + 3 = 1483$

Example 3

The same number of landscaping bricks is stacked on each of 4 pallets. The total weight of the pallets is 3 tons. What is the weight in pounds of each pallet?

First we find the number of pounds in 3 tons. Each ton is 2 thousand pounds, so 3 tons is 6 thousand pounds. Now we find the weight of each pallet of bricks by dividing 6000 by 4.

```
  1500
4)6000
  4
  20
  20
   000
```

We find that each pallet of bricks weighs **1500 pounds.**

Lesson Practice

a. List the four steps of division and draw the division diagram.

a. Divide, multiply, subtract, bring down

Divide:

b. $4\overline{)815}$ 203 R 3 **c.** $5\overline{)4152}$ 830 R 2

Divide. Show your answer with a remainder.

d. $6\overline{)5432}$ 905 R 2 **e.** $7\overline{)845}$ 120 R 5

English Learners

Say, ***"A pallet is a kind of low, portable platform or stand. When products are made in a factory, they are usually packed together in boxes and stored on pallets. The pallets are then used to move the products to stores."***

Ask for volunteers to draw a picture on the board of a pallet with boxes stacked on it.

New Concept *(Continued)*

Example 2

Active Learning

Before you discuss the solution, remind students that correctly placing the first digit of the quotient is an essential division skill. Then ask:

"To divide 1483 by 4, where will the first digit in the quotient be placed? Explain why." In the hundreds place; the divisor (4) is greater than the first digit in the dividend (1). So we regroup 1 thousand and 4 hundreds as 14 hundreds, then divide again.

Extend the **Justify** question by asking:

"How many operations are used to check a quotient that does not include a remainder? Explain your answer." One operation—multiplication—is used; Multiply the quotient and the divisor, and then compare the result to the dividend.

"Explain how estimation could be used to check this quotient." Sample: Change 1483 to 1600 because 1600 is divisible by 4; a reasonable estimate is $1600 \div 4$ or 400.

Extend the Example

Challenge advanced learners by asking them to divide 1483 by 3 and then by 5.
494 R 1; 296 R 3

Example 3

Error Alert

Remind students to read problems carefully by pointing out that the weight is given in tons, and the answer is to be given in pounds.

As you discuss the solution, emphasize the fact that when there are no more nonzero digits to bring down from the dividend, we complete the division by writing zeros in the quotient.

Lesson Practice

Guided Practice

Use these problems as guided practice to check the students' understanding of today's concept.

Problem b

Some students may find it helpful if you complete this division on the board or overhead as a class activity. Invite volunteers to explain or demonstrate each of the steps that must be completed to find the quotient.

Problems c–e

Error Alert

Before students begin the arithmetic, ask them to explain where the first digit in each quotient will be placed.

(continued)

New Concept *(Continued)*

Closure

The questions below help assess the concepts taught in this lesson.

"To divide a number, how many times are the four steps of division repeated?" as many times as needed; until all of the digits in the dividend have been brought down

"Give two reasons why a quotient sometimes includes one or more zeros." If one digit is brought down from the dividend and the division cannot continue until a second digit is brought down, we write a zero in the quotient. If the only digits in a dividend that can be brought down are zeros, we write zeros in the quotient to complete the division.

Write $3275 \div 8$ and $650 \div 5$ on the board or overhead and ask students to find each quotient. $3275 \div 8 = 409 \text{ R } 3$; $650 \div 5 = 130$

Written Practice

Math Conversations

Independent Practice and Discussions to Increase Understanding

Problem 3

Challenge students to use only mental math to answer this question:

"Suppose Daniella reads 20 pages each day for one month. Is 6000 pages a reasonable estimate of the number of pages she will read during that month? Explain why or why not." No; sample: There are about 30 days in a month, and the product of 30×20 can be found by writing two zeros after the product of 3×2; A reasonable estimate is 30×20 or 600 pages.

Problem 5

Extend the Problem

Give students an opportunity to review triangle classifications by asking:

"Why is this triangle an isosceles triangle?" The triangle has at least two sides of equal length.

(continued)

Divide mentally:

f. $5\overline{)1500}$ 300 **g.** $4\overline{)2000}$ 500

h. Find the missing factor in the equation $3m = 1200$. $m = 400$

Written Practice

Distributed and Integrated

*1. (62, 80) Mr. Carson bought 2 packages of turkey. They weighed 3.24 kg and 2.26 kg. To the nearest tenth, how much did the packages weigh altogether? 5.5 kilograms

2. (28) **Justify** On the package there were two 39¢ stamps, two 20¢ stamps, and one 15¢ stamp. Altogether, how much did the stamps on the package cost? Explain why your answer is reasonable. $1.33; sample: 40¢ + 40¢ + 20¢ + 20¢ + 15¢ = 135¢, or $1.35, which is close to $1.33.

▸ 3. (39, 71) Daniella read 20 pages each day. How many pages did she read in 2 weeks? 280 pages

4. (42) In the first track meet of the season, Wyatt's best triple jump measured 36 feet. What was the distance of that jump in yards? 12 yards

▸ 5. (20, 42) What is the perimeter of this isosceles triangle in centimeters? 7 cm

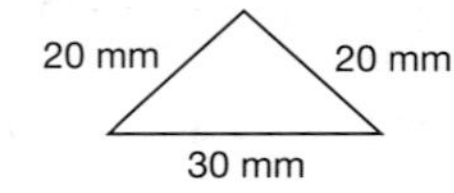

*6. (56, Inv. 6) **Multiple Choice** Which of these tallies represents a prime number? C

A 𝍸 III **B** 𝍸 𝍸
C 𝍸 𝍸 I **D** 𝍸 𝍸 II

▸ *7. (73) **Multiple Choice** About how much liquid is in this medicine dropper? A

A 2 milliliters **B** 2 liters
C 2 pints **D** 2 cups

8. (64) Solve for n: $87 + 0 = 87 \times n$ 1

▸ *9. (74) **Represent** One third of the 24 students finished early. How many students finished early? Draw a picture to illustrate the problem. 8 students

24 students
$\frac{1}{3}$ finished early. — 8 students
$\frac{2}{3}$ did not finish early. — 8 students, 8 students

Inclusion

Use this strategy if the student displays:

- Poor Retention.
- Difficulty with Multiple Steps.

Division with Zeros in Three Digit Answers (Pairs)

Materials: money manipulatives

- Read aloud, ***"Derrick has $354 and wants to divide it up equally among his five children. How many dollars will each child get?"***
- Have student use the money maniuplatives to make $354. Ask, ***"How many groups of 5 can you make out of $300?"*** 60 ***"How many groups of 5 can you make out of 50?"*** 10 ***"How many groups of 5 can you make out of 4?"*** 0 ***"What does the 4 represent?"*** the remainder ***"How many dollars will each child get?"*** 70

*10. a. **Multiple Choice** Sketch each of the triangles below. Which of (81) these triangles does *not* exist? C

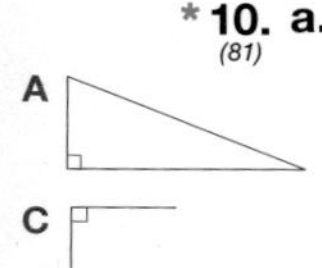

A a scalene right triangle B an isosceles right triangle
C an equilateral right triangle D an equilateral acute triangle

b. **Justify** Explain why the triangle you chose does not exist. Sample: A triangle that is equilateral has three acute angles. It cannot have any right angles.

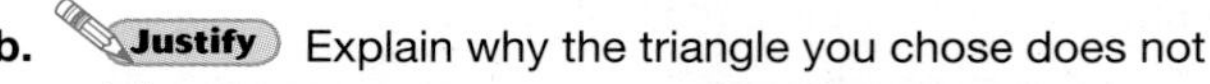

11. (28, 51) $478.63 + $ 32.47 = $511.10

12. (52) 137,140 − 129,536 = 7604

13. (28, 52) $60.00 − $24.38 = $35.62

►*14. (71) 72×90 6480

15. (71) 28×50 = 1400

*16. (71) 25×40 = 1000

17. (59) $4.76 × 8 = $38.08

►*18. (59) 210×3 = 630

►*19. (59) 204×5 = 1020

20. (83) $4\overline{)3000}$ 750

21. (34, 79) $5n = 635$ 127

22. (75) $7\overline{)426}$ 60 R 6

23. (79) $8\overline{)3614}$ 451 R 6

24. (79) $\frac{2736}{6}$ 456

25. (74, 79, 83) How much is one fourth of $10.00? $2.50

*26. a. (82) **Conclude** Which of these letters has exactly one line of symmetry? T

Q R H T

b. Which of these letters has rotational symmetry? H

►*27. a. (18, 20, Inv. 3) **Represent** Draw a rectangle that is 5 cm long and 4 cm wide.

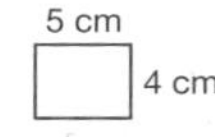

b. What is the perimeter and area of the rectangle you drew? 18 cm; 20 cm²

*28. a. (17, 82) **Conclude** In this polygon, which side appears to be parallel to side *BC*? side *AD* (or side *DA*)

► b. Copy this figure and draw its line of symmetry.

► c. Does this figure have rotational symmetry? No

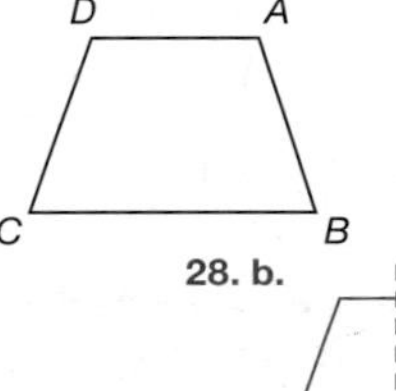

28. b.

Math Background

Using estimation is a good way to "catch" a missing zero in a quotient. If the divisor and quotient are rounded and multiplied, the result should be fairly close to the dividend. If a zero is missing from the quotient, the estimate will be far from the dividend.

In Example 2, the quotient for 1483 ÷ 4 is found to be 370 R 3. Rounding 370 to 400 and multiplying by 4 gives 1600, which is close to the dividend. Suppose the zero had been left out of the quotient, giving an answer of 37. Rounding and multiplying would have given an estimated dividend of 40 × 4, or 160. This is far from 1483, indicating that 37 is incorrect.

Written Practice *(Continued)*

Math Conversations *(cont.)*

Problem 7 Multiple Choice

Test-Taking Strategy

Discuss with students their understanding of capacity relationships and help them apply those relationships to solve the problem. For example, since the dropper cannot hold 2 cups of liquid, and 2 cups is less than 2 pints or 2 liters, answer choice **A** is the only reasonable choice.

Problem 9 Represent

Extend the Problem

"Explain how division can be used to check our answer." Finding $\frac{1}{3}$ of a number is the same as dividing the number by 3; Divide 24 by 3, and then compare answers.

Problems 14, 18, and 19

Remind students of the importance of checking their work, and then ask them to make an estimate of each product before finding the exact answer. Have them use the estimate to help decide the reasonableness of the exact answer after the arithmetic has been completed. Sample estimates:

problem **14:** $70 \times 90 = 6300$

problem **18:** $200 \times 3 = 600$

problem **19:** $200 \times 5 = 1000$

Problem 27a Represent

Manipulative Use

Students will need rulers to draw a rectangle that has the given dimensions. Some students may find it helpful to draw the rectangle on grid paper.

Problems 28b and 28c

Manipulative Use

For part **b,** encourage students to trace the figure, and then fold the tracing after cutting it out to help identify the line of symmetry.

For part **c,** some students will find it helpful to rotate the page so that they can see different orientations of the figure.

(continued)

Written Practice *(Continued)*

Math Conversations *(cont.)*

Problem 30 **Interpret**

Extend the Problem

Challenge your advanced learners to write a fraction in simplest form to represent the number of votes each candidate received. Gabriella: $\frac{1}{10}$, Brandon: $\frac{1}{5}$, Julian: $\frac{3}{10}$, Nevaeh: $\frac{2}{5}$

Errors and Misconceptions

Problem 5

Make sure students recognize that the dimensions of the triangle are given in millimeters but that the problem asks for an answer in centimeters.

Students must use the conversion 1 cm = 10 mm to change the dimensions of the sides to centimeters or change the perimeter in millimeters to centimeters.

Problem 29

Students can find the common multiple by counting by fours and counting by sixes.

*29. (55) **Analyze** Which two-digit number less than 20 is a multiple of both 4 and 6? 12

▸*30. (Inv. 5) **Interpret** This circle graph shows the results of an election for class president. Use the graph to answer the parts that follow.

Class Election Results

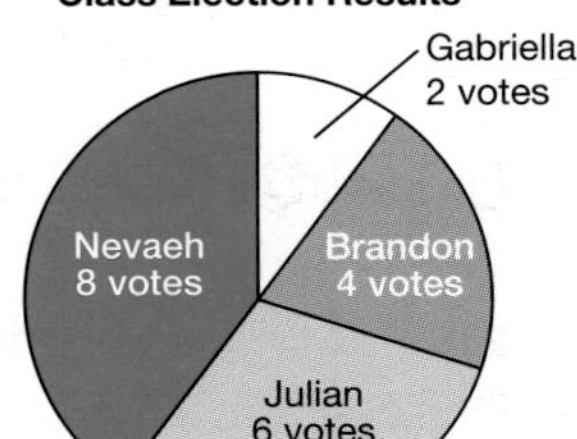

a. Which candidate won the election? How many votes did that candidate receive? Nevaeh; 8 votes

b. Altogether, how many votes were cast in the election? 20 votes

c. Which number is greater: the number of votes received by the winner or the sum of the number of votes received by all of the other candidates? The sum of the number of votes received by all of the other candidates

560 *Saxon Math* Intermediate 4

Division with zeros in three-digit quotients prepares students for:

- **Lesson 87,** solving division word problems that involve remainders.
- **Lesson 91,** estimating multiplication and division answers.

Planning & Preparation

• Multiplying by 10, 100, and 1000

Objectives

- Multiply a whole number by 10, 100, and 1000.
- Multiply dollars and cents by 10, 100, and 1000.
- Solve word problems involving multi-digit multiplication.

Prerequisite Skills

- Using the multiplication facts (0's, 1's, 2's, 5's).
- Multiplying dollars and cents by a one-digit number.
- Multiplying by multiples of 10.

Materials

Instructional Masters

- Power Up I Worksheet

Manipulative Kit

- Base ten blocks*

**optional*

California Mathematics Content Standards

NS 3.0, 3.3 Solve problems involving multiplication of multidigit numbers by two-digit numbers.

AF 1.0, 1.1 Use letters, boxes, or other symbols to stand for any number in simple expressions or equations (e.g., demonstrate an understanding and the use of the concept of a variable).

AF 1.0, 1.5 Understand that an equation such as $y = 3x + 5$ is a prescription for determining a second number when a first number is given.

MR 2.0, 2.4 Express the solution clearly and logically by using the appropriate mathematical notation and terms and clear language; support solutions with evidence in both verbal and symbolic work.

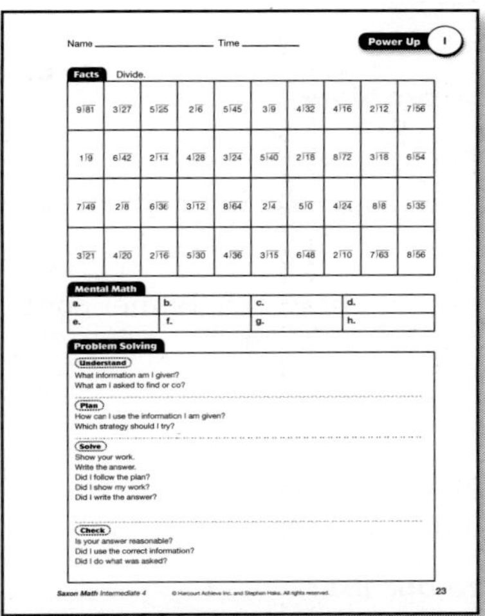

Power Up I Worksheet

Reaching All Special Needs Students

Special Education Students	At-Risk Students	English Learners	Advanced Learners
• Inclusion (TM) • Adaptations for Saxon Math	• Alternative Approach (TM) • Error Alert (TM) • Reteaching Masters • Refresher Lessons for California Standards	• English Learners (TM) • Developing Academic Language (TM) • English Learner Handbook	• Extend the Example (TM) • Extend the Problem (TM) • Online Activities

TM=Teacher's Manual

Developing Academic Language

Maintained
formula
product

English Learner
construction

Problem Solving Discussion

Problem

Tanner has three homework assignments to complete. One assignment is in math, one is in science, and one is in vocabulary. Tanner plans to finish one assignment before starting the next. What are the possible sequences in which he could complete the assignments?

Focus Strategy  **Make an Organized List**

Understand *Understand the problem.*

"What information are we given?"

Tanner must complete homework assignments in math, science, and vocabulary.

"What are we asked to do?"

We are asked to find the possible orders in which Tanner could complete the assignments.

Plan *Make a plan.*

"What problem-solving strategy can we use?"

We can *make an organized list* of the possible orders.

"What is a way we can organize our list?"

We can first list the possible orders that begin with math, then the possible orders that begin with science, and then the possible orders that begin with vocabulary.

Solve *Carry out the plan.*

"What does our list of the possible orders look like?"

We can use the abbreviations M for math, S for science, and V for vocabulary. Our list might look like this:

1. M, S, V	**3.** S, M, V	**5.** V, M, S
2. M, V, S	**4.** S, V, M	**6.** V, S, M

Check *Look back.*

"Does our answer fit the problem?"

Yes, because all six of the orders include each of the assignments for math, science, and vocabulary.

"Is it reasonable that there are six different orders in which Tanner could finish the assignments?"

There are three possible assignments Tanner could work on first. For each of these three possibilities, there are two orders in which Tanner could finish the other two assignments. Thus, there are $3 \times 2 = 6$ possible orders.

LESSON

84

• Multiplying by 10, 100, and 1000

California Mathematics Content Standards

NS 3.0, 3.3 Solve problems involving multiplication of multidigit numbers by two-digit numbers.

AF 1.0, 1.1 Use letters, boxes, or other symbols to stand for any number in simple expressions or equations (e.g., demonstrate an understanding and the use of the concept of a variable).

AF 1.0, 1.5 Understand that an equation such as $y = 3x + 5$ is a prescription for determining a second number when a first number is given.

facts Power Up I

count aloud Count down by quarters from 4 to $\frac{1}{4}$.

mental math Counting by fives from 1, 2, 3, 4, or 5, we find five different final-digit patterns: 1 and 6; 2 and 7; 3 and 8; 4 and 9; and 5 and 0. When a number ending in 5 is added to or subtracted from another number, the final digit of that number and of the answer will fit one of the five patterns. Look for the final-digit patterns as you solve problems **a–f.**

a. **Number Sense:** 22 + 5 27

b. **Number Sense:** 22 − 5 17

c. **Number Sense:** 38 + 5 43

d. **Number Sense:** 38 − 5 33

e. **Number Sense:** 44 + 5 49

f. **Number Sense:** 44 − 5 39

g. **Estimation:** Estimate the fraction of this circle that is shaded: About $\frac{2}{5}$

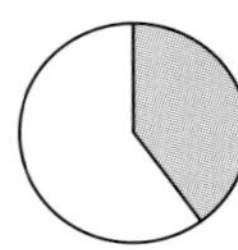

h. **Calculation:** $\sqrt{36}$, × 3, + 10, ÷ 4, − 1, ÷ 3 2

problem solving Choose an appropriate problem-solving strategy to solve this problem. Tanner has three homework assignments to complete. One assignment is in math, one is in science, and one is in vocabulary. Tanner plans to finish one assignment before starting the next. What are the possible sequences in which he could complete the assignments? M, S, V; M, V, S; S, M, V; S, V, M; V, M, S; V, S, M

Facts Divide.

$\overset{9}{9\overline{)81}}$	$\overset{9}{3\overline{)27}}$	$\overset{5}{5\overline{)25}}$	$\overset{3}{2\overline{)6}}$	$\overset{9}{5\overline{)45}}$	$\overset{3}{3\overline{)9}}$	$\overset{8}{4\overline{)32}}$	$\overset{4}{4\overline{)16}}$	$\overset{6}{2\overline{)12}}$	$\overset{8}{7\overline{)56}}$
$\overset{9}{1\overline{)9}}$	$\overset{7}{6\overline{)42}}$	$\overset{7}{2\overline{)14}}$	$\overset{7}{4\overline{)28}}$	$\overset{8}{3\overline{)24}}$	$\overset{8}{5\overline{)40}}$	$\overset{9}{2\overline{)18}}$	$\overset{9}{8\overline{)72}}$	$\overset{6}{3\overline{)18}}$	$\overset{9}{6\overline{)54}}$
$\overset{7}{7\overline{)49}}$	$\overset{4}{2\overline{)8}}$	$\overset{6}{6\overline{)36}}$	$\overset{4}{3\overline{)12}}$	$\overset{8}{8\overline{)64}}$	$\overset{2}{2\overline{)4}}$	$\overset{0}{5\overline{)0}}$	$\overset{6}{4\overline{)24}}$	$\overset{1}{8\overline{)8}}$	$\overset{7}{5\overline{)35}}$
$\overset{7}{3\overline{)21}}$	$\overset{5}{4\overline{)20}}$	$\overset{8}{2\overline{)16}}$	$\overset{6}{5\overline{)30}}$	$\overset{9}{4\overline{)36}}$	$\overset{5}{3\overline{)15}}$	$\overset{8}{6\overline{)48}}$	$\overset{5}{2\overline{)10}}$	$\overset{9}{7\overline{)63}}$	$\overset{7}{8\overline{)56}}$

Power Up

Facts

Distribute **Power Up I** to students. See answers below.

Count Aloud

Before students begin the Mental Math exercises, do these counting exercises as a class.

Mental Math

Encourage students to share different ways to mentally compute these exercises. Strategies for exercises are listed below.

a. Add Tens, then Add Ones
20 + 2 + 5 = 20 + 7 = 27

b. Subtract 2, then Subtract 3
22 − 2 = 20; 20 − 3 = 17

e. Add Tens, then Add Ones
40 + 4 + 5 = 40 + 9 = 49

f. Subtract 4, then Subtract 1
44 − 4 = 40; 40 − 1 = 39

Problem Solving

Refer to **Problem-Solving Strategy Discussion,** p. 561B.

New Concept

Active Learning

Encourage students to discuss, then form a generalization about the products of factors when one factor is 10, 100, or 1000. Sample: To multiply a number by 10, 100, or 1000, multiply the non-zero digits in the factors, and then attach one zero to the right of that product if a factor is 10, two zeros if a factor is 100, or three zeros if a factor is 1000.

Example 1

Make sure students recognize that they are to name each product using only mental math.

Error Alert

For part **b,** students should understand that since there are a total of two decimal places in the factors, there must be two decimal places in the product.

For part **c,** have students recall that if a number of cents is greater than 99¢, the number is not considered to be in simplest form and must be changed to dollars and cents.

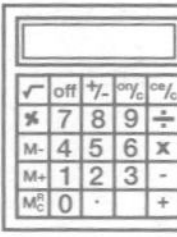

You may choose to have students use a calculator to prove their answer is correct in Example 1.

Example 2

Active Learning

The solution assumes that the product is found using mental math. Ask:

"Explain how mental math can be used to find the product of 2000 and 10." Since the factors have a total of four zeros, attach four zeros to the right of the product of 2 × 1.

Extend the Example

Challenge advanced learners to find how many pounds are in $10\frac{1}{2}$ tons. 21,000 pounds

(continued)

New Concept

To multiply a whole number by 10, we simply add a zero to the end of the number.

$$\begin{array}{r} 123 \\ \times \quad 10 \\ \hline 1230 \end{array}$$

When we multiply a whole number by 100, we add two zeros to the end of the number.

$$\begin{array}{r} 123 \\ \times \quad 100 \\ \hline 12{,}300 \end{array}$$

When we multiply a whole number by 1000, we add three zeros to the end of the number.

$$\begin{array}{r} 123 \\ \times \quad 1000 \\ \hline 123{,}000 \end{array}$$

When we multiply dollars and cents by a whole number, we remember to insert the decimal point two places from the right side of the product.

$$\begin{array}{r} \$1.23 \\ \times \quad 100 \\ \hline \$123.00 \end{array}$$

Thinking Skills

Generalize

If we were to multiply 15 by 1 million, how many zeros would we attach to the right of the product of 15 and 1?

6 zeros

Example 1

Multiply mentally:

a. 37 × 10 **b.** $6.12 × 100 **c.** 45¢ × 1000

a. The answer is "37" with one zero at the end:

370

b. The answer is "612" with two zeros at the end. We remember to place the decimal point and dollar sign:

$612.00

c. The answer is "45" with three zeros at the end. This makes 45,000¢, which in dollar form is

$450.00

Thinking Skills

Discuss

Why is the product of 100 and $6.12 *not* written as $6.1200?

When we multiply $6.12 by 100, the product should be greater 6.12 and 6.1200 are equal.

Alternative Approach: Using Manipulatives

Students may benefit from using base ten blocks to model multiplying by 10, 100, and 1000.

Money manipulatives can be used to model amounts when a factor is stated in dollars and/or cents. Remind students to convert a product that is greater than ninety-nine cents to dollars and cents.

Example 2

A cement company delivered 10 tons of cement to a construction site. How many pounds is that?

We know that 2000 lbs = 1 ton. We can multiply 2000 × 10 to find the number of pounds.

$$2000 \times 10 = 20{,}000$$

The cement company delivered in **20,000 lbs** of cement.

Generalize Write a formula for changing any number of tons to pounds. Use p for pounds and t for tons. Find the number of pounds in 7 tons. $p = 2000t$ or $2000t = p$; 14,000 lbs

Lesson Practice

Multiply mentally:

a. 365 × 10 3650 **b.** 52 × 100 5200 **c.** 7 × 1000 7000

d. \$3.60 × 10 \$36.00 **e.** 420 × 100 42,000 **f.** \$2.50 × 1000 \$2500.00

g. The table below shows the relationship between dimes and dollars. Write a formula to represent the relationship where d = dimes and l = dollars. $d = 10l$

Number of Dollars	1	2	3	4	5
Number of Dimes	10	20	30	40	50

Written Practice

Distributed and Integrated

1. (15, 16, Inv. 5) **Interpret** The line graph shows the average monthly temperatures during spring in Jacksonville, Florida. Use the graph to answer the parts that follow:

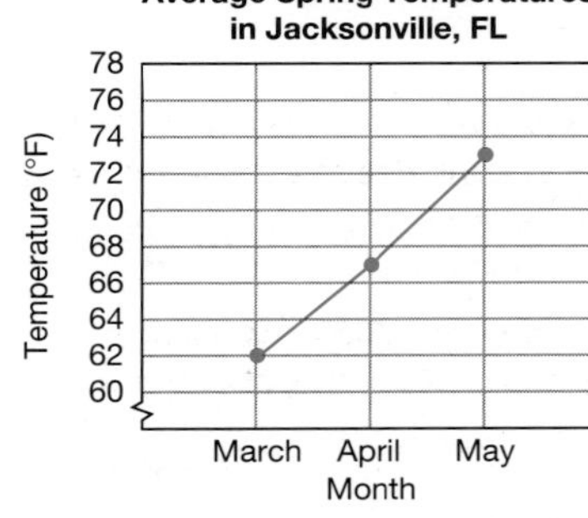

a. What is the average temperature during March in Jacksonville, Florida? During April? During May? 62°F; 67°F; 73°F

New Concept *(Continued)*

Lesson Practice

Guided Practice

Use these problems as guided practice to check the students' understanding of today's concept.

Problems a–f

All of the products are to be named using only mental math. Before students name the products, ask:

"How many zeros do we attach to a product when one factor is 10?" one zero

"How many zeros do we attach to a product when one factor is 100?" two zeros

"How many zeros do we attach to a product when one factor is 1000?" three zeros

Problems d and f Error Alert

If students have difficulty multiplying a decimal factor, explain that they can move the decimal point in the factor two places to the right, and multiply the factors as whole numbers. However, they must remember to move the decimal point two places to the left in the product.

Closure

The question below helps assess the concepts taught in this lesson.

"Explain how mental math can be used to name the product of two numbers when one number is 10, 100, or 1000." If one number is 10, write one zero to the right of the product of the non-zero digits; If one number is 100, write two zeros to the right of the product of the non-zero digits; If one number is 1000, write three zeros to the right of the product of the non-zero digits.

Math Background

One quick way to multiply a decimal number by 10, 100, or 1000 involves shifting the decimal point to the right. To multiply by 10, shift the decimal point one place to the right. To multiply by 100, shift the decimal point two places to the right. To multiply by 1000, shift the decimal point three places to the right. Here are some examples:

2.34 × 10 = 23.4

Decimal shifts **one** place right.

2.34 × 100 = 234

Decimal shifts **two** places right.

2.34 × 1000 = 2340

Decimal shifts **three** places right.

English Learners

Explain that **construction** is the way in which something is built or put together.

Ask:

"Does anyone know of somebody who helps build houses?"

"You could say that the person who helps build houses works in construction."

Ask:

"Name other types of constructions." Samples: Office buildings, parking lots, shopping malls, restaurants

Written Practice

Math Conversations

Independent Practice and Discussions to Increase Understanding

Problem 1 **Interpret**

Extend the Problem

Give students an opportunity to make predictions about the data by asking them to predict the average monthly temperature in February and in June. Encourage volunteers to explain how their predictions were made.

(continued)

Written Practice *(Continued)*

Math Conversations *(cont.)*

Problem 4

Extend the Problem

"Using the fewest number of bills and coins, what bills and coins should Shunsuke receive as change?" one $5 bill, four $1 bills, one dime, and three pennies

Problem 9 **Formulate**

Point out that the equation must contain at least one set of parentheses.

(continued)

b. Write a sentence that compares the average March temperature to the freezing temperature of water.

c. In Salt Lake City, Utah, the average May temperature is 14 degrees cooler than the average May temperature in Jacksonville, Florida. What is the average May temperature in Salt Lake City? 59°F

1. b. Sample: The average March temperature is 62° – 32° or 30° greater than the freezing temperature of water.

2. (53, 72) The 3-pound melon cost $1.44. What was the cost per pound? $0.48

3. (78) Jin spun all the way around in the air and dunked the basketball. Jin turned about how many degrees? About 360°

▸ ***4.** (28, 51, 52) Shunsuke bought a pair of shoes priced at $47.99. The sales tax was $2.88. Shunsuke gave the clerk $60.00. How much change should he receive? $9.13

5. (Inv. 3) **Analyze** If the perimeter of a square is 1 foot, how many inches long is each side? 3 in.

***6.** (80) The mass of a dollar bill is about 1 gram. Use this information to estimate the number of dollar bills it would take to equal 1 kilogram. About 1000 dollar bills

7. (74) **Represent** One fourth of the 64 balloons were red. How many balloons were red? Draw a picture to illustrate the problem. 16 balloons

7.

64 balloons

$\frac{1}{4}$ were red. { 16 balloons

16 balloons

$\frac{3}{4}$ were not red. { 16 balloons

16 balloons

***8.** (13, 60, Inv. 7) **a.** T'Marra knew that her trip would take about 7 hours. If she left at half past nine in the morning, around what time should she arrive? 4:30 p.m.

b. If T'Marra traveled 350 miles in 7 hours, then she traveled an average of how many miles each hour? 50 miles

c. Using your answer to part **b,** make a table to show how far T'Marra would travel at her average rate in 1, 2, 3, and 4 hours.

8. c.

Hours	Miles
1	50
2	100
3	150
4	200

▸ ***9.** (63) **Formulate** The product of 7 and 8 is how much greater than the sum of 7 and 8? Write an equation to show your work. $(7 \cdot 8) - (7 + 8) = 56 - 15$ or 41

10. (44) Compare: 3049 ⊜ 3049.0

Inclusion

Use this strategy if the student displays:

- Slow Learning Rate.
- Difficulty with Abstract Processing.

Multiplying by 10, 100, and 1000 (Pairs)

Materials: base ten blocks

- Write 8 × 1 on the board. Have students make 8 groups of 1. Ask, ***"What is 8 × 1?"*** 8
- Add a 0 to the problem on the board to make it 8 × 10. Have students make 8 groups of 10. Ask, ***"What is 8 × 10?"*** 80
- Add another 0 to the problem on the board to make 8 × 100. Ask prior to work with base ten blocks, ***"Can anyone guess what 8 × 100 is?"*** 800

  If students are not able to predict correctly have them gather 8 groups of 100. Finally, add another 0 to the problem on the board to make 8 × 1000. Ask, ***"What is 8 × 1000?"*** 8000
- Have students make problem that is a number multiplied by 1 and write the subsequent problems to show ×10, ×100 and ×100. The problems can be passed to a partner to work.

▸*11. (46) **Estimate** Shakura purchased a birthday present for each of two friends. Including sales tax, the cost of one present was \$16.61 and the cost of the other present was \$14.37. What is a reasonable estimate of the total cost of the presents? Explain your answer. Sample: Round to the nearest dollar; \$17 + \$14 = \$31

*12. (55, 84) What is the product of the fifth multiple of 2 and the eighth multiple of 6? $10 \times 48 = 480$

*13. (Inv. 8) **Represent** Draw and shade two circles to show that $\frac{3}{4} = \frac{6}{8}$.

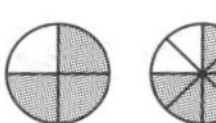

▸*14. (81) **Multiple Choice** Which of these words does *not* describe triangles *ABC* and *DEF*? D

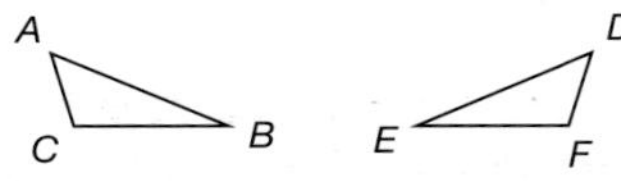

A similar **B** obtuse **C** scalene **D** isosceles

15. (9, 45) Find $0.625 - (0.5 + 0.12)$. Describe the steps in order. 0.005; sample: First add 0.5 and 0.12, which is $0.5 + 0.12 = 0.62$; Then subtract 0.62 from 0.625, which is $0.625 - 0.62 = 0.005$.

16. (84) Mentally find this product. 47×100 4700

17. (59) 328×4 1312

*18. (71) 43×30 1290

*19. (71) 35×40 1400

20. (79) $5\overline{)4317}$ 863 R 2

21. (79, 83) $8\overline{)\$40.00}$ \$5.00

22. (83) $6\overline{)3963}$ 660 R 3

23. (34, 79) $3a = 426$ 142

24. (79) $2524 \div 4$ 631

*25. (84) 60×100 6000

*26. (82) **Conclude** Below we show an equilateral triangle, an isosceles triangle, and a scalene triangle. Name the triangle that does not have reflective symmetry. scalene triangle

27. (4) $4 + 3 + 27 + 35 + 8 + n = 112$ 35

Written Practice *(Continued)*

Math Conversations *(cont.)*

Problem 11 Estimate

A variety of estimates are possible. After students complete their estimates, invite volunteers to share their estimates and explanations with the class.

Problem 14 Multiple Choice

Test-Taking Strategy

Point out that there is no test-taking rule that prohibits students from tracing triangle *ABC* and comparing the tracing to triangle *DEF* to help decide if the triangles are similar.

Also point out that there is no test-taking rule that prohibits students from comparing the angles of the given triangles to a known right angle, such as the square corner of a piece of paper, to help classify the angles.

Remind students that finding the term that does not describe the triangles can be accomplished by identifying all of the terms that do describe the triangles. The correct answer to the problem will be the term that was not identified.

(continued)

Written Practice *(Continued)*

Math Conversations *(cont.)*

Problem 29

Extend the Problem

Challenge students to make an organized list on the board or overhead of all the pairs of parallel and perpendicular edges.

Problem 30 Explain

Although the problem can be solved simply by looking at the *y*-axis, make sure students solve the problem by first writing the coordinates of the endpoints, and then subtracting the *y*-coordinates of those points.

Errors and Misconceptions

Problem 1b

Make sure students understand that because the graph displays Fahrenheit temperatures, the freezing temperature of water in degrees Celsius (0°C) cannot be a part of the comparison. Watch for opportunities to help students recall that the freezing temperature of water is 32°F.

Problem 6

Some students may need to be reminded that 1 kilogram is the same as 1000 grams.

Problem 8

Because T'Marra traveled at an average speed of 50 miles per hour, some students may assume that she traveled at exactly that speed for each hour of the trip. Point out that an average is only a representative measure of a whole. In other words, we only know that T'Marra traveled 350 miles in an elapsed time of 7 hours. We know nothing more. It is possible, for example, that she traveled at a speed greater than 50 miles per hour for a portion of her trip and stopped along the way to rest or eat. So, it is likely that she was not traveling at a speed of exactly 50 miles per hour for each moment of her trip.

***28.** (42, 45) **a.** Segment *BC* is 1.7 cm long. How many centimeters long is segment *AB?* 1.8 cm

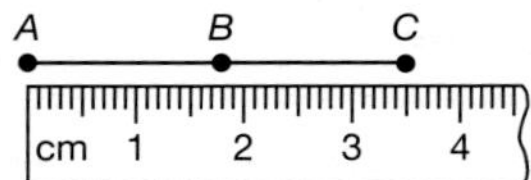

b. Write a decimal addition problem that is illustrated by the lengths of segments *AB, BC,* and *AC.* 1.8 + 1.7 = 3.5

▸*29. (17) **a.** Name a pair of parallel edges in the figure at right.
Sample: $\overline{AB}$ and $\overline{CD}$

b. Name a pair of perpendicular edges. Sample: $\overline{AC}$ and $\overline{CD}$

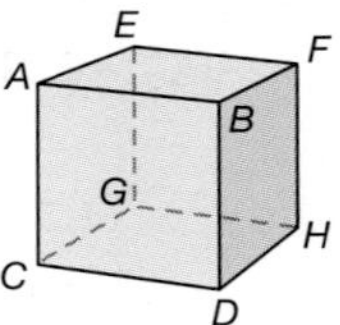

▸*30. (Inv. 7) **Explain** What is the length of segment *RT?* Explain your reasoning.
7 units; Count units or subtract *y*-coordinates; 9 − 2 = 7

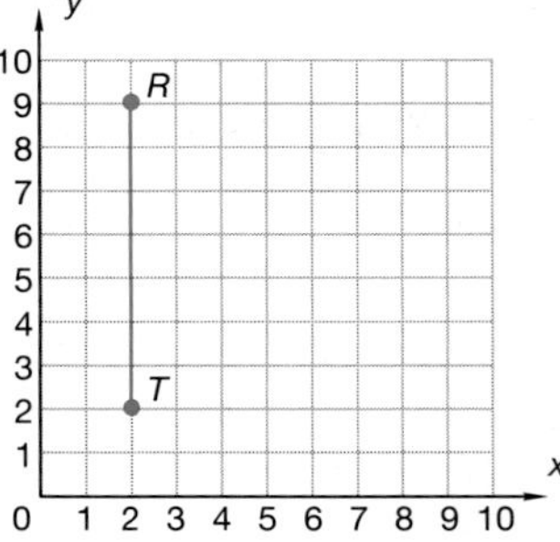

Looking Forward

Multiplying whole numbers and money amounts by 10, 100, and 1000 prepares students for:

- **Lesson 85,** multiplying two or more multiples of 10 and 100.
- **Lessons 86** and **88,** multiplying two-digit numbers.
- **Lesson 91,** estimating the answers to multiplication and division problems.
- **Lesson 104,** rounding whole numbers to the nearest hundred thousand and the nearest million.
- **Lesson 105,** factoring whole numbers.

Planning & Preparation

• Multiplying Multiples of 10 and 100, Part 2

Objectives

- Multiply two multiples of 10 or 100.
- Solve problems involving multi-digit problems.

Prerequisite Skills

- Finding patterns for multiplying a whole number by 10, 100, and 1000.
- Finding patterns for multiplying money amounts by 10, 100, and 1000.

Materials

Instructional Masters

- Power Up G Worksheet
- Lesson Activity 8*

Manipulative Kit

- Rulers
- Base ten blocks*

Teacher-provided materials

- Grid paper*

**optional*

California Mathematics Content Standards

NS 1.0, 1.2 Order and compare whole numbers and decimals to two decimal places.

NS 3.0, 3.3 Solve problems involving multiplication of multidigit numbers by two-digit number.

MR 3.0, 3.3 Develop generalizations of the results obtained and apply them in other circumstances.

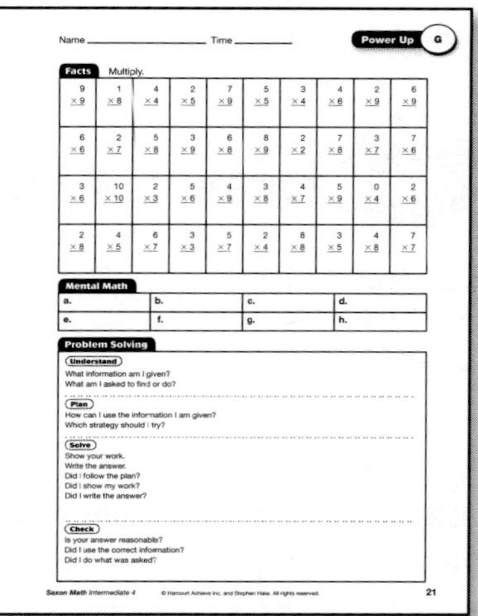
Name ____________ Time ________ **Power Up G**

Facts Multiply.

9 × 9	1 × 8	4 × 4	2 × 5	7 × 9	5 × 5	3 × 4	4 × 6	2 × 9	6 × 9
6 × 6	2 × 7	5 × 8	3 × 9	6 × 8	8 × 9	2 × 2	7 × 8	3 × 7	7 × 6
3 × 6	10 × 10	2 × 3	5 × 6	4 × 9	3 × 8	4 × 7	5 × 9	0 × 4	2 × 6
2 × 8	4 × 5	6 × 7	3 × 3	5 × 7	2 × 4	8 × 8	3 × 5	4 × 8	7 × 7

Mental Math

a.	b.	c.	d.
e.	f.	g.	h.

Problem Solving

Understand
What information am I given?
What am I asked to find or do?

Plan
How can I use the information I am given?
Which strategy should I try?

Solve
Show your work.
Write the answer.
Did I follow the plan?
Did I show my work?
Did I write the answer?

Check
Is your answer reasonable?
Did I use the correct information?
Did I do what was asked?

Saxon Math Intermediate 4 21

Power Up G Worksheet

Universal Access

Reaching All Special Needs Students

Special Education Students	At-Risk Students	English Learners	Advanced Learners
• Inclusion (TM) • Adaptations for Saxon Math	• Alternative Approach (TM) • Error Alert (TM) • Reteaching Masters • Refresher Lessons for California Standards	• English Learners (TM) • Developing Academic Language (TM) • English Learner Handbook	• Extend the Example (TM) • Extend the Problem (TM) • Online Activities

TM=Teacher's Manual

Developing Academic Language

Maintained	**English Learner**
factors	concentrated
product	

Problem Solving Discussion

Problem

The diagram at the right is called a *Venn diagram*. The circle on the left represents fruit, and the circle on the right represents vegetables. The *A* represents apples, which are fruit, and the *B* represents broccoli, which is a vegetable. The *C* represents cheese, which is neither a fruit nor a vegetable. Copy the diagram on your paper and place abbreviations for eggs, oranges, and green beans.

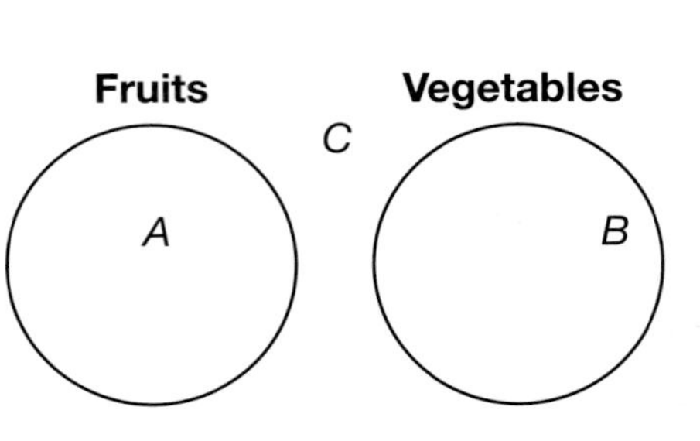

Focus Strategy

Draw a Picture or Diagram

Understand *Understand the problem.*

"What information are we given?"

We are shown a Venn diagram that has two circles and three letters. One circle represents fruit, and the other circle represents vegetables.

"If an abbreviation is placed outside both circles, what does that mean?"

It means that the food the abbreviation stands for is neither a fruit nor a vegetable.

"What are we asked to do?"

We are asked to copy the Venn diagram and place abbreviations for eggs, oranges, and green beans.

Plan *Make a plan.*

"What problem-solving strategy will we use to solve this problem?"

We will *draw a diagram.*

Solve *Carry out the plan.*

"Where should we place the abbreviations for eggs, oranges, and green beans?"

Eggs are neither a fruit nor a vegetable, so we place an *E* outside the circles. Oranges are a fruit, so we place an *O* inside the circle for fruits. Green beans are a vegetable, so we place *GB* inside the circle for vegetables.

"What should our diagram look like?"

The diagram might look like the diagram at the right.

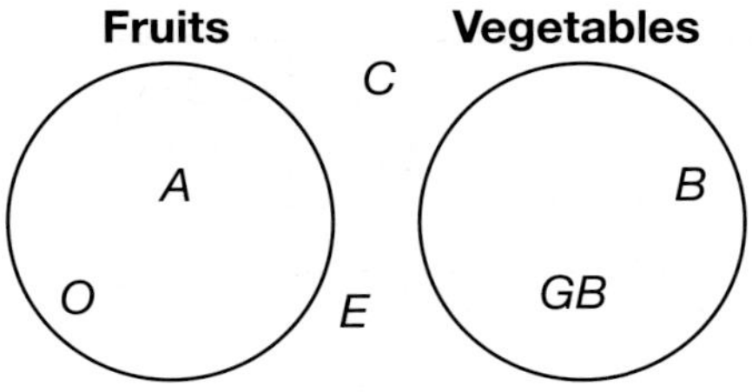

Check *Look back.*

"Did we complete the task?"

Yes. We drew a Venn diagram and placed abbreviations for eggs, oranges, and green beans.

LESSON
85

California Mathematics Content Standards

NS 1.0, 1.2 Order and compare whole numbers and decimals to two decimal places.

NS 3.0, 3.3 Solve problems involving multiplication of multidigit numbers by two-digit number.

MR 3.0, 3.3 Develop generalizations of the results obtained and apply them in other circumstances.

• Multiplying Multiples of 10 and 100, Part 2

facts Power Up G

mental math Use the fives pattern as you add in problems **a–c.**

a. **Number Sense:** 36 + 15 51

b. **Number Sense:** 47 + 25 72

c. **Number Sense:** 28 + 35 63

d. **Number Sense:** 40 × 40 × 10 16,000

e. **Money:** \$10.00 − \$2.75 \$7.25

f. **Time:** How many days is 8 weeks? 56 days

g. **Estimation:** Each bracelet costs \$2.99. Kim has \$11. Does she have enough money to buy 4 bracelets? No

h. **Calculation:** $\frac{1}{2}$ of 42, ÷ 3, + 10, − 3, ÷ 2, × 7 49

problem solving The diagram at right is called a *Venn diagram.* The circle on the left represents fruit, and the circle on the right represents vegetables. The *A* represents apples, which are a fruit, and the *B* represents broccoli, which is a vegetable. The *C* represents cheese, which is neither a fruit nor a vegetable. Copy the diagram on your paper and place abbreviations for eggs, oranges, and green beans.

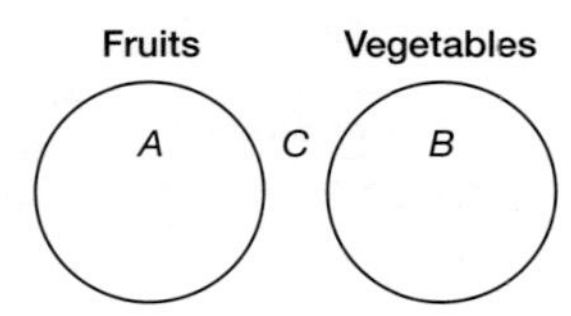

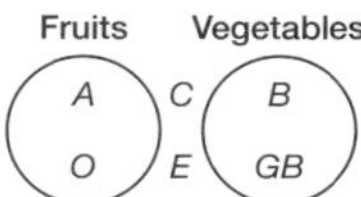

Power Up

Facts
Distribute **Power Up G** to students. See answers below.

Count Aloud
Before students begin the Mental Math exercises, do these counting exercises as a class.

Count by $\frac{1}{4}$'s from $\frac{1}{4}$ to 4 and back down to $\frac{1}{4}$.

Mental Math
Encourage students to share different ways to mentally compute these exercises. Strategies for exercises are listed below.

a. Add 10, then Add 5

36 + 10 = 46; 46 + 5 = 51

Add 20, then Subtract 5

36 + 20 = 56; 56 − 5 = 51

d. Attach 3 Zeros to 4 × 4 × 1

4 × 4 × 1 = 16; 40 × 40 × 10 = 16,000

e. Subtract \$3, then Add 25¢

\$10 − \$3 = \$7; \$7.00 + 25¢ = \$7.25

Problem Solving
Refer to **Problem-Solving Strategy Discussion,** p. 567B.

Facts Multiply.

9 × 9 81	1 × 8 8	4 × 4 16	2 × 5 10	7 × 9 63	5 × 5 25	3 × 4 12	4 × 6 24	2 × 9 18	6 × 9 54
6 × 6 36	2 × 7 14	5 × 8 40	3 × 9 27	6 × 8 48	8 × 9 72	2 × 2 4	7 × 8 56	3 × 7 21	7 × 6 42
3 × 6 18	10 × 10 100	2 × 3 6	5 × 6 30	4 × 9 36	3 × 8 24	4 × 7 28	5 × 9 45	0 × 4 0	2 × 6 12
2 × 8 16	4 × 5 20	6 × 7 42	3 × 3 9	5 × 7 35	2 × 4 8	8 × 8 64	3 × 5 15	4 × 8 32	7 × 7 49

New Concept

Explanation

Make sure students understand that the phrase "first digits of the factors" represents the non-zero digits.

Observation

Have students note that the number of zeros in the factors (there are two zeros altogether) are written to the right of the product of the nonzero digits.

Example 1

It is important for students to understand that we write two zeros to the right of the product of 6 × 8 because there are two zeros altogether in the factors 60 × 80.

Example 2

Error Alert

A common error when placing a decimal point in a product that represents dollars and cents is to place the decimal point by counting from left to right. Make sure students understand that the decimal point is placed by counting two places from right to left.

Example 3

Active Learning

To reinforce this concept, ask students:

"What four factors does the product of 400 × 700 represent?" 4 × 7 × 100 × 100

Extend the Example

Challenge your advanced learners to name other factors that have the same product as **4 × 7 × 100 × 100.** Samples 4 × 7 × 10 × 10 × 10 × 10; 4 × 70,000; 40 × 7000; 7 × 40,000; 70 × 4000

Lesson Practice

Guided Practice

Use these problems as guided practice to check the students' understanding of today's concept.

Problem a

"What multiplication fact can we use to find the product of 70 and 80 using only mental math?" 7 × 8 = 56

"Explain how we can find the product of 70 and 80 using only mental math." Write two zeros to the right of the product of 7 × 8; 70 × 80 = 5600

(continued)

New Concept

Thinking Skills

Analyze

Is the product of 40 and 50 written as 200, 2000, or 20,000? Explain your reasoning.

2000; sample: Attach 2 zeros to the right of the product of 4 and 5.

Once we have memorized the multiplication facts, we can multiply rounded numbers "in our head." To do this, we multiply the first digits of the factors and count zeros. Study the multiplication on the next page.

```
   40  ←┐
 × 30  ←┘ two zeros
 ____
  _ _
4 × 3 ┘ └ two zeros
```

To find the product of 40 and 30, we multiply 4 by 3 and then attach two zeros. The product is 4 × 3 × 10 × 10, or 1200.

Example 1

In the weightlifting room, a group of football players lifted 80 pounds of weights 60 different times. How many pounds of weight did the players lift altogether?

We think, "six times eight is 48." Since there is one zero in 60 and one zero in 80, we attach two zeros to 48. The product is 4800, so the total weight lifted was **4800 pounds.**

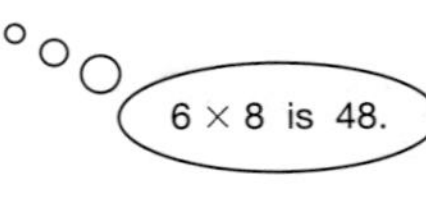

Example 2

Thinking Skills

Verify

Why do we attach three zeros when we multiply 30 by $7.00?

Sample: One zero represents multiplying by 3 tens, one zero represents the number of dimes, and one zero represents the number of pennies.

A store has 30 ping pong paddles for sale at $7.00 each. How much money will the store receive if all of the paddles are sold?

We think, "three times seven is 21." There are three zeros in the problem, so we attach three zeros to 21 to get 21,000. Since we multiplied dollars and cents, we insert the decimal point two places from the right and add a dollar sign. The product is $210.00, so the income will be **$210.**

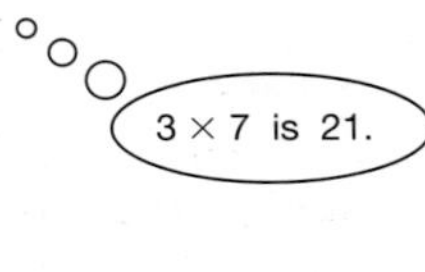

Math Background

Decimal numbers with one non-zero digit can also be multiplied mentally. To multiply 0.7 and 0.06, first multiply 7 × 6 to get 42. Now count the number of decimal places in the two factors. There's one in 0.7 and two in 0.06. The total, three, is the number of decimal places in the answer, so 0.7 × 0.06 = 0.042. Here are two more examples:

- To find 8 × 0.6, multiply 8 × 6 to get 48. The answer must have one decimal place, so it is 4.8.
- To find 0.04 × 0.005, multiply 4 × 5 to get 20. The answer must have five decimal places, so it is 0.00020. After the position of the decimal point has been determined, any unnecessary zeros at the end of the product can be dropped. The answer can be written as 0.0002.

Any unnecessary zeros should be dropped from the factors before multiplying. For example, to find 0.20 × 0.040, first rewrite the problem as 0.2 × 0.04.

Example 3

Multiply mentally: 400 × 700

We think, "Four times seven is 28." We attach four zeros and get **280,000.**

Connect How would we multiply 40 × 7000? What is the product?

4 × 7 = 28 and attach four zeros; 280,000

Lesson Practice

Multiply mentally:

a. 70 × 80 5600

b. 40 × 50 2000

c. 40 × $6.00 $240.00

d. 30 × 800 24,000

e. **Verify** Write >, <, or = to make this statement true:

300 × 200 (=) 30 × 2000

Written Practice *Distributed and Integrated*

1. (28) **Analyze** Three quarters, four dimes, two nickels, and seven pennies is how much money? $1.32

▶ ***2.** (Inv. 1, 79) **Formulate** Write a division word problem with a quotient of 630. See student work.

▶ ***3.** (76) **Explain** Gregory paid $1 for a folder and received 52¢ in change. If the tax was 3¢, how much did the folder cost without tax? Explain your thinking. 45¢; sample: Subtract 52¢ from $1 to find the total cost of the folder, which is 48¢; Next, subtract the tax to find the original cost; 48¢ − 3¢ = 45¢

4. (39) Ryan wrote each of his 12 spelling words five times. In all, how many words did he write? 60 words

5. (40) **Estimate** In the 2004 presidential election, 5992 voters in Blaine County, Idaho, voted for candidate John Kerry, and 4034 voters voted for candidate George Bush. Estimate the total number of votes those two candidates received, and explain your estimate. Sample: about 10,000 votes; Round each number of votes to the nearest thousand, then add; 6000 + 4000 = 10,000

6. (Inv. 6) What is the tally for 10? 𝍸 𝍸

7. (Inv. 4) Name the shaded part of this square

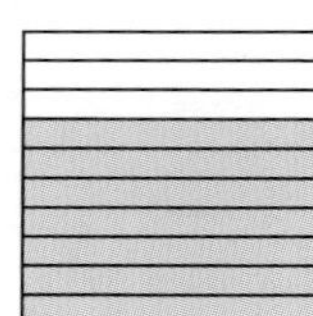

a. as a fraction. $\frac{7}{10}$

b. as a decimal number. 0.7

Inclusion

Use this strategy if the student displays:

- Slow Learning Rate.
- Difficulty Reading.

Multiplying Multiples of 10 and 100 (Individual)

Material: paper

- Read, ***"There are 20 oranges in a crate. If 30 crates are loaded on the truck, how many oranges are there?"***
- Have students draw a picture to solve this problem. Ask, ***"How many oranges are there?"*** 600

  Write the 2 × 3 on the board and ask for its product. Ask, ***"How many zeros are in the original numbers?"*** 2

  Tell students to add these two zeros to the number 6 to make 600.
- Read, ***"Jane reads 20 pages a day. If she reads for 40 days, how many total pages will she have read?"***
- Have students write the factors without zeros 2 × 4 and solve for the product. 8 Then ask, ***"How many zeros are in the factors?"*** 2

  Have students add these zeros to the 8 and ask, ***"How many total pages will Jane have read?"*** 800

New Concept *(Continued)*

Lesson Practice

Problem b
Error Alert

When the product of the non-zero digits is a multiple of 10, a common error is to write too few zeros to the right of the product because the product already contains one or more zeros. In problem **b,** for example, students must be sure to write two zeros to the right of the 20, the product of 5 × 4.

Closure The questions below help assess the concepts taught in this lesson.

"Explain how mental math can be used to name the product of two factors when one or both factors are multiples of 10." Count the number of zeros in the factors and then write that number of zeros to the right of the product of the non-zero digits.

"Name the product of 40 times 200 using only mental math." Write three zeros to the right of the product of 4 × 2; 4 × 2 = 8 and 40 × 200 = 8000

Written Practice

Math Conversations

Independent Practice and Discussions to Increase Understanding

Problem 2 **Formulate**

If students have difficulty identifying the dividend and the divisor, explain that they should choose a number for the divisor. The product of that number and the quotient (630) will be the dividend of the division.

Problem 3 **Explain**

Make sure that the explanations include the fact that subtraction must be used twice—once to find the cost of the folder including tax, and once to find the cost of the folder not including tax.

(continued)

Written Practice *(Continued)*

Math Conversations *(cont.)*

Problem 9

Students should use arithmetic instead of a ruler to compute the length of segment *CD*. After the length has been computed, invite them to use a ruler and measure segment *CD* to check their work.

Problem 12

To maintain alignment of the decimal points, some students may find it helpful to write the subtraction on grid paper or on lined paper turned sideways.

Problem 15

Before students perform the arithmetic, ask:

"Is 1000 a reasonable estimate of the exact product? Explain why or why not."

Yes; sample: 47 rounds to 50, and $50 \times 20 = 1000$.

Problem 23

Make sure students recall that none of the sides of a scalene triangle have the same length.

Problems 24 a and b **Represent**

Manipulative Use

Students will need a ruler to complete part **a,** and some students may find it helpful to draw the square on grid paper.

As students complete part **b,** remind them to think of half as division by 2. They can then calculate the area of one half of the square, regardless of how it has been divided, by dividing the area of the square (16 square centimeters) by 2.

(continued)

8. (74) **Represent** One sixth of the 48 crayons are in the box. How many crayons are in the box? Draw a picture to illustrate the problem. 8 crayons

8. 48 crayons

$\frac{1}{6}$ are in the box.	8 crayons
$\frac{5}{6}$ are not in the box.	8 crayons
	8 crayons
	8 crayons
	8 crayons
	8 crayons

9. (33, 42) Segment *AB* is 32 mm long. Segment *BC* is 26 mm long. Segment *AD* is 91 mm long. How many millimeters long is segment *CD?* 33 mm

A B C D

***10.** (41) Which digit in 6.120 is in the hundredths place? 2

11. (73, 80) **Estimate** If a pint of water weighs about one pound, then about how many pounds does a quart of water weigh? About 2 pounds

***12.** (45) $4.32 - 0.43$ 3.89

13. (Inv. 3, 63, 65) $5^2 + \sqrt{25} + n = 30$ 0

14. (59) $\$6.08 \times 8$ \$48.64

***15.** (71) 47×20 940

***16.** (85) 300×20 6000

17. (71) 53×30 1590

***18.** (71) 63×40 2520

19. (84) 100×32 3200

20. (79) $4\overline{)3456}$ 864

21. (79) $8n = 6912$ 864

22. (79, 83) $7\overline{)\$50.40}$ \$7.20

***23.** (81) Draw a right, scalene triangle.

23. 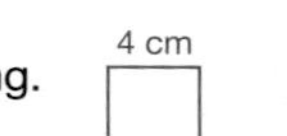

24. (18, 19, Inv. 3) **Represent** **a.** Draw a square with sides 4 cm long.

b. Shade half of the square you drew. How many square centimeters did you shade? 4 cm ; 8 sq. cm

***25.** (Inv. 4) **Represent** Write twenty-one hundredths as a fraction and as a decimal number. $\frac{21}{100}$; 0.21

Alternative Approach: Using Manipulatives

To help students understand the concept of multiplying multiples of 10, and 100, have them use base ten blocks to model multiplication.

Have students model 40×30 using base ten blocks. $40 \times 0 = 0$ ones; 40×3 tens $= 120$ tens and regrouping gives 1 thousand, 2 hundred, 0 tens. Add the ones, tens, hundreds, and thousands to get 1 thousand, 2 hundreds, 0 tens, 0 ones or 1200. Have students model other examples.

English Learners

When food is **concentrated,** it means that something was removed for packaging or transportation purposes.

For example, orange juice is often concentrated which means that water was removed and we have to add water in order to make it drinkable.

Ask:

"What other things are concentrated?"

Samples: cranberry juice, soap

*26. (53, 72) **Explain** Emma mixed two quarts of orange juice from frozen concentrate. She knows 1 quart is equal to 32 fluid ounces. The small juice glasses Emma is filling each have a capacity of 6 fluid ounces. How many juice glasses can Emma fill? Explain your answer.
10; sample: Since 32 + 32 = 64, and 64 ÷ 6 = 10 R 4, Emma can fill 10 glasses. The remainder represents 4 ounces of juice, which is not enough to fill another glass.

▸*27. (17, 82) **Multiple Choice** Use the polygons below to answer parts **a–d.**

A **B** **C** **D**

a. Which of these polygons has no lines of symmetry? D

b. Which two of these polygons have rotational symmetry? A and C

c. Which polygon does not have any parallel sides? A

d. Which polygons do not have any perpendicular sides? A and B

▸ 28. (78) How many degrees does the minute hand of a clock turn in half an hour? 180°

*29. (44) Compare: 4.2 ⓔ 4.200

*30. (Inv. 5) Use the pictograph below to answer the questions that follow:

Animal	Typical Weight (in pounds)
Alligator	
Porpoise	
Wild Boar	
Seal	

Key: = 100 pounds

a. What amount of weight does each symbol represent? 100 pounds

b. Write the typical weights of the animals in order from least to greatest. 100 lb, 150 lb, 200 lb, 300 lb

c. **Connect** Write a sentence that compares the weights of two animals. Sample: An alligator typically weighs half as much as a wild boar.

Written Practice (Continued)

Math Conversations *(cont.)*

Problem 27 Multiple Choice

Test-Taking Strategy

Remind students that test questions will not always involve computation. To help decide which figures have no lines of symmetry, students can trace the figures. To help decide which figures have rotational symmetry, students can rotate the page on which the figures are shown.

Problem 28

Extend the Problem

Ask students to name the number of degrees the minute hand turns in 15 minutes, in 45 minutes, and in one hour. 15 minutes, 90°; 45 minutes, 270°; one hour, 360°

Errors and Misconceptions

Problem 1

Some students may benefit from using money manipulatives, if available, to find the value of the coins. Provide these students with 3 quarters, 4 dimes, 2 nickels, and 7 pennies.

Problem 29

Make sure students do not compare the numbers by comparing the number of digits in each number. Students who compare in this way will decide that 4.2 < 4.200. Demonstrate for these students that two zeros can be attached to 4.2, or two zeros can be erased from 4.200, to help compare the numbers and identify them as equivalent decimal numbers.

Looking Forward

Multiplying two or more multiples of 10 and 100 prepares students for:

- **Lessons 86** and **88,** multiplying two two-digit numbers.
- **Lesson 91,** estimating the answers to multiplication and division problems.
- **Lesson 104,** rounding whole numbers to the nearest hundred thousand and the nearest million.
- **Lesson 105,** factoring whole numbers.

Cumulative Assessments and Test-Day Activity

Assessments

Distribute **Power-Up Test 16** and **Cumulative Test 16** to each student. Have students complete the **Power-Up Test** first. Allow 10 minutes. Then have students work on the **Cumulative Test**.

Test-Day Activity

The remaining class time can be spent on the **Test-Day Activity 8.** Students can begin the activity in class and complete it as homework.

California Mathematics Content Standards

SDAP 2.0, 2.1 Represent all possible outcomes for a simple probability situation in an organized way (e.g., tables, grids, tree diagrams)

MR 2.0, 2.4 Express the solution clearly and logically by using the appropriate mathematical notation and terms and clear language; support solutions with evidence in both verbal and symbolic work.

Planning & Preparation

• Multiplying Two Two-Digit Numbers, Part 1

Objectives

- Multiply a two-digit number by a two-digit number, without regrouping.
- Solve problems involving multi-digit problems.

Prerequisite Skills

- Multiplying a three-digit number by a one-digit number with and without regrouping.
- Multiplying dollars and cents by a one-digit number.
- Multiplying by multiples of 10.

Materials

Instructional Masters

- Power Up G Worksheet
- Lesson Activity 8*

Manipulative Kit

- Base ten blocks*

Teacher-provided materials

- Grid paper*

*optional

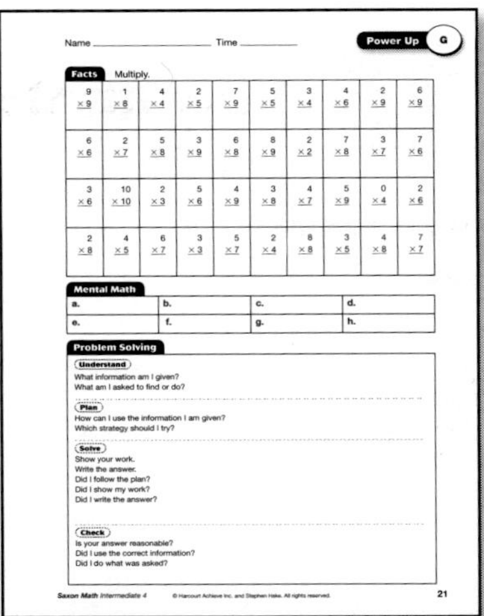

Power Up G Worksheet

Universal Access

Reaching All Special Needs Students

Special Education Students	At-Risk Students	English Learners	Advanced Learners
• Inclusion (TM) • Adaptations for Saxon Math	• Alternative Approach (TM) • Error Alert (TM) • Reteaching Masters • Refresher Lessons for California Standards	• English Learners (TM) • Developing Academic Language (TM) • English Learner Handbook	• Extend the Example (TM) • Extend the Problem (TM) • Online Activities

TM=Teacher's Manual

Developing Academic Language

New	Maintained	English Learner
partial product	multiply	partial

Problem Solving Discussion

Problem

Josh will flip a coin three times in a row. On each flip, the coin will either land "heads" or "tails." If the coin were to land heads up each time, the combination of flips would be heads, heads, heads, which can be abbreviated as HHH. Find all the possible combinations of heads and tails Josh can get with three coin flips.

Focus Strategies

Draw a Picture or Diagram

Make an Organized List

Understand *Understand the problem.*

"What information are we given?"

Josh will flip a coin three times in a row.

"What are we asked to do?"

We are asked to find all the possible combinations of heads and tails from three coin flips.

Plan *Make a plan.*

"What problem-solving strategy can we use?"

We can *make an organized list* in the form of a tree diagram.

"How can we abbreviate the names of the flips in our tree diagram?"

We can use H for heads and T for tails.

Solve *Carry out the plan.*

"What will our tree diagram look like?"

Our tree diagram might look like this:

Flip 1	Flip 2	Flip 3	Outcome
H	H	H	HHH
		T	HHT
	T	H	HTH
		T	HTT
T	H	H	THH
		T	THT
	T	H	TTH
		T	TTT

"How many possible outcomes are there for the three flips of a coin?"

Our diagram shows us that there are 8 possible outcomes.

Check *Look back.*

"Did we complete the task?"

Yes. We listed the 8 outcomes that are possible from three flips of a coin.

"Are our answers reasonable?"

Each outcome that we listed is a possible combination of heads and tails for three coin flips.

"If we acted out this problem with a real coin, would we find the same results?"

Eventually, all eight orders would occur in an experiment, but it might take us a long time to get all eight results. Our tree diagram shows the possible outcomes. Each outcome is equally likely, but that does not mean we can predict when a particular outcome will happen.

Facts
Distribute **Power Up G** to students. See answers below.

Count Aloud
Before students begin the Mental Math exercises, do these counting exercises as a class.

Count by 9's from 9 to 63 and back to 9.

Mental Math
Encourage students to share different ways to mentally compute these exercises. Strategies for exercises are listed below.

c. Subtract 40, then Subtract 5
$84 - 40 = 44;\ 44 - 5 = 39$
Subtract 50, then Add 5
$84 - 50 = 34;\ 34 + 5 = 39$

d. Apply the Distributive Property
$30 \times (20 + 5) = 600 + 150 = 750$
Triple the Product of 25 × 10
$25 \times 10 = 250;\ 250 \times 3 = 750$

Problem Solving
Refer to **Problem-Solving Strategy Discussion,** p. 572B.

New Concept

Generalize

Lead students to generalize from the example that the number of digits in the number they are multiplying by is the number of partial products that the multiplication will produce. For example, multiplying by a two-digit number will produce two partial products, multiplying by a three-digit number will produce three partial products, and so on.

(continued)

LESSON 86

California Mathematics Content Standards

SDAP 2.0, 2.1 Represent all possible outcomes for a simple probability situation in an organized way (e.g., tables, grids, tree diagrams)

MR 2.0, 2.4 Express the solution clearly and logically by using the appropriate mathematical notation and terms and clear language; support solutions with evidence in both verbal and symbolic work.

• Multiplying Two Two-Digit Numbers, Part 1

Power Up

facts Power Up G

mental math Use the fives pattern as you subtract in problems **a–c.**

a. Number Sense: 41 − 15 26

b. Number Sense: 72 − 25 47

c. Number Sense: 84 − 45 39

d. Number Sense: 25 × 30 750

e. Money: Bridget spent $6.54. Then she spent $2.99 more. Altogether, how much did Bridget spend? $9.53

f. Time: Mirabel's speech lasted 2 minutes 20 seconds. How many seconds is that? 140 seconds

g. Estimation: Kione purchased two DVDs for $18.88 each. Estimate the total cost of the DVDs. $38

h. Calculation: $\frac{1}{10}$ of 60, × 4, ÷ 2, × 5 60

H — H — H HHH
H — H — T HHT
H — T — H HTH
H — T — T HTT
T — H — H THH
T — H — T THT
T — T — H TTH
T — T — T TTT

problem solving Choose an appropriate problem-solving strategy to solve this problem. Josh will flip a coin three times in a row. On each flip, the coin will either land on "heads" or "tails." If the coin were to land heads up each time, the combination of flips would be heads, heads, heads, which can be abbreviated as HHH. Find all the possible combinations of heads and tails Josh can get with three coin flips.

We use three steps to multiply by a two-digit number. First we multiply by the ones digit. Next we multiply by the tens digit. Then we add the products. To multiply 34 by 12, for example, we multiply 34 by 2 and then multiply 34 by 10. Then we add the products.

Facts Multiply.

9 × 9 81	1 × 8 8	4 × 4 16	2 × 5 10	7 × 9 63	5 × 5 25	3 × 4 12	4 × 6 24	2 × 9 18	6 × 9 54
6 × 6 36	2 × 7 14	5 × 8 40	3 × 9 27	6 × 8 48	8 × 9 72	2 × 2 4	7 × 8 56	3 × 7 21	7 × 6 42
3 × 6 18	10 × 10 100	2 × 3 6	5 × 6 30	4 × 9 36	3 × 8 24	4 × 7 28	5 × 9 45	0 × 4 0	2 × 6 12
2 × 8 16	4 × 5 20	6 × 7 42	3 × 3 9	5 × 7 35	2 × 4 8	8 × 8 64	3 × 5 15	4 × 8 32	7 × 7 49

Thinking Skills

Evaluate

Can the expression (2 × 34) + (10 × 34) be used to represent the vertical form of 34 × 12? Explain why or why not.

Yes; The expression shows the steps of the multiplication algorithm when the factors are arranged vertically.

34 × 2 =	68	partial product
34 × 10 =	340	partial product
34 × 12 =	408	total product

It is easier to write the numbers one above the other when we multiply, like this:

$$\begin{array}{r} 34 \\ \times\ 12 \\ \hline \end{array}$$

Method 1: First we multiply 34 by 2 and write the answer.

$$\begin{array}{r} 34 \\ \times\ 12 \\ \hline 68 \end{array}$$

Next we multiply 34 by 1. This 1 is actually 10, so the product is 340. We write the answer, and then we add the results of the two multiplication problems and get 408.

$$\begin{array}{r} 34 \\ \times\ 12 \\ \hline 68 \\ 340 \\ \hline 408 \end{array}$$

Method 2: An alternate method would be to omit the zero from the second multiplication. Using this method, we position the last digit of the second multiplication in the second column from the right. The empty place is treated like a zero when adding.

$$\begin{array}{r} 34 \\ \times\ 12 \\ \hline 68 \\ 34\ \ \\ \hline 408 \end{array}$$

Example

Multiply: $\begin{array}{r} 31 \\ \times\ 23 \\ \hline \end{array}$

First we multiply 31 by 3.

$$\begin{array}{r} 31 \\ \times\ 23 \\ \hline 93 \end{array}$$

English Learners

Say, ***"The term partial product refers to a product found in one step of a multi-step multiplication process. Partial refers to a part, rather than the whole."***

Ask, ***"What is a partially finished project?"*** A project that someone has finished part of but not all.

Ask students to share sentences of their own that include the word *partial* or *partially.*

New Concept *(Continued)*

Math-to-Math Connection

Remind students that the Commutative Property of Multiplication states that the order of two factors can be changed without changing the product of those factors. Point out that one way to apply the property in this lesson is for students to check their work by reversing the order of the factors and multiplying a second time. If the order of the factors is reversed, the partial products will change, but the product will not. For example:

$$\begin{array}{r} 34 \\ \times\ 12 \\ \hline 68 \\ +\ 340 \\ \hline 408 \end{array} \qquad \begin{array}{r} 12 \\ \times\ 34 \\ \hline 48 \\ +\ 360 \\ \hline 408 \end{array}$$

Error Alert

If students have difficulty maintaining correct alignment of the digits, have them use grid paper, lined paper turned sideways, or a copy of **Lesson Activity Master 8**.

Active Learning

After discussing both methods, invite students to compare and contrast the methods. Then have them name the method they prefer and explain why they prefer that method.

Example

Before discussing the solution, ask:

"How many partial products will the multiplication 31 times 23 produce? Explain how you know." Two; The number of partial products is the same as the number of digits in the number we are multiplying by; Since 23 is a two-digit number, there will be two partial products.

Extend the Example

Challenge your advanced learners by having them multiply 310 × 28, then have them explain how many partial products it will produce.

(continued)

New Concept *(Continued)*

Lesson Practice

Guided Practice

Use these problems as guided practice to check the students' understanding of today's concept.

Problems a–h

Error Alert

Before students complete problems **a–h,** ask them to name the number of partial products each multiplication will produce. Each multiplication will produce two partial products.

Closure The questions below help assess the concepts taught in this lesson.

"Explain how you know the number of partial products a multiplication will produce. Then give an example to support your answer." The number of partial products is the same as the number of digits in the number we are multiplying by; See student work.

Written Practice

Math Conversations

Independent Practice and Discussions to Increase Understanding

Problem 1 **(Analyze)**

For problem **a,** ask:

"What operation does the phrase 'in all' suggest? Explain why you named that operation." Addition; "in all" represents a total, and addition is used to find a total.

For problem **c,** ask:

"Is Maritza cutting all of the sandwiches in half, or only some of the sandwiches?" Some of the sandwiches

"Which sandwiches is Maritza cutting in half?" The tuna sandwiches

"What operation should we use to find the answer?" Multiply the number of tuna sandwiches by 2 or add the number of tuna sandwiches to itself.

(continued)

Now we multiply 31 by 2. Since this 2 is actually 20, we write the last digit of the product in the tens column. Then we add to get **713.**

$$\begin{array}{r} 31 \\ \times\ 23 \\ \hline 93 \\ 62 \\ \hline 713 \end{array} \quad \text{or} \quad \begin{array}{r} 31 \\ \times\ 23 \\ \hline 93 \\ 620 \\ \hline 713 \end{array}$$

Lesson Practice Multiply:

a. 32×23 736
b. 25×32 800
c. 43×12 516
d. 34×21 714
e. 32×32 1024
f. 22×14 308
g. 13×32 416
h. 33×33 1089

Written Practice

Distributed and Integrated

▸ *__1.__ (76) **(Analyze)** Use this information to answer parts **a–c.**

Maritza invited 2 friends over for lunch. She plans to make 2 tuna sandwiches, a bologna sandwich, and 3 chicken sandwiches.

a. How many sandwiches will Maritza make in all? 6

b. Including Maritza, each person can have how many sandwiches? 2

c. If Maritza cuts each tuna sandwich in half, how many halves will there be? 4

2. (53, 79) Five pounds of grapes cost $2.95. What is the cost per pound? $0.59 per pound

▸ *__3.__ (20, 42, 50) If each side of a hexagon is 4 inches long, what is the perimeter of the hexagon in feet? 2 ft

4. (27, 52) **(Represent)** Four hundred fifty-seven thousand is how much greater than three hundred eighty-four thousand, nine hundred seventy-six? 72,024

*__5.__ (Inv. 4) Three brands of whole-grain cereal cost $4.68, $4.49, and $4.71. Arrange these prices in order from least to greatest. $4.49, $4.68, $4.71

Math Background

Multiplying 34 × 12 involves adding the partial products 34 × 2 and 34 × 10. But notice that finding each of these products also involves adding two partial products. Specifically, to find 34 × 2 we add 2 × 4 and 2 × 30, and to find 34 × 10 we add 10 × 4 and 10 × 30.

In general, we can multiply two two-digit numbers by writing both numbers in expanded form and then multiplying each term of one number by each term of the other. For example, the product of 36 × 24 can be found as shown below:

$$\begin{aligned}(\mathbf{30} + \mathbf{6})(20 + 4) &= \mathbf{30} \cdot 20 + \mathbf{30} \cdot 4 + \mathbf{6} \cdot 20 + \mathbf{6} \cdot 4 \\ &= 600 + 120 + 120 + 24 \\ &= 864\end{aligned}$$

▶ *6. (61, 62) **Estimate** Lauren saw that a spindle of 50 blank CDs costs $9.79. Estimate the cost for Lauren to buy 100 blank CDs. Explain your answer. Sample: about $20; Since 100 is 50 + 50. Lauren needs to buy two spindles. Each spindle costs about $10, and 2 × $10 = $20.

7. (Inv. 4) Name the shaded part of the large square

a. as a fraction. $\frac{7}{100}$

b. as a decimal number. 0.07

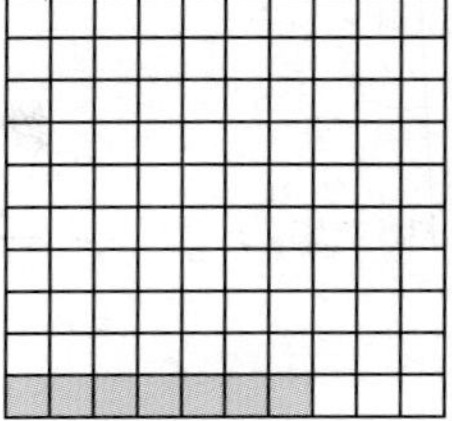

8. (32) **Represent** Use words to write $7572\frac{1}{8}$. seven thousand, five hundred seventy-two and one eighth

▶ *9. (74) **Represent** At Kelvin's school, one fifth of the 80 fourth grade students ride the bus to and from school each day. How many fourth grade students ride the bus? Draw a picture to illustrate the problem. 16 students

9.

	80 students
$\frac{4}{5}$ do not ride the bus.	16 students
	16 students
	16 students
	16 students
$\frac{1}{5}$ ride the bus.	16 students

*10. (76) **Analyze** Josh has $46 in his bank account. He wrote a check for $53. What number represents his account balance? −$7

11. (13) Franca's trip only lasted for a couple of hours. According to the clocks shown below, exactly how long did the trip take? 2 hours 15 minutes

Began

Finished

*12. (60) **Justify** James traveled 301 miles in 7 hours. He traveled an average of how many miles per hour? Explain your reasoning. 43 miles per hour; sample: I used compatible numbers; 280 ÷ 7 = 40

▶*13. (51, 52, 59) Martino bought 3 folders priced at $1.99 each. Sales tax was 33¢. He paid with a $20 bill. How much money should he get back? $13.70

14. (28) $25 + $2.75 + $15.44 + 27¢ $43.46

Inclusion

Use this strategy if the student displays:

- Slow Learning Rate.
- Difficulty with Multiple Steps.

Multiplying Two Two-Digit Numbers, Part 1 (Individual)

Material: Lesson Activity Master 8 (grid paper)

- Write 24 × 22 on the board. Then have students rewrite it as two partial products: 24 × 2 and 24 × 20 using the grid paper to align the digits. Ask, **"What is 24 × 2?"** 48 Then have students find the product of 24 and 20.
- Remind students to remember the properties of multiplying numbers with a zero. Ask, **"What is 24 × 20?"** 480
- Tell students that both partial products need to be combined to find the final product. Have students add the numbers. Ask, **"What is the product of 24 × 22?"** 528
- Have students work in pairs to find the partial products and final products of the following problems: 15 × 27; 32 × 44

Written Practice *(Continued)*

Math Conversations *(cont.)*

Problem 3

"How many sides does a hexagon have?" six sides

"How can we use addition to find the perimeter of the hexagon?" Add 4 inches six times

"How can we use multiplication to find the perimeter of the hexagon?" Multiply 4 inches by 6

Make sure students recognize that the answer is to be given in feet, not inches.

Problem 6 **Estimate**

Extend the Problem

Invite volunteers to explain how to estimate the cost of one CD. Sample: Round $9.79 to $10, change $10 to 1000¢, and then divide 1000¢ by 50; Each CD costs about 20¢.

Problem 9 **Represent**

After the pictures have been completed, ask students to name an operation that can be used to check their work and to explain how that operation can be used. Sample: division; Finding $\frac{1}{5}$ of 80 is the same as dividing 80 by 5 (80 ÷ 5 = 16).

Problem 13

Extend the Problem

Challenge advanced learners to name the least number of coins and bills Martino should receive as change. One $10 bill, three $1 bills, two quarters, and two dimes

(continued)

Written Practice *(Continued)*

Math Conversations *(cont.)*

Problem 15

"What operation is used to find a missing addend?" subtraction

Problem 20

Extend the Problem

Before completing the arithmetic, challenge your advanced learners to explain how to estimate a range for the exact answer. Sample: Round 368 up and down, and then multiply; A reasonable range for the exact answer is 300 × 4 or 1200 to 400 × 4 or 1600.

Record the range, and after the arithmetic has been completed, ask students to use the range to decide if the exact answer is reasonable. (The exact answer is reasonable if it is within the range.)

Problem 29 Verify

Before students solve the problems, ask:

"What does it mean if a figure has line symmetry?" Sample: The two halves of the figure match exactly if it is folded in half; One half of the figure is a reflection of the other half.

"What does it mean if a figure has rotational symmetry?" Sample: The figure will match its original position in less than one full turn.

Errors and Misconceptions

Problem 28

Students who write 0.75 or 0.750 as the answer did not follow the order of operations by completing the operation inside the parentheses first. Instead, these students completed the operations in order from left to right.

Remind these students that whenever parentheses are present in an expression or in an equation, the operation in parentheses must be completed first.

▸*15. (8, 45) $m + 0.26 = 6.2$ 5.94

16. (45, 52) \$100 − \$89.85 \$10.15

17. (84) 65 × 1000 65,000

18. (71) 42 × 30 1260

19. (86) 21 × 17 357

▸*20. (59) 368 × 4 = 1472

*21. (85) 4000 × 20 = 80,000

22. (59) \$4.79 × 6 = \$28.74

23. (83) $9\overline{)918}$ 102

24. (34, 69) $5r = 485$ 97

25. (83) $6\overline{)482}$ 80 R 2

26. (79) \$50.00 ÷ 8 \$6.25

27. (83) 2100 ÷ 7 300

28. (9, 45) 0.875 − (0.5 + 0.375) 0

▸*29. (82) a. **Verify** Which of these letters has two lines of symmetry? H

H A P P Y

b. Which of these letters has rotational symmetry? H

*30. (81) **Represent** Draw a triangle that has two perpendicular sides. What type of triangle did you draw? Sample: right triangle

Alternative Approach: Using Manipulatives

To help students understand the concept of multiplying two two-digit numbers, have them use base ten blocks to model multiplication. Have students model 34 × 12. Students should model 34 as 3 tens 4 ones and show 12 groups of each. Have students combine the ones and regroup and combine tens and regroup.

Have students model other examples.

Looking Forward

Multiplying two-digit numbers prepares students for:

- **Lesson 88,** multiplying two-digit numbers.
- **Lesson 91,** estimating the answers to multiplication and division problems.
- **Lesson 104,** rounding whole numbers to the nearest hundred thousand and the nearest million.
- **Lesson 105,** factoring whole numbers.

Planning & Preparation

California Mathematics Content Standards

NS 3.0, 3.4 Solve problems involving division of multidigit numbers by one-digit numbers.

MR 1.0, 1.1 Analyze problems by identifying relationships, distinguishing relevant from irrelevant information, sequencing and prioritizing information, and observing patterns.

• Remainders in Word Problems

Objectives

- Solve division word problems that involve remainders.
- Interpret the remainder for a division word problem.

Prerequisite Skills

- Using compatible numbers to find a reasonable estimate to a division word problem.
- Analyzing a problem and choosing the information needed to solve a problem.

Materials

Instructional Masters

- Power Up G Worksheet
- Lesson Activity 8*

Manipulative Kit

- Two-color counters*

Teacher-provided materials

- Grid paper*

**optional*

Power Up G Worksheet

Universal Access

Reaching All Special Needs Students

Special Education Students	At-Risk Students	English Learners	Advanced Learners
• Inclusion (TM) • Adaptations for Saxon Math	• Alternative Approach (TM) • Error Alert (TM) • Reteaching Masters • Refresher Lessons for California Standards	• English Learners (TM) • Developing Academic Language (TM) • English Learner Handbook	• Extend the Example (TM) • Extend the Problem (TM) • Online Activities

TM=Teacher's Manual

Developing Academic Language

Maintained
divide
remainder

English Learner
short stack

Problem Solving Discussion

Problem

Sandra bought a CD priced at $12.95. Sales tax was $1.10. She paid for her purchase with a $10 bill and a $5 bill. Sandra got back five coins (not including a half-dollar). What were the coins Sandra should have received in change?

Focus Strategies

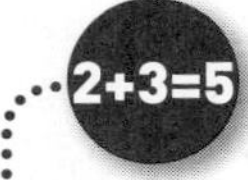

Write a Number Sentence or Equation

Guess and Check

Understand *Understand the problem.*

"What information are we given?"

1. A CD was priced at $12.95.
2. Sales tax was $1.10.
3. A $10 bill and a $5 bill were used to pay for the CD.
4. Five coins (not including a half-dollar) were given in change.

"What are we asked to do?"

We are asked to find the five coins that Sandra received in change.

Plan *Make a plan.*

"What problem-solving strategies can we use to solve this problem?"

We can *write number sentences* to find the total cost of the CD (price plus tax) and to find how much change Sandra should receive. Then we can use *guess and check* to find the coins.

Solve *Carry out the plan.*

"What was the total cost of the CD?"

$12.95 + $1.10 = $14.05

"How much change should Sandra have received?"

Sandra paid with a $10 bill and a $5 bill, which is $15 altogether. To find the amount of change Sandra should have received, we subtract: $15.00 – $14.05 = $0.95.

"Now we know we are looking for five coins that total 95¢. We know that none of the coins are half-dollars. Do you think that Sandra received some quarters in change?"

Yes. She must have received some quarters, because we cannot make 95¢ from any combination of five dimes, nickels, or pennies.

We might guess 2 quarters (50¢), which would leave us 45¢ to make up with 3 other coins. This can be done with 1 more quarter and 2 dimes. The change Sandra received would be 3 quarters and 2 dimes.

We might have originally guessed 3 quarters (75¢), which would have left us to make up 20¢ with 2 other coins (2 dimes). Either way, our answer is the same.

Check *Look back.*

"What five coins should Sandra have received in change?"

3 quarters and 2 dimes

"Is our answer reasonable?"

We know that our answer is reasonable by adding the price of the CD, the tax, and the change: $12.95 + $1.10 + $0.95 = $15.00, which is the amount Sandra paid.

LESSON 87

California Mathematics Content Standards

NS 3.0, 3.4 Solve problems involving division of multidigit numbers by one-digit numbers.

MR 1.0, 1.1 Analyze problems by identifying relationships, distinguishing relevant from irrelevant information, sequencing and prioritizing information, and observing patterns.

• Remainders in Word Problems

Power Up

facts Power Up G

mental math Use the fives pattern as you add or subtract in problems **a–c.**

a. Number Sense: 83 − 15 68

b. Number Sense: 29 + 35 64

c. Number Sense: 76 + 15 91

d. Fractional Part: Corey figures that about $\frac{1}{2}$ of the calories he consumes are from carbohydrates. Corey consumes about 2000 calories each day. About how many of those calories are from carbohydrates? 1000 calories

e. Measurement: How many inches is one yard? 36 in.

f. Time: Which day of the week is 71 days after Monday? Tuesday

g. Estimation: Jayla has run $\frac{1}{2}$ mile in 4 minutes 57 seconds. If she can continue running at the same pace, about how long will it take Jayla to run one full mile? About 10 min

h. Calculation: $5^2 + 5^2$, + 6, ÷ 8 7

problem solving Choose an appropriate problem-solving strategy to solve this problem. Sandra bought a CD priced at $12.95. Sales tax was $1.10. She paid for her purchase with a $10 bill and a $5 bill. Sandra got back five coins (not including a half-dollar). What were the coins Sandra should have received in change? 3 quarters and 2 dimes

New Concept

We have practiced solving "equal groups" problems using division. In these problems, there were no remainders from the division. In this lesson we will begin practicing division word problems that involve remainders. When solving these problems, we must be careful to identify exactly what the question is asking.

Facts Multiply.

9 × 9 = 81	1 × 8 = 8	4 × 4 = 16	2 × 5 = 10	7 × 9 = 63	5 × 5 = 25	3 × 4 = 12	4 × 6 = 24	2 × 9 = 18	6 × 9 = 54
6 × 6 = 36	2 × 7 = 14	5 × 8 = 40	3 × 9 = 27	6 × 8 = 48	8 × 9 = 72	2 × 2 = 4	7 × 8 = 56	3 × 7 = 21	7 × 6 = 42
3 × 6 = 18	10 × 10 = 100	2 × 3 = 6	5 × 6 = 30	4 × 9 = 36	3 × 8 = 24	4 × 7 = 28	5 × 9 = 45	0 × 4 = 0	2 × 6 = 12
2 × 8 = 16	4 × 5 = 20	6 × 7 = 42	3 × 3 = 9	5 × 7 = 35	2 × 4 = 8	8 × 8 = 64	3 × 5 = 15	4 × 8 = 32	7 × 7 = 49

Power Up

Facts

Distribute **Power Up G** to students. See answers below.

Count Aloud

Before students begin the Mental Math exercises, do these counting exercises as a class.

Count by 6's from 18 to 66 and back to 18.

Mental Math

Encourage students to share different ways to mentally compute these exercises. Strategies for exercises are listed below.

a. Subtract 10, then Subtract 5

83 − 10 = 73; 73 − 5 = 68

Subtract 20, then Add 5

83 − 20 = 63; 63 + 5 = 68

b. Add 30, then Add 5

29 + 30 = 59; 59 + 5 = 64

Add Tens and Add Ones

20 + 30 + 9 + 5 = 50 + 14 = 64

Problem Solving

Refer to **Problem-Solving Strategy Discussion**, p. 577B.

New Concept

Discussion

This lesson introduces the skill of interpreting the remainder. For example, have students suppose that all of the desks in their classroom were arranged in rows of six (or any other number that produces a remainder when the number of chairs altogether is divided by the number in each row). How many full rows of six desks would be formed? How many desks will be in the row that is not full? Including complete rows of six and the remaining desks, how many rows would be formed altogether? Lead students to understand that when we divide to solve a problem, the answer may be the quotient, it may be the remainder, or it may be both the quotient and the remainder.

(continued)

New Concept (Continued)

Example

Active Learning

To have students model this example, distribute 100 unit cubes to each group of students and ask them to arrange the cubes in groups of 6.

Error Alert

Make sure students understand that each question asks for different information.

Extend the Example

Challenge advanced learners to determine how many bottles would be left over if the packer has to place 200 bottles into a box that holds 6 bottles each. 2 bottles

Lesson Practice

Guided Practice

Use these problems as guided practice to check the students' understanding of today's concept.

Problems a and b **Interpret**

After students complete the arithmetic for parts **a** and **b**, ask:

"For problem a, what part of the quotient is not included in the answer?" the remainder

"For problem b, does the remainder of the division affect the answer? Explain why or why not." Yes; 2 students represent the remainder. In order for all of the students to go on the trip, the quotient (which represents the number of cars that are needed) must be increased by 1.

Extend the Problem

Ask your students to determine the number of minivans your class would need to go on a field trip, assuming that each minivan would carry 7 students.

Problems c–e

Error Alert

Before solving these problems, make sure students identify 7 R 3 as the quotient of the division.

(continued)

Example

The packer needs to place 100 bottles into boxes that hold 6 bottles each.

a. How many boxes can be filled?

b. How many bottles will be left over?

c. How many boxes are needed to hold all the bottles?

Each of these questions asks for different information. To answer the questions, we begin by dividing 100 by 6.

$$\begin{array}{r} 16 \text{ R } 4 \\ 6\overline{)100} \\ \underline{6} \\ 40 \\ \underline{36} \\ 4 \end{array}$$

The result "16 R 4" means that the 100 bottles can be separated into 16 groups of 6 bottles. There will be 4 extra bottles.

a. The bottles can be separated into 16 groups of 6 bottles, so **16 boxes** can be filled.

b. The 4 remaining bottles do not completely fill a box. So after filling 16 boxes, there will still be **4 bottles** left over.

c. Although the 4 remaining bottles do not completely fill a box, another box is needed to hold them. Thus, **17 boxes** are needed to hold all the bottles.

Lesson Practice **Interpret** Use the statements below to answer problems **a–e.**

Tomorrow 32 students are going on a field trip. Each car can carry 5 students.

a. How many cars can be filled? 6 cars

b. How many cars will be needed? 7 cars

Tendai found 31 quarters in his bank. He made stacks of 4 quarters each.

c. How many stacks of 4 quarters did he make? 7 stacks

d. How many extra quarters did he have? 3 quarters

e. If Tendai made a short stack with the extra quarters, how many stacks would he have in all? 8 stacks

English Learners

Say, ***"We sometimes talk about stacks of quarters that contain 4 quarters each. We sometimes refer to a short stack of quarters (or some other type of coin). A short stack of coins is less than one dollar. How many quarters are in a short stack?"*** Between 1 and 3

Ask, ***"How much could a short stack of dimes be worth?"*** 10¢, 20¢, 30¢, 40¢, 50¢, 60¢, 70¢, 80¢, or 90¢

Alternative Approach: Using Manipulatives

To help students develop understanding of remainders, have them use counters to model word problems about equal groups.

Have students use counters to model each problem in the Lesson Practice. Have students explain what to do with the remainder and why in some problems, the quotient is increased by 1.

Written Practice *Distributed and Integrated*

▸ *1. (87) Ninety-one students are divided as equally as possible among 3 classrooms.

a. How many classrooms have exactly 30 students? 2 classrooms

b. How many classrooms have 31 students? 1 classroom

▸ 2. (39) **Analyze** a. 1970 it cost 6¢ to mail a letter. How much did it cost to mail twenty letters in 1970? $1.20

b. How much does it cost to mail twenty letters today? See student work.

3. (Inv. 2) **Represent** Point *A* represents what number on this number line? 120

A

0 100 200

4. (52) George Washington was president of the United States of America until 1796. How many years has it been since his presidency? See student work.

5. (80) A $1 bill weighs about 1 gram. How much would a $5 bill weigh? About 1 gram

6. (Inv. 4) Name the shaded part of the large square

a. as a fraction. $\frac{9}{10}$

b. as a decimal number. 0.9

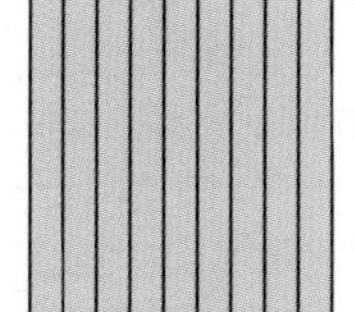

▸ *7. (64, Inv. 7) **Evaluate** If $y = 4x + 5$, then what is y when $x = 4$, 5, and 6? 21, 25, 29

*8. (82) a. A regular pentagon has how many lines of symmetry? 5 lines

b. **Justify** Does a regular pentagon have rational symmetry? How do you know? Yes; As the pentagon is rotated, it shows itself in its original position five times before in one full turn.

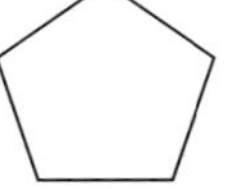

▸ *9. (74) **Represent** One half of the 32 chess pieces were still on the board. How many chess pieces were still on the board? Draw a picture to illustrate the problem. 16 chess pieces

9. 32 chess pieces

$\frac{1}{2}$ on the board: 16 chess pieces

$\frac{1}{2}$ not on board: 16 chess pieces

Inclusion

Use this strategy if the student displays:

- Difficulty Reading.
- Difficulty with Abstract Processing.

Remainders in Word Problems (Individual)

Material: Lesson Activity Master 8 (grid paper)

- Read, ***"There were 14 runners in a race. All runners were placed in teams of 4. How many teams of four were formed?"***
- Have students shade 14 squares on the grid paper and loop groups of 4. Ask, ***"How many teams of 4 are there?"*** 3 ***"How many runners do not have a team?"*** 2
- Read, ***"21 students are going on a field trip. Each school bus will hold 12 students. How many school buses are needed?"***
- Have students shade 21 squares on the grid paper and circle groups of 12. Ask, ***"How many buses will be filled?"*** 1 ***"How many students are remaining?"*** 9 ***" "How many buses will be needed to take all of the students?"*** 2

New Concept *(Continued)*

Closure **The question below helps assess the concepts taught in this lesson.**

"Tennis balls are sold in containers called sleeves. Each sleeve contains three balls. Suppose a tennis coach has 28 tennis balls. What is the least number of sleeves the coach could have purchased? Explain your answer." 10 sleeves; The quotient of the division 28 ÷ 3 is 9 R 1. A purchase of 9 sleeves would result in only 27 tennis balls, so the coach must have purchased at least 10 sleeves.

"Write a division problem that involves equal groups and has the remainder of the division as the answer." Sample: If 11 chairs are arranged in rows of 4, how many chairs will be in the row that is not full?

Written Practice

Math Conversations

Independent Practice and Discussions to Increase Understanding

Problem 1

Make sure students recognize that the meaning of the phrase "as equally as possible" is different from the meaning of the word "equally." In this problem, 91 is not divisible by 3, so it is not possible for the same number of students to be in each classroom.

Problem 2 **Analyze**

Extend the Problem

You can extend this problem by having advanced learners determine the cost of sending 20 letters today. Students should multiply the current cost of a first-class stamp by 20.

Problem 7 **Evaluate**

Make sure students understand that they must make three different substitutions for x, and after each substitution, follow the order of operations and simplify the equation to solve for y.

Problem 9 **Represent**

After the pictures have been completed, ask students to name an operation that can be used to check their work and to explain how that operation can be used. Sample: division; Finding $\frac{1}{2}$ of 32 is the same as dividing 32 by 2 ($32 \div 2 = 16$).

(continued)

Written Practice *(Continued)*

Math Conversations *(cont.)*

Problem 13

Extend the Problem

"Suppose Connor had turned 360° clockwise instead of turning 90° counterclockwise. In which direction would he have been facing after the turn?" west

Problems 21 and 22

Ask students to make an estimate of each product before completing the arithmetic, and then use the estimates to help decide the reasonableness of the exact answers. Sample:
problem **21:** $15 \times 20 = 300$
problem **22:** $5000 \times 4 = 20{,}000$

Problems 28 and 29

The products are to be named using only mental math. Before students name the products, ask:

"How many zeros do we attach to a product when one factor is 1000?" three zeros

"How many zeros do we attach to a product when one factor is 100?" two zeros

Errors and Misconceptions

Problem 3

Make sure that students who do not identify the location of point A can correctly identify the interval of the number line. Point out that because the distance from 0 to 100 (and from 100 to 200) is divided into five equal parts, each tick mark represents 20 because $100 \div 5 = 20$.

Problem 5

Watch for students who reason incorrectly and decide that the weight of a \$5 bill is five times the weight of a \$1 bill.

Problem 13

If students answer incorrectly, place "N-E-S-W" labels on the classroom walls, or suggest that students draw a diagram on a sheet of paper and then act out this problem.

10. (13) Miriam left home at 10:30 a.m. She traveled for 7 hours. What time was it when she arrived? 5:30 p.m.

11. (58, 71) Maureo traveled 42 miles in 1 hour. If he kept going at the same speed, how far would he travel in 20 hours? 840 mi

***12.** (52) Violet gave the cashier \$40 for a toaster that cost \$29.99 plus \$1.80 in tax. What was her change? Write an equation to solve the problem. \$8.21; $\$40 - (\$29.99 + \$1.80) = c$

▶ ***13.** (78) Alvin faced the sun as it set in the west, then turned 90° counterclockwise and headed home. In what direction was Alvin heading after he turned? south

14. (4) $n + 8 + 2 + 3 + 5 + 2 = 24$ 4

15. (9, 45) $4.12 - (3.6 + 0.2 + 0.12)$ 0.2 or 0.20

16. (28, 52) $\$18 - \$15.63$ \$2.37

17. (28, 51) $\$15.27 + \$85.75$ \$101.02

18. (Inv. 3, 65) $2^3 \times \sqrt{25}$ 40

19. (85) 30×90 2700

20. (59) $\$7.50 \times 8$ \$60.00

▶ ***21.** (86) 14×22 308

▶ ***22.** (59) 5126×4 20,504

23. (71) 74×40 2960

24. (79) $4\overline{)\$6.36}$ \$1.59

25. (83) $5\overline{)800}$ 160

26. (72) $473 \div 8$ 59 R 1

27. (34, 83) $3m = 1800$ 600

▶ ***28.** (84) 16×1000 16,000

▶ ***29.** (84) 263×100 26,300

30. (66) Find the perimeter and area of this rectangle. 140 ft; 1000 ft^2

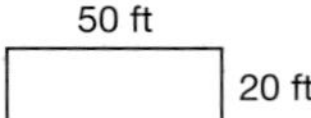

Looking Forward

Solving division word problems that involve remainders prepares students for:

- **Lesson 89,** mixed numbers and improper fractions.
- **Lesson 91,** estimating multiplication and division answers
- **Lesson 92,** comparing and ordering fractions and decimals.
- **Lesson 94,** two-step problems about fractions of a group.
- **Lesson 98,** fractions equal to 1 and to $\frac{1}{2}$
- **Lesson 99,** changing improper fractions to whole or mixed numbers.
- **Lesson 100,** adding and subtracting fractions with common denominators.
- **Lesson 103,** finding equivalent fractions.
- **Lesson 106,** reducing fractions.
- **Lesson 111,** simplifying fractions.
- **Lesson 112,** renaming fractions.
- **Lesson 113,** finding a common denominator and renaming fractions.

Planning & Preparation

• Multiplying Two Two-Digit Numbers, Part 2

Objectives
- Multiply a two-digit number by a two-digit number, without regrouping.
- Solve problems involving multi-digit problems.
- Estimate a product for a multiplication word problem.

Prerequisite Skills
- Using the multiplication algorithm to multiply a two-digit number by a one-digit number.
- Multiplying dollars and cents by a one-digit number.
- Multiplying by multiples of 10.

Materials
Instructional Masters
- Power Up G Worksheet
- Lesson Activity 8

Manipulative Kit
- Money manipulatives, base ten blocks*

Teacher-provided materials
- Grid paper

**optional*

California Mathematics Content Standards

NS 1.0, 1.3 Round whole numbers through the millions to the nearest ten, hundred, thousand, ten thousand, or hundred thousand.

MR 2.0, 2.6 Make precise calculations and check the validity of the results from the context of the problem.

MR 3.0, 3.1 Evaluate the reasonableness of the solution in the context of the original situation.

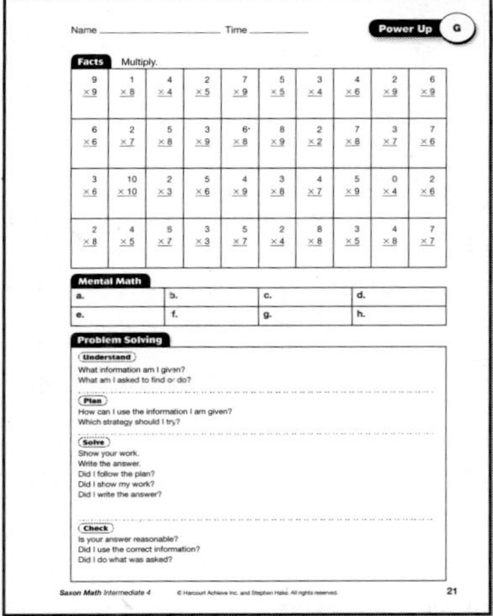

Power Up G Worksheet

Lesson Activity 8

Universal Access

Reaching All Special Needs Students

Special Education Students	At-Risk Students	English Learners	Advanced Learners
• Inclusion (TM) • Adaptations for Saxon Math	• Alternative Approach (TM) • Error Alert (TM) • Reteaching Masters • Refresher Lessons for California Standards	• English Learners (TM) • Developing Academic Language (TM) • English Learner Handbook	• Extend the Example (TM) • Extend the Problem (TM) • Online Activities

TM=Teacher's Manual

Developing Academic Language

Maintained
Commutative Property of Multiplication
partial product

English Learner
reception

Problem Solving Discussion

Problem

Tandy wants to know the circumference of (the distance around) her bicycle tire. She has some string and a meterstick. How can Tandy measure the circumference of the tire in centimeters?

Focus Strategies

Make It Simpler

Act It Out or Make a Model

Understand *Understand the problem.*

"What are we asked to do?"

We are asked to explain how the circumference of a bicycle tire can be measured with string and a meter stick.

"Is the circumference of a bicycle tire a straight line or a curve?"

The circumference of a bicycle tire forms a curve. We cannot use a meter stick to measure a curve; however, we can wrap a string around a curve and then measure the string.

Plan *Make a plan.*

"What problem-solving strategy can we use to solve the problem?"

We can *make the problem* simpler by finding a way to measure a curve with a meter stick, which has a straight edge. We will describe how to *act out the problem.*

Solve *Carry out the plan.*

"How can Tandy use a piece of string and a meter stick to measure the distance around the bicycle tire?"

Tandy could wrap the string around the tire and mark the place where the string goes once around (or cut the string at that place). Then Tandy could place the string along a meterstick and measure the length of the string (or to the place that was marked) in centimeters.

"If the string were longer than the meter stick, how would Tandy measure the full length of the string?"

She could mark the string at the place where it is 100 centimeters long, and then place that mark at the 0 cm end of the meter stick. Then, she could measure the remaining string length in centimeters and add the measurement to 100 centimeters.

"Will the measurement of the string equal the circumference of the tire?"

Yes. The length of string that Tandy marks off would be equal to the distance around the tire.

Check *Look back.*

"Is our answer reasonable?"

We know that our answer is reasonable, because if we were to wrap a string once around a tire, that length of the string would equal the circumference of the tire.

LESSON 88

California Mathematics Content Standards

NS 1.0, 1.3 Round whole numbers through the millions to the nearest ten, hundred, thousand, ten thousand, or hundred thousand.

MR 2.0, 2.6 Make precise calculations and check the validity of the results from the context of the problem.

MR 3.0, 3.1 Evaluate the reasonableness of the solution in the context of the original

• Multiplying Two Two-Digit Numbe…

Monday

PowerUp problem from Ls 87

facts

mental math

…? 8 pt

…after Monday?

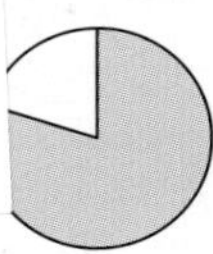

h. Calculation: $\sqrt{81}$, ÷ 3, × 25, + 75, × 2 300

problem solving

Choose an appropriate problem-solving strategy to solve this problem. Tandy wants to know the circumference of (the distance around) her bicycle tire. She has some string and a meterstick. How can Tandy measure the circumference of the tire in centimeters? Sample: Tandy can wrap the string around the tire and then mark or cut the place where the string meets itself. Then Tandy can use the meterstick to count full meter lengths and any remaining centimeters. The total measurement will be the circumference of the tire.

Recall the three steps for multiplying two two-digit numbers:

Step 1: Multiply by the ones digit.

Step 2: Multiply by the tens digit.

Step 3: Add to find the total.

Facts Multiply.

9 × 9 81	1 × 8 8	4 × 4 16	2 × 5 10	7 × 9 63	5 × 5 25	3 × 4 12	4 × 6 24	2 × 9 18	6 × 9 54
6 × 6 36	2 × 7 14	5 × 8 40	3 × 9 27	6 × 8 48	8 × 9 72	2 × 2 4	7 × 8 56	3 × 7 21	7 × 6 42
3 × 6 18	10 × 10 100	2 × 3 6	5 × 6 30	4 × 9 36	3 × 8 24	4 × 7 28	5 × 9 45	0 × 4 0	2 × 6 12
2 × 8 16	4 × 5 20	6 × 7 42	3 × 3 9	5 × 7 35	2 × 4 8	8 × 8 64	3 × 5 15	4 × 8 32	7 × 7 49

Power Up

Facts

Distribute **Power Up G** to students. See answers below.

Count Aloud

Before students begin the Mental Math exercises, do these counting exercises as a class.

Count by $\frac{1}{3}$'s from $\frac{1}{3}$ to 5 and back to $\frac{1}{3}$.

Mental Math

Encourage students to share different ways to mentally compute these exercises. Strategies for exercises are listed below.

a. Subtract 40, then Add 2

85 − 40 = 45; 45 + 2 = 47

Subtract 5 from 85 and from 38

85 − 5 = 80; 38 − 5 = 33; 80 − 33 = 47

b. Attach 2 Zeros to 4 × 2 × 1

4 × 2 × 1 = 8; 4 × 20 × 10 = 800

Multiply from Left to Right

4 × 20 = 80; 80 × 10 = 800

Problem Solving

Refer to **Problem-Solving Strategy Discussion**, p. 581B.

New Concept

Instruction

Before beginning the lesson, have students recall that the number of partial products in a multiplication is related to the number of digits in the number we are multiplying by. For example, there will be two partial products if the number we are multiplying by is a two-digit number.

The new concept that is presented in this lesson is regrouping when multiplying.

(continued)

New Concept *(Continued)*

Example 1

Error Alert

As you discuss Step 1, make sure students understand why the digit 4 is carried to the tens place. Point out that the digit 4 represents 4 tens and it is carried to the tens place because the product of 7 × 6 is 42, which must be regrouped as 4 tens 2 ones.

Also point out that after the first partial product is complete, it is a good idea to cross off the 4 so that it will not be used when finding other partial products. As you discuss Step 2, have students note that the regrouped 1 was rewritten above the regrouped 4 to show that it belongs to a different partial product.

Example 2

Before discussing the solution, remind students of the importance of checking their work. Then invite several volunteers to demonstrate on the board how to make an estimate of the exact answer. Sample: Round 46 to 50 and round 72 to 70, then multiply; A reasonable estimate is 50 × 70 or 3500.

Extend the Example

Challenge your advanced learners by asking them to compare the exact answer to the estimate and to explain if the exact answer is reasonable. Sample: The exact answer is reasonable because 3312 is close to 3500.

(continued)

Example 1

A college auditorium has 27 rows of seats and 46 seats in each row. How many people can be seated in the auditorium?

Thinking Skills

Justify

How can we check the answer?

Sample: Apply the Commutative Property: (6 × 27) + (40 × 27); 162 + 1080 = 1242

The first step is to multiply 46 by 7. The result is 322. This is not the final product. It is called a partial product.

Step 1:

```
   4
  46
× 27
 322
```

The second step is to multiply 46 by the 2 of 27. Since we are actually multiplying by 20, we place a zero in the ones place or shift this partial product one place to the left.

Step 2 and Step 3:

```
    1            1
    4            4
   46           46
 × 27    or   × 27
  322          322
  92           920
 1242         1242
```

The third step is to add the partial products. The final product is 1242.

We find that **1242 people** can be seated.

Example 2

A golf course has 46 different viewer mounds. Each mound can seat an average of 72 viewers. How many viewers in all can be seated on the mounds?

First we multiply 46 by 2.

```
   1
  46
× 72
  92
```

Next we multiply 46 by 7 and then add the partial products.

```
    4            4
    1            1
   46           46
 × 72    or   × 72
   92           92
 322          3220
 3312         3312
```

We find that **3312 viewers** can be seated.

Math Background

We can make an area model to illustrate the multiplication algorithm. The product 46 × 27 is the area of a rectangle with side lengths 46 and 27. We can draw a horizontal segment that breaks the rectangle into smaller rectangles and divides the side of length 27 into segments of length 20 and 7. The area of the larger rectangle is the sum of the areas of the two smaller rectangles: 46 × 27 = 46 × 7 + 46 × 20. These are the same two products we find when we use the multiplication algorithm.

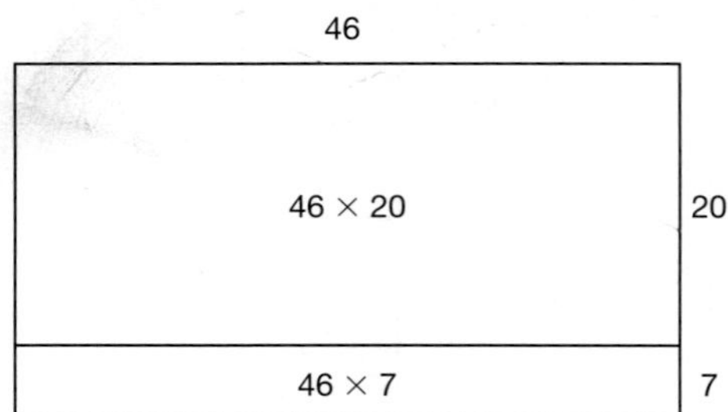

Example 3

Adelio estimated the product of 86 × 74 to be 6300. Did Adelio make a reasonable estimate?

Before multiplying, we round 86 to 90 and round 74 to 70. Since 90 × 70 = 6300, Adelio's estimate is reasonable. (The exact product is 6364.)

Lesson Practice

Multiply:

a. 38 × 26 = 988 **b.** 49 × 82 = 4018 **c.** 84 × 67 = 5628 **d.** 65 × 48 = 3120

e. Mya is renting 21 tables for a reception. The rental charge is $29 per table. Explain how Mya can make a reasonable estimate of the total cost. Sample: Mya can round $29 to $30 and round 21 to 20; A reasonable estimate is $600 because $30 × 20 = $600.

Written Practice

Distributed and Integrated

1. (28, 51, 52) Joel gave the clerk a $5 bill to pay for a half gallon of milk that cost $1.06 and a box of cereal that cost $2.39. How much change should he receive? $1.55

***2.** (77) What fraction of the letters in the following word are A's? $\frac{4}{7}$

ALABAMA

3. (39) Melba planted 8 rows of apple trees. There were 15 trees in each row. How many trees did she plant? 120 trees

4. (53, 69) A ruble is a Russian coin. If four pounds of beets costs one hundred fifty-six rubles, what is the cost in rubles of each pound of beets? 39 rubles

***5.** (80) **a.** This scale shows a mass of how many grams? 550 g

b. **Explain** Would this fruit have the same mass on another planet? Explain why. Yes; sample: Mass is the same on all the planets because mass does not depend on the force of gravity.

English Learners

Say, ***"A reception** is a small, usually formal, gathering held to celebrate an event or introduce one or more people."*

Ask how many students have attended a wedding. Explain that the guests are usually introduced to the bride and groom after the wedding ceremony. This is a type of **reception.**

New Concept *(Continued)*

Example 3

Active Learning

As you discuss the solution, ask:

"To find the product of 90 × 70, why do we attach two zeros to the right of the product of 9 × 7?" Whenever one or both factors are multiples of 10, we write the same number of zeros in the product as there are in the factors.

Lesson Practice

Guided Practice

Use these problems as guided practice to check the students' understanding of today's concept.

Problems a–d

Before students perform the arithmetic, ask:

"After we find a first partial product in a multiplication, why is it a good idea for us to cross off any numbers that we carried?" Sample: to prevent those numbers from being used when we find the second partial product

"How many partial products will each multiplication produce?" two

Problems a–d

Error Alert

Verify that students are accurately lining up columns as they complete problem **a**. If they are not, provide grid paper or copies of **Lesson Activity Master 8** to help them organize the alignment of the place values.

Closure

The questions below help assess the concepts taught in this lesson.

Write the multiplication 25 × 52 on the board or overhead and then ask:

"Describe the regroupings that must be completed to find the product of 25 and 52. Then name the product." In the first partial product, 10 ones are regrouped as 1 ten, and the digit 1 is carried. In the second partial product, 25 tens is regrouped as 2 hundreds 5 tens, and the digit 2 is carried. The product of 25 × 52 is 1300.

Written Practice

Math Conversations

Independent Practice and Discussions to Increase Understanding

Problem 7 Interpret

Make sure students recognize that they are dividing 100 by 6. Ask students to explain why there aren't 17 packages even though there are balls remaining. Sample: If we fill 17 packages, we would have a partial container. People don't buy packages of balls that aren't full.

Problem 11 Classify

Extend the Problem

After completing each part, ask students to explain why the statement is true or false.

(continued)

6. Name the shaded part of the large square (Inv. 4)

a. as a fraction. $\frac{11}{100}$

b. as a decimal number. 0.11

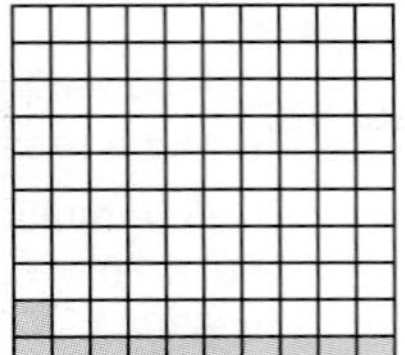

▸ ***7.** Interpret Peter packed 6 table-tennis balls in each package. There were 100 table-tennis balls to pack. (87)

a. How many packages did he fill? 16 packages

b. How many table-tennis balls were left over? 4 table-tennis balls

***8.** List Write the factors of 35. 1, 5, 7, 35 (55)

9. Represent Bactrian camels have 2 humps. One third of the 24 camels were Bactrian. How many camels were Bactrian? Draw a picture to illustrate the problem. 8 camels (74)

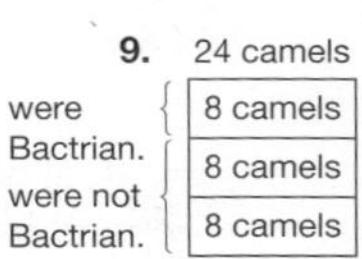

10. A quart is a quarter of a gallon. A quart is what decimal part of a gallon? 0.25 (Inv. 4, 73)

▸ ***11.** Classify For each statement, write either *true* or *false*: (81)

a. Every right triangle has perpendicular sides. true

b. Every isosceles triangle is also an equilateral triangle. false

***12. a.** Represent Seventy-one of the one hundred students in the school were girls. Girls made up what fraction of the students in the school? $\frac{71}{100}$ (Inv. 4)

b. Represent Write your answer for part **a** as a decimal number. Then use words to name the number. 0.71; seventy-one hundredths

***13.** Which digit in 1.875 is in the tenths place? 8 (41)

***14.** If $y = 2x - 3$, what is y when x is 5? 7 (64)

15. Tyler traveled 496 miles in 8 hours. He traveled an average of how many miles per hour? 62 miles per hour (60, 68)

Inclusion

Use this strategy if the student displays:

- Slow Learning Rate.
- Difficulty with Multiple Steps

Multiplying Two Two-Digit Numbers, Part 2 (Small Group)

Material: money manipulatives

- Read, ***"Each child in the class has $25 to spend at the carnival. If there are 21 students, how much money does the class have?"***
- Have students set up the problem. Ask, ***"What is the first partial product to find?"*** 25 × 1 Have students use their money to find the first partial product and write it under the problem.
- Ask, ***"What is the second partial product to find?"*** 25 × 20 Tell students to find the answer using money manipulatives to model 25 × 2 and to show how to write the answer.
- Ask, ***"What number should go in the empty space next to 50?"*** 0 If students don't know remind them of the number removed from the second partial product problem. Model adding the zero and combining the partial products.

584 ***Saxon Math*** *Intermediate 4*

*16. Find 8.3 − (1.74 + 0.9). Describe the steps in order. 5.66 (9, 45)

16. Add: 1.74 + 0.9 = 2.64 Subtract: 8.3 − 2.64 = 5.66

17. 63 × 1000 63,000 (84)

18. 80 × 50¢ $40.00 (85)

19. (11)
$$\begin{array}{r} 37 \\ 81 \\ 45 \\ 139 \\ 7 \\ 15 \\ +\ 60 \\ \hline 384 \end{array}$$

*20. (88)
$$\begin{array}{r} 52 \\ \times\ 15 \\ \hline 780 \end{array}$$

*21. (88)
$$\begin{array}{r} 36 \\ \times\ 27 \\ \hline 972 \end{array}$$

22. $2\overline{)714}$ 357 (79)

23. $6\overline{)789}$ 131 R 3 (79)

24. $3n = 624$ 208 (34, 79)

25. $5 + w = 5^2$ 20 (64, 65)

*26. (Inv. 7) **Model** Write five ordered pairs for the equation $y = 2x$. Then use **Lesson Activity 8** to graph the ordered pairs. See student work.

*27. (43) **Analyze** Write these numbers in order from least to greatest: $\frac{3}{100}, \frac{1}{10}, 1\frac{4}{10}, 2.06$

$$\frac{1}{10}, 2.06, 1\frac{4}{10}, \frac{3}{100}$$

28. (Inv. 3) A room is 5 yards long and 4 yards wide. How many square yards of carpeting are needed to cover the floor? 20 yd^2

29. (18, 42) The radius of this circle is 15 millimeters. The diameter of the circle is how many centimeters? 3 cm

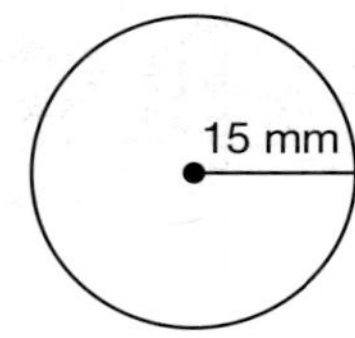

*30. (17, 82) a. **Verify** Which of these letters has two lines of symmetry? X

V W X Y Z

b. **Verify** Which two letters have rotational symmetry? X and Z

c. **Multiple Choice** The angle formed by the letter V illustrates what kind of angle? A

A acute **B** right **C** obtuse **D** straight

Alternative Approach: Using Manipulatives

Provide students with base ten blocks or money manipulatives to help them estimate the product of two two-digit numbers.

Have students compare the product they compute with their estimate in order to check for reasonableness.

Looking Forward

Multiplying two two-digit numbers prepares students for:

- **Lesson 91,** estimating the answers to multiplication and division problems.
- **Lesson 104,** rounding whole numbers to the nearest hundred thousand and the nearest million.
- **Lesson 105,** factoring whole numbers.

Written Practice *(Continued)*

Math Conversations *(cont.)*

Problem 20

Before completing the arithmetic, challenge your advanced learners to explain how to estimate a range for the exact answer.

Sample: Round 52 to 50, change 15 to 10 and to 20, and then multiply; A reasonable range for the exact answer is 50 × 10 or 500 to 50 × 20 or 1000.

Problems 30 a and b Verify

For part **a,** suggest that students trace each letter and then draw the lines of symmetry.

For part **b,** suggest that students turn the tracing or the page to help identify the letters that have rotational symmetry.

Problem 30c Multiple Choice

Test-Taking Strategy

Encourage students to infer what the answer is by comparing the angle formed by the letter "V" to a right angle. (Since the given angle is less than that of a right or 90° angle, the correct answer must be choice **A** because all of the other answer choices represent angles that are greater than or equal to a right angle.)

Errors and Misconceptions

Problem 5

If the scale is not familiar to some students, explain that we find the number that each tick mark represents the same way we find the number that each tick mark represents on a number line—we identify the number of equal parts between two given numbers, then divide. For this scale, the distance between 0 and 200, 200 and 400, and so on, is divided into 4 equal parts. Therefore, each tick mark represents 200 ÷ 4 or 50 more than the tick mark to its right or 50 less than the tick mark to its left.

Problem 16

Students who write 7.46 as the answer did not follow the order of operations by completing the operation inside the parentheses first. Instead, these students completed the operations in order from left to right.

Remind these students that whenever parentheses are present in an expression or in an equation, the operation in parentheses must be completed first.

Planning & Preparation

• Mixed Numbers and Improper Fractions

Objectives
- Rename mixed numbers as improper fractions.
- Draw models to show mixed numbers and their equivalent improper fractions.

Prerequisite Skills
- Multiplying dollars and cents by a one-digit number.
- Multiplying by multiples of 10.

Materials
Instructional Masters
- Power Up G Worksheet
- Instructional Transparency 9*

Manipulative Kit
- Rulers
- Fraction circles*

Teacher-provided materials
- Fraction manipulatives from Investigation 8
- Fraction bars, scissors*

**optional*

California Mathematics Content Standards

NS 1.0, 1.5 Explain different interpretations of fractions, for example, parts of a whole, parts of a set, and division of whole numbers by whole numbers; explain equivalents of fractions (see Standard 4.0).

NS 1.0, 1.7 Write the fraction represented by a drawing of parts of a figure; represent a given fraction by using drawings; and relate a fraction to a simple decimal on a number line.

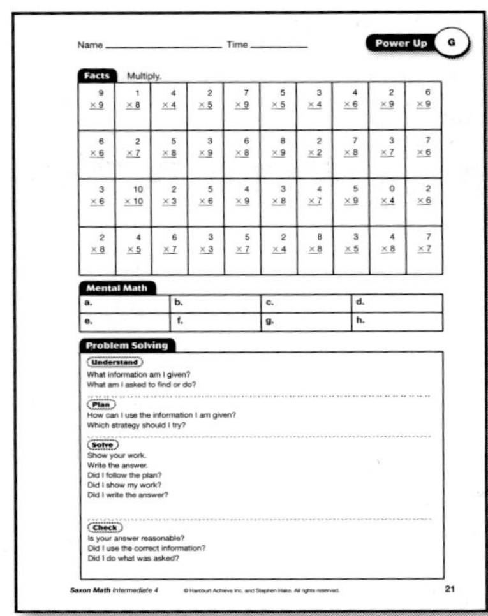

Power Up G Worksheet

Universal Access

Reaching All Special Needs Students

Special Education Students	At-Risk Students	English Learners	Advanced Learners
• Inclusion (TM) • Adaptations for Saxon Math	• Error Alert (TM) • Reteaching Masters • Refresher Lessons for California Standards	• English Learners (TM) • Developing Academic Language (TM) • English Learner Handbook	• Extend the Example (TM) • Extend the Problem (TM) • Online Activities

TM=Teacher's Manual

Developing Academic Language

New	Maintained	English Learner
improper fractions	denominator fraction mixed number numerator	improper

Problem Solving Discussion

Problem

In this Venn diagram, the circle on the left represents multiples of 3. The circle on the right represents even numbers. The number 6 is both a multiple of 3 and an even number, so it is placed within the space created by the overlap of the two circles. The number 4 is placed within the circle for even numbers but outside the overlap, since 4 is not a multiple of 3. The number 1 is placed outside both circles because it is not a multiple of 3 and it is not even. Copy the Venn diagram on your paper, and place the numbers 9, 10, 11, and 12.

Multiples of 3
Even Numbers
6
4
1

Focus Strategy  Draw a Picture or Diagram

Understand ***Understand the problem.***

"What information are we given?"

We are shown a Venn diagram that has two overlapping circles and three numbers (6, 4, and 1).

"What do the two circles stand for?"

One circle stands for multiples of 3, and the other circle stands for even numbers.

"Why do the two circles overlap?"

The two circles overlap because some numbers are even and are multiples of 3 as well. Those numbers belong in the overlap of the Venn diagram.

"What are we asked to do?"

We are asked to copy the Venn diagram and place the numbers 9, 10, 11, and 12.

Plan ***Make a plan.***

"What problem-solving strategy will we use to solve this problem?"

We will *draw a diagram.*

Solve ***Carry out the plan.***

"Where should we place the numbers 9, 10, 11, and 12?"

The number 9 is not even, but it is a multiple of 3.

The number 10 is even, but it is not a multiple of 3.

The number 11 is neither even nor a multiple of 3.

The number 12 is both even and a multiple of 3.

We place the numbers in the appropriate regions of the Venn diagram.

"What should our diagram look like?"

The diagram might look like the diagram at right.

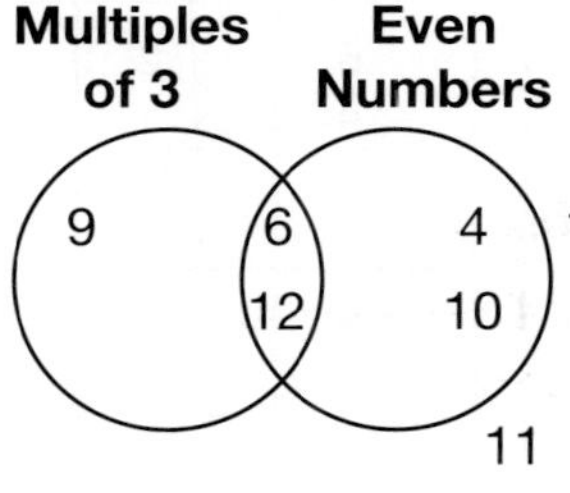

Check ***Look back.***

"Did we complete the task?"

Yes. We drew a Venn diagram of the multiples of 3 and even numbers and placed the numbers 9, 10, 11, and 12 in the diagram.

Facts

Distribute **Power Up G** to students. See answers below.

Count Aloud

Before students begin the Mental Math exercises, do these counting exercises as a class.

Count up by 8's from 24 to 72 and back to 24.

Mental Math

Encourage students to share different ways to mentally compute these exercises. Strategies for exercises are listed below.

a. Attach 3 Zeros to 25 × 1
$25 \times 1 = 25$; $25 \times 1000 = 25{,}000$
Use a Word Name
25×1 thousand $= 25$ thousand $= 25{,}000$

c. Divide by 4
$\frac{1}{4}$ of $\$40 = \$40 \div 4 = \$10$

f. Subtract \$6, then Subtract 75¢
$\$10 - \$6 = \$4$; $\$4 - 75¢ = \$3.25$

Problem Solving

Refer to **Problem-Solving Strategy Discussion**, p. 586B.

LESSON 89

• Mixed Numbers and Improper Fractions

California Mathematics Content Standards

NS 1.0, 1.5 Explain different interpretations of fractions, for example, parts of a whole, parts of a set, and division of whole numbers by whole numbers; explain equivalents of fractions (see Standard 4.0)

NS 1.0, 1.7 Write the fraction represented by a drawing of parts of a figure; represent a given fraction by using drawings; and relate a fraction to a simple decimal on a number line.

Power Up

facts Power Up G

mental math

a. **Number Sense:** 25×1000 25,000

b. **Number Sense:** $58 + 35$ 93

c. **Fractional Part:** Alonso needs to collect $\frac{1}{4}$ of \$40. What is $\frac{1}{4}$ of \$40? \$10

d. **Time:** What day is 71 days after Wednesday? Thursday

e. **Measurement:** How many feet is 6 yards? 18 ft

f. **Money:** The book cost \$6.75. If Daina paid for the book with a \$10 bill, then how much change should she receive? \$3.25

g. **Estimation:** The total cost for 6 picture frames was \$41.94. Round this amount to the nearest dollar and then divide by 6 to estimate the cost of each frame. \$7

h. **Calculation:** $\sqrt{1}$, $\times 1$, $\div 1$, $- 1 + 1$ 1

problem solving

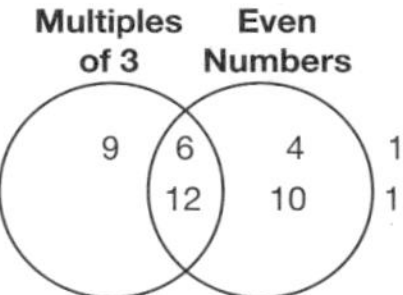

In this Venn diagram, the circle on the left represents multiples of 3. The circle on the right represents even numbers. The number 6 is both a multiple of 3 and an even number, so it is placed within the space created by the overlap of the two circles. The number 4 is placed within the circle for even numbers but outside the overlap, since 4 is not a multiple of 3. The number 1 is placed outside both circles because it is not a multiple of 3 and it is not even. Copy the Venn diagram on your paper, and place the numbers 9, 10, 11, and 12.

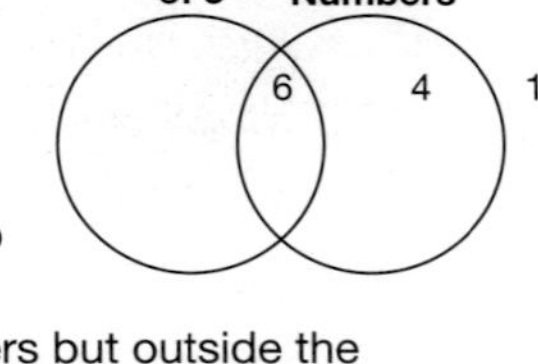

Facts Multiply.

9 × 9 = 81	1 × 8 = 8	4 × 4 = 16	2 × 5 = 10	7 × 9 = 63	5 × 5 = 25	3 × 4 = 12	4 × 6 = 24	2 × 9 = 18	6 × 9 = 54
6 × 6 = 36	2 × 7 = 14	5 × 8 = 40	3 × 9 = 27	6 × 8 = 48	8 × 9 = 72	2 × 2 = 4	7 × 8 = 56	3 × 7 = 21	7 × 6 = 42
3 × 6 = 18	10 × 10 = 100	2 × 3 = 6	5 × 6 = 30	4 × 9 = 36	3 × 8 = 24	4 × 7 = 28	5 × 9 = 45	0 × 4 = 0	2 × 6 = 12
2 × 8 = 16	4 × 5 = 20	6 × 7 = 42	3 × 3 = 9	5 × 7 = 35	2 × 4 = 8	8 × 8 = 64	3 × 5 = 15	4 × 8 = 32	7 × 7 = 49

New Concept

Here we show a picture of $1\frac{1}{2}$ shaded circles. Each whole circle has been divided into two half circles.

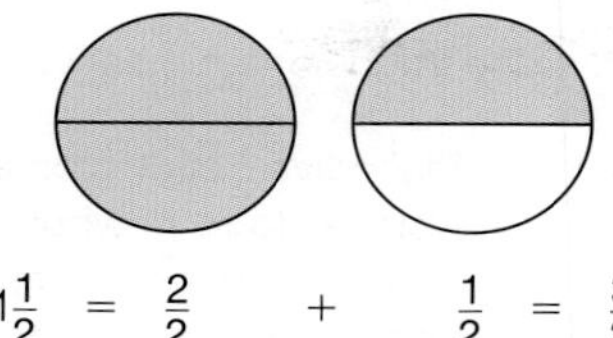

$$1\frac{1}{2} = \frac{2}{2} + \frac{1}{2} = \frac{3}{2}$$

> **Math Language**
> A **proper fraction** is a fraction whose numerator is less than the denominator.

We see from the picture that $1\frac{1}{2}$ is the same as three halves, which is written as $\frac{3}{2}$. The numerator is greater than the denominator, so the fraction $\frac{3}{2}$ is greater than 1. Fractions that are greater than or equal to 1 are called **improper fractions.** In this lesson we will draw pictures to show mixed numbers and their equivalent improper fractions.

Example 1

Draw circles to show that $2\frac{3}{4}$ equals $\frac{11}{4}$.

We begin by drawing three circles. The denominator of the fraction part of $2\frac{3}{4}$ is four, so we divide all the circles into fourths and shade $2\frac{3}{4}$ of them.

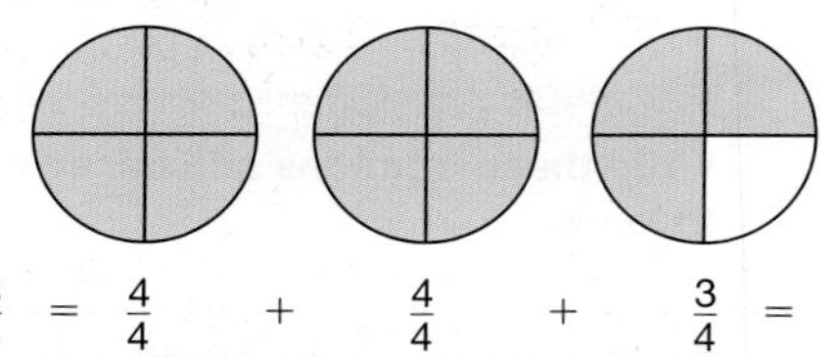

$$2\frac{3}{4} = \frac{4}{4} + \frac{4}{4} + \frac{3}{4} = \frac{11}{4}$$

We count 11 shaded fourths. The drawing shows that $2\frac{3}{4}$ equals $\frac{11}{4}$.

New Concept

Observation

You might choose to use an overhead projector and the overhead fraction circles to help students visualize that $1\frac{1}{2} = \frac{3}{2}$.

Example 1

Active Learning

Draw this example on the board or on an overhead projector and ask the class to help you count the shaded sections. Point to each shaded section as you count.

Extend the Example

Challenge your advanced learners by asking:

"What fractional part of the whole remains unshaded?" $\frac{1}{4}$

"If all three circles were shaded, what improper fraction would represent this fact?" $\frac{12}{4}$

(continued)

Math Background

Here is a shortcut for changing a mixed number to an improper fraction: Multiply the whole number part by the denominator and then add the numerator.

The result is the numerator of the improper fraction. The denominator stays the same. Here is an example:

$$2\frac{3}{4} = \frac{4 \times 2 + 3}{4} = \frac{11}{4}$$

Why does this work? Multiplying 2 by 4 gives us 8—the number of fourths in 2. Adding 3 adds the 3 fourths from the original mixed number. The result is 11, so there are 11 fourths in all. This can be written as the improper fraction $\frac{11}{4}$. Similar reasoning applies to any mixed number.

New Concept *(Continued)*

Activity

Overhead fraction circles can be used to guide students through the activity. Overhead fraction tiles can also be used to show a different representation of fractions.

Example 2

Generalize

As you discuss the fact that $\frac{7}{5}$ is greater than $\frac{4}{5}$, lead students to generalize that when the denominators of two or more fractions are the same, we can compare the fractions by comparing the numerators.

Error Alert

As you discuss the fact that $\frac{7}{4}$ is greater than $\frac{7}{5}$, make sure students understand the connection to unit fractions (unit fractions are those that have a numerator of 1), and generalize that if the numerators of two or more fractions are 1, the fraction with the greatest denominator is the least fraction and the fraction with the least denominator is the greatest fraction. To reinforce this generalization, offer the following money analogy:

"What is the value of $\frac{1}{2}$ of a dollar?" 50¢

"What is the value of $\frac{1}{4}$ of a dollar?" 25¢

"Both numerators are 1, but the denominators are different. Which amount of money is greater, $\frac{1}{4}$ of a dollar—the fraction with the greatest denominator, or $\frac{1}{2}$ of a dollar—the fraction with the least denominator?" The fraction with the least denominator is the greatest amount of money.

Extend the Example

Challenge advanced learners to demonstrate a way to check the answer. Sample: Change each fraction or mixed number to a decimal number in hundredths, then compare; since $1\frac{2}{5} = 1.40$, $\frac{4}{5} = 0.80$, and $1\frac{3}{4} = 1.75$, we find that $1.75 > 1.40 > 0.80$, so $1\frac{3}{4} > 1\frac{2}{5} > \frac{4}{5}$.

(continued)

Modeling Mixed Numbers and Improper Fractions

Material needed:

- fraction manipulatives from **Lesson Activities 11** and **12**

Use fraction manipulatives to perform the following activities:

a. Place five $\frac{1}{2}$ circles on a desk. Then arrange four of the $\frac{1}{2}$ circles to form whole circles. Draw a picture of the whole and part circles you formed, and write the improper fraction and mixed number represented by the five $\frac{1}{2}$ circles. $\frac{5}{2} = 2\frac{1}{2}$

b. Place one more $\frac{1}{2}$ circle on the desk to complete another circle. Write the improper fraction and whole number represented. $\frac{6}{2} = 3$

c. Clear the desk of $\frac{1}{2}$ circles and place seven $\frac{1}{4}$ circles on the desk. Fit the pieces together to form a whole circle and part of a circle. Draw a picture, and write the improper fraction and mixed number represented. $\frac{7}{4} = 1\frac{3}{4}$

d. Place one more $\frac{1}{4}$ circle on the desk to complete another circle. Write the improper fraction and whole number represented. $\frac{8}{4} = 2$

Example 2

Write these fractions and mixed numbers in order from greatest to least.

$$1\frac{2}{5}, \frac{4}{5}, 1\frac{3}{4}$$

We start by writing the mixed numbers as fractions.

$$1\frac{2}{5} = \frac{5}{5} + \frac{2}{5} \text{ or } \frac{7}{5}$$

We have two fractions that are fifths: $\frac{7}{5}$ and $\frac{4}{5}$. We can see that $\frac{7}{5}$ is greater than $\frac{4}{5}$.

We write $\frac{7}{5}, \frac{4}{5}$.

English Learners

Explain to students that the word **improper** means not belonging or not correct. Say:

"In math we have improper fractions. These are fractions that are not in the correct form. The correct, or proper, form of the improper fraction $\frac{12}{3}$ is 4."

"It is improper to play baseball inside the house, because baseball is meant to be played outside."

Ask:

"Can you think of other times something might be improper?" Samples: wearing casual clothes to a special occasion, talking when someone else is, etc.

Now we can write $1\frac{3}{4}$ as a fraction.

$$1\frac{3}{4} = \frac{4}{4} + \frac{3}{4} \text{ or } \frac{7}{4}$$

Finally we compare fifths and fourths.

Since $\frac{1}{4}$ is greater than $\frac{1}{5}$, then $\frac{7}{4}$ is greater than $\frac{7}{5}$.

We write $\frac{7}{4}, \frac{7}{5}, \frac{4}{5}$.

Discuss Why did we use $\frac{5}{5}$ to change $1\frac{2}{5}$ to $\frac{7}{5}$?

Sample: The fraction part of the mixed number is fifths, we use the same denominator

Lesson Practice

a. Draw circles to show that $1\frac{3}{4} = \frac{7}{4}$.

b. Draw circles to show that $2\frac{1}{2} = \frac{5}{2}$.

c. Draw circles to show that $1\frac{1}{3} = \frac{4}{3}$.

d. Write these numbers from greatest to least.

$$\frac{5}{2}, \frac{3}{4}, 1\frac{1}{4}$$ $\frac{5}{2}, 1\frac{1}{4}, \frac{3}{4}$

Written Practice

Distributed and Integrated

1. (Inv. 6) **Interpret** Use this tally sheet to answer parts **a–c.**

Results of Class Election

Candidate	Tally
Irma	𝍸 II
Hamish	𝍸 I
Thanh	𝍸 III
Marisol	𝍸 𝍸 II

a. Who was second in the election? Thanh

b. Who received twice as many votes as Hamish? Marisol

c. Altogether, how many votes were cast? 33 votes

2. (Inv. 4) Write these amounts in order from greatest to least: $2.03, $1.48, $1.45, $0.99

$1.45 $2.03 $0.99 $1.48

3. (14, 16) **Formulate** The Osage River in Kansas is 500 miles long. The Kentucky River is 259 miles long. How many miles longer is the Osage River? Write and solve an equation. Sample: $500 - 259 = m$; 241 miles

New Concept *(Continued)*

Lesson Practice

Guided Practice

Use these problems as guided practice to check the students' understanding of today's concept.

Problems a–c

Before solving each problem, ask students to name the number of circles that must be drawn, and name the number of equal parts those circles will be divided into. For each number that is named, have students explain why they named that number.

Invite students to use their fraction pieces to check their work.

Problem c

Error Alert

If some students have difficulty dividing a circle into thirds, use **Instructional Transparency 9** to demonstrate how visualizing the 12 numbers on a clock can help. Point out to students that since 12 divided by 3 is 4, a radius can be drawn from the center of the circle to every fourth number and the result will be a circle divided into thirds.

Closure

The question below helps assess the concepts taught in this lesson.

"What improper fraction is equal to $3\frac{3}{4}$? Draw circles to support your answer." $\frac{15}{4}$ Students should draw four circles and divide each circle into 4 equal parts, and then they should shade 3 circles and 3 parts of the fourth circle.

Inclusion

Use this strategy if the student displays:

- Difficulty with Large Group Instruction.
- Difficulty with Abstract Process.

Mixed Numbers and Improper Fractions (Pairs)

Materials: paper, fraction circles

- Draw [circles] on the board and ask, ***"How many whole circles are shown?"*** 1 ***"How many parts are in each circle?"*** 4 ***"What fraction is shown in the partial shaded circle?"*** $\frac{1}{4}$
- Write the mixed number $1\frac{1}{4}$ on the board. (Write corresponding number under corresponding circle)
- Using the same picture as students to make a fraction out of the whole circle. Ask, ***"How many parts are shaded in the whole circle?"*** 4 ***"How many total parts are there?"*** 4
- Erase the 1 under the whole circle and write $\frac{4}{4}$. Then tell students to combine the total number of shaded parts to get $\frac{5}{4}$.
- Have students create a picture of a whole number and fraction using their fraction circles. Students can pass their picture to a partner to write the mixed number and improper fraction.

Written Practice

Math Conversations

Independent Practice and Discussions to Increase Understanding

Problem 5 **Analyze**

Make sure students understand that the phrase "as equally as possible" suggests that not all of the teams will have the same number of players.

Problem 6 **Conclude**

Extend the Problem

After completing each problem, ask students to explain why the statement is true or false.

Problem 8

Extend the Problem

"Suppose that we change 88 to 85 and 59 to 55. Explain how we could estimate the product of 85 and 55." See student work.

If the explanations describe rounding both factors up or rounding both factors down, point out that because both factors are halfway between the nearest multiples of 10, rounding one factor up and rounding one factor down will produce a very good estimate. $90 \times 50 = 4500$ and $80 \times 60 = 4800$; The exact product of 85×55 is 4675.

Problem 10

"What does each tick mark on the number line represent? Explain how you know." Each tick mark represents 10 more than the tick mark to its left and 10 less than the tick mark to its right because the distance from 600 to 700 is divided into ten equal parts, and $(700 - 600) \div 10 = 10$.

(continued)

*4. (77) What fraction of the letters in the following word are I's? $\frac{4}{11}$

MISSISSIPPI

▸ *5. (87) **Analyze** The coach divided 33 players as equally as possible into 4 teams.

a. How many teams had exactly 8 players? 3 teams

b. How many teams had 9 players? 1 team

▸ *6. (81) **Conclude** Write *true* or *false* for parts **a–d.**

a. All equilateral triangles are also equiangular. true

b. A right triangle could have more than one right angle. false

c. An equilateral triangle is also an isosceles triangle. true

d. All triangles are polygons. true

7. (Inv. 4, 77) Name the shaded part of this group

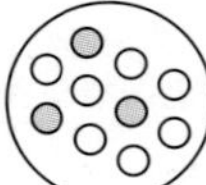

a. as a fraction. $\frac{3}{10}$

b. as a decimal number. 0.3

▸ *8. (88) Estimate the product of 88 and 59. Then find the exact product. 5400; 5192

9. (RF12) Sue's birthday is May 2. Her birthday will be on what day of the week in the year 2045? Tuesday

MAY 2045

S	M	T	W	T	F	S
	1	2	3	4	5	6
7	8	9	10	11	12	13
14	15	16	17	18	19	20
21	22	23	24	25	26	27
28	29	30	31			

▸ *10. (Inv. 2) Point W represents what number on this number line? 650

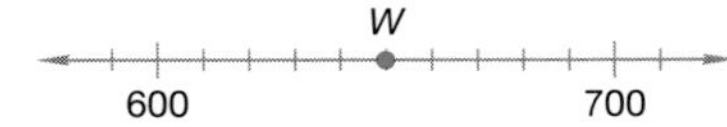

11. (28, 51) $32.63 + $42 + $7.56
$82.19

12. (9, 51, 52) $86.45 − ($74.50 + $5)
$6.95

590 ***Saxon Math** Intermediate 4*

13. 83×40 (71) 3320

14. 1000×53 (84) 53,000

15. 200×800 (85) 160,000

*16. (88) $\begin{array}{r} 32 \\ \times\ 16 \\ \hline 512 \end{array}$

*17. (88) $\begin{array}{r} 67 \\ \times\ 32 \\ \hline 2144 \end{array}$

18. (59) $\begin{array}{r} \$8.95 \\ \times\ \ \ \ 4 \\ \hline \$35.80 \end{array}$

19. $3\overline{)625}$ (83) 208 R 1

20. $4\overline{)714}$ (79) 178 R 2

21. $6\overline{)1385}$ (83) 230 R 5

22. $\frac{900}{5}$ (83) 180

23. $3748 \div 9$ (79) 416 R 4

24. $8m = \$28.56$ (34, 79) \$3.57

▶ *25. (89) **Represent** This circle shows that $\frac{2}{2}$ equals 1. Draw a circle that shows that $\frac{3}{3}$ equals 1.

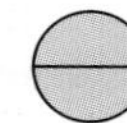

26. (66) Find the perimeter and area of this rectangle. 180 mi; 2000 mi²

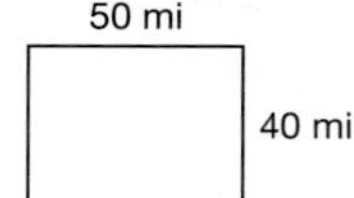

▶ *27. (70, 81, 82) **a.** Draw two congruent isosceles triangles.

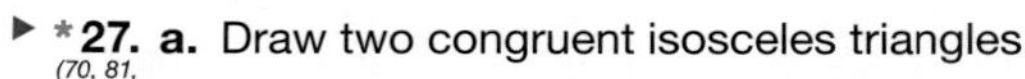

27. a. Sample:

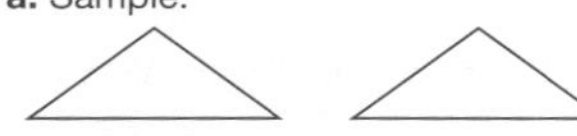

b. Draw the line of symmetry on one of the figures you created.

27. b. Sample:

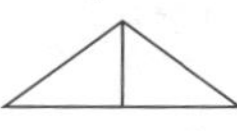

▶ *28. (44) Compare: 0.5 ⊜ 0.50

*29. (42) Kelly ran and jumped 9 ft 6 in. How many inches did Kelly jump? 114 in.

Written Practice *(Continued)*

Math Conversations *(cont.)*

Problem 25 **Represent**

When dividing a circle into thirds, some students may find it helpful to think of the numbers on the face of a clock. Encourage these students to draw a circle, label a point at the center of the circle, and then to draw radii from that point to 4 o'clock, to 8 o'clock, and to 12 o'clock.

Problem 27a

The simplest way for students to draw two congruent isosceles triangles is to use a ruler and draw one triangle, and then trace it.

Problem 28

Watch for opportunities to remind students that they can attach a zero in the hundredths place of 0.5, or drop a zero from the hundredths place of 0.50, because the values of the numbers do not change.

(continued)

Written Practice *(Continued)*

Errors and Misconceptions

Problem 1

If students have difficulty solving the problem, suggest that they first determine the number each tally represents: Irma, 7; Hamish, 6; Thanh, 8; Marisol, 12.

Problem 27b

Encourage students who have difficulty identifying lines of symmetry to trace one of the triangles, cut it out, and then fold it into two parts in a variety of ways. Explain that whenever a fold divides a figure into two identical (congruent) parts, the fold line is a line of symmetry.

***30.** (58, Inv. 7) The table shows the relationship between the number of hours Aidan works and the amount of money he earns.

Number of Hours Worked	Income Earned (in dollars)
1	19
2	38
3	57
4	76
5	95

a. **Generalize** Write a word sentence that describes the relationship of the data. Sample: Aidan earns $19 for each hour he works.

b. **Predict** Aidan works 40 hours each week. What is a reasonable estimate of the amount of income he earns each week? Explain your answer. Sample: I rounded $19 to $20, and then multiplied by 40; A reasonable estimate is $20 × 40, or $800.

592 ***Saxon Math*** *Intermediate 4*

Looking Forward

Renaming and modeling mixed numbers and improper fractions prepares students for:

- **Lesson 92,** comparing and ordering fractions and decimals.
- **Lesson 94,** solving two-step problems that involve a fraction of a group.
- **Lesson 98,** identifying and writing fractions equal to 1 and to $\frac{1}{2}$.
- **Lesson 99,** changing improper fractions to whole or mixed numbers.
- **Lesson 100,** adding and subtracting fractions with common denominators.
- **Lesson 103,** finding equivalent fractions.
- **Lesson 106,** writing the reduced form of a fraction.
- **Lessons 111–113,** simplifying and renaming fractions, and finding a common denominator.

Planning & Preparation

• Classifying Quadrilaterals

Objectives

- Describe the attributes of different types of quadrilaterals.
- Classify and draw quadrilaterals by their attributes.
- Identify line and rotational symmetry for quadrilaterals.

Prerequisite Skills

- Drawing triangles and rectangles with given side measurements.
- Describing and drawing acute, obtuse, right, and straight angles.
- Locating a line of symmetry for a figure.

Materials

Instructional Masters

- Power Up I Worksheet
- Lesson Activity 25
- Lesson Activity 21*

Manipulative Kit

- Mirrors

Teacher-provided materials

- Straws or other straight objects, grid paper, scissors*

**optional*

California Mathematics Content Standards

MG 3.0, 3.1 Identify lines that are parallel and perpendicular.

MG 3.0, 3.4 Identify figures that have bilateral and rotational symmetry.

MG 3.0, 3.5 Know the definitions of a right angle, an acute angle, and an obtuse angle. Understand that 90°, 180°, 270°, and 360° are associated, respectively, with $\frac{1}{4}$, $\frac{1}{2}$, $\frac{3}{4}$, and full turns.

MG 3.0, 3.8 Know the definition of different quadrilaterals (e.g., rhombus, square, rectangle, parallelogram, trapezoid).

MR 2.0, 2.3 Use a variety of methods, such as words, numbers, symbols, charts, graphs, tables, diagrams, and models, to explain mathematical reasoning.

Power Up I Worksheet

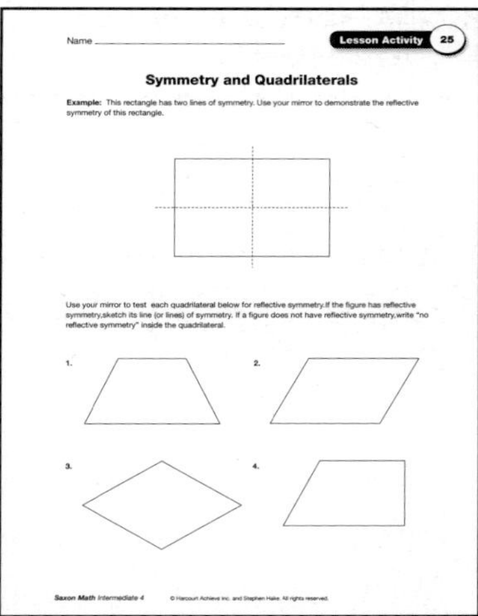
Lesson Activity 25

Symmetry and Quadrilaterals

Lesson Activity 25

Universal Access

Reaching All Special Needs Students

Special Education Students	At-Risk Students	English Learners	Advanced Learners
• Inclusion (TM) • Adaptations for Saxon Math	• Alternative Approach (TM) • Error Alert (TM) • Reteaching Masters • Refresher Lessons for California Standards	• English Learners (TM) • Developing Academic Language (TM) • English Learner Handbook	• Extend the Example (TM) • Extend the Problem (TM) • Online Activities

TM=Teacher's Manual

Developing Academic Language

New	Maintained	English Learner
parallelogram	angles	board
rhombus	line segments	
trapezoid	parallel	
	perpendicular	
	rectangle	

Problem Solving Discussion

Problem

A half-ton pickup truck can carry a load weighing half of a ton. How many 100-pound sacks of cement can a half-ton pickup truck carry?

Focus Strategies

ABC **Make It Simpler**

2+3=5 **Write a Number Sentence or Equation**

Understand *Understand the problem.*

"What information are we given?"

A half-ton pickup truck can carry a load weighing half of a ton.

"What are we asked to do?"

We are asked to find how many 100-pound sacks of cement a half-ton truck can carry.

Plan *Make a plan.*

"How can we use the information we know to solve the problem?"

We need to use consistent units of weight. The weight of the cement sacks is given in pounds, so we need to calculate how many pounds the truck can carry.

"What do we predict our answer will be in the range of?"

Discuss predictions as a class.

Solve *Carry out the plan.*

"How many pounds are in 1 ton?"

One ton is 2000 pounds.

"The pickup truck can carry half a ton. How many pounds are in half of a ton?"

Half of a ton is 1000 pounds.

"How many 100-pound sacks of cement would it take to total 1000 pounds?"

It would take ten 100-pound sacks of cement to total 1000 pounds.

"How many 100-pound sacks of cement can a half-ton pickup truck carry?"

A half-ton pickup truck can carry 10 sacks of cement that weigh 100 pounds each.

Check *Look back.*

"Is our solution reasonable?"

Yes. We know that our answer is reasonable because ten 100-pound sacks of cement weigh a total of 10×100 lb $= 1000$ lb, which is half of a ton.

"What problem-solving strategies did we use, and how did they help us?"

We can say that we *made the problem simpler* by changing the half ton measurement into pounds so that we used the same weight units as the cement sacks. We *wrote a number sentence* to confirm that 10 sacks of cement weigh 1000 pounds.

• Classifying Quadrilaterals

California Mathematics Content Standards

MG 3.0, 3.1 Identify lines that are parallel and perpendicular.

MG 3.0, 3.5 Know the definitions of a right angle, an acute angle, and an obtuse angle. Understand that 90°, 180°, 270°, and 360° are associated, respectively, with $\frac{1}{4}$, $\frac{1}{2}$, $\frac{3}{4}$, and full turns.

MG 3.0, 3.8 Know the definition of different quadrilaterals (e.g., rhombus, square, rectangle, parallelogram, trapezoid).

Power Up

facts Power Up I

mental math Find half of each number in problems **a–d.**

a. Number Sense: 40 20

b. Number Sense: 48 24

c. Number Sense: 64 32

d. Number Sense: 86 43

e. Number Sense: 75 + 37 112

f. Money: Taylor bought scissors for \$3.54 and glue for \$2.99. What was the total cost? \$6.53

g. Estimation: Choose the more reasonable estimate for the mass of 500 sheets of copy paper: 2 grams or 2 kilograms. 2 kg

h. Calculation: $\sqrt{49}$, × 2, + 7, ÷ 3, × 7 49

problem solving Choose an appropriate problem-solving strategy to solve this problem. A half-ton pickup truck can carry a load weighing half of a ton. How many 100-pound sacks of cement can a half-ton pickup truck carry? 10 sacks

New Concept

Recall from Lesson 50 that a quadrilateral is a polygon with four sides. In this lesson we will practice recognizing and naming different types of quadrilaterals. On the following page, we show four different types.

Facts Divide.

9)81 9	3)27 9	5)25 5	2)6 3	5)45 9	3)9 3	4)32 8	4)16 4	2)12 6	7)56 8
1)9 9	6)42 7	2)14 7	4)28 7	3)24 8	5)40 8	2)18 9	8)72 9	3)18 6	6)54 9
7)49 7	2)8 4	6)36 6	3)12 4	8)64 8	2)4 2	5)0 0	4)24 6	8)8 1	5)35 7
3)21 7	4)20 5	2)16 8	5)30 6	4)36 9	3)15 5	6)48 8	2)10 5	7)63 9	8)56 7

Power Up

Facts

Distribute **Power Up I** to students. See answers below.

Count Aloud

Before students begin the Mental Math exercises, do these counting exercises as a class.

Count by 5's from 35 to 80 and back to 35.

Mental Math

Encourage students to share different ways to mentally compute these exercises. Strategies for exercises are listed below.

a. Divide Tens by 2

4 tens ÷ 2 = 2 tens = 20

b. Divide Tens and Divide Ones

40 ÷ 2 = 20 and 8 ÷ 2 = 4; 20 + 4 = 24

e. Add 40, then Subtract 3

75 + 40 = 115; 115 − 3 = 112

Add 30, then Add 7

75 + 30 = 105; 105 + 7 = 112

Problem Solving

Refer to **Problem-Solving Strategy Discussion**, p. 593B.

New Concept

Instruction

Remind students that the prefix *quad–* means "four" and explain that the term *lateral* can be thought of as "sides."

(continued)

New Concept *(Continued)*

Active Learning

Ask students to study the five different quadrilaterals. Then ask comparison questions such as those shown below to help focus attention on how the quadrilaterals are different.

"Why aren't all rectangles also squares?" A rectangle does not necessarily have four sides of equal length, but every square always has four sides of equal length.

"Why aren't all parallelograms also rectangles?" A parallelogram does not necessarily have four right angles, but every rectangle always has four right angles.

Example 1

Connection

Point out that trapezoids are not parallelograms and parallelograms are not trapezoids, but that both trapezoids and parallelograms are quadrilaterals.

Example 2

Extend the Example

Challenge your advanced learners by asking:

"What figures can we form if we draw two parallel line segments that are the same length and then connect the endpoints?" Possible figures include a square, a rhombus, a rectangle, and a parallelogram.

(continued)

Thinking Skills

Verify

Why does a square have so many names?

Sample: A square is a parallelogram because it has parallel sides; A square is a rectangle because it has perpendicular sides and four right angles; A square is a rhombus because it has congruent sides.

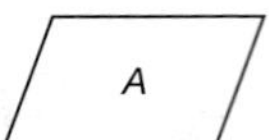

parallelogram

B
parallelogram
rhombus

C
parallelogram
rectangle

D
parallelogram
rhombus
rectangle
square

E
trapezoid

A **parallelogram** is a quadrilateral with *two* pairs of parallel sides. Figures *A, B, C,* and *D* each have two pairs of parallel sides, so all four figures are parallelograms. A **trapezoid** is a quadrilateral with exactly *one* pair of parallel sides. Figure *E* is not a parallelogram; it is a trapezoid.

A **rectangle** is a special type of parallelogram that has four right angles. Figures *C* and *D* are rectangles. A **rhombus** is a special type of parallelogram whose sides are equal in length. Figure *B* is a rhombus, as is figure *D*. A **square** is a regular quadrilateral. Its sides are equal in length, and its angles are all right angles. Figure *D* is a square. It is also a parallelogram, a rhombus, and a rectangle.

Example 1

Which of these quadrilaterals is *not* a parallelogram?

G　H　I

We look for pairs of parallel sides. A parallelogram has two pairs of parallel sides. Figures *F, G,* and *I* each have two pairs of parallel sides. **Figure *H*** has only one pair of parallel sides, so it is a trapezoid, not a parallelogram.

Example 2

Draw two parallel line segments of different lengths. Then form a quadrilateral by drawing two line segments that connect the endpoints. What type of quadrilateral did you make?

First we draw two parallel line segments of different lengths.

Then we connect the endpoints with line segments to form a quadrilateral.

We see that this quadrilateral is a **trapezoid.**

Alternative Approach: Using Manipulatives

To help the students build an understanding of the concept of classifying quadrilaterals, have students use straws or other straight objects to model the terms: parallel sides, perpendicular sides, opposite sides, right angle, acute angle, and obtuse angles.

Example 3

> **Thinking Skills**
>
> **Model**
>
> Find a quadrilateral in your classroom. Identify and describe the parallel, perpendicular, and intersecting segments in the quadrilateral.

Sample: Parallel segments stay the same distance apart and do not intersect. Perpendicular segments intersect at right angles. Intersecting segments share a common point.

Which of the following quadrilaterals has sides that are *not* parallel or perpendicular?

A

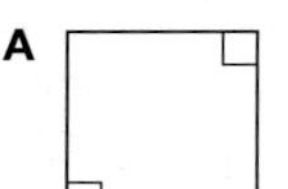

B

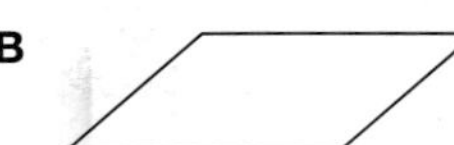

C

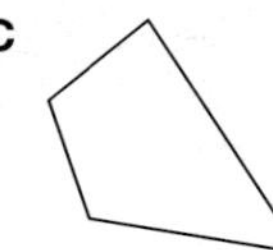

D

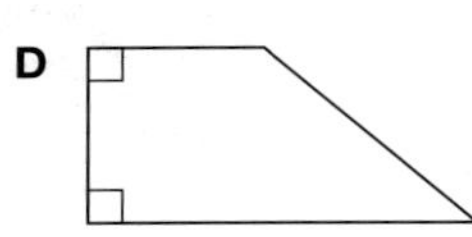

We will consider the relationships between the sides of each quadrilateral.

A The opposite sides are parallel, and the adjacent sides are perpendicular.

B The opposite sides are parallel, and the adjacent sides intersect but are not perpendicular.

C There are no parallel or perpendicular sides.

D One pair of opposite sides is parallel, and another side is perpendicular to the parallel sides.

Only **figure C** has sides that are not parallel or perpendicular.

Example 4

Describe the angles in each of the quadrilaterals in Example 3.

Figure **A** appears to be a square; it has **four right angles.**

Figure **B** is a parallelogram; it has **two acute angles and two obtuse angles.**

Figure **C** is a quadrilateral with **two obtuse angles and two acute angles.**

Figure **D** is a trapezoid with **two right angles, one acute angle, and one obtuse angle.**

New Concept *(Continued)*

Example 3

Instruction

As you discuss figure **A**, have students note that the small square that is located at two vertices of the figure indicates that each angle is a right angle. Make sure students understand that if an angle is a right angle, the line segments or rays that form the sides of the angle are perpendicular. Because figure **A** also has parallel sides, it does not meet either condition that was established in the problem.

Error Alert

As you discuss figure **B**, remind students that they are looking for a figure that does not have parallel sides.

As you discuss figure **D**, help students recognize that it is similar to figure **A** in the sense that both figures do not meet either of the conditions that were established in the problem.

Example 4

Extend the Example

"Name another quadrilateral that has 4 right angles." Rectangle and square

"Name 2 other quadrilaterals that could have 2 acute and 2 obtuse angles." Rhombus and trapezoid

(continued)

Inclusion

Use this strategy if the student displays:

- Slow Learning Rate.
- Poor Retention.

Classifying Quadrilaterals (Individual)

Materials: 1-inch grid paper, scissors

- Cut out four or more figures ahead of class. Include a square, a rectangle that is not a square, a rhombus that is not a square, a trapezoid or two, and possibly a parallelogram that is not a rectangle. Ask students questions about the figures such as:

  "Which figures have four right angles? What is the name for these shapes?" Rectangles and squares

  "Which figures have four sides the same length? What is the name for these shapes?" Rhombuses and squares

  "Which figure is a rectangle and a rhombus?" Square

  "Which figures have parallel sides?" All

  "Which figure has only one pair of parallel sides?" Trapezoid

  "Which figures haves two pairs of parallel sides? What is the name for these figures?" Squares, rectangles, rhombuses, parallelograms

New Concept (Continued)

Activities 1 and 2

After the activities have been completed, invite volunteers to share their drawings and their explanations with the class.

Lesson Practice

Guided Practice

Use these problems as guided practice to check the students' understanding of today's concept.

Problems a–d **Classify**

Suggest that students look for pairs of parallel sides, right angles, and equal-length sides to help classify each figure.

Problems a–d
Extend the Problem

Ask students to identify real-world objects they have seen with the shapes shown. Samples: buildings, gift boxes, etc.

Problem e

An alternative to having students write lengthy descriptions is to have a class discussion about the relationships.

Problems a–d
Error Alert

Remind students that more than one description may apply to each figure.

Closure The questions below help assess the concepts taught in this lesson.

"Name five different quadrilaterals." Square, rhombus, rectangle, parallelogram, trapezoid

"Which quadrilaterals have at least one pair of parallel sides?" Square, rhombus, rectangle, parallelogram, trapezoid

"Which quadrilaterals have two pairs of parallel sides?" Square, rhombus, rectangle, parallelogram

"Which quadrilaterals have four right angles?" Rectangles and squares

Activity 1

Quadrilaterals in the Classroom

Look around the room for quadrilaterals. Find examples of at least three different types of quadrilaterals illustrated in the beginning of this lesson. Draw each example you find, and next to each picture, name the object you drew and its shape. Then describe how you know that the object is the shape you named and describe the relationships of the sides of each quadrilateral.

Activity 2

Symmetry and Quadrilaterals

Materials needed:
- **Lesson Activity 25**
- mirror or reflective surface

If a figure can be divided into mirror images by a line of symmetry, then the figure has reflective symmetry. A mirror can help us decide if a figure has reflective symmetry. If we place a mirror upright along a line of symmetry, the half of the figure behind the mirror appears in the reflection of the other half. Use a mirror to discover which figures in **Lesson Activity 25** have reflective symmetry. If you find a figure with reflective symmetry, draw its line (or lines) of symmetry.

Lesson Practice

a. Parallelogram, rhombus, rectangle, square
b. parallelogram
c. parallelogram, rectangle
d. trapezoid
e. Sample: Figure **a** has four right angles and two pairs of parallel sides. The parallel side pairs are perpendicular.
f.

Classify Describe each quadrilateral as a trapezoid, parallelogram, rhombus, rectangle, or square. (More than one description may apply to each figure.)

a. 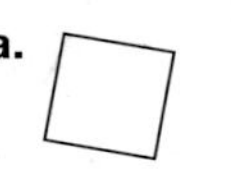 **b.** 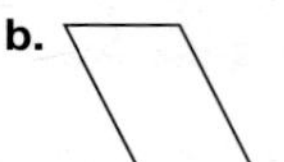 **c.** 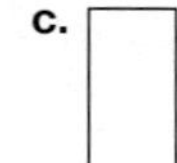 **d.** 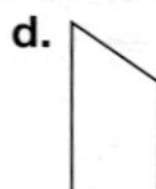

e. Describe the angles in figures **a–d** and the relationships between the sides.

f. Draw two parallel line segments that are the same length. Then make a quadrilateral by drawing two more parallel line segments that connect the endpoints. Is your quadrilateral a parallelogram? Why or why not? Yes, they have two pairs of parallel lines; Therefore, it is a parallelogram.

Written Practice

Distributed and Integrated

▸ *1. (RF12) **Analyze** What is the total number of days in the first three months of a leap year? 91 days

▸ *2. (87) Thirty-two desks were arranged as equally as possible in 6 rows.

a. How many rows had exactly 5 desks? 4 rows

b. How many rows had 6 desks? 2 rows

*3. (64, Inv. 7) **Evaluate** If $y = 3x + 6$, then what is y when $x = 4$, 5, and 6? 18, 21, 24

▸ *4. (87) **Analyze** Carmen separated the 37 math books as equally as possible into 4 stacks.

a. How many stacks had exactly 9 books? 3 stacks

b. How many stacks had 10 books? 1 stack

*5. (90) **Conclude** Write *true* or *false* for parts **a–e.**

a. All rectangles have four right angles. true

b. Some squares are rectangles. false

c. All trapezoids are rhombuses. false

d. All rectangles are parallelograms. true

e. Some parallelograms have no right angles. true

6. (Inv. 4) **a.** What decimal number names the shaded part of the large square at right? 0.05

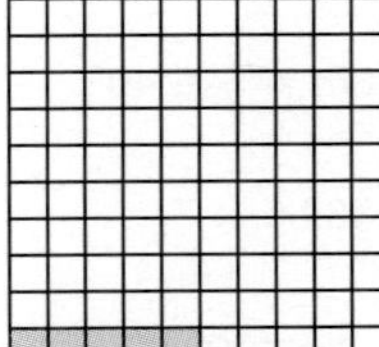

b. What decimal number names the part that is not shaded? 0.95

▸ *7. (87) **Explain** Near closing time, 31 children and adults are waiting in line to board a ride at an amusement park. Eight people board the ride at one time. How many people will be on the last ride of the day? Explain your answer. 7 people; sample: $31 \div 8 = 3$ R 7; 3 represents the number of full rides, and 7 represents the number of people on the last ride.

English Learners

To **board** means to enter or get on, as in a plane. Ask students if they have ever been in an airport or bus station and heard someone say:

"We will be boarding in 20 minutes."

Explain that this means passengers can begin getting on the bus or plane in 20 minutes.

Ask:

"What other things do people board?"

Samples: trains, roller coasters, boats

Written Practice

Math Conversations

Independent Practice and Discussions to Increase Understanding

Problem 1 Analyze

You may need to remind students that January has 31 days, February has 29 days in a leap year, and March has 31 days.

Extend the Problem

Ask students:

"Is the average number of days in those months a whole number? Use mental math to decide, and explain why or why not." No; sample: 91 is not divisible by 3 because $3 \times 30 = 90$ and $3 \times 31 = 93$.

Problems 2 and 4

Make sure students recognize that the meaning of the phrase as *equally as possible* is different from the meaning of the word *equally.* In problem **2,** 32 is not divisible by 6, so it is not possible for the same number of desks to be in each row. In problem **4,** 37 is not divisible by 4, so it is not possible for the same number of books to be in each stack.

Problem 7 Explain

Students must ignore the quotient and write the remainder to solve the problem correctly.

(continued)

Written Practice *(Continued)*

Math Conversations *(cont.)*

Problem 11

"What is a word that means the same as "median?" Sample: middle

"How must numbers be arranged before we can identify the median of the numbers?" From least to greatest or from greatest to least

Problems 16 and 17

Before they complete the arithmetic, ask students to estimate each product and then to compare the exact answers to the estimates to decide if the answers are reasonable.

(continued)

8. (40) Round 3874 to the nearest thousand. 4000

9. (73) **Estimate** Alicia opened a liter of milk and poured half of it into a pitcher. About how many milliliters of milk did she pour into the pitcher? About 500 mL

10. (13) The sun was up when Mark started working. It was dark when he stopped working later in the day. How much time had gone by? 9 hours 10 minutes

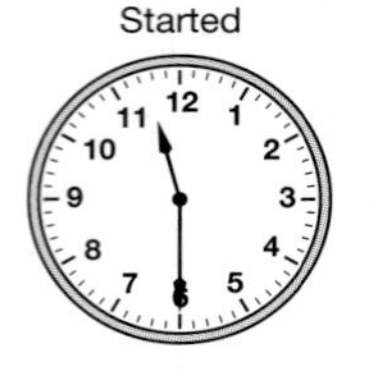

▶ *11. (Inv. 6) For five days Pilar recorded the high temperature. The temperatures were 79°F, 82°F, 84°F, 81°F, and 74°F. What was the median temperature for those five days? 81°F

12. (60, 69) **Explain** Leena drove 368 miles in 8 hours. If she drove the same number of miles each hour, how far did she drive each hour? Explain how you found your answer. 46 miles each hour; sample: I divided 368 miles by 8 hours.

13. (51) $496{,}325 + 3{,}680$ — 500,005

14. (52) $\$36.00 - \$30.78$ — \$5.22

15. (11, 28) \$12.45 + \$1.30 + \$2.00 + \$0.25 + \$0.04 + \$0.32 + \$1.29 — \$17.65

▶ *16. (88) 26×24 — 624

▶ *17. (88) 25×25 — 625

18. (34, 83) $8m = \$16.40$ — \$2.05

19. (85) 60×300 — 18,000

20. (59) $\$8.56 \times 7$ — \$59.92

21. (83) $7\overline{)845}$ — 120 R 5

22. (79) $9\overline{)1000}$ — 111 R 1

23. (69) $\frac{432}{6}$ — 72

24. (89) **Represent** Draw and shade a circle that shows that $\frac{4}{4}$ equals 1.

25. (Inv. 3) The wall was 8 feet high and 12 feet wide. How many square feet of wallpaper were needed to cover the wall? 96 ft^2

26. (Inv. 6) **Analyze** Below are Tene's scores on the first seven games. Refer to these scores to answer parts **a–c.**

85, 85, 100, 90, 80, 100, 85

a. Rearrange the scores so that the scores are in order from lowest to highest. 80, 85, 85, 85, 90, 100, 100

b. In your answer to part **a,** which score is the median score in the list? 85

c. In the list of game scores, which score is the mode? 85

*27. (61) **Estimate** What is a reasonable estimate of the number in each group when 912 objects are separated into 3 equal groups? Explain why your estimate is reasonable. Sample: A reasonable estimate is 300 because 912 is close to 900, and $900 \div 3 = 300$.

*28. (53) According to many health experts, a person should drink 64 ounces of water each day. If Shankeedra's glass holds 8 ounces of water, how many glasses of water should she drink in one day? 8 glasses

► *29. (56) Arthur told his classmates that his age in years is a single-digit odd number greater than one. He also told his classmates that his age is not a prime number. How old is Arthur? 9 years old

► *30. (64) If $y = 3x - 1$, what is y when x is 2? 5

Written Practice *(Continued)*

Math Conversations *(cont.)*

Problem 29

Make sure students understand that because Arthur's age is a single-digit number, the only possible numbers that can represent his age in years are 1, 2, 3, 4, 5, 6, 7, 8, or 9.

Problem 30

Extend the Problem

Challenge your advanced learners to name the value of x when $y = 0$. $x = \frac{1}{3}$

Errors and Misconceptions

Problem 26a

When students rewrite data, common errors involve writing the data incorrectly and forgetting to write one or more data values. Remind students that it is important to check their work by comparing the rewritten data to the given data whenever they rewrite a problem.

Problem 26b

Help students who name 90 as the answer recognize that the phrase, "In your answer to part a" means that they were to identify the middle value of the data (85) after the data were arranged from lowest to highest.

Looking Forward

Classifying quadrilaterals prepares students for:

- **Lesson 96,** classifying geometric solids by their vertices, edges, and faces.
- **Lesson 97,** making three-dimensional models of rectangular and triangular prisms.
- **Lesson 108,** identifying the attributes of geometric solids.
- **Lesson 109,** describing the attribute of pyramids.
- **Lesson 114,** determining the perimeter and area of complex figures.

Cumulative Assessments and Performance Task

Assessments

Distribute **Power-Up Test 17** and **Cumulative Test 17** to each student. Have students complete the **Power-Up Test** first. Allow 10 minutes. Then have students work on the **Cumulative Test.**

Performance Task

The remaining class time can be spent on **Performance Task 9.** Students can begin the task in class or complete it during another class period.

Flexible Grouping

Flexible grouping gives students an opportunity to work with other students in an interactive and encouraging way. The choice for how students are grouped depends on the goals for instruction, the needs of the students, and the specific learning activity.

Assigning Groups

Group members can be randomly assigned, or can be assigned based on some criteria such as grouping students who may need help with a certain skill or grouping students to play specific roles in a group (such as recorder or reporter).

Types of Groups

Students can be paired or placed in larger groups. For pairing, students can be assigned partners on a weekly or monthly basis. Pairing activities are the easiest to manage in a classroom and are more likely to be useful on a daily basis.

Flexible Grouping Ideas

Lesson 83, Example 2
Materials: paper

Divide students into groups of 4. Have students choose a partner from the group. Write two division problems with zeros in the answer on the board.

- Each student should choose one of the problems to answer.
- The student who did not choose the problem will interview the other by asking questions about how to solve the problem. (Example: Can you divide into the first digit?)
- After both students have interviewed each other and solved the problems, they must share their answers with the group and compare solutions.

Lesson 86, Example
Materials: paper

After guiding the students through the example, write three similar multiplication problems on the board. Divide the students into groups of 4.

- Have the groups work together to solve the first problem.
- Have the groups divide into pairs to solve the second problem.
- Direct students to work on the last problem independently and then check their solutions with the group.

Lesson 87, Example
Materials: paper

Have students form pairs to discuss solving word problems that involve division with remainders.

- Direct the students to look at the example without reading the answers below. Then instruct students to think about how to solve the problem.
- Then have students work in pairs to solve the problem. Have volunteers share their solutions with the class.

Planning & Preparation

• Analyzing Relationships

Objectives

- Given a horizontal or vertical line, name the coordinates of a point on the line.
- Subtract the x-coordinate and y-coordinate to determine the length of a line.
- Extend a table of values to show the relationship between two quantities.
- Write a set of ordered pairs for an equation such as $y = 3x + 2$.
- Graph an equation such as $y = 3x + 2$.

Prerequisite Skills

- Identifying lines and line segments.
- Naming points on a number line.
- Drawing number lines with a given scale.

Materials

Instructional Masters

- Lesson Activity 26

Teacher-provided materials

- Coordinate plane

California Mathematics Content Standards

AF 1.0, 1.3 Use parentheses to indicate which operation to perform first when writing expressions containing more than two terms and different operations.

AF 1.0, 1.4 Use and interpret formulas (e.g., area = length × width or $A = lw$) to answer questions about quantities and their relationships.

AF 1.0, 1.5 Understand that an equation such as $y = 3x + 5$ is a prescription for determining a second number when a first number is given.

MG 2.0, 2.1 Draw the points corresponding to linear relationships on graph paper (e.g., draw 10 points on the graph of the equation $y = 3x$ and connect them by using a straight line).

MG 2.0, 2.2 Understand that the length of a horizontal line segment equals the difference of the x–coordinates.

MG 2.0, 2.3 Understand that the length of a vertical line segment equals the difference of the y–coordinates.

MR 2.0, 2.2 Apply strategies and results from simpler problems to more complex problems.

MR 2.0, 2.6 Make precise calculations and check the validity of the results from the context of the problem.

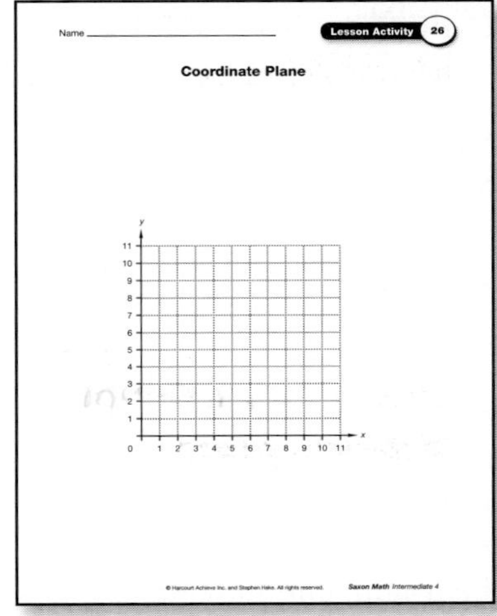

Lesson Activity 26

Reaching All Special Needs Students

Special Education Students	At-Risk Students	English Learners	Advanced Learners
• Inclusion (TM) • Adaptations for Saxon Math	• Reteaching Masters • Refresher Lessons for California Standards	• English Learners (TM) • Developing Academic Language (TM) • English Learner Handbook	• Extend the Problem (TM) • Investigate Further (SE) • Online Activities

TM=Teacher's Manual
SE=Student Edition

Developing Academic Language

New	Maintained	English Learner
endpoint	coordinates ordered pairs	axis

Analyzing Relationships

In this investigation, students will plot and locate points in Quadrant I of the coordinate plane, graph equations, and use the coordinates of endpoints to determine the lengths of horizontal and vertical line segments.

Materials:

- Each student will need 3 copies of **Lesson Activity Master 26** to complete the graphing activities in this investigation.

Discussion

Introduce the lesson by discussing the characteristics of the coordinate plane. Guide the discussion to include these concepts:

- The coordinate plane is created by the intersection of perpendicular number lines. The horizontal number line is called the *x*-axis, and the vertical number line is called the *y*-axis.
- The axes intersect at a point called the *origin*.
- An ordered pair of the form (x, y) consists of two coordinates and identifies the location a point in the plane. The *x*-coordinate of the ordered pair describes horizontal distance from the origin along the *x*-axis. The *y*-coordinate of the ordered pair describes vertical distance from the origin along the *y*-axis.
- The coordinates (0, 0) describe the location of the origin.
- Points are plotted or located by starting at the origin, and moving to the right, and then moving up. (This investigation is limited to the first quadrant of the coordinate plane; there are four quadrants altogether).

Instruction

Make sure students understand that we can find the length of horizontal line segment *PS* (without the assistance of numbers on the *x*- and *y*-axes) by subtracting the *x*-coordinates of the endpoints.

Lead students to generalize from the example art that to find the length of a horizontal line segment, we subtract the *x*-coordinates of the endpoints, and to find the length of a vertical line segment, we subtract the y-coordinates of the endpoints.

Use graphing software to graph a set of ordered pairs from an equation. Have students find the distance between two points on a vertical line or horizontal line.

(continued)

California Mathematics Content Standards

- **MG 2.0, 2.1** Draw the points corresponding to linear relationships on graph paper (e.g., draw 10 points on the graph of the equation $y = 3x$ and connect them by using a straight line).
- **MG 2.0, 2.2** Understand that the length of a horizontal line segment equals the difference of the *x*-coordinates.
- **MG 2.0, 2.3** Understand that the length of a vertical line segment equals the difference of the *y*-coordinates.
- **MR 2.0, 2.2** Apply strategies and results from simpler problems to more complex problems.

Focus on

Analyzing Relationships

In Investigation 7, we learned how to count segments or subtract coordinates to find the length of a side of a polygon that is drawn on a coordinate graph. In this investigation, we will subtract coordinates to find the length of a segment.

For segment *PS* below, we see that the coordinates of each *endpoint* are given. Because the coordinates are given, we can find the length of the segment without seeing the numbers on the *x*-axis and *y*-axis. Since segment *PS* is horizontal, the *y*-coordinates are always 6. So, we subtract the *x*-coordinates to find its length.

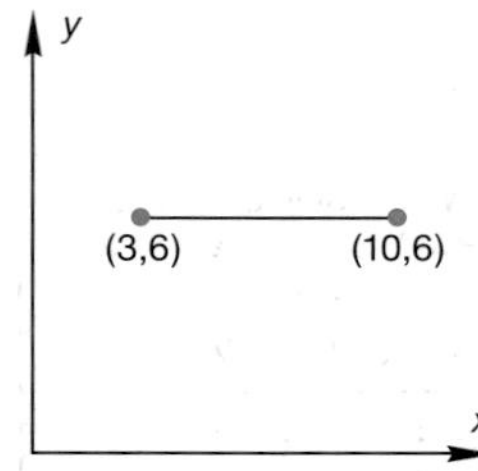

The *x*-coordinates of the endpoints are 10 and 3. Since $10 - 3 = 7$, the length of segment *PS* is 7 units.

1. **Explain** What is the length of segment *TR?* Explain your thinking.
9 units; Subtract the *y*-coordinates; $10 - 1 = 9$

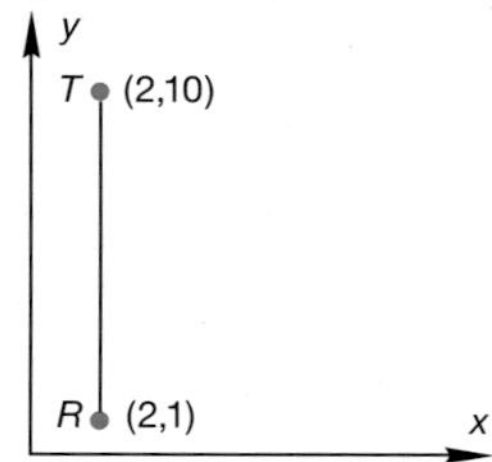

In Investigation 7 we also learned how to graph an equation such as $y = 2x + 1$. In the graph below, we can see that the line passes through the *y*-axis at 1. We can also see that the line $y = 2x + 2$ passes through the *y*-axis at 2.

Inclusion

Use this strategy if the student displays:

- Poor Retention.
- Slow Learning Rate.

Analyzing and Graphing Equations (Individual)

Materials: grid paper, ruler, string, scissors

- Have students draw points at (5, 8) and (1, 8). Tell place a piece of string on (1, 8) and extend it to (5, 8). Then cut the string the length of this distance. Have students measure the string in centimeters. Ask, ***"How many units long is the string?"*** 4 cm
- Write the points on the board and have students to subtract the x values (5 – 1) or (1 – 5). Remind students that a distance is never negative so they should remove a negative sign if they get one.
- Ask, ***"What is the difference in x values?"*** 4 Have students do the same with the y values and ask, ***"What is the difference in y values?"*** 0 Tell students to form a subtraction with these numbers 40 and ask, ***"What is the distance of the segment formed by these two points?"*** 4

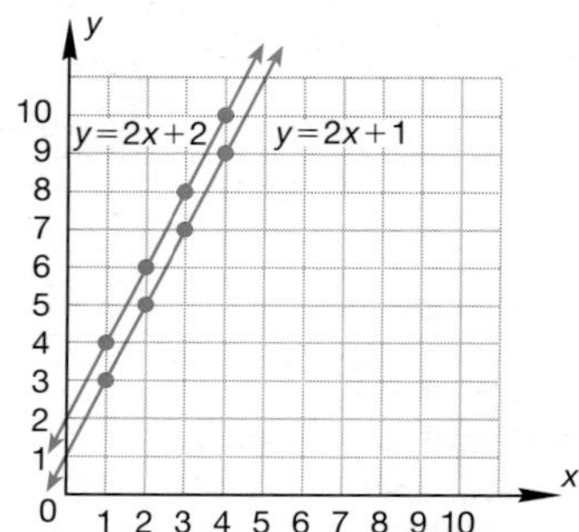

2. **Predict** Where will the line $y = 2x + 3$ cross the y-axis? 3 or (0, 3)

▸ 3. **Model** Write a set of ordered pairs for $y = 2x + 3$. Then use **Lesson Activity 26** to graph the line and check your prediction in problem **2.** For $x = 1$, 2, and 3, the ordered pairs are (1, 5), (2, 7), and (3, 9); See student work.

We have already studied how to make ordered pairs for a horizontal line such as $y = 5$. Another type of line we can make ordered pairs for is a vertical line. This line is the graph of $x = 5$.

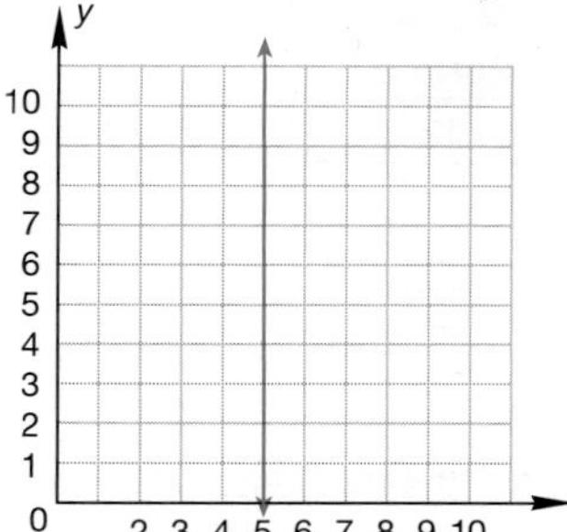

For every walue of y, the value of x will always be 5. We can make a list of ordered pairs for this line.

$x = (0 \cdot y) + 5$

x	y
5	1
5	2
5	3

The table tells us that the points (5,1), (5, 2), and (5, 3) are points on the line $x = 5$.

▸ 4. **Connect** Write the coordinates of another point that is on this line. Sample: (5, 4)

▸ 5. **Discuss** Do the coordinates (6, 3) represent a point on this line? Explain why or why not. No; sample: The x-coordinate of every point on the line is 5.

▸ 6. **Model** Draw the graph of $x = 7$. Name the coordinates of three points on the line. Sample: (7, 0), (7, 1), (7, 2); See student work.

We have been writing equations to show the relationship of two quantities. Graphs can also be used to display relationships of two quantities. Sample: The equations are different ways to represent the same line.

English Learners

An **axis** is a straight line around which a geometric figure, such as the earth, turns.

Explain that it also has other meanings, in mathematics, it is one of the lines of a coordinate grid that is used to measure distances.

Say:

"We can plot numbers on an x-axis and y-axis to solve problems about relationships."

Ask:

"What kind of information can you plot on an x- and y-coordinate system?" See student work.

Math Conversations

Independent Practice and Discussions to Increase Understanding

Problem 1 Explain

Some students may find it helpful if you write the coordinates of the endpoints as shown below.

(2, 10) (2, 1)
↑ ↑ ↑ ↑
x y x y

Connection

Write the equations of the lines $y = 2x + 1$ and $y = 2x + 2$ on the board or overhead, including two arrows, as shown below.

$y = 2x + 1$ ↑ $y = 2x + 2$ ↑

Help students make the connection that the last number in each equation identifies the point where the graph of the equation intersects the y-axis.

Problem 3 Model

Students should write at least three ordered pairs by substituting different values for x.

Active Learning

Remind students that after each substitution, two operations will be present in the equation. Then ask:

"What operations are present in the equation y = 2x + 3?" Multiplication and addition

"To simplify the equation and solve for y, which operation must we complete first? Explain why." Multiplication; The order of operations states that multiplication is completed before addition.

Instruction

Make sure students understand that the equation $x = 5$ is the same as $x = (0 \cdot y) + 5$ because the product of zero and any number is 0. So $x = 5$ is just a simpler way to write $x = (0 \cdot y) + 5$.

Problem 4 Connect

Extend the Problem

Challenge advanced learners to describe two different ways to name a point on the line. Sample: Place a point on the line and write the coordinates of the point; Substitute a number for y into the equation $x = (0 \cdot y) + 5$ and solve for x.

(continued)

Math Conversations *(cont.)*

Problem 5 Discuss

Extend the Problem

Challenge students to describe two different ways to decide if (6, 3) is a point on the line. Sample: Plot a point at (6, 3); substitute 6 for x and 3 for y into the equation $x = (0 \cdot y) + 5$, then simplify and decide if the equation is a true statement. (The statement is not true.)

Problem 6 Model

Have students use **Lesson Activity Master 26** to graph the equation.

To better understand that every point on the line has an x-coordinate of 7, students may find it helpful to substitute a variety of numbers for y into the equation $x = (0 \cdot y) + 7$.

Problem 7 Generalize

Make sure students can infer from the table that the number of cups is twice the number of pints.

Problem 8 Represent

To graph the relationship, students should assume that the pairs of numbers in the table represent the coordinates of points on the line, and label the x-axis as "pints" and the y-axis as "cups."

Problem 10

To help students identify a relationship, ask them to think about equivalent units of capacity, length, and weight in which one unit is twice as numerous as the other. To help them get started thinking in this way, point out that nickels and dimes is one such relationship—for an amount of money such as 50¢ (for example), the number of nickels is twice the number of dimes.

Extend the Problem

Ask advanced learners to find the total earnings Kanoni will make if she works on the garden for 6 hours, but does not receive the flat fee. Have them explain how they found their answer using an equation. $18; $y = 3x + 0$

▸ **7.** Generalize This table shows the relationship between pints and cups. Complete the table. Then write a formula that can be used for changing pints to cups. In your formula, use c for cups and p for pints.
$c = 2p$ or $2p = c$

Pints	1	2	3	4	5
Cups	2	4	6	8	10

▸ **8.** Represent Use **Lesson Activity 26** to graph the equation. See student work.

9. Discuss How is the graph you made similar to a graph of $y = 2x$?

▸ **10.** Name a relationship of two measures that can be graphed using an equation similar to $y = 2x$. Sample: quarts to pints ($y = 2x$); yards to feet ($y = 3x$); pounds to ounces ($y = 16x$)

a. Kanoni received a flat fee of $9 when she planted flowers, plus an additional $3 per hour for every hour she planted flowers. How much would she earn if it took her 5 hours to plant flowers?

Copy and extend the table to the right to find Kanoni's earnings.

Hours Worked	Money Earned
1	12
2	15
3	18
4	21
5	24

Use the table to make a graph showing the relationship between hours worked and money made. Write the equation that the graph represents. Sample: $y = 3x + 9$

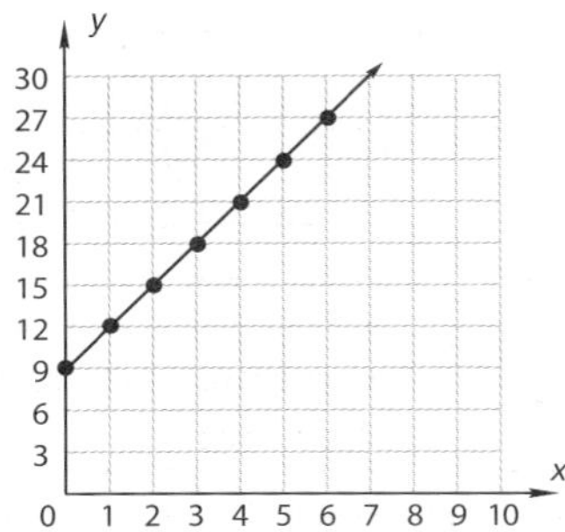

Looking Forward

Extending a table of values to show the relationship between two quantities, and graphing equations such as $y = 3x + 2$ prepares students for:

- **Lesson 92,** comparing and ordering fractions and decimals using a number line.
- **Investigation 10,** graphing equations such as $y = 3x + 2$.

Lesson Planner

Lesson	New Concepts	Materials	Resources
91	• Estimating Multiplication and Division Answers		• Power Up I Worksheet
92	• Comparing and Ordering Fractions and Decimals	• Manipulative Kit: rulers	• Power Up I Worksheet
93	• Two-Step Problems	• Manipulative Kit: rulers • Grid paper	• Power Up I Worksheet • Lesson Activity 8
94	• Two-Step Problems About a Fraction of a Group	• Manipulative Kit: rulers	• Power Up H Worksheet
95	• Describing Data	• Manipulative Kit: rulers	• Power Up H Worksheet
Cumulative Assessment			• Cumulative Test 18 • Test-Day Activity 9
96	• Geometric Solids		• Power Up H Worksheet • Lesson Activity 27
97	• Constructing Prisms	• Manipulative Kit: Relational GeoSolids • Scissors, tape, glue, grid paper	• Power Up H Worksheet • Lesson Activities 28–30 • Lesson Activity 21
98	• Fractions Equal to 1 and Fractions Equal to $\frac{1}{2}$	• Fraction manipulatives from Investigation 8	• Power Up H Worksheet
99	• Changing Improper Fractions to Whole Numbers or Mixed Numbers	• Manipulative Kit: rulers • Fraction manipulatives from Investigation 8	• Power Up J Worksheet
100	• Adding and Subtracting Fractions with Common Denominators		• Power Up J Worksheet
Cumulative Assessment			• Cumulative Test 19 • Performance Task 10
Inv. 10	• Graphing Relationships	• Grid paper	• Lesson Activity 8

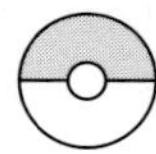
All resources are also available on the Resources and Planner CD.

Additional Resources

- Instructional Masters
- Reteaching Masters
- Refresher Lessons for California Standards
- Calculator Activities
- Resources and Planner CD
- Assessment Guide
- Performance Tasks
- Instructional Transparencies
- Answer Key CD
- Power Up Workbook
- Written Practice Workbook

Math Highlights

Enduring Understandings — The "Big Picture"

After completing Section 10, students will understand that:

- Median, range, and mode are all used to describe data.
- There are many ways to write a fraction equal to one.
- Fractions with common denominators can be added and subtracted.
- Three dimensional prisms are constructed from nets.

Essential Questions

- How are the median and range for data different?
- In a fraction equal to one, what is true about the numerator and denominator?
- What is a common denominator?
- What is a prism net?

Math Content Highlights	Math Processes Highlights
Number Sense • Estimating Multiplication and Division Answers *Lesson 91* • Compare and Order Fractions and Decimals *Lesson 92* • Fractions Equal to 1 and to $\frac{1}{2}$ *Lesson 98* • Changing Improper Fractions to Whole Numbers or Mixed Numbers *Lesson 99* • Adding and Subtracting Fractions *Lesson 100* **Algebraic Thinking** • Two-Step Problems *Lesson 93* • Two-Step Problems About Fractions of a Group *Lesson 94* **Geometry and Measurement** • Geometric Solids *Lesson 96* • Constructing Prisms *Lesson 97* • Graphing Relationships *Investigation 10* **Data Analysis, Statistics, and Probability** • Describing Data *Lesson 95*	**Problem Solving** • Strategies – Draw a Picture or Diagram *Lessons 91, 96, 98* – Find or Extend a Pattern *Lessons 92, 94* – Make an Organized List *Lessons 96, 98* – Make It Simpler *Lessons 97, 99, 100* – Use Logical Reasoning *Lessons 93, 97* – Work Backwards *Lesson 99* – Write a Number Sentence or Equation *Lesson 95* • Real-World Applications *Lessons 91, 95, 98, 100* **Communication** • Discuss *Lessons 91, 92, 93, 94, 95, 97, 99, 100* • Explain *Lessons 91, 92, 93, 94, 95, 96, 97, 99, 100, Investigation 10* • Formulate *Lesson 96* **Connections** • Math to Math – Algebra and Statistics *Lesson 95, Investigation 10* – Fractions and Problem Solving *Lessons 93, 94, 98, 99, 100* – Measurement and Geometry *Lessons 96, 97* • Math and Other Subjects – Math and History *Lessons 93, 99* – Math and Geography *Lessons 94, 95* – Math and Science *Lessons 94, 100* – Math and Sports *Lessons 91, 92, 93, 96, 100* **Representation** • Model *Lessons 97, 98, 99, Investigation 10* • Represent *Lessons 91, 92, 93, 94, 95, 96, 97, 98, 99, 100, Investigation 10* • Formulate an Equation *Investigation 10* • Using Manipulative/Hands On *Lessons 91, 92, 93, 94, 95, 96, 97, 98, 99, 100*

Universal Access

Support for universal access is included with each lesson. Specific resources and features are listed on each lesson planning page. Features in the Teacher's Manual to customize instruction include the following:

Teacher's Manual Support

Alternative Approach	Provides a different path to concept development. *Lessons 92, 94–98, 100*
Manipulative Use	Provides alternate concept development through the use of manipulatives. *Lessons 91–100*
Flexible Grouping	Provides suggestions for various grouping strategies tied to specific lesson examples. *TM page 665A*
Inclusion	Provides ideas for including all students by accommodating special needs. *Lessons 91–100, Inv. 10*
Developing Academic Language	Provides a list of new and maintained vocabulary words along with words that might be difficult for English learners. *Lessons 91–100, Inv. 10*
English Learners	Provides strategies for teaching specific vocabulary that may be difficult for English learners. *Lessons 91–100, Inv. 10*
Errors and Misconceptions	Provides information about common misconceptions students encounter with concepts. *Lessons 91–100*
Extend the Example	Provides additional concept development for advanced learners. *Lessons 91–96, 98, 100*
Extend the Problem	Provides an opportunity for advanced learners to broaden concept development by expanding on a particular problem approach or context. *Lessons 91–100, Inv. 10*
Early Finishers	Provides additional math concept extensions for advanced learners at the end of the Written Practice. *Lesson 91*
Investigate Further	Provides further depth to concept development by providing additional activities for an investigation. *Investigation 10*

Additional Resources

The following resources are also available to support universal access:

- Adaptations for Saxon Math
- English Learner Handbook
- Online Activities
- Performance Tasks
- Refresher Lessons for CA Standards
- Reteaching Masters

Technology

Student Resources

- Student Edition eBook
- Calculator Activities
- Online Resources at **www.SaxonMath.com/Int4ActivitiesCA**

Teacher Resources

- Resources and Planner CD
- Test and Practice Generator CD
- Monitoring Student Progress: eGradebook CD
- Teacher's Manual eBook CD
- Answer Key CD
- Adaptations for Saxon Math CD
- Online Resources at **www.SaxonMath.com**

Cumulative Assessment

The assessments in Saxon Math are frequent and consistently placed to offer a regular method of ongoing testing.

Power-Up Test: Allow no more than ten minutes for this test of basic facts and skills.

Cumulative Test: Next, administer this test, which checks mastery of concepts in previous lessons.

Test-Day Activity and Performance Task: The remaining class time can be spent on these activities. Students can finish the Test-Day Activity for homework. Advanced learners can complete the extended Performance Task in another class period.

After Lesson 95

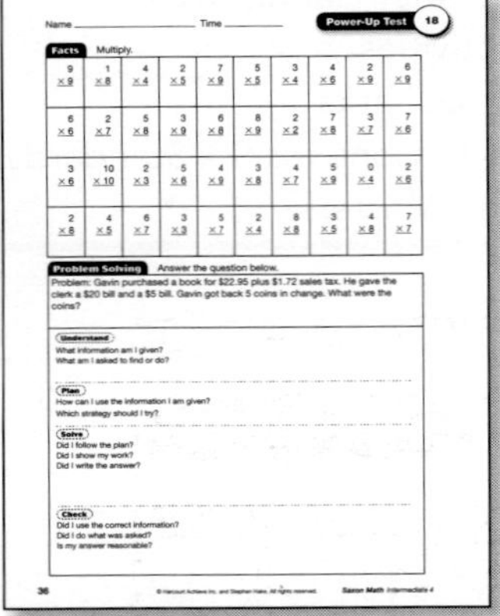

Power-Up Test 18

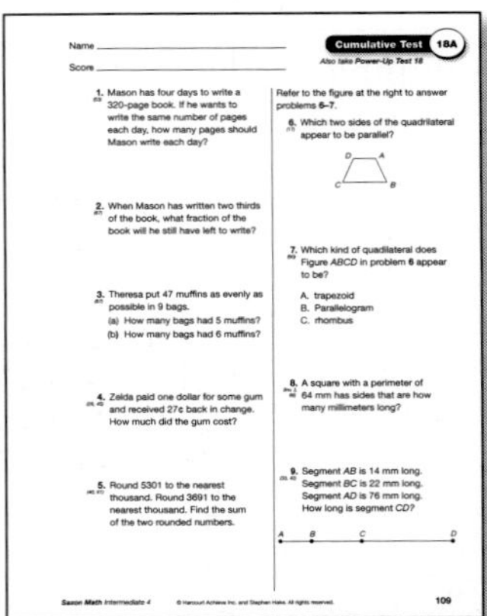

Cumulative Test 18

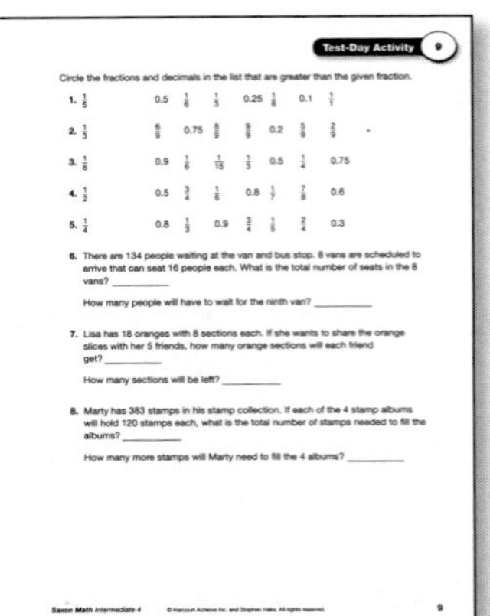

Test-Day Activity 9

After Lesson 100

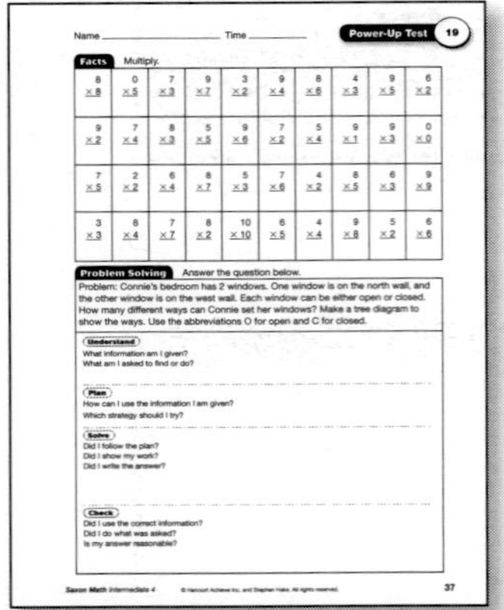

Power-Up Test 19

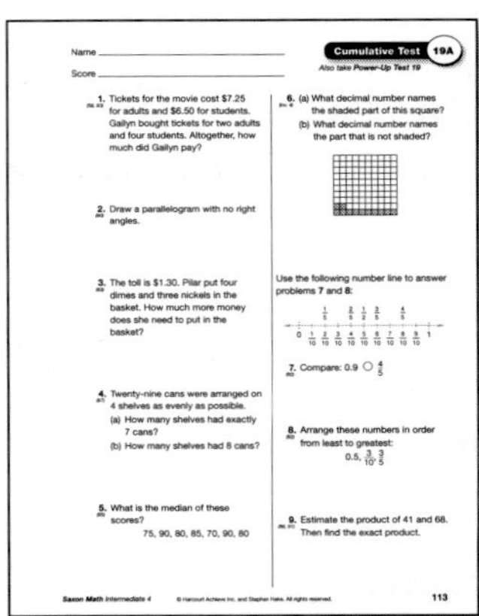

Cumulative Test 19

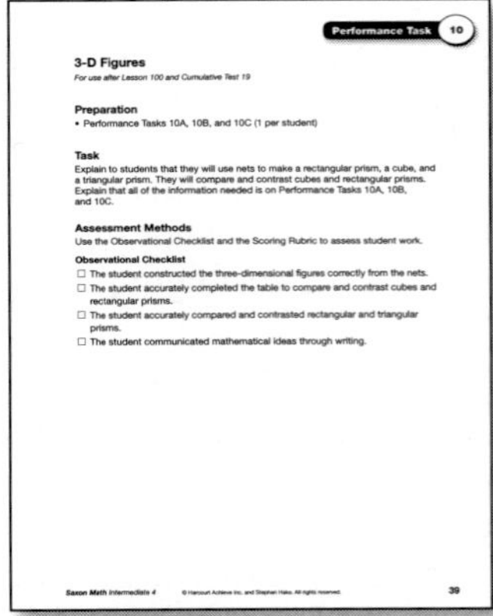

Performance Task 10

Evidence of Learning — What Students Should Know

By the conclusion of Section 10, students should be able to demonstrate the following competencies through the Cumulative Assessments, which are correlated to the California Mathematics Standards:

- Calculate the range, median, and mode for a set of numbers. **SDAP 1.2, MR 2.3**
- Compare and order fractions and decimals. **NS 1.6, NS 1.7, NS 1.9, MR 2.3**

Reteaching

Students who score below 80% on assessments may be in need of reteaching. Refer to the Reteaching Masters for reteaching opportunities for every lesson.

Benchmarking and Tracking the California Mathematics Standards

Benchmark Tests

Benchmark Tests correlated to lesson concepts allow you to assess student progress after every 20 lessons. An End-of-Course Test is a final benchmark test of the complete textbook. The Benchmark Tests are available in the Assessment Guide.

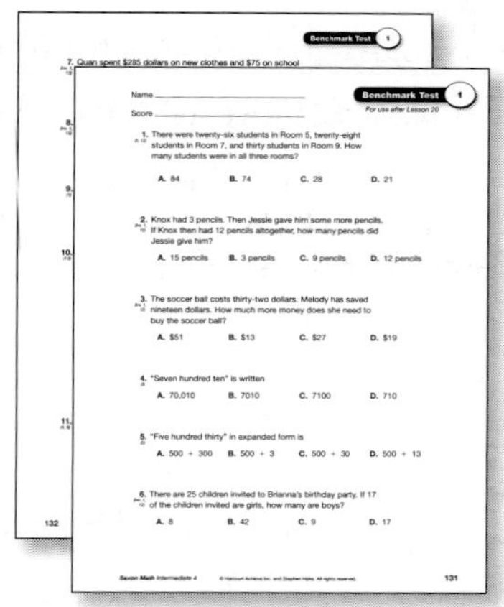

Monitoring Student Progress: eGradebook CD

To track California Standards mastery, enter students' scores on Cumulative Tests and Benchmark Tests into the Monitoring Student Progress: eGradebook CD. Use the report titled *Benchmark Standards Report* to determine which California Standards were assessed and the level of mastery for each student. Generate a variety of other reports for class tracking and more.

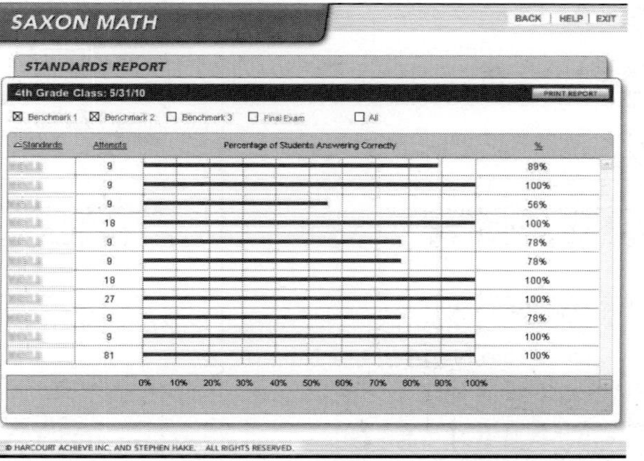

Test and Practice Generator CD

Test items also available in Spanish.

The Test and Practice Generator is an easy-to-manage benchmarking and assessment tool that creates unlimited practice and tests in multiple formats and allows you to customize questions or create new ones. A variety of reports are available to track student progress toward mastery of the California Standards throughout the year.

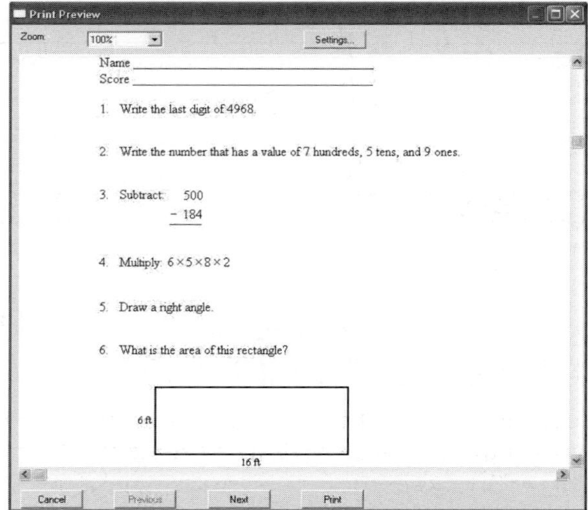

Content Trace

Lesson	New Concepts	Practiced	Assessed	Looking Forward
91	• Estimating Multiplication and Division Answers	Lessons 91, 92, 93, 94, 95, 97, 100, 101, 107, 108, 113	Tests 19, 20	Lessons 92, 102, 104, 105, 107
92	• Comparing and Ordering Fractions and Decimals	Lessons 92, 93, 94, 95, 97, 100	Test 19	Lessons 94, 98, 99, 100, 103, 106, 111, 112, 113
93	• Two-Step Problems	Lessons 93, 94, 95, 96, 97, 98, 99, 100, 102, 103, 104, 105, 106, 107, 108, 109, 110, 112, 114	Tests 19, 20, 21	Lessons 94, 95
94	• Two-Step Problems About a Fraction of a Group	Lessons 94, 95, 96, 97, 98, 99, 100, 101, 102, 103, 104, 105, 106, 109, 110, 111, 113, 114	Tests 19, 20, 21	Lessons 98, 99, 100, 103, 106, 111, 112, 113
95	• Describing Data	Lessons 95, 96, 97, 98, 99, 100, 103, 105, 112	Tests 19, 20	Investigation 10
96	• Geometric Solids	Lessons 96, 97, 98, 99, 100, 103, 105, 106, 108, 111, 112, 114	Test 20	Lessons 97, 108, 109, 114
97	• Constructing Prisms	Lessons 97, 98, 99, 100, 101, 106	Benchmark Test 5	Lessons 108, 109, 114
98	• Fractions Equal to 1 and Fractions Equal to $\frac{1}{2}$	Lessons 98, 99, 100, 101, 102, 103, 105, 108, 109, 110, 111, 113, 114	Tests 20, 21	Lessons 99, 100, 103, 106, 111, 112, 113
99	• Changing Improper Fractions to Whole Numbers or Mixed Numbers	Lessons 99, 100, 101, 102, 103, 104, 106	Tests 20, 22	Lessons 100, 106, 111, 112, 113
100	• Adding and Subtracting Fractions with Common Denominators	Lessons 100, 101, 102, 103, 104, 105, 106, 107, 108, 109, 110, 111, 113, 114	Test 21	Lessons 106, 111, 112, 113
Inv. 10	• Graphing Relationships	Lessons 102, 103, 104, 108, 111	Test 20	***Saxon Math*** *Intermediate 5*

Planning & Preparation

• Estimating Multiplication and Division Answers

California Mathematics Content Standards

NS 1.0, 1.3 Round whole numbers through the millions to the nearest ten, hundred, thousand, ten thousand, or hundred thousand.

NS 3.0, 3.4 Solve problems involving division of multidigit numbers by one-digit numbers.

MR 2.0, 2.1 Use estimation to verify the reasonableness of calculated results.

MR 2.0, 2.6 Make precise calculations and check the validity of the results from the context of the problem.

Objectives

- Estimate the answers to multiplication and division problems.
- Solve word problems involving multi-digit multiplication and division.

Prerequisite Skills

- Rounding numbers to the nearest ten and hundred using a number line.
- Estimating solutions to multiplication word problems using rounding.
- Using a number line to round numbers to the nearest thousand.
- Using compatible numbers to estimate a quotient.

Materials

Instructional Masters

- Power Up I Worksheet

Manipulative Kit

- Fraction circles, money manipulatives*

**optional*

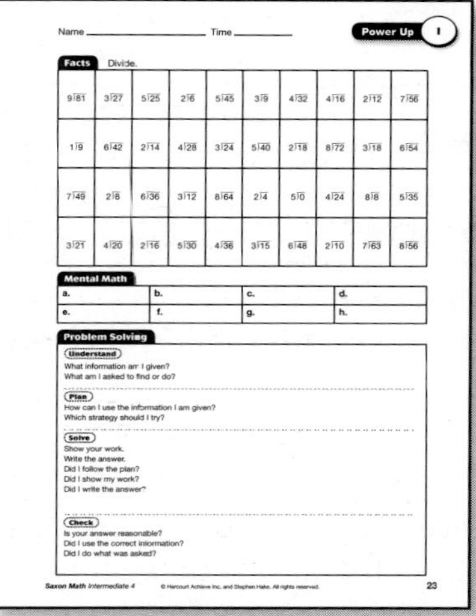

Power Up I Worksheet

Universal Access

Reaching All Special Needs Students

Special Education Students	At-Risk Students	English Learners	Advanced Learners
• Inclusion (TM) • Adaptations for Saxon Math	• Error Alert (TM) • Reteaching Masters • Refresher Lessons for California Standards	• English Learners (TM) • Developing Academic Language (TM) • English Learner Handbook	• Extend the Example (TM) • Extend the Problem (TM) • Early Finisher (SE) • Online Activities

TM=Teacher's Manual
SE=Student Edition

Developing Academic Language

Maintained	English Learner
estimate	ferry
multiply	
product	
quotient	

Problem Solving Discussion

Problem

There were two gallons of punch for the class party. The punch was served in 8-ounce cups. Two gallons of punch was enough to fill how many cups? (Remember that 16 ounces is a pint, two pints is a quart, two quarts is a half gallon, and two half gallons is a gallon.)

Focus Strategy  **Draw a Picture or Diagram**

Understand ***Understand the problem.***

"What information are we given?"

Two gallons of punch was served in 8-ounce cups. We are given a list of equivalent measures that relate ounces, pints, quarts, half gallons, and gallons.

"What are we asked to do?"

We are asked to find how many 8-ounce cups can be filled with 2 gallons of punch.

Plan ***Make a plan.***

"How can we use the information we know to solve the problem?"

We need to find how many 8-ounce cups are in one gallon. Then we can double that number to find how many cups of punch could be filled.

"What diagram can we use to help us see the relationships among cups, pints, quarts, and gallons?"

We can use this diagram (also used in Lesson 64 Problem Solving) to remind us that there are 2 cups in each pint, 2 pints in each quart, and 4 quarts in a gallon:

Solve ***Carry out the plan.***

"In the problem, we are told that 16 ounces equals a pint. How many ounces are in 1 cup?"

One cup is half of a pint. Half of 16 ounces is 8 ounces, so 1 cup equals 8 ounces, which is the capacity of the punch cups.

"How many 8-ounce cups equal 2 gallons?"

In our diagram, we count 16 cups in 1 gallon. This means that 2 gallons is 2×16 cups, or 32 cups. We find that 2 gallons of punch was enough to fill 32 cups.

Check ***Look back.***

"Is our answer reasonable?"

We know that our answer is reasonable, because each pint of punch is enough to fill two 8-ounce cups. There are 8 pints in 1 gallon. So 1 gallon can fill 16 cups, and 2 gallons can fill double that amount, which is 32 cups.

Alternate Strategy
Write a Number Sentence

Students can write number sentences to solve this problem. They can use a pattern of doubling to find the number of cups in each successively larger measurement:

1 pint = 2 cups
1 quart = 2×2 cups = 4 cups
1 half gallon = 2 quarts = 2×4 cups = 8 cups
1 gallon = 2 half gallons = 2×8 cups = 16 cups
2 gallons = 2×16 cups = 32 cups

LESSON

91

• Estimating Multiplication and Division Answers

California Mathematics Content Standards

NS 1.0, 1.3 Round whole numbers through the millions to the nearest ten, hundred, thousand, ten thousand, or hundred thousand.

NS 3.0, 3.4 Solve problems involving division of multidigit numbers by one-digit numbers.

MR 2.0, 2.1 Use estimation to verify the reasonableness of calculated results.

MR 2.0, 2.6 Make precise calculations and check the validity of the results from the context of the problem.

facts Power Up I

mental math Find half of each number in problems **a–d.**

a. Number Sense: 24 12

b. Number Sense: 50 25

c. Number Sense: 46 23

d. Number Sense: 120 60

e. Money: The apples cost $3.67. Lindsay paid for them with a $5 bill. How much change should she receive? $1.33

f. Estimation: About how many feet is 298 yards? (*Hint:* Round the number of yards to the nearest hundred yards before mentally calculating.) 900 ft

g. Calculation: 6×7, $-\ 2$, $+\ 30$, $+\ 5$, $\div\ 3$ 25

h. Simplify: $4 - 2 \div 2$ 3

problem solving Choose an appropriate problem-solving strategy to solve this problem. There were two gallons of punch for the class party. The punch was served in 8-ounce cups. Two gallons of punch was enough to fill how many cups? (Remember that 16 ounces is a pint, two pints is a quart, two quarts is a half gallon, and two half gallons is a gallon.) 32 cups

Facts Divide.

9 9)81	9 3)27	5 5)25	3 2)6	9 5)45	3 3)9	8 4)32	4 4)16	6 2)12	8 7)56
9 1)9	7 6)42	7 2)14	7 4)28	8 3)24	8 5)40	9 2)18	9 8)72	6 3)18	9 6)54
7 7)49	4 2)8	6 6)36	4 3)12	8 8)64	2 2)4	0 5)0	6 4)24	1 8)8	7 5)35
7 3)21	5 4)20	8 2)16	6 5)30	9 4)36	5 3)15	8 6)48	5 2)10	9 7)63	7 8)56

Facts

Distribute **Power Up I** to students. See answers below.

Count Aloud

Before students begin the Mental Math exercises, do these counting exercises as a class.

Count up and down by twos from 14 to 63.

Mental Math

Encourage students to share different ways to mentally compute these exercises. Strategies for exercises are listed below.

a. Use a Multiplication Fact

Since $12 \times 2 = 24$, $\frac{1}{2}$ of $24 = 12$.

Use Repeated Addition

Since $12 + 12 = 24$, $\frac{1}{2}$ of $24 = 12$.

d. Use a Division Pattern

Since $12 \div 2 = 6$, $120 \div 2 = 60$.

Use Repeated Addition

Since $60 + 60 = 120$, $\frac{1}{2}$ of $120 = 60$.

Problem Solving

Refer to **Problem-Solving Strategy Discussion,** p. 603H.

New Concept

Instruction

Remind students of the importance of always taking time to check their work. In this lesson, they will learn how rounding and compatible numbers can be used to check products and quotients.

Example 1

Error Alert

Multiplying 43 × 29 and not shifting the second partial product is likely to result in an incorrect product of 203, as shown below.

$$\begin{array}{r} 29 \\ \times\ 43 \\ \hline 87 \\ +\ 116 \\ \hline 203 \end{array}$$

Lead students to conclude that an estimate would alert them to this error (and to a variety of other errors as well).

Point out that being able to estimate a multiplication or division answer is also helpful when a calculator is used to find a product or quotient. A common calculator error is to input numbers incorrectly without realizing it. When we do the math on paper, we can find our mistakes but we cannot do this on a calculator.

Example 2

Active Learning

The solution describes rounding 42 to 40 and 53 to 50, and does not show the arithmetic of finding the product (2000) because it is assumed that the product will be found using mental math. Point out that 40 and 50 are both multiples of 10, then say:

"Explain how we can find the product of two factors that are multiples of 10 using only mental math." Write the number of zeros in the factors to the right of the product of the nonzero digits.

"The factors 40 and 50 are multiples of 10. Explain how to find the product of the factors using only mental math." Since there are two zeros in the factors, we write two zeros to the right of the product of the nonzero digits; 4 × 5 = 20 and 40 × 50 = 2000

Example 3

Extend the Example

Challenge advanced learners to estimate the number of chairs each truck will carry if the company sent 9 trucks. Each truck will carry about 200 chairs.

(continued)

New Concept

Estimation can help prevent mistakes. If we estimate the answer, we can tell whether our answer is reasonable.

Example 1

Luke multiplied 43 by 29 and got 203. Is Luke's answer reasonable?

We estimate the product of 43 and 29 by multiplying the rounded numbers 40 and 30.

$$40 \times 30 = 1200$$

Luke's answer of 203 and our estimate of 1200 are very different, so Luke's answer is **not reasonable.** He should check his work.

Discuss What is the exact product? Is the exact product close to 1200? 43 × 29 = 1247; Yes, 1247 is close to 1200.

Example 2

An auditorium has 42 rows of seats. There are 53 seats in each row. The sales department sold 2000 tickets. Will all the people with a ticket have a seat or will they need to bring in extra chairs?

Since we do not need an exact answer, we can estimate the product by rounding each number to the nearest ten and then multiplying.

42 rounds to 40
53 rounds to 50

Now we can multiply. 40 × 50 = 2000

There are about 2000 seats in the auditorium. **All the people with tickets will have a seat.**

Discuss How can we decide if the estimate is reasonable?

Sample: Since both numbers were rounded down, the estimate is lower than the actual number of seats. So, there are more seats than tickets sold.

Inclusion

Use this strategy if the student displays:

- Slow Learning Rate.
- Difficulty with Abstract Processing.

Estimating Multiplication and Division Answers (Small Group)

Material: money manipulatives

- Read, ***"Thomas wanted to buy bubble gum at the grocery store. Each piece was 13¢. Estimate how much it would cost if he bought 27 pieces."***
- Tell students to write the multiplication problem on their paper. Then ask, ***"What is 13¢ estimated?"*** 10¢ ***"What is 27 estimated?"*** 30

  Have students use their money to make 27 groups of dimes. Then ask, ***"About how much money will Thomas owe?"*** $3
- Write on the board and have partners work together on the following: **"Susan multiplied 34 × 38 and got 1592. Is Susan's answer reasonable?"**
- Have students estimate the original problem and determine if the estimated answer is close enough to Susan's answer.

Example 3

Thinking Skills

Estimate

How would you estimate the quotient of 184 ÷ 6?

Sample: 180 ÷ 6 = 30

One company sent 6 trucks with a delivery of 1845 chairs for a new hotel. Estimate the number of chairs each truck will carry.

We choose a number close to 1845 that is easily divided by 6. We know that 18 is a multiple of 6, so 1800 is a compatible dividend. We can calculate mentally: "18 hundred divided by 6 is 3 hundred."

$$1800 \div 6 = 300$$

Each truck will carry about **300 chairs.**

Lesson Practice

Estimate each product or quotient. Then find the exact answer.

a. 58 × 23 1200; 1334 **b.** 49 × 51 2500; 2499 **c.** 61 × 38 2400; 2318 **d.** 1845 ÷ 9 200; 205

e. **Estimate** A ferry can carry 843 people. About how many people can the ferry carry on a round trip? About 1600 people; 800 × 2 = 1600 people

Written Practice

Distributed and Integrated

*1. (Inv. 5) **Interpret** Use the information in this circle graph to answer parts **a–d**.

Activities of 100 Children at the Park

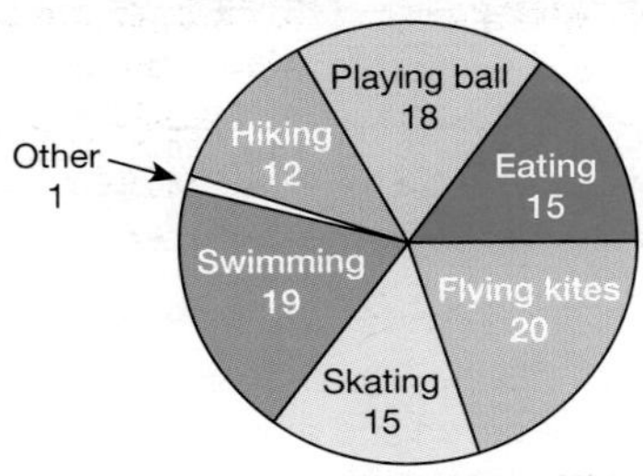

▸ **a.** Altogether, how many children were at the park? 100 children

b. How many children were not swimming? 81 children

c. How many children were either hiking or skating? 27 children

d. How many more children were flying kites than were swimming? 1 more child

*2. (56) **Justify** Name a prime number that is a factor of 115. Explain how you know it is prime. 5 or 23; They have only themselves and 1 as factors.

English Learners

Explain that a **ferry** is a boat used to carry people across a river or other body of water.

Ask, ***"Who do you think would be more likely to take a ferry to work: people in California, or in New Mexico?"*** People in California

Have students discuss ferries and other types of boats they have seen or ridden on.

Math Background

We can estimate a product of two two-digit numbers by rounding both factors to the nearest 10. Another strategy involves finding a range into which the product must fall. To do this, find the lower bound by rounding both factors down, and find the upper bound by rounding both factors up. The actual product must fall between the bounds. Consider the product of 43 × 29:

Upper bound: 50 × 30 = 1500

Lower bound: 40 × 20 = 800

The product is between 800 and 1500.

New Concept *(Continued)*

Lesson Practice

Guided Practice

Use these problems as guided practice to check the students' understanding of today's concept.

Problems a–d **Estimate**

The rounded numbers that were used to produce the estimates are shown below:

a. 60 × 20
b. 50 × 50
c. 60 × 40
d. 1800 ÷ 9

Problem d
Error Alert

If students choose to round to the nearest ten and round 1845 to 1850, they will find that 9 will not divide 1850 evenly (1850 ÷ 9 = 205 R 5). Remind students that whenever possible, an estimate is to be completed using only mental math.

Closure

The questions below help assess the concepts taught in this lesson.

"Why is it important to make an estimate of what an exact answer will be?" Sample: The estimate is used to help decide if the exact answer is reasonable.

"What should we do if we find that an estimate is very different from an exact answer?" Sample: Look for an error in the computation that produced the exact answer or the estimate.

"Explain how to make a reasonable estimate of the product of 18 × 71." Sample: Round 18 to 20 and round 71 to 70; A reasonable estimate is 20 × 70, or 1400.

Written Practice

Math Conversations

Independent Practice and Discussions to Increase Understanding

Problem 1a **Interpret**

Make sure students recognize that the answer can be found in the title of the graph.

(continued)

Written Practice *(Continued)*

Math Conversations *(cont.)*

Problem 3a **Analyze**

"To simplify this expression, we must perform the operation inside parentheses first, which is subtraction. After we subtract, which operation will we perform next? Explain why." Divide; sample: After we subtract, two operations—addition and division—will be present, and the order of operations states that we must divide before we add.

Problem 5

Encourage students to complete the estimate using only mental math. Because 40 and 400 are multiples of 10, the product of 40×400 can be found by attaching three zeros to the product of 4×4; $40 \times 400 = 16{,}000$

Problem 7

Manipulative Use

Students may use fraction pieces to help solve the problem or to check their answer.

Problem 12 **Conclude**

Extend the Problem

If students conclude that a statement is false, ask them to include an explanation or sketch to support the conclusion.

(continued)

MDAS

*3. (63) **Analyze** Simplify each expression. Remember to use the order of operations.

a. $4 + (15 - 5) \div 2$ 9 4+5 4 + 10 ÷ 2 5

b. $(36 \div 3) - (2 \times 4)$ 4

4. (Inv. 4) Write each mixed number as a decimal:

a. $3\frac{5}{10}$ 3.5

b. $14\frac{21}{100}$ 14.21

c. $9\frac{4}{100}$ 9.04

*5. (91) Estimate the product of 39 and 406. Then find the exact product. 16,000; 15,834

*6. (64) If $y = 4x - 2$, what is y when x is 4? 14

*7. (57) Write these fractions in order from least to greatest: $\frac{1}{2}, \frac{5}{8}, \frac{3}{4}$

$\frac{3}{4}$ $\frac{1}{2}$ $\frac{5}{8}$

8. (27) Compare: 2 thousand (<) 24 hundreds

Refer to the rectangle below to answer problems **9** and **10.**

30 mm

10 mm

9. (20, 42) What is the perimeter of the rectangle

a. in millimeters? 80 mm

b. in centimeters? 8 cm

10. (42, 66) What is the area of the rectangle

a. in square millimeters? 300 mm^2

b. in square centimeters? 3 cm^2

11. (13) Santos figured the trip would take seven and a half hours. He left at 7 a.m. At what time does he think he will arrive? 2:30 p.m.

*12. (70, 81, 90) **Conclude** Write *true* or *false* for parts **a–e.**

a. All squares are rectangles. true

b. All trapezoids are quadrilaterals. true

c. All equilateral triangles are congruent. false

d. All triangles have at least one right angle. false

e. All squares are similar. true

Teacher Tip

Keep a supply of graph paper available for students to use in solving multi-digit multiplication and division problems. Encourage students to write each digit in a single "box."

13. (71) 25×40 1000

14. (28, 38) 98¢ × 7 $6.86

15. (Inv. 3) $\sqrt{36} \times \sqrt{4}$ 12

16. (65) $\frac{3^3}{3}$ 9

17. (88) 36×34 1224

▶ **18.** (88) 35×35 1225

19. (4) 4 + 2 + 1 + 3 + 4 + 7 + 2 + 2 + 3 + 4 + x = 42 10

20. (34, 79) $8m = \$70.00$ $8.75

21. (83) $6\overline{)1234}$ 205 R 4

22. (79) $800 \div 7$ 114 R 2

23. (79) $487 \div 3$ 162 R 1

24. (28) $2.74 + $0.27 + $6 + 49¢ $9.50

25. (9, 45) $9.48 - (3.7 + 2.36)$ 3.42

▶***26.** (89) **Represent** Draw and shade circles to show that $2\frac{1}{3}$ equals $\frac{7}{3}$.

***27.** (Inv. 6) **Analyze** Listed below are the number of points Amon scored in his last nine basketball games, which range from 6 to 10. Refer to these scores to answer parts **a–c.**

8, 7, 7, 8, 6, 10, 9, 10, 7

a. What is the mode of the scores? 7

b. What is the median of the scores? 8

c. Are there any outliers? No

28. (17) Each school day, Brent's second class begins at 9:00 a.m. What kind of angle is formed by the minute hand and the hour hand of a clock at that time? right angle

***29.** (87) **Explain** Thirty-one students are entering a classroom. The desks in the classroom are arranged in rows with 7 desks in each row. If the students fill the first row of desks, then fill the second row of desks, and so on, how many full rows of students will there be? How many students will sit in a row that is not full? Explain your answer. 4 rows; 3 students; sample: The quotient of $31 \div 7$ is 4 R 3; 4 represents the number of full rows, and the remainder 3 represents the number of students in an incomplete row.

Written Practice *(Continued)*

Math Conversations *(cont.)*

Problem 18

Extend the Problem

"Explain how to make a reasonable estimate of the product." See student work.

Watch for an opportunity to explain that because both factors are halfway between the nearest multiples of 10, rounding one factor up and rounding one factor down will produce a very good estimate: $40 \times 30 = 1200$, and the exact product of 35×35 is 1225

You may have the students use a calculator to check their answers.

Problem 26 **Represent**

When dividing a circle into thirds, some students may find it helpful to think of the numbers on the face of a clock. Encourage these students to draw a circle, label a point at the center of the circle, and then to draw radii from that point to 4 o'clock, to 8 o'clock, and to 12 o'clock.

(continued)

Written Practice *(Continued)*

Math Conversations *(cont.)*

Problem 30 Conclude

Some students may find it helpful if you remind them that all points on the coordinate plane are ordered pairs of the form (x, y), and we can subtract coordinates to find the lengths of horizontal or vertical line segments.

Errors and Misconceptions

Problem 2

If students use a *guess and check* strategy to identify a prime factor of 115, explain that divisibility rules offer an organized alternative. Point out, for example, that 115

- is not divisible by 2 because it is not an even number.
- is not divisible by 3 because the sum of its digits is not divisible by 3.
- is not divisible by 4 because multiples of 4 are even numbers.
- is divisible by 5 because the digit in the ones place is 5.

Problem 27a

Explain to those students who answer 8 or 10 that although 7, 8, and 10 occur more than once, 7 occurs more often than either 8 or 10.

Remind all of your students that a set of numbers will not have a mode if all of the numbers in the set appear the same number of times. Also remind them that a set of numbers may have more than one mode. For example, if the given scores in problem **27** included an additional 10, for a total of three 10's altogether, then there would be two modes, 7 and 10.

Problem 27b

The students who name 6 as the median did not rewrite the scores from least to greatest or from greatest to least. Remind these students that data must be ordered before the median of the data can be determined.

Students may use either division or multiplication concepts to solve the salad problem. They may use a combination. Ask students to explain which operation(s) they used to solve the problem and why.

▸* **30.** (Inv. 9) Conclude What is the length of this segment? Explain your reasoning.
5 units; Since it is a horizontal segment, we subtract the x-coordinates, $6 - 1 = 5$.

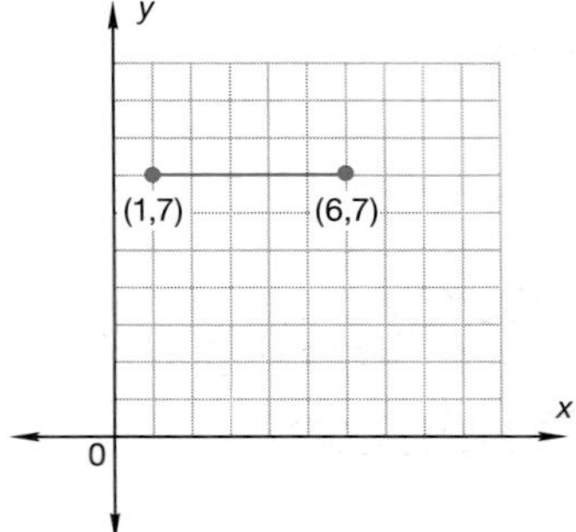

Real-World Connection

Mrs. Collins has to make some salads for 4 friends and herself. She has two salad recipes to choose from—one for a *garden salad* and one for a *spinach salad*. She has the following ingredients to work with: 24 tomatoes, 30 mushroom slices, 16 ounces of carrots, 36 ounces of lettuce, and 50 ounces of spinach.

Garden Salad for 1 person:	Spinach Salad for 1 person:
4 mushroom slices 1 ounce of carrots 4 tomatoes 7 ounces of lettuce	6 mushroom slices 3 ounces of carrots 5 tomatoes 9 ounces of spinach

a. Does Mrs. Collins have enough ingredients to make 5 *garden salads*? Yes

b. Which ingredient does Mrs. Collins not have enough of to make 5 *spinach salads*? tomatoes

c. Does Mrs. Collins have enough ingredients to make 3 *spinach salads* and 2 *garden salads*? Yes

Looking Forward

Estimating multiplication and division answers prepares students for:

- **Lesson 93,** translating and solving two-step word problems by drawing a picture or listing the information given.
- **Lesson 102,** using the Distributive Property to solve multiplication problems.
- **Lesson 107,** multiplying a three-digit number by a two-digit number.
- **Lesson 111,** multiplying three-digit numbers by a two-digit number ending in zero.

Planning & Preparation

• Comparing and Ordering Fractions and Decimals

Objectives

- Compare and order fractions and decimals using a number line.
- Identify equivalent fractions using a number line.

Prerequesite Skills

- Writing a decimal and a fraction for a point on a number line.
- Using models to compare and order fractions and decimals.
- Using fraction manipulatives to model equivalent fractions.

Materials

Instructional Masters

- Power Up I Worksheet
- Lesson Activity 8*
- Lesson Activity 14*

Manipulative Kit

- Rulers
- Fraction circles*

Teacher-provided materials

- Grid paper, number line*

**optional*

California Mathematics Content Standards

NS 1.0, 1.6 Write tenths and hundredths in decimal and fraction notations and know the fraction and decimal equivalents for halves and fourths (e.g., $\frac{1}{2} = 0.5$ or $.50$; $\frac{7}{4} = 1\frac{3}{4} = 1.75$).

NS 1.0, 1.7 Write the fraction represented by a drawing of parts of a figure; represent a given fraction by using drawings; and relate a fraction to a simple decimal on a number line.

NS 1.0, 1.9 Identify on a number line the relative position of positive fractions, positive mixed numbers, and positive decimals to two decimal places.

MR 2.0, 2.3 Use a variety of methods, such as words, numbers, symbols, charts, graphs, tables, diagrams, and models, to explain mathematical reasoning.

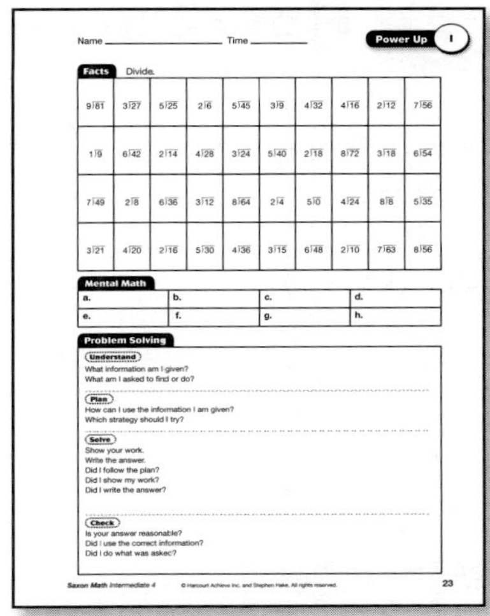

Power Up I Worksheet

Universal Access

Reaching All Special Needs Students

Special Education Students	At-Risk Students	English Learners	Advanced Learners
• Inclusion (TM) • Adaptations for Saxon Math	• Alternative Approach (TM) • Error Alert (TM) • Reteaching Masters • Refresher Lessons for California Standards	• English Learners (TM) • Developing Academic Language (TM) • English Learner Handbook	• Extend the Example (TM) • Extend the Problem (TM) • Online Activities

TM=Teacher's Manual

Developing Academic Language

Maintained	**English Learner**
benchmark	tiles
denominator	
fractions	
number line	

Problem Solving Discussion

Problem

Below we show the first five terms of a sequence. The terms of the sequence increase from left to right. Estimate how many terms will be in the sequence when it reaches a number that is 500 or greater. Then check your estimate by continuing the sequence until you reach a number that is 500 or greater.

1, 2, 4, 8, 16, ...

Focus Strategy  **Find/Extend a Pattern**

Understand *Understand the problem.*

"What information are we given?"

We are shown the first five terms of a sequence.

"What are we asked to do?"

We are asked to estimate how many terms will be in the sequence when it reaches a number that is 500 or greater. Then we are asked to check our estimate by extending the sequence.

Plan *Make a plan.*

"What problem-solving strategy can we use?"

We will *find a pattern* that describes the sequence. Then we will *extend the pattern.*

Solve *Carry out the plan.*

"How many terms do you estimate will be in the sequence when it reaches a number that is 500 or greater?"

Discuss student estimates.

"What pattern do you see in the sequence?"

Discuss student responses. If necessary, prompt students by asking the following question.

"What number do we multiply each term by to find the next term in the sequence?"

Each term is double the previous term, so we multiply by 2.

"What numbers do we find when we extend the sequence until we reach 500 or greater?"

32, 64, 128, 256, 512

"How many terms are in the sequence up through 512?"

There are 10 terms in the sequence.

"How close was your estimate?"

Discuss student responses and the effects of doubling numbers.

Check *Look back.*

"Did we complete the task?"

Yes. We estimated the number of terms in the sequence and then checked our estimate by *extending the pattern.*

LESSON 92

• Comparing and Ordering Fractions and Decimals

California Mathematics Content Standards

NS 1.0, 1.6 Write tenths and hundredths in decimal and fraction notations and know the fraction and decimal equivalents for halves and fourths (e.g., $\frac{1}{2}$ = 0.5 or .50; $\frac{7}{4}$ = $1\frac{3}{4}$ = 1.75).

NS 1.0, 1.7 Write the fraction represented by a drawing of parts of a figure; represent a given fraction by using drawings; and relate a fraction to a simple decimal on a number line.

NS 1.0, 1.9 Identify on a number line the relative position of positive fractions, positive mixed numbers, and positive decimals to two decimal places.

Power Up

facts Power Up I

mental math Find half of a product in problems **a–c.**

a. Number Sense: half of 10 × 12   60

b. Number Sense: half of 10 × 24   120

c. Number Sense: half of 10 × 480   2400

d. Money: The art supplies cost $17.50. Adam paid with a $20 bill. How much change should he receive? $2.50

e. Estimation: About what fraction of the circle is shaded? About what fraction of the circle is not shaded?   About $\frac{1}{10}$; about $\frac{9}{10}$

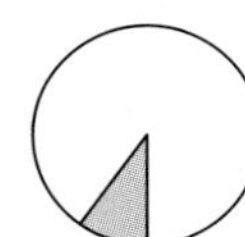

f. Calculation: $\frac{1}{4}$ of 40, × 2, + 4, ÷ 3   8

g. Simplify: 5 + 3 × 3   14

problem solving Choose an appropriate problem-solving strategy to solve this problem. Below we show the first five terms of a sequence. The terms of the sequence increase from left to right. Estimate how many terms will be in the sequence when it reaches a number that is 500 or greater. Then check your estimate by continuing the sequence until you reach a number that is 500 or greater.

1, 2, 4, 8, 16, ...

See student work; 32, 64, 128, 256, 512

Facts Divide.

9 9)81	9 3)27	5 5)25	3 2)6	9 5)45	3 3)9	8 4)32	4 4)16	6 2)12	8 7)56
9 1)9	7 6)42	7 2)14	7 4)28	8 3)24	8 5)40	9 2)18	9 8)72	6 3)18	9 6)54
7 7)49	4 2)8	6 6)36	4 3)12	8 8)64	2 2)4	0 5)0	6 4)24	1 8)8	7 5)35
7 3)21	5 4)20	8 2)16	6 5)30	9 4)36	5 3)15	8 6)48	5 2)10	9 7)63	7 8)56

Power Up

Facts

Distribute **Power Up I** to students. See answers below.

Count Aloud

Before students begin the Mental Math exercises, do these counting exercises as a class.

Count up and down by sixes from 18 to 60.

Mental Math

Encourage students to share different ways to mentally compute these exercises. Strategies for exercises are listed below.

a. Find 10 × (12 ÷ 2)

10 × (12 ÷ 2) = 10 × 6 = 60

Find (10 ÷ 2) × 12

(10 ÷ 2) × 12 = 5 × 12 = 60

d. Count On to $20

$17.50 to $18 = 50¢; $18 to $20 = $2; 50¢ + $2 = $2.50

Count Back to $17.50

$20 to $18 = $2; $18 to $17.50 = 50¢; $2 + 50¢ = $2.50

Problem Solving

Refer to **Problem-Solving Strategy Discussion,** p. 609B.

New Concept

Explanation

In this lesson, students will learn how number lines can be used to compare and order fractions and decimal numbers.

Active Learning

After you discuss the first number line in the lesson and students learn that the order of the fractions from least to greatest is $\frac{2}{5}$, $\frac{1}{2}$, and $\frac{7}{10}$, say:

"Which fraction is least?" $\frac{2}{5}$

"Where on the number line is $\frac{2}{5}$ located when compared to the other two fractions?" $\frac{2}{5}$ is the fraction that is farthest to the left.

"Which fraction is greatest?" $\frac{7}{10}$

"Where on the number line is $\frac{7}{10}$ located when compared to the other two fractions?" $\frac{7}{10}$ is the fraction that is farthest to the right.

"What generalization about left and right on a number line can we use to compare two or more fractions?"

Lead students to conclude that on a number line, the fraction farthest to the left is least and the fraction farthest to the right is greatest.

Example 1

Explanation

Point out that in order to compare fractions that have denominators of 2, 4, and 8, we use a number line in eighths because we can put halves and fourths on a number line divided into eighths.

Lead students to conclude that whenever we draw a number line to compare fractions, we choose the greatest denominator for the interval of the number line. In Example 1, the greatest denominator is 8, so we use a number line in eighths.

(continued)

New Concept

Since Lesson 57, we have been comparing and ordering fractions with different denominators using pictures and diagrams. We can also use number lines to compare and order fractions with different denominators.

We can use this number line to write the fractions $\frac{1}{2}$, $\frac{2}{5}$, and $\frac{7}{10}$ in order from least to greatest. We can use $\frac{5}{10}$ as a benchmark for comparing all three fractions.

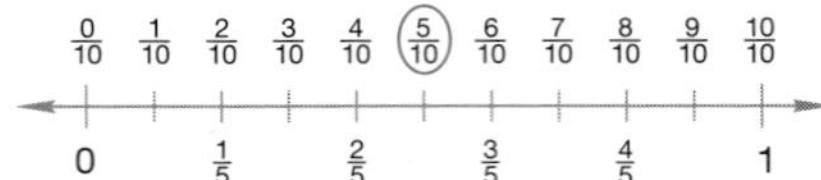

We know that $\frac{5}{10}$ is one half of a whole region.

$$\frac{5}{10} = \frac{1}{2}$$

On the number line we can see that $\frac{2}{5}$ is equivalent to $\frac{4}{10}$, so $\frac{2}{5}$ is less than $\frac{1}{2}$.

We can also see that $\frac{7}{10}$ is greater than $\frac{1}{2}$.

The fractions written in order from least to greatest are:

$$\mathbf{\frac{2}{5}, \frac{1}{2}, \frac{7}{10}}$$

Example 1

Use this number line to write these fractions in order from greatest to least:

$$\mathbf{\frac{3}{8}, \frac{1}{2}, \frac{3}{4}}$$

We can see on this number line that $\frac{2}{4}$ and $\frac{4}{8}$ are halfway between 0 and 1. This means that both $\frac{2}{4}$ and $\frac{4}{8}$ are equal to $\frac{1}{2}$. We can use this fact to compare all three numbers.

$$\frac{3}{8} < \frac{1}{2}, \quad \frac{3}{4} > \frac{1}{2}$$

610 ***Saxon Math*** *Intermediate 4*

Alternative Approach: Using Manipulatives

Some students may find it difficult to use number lines to solve some of the examples. Have these students draw pictures or use fraction manipulatives to represent fractions. Guide them as they transfer the information from the number line to a picture.

It is important for students to understand that the pictures they draw or make for each pair of fractions must be drawn using the same scale. That is, the picture or manipulative representing $\frac{1}{2}$ must be the same size as that representing $\frac{2}{4}$ or $\frac{3}{6}$.

The fractions written in order from greatest to least are:

$$\frac{3}{4}, \frac{1}{2}, \frac{3}{8}$$

Verify What number did we use as a benchmark for comparing? $\frac{1}{2}$

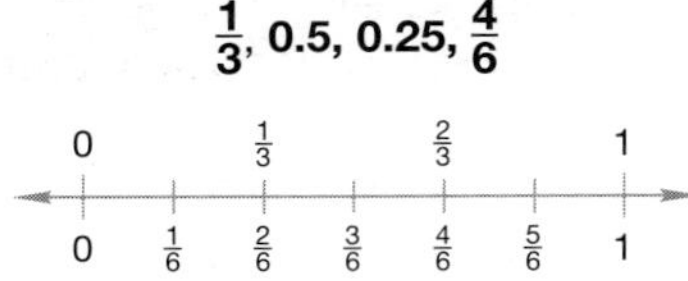

Example 2

Use this number line to write these fractions and decimals in order from least to greatest.

$$\frac{1}{3}, 0.5, 0.25, \frac{4}{6}$$

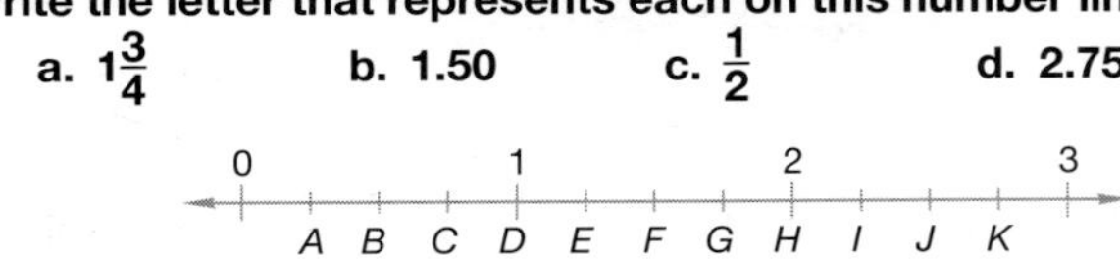

We can see on this number line that $\frac{3}{6}$ is halfway between 0 and 1. This means that $\frac{3}{6}$ is equal to $\frac{1}{2}$.

Since $0.5 = \frac{1}{2}$ and $\frac{1}{3}$ is less than $\frac{1}{2}$, then $\frac{1}{3}$ is less than 0.5.

Since $\frac{4}{6}$ is greater than $\frac{3}{6}$, then $\frac{4}{6}$ is greater than 0.5.

Now, we write $\frac{4}{6} > 0.5 > \frac{1}{3}$.

If we change 0.25 to the fraction $\frac{1}{4}$, we can compare $\frac{1}{3}$ and $\frac{1}{4}$ and we know that $\frac{1}{3} > \frac{1}{4}$.

These numbers written in order from least to greatest are:

$$0.25, \frac{1}{3}, 0.5, \frac{4}{6}$$

Discuss Why did we use $\frac{1}{2}$ as a benchmark for comparing?

Sample: It is easy to sort the numbers as greater than $\frac{1}{2}$ and less than $\frac{1}{2}$.

Example 3

Write the letter that represents each on this number line:

a. $1\frac{3}{4}$ **b.** 1.50 **c.** $\frac{1}{2}$ **d.** 2.75

0 1 2 3

A B C D E F G H I J K

On this number line, there are four segments between 0 and 1, 1 and 2, and 2 and 3. This means that this number line is divided into fourths.

a. Since each unit segment equals $\frac{1}{4}$, we count three segments after 1 and see that the letter ***G*** represents $1\frac{3}{4}$.

b. The letter *F* is halfway between 1 and 2, so ***F*** represents 1.50.

New Concept *(Continued)*

Example 2

Connection

It is important for students to note in this example that the number line is used to compare only three $\left(\frac{1}{3}, 0.5, \text{and } \frac{4}{6}\right)$ of the four numbers. Point out that because the number line shows thirds and sixths, it is not used to compare 0.25, which is equivalent to $\frac{1}{4}$. However, we use the unit fraction generalization shown below to compare $\frac{1}{4}$ to $\frac{1}{3}$:

- If the numerator of two or more fractions is 1, the fraction with the greater denominator is the lesser fraction and the fraction with the lesser denominator is the greater fraction.

Explain that the generalization is used to decide that on the number line, $\frac{1}{4}$ will be to the left of $\frac{1}{3}$.

Example 3

Error Alert

Remind students that each letter on this number line represents a number. Point out, for example, that *H* represents 2 and *D* represents 1, and we can say that *H* subtract *D* is 1.

Extend the Example

Challenge advanced learners to use only letters and addition signs to write an expression that has a sum of 10.

Sample: $K + I + H + G + E$

(continued)

Inclusion

Use this strategy if the student displays:

- Slow Learning Rate.
- Difficulty with Abstract Processing.

Compare and Order Fractions and Decimals (Pairs)

Materials: number lines, fraction manipulatives

- Write $\frac{1}{3}, \frac{4}{6}, 1, \frac{1}{2}$ on the board. Have students determine how to change $\frac{1}{3}$ and $\frac{1}{2}$ into fractions with a denominator of 6 using fraction manipulatives. Ask, ***"What are $\frac{1}{3}$ and $\frac{1}{2}$ in terms of sixths?"*** $\frac{2}{6}$ and $\frac{3}{6}$
- Have students use a number line to put the fractions in order from least to greatest. Remind students that all fractions must have the same denominator in order to compare them.
- Write 0.5, $\frac{3}{4}$, 2, 2.25 on the board. Have students use a number line to order the numbers from least to greatest. Remind students that fractions and decimals should be changed into the same form to compare them. Have student change the fraction $\frac{3}{4}$ to a decimal. Ask, ***"What is $\frac{3}{4}$ in decimal form?"*** 0.75 ***"What number is the smallest?"*** 0.5

New Concept *(Continued)*

Lesson Practice

Guided Practice

Use these problems as guided practice to check the students' understanding of today's concept.

Problems a–d

"Explain how we can decide what each tick mark on this number line represents." Since the distance from 0 to 1, 1 to 2, and so on, is divided into three equal parts or segments, the number line is in thirds. Each tick mark is $\frac{1}{3}$ more than the tick mark to its left and $\frac{1}{3}$ less than the tick mark to its right.

Problem c
Error Alert

Point out that to find the letter that represents the number closest to 2.92, students must first identify the two letters on the number line that 2.92 is between. Since *H* represents 2.75 and *I* represents 3, 2.92 is between *H* and *I*. Once that determination has been made, students can use subtraction to compare the distance to *H* and to *I*.

Closure The questions below help assess the concepts taught in this lesson.

"Look again at the number line in Example 3. What letter represents the mixed number $1\frac{1}{4}$?" *E*

"What letter represents the decimal number two and five tenths, or two point five?" *J*

Written Practice

Math Conversations

Independent Practice and Discussions to Increase Understanding

Problem 1 Represent

Extend the Problem

"To divide a circle into four equal parts, we draw two diameters of the circle. The intersection of the diameters form right angles. What one word describes the relationship of one diameter to the other?" perpendicular

Problem 2 Analyze

One way for students to complete the comparison is to compare each number to 1: because $\frac{3}{5}$ is less than 1, $\frac{3}{5}$ is the least number, and because $\frac{6}{5}$ is farther to the right of 1 than 1.01, $\frac{6}{5}$ is the greatest number.

(continued)

$\frac{7}{4} = \frac{4}{4} + \frac{3}{4}$ or $1\frac{3}{4}$;
$2.30 > 1\frac{3}{4}$

c. The letter *B* is halfway between 0 and 1, so ***B*** represents $\frac{1}{2}$.

d. We count three segments after 2, so the letter ***K*** represents 2.75.

Connect Use this number line to compare $\frac{7}{4}$ and 2.30.

Lesson Practice

Analyze Use this number line to answer problems **a–d**.

a. Which letter represents $1\frac{2}{3}$? *E*

b. Which letter represents $\frac{1}{3}$? *A*

c. Which letter represents the number closest to 2.92? *I*

d. Which letter represents $\frac{10}{3}$? *J*

Verify Write *true* or *false* for each problem. Use the number lines in this lesson to help you.

e. $\frac{5}{3} > 1\frac{1}{3}$ true

f. $\frac{6}{4} < 2.5$ true

g. $\frac{3}{5} > 0.75$ false

h. $1\frac{2}{8} < \frac{11}{8}$ true

Written Practice

Distributed and Integrated

***1.** (89) **Represent** Draw and shade circles to show that $\frac{10}{4} = 2\frac{1}{2}$.

***2.** (92) **Analyze** Write these numbers in order from greatest to least. Use the number line on page 611 if needed. $\frac{6}{5}$, 1.01, $\frac{3}{5}$

$\frac{3}{5}$, 1.01, $\frac{6}{5}$

3. (27) Compare. Write >, <, or =.

a. 206,353 ⓒ< 209,124

b. 518,060 ⓒ> 518,006

4. (27) Write these numbers in order from greatest to least: 120,044; 102,757; 96,720; 89,611

89,611 120,044 102,757 96,720

5. (Inv. 4, 43) **Represent** Write each mixed number as a decimal:

a. $5\frac{31}{100}$ 5.31

b. $16\frac{7}{10}$ 16.7

c. $5\frac{7}{100}$ 5.07

*6. (87) **Explain** 33 people are waiting for a boat ride. Each boat holds 6 people. If five boats arrive together, how many people will have to wait for the sixth boat? How did you find your answer? 3 people; 33 ÷ 6 = 5 R 3; 6 people got into each of the 5 boats and 3 people have to wait for the sixth boat.

▶ *7. (78) **Analyze** Jim spun all the way around in the air and dunked the basketball. How many degrees did Jim turn? 360 degrees

8. (Inv. 4) **Represent** Use words to write 7.68. seven and sixty-eight hundredths

9. (Inv. 4) **Represent** Use words to write 76.8. seventy-six and eight tenths

▶*10. (91) **Explain** Armando estimated that the exact product of 78 and 91 was close to 720. Did Armando make a reasonable estimate? Explain why or why not. No; sample: I rounded each factor to the nearest ten, then I multiplied; A reasonable estimate is 80 × 90 or 7200.

11. (Inv. 4) **Connect** Name the number of shaded squares below:

a. as a mixed number. $1\frac{3}{10}$

b. as a decimal. 1.3

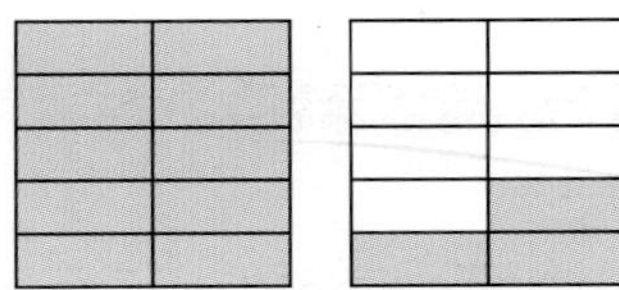

▶*12. (90) **Represent** Draw a quadrilateral with exactly two right angles.

13. (13) Makayla's school day ends 5 hours 20 minutes after the time shown on the clock. What time does Makayla's school day end? 3:00 p.m.

14. (58, 60) Mr. Romano could bake 27 pizzas in 3 hours.

a. How many pizzas could he bake in 1 hour? 9 pizzas

b. How many pizzas could he bake in 5 hours? 45 pizzas
(*Hint:* Multiply the answer to part **a** by 5.)

15. (45) 3.65 + 4.2 + 0.62 8.47

16. (28, 52) $13.70 − $6.85 $6.85

Written Practice *(Continued)*

Math Conversations *(cont.)*

Problem 7 Analyze

Make sure students understand that the phrase "spun all the way around" indicates that Jim made a full or complete turn.

Problem 10 Explain

Remind students who round 78 to 80 and round 91 to 90 that the product of 80 × 90 can be found using mental math by attaching two zeros to the product of 8 × 9.

Problem 12 Represent

Manipulative Use

Students will need rulers to draw the quadrilateral. Because the quadrilateral is to have two right angles, students may find it helpful to complete the drawing on grid paper.

(continued)

Written Practice (Continued)

Math Conversations (cont.)

Problem 26

Make sure students recognize that they must substitute 4 for x, and then follow the order of operations to solve for y.

Problem 28

Extend the Problem

"This set consists of seven numbers. When we look for the median of the numbers, how many numbers will we find in the middle of the set?" one

"Would your answer change if the set contained six numbers instead of seven? Explain why or why not." Yes; sample: If a set has an even amount of numbers, then there are two middle numbers.

Problem 29b (Estimate)

Before students round 65.25 to the nearest whole number, ask:

"What place in a number represents rounding to the nearest whole number?" The ones place

Errors and Misconceptions

Problem 18

Explain to those students who name 783¢ as the answer that 100 or more cents is not considered to be an answer in simplest form. Then ask:

"We can change cents to dollars by moving the decimal point. In which direction does the decimal point move?" To the left

"How many places to the left does the decimal point move?" two places

Ask students to rewrite 783¢ as dollars and cents. $7.83

Problem 26

Prior to finding the value of y when $x = 4$, some students may find it helpful if you demonstrate by substitution that $y = 7$ when $x = 2$ and $y = 9$ when $x = 3$.

17. (85) 26×100 2600

18. (28, 38) 9 × 87¢ $7.83

19. (88) 14×16 224

20. (65, 88) 15^2 225

21. (69) $\frac{456}{6}$ 76

22. (71) 47×60 2820

23. (34, 83) $6x = 4248$ 708

24. (79) $1\overline{)163}$ 163

25. (79, 83) 5)$49.00 $9.80

▸ ***26.** (64, Inv. 7) This table represents the equation $y = 2x + 3$ and shows the values of y when x is 2 and when x is 3. What is y when x is 4? 11

$y = 2x + 3$

x	y
2	7
3	9
4	?

27. (Inv. 3, 84) How many one-foot-square tiles are needed to cover the floor of a room that is 15 feet long and 10 feet wide? 150 square tiles

▸ ***28.** (Inv. 6) Find the median and mode of this set of numbers: median: 3; mode: 1

1, 1, 2, 3, 5, 8, 13

***29.** (22, 46, 62) (Estimate) Round each number to the given place:

a. Round 65.25 to the nearest ten. 70

▸ **b.** Round 65.25 to the nearest whole number. 65

c. Round 65.25 to the nearest tenth. 65.3

***30.** (63) (Explain) If $p + 50 = r + 50$, is the equation below true? Why or why not? Yes

$$p \div 2 = r \div 2$$

$p = r$ because equals added to equals are equal; Therefore $p \div 10 = r \div 10$ because equals divided by equals are equal.

614 Saxon Math Intermediate 4

English Learners

Explain to students that **tiles** are thin pieces of material used for covering surfaces, especially floors, walls, and kitchen counters. Add that tiles are usually square and painted or glazed.

Ask:

"What other materials can be used in place of tile to cover floors?"
Samples: carpet, hardwood, linoleum

Have students notice if there are any tiles in any part of their homes.

Looking Forward

Comparing and ordering fractions and decimals prepares students for:

- **Lesson 94,** solving two-step problems that involve a fraction of a group.
- **Lesson 98,** identifying and writing fractions equal to 1 and to $\frac{1}{2}$.
- **Lesson 99,** changing improper fractions to whole or mixed numbers.
- **Lesson 100,** adding and subtracting fractions with common denominators.
- **Lesson 103,** finding equivalent fractions.
- **Lesson 106,** writing the reduced form of a fraction.
- **Lessons 112–113,** adding and subtracting fractions and mixed numbers with common denominators and renaming fractions whose denominators are not equal by using a common denominator of the fractions.

Planning & Preparation

• Two-Step Problems

Objectives

- Translate and solve two-step word problems by drawing a picture or listing the information given.
- Describe the relationship between ordered pairs in a table.

Prerequisite Skills

- Analyzing a problem and choosing the information needed to solve it.
- Finding the total cost of a purchase including sales tax.
- Finding all possible combinations of a set.

Materials

Instructional Masters

- Power Up I Worksheet
- Lesson Activity 8

Manipulative Kit

- Rulers
- Money manipulatives, two-color counters*

Teacher-provided materials

- Grid paper

**optional*

California Mathematics Content Standards

NS 3.0, 3.4 Solve problems involving division of multidigit numbers by one-digit numbers.

AF 1.0, 1.3 Use parentheses to indicate which operation to perform first when writing expressions containing more than two terms and different operations.

AF 1.0, 1.5 Understand that an equation such as $y = 3x + 5$ is a prescription for determining a second number when a first number is given.

MG 1.0, 1.1 Measure the area of rectangular shapes by using appropriate units, such as square centimeter (cm^2), square meter (m^2), square kilometer (km^2), square inch (in^2), square yard (yd^2), or square mile (mi^2).

MR 1.0, 1.2 Determine when and how to break a problem into simpler parts.

MR 2.0, 2.5 Indicate the relative advantages of exact and approximate solutions to problems and give answers to a specified degree of accuracy.

MR 3.0, 3.2 Note the method of deriving the solution and demonstrate a conceptual understanding of the derivation by solving similar problems.

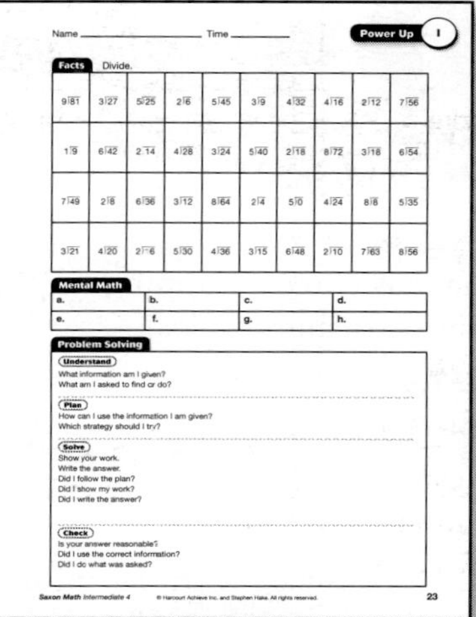

Power Up I Worksheet

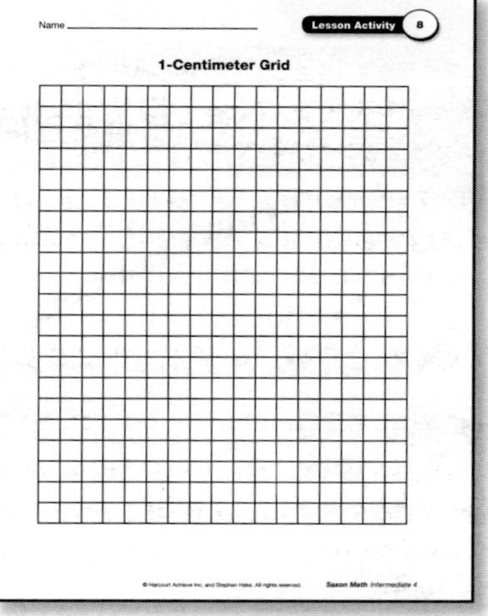

Lesson Activity 8

Universal Access

Reaching All Special Needs Students

Special Education Students	At-Risk Students	English Learners	Advanced Learners
• Inclusion (TM) • Adaptations for Saxon Math	• Error Alert (TM) • Reteaching Masters • Refresher Lessons for California Standards	• English Learners (TM) • Developing Academic Language (TM) • English Learner Handbook	• Extend the Example (TM) • Extend the Problem (TM) • Online Activities

TM=Teacher's Manual

Developing Academic Language

Maintained
divide
equation
number line
segment

English Learner
address

Problem Solving Discussion

Problem

In this Venn diagram, the circle on the left represents animals with the ability to fly, and the circle on the right represents birds. The *R* in the overlapping portion of the circles represents robins, which are birds that can fly. The *O* represents ostriches, which are birds that cannot fly. The *B* represents bats, which can fly but are not birds. The *W* represents whales, which are not birds and cannot fly. Copy the Venn diagram on your paper, and place an abbreviation for a penguin, eagle, goldfish, and cat.

Animals with Ability to Fly
Birds
B R O W

Focus Strategy  **Use Logical Reasoning**

Understand ***Understand the problem.***

"What information are we given?"

We are shown a Venn diagram that has two overlapping circles and four abbreviations (for bats, robins, ostriches, and whales).

"What do the two circles stand for?"

One circle stands for animals with the ability to fly, and the other circle stands for birds.

"Why do the two circles overlap?"

The two circles overlap because some animals with the ability to fly are also birds. The overlap is a place to represent those animals.

"What are we asked to do?"

We are asked to copy the Venn diagram and place an abbreviation for a penguin, eagle, goldfish, and cat.

Plan ***Make a plan.***

"What problem-solving strategy will we use to solve this problem?"

We will *draw a diagram.*

Solve ***Carry out the plan.***

"What categories do penguins, eagles, goldfish, and cats belong to? Where should we place the abbreviations?"

Eagles are birds that can fly, so we place an *E* in the overlap. Penguins are birds that cannot fly, so we place a *P* in the right-hand circle but outside the overlap. Goldfish and cats do not have the ability to fly, and they are not birds, so we place a *G* and a *C* outside the circles.

"What should our diagram look like?"

Our diagram might look like the diagram at right.

Animals with Ability to Fly
Birds
B R E O P W G C

Check ***Look back.***

"Did we complete the task?"

Yes. We drew a Venn diagram that shows the relationship between birds and the set of all animals with the ability to fly. We placed abbreviations for eagles, penguins, goldfish, and cats.

LESSON 93

• Two-Step Problems

California Mathematics Content Standards

NS 3.0, 3.4 Solve problems involving division of multidigit numbers by one-digit numbers.
AF 1.0, 1.5 Understand that an equation such as $y = 3x + 5$ is a prescription for determining a second number when a first number is given.
MR 2.0, 2.5 Indicate the relative advantages of exact and approximate solutions to problems and give answers to a specified degree of accuracy.

Power Up

facts Power Up I

mental math Find half of a product in problems **a–c.**

a. Number Sense: half of 10×18 90
b. Number Sense: half of 10×44 220
c. Number Sense: half of 10×260 1300
d. Time: How many minutes are in $1\frac{1}{2}$ hours? 90 min
e. Measurement: How many quarts is 3 gallons? 12 qt
f. Estimation: About how many feet is 1989 yards? 6000 ft
g. Calculation: 3^2, $+ 1$, $\times 5$, $- 1$, $\sqrt{}$ 7
h. Simplify: $6 - 3 \div 3$ 5

problem solving

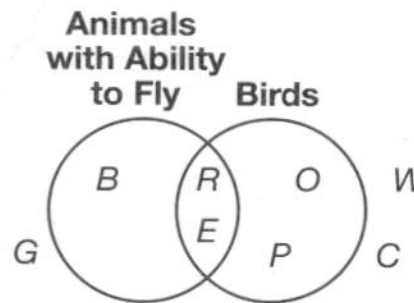

In this Venn diagram, the circle on the left represents animals with the ability to fly, and the circle on the right represents birds. The *R* in the overlapping portion of the circles represents robins, which are birds that can fly. The *O* represents ostriches, which are birds that cannot fly. The *B* represents bats, which can fly but are not birds. The *W* represents whales, which are not birds and cannot fly. Copy the Venn diagram on your paper, and place an abbreviation for a penguin, eagle, goldfish and cat.

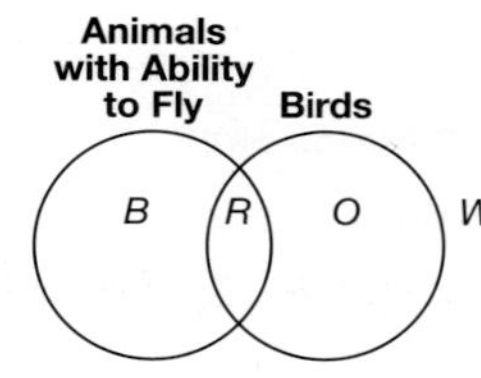

Facts Divide.

9 9)81	9 3)27	5 5)25	3 2)6	9 5)45	3 3)9	8 4)32	4 4)16	6 2)12	8 7)56
9 1)9	7 6)42	7 2)14	7 4)28	8 3)24	8 5)40	9 2)18	9 8)72	6 3)18	9 6)54
7 7)49	4 2)8	6 6)36	4 3)12	8 8)64	2 2)4	0 5)0	6 4)24	1 8)8	7 5)35
7 3)21	5 4)20	8 2)16	6 5)30	9 4)36	5 3)15	8 6)48	5 2)10	9 7)63	7 8)56

Power Up

Facts

Distribute **Power Up I** to students. See answers below.

Count Aloud

Before students begin the Mental Math exercises, do these counting exercises as a class.

Count up and down by nines from 27 to 90.

Mental Math

Encourage students to share different ways to mentally compute these exercises. Strategies for exercises are listed below.

a. Find $10 \times (18 \div 2)$
$10 \times (18 \div 2) = 10 \times 9 = 90$
Divide 10×18 by 2
$10 \times 18 = 180$; $180 \div 2 = 90$

b. Find $10 \times (44 \div 2)$
$10 \times (44 \div 2) = 10 \times 22 = 220$
Divide 10×44 by 2
$10 \times 44 = 440$; $440 \div 2 = 220$

Problem Solving

Refer to **Problem-Solving Strategy Discussion,** p. 615B.

New Concept

Active Learning

Ask students to name as many problem solving strategies as they can. Invite a volunteer to list the strategies on the board, and make sure the list includes:

Act It Out or Make a Model
Use Logical Reasoning
Draw a Picture or Diagram
Write a Number Sentence or Equation
Make It Simpler
Find/Extend a Pattern
Make an Organized List
Guess and Check
Make or Use a Table, Chart, or Graph
Work Backwards

Point out that many of the strategies will be used to solve the two-step word problems in today's lesson.

Example 1

Students will need to use logical reasoning to solve this problem. Encourage them to look at the problem as a puzzle that needs to be solved, and then point out that organizing the pieces of a puzzle can make it easier to solve the whole puzzle.

Instruction

Because some students will find it helpful to use abbreviations and symbols when listing the information given in a problem, you may want to demonstrate how this can be done. On the board or overhead, write, "Blanca is 9 years old," and under that, write, "$B = 9$." Then write, "Ali is 2 years younger than Blanca," and under that, "$A = B - 2$." Finally, write, "Jim is 5 years older than Ali," and under that, "$J = A + 5$."

Example 2

Point out that in this problem, students are finding the average cost of a pound of apples.

(continued)

New Concept

We have practiced two-step word problems that involve finding total costs (including tax) and change back. Starting with this lesson, we will practice other kinds of two-step problems. Writing down the given information and using problem-solving strategies is often helpful in solving these problems.

Reading Math

When we translate a problem, we identify the goal and list the steps.

Goal: Find Jim's age.

Step 1: Find Ali's age.

Step 2: Find Jim's age.

Then we use the steps to make a plan.

Example 1

Jim is 5 years older than Ali. Ali is 2 years younger than Blanca. Blanca is 9 years old. How old is Jim?

We will use two steps to solve the problem. First we will use Blanca's age to find Ali's age. Then we will use Ali's age to calculate Jim's age. We write down the given information.

Blanca is 9 years old.

Ali is 2 years younger than Blanca.

Jim is 5 years older than Ali.

We know that Blanca is 9 years old. Ali is 2 years younger than Blanca, so Ali is $9 - 2$, or 7 years old. Jim is 5 years older than Ali, so Jim is $7 + 5$, or **12 years old.**

Thinking Skills

Verify

What are the two steps needed to find the cost of each pound?

1. Find the cost of all the apples.
2. Find the cost of one pound.

Example 2

Ja'Von paid for 5 pounds of apples with a $10 bill. His change was $6. What was the cost of each pound of apples?

We begin by finding how much all 5 pounds of apples cost. If Ja'Von paid for the apples with a $10 bill and received $6 in change, then all 5 pounds must have cost $4.

$$\begin{array}{rl} \$10 & \text{amount paid} \\ -\ \$\ 6 & \text{change} \\ \hline \$\ 4 & \text{cost of 5 pounds of apples} \end{array}$$

To find the cost of each pound of apples, we divide $4 by 5.

$$\begin{array}{r} \$0.80 \\ 5\overline{)\$4.00} \\ \underline{4\,0} \\ 00 \\ \underline{0} \\ 0 \end{array}$$

Each pound of apples cost **$0.80.**

Teacher Tip

Remind students that they may get and use the money manipulatives to help them understand and solve problems.

Example 3

Maribella feeds her pet rabbit 2 ounces of lettuce each day. In how many days does her rabbit eat a pound of lettuce? How many pounds of lettuce does the rabbit eat in 4 months?

A pound is 16 ounces. At 2 ounces per day, the rabbit eats a pound of lettuce every **8 days.**

$$16 \div 2 = 8$$

A month is about 30 days, so 4 months is 4×30 days, which is 120 days. We divide 120 days into groups of 8 days to find the number of pounds of lettuce the rabbit eats.

$$120 \div 8 = 15$$

In 4 months, the rabbit eats about **15 pounds** of lettuce.

Example 4

Point *B* represents which number on this number line?

A, B, C; 0, 100, 200

Sometimes two-step problems are not word problems. We can solve problems like this with two or three steps of arithmetic.

We see that the distance from point *A* to point *C* is 100.

Step 1: $200 - 100 = 100$

The distance is divided into 4 segments. By dividing 100 by 4, we find that each segment is 25.

Step 2: $100 \div 4 = 25$

Step 3: If we count by 25's from 100, point *A* to point *B*, we find that point *B* represents **175.** Since point *B* is one segment from point *C*, we can check the answer by counting back 25 from 200. The result is 175, which is our original answer.

Discuss How could we use the *guess and check* strategy to solve this problem?

Sample: First try counting by 20's from 100 to 200; 180 is too small. Then try counting by 25's from 100 to 200; Each segment is 25.

New Concept *(Continued)*

Example 3

Error Alert

As you discuss the solution, have students note that the computation $16 \div 2$ produces an exact answer. Point out, however, that because the number of days in a month is not always 30, an answer that is computed using 30 represents an estimate. So the answer to the second step of the problem—found by multiplying 4×30 and then dividing the product by 8—represents an estimate.

Example 4

Connection

In Step 2 of the solution, make sure students recognize that the quotient of the division represents the interval of the number line. In other words, because $100 \div 4 = 25$, the tick marks of the number line can be labeled by skip counting by 25's, beginning at 0.

Extend the Example

Challenge your advanced learners to suppose that points *A, B,* and *C* were reflected across zero, and then name the integer that the reflection of each point would represent. *A:* –100; *B:* –175; *C:* –200

(continued)

Inclusion

Use this strategy if the student displays:

- Poor Retention.
- Difficulty with Abstract Processing.

Two-Step Word Problems (Small Group)

Material: counters

- Read, ***"There are 6 children participating in a play. If each child sings 3 songs and there are 5 performances, how many total songs will be sung?"***
- Have children identify the operation that the problem dictates and ask, ***"What is the first problem in this word problem?*** 6×3
- Have children use the counters to display 6×3. Then ask, ***"Using your answer what is the second problem to be performed?"*** 18×5 Have children use their counters to display 18×5. Ask, ***"How many total songs will be sung?"*** 90
- Have students write a two-step problem and exchange it with a partner to work.

New Concept *(Continued)*

Example 5

Before discussing the solution, point out that the letters x and y in the equation represent missing numbers, and that the goal in solving the equation is to find the value of y by substituting a given number for x ($x = 3$).

As you discuss the solution, make sure students can recognize that the expression $2x + 1$ represents two operations—multiplication and addition.

It is important for students to recall that if multiplication and addition are both present in an expression, the order of operations states that the multiplication is performed first. (First we use multiplication to find the product of 2×3, and then we add 1 to that product.)

Lesson Practice

Guided Practice

Use these problems as guided practice to check the students' understanding of today's concept.

Problem a

"The first step we must complete is to find the cost of 4 pounds of peaches. What operation should we use to find the cost?" subtraction

"Once we know the cost of 4 pounds of peaches, what operation should we use to find the cost of one pound? Explain why you named that operation." Division; We must divide the cost into 4 equal parts, and each part will represent one pound of peaches.

Problem e

"What two operations are present in the expression 3x + 2?" Multiplication and addition

"After we substitute 4 for x, which operation do we complete first?" multiplication

Problem e
Error Alert

As students substitute 4 for x in the expression $3x$, watch for the common error of rewriting $3x$ as 34.

(continued)

Example 5

If $y = 2x + 1$, then what is y when $x = 3$?

The equation $y = 2x + 1$ shows us how to find the number that y equals when we know what x equals.

The equation means, "To find y, multiply x by 2 and then add 1."

In this equation x is 3, so we multiply 2 times 3 and then add 1.

$$y = (2 \times 3) + 1$$
$$y = 6 + 1$$
$$y = 7$$

When x is 3, y is **7.**

Represent What is y when x is 5?

We can write these values in a table to find the answer.

2x + 1 = y

x	y
3	7
4	9
5	11

When x is 5, y is **11.**

Predict What is y when $x = 10$? Explain how you know. 21; Multiply 2 and x, then add 1; $(2 \times 10) + 1 = 21$

Lesson Practice

a. Kim paid for 4 pounds of peaches with a $5 bill. She got $3 back. What was the cost of each pound of peaches? (*Hint:* First find the cost of 4 pounds of peaches.) $0.50

b. The perimeter of this square is 12 inches. What is the area of the square? (*Hint:* First find the length of each side.) 9 sq. in.

G = 2 + Shin
O = 13
O = G − 10

c. Orlando is 10 years younger than Gihan and Gihan is 2 years older than Shaniqua. If Orlando is 13 years old, how old is Shaniqua? (*Hint:* First find how old Gihan is.) 21 years old

d. Point N represents what number on this number line? 460

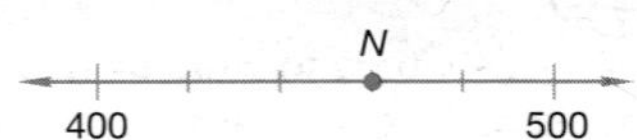

e. If $y = 3x + 2$, what is y when x is 4? 14

f. Mr. Simmons is 5 ft 10 in. tall. How many inches is 5 ft 10 in.? 70 in.

Math Background

The equation $y = 2x + 1$, is a *linear equation.* If we were to plot pairs of (x, y) values that satisfy the equation, they would fall exactly in a straight line. Any equation of the form $y = mx + b$, where m and b are fixed numbers, is a linear equation. The values of m and b tell us a lot about the line:

- If the value of m is positive, the line slants up from left to right. If the value of m is negative, the lines slant down from left to right.
- For positive values of m, the greater m is, the steeper the line is. For example, the graph of $y = 5x + 1$ is steeper than the graph of $y = 2x + 1$.
- The value of b tells us where the line crosses the y-axis (the vertical axis). The graph of $y = 2x + 1$ crosses the y-axis at 1. This is also called the *y-intercept.*

Written Practice *Distributed and Integrated*

▶ *1. (87) Fifty-three family photographs are being arranged in a photo album. The album has 12 pages altogether, and 6 photographs can be placed on each page.

a. How many full pages of photographs will be in the album? 8 pages

b. How many photographs will be on the page that is not full? 5 photographs

c. How many pages in the album will be empty? 3 pages

2. (61) **Estimate** Abraham Lincoln was born in 1809. He gave the Gettysburg Address in 1863. About how old was he when he gave the Gettysburg Address? About 50 years old

▶ *3. (93) **Analyze** The parking lot charges $1.25 to park a car for the first hour. It charges 75¢ for each additional hour. How much does it cost to park a car in the lot for 3 hours? $2.75

▶ *4. (74) **Represent** Two thirds of the team's 45 points were scored in the second half. How many points did the team score in the second half? Draw a picture to illustrate the problem. 30 points

4.

	45 points
$\frac{2}{3}$ scored in second half	15 points
	15 points
$\frac{1}{3}$ not scored in second half	15 points

*5. (28) Something is wrong with the sign to the right. Show two different ways to correct the error. $0.75; 75¢

6. (28) **Analyze** What is the value of 3 $10 bills, 4 $1 bills, 5 dimes, and 2 pennies? $34.52

7. (40, Inv. 4) **Represent** Use words to write 6412.5, and then round it to the nearest thousand. six thousand, four hundred twelve and five tenths; 6000

English Learners

Explain to your students that one meaning of the word **address** is a speech or written statement. Say:

"President Lincoln gave a speech, the Gettysburg Address, during the Civil War."

Ask:

"What other things might you give an address for?" Samples: talking about a book, presenting information to the class, etc.

New Concept *(Continued)*

Closure

The questions below help assess the concepts taught in this lesson.

"What are the names of several strategies you can use to help solve word problems?" Sample: *Act It Out or Make a Model; Use Logical Reasoning; Draw a Picture or Diagram; Write a Number Sentence or Equation; Make It Simpler; Find/Extend a Pattern; Make an Organized List; Guess and Check; Make or Use a Table, Chart, or Graph*

List the strategies named by students on the board or overhead, and then encourage them to describe one or more examples of problems that can be solved using each strategy.

Written Practice

Math Conversations

Independent Practice and Discussions to Increase Understanding

Problem 1

Students must interpret the division $53 \div 6 = 8$ R 5 to solve parts **a–c.**

To solve part **a,** students must infer that the quotient (8) represents the number of full pages.

To solve part **b,** students must infer that the remainder (5) represents the number of photographs on the page of the album that is not full.

To solve part **c,** students must infer that the quotient is increased to 9 (the number of pages that will contain photographs) and then subtracted from 12 (the number of pages altogether).

Problem 3 **Analyze**

Extend the Problem

Challenge your advanced learners to write an equation that can be used to find the cost for one or more hours. Sample: $c = \$0.50 + \$0.75h$ where c represents the cost in dollars and h represents the number of hours the car will be parked.

Problem 4 **Represent**

Extend the Problem

"How can we use division, and then use multiplication, to check our answer?" Use division to find $\frac{1}{3}$ of 45 points (45 points $\div$ 3 = 15 points), and find $\frac{2}{3}$ of 45 points by multiplying 15 points by 2 (15 points $\times$ 2 = 30 points). Then compare the answers.

(continued)

Written Practice *(Continued)*

Math Conversations *(cont.)*

Problem 11

Remind students who round 39 to 40 and round 41 to 40 that the product of 40 × 40 can be found using mental math by attaching two zeros to the right of the product of 4 × 4.

Problem 13 Explain

Make sure students recognize that $1\frac{2}{4}$ and $\frac{6}{5}$ can be compared without using arithmetic if $1\frac{2}{4}$ is changed to the improper fraction $\frac{6}{4}$ because the fractions will have the same numerator. Then ask:

"What generalization can we use to compare two fractions such as $\frac{6}{4}$ and $\frac{6}{5}$ when the numerators of the fractions are the same?" If two fractions have the same numerator, the fraction with the greater denominator is the lesser fraction and the fraction with the lesser denominator is the greater fraction.

Students should conclude that $\frac{6}{4}$ is greater than $\frac{6}{5}$ or $\frac{6}{5}$ is less than $\frac{6}{4}$.

(continued)

8. (61) Estimate Last year, 5139 people attended an outdoor jazz festival. This year, 6902 people attended the festival. Estimate the total attendance during those years and explain why your estimate is reasonable. Sample: 12,000 is a reasonable estimate because 5139 rounded to the nearest thousand is 5000, 6902 rounded to the nearest thousand is 7000, and 5000 + 7000 = 12,000.

9. (73, 77) **a.** Cooper opened a 1-gallon bottle of milk and poured out 1 quart. How many quarts of milk were left in the bottle? 3 quarts

b. What fraction of the milk was left in the bottle? $\frac{3}{4}$ gallon

***10.** (82) **Multiple Choice** Which of the following figures has exactly 4 lines of symmetry? Copy the figure and draw the lines of symmetry. B

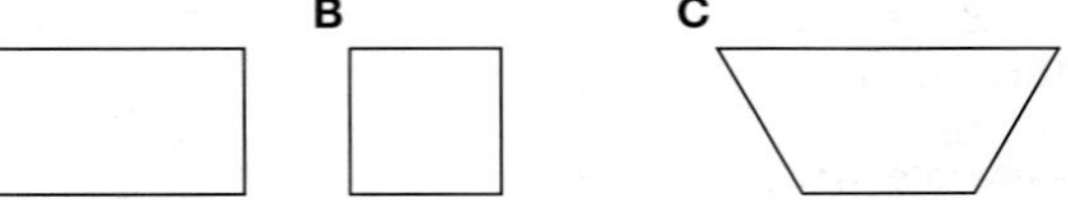

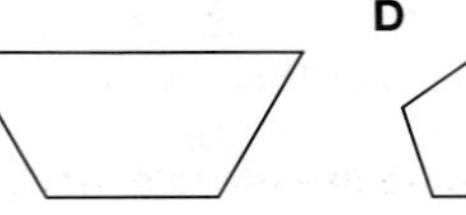

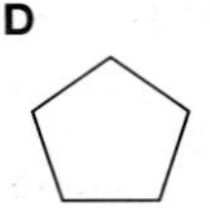

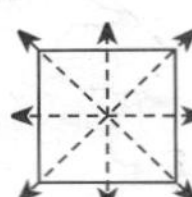

▶ ***11.** (91) Estimate the product of 39 and 41. Then find the exact product. 1600; 1599

***12.** (78) Estimate Felicia slowly gave the doorknob a quarter turn counterclockwise. About how many degrees did she turn the doorknob? About 90°

▶ ***13.** (92) Explain Write these numbers in order from greatest to least. Explain your thinking. 1.55, $1\frac{2}{4}$, $\frac{6}{5}$; $1\frac{2}{4} = \frac{6}{4}$ and $\frac{6}{4}$ is greater than $\frac{6}{5}$; $1\frac{2}{4} = 1\frac{1}{2}$ and 1.55 is greater than $1\frac{1}{2}$.

$$\frac{6}{5}, 1.55, 1\frac{2}{4}$$

14. (28, 51) \$68.57 + \$36.49 = \$105.06

15. (28, 52) \$100.00 − \$5.43 = \$94.57

16. (11) 15 + 24 + 36 + 75 + 21 + 8 + 36 + 420 = 635

17. (86) 12 × 12 = 144

18. (59) \$5.08 × 7 = \$35.56

19. (65, 85) 50^2 2500

20. (Inv. 3) $\sqrt{144}$ 12

21. (9, 45) 12.08 − (9.61 − 2.4) 4.87

22. (88) 49 × 51 2499

23. (88) 33 × 25 825

24. (83) $\frac{848}{8}$ 106

25. (34, 83) $9w = 6300$ 700

▸***26.** (89) **Represent** Draw and shade circles to show that $2\frac{2}{3}$ equals $\frac{8}{3}$.

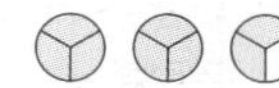

▸***27.** (18, 20, 66) **Represent** Draw a rectangle that is three inches long and one inch wide. Then find the perimeter and the area. 8 in.; 3 in^2

3 in. / 1 in.

▸***28.** (64, Inv. 7) This table represents the equation $y = 3x + 1$ and shows the values of y when x is 3 and when x is 4.

a. What is y when x is 5? 16

b. Use **Lesson Activity 26** to graph the equation.
See student work.

$y = 3x + 1$

x	y
3	10
4	13
5	?

***29.** (17) **Classify** Refer to this triangle for parts **a** and **b.**

a. Describe the angles as acute, right, or obtuse.
Angles A and B are acute; Angle C is right.

b. Which sides are perpendicular?
Segment AC is perpendicular to segment CB.

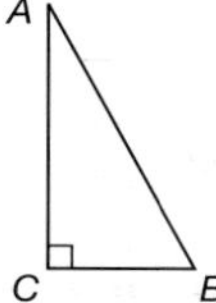

***30.** (90) **Classify** Write as many different names for this figure as you can. Quadrilateral, parallelogram, rhombus

Solving two-step word problems by drawing a picture or listing given information prepares students for:

- **Lesson 94,** solving two-step problems about a fraction of a group.
- **Lesson 95,** finding the median, mode, and range of a set of data.

Written Practice *(Continued)*

Math Conversations *(cont.)*

Problem 26 Represent

Manipulative Use

Invite students to use their fraction manipulatives to check their answers.

Problem 27 Represent

Manipulative Use

Students will need rulers to draw the rectangle. Some students will find it helpful to complete their drawings on grid paper.

Problem 28

Students will need a copy of **Lesson Activity Master 26** to graph the equation.

Prior to finding the value of y when $x = 5$, some students may find it helpful if you demonstrate by substitution that $y = 10$ when $x = 3$ and $y = 13$ when $x = 4$.

Errors and Misconceptions

Problem 5

Make sure students recognize that two money symbols are present in the amount \$0.75¢. If students have difficulty understanding why it is not correct to use two symbols, write "\$0.75" and "0.75¢" on the board. Explain that because the decimal number 0.75 is less than 1, the amount \$0.75 represents an amount that is less than one dollar ($\frac{75}{100}$ of a dollar, or 75¢), and explain that the amount 0.75¢ represents an amount that is less than one cent ($\frac{75}{100}$, or $\frac{3}{4}$ of a penny).

Remind students that it is not reasonable to label an amount with two different units.

Problem 30

Make sure students understand that because the equals sign is present, the quantity on one side of the equation must be equal to the quantity on the other side, and the only way for this to happen is for p and r to represent the same number. Point out that if p and r represent two different numbers, the equation is no longer true.

Planning & Preparation

• Two-Step Problems About a Fraction of a Group

Objectives

- Solve two-step problems that involve a fraction of a group.

Prerequisite Skills

- Using a fraction to find a portion of a group.
- Using fraction manipulatives to model, compare, and order equivalent fractions.
- Translating and solving two-step word problems by drawing a picture or listing the information given.

Materials

Instructional Masters

- Power Up H Worksheet
- Lesson Activity 8*

Manipulative Kit

- Rulers
- Fraction circles, two-color counters*

Teacher-provided materials

- Grid paper, red pencils*

*optional

California Mathematics Content Standards

NS 1.0, 1.5 Explain different interpretations of fractions, for example, parts of a whole, parts of a set, and division of whole numbers by whole numbers; explain equivalents of fractions (see Standard 4.0).

NS 1.0, 1.7 Write the fraction represented by a drawing of parts of a figure; represent a given fraction by using drawings; and relate a fraction to a simple decimal on a number line.

MR 1.0, 1.2 Determine when and how to break a problem into simpler parts.

MR 2.0, 2.3 Use a variety of methods, such as words, numbers, symbols, charts, graphs, tables, diagrams, and models, to explain mathematical reasoning.

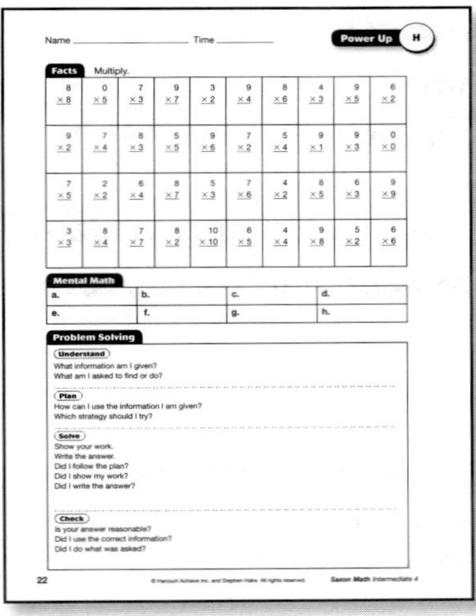

Power Up H Worksheet

Universal Access

Reaching All Special Needs Students

Special Education Students	At-Risk Students	English Learners	Advanced Learners
• Inclusion (TM) • Adaptations for Saxon Math	• Alternative Approach (TM) • Error Alert (TM) • Reteaching Masters • Refresher Lessons for California Standards	• English Learners (TM) • Developing Academic Language (TM) • English Learner Handbook	• Extend the Example (TM) • Extend the Problem (TM) • Online Activities

TM=Teacher's Manual

Developing Academic Language

Maintained	English Learner
diagram	contestant
fraction	
mass	
weight	

Problem Solving Discussion

Problem

Find the next five numbers in this sequence. Then describe the sequence in words.

..., 64, 32, 16, 8, __, __, __, __, __, ...

Focus Strategy  **Find/Extend a Pattern**

Understand *Understand the problem.*

"What information are we given?"

We are shown four terms of a sequence.

"What are we asked to do?"

We are asked to find the next five terms and to describe the sequence in words.

"Do the numbers increase or decrease in this sequence?"

The numbers decrease from left to right.

Plan *Make a plan.*

"What problem-solving strategy can we use to solve this problem?"

We can *find a pattern*, which means we need to find the rule for the sequence. Then we can use the rule to *extend the pattern*.

Solve *Carry out the plan.*

"How much do we count down to get from the first term to the second term?"

The first term is 64, and the second term is 32. Sixty-four minus 32 is 32.

"How much do we count down to get from the second term to the third term?"

The second term is 32, and the third term is 16. Thirty-two minus 16 is 16.

"Do the terms of the sequence count down by a constant amount?"

No. The decrease of the terms does not follow a counting down rule.

"What is a rule that describes the pattern of this sequence?"

The second term (32) is half of the first term (64). The third term (16) is half of the second term (32). We see that the fourth term is 8, which is half of 16. It appears that each term of the sequence is half of the previous term.

"What are the next five terms of the sequence?"

We continue the sequence by halving the terms: 4, 2, 1, $\frac{1}{2}$, and $\frac{1}{4}$.

Check *Look back.*

"Are our answers reasonable?"

We know that our answers are reasonable because 4 is half of 8, 2 is half of 4, 1 is half of 2, $\frac{1}{2}$ is half of 1, and $\frac{1}{4}$ is half of $\frac{1}{2}$.

"How can we describe this sequence using words?"

Each term of the sequence is half of the preceding term.

Power Up

Facts

Distribute **Power Up H** to students. See answers below.

Count Aloud

Before students begin the Mental Math exercises, do these counting exercises as a class.

Count up and down by fives from 25 to 65.

Mental Math

Encourage students to share different ways to mentally compute these exercises. Strategies for exercises are listed below.

a. Decompose 16

$5 \times (10 + 6) = 50 + 30 = 80$

Double 5 × 8

$5 \times 8 = 40;\ 40 \times 2 = 80$

c. Decompose 28

$5 \times (20 + 8) = 100 + 40 = 140$

Subtract 5 × 2 from 5 × 30

$(5 \times 30) - (5 \times 2) = 150 - 10 = 140$

Problem Solving

Refer to **Problem-Solving Strategy Discussion,** p. 622B.

New Concept

Instruction

Introduce the lesson by pointing out that problem-solving strategies can be used to solve two-step word problems involving fractions of a group.

(continued)

• Two-Step Problems About a Fraction of a Group

California Mathematics Content Standards

NS 1.0, 1.5 Explain different interpretations of fractions, for example, parts of a whole, parts of a set, and division of whole numbers by whole numbers; explain equivalents of fractions (see Standard 4.0).

NS 1.0, 1.7 Write the fraction represented by a drawing of parts of a figure; represent a given fraction by using drawings; and relate a fraction to a simple decimal on a number line.

MR 1.0, 1.2 Determine when and how to break a problem into simpler parts.

Power Up

facts Power Up H

mental math Five is half of 10. To multiply by 5, we can multiply by half of 10. For example, 5×12 equals half of 10×12. Find each product by multiplying by "half of 10" in problems **a–d.**

a. Number Sense: 5×16 80

b. Number Sense: 5×24 120

c. Number Sense: 5×28 140

d. Number Sense: 5×64 320

e. Measurement: A *stone* is a British unit of weight equal to 14 pounds. Two stone is 28 pounds, 3 stone is 42 pounds, and so on. How many pounds is 10 stone? 140 lb

f. Estimation: Lydia walked 1 km in 608 seconds. About how many minutes did it take her to walk 1 km? About 10 min

g. Calculation: $\frac{1}{10}$ of 40, $\times$ 10, + 5, $\div$ 5 9

h. Simplify: $8 + 2 \times 2$ 12

problem solving Choose an appropriate problem-solving strategy to solve this problem. Find the next five numbers in this sequence. Then describe the sequence in words. 4, 2, 1, $\frac{1}{2}$, $\frac{1}{4}$; Each number is one half the preceding number in the sequence.

..., 64, 32, 16, 8, ____, ____, ____, ____, ____, ...

New Concept

The word problems in this lesson are two-step problems involving fractions of a group. First we divide to find the number in one part. Then we multiply to find the number in more than one part.

Facts Multiply.

8 × 8 = 64	0 × 5 = 0	7 × 3 = 21	9 × 7 = 63	3 × 2 = 6	9 × 4 = 36	8 × 6 = 48	4 × 3 = 12	9 × 5 = 45	6 × 2 = 12
9 × 2 = 18	7 × 4 = 28	8 × 3 = 24	5 × 5 = 25	9 × 6 = 54	7 × 2 = 14	5 × 4 = 20	9 × 1 = 9	9 × 3 = 27	0 × 0 = 0
7 × 5 = 35	2 × 2 = 4	6 × 4 = 24	8 × 7 = 56	5 × 3 = 15	7 × 6 = 42	4 × 2 = 8	8 × 5 = 40	6 × 3 = 18	9 × 9 = 81
3 × 3 = 9	8 × 4 = 32	7 × 7 = 49	8 × 2 = 16	10 × 10 = 100	6 × 5 = 30	4 × 4 = 16	9 × 8 = 72	5 × 2 = 10	6 × 6 = 36

Example 1

Thinking Skills

Verify

What are the two steps needed to find the number of campers who wore green jackets?

1. Find the number of campers in each group.
2. Find the number of campers who wore green jackets.

There were 30 campers in the state park. Two thirds of them wore green jackets. How many campers wore green jackets?

The word *thirds* tells us there were 3 equal groups. First we find the number of campers in each group. Since there were 30 campers in all, we divide 30 by 3.

$$3\overline{)30}\quad = 10$$

There were 10 campers in each group. We draw this diagram:

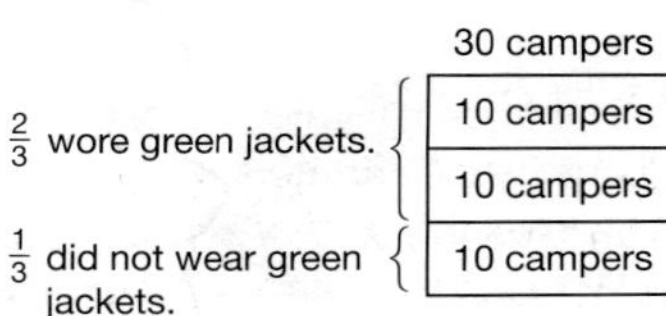

Two thirds wore green jackets. In two groups there were 2×10 campers or **20 campers** who wore green jackets. We also see that one group did not wear green jackets, so 10 campers did not wear green jackets.

Example 2

The force of gravity on Mars is about $\frac{2}{5}$ the force of gravity on Earth. A rock brought back to Earth from Mars weighs 50 pounds. How much did the rock weigh on Mars?

The mass of the rock is the same on Earth as it was on Mars because it is the same amount of rock. However, Earth is more massive than Mars, so the force of gravity is greater on Earth. The rock on Mars weighed only $\frac{2}{5}$ of its weight on Earth. To find $\frac{2}{5}$ of 50 pounds, we first find $\frac{1}{5}$ of 50 pounds by dividing 50 pounds by 5.

$$50 \text{ pounds} \div 5 = 10 \text{ pounds}$$

50 pounds

weight of the rock on Mars { 10 pounds, 10 pounds

10 pounds

10 pounds

10 pounds

Math Background

Finding a fraction of a number is the same as multiplying the number by the fraction.

For example, $\frac{2}{3}$ of 30 is the same as $\frac{2}{3} \times 30$.

We multiply fractions by multiplying the numerators and multiplying the denominators.

$\frac{2}{3}$ of $30 = \frac{2}{3} \times 30 = \frac{2}{3} \times \frac{30}{1} = \frac{60}{3}$

Recall that $\frac{60}{3} = 60 \div 3 = 20$. So, $\frac{2}{3}$ of $30 = 20$.

Alternative Approach: Using Manipulatives

Have students use two-color counters to model two-step problems about a fraction of a group.

In Example 1, give students 30 counters to represent the campers. Since two thirds of the campers wore green jackets, have students use the red side of the counter to represent these campers and the yellow side to represent the campers who did not wear green jackets. Have them arrange the counters into 3 equal groups. Ask students, ***"How many campers are in each group? How many campers wore green jackets?"*** 10 in each group; 20 wore green jackets. Have students model other examples.

New Concept *(Continued)*

Example 1

Discussion

As you discuss the solution, point out that the numerator of $\frac{2}{3}$ shows how many groups wore green jackets, the numerator of $\frac{1}{3}$ shows how many groups did not, and the denominator of the fractions shows the number of equal groups.

After discussing the solution, make sure students understand that to find the number of campers that represented $\frac{2}{3}$, they first found the number of campers that represented $\frac{1}{3}$. The number of campers representing $\frac{1}{3}$ (10) was then doubled to find the number of campers that represented $\frac{2}{3}$.

Students should generalize from the example that in order to find a number that represents more than one part of a whole, they must first find the number that represents one part of the whole.

Error Alert

Encourage students to check their work. Invite volunteers to explain how they can check their answer.

Example 2

Active Learning

After reading the problem, ask:

"Will the weight of the rock on Mars be more or less than the weight of the rock on Earth? Explain why." Less; sample: The weight of the rock on Mars is $\frac{2}{5}$ of the weight of the rock on Earth, which is 50 pounds. Since $\frac{2}{5}$ represents only a part of 50 pounds, the weight of the rock on Mars will be less than 50 pounds.

Extend the Example

After discussing the solution, ask your advanced learners to describe a method that can be used to solve problems that involve finding more than one part of a whole. Sample: To find a number that represents more than one part of a whole, first find the number that represents one part of the whole. Then use multiplication or addition to find more than one part of the whole.

(continued)

New Concept (Continued)

Lesson Practice

Guided Practice

Use these problems as guided practice to check the students' understanding of today's concept.

Problem a **Represent**

To help students begin, ask:

"What does the numerator of the fraction $\frac{3}{4}$ represent?" The number of groups of checkers that were still on the board

"What does the denominator of the fraction $\frac{3}{4}$ represent?" The number of equal groups the whole (or 24 checkers) is divided into

Problems a–c **Represent**

Error Alert

Encourage students to use addition to check their work. The number that each diagram represents altogether should be the same as the sum of the numbers that each part of the diagram represents. For example, after completing problem **a**, students should compare 24 to the sum of 6 + 6 + 6 + 6.

Closure

The questions below help assess the concepts taught in this lesson.

"Explain how to find $\frac{3}{4}$ of a number." Sample: Divide the whole into four equal parts. Find the number that each of those parts represent, and then multiply that number by 3 or use that number as an addend three times.

"Draw a diagram to find $\frac{3}{4}$ of 24. $\frac{3}{4}$ of 24 is 18." See student work.

Written Practice

Math Conversations

Independent Practice and Discussions to Increase Understanding

Problem 5 **Represent**

For part **a**, ask:

"We will draw a rectangle and divide it into equal parts to illustrate this problem. Into how many equal parts should we divide the rectangle? Explain how you know." Four; The denominator of a fraction represents the number of equal parts into which a whole is divided.

(continued)

Sample: Weight is related to the force of gravity, and the force of gravity on Mars is less than the force of gravity on Earth, so the weight of the rock is greater on Earth. The mass of the rock is the same on each planet.

Each fifth is 10 pounds, so $\frac{2}{5}$ is 20 pounds. We find that the rock that weighs 50 pounds on Earth weighed only **20 pounds** on Mars.

Discuss Why did the weight of the rock change when it was brought to Earth? How does the mass of the rock on Mars compare to the mass of the rock on Earth?

Lesson Practice

Represent Diagram problems **a** and **b**. Then answer the question.

a. 24 checkers

$\frac{1}{4}$ off the board	6 checkers
$\frac{3}{4}$ on the board	6 checkers
	6 checkers
	6 checkers

b. 30 students

$\frac{2}{5}$ studied for more than one hour.	6 students
	6 students
$\frac{3}{5}$ did not study for more than one hour.	6 students
	6 students
	6 students

a. Three fourths of the 24 checkers were still on the board. How many checkers were still on the board? 18 checkers

b. Two fifths of 30 students studied more than one hour for a test. How many students studied for more than one hour? 12 students

c. The force of gravity on Mercury is about $\frac{1}{3}$ the force of gravity on Earth. How much would a tire weigh on Mercury, if it weighs 39 lb on Earth? Would the mass be the same? Why or why not? 13 lb; The mass would be the same, because mass is the same no matter where you are.

Written Practice

Distributed and Integrated

1. (42, 75) One hundred fifty feet equals how many yards? 50 yards

2. (93) Tammy gave the clerk \$6 to pay for a book. She received 64¢ in change. Tax was 38¢. What was the price of the book? \$4.98

***3.** (93) DaJuan is 2 years older than Rebecca. Rebecca is twice as old as Dillon. DaJuan is 12 years old. How old is Dillon? (*Hint:* First find Rebecca's age.) 5 years old

4. (Inv. 4, 43) Write each decimal as a mixed number:

a. 3.29 $3\frac{29}{100}$ **b.** 32.9 $32\frac{9}{10}$ **c.** 3.09 $3\frac{9}{100}$

▸ ***5.** (44, 94) **Represent** **a.** Three fourths of the 84 contestants guessed incorrectly. How many contestants guessed incorrectly? Draw a picture to illustrate the problem. 63 contestants

b. What decimal number represents the contestants who guessed incorrectly? 0.75

5. 84 contestants

$\frac{3}{4}$ guessed incorrectly.	21 contestants
	21 contestants
	21 contestants
$\frac{1}{4}$ did not guess incorrectly.	21 contestants

English Learners

A **contestant** is a person who participates in a competition or contest.

Ask students to explain why they think the word is appropriately named. Sample: because a contestant is someone who competes in a contest

Ask students if they watch any television shows that have contestants in them.

*6. (21) **Analyze** In February, Fairbanks, Alaska, has an average high temperature of 7°F and an average low temperature of −14°F. How many degrees difference are these two temperatures? 21 degrees

7. (18, 42) **a.** What is the diameter of this circle? 1 in.

b. What is the radius of this circle? $\frac{1}{2}$ in.

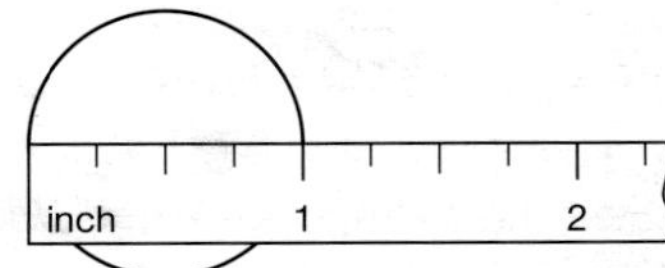

8. (Inv. 4) **Represent** Use words to write 8.75. eight and seventy-five hundredths

▶ *9. (91) **Estimate** Three students each made a different estimate of the quotient 2589 ÷ 9. Paulo's estimate was 30, Carter's estimate was 300, and Allison's estimate was 3000. Which student made the best estimate? Explain your answer. Carter made the best estimate; sample: 27 is divisible by 9, so 2700 is divisible by 9; Since 2589 is close to 2700, divide 2700 by 9.

*10. (Inv. 6) The first five odd counting numbers are 1, 3, 5, 7, and 9. Find the median of these five numbers. 5

*11. (92) **Explain** Write these numbers in order from least to greatest. Explain your thinking. $\frac{14}{10}$, 1.5, $\frac{7}{4}$; Sample: Change the numbers to mixed numbers and order them on a number line. $\frac{7}{4}$, 1.5, $\frac{14}{10}$

▶*12. (90) **Multiple Choice** Use the polygons below to answer parts **a–c.**

A 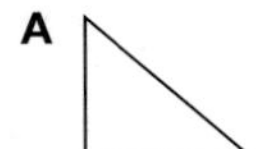 B  C 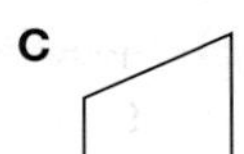 D 

a. Which of these polygons is a parallelogram? B

b. Which polygon(s) appear to have at least one obtuse angle? C and D

c. Which polygon does not appear to have any perpendicular sides? D

13. (9, 28, 52) \$16.25 − (\$6 − 50¢) \$10.75

14. (38) 5 × 7 × 9 315

15. (59) \$7.83 × 6 \$46.98

16. (84) 54 × 1000 54,000

Inclusion

Use this strategy if the student displays:

- Difficulty with Large Group Instruction.
- Difficulty with Abstract Processing.

Two-Step Problems About a Fraction of a Group (Individual)

Materials: grid paper, red pencil

- Read, ***"There are 28 students in a class. $\frac{3}{4}$ of them wore jeans to school today. How many students wore jeans?"***
- Tell students to outline 30 boxes on the grid paper. Ask, ***"How many groups are the students divided into?"*** 4
- Have students divide and outline (in red) the boxes into four groups. Ask, ***"How many Groups wore jeans?"*** 3 Have students shade the boxes in 3 of the red outlined groups. Ask, ***"How many students work jeans?"*** 21
- Write on the board and have students work in pairs to solve. Read ***"$\frac{2}{3}$ of the plants in the garden bloomed on the first day of spring. If there were 63 plants, how many bloomed?"***

Written Practice *(Continued)*

Math Conversations *(cont.)*

Extend the Problem

"How can we use division, and then use multiplication, to check our answer?" Use division to find $\frac{1}{4}$ of 84 (84 ÷ 4 = 21), and then find $\frac{3}{4}$ by subtracting that number from 84 or by multiplying that number by 3. Then compare the answers.

For part **b,** ask:

"Explain how to change the fraction $\frac{3}{4}$ to a decimal number." Divide 3 by 4; 3 ÷ 4 = 0.75

Problem 9 **Estimate**

Before students solve the problem, invite a volunteer to explain how using compatible numbers to make an estimate is different from using rounding. Rounding involves a specific place value, such as hundreds or thousands; Using compatible numbers involves choosing numbers that are easy to compute mentally, regardless of a specific place value.

Encourage students to complete their estimates using only mental math.

Problem 12 **Multiple Choice**

Test-Taking Strategy

Explain that students can use the idea that parallelograms are quadrilaterals and that quadrilaterals have four sides to immediately identify choices **A** and **D** as incorrect answers to part **a.**

(continued)

Written Practice *(Continued)*

Math Conversations *(cont.)*

Problem 26 Represent

Manipulative Use

Encourage students to use their fraction manipulatives to check their work.

Problem 27 Analyze

Make sure students infer that because the distance around the square is 40 cm and each of the four sides of the square have the same length, the length of one side of the square can be found by dividing 40 cm by 4.

Problem 28 Represent

Manipulative Use

Students can trace this figure or draw a larger or smaller version of it using a ruler.

Problem 30 Analyze

Point out that writing a check is a way of spending money, and make sure students can conclude that because Madison spent more money than she had, the balance in her account must be a negative number.

Errors and Misconceptions

Problem 2

If students have difficulty finding the cost of the book, suggest that they work backward to solve the problem. Subtracting 64¢ from \$6.00 equals \$5.36, the price of the book including tax. Subtracting 38¢ from \$5.36 equals the price of the book before tax.

Problem 23

When simplifying fractions, students may not think of a fraction bar as a grouping symbol. This expression provides an opportunity for you to remind students that in addition to representing division, a fraction bar also represents a grouping symbol. Operations both above and below the grouping symbol must be completed before dividing.

17. (88) 45×45 2025

18. (71) 32×40 1280

19. (88) 46×44 2024

20. (83) $6\overline{)3625}$ 604 R 1

21. (83) $5\overline{)3000}$ 600

22. (34, 79) $7n = 987$ 141

23. (Inv. 3, 65, 83) $\frac{10^3}{\sqrt{25}}$ 200

24. (79) \$13.76 ÷ 8 \$1.72

25. (68) $\frac{232}{4}$ 58

▶***26.** (89) Represent Draw and shade a circle to show that $\frac{8}{8}$ equals 1.

▶***27.** (31, 66) Analyze The perimeter of the square at right is 40 cm. What is the area of this square? 100 cm^2

▶ **28.** (70, 82) Represent Draw a triangle that is similar to this isosceles triangle. Then draw its line of symmetry.

***29.** (28, 44) **a.** Compare: 0.25 ⊜ 0.250

b. Compare: \$0.25 ⊜ 25¢

▶***30.** (76) Analyze Madison had \$100 in the bank. She wrote a check for \$145. What number represents the balance of her account? −\$45

Looking Forward

Solving two-step problems that involve a fraction of a group prepares students for:

- **Lesson 98,** identifying and writing fractions equal to 1 and to $\frac{1}{2}$.
- **Lesson 99,** changing improper fractions to whole or mixed numbers.
- **Lesson 100,** adding and subtracting fractions with common denominators.
- **Lesson 103,** finding equivalent fractions.
- **Lesson 106**, writing the reduced form of a fraction.
- **Lessons 112–113,** adding and subtracting fractions and mixed numbers with common denominators and renaming fractions whose denominators are not equal by using a common denominator of the fractions.

California Mathematics Content Standards

AF 1.0, 1.3 Use parentheses to indicate which operation to perform first when writing expressions containing more than two terms and different operations.

SDAP 1.0, 1.1 Formulate survey questions; systematically collect and represent data on a number line; and coordinate graphs, tables, and charts.

SDAP 1.0, 1.2 Identify the mode(s) for sets of categorical data and the mode(s), median, and any apparent outliers for numerical data sets.

MR 2.0, 2.3 Use a variety of methods, such as words, numbers, symbols, charts, graphs, tables, diagrams, and models, to explain mathematical reasoning.

Planning & Preparation

• Describing Data

Objectives

- Find the median of a set of numbers.
- Find the range of a set of numbers.
- Find the mode(s) of a set of numbers.

Prerequisite Skills

- Finding the difference of three-digit numbers with regrouping.
- Listing a set of numbers in order from least to greatest.

Materials

Instructional Masters

- Power Up H Worksheet
- Lesson Activity 8*

Manipulative Kit

- Rulers
- Fraction circles, two-color counters*

Teacher-provided materials

- Grid paper, index cards*

**optional*

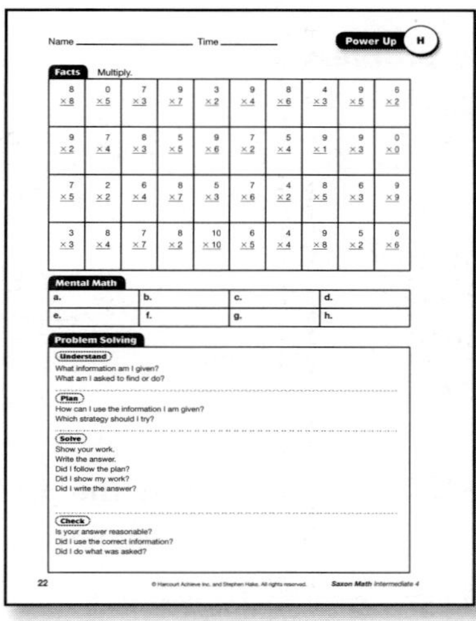

Power Up H Worksheet

Reaching All Special Needs Students

Special Education Students	At-Risk Students	English Learners	Advanced Learners
• Inclusion (TM) • Adaptations for Saxon Math	• Alternative Approach (TM) • Error Alert (TM) • Reteaching Masters • Refresher Lessons for California Standards	• English Learners (TM) • Developing Academic Language (TM) • English Learner Handbook	• Extend the Example (TM) • Extend the Problem (TM) • Online Activities

TM=Teacher's Manual

Developing Academic Language

New	Maintained	English Learner
range	line plot	affect
	median	
	mode	
	outlier	
	table	

Problem Solving Discussion

Problem

On February 4, Edgar remembered that his two library books were due on January 28. The fine for late books is 15¢ per book per day. If he returns the books on February 4, what will be the total fine?

Focus Strategy  **Write a Number Sentence or Equation**

Understand *Understand the problem.*

"What information are we given?"

Two library books were due on January 28.

The fine for late books is 15¢ per day.

Both books will be returned on February 4.

"What are we asked to do?"

We are asked to calculate Edgar's total library fine.

Plan *Make a plan.*

"How can we use the information we know to solve the problem?"

We can count the number of days the books are late. Then we can *write a number sentence* to calculate Edgar's fine.

Solve *Carry out the plan.*

"For which dates in January will Edgar be charged a late fine?"

January 29, 30, and 31

"For which dates in February will Edgar be charged a late fine?"

February 1, 2, 3, and 4

"How can we calculate Edgar's total late fine?"

The library fine for each book is 15¢ per day. This means the late fine for 2 books is 30¢ per day.

"What is a number sentence that we can use to calculate the total fine?"

Fine = 30¢ × 7 = $2.10

Check *Look back.*

"Is our answer reasonable?"

We know that our answer is reasonable, because January 29 through February 4 is a total of 7 days that the books will be counted as late. The fine for each book is 15¢ per day, so the total fine on 2 books is 30¢ per day. Thirty cents per day for 7 days is a total of 7 × 30¢, which is $2.10

"What is another way we could have solved the problem?"

We could have multiplied 15¢ by the number of days late to find the total fine for each book (7 × 15¢ = $1.05). Then we could have doubled that amount because Edgar had 2 books that were overdue (2 × $1.05 = $2.10).

Alternate Strategy

Make or Use a Chart, Table, or Graph

Students may use a calendar to find that February 4 is 1 week after January 28. One week is 7 days. Students can make a table to show the total late fine for each day.

LESSON 95

• Describing Data

California Mathematics Content Standards

AF 1.0, 1.3 Use parentheses to indicate which operation to perform first when writing expressions containing more than two terms and different operations.

SDAP 1.0, 1.1 Formulate survey questions; systematically collect and represent data on a number line; and coordinate graphs, tables, and charts.

SDAP 1.0, 1.2 Identify the mode(s) for sets of categorical data and the mode(s), median, and any apparent outliers for numerical data sets.

Power Up

facts Power Up H

mental math Find each product by multiplying by "half of 10" in problems **a–c.**

a. Number Sense: 5 × 46 230

b. Number Sense: 5 × 62 310

c. Number Sense: 5 × 240 1200

d. Money: The price of the blouse is \$24.87. Sales tax is \$1.95. What is the total cost? \$26.82

e. Measurement: The large glass of water weighed half a kilogram. How many grams is half a kilogram? 500 g

f. Estimation: The package of 10 pencils costs \$1.98. Round that price to the nearest dollar and then divide by 10 to estimate the cost per pencil. 20¢

g. Calculation: $\sqrt{4}$, × 7, + 1, + 10, $\sqrt{\ }$, − 4 1

h. Simplify: 10 − 6 ÷ 2 7

problem solving Choose an appropriate problem-solving strategy to solve this problem. On February 4, Edgar remembered that his two library books were due on January 28. The fine for late books is 15¢ per book per day. If he returns the books on February 4, what will be the total fine? \$2.10

New Concept

The median of a set of numbers is the middle number when the numbers are arranged in order of size. When there is an even set of numbers, the median is the sum of the two middle numbers divided by two.

Facts Multiply.

8 × 8 64	0 × 5 0	7 × 3 21	9 × 7 63	3 × 2 6	9 × 4 36	8 × 6 48	4 × 3 12	9 × 5 45	6 × 2 12
9 × 2 18	7 × 4 28	8 × 3 24	5 × 5 25	9 × 6 54	7 × 2 14	5 × 4 20	9 × 1 9	9 × 3 27	0 × 0 0
7 × 5 35	2 × 2 4	6 × 4 24	8 × 7 56	5 × 3 15	7 × 6 42	4 × 2 8	8 × 5 40	6 × 3 18	9 × 9 81
3 × 3 9	8 × 4 32	7 × 7 49	8 × 2 16	10 × 10 100	6 × 5 30	4 × 4 16	9 × 8 72	5 × 2 10	6 × 6 36

LESSON 95

Power Up

Facts

Distribute **Power Up H** to students. See answers below.

Count Aloud

Before students begin the Mental Math exercises, do these counting exercises as a class.

Count up and down by twelves from 24 to 144.

Mental Math

Encourage students to share different ways to mentally compute these exercises. Strategies for exercises are listed below.

a. Add 5 × 6 to 5 × 40

$(5 \times 40) + (5 \times 6) = 200 + 30 = 230$

Subtract 5 × 4 from 5 × 50

$(5 \times 50) - (5 \times 4) = 250 - 20 = 230$

b. Decompose 62

$5 \times (60 + 2) = 300 + 10 = 310$

Add 5 × 2 to 5 × 60

$(5 \times 60) + (5 \times 2) = 300 + 10 = 310$

Problem Solving

Refer to **Problem-Solving Strategy Discussion**, p. 627B.

New Concept

Explanation

In this lesson, students will learn that a median, a mode, and a range are ways to describe a set of data.

(continued)

New Concept *(Continued)*

Example 1

As you discuss the solution, point out that although the scores are shown ordered from lowest to highest, they also can be ordered from highest to lowest—both ways of ordering the scores will produce the same median.

It is important for students to understand the concept that is addressed in the **Discuss** question. The median of those two middle values is the average of those values, which is found by dividing the sum of the values by 2 or finding a number halfway between the two numbers.

Active Learning

Ask:

"What could we do to find the median if a set of numbers does not have one middle number?" Sample: Find, the two middle numbers and determine the half-way point between the two.

For example, the set of numbers 1, 6, 8, 10, 15, 16 has no middle number. We can look at 8 and 10 to find the median.

"What number is between 8 and 10?" 9

Example 2

Explain that finding a range involves comparing the values in the data set and identifying the greatest and least values.

Error Alert

Make sure students understand that it is not necessary to order the data from least to greatest or from greatest to least to find a range.

Example 3

In this example, the data have one mode. The **Discuss** question gives students an opportunity to learn that data may have two modes. Also point out that a data set may have more than two modes, or no mode at all.

Extend the Example

Challenge your advanced learners to write a set of numbers that have the same median, mode, and range, and then share those numbers with the class. Sample: The median, mode, and range of {1, 2, 2, 2, 3} is 2.

(continued)

Example 1

Find the median of Ian's seven game scores.

80, 85, 85, 10, 90, 90, 85

The median score is the middle score. To find the median score, we arrange the scores in order. We begin with the lowest score.

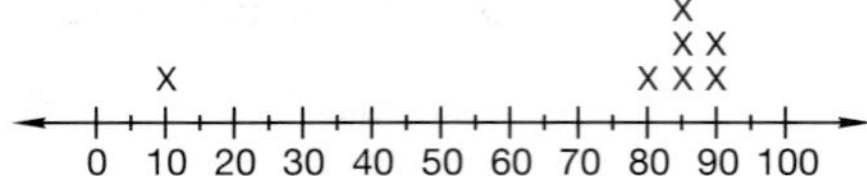

We see that the median score is **85.**

Discuss Explain how to find the median of the following set of numbers.

5, 4, 3, 8, 7, 7

Sample: The median is 6 because $(5 + 7) \div 2 = 6$.

Notice that the low score of 10 does not affect the median. A score that is far from the other scores is called an outlier. Outliers generally have little or no effect on the median. Below we have placed these scores on a line plot. We see that most of the scores are close together.

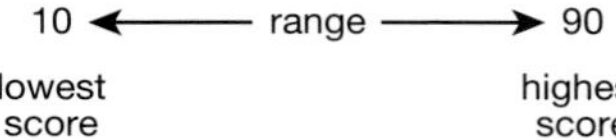

The outlier is far away from the other scores.

The range of a set of numbers is the difference between the largest and the smallest numbers in a list. To calculate the range of a list, we subtract the smallest number from the largest number.

Example 2

Find the range of Ian's seven game scores.

80, 85, 85, 10, 90, 90, 85

The scores vary from a low of 10 to a high of 90. The range is the difference of the high and low scores. We subtract 10 from 90 and find that the range is **80.**

The mode of a set of numbers is the number that occurs most often.

Math Background

Consider this data set: 2, 2, 4, 4, 4, 5, 5, 6. The mean and median of this data set are both 4.

Now, we'll replace the 6 with 30: 2, 2, 4, 4, 4, 5, 5, 30. The mean has increased to 7. However, the median has not changed; it is still 4. Note that the median would be 4 even if we had replaced the 6 with 30,000.

In statistics, the median is referred to as a *robust* measure. This means that it is not affected by extreme data values. The mean is not nearly as robust as the median, however. If we replaced the 6 with 30,000, the mean would increase to 3750.75.

English Learners

Explain to your students that to **affect** means to act on or change. Say:

"Practicing a musical instrument affects how well you can play the instrument."

Ask:

"What can you do to affect how well you do in math?" Samples: do your homework, try to understand, ask questions, etc.

Example 3

Find the mode of Ian's seven game scores.

80, 85, 85, 10, 90, 90, 85

We see that the score of 85 appears three times. No other score appears more than twice. So the mode is **85**.

Discuss What is the mode of the following set of numbers?

5, 5, 3, 6, 8, 7, 7

The data have two modes, 5 and 7.

Collecting Data

Materials needed:

- paper and pencil

Use a sheet of paper for recording data from a survey. Then take a survey of ten friends. Use this question or one of your own:

How many bicycles do you have in your home?

a. Record the data in a table.

b. Use the data to make a line plot.

c. Write the median and mode. See student work.

Lesson Practice

a. **Analyze** Find the median, mode, and range of Raquel's game points shown below. Is there an outlier in this set of points? Median, 90; mode, 90; range, 50; outlier, 50

50, 80, 90, 85, 90, 95, 90, 100

b. Find the median, mode, and range of this set of numbers: Median, 30; mode, 31; range, 6

31, 28, 31, 30, 25

c. **Explain** Find the median of these temperatures. Explain how you found your answer.

75°, 80°, 80°, 90°, 95°, 100°

c. The median is 85. There is an even number of temperatures, so there is no one middle temperature. The sum of the two middle temperatures, 80 and 90, divided by two is 85.

d. **Interpret** Every X on this line plot stands for the age of a child attending a party. How many children attended the party? What is the mode of the ages? 12 children; 10 years old

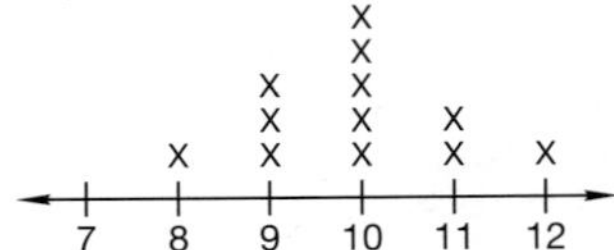

Alternative Approach: Using Manipulatives

Give each student or group of students 7 index cards. Have them write the following numbers on the cards (one per card): 12, 10, 9, 11, 11, 11, 10. Explain that these numbers represent the ages in a group of students.

Have students arrange the cards in order from least to greatest in a horizontal row. 9, 10, 10, 11, 11, 11, 12 To find the range, have students select the cards on each end (smallest and largest numbers) and find the difference between them. Ask, ***"What is the range of this set of data?"*** 12 − 9 = 3

To find the mode, have students select the cards with the numbers that appear most often. Ask, ***"What is the mode of this set of data?"*** The mode of this set of data is 11.

To find the median, have students start at each end with the smallest and largest numbers and flip the cards face down at the same time. Continue until one card is left. The card in the middle that is left face up is the median. Point out that there are three cards on each side of this median. Ask students, ***"What is the median of this set of data?"*** 11

New Concept *(Continued)*

Activity

As you discuss the activity, encourage students to suggest a variety of questions that could be asked in place of the given question.

If students survey friends and relatives from outside the classroom, invite volunteers to share their findings with the class.

Lesson Practice

Guided Practice

Use these problems as guided practice to check the students' understanding of today's concept.

Problem a **Analyze**

To help students get started, have them look at the data set in part **a.** Then ask:

"Is the number of scores in this data set odd or even?" even

"To calculate the median, how many scores will we find in the middle after we arrange the scores in order from least to greatest or from greatest to least?" two

"Explain how to find the median of the two middle scores." Divide the sum of the scores by 2.

"What operation should we use to calculate the range of the scores?" subtraction

Problem d
Error Alert

Make sure students understand that it is not usually necessary to complete a pencil-and-paper computation to identify a mode. This is especially true with line plots because the mode of a line plot is simply the tallest column, or the tallest columns when two or more columns have the same height.

Closure **The question below helps assess the concepts taught in this lesson.**

"Explain how to find the median, the mode, and the range of a data set that contains six numbers." Median: Arrange the numbers in order and then find the average of the two middle numbers by dividing the sum of the numbers by 2; mode: Name the number (if any) or numbers that appear most often; range: Subtract the least number from the greatest.

Written Practice

Math Conversations

Independent Practice and Discussions to Increase Understanding

Problem 1 (Interpret)

Before students solve parts **a–c,** invite volunteers to describe the different labels of the table, such as its title and the headings for each column, and have them identify the information that is given in each row.

Before students complete part **a,** make sure that they recognize that the rainfall data are inches, but that the unit described in part **a** is feet.

"Explain how we can change a number of inches to feet." Sample: Divide the number of inches by 12; The quotient will represent the number of feet, and if there is a remainder, the remainder will represent the number of inches.

To complete part **c,** students will need to estimate the heights of four of the five bars. Prior to drawing the bars, discuss with students different ways to make reasonable estimates of the heights. Some students will find it helpful to copy and complete the graph on grid paper.

Problem 2 (Represent)

"We will draw a shape and divide it into equal parts to illustrate this problem. Into how many equal parts should we divide the shape? Explain how you know." Six; The denominator of the fraction $\frac{5}{6}$ represents the number of equal parts into which the whole or 288 marchers is divided.

(continued)

e. (Verify) Is there an outlier in the data in problem **d**? Why or why not? No; All of the data is clustered together.

Distributed and Integrated

▸ *1. (Inv. 5) (Interpret) Use the information in this table to answer parts **a–c.**

Average Yearly Rainfall

City	Rainfall (in inches)
Boston	43
Chicago	36
Denver	16
Houston	48
San Francisco	20

a. Which cities listed in the table average less than 2 feet of rain per year? Denver and San Francisco

b. One year Houston received 62 inches of rain. This was how much more than its yearly average? 14 inches

c. Copy and complete this bar graph to show the information in the rainfall table:

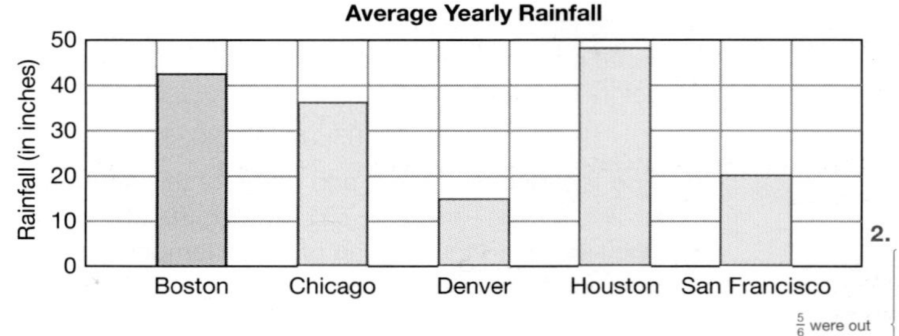

▸ *2. (94) (Represent) Five sixths of the 288 marchers were out of step. How many marchers were out of step? Draw a picture to illustrate the problem. 240 marchers

2. 288 marchers
$\frac{5}{6}$ were out of step.: 48 marchers, 48 marchers, 48 marchers, 48 marchers, 48 marchers
$\frac{1}{6}$ were not out of step.: 48 marchers

*3. (28) (Represent) Something is wrong with this sign. Draw two different signs that show how to correct the error.

WATER
.99¢
per gallon

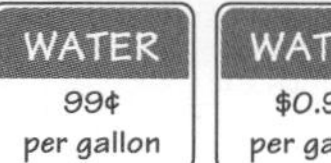

Inclusion

Use this strategy if the student displays:

- Poor Retention.
- Difficulty with Abstract Processing.

Describing Data (Small Group)

Material: counters

- Write: 3, 3, 3, 5, 6, 1, 7 on the board. Tell students that this is set of data representing the ages of some siblings in the class. Instruct students to write the numbers in order from least to greatest? Ask, ***"What is the difference or range between the greatest number and the least number in the data set?"*** 6
- Tell students to find the number in the middle and ask, ***"What is the median or middle number?"*** 3
- Have students add up all the numbers. Ask, ***"What is the total of all the numbers?"*** 28 ***"How many total numbers are there?"*** 7 ***"What number is the mode or occurs most?"*** 3

4. What is the radius of this circle in millimeters? 10 mm
(18, 42)

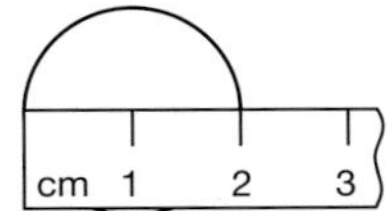

***5.** **Verify** Write *true* or *false* for each parts **a–c.**
(92)

a. $\frac{7}{6} > \frac{7}{4}$ false

b. $\frac{7}{10} > 0.5$ true

c. $1\frac{4}{6} < 1\frac{5}{10}$ false

▶ ***6.** Estimate the product of 88 and 22. Then find the actual product.
(91) 1800; 1936

7. Apples were priced at 53¢ per pound. What was the cost of 5 pounds of apples? $2.65
(39)

8. **Represent** Write the number 3708 in expanded form. Then use words to write the number. 3000 + 700 + 8; three thousand, seven hundred eight
(27)

9. The top of a doorway is about two meters from the floor. Two meters is how many centimeters? 200 cm
(42)

▶***10.** Four pounds of pears cost $1.20. What did 1 pound of pears cost? What did 6 pounds of pears cost? $0.30; $1.80
(93)

11. Mike drove his car 150 miles in 3 hours. What was his average speed in miles per hour? 50 miles per hour
(60)

12. (28, 52) $46.00 − $45.56 = $0.44

13. (52) 10,165 − 856 = 9309

14. (11, 28, 51) $0.63 + $1.49 + $12.24 + $0.38 + $0.06 + $5.00 + $1.20 = $21.00

15. (65, 85) 70^2 4900

16. (86) 71×69 4899

17. (83) $4\overline{)\$30.00}$ $7.50

18. (72) $3\overline{)263}$ 87 R 2

19. (34, 79) $5x = 4080$ 816

20. (69) $\frac{344}{8}$ 43

Written Practice *(Continued)*

Math Conversations *(cont.)*

Problem 6

Remind students who round 88 to 90 and round 22 to 20 that the product of 90 × 20 can be found using mental math by attaching two zeros to the right of the product of 9 × 2.

Problem 10

After the problem has been solved, point out that finding the cost of 1 pound of pears when the cost of 4 pounds is known is the same as finding the average cost per pound of the pears.

Problem 25

Before students complete any arithmetic, ask:

"To find a median, we must first arrange the numbers in order. This set of numbers contains five numbers. How many numbers should we find in the middle of the set after we arrange the numbers in order?" one number

"How many modes can a data set have?" None, one, or more than one

"What operation is used to find a range?" subtraction

Problem 26 Represent

Manipulative Use

Encourage students to use their fraction manipulatives to check their work.

Problem 27 Represent

Manipulative Use

Students will need a ruler to draw the square. Some students may find it helpful to complete the drawing on grid paper.

Extend the Problem

Ask your advanced learners to identify the operation they used to solve the problem, and then explain how a different operation can be used to check their answer. Sample: I multiplied 4 cm by 4 to solve the problem, and I can add 4 cm + 4 cm + 4 cm + 4 cm to check the answer.

(continued)

Written Practice (Continued)

Math Conversations (cont.)

Problem 30 (Analyze)

Some students will have difficulty solving this problem. To help those students, ask them to trace the figure, and then point to the three different shapes the figure contains —one large square in the middle, eight smaller squares around the perimeter, and eight triangles.

Lead students to understand that we cannot solve the problem until the figure is divided into equal parts. Then ask them to draw the two diagonals of the large square in the center of the figure, and then draw one diagonal in each of the other eight squares. The result will be a figure that is divided into 28 equal parts (or 28 congruent triangles).

Errors and Misconceptions

Problem 3

Make sure students are able to recognize the amount on the sign as $\frac{99}{100}$ of a cent (in other words, almost, but not quite, one penny).

Problem 4

Students who give the answer as 2 mm have neglected two important pieces of information:

- The ruler shows the diameter in centimeters.
- A radius is half of a diameter.

Review with these students the importance of looking for details in, and making inferences from, a given diagram.

Problem 15

Multiplying the base (70) by the exponent (2) will result in an incorrect answer of 140. Remind students who give 140 as the answer that an exponent represents the number of times that the other number (e.g. the base) is used as a factor, and then ask them to write 70^2 as the product of two identical factors. $70 \cdot 70$

Also point out that because 70 is a multiple of 10, the product of $70 \cdot 70$ can be found using mental math.

Problem 24

Students who give the answer as 3.24 simplified the expression by working from left to right instead of completing the operation in parentheses first.

21. (71) 37×60 2220

22. (88) 56×42 2352

23. (59) $\$5.97 \times 8$ \$47.76

24. (45) $10.00 - (4.46 - 2.3)$ 7.84

▶***25.** (95) Find the median, mode, and range of this set of numbers:
median, 3; mode, 1; range, 5

3, 1, 4, 1, 6

▶***26.** (89) (Represent) Draw and shade circles to show that 2 equals $\frac{4}{2}$.

▶***27.** (18, 66) **a.** (Represent) Draw a square with sides 4 cm long.
4 cm

b. Find the perimeter and the area of the square you drew.
16 cm; 16 sq. cm

***28.** (Inv. 9) Graph the equation $x = 3$. Name two points on the line.
See student work.

***29.** (64, 93) If $y = 6x - 4$, what is y when

a. x is 5? 26 **b.** x is 8? 44

▶***30.** (67) (Analyze) In this pattern of loose tiles, there are triangles and squares.

a. How many same-sized triangles as the shaded triangle, are there? 8

b. What fractional part of the whole design is the shaded triangle? $\frac{1}{28}$

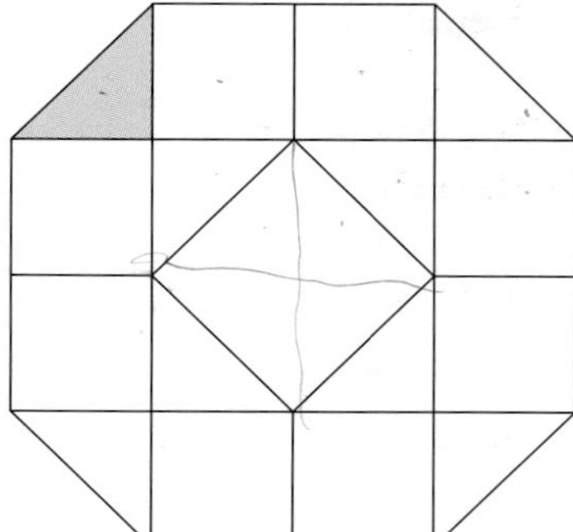

Looking Forward

Finding the median, mode, and range of a set of data prepares students for:

- **Investigation 10,** graphing relationships.

Cumulative Assessment and Test-Day Activity

Assessment

Distribute **Power-Up Test 18** and **Cumulative Test 18** to each student. Have students complete the **Power-Up Test** first. Allow 10 minutes. Then have students work on the **Cumulative Test.**

Test-Day Activity

The remaining class time can be spent on **Test-Day Activity 9.** Students can begin the activity in class and complete it as homework.

Planning & Preparation

California Mathematics Content Standards

MG 3.0, 3.6 Visualize, describe, and make models of geometric solids (e.g., prisms, pyramids) in terms of the number and shape of faces, edges, and vertices; interpret two-dimensional representations of three-dimensional objects; and draw patterns (of faces) for a solid that, when cut and folded, will make a model of the solid.

• Geometric Solids

Objectives

- Classify geometric solids by their vertices, edges, and faces.

Prerequisite Skills

- Classifying and drawing quadrilaterals by their characteristics.
- Finding examples of different quadrilaterals in the real world.

Materials

Instructional Masters

- Power Up H Worksheet
- Lesson Activity 27

Manipulative Kit

- Relational GeoSolids, fraction circles*

Teacher-provided materials

- Containers of different shapes and sizes, poster board, magazines, colored pencils*

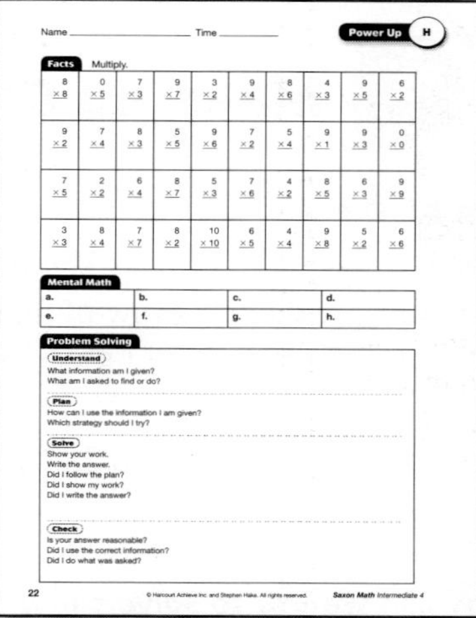

Power Up H Worksheet

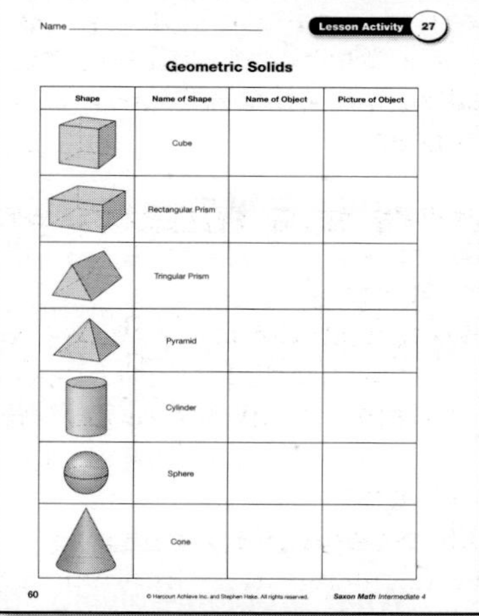

Lesson Activity 27

Universal Access

Reaching All Special Needs Students

Special Education Students	At-Risk Students	English Learners	Advanced Learners
• Inclusion (TM) • Adaptations for Saxon Math	• Alternative Approach (TM) • Error Alert (TM) • Reteaching Masters • Refresher Lessons for California Standards	• English Learners (TM) • Developing Academic Language (TM) • English Learner Handbook	• Extend the Example (TM) • Extend the Problem (TM) • Online Activities

TM=Teacher's Manual

Developing Academic Language

New		Maintained	English Learner
apex	geometric solids	vertex	funnel
cone	pyramid		
cube	rectangular prism		
cylinder	sphere		
edge	triangular prism		
face			

Problem Solving Discussion

Problem

There are three light switches that each control a row of lights in the classroom—a row in front, a row in the middle, and a row in back. Make a tree diagram to find the different ways the rows of lights can be turned on or off. Use the tree diagram to count the total number of combinations.

Focus Strategies

Draw a Picture or Diagram

1. 2. 3. **Make an Organized List**

Understand *Understand the problem.*

"What information are we given?"

There are three light switches: a switch for the front row of lights, a switch for the middle row of lights, and a switch for the back row of lights.

"What are we asked to do?"

We are asked to find all the different ways the rows of lights can be turned on or off.

Plan *Make a plan.*

"What problem-solving strategy can we use to solve the problem?"

We can *make an organized list* by *drawing a tree diagram.*

Solve *Carry out the plan.*

"What will our tree diagram look like?"

For each row of lights, the possibilities are on and off. We start our tree diagram by writing these two possibilities for the front row of lights. We draw two branches from "on" and two branches from "off" to show the possibilities for the middle row of lights. Then we draw two more branches from each combination to show the possibilities for the back row of lights. Our tree diagram might look like this.

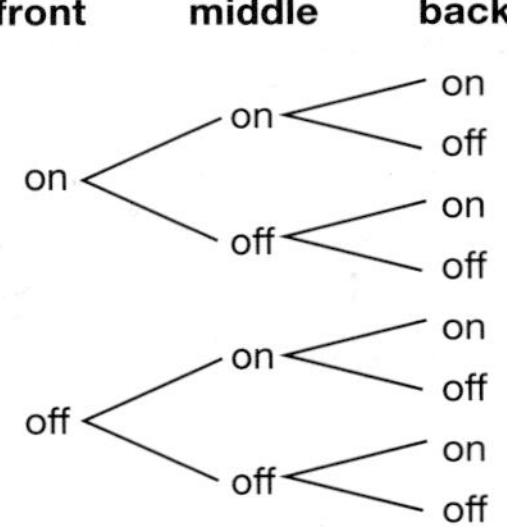

"How many different ways are there for the classroom lights to be turned on or off?"

Our diagram shows us that there are 8 combinations.

Check *Look back.*

"Did we complete the task?"

Yes. We made a tree diagram to count the ways three rows of lights could be turned on or off. There are 8 combinations.

"Is our answer reasonable? How can we use multiplication to explain why there are 8 possible combinations?"

It is reasonable that there are 8 ways. There are 2 possibilities for the front row (on or off). For each of these 2 possibilities, the middle row can be either on or off. So there are $2 \times 2 = 4$ combinations for the front and middle rows of lights. For each of the 4 possible combinations for the front and middle rows, the back row can be either on or off. So there are $4 \times 2 = 8$ combinations altogether.

"How is this problem similar to listing the outcomes of three consecutive coin flips?"

In each problem, there are two possible outcomes for each of three events. In the coin-flip problem, the outcomes are heads and tails. In the light-switch problem, the outcomes are on and off.

LESSON 96

• Geometric Solids

California Mathematics Content Standards

MG 3.0, 3.6 Visualize, describe, and make models of geometric solids (e.g., prisms, pyramids) in terms of the number and shape of faces, edges, and vertices; interpret two-dimensional representations of three-dimensional objects; and draw patterns (of faces) for a solid that, when cut and folded, will make a model of the solid.

Power Up

facts Power Up H

mental math Find half of a product in problems **a–c.**

a. Number Sense: half of 100 × 12 600

b. Number Sense: half of 100 × 24 1200

c. Number Sense: half of 100 × 48 2400

d. Money: The salad cost \$4.89. Ramona paid for it with a \$10 bill. How much change should she receive? \$5.11

e. Geometry: The angles of the triangle measured 47°, 43°, and 90°. What is the sum of the angle measures? 180°

f. Estimation: In 10 minutes, Tevin counted 25 cars that drove through the intersection. About how many cars might Tevin expect to count in 20 minutes? 50 cars

g. Calculation: 16 ÷ 2, − 6, × 2, $\sqrt{\ }$ 2

h. Simplify: 1 + 5 × 3 16

front middle back
on — on — on / off
on — off — on / off
off — on — on / off
off — off — on / off

problem solving There are three light switches that each control a row of lights in the classroom—a row in front, a row in the middle, and a row in back. Make a tree diagram to find the different ways the rows of lights can be turned on or off. Use the tree diagram to count the total number of combinations. 8 combinations

New Concept

Figures such as triangles, rectangles, and circles are flat shapes that cover an area but do not take up space. They have length and width but not depth. Objects that take up space are things such as cars, basketballs, desks, and houses. People also take up space.

Facts Multiply.

8 × 8 64	0 × 5 0	7 × 3 21	9 × 7 63	3 × 2 6	9 × 4 36	8 × 6 48	4 × 3 12	9 × 5 45	6 × 2 12
9 × 2 18	7 × 4 28	8 × 3 24	5 × 5 25	9 × 6 54	7 × 2 14	5 × 4 20	9 × 1 9	9 × 3 27	0 × 0 0
7 × 5 35	2 × 2 4	6 × 4 24	8 × 7 56	5 × 3 15	7 × 6 42	4 × 2 8	8 × 5 40	6 × 3 18	9 × 9 81
3 × 3 9	8 × 4 32	7 × 7 49	8 × 2 16	10 × 10 100	6 × 5 30	4 × 4 16	9 × 8 72	5 × 2 10	6 × 6 36

Power Up

Facts

Distribute **Power Up H** to students. See answers below.

Count Aloud

Before students begin the Mental Math exercises, do these counting exercises as a class.

Count up and down by fours from 24 to 52.

Mental Math

Encourage students to share different ways to mentally compute these exercises. Strategies for exercises are listed below.

a. Divide 100 × 12 by 2

(100 × 12) ÷ 2 = 1200 ÷ 2 = 600

Find 100 × (12 ÷ 2)

100 × (12 ÷ 2) = 100 × 6 = 600

d. Count On

\$4.89 to \$5 is 11¢ and \$5 to \$10 is \$5; 11¢ + \$5 = \$5.11

Count Back

\$10 to \$5 is \$5 and \$5 to \$4.89 is 11¢; \$5 + 11¢ = \$5.11

Problem Solving

Refer to **Problem-Solving Strategy Discussion,** p. 633B.

New Concept

Observation

Introduce the lesson by inviting students to search the classroom for examples of the geometric solids that are shown in the chart.

As each of the geometric solids in this less... are described and discussed, displa... of the solid using Relational Ge...

Example 1

Active Learning

After they name the shapes, say:

"Give some examples of a sphere, ... and cone." Samples: sphere; kickbal... cube; dot cube; cone; party hat

Extend the Example

Have your advanced learners name real-world examples of a pyramid and a triangular prism.

Example 2

Use an unopened container, such as a can of soup or vegetables, to illustrate the shape of a cylinder. If possible, display a variety of containers of different sizes, such as a can of soup and a can of tuna.

(continued)

LS 96 Math 11^30 - 12^30

Geometric shapes that take up space are called **geometric solids.** The chart below shows the names of some geometric solids.

Geometric Solids

Shape	Name
	Cube and rectangular prism
	Rectangular prism (or rectangular solid)
	Triangular prism
	Pyramid
	Cylinder
	Sphere
	Cone

...e:

b.

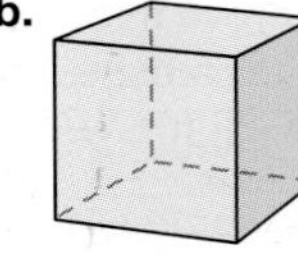

c.

We compare each shape with the chart.

a. sphere **b. cube** **c. cone**

Example 2

What is the shape of a soup can?

A soup can has the shape of a **cylinder.**

A flat surface of a solid is called a **face.** Two faces meet at an **edge.** Three or more edges meet at a corner called a **vertex** (plural: *vertices*).

face

edge

vertex

Alternative Approach: Using Manipulatives

To help students visualize the different parts of three-dimensional figures, show students different geometric solids from the classroom or using the Relational Geosolids. Have them identify the number of faces, edges, and vertices.

A circular cylinder has one curved surface and two flat circular surfaces. A cone has one curved surface and one flat circular surface. The pointed end of a cone is its **apex.** A sphere has no flat surfaces.

Example 3

a. How many faces does a box have?

b. How many vertices does a box have?

c. How many edges does a box have?

Find a closed, rectangular box in the classroom (a tissue box, for example) to answer the questions.

a. 6 faces (top, bottom, left, right, front, back)

b. 8 vertices (4 around the top, 4 around the bottom)

c. 12 edges (4 around the top, 4 around the bottom, and 4 running from top to bottom)

Geometric Solids in the Real World

Material needed:

- **Lesson Activity 27**

Looking around us, we see examples of the geometric solids shown in the table of this lesson. With some objects, two or more shapes are combined. For example, in a building we might see a triangular prism and a rectangular prism.

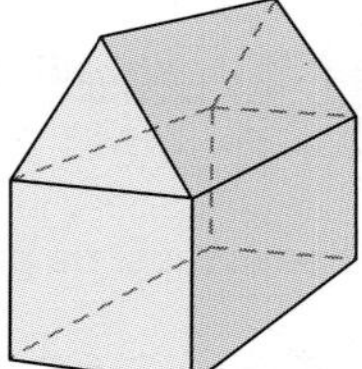

Complete **Lesson Activity 27** by finding and naming an object for each shape. Then draw a picture of each object on the page.

Math Background

A *prism* is any solid with parallel bases that are congruent polygons and faces that are parallelograms. A prism is named for the shape of its bases. For example, a triangular prism has bases that are triangles. If the lateral faces of a prism are rectangles, then the prism is a *right prism.* When a right prism sits on a base, it extends straight up, perpendicular to the surface it is on. If the lateral faces are non-rectangular parallelograms, then the prism is an *oblique prism.* When an oblique prism sits on a base, it slants to one side.

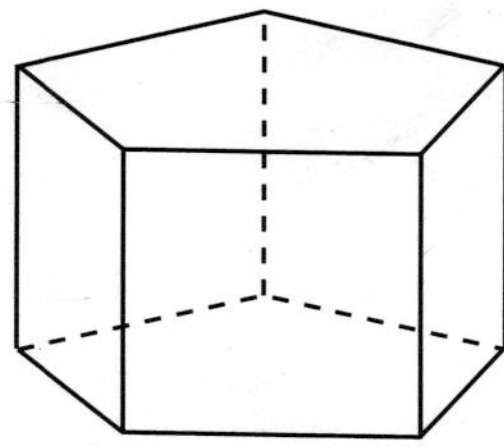

right pentagonal prism

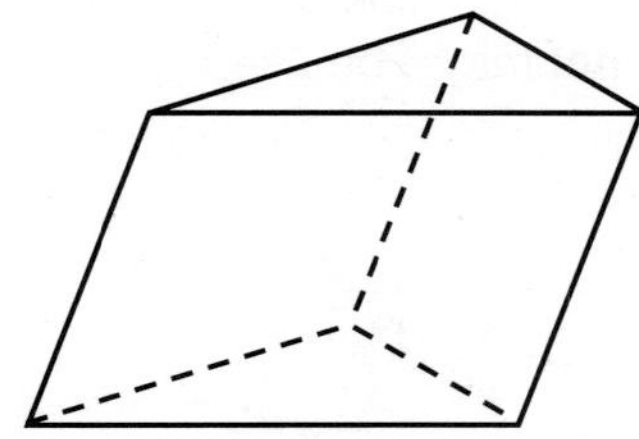

oblique triangular prism

New Concept *(Continued)*

Example 3

Use a rectangular box, such as an empty tissue box or an empty cereal box, to illustrate the shape of a rectangular prism.

If necessary, cut the box apart to give students an opportunity to recognize and count the different faces of the box.

Error Alert

Make sure students understand the meanings of faces, vertices, and edges before they answer each problem. You might have them draw and label a cube on an index card.

(continued)

New Concept *(Continued)*

Lesson Practice

Guided Practice

Use these problems as guided practice to check the students' understanding of today's concept.

Problems a–d Manipulative Use

Some students may find it helpful if you provide them with an example of each solid to examine.

Problem f Manipulative Use

Encourage interested students to examine a pyramid model before they complete the problem.

Problem e
Error Alert

Make sure students can recognize that unlike the faces of a rectangular solid, all of the faces of a pyramid (except for one—the base) meet at one point.

Closure The questions below help assess the concepts taught in this lesson.

"How is a polygon different than a solid?" Sample: Polygons are flat, two-dimensional, and do not take up space; Solids are three-dimensional, take up space, and are not flat.

"Name four different polygons and four different solids." Sample: triangle, rectangle, square, hexagon; cube, cylinder, pyramid, cone

Lesson Practice

In problems **a–d,** name the shape of the object listed:

a. basketball sphere

b. shoebox rectangular solid

c. funnel cone

d. juice can cylinder

e. The figure at right is the same shape as several Egyptian landmarks. What is the shape? pyramid

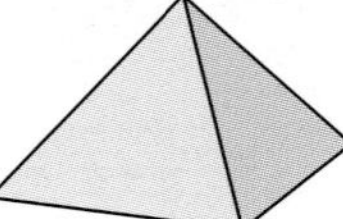

f. The figure in problem **e** has a square base. How many faces does the figure have? How many edges? How many vertices? 5 faces; 8 edges; 5 vertices

Use the rectangular prism to answer problems **g–h**.

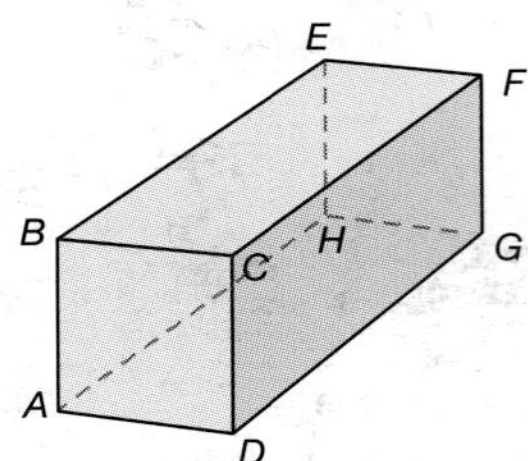

g. Name the front face and the back face. Are the two faces congruent? Sample: *ABCD* and *EFGH*; yes

h. Name two faces that share edge *CD*. Are the two faces perpendicular? Sample: *ABCD* and *CFGD*; yes

Written Practice

Distributed and Integrated

*1. (87) **Analyze** All 110 books must be packed in boxes. Each box will hold 8 books.

a. How many boxes can be filled? 13 boxes

b. How many boxes are needed to hold all the books? 14 boxes

636 *Saxon Math Intermediate 4*

English Learners

Explain that a **funnel** is used to help pour liquid from one container to another. If possible, display a funnel for students.

Explain that a **funnel** might be made of thick paper, plastic, or metal.

Ask students if they have ever seen anyone pour oil into an engine with a cone-like object. Have students think of any other ways that a **funnel** might be used.

▶ *2. (63) **Formulate** What number is five more than the product of six and seven? Write an expression. 47; $(6 \times 7) + 5$

▶ *3. (93) **Explain** Sergio paid $7 for the tape. He received a quarter and two dimes as change. Tax was 42¢. What was the price of the tape? Explain how you found your answer. $6.13; sample: Since a quarter and two dimes equal 45¢, I added 45¢ and 42¢ then subtracted the sum from $7.

*4. (94) **Represent** Four fifths of the 600 gymnasts did back handsprings. How many gymnasts did back handsprings? Draw a picture to illustrate the problem. 480 gymnasts

4. 600 gymnasts

$\frac{4}{5}$ did back handsprings.	120 gymnasts
	120 gymnasts
	120 gymnasts
	120 gymnasts
$\frac{1}{5}$ did not do back handsprings.	120 gymnasts

*5. (87) **Explain** Mrs. Tyrone is arranging 29 desks into rows. If she starts by putting 8 desks in each row, how many desks will be in the last row? Explain how you know. 5 desks; sample: The quotient of $29 \div 8$ is 3 R 5; 3 represents the number of complete rows of 8 desks, and 5 represents the number of desks in the incomplete row.

6. (28) **Analyze** What is the value of two $100 bills, five $10 bills, four $1 bills, 3 dimes, and 1 penny? $254.31

7. (42) a. Find the length of the line segment in millimeters. 35 mm

b. Find the length of the line segment in centimeters. Write the answer as a decimal number. 3.5 cm

mm 10 20 30 40

cm 1 2 3 4

8. (Inv. 4) **Represent** Use words to write 12.67. twelve and sixty-seven hundredths

▶ *9. (40, 46) a. Round 3834 to the nearest thousand. 4000

b. Round 38.34 to the nearest whole number. 38

10. (18, 42) The diameter of a circle is 1 meter. What is the radius of the circle in centimeters? 50 cm

*11. (27, 51) Find the sum of two hundred eighty-six thousand, five hundred fourteen and one hundred thirty-seven thousand, two. 423,516

Inclusion

Use this strategy if the student displays:

- Poor Retention.
- Slow Learning Rate.

Geometric Solids (Whole Group)

Materials: poster board, magazines, and colored pencils

- Post the chart to the right on the board.
- Create a poster board for each type of geometric solid. Have students use magazines to find real-word examples of the geometric solids, cut them out, and paste them on the poster boards. Display poster boards around the room.

Geometric Solids

Shape	Name
	Cube and rectangular prism
	Rectangular prism (or rectangular solid)
	Triangular prism
	Pyramid
	Cylinder
	Sphere
	Cone

Written Practice

Math Conversations

Independent Practice and Discussions to Increase Understanding

Problem 2 Formulate

Extend the Problem

Although some students may write the expression $(6 \times 7) + 5$ to solve the problem, explain that another correct expression is $5 + (6 \times 7)$ because addition is commutative, and $5 + (7 \times 6)$ is also correct because multiplication is commutative.

The Commutative Properties of Addition and Multiplication can be used to write many different expressions to represent the product of 6 and 7 increased by 5. Challenge your advanced students to write as many of the expressions as they can. Sample: $(6 \times 7) + 5$; $5 + (6 \times 7)$; $(7 \times 6) + 5$; $5 + (7 \times 6)$; $6 \times 7 + 5$; $5 + 6 \times 7$; $7 \times 6 + 5$; $5 + 7 \times 6$; $6(7) + 5$; $5 + 6(7)$; $7(6) + 5$; $5 + 7(6)$

Problem 3 Explain

Some students may find it helpful if you suggest that they work backward to find the price of the tape.

Problem 9

Before students complete part **a**, ask:

"Why is the digit in the hundreds place of a number important when we round the number to the nearest thousand?" If the digit in the hundreds place is less than 5, the digit in the thousands place does not change; If the digit in the hundreds place is 5 or more, the digit in the thousands place is increased by 1.

Before students complete part **b**, ask:

"When we round to the nearest whole number, which place in a number are we rounding to?" The ones place

(continued)

Written Practice *(Continued)*

Math Conversations *(cont.)*

Problem 14

Manipulative Use

Encourage interested students to examine a triangular prism model before they complete the problem.

Problems 19–20 and 22–25

Remind students of the importance of checking their work, and then ask them to make an estimate of each product or quotient. After finding the exact answers, students should use the estimates to help decide the reasonableness of those answers.

Problem 28

Manipulative Use

Encourage students to use their fraction manipulatives to check their work.

Problem 29

Make sure students understand that because 1 m = 100 cm, any number of centimeters can be changed to meters by dividing the number of centimeters by 100. Dividing by 100 produces the same result as moving the decimal point two places to the left.

Students may be interested to learn that the player is about 83 inches, or 6 feet 11 inches, tall.

Errors and Misconceptions

Problem 1

The scenario requires students to interpret the remainder of the division. For part **a**, the answer is 13, the quotient. For part **b**, students must infer that 13 is increased to 14 because the quotient includes a remainder.

Problem 6

A common error when using pencil-and-paper addition to find the value of bills and coins is to not maintain correct alignment of the place values. Remind students that they can use grid paper or lined paper turned sideways to maintain alignment whenever they add or subtract decimal numbers.

12. (93) Seven pairs of beach sandals cost \$56. What is the cost of one pair? What is the cost of ten pairs? \$8; \$80

* **13.** (95) **Interpret** Find the median, mode, range, and any outliers of this data: Median: 30, mode: 28, range: 49, outlier: 1

1, 32, 44, 28, 50, 28

▶* **14.** (96) This triangular prism has a rectangular base. How many vertices does it have? 6

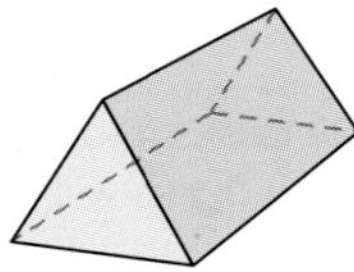

15. (45) $7.48 - (6.47 + 0.5)$ 0.51

16. (85) 40×50 2000

17. (86) 41×49 2009

18. (Inv. 3, 65) $2^3 \times 5 \times \sqrt{49}$ 280

▶ **19.** (88) 32×17 544

▶ **20.** (71) 38×40 1520

21. (4) $7 + 4 + 6 + 8 + 5 + 2 + 7 + 3 + k = 47$ 5

▶ **22.** (69) $8\overline{)360}$ 45

▶ **23.** (83) $4\overline{)810}$ 202 R 2

▶ **24.** (83) $7\overline{)356}$ 50 R 6

▶ **25.** (34, 79) $6n = \$4.38$ \$0.73

26. (79) $7162 \div 9$ 795 R 7

27. (83) $\frac{1414}{2}$ 707

▶* **28.** (89) Draw and shade circles to show that 2 equals $\frac{8}{8}$.

▶* **29.** (42) The basketball player was 211 centimeters tall. Write the height of the basketball player in meters. 2.11 m

30. (66, 84) How many square yards of carpeting are needed to cover the floor of a classroom that is 15 yards long and 10 yards wide? 150 yd^2

638 **Saxon Math** *Intermediate 4*

Looking Forward

Classifying geometric solids by their vertices, edges, and faces prepares students for:

- **Lesson 97,** making three-dimensional models of rectangular and triangular prisms.
- **Lesson 108,** identifying the attributes of geometric solids.
- **Lesson 109,** describing the attributes of pyramids.
- **Lesson 114,** determining the perimeter and area of complex figures.

Planning & Preparation

• Constructing Prisms

Objectives

- Construct three-dimensional models of rectangular and triangular prisms.
- Draw a net that can be used to make a prism.
- Identify faces, edges, and vertices.
- Identify acute, obtuse, and right angles.
- Identify intersecting, perpendicular, and parallel faces.
- Compare and contrast rectangular and triangular prisms.

Prerequisite Skills

- Identifying, drawing, and describing lines, rays, and line segments.
- Identifying and drawing parallel lines and segments.
- Identifying and drawing pairs of intersecting lines and segments that are perpendicular or oblique.

Materials

Instructional Masters

- Power Up H Worksheet
- Lesson Activities 28–30
- Lesson Activity 21

Manipulative Kit

- Relational GeoSolids
- Fraction circles

Teacher-provided materials

- Scissors, tape, glue, grid paper
- Construction paper, empty cardboard boxes*

**optional*

California Mathematics Content Standards

MG 3.0, 3.1 Identify lines that are parallel and perpendicular.

MG 3.0, 3.3 Identify congruent figures.

MG 3.0, 3.5 Know the definitions of a right angle, an acute angle, and an obtuse angle. Understand that 90°, 180°, 270°, and 360° are associated, respectively, with $\frac{1}{4}$, $\frac{1}{2}$, $\frac{3}{4}$, and full turns.

MG 3.0, 3.6 Visualize, describe, and make models of geometric solids (e.g., prisms, pyramids) in terms of the number and shape of faces, edges, and vertices; interpret two-dimensional representations of three-dimensional objects; and draw patterns (of faces) for a solid that, when cut and folded, will make a model of the solid.

MR 2.0, 2.3 Use a variety of methods, such as words, numbers, symbols, charts, graphs, tables, diagrams, and models, to explain mathematical reasoning.

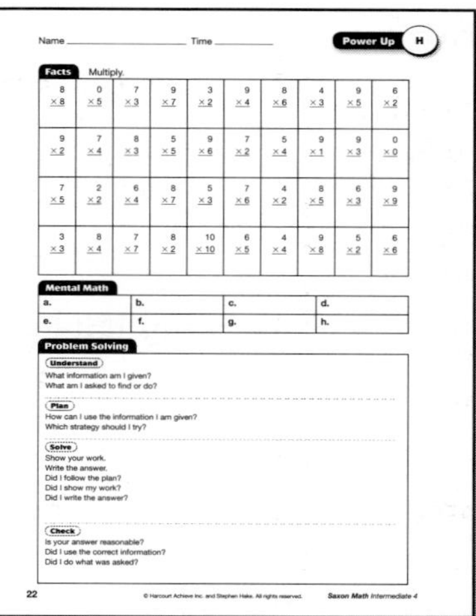

Power Up H Worksheet

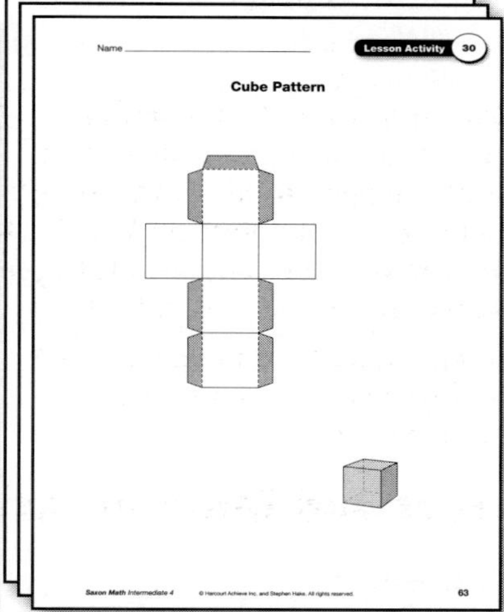

Lesson Activities 21, 28–30

Universal Access

Reaching All Special Needs Students

Special Education Students	At-Risk Students	English Learners	Advanced Learners
• Inclusion (TM) • Adaptations for Saxon Math	• Alternative Approach (TM) • Error Alert (TM) • Reteaching Masters • Refresher Lessons for California Standards	• English Learners (TM) • Developing Academic Language (TM) • English Learner Handbook	• Extend the Problem (TM) • Online Activities

TM=Teacher's Manual

Developing Academic Language

New	Maintained	English Learner
net	rectangular prism rectangular solid	seam

Problem Solving Discussion

Problem

There are 365 days in a common year, which is about 52 weeks. However, since 52 weeks is exactly 364 days, a year does not start on the same day of the week as the start of the preceding year. If a common year starts on a Tuesday, on what day of the week will the following year begin?

Focus Strategies

Use Logical Reasoning

Make It Simpler

Understand *Understand the problem.*

"What information are we given?"

1. There are 365 days in a common year, which is about 52 weeks.
2. Fifty-two weeks is exactly 364 days.
3. A year does not start on the same day of the week as the start of the preceding year.

"What are we asked to do?"

We are asked to find the day of the week a year begins if it follows a common year that began on Tuesday.

Plan *Make a plan.*

"What problem-solving strategies can we use to solve the problem?"

We can *use logical reasoning* to *make it simpler.*

Solve *Carry out the plan.*

"What day is one week after Tuesday?"

Tuesday

"What day is 52 weeks after Tuesday?"

Tuesday

"A common year is how many days more than 52 weeks?"

A common year is 365 days, and 52 weeks is 364 days. Thus, a common year is 1 day more than 52 weeks.

"If a common year starts on Tuesday, what day of the week will the next year begin on?"

It will begin 52 weeks and 1 day after Tuesday, which is **Wednesday.**

Check *Look back.*

"Is our answer reasonable?"

Yes. We know that our answer is reasonable because a common year is 52 weeks and 1 day. The extra day pushes back the start of the following year by 1 day.

"What problem-solving strategies did we use, and how did they help us?"

We *used logical reasoning* to determine that the extra day in a common year means the next year will begin 1 day of the week later. This means we *made the problem simpler* than if we had used a calendar or counted the days. We might also say that we *extended a pattern*, since the days of the week repeat every 7 days.

Alternate Strategy
Make or Use a Chart, Table, or Graph

Students may use a calendar of a common year (not a leap year) to solve the problem.

LESSON 97

• Constructing Prisms

California Mathematics Content Standards

MG 3.0, 3.5 Know the definitions of a right angle, an acute angle, and an obtuse angle. Understand that 90°, 180°, 270°, and 360° are associated, respectively, with $\frac{1}{4}$, $\frac{1}{2}$, $\frac{3}{4}$, and full turns.

MG 3.0, 3.6 Visualize, describe, and make models of geometric solids (e.g., prisms, pyramids) in terms of the number and shape of faces, edges, and vertices; interpret two-dimensional representations of three-dimensional objects; and draw patterns (of faces) for a solid that, when cut and folded, will make a model of the solid.

facts Power Up H

mental math Fifty is half of 100. Find each product by multiplying by half of 100 in problems **a–d.**

a. Number Sense: 50 × 16 800

b. Number Sense: 50 × 44 2200

c. Number Sense: 50 × 26 1300

d. Number Sense: 50 × 68 3400

e. Money: The groceries cost $32.48 and the magazine cost $4.99. What was the total cost? $37.47

f. Estimation: Each box is 30.5 cm tall. Estimate the height (using cm) of a stack of 6 boxes. 180 cm

g. Calculation: 200 ÷ 2, ÷ 2, ÷ 2 25

h. Simplify: 20 − 10 ÷ 5 18

problem solving Choose an appropriate problem-solving strategy to solve this problem. There are 365 days in a common year, which is about 52 weeks. However, since 52 weeks is exactly 364 days, a year does not start on the same day of the week as the start of the preceding year. If a common year starts on a Tuesday, on what day of the week will the following year begin? Wednesday

In Lesson 96 we named solids by their shapes. In this lesson we will focus our attention on understanding rectangular prisms and triangular prisms.

Power Up

Facts

Distribute **Power Up H** to students. See answers below.

Count Aloud

Before students begin the Mental Math exercises, do these counting exercises as a class.

Count up and down by tens from 20 to 110.

Mental Math

Encourage students to share different ways to mentally compute these exercises. Strategies for exercises are listed below.

a. Find (100 × 16) ÷ 2
(100 × 16) ÷ 2 = 1600 ÷ 2 = 800

b. Find (100 × 44) ÷ 2
(100 × 44) ÷ 2 = 4400 ÷ 2 = 2200

c. Find (100 × 26) ÷ 2
(100 × 26) ÷ 2 = 2600 ÷ 2 = 1300

d. Find (100 × 68) ÷ 2
(100 × 68) ÷ 2 = 6800 ÷ 2 = 3400

Problem Solving

Refer to **Problem-Solving Strategy Discussion,** p. 639B.

Facts Multiply.

8 × 8 64	0 × 5 0	7 × 3 21	9 × 7 63	3 × 2 6	9 × 4 36	8 × 6 48	4 × 3 12	9 × 5 45	6 × 2 12
9 × 2 18	7 × 4 28	8 × 3 24	5 × 5 25	9 × 6 54	7 × 2 14	5 × 4 20	9 × 1 9	9 × 3 27	0 × 0 0
7 × 5 35	2 × 2 4	6 × 4 24	8 × 7 56	5 × 3 15	7 × 6 42	4 × 2 8	8 × 5 40	6 × 3 18	9 × 9 81
3 × 3 9	8 × 4 32	7 × 7 49	8 × 2 16	10 × 10 100	6 × 5 30	4 × 4 16	9 × 8 72	5 × 2 10	6 × 6 36

New Concept

Observation

As each of the geometric solids in this lesson are described and discussed, display a model of the solid using Relational GeoSolids, or pass the models around the classroom for students to examine.

Problem 1

Error Alert

If students are not sure what a "panel" is, explain that it is a face of the box. The number of panels of a cereal box is the same as the number of its faces.

Problem 3

Manipulative Use

Ask students to hold a rectangular prism so that they can see that only three panels or faces are visible from any perspective. In place of holding a prism, students can use a closed textbook and vary its orientation while holding it.

Active Learning

If possible, distribute an empty box, such as a cereal box, to each student or group of students. Have students cut the box apart to model the diagram. Before they begin cutting, have students note that only seven cuts are needed to flatten the box.

Activity

Extend the Activity

An alternative to having your advanced learners construct the shapes during math class is to have them construct them during an art class without the **Lesson Activity Masters.** Regardless of where they are constructed, you may want to have students work in groups of two or three to speed up the construction.

Extra copies of **Lesson Activity Masters 28, 29,** and **30** can be used to make additional shapes if needed.

(continued)

Consider the shape of a cereal box. The shape is called a rectangular prism (or rectangular solid). Every panel (side) of a closed cereal box is a rectangle.

If an empty cereal box or similar container is available, you may refer to it to answer the following questions:

1. A closed cereal box has how many panels? 6 panels
2. What words could we use to refer to these panels? Front, back, top, bottom, left, right
3. Without a mirror, what is the largest number of panels that can be seen at one time? 3 panels
4. Two panels meet at a fold, or seam, in the cardboard. Each fold is an edge. A closed cereal box has how many edges? 12 edges
5. Three edges meet at each corner, or vertex, of the box. A closed cereal box has how many vertices? 8 vertices

If we tape an empty cereal box closed and cut it along seven edges, we can "flatten out" the container, as shown below.

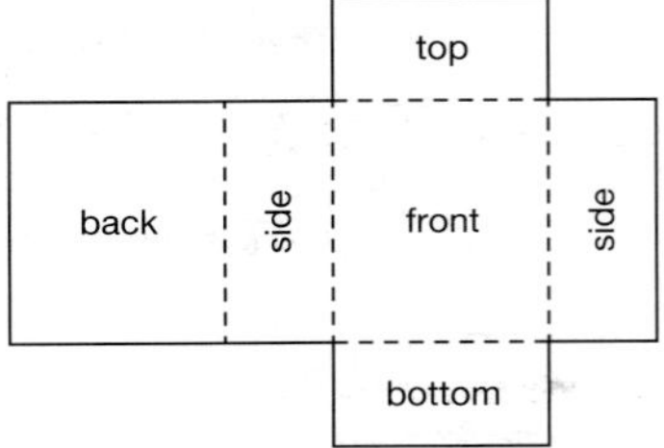

We can see the six rectangles that formed the panels of the closed box. We will use nets like this one to construct the models of solids.

Math Language

A **net** is a 2-dimensional representation of a 3-dimensional geometric figure.

Constructing Prisms

Materials needed:

- **Lesson Activities 28, 29,** and **30**
- scissors
- tape or glue

English Learners

Explain to your students that a **seam** is formed by two pieces of material that are joined. Say:

"A cereal box is made of a flat piece of cardboard that is cut, folded, and glued together. If you look carefully at a cereal box, you can find the seams where the pieces of cardboard are glued together."

Ask:

"Can you find a seam on your pants or shirt where two pieces of material are sewn together?"

We can make models of cubes, rectangular prisms, and triangular prisms by cutting, folding, and taping nets of shapes to form 3-dimensional figures. Use **Lesson Activities 28, 29,** and **30** to construct two rectangular prisms, two triangular prisms, and two cubes. Then study those figures to answer the questions in Lesson Practice.

Lesson Practice

Discuss Refer to the cube to answer problems **a–e.**

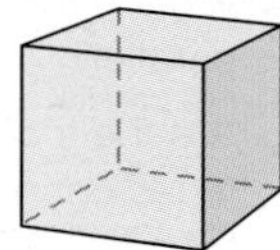

a. What is the shape of each face? square

b. Is each face parallel to an opposite face? Yes

c. Is each edge parallel to at least one other edge? Yes

d. Is each edge perpendicular to at least one other edge? Yes

e. What type of angle is formed by every pair of intersecting edges? right angle

Refer to the rectangular prism below to answer problems **f–j.**

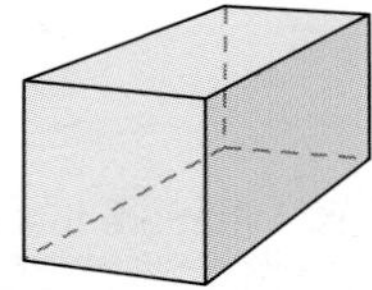

f. What is the shape of each face? rectangle

g. Is each face parallel to the opposite face? Yes

h. Is each edge parallel to at least one other edge? Yes

i. Is each edge perpendicular to at least one other edge? Yes

j. What type of angle is formed by every pair of intersecting edges? right angle

Math Background

There are 11 possible nets for a cube. They are pictured below:

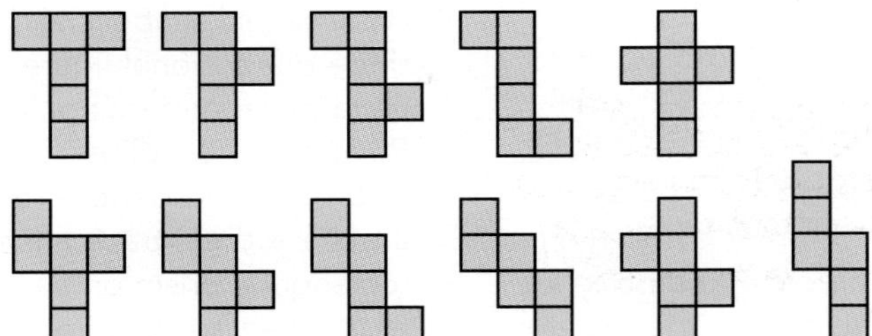

New Concept *(Continued)*

Lesson Practice

Guided Practice

Use these problems as guided practice to check the students' understanding of today's concept.

Problems a–t

Have students use the solids that were constructed in the activity to solve parts **a–t.**

Problem b

To emphasize opposite parallel faces, have students choose three different crayons or colored pencils, and then color pairs of opposite faces the same color.

Problem g

To emphasize opposite parallel faces, have students choose three different crayons or colored pencils, and then color pairs of opposite faces the same color.

(continued)

New Concept (Continued)

Lesson Practice

Problems l and q

To emphasize the parallel triangular faces, have students color the two triangles the same color.

Have students use drawing software to draw geometric solids. Then have them identify parallel or perpendicular faces by using the paint function to fill them with different colors.

Problem t

Point out that of the five faces of a triangular prism, two faces are also classified as bases. The bases of a triangular prism are its triangular faces. Students may be interested to learn that because the bases of the prism used to solve problems **p–t** are right triangles, the prism is classified as a right triangular prism.

Problem f

Error Alert

Although the front and back faces of the prism are squares, it is not correct to label all of the faces as squares. Since a square is also classified as a rectangle, all the faces of the prism are rectangles.

Closure

The questions below help assess the concepts taught in this lesson.

"How is a cube similar to a rectangular prism? How is it different?" Sample: (similar) Each is a solid with 6 faces and each has congruent and parallel opposite faces; (different) A cube has 6 congruent faces, but a rectangular prism can have 2, 4, or 6 congruent faces.

"Describe a triangular prism." Sample: A triangular prism is a solid that has three rectangular faces and two triangular faces; The triangular faces are congruent and parallel; The rectangular faces are not parallel.

Refer to the triangular prism with two faces that are equilateral triangles to answer problems **k–o.**

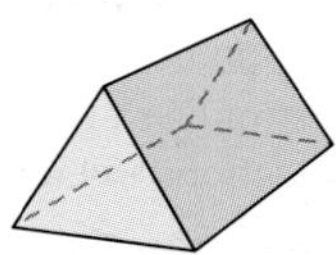

k. What are the shapes of the five faces? Two triangles, three rectangles

l. Are the triangular faces parallel? Are the rectangular faces parallel? The triangular faces are parallel; The rectangular faces are not parallel.

m. Are the triangular faces congruent? Are the rectangular faces congruent? The triangles are congruent; The rectangles are congruent.

n. Do you find pairs of edges that are parallel? That are perpendicular? That intersect but are not perpendicular? Yes; yes; yes

o. What types of angles are formed by the intersecting edges? Right angles and acute angles

Refer to the triangular prism with two faces that are right triangles to answer problems **p–t.**

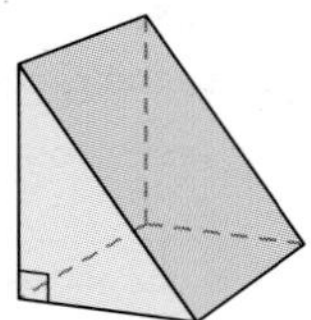

p. What are the shapes of the five faces? Two right triangles, three rectangles

q. Which faces are parallel? The triangular faces

r. Are the triangular faces congruent? Are the rectangular faces congruent? The triangles are congruent; The rectangles are not congruent.

s. Are there pairs of edges that are parallel? Perpendicular? Intersecting but not perpendicular? Yes; yes; yes

t. What types of angles are formed by the intersecting edges? Right angles and acute angles

u. (Verify) One of these nets could be cut out and folded to form a cube. The other will not form a cube. Which net will form a cube? Net 1

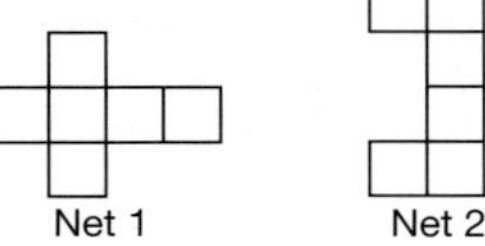

Inclusion

Use this strategy if the student displays:

- Difficulty with Abstract Processing.
- Slow Learning Rate.

Constructing Prisms (Small Group)

Materials: 4 or 5 cardboard boxes, construction paper, scissors, tape

- Divide children in groups and pass out a cardboard box to each student. Have students work together to unfold the cardboard boxes into their net shape. One side of the boxes will need to be cut so that it can unfold. Have students draw the net on construction paper.
- Have students draw a net shape on construction paper, and then build the prism. Students can decorate their prisms as they choose. Display around the classroom.

Alternative Approach: Using Manipulatives

To help students picture the two-dimensional shapes used to make a three-dimensional figure, show them the rectangular and triangular prisms from the Relational Geosolids. Give each student or group of students a rectangular prism and have them trace each face of the rectangular prism on paper. Ask students to label each plane figure found in the faces of the solid.

Ask, ***"What are the faces of a rectangular prism?"*** Squares and rectangles

Repeat the activity using a triangular prism.

v. **Model** Use 1-inch grid paper to draw a different net that will fold into a cube. Cut it out and fold it up to check your work. See student work.

Written Practice

Distributed and Integrated

1. (RF6, 68) **Analyze** Find an even number between 79 and 89 that can be divided by 6 without a remainder. 84

2. (13, 37) How many minutes is 3 hours? 180 minutes

***3.** (93) Victor has $8. Dana has $2 less than Victor. How much money do they have altogether? $14

▸ **4.** (Inv. 4) **Represent** Write each fraction or mixed number as a decimal number:

a. $\frac{3}{10}$ 0.3 **b.** $4\frac{99}{100}$ 4.99 **c.** $12\frac{1}{100}$ 12.01

▸ ***5.** (94) **Represent** Five eighths of the 40 students wore school colors. How many students wore school colors? Draw a picture to illustrate the problem. 25 students

5. 40 students

$\frac{5}{8}$ wore school colors.	5 students
	5 students
	5 students
	5 students
	5 students
$\frac{3}{8}$ did not wear school colors.	5 students
	5 students
	5 students

6. (18, 42) **a.** What is the diameter of this circle in centimeters? 3 cm

b. What is the radius of this circle in centimeters? 1.5 cm

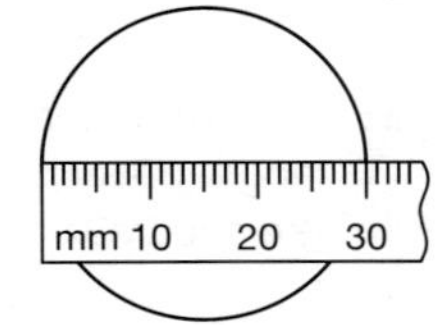

7. (18) The radius of a circle is what fractional part of the diameter? $\frac{1}{2}$

8. (91) Estimate the product of 49 and 68. Then find the actual product. 3500; 3332

▸ ***9.** (87) **Explain** Pavan has filled a pitcher with iced tea for two guests and himself. The capacity of the pitcher is two quarts. How many 10-ounce glasses of iced tea can be poured from the pitcher? Explain your answer.
6 glasses; sample: Two quarts is the same as 32 + 32, or 64 ounces, and 64 ÷ 10 = 6 R 4.

Written Practice

Math Conversations

Independent Practice and Discussions to Increase Understanding

Problem 4 **Represent**

"In a decimal number, what are the names of the first two places to the right of the decimal point?" tenths, hundredths

"How many places to the right of the decimal point does a decimal number in tenths have? In hundredths?" one; two

Problem 5 **Represent**

Extend the Problem

Challenge your advanced learners to explain or demonstrate a number of ways to use pencil-and-paper arithmetic to check the answer. Sample: One eighth of a number is the same as dividing the number by 8; 40 students ÷ 8 = 5 students. Since 5 students represent $\frac{1}{8}$ of the class, multiply that number of students by 5 to find the number of students in $\frac{5}{8}$ of the class; 5 students × 5 = 25 students

Problem 9 **Explain**

"This problem contains extra information. What information will we not use to solve the problem?" The number of people

"What equivalent capacity relationship must we know to solve the problem?" 1 quart = 32 ounces

(continued)

Written Practice *(Continued)*

Math Conversations *(cont.)*

Problem 12 Analyze

Extend the Problem

Challenge your advanced learners with this question:

"Suppose that one more game score was added to the list so that there were 9 scores altogether. If the range of the scores does not change, what scores could be added to the list? Explain your answer." Any score greater than or equal to 80 and less than or equal to 100 could be added to the list. The range of the list is found using 100, the greatest number, and 80, the least number. Any score less than 80 or greater than 100 would change the range of the scores.

Problem 24 Represent

Manipulative Use

Encourage students to use their fraction manipulatives to check their work.

Problem 26

Remind students that one way for them to check their answer is to use division because a fraction bar is a symbol for division.

(continued)

*10. (92) **Estimate** Which letter represents the number closest to 3.5? *B*

(Number line from 3 to 4 with points A, B, E)

*11. (93) Gretchen paid $20 for five identical bottles of fruit juice. She received $6 in change. What was the price of one bottle of juice? $2.80

►*12. (95) **Analyze** Find the median, mode, and range of Vonda's game scores. (Since there is an even number of scores, the median is the average of the two middle scores.) Median, 95; mode, 100; range, 20

100, 80, 90, 85, 100, 90, 100, 100

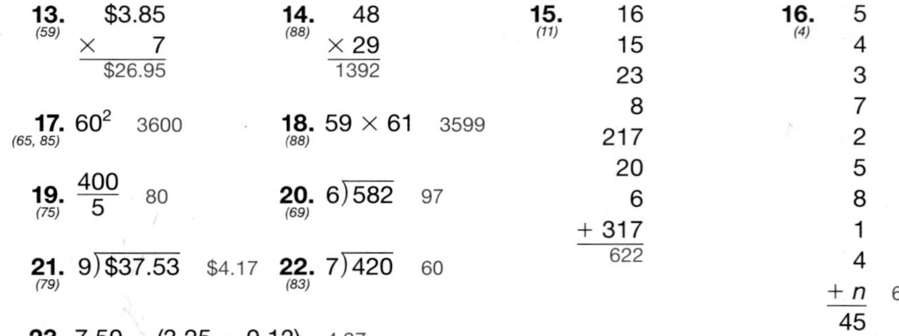

13. (59) $\$3.85 \times 7$ = $26.95

14. (88) 48×29 = 1392

15. (11) 16 + 15 + 23 + 8 + 217 + 20 + 6 + 317 = 622

16. (4) 5 + 4 + 3 + 7 + 2 + 5 + 8 + 1 + 4 + n = 45 n = 6

17. (65, 85) 60^2 3600

18. (88) 59×61 3599

19. (75) $\frac{400}{5}$ 80

20. (69) $6\overline{)582}$ 97

21. (79) $9\overline{)\$37.53}$ $4.17

22. (83) $7\overline{)420}$ 60

23. (9, 45) $7.50 - (3.25 - 0.12)$ 4.37

►*24. (89) **Represent** Draw and shade circles to show that $3\frac{3}{4}$ equals $\frac{15}{4}$.

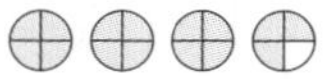

25. (20, 66) The perimeter of this square is 20 inches. What is the length of each side of the square? What is the area of the square? 5 in.; 25 in^2

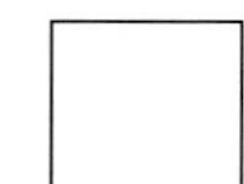

►*26. (89) Write a fraction equal to 1 with a denominator of 8. $\frac{8}{8}$

*27. Which of the following nets folds up into a triangular prism? B
(97)

A

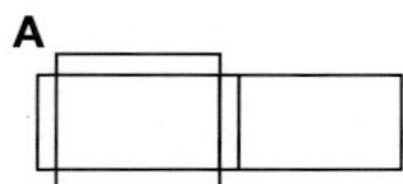

B

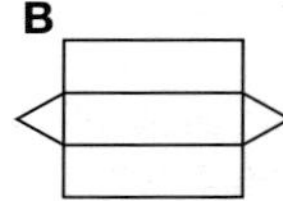

C

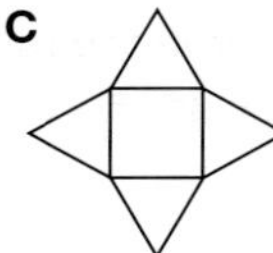

D

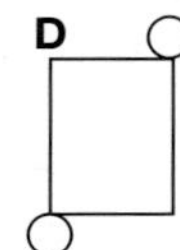

*28. Songhi measured the paper in her notebook and found that it was 28 cm long. Write the length of her paper in meters. 0.28 m
(42)

▶*29. **Estimate** Round $12\frac{5}{12}$ to the nearest whole number. 12
(92)

▶*30. a. **Classify** What is the geometric name for the shape of a cereal box? Rectangular prism (or rectangular solid)
(96)

b. How many edges does this box have? 12 edges

c. Describe the angles. All right angles

Making three-dimensional models of rectangular and triangular prisms prepares students for:

- **Lesson 108,** identifying the attributes of geometric solids.
- **Lesson 109,** describing the attributes of pyramids.
- **Lesson 114,** determining the perimeter and area of complex figures.

Written Practice *(Continued)*

Math Conversations *(cont.)*

Problem 29 Estimate

If students need assistance solving the problem, ask:

"What two consecutive whole numbers is the mixed number $12\frac{5}{12}$ between?"
12 and 13

"What mixed number is halfway between 12 and 13?" $12\frac{1}{2}$ or $12\frac{6}{12}$

"What mixed number should we compare $12\frac{5}{12}$ to?" $12\frac{1}{2}$ or $12\frac{6}{12}$

Problem 30

Manipulative Use

If students find it difficult to visualize a cereal box, have them inspect a rectangular prism.

Errors and Misconceptions

Problem 10

Because there are an odd number of smaller tick marks between the tick marks at 3 and 4, students should conclude that the middle tick mark represents 3.5.

Problem 11

Students who give an answer of $4 ignored the amount of change Gretchen received from her purchase. Point out to these students that $20 is not the total cost of the juice, and then ask them to name the total cost. $\$20 - \$6 = \$14$

Problem 27

Choices **A** and **B** can be folded to form a prism. However, only net **B** can be folded to form a *triangular* prism.

Planning & Preparation

• Fractions Equal to 1 and Fractions Equal to $\frac{1}{2}$

Objectives

- Identify and write fractions that are equal to 1.
- Identify and write fractions that are equal to $\frac{1}{2}$.

Prerequisite Skills

- Using fraction manipulatives to model, compare, and order equivalent fractions.
- Comparing fractions with different denominators using pictorial models and manipulatives.
- Using fraction manipulatives to compare fractions with different denominators.

Materials

Instructional Masters

- Power Up H Worksheet
- Lesson Activity 21*

Manipulative Kit

- Overhead fraction circles, fraction circles*

Teacher-provided materials

- Fraction manipulatives from Investigation 8
- Grid paper, colored pencils*

**optional*

California Mathematics Content Standards

NS 1.0, 1.4 Decide when a rounded solution is called for and explain why such a solution may be appropriate.

NS 1.0, 1.5 Explain different interpretations of fractions, for example, parts of a whole, parts of a set, and division of whole numbers by whole numbers; explain equivalents of fractions (see Standard 4.0).

NS 1.0, 1.7 Write the fraction represented by a drawing of parts of a figure; represent a given fraction by using drawings; and relate a fraction to a simple decimal on a number line.

NS 1.0, 1.9 Identify on a number line the relative position of positive fractions, positive mixed numbers, and positive decimals to two decimal places.

MG 1.0, 1.1 Measure the area of rectangular shapes by using appropriate units, such as square centimeter (cm^2), square meter (m^2), square kilometer (km^2), square inch (in^2), square yard (yd^2), or square mile (mi^2).

MR 2.0, 2.3 Use a variety of methods, such as words, numbers, symbols, charts, graphs, tables, diagrams, and models, to explain mathematical reasoning.

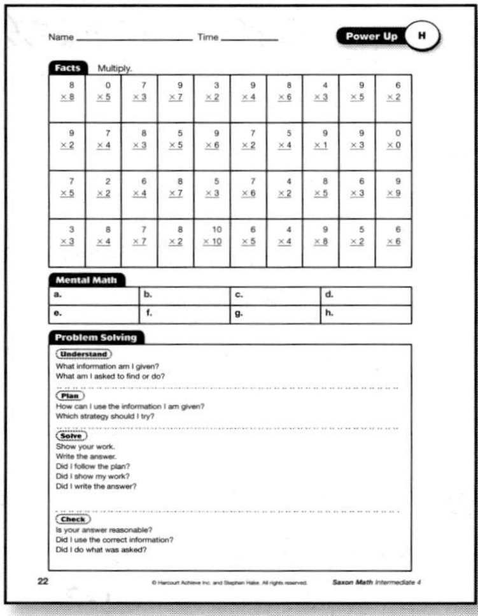

Power Up H Worksheet

Universal Access

Reaching All Special Needs Students

Special Education Students	At-Risk Students	English Learners	Advanced Learners
• Inclusion (TM) • Adaptations for Saxon Math	• Alternative Approach (TM) • Error Alert (TM) • Reteaching Masters • Refresher Lessons for California Standards	• English Learners (TM) • Developing Academic Language (TM) • English Learner Handbook	• Extend the Example (TM) • Extend the Problem (TM) • Online Activities

TM=Teacher's Manual

Developing Academic Language

Maintained	English Learner
denominator	checkup
fraction	
numerator	

Problem Solving Discussion

Problem

To get to the room where he will have his yearly medical checkup, Jerome will walk through three doors—a door into the doctor's office building, a door into the waiting room, and a door into the checkup room. Each door might be either open or closed when Jerome gets to it. List the possible combinations of open and closed doors that Jerome might encounter on his way into the checkup room. Use the abbreviations O for "open" and C for "closed."

Focus Strategies

Make an Organized List

Draw a Picture or Diagram

Understand *Understand the problem.*

"What information are we given?"

Jerome will walk through three doors. Each door can be either open or closed.

"What are we asked to do?"

We are asked to list the possible combinations of open and closed doors.

Plan *Make a plan.*

"What problem-solving strategy can we use to solve the problem?"

We can *make an organized list* in the form of a tree diagram.

"What abbreviations will we use to describe the doors?"

We will use O for "open" and C for "closed."

Solve *Carry out the plan.*

"What will our tree diagram look like?"

For each door, the possibilities are open and closed. We start our tree diagram by writing the abbreviations O and C for the first door. We draw two branches from O and two branches from C to show the possibilities for the second door. Then we draw two more branches from each combination to show the possibilities for the third door.

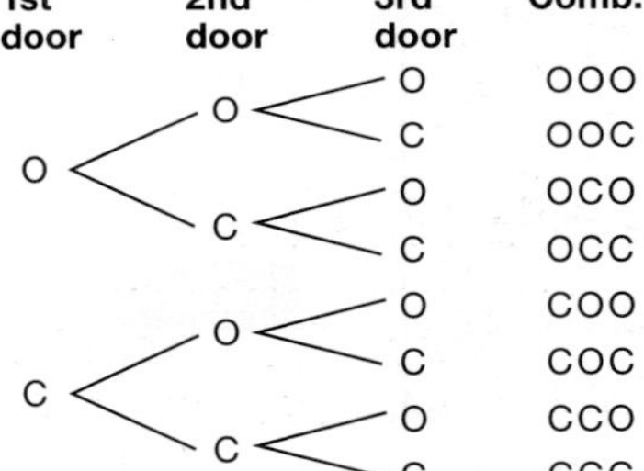

"How many combinations are possible?"

Our diagram shows that there are 8 ways Jerome could encounter the doors.

Check *Look back.*

"What are the possible combinations of doors that Jerome could encounter?"

OOO, OOC, OCO, OCC, COO, COC, CCO, CCC

"Is it reasonable that there are 8 possible combinations?"

Yes. There are two possibilities for the first door. For each of these two possibilities, there are two possibilities for the second door. So there are $2 \times 2 = 4$ combinations for the first two doors. For each of these combinations, there are two possibilities for the third door. So there are $2 \times 4 = 8$ combinations for all three doors.

"What multiplication problem can we use to find the number of combinations?"

We can multiply the number of possibilities for each of the three doors: $2 \times 2 \times 2 = 8$.

Alternate Strategy

Write a Number Sentence or Equation

Explain to students that they can also *write a number sentence* to find the number of combinations. Each of the three doors has two possibilities, so the equation $2 \times 2 \times 2 = 8$ can be used to find the number of combinations.

Power Up

Facts

Distribute **Power Up H** to students. See answers below.

Count Aloud

Before students begin the Mental Math exercises, do these counting exercises as a class.

Count up and down by threes from 21 to 63.

Mental Math

Encourage students to share different ways to mentally compute these exercises. Strategies for exercises are listed below.

a. Double 3 and Divide 14 by 2
$3 \times 2 = 6$ and $14 \div 2 = 7$; $6 \times 7 = 42$

b. Double 4 and Divide 16 by 2
$4 \times 2 = 8$ and $16 \div 2 = 8$; $8 \times 8 = 64$

c. Double 5 and Divide 22 by 2
$5 \times 2 = 10$ and $22 \div 2 = 11$; $10 \times 11 = 110$

d. Double 50 and Divide 24 by 2
$50 \times 2 = 100$ and $24 \div 2 = 12$; $100 \times 12 = 1200$

Problem Solving

Refer to **Problem-Solving Strategy Discussion,** p. 646B.

LESSON 98

• Fractions Equal to 1 and Fractions Equal to $\frac{1}{2}$

California Mathematics Content Standards

NS 1.0, 1.4 Decide when a rounded solution is called for and explain why such a solution may be appropriate.
NS 1.0, 1.7 Write the fraction represented by a drawing of parts of a figure; represent a given fraction by using drawings; and relate a fraction to a simple decimal on a number line.
NS 1.0, 1.9 Identify on a number line the relative position of positive fractions, positive mixed numbers, and positive decimals to two decimal places.

Power Up

facts Power Up H

mental math We can double one factor of a multiplication and take one half of the other factor to find a product.

$$4 \times 18$$
double ↓ ↓ half
$$8 \times 9 = 72$$

Find each product by the "double and half" method in problems **a–d.**

a. Number Sense: 3×14 42

b. Number Sense: 4×16 64

c. Number Sense: 5×22 110

d. Number Sense: 50×24 1200

e. Money: \$1.00 − 42¢ 58¢

f. Estimation: Choose the more reasonable estimate for the height of a ceiling: 250 cm or 250 m. 250 cm

g. Calculation: 6^2, + 4, − 30, × 10 100

h. Simplify: $25 - 5 \times 5$ 0

problem solving Choose an appropriate problem-solving strategy to solve this problem. To get to the room where he will have his yearly medical checkup, Jerome will walk through three doors—a door into the doctor's office building, a door into the waiting room, and a door into the checkup room. Each door might be either open or closed when Jerome gets to it. List the possible combinations of open and closed doors that Jerome might encounter on his way into the checkup room. Use the abbreviations O for "open" and C for "closed." 8 possible combinations: OOO, OOC, OCO, OCC, COO, COC, CCO, CCC

Facts Multiply.

8 × 8 64	0 × 5 0	7 × 3 21	9 × 7 63	3 × 2 6	9 × 4 36	8 × 6 48	4 × 3 12	9 × 5 45	6 × 2 12
9 × 2 18	7 × 4 28	8 × 3 24	5 × 5 25	9 × 6 54	7 × 2 14	5 × 4 20	9 × 1 9	9 × 3 27	0 × 0 0
7 × 5 35	2 × 2 4	6 × 4 24	8 × 7 56	5 × 3 15	7 × 6 42	4 × 2 8	8 × 5 40	6 × 3 18	9 × 9 81
3 × 3 9	8 × 4 32	7 × 7 49	8 × 2 16	10 × 10 100	6 × 5 30	4 × 4 16	9 × 8 72	5 × 2 10	6 × 6 36

New Concept

Each of the following circles is divided into parts. Together, the parts of each circle make up a whole.

We see that 2 halves is the same as 1 whole. We also see that 3 thirds, 4 fourths, and 5 fifths are ways to say 1 whole. If the numerator (top number) and the denominator (bottom number) of a fraction are the same, the fraction equals 1.

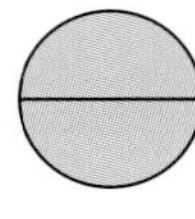
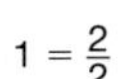
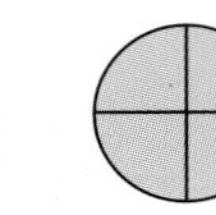
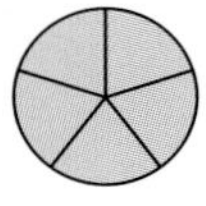

$1 = \frac{2}{2}$ $1 = \frac{3}{3}$ $1 = \frac{4}{4}$ $1 = \frac{5}{5}$

Example 1

Which of these fractions equals 1?

$\frac{1}{6}$ $\frac{5}{6}$ $\frac{6}{6}$ $\frac{7}{6}$

A fraction equals 1 if its numerator and denominator are equal. The fraction equal to 1 is $\frac{6}{6}$.

Model Use fraction manipulatives to verify that $\frac{6}{6} = 1$.

See student work.

Example 2

Write a fraction equal to 1 that has a denominator of 7.

A fraction equals 1 if its numerator and denominator are the same. If the denominator is 7, the numerator must also be 7. We write $\frac{7}{7}$.

If the numerator of a fraction is half the denominator, then the fraction equals $\frac{1}{2}$. Notice below that the top number of each fraction illustrated is half of the bottom number of the fraction.

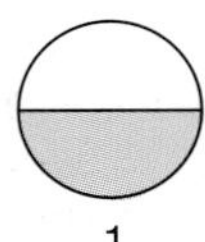
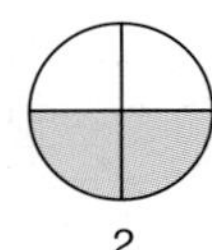
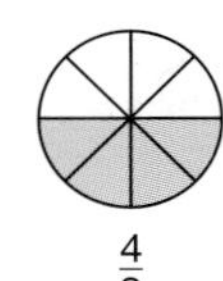

$\frac{1}{2}$ $\frac{2}{4}$ $\frac{3}{6}$ $\frac{4}{8}$

New Concept

Observation

Some students may find it helpful if you display the *Basic Fraction Circles* poster as you complete this lesson.

Active Learning

Point out that $\frac{2}{2}$, $\frac{3}{3}$, $\frac{4}{4}$, and $\frac{5}{5}$ are examples of equivalent fractions. Write the term 'equivalent fractions' on the board or overhead and explain that equivalent fractions are different names for the same number (which in this case is 1).

Invite students to name other examples of fractions that are equal to 1. Then ask:

"How many fractions can we name that are equal to 1?" An infinite number; too many to count

Manipulative Use

The circles showing halves, thirds, fourths, and fifths can be modeled using overhead fraction circles.

Example 1

Connection

After discussing the solution, explain that another way to show that $\frac{6}{6}$ is equal to 1 is to complete the division $6 \div 6$. Remind students we can use division because a fraction bar is a symbol for division.

Example 2

Active Learning

Invite a volunteer to sketch and shade a circle on the board or overhead to model the example.

(continued)

English Learners

A **checkup** is an examination of someone or something.

Explain that sometimes the checkup is a medical one and then it is called a medical checkup.

Ask students if they have ever been to the doctor for a medical checkup.

Ask:

"What are some things the Doctor or nurse did to you?" Samples: They weighed me, checked my blood pressure, listened to my heartbeat, etc.

Alternative Approach: Using Manipulatives

To help students visualize fractions that are equal to 1 and fractions that are equal to $\frac{1}{2}$, have them use 1-inch grid paper for the following activity.

- Have students draw a 4×4 square on the grid paper. Have them shade $\frac{1}{2}$ of it. Ask:

"How many of the small squares did you shade? How many are not shaded?"
8; 8

Ask students to draw a 6×6 square and a 8×8 square and find other fractions equal to $\frac{1}{2}$. Then repeat the activity with the same squares, asking students to find fractions equal to 1.

New Concept *(Continued)*

Example 3

Encourage students to complete the comparisons using only mental math by comparing each numerator to its denominator.

Example 4

Extend the Example

Ask advanced learners to name the number of eighths that are equivalent to $\frac{1}{2}$. 4 eighths

Example 5

Error Alert

Make sure students understand that the first step in rounding a mixed number to a whole number is to identify the two consecutive whole numbers the mixed number is between. The second step is to compare the given number to the mixed number that is halfway between the two consecutive whole numbers.

(continued)

If the numerator is less than half the denominator, the fraction is less than $\frac{1}{2}$. If the numerator is greater than half the denominator, the fraction is greater than $\frac{1}{2}$.

Model Use fraction manipulatives to verify that $\frac{5}{10} = \frac{1}{2}$. See student work.

Example 3

a. Which fraction below equals $\frac{1}{2}$?

b. Which is less than $\frac{1}{2}$?

c. Which is greater than $\frac{1}{2}$?

$$\frac{3}{7} \qquad \frac{6}{12} \qquad \frac{5}{9}$$

a. Since 6 is half of 12, the fraction equal to $\frac{1}{2}$ is $\frac{6}{12}$.

b. Since 3 is less than half of 7, the fraction less than $\frac{1}{2}$ is $\frac{3}{7}$.

c. Since 5 is greater than half of 9, the fraction greater than $\frac{1}{2}$ is $\frac{5}{9}$.

Example 4

Compare: $\frac{3}{8} \bigcirc \frac{1}{2}$

Since 3 is less than half of 8, we know that $\frac{3}{8}$ is less than $\frac{1}{2}$.

$$\frac{3}{8} < \frac{1}{2}$$

Represent Make a sketch that proves the answer is correct.

Sample:

Example 5

Round $6\frac{7}{10}$ to the nearest whole number.

Halfway between 6 and 7 is $6\frac{1}{2}$. We know that $6\frac{7}{10}$ is greater than $6\frac{1}{2}$ because $\frac{7}{10}$ is greater than $\frac{5}{10}$, which equals $\frac{1}{2}$.

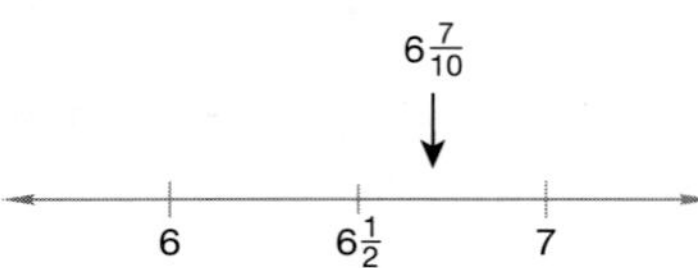

This means $6\frac{7}{10}$ rounds to **7**.

Inclusion

Use this strategy if the student displays:

- Difficulty with Abstract Processing.
- Slow Learning Rate.

Fractions Equal to 1; Fractions Equal to $\frac{1}{2}$ (Small Group)

Materials: fraction circles; paper; colored pencils

- Have students display fraction circles on their table. Tell students to draw the fractions $\frac{4}{4}$, $\frac{6}{6}$ and $\frac{8}{8}$ on paper. At the top of the paper have the students write a large 1 to label the fractions on the page a whole.
- Using the same fraction circles, have students remove $\frac{1}{2}$ of it. Have students show $\frac{4}{4}$ but take away half of it and explain that $\frac{1}{2}$ of $\frac{4}{4}$ is $\frac{2}{4}$.
- Do the same for $\frac{6}{6}$ and $\frac{8}{8}$. Ask, ***"What is half of $\frac{6}{6}$?"*** $\frac{3}{6}$ ***"What is half of $\frac{8}{8}$?"*** $\frac{4}{8}$

Example 6

Estimate the perimeter and area of this rectangle.

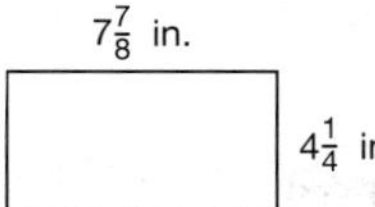

First we round each dimension to the nearest whole number of inches. Since $\frac{7}{8}$ is greater than $\frac{1}{2}$, we round $7\frac{7}{8}$ in. up to 8 in. Since $\frac{1}{4}$ is less than $\frac{1}{2}$, we round $4\frac{1}{4}$ in. down to 4 in. Then we use 8 in. and 4 in. to estimate the perimeter and area.

Perimeter: 8 in. + 4 in. + 8 in. + 4 in. = **24 in.**

Area: 8 in. × 4 in. = **32 sq. in.**

Lesson Practice

a. Write a fraction equal to 1 that has a denominator of 6. $\frac{6}{6}$

b. **Multiple Choice** Which of these fractions equals 1? C

A $\frac{1}{10}$ **B** $\frac{9}{10}$ **C** $\frac{10}{10}$ **D** $\frac{11}{10}$

What fraction name for 1 is shown by each picture?

c. 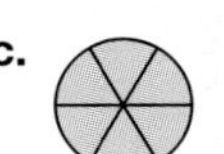 $\frac{6}{6}$

d. 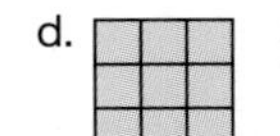 $\frac{9}{9}$

e. Write a fraction equal to $\frac{1}{2}$ with a denominator of 12. $\frac{6}{12}$

f. Compare: $\frac{9}{20} \bigcirc \frac{1}{2}$ <

g. **Estimate** Round $5\frac{3}{8}$ to the nearest whole number. 5

h. Estimate the perimeter and area of a rectangle that is $6\frac{3}{4}$ in. long and $4\frac{3}{8}$ in. wide. 22 in.; 28 sq. in.

Written Practice

Distributed and Integrated

▶ *1. (20, 31, 66) **a.** **Analyze** If the perimeter of a square is 280 feet, how long is each side of the square? 70 ft

b. What is the area? 4900 ft^2

c. Give the dimensions of another rectangle that has the same perimeter, 280 ft, and an area greater than 100 ft^2 and less than 150 ft^2. 139 ft by 1 ft

Math Background

The ideas in this lesson can be extended to other fractions as well. For example, the fractions below are all equivalent to $\frac{1}{4}$ because the numerator is a fourth of the denominator.

$$\frac{2}{8} \quad \frac{3}{12} \quad \frac{4}{16} \quad \frac{5}{20}$$

We can compare a fraction to $\frac{1}{4}$ by determining whether its numerator is more or less than a fourth of its denominator. For example, $\frac{3}{8} > \frac{1}{4}$ because 3 is more than one fourth of 8 and $\frac{5}{24} < \frac{1}{4}$ because 5 is less than a fourth of 24.

New Concept *(Continued)*

Example 6

Error Alert

Remind students that whenever addition is used to find the perimeter of a rectangle, the addition must include four addends. In other words, the length and the width are each used twice.

Also remind students that calculations of area are to include a 'square units' label.

Lesson Practice

Guided Practice

Use these problems as guided practice to check the students' understanding of today's concept.

Problems c and d

"When we write a fraction to represent a picture, what does the denominator of the fraction represent?" The number of equal parts into which the picture is divided

"What does the numerator represent?" The number being named (the number of shaded parts)

Problem g **Estimate**

To help students complete the rounding, ask:

"What two consecutive whole numbers is the mixed number $5\frac{3}{8}$ between?" 5 and 6

"To what mixed number should we compare $5\frac{3}{8}$?" $5\frac{1}{2}$ or $5\frac{4}{8}$

Problem h Extend the Problem

Challenge your advanced learners to find the exact perimeter of the rectangle. 22.25 or $22\frac{1}{4}$ in.

Problems a and b

Error Alert

Encourage students to use their fraction pieces to help solve these problems or to check their work.

Closure

The questions below help assess the concepts taught in this lesson.

"Explain how to write a fraction that is equivalent to 1 and then name three fractions that are equivalent to 1." Sample: Write the same number for the numerator and the denominator of the fraction; $\frac{2}{2}$, $\frac{3}{3}$, $\frac{4}{4}$

"Explain how to write a fraction that is equivalent to $\frac{1}{2}$ and then name three fractions that are equivalent to $\frac{1}{2}$." Sample: Write a number for the numerator, and then double the numerator and write that number as the denominator; $\frac{2}{4}$, $\frac{3}{6}$, $\frac{4}{8}$

Written Practice

Math Conversations

Independent Practice and Discussions to Increase Understanding

Problem 1

Before students solve problems **a** and **b**, you might choose to ask them to write a formula that can be used to find the perimeter of the rectangle, and a formula that can be used to find its area. Since a number of formulas are possible, invite volunteers to share their work and to write their formulas on the board or overhead. Sample: $P = (2 \cdot l) + (2 \cdot w)$ where l = length and w = width; $A = s \cdot s$ where s = the length of a side.

Some students may find it helpful if you discuss part **c** as a class and then solve the problem as a class activity.

Problem 4 (Represent)

Remind students of the importance of checking their work, and point out that an estimate is often a good way to check an answer. Then before completing the arithmetic, invite students to share different ways to estimate the exact answer. Sample: We must find $\frac{3}{5}$ of 60 to solve the problem. Since $\frac{3}{5}$ is a little more than $\frac{1}{2}$, a little more than $\frac{1}{2}$ of 60 trees is the answer; 35 trees is a good estimate.

After the arithmetic has been completed, remind students to compare their exact answers to their estimates to help decide the reasonableness of those answers.

Problem 6

"When we write a fraction to represent the shaded part of a circle, what does the denominator of the fraction represent?"
The number of equal parts into which the whole is divided

"What does the numerator represent?"
The number of shaded parts

Problem 9 (Represent)

Encourage students to use their fraction manipulatives to check their work.

(continued)

*2. (RF12, 87) There are 365 days in a common year. How many full weeks are there in 365 days? 52 full weeks

*3. (87, 93) Nia passed out crayons to 6 of her friends. Each friend received 3 crayons. There were 2 crayons left for Nia. How many crayons did Nia have when she began? 20 crayons

▸ *4. (94) (Represent) Three fifths of the 60 trees in the orchard were more than 10 feet tall. How many trees were more than 10 feet tall? Draw a picture to illustrate the problem. 36 trees

4. 60 trees

$\frac{3}{5}$ were more than 10 ft tall.	12 trees
	12 trees
	12 trees
$\frac{2}{5}$ were less than 10 ft tall.	12 trees
	12 trees

5. (42) **a.** Find the length of this line segment in millimeters. 43 mm

b. Find the length of the line segment in centimeters. Write the answer as a decimal number. 4.3 cm

mm 10 20 30 40 50

cm 1 2 3 4 5

▸ *6. (98) What fraction name for 1 is shown by this circle? $\frac{8}{8}$

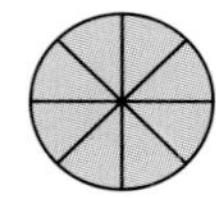

*7. (22, 40) Round $350,454 to the nearest thousand, to the nearest hundred, and to the nearest ten. $350,000; $350,500; $350,450

*8. (Inv. 4, 43, 92) Copy this number line. Then place a dot at $\frac{1}{2}$ and label the dot point *A*. Place a dot at 1.3 and label the dot point *B*. Place a dot at $1\frac{7}{10}$ and label the dot point *C*.

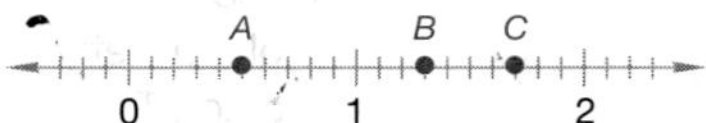

▸ *9. (89) (Represent) Change the improper fraction $\frac{5}{4}$ to a mixed number. Draw a picture to show that the improper fraction and the mixed number are equal. $1\frac{1}{4}$;

650 *Saxon Math* Intermediate 4

10. (95)  The bar graph shows the number of students in fourth grade at Sebastian's school. Use the graph to answer the questions that follow.

The Number of 4th Graders at Sebastian's School

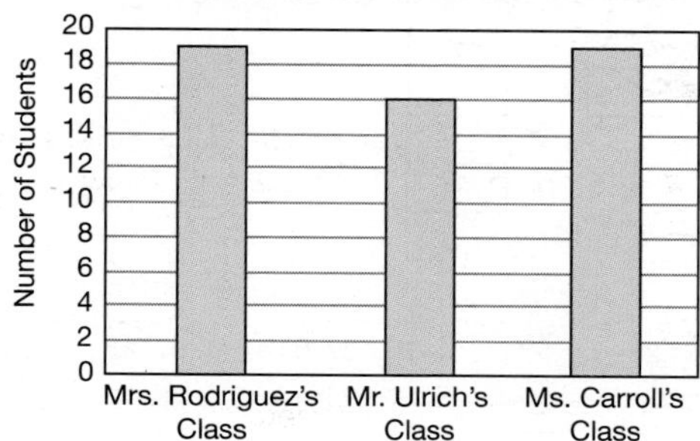

a. How many fewer students are in Mr. Ulrich's class than in Ms. Carroll's class or in Mrs. Rodriguez's class? 3 fewer students

b. Altogether, how many fourth grade students does the bar graph represent? 54 students

▸ **c.** Which measure of the data is greater: the range or the median? Explain your answer. Median; sample: The median is the middle number (19). The range is 3 because the difference of the greatest and least numbers is 19 − 16.

11. (39, 71) The baker used 30 pounds of flour each day to make bread. How many pounds of flour did the baker use in 73 days? 2190 lb

12. (53, 69) The chef used 132 pounds of potatoes every 6 days. How many pounds of potatoes were used each day? 22 lb

***13.** (95) Interpret Jeremy asked 8 friends what type of dog is their favorite. The results of his survey are below. What is the mode of this data? Boston Terrier and Poodle

German Shepard	Poodle
Boston Terrier	Golden Retriever
Irish Setter	Boston Terrier
Dachshund	Poodle

Written Practice (Continued)

Math Conversations (cont.)

Problem 10c Interpret

Extend the Problem

Offer the following challenge to your students:

"If one new student enrolled in Mr. Ulrich's class, would the median number of students in the fourth grade change? Would the range of the data change? Explain your answers." No; yes; sample: The median would not change because 19 is the median of 19, 19, and 17; The range would change because the subtraction 19 − 17 would be used to find the range.

(continued)

Written Practice *(Continued)*

Math Conversations *(cont.)*

Problem 18

Remind students that an exponent represents the number of times a base is used as a factor, and then ask them to rewrite and simplify the expressions below for additional practice.

3^3 $3 \cdot 3 \cdot 3 = 27$ 2^5 $2 \cdot 2 \cdot 2 \cdot 2 \cdot 2 = 32$

Problem 28

If students do not know that 1 gallon = 128 fluid ounces, explain that they can still solve the problem by applying the capacity relationships they do know. For example, if they know that 1 quart = 32 ounces and 4 quarts = 1 gallon, the number of ounces that are equal to 1 gallon would be 4 × 32, or 128. Knowing that, the division 128 ÷ 8 can be used to solve the problem.

Errors and Misconceptions

Problem 15

Students must recognize that because two amounts represent dollars, and one amount represents dollars and cents, a decimal point will need to be placed to the right of the dollar amounts for the amounts to be aligned properly for adding and subtracting.

Problem 20

Remind those students who wrote 474¢ as the answer that any number of cents that is greater than 99¢ is not considered to be in simplest form.

Also make sure those students understand that because $1 = 100¢, an amount in cents can be changed to dollars by moving the decimal point two places to the left and writing a dollar sign.

*14. (96, 97) **a.** What is another name for this rectangular prism? cube

b. How many edges does it have? 12

c. Which of the following nets will fold up to make the figure? Net 1

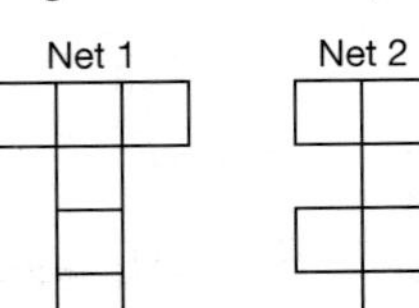

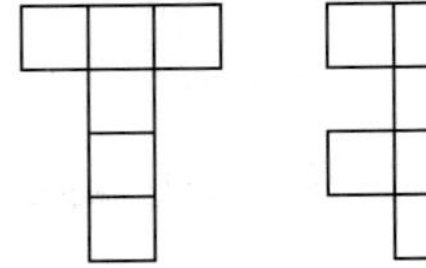

15. (9, 28, 52) $80 − ($63.72 + $2) $14.28

16. (52) 37,614 − 29,148 8466

17. (64) $9w = 9 \cdot 26$ 26

► 18. (65) 3^4 81

19. (84) 24 × 1000 24,000

20. (28, 38) 79¢ × 6 $4.74

21. (85) 50×50 = 2500

22. (86) 51×49 = 2499

23. (88) 47×63 = 2961

24. (79) $4\overline{)810}$ 202 R 2

25. (69) $5\overline{)490}$ 98

26 (72) $6\overline{)362}$ 60 R 2

27. (Inv. 3, 83) $1435 \div \sqrt{49}$ 205

►*28. (73) **a.** **Analyze** How many 8-ounce cups of milk can be poured from one gallon of milk? 16 cups

b. Write a formula to change any number of gallons to cups. Use g for gallons and c for cups. $16g = c$ or $c = 16g$

*29. (98) Round $16\frac{5}{8}$ to the nearest whole number. 17

*30. (98) Estimate the area of a window with the dimensions shown: 12 ft²

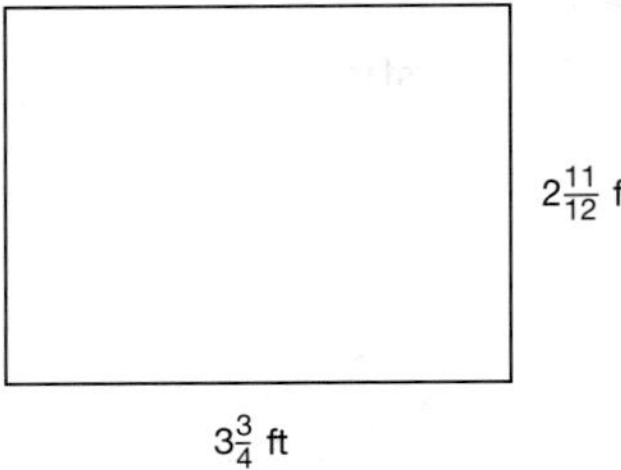

Looking Forward

Identifying and writing fractions equal to 1 and to $\frac{1}{2}$ prepares students for:

- **Lesson 99,** changing improper fractions to whole or mixed numbers.
- **Lesson 100,** adding and subtracting fractions with common denominators.
- **Lesson 103,** finding equivalent fractions.
- **Lesson 106,** writing the reduced form of a fraction.
- **Lessons 112–113,** adding and subtracting fractions and mixed numbers with common denominators and renaming fractions whose denominators are not equal by using a common denominator of the fractions.

Planning & Preparation

• Changing Improper Fractions to Whole Numbers or Mixed Numbers

Objectives

- Write an improper fraction as a whole number or a mixed number.
- Write an improper fractions as a decimal.

Prerequisite Skills

- Using a number line to locate and name mixed numbers.
- Writing improper fractions using pictorial models.

Materials

Instructional Masters

- Power Up J Worksheet
- Lesson Activity 8*

Manipulative Kit

- Rulers
- Overhead fraction circles, color tiles, money manipulatives, safety compasses, fraction circles*

Teacher-provided materials

- Fraction manipulatives from Investigation 8
- Grid paper, jars or circle cutouts*

**optional*

California Mathematics Content Standards

NS 1.0, 1.5 Explain different interpretations of fractions, for example, parts of a whole, parts of a set, and division of whole numbers by whole numbers; explain equivalents of fractions (see Standard 4.0).

NS 1.0, 1.6 Write tenths and hundredths in decimal and fraction notations and know the fraction and decimal equivalents for halves and fourths (e.g., $\frac{1}{2} = 0.5$ or $.50$; $\frac{7}{4} = 1\frac{3}{4} = 1.75$).

NS 1.0, 1.7 Write the fraction represented by a drawing of parts of a figure; represent a given fraction by using drawings; and relate a fraction to a simple decimal on a number line.

MR 2.0, 2.3 Use a variety of methods, such as words, numbers, symbols, charts, graphs, tables, diagrams, and models, to explain mathematical reasoning.

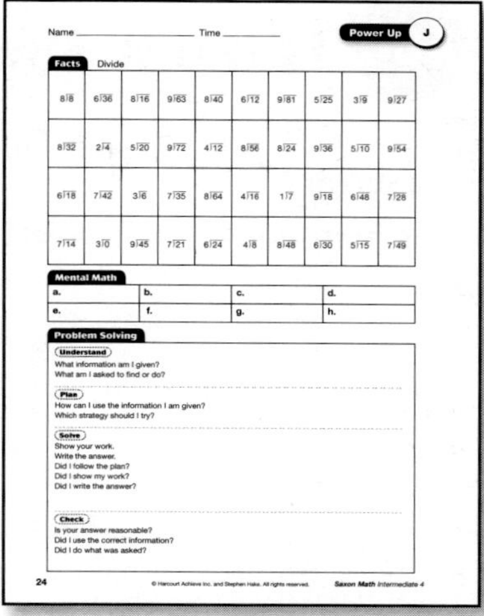

Name __________ Time ______ **Power Up J**

Facts Divide

$8\overline{)8}$	$6\overline{)36}$	$8\overline{)16}$	$9\overline{)63}$	$8\overline{)40}$	$6\overline{)12}$	$9\overline{)81}$	$5\overline{)25}$	$3\overline{)9}$	$9\overline{)27}$
$8\overline{)32}$	$2\overline{)4}$	$5\overline{)20}$	$9\overline{)72}$	$4\overline{)12}$	$8\overline{)56}$	$8\overline{)24}$	$9\overline{)36}$	$5\overline{)10}$	$9\overline{)54}$
$6\overline{)18}$	$7\overline{)42}$	$3\overline{)6}$	$7\overline{)35}$	$8\overline{)64}$	$4\overline{)16}$	$1\overline{)7}$	$9\overline{)18}$	$6\overline{)48}$	$7\overline{)28}$
$7\overline{)14}$	$3\overline{)0}$	$9\overline{)45}$	$7\overline{)21}$	$6\overline{)24}$	$4\overline{)8}$	$8\overline{)48}$	$6\overline{)30}$	$5\overline{)15}$	$7\overline{)49}$

Mental Math

a.	b.	c.	d.
e.	f.	g.	h.

Problem Solving

Understand
What information am I given?
What am I asked to find or do?

Plan
How can I use the information I am given?
Which strategy should I try?

Solve
Show your work.
Write the answer.
Did I follow the plan?
Did I show my work?
Did I write the answer?

Check
Is your answer reasonable?
Did I use the correct information?
Did I do what was asked?

24 *Saxon Math Intermediate 4*

Power Up J Worksheet

Universal Access

Reaching All Special Needs Students

Special Education Students	At-Risk Students	English Learners	Advanced Learners
• Inclusion (TM) • Adaptations for Saxon Math	• Error Alert (TM) • Reteaching Masters • Refresher Lessons for California Standards	• English Learners (TM) • Developing Academic Language (TM) • English Learner Handbook	• Extend the Problem (TM) • Online Activities

TM=Teacher's Manual

Developing Academic Language

Maintained
decimal
division
improper fraction
mixed number

English Learner
im- (prefix)

Problem Solving Discussion

Problem

Danae can walk twice as fast as she can swim. She can run twice as fast as she can walk. She can ride a bike twice as fast as she can run. If Danae can ride her bike a quarter mile in one minute, how long would it take her to swim a quarter mile?

Focus Strategies

Work Backwards

ABC Make It Simpler

Understand *Understand the problem.*

"How can we list the four activities from slowest to fastest?"

Swim, walk, run, and bike

"What are we asked to do?"

We are asked to find how long it would take for Danae to swim a quarter mile.

Plan *Make a plan.*

"What problem-solving strategy can we use to solve the problem?"

We can *work backwards.* First, we need to find how long it would take Danae to run a quarter mile. Then we can find how long it would take her to walk a quarter mile, and then we can find how long it would take her to swim a quarter mile.

Solve *Carry out the plan.*

"Danae runs slower than she rides her bike. So will it take her more time or less time to run a quarter mile than to bike the same distance?"

Since she runs slower, it will take her longer to run a quarter mile.

"How long would it take Danae to run a quarter mile?"

Danae rides her bike twice as fast as she can run. This means it would take Danae twice as long to run a quarter mile as to ride her bike the same distance. Thus, it would take Danae 2×1 minute, or 2 minutes, to run a quarter mile.

"How long would it take Danae to walk a quarter mile?"

It would take Danae twice as long to walk a quarter mile as to run the same distance. Thus, it would take Danae 2×2 minutes, or 4 minutes, to walk a quarter mile.

"How long would it take Danae to swim a quarter mile?"

It would take Danae twice as long to swim a quarter mile as to walk the same distance. Thus, it would take Danae 2×4 minutes, or 8 minutes, to swim a quarter mile.

Check *Look back.*

"Is our answer reasonable?"

When Danae travels slower, it takes her longer to travel a quarter mile than when she travels faster. It makes sense that it would take Danae 8 times as long to swim a quarter mile as to ride her bike that distance, since swimming is slower than biking.

"What problem-solving strategies did we use, and how did they help us?"

We broke the problem into smaller parts (*made it simpler*) by *working backwards* step by step.

LESSON 99

• Changing Improper Fractions to Whole Numbers or Mixed Numbers

California Mathematics Content Standards

NS 1.0, 1.5 Explain different interpretations of fractions, for example, parts of a whole, parts of a set, and division of whole numbers by whole numbers; explain equivalents of fractions (see Standard 4.0).

NS 1.0, 1.6 Write tenths and hundredths in decimal and fraction notations and know the fraction and decimal equivalents for halves and fourths (e.g., $\frac{1}{2}$ = 0.5 or .50; $\frac{7}{4} = 1\frac{3}{4}$ = 1.75).

NS 1.0, 1.7 Write the fraction represented by a drawing of parts of a figure; represent a given fraction by using drawings; and relate a fraction to a simple decimal on a number line.

facts Power Up J

mental math Find each product by the "double and half" method in problems **a–c.**

a. Number Sense: 3 × 18 54

b. Number Sense: 15 × 60 900

c. Number Sense: 50 × 48 2400

d. Money: Shawntay had $5.00. He spent $1.75 on a birthday card for his brother. How much does he have left? $3.25

e. Fractional Part: What is $\frac{1}{5}$ of 100? 20

f. Estimation: Brittany used $11\frac{3}{4}$ inches of tape to wrap one gift. About how much tape will she need to wrap five more gifts that are the same size as the first? 60 in. or 5 ft

g. Calculation: $\sqrt{25}$, ÷ 5, + 6, × 2, − 11 3

h. Simplify: 1 + (2 × 3) 7

problem solving Choose an appropriate problem-solving strategy to solve this problem. Danae can walk twice as fast as she can swim. She can run twice as fast as she can walk. She can ride a bike twice as fast as she can run. If Danae can ride her bike a quarter mile in one minute, how long would it take her to swim a quarter mile? 8 min

If the numerator of a fraction is equal to or greater than the denominator, the fraction is an improper fraction. All of these fractions are improper fractions:

$$\frac{3}{2} \quad \frac{5}{4} \quad \frac{10}{3} \quad \frac{9}{4} \quad \frac{5}{5}$$

Facts Divide

1 8)8	6 6)36	2 8)16	7 9)63	5 8)40	2 6)12	9 9)81	5 5)25	3 3)9	3 9)27
4 8)32	2 2)4	4 5)20	8 9)72	3 4)12	7 8)56	3 8)24	4 9)36	2 5)10	6 9)54
3 6)18	6 7)42	2 3)6	5 7)35	8 8)64	4 4)16	7 1)7	2 9)18	8 6)48	4 7)28
2 7)14	0 3)0	5 9)45	3 7)21	4 6)24	2 4)8	6 8)48	5 6)30	3 5)15	7 7)49

Power Up

Facts

Distribute **Power Up J** to students. See answers below.

Count Aloud

Before students begin the Mental Math exercises, do these counting exercises as a class.

Count up and down by nines from 18 to 72.

Mental Math

Encourage students to share different ways to mentally compute these exercises. Strategies for exercises are listed below.

a. Double 3 and Halve 18
3 × 2 = 6 and 18 ÷ 2 = 9; 6 × 9 = 54

b. Double 15 and Halve 60
15 × 2 = 30 and 60 ÷ 2 = 30;
30 × 30 = 900

d. Subtract $1, then Subtract 75¢
$5 − $1 = $4; $4 − 75¢ = $3.25

Subtract $2, then Add 25¢
$5 − $2 = $3; $3 + 25¢ = $3.25

Problem Solving

Refer to **Problem-Solving Strategy Discussion,** p. 653B.

New Concept

Instruction

Some students may assume that for a fraction to be improper, the numerator must be greater than the denominator. Have students note the fraction $\frac{5}{5}$ in the list of fractions, and make sure that they understand that an improper fraction can have the same numerator and denominator.

Example 1

Manipulative Use

On the board or overhead, demonstrate how to write and complete the division that is used to write $\frac{13}{5}$ as a mixed number. Then use overhead fraction circles to demonstrate that $2\frac{3}{5}$ and $\frac{13}{5}$ are equal.

Extend the Example

Challenge your advanced learners by saying: ***"Write $4\frac{6}{7}$ as an improper fraction."*** $\frac{34}{7}$

Example 2

Error Alert

Some students will benefit if you explain how visualizing the face of a clock can be used to help divide a circle into a variety of equal parts. For example, explain that since there are 60 minutes in an hour, the division 60 ÷ 5 can be used to divide a circle into five equal parts, or fifths. Since 60 ÷ 5 = 12, students can draw a circle and visualize it as a clock face and then make a mark for every 12 minutes on the clock.

Active Learning

Invite volunteers to demonstrate on the board or overhead how the technique described above can be used to divide a circle into other equal parts, such as sixths, tenths, or twelfths.

(continued)

Model Use fraction manipulatives to show $\frac{3}{2}$ and $\frac{5}{4}$ as mixed numbers. $\frac{3}{2} = 1\frac{1}{2}$ and $\frac{5}{4} = 1\frac{1}{4}$

To write an improper fraction as a whole or mixed number, we divide to find out how many wholes the improper fraction contains. If there is no remainder, we write the improper fraction as a whole number. If there is a remainder, the remainder becomes the numerator in a mixed number.

Example 1

Write $\frac{13}{5}$ as a mixed number. Draw a picture to show that the improper fraction and mixed number are equal.

To find the number of wholes, we divide.

$$\begin{array}{r} 2 \\ 5\overline{)13} \\ \underline{10} \\ 3 \end{array}$$

2 ← wholes
3 ← remainder of 3

This division tells us that $\frac{13}{5}$ equals two wholes with three fifths left over. We write this as $2\frac{3}{5}$. We can see that $\frac{13}{5}$ equals $2\frac{3}{5}$ if we draw a picture.

$$\frac{13}{5} = \frac{5}{5} + \frac{5}{5} + \frac{3}{5} = 2\frac{3}{5}$$

Example 2

Write $\frac{10}{3}$ as a mixed number. Then draw a picture to show that the improper fraction and mixed number are equal.

First we divide.

$$\begin{array}{r} 3 \\ 3\overline{)10} \\ \underline{9} \\ 1 \end{array}$$

From the division we see that there are three wholes. One third is left over. We write $3\frac{1}{3}$. Then we draw a picture to show that $\frac{10}{3}$ equals $3\frac{1}{3}$.

English Learners

The **"im"** at the beginning of the word improper makes the word mean **"the opposite of, or not proper."**

Ask, ***"What do these words means: imperfect, imbalance, impolite?"*** not perfect, not in balance, the opposite of polite

Discuss with students that not every word that begins with the letters **"im"** carries the meaning *the opposite* of or not.

Ask, ***"Which of these words includes the idea 'the opposite of' or 'not': imagine, improve, impossible?"*** impossible

Have students think of other words that begin with 'im" and determine whether the word carries the idea "the opposite of."

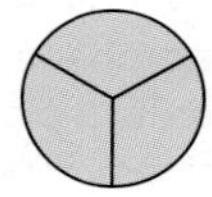 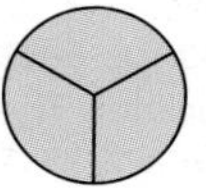 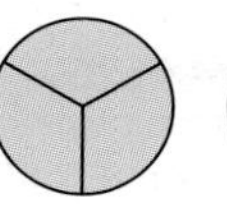 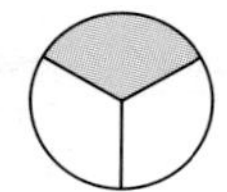

$\frac{10}{3} = 3\frac{1}{3}$

Sample: Dividing 10 blocks of modeling clay among 3 children; Each child will receive $3\frac{1}{3}$ blocks of clay.

Formulate Give a real-world example for dividing items into groups of $3\frac{1}{3}$.

Example 3

Write $\frac{12}{4}$ as a whole number. Then draw a picture to show that the improper fraction and whole number are equal.

First we divide.

$$\begin{array}{r} 3 \\ 4\overline{)12} \\ \underline{12} \\ 0 \end{array}$$

We have three wholes and no remainder. Our picture looks like this:

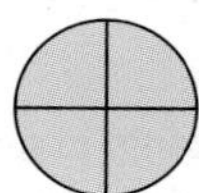 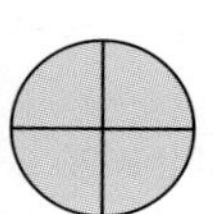 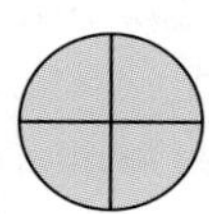

$\frac{12}{4} = \mathbf{3}$

Discuss Explain how $\frac{4}{4}$ is related to $\frac{12}{4}$. $\frac{4}{4} + \frac{4}{4} + \frac{4}{4} = \frac{12}{4}$

Example 4

Write each improper fraction as a decimal.

a. $\frac{7}{4}$ **b.** $\frac{17}{10}$

a. We can change $\frac{7}{4}$ to a mixed number.

$$\frac{7}{4} = \frac{4}{4} + \frac{3}{4} \text{ or } 1\frac{3}{4}$$

We know that $\frac{3}{4}$ is 0.75, so $1\frac{3}{4}$ is **1.75.**

b. We can write $\frac{17}{10}$ as a mixed number.

$$\frac{17}{10} = \frac{10}{10} + \frac{7}{10} \text{ or } 1\frac{7}{10}$$

We know that $1\frac{7}{10}$ is also written as **1.7.**

New Concept *(Continued)*

Example 3

Math-to-Math Connection

Have students recall that we can use division to write $\frac{12}{4}$ as a whole number because a fraction bar is a symbol for division.

Students may be interested to learn that in addition to being a symbol for division, a fraction bar is also a grouping symbol. To demonstrate this concept, you might challenge students to simplify the improper fraction $\frac{7+2}{3}$, which simplifies to 3 because $9 \div 3 = 3$. Point out that in this example, the fraction bar functions as a set of parentheses: when parentheses are present, the operation in parentheses must be completed first. The same idea is true about the fraction bar: the operation above (or below) the bar must be completed first.

(continued)

Math Background

As shown in the lesson, an improper fraction can be converted to a mixed number by dividing the numerator by the denominator. Another method involves writing the improper fraction as a sum involving as many fractions equal to 1 as possible.

For example, to convert $\frac{10}{3}$ to a mixed number, we write the improper fraction as a sum with as many addends as $\frac{3}{3}$ (which is equal to 1) as possible. $\frac{10}{3} = \frac{3}{3} + \frac{3}{3} + \frac{3}{3} + \frac{1}{3} = 1 + 1 + 1 + \frac{1}{3} = 3\frac{1}{3}$

Teacher Tip

Make compasses available to students to use during the lesson. Some round jar tops or circle cutouts will be helpful for students to trace to make circles.

New Concept *(Continued)*

Lesson Practice

Guided Practice

Use these problems as guided practice to check the students' understanding of today's concept.

Problems b and d

Make sure students conclude that a whole number is the simplest form of each improper fraction.

Problems a–d
Error Alert

Encourage students to use their fraction manipulatives to check their work.

Closure The questions below help assess the concepts taught in this lesson.

"Draw a picture or use your fraction manipulatives to show the mixed number that $\frac{11}{6}$ is equal to." $\frac{11}{6} = 1\frac{5}{6}$; The pictures or manipulative arrangements should show two circles each divided into six equal parts, with one complete circle shaded and five parts of the other circle shaded.

"Explain how division can be used to change an improper fraction to a whole or mixed number, and give an example to support your answer." Divide the numerator by the denominator; sample: $\frac{20}{4} = 20 \div 4 = 5$

Written Practice

Math Conversations

Independent Practice and Discussions to Increase Understanding

Problem 4 **Represent**

Manipulative Use

One way for students to check their answers is to use colored tiles to represent $\frac{1}{4}$ and $\frac{3}{4}$.

Problem 6

After writing the fraction, remind students that division can be used to check their answers because a fraction bar is a symbol for division.

(continued)

Lesson Practice

Represent Change each improper fraction to a whole number or to a mixed number. Then draw a picture to show that the improper fraction is equal to the number you wrote.

a. $\frac{7}{2}$ $3\frac{1}{2}$ **b.** $\frac{12}{3}$ 4 **c.** $\frac{8}{3}$ $2\frac{2}{3}$ **d.** $\frac{15}{5}$ 3

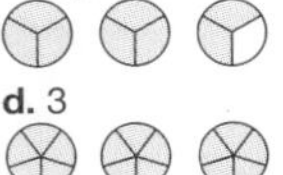

Analyze Write each improper fraction as a decimal:

e. $\frac{7}{2}$ 3.5 **f.** $\frac{19}{10}$ 1.9

Written Practice

Distributed and Integrated

1. (87) How many 6¢ erasers can be bought with 2 quarters? 8 erasers

2. (29) Two quarters are what fractional part of a dollar? $\frac{2}{4}$ or $\frac{1}{2}$

3. (93) Jason has \$8. Parisa has \$2 more than Jason. How much money do they have altogether? \$18

▸ ***4.** (94) **Represent** Three fourths of the 20 students in a class participate in an after-school activity. What number of students participate? Draw a picture to illustrate and solve the problem. 15 students

4. 20 students

$\frac{1}{4}$ do not participate.	5 students
$\frac{3}{4}$ participate.	5 students
	5 students
	5 students

***5.** (95) **Interpret** Bethany surveyed twelve friends and asked them the number of times they saw a movie in a theater last month. She recorded the results on the number line below.

Number of Movies in a Theater

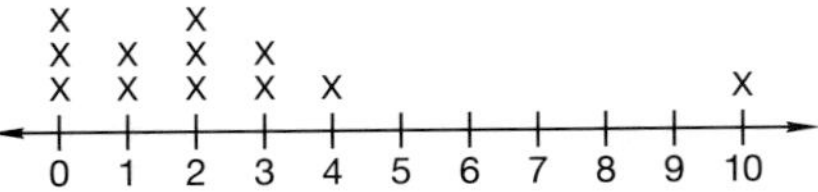

a. **Interpret** Is there an outlier? If yes, name it. Yes; 10

b. **Explain** How can you find the median for this data? Sample: Write the numbers in order and find the middle number; 2 is the median

c. **Verify** What is the mode? Explain how you know. Two modes: 0 and 2; sample: They each have the same number and more X's than the other numbers.

d. What is the range of this data? 10

▸ ***6.** (98) Write a fraction equal to one that has a denominator of 10. $\frac{10}{10}$

Inclusion

Use this strategy if the student displays:

- Difficulty with Abstract Processing.
- Slow Learning Rate.

Changing Improper Fractions to Whole Number or Mixed Numbers (Small Group)

Materials: fraction circles, paper

- Write $\frac{13}{4}$ on the board. Have students work in groups to display the improper fraction using the fraction circles. Ask, ***"How many whole fractions are made?"*** 3 ***"How many parts are leftover?"*** 1 out of 4

  Write $= 3\frac{1}{4}$ on the board next to the improper fraction.

- Write $\frac{18}{6}$ on the board. Have students draw a picture to represent the improper fraction. Ask, ***"How many wholes are made?"*** 3 ***"How many are leftover?"*** none

  Write = 3 on the board next to the improper fraction.

7. (Inv. 4) **Represent** Write 86.74 with words. eighty-six and seventy-four hundredths

▶ ***8.** (61) **Estimate** There are many ways to make an estimate. Describe two different ways to estimate the difference of 496 subtracted from 605. Sample: Round to the nearest hundred and round to the nearest ten; $600 - 500 = 100$, and $610 - 500 = 110$

***9.** (99) Change each improper fraction to a whole number or a mixed number:

a. $\frac{9}{5}$ $1\frac{4}{5}$ **b.** $\frac{9}{3}$ 3 **c.** $\frac{9}{2}$ $4\frac{1}{2}$

d. Write each number in order from greatest to least as improper fractions. $\frac{9}{2}, \frac{9}{3}, \frac{9}{5}$

▶ ***10.** (61, 76) **Estimate** Soon after James Marshall discovered gold at John Sutter's mill in California on January 24, 1848, the "gold rush" began. If 2450 people came in 5 days, about how many came each day? About how many people came in 1 week? About 500 people; about 3500 people

11. (42) Find the length of this segment to the nearest tenth of a centimeter. Write the length as a decimal number. 4.3 cm

cm 1 2 3 4 5

***12.** (93) A miner bought 6 bags of flour for $4.20 per bag and 8 pounds of salt for 12¢ per pound. How much money did the miner spend? $26.16

▶ ***13.** (41, 62) **a.** Which digit in 86.74 is in the tenths place? 7

b. Is 86.74 closer to 86.7 or 86.8? 86.7

▶ **14.** (90) Draw a trapezoid. Sample:

15. (9, 45) $4.86 - (2.8 + 0.56)$ 1.5

16. (65, 85) 30^2 900

17. (88) 54×29 1566

***18.** (69) $5\overline{)230}$ 46

19. (83) $7\overline{)2383}$ 340 R 3

***20.** (82) Which letters in **MATH** have one line of symmetry? Which has two lines of symmetry? Which has rotational symmetry? M, A, and T have one line of symmetry; H has two lines of symmetry; H has rotational symmetry.

Written Practice *(Continued)*

Math Conversations *(cont.)*

Problem 8 Estimate

Because students are likely to make a number of different estimates, invite volunteers to share their estimates and explanations with the class. After each estimate that is presented, ask students to describe the method that was used to produce the estimate (for example, rounding or using compatible numbers).

Problem 10 Estimate

Students may be interested to learn that James Marshall was a carpenter who discovered the gold in the form of nuggets on the bottom of the stream while he was building a sawmill for John Sutter.

Problem 13a

Ask students to name the place value of each digit in the number. 8, tens; 6, ones; 7, tenths; 4, hundredths

Problem 14

Manipulative Use

Each student will need a ruler to draw the trapezoid, and some may find it helpful to draw on grid paper.

Make sure students understand that a trapezoid is a quadrilateral that has one pair of parallel sides.

(continued)

Written Practice *(Continued)*

Math Conversations *(cont.)*

Problem 21

Before students begin the division, ask:

"Is 70 a reasonable estimate of the quotient? Explain why or why not."
Yes; sample: $70 \times 5 = 350$, and 350 is close to 372

Problem 28a

Extend the Problem

Remind students of the importance of checking their work, and then ask them to check their work using a method that is different than the method that was used to find the answer. Sample: $P = 300 \text{ ft} + 200 \text{ ft} + 300 \text{ ft} + 200 \text{ ft} = 1000 \text{ ft}$; check: $2(300 \text{ ft}) + 2(200 \text{ ft}) = 600 \text{ ft} + 400 \text{ ft} = 1000 \text{ ft}$

Problem 30 Interpret

If some students are not familiar with this type of chart, explain that each number at the intersection of a row and a column represents the distance in miles between those two cities. Also provide students with an example, such as:

"To find the distance between St. Louis and Boston, follow the St. Louis row to the Boston column, and then read the number. The number (which is 1141) represents the distance in miles between St. Louis and Boston."

Errors and Misconceptions

Problem 2

If students solve the problem by changing both amounts to cents, explain that an alternative way to solve the problem (or a way for them to check their work) is to change $1 to 4 quarters, and then find the fraction of 4 quarters that 2 quarters represents.

Problem 12

Make sure students recognize 6 bags and 8 pounds must be used to solve the problem.

▸***21.** (72) $372 \div 5$ 74 R 2

22. (34, 79) $8c = \$5.76$ $0.72

23. (11) 12 + 26 + 13 + 35 + 110 + 8 + 15 = 219

24. (51) 351,426 + 449,576 = 801,002

25. (52) $50.00 − $49.49 = $0.51

26. (59) $12.49 × 8 = $99.92

27. (88) 73 × 62 = 4526

▸***28.** (20) **a.** A field is 300 feet long and 200 feet wide. How many feet of fencing would be needed to go around the field? 1000 ft

300 ft
200 ft

b. **Explain** Is this problem about perimeter or area? How do you know? Perimeter; sample: Perimeter is the measure of distance around.

***29.** (96, 97) **a.** Name a geometric solid that has no vertices. sphere

b. **Justify** Can a rectangular prism have no congruent faces? Why or why not? No; sample: A rectangular prism must have a congruent top and bottom. All of the sides must be congruent to each other so when it folds up it will have right angles, and perpendicular faces and edges.

▸***30.** (RF13) **Interpret** Use this chart to answer parts **a–c.**

Mileage Chart

	Atlanta	Boston	Chicago	Kansas City	Los Angeles	New York City	Wash., D.C.
Chicago	674	963		499	2054	802	671
Dallas	795	1748	917	489	1387	1552	1319
Denver	1398	1949	996	600	1059	1771	1616
Los Angeles	2182	2979	2054	1589		2786	2631
New York City	841	206	802	1198	2786		233
St. Louis	541	1141	289	257	1845	948	793

a. The distance from Los Angeles to Boston is how much greater than the distance from Los Angeles to New York City? 193 mi

b. Rebecca is planning a trip from Chicago to Dallas to Los Angeles to Chicago. How many miles will her trip be? 4358 mi

c. There are three empty boxes in the chart. What number would go in these boxes? 0

Changing improper fractions to whole or mixed numbers prepares students for:

- **Lesson 100,** adding and subtracting fractions with common denominators.
- **Lesson 106,** writing the reduced form of a fraction.
- **Lessons 112–113,** adding and subtracting fractions and mixed numbers with common denominators and renaming fractions whose denominators are not equal by using a common denominator of the fractions.

Planning & Preparation

• Adding and Subtracting Fractions with Common Denominators

Objectives
- Add fractions with common denominators.
- Subtract fractions with common denominators.

Prerequisite Skills
- Subtracting two numbers and using addition to check the answer.
- Using addition and subtraction fact families to write addition and subtraction facts.
- Converting improper fractions to whole or mixed numbers.

Materials

Instructional Masters
- Power Up J Worksheet
- Lesson Activity 8*

Manipulative Kit
- Rulers, fraction circles*

Teacher-provided materials
- Grid paper*

California Mathematics Content Standards

NS 1.0, 1.5 Explain different interpretations of fractions, for example, parts of a whole, parts of a set, and division of whole numbers by whole numbers; explain equivalents of fractions (see Standard 4.0).

NS 1.0, 1.7 Write the fraction represented by a drawing of parts of a figure; represent a given fraction by using drawings; and relate a fraction to a simple decimal on a number line.

MR 2.0, 2.6 Make precise calculations and check the validity of the results from the context of the problem.

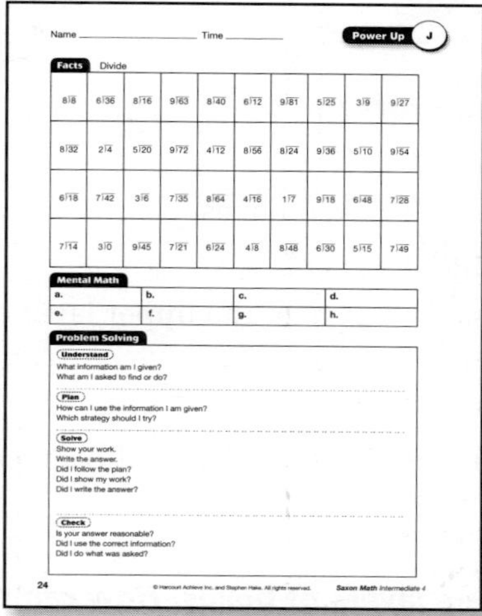

Name ______________ Time ________ **Power Up J**

Facts Divide

8)8	6)36	8)16	9)63	8)40	6)12	9)81	5)25	3)9	9)27
8)32	2)4	5)20	9)72	4)12	8)56	8)24	9)36	5)10	9)54
6)18	7)42	3)6	7)35	8)64	4)16	1)7	9)18	6)48	7)28
7)14	3)0	9)45	7)21	6)24	4)8	8)48	6)30	5)15	7)49

Mental Math

a.	b.	c.	d.
e.	f.	g.	h.

Problem Solving

Understand
What information am I given?
What am I asked to find or do?

Plan
How can I use the information I am given?
Which strategy should I try?

Solve
Show your work.
Write the answer.
Did I follow the plan?
Did I show my work?
Did I write the answer?

Check
Is your answer reasonable?
Did I use the correct information?
Did I do what was asked?

24 *Saxon Math Intermediate 4*

Power Up J Worksheet

Universal Access

Reaching All Special Needs Students

Special Education Students	At-Risk Students	English Learners	Advanced Learners
• Inclusion (TM) • Adaptations for Saxon Math	• Alternative Approach (TM) • Error Alert (TM) • Reteaching Masters • Refresher Lessons for California Standards	• English Learners (TM) • Developing Academic Language (TM) • English Learner Handbook	• Extend the Example (TM) • Extend the Problem (TM) • Online Activities

TM=Teacher's Manual

Developing Academic Language

Maintained	**English Learner**
denominator	hike
mixed number	
numerator	

Problem Solving Discussion

Problem

Franklin's family is moving to a new house, and they have packed their belongings in identical boxes. The picture at right represents the stack of boxes that is inside the moving truck. How many boxes are in the stack?

Focus Strategy

Make It Simpler

Understand *Understand the problem.*

"What information are we given?"

We are shown a picture of identical, stacked boxes.

"Can we see all the boxes in the picture?"

No. However, we can assume that the boxes in the upper layer are supported by boxes in the lower layers.

"What are we asked to do?"

We are asked to find how many boxes are in the stack altogether.

Plan *Make a plan.*

"In the picture, we can see three layers of boxes. How can this help us find the total number of boxes in the stack?"

If we can find how many boxes are in each layer, we can multiply by 3 to find the total number of boxes.

Solve *Carry out the plan.*

"How many boxes are in the top layer?"

If we look at the top layer of boxes, we see 4 boxes along the front and 3 boxes along the side. Four rows of 3 boxes means there are 4×3 boxes $= 12$ boxes in the top layer.

"Altogether, how many boxes are in the stack?"

The middle and bottom layers contain the same number of boxes as the top layer. Since there are three layers of boxes, we find that there are 3×12 boxes $= 36$ boxes in the stack altogether.

Check *Look back.*

"Is our answer reasonable?"

We know our answer is reasonable because three layers of 12 boxes each is 36 boxes altogether.

Alternate Strategy

Act It Out or Make a Model

Students can use unit cubes to make a model of the three layers of boxes. Then they can count the number of unit cubes used to make the model to find the total number of boxes stacked in the moving truck.

• Adding and Subtracting Fractions with Common Denominators

California Mathematics Content Standards

NS 1.0, 1.5 Explain different interpretations of fractions, for example, parts of a whole, parts of a set, and division of whole numbers by whole numbers; explain equivalents of fractions (see Standard 4.0).

NS 1.0, 1.7 Write the fraction represented by a drawing of parts of a figure; represent a given fraction by using drawings; and relate a fraction to a simple decimal on a number line.

MR 2.0, 2.6 Make precise calculations and check the validity of the results from the context of the problem.

facts Power Up J

mental math Find each product by the "double and half" method in problems **a–c.**

a. Number Sense: 4 × 14 56

b. Number Sense: 25 × 80 2000

c. Number Sense: 50 × 64 3200

d. Money: Cooper paid for a lawn sprinkler that cost $8.16 with a $10 bill. How much change should he receive? $1.84

e. Geometry: What is the diameter of a wheel that has a radius of 14 inches? 28 in.

f. Estimation: Estimate 19 × 41 by rounding each number to the nearest ten before multiplying. 800

g. Calculation: 15 – 9, square the number, ÷ 4, – 8 1

h. Simplify: 10 – (4 ÷ 2) 8

problem solving Franklin's family is moving to a new house, and they have packed their belongings in identical boxes. The picture at right represents the stack of boxes that is inside the moving truck. How many boxes are in the stack?

Focus Strategy: Make It Simpler

Understand We are shown a picture of identical, stacked boxes. We assume that boxes in the upper layer are supported by boxes in the lower layers. We are asked to find how many boxes are in the stack altogether.

Facts Divide

1 8)8	6 6)36	2 8)16	7 9)63	5 8)40	2 6)12	9 9)81	5 5)25	3 3)9	3 9)27
4 8)32	2 2)4	4 5)20	8 9)72	3 4)12	7 8)56	3 8)24	4 9)36	2 5)10	6 9)54
3 6)18	6 7)42	2 3)6	5 7)35	8 8)64	4 4)16	7 1)7	2 9)18	8 6)48	4 7)28
2 7)14	0 3)0	5 9)45	3 7)21	4 6)24	2 4)8	6 8)48	5 6)30	3 5)15	7 7)49

Power Up

Facts

Distribute **Power Up J** to students. See answers below.

Count Aloud

Before students begin the Mental Math exercises, do these counting exercises as a class.

Count up and down by fours from 24 to 52.

Mental Math

Encourage students to share different ways to mentally compute these exercises. Strategies for exercises are listed below.

b. Double 25 and Divide 80 by 2
25 × 2 = 50 and 80 ÷ 2 = 40;
50 × 40 = 2000

c. Double 50 and Divide 64 by 2
50 × 2 = 100 and 64 ÷ 2 = 32;
100 × 32 = 3200

d. Subtract $8, then Subtract 16¢
$10 – $8 = $2; $2 – 16¢ = $1.84

Subtract $9, then Add 84¢
$10 – $9 = $1; $1 + 84¢ = $1.84

Problem Solving

Refer to **Problem-Solving Strategy Discussion,** p. 659B.

New Concept

Observation

Use overhead fraction circles to demonstrate adding and subtracting fractions with common denominators.

Example 1

Error Alert

Emphasize that only the numerators of the fractions are added or subtracted.

To help remind students that the denominators are not added, you can rewrite the examples in this lesson using the word form of the denominators. For example, the fractions in Example 1 can be rewritten:

3 fifths
+ 1 fifth
4 fifths

(continued)

Plan In the picture, we can see three layers of boxes. If we can find how many boxes are in each layer, we can multiply by 3 to find the total number of boxes.

Solve If we look at the top layer of boxes, we see 4 boxes along the front and 3 boxes along the side. Four rows of 3 boxes means there are 4×3 boxes = 12 boxes in the top layer. The middle and bottom layers contain the same number of boxes as the top layer. Since there are three layers of boxes, we find that there are 3×12 boxes = **36 boxes** in the stack altogether.

Check We know our answer is reasonable because three layers of 12 boxes each is 36 boxes altogether. If we have blocks or unit cubes, we can check our answer by modeling the problem.

New Concept

To add fractions, it helps to think of the numerators as objects, like apples. Just as 1 apple plus 1 apple equals 2 apples, 1 third plus 1 third equals 2 thirds.

1 apple + 1 apple = 2 apples

1 third + 1 third = 2 thirds

$$\frac{1}{3} + \frac{1}{3} = \frac{2}{3}$$

When we add fractions, we add the numerators (top numbers). We do not add the denominators (bottom numbers).

Example 1

Blake mixed $\frac{3}{5}$ of a pound of cashews with $\frac{1}{5}$ of a pound of pecans. What is the weight in pounds of the cashew and pecan mixture?

We add only the top numbers. Three fifths plus one fifth is four fifths. The weight of the cashew and pecan mixture is **$\frac{4}{5}$ of a pound.**

$$\frac{3}{5} + \frac{1}{5} = \frac{4}{5}$$

Math Background

When we add mixed numbers, the fraction part of the sum is sometimes greater than 1. We can either adjust the answer when we are done adding, or we can regroup as we do when we add whole numbers. Both methods are demonstrated below.

Method 1

(A) Add fractions and whole numbers separately.

$$3\frac{4}{5} + 1\frac{3}{5} = 4\frac{7}{5}$$

(B) Adjust the answer so it is in the proper form.

$$3\frac{4}{5} + 1\frac{3}{5} = 4\frac{7}{5} = 5\frac{2}{5}$$

Method 2

(A) Add the fractions. The result is $\frac{7}{5}$. Write $\frac{2}{5}$ as the fraction part of the answer and carry $\frac{5}{5}$, or 1, to the whole-number column.

$$\begin{array}{r} 1 \\ 3\frac{4}{5} \\ +\ 1\frac{3}{5} \\ \hline \frac{2}{5} \end{array}$$

(B) Add the whole numbers.

$$\begin{array}{r} 1 \\ 3\frac{4}{5} \\ +\ 1\frac{3}{5} \\ \hline 5\frac{2}{5} \end{array}$$

Likewise, when we subtract fractions, we subtract only the numerators. The denominator does not change. For example, five sevenths minus two sevenths is three sevenths.

$$\frac{5}{7} - \frac{2}{7} = \frac{3}{7}$$

Example 2

To make a small bow for a present, Sakura cut $\frac{1}{5}$ of a yard of ribbon from a length of ribbon that was $\frac{3}{5}$ of a yard long. What is the length of the ribbon that was not used for the bow?

We subtract only the numerators. Three fifths minus one fifth is two fifths.The length of the ribbon not used for the bow is **$\frac{2}{5}$ of a yard.**

$$\frac{3}{5} - \frac{1}{5} = \frac{2}{5}$$

Discuss How can we check the answer?

Sample: Add $\frac{2}{5}$ and $\frac{1}{5}$, and then compare the sum to $\frac{3}{5}$.

Recall that a mixed number is a whole number plus a fraction, such as $2\frac{3}{5}$. To add mixed numbers, we add the fraction parts and then the whole-number parts.

Example 3

Add: $2\frac{3}{5} + 3\frac{1}{5}$

It is helpful to write the numbers one above the other. First we add the fractions and get $\frac{4}{5}$. Then we add the whole numbers and get 5. The sum of the mixed numbers is **$5\frac{4}{5}$.**

$$\begin{array}{r} 2\frac{3}{5} \\ +\ 3\frac{1}{5} \\ \hline 5\frac{4}{5} \end{array}$$

Example 4

Subtract: $5\frac{2}{3} - 1\frac{1}{3}$

We subtract the second number from the first number. To do this, we write the first number above the second number. We subtract the fractions and get $\frac{1}{3}$. Then we subtract the whole numbers and get 4. The difference is **$4\frac{1}{3}$.**

$$\begin{array}{r} 5\frac{2}{3} \\ -\ 1\frac{1}{3} \\ \hline 4\frac{1}{3} \end{array}$$

Example 5

In the race Martin rode his bike $7\frac{1}{2}$ miles and ran $2\frac{1}{2}$ miles. Altogether, how far did Martin ride his bike and run?

This is a story about combining. We add $7\frac{1}{2}$ miles and $2\frac{1}{2}$ miles. The two half miles combine to make a whole mile. The total distance is **10 miles.**

$$\begin{array}{r} 7\frac{1}{2} \\ +\ 2\frac{1}{2} \\ \hline 9\frac{2}{2} \end{array} = 10$$

Alternative Approach: Using Manipulatives

To help students understand adding and subtracting fractions with common denominators, have them model problems using fraction manipulatives.

Display the problem $\frac{1}{4} + \frac{2}{4}$. Have students line up one of the $\frac{1}{4}$ fraction pieces. Then have them line up two more of the $\frac{1}{4}$ fraction pieces. Ask students, ***"How many $\frac{1}{4}$ fraction pieces are there all together?"*** Three $\frac{1}{4}$ pieces

Explain to the students that the answer is $\frac{3}{4}$.

Display the problem $\frac{7}{8} - \frac{4}{8}$. Have students line up seven of the $\frac{1}{8}$ fraction pieces. Then have them take away four of the $\frac{1}{8}$ pieces. Ask students, ***"How many $\frac{1}{8}$ fraction pieces are left?"*** Three $\frac{1}{8}$ pieces

Explain to the students that the answer is $\frac{3}{8}$. Have students show other examples.

New Concept *(Continued)*

Example 2

Connection

After students answer the **Discuss** question, point out that addition and subtraction are inverse operations. Explain that when two operations are inverse operations, one operation undoes the other. The answer for Example 2 was found using subtraction, and it can be checked using addition.

Example 3

Extend the Example

Challenge your advanced learners to explain why the fraction part of $5\frac{4}{5}$ is a fraction in simplest form. The only number that can divide both the numerator and the denominator is 1.

Example 5

Active Learning

Have students note in this example that the sum of two mixed numbers is not always a sum in simplest form. Then ask:

"Why does $9\frac{2}{2}$ simplify to 10?" Sample: Since a fraction bar represents division, $\frac{2}{2}$ can be rewritten as $2 \div 2$, which has a quotient of 1 because any number divided by itself is 1; So $9\frac{2}{2}$ is the same as $9 + 1$, and $9 + 1 = 10$.

Lesson Practice

Guided Practice

Use these problems as guided practice to check the students' understanding of today's concept.

Problems a–l

Prior to completing the exercises, ask students to explain, in a general way, how to find the sum or difference of two fractions that have the same denominator. Sample: Write the sum or difference of the numerators over the common denominator, and then simplify, if possible.

Also ask students to explain, in a general way, how to find the sum or difference of two mixed numbers whose fraction parts have the same denominator. Sample: First add the fractions by writing the sum of the numerators over the common denominator. Then add the whole numbers and simplify the answer if possible.

(continued)

New Concept *(Continued)*

Lesson Practice

Problems a–l
Error Alert

A common error when adding fractions with common denominators is to write the sum of the denominators.

Closure

The questions below help assess the concepts taught in this lesson.

"Write two fractions that have the same denominator. Name the sum or difference of those fractions and explain how you found the answer." Sample: $\frac{1}{9} + \frac{4}{9} = \frac{1 + 4}{9} = \frac{5}{9}$; Write the sum of the numerators as the numerator of a fraction that has a denominator of 9.

"Explain how to add two mixed numbers whose fraction parts have the same denominator. Include an example to support your answer." Sample: $4\frac{1}{3} + 5\frac{1}{3} = \frac{1 + 1}{3} + 4 + 5 = 9\frac{2}{3}$; Write the sum of the numerators as the numerator of a fraction that has a denominator of 3, and then add the whole numbers.

Written Practice

Math Conversations

Independent Practice and Discussions to Increase Understanding

Problem 2

Manipulative Use

Each student will need a ruler to draw the triangle, and some students will find it helpful to draw on grid paper.

Make sure students understand that after the right angle is labeled *C*, the letter *A* can be used to name either of the other two angles of the triangle.

Extend the Problem

Ask students to classify each of the non-right angles of their triangles. The two non-right angles of a right triangle are acute angles.

Problem 4 **Represent**

Before completing the arithmetic, ask students to explain why an estimate of the exact answer should be more than 14 students. Sample: Since $\frac{5}{7}$ is greater than $\frac{1}{2}$, $\frac{5}{7}$ of 28 students will be greater than $\frac{1}{2}$ of 28, or 14 students.

(continued)

Lesson Practice

Find each sum or difference:

a. $\frac{1}{3} + \frac{1}{3}$ $\frac{2}{3}$
b. $\frac{1}{4} + \frac{2}{4}$ $\frac{3}{4}$
c. $\frac{3}{10} + \frac{4}{10}$ $\frac{7}{10}$

d. $\frac{2}{3} - \frac{1}{3}$ $\frac{1}{3}$
e. $\frac{3}{4} - \frac{2}{4}$ $\frac{1}{4}$
f. $\frac{9}{10} - \frac{6}{10}$ $\frac{3}{10}$

g. $2\frac{1}{4} + 4\frac{2}{4}$ $6\frac{3}{4}$
h. $5\frac{3}{8} + 1\frac{2}{8}$ $6\frac{5}{8}$
i. $8 + 1\frac{2}{5}$ $9\frac{2}{5}$

j. $4\frac{3}{5} - 1\frac{1}{5}$ $3\frac{2}{5}$
k. $9\frac{3}{4} - 4\frac{2}{4}$ $5\frac{1}{4}$
l. $12\frac{8}{9} - 3\frac{3}{9}$ $9\frac{5}{9}$

m. How much is three eighths plus four eighths? $\frac{7}{8}$

n. The troop hiked to the end of the trail and back. If the trail was $3\frac{1}{2}$ miles long, how far did the troop hike? 7 miles

Written Practice

Distributed and Integrated

***1.** (76, 100) Use this information to answer parts **a–c.**

Nara has 6 cats. Each cat eats $\frac{1}{2}$ can of food each day. Cat food costs 47¢ per can.

a. How many cans of cat food are eaten each day? 3 cans

b. How much does Nara spend on cat food per day? $1.41

c. How much does Nara spend on cat food in a week? $9.87

▸ ***2.** (17, 50, 81) **a.** Sketch a right triangle. Label the vertices *A*, *B*, and *C*, so that *C* is at the right angle.

2. a. Sample:

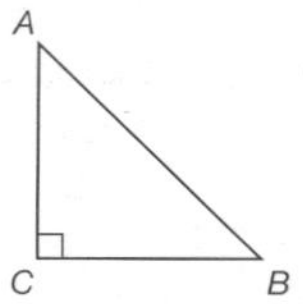

b. Name two segments that are perpendicular. Segment *AC* and segment *BC*

c. Name two segments that intersect but are not perpendicular. Segment *AB* and either segment *AC* or segment *BC*

d. Can a triangle have two parallel sides? No

3. (20, 66, 85) If the perimeter of a square classroom is 120 feet, then how long is each side of the classroom? What is the area of the classroom? 30 ft; 900 ft^2

▸ ***4.** (94) **Represent** Math was the favorite class of five sevenths of the 28 students. Math was the favorite class of how many students? Draw a picture to illustrate the problem. 20 students

4.

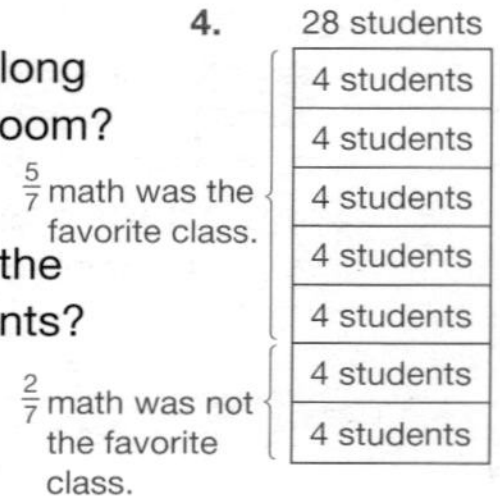

English Learners

To **hike** means to go on a long walk, especially in a wooded area where there are trails.

Ask students why people might go on hikes? Sample: to exercise, for fun, to be close to nature

Have students share a favorite hiking place with another student.

*5. **Interpret** Name the median, mode and range of this data.
(95)

14, 23, 34, 51, 63, 23, 14, 23, 45

Median: 23, mode: 23, range: 49

▶ *6. **Conclude** Use this geometric solid to answer parts **a–c.**
(96, 97)

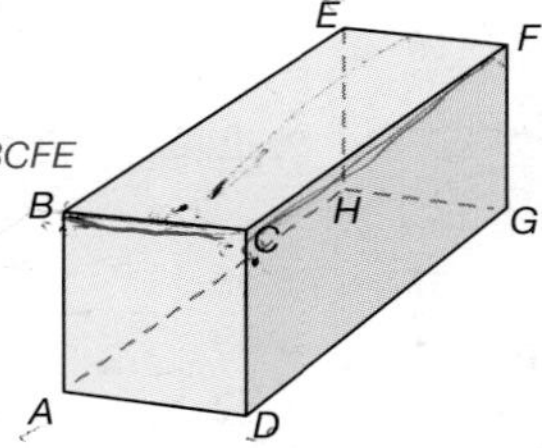

a. What is the name of this geometric solid? Rectangular prism

b. Name two faces that share (the edge) $\overline{BC}$. *ABCD* and *BCFE*

c. Name three faces that share the same vertex. Sample: *ABCD*, *CBEF*, and *CDGF*

7. If the radius of a circle is $1\frac{1}{2}$ inches, then what is the diameter of the circle? 3 in.
(18, 100)

8. **Represent** Use words to write 523.43. five hundred twenty-three and forty-three hundredths
(Inv. 4)

9. **Estimate** Colin used rounding to estimate the product of 61 and 397. What estimate did Colin make? Explain your answer.
(91)
24,000; sample: I rounded to the nearest ten; 61 rounds to 60 and 397 rounds to 400, so $60 \times 400 = 24{,}000$

▶*10. Change each improper fraction to a whole number or a mixed number:
(99)

a. $\frac{10}{10}$ 1 **b.** $\frac{10}{5}$ 2 **c.** $\frac{10}{3}$ $3\frac{1}{3}$

d. Write each number in order from least to greatest as improper fractions. $\frac{10}{10}, \frac{10}{5}, \frac{10}{3}$

*11. LaTonya went to the fair with $20. She paid $6.85 for a necklace and $4.50 for lunch. Then she bought a soft drink for 75¢. How much money did she have left? $7.90
(93)

▶*12. **Explain** Clara bought two dolls priced at $7.40 each. The tax was 98¢. She paid the clerk with a $20 bill. How much change did she get back? Explain why your answer is reasonable. $4.22; sample: I multiplied to find the price of two dolls, added the tax to the product, and then subtracted the sum from $20; $7.40 × 2 = $14.80 + $.98 = $15.78; $20 − $15.78 = $4.22
(93)

13. The big truck that transported the Ferris wheel could go only 140 miles in 5 hours. What was the truck's average speed in miles per hour?
(60)
28 miles per hour

*14. Compare: $\frac{49}{100}$ ⓧ $\frac{1}{2}$ — answer: $\frac{49}{100} < \frac{1}{2}$
(92, 98)

Written Practice (Continued)

Math Conversations *(cont.)*

Problem 6 **Conclude**

Challenge interested students to list all of the perpendicular faces of the prism and all of the parallel faces of the prism, and then compare lists.

Problem 10

"What operation does a fraction bar represent?" division

Problem 12 **Explain**

After the problem has been solved, ask students to name the bills and coins Clara is likely to have received. Four $1 bills, two dimes, and two pennies

(continued)

Inclusion

Use this strategy if the student displays:

- Difficulty with Large Group Instruction.
- Slow Learning Rate.

Adding and Subtracting Fractions with Common Denominators (Small Group)

Materials: fraction circles, paper

- Read, ***"Ella weighed the books in her bag. Her math book weighed $\frac{5}{8}$ of a pound and her science workbook weighed $\frac{3}{8}$ of a pound. How much did the books in her bag weigh?"***
- Model writing an addition problem $\frac{3}{8} + \frac{5}{8} =$ Ask, ***"Are the denominators the same?"*** Yes

  Tell students that if the denominators are the same that the numerators can be added. Ask, ***"What is 3 + 5?"*** 8 ***"When combining both groups does the denominator change?"*** No
- Write $= \frac{8}{8}$ on the board next to the problem. Remind students that only the numerators are added in fraction problems.
- Write $2\frac{2}{5} + 1\frac{3}{5} =$ on the board. Have students work with a partner to add the whole number and then the fractions to find the mixed number answer.

Written Practice *(Continued)*

Math Conversations *(cont.)*

Problem 15b

To help students complete the rounding, ask:

"What two consecutive whole numbers is twelve and twenty-five hundredths between?" 12 and 13

Problem 16b (Estimate)

Ask students to include an explanation with their answer.

Problems 23 and 26

Remind students of the importance of checking their work, and then ask them to make an estimate of each quotient and use it to help decide the reasonableness of the exact answer. Sample estimates:
problem **23**: $4500 \div 5 = 900$
problem **26**: $560 \div 7 = 80$

Problem 29 Multiple Choice

Test-Taking Strategy

Make sure students can recognize that because $5\frac{3}{5}$ is between 5 and 6, and $6\frac{3}{4}$ is between 6 and 7, the sum of the mixed numbers is between the sums of the whole numbers.

$$\begin{array}{r} 5 \\ +\ 6 \\ \hline 11 \end{array} \qquad \begin{array}{r} 5\frac{3}{5} \\ +\ 6\frac{3}{4} \\ \hline \end{array} \qquad \begin{array}{r} 6 \\ +\ 7 \\ \hline 13 \end{array}$$

Problem 30

Students may be interested to learn that at birth, an African bush elephant calf weighs about 200 pounds. The African bush elephant has no natural enemies, but it is hunted for its ivory tusks. Although most countries have banned the ivory trade, illegal hunting has caused this mammal to be placed on the endangered species list.

Errors and Misconceptions

Problem 1c

A common error when solving problems involving a number of weeks is to assume that each week represents 5 days because the length of a school week is 5 days. Explain to students that the length of a week depends on the context of the word problem. In other words, it depends on what the word problem is describing. In problem **1c,** make sure students understand that each week represents 7 days because Nara's cat eats each day.

Problem 14

Remind students that it can be very difficult to compare fractions if the fractions have different denominators, and then have them recall that multiplying a fraction by another name for 1 can help them change a fraction such as $\frac{1}{2}$ to $\frac{50}{100}$ $\left(\frac{1}{2} \times \frac{50}{50} = \frac{50}{100}\right)$.

***15.** (46) **a.** (Estimate) Round $12.25 to the nearest dollar. $12

▸ **b.** Round 12.25 to the nearest whole number. 12

***16.** (41, 62) **a.** Which digit in 36.47 is in the tenths place? 4

▸ **b.** (Estimate) Is 36.47 closer to 36.4 or to 36.5? 36.5

17. (45) $\begin{array}{r} 73.48 \\ 5.63 \\ +\ 17.9 \\ \hline 97.01 \end{array}$ **18.** (28) $\begin{array}{r} \$65.00 \\ -\ \$29.87 \\ \hline \$35.13 \end{array}$ **19.** (52) $\begin{array}{r} 24{,}375 \\ -\ 8{,}416 \\ \hline 15{,}959 \end{array}$ **20.** (59) $\begin{array}{r} \$3.68 \\ \times\ 9 \\ \hline \$33.12 \end{array}$

21. (88) 89×91 8099 **22.** (79) $6\overline{)3210}$ 535 ▸***23.** (83) $5\overline{)4300}$ 860

24. (79) $6\overline{)\$57.24}$ $9.54 **25.** (69) $765 \div 9$ 85 ▸***26.** (72) $563 \div 7$ 80 R 3

***27.** (63, 65, 85) (Evaluate) Find the value of n^2 when n is 90. 8100

***28.** (Inv. 3) (Evaluate) Find the value of $\frac{m}{\sqrt{m}}$ when m is 36. 6

▸***29.** (98) **a.** **Multiple Choice** The sum of $6\frac{3}{4}$ and $5\frac{3}{5}$ is between which two numbers? D

A 5 and 7 **B** 30 and 40 **C** 0 and 2 **D** 11 and 13

b. Explain your answer for part **a.** Sample: The sum is greater than 6 + 5 and less than 7 + 6.

▸ **30.** (59, 80, 84) The African bush elephant is the heaviest land mammal on Earth. Even though it eats only twigs, leaves, fruit, and grass, an African bush elephant can weigh 7 tons. Seven tons is how many pounds? 14,000 pounds

---

Looking Forward

Adding and subtracting fractions with common denominators prepares students for:

- **Lesson 106,** writing the reduced form of a fraction.
- **Lessons 111–113,** simplifying and renaming fractions, and finding a common denominator.

Cumulative Assessments and Performance Task

Assessments

Distribute **Power-Up Test 19** and **Cumulative Test 19** to each student. Have students complete the **Power-Up Test** first. Allow 10 minutes. Then have students work on the **Cumulative Test.**

Performance Task

The remaining class time can be spent on **Performance Task 10.** Students can begin the task in class or complete it during another class period.

Flexible Grouping

Flexible grouping gives students an opportunity to work with other students in an interactive and encouraging way. The choice for how students are grouped depends on the goals for instruction, the needs of the students, and the specific learning activity.

Assigning Groups

Group members can be randomly assigned, or can be assigned based on some criteria such as grouping students who may need help with a certain skill or grouping students to play specific roles in a group (such as recorder or reporter).

Types of Groups

Students can be paired or placed in larger groups. For pairing, students can be assigned partners on a weekly or monthly basis. Pairing activities are the easiest to manage in a classroom and are more likely to be useful on a daily basis.

Flexible Grouping Ideas

Lesson 94, Example 1
Materials: counters, paper

Divide students into groups of 4. The groups should be of varying abilities. Assign each student a number: 1, 2, 3, or 4.

- Have students read Example 1 without looking at the solution. Direct students to work together to solve the problem using the counters.
- Any member of the group should be able to present the answer to the problem and explain how they solved it.
- The teacher then calls out a student number, and each student assigned that number must present his or her group's solution and strategy for solving the problem.

Lesson 96, Example 3
Materials: Relational GeoSolids, paper

Divide students into groups of 4. Have each group decide who is going to be the Leader, the Recorder, the Checker, and the Presenter.

- After guiding students through Example 3, instruct the students to create a table that will reflect the number of faces, sides, and vertices of the rectangular solid. Then have the students look at the solids mentioned on page 634 and add their information to the table.
- The Leader should make sure all group members are on task. The Checker will check that all solids are added to the table.
- The Recorder will write the information in the table with the help of the group. The Presenter will present the group's table to the class.

Lesson 98, Example 1
Materials: counters, paper

Students will work independently and then in pairs to reinforce fractions that equal 1.

- Have students read Example 1. Then instruct them to use the counters to verify that $\frac{6}{6} = 1$.
- Have students form pairs and model how they verified the fraction.
- The students should ask their partners to explain their thinking.

Lesson 100, Example 1
Materials: fraction circles, fraction bars, counters

Have students individually model how to answer Example 1. They can use fraction circles, fraction bars, or counters. Then divide the students into groups of 4.

- Have students take turns telling the group the strategy they used to solve the problem. All strategies are acceptable.
- One student from the group should be chosen as the Recorder. The group should work together to write a summary of the strategies that were used.

Planning & Preparation

• Graphing Relationships

Objectives

- Given a horizontal or vertical line, name the coordinates of a point on the line.
- Subtract the x-coordinate and y-coordinate to determine the length of a line.
- Write a set of ordered pairs for an equation such as $y = 3x + 2$.
- Graph an equation such as $y = 3x + 2$.

Prerequisite Skills

- Locating and plotting points in Quadrant I.
- Subtracting the x-coordinates to determine the length of a horizontal line segment.
- Subtracting the y-coordinates to determine the length of a vertical line segment.
- Graphing points that will form a polygon.

Materials

Instructional Masters

- Lesson Activity 8

Manipulative Kit

- Two-color counters*

Teacher-provided materials

- Grid paper
- Index cards*

**optional*

California Mathematics Content Standards

AF 1.0, 1.1 Use letters, boxes, or other symbols to stand for any number in simple expressions or equations (e.g., demonstrate an understanding and the use of the concept of a variable).

AF 1.0, 1.4 Use and interpret formulas (e.g., area = length × width or $A = lw$) to answer questions about quantities and their relationships.

AF 1.0, 1.5 Understand that an equation such as $y = 3x + 5$ is a prescription for determining a second number when a first number is given.

MG 2.0, 2.1 Draw the points corresponding to linear relationships on graph paper (e.g., draw 10 points on the graph of the equation $y = 3x$ and connect them by using a straight line).

MG 2.0, 2.2 Understand that the length of a horizontal line segment equals the difference of the x–coordinates.

MG 2.0, 2.3 Understand that the length of a vertical line segment equals the difference of the y–coordinates.

SDAP 1.0, 1.3 Interpret one- and two-variable data graphs to answer questions about a situation.

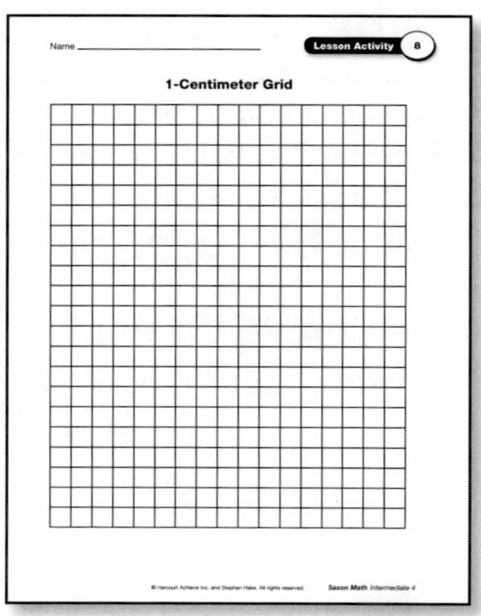

Lesson Activity 8

Universal Access

Reaching All Special Needs Students

Special Education Students	At-Risk Students	English Learners	Advanced Learners
• Inclusion (TM) • Adaptations for Saxon Math	• Error Alert (TM) • Reteaching Masters • Refresher Lessons for California Standards	• English Learners (TM) • Developing Academic Language (TM) • English Learner Handbook	• Extend the Problem (TM) • Investigate Further (SE) • Online Activities

TM=Teacher's Manual
SE=Student Edition

Developing Academic Language

Maintained	English Learner
coordinates	function
equation	
formula	
graph	
ordered pair	
table	

Focus on

Graphing Relationships

California Mathematics Content Standards

MG 2.0, 2.1 Draw the points corresponding to linear relationships on graph paper (e.g., draw 10 points on the graph of the equation $y = 3x$ and connect them by using a straight line).

MG 2.0, 2.2 Understand that the length of a horizontal line segment equals the difference of the x-coordinates.

MG 2.0, 2.3 Understand that the length of a vertical line segment equals the difference of the y-coordinates.

SDAP 1.0, 1.3 Interpret one-and two-variable data graphs to answer questions about a situation.

Graphs can also be used to display relationships between two quantities, such as pay and time worked.

Suppose Dina has a job that pays $10 per hour. This table shows the total pay Dina would receive for 1, 2, 3, or 4 hours of work.

1. Represent Copy and extend the table to show Dina's pay for each hour up to 8 hours of work.

Pay Schedule

Hours Worked	Total Pay
1	$10
2	$20
3	$30
4	$40
5	$50
6	$60
7	$70
8	$80

The graph below shows the same relationship between hours worked and total pay. Each dot on the graph represents both a number of hours and an amount of pay.

If Dina works more hours, she earns more pay. We say that her total pay is a function of the number of hours she works. Since Dina's total pay depends on the number of hours she works, we make "Total Pay" the vertical scale and "Total Hours" the horizontal scale.

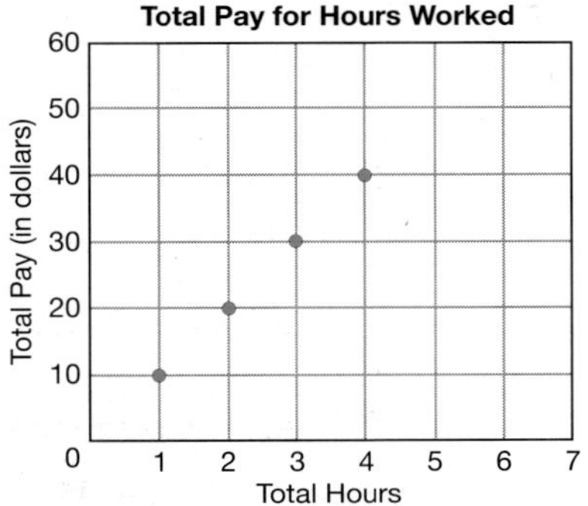

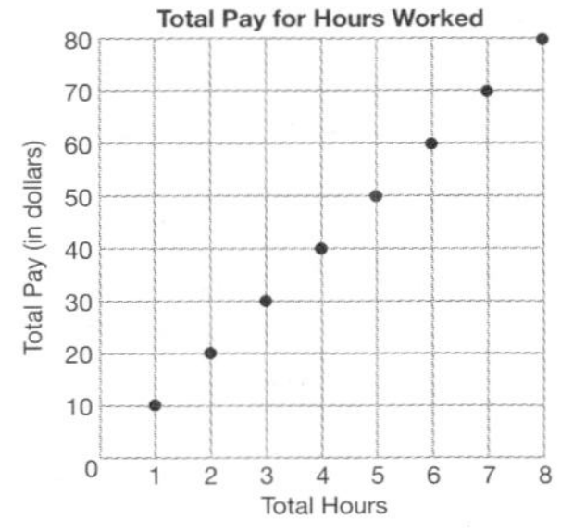

2. Represent Copy the graph. Extend the sides of the graph to include 8 hours and $80. Then graph (draw) the dots for Dina's total pay for each hour up to 8 hours.

English Learners

Saying that Dina's pay is a **function** of the number of hours she works means that how much Dina is paid is directly related to how many hours she works.

Ask students to explain the relationship between how many minutes they ride a bike at a steady speed and how far they ride.

Teacher Tip

You might present the concept of graphs simply as a way to express a relationship. Have volunteers draw graphs that describe such situations as: Maya likes to practice free throws every day after school. She shoots 15 baskets in fifteen minutes. Show how many baskets Maya shoots in 1 day, 2 days, up to 5 days.

INVESTIGATION 10

Graphing Relationships

In this investigation, students will learn to extend a table of values that shows the relationship between two quantities, represent the values with an equation and a graph of the equation, and locate points on the coordinate plane.

Materials:

- Each student will need a copy of **Lesson Activity Master 26** to complete the graphing activity in this investigation.

Explanation

Explain that the table shows the relationship of the number of hours Dina works and the amount of income she earns.

Math Conversations

Independent Practice and Discussions to Increase Understanding

Problem 1 Represent

"What pattern can be seen that will help us extend the table?" Sample: As the number of hours worked increases by 1, the total pay increases by $10.

Instruction

As you discuss the graph, ask students to name the location of each point, and help them infer that the points on the graph represent the pairs of numbers in the table.

Lead students to conclude that data in a table can often be displayed in a graph.

Problem 2

Error Alert

Make sure that the completed graphs have points at (1, 10), (2, 20), (3, 30), (4, 40), (5, 50), (6, 60), (7, 70), and (8, 80).

(continued)

Math Conversations *(cont.)*

Connection

As you discuss the graph of Rosita's hike, review the title and axes of the graph, and call attention to how the points on the graph represent the values in the table. Then point out that the graph consists of points connected by a line because Rosita's hike is an example of *continuous* data—at any time during her hike, she was a distance from the starting point, and we connect the points on the graph to show this continuous relationship of time and distance.

Problem 3 **Interpret**

Error Alert

If students have difficulty reading the graph, suggest that they use an index card and align the length and the width of the card with the horizontal and vertical axes of the graph. The card can then be moved up or to the right to help read the horizontal and vertical scales for any distance or time.

Activity

Some students will find it helpful to draw the graphs on grid paper.

After the activity has been completed, invite volunteers to display their graphs and describe the relationship of the data the graphs represent.

(continued)

The following table and graph show how many miles Rosita hiked at 4 miles per hour:

Miles Hiked
(at 4 mi per hr)

Hours	Miles
1	4
2	8
3	12

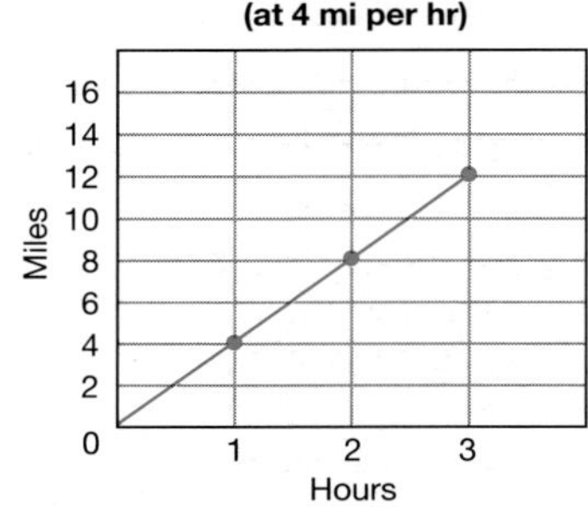

The dots indicate how far Rosita hiked in one, two, and three hours. However, every second Rosita hiked, she was hiking a small part of a mile. We show this progress by drawing a line through the dots. Every point on a line represents a distance hiked for a given time.

For example, straight up from $1\frac{1}{2}$ hours is a point on the line at 6 miles.

▸ **3.** **Interpret** Use the graph to find the distance Rosita hiked in $2\frac{1}{2}$ hours. 10 miles

4. **Analyze** What multiplication formula could you write to represent the relationship between the two sets of data? Sample: the numbers of hours × 4 = the number of miles hiked, or $4n$ = miles hiked

5. **Verify** Use your formula to find the number of miles Rosita would hike in 5 hours. 4 × 5 = 20 miles

Activity

Graphing Pay Rates

Formulate Work with a partner and agree on an hourly rate of pay for a selected job. Then create a table to display a pay schedule showing the total pay for 1, 2, 3, 4, 5, 6, 7, and 8 hours of work at the agreed rate of pay. Use the pay schedule to create a graph that shows the relationship represented by the table. Write an equation to represent the data. See student work.

Inclusion

Use this strategy if the student displays:

- Difficulty with Abstract Processing.
- Slow Learning Rate.

Analyzing and Graphing Relationships (Individual)

Materials: Lesson Activity Master 26, two-color counters

- Sketch a coordinate plane on the board and nearby write (x, y). Tell students that a coordinate plane is like a map and that (x, y) is like an address. Label the x-axis and the y-axis and emphasize that the x-axis runs sideways and the y-axis runs up and down.
- Have students locate where the x-axis and y-axis meet and have them call that point the origin. Tell students that the coordinates or address of the origin is (0, 0).
- Write (2, 3) on the board. Tell students that the coordinates (2, 3) name the location of a point on the plane. Traveling to (2, 3) from the origin is like driving on two roads. First we take the x-road from the origin to 2. From there we turn and go up to the line that goes through 3 on the y-axis. Demonstrate the movement from (0, 0) along the x-axis to (2, 0) and then up to (2, 3).
- Select other points for students to locate. For each point have students begin at the origin, travel first on the x-axis and then up the y-axis, tracing the route with a finger. Monitor student work and continue to select points for students to locate until they are successful.

We can represent similar relationships using equations and graphs.

Suppose a rug cleaning machine can be rented for $2 per hour plus a $10 rental fee. How much would it cost to rent the machine for 3 hours? The hourly rate will be applied to part of an hour.

We can write an equation to represent this problem.

$$\$2 \text{ per hour} + \$10 \text{ rental fee} = \text{total cost}$$

$$2h + 10 = t$$

We can create a set of ordered pairs for 1, 2, and 3 hours.

$2h + 10 = t$

h	t
1	12
2	14
3	16

Now we can graph the ordered pairs. 24

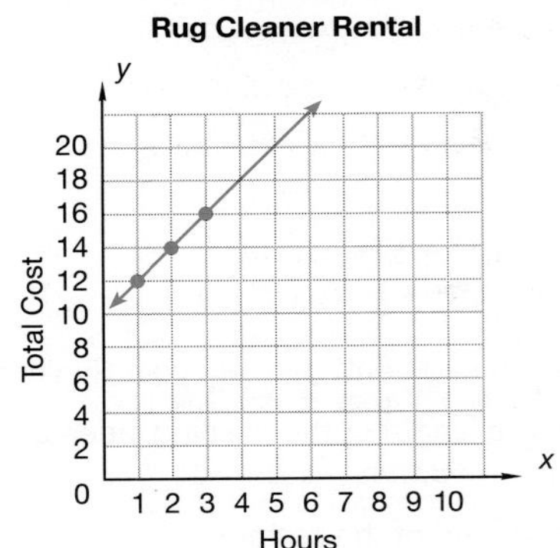

▸ **6.** **Interpret** Use the graph to find the total cost of renting the machine for $5\frac{1}{2}$ hours. $21

▸ **7.** **Analyze** Use the equation to find the cost of renting the machine for 1 full day. $58

Math Conversations *(cont.)*

Explanation

Explain that the cost of renting a rug cleaning machine is an example of a relationship that can be described in a table, by an equation, and by a graph of the equation.

Active Learning

Have students compare the equation and the data in the table to the graph of the data, and then ask:

"The graph of the equation does not begin at zero. Why not?" Sample: There is a fixed charge (or flat fee) for renting the machine regardless of the number of hours the machine is rented for. Since this amount is $10, the graph of the equation must begin at $10 because that amount represents the least possible cost of renting the machine.

Problem 6 **Interpret**

Because no grid lines of the graph exist at $(5\frac{1}{2}, 21)$, students must make an estimate of the cost; any estimate greater than $20 and less than $22 is a reasonable estimate.

Problem 7 **Analyze**

Make sure students recognize that the phrase "1 full day" represents 24 hours.

(continued)

Math Background

The coordinate plane consists of two axes and four quadrants, with the center point at (0, 0) called the *origin*. Each point in the plane can be named with only two numbers. The horizontal number line is known as the *x*-axis or *abscissa*. The vertical number line is the *y*-axis or *ordinate*. Points can be plotted on the plane when both an *x*- and a *y*-coordinate are known.

The first quadrant is in the upper right, or northeast, position. In the first quadrant, both the *x*- and *y*-values are positive. We know this because numbers to the right of the origin have positive *x*-values and numbers above the origin have positive *y*-values. Numbers to the left of the origin have negative *x*-values and numbers below the origin have negative *y*-values. The second quadrant is in the northwest position, the third in the southwest, and the fourth in the southeast. In the third quadrant, both the *x*- and *y*-values are negative.

Math Conversations *(cont.)*

Problem 8a **Formulate**

If some students have difficulty writing an equation to represent the relationship, explain that they should use h to represent the number of hours and p to represent the pay in dollars. Then refer them to the rug cleaning equation that is shown earlier in this investigation, and help them make the connection that the rug cleaning equation and the equation they are to write for problem **8a** both involve a fixed fee and a cost per hour. Because of this connection, students can use the rug cleaning equation as a model for writing an equation to represent the cost of hiring a clown for the party.

Problems 9–11

In order for students to correctly solve problem **11,** they must correctly solve problems **9** and **10.** Remind students that axes labels such as 1, 2, 3, and so on, are not needed to find the length of horizontal and vertical segments on the coordinate plane. If necessary, point out that when we know the coordinates of the endpoints of the segments, we find the lengths by subtracting the x- or the y-coordinates.

Problem a
Extend the Problem

Challenge advanced learners to name the coordinates of the midpoint of the base. The *midpoint* is the point halfway between the endpoints. $(4\frac{1}{2}, 6)$

Problem a
Error Alert

Make sure students understand that if they know the length of one side of the triangle, they know the lengths of all three sides because the triangle is an equilateral triangle.

8. Use this problem to answer parts **a–c.**

Mrs. Becker hired a student clown for a children's party. The clown charges $4 per hour plus a $2 traveling fee. The hourly rate is applied to part of an hour.

▸ **a.** **Formulate** Write an equation to represent the relationship between hours and pay for any number of hours. $4h + 2 = p$

b. **Evaluate** Use the equation to make a set of ordered pairs for 1, 2, and 3 hours. (1, 6), (2, 10), (3, 14)

c. **Model** Graph the ordered pairs and draw a line to represent the equation. See student work.

The two segments below represent opposite sides of a rectangle:

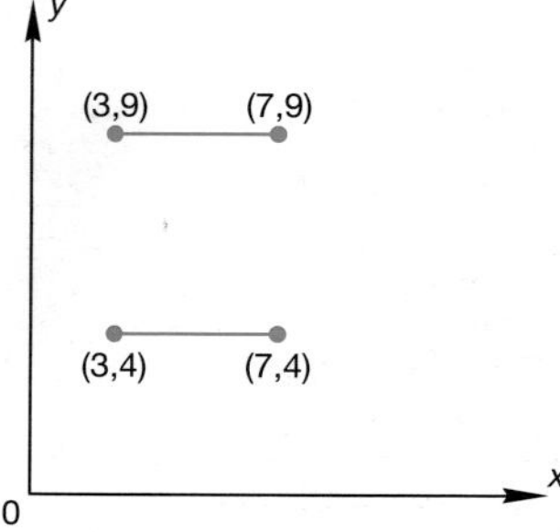

▸ **9.** **Interpret** What is the length of each segment? Explain your thinking. 4 units; Subtract the x-coordinates.

▸ **10.** **Explain** How can you determine the length of the missing sides of the rectangle? For a vertical segment, subtract the y-coordinates

▸ **11.** **Analyze** What is the perimeter and area of the rectangle? P = 18 units, A = 20 square units

a. How can you subtract coordinates to determine the perimeter of this equilateral triangle?

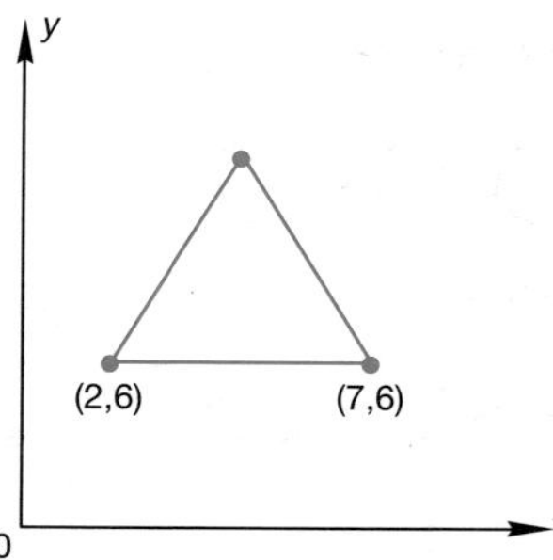

Sample: Subtract the x-coordinates, $7 - 2 = 5$, then multiply 3×5, $P = 15$ units.

Graphing Relationships will be further developed in ***Saxon Math*** *Intermediate 5.*

Lesson Planner

Lesson	New Concepts	Materials	Resources
101	• Formulas	• Grid paper	• Power Up J Worksheet • Lesson Activity 8
102	• The Distributive Property	• Grid paper	• Power Up A Worksheet • Lesson Activity 8
103	• Equivalent Fractions		• Power Up A Worksheet
104	• Rounding Whole Numbers Through Hundred Millions	• Grid paper	• Power Up A Worksheet • Lesson Activity 8
105	• Factoring Whole Numbers	• Manipulative Kit: rulers	• Power Up A Worksheet
Cumulative Assessment			• Cumulative Test 20 • Test-Day Activity 10
106	• Reducing Fractions	• Manipulative Kit: rulers	• Power Up A Worksheet
107	• Multiplying a Three-Digit Number by a Two-Digit Number	• Manipulative Kit: rulers	• Power Up B Worksheet
108	• Analyzing Prisms		• Power Up B Worksheet
109	• Constructing Pyramids	• Grid paper, scissors, tape, glue	• Power Up B Worksheet • Lesson Activity 31 • Lesson Activity 8
110	• Simple Probability		• Power Up B Worksheet
Cumulative Assessment			• Cumulative Test 21 • Performance Task 11
Inv. 11	• Probability Experiments	• Manipulative Kit: dot cubes	• Lesson Activity 32

All resources are also available on the Resources and Planner CD.

Additional Resources

- Instructional Masters
- Reteaching Masters
- Refresher Lessons for California Standards
- Calculator Activities
- Resources and Planner CD
- Assessment Guide
- Performance Tasks
- Instructional Transparencies
- Answer Key CD
- Power Up Workbook
- Written Practice Workbook

Math Highlights

Enduring Understandings — The "Big Picture"

After completing Section 11, students will understand that:

- All whole numbers have prime factors.
- Generally, all fractions should be written in reduced form.
- Pyramids are constructed from nets.
- Probability of an event can be stated as a fraction.

Essential Questions

- What is a prime factor?
- How do I reduce a fraction?
- How is a prism net similar to a pyramid net?
- What is probability?

Math Content Highlights	Math Processes Highlights
Number Sense • **The Distributive Property** *Lesson 102* • **Equivalent Fractions** *Lesson 103* • **Rounding Whole Numbers Through Hundred Millions** *Lesson 104* • **Factoring Numbers** *Lesson 105* • **Reducing Fractions** *Lesson 106* • **Multiplying a Three-Digit Number by a Two-Digit Number** *Lesson 107* **Algebraic Thinking** • **Formulas** *Lesson 101* • **Factoring Numbers** *Lesson 105* • **Solving Word Problems Involving Multi-Digit Multiplication** *Lesson 107* **Geometry and Measurement** • **Analyzing Prisms** *Lesson 108* • **Constructing Pyramids** *Lesson 109* **Data Analysis, Statistics, and Probability** • **Probability** *Lesson 110, Investigation 11*	**Problem Solving** • **Strategies** – **Act It Out or Make a Model** *Lesson 102* – **Find or Extend a Pattern** *Lessons 105, 108* – **Make an Organized List** *Lesson 109* – **Make It Simpler** *Lessons 104, 110* – **Use Logical Reasoning** *Lessons 102, 103, 106, 107* – **Write a Number Sentence or Equation** *Lessons 101, 103, 104, 106, 107, 110* • **Real-World Applications** *Lessons 101, 109* **Communication** • **Discuss** *Lesson 106* • **Explain** *Lessons 101, 102, 104, 105, 106, 107, 108, 109, 110, Investigation 11* • **Formulate** *Lesson 102* **Connections** • **Math to Math** – **Number Sense and Algebra** *Lessons 100, 101* – **Measurement and Geometry** *Lessons 108, 109* – **Probability and Statistics** *Lesson 110, Investigation 11* • **Math and Other Subjects** – **Math and History** *Lesson 107* – **Math and Geography** *Lessons 102, 107* – **Math and Science** *Lesson 109* – **Math and Sports** *Lessons 103, 104, 105, 107, 108* **Representation** • **Model** *Lessons 101, 102, 109, Investigation 11* • **Represent** *Lessons 101, 102, 103, 104, 105, 106, 107, 108, 109, 110, Investigation 11* • **Formulate an Equation** *Lessons 101, 103, 104* • **Using Manipulative/Hands On** *Lessons 101, 102, 103, 104, 105, 106, 107, 108, 109, 110*

Universal Access

Support for universal access is included with each lesson. Specific resources and features are listed on each lesson planning page. Features in the Teacher's Manual to customize instruction include the following:

Teacher's Manual Support

Alternative Approach	Provides a different path to concept development. *Lessons 102, 104–106, 108, 110*
Manipulative Use	Provides alternate concept development through the use of manipulatives. *Lessons 101–104, 107, 109*
Flexible Grouping	Provides suggestions for various grouping strategies tied to specific lesson examples. *TM page 727A*
Inclusion	Provides ideas for including all students by accommodating special needs. *Lessons 101–110, Inv. 11*
Developing Academic Language	Provides a list of new and maintained vocabulary words along with words that might be difficult for English learners. *Lessons 101–110, Inv. 11*
English Learners	Provides strategies for teaching specific vocabulary that may be difficult for English learners. *Lessons 101–110, Inv. 11*
Errors and Misconceptions	Provides information about common misconceptions students encounter with concepts. *Lessons 101–110*
Extend the Example	Provides additional concept development for advanced learners. *Lessons 101–110*
Extend the Problem	Provides an opportunity for advanced learners to broaden concept development by expanding on a particular problem approach or context. *Lessons 101–110, Inv. 11*
Early Finishers	Provides additional math concept extensions for advanced learners at the end of the Written Practice. *Lessons 101, 102, 109*
Investigate Further	Provides further depth to concept development by providing additional activities for an investigation. *Investigation 11*

Additional Resources

The following resources are also available to support universal access:

- Adaptations for Saxon Math
- English Learner Handbook
- Online Activities
- Performance Tasks
- Refresher Lessons for CA Standards
- Reteaching Masters

Student Resources

- Student Edition eBook
- Calculator Activities
- Online Resources at www.SaxonMath.com/Int4ActivitiesCA

Teacher Resources

- Resources and Planner CD
- Test and Practice Generator CD
- Monitoring Student Progress: eGradebook CD
- Teacher's Manual eBook CD
- Answer Key CD
- Adaptations for Saxon Math CD
- Online Resources at www.SaxonMath.com

Cumulative Assessment

The assessments in Saxon Math are frequent and consistently placed to offer a regular method of ongoing testing.

Power-Up Test: Allow no more than ten minutes for this test of basic facts and skills.

Cumulative Test: Next, administer this test, which checks mastery of concepts in previous lessons.

Test-Day Activity and Performance Task: The remaining class time can be spent on these activities. Students can finish the Test-Day Activity for homework. Advanced learners can complete the extended Performance Task in another class period.

After Lesson 105

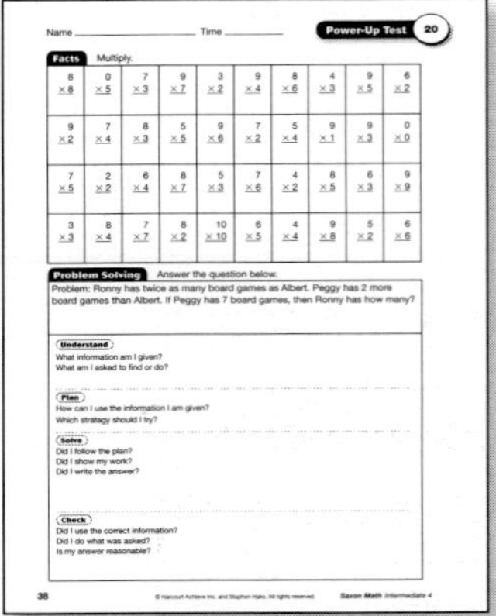
Power-Up Test 20

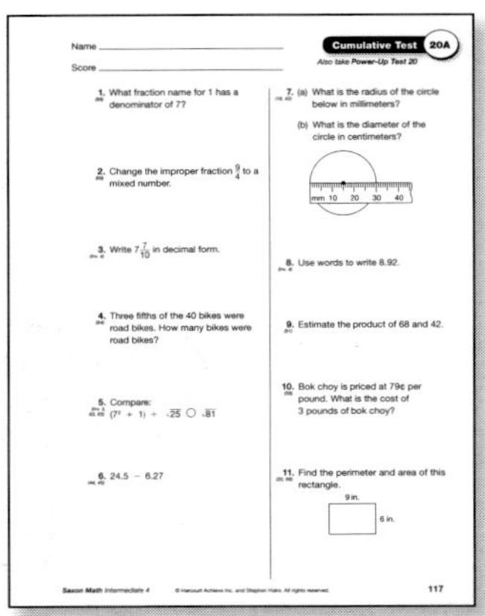
Cumulative Test 20

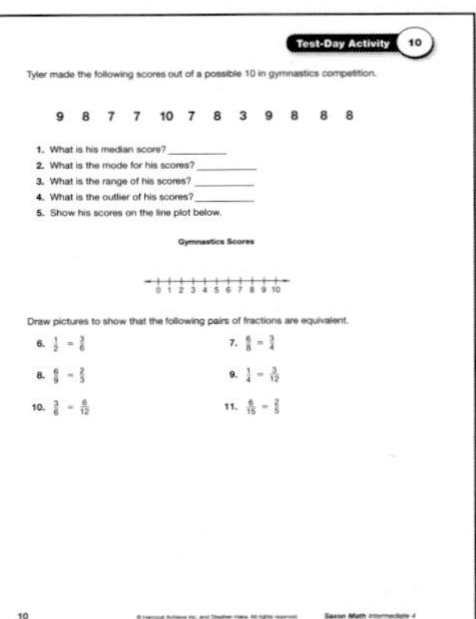
Test-Day Activity 10

After Lesson 110

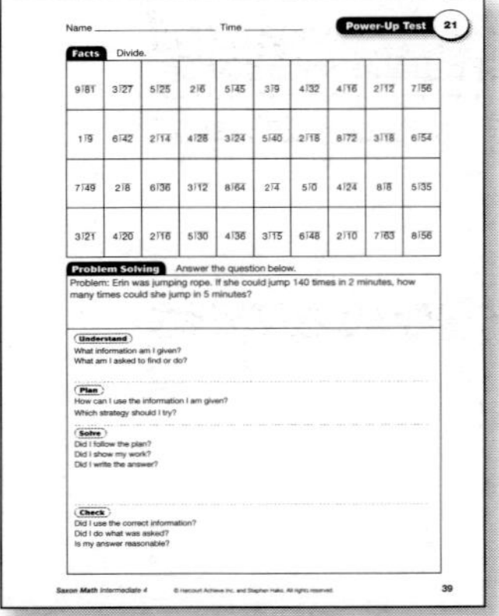
Power-Up Test 21

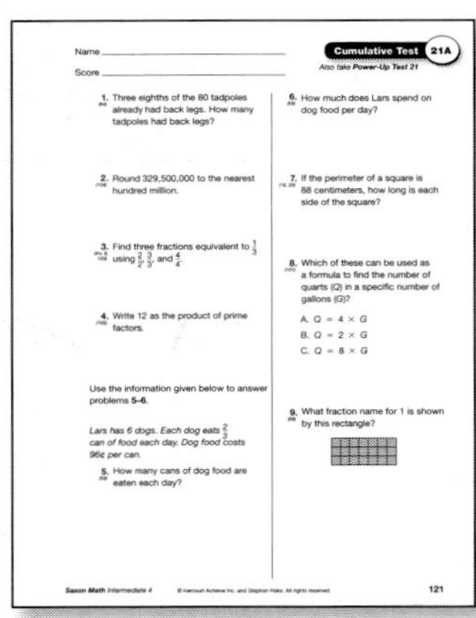
Cumulative Test 21

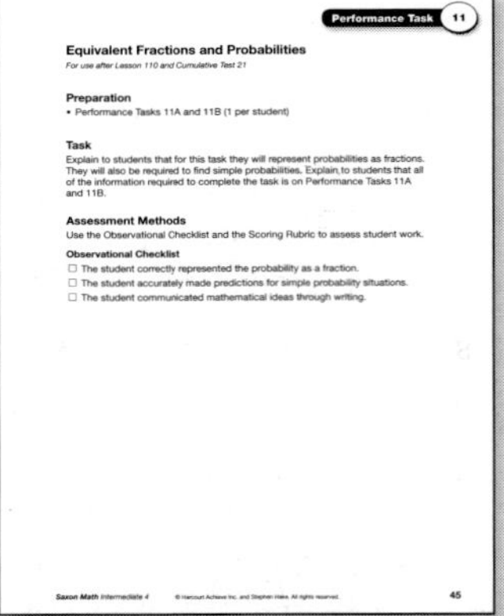
Performance Task 11

Evidence of Learning — What Students Should Know

By the conclusion of Section 11, students should be able to demonstrate the following competencies through the Cumulative Assessments, which are correlated to the California Mathematics Standards:

- Utilize a given formula to find an unknown amount. **AF 1.1, AF 1.4, MR 2.2, MR 2.3**
- Identify fractions equal to one. **NS 1.5, NS 1.7, MR 2.3**
- Understand the concept of and identify the radius and diameter of a circle. **MG 3.2**

Reteaching

Students who score below 80% on assessments may be in need of reteaching. Refer to the Reteaching Masters for reteaching opportunities for every lesson.

Benchmarking and Tracking the California Mathematics Standards

Benchmark Tests

Benchmark Tests correlated to lesson concepts allow you to assess student progress after every 20 lessons. An End-of-Course Test is a final benchmark test of the complete textbook. The Benchmark Tests are available in the Assessment Guide.

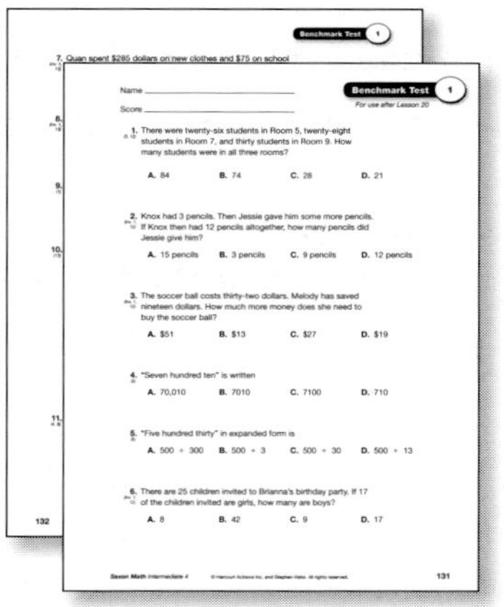

Benchmark Test 1

7. Quan spent $285 dollars on new clothes and $75 on school

Name ______________________

Score ______________________

Benchmark Test 1

For use after Lesson 20

1. There were twenty-six students in Room 5, twenty-eight students in Room 7, and thirty students in Room 9. How many students were in all three rooms?

   A. 84 B. 74 C. 28 D. 21

2. Knox had 3 pencils. Then Jessie gave him some more pencils. If Knox then had 12 pencils altogether, how many pencils did Jessie give him?

   A. 15 pencils B. 3 pencils C. 9 pencils D. 12 pencils

3. The soccer ball costs thirty-two dollars. Melody has saved nineteen dollars. How much more money does she need to buy the soccer ball?

   A. $51 B. $13 C. $27 D. $19

4. "Seven hundred ten" is written

   A. 70,010 B. 7010 C. 7100 D. 710

5. "Five hundred thirty" in expanded form is

   A. 500 + 300 B. 500 + 3 C. 500 + 30 D. 500 + 13

6. There are 25 children invited to Brianna's birthday party. If 17 of the children invited are girls, how many are boys?

   A. 8 B. 42 C. 9 D. 17

132

Saxon Math Intermediate 4 © Harcourt Achieve Inc. and Stephen Hake. All rights reserved. 131

Monitoring Student Progress: eGradebook CD

To track California Standards mastery, enter students' scores on Cumulative Tests and Benchmark Tests into the Monitoring Student Progress: eGradebook CD. Use the report titled *Benchmark Standards Report* to determine which California Standards were assessed and the level of mastery for each student. Generate a variety of other reports for class tracking and more.

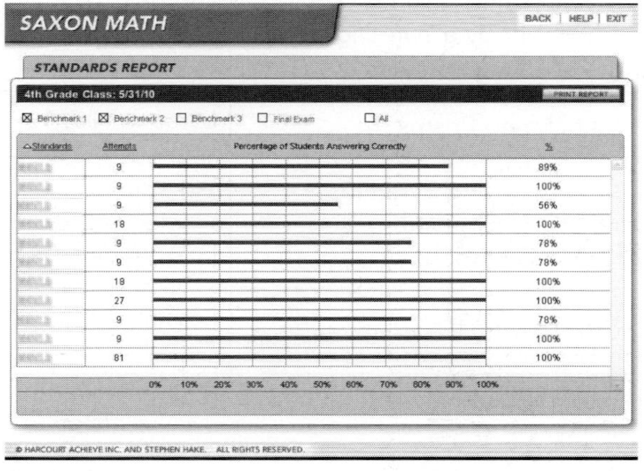

SAXON MATH BACK | HELP | EXIT

STANDARDS REPORT

4th Grade Class: 5/31/10 PRINT REPORT

☒ Benchmark 1 ☒ Benchmark 2 ☐ Benchmark 3 ☐ Final Exam ☐ All

Standards	Attempts	Percentage of Students Answering Correctly	%
[illegible]	9		89%
[illegible]	9		100%
[illegible]	9		56%
[illegible]	18		100%
[illegible]	9		78%
[illegible]	9		78%
[illegible]	18		100%
[illegible]	27		100%
[illegible]	9		78%
[illegible]	9		100%
[illegible]	81		100%

0% 10% 20% 30% 40% 50% 60% 70% 80% 90% 100%

© HARCOURT ACHIEVE INC. AND STEPHEN HAKE. ALL RIGHTS RESERVED.

Test and Practice Generator CD

Test items also available in Spanish.

The Test and Practice Generator is an easy-to-manage benchmarking and assessment tool that creates unlimited practice and tests in multiple formats and allows you to customize questions or create new ones. A variety of reports are available to track student progress toward mastery of the California Standards throughout the year.

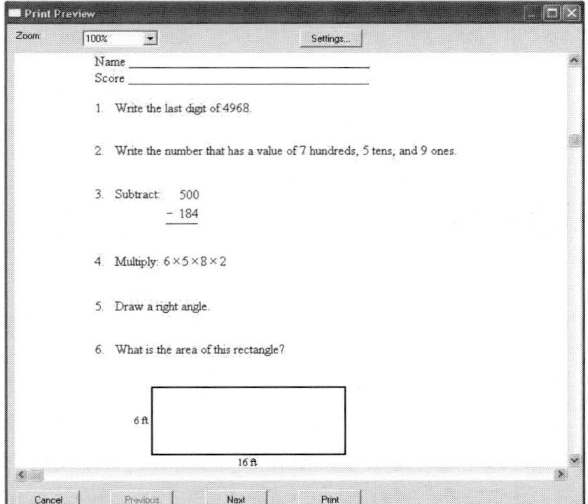

Print Preview

Zoom: 100% Settings...

Name ______________________

Score ______________________

1. Write the last digit of 4968.
2. Write the number that has a value of 7 hundreds, 5 tens, and 9 ones.
3. Subtract: 500 − 184
4. Multiply: $6 \times 5 \times 8 \times 2$
5. Draw a right angle.
6. What is the area of this rectangle?

6 ft

16 ft

Cancel Previous Next Print

Content Trace

Lesson	New Concepts	Practiced	Assessed	Looking Forward
101	• Formulas	Lessons 101, 102, 103, 104, 107, 111, 112, 113	Test 21	Lessons 109, 114
102	• The Distributive Property	Lessons 103, 104, 105, 107, 108	Test 9	Lesson 104
103	• Equivalent Fractions	Lessons 103, 104, 105, 106, 107, 110, 113	Test 21	Lessons 106, 111, 112, 113
104	• Rounding Whole Numbers Through Hundred Millions	Lessons 104, 106, 107, 109, 112, 113, 114	Test 21	Lessons 105, 107
105	• Factoring Whole Numbers	Lessons 105, 106, 108, 109, 110	Test 21	***Saxon Math*** *Intermediate 5*
106	• Reducing Fractions	Lessons 106, 107, 108, 109, 110, 111, 112, 113, 114	Test 22	Lessons 111, 112, 113
107	• Multiplying a Three-Digit Number by a Two-Digit Number	Lessons 107, 108, 109, 110, 111, 112, 113, 114	Test 22	***Saxon Math*** *Intermediate 5*
108	• Analyzing Prisms	Lessons 108, 109, 110, 111, 112	Test 21	Lessons 109, 114
109	• Constructing Pyramids	Lessons 109, 110, 111, 112, 114	Test 22	Lesson 114
110	• Simple Probability	Lessons 110, 111, 112, 113, 114	Test 22	Investigation 11
Inv. 11	• Probability Experiments	Lessons 111, 112, 113, 114	Test 22	***Saxon Math*** *Intermediate 5*

Planning & Preparation

• Formulas

Objectives

- Use formulas to find area and perimeter.
- Use formulas to solve problems about sales tax.

Prerequisite Skills

- Recognizing that perimeter is the distance around a figure.
- Using tiles to represent perimeter and area of different figures.
- Solving problems that involve multiplication.

Materials

Instructional Masters

- Power Up J Worksheet
- Lesson Activity 8

Manipulative Kit

- Money manipulatives*

Teacher-provided materials

- Grid paper
- Fraction manipulatives from Investigation 8, scissors, index cards*

**optional*

California Mathematics Content Standards

NS 1.0, 1.8 Use concepts of negative numbers (e.g., on a number line, in counting, in temperature, in "owing").

AF 1.0, 1.1 Use letters, boxes, or other symbols to stand for any number in simple expressions or equations (e.g., demonstrate an understanding and the use of the concept of a variable).

AF 1.0, 1.4 Use and interpret formulas (e.g., area = length × width or $A = lw$) to answer questions about quantities and their relationships.

MR 2.0, 2.2 Apply strategies and results from simpler problems to more complex problems.

MR 2.0, 2.3 Use a variety of methods, such as words, numbers, symbols, charts, graphs, tables, diagrams, and models, to explain mathematical reasoning.

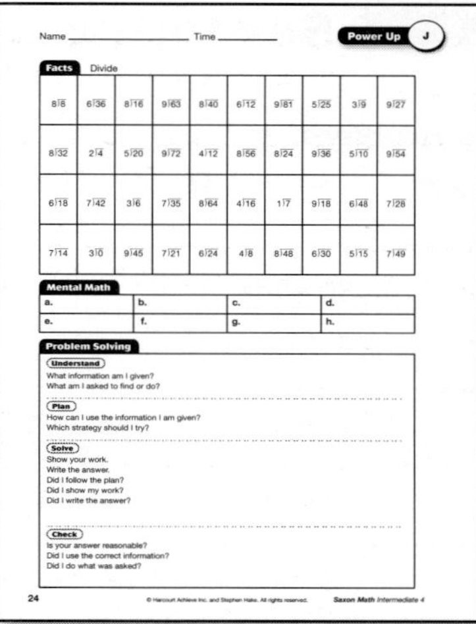

Power Up J Worksheet

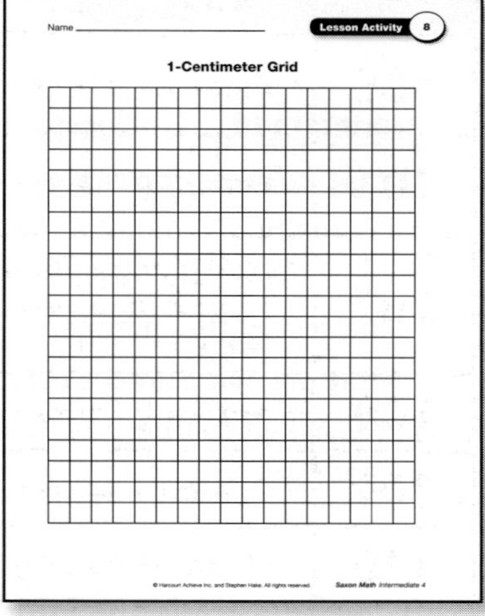

Lesson Activity 8

Universal Access

Reaching All Special Needs Students

Special Education Students	At-Risk Students	English Learners	Advanced Learners
• Inclusion (TM) • Adaptations for Saxon Math	• Error Alert (TM) • Reteaching Masters • Refresher Lessons for California Standards	• English Learners (TM) • Developing Academic Language (TM) • English Learner Handbook	• Extend the Example (TM) • Early Finisher (SE) • Online Activities

TM=Teacher's Manual
SE=Student Edition

Developing Academic Language

Maintained	**English Learner**
area	tax
formula	
perimeter	

Problem Solving Discussion

Problem

Congress meets in Washington, D.C., to make laws for the United States. The 535 members of the U.S. Congress are divided into two groups—representatives and senators. There are 2 senators from each of the 50 states. The rest of the people in U.S. Congress are representatives. How many senators are there? How many representatives are there?

Focus Strategy 2+3=5 **Write a Number Sentence or Equation**

Understand *Understand the problem.*

"What information are we given?"

1. There are 535 members of Congress.
2. There are 2 senators from each of the 50 states.
3. The rest of the members are representatives.

"What are we asked to do?"

We are asked to find how many senators and how many representatives are in Congress.

Plan *Make a plan.*

"How can we use the information we know to solve the problem?"

We can first find how many senators are in Congress. Then we can *write a number sentence* to find how many representatives are in Congress.

Solve *Carry out the plan.*

"How many senators are in Congress?"

There are 2 senators from each of the 50 states. Thus, there are 50×2 senators, or 100 senators, in Congress.

"What number sentence can we write to find the number of representatives?"

We might write a number sentence that follows a some, some more pattern:

Some + some more = total

100 senators + R representatives = 535 members of Congress

We can find the number of representatives by subtracting 100 from 535:

$535 - 100 = 435$ representatives

Check *Look back.*

"Did we complete the task?"

Yes. We found that there are 100 senators and 435 representatives in Congress.

"Is our answer reasonable?"

We know that our answer is reasonable, because 2 senators from each state is 100 senators altogether. Also, 100 senators plus 435 representatives is a total of 535 members of Congress. This number matches the number we were given in the problem.

LESSON 101

• Formulas

California Mathematics Content Standards

- **NS 1.0, 1.8** Use concepts of negative numbers (e.g., on a number line, in counting, in temperature, in "owing").
- **AF 1.0, 1.4** Use and interpret formulas (e.g., area = length × width or $A = lw$) to answer questions about quantities and their relationships.
- **MR 2.0, 2.2** Apply strategies and results from simpler problems to more complex problems.

facts Power Up J

mental math Thinking of quarters can make mentally adding and subtracting numbers ending in 25, 50, and 75 easier. Use this strategy to solve problems **a–c.**

a. **Number Sense:** 350 + 175 525

b. **Number Sense:** 325 − 150 175

c. **Number Sense:** 175 + 125 300

d. **Money:** Each ticket costs $10.00 if purchased at the concert hall. A ticket costs $1.95 less if it is purchased in advance. What is the advance price for a ticket? $8.05

e. **Time:** The year 2011 begins on a Saturday. On what day of the week will the year 2012 begin? Sunday

f. **Estimation:** Estimate 24 × 21. Round 24 to 25, round 21 to 20, and then multiply. 500

g. **Calculation:** $\frac{1}{10}$ of 70, − 5, × 50, $\sqrt{\ }$ 10

h. **Simplify:** 3 × (1 + 1) 6

problem solving Choose an appropriate problem-solving strategy to solve this problem. Congress meets in Washington, D.C., to make laws for the United States. The 535 members of the U.S. Congress are divided into two groups—representatives and senators. There are 2 senators from each of the 50 states. The rest of the people in the U.S. Congress are representatives. How many senators are there? How many representatives are there? 100 senators; 435 representatives

Facts Divide

1 8)8	6 6)36	2 8)16	7 9)63	5 8)40	2 6)12	9 9)81	5 5)25	3 3)9	3 9)27
4 8)32	2 2)4	4 5)20	8 9)72	3 4)12	7 8)56	3 8)24	4 9)36	2 5)10	6 9)54
3 6)18	6 7)42	2 3)6	5 7)35	8 8)64	4 4)16	7 1)7	2 9)18	8 6)48	4 7)28
2 7)14	0 3)0	5 9)45	3 7)21	4 6)24	2 4)8	6 8)48	5 6)30	3 5)15	7 7)49

Power Up

Facts
Distribute **Power Up J** to students. See answers below.

Count Aloud
Before students begin the Mental Math exercises, do these counting exercises as a class.

Count up and down by tens from 20 to 120.

Mental Math
Encourage students to share different ways to mentally compute these exercises. Strategies for exercises are listed below.

a. Add 100, then Add 75
350 + 100 = 450; 450 + 75 = 525
Add 200, then Subtract 25
350 + 200 = 550; 550 − 25 = 525

b. Subtract 100, then Subtract 50
325 − 100 = 225; 225 − 50 = 175
Subtract 200, then Add 50
325 − 200 = 125; 125 + 50 = 175

Problem Solving
Refer to **Problem-Solving Strategy Discussion,** p. 669H.

New Concept

Instruction

As you discuss the different formulas, remind students that expressions such as lw, $2l$, $2w$, $3y$, and $4g$ represent the product of two factors.

Error Alert

Point out that because some formulas contain more than one operation (such as $P = 2l + 2w$), it is important for students to follow the order of operations after the substitutions have been made.

Example 1

Active Learning

"What operation was used to solve this problem?" addition

"To check the answer, what operation should be used?" subtraction

Ask your students to demonstrate on the board or overhead two different subtractions that can be used to check the answer. Sample: Subtract $1.40 from $29.30 and compare the result to $27.90; Subtract $27.90 from $29.30 and compare the result to $1.40.

(continued)

New Concept

We have been using formulas to find area and perimeter.

$$A = lw \qquad P = 2l + 2w$$

We also have been writing formulas to convert from one unit of measure to another.

Feet and Yards	Quarts and Gallons
$f = 3y$	$q = 4g$

Any situation where the relationship between two quantities is constant can be represented with a formula. We can solve problems using these formulas:

Total Cost (T) = Original Price (P) + Sales Tax (S)

Profit (or Loss) (P) = Sales (S) − Expenses (E)

Total Miles (T) = Total Gallons of Fuel (G) × Miles per Gallon (M)

Distance (D) = Speed (S) × Time (T)

Example 1

A hat cost $27.90. The tax is $1.40. What is the total cost of the hat?

We can solve any sales tax problem using this formula:

Total Cost (T) = Original Price (P) + Sales Tax (S) or $T = P + S$

$$T = \$27.90 + \$1.40$$
$$= \$29.30$$

The total cost of the hat is **$29.30.**

Example 2

Lisa spent $25 on supplies to make 20 bracelets. She sold them for $35. What was her profit?

We can use the formula

Profit (P) = Sales (S) − Expenses (E) or $P = S - E$

$$P = \$35 - \$25$$
$$= \$10$$

Lisa's profit was **$10.**

Connect Suppose Lisa sold the bracelets for $20. What would her profit be? None; She would have had a loss of $5.

English Learners

Explain that a **tax** is a payment, usually a percentage of the price of something, added on to the original purchase price. Money from taxes support the government.

Ask, ***"If the tax was 8¢, how much would the gloves cost if they are marked $2?"*** $2 + $0.08 = $2.08

Explain to students that there are different tax rates in different parts of the country.

Math Background

The formulas to find the area and perimeter of a rectangle are:

$$A = lw \qquad P = 2l + 2w$$

The formulas to find area and perimeter of a circle are:

$$A = \pi r^2 \qquad P = 2\pi r$$

Example 3

Ed's car holds 20 gallons of gasoline. The car dealer told him he could drive 17 miles on each gallon of gas. How far can Ed drive on a full tank?

For this problem we use the formula

Total Miles (T) = Total Gallons of Fuel (G) × Miles per Gallon (M) or $T = G \times M$

$$T = 20 \times 17$$
$$= 340$$

Ed can drive **340 miles** on a full tank.

Lesson Practice

Generalize Write a formula to solve each problem:

a. Genevieve drove for 4 hours at a speed of 50 miles per hour. How far did she drive? 200 miles; $D = S \times T$; $4 \times 50 = 200$

b. At the end of a week, one store had expenses of $1000 and sales of $800. What number would represent the week's record of sales and expenses? Explain why. −$200; Expenses were $200 higher than sales.

c. Mary Beth ran 6 kilometers. How many meters did she run? 6000 m; $1000k = m$

d. A car can be driven 95 miles on 5 gallons of gas. How far can it be driven on 1 gallon of gas? 19 miles; $T = G \times M$; $5 \times M = 95$ or $95 \div 5 = M$

Written Practice

Distributed and Integrated

▸ *1. (28, 39, 52) **Justify** Haley bought 5 tickets for $2.75 each. She paid for them with a $20 bill. How much change should she receive? Explain why your answer is reasonable. $6.25; sample: $2.75 is close to $3, $3 × 5 = $15, and $20 − $15 = $5, which is close to $6.25.

2. (87) If fifty cents is divided equally among 3 friends, there will be some cents left. How many cents will be left? 2 cents

3. (10) What is the difference when four hundred nine is subtracted from nine hundred four? 495

▸ *4. (94) **Represent** Two fifths of the 45 stamps were from Brazil. How many stamps were from Brazil? Draw a picture to illustrate the problem. 18 stamps

4. 45 stamps

$\frac{2}{5}$ were from Brazil.	9 stamps
	9 stamps
$\frac{3}{5}$ were not from Brazil.	9 stamps
	9 stamps
	9 stamps

Teacher Tip

Explain that using a formula to solve a problem is like following a recipe in cooking. Both tell you what steps to follow and in what order.

New Concept *(Continued)*

Example 3

Extend the Example

Write the following information on the board or overhead:

Car 1	Car 2
120,000 mi	120,000 mi
25 mpg	20 mpg
$3/gal	$3/gal

Explain that two owners of new cars plan to drive their cars for 120,000 miles. Car 1 uses 1 gallon of fuel every 25 miles and Car 2 uses 1 gallon every 20 miles. Challenge advanced learners to find the total cost of fuel for each car if the average cost of a gallon of fuel is $3. Car 1: $14,400; Car 2: $18,000

Lesson Practice

Guided Practice

Use these problems as guided practice to check the students' understanding of today's concept.

Problems a and b

If students have difficulty identifying a formula that can be used to solve either problem, ask them to use one of the formulas that are shown in the beginning of the lesson.

Problem d

Point out that the number of miles a car can travel using one gallon of fuel is a concept known as *fuel economy*.

Problem c

Error Alert

You may need to remind some students that 1 kilometer = 1000 meters.

Closure **The questions below help assess the concepts taught in this lesson.**

"Name a formula and explain how that formula is used to solve a problem."

Sample: The formula $A = lw$ is used to find the area of a rectangle; Substitute the length of the rectangle for l and substitute its width for w, and then find the product of those numbers.

Written Practice

Math Conversations

Independent Practice and Discussions to Increase Understanding

Problem 1 (Justify)

Make sure students recognize that this is a two-step problem; Before the amount of change can be determined, the total cost of the tickets ($5 \times \$2.75 = \$13.75$) must be known.

After students complete the problem, invite volunteers to share reasons why their answers are reasonable.

Problem 4 (Represent)

Invite a volunteer to demonstrate how pencil-and-paper arithmetic can be used to check the answer. Sample: One-fifth of a number is the same as dividing the number by 5; 45 stamps ÷ 5 = 9 stamps. Since 9 stamps represents $\frac{1}{5}$ of the stamps, double that number of stamps to find the number of stamps that $\frac{2}{5}$ represents: 9 stamps × 2 = 18 stamps

Problem 5

Manipulative Use

Encourage students to use their fraction manipulatives to check their work.

Problem 6 (Formulate)

Although the formulas may vary, each should represent the product of two factors. You might choose to have students list the formulas on the board, and then discuss with them how the formulas are alike and different.

Problem 7 (Model)

Encourage students to cut and fold their designs to check their work.

Problem 10 Multiple Choice

Test-Taking Strategy

Before students solve the problem, ask:

"When a fraction is equal to 1, how does the numerator of the fraction compare to the denominator?" Sample: The numerator and the denominator are identical.

Problem 13 (Explain)

Invite a volunteer to explain how the problem can be solved using only mental math.

(continued)

▶ *5. (19, 98) **a.** The quesadilla was cut into 10 equal slices. The entire sliced quesadilla shows what fraction name for 1? $\frac{10}{10}$

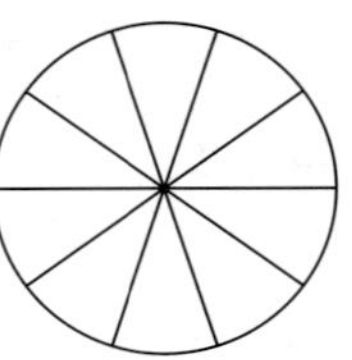

b. Two slices of the quesadilla is what fractional part of the whole quesadilla? $\frac{2}{10}$ or $\frac{1}{5}$

▶ *6. (58, 101) (Formulate) If a car gets 15 miles per gallon, how many miles can the car go on 15 gallons? Write a formula to solve the problem. $T = G \times M$; 15 × 15 = 225, 225 miles

▶ *7. (97) (Model) Use grid paper to draw a net that can be folded into a rectangular prism. See student work.

8. (40) (Estimate) Round 5167 to the nearest thousand. 5000

*9. (99) Change the improper fraction $\frac{9}{4}$ to a mixed number. $2\frac{1}{4}$

▶*10. (98) **Multiple Choice** Which of these fractions is *not* equal to 1? C

A $\frac{12}{12}$ **B** $\frac{11}{11}$ **C** $\frac{11}{10}$ **D** $\frac{10}{10}$

11. (38, 39, 76) In the summer of 1926, there were only 17 stores in the town. Today there are 8 times as many stores in the town. How many stores are in the town today? 136 stores

12. (91) (Estimate) The wagon train took 9 days to make the 243-mile journey. About how many miles did it travel per day? About 30 miles; 270 ÷ 9

▶*13. (100) (Explain) On Saturday Jacinda played outside for $1\frac{1}{2}$ hours and played board games for $2\frac{1}{2}$ hours. Altogether, how much time did Jacinda spend playing outside and playing board games? Explain how you found your answer. 4 hours; sample: I added $1\frac{1}{2}$ hours to $2\frac{1}{2}$ hours and the sum is 4 hours.

▶*14. (98) (Estimate) Round $8\frac{21}{100}$ to the nearest whole number. 8

15. (45) $36.31 - 7.4$ = 28.91

*16. (100) $\frac{5}{8} + \frac{2}{8}$ $\frac{7}{8}$

17. (4) $6 + 5 + 4 + 3 + n = 25$ 7

*18. (100) $\frac{9}{10} - \frac{2}{10}$ $\frac{7}{10}$

*19. (100) $3\frac{2}{5} + 1\frac{1}{5}$ $4\frac{3}{5}$

Inclusion

Use this strategy if the student displays:

- Poor Retention.
- Slow Learning Rate.

Formulas (Individual)

Materials: index card

- Have students copy the following formulas on their index cards:
  A = *lw* **P** = 2*l* + 2*w*
  Feet and Yards *f* = 3*y*
  Quarts and Gallons *q* = 4*g*
  Total Cost (*T*) = Original Price *(P)* + Sales Tax *(S)*
  Profit (or Loss) (*P*) = Sales *(S)* − Expenses *(E)*
  Total Miles (*T*) = Total Gallons of Fuel *(G)* × Miles per Gallon *(M)*
  Distance (*D*) = Speed *(S)* × Time *(T)*
- Read aloud and write on the board ***"A basketball costs $21.95. The sales tax on the ball is $2.08. What is the total cost of the ball?"*** Have students locate the formula to use to solve the problem. Ask, ***"What needs to be added together to find the total cost?"*** Original price and sales tax ***"What is the total cost?"*** $24.03
- Write problems on the board that require the use of each formula and have students work with a partner to solve.

20. 27×32 864
(88)

21. 62×15 930
(88)

22. $7^2 + \sqrt{49}$ 56
(Inv. 3, 65)

▸*23. $5\overline{)460}$ 92
(69)

24. $9\overline{)\$27.36}$ \$3.04
(83)

25. $6w = 2316$ 386
(34, 79)

26. $1543 \div 7$ 220 R 3
(83)

*27. $532 \div 6$ 88 R 4
(72)

28. $\frac{256}{8}$ 32
(69)

*29. a. How many square feet of shingles are needed to cover a rectangular roof that is 40 feet wide and 60 feet long? 2400 square feet
(Inv. 3, 85)

b. Is this problem about area or perimeter? How do you know? Area; sample: Area covers a surface like shingles cover a roof.

30. Troy walked $2\frac{1}{5}$ miles on Monday. He walked $3\frac{4}{5}$ miles on Wednesday. How many more miles did Troy walk on Wednesday than on Monday? $1\frac{3}{5}$ miles
(100)

Real-World Connection

What is the length of the line segment on the grid? Explain how you found your answer.

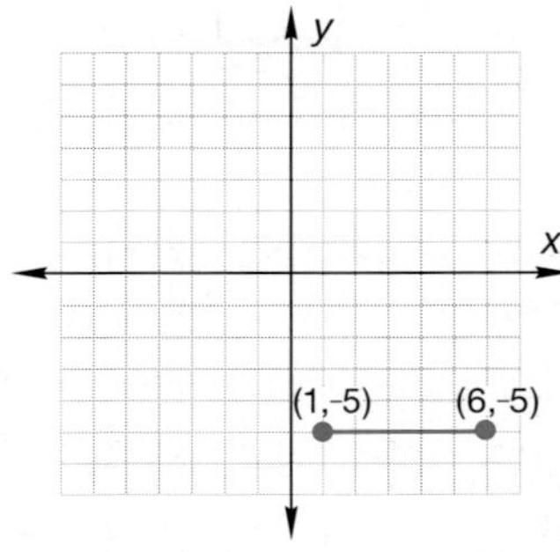

5 units; sample: Since this is a horizontal line segment, the y-coordinates are the same. We subtract the x-coordinates to find the length of the segment. 6 – 1 = 5

Using formulas to find area and perimeter prepares students for:

- **Lesson 114,** determining the perimeter and area of complex figures.

Written Practice *(Continued)*

Math Conversations *(cont.)*

Problem 14 Estimate

"When we round $8\frac{21}{100}$ to the nearest whole number, there are only two possible answers. What are those answers?" 8 or 9

"Explain how to decide which number—8 or 9—is the correct answer." Sample: Compare $8\frac{21}{100}$ to the mixed number that is halfway between 8 and 9. Since that mixed number is $8\frac{50}{100}$, and $8\frac{21}{100}$ is less than $8\frac{50}{100}$, the correct answer is 8.

Problem 23

Extend the Problem

Challenge an advanced learner to explain how the division can be completed using only mental math.

Errors and Misconceptions

Problem 13

Ask students who do not reduce $3\frac{2}{2}$ hours to name the operation that a fraction bar represents. division

Then ask them to name the quotient that $2 \div 2$ represents. 1

Conclude by asking them to name the simplest form of $3\frac{2}{2}$ hours. 4 hours

Problem 16

"What mistake can be made when we add two fractions that have the same denominator?" Add the denominators

Problem 18

"What mistake can be made when we subtract two fractions that have the same denominator?" Subtract the denominators

Explain to students that even though the points are negative numbers, we can still find the length of the segment by subtracting 6 – 1.

Planning & Preparation

• The Distributive Property

Objectives

- Use the Distributive Property to solve multiplication problems.
- Relate the Distributive Property to division.

Prerequisite Skills

- Drawing an array to model a multiplication problem.
- Taking steps in order from left to right in a problem with more than one addition or subtraction step.

Materials

Instructional Masters

- Power Up A Worksheet
- Lesson Activity 8

Manipulative Kit

- Two-color counters, base ten blocks*

Teacher-provided materials

- Grid paper
- Fraction manipulatives from Investigation 8*

**optional*

California Mathematics Content Standards

NS 3.0, 3.1 Demonstrate an understanding of, and the ability to use, standard algorithms for the addition and subtraction of multidigit numbers.

NS 3.0, 3.2 Demonstrate an understanding of, and the ability to use, standard algorithms for multiplying a multidigit number by a two-digit number and for dividing a multidigit number by a one-digit number; use relationships between them to simplify computations and to check results.

AF 1.0, 1.2 Interpret and evaluate mathematical expressions that now use parentheses.

AF 1.0, 1.3 Use parentheses to indicate which operation to perform first when writing expressions containing more than two terms and different operations.

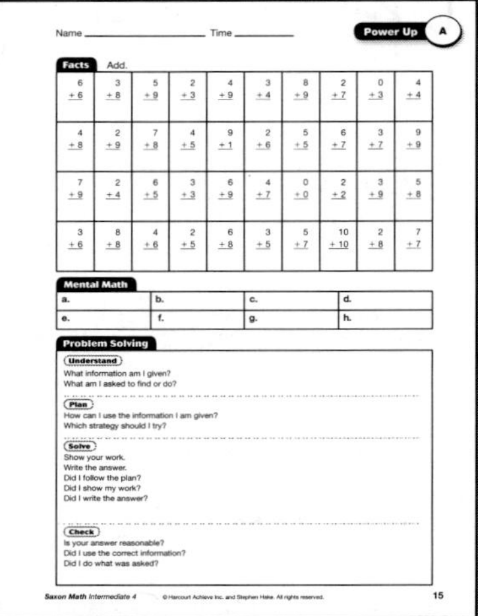

Name ______ Time ______ **Power Up A**

Facts Add.

6 + 6	3 + 8	5 + 9	2 + 3	4 + 9	3 + 4	8 + 9	2 + 7	0 + 3	4 + 4
4 + 8	2 + 9	7 + 8	4 + 5	9 + 1	2 + 6	5 + 5	6 + 7	3 + 7	9 + 9
7 + 9	2 + 4	6 + 5	3 + 3	6 + 9	4 + 7	0 + 0	2 + 2	3 + 9	5 + 8
3 + 6	8 + 8	4 + 6	2 + 5	6 + 8	3 + 5	5 + 7	10 + 10	2 + 8	7 + 7

Mental Math

a.	b.	c.	d.
e.	f.	g.	h.

Problem Solving

Understand
What information am I given?
What am I asked to find or do?

Plan
How can I use the information I am given?
Which strategy should I try?

Solve
Show your work.
Write the answer.
Did I follow the plan?
Did I show my work?
Did I write the answer?

Check
Is your answer reasonable?
Did I use the correct information?
Did I do what was asked?

Saxon Math Intermediate 4 © Harcourt Achieve Inc. and Stephen Hake. All rights reserved. 15

Power Up A Worksheet

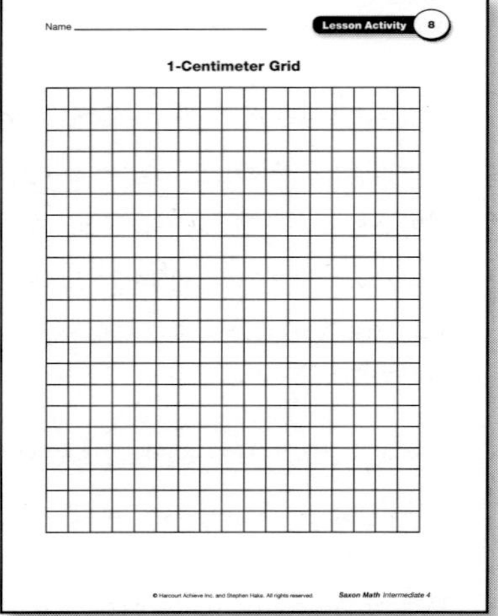

Name ______ **Lesson Activity 8**

1-Centimeter Grid

© Harcourt Achieve Inc. and Stephen Hake. All rights reserved. *Saxon Math Intermediate 4*

Lesson Activity 8

Universal Access

Reaching All Special Needs Students

Special Education Students	At-Risk Students	English Learners	Advanced Learners
• Inclusion (TM) • Adaptations for Saxon Math	• Alternative Approach (TM) • Error Alert (TM) • Reteaching Masters • Refresher Lessons for California Standards	• English Learners (TM) • Developing Academic Language (TM) • English Learner Handbook	• Extend the Example (TM) • Early Finisher (SE) • Online Activities

TM=Teacher's Manual
SE=Student Edition

Developing Academic Language

New	**Maintained**	**English Learner**
Distributive Property	parentheses partial product quotient	statement

Problem Solving Discussion

Problem

Nalo said, "An inch is less than $\frac{1}{10}$ of a foot." Write a short paragraph explaining why you agree or disagree with Nalo's statement.

Focus Strategies

Act It Out or Make a Model

Use Logical Reasoning

Understand *Understand the problem.*

"What is Nalo's claim about the length of an inch?"

Nalo says that an inch is less than $\frac{1}{10}$ of a foot.

"What are we asked to do?"

We are asked to write a short paragraph explaining why we agree or disagree with Nalo's claim.

Plan *Make a plan.*

"What problem-solving strategies can we use to help us find whether Nalo is correct?"

We can *use a model* to help us visualize what Nalo is stating. We can also *use logical reasoning.*

Teacher Note: Ask students to say whether they think Nalo is correct and to explain their reasoning. Discuss student responses as a class.

Solve *Carry out the plan.*

"What common classroom tool shows a length of 1 foot?"

A ruler

"One inch is what fraction of 1 foot?"

There are 12 inches in a foot, so 1 inch is $\frac{1}{12}$ of a foot.

"If we were to divide a foot into 10 parts (tenths) instead of 12 inches, would each of the 10 parts be shorter than 1 inch or longer than 1 inch?"

The more pieces we divide a specific length into, the smaller the pieces get. So $\frac{1}{10}$ of a foot is longer than an inch, which is $\frac{1}{12}$ of a foot.

"Is Nalo's statement true? Explain why or why not."

Yes, Nalo's statement is true. If we take a specific length and divide it into more and more equal parts, the parts become smaller and smaller. An inch is one of 12 equal parts of a foot. Since 12 parts is more than 10 parts, $\frac{1}{12}$ of a foot is less than $\frac{1}{10}$ of a foot.

Check *Look back.*

"Is our answer reasonable?"

We know our answer is reasonable because $\frac{1}{12}$ is a smaller fraction than $\frac{1}{10}$.

Power Up

Facts
Distribute **Power Up A** to students. See answers below.

Count Aloud
Before students begin the Mental Math exercises, do these counting exercises as a class.

Count up and down by fives from 30 to 75.

Mental Math
Encourage students to share different ways to mentally compute these exercises. Strategies for exercises are listed below.

a. Subtract 200, then Add 25
$425 - 200 = 225$; $225 + 25 = 250$
Subtract 100, then Subtract 75
$425 - 100 = 325$; $325 - 75 = 250$

b. Decompose 18
$(4 \times 10) + (4 \times 8) = 40 + 32 = 72$
Subtract 4 × 2 from 4 × 20
$(4 \times 20) - (4 \times 2) = 80 - 8 = 72$

Problem Solving
Refer to **Problem-Solving Strategy Discussion,** p. 674B.

California Mathematics Content Standards

NS 3.0, 3.1 Demonstrate an understanding of, and the ability to use, standard algorithms for the addition and subtraction of multidigit numbers.

NS 3.0, 3.2 Demonstrate an understanding of, and the ability to use, standard algorithms for multiplying a multidigit number by a two-digit number and for dividing a multidigit number by a one-digit number; use relationships between them to simplify computations and to check results.

AF 1.0, 1.2 Interpret and evaluate mathematical expressions that now use parentheses.

• The Distributive Property

Power Up

facts Power Up A

mental math

a. **Number Sense:** 425 − 175 250

b. **Number Sense:** 4 × 18 72

c. **Money:** Gabriella purchased a sandwich for $3.65 and a beverage for $0.98. What was the total price? $4.63

d. **Geometry:** How many vertices do 4 hexagons have? 24 vertices

e. **Time:** The year 2012 begins on a Sunday. On what day of the week will the year 2013 begin? (Remember that 2012 is a leap year.) Tuesday

f. **Estimation:** Estimate 19 × 31 by rounding one number up and the other number down. 600

g. **Calculation:** 4 × 5, − 5, + 6, ÷ 7 3

h. **Simplify:** 12 ÷ (6 − 2) 3

problem solving Choose an appropriate problem-solving strategy to solve this problem. Nalo said, "An inch is less than $\frac{1}{10}$ of a foot." Write a short paragraph explaining why you agree or disagree with Nalo's statement. Sample: Nalo's statement is true. If a foot were divided into 10 equal parts, each part would be $\frac{1}{10}$ of a foot. An inch is one of 12 equal parts. If we take a specific length and divide it into more and more parts, the smaller the parts become. Since 12 parts is a greater amount than 10 parts, $\frac{1}{12}$ of a foot is less than $\frac{1}{10}$, of a foot.

New Concept

The multiplication algorithm is based on the **Distributive Property.** The Distributive Property applies to multiplication problems such as 23 × 14. According to the Distributive Property:

$$23 \times 14 = 23(10 + 4)$$

Facts Add.

6 + 6 12	3 + 8 11	5 + 9 14	2 + 3 5	4 + 9 13	3 + 4 7	8 + 9 17	2 + 7 9	0 + 3 3	4 + 4 8
4 + 8 12	2 + 9 11	7 + 8 15	4 + 5 9	9 + 1 10	2 + 6 8	5 + 5 10	6 + 7 13	3 + 7 10	9 + 9 18
7 + 9 16	2 + 4 6	6 + 5 11	3 + 3 6	6 + 9 15	4 + 7 11	0 + 0 0	2 + 2 4	3 + 9 12	5 + 8 13
3 + 6 9	8 + 8 16	4 + 6 10	2 + 5 7	6 + 8 14	3 + 5 8	5 + 7 12	10 + 10 20	2 + 8 10	7 + 7 14

Reading Math

When a number is directly in front of a set of parentheses it means multiply that number by the number or numbers inside the parentheses. We read 5(4) as 5 times 4. We read 5(4 + 2) as (5 × 4) + (5 × 2).

When we multiply each addend and then add the products, we are using the same approach as the multiplication algorithm.

$$\begin{aligned} 23(10 + 4) &= (23 \times 10) + (23 \times 4) \\ &= 230 + 92 \\ &= 322 \end{aligned}$$

$$\begin{array}{r} 23 \\ \times\ 14 \\ \hline 92 \\ +\ 230 \\ \hline 322 \end{array}$$

This method matches the partial products of the multiplication algorithm.

We can also use the Distributive Property to check a division problem.

$$\begin{aligned} 84 \div 4 &= (80 \div 4) + (4 \div 4) \\ &= 20 + 1 \\ &= 21 \end{aligned}$$

$$\begin{array}{r} 21 \\ 4\overline{)84} \\ \underline{80} \\ 04 \\ \underline{4} \\ 0 \end{array}$$

This method matches the partial products of the division algorithm.

Example 1

Nina wants to multiply 35 by 25. Use the Distributive Property to find the product.

First we rewrite the factors using parentheses and the expanded form. Then we solve the equation.

$$\begin{aligned} 35(20 + 5) &= (35 \times 20) + (35 \times 5) \\ &= 700 + 175 \\ &= 875 \end{aligned}$$

The product is **875.**

Example 2

Jose divided 126 by 3. Use the Distributive Property to check his answer.

$$\begin{array}{r} 42 \\ 3\overline{)126} \\ \underline{12} \\ 06 \\ \underline{6} \\ 0 \end{array}$$

$$\begin{aligned} 126 \div 3 &= (120 \div 3) + (6 \div 3) \\ &= 40 + 2 \\ &= 42 \end{aligned}$$

The quotient **42** is correct.

English Learners

Explain that a **statement** is something that is stated or said.

"If I say, 'An addend is any number added to one or more numbers to find a sum,' is this a statement?" Yes

Say:

"Does a statement have to be true?" Not necessarily

Explain that a **statement** could be true or false.

Math Background

The Distributive Property states that $a(b + c) = ab + ac$ for any numbers a, b, and c. We can visualize this in terms of the area of the large rectangle below. The rectangle is made up of two smaller rectangles. To find the area of the large rectangle, we could multiply its dimensions: $a(b + c)$. We could also find the area by adding the areas of the two smaller rectangles: $ab + ac$. These areas must be equal, so $a(b + c) = ab + ac$.

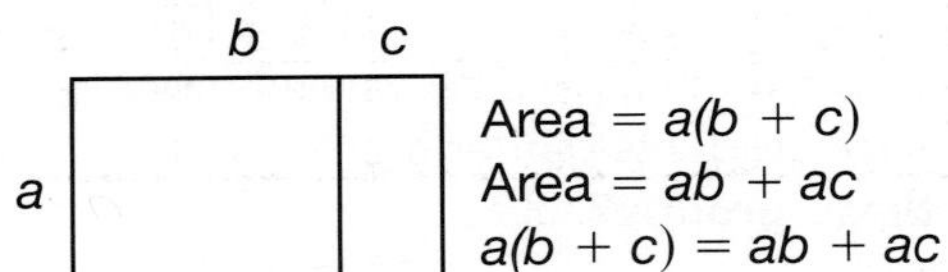

New Concept

Instruction

In this lesson, students will learn about the relationship shared by the multiplication algorithm and the Distributive Property.

Explanation

When we apply the Distributive Property to multiply 23 × 14, we rewrite the factors as 23(10 + 4), and we find the product of 23 and 10, we find the product of 23 and 4, and then we find the sum of the products.

When we use the multiplication algorithm to multiply 23 and 14, we rewrite the factors vertically, and we find the product of 4 and 23, we find the product of 10 and 23, and then we find the sum of the products.

Lead students to conclude that both methods produce the same result because the multiplication algorithm is based on the Distributive Property.

Example 1

Extend the Example

Challenge your advanced learners by asking:

"Use the Distributive Property and the multiplication algorithm to find the product of 64 and 75."

Error Alert

Make sure students understand that when the Distributive Property is used to find the product of two factors, we first write the expanded form of the number we are multiplying by. In this example, the expanded form of 25, the number we are multiplying by, is 20 + 5.

Example 2

Active Learning

After discussing the solution, invite a student to describe another way to check the answer, and include the words 'dividend,' 'divisor,' and 'quotient' in the description. Sample: Compare the product of the divisor and the quotient to the dividend.

Explanation

When we use the Distributive Property to check a quotient, we must break the dividend into two parts that are each divisible by the divisor. In this example, point out that the divisor is 3, and we rewrite the dividend (126) as 120 + 6 because both 120 and 6 are divisible by 3.

(continued)

New Concept *(Continued)*

Lesson Practice

Guided Practice

Use these problems as guided practice to check the students' understanding of today's concept.

Problems a and b **Connect**

Make sure students recall that when the Distributive Property is used to find the product of two factors, we write the expanded form of the number we are multiplying by. For part **a**, 42×16 is rewritten as $42(10 + 6)$, and for part **b**, 38×12 is rewritten as $38(10 + 2)$.

Problem c **Justify**

Error Alert

Remind students that using the Distributive Property to check involves breaking the dividend (245) into two parts that are each divisible by the divisor (5). If students have difficulty choosing two numbers, remind them that numbers ending in 0 or 5 are divisible by 5.

Closure

The questions below help assess the concepts taught in this lesson.

Write "24×12" on the board or overhead. Then ask:

"Demonstrate how the Distributive Property and the multiplication algorithm can each be used to find the product of 24 and 12."

$24 \times 12 = 24(10 + 2) = 240 + 48 = 288$

$$\begin{array}{r} 24 \\ \times\ 12 \\ \hline 48 \\ 240 \\ \hline 288 \end{array}$$

Written Practice

Math Conversations

Independent Practice and Discussions to Increase Understanding

Problem 1 **Explain**

After students identify the first step in solving the problem, have them name the remaining step or steps that will need to be performed to find the cost of 1 pound of oranges. After subtraction is used to find the cost of 8 pounds of oranges, division is used to find the cost of 1 pound.

(continued)

Lesson Practice

Connect Use the Distributive Property to find each product. See student work.

a. 42×16 672 **b.** 38×12 456

c. **Justify** Divide 245 by 5. Then, use the Distributive Property to check the answer. 49

Written Practice

Distributed and Integrated

▸ *1. (93) **Explain** Cody bought 8 pounds of oranges. He gave the storekeeper a $5 bill and received $1.96 in change. What did 1 pound of oranges cost? What is the first step in solving this problem? $0.38; finding how much *all* the oranges cost

2. (63) **Formulate** What number is six less than the product of five and four? Write an expression. 14; $(5 \times 4) - 6$

3. (94) Two thirds of the 12 guitar strings were out of tune. How many guitar strings were out of tune? Draw a picture to illustrate the problem. 8 guitar strings

3. 12 strings
$\frac{2}{3}$ were out of tune. — 4 strings, 4 strings
$\frac{1}{3}$ were not out of tune. — 4 strings

*4. (47, 48) **Represent** Use digits to write eight million, nine hundred forty-five thousand in standard form. Then, round it to the nearest ten thousand. 8,945,000; 8,950,000

▸ *5. (43, 45) **Connect** What is the sum of the numbers labeled *A* and *B* on the number line below? 0.87

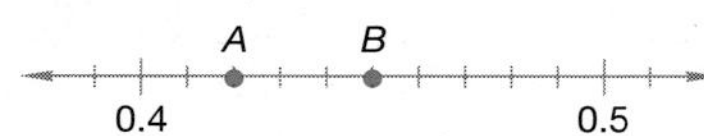

▸ *6. (98) Write a fraction equal to 1 and that has a denominator of 5. $\frac{5}{5}$

7. (32) **Represent** Use words to write $397\frac{3}{4}$. three hundred ninety-seven and three fourths

8. (61) Estimate the sum of 4178 and 6899 by rounding both numbers to the nearest thousand before adding. 11,000

▸ *9. (99) Change each improper fraction to a whole number or a mixed number:

a. $\frac{7}{3}$ $2\frac{1}{3}$ **b.** $\frac{8}{4}$ 2 **c.** $\frac{9}{5}$ $1\frac{4}{5}$

Inclusion

Use this strategy if the student displays:

- Difficulty with Large Group Instruction.
- Difficulty with Abstract Processing.

The Distributive Property (Pairs)

Material: counters

- Write 3×11 on the board. Tell students to use counters to make 3 groups of 11. Ask, ***"What is the product of 3 × 11?"*** 33
- Have students return counters and ask, ***"What two numbers added together make 11?"*** Sample (10, 1)
- Write on the board $3 \times 11 = 3\,(10 + 1)$. Tell students that the 3 next to the parentheses means to multiply 3 by each number inside of the groups. Then write $= (3 \times 10) + (3 \times 1)$. Have students gather 3 groups of 10 and then 3 groups of 1. Ask, ***"What is the total of these groups?"*** 33

  Tell students that breaking down 3×11 into $3\,(10 + 1)$ is called the Distributive Property.
- Have students work with a partner to break down 4×13 using the Distributive Property.

676 **Saxon Math** *Intermediate 4*

▸* **10.** (58, 93) For the first 3 hours, the hikers hiked at 3 miles per hour. For the next 2 hours they hiked at 4 miles per hour. If the total trip was 25 miles, how far did they still have to go? 8 miles

* **11.** (42, 101) **a.** What fractional part of yard is a foot? $\frac{1}{3}$

b. (Formulate) Write a formula for changing any number of yards to feet. $3y = f$ or $f = 3y$

▸* **12.** (Inv. 10) (Model) Graph the relationship between yards and feet for 1, 2, and 3 yards. See student work.

13. (45) $41.6 + 13.17 + 9.2$ 63.97

14. (8, 45) $h + 8.7 = 26.47$ 17.77

▸* **15.** (100) $6\frac{3}{8} + 4\frac{2}{8}$ $10\frac{5}{8}$

▸* **16.** (100) $4\frac{7}{10} - 1\frac{6}{10}$ $3\frac{1}{10}$

▸* **17.** (102) We may write 48 as 40 + 8. Use the Distributive Property to find 5(40 + 8). $200 + 40 = 240$

* **18.** (100) (Analyze) Two fifths of the students rode the bus, and one fifth traveled by car. What fraction of the students either rode the bus or traveled by car? $\frac{3}{5}$

19. (38) $\$0.48 \times 5$ \$2.40

20. (65, 85) 80^2 6400

21. (Inv. 3) $\sqrt{25} \times \sqrt{25}$ 25

22. (34, 79) $4d = \$6.36$ \$1.59

* **23.** (79) $2\overline{)520}$ 260

24. (69) $\frac{175}{5}$ 35

25. (66, 101) What is the perimeter and area of this square? Use formulas to solve the problem. 40 in.; 100 in^2

10 in.

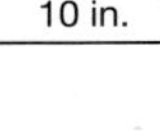

Alternative Approach: Using Manipulatives

To help students understand the concept of using the Distributive Property to multiply, have them use base ten blocks to model the multiplication.

Display the problem 3×17. Ask students to model 17 as 1 ten and 7 ones. Explain to students that *times* 3 means to show 3 groups of 1 ten and 7 ones. Have students put all of the ones in one group and all of the tens in another group. Instruct students to find the total for each group, regroup if necessary, and write how many are in each group. 5 tens 1 one or 51
$30 + 21 = 51$

Written Practice (Continued)

Math Conversations (cont.)

Problem 5 (Connect)

"On this number line, the distance between 0.4 and 0.5 is divided into 10 equal parts. What does that fact tell us about the number that each tick mark represents? Explain your answer." Sample: The tick marks represent hundredths; Each tick mark is one hundredth more than the tick mark to its left and one hundredth less than the tick mark to its right.

Problem 6

"What is the quotient when any number is divided by itself?" 1

Problem 9

Manipulative Use

Encourage students to use their fraction manipulatives to check their answers.

Problem 10

Make sure students recognize that more than one step is needed to find the answer.

Problem 12 (Model)

Students should use the formula $f = 3y$ and generate three ordered pairs to plot by substituting 1, 2, and 3 for y and then solving for f.

Problems 15 and 16

Before students complete the arithmetic, ask them to name an operation that can be used to check each answer. Problem **15** is addition; Use subtraction to check. Problem **16** is subtraction; Use addition to check.

Instruct students to include a check of the answer along with each answer.

Problem 17

Extend the Problem

"How many partial products will the expression 5(40 + 8) produce?" two

"How many partial products would 5 × 2(40 + 8) produce?" two

(continued)

Written Practice *(Continued)*

Math Conversations *(cont.)*

Problem 26b Analyze

To locate points on the coordinate plane, make sure students recall that we begin at the origin and move to the right, and then move up.

Problem 28 Interpret

"How many degrees does each horizontal line on the graph represent? Explain how you know." The distance between 60° and 70°, or between 70° and 80°, represents 10° and is divided into 5 equal parts, so each line represents 10° ÷ 5, or 2°.

(continued)

* **26.** (Inv. 9, Inv. 10) **Analyze** Use this coordinate graph to solve parts **a** and **b.**

a. Which coordinates can you subtract to find the length of this segment? What is the length? *y* coordinates, 8 − 1 = 7 units

▸ **b.** Name three points on this segment. Sample: (7, 8), (7, 1), (7, 5)

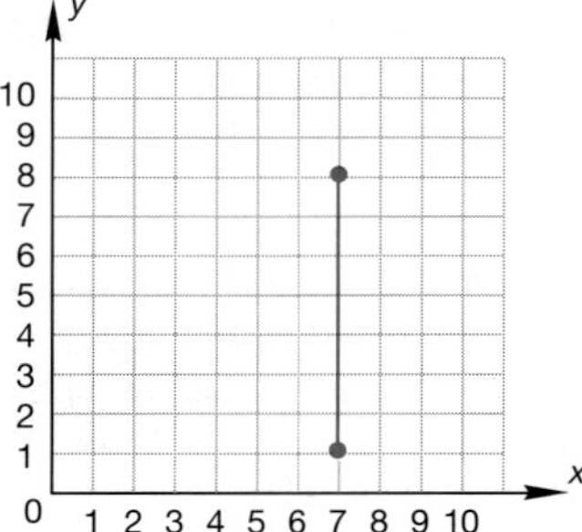

* **27.** (42) The tabletop was 76 cm above the floor. The tabletop was how many meters above the floor? 0.76 m

▸* **28.** (Inv. 5, Inv. 6) 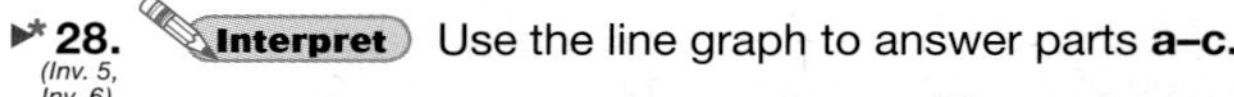 **Interpret** Use the line graph to answer parts **a–c.**

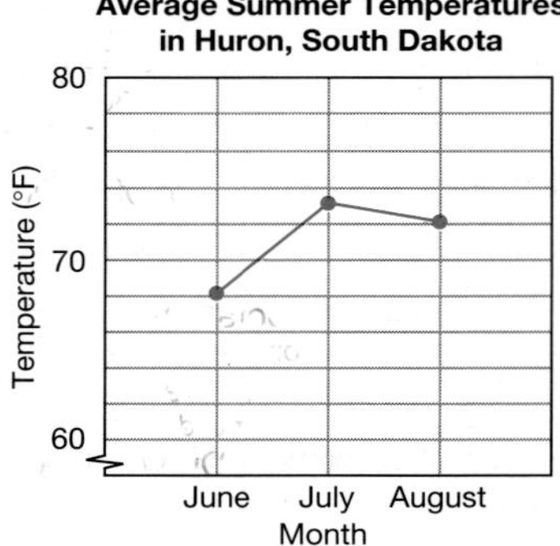

a. Write the names of the months in order from warmest to coolest. July, August, June

b. How many degrees warmer is the average temperature during July than the average temperature during June? 5° warmer

c. Explain how to find the median temperature. Sample: Write the temperatures in order: 68°F, 72°F, 73°F; The median is the middle number, 72°F.

678 ***Saxon Math*** *Intermediate 4*

*29. There were $3\frac{4}{5}$ pitas in the chef's kitchen. Then the chef removed $1\frac{3}{5}$ of the pitas. How many potpies remained in the chef's kitchen? $2\frac{1}{5}$ pitas
(100)

▸*30. **Multiple Choice** The mixed numbers $5\frac{3}{8}$ and $7\frac{4}{5}$ do not have common denominators, but we know their sum is between which two numbers? B
(98)

A 14 and 16 **B** 12 and 14
C 10 and 12 **D** 5 and 8

Real-World Connection

Platonic solids, named after the Greek philosopher Plato, are a famous group of three-dimensional figures. The most commonly known Platonic solid is the cube (also called a hexahedron). The cube is, of course, based on a square and has 6 square faces. There are 3 Platonic solids based on a triangle, however, and 1 Platonic solid based on a pentagon. Refer to the table below.

Platonic Solid	Base Polygon	Faces	Edges	Vertices
Tetrahedron	Triangle	4	6	4
Cube	Square	6	12	8
Octahedron	Triangle	8	12	6
Dodecahedron	Pentagon	12	30	20
Icosahedron	Triangle	20	30	12

a. Which Platonic solid has the greatest number of vertices? Which has the fewest? icosahedron; tetrahedron

b. Name a major difference between an octagon and an octahedron. An octagon is a 2-d figure while an octahedron is a 3-d figure; See student work.

c. Is an icosahedron always larger in size than a cube? Why? No; A larger number faces does not necessarily mean a larger 3-d figure

d. What is another name for a tetrahedron? Draw a model of a tetrahedron. Triangular pyramid; See student work.

Using the Distributing Property to solve for multiplication problems prepares students for:

- **Lesson 107,** multiplying a three-digit number by a two-digit number.

Written Practice *(Continued)*

Math Conversations *(cont.)*

Problem 30 Multiple Choice

Test-Taking Strategy

Make sure students recognize that rounding can be used to find the range of possible answers.

Errors and Misconceptions

Problem 10

If students give an incorrect answer, have them check their work by reviewing each step of their solution. For the first three hours, the hikers hiked 9 miles. During the next two hours, the hikers hiked 8 miles. At that time, they had hiked 9 miles + 8 miles, or 17 miles, altogether.

Problem 14

Make sure students recognize this problem as a missing-addend problem. If they cannot identify the operation that is used to solve the problem, ask them to consider this simpler problem:

"What number plus 2 is 5?"

Ask students to name the answer (3) and operation that can be used to find the answer (subtraction; 5 − 2), and then have them use that same operation to solve for *h* in problem **14.**

Encourage early finishers to research Platonic solids and Archimedean solids on the Internet or in a library. Challenge advanced learners with the following:

"What common piece of sports equipment resembles the Archimedean solid known as a truncated iscosahedron?" soccer ball

Thinking About Multiplying Two-Digit Numbers

Use this page to enhance conceptual understanding of key mathematical concepts.

Guided Instruction

Go through the presentation on the student page with the class. Help students see that the rectangle is divided into smaller rectangles that have the expanded form of the two factors as the lengths of their sides. Make sure students understand that the multiplication in each smaller rectangle represents the area of that rectangle. Then lead students through adding the individual areas to find the total area of the large rectangle.

Write the following on the board:

$$\begin{array}{r} 23 \\ \times\ 14 \\ \hline 92 \\ \underline{230} \\ 322 \end{array}$$

Point out that you used a zero to show the place value of the second partial product in the multiplication. Ask how the partial products are related to the areas of the smaller rectangles. 92 is the sum of 80 + 12, the areas of the rectangles with a side of 4, and it is the product of 4 × 23. 230 is the sum of 200 + 30, the areas of the rectangles with a side of 10, and it is the product of 10 × 23.

Extending the Concept

Although not mentioned on the student page, the Distributive Property is applied in this example, because it allows the large rectangle to be divided into smaller rectangles.

Students may ask if it is necessary to use the expanded form of the numbers to divide the rectangle. Explain that the numbers could be decomposed in any way but using expanded form makes the computation simpler.

Closure

The question below helps assess the concepts taught in this lesson.

"Why can we use rectangle models to show both multiplication and division?" Sample: The area of a rectangle and the side lengths of a rectangle can be related using either a multiplication sentence or a division sentence.

California Mathematics Content Standards

NS 3.0, 3.2 Demonstrate an understanding of, and the ability to use, standard algorithms for multiplying a multidigit number by a two-digit number and for dividing a multidigit number by a one-digit number; use relationships between them to simplify computations and to check results.

MR 3.0, 3.2 Note the method of deriving the solution and demonstrate a conceptual understanding of the derivation by solving similar problems.

• Thinking About Multiplying Two-Digit Numbers

We can use a rectangle model to represent a multiplication problem. Let's look at 14 × 23.

We use expanded form to rewrite each of the factors.

14 = 10 + 4

23 = 20 + 3

Then we label the sides of a rectangle with the expanded form of the two factors. We multiply to find the area of each of the four rectangles that make up our larger rectangle.

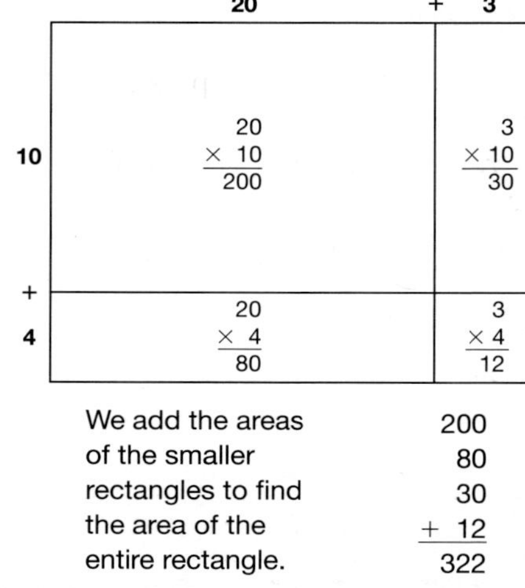

We add the areas of the smaller rectangles to find the area of the entire rectangle.

$$\begin{array}{r} 200 \\ 80 \\ 30 \\ +\ 12 \\ \hline 322 \end{array}$$

Explain Describe how you would draw a rectangle model for multiplying 24 × 48. Sample: Draw a rectangle, make four parts and use the expanded forms of 24 and 48 to label the sides.

Apply Draw a rectangle model and use it to multiply 24 × 48.

	40	+ 8
20	20 × 40 = 800	20 × 8 = 160
+ 4	4 × 40 = 160	4 × 8 = 32

$$\begin{array}{r} 800 \\ 160 \\ 160 \\ +\ 32 \\ \hline 1152 \end{array}$$

Planning & Preparation

• Equivalent Fractions

Objectives
- Use pictures to show that two fractions are equivalent.
- Find fractions that are equivalent to a given fraction.

Prerequisite Skills
- Drawing and shading pictures of fractions representing halves, thirds, and fourths.
- Using fraction manipulatives to model, compare, and order equivalent fractions.
- Representing and comparing fractions equal to one half using pictorial models.
- Comparing fractions to the nearest half.

Materials
Instructional Masters
- Power Up A Worksheet

Manipulative Kit
- Relational GeoSolids*

Teacher-provided materials
- Fraction manipulatives from Investigation 8, fraction bars, construction paper*

**optional*

California Mathematics Content Standards

NS 1.0, 1.5 Explain different interpretations of fractions, for example, parts of a whole, parts of a set, and division of whole numbers by whole numbers; explain equivalents of fractions (see Standard 4.0).

NS 1.0, 1.7 Write the fraction represented by a drawing of parts of a figure; represent a given fraction by using drawings; and relate a fraction to a simple decimal on a number line.

MG 3.0, 3.4 Identify figures that have bilateral and rotational symmetry.

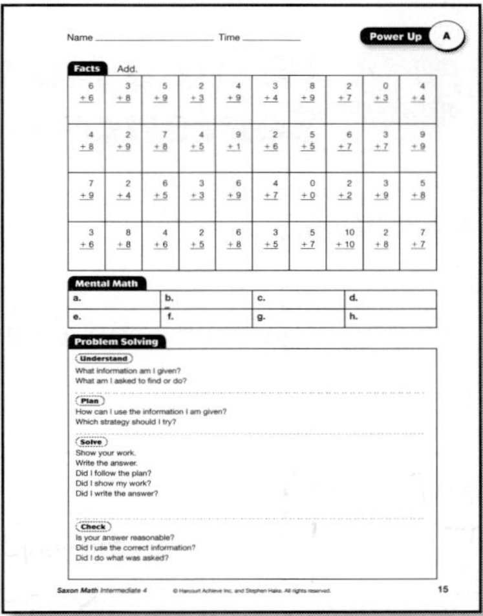
Name ____________ Time ________ **Power Up A**

Facts Add.

6 + 6	3 + 8	5 + 9	2 + 3	4 + 9	3 + 4	8 + 9	2 + 7	0 + 3	4 + 4
4 + 8	2 + 9	7 + 8	4 + 5	9 + 1	2 + 6	5 + 5	6 + 7	3 + 7	9 + 9
7 + 9	2 + 4	6 + 5	3 + 3	6 + 9	4 + 7	0 + 0	2 + 2	3 + 9	5 + 8
3 + 6	8 + 8	4 + 6	2 + 5	6 + 8	3 + 5	5 + 7	10 + 10	2 + 8	7 + 7

Mental Math

a.	b.	c.	d.
e.	f.	g.	h.

Problem Solving

Understand
What information am I given?
What am I asked to find or do?

Plan
How can I use the information I am given?
Which strategy should I try?

Solve
Show your work.
Write the answer.
Did I follow the plan?
Did I show my work?
Did I write the answer?

Check
Is your answer reasonable?
Did I use the correct information?
Did I do what was asked?

Saxon Math Intermediate 4 © Harcourt Achieve Inc. and Stephen Hake. All rights reserved. 15

Power Up A Worksheet

Universal Access

Reaching All Special Needs Students

Special Education Students	At-Risk Students	English Learners	Advanced Learners
• Inclusion (TM) • Adaptations for Saxon Math	• Error Alert (TM) • Reteaching Masters • Refresher Lessons for California Standards	• English Learners (TM) • Developing Academic Language (TM) • English Learner Handbook	• Extend the Example (TM) • Extend the Problem (TM) • Online Activities

TM=Teacher's Manual

Developing Academic Language

Maintained	**English Learner**
equivalent	portion
fraction	
multiply	

Problem Solving Discussion

Problem

A square has 90° rotational symmetry because for every 90° it is turned, it matches its original position. A regular pentagon has rotational symmetry of 72°. Does a regular octagon have rotational symmetry? If so, what degree of rotational symmetry does it have?

Focus Strategies

Use Logical Reasoning

2+3=5 Write a Number Sentence or Equation

Understand *Understand the problem.*

"What information are we given?"

We are told that a square has 90° rotational symmetry and a regular pentagon has 72° rotational symmetry.

"What are we asked to do?"

We are asked to determine if a regular octagon has rotational symmetry and if so, what degree.

Plan *Make a plan.*

"What problem-solving strategy will we use?"

We will *use logical reasoning* to help us *write an equation.*

"We know that a square has 4 equal sides, and a regular pentagon has 5 equal sides. We also know that one full turn is equal to 360°. How might this information help us?"

We know that a square would have to make four 90° turns to make one full turn because $360 \div 4 = 90$. We also know that a regular pentagon would have to make five 72° turns to make one full turn because $360 \div 5 = 72$. If we determine the number of sides a regular octagon has, we can divide 360° by that number.

Solve *Carry out the plan.*

"How many equal sides does a regular octagon have?"

8

"How can we find the degree of rotational symmetry needed for an octagon to match its original position?"

We can divide one full turn, 360°, into 8 equal increments.

$$360° \div 8 = 45°$$

Check *Look back.*

"Is our answer reasonable?"

We know that our answer is reasonable because 45° multiplied by eight sides is 360° or one full turn.

LESSON 103

• Equivalent Fractions

California Mathematics Content Standards

NS 1.0, 1.5 Explain different interpretations of fractions, for example, parts of a whole, parts of a set, and division of whole numbers by whole numbers; explain equivalents of fractions (see Standard 4.0).

NS 1.0, 1.7 Write the fraction represented by a drawing of parts of a figure; represent a given fraction by using drawings; and relate a fraction to a simple decimal on a number line.

Power Up

facts Power Up A

mental math

a. **Number Sense:** 450 − 175 275

b. **Number Sense:** 50 × 42 2100

c. **Money:** Casius gave the clerk $2.00 for lemons that cost $1.62. How much change should he receive? 38¢

d. **Time:** Which date occurs only once every four years? February 29

e. **Powers/Roots:** $2^3 \div 2$ 4

f. **Estimation:** Micalynn purchased 4 toothbrushes for $11.56. Round this amount to the nearest dollar and then divide by 4 to estimate the cost per toothbrush. $3

g. **Calculation:** $\sqrt{36}$, × 3, + 2, ÷ 10, − 1 1

h. **Simplify:** $4 - a$ when $a = 3$ 1

problem solving

Choose an appropriate problem-solving strategy to solve this probelm. A square has 90° rotational symmetry because for every 90° it is turned, it matches its original position. A regular pentagon has rotational symmetry of 72°. Does a regular octagon have rotational symmetry? If so, what degree of rotational symmetry does it have? Yes; 45°

Facts Add.

6 + 6 = 12	3 + 8 = 11	5 + 9 = 14	2 + 3 = 5	4 + 9 = 13	3 + 4 = 7	8 + 9 = 17	2 + 7 = 9	0 + 3 = 3	4 + 4 = 8
4 + 8 = 12	2 + 9 = 11	7 + 8 = 15	4 + 5 = 9	9 + 1 = 10	2 + 6 = 8	5 + 5 = 10	6 + 7 = 13	3 + 7 = 10	9 + 9 = 18
7 + 9 = 16	2 + 4 = 6	6 + 5 = 11	3 + 3 = 6	6 + 9 = 15	4 + 7 = 11	0 + 0 = 0	2 + 2 = 4	3 + 9 = 12	5 + 8 = 13
3 + 6 = 9	8 + 8 = 16	4 + 6 = 10	2 + 5 = 7	6 + 8 = 14	3 + 5 = 8	5 + 7 = 12	10 + 10 = 20	2 + 8 = 10	7 + 7 = 14

Power Up

Facts

Distribute **Power Up A** to students. See answers below.

Count Aloud

Before students begin the Mental Math exercises, do these counting exercises as a class.

Count up and down by twos from 8 to 32.

Mental Math

Encourage students to share different ways to mentally compute these exercises. Strategies for exercises are listed below.

a. Subtract 200, then Add 25

450 − 200 = 250; 250 + 25 = 275

Subtract 100, then Subtract 75

450 − 100 = 350; 350 − 75 = 275

b. Double 50 and Divide 42 by 2

50 × 2 = 100 and 42 ÷ 2 = 21; 100 × 21 = 2100

Decompose 42

50 × (40 + 2) = 2000 + 100 = 2100

Problem Solving

Refer to **Problem-Solving Strategy Discussion**, p. 681B.

New Concept

Observation

Display the *Basic Fraction Circles* poster during today's lesson.

Manipulative Use

Use overhead fraction circles to model the fractions that are equivalent to $\frac{1}{2}$, and to model the equivalent fractions that are presented in the three examples.

Example 1

Error Alert

Make sure students understand that when a fraction is used to describe the shaded portion of a whole, the denominator of the fraction represents the number of equal parts into which the whole is divided, and the numerator represents the number of shaded parts.

Example 2

Active Learning

After discussing the example, ask:

"What does it mean when two fractions are equivalent?" Sample: The fractions are different ways to name the same amount.

Connection

It is very important for students to understand that multiplication by 1, in any form, does not change the value of the original fraction. Reinforce this concept often as you complete the remainder of the lesson.

(continued)

New Concept

Math Language

Equivalent is another word for equal. For example, $\frac{1}{2}$ and $\frac{2}{4}$ are equivalent fractions, and $\frac{1}{2}$ and $\frac{2}{4}$ are equal fractions.

Equal portions of each circle below have been shaded. We see that different fractions are used to name the shaded portions.

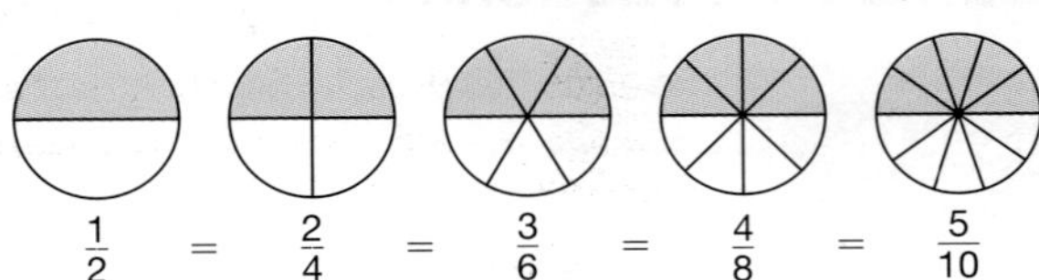

$$\frac{1}{2} = \frac{2}{4} = \frac{3}{6} = \frac{4}{8} = \frac{5}{10}$$

These fractions all name the same amount. Different fractions that name the same amount are called **equivalent fractions.**

Example 1

The rectangle on the left has three equal parts. We see that two parts are shaded, so two thirds of the figure is shaded.

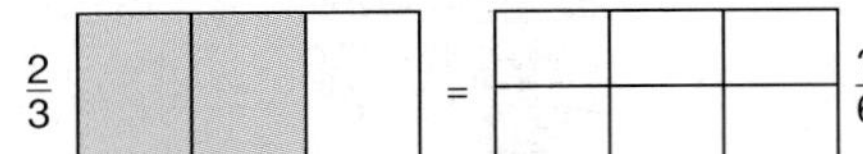

The rectangle on the right has six equal parts. How many parts must be shaded so that the same fraction of this rectangle is shaded?

We see that **four parts** out of six must be shaded. This means two thirds is the same as four sixths.

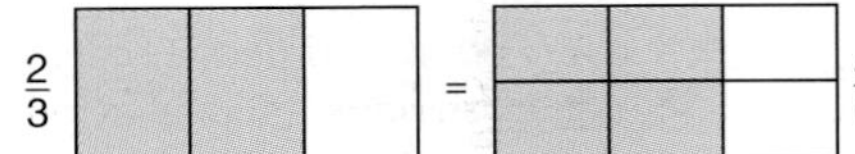

$\frac{2}{3}$ and $\frac{4}{6}$ are equivalent fractions.

Example 2

What equivalent fractions are shown at right?

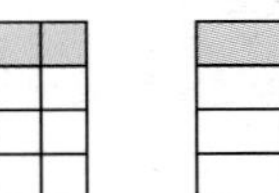

An equal portion of each rectangle is shaded. The rectangles shown are equal.

$$\frac{2}{8} = \frac{1}{4}$$

English Learners

Explain to your students that a **portion** is a piece of something. Say:

"When we have dinner we get a portion of the meal our family has."

Ask:

"What portion of a gallon is 2 quarts?" $\frac{1}{2}$

Thinking Skills

Verify

What property states that we can multiply any number by 1 and the answer is that number?

Identity Property of Multiplication

We remember that when we multiply a number by 1, the answer equals the number we multiplied.

$$2 \times 1 = 2 \qquad 2000 \times 1 = 2000 \qquad \frac{1}{2} \times 1 = \frac{1}{2}$$

We also remember that there are many ways to write "1."

$$1 = \frac{2}{2} = \frac{3}{3} = \frac{4}{4} = \frac{5}{5} = \frac{6}{6} = \ldots$$

We can use these two facts to find equivalent fractions. If we multiply a fraction by a fraction name for 1, the product is an equivalent fraction.

$$\frac{1}{2} \times \frac{2}{2} = \frac{2}{4} \qquad \begin{matrix}(1 \times 2 = 2)\\(2 \times 2 = 4)\end{matrix}$$

By multiplying $\frac{1}{2}$ by $\frac{2}{2}$, which is a fraction name for 1, we find that $\frac{1}{2}$ equals $\frac{2}{4}$. Notice that we multiply numerator by numerator and denominator by denominator. We can find other fractions equal to $\frac{1}{2}$ by multiplying by other fraction names for 1:

$$\frac{1}{2} \times \frac{3}{3} = \frac{3}{6} \qquad \frac{1}{2} \times \frac{4}{4} = \frac{4}{8} \qquad \frac{1}{2} \times \frac{5}{5} = \frac{5}{10}$$

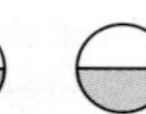

Example 3

Find four fractions equal to $\frac{1}{3}$ by multiplying $\frac{1}{3}$ by $\frac{2}{2}$, $\frac{3}{3}$, $\frac{4}{4}$, and $\frac{5}{5}$.

$$\frac{1}{3} \times \frac{2}{2} = \mathbf{\frac{2}{6}} \qquad \frac{1}{3} \times \frac{3}{3} = \mathbf{\frac{3}{9}}$$

$$\frac{1}{3} \times \frac{4}{4} = \mathbf{\frac{4}{12}} \qquad \frac{1}{3} \times \frac{5}{5} = \mathbf{\frac{5}{15}}$$

Each of our answers is a fraction equal to $\frac{1}{3}$.

Lesson Practice Name the equivalent fractions shown:

a. 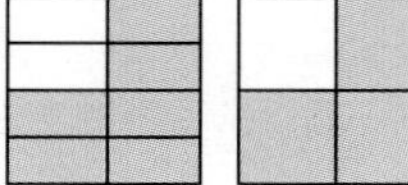 $\frac{6}{8} = \frac{3}{4}$

b. 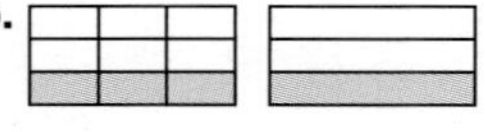 $\frac{3}{9} = \frac{1}{3}$

New Concept (Continued)

Example 3

Extend the Example

Lead students to generalize from this example that every fraction has an infinite number of equivalent fractions. Challenge your advanced learners by asking:

"In this example, we see how two halves, three thirds, four fourths, and five fifths can be used to find fractions that are equivalent to $\frac{1}{3}$. How can we find more fractions that are equivalent to $\frac{1}{3}$?" Multiply $\frac{1}{3}$ by other fractions that have the same numerator and denominator, such as $\frac{6}{6}$, $\frac{7}{7}$, $\frac{8}{8}$, and so on.

(continued)

Math Background

Finding equivalent fractions is useful when we want to compare fractions.

For example, suppose we want to compare $\frac{5}{9}$ and $\frac{7}{12}$ If we rewrite these fractions as equivalent fractions with the same denominator, we can easily determine which is greater. We will use the denominator 36 because it is a multiple of both 9 and 12. To write $\frac{5}{9}$ as an equivalent fraction with a denominator of 36, we multiply it by $\frac{4}{4}$. To write $\frac{7}{12}$ as an equivalent fraction with a denominator of 36, we multiply by $\frac{3}{3}$.

$$\frac{5}{9} \times \frac{4}{4} = \frac{20}{36} \qquad \frac{7}{12} \times \frac{3}{3} = \frac{21}{36}$$

Because $\frac{21}{36} > \frac{20}{36}$ we know that $\frac{7}{12} > \frac{5}{9}$.

New Concept (Continued)

Lesson Practice

Guided Practice
Use these problems as guided practice to check the students' understanding of today's concept.

Problems c–e Manipulative Use
Instead of drawing pictures to solve the problems, you might choose to have students use their fraction manipulatives.

If students draw pictures, emphasize the importance of drawing pairs of rectangles (or circles) that are the same size, and encourage them to use their fraction manipulatives to check their drawings.

Problems f–i
Error Alert
As they work, remind the students that multiplying a fraction by $\frac{2}{2}$, $\frac{3}{3}$, $\frac{4}{4}$, or $\frac{5}{5}$ is the same as multiplying the fraction by 1.

Closure **The questions below help assess the concepts taught in this lesson.**

"What does it mean when two fractions are equivalent?" Sample: The fractions are equal; They are different names for the same amount.

Write "$\frac{2}{3} \times \frac{4}{4}$" on the board or overhead. Then ask:

"Will multiplying the fraction two thirds by four fourths change the value of two thirds? Explain why or why not." No; $\frac{4}{4}$ is another name for 1, and multiplying a number by 1 does not change the value of the number.

Written Practice

Math Conversations

Independent Practice and Discussions to Increase Understanding

Problem 2

It is important for students to understand that when more than one operation is present in an equation, the order in which those operations are performed is very important. In other words, more than one answer may be possible, depending on which operation is performed first.

A number of different expressions can be written to represent the number that is six less than the sum of seven and eight; invite volunteers to list different expressions on the board.

(continued)

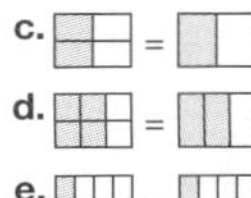

Draw pictures to show that the following pairs of fractions are equivalent:

c. $\frac{2}{4} = \frac{1}{2}$ **d.** $\frac{4}{6} = \frac{2}{3}$ **e.** $\frac{2}{8} = \frac{1}{4}$

Find four equivalent fractions for each fraction below. To do this, multiply each fraction by $\frac{2}{2}$, $\frac{3}{3}$, $\frac{4}{4}$, and $\frac{5}{5}$.

f. $\frac{1}{4}$ $\frac{2}{8}, \frac{3}{12}, \frac{4}{16}, \frac{5}{20}$ **g.** $\frac{5}{6}$ $\frac{10}{12}, \frac{15}{18}, \frac{20}{24}, \frac{25}{30}$ **h.** $\frac{2}{5}$ $\frac{4}{10}, \frac{6}{15}, \frac{8}{20}, \frac{10}{25}$ **i.** $\frac{1}{10}$ $\frac{2}{20}, \frac{3}{30}, \frac{4}{40}, \frac{5}{50}$

Written Practice

Distributed and Integrated

1. (Inv. 5) **Interpret** The pictograph shows the number of motor vehicles that were driven past Cruz's home during 1 hour. Use the pictograph to answer the questions that follow.

Type of Vehicle	Number of Vehicles
Cars	6 symbols
Trucks	2 symbols
Mopeds	half symbol
Motorcycles	1 and a half symbols

Key:  = 4 vehicles

a. What kind of vehicle was driven past Cruz's home two times? moped

b. Write a word sentence that compares the number of trucks to the number of cars. Sample: The number of trucks was $\frac{1}{3}$ of the number of cars.

c. Suppose ten bicyclists rode past Cruz's house. How many symbols would be needed to show the number of bicycles in the pictograph? Explain your answer. $2\frac{1}{2}$ symbols; sample: Each symbol represents 4 vehicles, and $10 \div 4 = 2\frac{1}{2}$.

▶ ***2.** (63) What number is six less than the sum of seven and eight? Write an expression. 9; $(7 + 8) - 6$

▶ ***3.** (94) Nell read three tenths of 180 pages in one day. How many pages did she read in one day? 54 pages

Inclusion

Use this strategy if the student displays:

- Poor Retention.
- Slow Learning Rate.

Equivalent Fractions (Individual)

Material: construction paper

- Pass out construction paper. Have student fold one piece in half and open it up. Ask, ***"What fraction does each side represent?"*** $\frac{1}{2}$
  Tell students to write $\frac{1}{2}$ on each side and refold the paper.
- Then have students fold it in half again and open it up. Ask, ***"What fraction does each side represent now?"*** $\frac{2}{4}$
  Have students write $= \frac{2}{4}$ next to the $\frac{1}{2}$ on each side and fold the paper back into fourths.
- Finally have the students fold the paper in half again and open it up. Ask, ***"What is another name for $\frac{1}{2}$ and $\frac{2}{4}$?"*** $\frac{4}{8}$
  Have students write $= \frac{4}{8}$ next to the other fractions.
- Pass out another piece of construction paper and have students fold it in thirds and label each section. Then have students fold it in half. Repeat the questioning and labeling for $\frac{1}{3}$ or $\frac{2}{6}$.

4. a. (21) The thermometer shows the temperature of a warm October day in Buffalo, New York. What temperature does the thermometer show? 67°F

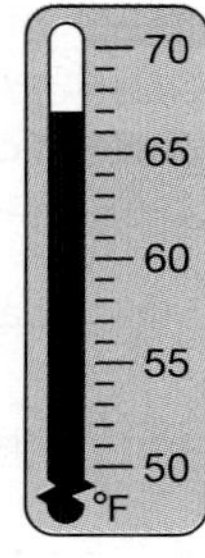

b. On a cold day in January an afternoon temperature could be 19°F. If the temperature dropped 22 degrees overnight, what would the temperature be? −3°F

5. (98) A circular disk, divided into 8 equal pieces, represents what fraction name for 1? $\frac{8}{8}$

6. a. (18, 42) What is the diameter of this dime? 18 mm

b. What is the radius of the dime? 9 mm

c. What is the diameter of the dime in centimeters? 1.8 cm

7. (37, 38, 39) There are 11 players on a football team, so when two teams play, there are 22 players on the field at one time. Across the county on a Friday night in October, many games are played. The table shows the number of players on the field for a given number of games. How many players are on the field in 5 games? 10 games? 110 players; 220 players

Number of games	1	2	3	4	5
Number of players	22	44	66	88	?

8. (13) Rick left home at the time shown on the clock and arrived at a friend's house 15 minutes later. At what time did Rick arrive at his friend's house? 4:09 p.m.

▶ ***9.** (99) **Represent** Change the improper fraction $\frac{5}{2}$ to a mixed number. Draw a picture that shows that the improper fraction and the mixed number are equal. $2\frac{1}{2}$;

Written Practice *(Continued)*

Math Conversations *(cont.)*

Problem 3

Some students may find it helpful to draw a picture (such as a rectangle) to solve this problem. Make sure these students recognize that the denominator of the fraction describes the number of equal parts the picture is to be divided into. After the division of 180 by 10, students should conclude that each equal part of the picture represents 18 pages.

Problem 9 **Represent**

Make sure students recall the importance of drawing shapes (such as rectangles or circles) that are congruent, and encourage them to use their fraction manipulatives to check their drawings.

(continued)

Written Practice *(Continued)*

Math Conversations *(cont.)*

Problem 10

Extend the Problem

Challenge your students to write an equation that can be used to find the number of push-ups (p) for any number of days (d).
Sample: $p = 2d + 10$

Problem 11 Interpret

The points can be identified two ways:

- Name two points on the line that are located at the intersection of two grid lines.
- Choose two numbers for x and for each number, solve the given equation for y.

A way for students to check their work is to use one method to solve the problem and the other method to check their answers.

Problem 14

Make sure students recognize that applying the Distributive Property will produce two products (5×60, or 300, and 5×3, or 15).

Problem 18 Multiple Choice

Test-Taking Strategy

Remind students to always read test questions carefully, and to reread the questions a second time when necessary.

It is important for students to understand that the condition "two pairs" eliminates answer choice **C** and the condition "certain" eliminates choices **A** and **D**.

(continued)

▸***10.** (11, 76, Inv. 10) Use the information below to answer parts **a** and **b**.

Chico did 12 push-ups on the first day. On each of the next four days, he did two more push-ups than he did the day before.

a. Altogether, Chico did how many push-ups in five days? 80

b. Make a table to represent the problem.

10b.

Day	1	2	3	4	5
Number of Push-ups	12	14	16	18	20

▸***11.** (Inv. 9, Inv. 10) Interpret Name two points on this line. Sample: (1, 4), (3, 8)

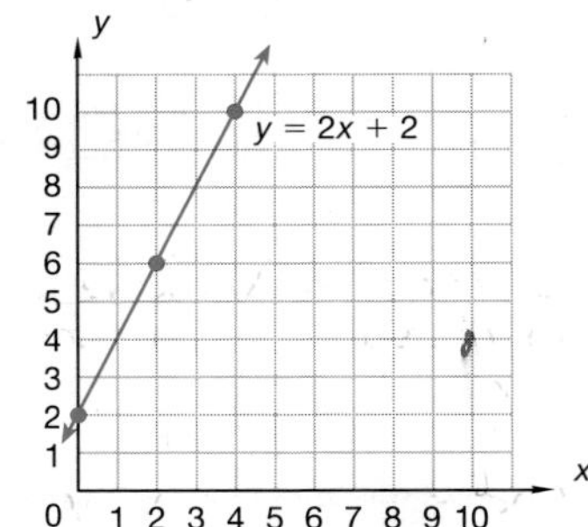

***12.** (64, 93) Analyze There are blue, orange, and grey marbles in a bag. There are twice as many orange marbles as there are blue marbles. There are two less grey marbles than orange. If there are 8 grey marbles, then how many blue are there? 5 blue

***13.** (103) Find three fractions equivalent to $\frac{2}{3}$ by multiplying $\frac{2}{3}$ by $\frac{2}{2}$, $\frac{3}{3}$, and $\frac{10}{10}$. $\frac{4}{6}, \frac{6}{9}, \frac{20}{30}$

▸***14.** (102) Since 63 equals 60 + 3, we may find 5×63 by finding 5(60 + 3). Use the Distributive Property to find 5(60 + 3). 300 + 15 = 315

***15.** (63, 88) Find ac when a is 18 and c is 22. 396

***16.** (101) Formulate A store owner had expenses of $12,000 and sales of $8000. Write a formula to show the profit or loss. Profit = Sales − Expenses, $8,000 − $12,000 = −$4,000

17. (Inv. 6, 95) Find the median, mode, and range of this set of scores:

100, 100, 95, 90, 90, 80, 80, 80, 60

Median, 90; mode, 80; range, 40

▸***18.** (90) **Multiple Choice** If a quadrilateral has two pairs of parallel sides, then the quadrilateral is certain to be a ______. B

A rectangle **B** parallelogram
C trapezoid **D** square

19. (8, 45) $v + 8.5 = 24.34$ 15.84

20. (45) $26.4 - 15.18$ 11.22

21. (23) $4 \times 3 \times 2 \times 1$ 24

22. (71) 26×30 780

23. (79, 83) $8\overline{)\$16.48}$ \$2.06

***24.** (34, 85) $10n = 250$ 25

***25.** (100) $\frac{5}{12} + \frac{6}{12}$ $\frac{11}{12}$

***26.** (100) $\frac{8}{12} - \frac{3}{12}$ $\frac{5}{12}$

27. (Inv. 3) How many square feet of paper are needed to cover a bulletin board that is 3 feet tall and 6 feet wide? 18 sq. ft

***28.** (93, 100) The bread recipe calls for $7\frac{1}{2}$ cups of flour to make 2 loaves of bread. The baker wants to make 4 loaves of bread. How many cups of flour does the baker need? 15 cups of flour

►***29.** (96) The backpackers camped in a tent. Refer to the figure at right to answer parts **a–c.**

a. The tent has the shape of what geometric solid? triangular prism

b. Including the bottom, how many faces does it have? 5 faces

c. How many edges does it have? 9 edges

► **30.** (19, 76) The flag of the United States has thirteen stripes. Six of the stripes are white, and the rest of the stripes are red.

a. How many red stripes are on the American flag? 7 red stripes

b. What fraction of the stripes on the American flag are white? $\frac{6}{13}$

c. What fraction of the stripes on the American flag are red? $\frac{7}{13}$

Written Practice *(Continued)*

Math Conversations *(cont.)*

Problem 29

Manipulative Use

Give students who have difficulty solving this problem an opportunity to inspect a triangular prism using Relational GeoSolids.

Problem 30

Real-World Connection

Students may be interested to learn that in 1818, Congress established what the colors and the number of stars and stripes for the American flag would be. White symbolizes purity and innocence, red symbolizes hardiness and valor, and blue symbolizes vigilance.

Errors and Misconceptions

Problem 2

Make sure students can infer from this problem that 6 must be written at the end of the expression because 6 is to be subtracted from $7 + 8$. It is not correct to write 6 at the beginning of the expression, as in $6 - (7 + 8)$, because the expression would represent the sum of $7 + 8$ being subtracted from 6.

In the answer $(7 + 8) - 6$, the parentheses are optional because without them, the expression would still be simplified by working from left to right. So $7 + 8 - 6$ is also a correct answer.

Finding equivalent fractions prepares students for:

- **Lesson 106,** reducing fractions.
- **Lesson 111,** simplifying fractions.
- **Lesson 112,** renaming fractions.
- **Lesson 113,** finding a common denominator and renaming fractions.

Use Equivalent Fractions to Find Common Denominators

Use this page to enhance conceptual understanding of key mathematical concepts.

Guided Instruction

The first method described on this page can be used to add or subtract any two fractions. However this method can result in denominators that are larger than necessary, resulting in answers that need to be simplified.

The second method can be more efficient. Ask students to solve the second problem using the first process to demonstrate the need to simplify the sum.

Extending the Concept

Some students may be interested in knowing why it is true that a common denominator for adding two fractions can always be found by multiplying the denominators of the fractions.

Add: $\frac{a}{b} + \frac{c}{d}$

We can show that

$\frac{a}{b} = \frac{ad}{bd}$, because $\frac{d}{d} = 1$ and

$\frac{c}{d} = \frac{bc}{bd}$, because $\frac{b}{b} = 1$

Then we can write:

$\frac{ad}{bd} + \frac{bc}{bd} = \frac{ad + bc}{bd}$

You might point out that:

- The numerator of the answer is the sum of the product of the first original numerator times the second original denominator and the product of the second original numerator times the first original denominator.
- The denominator of the answer is the product of the two original denominators.

Closure **The question below helps assess the concepts taught in this lesson.**

"Why is it always possible to rewrite two fractions so that they have the same denominator?" Sample: You can look for a common factor or common multiple, but if you can't find one, you can always multiply the two denominators.

California Mathematics Content Standards

NS 1.0, 1.5 Explain different interpretations of fractions, for example, parts of a whole, parts of a set, and division of whole numbers by whole numbers; explain equivalents of fractions (see Standard 4.0).

MR 1.0, 1.1 Analyze problems by identifying relationships, distinguishing relevant from irrelevant information, sequencing and prioritizing information, and observing patterns.

• Use Equivalent Fractions to Find Common Denominators

Equivalent fractions are fractions that represent the same number.

When we add or subtract fractions, we write the fractions with common denominators first. There are a few ways to do this.

Method 1 Multiply the denominators.

$\frac{2}{3} + \frac{1}{5}$	We want the fractions to have the same denominator.
$3 \times 5 = 15$	We multiply the denominators to find the common denominator.
$\frac{2 \times 5}{3 \times 5}$ and $\frac{1 \times 3}{5 \times 3}$	We must multiply the numerator and denominator by the same number.
$\frac{10}{15} + \frac{3}{15} = \frac{13}{15}$	The two fractions now have a common denominator of 15. Now we add.

Method 2 Find the least common multiple of each denominator.

$\frac{1}{6} + \frac{3}{4}$	We want the fractions to have the same denominator.
$\frac{1}{6} \cdot \frac{2}{2} + \frac{3}{4} \cdot \frac{3}{3}$	12 is a multiple of 6 and 4. We can use 12 for the common denominator instead of 24.
$\frac{2}{12} + \frac{9}{12} = \frac{11}{12}$	The two renamed fractions have the same denominator. We can add.

Apply Decide the best way to find a common denominator.

a. $\frac{3}{4} - \frac{5}{12}$

a. find the LCM of the denominators

b. $\frac{3}{5} + \frac{1}{3}$

b. find the product of the denominators

California Mathematics Content Standards

NS 1.0, 1.1 Read and write whole numbers in the millions.

NS 1.0, 1.3 Round whole numbers through the millions to the nearest ten, hundred, thousand, ten thousand, or hundred thousand.

MR 2.0, 2.3 Use a variety of methods, such as words, numbers, symbols, charts, graphs, tables, diagrams, and models, to explain mathematical reasoning.

Planning & Preparation

• Rounding Whole Numbers Through Hundred Millions

Objectives

- Round whole numbers to the nearest hundred thousand and the nearest million.

Prerequisite Skills

- Using words and digits to name numbers through hundred thousands.
- Reading, comparing, and ordering numbers through hundred millions.
- Rounding numbers to the nearest ten and hundred using a number line.
- Using a number line to round numbers to the nearest thousand.

Materials

Instructional Masters

- Power Up A Worksheet
- Lesson Activity 8
- Lesson Activity 21*

Manipulative Kit

- Base ten blocks*

Teacher-provided materials

- Centimeter grid paper
- Fraction manipulatives from Investigation 8, place-value workmat, place-value chart, one inch grid paper*

**optional*

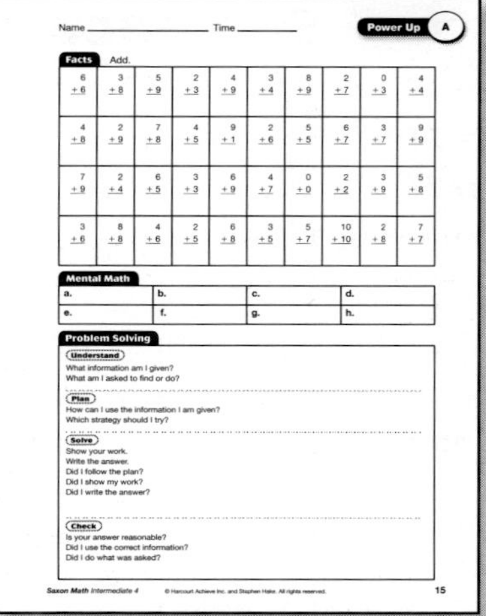

Power Up A Worksheet

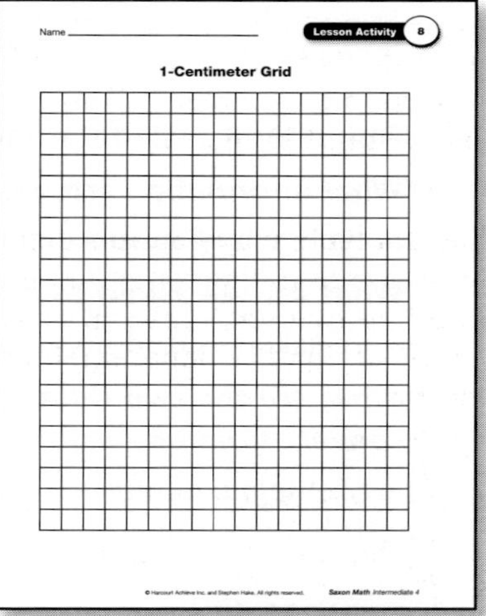

Lesson Activity 8

Universal Access

Reaching All Special Needs Students

Special Education Students	At-Risk Students	English Learners	Advanced Learners
• Inclusion (TM) • Adaptations for Saxon Math	• Alternative Approach (TM) • Error Alert (TM) • Reteaching Masters • Refresher Lessons for California Standards	• English Learners (TM) • Developing Academic Language (TM) • English Learner Handbook	• Extend the Example (TM) • Extend the Problem (TM) • Online Activities

TM=Teacher's Manual

Developing Academic Language

Maintained	**English Learner**
hundred thousand	touchdown
million	
ten thousand	

Problem Solving Discussion

Problem

Todd rode his bicycle down his 50-foot driveway and counted eight full turns of the front wheel. How many times will the front wheel turn if he rides 100 yards?

Focus Strategies

ABC **Make It Simpler**

2+3=5 **Write a Number Sentence or Equation**

Understand *Understand the problem.*

"What information are we given?"

A bicycle wheel makes eight full turns in 50 feet.

"What are we asked to do?"

We are asked to find how many times the wheel would turn in 100 yards.

"What are the two different units of length in the problem? How can we convert from one unit to the other?"

The problem contains a measurement in feet and a measurement in yards. We can multiply the number of yards by 3 to find the number of feet.

Plan *Make a plan.*

"How can we use the information we know to solve the problem?"

We can find how many feet are in 100 yards. Then we can find how many 50-foot driveways would equal 100 yards.

"What do we anticipate our answer will be in the range of?"

Discuss student responses.

Solve *Carry out the plan.*

"How many feet are in 100 yards?"

100×3 feet $= 300$ feet

"How many 50-foot driveways would it take to equal 300 feet?"

This is an equal-groups problem. We can think, "What number times 50 feet equals 300 feet?" Since $6 \times 50 = 300$, we find that six 50-foot driveways equal 300 feet.

"How many full turns would the wheel make over a distance of 100 yards?"

The wheel turns eight times when Todd rides it down the 50-foot driveway. One hundred yards is six times as long as the driveway, so the wheel would turn 6×8 times, or 48 times, if Todd were to ride his bike 100 yards.

Check *Look back.*

"Is our answer reasonable?"

We know that our answer is reasonable because 100 yards is six times the length of Todd's driveway. Todd's bicycle wheel makes eight full turns along the driveway, so it would make $6 \times 8 = 48$ full turns in 300 feet.

"Does our answer match our estimates?"

Discuss student estimates and why they were close to or far from the actual answer.

LESSON 104

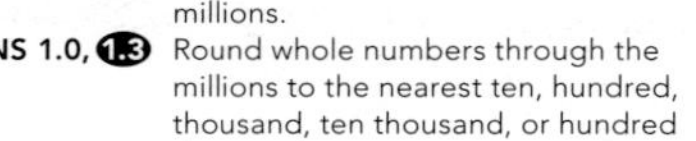

California Mathematics Content Standards

NS 1.0, 1.1 Read and write whole numbers in the millions.

NS 1.0, 1.3 Round whole numbers through the millions to the nearest ten, hundred, thousand, ten thousand, or hundred thousand.

MR 2.0, 2.3 Use a variety of methods, such as words, numbers, symbols, charts, graphs, tables, diagrams, and models, to explain mathematical reasoning.

• Rounding Whole Numbers Through Hundred Millions

Power Up

facts Power Up A

mental math Think of one cent more or less than quarters in problems **a–c.**

a. Number Sense: 425 + 374 799

b. Number Sense: 550 − 324 226

c. Number Sense: \$4.49 + \$2.26 \$6.75

d. Number Sense: 15 × 40 600

e. Time: Each section of the test takes 25 minutes. There is a 5-minute break between sections. If the class starts the test at 9:00 a.m., how many sections can the class finish by 10:30 a.m.? 3 sections

f. Estimation: Estimate 35 × 25. Round 35 to 40, round 25 down to 20, and then multiply. 800

g. Calculation: 2 × 2, square the number, + 4, ÷ 5, − 4 0

h. Simplify: $2b$ when $b = 5$ 10

problem solving Choose an appropriate problem-solving strategy to solve this problem. Todd rode his bicycle down his 50-foot driveway and counted eight full turns of the front wheel. How many times will the front wheel turn if he rides 100 yards? 48 times

New Concept

In this lesson we will practice rounding large numbers to the nearest ten thousand, the nearest hundred thousand, and so on through the nearest hundred million.

Recall the locations of the whole-number place values through hundred millions:

Facts Add.

6 + 6 12	3 + 8 11	5 + 9 14	2 + 3 5	4 + 9 13	3 + 4 7	8 + 9 17	2 + 7 9	0 + 3 3	4 + 4 8
4 + 8 12	2 + 9 11	7 + 8 15	4 + 5 9	9 + 1 10	2 + 6 8	5 + 5 10	6 + 7 13	3 + 7 10	9 + 9 18
7 + 9 16	2 + 4 6	6 + 5 11	3 + 3 6	6 + 9 15	4 + 7 11	0 + 0 0	2 + 2 4	3 + 9 12	5 + 8 13
3 + 6 9	8 + 8 16	4 + 6 10	2 + 5 7	6 + 8 14	3 + 5 8	5 + 7 12	10 + 10 20	2 + 8 10	7 + 7 14

Power Up

Facts

Distribute **Power Up A** to students. See answers below.

Count Aloud

Before students begin the Mental Math exercises, do these counting exercises as a class.

Count up and down by sevens from 28 to 63.

Mental Math

Encourage students to share different ways to mentally compute these exercises. Strategies for exercises are listed below.

a. Add 100's, then 10's, then 1's

(400 + 300) + (20 + 70) + (5 + 4) = 700 + 90 + 9 = 799

Subtract 25 and Add 25

425 − 25 = 400; 374 + 25 = 399; 400 + 399 = 799

d. Attach One Zero to 15 x 4

15 × 4 = 60; 15 × 40 = 600

Decompose 15

40 × (10 + 5) = 400 + 200 = 600

Problem Solving

Refer to **Problem-Solving Strategy Discussion**, p. 689B.

New Concept

Math Language

This lesson presents an excellent opportunity to have students practice reading numbers aloud.

Manipulative Use

You may wish to display the *Place-Value Chart* poster as you discuss rounding whole numbers with students.

(continued)

New Concept *(Continued)*

Example 1

Active Learning

As you discuss the solution, write the number 12,500,000 on the board or overhead and point out that it is the number that is halfway between 12 million and 13 million.

Ask students to explain why 12,876,250 is rounded up to the next million. Sample: 12,876,250 is to the right of 12,500,000 on a number line and thus greater than 12,500,000.

Examples 2 and 3

As you discuss the solutions to Examples 2 and 3, lead students to these generalizations:

- If the digit to the right of the rounding place is less than 5, the digit in the rounding place does not change, and all digits to the right of that place are changed to zero.
- If the digit to the right of the rounding place is 5 or more, the digit in the rounding place is increased by 1 and all digits to the right of that place are changed to zero.

Extend the Example

Challenge your advanced learners to round 216,458,500 to the nearest hundred millions. 200,000,000

Error Alert

If students find it difficult to identify the place values of a number, suggest that they read the number aloud.

Explanation

The two strategies presented in the examples in this lesson both represent correct ways to round numbers. Encourage students to choose the strategy they are most comfortable with to solve problems that involve rounding. Also encourage them to use one strategy to solve a rounding problem, and use a different strategy to check their work.

Students can explore the Internet to find examples of numbers through hundred millions. These will most likely be values in science (e.g. diameter of the earth). Then have them round the numbers to the nearest ten millions, millions, and hundred thousands.

(continued)

Whole Number Place Values

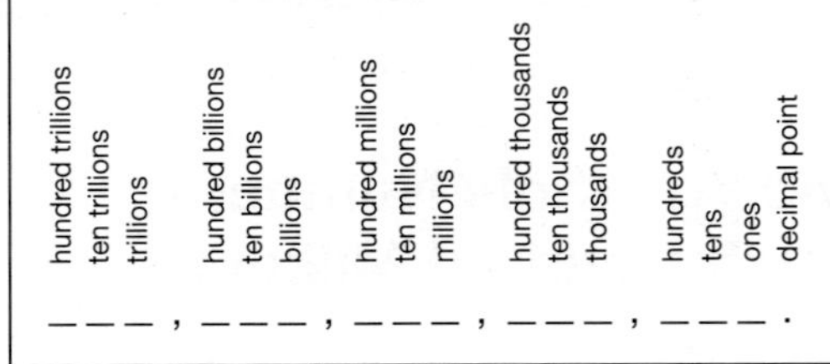

After rounding to the nearest ten thousand, each place to the right of the ten-thousands place will be zero.

Analyze How is the value of each place related to the value of the place to its right? Sample: Each place is 10 times greater than the place to its right.

Example 1

Round 12,876,250 to the nearest million.

The number begins with "twelve million." Counting by millions from 12 million, we say "twelve million, thirteen million," and so on. We know that 12,876,250 is between 12 million and 13 million. Since 12,876,250 is more than halfway to 13 million, we round up to **13,000,000.**

Example 2

Round 16,458,500 to the nearest hundred thousand.

Since we want to round to the nearest hundred thousand, we look at the place to the right of the hundred thousands place—the ten thousands place.

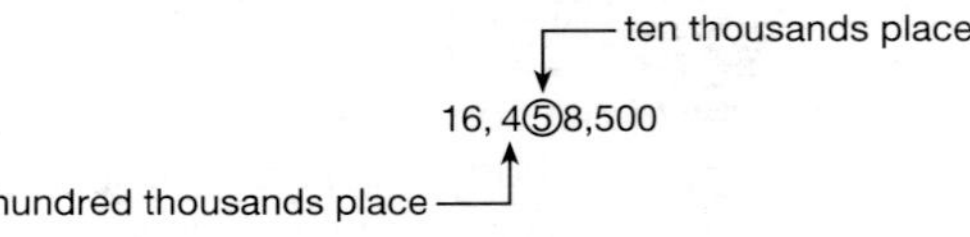

The digit in the ten thousands place is 5 so we add 1 to the digit in the hundred thousands place. All the digits to the right of the hundred thousands place become zeros.

To the nearest hundred thousand, 16,458,500 rounds to **16,500,000.**

Math Background

A method for rounding a whole number to any place is to underline the digit in the place you are rounding to. Then look at the digit to the right of the underlined digit, and consider the following:

- If it is less than 5, change all the digits to the right of the underlined digits to 0.
- If it is 5 or greater, increase the underlined digit by 1 and change all the digits to the right of the underlined digit to 0.

For example, to round 384,321 to the nearest ten thousand, underline the 8: 3<u>8</u>4,321. The digit to the right of 8 is 4, which is less than 5. Change the digits to the right of 8 to 0 to get 380,000.

To round 2754 to the nearest hundred, underline the 7: 2<u>7</u>54. The digit to the right of 7 is 5, which is 5 or greater. So, increase 7 to 8 and change the digits to the right to 0s. The rounded number is 2800.

Example 3

Round 237,984,000 to the nearest hundred million.

Since we want to round to the nearest hundred million, we look at the place to the right of the hundred millions place—the ten millions place.

2③7,984,000 (ten millions place: 3; hundred millions place: 2)

The digit in the ten millions place is 3 so we leave the digit in the hundred millions place unchanged. All the digits to the right of the hundred millions place become zeros.

To the nearest hundred million, 237,984,000 rounds to **200,000,000.**

Lesson Practice

a. Round 2,156,324 to the nearest million. 2,000,000

b. Round 28,376,000 to the nearest ten million. 30,000,000

c. Round 412,500,000 to the nearest hundred million. 400,000,000

Estimate Round each number to the nearest hundred thousand:

d. 5,346,891 5,300,000 **e.** 75,965,000 76,000,000 **f.** 350,525,000 350,500,000

Written Practice

Distributed and Integrated

► ***1.** (87) **Analyze** Eighty students were divided among three classrooms as equally as possible. Write three numbers to show how many students were in each of the three classrooms. 26, 27, 27

***2.** (63) **Formulate** When the sum of three and four is subtracted from the product of three and four, what is the difference? Write an equation to solve the problem. 5; $(3 \times 4) - (3 + 4) = d$

3. (93) **Explain** Irma is twice as old as her sister and three years younger than her brother. Irma's sister is six years old. How old is Irma's brother? What is the first step? 15 years old; First find Irma's age.

► ***4.** (94) Four ninths of 513 fans cheered when the touchdown was scored. How many fans cheered? 228 fans

English Learners

Explain to your students that a **touchdown** is when a football team scores by taking the ball to the end zone. Ask:

"Do you know how many points a team scores if they make a touchdown?" 6 points

Ask:

"Are there any other types of touchdowns?" Samples: when airplanes land, in rugby

New Concept *(Continued)*

Lesson Practice

Guided Practice

Use these problems as guided practice to check the students' understanding of today's concept.

Problem a

To help students get started, ask:

"What place value are we to round this number to?" millions

"What numbers in millions is this number between?" 2 million and 3 million

"How do we decide which number—2 million or 3 million—is the correct answer?" Sample: Since 2,156,324 is closer to 2 million than 3 million, the correct answer is 2 million.

Problem c

Write the number 27,399 on the board or overhead and then ask your students to state two different place values that make the sentence below true.

"If we round this number to the _____ place and to the _____ place, the result will be the same number." hundreds; tens

Problems d–f **Estimate**

Error Alert

If students are having difficulty finding the place values of the numbers, have them refer to the *Place-Value Chart* poster.

Closure

The questions below help assess the concepts taught in this lesson.

Write the number 349,850 on the board or overhead. Then say:

"Explain how to round this number to the nearest thousand." Sample: Counting by thousands, 349,850 is between 349,000 and 350,000. The number halfway between 349,000 and 350,000 is 349,500. Since 349,850 is greater than 349,500, we round to 350,000.

Written Practice

Math Conversations

Independent Practice and Discussions to Increase Understanding

Problem 1 (Analyze)

After students read the problem and understand that division is used to find the answer, ask them to decide if 80 is divisible by 3. No Then help them conclude that because 80 ÷ 3 includes a remainder, it will not be possible to have the same number of students in each classroom.

Problem 4

Some students may find it helpful to draw a picture (such as a rectangle) to solve this problem. Make sure these students recognize that the denominator of the fraction describes the number of equal parts the picture is to be divided into. After the division of 513 by 9, students should conclude that each equal part in the picture represents 57 cheering fans.

Problem 5 (Connect)

Extend the Problem

Have students recall that multiplying a number by 1 does not change the value of the number. Then ask:

"What name for 1 can we multiply $\frac{1}{2}$ by to change $\frac{1}{2}$ to $\frac{3}{6}$?" $\frac{3}{3}$

"What name for 1 can we multiply $\frac{1}{2}$ by to change $\frac{1}{2}$ to $\frac{4}{8}$?" $\frac{4}{4}$

Remind students that $\frac{3}{3}$ and $\frac{4}{4}$ are equivalent to 1 because a fraction bar is a symbol for division, and any number divided by itself is 1.

Problem 9

Manipulative Use

Encourage students to use their fraction pieces to solve the problem or to check their work.

Problem 11

Extend the Problem

Ask students to name the change Kia should receive if she paid with a ten-dollar bill. Name as few bills and coins as possible. One $1 bill, one dime, one nickel, two pennies

(continued)

▸ *5. (103) (Connect) These circles show fractions equivalent to $\frac{1}{2}$. Name the fractions shown. $\frac{3}{6}$, $\frac{4}{8}$

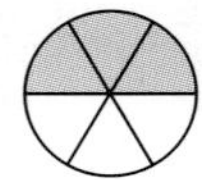
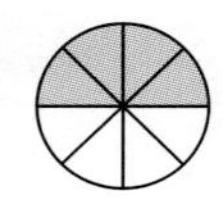

*6. (102) (Analyze) Use the Distributive Property to multiply 34 and 65. $34(60 + 5) = (34 \times 60) + (34 \times 5)$ $= 2040 + 170$ $= 2210$

*7. (104) (Represent) Round each number to the given place:

a. Round 13,458,912 to the nearest ten million. 10,000,000

b. Round 13,458,912 to the nearest million. 13,000,000

c. Round 13,458,912 to the nearest hundred thousand. 13,500,000

d. Round 13,458,912 to the nearest ten thousand. 13,460,000

*8. (61) (Explain) In a sporting goods store, an aluminum baseball bat sells for $38.49, a baseball sells for $4.99, and a baseball glove sells for $24.95. What is a reasonable estimate of the cost of a bat, a glove, and two baseballs? Explain why your estimate is reasonable. Sample: I used compatible numbers; Since $38.49 is close to $40, $4.99 × 2 is close to $5 × 2, and $24.95 is close to $25, $40 + $10 + $25, or $75, is a reasonable estimate.

▸ *9. (99) Change the improper fraction $\frac{5}{2}$ to a mixed number. $2\frac{1}{2}$

10. (60) Paul ran 7 miles in 42 minutes. What was the average number of minutes it took Paul to run one mile? 6 minutes

▸ 11. (101) Kia bought 3 scarves priced at $2.75 each. Tax was 58 cents. How much did she pay for the scarves? Write a formula to solve the problem. $8.83; Original + Tax = Total Cost

12. (93) (Analyze) Two tickets for the play cost $26. At that rate, how much would twenty tickets cost? $260

*13. (100) Dawn is $49\frac{1}{2}$ inches tall. Tim is $47\frac{1}{2}$ inches tall. Dawn is how many inches taller than Tim? 2 inches

14. (45) $7.43 + 6.25 + 12.7$ 26.38

15. (8, 45) $q + 7.5 = 14.36$ 6.86

16. (85) 90×800 720,000

17. (28, 38) $f \times 73¢$ if $f = 8$ $5.84

18. (23) $7 \times 6 \times 5 \times 0$ 0

19. (65, 88) 15^2 225

Inclusion

Use this strategy if the student displays:

- Difficulty with Large Group Instruction.
- Slow Learning Rate.

Rounding Whole Numbers (Individual)

Material: place-value mat

- Copy the place value chart on to mats if possible or onto the board.

Whole Number Place Values

hundred trillions	ten trillions	trillions	,	hundred billions	ten billions	billions	,	hundred millions	ten millions	millions	,	hundred thousands	ten thousands	thousands	,	hundreds	tens	ones	decimal point
___	___	___	,	___	___	___	,	___	___	___	,	___	___	___	,	___	___	___	.

- Write 359,021 on the board. Ask, ***"What group do we look at when rounding to the ten-thousands?"*** thousands ***"Are there more than 5 in this group?"*** Yes
- Have students round up by adding 1 to the ten-thousand group and placing zeros to the right of it. Ask, ***"What is 359, 021 rounded to the ten-thousands?"*** 360,000
- Using the chart have students work together with a partner to round 446,291 to the thousands place and then again to the hundred thousands place.

20. 60×5^2 1500
(65, 71)

21. $\sqrt{49} \times \sqrt{49}$ 49
(Inv. 3)

▶*22. $5\frac{1}{3} + 3\frac{1}{3}$ $8\frac{2}{3}$
(100)

▶*23. $4\frac{4}{5} - 3\frac{3}{5}$ $1\frac{1}{5}$
(100)

▶*24. $\frac{1242}{6}$ 207
(83)

*25. $4\overline{)3000}$ 750
(83)

26. This square has a perimeter of 8 cm. Find the length of each side. Then find the area of the square. 2 cm; 4 cm²
(20, 66)

▶*27. Refer to this bus schedule to answer parts **a–c.**
(RF13, 13)

Route 346

Destination	Arrival Time	Arrival Time	Arrival Time
	6:43 a.m.	7:25 a.m.	3:45 p.m.
5th & Western	6:50 a.m.	7:32 a.m.	3:50 p.m.
5th & Cypress	6:54 a.m.	7:36 a.m.	3:55 p.m.
Cypress & Hill	7:01 a.m.	7:43 a.m.	4:03 p.m.
Hill & Lincoln	7:08 a.m.	7:50 a.m.	4:12 p.m.
Lincoln & 5th	7:16 a.m.	7:58 a.m.	4:20 p.m.

a. Ella catches the 6:50 a.m. bus at 5th and Western. When can she expect to arrive at Hill and Lincoln? 7:08 a.m.

b. If the bus runs on schedule, how many minutes is her ride? 18 min

c. If Ella misses the 6:50 a.m. bus, then when can she catch the next Route 346 bus at that corner? 7:32 a.m.

28. When Xena says a number, Yoli doubles the number and adds 3. Xena and Yoli record their numbers in a table.
(64, 93)

X	1	2	5	7
Y	5	7	13	17

a. **Predict** What number does Yoli say if Xena says 11? 25

b. **Generalize** Write an equation that shows the relationship of X and Y.
$Y = 2X + 3$

Alternative Approach: Using Manipulatives

Provide students with place-value charts to help them name and work with larger numbers in the lesson. Encourage students to write or paste a copy of a place-value chart in their math notebooks.

Teacher Tip

Make 1-inch grid paper available for students when working with writing large numbers. Advise students to put either one digit or a comma in its own box as they write large numbers.

Written Practice *(Continued)*

Math Conversations *(cont.)*

Problems 22 and 23

"A mixed number is made up of a fraction and a whole number. When we add or subtract mixed numbers, which part of those numbers do we add or subtract first?" The fractions

Problem 24

Extend the Problem

Challenge your advanced learners to describe different ways that the answer can be checked using only mental math. Sample: Break apart 207 to 200 + 7, then multiply, add, and compare the result to the dividend; $6(200 + 7) = 1200 + 42 = 1242$

Problem 27

Some students may find it helpful if you explain how the schedule is read.

(continued)

Written Practice (Continued)

Math Conversations (cont.)

Problem 30 Represent

The following sample graph is provided to help guide students:

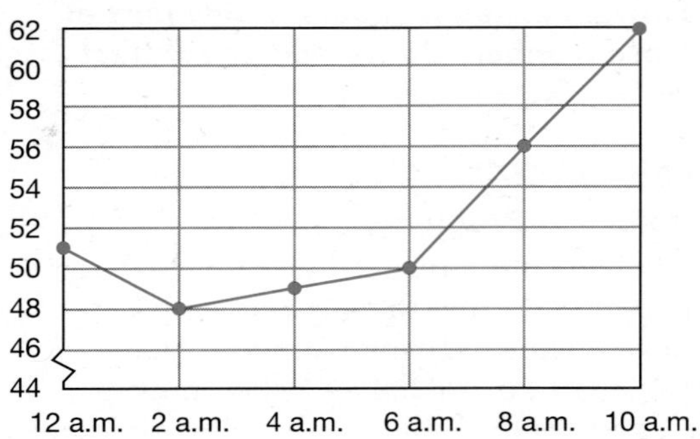

Errors and Misconceptions

Problem 1

A common error when solving problems of this nature is to assign the remainder of the division to one group. For example, when dividing 80 students among 3 classrooms, 26 students will be assigned to each classroom because $80 \div 3 = 26$ R 2, and the two students who are represented by the remainder are assigned to the same classroom.

Make sure students understand that the phrase "as equally as possible" requires them to compensate for the remainder by assigning 1 student to each of two classrooms because classrooms numbering 26, 27, and 27 are more equal in number than classrooms numbering 26, 26, and 28.

*29. (Inv. 10) **Interpret** Use the graph below to solve parts **a–b.**

a. Kyle earns $5 per hour packing boxes. How long will it take him to earn $50? 10 hours

b. Write an equation to show the relationship between hours and dollars. $5h = d$ where h = hours and d = dollars

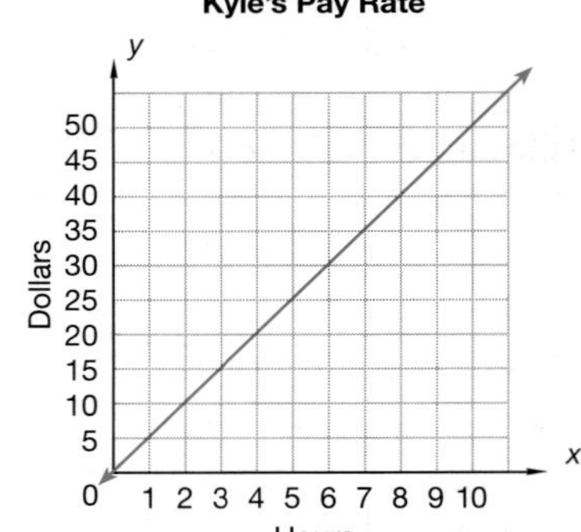

*30. (Inv. 5) **Represent** A variety of morning times and temperatures are shown in the table below:

Morning Temperatures

Time	Temperature (°F)
12:00 a.m.	51
2:00 a.m.	48
4:00 a.m.	49
6:00 a.m.	50
8:00 a.m.	56
10:00 a.m.	62

Display the data in a line graph. Then write one statement that describes the data. See student work; sample: The temperature decreased and then increased.

Rounding whole numbers to the nearest hundred thousand and the nearest million prepares students for:

- **Lesson 107,** multiplying a three-digit number by a two-digit number.

Planning & Preparation

• Factoring Whole Numbers

Objectives
- Factor whole numbers different ways.
- Find the prime factors of whole numbers.

Prerequisite Skills
- Drawing arrays and area models to represent factors of a given number.
- Distinguishing between prime and composite numbers.
- Using division to find a missing factor.

Materials
Instructional Masters
- Power Up A Worksheet
- Lesson Activity 8*

Manipulative Kit
- Rulers
- Color tiles*

Teacher-provided materials
- Grid paper*

**optional*

California Mathematics Content Standards

NS 4.0, 4.1 Understand that many whole numbers break down in different ways (e.g., 12 = 4 × 3 = 2 × 6 = 2 × 2 × 3).

NS 4.0, 4.2 Know that numbers such as 2, 3, 5, 7, and 11 do not have any factors except 1 and themselves and that such numbers are called prime numbers.

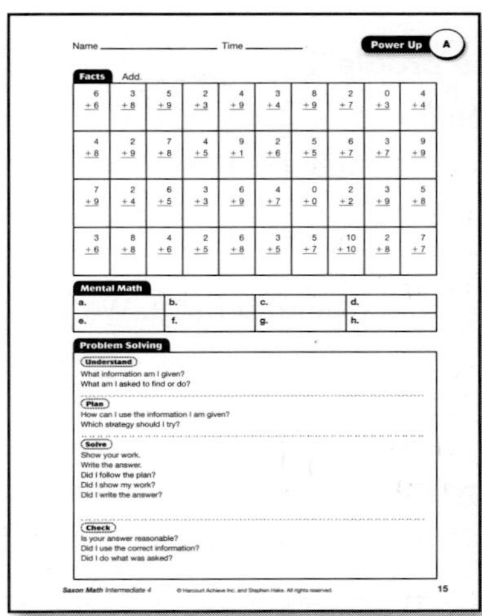
Name Time
Power Up A
Facts Add.
Mental Math
Problem Solving
Understand
Plan
Solve
Check

Power Up A Worksheet

Universal Access

Reaching All Special Needs Students

Special Education Students	At-Risk Students	English Learners	Advanced Learners
• Inclusion (TM) • Adaptations for Saxon Math	• Alternative Approach (TM) • Error Alert (TM) • Reteaching Masters • Refresher Lessons for California Standards	• English Learners (TM) • Developing Academic Language (TM) • English Learner Handbook	• Extend the Example (TM) • Extend the Problem (TM) • Online Activities

TM=Teacher's Manual

Developing Academic Language

New	Maintained	English Learner
prime factors	factors product	prime

Problem Solving Discussion

Problem

This sequence has an alternating pattern. Copy this sequence on your paper, and continue the sequence to 18. Then describe the pattern in words.

0, 5, 3, 8, 6, 11, 9, 14, ...

Focus Strategy

Find/Extend a Pattern

Understand *Understand the problem.*

"What information are we given?"

We are given the first eight terms of a sequence. We are told that the sequence has an alternating pattern.

"What are we asked to do?"

We are asked to copy the sequence and extend it to 18. We are also asked to describe the pattern in words.

Plan *Make a plan.*

"What problem-solving strategy will we use to solve the problem?"

We will *find a pattern* and then *extend the pattern.*

Solve *Carry out the plan.*

"How can we find the pattern?"

We can find the increase or decrease that occurs between consecutive terms of the pattern:

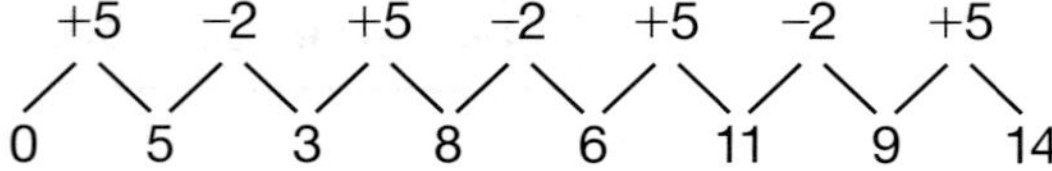

"What is the pattern for the sequence?"

The pattern alternates between an increase of 5 and a decrease of 2.

"What are the next five terms of the sequence?"

We continue the alternating pattern:

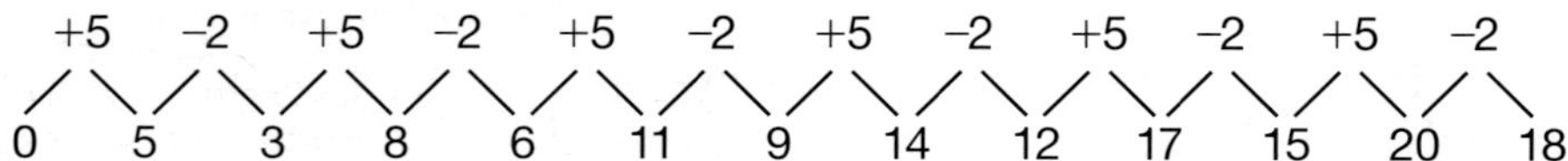

Check *Look back.*

"Did we complete the task that was assigned?"

Yes. We continued the sequence to 18 by finding the next five terms. The next five terms are 12, 17, 15, 20, 18.

"How would you describe the pattern in words?"

The pattern to the sequence is "increase by five, then decrease by two."

LESSON 105

• Factoring Whole Numbers

California Mathematics Content Standards

NS 4.0, 4.1 Understand that many whole numbers break down in different ways (e.g., 12 = 4 × 3 = 2 × 6 = 2 × 2 × 3).

NS 4.0, 4.2 Know that numbers such as 2, 3, 5, 7, and 11 do not have any factors except 1 and themselves and that such numbers are called prime numbers.

Power Up

facts Power Up A

mental math Think of one cent more or less than quarters in problems **a–c.**

a. **Number Sense:** 126 + 375 501

b. **Number Sense:** 651 − 225 426

c. **Number Sense:** \$6.51 + \$2.75 \$9.26

d. **Money:** The atlas cost \$16.25. Amol paid for it with a \$20 bill. How much change should he receive? \$3.75

e. **Measurement:** Fran drank $1\frac{1}{2}$ quarts of water. How many pints did she drink? 3 pt

f. **Estimation:** Estimate 32 × 28. 900

g. **Calculation:** 40 ÷ 4, × 6, + 4, $\sqrt{\ }$, − 8 0

h. **Simplify:** $d + 6$ when $d = 8$ 14

problem solving Choose an appropriate problem-solving strategy to solve this problem. This sequence has an alternating pattern. Copy this sequence on your paper, and continue the sequence to 18. Then describe the pattern in words. 12, 17, 15, 20, 18; Increase by five, then decrease by two.

0, 5, 3, 8, 6, 11, 9, 14, ...

New Concept

Math Language

Recall that a prime number is a number that has only two factors itself and 1.

We have learned to write a number as the product to two factors.

24 = 1 × 24, 2 × 12, 3 × 8, and 4 × 6

Today, we will learn how to write a number as the product of three or more factors.

Facts Add.

6 + 6 12	3 + 8 11	5 + 9 14	2 + 3 5	4 + 9 13	3 + 4 7	8 + 9 17	2 + 7 9	0 + 3 3	4 + 4 8
4 + 8 12	2 + 9 11	7 + 8 15	4 + 5 9	9 + 1 10	2 + 6 8	5 + 5 10	6 + 7 13	3 + 7 10	9 + 9 18
7 + 9 16	2 + 4 6	6 + 5 11	3 + 3 6	6 + 9 15	4 + 7 11	0 + 0 0	2 + 2 4	3 + 9 12	5 + 8 13
3 + 6 9	8 + 8 16	4 + 6 10	2 + 5 7	6 + 8 14	3 + 5 8	5 + 7 12	10 + 10 20	2 + 8 10	7 + 7 14

Power Up

Facts

Distribute **Power Up A** to students. See answers below.

Count Aloud

Before students begin the Mental Math exercises, do these counting exercises as a class.

Count up and down by elevens from 33 to 110.

Mental Math

Encourage students to share different ways to mentally compute these exercises. Strategies for exercises are listed below.

a. Subtract 1, then Add 1

126 − 1 = 125; 125 + 375 = 500; 500 + 1 = 501

b. Subtract 1, then Add 1

651 − 1 = 650; 650 − 225 = 425; 425 + 1 = 426

d. Count On

\$16.25 to \$17 is 75¢; \$17 to \$20 is \$3; 75¢ + \$3 = \$3.75

Count Back

\$20 − \$3 = \$17; \$17 − 75¢ = \$16.25; \$3 + 75¢ = \$3.75

Problem Solving

Refer to **Problem-Solving Strategy Discussion,** p. 695B.

New Concept

Active Learning

As you discuss the different ways that 24 can be rewritten as the product of two or more factors, ask students to identify the various factors and compare them to 24 using terms such as "greater than," "less than," or "equal to."

Conclude your discussion by asking students to state a generalization about the factors of a number. Sample: All of the factors of a number are less than or equal to the number; A factor of a number is never greater than the number.

(continued)

New Concept *(Continued)*

Example 1

Explain that whenever students are asked to write all of the different factor pairs of a number, it is helpful to find those factors in an organized way. For example, begin with 1. Since we know that every number is divisible by 1, write the factor pair. Next, decide if the number is odd or even. If it is even, write the factor pair that includes 2 and test for divisibility by other multiples of 2 such as 4, 6, and 8. To test for divisibility by 3, decide if the sum of the factors is divisible by 3. If it is, write the factor pairs and then test for divisibility by other multiples of 3, such as 6 and 9.

Lead students to conclude that working in an organized way will reduce the likelihood that one or more factor pairs are overlooked.

Extend the Example

Challenge your advanced learners by asking them to list all the factors of 48. 1, 2, 3, 4, 6, 8, 12, 16, 24, 48

Example 2

Have students note that the factor pair of 2 and 20 was used to begin the tree, and then explain that we instead could have used any factor pairs of 40, such as 5 and 8, or 4 and 10, for example.

Discussion

After you discuss the solution, make sure students understand that whenever we write the prime factorization of a number (such as $2 \times 2 \times 2 \times 5$), we write the factors in order from least to greatest.

Error Alert

Although any factor pair can be used to begin the tree, the likelihood of mistakes may be reduced if students choose a factor pair in which the factors are close together, such as 5 and 8 or 4 and 10. These factor pairs produce a more "balanced" tree in which the branches are more likely to be similar lengths. When the branches are not similar lengths, students may be more likely to overlook factors that are at the ends of branches elsewhere in the tree.

(continued)

Below are some ways we can write 24 as the product of three factors.

$$24 = 2 \times 2 \times 6,\ 1 \times 12 \times 2, \text{ and } 2 \times 3 \times 4$$

Another way to write 24 is as the product of *prime factors.*

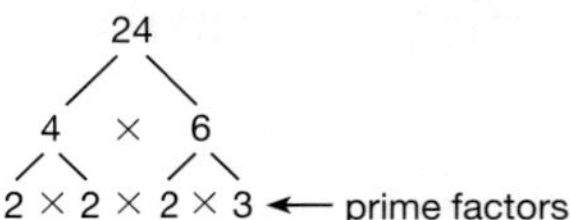

Example 1

Write 40 as the product of two factors in as many different ways as you can. Then list all the factors of 40.

We know that 1 is a factor of every number, so, we start with 1 and 40.

Since 40 is an even number, we know that 2 is a factor, $2 \times 20 = 40$.

Since 40 ends with a zero, we know that 5 and 10 are factors.

$$5 \times 8 = 40 \qquad 4 \times 10 = 40$$

We check and find that 3, 6, 7, and 9 are not factors of 40.

The factor pairs of 40 are, **1 × 40, 2 × 20, 4 × 10, and 5 × 8.** The factors of 40 are, **1, 2, 4, 5, 8, 10, 20, and 40.**

Example 2

Write 40 as the product of prime factors.

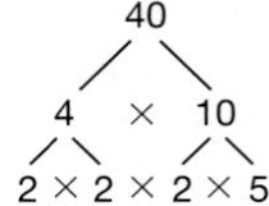

We start by finding two factors for 40 such as, 2 and 20.

Since 2 is a prime number, find two factors for 20 such as, 2 and 10.

Again, 2 is a prime number, find two factors for 10 such as, 2 and 5. Both 2 and 5 are prime numbers.

The number 40 is a product of the prime factors:

$$\mathbf{2 \times 2 \times 2 \times 5}$$

English Learners

Explain to students that **prime** can have other meanings and uses, as in *prime beef* or *prime minister.*

Prime beef means it's the best or top quality beef. A *prime minister* is the first or highest minister (leader) in some countries.

Teacher Tip

In the classroom, students can use colored tiles to model and list the factors of a number. At home, students might use such common household items as paper clips or toothpicks to model the factors of a number.

Lesson Practice

Analyze Write each number as a product of two numbers in as many different ways as you can:

a. 16 $1 \times 16, 2 \times 8, 4 \times 4$ **b.** 20 $1 \times 20, 2 \times 10, 4 \times 5$

c. **Verify** Write 27 as the product of prime factors. $3 \times 3 \times 3$

Written Practice

Distributed and Integrated

▸ *1. (13, 71, 85) **a.** Five minutes is equal to how many seconds? (*Hint:* There are 60 seconds in each minute.) 300 seconds

▸ **b.** Sixty minutes is how many seconds? 3600 seconds

*2. (93) **Explain** Trevor, Ann, and Lee were playing marbles. Ann had twice as many marbles as Trevor had, and Lee had 5 more marbles than Ann had. Trevor had 9 marbles. How many marbles did Lee have? What is the first step? 23 marbles; First find how many marbles Ann had.

3. (39) On each of 5 bookshelves there are 44 books. How many books are on all 5 bookshelves? 220 books

▸ *4. (67, 94) **a.** Nine tenths of the 30 students remembered their homework. How many students remembered their homework? 27 students

b. What fractional part of the students did not remember their homework? $\frac{1}{10}$

5. (43) For parts **a–c,** refer to this number line:

a. The number for point *A* is what fraction? $\frac{23}{100}$

b. The number for point *B* is what decimal number? 0.07

c. The number for point *C* is what fraction? $\frac{1}{10}$

6. (98) What fraction name for 1 has a denominator of 3? $\frac{3}{3}$

New Concept *(Continued)*

Lesson Practice

Guided Practice

Use these problems as guided practice to check the students' understanding of today's concept.

Problems a and b **Analyze**

Encourage students to find the factor pairs in an organized way. For example, explain that they should write the factor pair that includes 1 because every number is divisible by 1; Write the factor pair that includes 2 if the number is an even number; test the number for divisibility by 3, and so on.

Problem c **Verify**

Error Alert

Ask students to check their answer by comparing the product of the factors they wrote to 27, the number that was factored.

Closure

The questions below help assess the concepts taught in this lesson.

"How do the factors of a number compare to the number itself? Include the terms 'greater than,' 'less than,' or 'equal to' in your answer." Sample: The factors of a number are less than or equal to the number; The factors of a number are never greater than the number.

"Write all of the factor pairs whose product is 32." 1×32; 2×16; 4×8

"Write 18 as the product of prime factors." $2 \times 3 \times 3$

Math Background

Because factors come in pairs, it might seem that all numbers will have an even number of factors. However, a square number—a number equal to the product of a whole number and itself—has an odd number of factors.

In addition, consider all the factor pairs for 36: 1×36, 2×18, 3×12, 4×9, and 6×6.

Since the last pair of factors uses the same factor twice, it adds only one factor to the list of factors. This means 36 has an odd number of factors.

Specifically, it has 9 factors: 1, 2, 3, 4, 6, 9, 12, 18, and 36.

Alternative Approach: Using Manipulatives

Have students use colored tiles to make arrays to find all the factors of a given number.

Ask, ***"How can you tell if a number is a prime number?"*** If only two arrays can be made for a given number which shows one group of that number or that number of groups of one, then it is a prime number.

Written Practice

Math Conversations

Independent Practice and Discussions to Increase Understanding

Problems 1a and 1b

After students complete the arithmetic, ask them to name an operation that can be used to check each answer, and then use that operation to check the answer. Sample:
part **a:** division ($300 \div 5$ or $300 \div 60$)
part **b:** division ($3600 \div 60$)

(continued)

Written Practice (Continued)

Math Conversations (cont.)

Problem 4

Before they solve part **a**, remind students of the importance of checking their work, and then ask them to explain why we can expect the exact answer to be close to 30. Sample: We are finding a fractional part of a whole. Since $\frac{9}{10}$ is close to $\frac{10}{10}$, which is another name for 1, the answer will be close to the whole, which is 30 students.

For part **b**, ask students to explain why we can expect the exact answer to be close to zero. Sample: We are finding a fractional part of a whole. Since $\frac{1}{10}$ is close to $\frac{0}{10}$, which is another name for zero, the answer will be close to zero.

Problem 7

Extend the Problem

"What name for 1 can we multiply $\frac{1}{2}$ by to change $\frac{1}{2}$ to $\frac{5}{10}$?" $\frac{5}{5}$

"Why does multiplying $\frac{1}{2}$ by $\frac{5}{5}$ produce an equivalent fraction?" $\frac{5}{5}$ is another name for 1, and multiplying a number by 1 does not change the value of the number.

Problems 16–18

Before students complete the arithmetic, invite a volunteer to explain how to add and subtract fractions and mixed numbers that have common denominators.

(continued)

▸ *7. What equivalent fractions are shown below? $\frac{5}{10} = \frac{1}{2}$
(103)

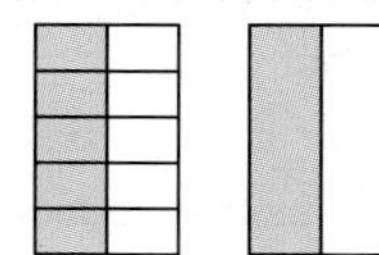

*8. **Represent** Draw a picture to show that $\frac{6}{8}$ and $\frac{3}{4}$ are equivalent fractions.
(Inv. 8, 103)

9. Below is a golf scorecard for 9 holes of miniature golf:
(Inv. 6, 95)

Putt 'N' Putt

Player	1	2	3	4	5	6	7	8	9	Total
Michelle	6	7	5	2	4	1	3	5	3	36
Mathea	5	4	4	3	4	3	2	5	3	33

What was Michelle's median score? What was the mode? Median: 4; mode: 3 and 5

10. It was 11:00 a.m., and Sarah had to clean the laboratory by 4:20 p.m. How much time did she have to clean the lab? 5 hours 20 minutes
(13)

*11. Draw a quadrilateral that has two sides that are parallel, a third side that is perpendicular to the parallel sides, and a fourth side that is not perpendicular to the parallel sides. What type of quadrilateral did you draw? trapezoid
(17, 50)

11. Sample:

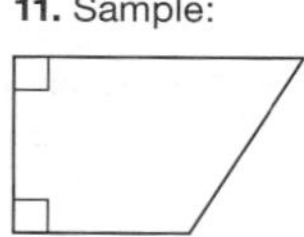

12. The factors of 10 are 1, 2, 5, 10. The factors of 15 are 1, 3, 5, 15. Which number is the largest factor of both 10 and 15? 5
(105)

13. **List** What are the prime factors of 8. $2 \times 2 \times 2$
(105)

14. $4.3 + 12.6 + 3.75$ 20.65
(45)

15. $364.1 - 16.41$ 347.69
(45)

▸*16. $\frac{5}{8} + \frac{2}{8}$ $\frac{7}{8}$
(100)

▸*17. $\frac{3}{5} + \frac{1}{5}$ $\frac{4}{5}$
(100)

▸*18. $1\frac{9}{10} - 1\frac{2}{10}$ $\frac{7}{10}$
(100)

19. 60×800 48,000
(85)

20. 73×48 3504
(88)

21. $9 \times 78¢$ $7.02
(28, 38)

22. 10^3 1000
(65, 85)

23. $4x = 3500$ 875
(34, 79)

24. $\frac{4824}{8}$ 603
(83)

*25. $6\overline{)540}$ 90
(75)

*26. $8\overline{)463}$ 57 R7
(72)

Inclusion

Use this strategy if the student displays:

- Difficulty with Abstract Processing.
- Difficulty with Large Group Instruction.

Factoring Whole Numbers (Individual)

Material: Lesson Activity Master 8 (grid paper)

- Write 20 on the board. Draw a 4×5 array. Label sides and tell students 4 and 5 are factors of 20.
- Have students draw the other arrays of 20. (Possible arrays include 10 by 2 and 20×1.) Ask, ***"What are all the factors of 20?"*** 1, 2, 4, 5, 10, 20
- If time permits, draw a factor tree on the board for 20.

*27. (RF14) Estimate the perimeter and area of this figure. Each small square represents one square inch. 16 in.; 16 sq. in.

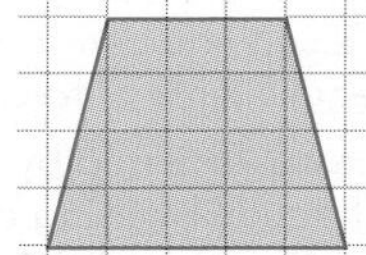

*28. (18, Inv. 4) **Represent** Draw a rectangle that is 4 cm long and 1 cm wide. Then shade 0.25 of it.

4 cm
1 cm

29. (96) **Multiple Choice** Which of the following is a cylinder? C

A 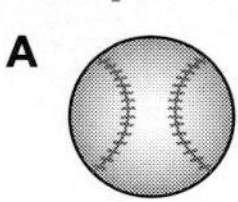

B 

C 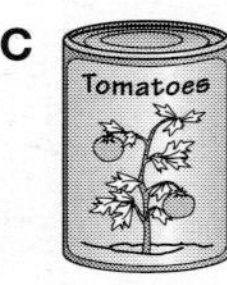

D 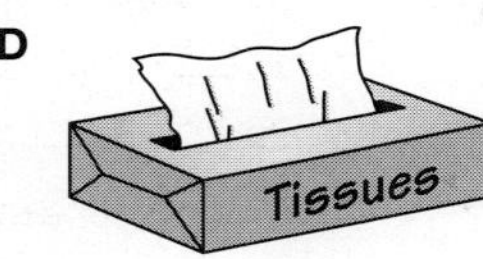

▶*30. (102) **Analyze** Hans divided 356 by 4 and checked his answer using the Distributive Property. Show how to check his answer with the Distributive Property.

$356 \div 4 = (300 \div 4) + (56 \div 4)$
$= 75 + 14$
$= 89$

Looking Forward

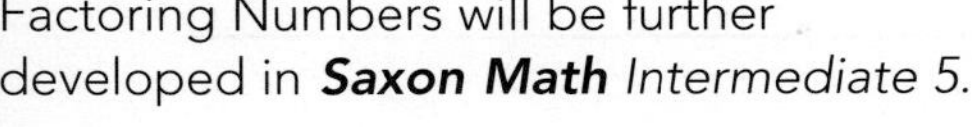

Factoring Numbers will be further developed in ***Saxon Math*** *Intermediate 5.*

Cumulative Assessments and Test-Day Activity

Assessments

Distribute **Power-Up Test 20** and **Cumulative Test 20** to each student. Have students complete the **Power-Up Test** first. Allow 10 minutes. Then have students work on the **Cumulative Test.**

Test-Day Activity

The remaining class time can be spent on the **Test-Day Activity 10.** Students can begin the activity in class and complete it as homework.

Written Practice *(Continued)*

Math Conversations *(cont.)*

Problem 30 Analyze

Before students begin the arithmetic, remind them that to use the Distributive Property, they must break apart the dividend (356) into two numbers that are each divisible by the divisor (4).

If students have difficulty finding two numbers, point out that every multiple of 100 is divisible by 4. So 100 and 356 − 100, 200 and 356 − 200, and 300 and 356 −300 are three ways to break apart the dividend.

Errors and Misconceptions

Problem 2

Make sure students recognize the fact that "Trevor had 9 marbles" as the fact that is used to find the number of marbles that Ann and Lee had. Also make sure students recognize that the number of marbles Lee had cannot be determined until the number of marbles Ann had is known. So to find the solution, students must first find the number of marbles Ann had.

Problem 11

If students seem overwhelmed by the number of characteristics the figure is to have, suggest that they informally sketch a variety of figures. Once they complete a sketch of a figure that has all of the characteristics, they can use a ruler to duplicate the figure with precision.

Problem 23

Make sure students recognize that the expression $4x$ represents the product of two factors; one factor is 4 and the other is unknown. Also make sure they understand that division is used to find an unknown or missing factor.

Planning & Preparation

• Reducing Fractions

Objectives

- Write the reduced form of a fraction.

Prerequisite Skills

- Using pictures to name fractions.
- Identifying multiples of a given number.
- Identifying factors of a given number.
- Distinguishing between prime and composite numbers.

Materials

Instructional Masters

- Power Up A Worksheet

Manipulative Kit

- Rulers
- Fraction circles, color tiles*

**optional*

California Mathematics Content Standards

NS 1.0, 1.5 Explain different interpretations of fractions, for example, parts of a whole, parts of a set, and division of whole numbers by whole numbers; explain equivalents of fractions (see Standard 4.0).

NS 1.0, 1.7 Write the fraction represented by a drawing of parts of a figure; represent a given fraction by using drawings; and relate a fraction to a simple decimal on a number line.

NS 4.0, 4.2 Know that numbers such as 2, 3, 5, 7, and 11 do not have any factors except 1 and themselves and that such numbers are called prime numbers.

MR 2.0, 2.3 Use a variety of methods, such as words, numbers, symbols, charts, graphs, tables, diagrams, and models, to explain mathematical reasoning.

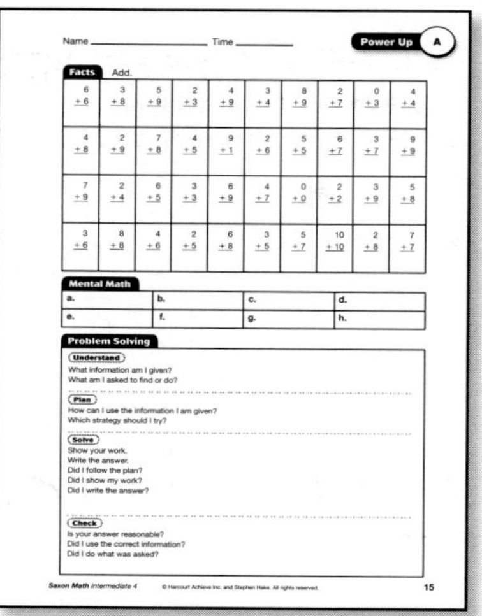

Power Up A Worksheet

Reaching All Special Needs Students

Special Education Students	At-Risk Students	English Learners	Advanced Learners
• Inclusion (TM) • Adaptations for Saxon Math	• Alternative Approach (TM) • Error Alert (TM) • Reteaching Masters • Refresher Lessons for California Standards	• English Learners (TM) • Developing Academic Language (TM) • English Learner Handbook	• Extend the Example (TM) • Extend the Problem (TM) • Online Activities

TM=Teacher's Manual

Developing Academic Language

Maintained	English Learner
denominator	board
numerator	
reduce	

Problem Solving Discussion

Problem

Two cups make a pint. Two pints make a quart. Two quarts make a half gallon, and two half gallons make a gallon. A pint of water weighs about one pound. Find the approximate weight of a cup, a quart, a half gallon, and a gallon of water.

Focus Strategies

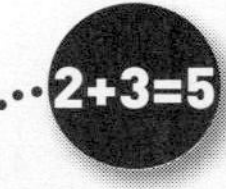

Write a Number Sentence or Equation

Use Logical Reasoning

Understand *Understand the problem.*

"What equivalent measures are we given?"

2 cups = 1 pint

2 pints = 1 quart

2 quarts = 1 half gallon

2 half gallons = 1 gallon

"What are we told about the weight of a pint of water?"

A pint of water weighs about one pound.

"What are we asked to do?"

We are asked to find the approximate weight of a cup, a quart, a half gallon, and a gallon of water.

Plan *Make a plan.*

"How can we use the information we know to solve the problem?"

We know how much a pint weighs (about 1 pound), so we need to find how many pints are in each of the other measurements.

Solve *Carry out the plan.*

"About how much does a cup of water weigh?"

There are 2 cups in a pint, so each cup is $\frac{1}{2}$ of a pint. This means that a cup of water weighs about $\frac{1}{2}$ pound ($\frac{1}{2} \times 1$ pound $= \frac{1}{2}$ pound).

"About how much does a quart of water weigh?"

There are 2 pints in a quart, so a quart of water weighs about 2 pounds (2×1 pound $= 2$ pounds).

"About how much does a half gallon of water weigh?"

There are 2 quarts in a half gallon, so a half gallon of water weighs about 4 pounds (2×2 pounds $= 4$ pounds).

"About how much does a gallon of water weigh?"

There are 2 half gallons in a gallon, so a gallon of water weighs about 8 pounds (2×4 pounds $= 8$ pounds).

Check *Look back.*

"Are our answers reasonable?"

It is reasonable that a cup weighs less than 1 pound, since a cup is half as much as a pint. It is reasonable that a quart, half gallon, and gallon all weigh more than 1 pound, since they are larger measurements than a pint.

Alternate Strategy

Draw a Picture or Diagram

To help students visualize the solution to the problem, have them *draw a picture or diagram* to show the relationship between a pint and the other units of capacity.

Facts
Distribute **Power Up A** to students. See answers below.

Count Aloud
Before students begin the Mental Math exercises, do these counting exercises as a class.

Count up and down by fours from 20 to 48.

Mental Math
Encourage students to share different ways to mentally compute these exercises. Strategies for exercises are listed below.

a. Divide 24 by 2

$24 \div 2 = 12$

Use a Related Fact

Since $12 \times 2 = 24$, $24 \div 2 = 12$.

c. Divide 24 by 4

$24 \div 4 = 6$

Use a Related Fact

Since $6 \times 4 = 24$, $24 \div 4 = 6$.

Problem Solving
Refer to **Problem-Solving Strategy Discussion,** p. 700B.

New Concept

Explanation

Remind students that in Lesson 103, they learned to write equivalent fractions by multiplying a fraction by a fraction that is equal to 1. Explain to students that in this lesson, they will learn to write an equivalent fraction by dividing a fraction by a fraction that is equal to 1.

Active Learning

Divide students into small groups. Distribute fraction circles to each group and ask them to demonstrate that $\frac{4}{6}$ is equivalent to $\frac{2}{3}$.

Math Language

Point out that using division to write an equivalent fraction is sometimes called *reducing a fraction, writing a fraction in lowest terms, or writing a fraction in simplest form.*

(continued)

LESSON 106

• Reducing Fractions

California Mathematics Content Standards

NS 1.0, 1.7 Write the fraction represented by a drawing of parts of a figure; represent a given fraction by using drawings; and relate a fraction to a simple decimal on a number line.

NS 4.0, 4.2 Know that numbers such as 2, 3, 5, 7, and 11 do not have any factors except 1 and themselves and that such numbers are called prime numbers.

MR 2.0, 2.3 Use a variety of methods, such as words, numbers, symbols, charts, graphs, tables, diagrams, and models, to explain mathematical reasoning.

Power Up

facts Power Up A

mental math Find each fraction of 24 in problems **a–c.**

a. **Fractional Part:** $\frac{1}{2}$ of 24 12

b. **Fractional Part:** $\frac{1}{3}$ of 24 8

c. **Fractional Part:** $\frac{1}{4}$ of 24 6

d. **Number Sense:** 4×18 72

e. **Money:** Stefano has $3.75 in his pocket and $4.51 in his piggy bank. Altogether, how much money does Stefano have? $8.26

f. **Estimation:** Estimate 62×19. 1200

g. **Calculation:** 5^2, $+ 10$, $- 3$, $\div 4$, $\times 2$ 16

h. **Simplify:** $e \div 3$ when $e = 30$ 10

problem solving Choose an appropriate problem-solving strategy to solve this problem. Two cups make a pint. Two pints make a quart. Two quarts make a half gallon, and two half gallons make a gallon. A pint of water weighs about one pound. Find the approximate weight of a cup, a quart, a half gallon, and a gallon of water.
cup: $\frac{1}{2}$ lb; quart: 2 lb; half gallon: 4 lb; gallon: 8 lb

Recall from Investigation 8 that when we *reduce* a fraction, we find an equivalent fraction written with smaller numbers or **lowest terms.** The picture below shows $\frac{4}{6}$ reduced to $\frac{2}{3}$.

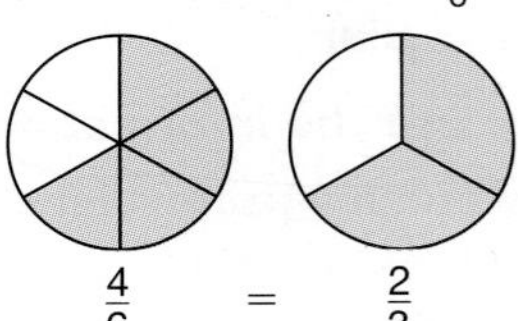

$\frac{4}{6} = \frac{2}{3}$

Facts Add.

6 + 6 12	3 + 8 11	5 + 9 14	2 + 3 5	4 + 9 13	3 + 4 7	8 + 9 17	2 + 7 9	0 + 3 3	4 + 4 8
4 + 8 12	2 + 9 11	7 + 8 15	4 + 5 9	9 + 1 10	2 + 6 8	5 + 5 10	6 + 7 13	3 + 7 10	9 + 9 18
7 + 9 16	2 + 4 6	6 + 5 11	3 + 3 6	6 + 9 15	4 + 7 11	0 + 0 0	2 + 2 4	3 + 9 12	5 + 8 13
3 + 6 9	8 + 8 16	4 + 6 10	2 + 5 7	6 + 8 14	3 + 5 8	5 + 7 12	10 + 10 20	2 + 8 10	7 + 7 14

Not all fractions can be reduced. Only a fraction whose numerator and denominator can be divided by the same number can be reduced. Since both the numerator and denominator of $\frac{4}{6}$ can be divided by 2, we can reduce the fraction $\frac{4}{6}$.

To reduce a fraction, we will use a fraction that is equal to 1. To reduce $\frac{4}{6}$, we will use the fraction $\frac{2}{2}$. We divide both 4 and 6 by 2, as shown.

$$\frac{4}{6} = \frac{4 \div 2}{6 \div 2} = \frac{2}{3}$$

Example

Thinking Skills

Discuss

How do we know that both 6 and 8 are divisible by 2?

They are even numbers, and all even numbers are divisible by 2.

Write the reduced form of each fraction:

a. $\frac{6}{8}$ **b.** $\frac{3}{6}$ **c.** $\frac{6}{7}$

a. The numerator and denominator are 6 and 8. These numbers can be divided by 2. That means we can reduce the fraction by dividing 6 and 8 by 2.

$$\frac{6}{8} = \frac{6 \div 2}{8 \div 2} = \mathbf{\frac{3}{4}}$$

$\frac{6}{8} = \frac{3}{4}$

b. The numerator and denominator are 3 and 6. These numbers can be divided by 3, so we reduce $\frac{3}{6}$ by dividing both 3 and 6 by 3.

$$\frac{3}{6} = \frac{3 \div 3}{6 \div 3} = \mathbf{\frac{1}{2}}$$

$\frac{3}{6} = \frac{1}{2}$

Math Background

The greatest common factor, or GCF, of two numbers is the greatest factor they have in common. In other words, it is the greatest number that divides both numbers evenly. For example, the greatest common factor of 14 and 21 is 7, and the greatest common factor of 12 and 30 is 6. To reduce a fraction completely (to *lowest terms*) in one step, divide the numerator and denominator by their GCF. Below we reduce $\frac{14}{21}$ and $\frac{12}{30}$.

$$\frac{14 \div 7}{21 \div 7} = \frac{2}{3} \qquad \frac{2 \div 6}{30 \div 6} = \frac{12}{5}$$

When two numbers have no factors in common except 1, we say they are *relatively prime*. If the numerator and denominator of a fraction are relatively prime, then the fraction cannot be reduced.

New Concept *(Continued)*

Example

It is very important for students to understand that the number chosen to divide by must be a factor of both the numerator and the denominator. If students need to review factors, demonstrate how a list can be used to identify the factors of 6 and 8 (the numerator and denominator of the fraction in part **a**). Write on the board or overhead, "The factors of 6 are 1, 2, 3, 6. The factors of 8 are 1, 2, 4, 8."

Circle "2" in each list. Then explain that the fraction $\frac{6}{8}$ can be simplified by dividing each number by 2 because 2 is a factor of each number.

Extend the Example

Challenge advanced learners by asking them to explain how the fraction $\frac{8}{12}$ can be simplified. The number and denominator can both be divided by 4, thus the fraction $\frac{8}{12}$ can be reduced to $\frac{2}{3}$.

Error Alert

As you discuss part **b,** remind students that the numerator (3) and the denominator (6) can both be divided by 3 because 3 is a factor of each number. Also point out that although 2 is a factor of the denominator 6, 2 is not a factor of the numerator 3, so we do not divide by $\frac{2}{2}$ to reduce $\frac{3}{6}$.

Generalize

Lead students to generalize from your discussion of part **c** that whenever 1 is the only common factor of a numerator and a denominator, the fraction cannot be reduced.

(continued)

New Concept (Continued)

Lesson Practice

Guided Practice

Use these problems as guided practice to check the students' understanding of today's concept.

Problems a–h

Before students begin the arithmetic for each problem, ask them to name the numerator of the fraction, name the denominator of the fraction, and name the greatest number that is a factor of both the numerator and the denominator. The greatest factors are as follows: **a:** 2; **b:** 2; **c:** 3; **d:** 1; **e:** 2; **f:** 2; **g:** 3; **h:** 1

Problem h Extend the Problem

Ask students:

"Suppose that the numerator of a fraction is a prime number, and the denominator of the fraction is a greater prime number. What is true about the fraction? Explain your answer." The fraction cannot be reduced; The only factor that prime numbers have in common is 1.

Problems d and h
Error Alert

Make sure students understand that a fraction cannot be reduced if the only common factor of its numerator and its denominator is 1.

Closure The questions below help assess the concepts taught in this lesson.

"The fraction $\frac{5}{10}$ can be reduced. Explain how to reduce $\frac{5}{10}$." Sample: Name a number that is greater than 1 and is a factor of both 5 and of 10, and then divide the numerator and the denominator of $\frac{5}{10}$ by that number; $\frac{5}{10} = \frac{5 \div 5}{10 \div 5} = \frac{1}{2}$

c. The numerator is 6 and the denominator is 7. The only number that divides 6 and 7 is 1. Dividing the terms of a fraction by 1 does not reduce the fraction.

$$\frac{6}{7} = \frac{6 \div 1}{7 \div 1} = \frac{6}{7}$$

The fraction $\frac{6}{7}$ cannot be reduced.

Justify Which number, 6 or 7, is prime? Explain why. 7 is a prime number because it has exactly two factors, itself and 1; The factors of 6 are 1, 2, 3, and 6.

Lesson Practice

Write the reduced form of each fraction:

a. $\frac{2}{4}$ $\frac{1}{2}$ **b.** $\frac{2}{6}$ $\frac{1}{3}$ **c.** $\frac{3}{9}$ $\frac{1}{3}$ **d.** $\frac{3}{8}$ $\frac{3}{8}$

e. $\frac{2}{10}$ $\frac{1}{5}$ **f.** $\frac{4}{10}$ $\frac{2}{5}$ **g.** $\frac{9}{12}$ $\frac{3}{4}$ **h.** $\frac{9}{10}$ $\frac{9}{10}$

i. $\frac{2}{8}$ $\frac{1}{4}$ **j.** $\frac{5}{10}$ $\frac{1}{2}$ **k.** $\frac{10}{12}$ $\frac{5}{6}$ **l.** $\frac{6}{10}$ $\frac{3}{5}$

Written Practice

Distributed and Integrated

*1. (76, 93) Use the following information to answer parts **a** and **b**.

One fence board costs 90¢. It takes 10 boards to build 5 feet of fence.

▸ **a.** How many boards are needed to build 50 feet of fence? 100 boards

b. How much will the boards cost altogether? $90.00

2. (66) Use a formula to find the perimeter and area of this rectangle. 16 cm; 15 cm^2

3 cm
5 cm

3. (42) **a.** Find the length of this line segment in millimeters. 34 mm

b. Find the length of the segment in centimeters. 3.4 cm

mm 10 20 30 40 50

cm 1 2 3 4 5

English Learners

A **board** is a piece of wood, usually long and thin that is used for a variety of things.

Explain that **boards** of all shapes and sizes can be used to make anything from houses to cutting **boards**.

Ask:

"What other things do people make with boards?" Sample: tables, benches, fences, dog houses

Alternative Approach: Using Manipulatives

To help students understand the concept of reducing fractions, have them use fraction manipulatives to model fractions.

Display the fraction $\frac{4}{10}$. Explain to students that we can find an equivalent fraction written with smaller numbers. Have students line up four $\frac{1}{10}$ fraction manipulatives below a 1-whole fraction manipulative. Have students line up two $\frac{1}{5}$ pieces under the four $\frac{1}{10}$ pieces to show that the two fractions are equivalent. Explain to the students that the fraction $\frac{4}{10}$ can be reduced to $\frac{2}{5}$. Have students show other examples.

▶ *4. (94) Five ninths of the 36 horses were gray. How many of the horses were gray? 20 horses

▶ *5. (99) Change each improper fraction to a whole number or a mixed number:

a. $\frac{15}{2}$ $7\frac{1}{2}$ b. $\frac{15}{3}$ 5 c. $\frac{15}{4}$ $3\frac{3}{4}$

*6. (56) Angelina's mom is more than 32 years old but less than 40 years old, and her age in years is a prime number. How old is Angelina's mom? 37 years old

*7. (Inv. 8, 103) What equivalent fractions are shown at right? $\frac{1}{2} = \frac{6}{12}$

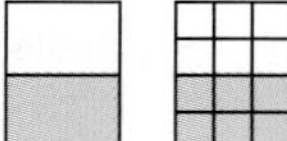

*8. (50, 82, 90) A regular polygon has all sides the same length and all angles the same measure.

▶ a. Draw a regular quadrilateral. Show all the lines of symmetry. 8. a.

b. A regular quadrilateral has how many lines of symmetry? 4

c. Does a regular quadrilateral have rotational symmetry? Yes

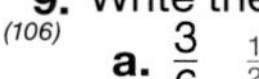

*9. (106) Write the reduced form of each fraction:

a. $\frac{3}{6}$ $\frac{1}{2}$ b. $\frac{4}{6}$ $\frac{2}{3}$ c. $\frac{6}{12}$ $\frac{1}{2}$

▶*10. (105) List What are the prime factors of 30? $2 \times 3 \times 5$

11. (93) T-shirts were priced at $5 each. Yoshi had $27 and bought 5 T-shirts. Tax was $1.50. How much money did he have left? $0.50

▶*12. (100) $3\frac{3}{9} + 4\frac{4}{9}$ $7\frac{7}{9}$

▶*13. (100) $\frac{1}{7} + \frac{2}{7} + \frac{3}{7}$ $\frac{6}{7}$

14. (45) 37.2 + 135.7 + 10.62 + 2.47 + 14.0 = 199.99

▶*15. (100) $\frac{11}{12} - \frac{10}{12}$ $\frac{1}{12}$

▶*16. (100) $\frac{8}{10} - \frac{5}{10}$ $\frac{3}{10}$

17. (88) 48×36 = 1728

18. (88) 72×58 = 4176

19. (59) $\$4.08 \times 7$ = $28.56

Inclusion

Use this strategy if the student displays:

- Difficulty with Abstract Processing.
- Slow Learning Rate.

Reducing Fractions

Material: Lesson Activity Master 8 (grid paper)

- Write $\frac{4}{6}$ on the board. Have students draw all possible arrays for 4 and 6. Ask, ***"What are the factors of 4?"*** 1, 2, 4 ***"What are the factors of 6?"*** 1, 2, 3, 6
- Tell students to circle the factors that 4 and 6 have in common. Ask, ***"What is the Greatest Common Factor of both numbers?"*** 2
- Tell students that if both numbers in a fraction have a common factor other than 1 it is not in simplest form and needs to be reduced. Write $\frac{4 \div 2}{6 \div 2} = \frac{2}{3}$ and tell students that to simplify you divide BOTH numbers by their greatest common factor.
- Write $\frac{10}{15}$ on the board and have students find the factors of both numbers. Ask, ***"What is the greatest common factor of 10 and 15?"*** 5 Have students reduce the fraction and ask, ***"What does $\frac{10}{15}$ simplify to?"*** $\frac{2}{3}$

Written Practice

Math Conversations

Independent Practice and Discussions to Increase Understanding

Problem 1a

This is a multiple-step problem. Ask the following questions if students have difficulty finding the solution:

"How many boards does it take to build 5 feet of fence?" 10 boards

Write "10 boards ÷ 5 feet" on the board or overhead. Then say:

"Explain what the quotient of the division 10 boards divided by 5 feet tells us." The quotient tells us that 2 boards are needed to build 1 foot of fence.

"Since we know that 2 boards are needed to build every foot of fence, how can we find the number of boards that would be needed to build 50 feet of fence?" Multiply 50 by 2.

Problem 4

Some students may find it helpful to draw a picture (such as a rectangle) to solve this problem. Make sure these students recognize that the denominator of the fraction describes the number of equal parts the picture is to be divided into. After the division of 36 by 9, students should conclude that each equal part of the picture represents 4 horses.

Alternate Method

Some students may find it helpful to use cubes or tiles to model the division of 36 into 9 equal groups.

Problem 5

"What operation does a fraction bar represent?" division

"Explain how to change an improper fraction to a mixed number." Divide the numerator by the denominator and then write the quotient in simplest form.

Problem 8a

A regular quadrilateral is a square.

Problem 10 List

Before students list the factors, ask:

"What are the first five prime numbers?" 2, 3, 5, 7, 11

Point out that some of the numbers that were named are prime factors of 30.

(continued)

Written Practice *(Continued)*

Math Conversations *(cont.)*

Problems 12, 13, 15, and 16

After the addition or the subtraction has been completed for each problem, ask:

"Can our answer be reduced? Explain why or why not." No; sample: The only common factor of the numerator and the denominator is 1.

Problem 30 **Explain**

Make sure students understand that they are to provide a reasonable estimate of the area and not an exact area.

Errors and Misconceptions

Problem 10

If students use a factor tree to find the prime factors, make sure they recall that a factor pair whose product is 30 (such as 5×6 or 2×15, for example) should be used to begin the tree.

Problems 17–22

Some students may not take time to check their work unless they are asked to do so. Explain to your students that with a little practice, it takes very little time to make a reasonable estimate of many different kinds of answers. Then work with them to quickly make an estimate of each product in problems **17–22**, and compare those estimates to the exact answers after completing the arithmetic. Sample:

problem **17:**	50×40; Write two zeros to the right of the product of 5×4.
problem **18:**	70×60; Write two zeros to the right of the product of 7×6.
problem **19:**	$\$4 \times 7 = \$28$
problem **20:**	$25 + 25 = 50$
problem **21:**	$36 - 4 = 32$
problem **22:**	$80 \div 2 = 40$ or $100 \div 2 = 50$

20. (45) $25.42 + 24.8$ 50.22

21. (45) $36.2 - 4.27$ 31.93

***22.** (68) $90 \div 2$ 45

23. (100) $\frac{5}{8} - \frac{5}{8}$ 0

24. (79) $7\overline{)2549}$ 364 R 1

***25.** (79) $\$19.40 \div 4$ $4.85

***26.** (106) Write the reduced form of each fraction.

a. $\frac{6}{9}$ $\frac{2}{3}$ **b.** $\frac{2}{12}$ $\frac{1}{6}$ **c.** $\frac{10}{15}$ $\frac{2}{3}$

***27.** (96, 97) **a.** What is the geometric name for the shape of this box? rectangular prism

b. True or false: All of the opposite faces of the box are parallel. true

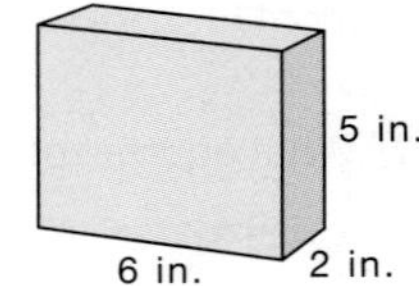

***28.** (104) **Represent** Round each number to the given place:

a. Round 241,679,500 to the nearest hundred million. 200,000,000

b. Round 241,679,500 to the nearest ten million. 240,000,000

c. Round 241,679,500 to the nearest million. 242,000,000

d. Round 241,679,500 to the nearest hundred thousand. 241,700,000

***29.** (64) **Evaluate** If $y = 2x + 8$, what is y when x is 4, 5, and 6? 16, 18, 20

▸***30.** (RF14) **Explain** Estimate the perimeter and area of this shoe print. Each small square represents one square inch. Describe the method you used. About 25 sq. in.; See student work.

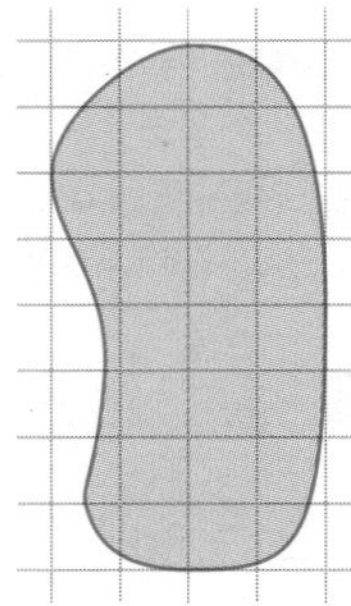

Writing the reduced form of a fraction prepares students for:

- **Lessons 112–113,** adding and subtracting fractions and mixed numbers with common denominators and renaming fractions whose denominators are not equal by using a common denominator of the fractions.

Planning & Preparation

California Mathematics Content Standards

NS 3.0, 3.3 Solve problems involving multiplication of multidigit numbers by two-digit numbers.

MR 2.0, 2.3 Use a variety of methods, such as words, numbers, symbols, charts, graphs, tables, diagrams, and models, to explain mathematical reasoning.

• Multiplying a Three-Digit Number by a Two-Digit Number

Objectives

- Multiply a three-digit number by a two-digit number.
- Multiply dollars and cents by a two-digit number.
- Solve word problems involving multi-digit multiplication.

Prerequisite Skills

- Using the multiplication algorithm to multiply a two-digit number by a one-digit number.
- Multiplying a three-digit number by a one-digit number with and without regrouping.
- Multiplying dollars and cents by a one-digit number.
- Multiplying by multiples of 10.

Materials

Instructional Masters

- Power Up B Worksheet

Manipulative Kit

- Rulers
- Two-color counters, base ten blocks*

Teacher-provided materials

- Fraction manipulatives from Investigation 8*

**optional*

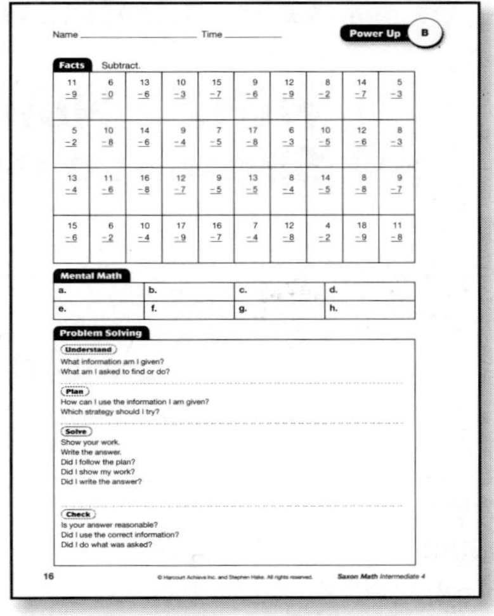

Power Up B Worksheet

Universal Access

Reaching All Special Needs Students

Special Education Students	At-Risk Students	English Learners	Advanced Learners
• Inclusion (TM) • Adaptations for Saxon Math	• Error Alert (TM) • Reteaching Masters • Refresher Lessons for California Standards	• English Learners (TM) • Developing Academic Language (TM) • English Learner Handbook	• Extend the Example (TM) • Extend the Problem (TM) • Online Activities

TM=Teacher's Manual

Developing Academic Language

Maintained	**English Learner**
multiply	ignore
product	

Problem Solving Discussion

Problem

In parts of the country where "daylight savings time" is observed, we follow the rule "spring forward, fall back." This rule means we turn the clock forward one hour in the spring and back one hour in the fall. Officially, clocks are reset at 2 a.m. on a Sunday. How many hours long are each of those Sundays when the clocks are reset?

Focus Strategies

Use Logical Reasoning

2+3=5 **Write a Number Sentence or Equation**

Understand *Understand the problem.*

"What information are we given?"

When daylight savings time begins in the spring, we turn the clock forward one hour. When daylight savings time ends in the fall, we turn the clock back one hour. Clocks are officially reset at 2 a.m. on a Sunday.

"What are we asked to determine?"

We are asked to find how many hours are in a Sunday when we "spring forward" and how many hours are in a Sunday when we "fall back."

Plan *Make a plan.*

"What problem-solving strategy can we use to solve the problem?"

We can *use logical reasoning* and *write a number sentence.*

Solve *Carry out the plan.*

"How do we reset the clocks when we 'spring forward' one hour?"

At 2 a.m. we reset the clocks to 3 a.m. This means we skip over the hour between 2 a.m. and 3 a.m. In other words, we lose one hour because there are zero minutes between 2 a.m. and 3 a.m.

"How many hours long is a Sunday when we 'spring forward' one hour?"

24 hours − 1 skipped hour = 23 hours

"How do we reset the clocks when we 'fall back' one hour?"

At 2 a.m. we reset the clocks to 1 a.m. This means we repeat the hour between 1 a.m. and 2 a.m. In other words, we gain one hour when we "fall back."

"How many hours long is a Sunday when we 'fall back' one hour?"

24 hours + 1 repeated hour = 25 hours

Check *Look back.*

"Did we find the answer to the question that was asked?"

Yes. We found that there are 23 hours on the Sunday we "spring forward" and 25 hours on the Sunday we "fall back."

"Why do most states observe daylight savings time?"

By turning clocks ahead one hour during the summer, we shift all our daily activities to occur one hour earlier. This has the effect of shifting one hour of early-morning daylight to the evening. We can use the extra hour of daylight in the evening to enjoy outdoor activities and to save on energy costs (since there are fewer hours we need to use artificial lighting before we go to bed).

Alternate Strategy

Act It Out or Make a Model

If desired, use a demonstration clock to show the time changes that occur at the beginning and end of daylight savings time ("spring forward" and "fall back").

LESSON 107

California Mathematics Content Standards

NS 3.0, 3.3 Solve problems involving multiplication of multidigit numbers by two-digit numbers.

MR 2.0, 2.3 Use a variety of methods, such as words, numbers, symbols, charts, graphs, tables, diagrams, and models, to explain mathematical reasoning.

• Multiplying a Three-Digit Number by a Two-Digit Number

Power Up

facts Power Up B

mental math Find each fraction of 30 in problems **a–c.**

a. Fractional Part: $\frac{1}{2}$ of 30 15

b. Fractional Part: $\frac{1}{3}$ of 30 10

c. Fractional Part: $\frac{1}{5}$ of 30 6

d. Number Sense: 50×28 1400

e. Time: The soccer match ended at 1:15 p.m. The match had started $1\frac{1}{2}$ hours earlier. When did the match begin? 11:45 a.m.

f. Estimation: To estimate 26×19, round 26 down to 25, round 19 up to 20, and then multiply. 500

g. Calculation: 5×2, $\times 10$, $\div 2$, $- 1$, $\sqrt{\ }$ 7

h. Simplify: s^2 when $s = 3$ 9

problem solving Choose an appropriate problem-solving strategy to solve this problem. In parts of the country where "daylight savings time" is observed, we follow the rule "spring forward, fall back." This rule means we turn the clock forward one hour in the spring and back one hour in the fall. Officially, clocks are reset at 2 a.m. on a Sunday. How many hours long are each of those Sundays when the clocks are reset? Spring: 23 hours long; fall: 25 hours long

New Concept

We have learned to multiply a two-digit number by another two-digit number. In this lesson we will learn to multiply a three-digit number by a two-digit number.

Facts Subtract.

11 − 9 2	6 − 0 6	13 − 6 7	10 − 3 7	15 − 7 8	9 − 6 3	12 − 9 3	8 − 2 6	14 − 7 7	5 − 3 2
5 − 2 3	10 − 8 2	14 − 6 8	9 − 4 5	7 − 5 2	17 − 8 9	6 − 3 3	10 − 5 5	12 − 6 6	8 − 3 5
13 − 4 9	11 − 6 5	16 − 8 8	12 − 7 5	9 − 5 4	13 − 5 8	8 − 4 4	14 − 5 9	8 − 8 0	9 − 7 2
15 − 6 9	6 − 2 4	10 − 4 6	17 − 9 8	16 − 7 9	7 − 4 3	12 − 8 4	4 − 2 2	18 − 9 9	11 − 8 3

Power Up

Facts

Distribute **Power Up B** to students. See answers below.

Count Aloud

Before students begin the Mental Math exercises, do these counting exercises as a class.

Count up and down by sevens from 49 to 84.

Mental Math

Encourage students to share different ways to mentally compute these exercises. Strategies for exercises are listed below.

c. Divide 30 by 5

$30 \div 5 = 6$

Use a Related Fact

Since $6 \times 5 = 30$, $30 \div 5 = 6$.

d. Decompose 28

$50 \times (20 + 8) = 1000 + 400 = 1400$

Subtract 50 × 2 from 50 × 30

$(50 \times 30) - (50 \times 2) = 1500 - 100 = 1400$

Problem Solving

Refer to **Problem-Solving Strategy Discussion,** p. 705B.

New Concept

Discussion

You may choose to discuss Lessons 86 and 88 (Multiplying Two Two-Digit Numbers, Parts 1 and 2) or complete a two-digit by two-digit multiplication as a way of introducing this lesson.

Example 1

Active Learning

Remind students that whenever we multiply whole (or decimal) numbers, the number of digits in the number we are multiplying by indicates the number of partial products that will be produced during the multiplication. Ask students to multiply 364 by 24 and explain why it will produce two partial products. It will produce two partial products because 24 is a two-digit number.

(continued)

New Concept *(Continued)*

Error Alert

Some students may find it easier to maintain alignment of the factors, partial products, and the products in this example (and in this lesson) if the arithmetic is completed on grid paper or lined paper turned sideways.

Example 2

Explain to students that the digits 7 and 2 above the tens place represent regroupings from the partial products. Have students note that 7 belongs to the first partial product and 2 belongs to the second. Point out that after a partial product is written, it is a good idea to cross out any numbers that were written to represent regroupings. For example, crossing off regroupings before calculating the second partial product will help make sure that regrouping from the first partial product are not included in the second partial product.

Extend the Example

Challenge advanced learners to explain how the product can be named using only mental math. Sample: subtract $\$4 \times 2$ from $\$4 \times 40$, subtract $\$0.29 \times 2$ from $\$0.29 \times 40$, and then add; $\$4 \times 40 - \$4 \times 2 = \$152$, $\$0.29 \times 40 - \$0.29 \times 2 = \$11.02$, and $\$152 + \$11.02 = \$163.02$

Lesson Practice

Guided Practice

Use these problems as guided practice to check the students' understanding of today's concept.

Problems a–f

Finding the products will take some time. For this reason, you may want to encourage students to estimate to check their work for reasonability.

Problem b

Point out that writing 430 underneath 14 will produce three partial products. Remind students that the *Commutative Property of Multiplication* enables them to rearrange the order of two factors.

Problems d and f
Error Alert

Make sure students insert a comma in numbers that are 10,000 or more.

(continued)

Example 1

A bakery is open 364 days each year. On each of those days, the bakery owner bakes 24 loaves of bread. How many loaves of bread does the owner bake each year?

Thinking Skills

Justify

Why are there two partial products?

Multiplying by a two-digit number produces two partial products.

We write the three-digit number above the two-digit number so that the last digits in each number are lined up. We multiply 364 by 4. Next we multiply 364 by 2. Since this 2 is actually 20, we write the last digit of this product in the tens place, which is under the 2 in 24. Then we add and find that the owner bakes **8736 loaves of bread** each year.

$$\begin{array}{r} {}^{1} \\ {}^{21} \\ 364 \\ \times\ 24 \\ \hline 1456 \\ 728\ \\ \hline 8736 \end{array}$$

Example 2

During summer vacation, a school principal ordered 38 paperback dictionaries for the school bookstore. The cost of each dictionary was \$4.29. What was the total cost of the dictionaries?

Thinking Skills

Generalize

When one factor of a multiplication is dollars and cents, how many decimal places will be in the product? Name the places.

2 places; dimes (or tenths of a dollar) and pennies (or hundredths of a dollar)

We will ignore the dollar sign and decimal point until we are finished multiplying. First we multiply 429 by 8. Then we multiply 429 by 3 (which is actually 30), remembering to shift the digits of the product one place to the left. We add and find that the product is 16302. Now we write the dollar sign and insert the decimal point two places from the right. We find that the total cost of the dictionaries was **\$163.02.**

$$\begin{array}{r} {}^{2} \\ {}^{2\ 7} \\ \$4.29 \\ \times\ 38 \\ \hline 34.32 \\ 128.7\ \\ \hline \$163.02 \end{array}$$

Lesson Practice Multiply:

a. 235×24 5640 **b.** 14×430 6020 **c.** $\$1.25 \times 24$ \$30.00

d. $\begin{array}{r} 416 \\ \times\ 32 \\ \hline \end{array}$ 13,312 **e.** $\begin{array}{r} \$6.25 \\ \times\ 31 \\ \hline \end{array}$ \$193.75 **f.** $\begin{array}{r} 562 \\ \times\ 47 \\ \hline \end{array}$ 26,414

English Learners

Explain that the word **ignore** means to pay no attention to, or to not notice. Sometimes people **ignore** things or other people so that they can stay focused.

Write \$4.29 × 15.00 on the board or overhead.

Ask:

"If I asked you to multiply these numbers why would it be easier to ignore the dollar sign and decimals until you are finished multiplying?"

So we can focus on the multiplication.

Teacher Tip

Direct students' attention to a *Place-Value Chart* poster displayed in the classroom; this can help students correctly read multi-digit products.

Written Practice

Distributed and Integrated

1. (51, 52, 93) Carrie drove to visit her cousin, who lives 3000 miles away. If Carrie drove 638 miles the first day, 456 miles the second day, and 589 miles the third day, how much farther does she need to drive to get to her cousin's house? 1317 mi

2. (66, 101) Use a formula to find the perimeter and area of this square: 28 in.; 49 in^2

7 in.

7 in.

3. (20, 42) If the perimeter of a square is 2 meters, then each side is how many centimeters long? 50 cm

▸ ***4.** (104) **Represent** Round 917,250,000 to the nearest hundred million. 900,000,000

5. (40) Round 6843 to the nearest thousand. 7000

▸ ***6.** (106) Write the reduced form of each fraction:

a. $\frac{4}{5}$ $\frac{4}{5}$ **b.** $\frac{5}{10}$ $\frac{1}{2}$ **c.** $\frac{4}{10}$ $\frac{2}{5}$

7. (Inv. 4) **Represent** Write 374.25 using words. three hundred seventy-four and twenty-five hundredths

▸ ***8.** (19, Inv. 8, 103) **Represent** Draw a picture to show that $\frac{1}{2}$ and $\frac{4}{8}$ are equivalent fractions.

▸ ***9.** (103) **Connect** Write three fractions equivalent to $\frac{1}{4}$. Sample: $\frac{2}{8}$, $\frac{3}{12}$, $\frac{5}{20}$

10. (91) **Estimate** The concession stand at an elementary school basketball tournament earned a profit of $850 during a 3-day tournament. About how much profit was earned each day? $300

▸ ***11.** (15, 51) **Analyze** The explorer Zebulon Pike estimated that the mountain's height was eight thousand, seven hundred forty-two feet. His estimate was five thousand, three hundred sixty-eight feet less than the actual height. Today we call this mountain Pikes Peak. What is the height of Pikes Peak? 14,110 ft

Math Background

Decimal numbers are multiplied in a similar way as whole numbers. The only extra step is determining where to place the decimal point in the answer. If both factors are written without extra zeros at the end (4.3, rather than 4.30), the number of decimal places in the answer will be the total of the numbers of decimal places in the two factors. **Example: multiply 4.32 × 2.6**

- (A) Ignore the decimal point and multiply.

$$\begin{array}{r} 4.32 \\ \times\ 2.6 \\ \hline 2592 \\ 8640 \\ \hline 11232 \end{array}$$

- (B) There are two decimal places in 4.32 and one in 2.6. So, the answer has three decimal places. Place the decimal point accordingly.

$$\begin{array}{r} 4.32 \\ \times\ 2.6 \\ \hline 2592 \\ 8640 \\ \hline 11.232 \end{array}$$

New Concept (Continued)

Closure The questions below help assess the concepts taught in this lesson.

Write "135 × 21" on the board or overhead. Then say:

"Complete this multiplication. What is the product of 135 and 21?" 2835

Written Practice

Math Conversations

Independent Practice and Discussions to Increase Understanding

Problem 4 Represent

"What digit is in the hundred millions place?" 9

"How does the digit in the place to the right of the rounding place—the ten millions place—compare to 5?" The digit is 1 and 1 is less than 5.

"Since 1 is less than 5, what number do we round to? Explain why." 900,000,000; sample: When the digit in the place next to the rounding place is less than 5, the digit in the rounding place does not change, and we change all of the digits to the right of the rounding place to zero.

Problem 6

Before students begin the arithmetic for each problem, ask them to name the numerator of the fraction, the denominator of the fraction, and the greatest number that is a factor of both the numerator and the denominator. The greatest factors are as follows: **a,** 1; **b,** 5; **c,** 2.

Make sure students understand that $\frac{4}{5}$ cannot be reduced because the only common factor of 4 and 5 is 1.

Problem 8 Represent

Manipulative Use

Encourage students to use their fraction manipulatives to check their work.

(continued)

Written Practice *(Continued)*

Math Conversations *(cont.)*

Problem 9 Connect

"What does it mean when two fractions are equivalent?" Sample: The fractions are equal; They are different names for the same amount.

Have students recall that multiplying a number by 1 does not change the value of the number. Then ask:

"To write an equivalent fraction for $\frac{1}{4}$, what name for 1 can we multiply $\frac{1}{4}$ by? Explain your answer." Sample: $\frac{2}{2}$; Any fraction that has the same numerator and denominator is another name for 1.

Remind students that fractions such as $\frac{3}{3}$, $\frac{4}{4}$, $\frac{5}{5}$, and so on are equivalent to 1 because a fraction bar is a symbol for division, and any number divided by itself is 1.

Problem 11 Analyze

Real-World Connection

Students may be interested to learn that Pike's Peak was named after Zebulon Pike, an explorer born in 1779, who attempted to climb the mountain during an 1806 expedition of the southwestern United States. The mountain is one of six found in Colorado's Front Range.

Problems 14, 15, 19, and 20

Remind students of the importance of checking their work. Ask them to make an estimate of each answer either before or after the arithmetic has been completed, and then use the estimate to help decide the reasonableness of the exact answer.

Problem 23

Extend the Problem

Invite volunteers to share their estimates with the class and explain how those estimates were made.

(continued)

12. (83) $6\overline{)4837}$ 806 R 1

13. (Inv. 3, 79) $\frac{1372}{\sqrt{16}}$ 343

▶***14.** (83) $4\overline{)960}$ 240

▶***15.** (79) $5\overline{)1360}$ 272

16. (45) 30.07 − 3.7 26.37

17. (45) 46.0 − 12.46 33.54

18. (45) 37.15 + 6.84 + 1.29 + 29.1 + 3.6 = 77.98

▶***19.** (107) \$3.28 × 46 = \$150.88

▶***20.** (107) 345 × 25 = 8625

***21.** (100) $\frac{8}{15} + \frac{6}{15}$ $\frac{14}{15}$

***22.** (100) $4\frac{4}{5} - 1\frac{3}{5}$ $3\frac{1}{5}$

▶***23.** (RF14) Estimate the perimeter and area of this triangle. Each small square represents one square centimeter. About 18 cm; about 15 sq. cm

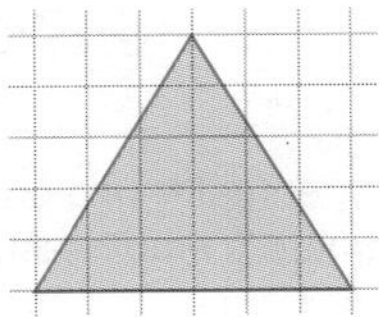

24. (1, 27) Conclude Write the next three numbers in this counting sequence: 40,000, 50,000, 60,000

. . ., 10,000, 20,000, 30,000, . . .

▶***25.** (17, 18, 81) **a. Multiple Choice** Which of these triangles appears to be an equilateral triangle? C

A B C D

b. Describe the angles in triangle **B.** One right and two acute angles

c. Describe the segments in triangle **B.** There are two perpendicular segments. The third segment intersects but is not perpendicular.

26. (78) **Multiple Choice** To remove the lid from the pickle jar, Nadir turned the lid counterclockwise two full turns. Nadir turned the lid about how many degrees? C

A 360° **B** 180° **C** 720° **D** 90°

▶ **27.** (82) **a.** Which of these letters has no lines of symmetry? K

M I C K E Y

Inclusion

Use this strategy if the student displays:

- Poor Retention.
- Difficulty with Large Numbers.

Multiplying a Three-Digit Number (Individual)

Material: none

- Write 255 × 16 on the board. Have students use the distributive property to breakdown 16 into 10 and 6. Write = 255 × (10 + 6). Have students multiply 255 by 10 and ask, ***"What is the product of 255 and 10?"*** 2550
- Then have students multiply 255 by 6 and ask, ***"What is the product of 255 and 6?"*** 1530 "***What final operation needs to be performed?"*** addition

  Have students add the two partial products and compare their answer with a peer.
- Read, ***"There are 18 classes. Each class needs 129 bottles of water. How many total bottles of water are needed?"*** Have students solve.

b. Which letter has rotational symmetry? I

*28. (20, 100) If each side of an equilateral triangle is $2\frac{1}{4}$ inches long, what is the perimeter of the triangle? $6\frac{3}{4}$ inches

*29. (55, 56, 105) **List** **a.** Write 35 as the product of two factors as many ways as possible. 1×35, 5×7

b. Write 35 as the product of prime factors. 5×7

▶*30. (102) **Verify** Use the Distributive Property to multiply 23 and 36. Show your work.

$$\begin{aligned} 23 \times 36 &= (23 \times 30) + (23 \times 6) \\ &= 690 + 138 \\ &= 828 \end{aligned}$$

Multiplying a Three-Digit Number by a Two-Digit Number will be developed in ***Saxon Math*** *Intermediate 5.*

Written Practice *(Continued)*

Math Conversations *(cont.)*

Problem 25 Multiple Choice

Test-Taking Strategy

Before students solve the problem, ask:

"If a triangle is an equilateral triangle, how do the lengths of its sides compare?" All of the sides of an equilateral triangle have the same length.

Problem 27a

Extend the Problem

Ask students to trace the letters that have lines of symmetry and draw all of the lines of symmetry for these letters.

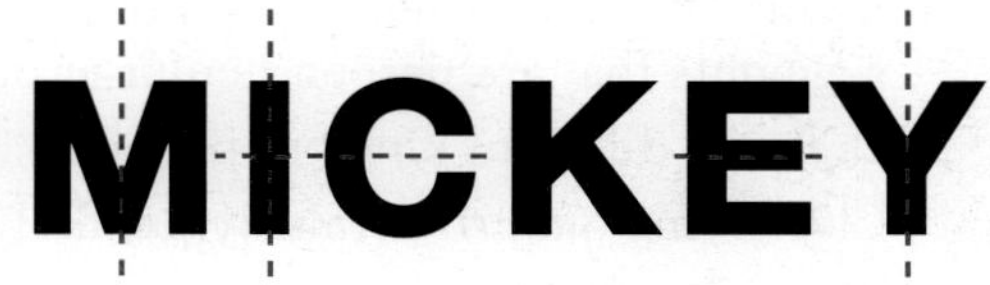

Problem 30 **Verify**

Make sure students recall that when the Distributive Property is used to find the product of two factors, we first write the expanded form of the number we are multiplying by. The expanded form of 36, the number we are multiplying by, is $30 + 6$.

Errors and Misconceptions

Problem 2

Watch for opportunities to remind students that linear measures, such as perimeter labeled as a number of units, and measures of area are labeled as a number of square units.

Problem 26

You may need to remind students that the measure in degrees of a full turn is 360°.

Planning & Preparation

• Analyzing Prisms

Objectives

- Visualize and describe different kinds of prisms.
- Identify congruent parts of geometric solids.
- Identify parallel and perpendicular faces of geometric solids.

Prerequisite Skills

- Identifying and drawing parallel lines and segments.
- Identifying and drawing pairs of intersecting lines and segments that are perpendicular or oblique.
- Drawing different kinds of polygons.
- Classifying quadrilaterals by parallel sides.

Materials

Instructional Masters

- Power Up B Worksheet

Manipulative Kit

- Relational GeoSolids*

**optional*

California Mathematics Content Standards

MG 3.0, 3.1 Identify lines that are parallel and perpendicular.

MG 3.0, 3.3 Identify congruent figures.

MG 3.0, 3.6 Visualize, describe, and make models of geometric solids (e.g., prisms, pyramids) in terms of the number and shape of faces, edges, and vertices; interpret two-dimensional representations of three-dimensional objects; and draw patterns (of faces) for a solid that, when cut and folded, will make a model of the solid.

MR 2.0, 2.3 Use a variety of methods, such as words, numbers, symbols, charts, graphs, tables, diagrams, and models, to explain mathematical reasoning.

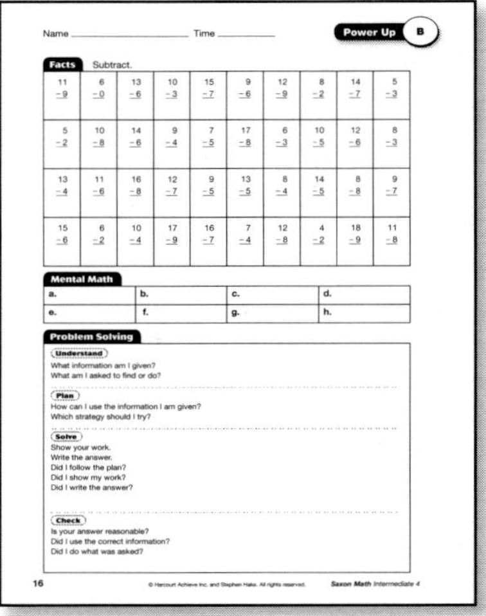

Name ______________ Time ________ **Power Up B**

Facts Subtract.

11 − 9	6 − 0	13 − 6	10 − 3	15 − 7	9 − 6	12 − 9	8 − 2	14 − 7	5 − 3
5 − 2	10 − 8	14 − 6	9 − 4	7 − 5	17 − 8	6 − 3	10 − 5	12 − 6	8 − 3
13 − 4	11 − 6	16 − 8	12 − 7	9 − 5	13 − 5	8 − 4	14 − 5	8 − 8	9 − 7
15 − 6	6 − 2	10 − 4	17 − 9	16 − 7	7 − 4	12 − 8	4 − 2	18 − 9	11 − 8

Mental Math

a.	b.	c.	d.
e.	f.	g.	h.

Problem Solving

Understand
What information am I given?
What am I asked to find or do?

Plan
How can I use the information I am given?
Which strategy should I try?

Solve
Show your work.
Write the answer.
Did I follow the plan?
Did I show my work?
Did I write the answer?

Check
Is your answer reasonable?
Did I use the correct information?
Did I do what was asked?

16 © Harcourt Achieve Inc. and Stephen Hake. All rights reserved. *Saxon Math Intermediate 4*

Power Up B Worksheet

Universal Access

Reaching All Special Needs Students

Special Education Students	At-Risk Students	English Learners	Advanced Learners
• Inclusion (TM) • Adaptations for Saxon Math	• Alternative Approach (TM) • Error Alert (TM) • Reteaching Masters • Refresher Lessons for California Standards	• English Learners (TM) • Developing Academic Language (TM) • English Learner Handbook	• Extend the Example (TM) • Extend the Problem (TM) • Online Activities

TM=Teacher's Manual

Developing Academic Language

New	Maintained	English Learner
hexagonal prism	congruent	reduce
octagonal prism	edges	
pentagonal prism	faces	
trapezoidal prism	parallel	
	perpendicular	
	rectangular prism	
	triangular prism	
	vertices	

Problem Solving Discussion

Problem

In this sequence, each term is the sum of the two preceding terms. Copy this sequence and find the next four terms.

1, 1, 2, 3, 5, 8, __, __, __, __, ...

Focus Strategy

Find/Extend a Pattern

Understand ***Understand the problem.***

"What information are we given?"

The first six terms of a sequence are 1, 1, 2, 3, 5, and 8.

Each term is the sum of the two preceding terms.

"What are we asked to do?"

We are asked to find the next four terms of the sequence.

Plan ***Make a plan.***

"What problem-solving strategy will we use to solve the problem?"

We will *extend the pattern.*

Solve ***Carry out the plan.***

"What term follows 8 in the sequence?"

We add 5 and 8 to get 13.

"What term follows 13 in the sequence?"

We add 8 and 13 to get 21.

"What term follows 21 in the sequence?"

We add 13 and 21 to get 34.

"What term follows 34 in the sequence?"

We add 21 and 34 to get 55.

Check ***Look back.***

"Did we complete the task that was assigned?"

Yes. We found that the next four terms of the sequence are 13, 21, 34, and 55.

"Are our answers reasonable?"

Yes. We know that our answers are reasonable because each term we found is the sum of the two previous terms in the sequence.

"What do you notice about the increase from term to term?"

We can *draw a diagram* to study the increase from one term to the next:

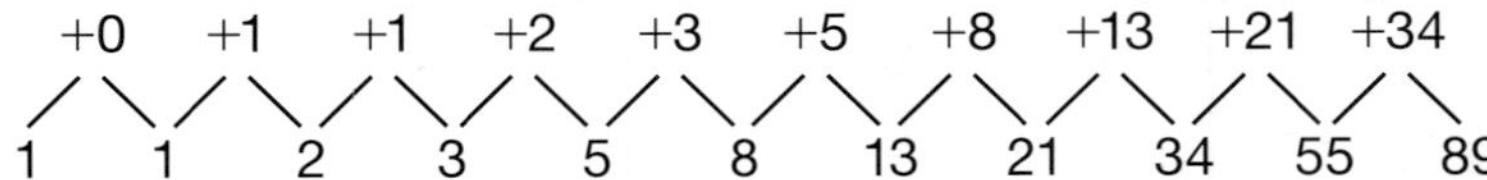

We find that the increase of the terms recreates the sequence.

"This sequence is called a Fibonacci sequence (pronounced FIH-buh-NAH-chee). It is named after a mathematician who lived in the 1200's. The numbers in a Fibonacci sequence have interesting properties that relate them to nature. For example, the number of petals on a flower is often a Fibonacci number."

Encourage students to research Fibonacci numbers and their connection to nature and the golden ratio.

Power Up

Facts

Distribute **Power Up B** to students. See answers below.

Count Aloud

Before students begin the Mental Math exercises, do these counting exercises as a class.

Count up and down by twelves from 12 to 96.

Mental Math

Encourage students to share different ways to mentally compute these exercises. Strategies for exercises are listed below.

a. Decompose 36
$(30 + 6) \div 2 = (30 \div 2) + (6 \div 2) =$
$15 + 3 = 18$

Divide 36 by 2
$36 \div 2 = 18$

d. Subtract 70, then Add 2
$83 - 70 = 13; 13 + 2 = 15$

Subtract 60, then Subtract 8
$83 - 60 = 23; 23 - 8 = 15$

Problem Solving

Refer to **Problem-Solving Strategy Discussion,** p. 710B.

New Concept

Active Learning

For each prism, ask students to point to each of the bases. If they have difficulty identifying the bases, explain that a prism has two bases, and the bases are parallel to each other, and congruent.

As students point to the bases, remind them that the bases of a prism can be any polygon, and that a base is not always the bottom of a prism.

Explanation

Make sure students notice the tick marks on the one base of the triangular prism, the rectangular prism, and the trapezoidal prism. Explain that the tick marks are symbols for congruency and indicate that the triangular bases are isosceles triangles, the rectangular bases are squares, and the trapezoidal bases are isosceles trapezoids.

(continued)

LESSON 108

California Mathematics Content Standards

MG 3.0, 3.1 Identify lines that are parallel and perpendicular.
MG 3.0, 3.3 Identify congruent figures.
MG 3.0, 3.6 Visualize, describe, and make models of geometric solids (e.g., prisms, pyramids) in terms of the number and shape of faces, edges, and vertices; interpret two-dimensional representations of three-dimensional objects; and draw patterns (of faces) for a solid that, when cut and folded, will make a model of the solid.

• Analyzing Prisms

facts Power Up B

mental math Find each fraction of 36 in problems **a–c.**

a. Fractional Part: $\frac{1}{2}$ of 36 18

b. Fractional Part: $\frac{1}{3}$ of 36 12

c. Fractional Part: $\frac{1}{4}$ of 36 9

d. Number Sense: 83 − 68 15

e. Geometry: What is the perimeter of a hexagon with sides that are each 5 cm long? 30 cm

f. Estimation: Camille is cutting lengths of yarn that are each $7\frac{3}{4}$ inches long. If she must cut 6 pieces of yarn, about how many inches of yarn will she need? 48 in. or 4 ft

g. Calculation: 10 ÷ 2, × 8, − 4, ÷ 6 6

h. Simplify: c^2 when $c = 4$ 16

problem solving Choose an appropriate problem-solving strategy to solve this problem. In this sequence, each term is the sum of the two preceding terms. Copy this sequence and find the next four terms.

1, 1, 2, 3, 5, 8, 13, 21, 34, 55, . . .

A **prism** is a three-dimensional solid with two congruent bases. These congruent bases are parallel. The shape of each pair of bases can be any polygon. The shape of the base determines the name of the prism. The word "base" does not mean the bottom of the figure. In each figure below, the bases are the front and back of the figure. However, the figures can be turned so that the bases are in different positions.

Facts Subtract.

11 − 9 = 2	6 − 0 = 6	13 − 6 = 7	10 − 3 = 7	15 − 7 = 8	9 − 6 = 3	12 − 9 = 3	8 − 2 = 6	14 − 7 = 7	5 − 3 = 2
5 − 2 = 3	10 − 8 = 2	14 − 6 = 8	9 − 4 = 5	7 − 5 = 2	17 − 8 = 9	6 − 3 = 3	10 − 5 = 5	12 − 6 = 6	8 − 3 = 5
13 − 4 = 9	11 − 6 = 5	16 − 8 = 8	12 − 7 = 5	9 − 5 = 4	13 − 5 = 8	8 − 4 = 4	14 − 5 = 9	8 − 8 = 0	9 − 7 = 2
15 − 6 = 9	6 − 2 = 4	10 − 4 = 6	17 − 9 = 8	16 − 7 = 9	7 − 4 = 3	12 − 8 = 4	4 − 2 = 2	18 − 9 = 9	11 − 8 = 3

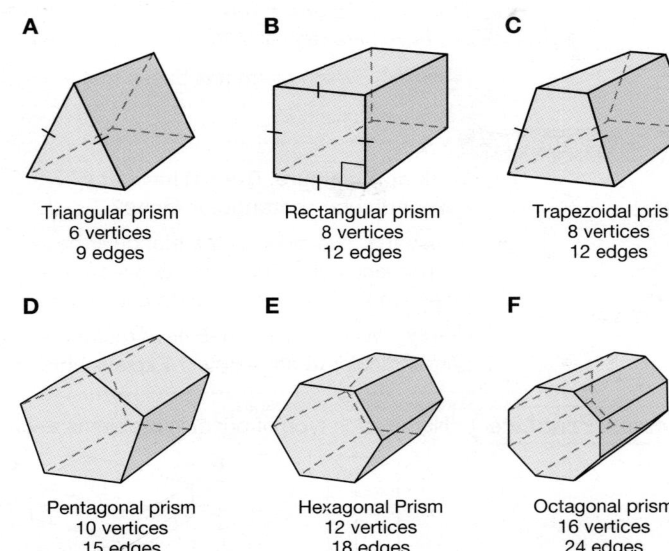

Analyze What shape is each pair of bases in prisms **A–F?** What shape are the faces that are not bases?

Isosceles triangles, squares, isosceles trapezoids,regular pentagons, regular hexagons, regular octagons; rectangles

Example 1

Which prisms A–F have parallel rectangular faces?

In figure **B,** if we consider the front and back of the rectangular prism as bases, then we see two other pairs of parallel rectangular faces. That is, the top and the bottom faces are parallel, and the left and right faces are also parallel. Also notice that opposite rectangular faces in figures **C, E,** and **F** are parallel. Any prism whose bases have parallel sides has parallel rectangular faces.

Conclude Do all regular polygons have parallel sides? Why or why not?

No; sample: Equilateral triangles and regular pentagons do not have parallel sides; The sides are parallel only when the regular polygon has an even number of sides.

Example 2

Which prisms A–F have congruent rectangular faces?

Prism A has 2 congruent rectangular faces since two sides of the triangular base are the same length.

Prism B has four congruent rectangular faces since its bases are squares.

Prism C has 2 congruent rectangular faces since its bases are trapezoids with two sides the same length.

New Concept *(Continued)*

Example 1

As students study the prisms to identify the parallel rectangular faces, point out that if two faces of a prism are parallel, the faces are opposite each other, and students should look for opposite faces.

Example 2

Error Alert

As students identify the prisms that have congruent rectangular faces, remind them that in order for two (or more than two) faces of a prism to be congruent, they must be exactly the same size and shape. In other words, they must be identical.

(continued)

Alternative Approach: Using Manipulatives

To help students identify the bases, faces, and edges of solid figures, have students model each term using a triangular prism. Show the students one of the bases of the prism. Ask:

"What kind of polygon forms the base of this prism?" triangle

Use colored self-stick notes to label the bases. Next show the students one of the rectangular-shaped faces. Ask:

"What kind of polygon is this?" rectangle

Label each rectangular face with a different colored self-stick note. Have students count all the self-stick notes (both colors) to identify the number of faces of the prism.

Then identify the edges and place a small, numbered self-stick note on each edge as you count them. Have students select a different solid figure and identify and count the bases, faces, and edges of the figure and record their answers.

New Concept (Continued)

Example 3

Extend the Example

Challenge your advanced learners by asking them to classify the prism. The prism is a right triangular prism.

Lesson Practice

Guided Practice

Use these problems as guided practice to check the students' understanding of today's concept.

Problem e

Encourage students who have difficulty identifying the pairs of parallel faces to use phrases such as "top and bottom," "front and back" and "left side and right side" as a way of recording their observations.

Problems a–c
Error Alert

Remind students that prisms are named for their bases, and prisms have two parallel congruent bases.

Problem g **Explain**
Error Alert

Remind students that the two bases of a prism must be parallel and congruent.

Closure

The questions below help assess the concepts taught in this lesson.

"How is a prism different than a polygon?" Sample: A polygon is a two-dimensional flat figure and a prism is a three-dimensional solid figure. For example, a polygon has a length and a width; A prism has a length, a width, and a height.

"Explain how prisms are named. Give an example to support your answer." All prisms have two parallel congruent bases, and are named for the shapes of those bases. For example, if the bases of a prism are rectangles, the prism is a rectangular prism.

Figures D, E, and F have all congruent rectangular faces since the bases are regular polygons.

Classify Which prism has bases that are rhombuses? Prism **B**, a square is a rhombus

Example 3

Look at this figure. Does it have any perpendicular rectangular faces?

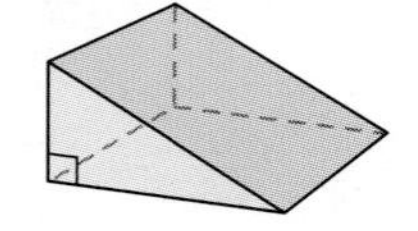

Notice that two sides of the triangular bases are perpendicular. Therefore, two rectangle faces are also perpendicular to each other.

Verify Which prisms **A–F** have rectangular faces that are perpendicular to each other? Explain why. Prism **B** because it has square or rectangular bases.

Lesson Practice Name each type of prism in problems **a–c**.

a. 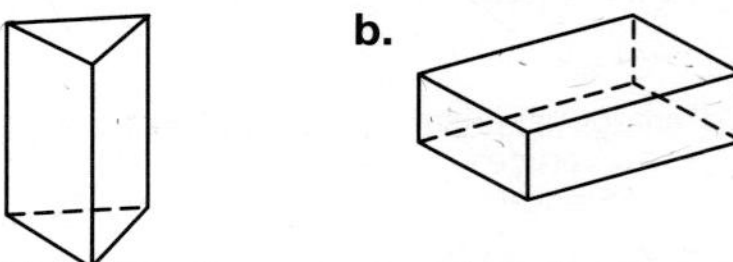 triangular prism

b. 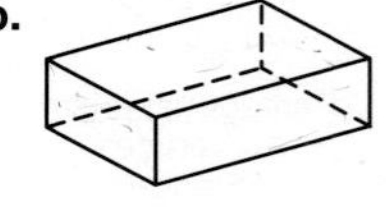 rectangular prism

c. 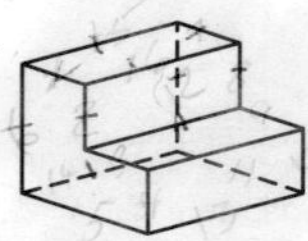 hexagonal prism

d. The prism in problem **a** has how many rectangular faces that are perpendicular to each other? none

e. A rectangular prism has how many pairs of parallel faces? 3

f. The prism in problem **c** has how many edges? 18

g. **Explain** Is this figure a prism? Explain your answer. No, the figure is not a prism because it does not have two parallel congruent bases.

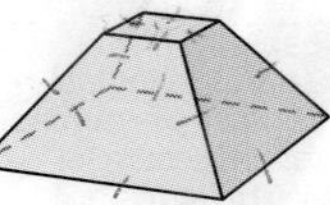

Written Practice

Distributed and Integrated

1. (93) **Justify** Tessa made 70 photocopies. If she paid 6¢ per copy and the total tax was 25¢, how much change should she have gotten back from a $5 bill? Is your answer reasonable? Why or why not? 55¢; sample: I know my answer is reasonable because $70 \times 6 = 420$; $420 + 25 = 445$; $500 - 445 = 55$

2. (20, Inv. 3) **a.** What is the area of this square? 36 sq. cm

b. What is the perimeter of the square? 24 cm

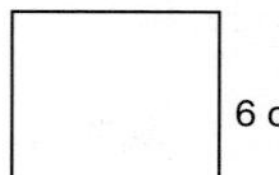

Math Background

There are different types of prisms. The prisms that have faces that are rectangles are called right prisms. Some prisms have faces that are non-rectangular parallelograms; these are called oblique prisms.

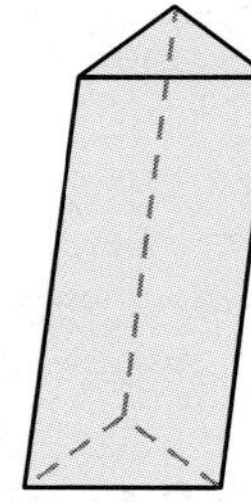

oblique triangular prism

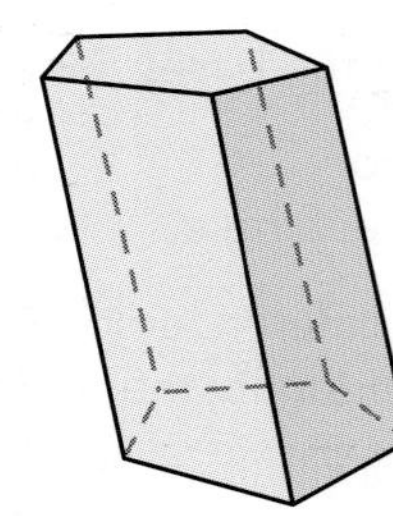

oblique pentagonal prism

*3. (93) Use the information below to answer parts **a** and **b.**

Walker has $9. Dembe has twice as much money as Walker. Chris has $6 more than Dembe.

a. How much money does Dembe have? $18

b. How much money does Chris have? $24

4. (25, 93, Inv. 10) Use this table to answer the questions that follow:

Number of Dumplings	12	24	36	48	60
Number of Dozens	1	2	3	4	5

a. Generalize Write a rule that describes the relationship of the data. Sample: To find the number of dumplings, multiply the number of dozens by 12.

b. Predict How many dumplings is 12 dozen dumplings? 144 dumplings

5. (93) Analyze There are 40 quarters in a roll of quarters. What is the value of 2 rolls of quarters? $20

6. (91) Estimate Lucio estimated that the exact quotient of 1754 divided by 9 was close to 20. Did Lucio make a reasonable estimate? Explain why or why not. No; sample: use compatible numbers; Since 1800 ÷ 9 = 200, the exact quotient will be close to 200.

▶ *7. (106) Write the reduced form of each fraction:

a. $\frac{2}{12}$ $\frac{1}{6}$ **b.** $\frac{6}{8}$ $\frac{3}{4}$ **c.** $\frac{3}{9}$ $\frac{1}{3}$

▶ **8.** (76, 93) Conclude The three runners wore black, red, and green T-shirts. The runner wearing green finished one place ahead of the runner wearing black, and the runner wearing red was not last. Who finished first? Draw a diagram to solve this problem. See student work; The runner wearing red was first.

*9. (106) Explain Reduce the fraction $\frac{6}{8}$. Explain your thinking. $\frac{3}{4}$; sample: Divide the numerator and the denominator by 2.

*10. (55, 56, 105) List **a.** Write 50 as the product of two factors as many ways as possible. 1 × 50, 2 × 25, 5 × 10

b. Write 50 as the product of prime factors. 2 × 5 × 5

Written Practice

Math Conversations

Independent Practice and Discussions to Increase Understanding

Problem 1 Justify

Make sure students recognize this problem as a multiple-step problem and understand how to find the total cost of the photocopies including tax. $4.45

Students are likely to give a variety of reasons why their answers are reasonable; invite volunteers to share their reasons with the class.

Problem 7

Before students begin the arithmetic for each problem, ask them to name the numerator of the fraction, the denominator of the fraction, and the greatest number that is a factor of both the numerator and the denominator. The greatest factors are as follows: **a:** 2; **b:** 2; **c:** 3.

Then ask:

"Explain how division can be used to reduce a fraction." Sample: Divide the numerator and the denominator by a factor of the numerator and the denominator.

"What is true if 1 is the only common factor of a numerator and a denominator?" The fraction cannot be reduced.

Problem 8 Conclude

The runner wearing red finished first, the runner wearing green finished second, and the runner wearing black finished third.

(continued)

English Learners

Explain that the common meaning of the word **reduce** is to make smaller in size, amount or number.

Ask:

"How can we reduce the amount of water in a glass?" Sample: Pour some water out of the glass.

Say, ***"When we reduce a fraction we do not make the fraction smaller, but we use smaller numbers to name the fraction."***

Ask:

"Explain how we reduce the fraction $\frac{4}{6}$." We divide the numerator and denominator by 2 and get $\frac{2}{3}$.

Inclusion

Use this strategy if the student displays:

- Poor Vision
- Poor Retention.

Analyzing Prisms (Whole Group)

Material: Relational GeoSolids

- Display and pass a triangular prism. Tell students to look at the faces, vertices, and edges. Ask, ***"How many faces does the prism have?"*** 5 ***"What shapes are they?"*** Rectangles and triangles ***"How many vertices does the prism have?"*** 6 ***"How many edges does the prism have?"*** 9
- Have students analyze each prism by making a chart. They should identify the number of faces, vertices and edges as well as the types of shapes used.

Written Practice *(Continued)*

Math Conversations *(cont.)*

Problem 11 Classify

Extend the Problem

"Which faces of the prism are congruent? the rectangular faces and the hexagonal bases

"How many pairs of faces are parallel? four pairs

"How many pairs of faces are perpendicular? twelve pairs

Problems 16–18

Remind students to make sure their answers are in simplest form. (The computations for problems **16, 17,** and **18** produce sums that can be simplified.)

Problems 20 and 21

Ask students to estimate each product and use the estimate to help decide the reasonableness of the exact answer. Sample:

problem **20:** 400×40; write three zeros after the product of 4×4.

problem **21:** 50×140; write two zeros after the product of 5×14.

Problem 27 Multiple Choice

Test-Taking Strategy

Help students understand that since 427,063 is between 400,000 and 500,000, choices **A** and **B** can immediately be eliminated, and since 427,063 is closer to 400,000 than to 500,000, choice **C** is the best answer.

Errors and Misconceptions

Problem 3

This problem can be solved by working forward. Students who attempt to find the answer for part **a** using the *work backwards* problem-solving strategy will find that the strategy cannot be used to find the answer. (The usefulness of the strategy depends on the order in which the data are given.)

Problem 30

The arithmetic students complete to simplify the expression must include two partial products. Completing the operation in parentheses first is not an application of the Distributive Property.

▸* **11.** (108) Classify Name this prism. hexagonal prism

a. How many vertices does it have? 12 vertices

b. How many edges does it have? 18 edges

c. How many faces does it have? 8 faces

12. (45) $4.62 + 16.7 + 9.8$ 31.12

13. (45) $14.62 - (6.3 - 2.37)$ 10.69

* **14.** (100) $\frac{3}{5} + \frac{1}{5}$ $\frac{4}{5}$

* **15.** (100) $16 + 3\frac{3}{4}$ $19\frac{3}{4}$

▸* **16.** (98, 100) $1\frac{2}{3} + 3\frac{1}{3}$ 5

▸* **17.** (98, 100) $\frac{2}{5} + \frac{3}{5}$ 1

▸* **18.** (98, 100) $7\frac{4}{5} + 7\frac{1}{5}$ 15

* **19.** (100) $6\frac{1}{3} + 3\frac{1}{3}$ $9\frac{2}{3}$

▸* **20.** (107) 372×39 14,508

▸* **21.** (107) 47×142 6674

* **22.** (Inv. 3, 59) $375 \times \sqrt{36}$ 2250

* **23.** (RF14) Estimate the area of this circle. Each small square represents one square centimeter. 28 sq. cm

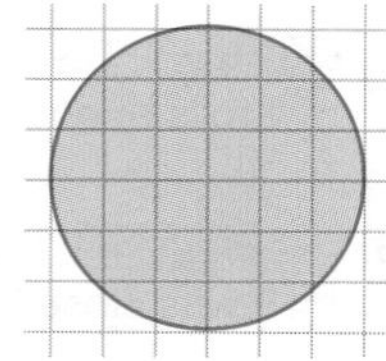

24. (34, 83) $8y = 4832$ 604

25. (65, 79) $\frac{2840}{2^3}$ 355

* **26.** (79) $3\overline{)963}$ 321

▸ **27.** (Inv. 2, 27) Represent Which arrow could be pointing to 427,063? C

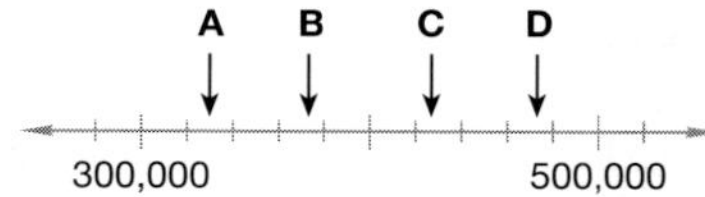

* **28.** (20, 100) If the length of each side of a square is $1\frac{1}{4}$ inches, then what is the perimeter of the square? 5 inches

29. (96) What is the geometric shape of a volleyball? sphere

* **30.** (102) Use the Distributive Property to multiply: 130

$$5(20 + 6)$$

714 ***Saxon Math** Intermediate 4*

Identifying the attributes of geometric solids prepares students for:

- **Lesson 109,** describing the attributes of pyramids.

Planning & Preparation

• Constructing Pyramids

Objectives

- Construct three-dimensional models of pyramids using nets.
- Draw a net that can be used to make a prism.
- Describe the attributes of pyramids.
- Compare and contrast pyramids and prisms.

Prerequisite Skills

- Classifying geometric solids by their sides, bases, and vertices.
- Finding real-world examples of geometric solids.
- Drawing triangles and rectangles with given side measurements.
- Drawing different kinds of polygons.

Materials

Instructional Masters

- Power Up B Worksheet
- Lesson Activity 8
- Lesson Activity 31

Manipulative Kit

- Relational GeoSolids*

Teacher-provided materials

- Grid paper, pyramid pattern, scissors, tape, glue
- Large construction paper*

**optional*

California Mathematics Content Standards

MG 3.0, 3.1 Identify lines that are parallel and perpendicular.

MG 3.0, 3.5 Know the definitions of a right angle, an acute angle, and an obtuse angle. Understand that 90°, 180°, 270°, and 360° are associated, respectively, with $\frac{1}{4}$, $\frac{1}{2}$, $\frac{3}{4}$, and full turns.

MG 3.0, 3.6 Visualize, describe, and make models of geometric solids (e.g., prisms, pyramids) in terms of the number and shape of faces, edges, and vertices; interpret two-dimensional representations of three-dimensional objects; and draw patterns (of faces) for a solid that, when cut and folded, will make a model of the solid.

MR 2.0, 2.3 Use a variety of methods, such as words, numbers, symbols, charts, graphs, tables, diagrams, and models, to explain mathematical reasoning.

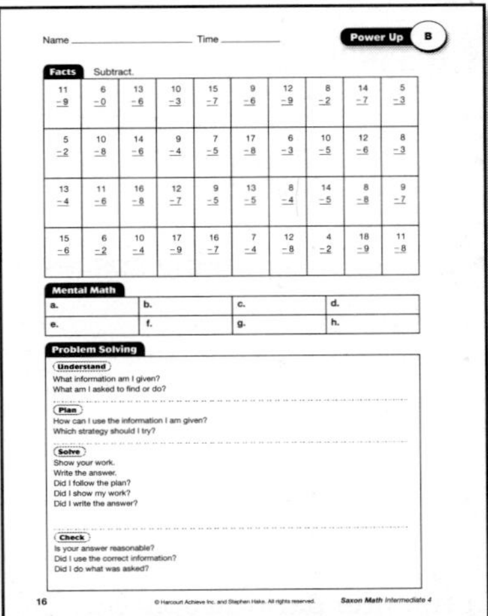

Power Up B Worksheet

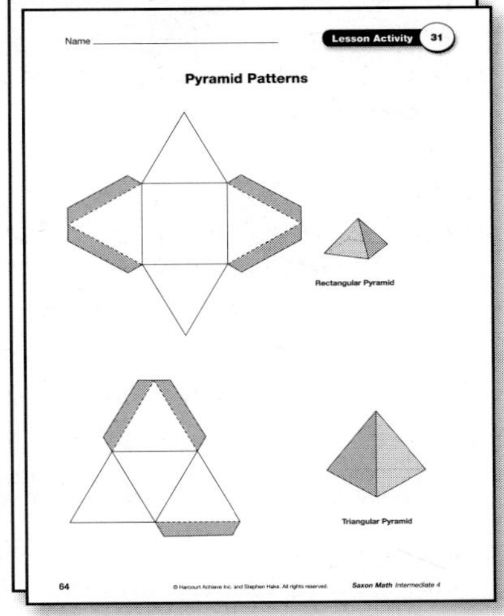

Lesson Activities 8 and 31

Universal Access

Reaching All Special Needs Students

Special Education Students	At-Risk Students	English Learners	Advanced Learners
• Inclusion (TM) • Adaptations for Saxon Math	• Error Alert (TM) • Reteaching Masters • Refresher Lessons for California Standards	• English Learners (TM) • Developing Academic Language (TM) • English Learner Handbook	• Extend the Problem (TM) • Early Finisher (SE) • Online Activities

TM=Teacher's Manual
SE=Student Edition

Developing Academic Language

Maintained
cone
cube
geometric solid
pyramid

English Learner
optical illusion

Problem Solving Discussion

Problem

There are four parking spaces (1, 2, 3, and 4) in the row nearest to the entrance of the building. Suppose only two of the four parking spaces are filled. What are the combinations of two parking spaces that could have cars in them?

Focus Strategy

Make an Organized List

Understand *Understand the problem.*

"What information are we given?"

There are four parking spaces numbered 1, 2, 3, and 4.

"What are we asked to do?"

We are asked to find the combinations of two parking spaces that could be filled.

Plan *Make a plan.*

"What problem-solving strategy can we use?"

We can *make an organized list* of the combinations.

"How can we organize our list?"

We can start by listing all the combinations that include parking space 1. Then we can find all the combinations that include parking space 2. Then we can find any remaining combinations that include parking spaces 3 and 4.

Solve *Carry out the plan.*

"What does our list look like?"

1-2, 1-3, 1-4
2-3, 2-4,
3-4

"Why did we not list '2-1,' '3-1,' '3-2,' '4-1,' '4-2,' or '4-3'?"

We do not list those combinations because they are repeats of the combinations 1-2, 1-3, 2-3, 1-4, 2-4, and 3-4, which we had already listed elsewhere. The order in which the parking spots are listed does not matter.

Check *Look back.*

"How many combinations of two parking spaces can be filled?"

There are 6 different ways that two of the four parking spots can be filled. The combinations are 1 and 2; 1 and 3; 1 and 4; 2 and 3; 2 and 4; and 3 and 4.

"Is our answer reasonable?"

We know that our answer is reasonable, because each combination lists two parking spaces that can be filled.

"What is another problem-solving strategy that we could use to help us solve the problem?"

We could *draw a picture or diagram.*

Alternate Strategy

Draw a Picture or Diagram

Students can also *draw a diagram* of the parking spaces to help them visualize the problem and find the combinations.

LESSON 109

• Constructing Pyramids

California Mathematics Content Standards

MG 3.0, 3.1 Identify lines that are parallel and perpendicular.

MG 3.0, 3.6 Visualize, describe, and make models of geometric solids (e.g., prisms, pyramids) in terms of the number and shape of faces, edges, and vertices; interpret two-dimensional representations of three-dimensional objects; and draw patterns (of faces) for a solid that, when cut and folded, will make a model of the solid.

Power Up

facts Power Up B

mental math Find each fraction of 40 in problems **a–c.**

a. **Fractional Part:** $\frac{1}{2}$ of 40 20

b. **Fractional Part:** $\frac{1}{4}$ of 40 10

c. **Fractional Part:** $\frac{1}{10}$ of 40 4

d. **Money:** Shelly gave the clerk a \$10 bill for a half gallon of milk that cost \$1.95. How much change should she receive? \$8.05

e. **Time:** Rashid was born on a Monday in April 2000. On what day of the week was his first birthday? Tuesday

f. **Estimation:** Estimate the area of the rectangle shown at right. 20 in²

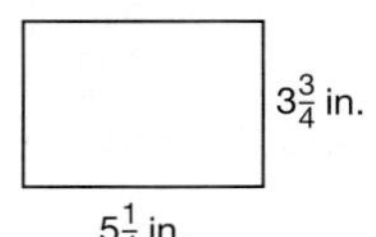

g. **Calculation:** $\sqrt{64}$, − 3, × 7, − 3, ÷ 8 4

h. **Simplify:** $39 - g^2$ when $g = 3$ 30

problem solving Choose an appropriate problem-solving strategy to solve this problem. There are four parking spaces (1, 2, 3, and 4) in the row nearest to the entrance of the building. Suppose only two of the four parking spaces are filled. What are the combinations of two parking spaces that could have cars in them? 1 and 2, 1 and 3, 1 and 4, 2 and 3, 2 and 4, 3 and 4

Power Up

Facts

Distribute **Power Up B** to students. See answers below.

Count Aloud

Before students begin the Mental Math exercises, do these counting exercises as a class.

Count up and down by fives from 50 to 105.

Mental Math

Encourage students to share different ways to mentally compute these exercises. Strategies for exercises are listed below.

b. Divide 40 by 4

$40 \div 4 = 10$

Find $\frac{1}{2}$ of $\frac{1}{2}$ of 40

$\frac{1}{2}$ of $40 = 20$; $\frac{1}{2}$ of $20 = 10$

d. Subtract \$2, then Add 5¢

\$10 − \$2 = \$8; \$8 + 5¢ = \$8.05

Subtract \$1, then Subtract 95¢

\$10 − \$1 = \$9; \$9 − 95¢ = \$8.05

Problem Solving

Refer to **Problem-Solving Strategy Discussion,** p. 715B.

Facts Subtract.

11 − 9 2	6 − 0 6	13 − 6 7	10 − 3 7	15 − 7 8	9 − 6 3	12 − 9 3	8 − 2 6	14 − 7 7	5 − 3 2
5 − 2 3	10 − 8 2	14 − 6 8	9 − 4 5	7 − 5 2	17 − 8 9	6 − 3 3	10 − 5 5	12 − 6 6	8 − 3 5
13 − 4 9	11 − 6 5	16 − 8 8	12 − 7 5	9 − 5 4	13 − 5 8	8 − 4 4	14 − 5 9	8 − 8 0	9 − 7 2
15 − 6 9	6 − 2 4	10 − 4 6	17 − 9 8	16 − 7 9	7 − 4 3	12 − 8 4	4 − 2 2	18 − 9 9	11 − 8 3

New Concept

Connection

As you discuss the examples of plane figures, remind students that plane figures are two-dimensional, flat shapes.

Error Alert

As you discuss the examples of geometric solids, contrast the characteristics of plane figures with those of the solids. Have students note that solids are three-dimensional and occupy space. In other words, a plane figure does not take up space; a solid figure does take up space.

Observation

Point out that the dotted lines of the cube, the pyramid, and the cone make these figures appear as if they have three dimensions. However, they do not have three dimensions because the paper they are drawn on has only two dimensions. Explain that these perspective lines produce a false visual impression is known as an *optical illusion.*

Activity

Active Learning

Some students may benefit from working with a partner. Ask students to cut out each pattern, make sure students understand that they are not to cut along the dotted lines of each pattern—the dotted lines are fold lines. Instead, students should cut around the perimeter of each pattern, and they may find it helpful if you display a cutout sample of one of the patterns.

Folding and gluing (or taping) carefully will help ensure that the solids have sharp edges and well-defined faces.

Have students construct nets of pyramids using drawing software. Then allow them to print and construct the pyramid.

(continued)

New Concept

Math Language

A **plane** is a 2-dimensional, flat surface that never ends. Lines and plane figures are found on planes.

Recall from Lesson 50 that geometric shapes such as triangles, rectangles, and circles have two dimensions—length and width—but they do not have depth. These kinds of figures occupy area, but they do not take up space. We call shapes such as these plane figures because they are confined to a plane.

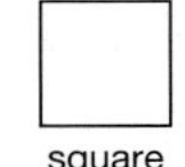
square

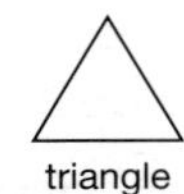
triangle

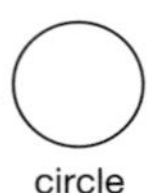
circle

Shapes that take up space are *geometric solids* such as cubes, pyramids, and cones. Geometric solids have three dimensions: length, width, and depth. Sometimes we simply call these shapes solids. Solids are not confined to a plane, so to draw them we try to create an optical illusion to suggest their shape.

Math Language

A pyramid is a three-dimensional solid with one base that can be any polygon. The base of a pyramid is not a face.

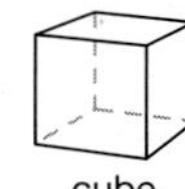
cube

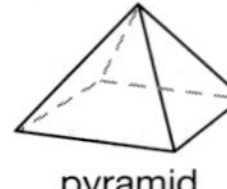
pyramid

cone

In Lesson 97 we studied models of rectangular prisms and triangular prisms. In this lesson we will study models of pyramids.

Constructing Models of Pyramids

Materials needed:

- **Lesson Activity 31**
- scissors
- glue or tape

Cut out the patterns for the pyramids. The shaded parts of each pattern are tabs to help hold the figures together. Fold the paper along the edges before you glue or tape the seams. You might want to work with a partner as you construct the models. Refer to the models to answer the following questions.

English Learners

Explain that an **optical illusion** is something that "tricks the eye." Point out the dotted lines in the drawings of a cube, a pyramid, and a cone. The dotted lines "trick the eye," or make the drawing seem to represent three dimensions when it has only two.

Ask students to look down a long, straight street the next time they are outdoors.

"What do you notice about the sides of the street the farther away you look?" Sample: they seem to get closer together

Ask students to describe other types of **optical illusions** with which they are familiar.

Math Background

Pyramids and prisms are types of polyhedra. A polyhedron is a solid with faces that are polygons joined at their edges. A regular polyhedron is a polyhedron whose faces are congruent, regular polygons and whose angles are congruent angles. There are only five regular polyhedra. They are pictured below:

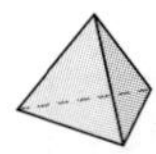
Tetrahedron

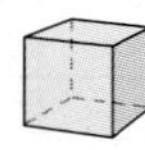
Cube

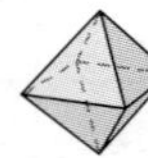
Octahedron

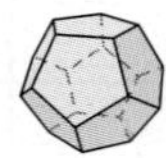
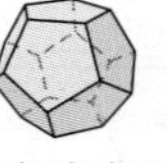
Dodecahedron

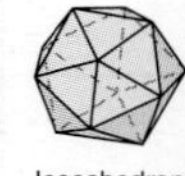
Icosahedron

Refer to the pyramid with a square base at right to answer problems **a–d.**

a. How many faces does the pyramid have, and what are their shapes? 5 faces; one square and four triangles

b. Does the pyramid have any parallel faces? No

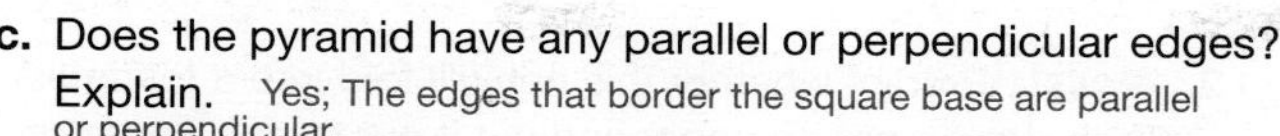

c. Does the pyramid have any parallel or perpendicular edges? Explain. Yes; The edges that border the square base are parallel or perpendicular.

d. In the pyramid above, what types of angles are formed by the intersecting edges? Acute and right angles

Refer to the pyramid with the triangular base at right to answer problems **e–h.**

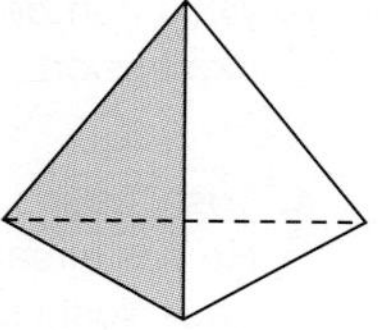

e. How many faces does the pyramid have and what are their shapes? 4 faces; all faces are (equilateral) triangles.

f. Does the pyramid have any parallel faces? No

g. Does the pyramid have any parallel or perpendicular edges? No

h. In the pyramid above, what types of angles are formed by intersecting edges? acute angles

Lesson Practice

a. **Verify** Which of these nets can be folded to form a pyramid? Net 1

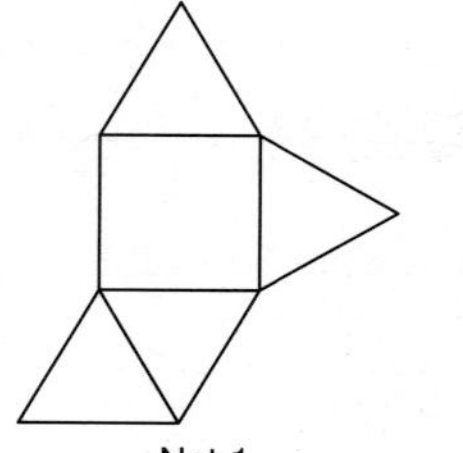

Net 1

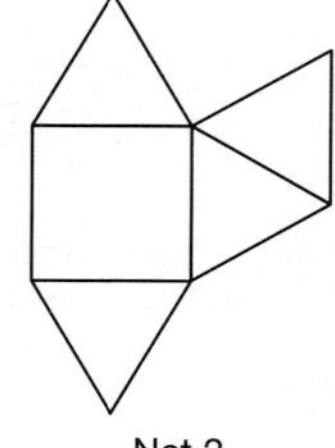

Net 2

b. **Model** Use grid paper to draw a net that will fold into a pyramid. Cut it out and fold it up to check your drawing. See student work.

Inclusion

Use this strategy if the student displays:

- Visual Impairment.
- Poor Retention.

Constructing Pyramids (Individual)

Materials: pyramids with square bases, large construction paper, scissors, and tape

- Pass out a constructed pyramid to each group. Have students unfold the pyramid into its net. Instruct students to trace the net of the pyramid on their paper. Ask, ***"What types of polygons do we see on a pyramid that has a square base?"*** Triangles and a square
- Have students cut apart the net image into the 5 polygons.
- If time permits, have students pass their shapes to a peer. Using the peer's shapes students reconstruct a pyramid. Ask, ***"How many faces, vertices and edges does this pyramid have?"***

New Concept *(Continued)*

Problems a–h Manipulative Use

Encourage students to use the models they constructed during the activity to solve these problems. Some students may benefit from numbering or coloring the faces of the models.

Extend the Activity

After students have completed the activity, invite advanced learners to name real-world objects they have seen (or read about) that look similar to the pyramid in this activity, and to the solids that appear elsewhere in this lesson.

Problems a–h
Error Alert

Make sure students understand how the perspective lines can be used to help count the faces and identify their shapes.

Lesson Practice

Guided Practice

Use these problems as guided practice to check the students' understanding of today's concept.

Problem b **Model**

To draw a net that will fold into a pyramid, the height of each triangle must be greater than one-half the length of a side of the square. To simplify this concept, ask students to make the height of the triangle the same as, or greater than, the length of a side of the square.

Problem b **Model**
Error Alert

The nets do not need to be folded precisely; The goal of the activity is to gain a sense of arrangements that can, and cannot, be folded to form a pyramid.

Closure

The questions below help assess the concepts taught in this lesson.

"Name three examples of plane figures and name three examples of geometric solids." Sample: square, triangle, circle; cube, pyramid, cone

"How are the figures and solids you named alike? How are they different?" Sample: (same) The figures have at least two dimensions; (different) Plane figures have two dimensions and do not take up space, and solid figures have three dimensions and take up space.

Written Practice

Math Conversations

Independent Practice and Discussions to Increase Understanding

Problem 2 (Model)

Remind students that even when points are in the negatives they can still find the length of a line segment. They find the length by subtracting 6 – (–4).

Problem 7 Multiple Choice

Test-Taking Strategy

Make sure students understand that since 356,420 is between 300,000 and 400,000, choice **D** (a number greater than 400,000) can immediately be eliminated, and since 356,420 is a little more than halfway between 300,000 to 400,000, choice **B** is the best answer.

Problem 8

Before students write the reduced form of each fraction, ask:

"What is the greatest number that divides both the numerator and the denominator?" **a:** 2; **b:** 3; **c:** 1 $\left(\frac{9}{16}\right.$ is already in reduced form$\left.\right)$

(continued)

Written Practice

Distributed and Integrated

1. (93) If a can of soup costs \$1.50 and serves 3 people, how much would it cost to serve soup to 12 people? \$6.00

▶ ***2.** (109) (Model) Predict whether this net will fold into a triangular pyramid. Then draw a net on paper and cut it out to see if your prediction was correct. See student work.

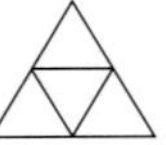

3. (63) What number is eight less than the product of nine and ten? Write an expression. 82; (9 × 10) − 8

4. (94) Yoshi needs to learn 306 new words for the regional spelling bee. He has already memorized $\frac{2}{3}$ of the new words. How many words does Yoshi still need to memorize? Draw a picture to illustrate the problem. 102 words

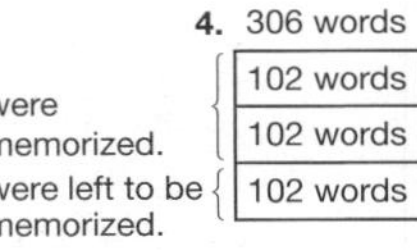

5. (42) **a.** Find the length of this line segment in centimeters. 3.7 cm

b. Find the length of the segment in millimeters. 37 mm

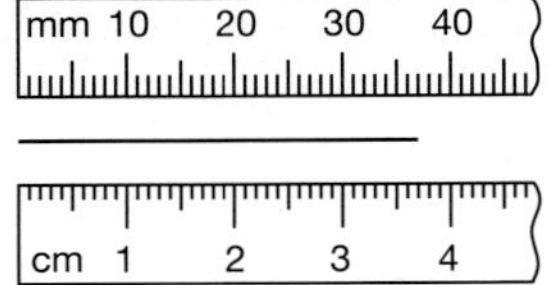

6. (27) (Represent) Use words to write 356,420. three hundred fifty-six thousand, four hundred twenty

▶ **7.** (Inv. 2, 27) (Represent) Which arrow could be pointing to 356,420? B

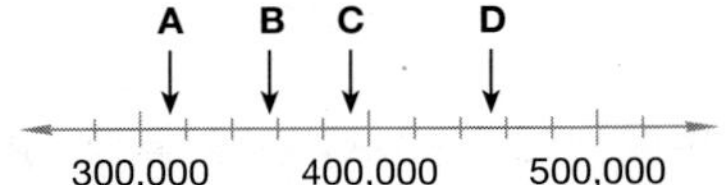

▶ ***8.** (106) Write the reduced form of each fraction:

a. $\frac{2}{6}$ $\frac{1}{3}$ **b.** $\frac{6}{9}$ $\frac{2}{3}$ **c.** $\frac{9}{16}$ $\frac{9}{16}$

718 **Saxon Math** *Intermediate 4*

*9. (Inv. 4, 106) **a.** There were 40 workers on the job. Of those workers, 10 had worked overtime. What fraction of the workers had worked overtime? (Remember to reduce the fraction.) $\frac{1}{4}$

b. What decimal part of the workers had worked overtime? 0.25

*10. (104) **Estimate** Round 14,563,900 to the nearest million. 15,000,000

▶*11. (105) **Explain** Reduce $\frac{10}{15}$. Explain your reasoning. $\frac{2}{3}$; sample: Divide the numerator and denominator by 5.

12. (11, 93) **Conclude** Jamar received $10 for his tenth birthday. Each year after that, he received $1 more than he did on his previous birthday. He saved all his birthday money. In all, how much birthday money did Jamar have on his fifteenth birthday? $75

*13. (100) **Analyze** Every morning Marta walks $2\frac{1}{2}$ miles. How many miles does Marta walk in two mornings? 5 miles

14. (45) $9.36 - (4.37 - 3.8)$ 8.79

15. (45) $24.32 - (8.61 + 12.5)$ 3.21

▶*16. (98, 100) $5\frac{5}{8} + 3\frac{3}{8}$ 9

▶*17. (100, 106) $6\frac{3}{10} + 1\frac{2}{10}$ $7\frac{1}{2}$

▶*18. (100) $8\frac{2}{3} - 5\frac{1}{3}$ $3\frac{1}{3}$

▶*19. (100, 106) $4\frac{3}{4} - 2\frac{1}{4}$ $2\frac{1}{2}$

*20. (107) 125×16 2000

*21. (107) $12 \times \$1.50$ $18.00

22. (34, 83) $6m = 3642$ 607

23. (69) $\$125 \div 5$ $25

▶*24. (79) $4\overline{)645}$ 161 R 1

25. (25, 34, 65) $3m = 6^2$ 12

26. (38, 63) **Evaluate** If n is 16, then what does $3n$ equal? 48

27. (21, 45) Dion's temperature is 99.8°F. Normal body temperature is about 98.6°F. Dion's temperature is how many degrees above normal body temperature? 1.2°F

Written Practice *(Continued)*

Math Conversations *(cont.)*

Problem 11 Explain

Extend the Problem

Challenge your advanced learners to reduce $\frac{24}{42}$ to simplest form. $\frac{4}{7}$

Problems 16–19

Remind students to make sure their answers are in simplest form. (The computations for problems **16, 17,** and **19** produce a sum or difference that can be simplified.)

Problem 24

Before students begin the arithmetic, ask:

"Is 15 a reasonable estimate of the quotient? Explain why or why not." No: sample: Round 645 to 600, then divide using a pattern; Since 60 ÷ 4 is 15, 600 ÷ 4 is 150, so the quotient will be close to 150.

(continued)

Written Practice *(Continued)*

Math Conversations *(cont.)*

Problem 28

Estimates may vary. Accept a range of reasonable estimates.

Problem 30 **Conclude**

Encourage interested students to inspect the triangular prism using Relational GeoSolids.

Errors and Misconceptions

Problem 8a

When division is used to reduce a fraction to simplest form, some students may write the division incorrectly, as shown below.

$$\frac{2}{6} \div \frac{2}{2}$$

It is incorrect to write the division in this way because (as students will learn in their future studies) to divide by a fraction, we multiply by the reciprocal of the fraction.

$$\frac{2}{6} \div \frac{2}{2} = \frac{2}{6} \cdot \frac{2}{2} = \frac{4}{12}$$

So the division simplifies to $\frac{2}{6} \div \frac{2}{2}$ simplifies to $\frac{4}{12}$ instead of the correct answer of $\frac{1}{3}$.

Make sure students understand that the method shown below is the correct way for them to write a division to reduce a fraction.

$$\frac{2}{6} = \frac{2 \div 2}{6 \div 2} = \frac{1}{3}$$

Problem 12

Make sure students determine that Jamar received \$10, \$11, \$12, \$13, \$14, and \$15 first.

Ask advanced learners:

"If I draw a diagonal line segment, could I subtract the x- and y-coordinates to find its length?" No, only the lengths of vertical and horizontal segments can be found by subtracting coordinates

▶***28.** *(RF14)* Estimate the perimeter and area of this piece of land. Each small square represents one square mile. 19 mi; 22 sq. mi

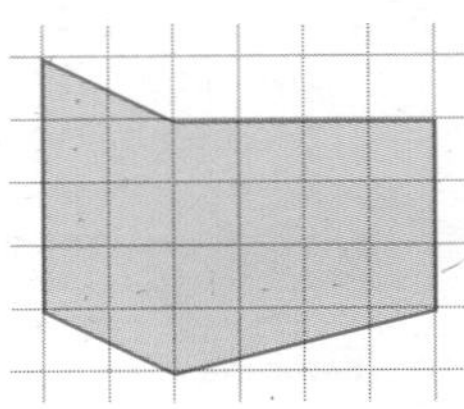

***29.** *(31)* **Analyze** Write the dimensions of a rectangle with a perimeter of 80 yd and an area of 400 yd^2. Square with side length 20 yd

▶***30.** *(108)* **Conclude** Use this figure to answer parts **a–d.**

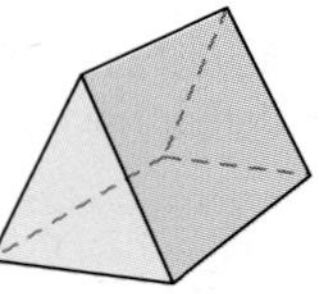

a. Name this figure. triangular prism

b. How many vertices does it have? 6 vertices

c. How many edges does it have? 9 edges

d. How many faces does it have? 5 faces

Early Finishers
Real-World Connection

What is the length of the line segment on the grid? Explain how you found your answer.

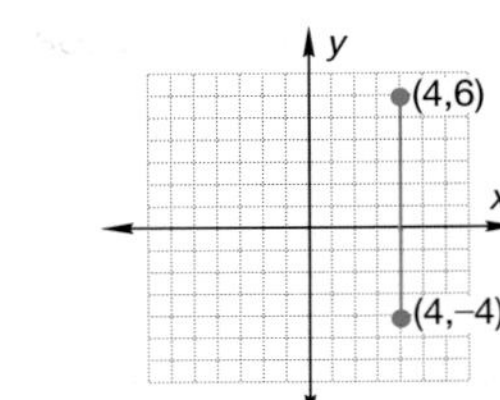

10 units; sample: Since this is a vertical line segment, the *x*-coordinates are the same. We subtract the *y*-coordinates to find the length of the segment. It is 6 units to zero and then 4 more units to −4. 6 − (−4) = 10

Constructing Pyramids will be further developed in ***Saxon Math*** *Intermediate 5.*

Planning & Preparation

California Mathematics Content Standards

SDAP 2.0, 2.1 Represent all possible outcomes for a simple probability situation in an organized way (e.g., tables, grids, tree diagrams).

SDAP 2.0, 2.2 Express outcomes of experimental probability situations verbally and numerically (e.g., 3 out of 4; $\frac{3}{4}$).

• Simple Probability

Objectives

- Make predictions for simple probability situations.
- Express the probability of an event verbally.
- Represent the probability of an event as a fraction.
- Record all the possible outcomes of an experiment in a table.

Prerequisite Skills

- Drawing a diagram to solve problems about a fraction of a group.
- Reading and writing fractions in number form and word form.

Materials

Instructional Masters

- Power Up B Worksheet

Manipulative Kit

- Money manipulatives, color tiles*

Teacher-provided materials

- Bag*

**optional*

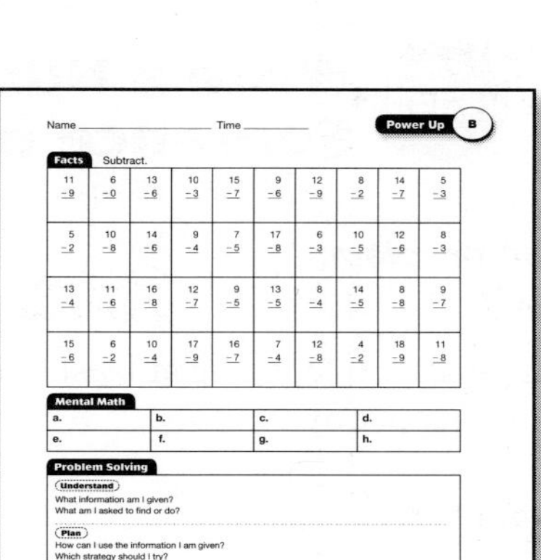

Power Up B Worksheet

Universal Access

Reaching All Special Needs Students

Special Education Students	At-Risk Students	English Learners	Advanced Learners
• Inclusion (TM) • Adaptations for Saxon Math	• Alternative Approach (TM) • Error Alert (TM) • Reteaching Masters • Refresher Lessons for California Standards	• English Learners (TM) • Developing Academic Language (TM) • English Learner Handbook	• Extend the Example (TM) • Extend the Problem (TM) • Online Activities

TM=Teacher's Manual

Developing Academic Language

New	Maintained	English Learner
certain	fraction	probability
outcome		

Problem Solving Discussion

Problem

Using at least one of each coin from a penny through a half-dollar, which nine coins would be needed to make exactly 99¢?

Focus Strategies

ABC **Make It Simpler**

2+3=5 **Write a Number Sentence or Equation**

Understand *Understand the problem.*

"What are we asked to do?"

We are asked to find nine coins that total 99¢, using at least one half-dollar, one quarter, one dime, one nickel, and one penny.

Plan *Make a plan.*

"What problem-solving strategy can we use?"

We can *make the problem simpler* by subtracting the values of the coins that we already know are part of the combination.

Solve *Carry out the plan.*

"What is the value of one half-dollar, one quarter, one dime, one nickel, and one penny?"

50¢ + 25¢ + 10¢ + 5¢ + 1¢ = 91¢

"How many coins total the 91¢?"

One of each kind of coin is five coins that total 91¢.

"How many coins are we still looking for? What is their total value?"

We are looking for four more coins that total 99¢ − 91¢ = 8¢.

"What four coins total 8¢?"

1 nickel and 3 pennies

"What is the combination of coins asked for in the problem?"

1 half-dollar, 1 quarter, 1 dime, 2 nickels, and 4 pennies

Check *Look back.*

"Did we find the answer to the question that was asked?"

Yes. We found the combination of nine coins that totals 99¢ and includes at least one of each coin.

"Is our answer reasonable?"

We know that our answer is reasonable because 1 half-dollar, 1 quarter, 1 dime, 2 nickels, and 4 pennies is a total of nine coins, and they have a total value of 50¢ + 25¢ + 10¢ + 10¢ + 4¢, which is 99¢.

LESSON **110**

California Mathematics Content Standards
SDAP 2.0, 2.2 Express outcomes of experimental probability situations verbally and numerically (e.g., 3 out of 4; $\frac{3}{4}$).

• Simple Probability

facts Power Up B

mental math Find each fraction of 100 in problems **a–c.**

a. Fractional Part: $\frac{1}{2}$ of 100 50

b. Fractional Part: $\frac{1}{4}$ of 100 25

c. Fractional Part: $\frac{1}{10}$ of 100 10

d. Number Sense: 5×46 230

e. Money: Doug purchased socks for \$4.37 and a hairbrush for \$2.98. How much did he spend? \$7.35

f. Estimation: Estimate the area of the rectangle shown at right. 18 in^2

$2\frac{3}{4}$ in.

$5\frac{3}{4}$ in.

g. Calculation: 12×3, $\sqrt{\ }$, $\div 2$, $\div 3$ 1

h. Simplify: $4 + h^2$ when $h = 4$ 20

problem solving Choose an appropriate problem-solving strategy to solve this problem. Using at least one of each coin from a penny through a half-dollar, which nine coins would be needed to make exactly 99¢? 4 pennies, 2 nickels, 1 dime, 1 quarter, and 1 half-dollar

Probability is a measure of how likely it is that an event (or combination of events) will occur. Probabilities are numbers between 0 and 1. An event that is **certain** to happen has a probability of 1. An event that is *impossible* has a probability of 0. If an event is uncertain to occur, then its probability is a fraction between 0 and 1.

Facts Subtract.

11 − 9 2	6 − 0 6	13 − 6 7	10 − 3 7	15 − 7 8	9 − 6 3	12 − 9 3	8 − 2 6	14 − 7 7	5 − 3 2
5 − 2 3	10 − 8 2	14 − 6 8	9 − 4 5	7 − 5 2	17 − 8 9	6 − 3 3	10 − 5 5	12 − 6 6	8 − 3 5
13 − 4 9	11 − 6 5	16 − 8 8	12 − 7 5	9 − 5 4	13 − 5 8	8 − 4 4	14 − 5 9	8 − 8 0	9 − 7 2
15 − 6 9	6 − 2 4	10 − 4 6	17 − 9 8	16 − 7 9	7 − 4 3	12 − 8 4	4 − 2 2	18 − 9 9	11 − 8 3

Power Up

Facts

Distribute **Power Up B** to students. See answers below.

Count Aloud

Before students begin the Mental Math exercises, do these counting exercises as a class.

Count up and down by fours from 16 to 56.

Mental Math

Encourage students to share different ways to mentally compute these exercises. Strategies for exercises are listed below.

c. Divide 100 by 10
$100 \div 10 = 10$
Use a Related Fact
Since $10 \times 10 = 100$, $100 \div 10 = 10$.

d. Decompose 46
$5 \times (40 + 6) = 200 + 30 = 230$
Subtract 5 × 4 from 5 × 50
$(5 \times 50) - (5 \times 4) = 250 - 20 = 230$

Problem Solving

Refer to **Problem-Solving Strategy Discussion,** p. 721B.

New Concept

Active Learning

As you discuss the concept that the probability of an event can range from 0 (impossible) to 1 (certain), ask students to suggest a variety of events that may have a probability of 0 or 1. Prompt the discussion by pointing out that the probability of tossing a dot cube and getting a result of 7 is an impossible event. Point out, however, that tossing the cube and getting a result of 1, 2, 3, 4, 5, or 6 is a certain event.

Then invite students to suggest a variety of events that are not impossible, but not certain, to happen. In other words, the probability of the event is greater than 0 and less than 1. Prompt the discussion by having students suppose that each of them placed a penny in the same paper bag, and then one penny was selected without looking. Point out that the probability of a student's penny being selected is not certain, but it is also not impossible.

Error Alert

Make sure students understand that different events have different numbers of outcomes, or results. For example, tossing a coin has two outcomes. Rolling a dot cube has six outcomes.

Example 1

Before discussing the solution, ask students to name the outcomes, and name the number of outcomes there are altogether. The outcomes are A, B, and C, and there are three outcomes altogether.

Extend the Example

Challenge advanced learners by asking:

"What is the probability of the spinner stopping on a consonant? Explain your answer." 2 out of 3 or $\frac{2}{3}$; Sample: The spinner has 3 possible outcomes, and 2 of those outcomes are consonants.

(continued)

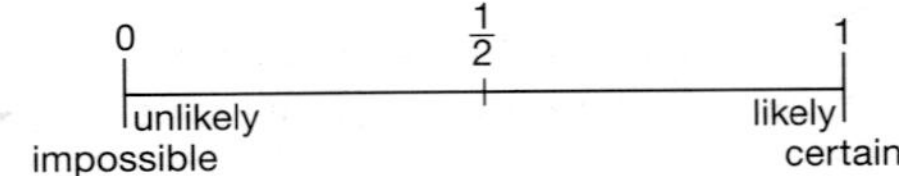

The more likely an event, the closer its probability is to 1.
The more unlikely an event, the closer its probability is to 0.

Suppose this nickel was tossed once. How might the coin land? Will it land heads up? Or will it land tails up?

The different ways the coin might land represent the outcomes of the toss. An **outcome** is a result. For a coin toss, there are two outcomes. It is just as likely for the coin to land heads up as it is to land tails up.

The probability of the coin landing heads up is "1 out of 2."
The probability of the coin landing tails up is "1 out of 2."

When probability is expressed as a fraction, we can read the fraction different ways. For example, if the probability of an event is $\frac{1}{2}$, we can read the probability as "1 out of 2" or "one half."

Example 1

Describe the probability of each outcome in a–c.

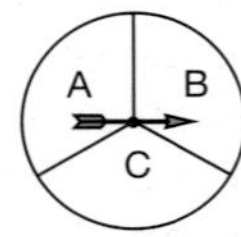

a. What is the probability of the spinner stopping on E?

b. What is the probability of the spinner stopping on a letter?

c. What is the probability of the spinner stopping on A?

a. Since there is no letter E on the spinner, it is impossible to land on the letter E. The probability is **0.**

b. Each section has a letter on it, so it is certain that the spinner will land on a letter. The probability is **1.**

c. Since the circle is divided into three equal parts, it is just as likely for the spinner to land on each of the letters. The probability of landing on A is **1 out of 3 or $\frac{1}{3}$.**

English Learners

Explain that **probability** deals with how *probable* or *likely* it is that something will happen.

If you live in a valley in Southern California, the **probability** of snow in December is very low.

Ask, ***"Where would the probability of snow in December be very likely?"*** Sample: In the mountains, in Minnesota, Maine

Students may discuss other common or rarely occurring events and state their probabilities.

722 *Saxon Math Intermediate 4*

Example 2

> **Thinking Skills**
>
> **Analyze**
>
> If two marbles are chosen from the bag each time, what are the possible outcomes? Show your answer using a table. See table below.

A brown paper bag contains black, blue, and white marbles that are the same size. The colors and number of each color are shown below. If one marble is chosen without looking, which color is most likely to be chosen?

4 black 3 white 5 blue

Since there are more yellow marbles than red or green marbles in the bag, **it is most likely that a blue marble will be chosen.**

Connect What color is least likely to be chosen? white

Lesson Practice

Marble 1	Marble 2
Black	Black
White	White
Blue	Blue
Black	White
Black	Blue
White	Blue

Analyze The spinner at the right is spun once.

a. Describe the probability of the spinner landing on B. Sample: 1 out of 4 one fourth

b. What is the probability of the spinner landing on C? Write a fraction to show your answer. $\frac{1}{4}$

c. What is the probability of the spinner landing on P? 0

d. Five pennies are placed in a bag. The year in which each penny was minted is shown below:

2006 1999 1976 1998 2007

Suppose you reach into the bag and choose a penny without looking. What fraction describes the probability that you will choose the 1976 penny? $\frac{1}{5}$

e. If a dime is dropped on the floor, what is the probability that it will land heads up? $\frac{1}{2}$

f. Chad printed his first name on a piece of paper. Then he cut out his name, cut apart the letters, and placed the letters in a bag. If Chad pulls one letter out of the bag, what is the probability that the letter will be a C? $\frac{1}{4}$

g. Read problem **f** again. Is it likely or unlikely that the letter Chad picks will be a consonant? likely

Distributed and Integrated

1. (94) Evan found 24 seashells. If he gave one fourth of them to his brother, how many did he keep? 18 seashells

2. (20) Rectangular Park is 2 miles long and 1 mile wide. Gordon ran around the park twice. How many miles did he run? 12 mi

2 mi

1 mi

Math Background

A possible result of an experiment is called an *outcome*. For example, when a coin is tossed, the outcomes are heads and tails. When a dot cube is rolled, the outcomes are 1, 2, 3, 4, 5, and 6.

An *event* is a set of possible outcomes. For example, when a dot cube is rolled, "rolling an even number" is the event {2, 4, 6}. If the outcomes of an experiment are equally likely to occur, then the probability of an event =

$$\frac{\text{number of outcomes in the event}}{\text{number of possible outcomes}}$$

For example, the probability of the event "tossing heads" is $\frac{1}{2}$ because there are only two possible outcomes and one of them is tossing heads. On the other hand, the probability of the event "rolling an even number" is $\frac{3}{6}$, or $\frac{1}{2}$, because there are 6 possible outcomes and three of them are even numbers.

New Concept *(Continued)*

Example 2

Error Alert

It is not correct for students to assume that because there are three colors of marbles in the bag, the probability of choosing a marble of one color is 1 out of 3. Make sure students understand that the probability would be 1 out of 3 if there was one red marble, one green marble, and one yellow marble in the bag. Point out, however, that there are 12 marbles in the bag, and since 5 of those marbles are yellow, the probability of choosing a yellow marble is 5 out of 12, or $\frac{5}{12}$, which is a greater fraction than $\frac{4}{12}$, the probability of choosing a red marble, and $\frac{3}{12}$, the probability of choosing a green marble.

Lesson Practice

Guided Practice

Use these problems as guided practice to check the students' understanding of today's concept.

Problem a **Analyze**

Help students get started by asking them to name the outcomes, and name the number of outcomes there are altogether. The outcomes are **A**, **B**, **C**, and **D**, and there are four outcomes altogether.

Problem c

Error Alert

Remind those students who write the probability as $\frac{0}{0}$ that a fraction bar represents division, and the fraction $\frac{0}{0}$ represents $0 \div 0$. Point out that division by zero is not possible, so we use 0 instead of $\frac{0}{0}$ to describe the probability of an impossible event.

Closure **The questions below help assess the concepts taught in this lesson.**

"What is the probability of an event that is certain to happen?" 1

"What is the probability of an event that can never happen?" 0

"When we work with probability, we work with outcomes. What is an outcome?" Sample: a result

"A number cube has faces numbered 1, 2, 3, 4, 5, and 6. What is the probability of an outcome of 4 if the cube is tossed once? Explain your answer." $\frac{1}{6}$; sample: The cube has six possible outcomes, and only one of those outcomes is 4.

Written Practice

Math Conversations

Independent Practice and Discussions to Increase Understanding

Problem 3

Extend the Problem

Write "$\frac{2}{42¢} = \frac{8}{c}$" on the board or overhead and point out that the equation models problem **3** because *c* represents the cost of 8 oranges if 2 oranges cost 42¢. Then challenge your advanced students by asking:

"How can we find c?" Sample: Since 2 × 4 = 8, multiply 42¢ by 4; *c* = 42¢ × 4 or 168¢, which is the same as $1.68

Problem 6 Multiple Choice

Test-Taking Strategy

Point out that test questions can sometimes be solved using only mental math. If students have difficulty choosing the correct answer to problem **6** using only mental math, explain that in order for a fraction to be equivalent to $\frac{1}{2}$, the numerator of the fraction will be half the denominator (or the denominator of the fraction will be double the numerator). Then encourage students to use mental math to compare the numerators and denominators of the given fractions. For example, since the numerator of $\frac{3}{6}$ (choice **A**) is half of the denominator (or since the denominator is double the numerator), $\frac{3}{6}$ is equivalent to $\frac{1}{2}$ and does not represent the correct answer.

Problem 7a

To focus students' attention on how these problems are solved, ask:

"What name for 1 will you use to find the missing number? Explain why." $\frac{6}{6}$; sample: To change the denominator 2 to 12, we multiply by 6, and we multiply the numerator by the same number.

Extend the Problem

"Does multiplying $\frac{1}{2}$ by $\frac{6}{6}$ change the value of $\frac{1}{2}$? Explain why or why not." No; $\frac{6}{6}$ is another name for 1, and multiplying a number by 1 does not change the value of the number.

(continued)

▸ **3.** If 2 oranges cost 42¢, how much would 8 oranges cost? $1.68
(93)

4. a. Represent Three fourths of the 64 baseball cards showed rookie players. How many of the baseball cards showed rookie players? Draw a picture to illustrate the problem. 48 baseball cards
(67, 94)

4.a. 64 cards

$\frac{3}{4}$ showed rookie players.	16 cards
	16 cards
	16 cards
$\frac{1}{4}$ didn't show rookie players.	16 cards

b. What fractional part of the baseball cards were not rookie players? $\frac{1}{4}$

5. Write these numbers in order from greatest to least: $7\frac{7}{10}$, 7.5, $7\frac{3}{10}$, 7.2
(Inv. 4, 43)

7.2 $7\frac{7}{10}$ $7\frac{3}{10}$ 7.5

▸ **6.** **Multiple Choice** Which of these fractions is *not* equivalent to $\frac{1}{2}$? C
(98)

A $\frac{3}{6}$ **B** $\frac{5}{10}$ **C** $\frac{10}{21}$ **D** $\frac{50}{100}$

***7.** Complete each equivalent fraction:
(103)

▸ **a.** $\frac{1}{2} = \frac{?}{12}$ 6 **b.** $\frac{1}{3} = \frac{?}{12}$ 4 **c.** $\frac{1}{4} = \frac{?}{12}$ 3

***8.** Write the reduced form of each fraction:
(106)

▸ **a.** $\frac{5}{10}$ $\frac{1}{2}$ **b.** $\frac{8}{15}$ $\frac{8}{15}$ **c.** $\frac{6}{12}$ $\frac{1}{2}$

9. Analyze Caleb paid 42¢ for 6 clips and 64¢ for 8 erasers. What was the cost of each clip and each eraser? What would be the total cost of 10 clips and 20 erasers? 7¢ per clip; 8¢ per eraser; $2.30
(93)

10.  Conclude There were 14 volunteers the first year, 16 volunteers the second year, and 18 volunteers the third year. If the number of volunteers continued to increase by 2 each year, how many volunteers would there be in the tenth year? Explain how you know. 32 volunteers; sample: I used a table and the equation *v* = 2*y* + 12, where *v* was the number of volunteers and *y* is the number of years.
(64, 93)

***11.** Represent Write the number 16 as the product of prime factors. 2 × 2 × 2 × 2
(105)

12. Predict A standard dot cube is rolled. What is the probability that the number rolled will be less than seven? 1
(110)

13. 47.14 − (3.63 + 36.3) 7.21
(9, 45)

14. 50.1 + (6.4 − 1.46) 55.04
(9, 45)

Inclusion

Use this strategy if the student displays:

- Difficulty with Abstract Processing.
- Difficulty with Reading.

Simple Probability (Pairs)

Material: coins

- Have students pair up and copy the chart shown:
- Give each pair a coin and have the students toss the coin 5 times each (total of 10) and record their results. Combine all results from groups.
- Ask students, ***"What is the chance that you will get a heads on a toss?"*** 1 out of 2. ***"What is the fraction that represents the probability that you will get a tails?"*** $\frac{1}{2}$
- Show students the class results and discuss how close they are to $\frac{1}{2}$.

Coin Toss #	Heads or Tails

▸*15. (98, 100) $\frac{2}{4} + \frac{1}{4} + \frac{1}{4}$ 1

▸*16. (100, 106) $4\frac{1}{6} + 1\frac{1}{6}$ $5\frac{1}{3}$

▸*17. (100, 106) $5\frac{3}{5} + 1\frac{2}{5}$ 7

▸*18. (100) $\frac{5}{6} + \frac{1}{6}$ 1

▸*19. (100, 106) $12\frac{3}{4} - 3\frac{1}{4}$ $9\frac{1}{2}$

▸*20. (100) $6\frac{1}{5} - 1\frac{1}{5}$ 5

*21. (107) 340 × 15 5100

*22. (107) 26 × 337 8762

*23. (107) 72 × 251 18,072

24. (83) $\frac{3550}{5}$ 710

*25. (79) 432 ÷ 3 144

26. (79) $9\overline{)5784}$ 642 R 6

▸*27. (RF13, 76) Karen is planning a trip to Los Angeles from Chicago for her vacation. She finds the following two round-trip flight schedules. Use this information to answer parts **a–c.**

Passengers: 1			Price: $246.00	
Flight number	Departure city	Date Time	Arrival city	Date Time
12A	ORD Chicago	7/21 06:11 PM	LAX Los Angeles	7/21 08:21 PM
46	LAX Los Angeles	7/28 06:39 PM	ORD Chicago	7/29 12:29 AM

Passengers: 1			Price: $412.00	
Flight number	Departure city	Date Time	Arrival city	Date Time
24	ORD Chicago	7/21 08:17 AM	LAX Los Angeles	7/21 10:28 AM
142	LAX Los Angeles	7/28 03:28 PM	ORD Chicago	7/28 09:18 PM

a. If Karen wants to arrive in Los Angeles in the morning, how much will she pay for airfare? $412.00

b. If Karen chooses the more economical round trip, when is her return flight scheduled to land? July 29 at 12:29 a.m.

c. **Multiple Choice** There is a 2-hour time difference between Chicago and Los Angeles. About how long does a flight between those cities last? B

A 2 hours **B** 4 hours **C** 6 hours **D** 8 hours

Alternative Approach: Using Manipulatives

To have students practice predicting outcomes, place 2 red, 5 blue, 2 green, and 1 yellow colored tiles in a bag.

Ask, ***"How many tiles are in the bag?*** 10 ***Which color(s) of tile would be the most likely, the least likely, and equally likely to be pulled based on probability?"*** Blue; yellow; red and green

Say, ***"Explain your answer."*** There are 10 color tiles in the bag. Half of them are blue, so blue is most likely. Only one tile is yellow, so it's the least likely. There are 2 green and 2 red tiles, so they're equally likely.

Written Practice *(Continued)*

Math Conversations *(cont.)*

Problem 8a

To help students recall how these problems are solved, ask:

"To reduce a fraction, we divide the numerator and the denominator by the same number. What number would you choose to divide both the numerator and the denominator of $\frac{5}{10}$ by? Explain why you chose that number." Divide by 5 because 5 is a factor of 5 and of 10.

Problems 15–20

Have students note that the same denominator is present in each problem. Then ask:

"What mistake can be made when we add or subtract fractions and mixed numbers that have the same denominator?" Add or subtract the denominators

Problem 27

Real-World Connection

Point out that all major airports are designated by unique airport codes. For example, "ORD" stands for Chicago O'Hare International Airport, and "LAX" stands for Los Angeles International Airport.

For part **b,** explain that "more economical" means "less expensive."

For part **c,** make sure students understand that because of the 2-hour time difference, it is necessary to add two hours to the difference in times from departure in Chicago to landing in Los Angeles.

(continued)

Written Practice *(Continued)*

Math Conversations *(cont.)*

Problem 28

Before solving the problem, invite volunteers to describe the sides of a dot cube. Sample: The sides have dots from 1–6.

Problem 30

Extend the Problem

"Which faces of the prism are congruent?" Sample: top and bottom; front and back; left side and right side

"How many pairs of faces are parallel?" three pairs

"How many pairs of faces are perpendicular?" twelve pairs

Errors and Misconceptions

Problem 2

Remind those students who named 6 miles as the answer to read problems carefully and a second time whenever necessary, and then point out that although the perimeter of the park is 6 miles, the problem states that Gordon ran around the park twice.

▸***28.** (110) Jenna is playing a board game. She has one dot cube and wants to roll a 5. What is the probability she rolls a 5 in one roll? $\frac{1}{6}$

***29.** (109) **Explain** Is this figure a pyramid? Why or why not?
No; A pyramid has only 1 base.

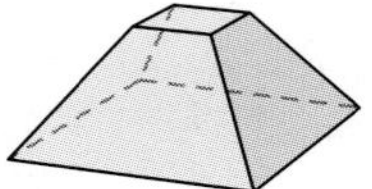

▸***30.** (108) **Analyze** Use this figure to for parts **a–c.**

a. **Classify** What is the geometric name for the shape of a cereal box? Rectangular solid (or rectangular prism)

b. How many edges does this box have? 12 edges

c. Describe the angles. All right angles

Looking Forward

Making predictions and representing probability prepares students for:

- **Investigation 11,** recording all possible outcomes of an event and finding the probability of an event occurring.

Cumulative Assessments and Performance Task

Assessments

Distribute **Power-Up Test 21** and **Cumulative Test 21** to each student. Have students complete the **Power-Up Test** first. Allow 10 minutes. Then have students work on the **Cumulative Test.**

Performance Task

The remaining class time can be spent on **Performance Task 11.** Students can begin the task in class or complete it during another class period.

Flexible Grouping

Flexible grouping gives students an opportunity to work with other students in an interactive and encouraging way. The choice for how students are grouped depends on the goals for instruction, the needs of the students, and the specific learning activity.

Assigning Groups

Group members can be randomly assigned, or can be assigned based on some criteria such as grouping students who may need help with a certain skill or grouping students to play specific roles in a group (such as recorder or reporter).

Types of Groups

Students can be paired or placed in larger groups. For pairing, students can be assigned partners on a weekly or monthly basis. Pairing activities are the easiest to manage in a classroom and are more likely to be useful on a daily basis.

Flexible Grouping Ideas

Lesson 102, Example 2
Materials: paper

Pair students before you teach Lesson 102. Then teach the lesson and stop before you go over Example 2.

- Have students read the example and discuss how to use the Distributive Property to divide.
- Have volunteers share their comments with the class.

Lesson 104, Example 3
Materials: paper

Have students form pairs to discuss rounding to the nearest million.

- Guide students through Example 3. Then write a similar number on the board. Instruct students to think about how to round the number to the nearest million.
- Then have students work in pairs to round and write the answer.
- Have volunteers share their solutions with the class.

Lesson 106, Example
Materials: paper

Divide students into groups of 4. Have students choose a partner from the group. On the board, write two fractions that can be reduced.

- Each student should choose one of the fractions to reduce.
- The student who did not choose the fraction will interview the other by asking questions about how to reduce the fraction. (Example: What is a common factor of both numbers?)
- After both students have interviewed each other and reduced the fractions, they must share their answers with the group and compare solutions.

Lesson 107, Example 1
Materials: paper

After guiding the students through Example 1, write three similar multiplication problems on the board. Divide the students into groups of 4.

- Have the groups work together to solve the first problem.
- Have the groups divide into pairs to solve the second problem.
- Direct students to work on the last problem independently and then check their solutions with the group.

Planning & Preparation

• Probability Experiments

Objectives

- Record all the possible outcomes for an experiment using a grid or tree diagram.
- Find the probability of an event.
- Express the probability of an event as a fraction.

Prerequisite Skills

- Relating fractions to percents that name hundredths.
- Identifying percent of a whole.

Materials

Instructional Masters
- Lesson Activity 32

Manipulative Kit
- Dot cubes

Teacher-provided materials
- 2 colored shirts, 3 hats*

  **optional*

California Mathematics Content Standards

SDAP 1.0, 1.1 Formulate survey questions; systematically collect and represent data on a number line; and coordinate graphs, tables, and charts.

SDAP 1.0, 1.3 Interpret one-and two-variable data graphs to answer questions about a situation.

SDAP 2.0, 2.1 Represent all possible outcomes for a simple probability situation in an organized way (e.g., tables, grids, tree diagrams).

SDAP 2.0, 2.2 Express outcomes of experimental probability situations verbally and numerically (e.g., 3 out of 4; $\frac{3}{4}$).

MR 1.0, 1.1 Analyze problems by identifying relationships, distinguishing relevant from irrelevant information, sequencing and prioritizing information, and observing patterns.

MR 2.0, 2.3 Use a variety of methods, such as words, numbers, symbols, charts, graphs, tables, diagrams, and models, to explain mathematical reasoning.

MR 2.0, 2.4 Express the solution clearly and logically by using the appropriate mathematical notation and terms and clear language; support solutions with evidence in both verbal and symbolic work.

MR 3.0, 3.3 Develop generalizations of the results obtained and apply them in other circumstances.

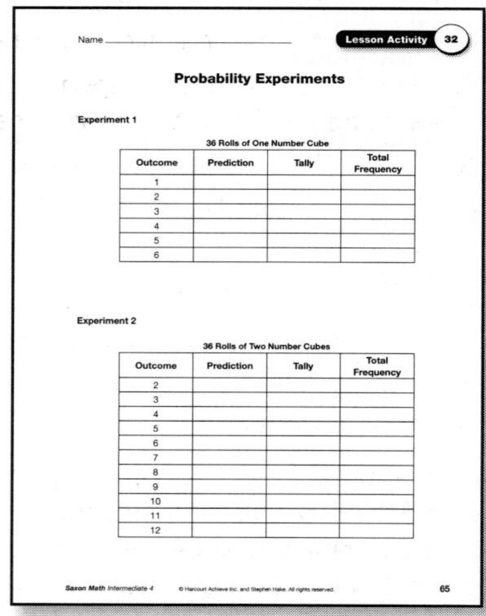

Name ______________________ **Lesson Activity 32**

Probability Experiments

Experiment 1

36 Rolls of One Number Cube

Outcome	Prediction	Tally	Total Frequency
1			
2			
3			
4			
5			
6			

Experiment 2

36 Rolls of Two Number Cubes

Outcome	Prediction	Tally	Total Frequency
2			
3			
4			
5			
6			
7			
8			
9			
10			
11			
12			

Saxon Math Intermediate 4 © Harcourt Achieve Inc. and Stephen Hake. All rights reserved. 65

Lesson Activity 32

Universal Access

Reaching All Special Needs Students

Special Education Students	At-Risk Students	English Learners	Advanced Learners
• Inclusion (TM) • Adaptations for Saxon Math	• Error Alert (TM) • Reteaching Masters • Refresher Lessons for California Standards	• English Learners (TM) • Developing Academic Language (TM) • English Learner Handbook	• Extend the Problem (TM) • Investigate Further (SE) • Online Activities

TM=Teacher's Manual
SE=Student Edition

Developing Academic Language

New	Maintained	English Learner
chance	certain	sector
probability	impossible	
sector	outcome	
	uncertain	

California Mathematics Content Standards
SDAP 1.0, 1.3 Interpret one-and two-variable data graphs to answer questions about a situation.
SDAP 2.0, 2.1 Represent all possible outcomes for a simple probability situation in an organized way (e.g., tables, grids, tree diagrams).
SDAP 2.0, 2.2 Express outcomes of experimental probability situations verbally and numerically (e.g., 3 out of 4; $\frac{3}{4}$).

Focus on

Probability Experiments

Many board games involve an element of **chance.** This means that when we spin a spinner, roll number cubes, or draw a card from a shuffled deck, we cannot know the outcome (result) of the event ahead of time. However, we can often find how *likely* a particular outcome is. The degree of likelihood of an outcome is called its probability.

Here we show a spinner. The face is divided into six equal parts called **sectors.** Each sector is $\frac{1}{6}$ of the face of the spinner. Assuming the spinner is balanced and fair, then a spin of the arrow can end up with the arrow pointing in any direction. The letter that names the sector where the arrow lands is the outcome of the spin. For the questions that follow, ignore the possibility that the arrow may stop on a line.

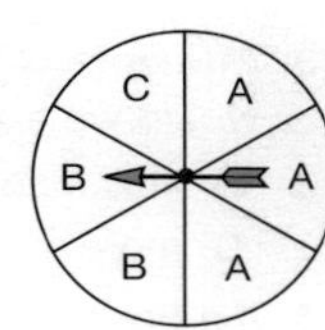

1. If the arrow is spun once, what outcomes are possible? A, B, or C
2. **Explain** On which letter is the arrow most likely to stop, and why?
3. **List** Write the possible outcomes of a spin in order from least likely to most likely. C, B, A
4. Which outcome of a spin is twice as likely as the outcome C? B
5. **Predict** If the arrow is spun many times, then about half the outcomes are likely to be which sector? A
6. **Multiple Choice** If the arrow is spun many times, then what fraction of the spins are likely to stop in sector C? A
   A $\frac{1}{6}$ **B** $\frac{1}{3}$ **C** $\frac{1}{2}$ **D** $\frac{5}{6}$
7. **Multiple Choice** In 60 spins, about how many times should we expect it to stop in sector C? B
   A about 6 times **B** about 10 times
   C about 20 times **D** about 30 times

2. The arrow is most likely to stop on A because the A sectors cover more of the spinner than the B sectors or the C sector.

Recall that probability of an outcome can be expressed as a number ranging from 0 to 1. An outcome that cannot happen has a probability of 0. An outcome that is certain to happen has a probability of 1. An outcome that could happen but is not certain to happen is expressed as a fraction between 0 and 1.

Use the spinner at right to answer problems **8–10.**

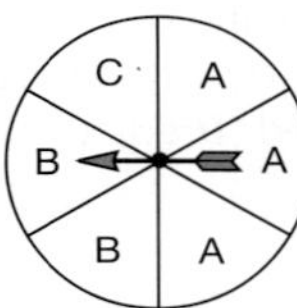

8. **Explain** What is the probability that the arrow will stop in sector D? Why? 0; The letter D is not on the spinner, so D is an impossible outcome.

Probability Experiments

In this investigation, students will explore combinations, name all of the outcomes of an event, and find the probabilities of various events, including

- rolling one dot cube 36 times.
- rolling two dot cubes 36 times and recording the sums that dot cubes produce.

Discussion

Have students recall that when a weather forecast describes a chance of precipitation, the forecast is describing the probability of precipitation. Then invite volunteers to tell what they recall about the concept of probability.

Instruction

As you discuss the spinner, explain that students can think of the spinner as a fraction circle of 6 sixths or one whole.

Error Alert

Make sure students understand that because each sector is the same size, the probability of the spinner stopping on any one of the six sectors is the same. However, because some sectors display the same letter, the letters represent the possible outcomes of spinning the spinner, and the probabilities of those possible outcomes are not the same.

Math Conversations

Independent Practice and Discussions to Increase Understanding

Problem 1

Make sure students understand that the outcomes are the results that can happen if the spinner is spun only once.

Problems 2 and 3

Error Alert

It is not correct for students to assume that simply because there are three letters on the spinner, the probability of the spinner stopping on a letter is 1 out of 3. It is important for students to understand that because

- 3 of 6 sectors represent an outcome of A, the probability of an outcome of A is 3 out of 6, or $\frac{1}{2}$.
- 2 of 6 sectors represent an outcome of B, the probability of an outcome of B is 2 out of 6, or $\frac{1}{3}$.
- 1 of 6 sectors represent an outcome of C, the probability of an outcome of C is 1 out of 6, or $\frac{1}{6}$.

(continued)

Math Conversations *(cont.)*

Instruction

Remind students that whenever we write a probability as a fraction, we write the fraction in simplest form.

Problem 4

Extend the Problem

"Which outcome is half as likely as outcome B?" outcome C

"How likely is outcome C when compared to outcome A?" $\frac{1}{3}$ as likely

Instruction

As you discuss the concept that the probability of an event ranges from 0 to 1, point out that the probability of most events is greater than 0 and less than 1.

Problem 9 Explain

Extend the Problem

Use this problem to lead advanced learners to generalize that the sum of the probabilities of all of the possible outcomes of an event is 1. Explain that for this spinner, $P(A) = \frac{3}{6}$, $P(B) = \frac{2}{6}$, and $P(C) = \frac{1}{6}$, and then write the addition $\frac{3}{6} + \frac{2}{6} + \frac{1}{6} = \frac{6}{6} = 1$ on the board or overhead to reinforce this concept.

Active Learning

Provide students with dot cubes to examine while solving problems **11–16.** If you do not have dot or number cubes, give students blank cubes and have them number the faces 1, 2, 3, 4, 5, and 6.

Problem 13

Extend the Problem

Challenge your students by asking:

"How could the cube be renumbered so that the outcome of rolling the cube once will always be a counting number, but never be a prime number or a composite number?" Change 2, 3, 4, 5, and 6 to 1

Problem 16 Multiple Choice

Test-Taking Strategy

Make sure students can generalize that the term "unlikely" represents a probability closer to 0 than to 1, and the term "very likely" represents a probability closer to 1 than to 0.

Activity

Experiment 1

Active Learning

Have students work in pairs to complete this experiment. Distribute a 1–6 dot cube to each pair of students.

To help manage the activity, you might choose to ask each pair of students to roll the cube in a confined area, such as on a tray or in the lid of a box.

(continued)

▸ **9.** Explain What is the probability that the outcome will be one of the first three letters of the alphabet? Why? **9.** 1; Every sector of the spinner is labeled with one of the first three letters of the alphabet, so that outcome is certain to happen.

10. What is the probability that the arrow will stop in sector C? $\frac{1}{6}$

Here we show a standard dot cube.

11. What numbers are represented by the dots on the faces of a dot cube? 1, 2, 3, 4, 5, and 6

12. Justify If a dot cube is rolled once, which number is most likely to end up on top? Why? **12.** None of the numbers is most likely to end up on top because each number is equally likely to end up on top after one roll.

▸ **13. Multiple Choice** If a dot cube is rolled many times, about how often would we expect to roll a number greater than 3? B

A less than half the time **B** about half the time
C more than half the time **D** none of the time

14. If a dot cube is rolled once, what is the probability of rolling a 7? 0

15. With one roll of a dot cube, what is the probability of rolling a 1? $\frac{1}{6}$

▸ **16. Multiple Choice** How would we describe the likelihood of rolling a 6 with one roll of a dot cube? C

A very likely **B** just as likely to roll a 6 as not to roll a 6
C unlikely **D** certain

Activity

Probability Experiments

Materials needed:
- **Lesson Activity 32**
- dot cubes

Experiment 1: Work with a partner for this experiment. You and your partner will roll one dot cube 36 times and tally the number of times each face of the dot cube turns up. You will record the results in the Experiment 1 table on **Lesson Activity 32.** (A copy of the table is shown on the next page.)

Predict Before starting the experiment determine all the possible outcomes. For this experiment there are 6 possible outcomes, 1, 2, 3, 4, 5 and 6. Then, predict the number of times each outcome will occur during the experiment. Write your predictions in the column labeled "Prediction."

English Learners

The words **sector** and **section** are related. They both refer to a part of something. A sector is a part of a circle sliced like a piece of a quesadilla.

Explain that the English language is made up of a large number of words. This is one reason there are usually a variety of ways to express an idea, each slightly different based on the words used.

Math Background

We can make an addition table showing the sum for every possible roll of two dot cubes. There are 36 different rolls.

+	1	2	3	4	5	6
1	1	3	4	5	6	7
2	3	4	5	6	7	8
3	4	5	6	7	8	9
4	5	6	7	8	9	10
5	6	7	8	9	10	11
6	7	8	9	10	11	12

We can use this table to find the probability of any sum. For example, the sum 4 appears in the table three times, indicating that 3 of the 36 possible dot-cube rolls have a sum of 4. The probability of getting a 4 is therefore $\frac{3}{36}$, which can be reduced to $\frac{1}{12}$.

36 Rolls of One Dot Cube

Outcome	Prediction	Tally	Total Frequency
1			
2			
3			
4			
5			
6			

Now begin rolling the dot cube. Make a tally mark for each roll in the appropriate box in the "Tally" column. When all groups have finished, report your results to the class. As a class, total the groups' tallies for each outcome, and write these totals in the boxes under "Total Frequency."

17. Make a bar graph using the data from your table. See student work.
18. **Conclude** What conclusions can you draw from the results of Experiment 1? See student work.
19. What was the mode for the outcomes of this experiment? See student work.
20. Is it easier to compare data using the bar graph or the table? See student work.

20. For the whole class, the frequency of the outcomes are likely to be roughly equal.

Experiment 2: In this experiment you and your group will roll a pair of dot cubes 36 times and tally the outcomes. For each roll the outcome will be the sum of the two numbers that end up on top. You will record your results in the Experiment 2 table on **Lesson Activity 32.**

Form groups so that each group can have two number cubes.

Predict Before starting the experiment, predict as a group the number of times each outcome will occur during the experiment. Write your predictions in the column labeled "Prediction."

36 Rolls of Two Dot Cubes

Outcome	Prediction	Tally	Total Frequency
2			
3			
4			
5			
6			
7			
8			
9			
10			
11			
12			

Math Conversations *(cont.)*

Before students begin the experiment, make sure that they predict (and record in the Prediction column of the chart) the number of times each outcome will occur. They should also check their predictions by making sure their sum is 36 (because the number cube will be rolled 36 times). Invite volunteers to share their predictions with the class, and explain how those predictions were made.

As they complete the activity, make sure that both students in each pair have the same opportunity to roll the cube and tally the results: each student rolls the cube 18 times and tallies the results 18 times.

Activity
Experiment 2
Active Learning

Have students work in groups of three to complete this activity. Distribute two 1–6 dot cubes to each group of students.Before students begin the activity, point out that there are 11 outcomes and make sure that students understand there are more than 6 outcomes because we are recording the sum of the dots or numbers. Give the groups an opportunity to discuss how to predict the outcomes before they write their predictions on the activity sheet in the column labeled "Prediction."

Suggest that students decide who will first roll the cubes, find the sum, and tally, before beginning the activity. To make sure that each group member has the same opportunity to perform all of the tasks, group members should switch tasks after 12 rolls.

(continued)

Inclusion

Use this strategy if the student displays:

- Difficulty with Large Group Instruction.
- Slow Learning Rate.

Probability Experiments (Whole Group)

Materials: 2 colored shirts, 3 hats

- Lay the clothing options out in the front of the room. Tell students that a student has a choice of what to wear and they need to find how many different arrangements they can choose from.
- Ask for a volunteer to come lay out one clothing option and write the combination on the board. Have students continue to come to the front to lay out different options.
- Using the same clothing options, create a tree diagram to show students another way of outlining the arrangements.

Math Conversations *(cont.)*

Problem 24 **Model**

Error Alert

Duplicate the table shown below on the board or overhead to help students recognize that there are six different ways in which two number cubes can produce a sum of 7.

First Cube	1	2	3	4	5	6
Second Cube	6	5	4	3	2	1

(continued)

Now begin rolling the dot cubes. Each time you roll a pair of dot cubes, make a tally mark in the appropriate box. When all groups have finished, report your results to the class. As a class, total the groups' tallies for each outcome and record these totals in the "Total Frequency" column.

21. What was the mode of the outcomes? Why?

22. Which outcome(s) occurred least frequently? Why?

23. What conclusions can you draw from the results of Experiment 2?

▸ **24.** **Model** What are all the possible combinations you could roll with a sum of 7 as the result? Explain.

21. For the class as a whole, 7 is the mode. There are more combinations of two dot cubes that total 7 than for any other outcome.

22. It is likely that 2 and 12 are the least frequent outcomes. There are fewer combinations of two dot cubes that total 2 and 12 than for any other outcome.

Investigate Further

23. The more combinations that add up to the outcome's number, the more likely that outcome is to happen. The lowest and highest numbers in the set of outcomes are least likely to happen, while those in the middle are most likely.

24. Sample: Although there are three number combinations (1 and 6, 2 and 5, 3 and 4), there are six dot cube combinations because each of the three number combinations can occur in two possible ways.

a. Logan brought two hats for a weekend trip: one navy blue and one black. He also brought three shirts: one red, one green, and one yellow. We can use a tree diagram to show all the possible combinations of shirts and hats he can wear.

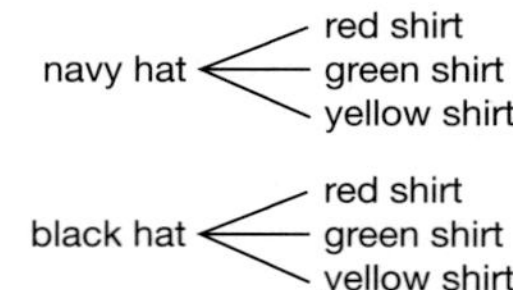

We can count the branches to see all the possible combinations. There are six combinations of hats and shirts.

Represent Logan brought three pairs of shorts: denim, brown, and black. Draw a tree diagram to show all the possible combinations of hats, shirts, and shorts. How many are there?
18 combinations; See student work.

b. There are two spinners shown below. Spinner A is labeled with letters and Spinner B is labeled with numbers.

Spinner A

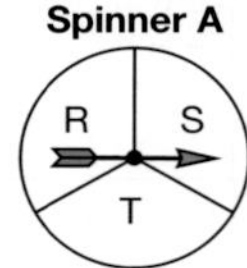

Spinner B

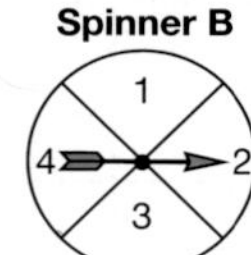

We can show all possible outcomes for the two spinners on a grid. We make a column for each possible letter and pair each possible number with them. We can see that there are 12 possible outcomes.

Outcomes for Spinners A and B

R, 1	S, 1	T, 1
R, 2	S, 2	T, 2
R, 3	S, 3	T, 3
R, 4	S, 4	T, 4

Interpret What is the probability of spinning the letter T and the number 4? $\frac{1}{12}$

Represent Use the grid to make a tree diagram of all the possible outcomes for the Spinners A and B. See student work.

Probability will be further developed in ***Saxon Math** Intermediate 5*.

Math Conversations *(cont.)*

Extend the Problem

If there is enough time, challenge volunteers to work together to make a list of all of the different ways two number cubes can produce the sums 2–12. You may also use this as an activity for advanced learners.

Sum	First Cube	Second Cube
2	1	1
3	1	2
	2	1
4	1	3
	2	2
	3	1
5	1	4
	2	3
	3	2
	4	1
6	1	5
	2	4
	3	3
	4	2
	5	1
7	1	6
	2	5
	3	4
	4	3
	5	2
	6	1
8	2	6
	3	5
	4	4
	5	3
	6	2
9	3	6
	4	5
	5	4
	6	3
10	4	6
	5	5
	6	4

Closure

The questions below help assess the concepts taught in this lesson.

"What does probability mean?" Sample: how likely it is that an outcome will occur

"How is probability like chance?" Sample: Both probability and chance are ways to tell how likely it is that something will happen.

"What did you learn from the two experiments?" Sample: You have to consider all the ways that an outcome can occur because outcomes are not always as simple as they seem to be.

Lesson Planner

Lesson	New Concepts	Materials	Resources 
111	• Multiplying Three-Digit Numbers	• Grid paper	• Power Up C Worksheet • Lesson Activity 8
112	• Simplifying Fraction Answers	• Manipulative Kit: rulers	• Power Up G Worksheet
113	• Renaming Fractions and Common Denominators	• Manipulative Kit: rulers	• Power Up I Worksheet
114	• Perimeter and Area of Complex Figures		• Power Up H Worksheet
Cumulative Assessment			• Cumulative Test 22 • Test-Day Activity 11

All resources are also available on the Resources and Planner CD.

Additional Resources

- Instructional Masters
- Reteaching Masters
- Refresher Lessons for California Standards
- Calculator Activities
- Resources and Planner CD
- Assessment Guide
- Performance Tasks
- Instructional Transparencies
- Answer Key CD
- Power Up Workbook
- Written Practice Workbook

Math Highlights

Enduring Understandings — The "Big Picture"

After completing Section 12, students will understand that:

- If two fractions have different denominators, they each can be rewritten with the same denominator.
- The area of a complex figure can be found by breaking it up into rectangles.

Essential Questions

- What is one method for finding a common denominator?
- If I add the areas of a figure's parts, does it equal the area of the whole figure?

Math Content Highlights	Math Processes Highlights
Number Sense • **Multiplying Three-Digit Numbers** *Lesson 111* • **Simplifying Fraction Answers** *Lesson 112* • **Renaming Fractions** *Lesson 113* • **Common Denominators** *Lesson 113* **Geometry and Measurement** • **Perimeter and Area of Complex Figures** *Lesson 114*	**Problem Solving** • **Strategies** – **Find or Extend a Pattern** *Lessons 112, 113* – **Guess and Check** *Lesson 111* – **Use Logical Reasoning** *Lesson 114* – **Work Backwards** *Lesson 114* – **Write a Number Sentence or Equation** *Lesson 111* • **Real-World Applications** *Lesson 111* **Communication** • **Discuss** *Lessons 111, 113* • **Explain** *Lessons 111, 112, 114* **Connections** • **Math to Math** – **Algebra and Geometry** *Lesson 114* – **Fractions and Number Sense** *Lessons 112, 113* – **Multiplication and Number Sense** *Lesson 111* • **Math and Other Subjects** – **Math and Geography** *Lessons 111, 112, 114* **Representation** • **Represent** *Lessons 111, 112, 113, 114* • **Using Manipulative/Hands On** *Lessons 111, 112, 113, 114*

Universal Access

Support for universal access is included with each lesson. Specific resources and features are listed on each lesson planning page. Features in the Teacher's Manual to customize instruction include the following:

Teacher's Manual Support

Alternative Approach	Provides a different path to concept development. *Lesson 114*
Manipulative Use	Provides alternate concept development through the use of manipulatives. *Lessons 113, 114*
Inclusion	Provides ideas for including all students by accommodating special needs. *Lessons 111–114*
Developing Academic Language	Provides a list of new and maintained vocabulary words along with words that might be difficult for English learners. *Lessons 111–114*
English Learners	Provides strategies for teaching specific vocabulary that may be difficult for English learners. *Lessons 111–114*
Errors and Misconceptions	Provides information about common misconceptions students encounter with concepts. *Lessons 111–114*
Extend the Example	Provides additional concept development for advanced learners. *Lessons 111–114*
Extend the Problem	Provides an opportunity for advanced learners to broaden concept development by expanding on a particular problem approach or context. *Lessons 111–114*
Early Finishers	Provides additional math concept extensions for advanced learners at the end of the Written Practice. *Lesson 113*

Additional Resources

The following resources are also available to support universal access:

- Adaptations for Saxon Math
- English Learner Handbook
- Online Activities
- Performance Tasks
- Refresher Lessons for CA Standards
- Reteaching Masters

Technology

Student Resources

- Student Edition eBook
- Calculator Activities
- Online Resources at **www.SaxonMath.com/Int4ActivitiesCA**

Teacher Resources

- Resources and Planner CD
- Test and Practice Generator CD
- Monitoring Student Progress: eGradebook CD
- Teacher's Manual eBook CD
- Answer Key CD
- Adaptations for Saxon Math CD
- Online Resources at **www.SaxonMath.com**

Cumulative Assessment

The assessments in Saxon Math are frequent and consistently placed to offer a regular method of ongoing testing.

Power-Up Test: Allow no more than ten minutes for this test of basic facts and skills.

Cumulative Test: Next, administer this test, which checks mastery of concepts in previous lessons.

Test-Day Activity and Performance Task: The remaining class time can be spent on these activities. Students can finish the Test-Day Activity for homework. Advanced learners can complete the extended Performance Task in another class period.

After Lesson 114

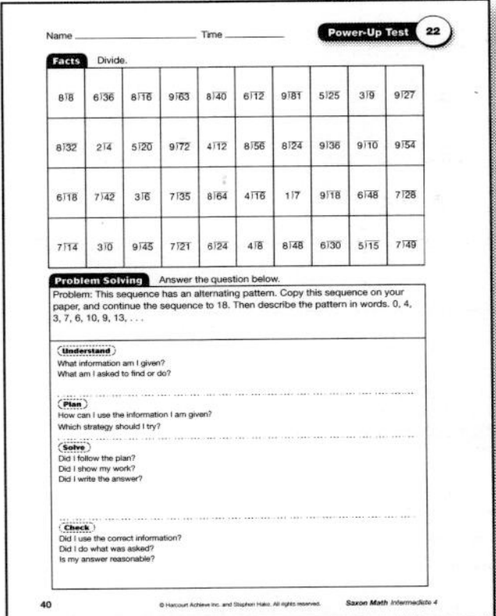

Name ______________ Time ________ **Power-Up Test 22**

Facts Divide.

$8\overline{)8}$	$6\overline{)36}$	$8\overline{)16}$	$9\overline{)63}$	$8\overline{)40}$	$6\overline{)12}$	$9\overline{)81}$	$5\overline{)25}$	$3\overline{)9}$	$9\overline{)27}$
$8\overline{)32}$	$2\overline{)4}$	$5\overline{)20}$	$9\overline{)72}$	$4\overline{)12}$	$8\overline{)56}$	$8\overline{)24}$	$9\overline{)36}$	$9\overline{)10}$	$9\overline{)54}$
$6\overline{)18}$	$7\overline{)42}$	$3\overline{)6}$	$7\overline{)35}$	$8\overline{)64}$	$4\overline{)16}$	$1\overline{)7}$	$9\overline{)18}$	$6\overline{)48}$	$7\overline{)28}$
$7\overline{)14}$	$3\overline{)0}$	$9\overline{)45}$	$7\overline{)21}$	$6\overline{)24}$	$4\overline{)8}$	$8\overline{)48}$	$6\overline{)30}$	$5\overline{)15}$	$7\overline{)49}$

Problem Solving Answer the question below.

Problem: This sequence has an alternating pattern. Copy this sequence on your paper, and continue the sequence to 18. Then describe the pattern in words. 0, 4, 3, 7, 6, 10, 9, 13, . . .

Understand
What information am I given?
What am I asked to find or do?

Plan
How can I use the information I am given?
Which strategy should I try?

Solve
Did I follow the plan?
Did I show my work?
Did I write the answer?

Check
Did I use the correct information?
Did I do what was asked?
Is my answer reasonable?

40 © Harcourt Achieve Inc. and Stephen Hake. All rights reserved. *Saxon Math Intermediate 4*

Power-Up Test 22

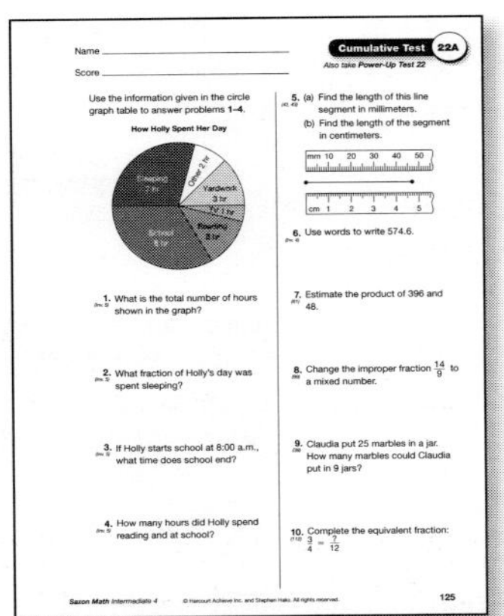

Name ______________ **Cumulative Test 22A**
Score ______________ *Also take Power-Up Test 22*

Use the information given in the circle graph table to answer problems **1–4**.

How Holly Spent Her Day

1. What is the total number of hours shown in the graph?
2. What fraction of Holly's day was spent sleeping?
3. If Holly starts school at 8:00 a.m., what time does school end?
4. How many hours did Holly spend reading and at school?
5. (a) Find the length of this line segment in millimeters.
   (b) Find the length of the segment in centimeters.
6. Use words to write 574.6.
7. Estimate the product of 396 and 48.
8. Change the improper fraction $\frac{14}{9}$ to a mixed number.
9. Claudia put 25 marbles in a jar. How many marbles could Claudia put in 9 jars?
10. Complete the equivalent fraction: $\frac{3}{4} = \frac{?}{12}$

Saxon Math Intermediate 4 © Harcourt Achieve Inc. and Stephen Hake. All rights reserved. 125

Cumulative Test 22

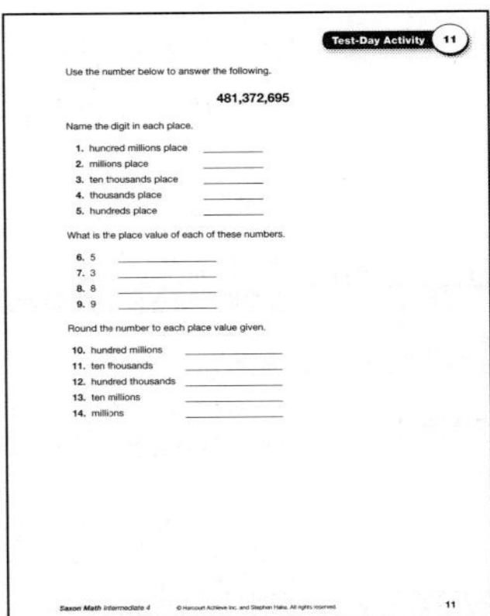

Test-Day Activity 11

Use the number below to answer the following.

481,372,695

Name the digit in each place.

1. hundred millions place ______
2. millions place ______
3. ten thousands place ______
4. thousands place ______
5. hundreds place ______

What is the place value of each of these numbers.

6. 5 ______
7. 3 ______
8. 8 ______
9. 9 ______

Round the number to each place value given.

10. hundred millions ______
11. ten thousands ______
12. hundred thousands ______
13. ten millions ______
14. millions ______

Saxon Math Intermediate 4 © Harcourt Achieve Inc. and Stephen Hake. All rights reserved. 11

Test Day Activity 11

Evidence of Learning — What Students Should Know

By the conclusion of Section 12, students should be able to demonstrate the following competencies through the Cumulative Assessments, which are correlated to the California Mathematics Standards:

- Describe the difference between a prism and a pyramid. **MG 3.6, MR 2.3**
- Express the probability of an event in various ways. **SDAP 1.3, SDAP 2.2, MR 2.3**

Reteaching

Students who score below 80% on assessments may be in need of reteaching. Refer to the Reteaching Masters for reteaching opportunities for every lesson.

Benchmarking and Tracking the California Mathematics Standards

Benchmark Tests

Benchmark Tests correlated to lesson concepts allow you to assess student progress after every 20 lessons. An End-of-Course Test is a final benchmark test of the complete textbook. The Benchmark Tests are available in the Assessment Guide.

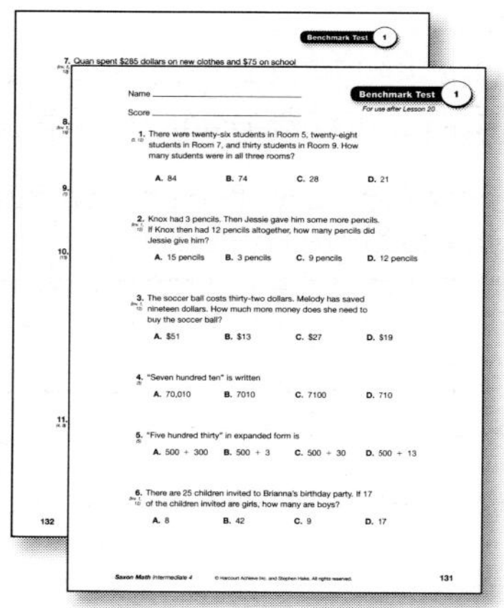
Benchmark Test 1

7. Quan spent $285 dollars on new clothes and $75 on school

8.

9.

10.

11.

132

Name ______

Score ______

Benchmark Test 1
For use after Lesson 20

1. There were twenty-six students in Room 5, twenty-eight students in Room 7, and thirty students in Room 9. How many students were in all three rooms?

A. 84 **B.** 74 **C.** 28 **D.** 21

2. Knox had 3 pencils. Then Jessie gave him some more pencils. If Knox then had 12 pencils altogether, how many pencils did Jessie give him?

A. 15 pencils **B.** 3 pencils **C.** 9 pencils **D.** 12 pencils

3. The soccer ball costs thirty-two dollars. Melody has saved nineteen dollars. How much more money does she need to buy the soccer ball?

A. $51 **B.** $13 **C.** $27 **D.** $19

4. "Seven hundred ten" is written

A. 70,010 **B.** 7010 **C.** 7100 **D.** 710

5. "Five hundred thirty" in expanded form is

A. 500 + 300 **B.** 500 + 3 **C.** 500 + 30 **D.** 500 + 13

6. There are 25 children invited to Brianna's birthday party. If 17 of the children invited are girls, how many are boys?

A. 8 **B.** 42 **C.** 9 **D.** 17

Saxon Math Intermediate 4 © Harcourt Achieve Inc. and Stephen Hake. All rights reserved. 131

Monitoring Student Progress: eGradebook CD

To track California Standards mastery, enter students' scores on Cumulative Tests and Benchmark Tests into the Monitoring Student Progress: eGradebook CD. Use the report titled *Benchmark Standards Report* to determine which California Standards were assessed and the level of mastery for each student. Generate a variety of other reports for class tracking and more.

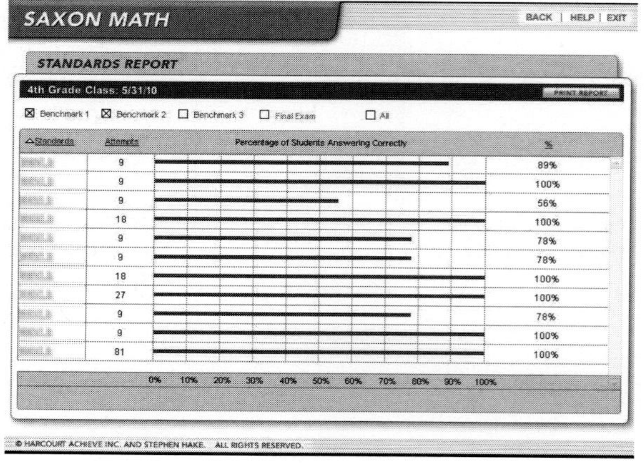
SAXON MATH BACK | HELP | EXIT

STANDARDS REPORT

4th Grade Class: 5/31/10 PRINT REPORT

☒ Benchmark 1 ☒ Benchmark 2 ☐ Benchmark 3 ☐ Final Exam ☐ All

Standards	Attempts	Percentage of Students Answering Correctly	%
[illegible]	9		89%
[illegible]	9		100%
[illegible]	9		56%
[illegible]	18		100%
[illegible]	9		78%
[illegible]	9		78%
[illegible]	18		100%
[illegible]	27		100%
[illegible]	9		78%
[illegible]	9		100%
[illegible]	81		100%

0% 10% 20% 30% 40% 50% 60% 70% 80% 90% 100%

© HARCOURT ACHIEVE INC. AND STEPHEN HAKE. ALL RIGHTS RESERVED.

Test and Practice Generator CD

Test items also available in Spanish.

The Test and Practice Generator is an easy-to-manage benchmarking and assessment tool that creates unlimited practice and tests in multiple formats and allows you to customize questions or create new ones. A variety of reports are available to track student progress toward mastery of the California Standards throughout the year.

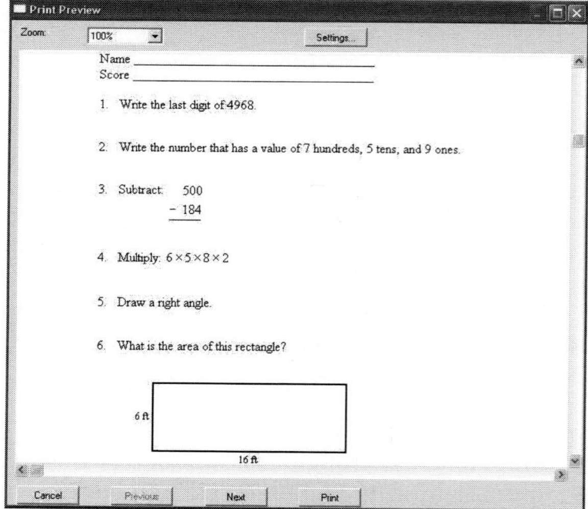
Print Preview

Zoom: 100% Settings...

Name ______

Score ______

1. Write the last digit of 4968.

2. Write the number that has a value of 7 hundreds, 5 tens, and 9 ones.

3. Subtract: $\begin{array}{r} 500 \\ -\ 184 \\ \hline \end{array}$

4. Multiply: $6 \times 5 \times 8 \times 2$

5. Draw a right angle.

6. What is the area of this rectangle?

6 ft

16 ft

Cancel Previous Next Print

Content Trace

Lesson	New Concepts	Practiced	Assessed	Looking Forward
111	• Multiplying Three-Digit Numbers	Lessons 111, 112	Test 22	Lessons 112, 113
112	• Simplifying Fraction Answers	Lessons 112, 113, 114	Test 22	Lesson 113
113	• Renaming Fractions and Common Denominators	Lessons 113, 114	Test 22	***Saxon Math*** *Intermediate 5*
114	• Perimeter and Area of Complex Figures	Lesson 114	Test 10	***Saxon Math*** *Intermediate 5*

Planning & Preparation

• Multiplying Three-Digit Numbers

Objectives
- Multiply a three-digit number by a two-digit number ending in zero.
- Multiply a three-digit number containing a zero by a two-digit number.

Prerequisite Skills
- Multiplying numbers by multiples of 10.
- Finding partial products.

Materials
Instructional Masters
- Power Up C Worksheet
- Lesson Activity 8

Manipulative Kit
- Base ten blocks*

Teacher-provided materials
- Grid paper
- Internet, almanac, atlas, place-value workmat, fraction bars*

**optional*

California Mathematics Content Standards

NS 3.0, 3.3 Solve problems involving multiplication of multidigit numbers by two-digit numbers.

MR 3.0, 3.2 Note the method of deriving the solution and demonstrate a conceptual understanding of the derivation by solving similar problems.

MR 3.0, 3.3 Develop generalizations of the results obtained and apply them in other circumstances.

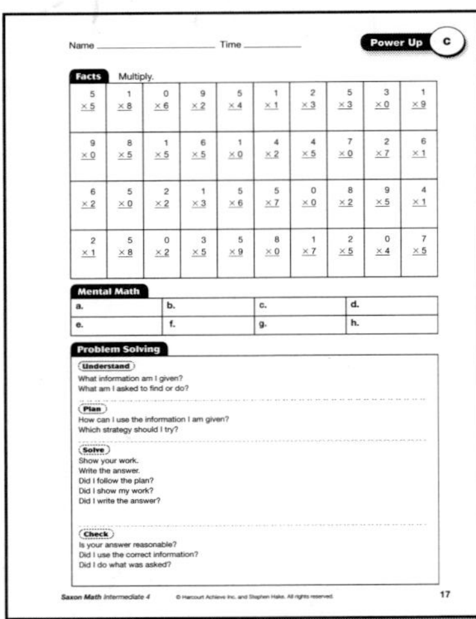
Power Up C Worksheet

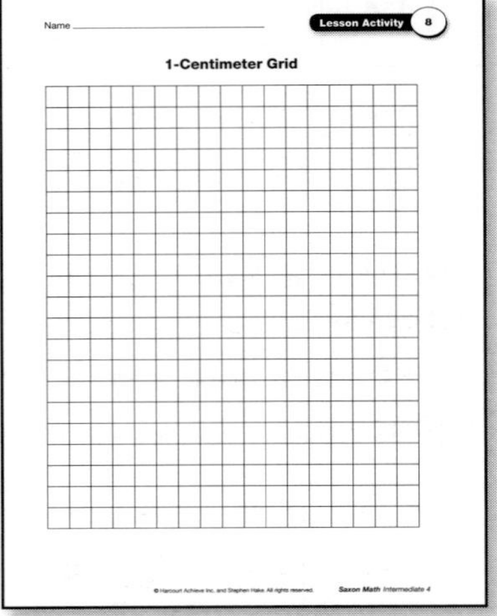
Lesson Activity 8

Universal Access

Reaching All Special Needs Students

Special Education Students	At-Risk Students	English Learners	Advanced Learners
• Inclusion (TM) • Adaptations for Saxon Math	• Alternative Approach (TM) • Error Alert (TM) • Reteaching Masters • Refresher Lessons for California Standards	• English Learners (TM) • Developing Academic Language (TM) • English Learner Handbook	• Extend the Example (TM) • Extend the Problem (TM) • Online Activities

TM=Teacher's Manual

Developing Academic Language

Maintained	**English Learner**
partial product	tutor

Problem Solving Discussion

Problem

Marco paid a dollar for an item that cost 54¢. He received four coins in change. What four coins did he receive?

Focus Strategies

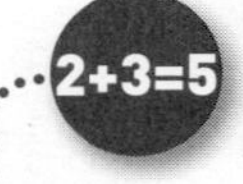
Write a Number Sentence or Equation

Guess and Check

Understand *Understand the problem.*

"What information are we given?"

Item costs 54¢.

Marco paid with $1.

He received four coins in change.

"What are we asked to do?"

We are asked to find the coins that Marco received.

Plan *Make a plan.*

"How can we use the information we know to solve the problem?"

We first need to find the value of the change that Marco received. We can do this by *writing a number sentence* to subtract 54¢ from $1. Then we can *guess and check* to find the coins.

Solve *Carry out the plan.*

"What is the value of the change Marco received?"

$1.00 – $0.54 = $0.46

"How can we make 46¢ with four coins?"

We might guess that one of the coins is a quarter (25¢). This would leave 46¢ – 25¢ = 21¢ for the other three coins. We can start a table to record our guesses.

HD	0
Q	1
D	2
N	0
P	1

"How can we make 21¢ with three coins?"

Two dimes and 1 penny have a total value of 21¢.

"What combination of four coins did Marco receive in change?"

Marco received 1 quarter, 2 dimes, and 1 penny in change.

Check *Look back.*

"Is our answer reasonable?"

We know that our answer is reasonable because 25¢ + 10¢ + 10¢ + 1¢ = 46¢. This is the amount of money Marco received in change.

"What is another way we could have solved this problem?"

We could have counted up the change like a cashier might do.

The cashier would need to use 1 penny to count up from 54¢ to 55¢.

The cashier could then use nickels, but it would mean using more coins than necessary to make the change. Instead of using nickels, the cashier can count up from 55¢ to 75¢ with 2 dimes.

"Which coin can the cashier use to count up from 75¢ to $1?"

1 quarter

Facts
Distribute **Power Up C** to students. See answers below.

Count Aloud
Before students begin the Mental Math exercises, do these counting exercises as a class.

Count up and down by fours from 16 to 56.

Mental Math
Encourage students to share different ways to mentally compute these exercises. Strategies for exercises are listed below.

a. Divide 60 by 3
$60 \div 3 = 20$

Use a Related Fact
Since $20 \times 3 = 60$, $60 \div 3 = 20$.

d. Decompose 46
$50 \times (40 + 6) = 2000 + 300 = 2300$

Subtract 50 × 4 from 50 × 50
$(50 \times 50) - (50 \times 4) = 2500 - 200 = 2300$

Problem Solving
Refer to **Problem-Solving Strategy Discussion,** p. 732B.

New Concept

Explanation
When the multiplication algorithm is used, the number of partial products is equal to the amount of digits in the number we are multiplying by. In this lesson, students will learn that if the number we are multiplying by is a multiple of 10, we can complete the multiplication by writing only one partial product.

(continued)

LESSON 111

• Multiplying Three-Digit Numbers

California Mathematics Content Standards

NS 3.0, 3.3 Solve problems involving multiplication of multidigit numbers by two-digit numbers.

MR 3.0, 3.2 Note the method of deriving the solution and demonstrate a conceptual understanding of the derivation by solving similar problems.

MR 3.0, 3.3 Develop generalizations of the results obtained and apply them in other circumstances.

facts Power Up C

mental math Find each fraction of 60 in problems **a–c.**

a. Fractional Part: $\frac{1}{3}$ of 60 20

b. Fractional Part: $\frac{2}{3}$ of 60 40

c. Fractional Part: $\frac{3}{3}$ of 60 60

d. Number Sense: 50×46 2300

e. Probability: With one roll of a dot cube, what is the probability of rolling a 4? $\frac{1}{6}$

f. Estimation: Estimate 49×21. 1000

g. Calculation: $\frac{1}{3}$ of 90, + 50, + 1, $\sqrt{\ }$, $\sqrt{\ }$, − 2 1

h. Simplify: $k^2 + 25$ when $k = 5$ 50

problem solving Choose an appropriate problem-solving strategy to solve this problem. Marco paid a dollar for an item that cost 54¢. He received four coins in change. What four coins did he receive? 1 quarter, 2 dimes, and 1 penny

When we multiply a three-digit number by a multiple of ten, we can find the product by doing only one multiplication instead of two.

$$\begin{array}{r} 243 \\ \times\ 20 \\ \hline \end{array}$$ We can rewrite the problem so the zero "hangs out" to the right. $$\begin{array}{r} 243 \\ \times\ \ \ 20 \\ \hline \end{array}$$

Facts Multiply.

5 × 5 25	1 × 8 8	0 × 6 0	9 × 2 18	5 × 4 20	1 × 1 1	2 × 3 6	5 × 3 15	3 × 0 0	1 × 9 9
9 × 0 0	8 × 5 40	1 × 5 5	6 × 5 30	1 × 0 0	4 × 2 8	4 × 5 20	7 × 0 0	2 × 7 14	6 × 1 6
6 × 2 12	5 × 0 0	2 × 2 4	1 × 3 3	5 × 6 30	5 × 7 35	0 × 0 0	8 × 2 16	9 × 5 45	4 × 1 4
2 × 1 2	5 × 8 40	0 × 2 0	3 × 5 15	5 × 9 45	8 × 0 0	1 × 7 7	2 × 5 10	0 × 4 0	7 × 5 35

```
 243
× 20
4860
```

Multiplying by 243 by 20 is the same as multiplying 243 by 10 and then by 2.

We multiply by 2. — We write the zero in the product to show that we multiplied by 10.

The product is **4860.**

Example 1

Multiply: 20 × 306

First we write the factors so the zero "hangs out."

```
  1
 306
×  20
6120
```

Step 2
We think 2 × 0 = 0 plus 1 = 1.
We write the 1 in the product.
We multiply by 3.

Step 1
We think 2 × 6 = 12. Write the 2 in the product and write the 1 ten above the 0.

The product is **6120.**

Example 2

Multiply: 24 × 406

Since there are two digits in the multiplier 24, we will have two partial products.

First we multiply by 4 ones. We think 4 × 6 = 24. Write the 4 in the product and write the 2 tens above the 0. Next, we multiply 0 by 4. 4 × 0 = 0 plus 2 = 2. Write the two in the tens place of the product. Then, we multiply the hundreds. 4 × 4 = 16.

Now we multiply by 2, which is really 20. We think 2 × 6 = 12. Write the 2 in the tens place of the product and write the 1 above the 0. Then we multiply 2 × 0 = 0 plus 1 = 1. Write the 1 in the product. Now we multiply 2 × 4 and write 8 in the product.

```
   1
   2
  406
×  24
 1624
 812
 9744
```

Finally, we add the partial products.

The product is **9744.**

Discuss Why did we move one place to the left when we multiplied by the 2 tens in 24?

Sample: We really multiplied by 20, so we moved one place to the left to show we multiplied by a multiple of 10.

New Concept *(Continued)*

Active Learning

Another way to describe the method in which a zero "hangs out" is to explain that it produces the same result as writing the number of zeros in the number we are multiplying by to the right of the product of the nonzero digits. In this example, there is one zero in the factor 20, and the product of the nonzero digits (243 × 2) is 486. Ask students to name the product of 243 × 20 and explain their answer. 4860; There is one zero written to the right of 486 because there is only one zero in the factor 20.

Example 2

Error Alert

It is not correct for students to assume that because the factor 406 contains a zero, the method shown in Example 1 (in which a zero 'hangs out') can be used to multiply 406 × 24. Make sure students understand that the method shown in Example 1 can only be used when one or both factors are multiples of 10. Point out that in this example, both factors are not multiples of 10, so we must use the multiplication algorithm to find the product.

Extend the Example

Remind advanced learners that the Commutative Property of Multiplication enables us to multiply two factors in any order. Then ask:

"In this example, we multiplied 406 by 24, which produced two partial products. Suppose that to check our work, we multiply 24 by 406. Will the multiplication produce the same number of partial products? Explain why or why not." No; sample: The number of partial products is the same as the number of digits in the number we are multiplying by, so the multiplication 24 × 406 will produce three partial products.

(continued)

New Concept *(Continued)*

Lesson Practice

Guided Practice

Use these problems as guided practice to check the students' understanding of today's concept.

Problems a–d

Have students note that the number we are multiplying by is a multiple of 10, and they may use the method shown in Example 1 to find each product.

Problems a–j

Error Alert

Remind students of the importance of checking their work. Then ask them to estimate each product and use the estimate to help decide the reasonableness of the exact answer.

Closure

The questions below help assess the concepts taught in this lesson.

Write "314 × 30" and "409 × 21" on the board or overhead. Then ask:

"Explain how we can find the product of 314 and 30 by writing only one partial product." Sample: Write 30 under 314 and let the zero "hang out." Write a zero after the product of 314 × 3.

Have students use the multiplication algorithm to find the product of 409 and 21. 314 × 30 = 9420; 409 × 21 = 8589

Written Practice

Math Conversations

Independent Practice and Discussions to Increase Understanding

Problem 3 **Represent**

Extend the Problem

Challenge your advanced learners to explain or demonstrate how pencil-and-paper arithmetic can be used to check the answer. Sample: One sixth of a number is the same as dividing the number by 6; 90 questions ÷ 6 = 15 questions. Since 15 questions represents $\frac{1}{6}$ of the total number of questions, we can multiply that number of questions by 5 to find the number of questions that $\frac{5}{6}$ represents. 15 questions × 5 = 75 questions

(continued)

Lesson Practice

a. 402 × 30 12,060
b. 543 × 40 21,720
c. 804 × 60 48,240
d. 320 × 50 16,000
e. 36 × 115 4140
f. 419 × 63 26,397
g. 102 × 12 1224
h. 404 × 25 10,100
i. 125 × 16 2000
j. 306 × 23 7038

Written Practice

Distributed and Integrated

1. (87) **Explain** Forty-five students are separated into four groups. The number of students in each group is as equal as possible. How many students are in the largest group? Explain your reasoning. 12 students; sample: Since the quotient of 45 ÷ 4 is 11 R 1, each of four groups includes 11 students, but one of those groups includes one additional student because the remainder of the division is 1.

2. (66, 101) Use the formulas to solve parts **a–b.**

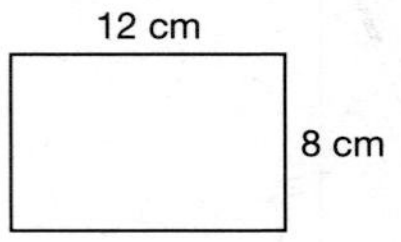

a. What is the area of this rectangle? 96 cm^2; $A = l \cdot w$

b. What is the perimeter of this rectangle? 40 cm; $P = 2l + 2w$

▸ ***3.** (94) **Represent** Iggy answered $\frac{5}{6}$ of the 90 questions correctly. How many questions did Iggy answer correctly? Draw a picture to illustrate the problem. 75 questions

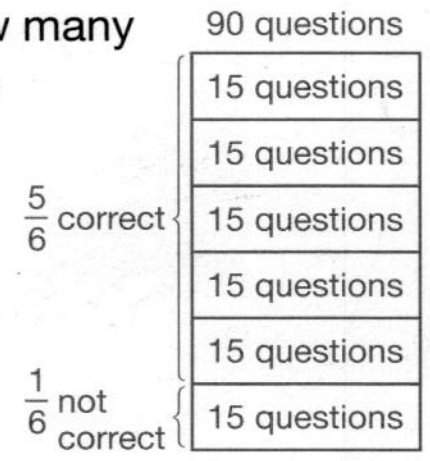

4. (96) Name the shape of each object:

a. roll of paper towels cylinder **b.** baseball sphere

***5.** (106) Write the reduced form of each fraction:

a. $\frac{3}{6}$ $\frac{1}{2}$ **b.** $\frac{5}{15}$ $\frac{1}{3}$ **c.** $\frac{8}{12}$ $\frac{2}{3}$

▸ ***6.** (110, Inv. 11) **Analyze** **a.** A box contains marbles that are the same size. There are 3 blue, 7 purple, and 5 red marbles in the box. If one marble is chosen without looking, which color is least likely to be chosen? blue

b. What number is least likely to be rolled on a number cube labeled 1, 2, 3, 4, 5, and 6? None

Inclusion

Use this strategy if the student displays:

- Poor Retention.
- Slow Learning Rate.

Multiplying Three Digit Numbers (Pairs)

Materials: base ten blocks and place-value mats (optional)

- Write 345 × 20 on the board. Tell students that if one of the factors is a multiple of 10, such as 20, then they can drop the zero and just multiply by the non-zero digit. Tell students to multiply 345 and 2.
- Students that struggle with multiplication can use base ten blocks and their place-value mats. Ask, ***"What is the product of 345 and 2?"*** 690 ***"How many zeros were dropped off the problem?"*** one zero

  Instruct students to add the zero onto the end of the product. Ask, ***"What is the product of 345 and 20?"*** 6900
- Have students work in pairs to solve the following problems: 550 × 40; 789 × 30

7. (49) Which digit is in the ten-millions place in 328,496,175? 2

8. (33) **Analyze** Draw a picture to help you solve this problem:

Winder is between Atlanta and Athens. It is 73 miles from Athens to Atlanta. It is 23 miles from Winder to Athens. How many miles is it from Winder to Atlanta? See student work; 50 mi

9. (13) Lyle volunteers after school as a tutor. Each afternoon he begins a tutoring session at the time shown on the clock and finishes three quarters of an hour later. What time does each tutoring session end? 4:10 p.m.

▶***10.** (21) In 1994, Caribou, Maine, had a record high temperature of 59°F in February. In 1955, Caribou's record low temperature in February was −41°F. What is the difference between these two record temperatures? 100 degrees

11. (45) $4.36 + 12.7 + 10.72$ 27.78

12. (9, 45) $8.54 - (4.2 - 2.17)$ 6.51

***13.** (100) $\frac{5}{9} + \frac{3}{9}$ $\frac{8}{9}$

***14.** (98, 100) $3\frac{2}{3} + 1\frac{1}{3}$ 5

15. (100) $4\frac{5}{8} + 1$ $5\frac{5}{8}$

***16.** (100) $7\frac{1}{4} + 1\frac{2}{4}$ $8\frac{3}{4}$

***17.** (100) $4\frac{4}{9} + 1\frac{1}{9}$ $5\frac{5}{9}$

***18.** (98, 100) $\frac{11}{12} + \frac{1}{12}$ 1

▶***19.** (107) 507×60 30,420

▶***20.** (107) 382×31 11,842

21. (111) 505×22 11,110

22. (79) $\frac{3731}{7}$ 533

23. (79) $9\overline{)5432}$ 603 R 5

***24.** (72) $6\overline{)548}$ 91 R 2

25. (Inv. 3) **Predict** The first five square numbers are 1, 4, 9, 16, and 25.

What is the eighth term of this sequence? Write an equation to support your answer. 64; sample: $8 \times 8 = 64$

▶***26.** (49) In the year 2006 the population of the United States reached three hundred million. Use digits to write the number in standard form. 300,000,000

English Learners

Explain to your students that a **tutor** is a person that helps other people learn things that they might not know or understand. Say:

"Sometimes it is helpful to find a math tutor to explain things again."

Ask:

"Do you think all tutors only teach school subjects? Give an example." No; sample: They may teach sewing, cooking, how to fix a car, etc.

Written Practice *(Continued)*

Math Conversations *(cont.)*

Problem 6 Analyze

For part **a**, make sure students understand that because the number of blue, purple, and red marbles is different, some colors are more likely to be chosen than others.

For part **b**, ask students to explain their answers.

Problem 10

If students have difficulty solving the problem, these questions offer them a simpler problem to solve.

"Suppose that a temperature decreased from 5° above zero to 0°. How many degrees did the temperature decrease?" 5°

"Suppose that the temperature then decreased from 0° to 5° below zero. How many degrees did the temperature decrease?" 5°

"What operation can we use to find the number of degrees the temperature decreased altogether? Explain your answer." Addition; $5° + 5° = 10°$

Problems 19 and 20

Ask students to make an estimate of each product, and then use the estimates to decide if the exact answers are reasonable. Sample:

problem **19:** Round 507 to 500; $500 \times 60 = 30,000$

problem **20:** Round 382 to 400 and 31 to 30; $400 \times 30 = 12,000$

Problem 26

Real-World Connection

You may wish to extend this problem by inviting students to use the Internet (at school, or at home with the permission of a family member), an almanac, or an atlas to find the population of your state. Ask students to round the population to the nearest million, or to the nearest hundred thousand for states with smaller populations.

(continued)

Written Practice *(Continued)*

Math Conversations *(cont.)*

Problem 27a Multiple Choice

Test-Taking Strategy

Remind students that a way to identify the term that does not name the shape is to identify those terms that do name the shape. The correct answer will be the term that is not identified.

Errors and Misconceptions

Problem 7

If students find it difficult to identify the place values of a number, suggest that they read the number aloud.

Problem 25

If students have difficulty identifying terms of the sequence, write the relationship shown below on the board or overhead. (This sequence uses exponents to represent the square numbers.)

1	4	9	16	25	...
1×1	2×2	3×3	4×4	5×5	
1^2	2^2	3^2	4^2	5^2	...

Point out that because the sequence uses exponents to represent the square numbers, students can use multiplication to continue the sequence.

▸ **27.** (17, 90) **a. Multiple Choice** Dacus built a square frame using two-by-fours, but when he leaned against it, the frame shifted to this shape. What word does *not* name this shape? D

A quadrilateral **B** parallelogram
C rhombus **D** trapezoid

b. Describe the angles. 2 acute angles and 2 obtuse angles

c. Describe the sides. 2 pairs of parallel sides

28. (20, 42) If the perimeter of a square is 6 centimeters, then each side is how many millimeters long? 15 mm

29. (96, 108, 109) A cube has how many more vertices than this pyramid? 3 more vertices

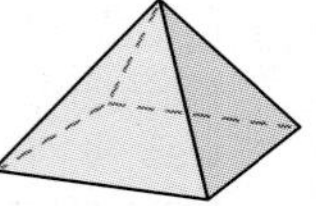

***30.** (Inv. 7, Inv. 9, Inv. 10) Three teaspoons are equal to one tablespoon. Use this relationship for parts **a–c.**

a. (Generalize) Write a formula for changing any number of tablespoons to teaspoons. Use t for teaspoons and b for tablespoons. $3b = t$, or $t = 3b$

b. (Evaluate) Write a set of ordered pairs for 1, 2, and 3 tablespoons. (1, 3), (2, 6), (3, 9)

c. (Represent) Graph the ordered pairs and draw a line to represent the equation. See student work.

Multiplying Three-Digit Numbers will be further developed in ***Saxon Math*** *Intermediate 5.*

Planning & Preparation

• Simplifying Fraction Answers

Objectives

- Write an answer that contains a fraction in the simplest form possible.
- Add and subtract fractions and mixed numbers with common denominators.

Prerequisite Skills

- Identifying factors of a given number.
- Writing the reduced form of a fraction.
- Converting improper fractions to whole or mixed numbers.

Materials

Instructional Masters

- Power Up G Worksheet

Manipulative Kit

- Rulers
- Fraction circles*

Teacher-provided materials

- Fraction bars*

**optional*

California Mathematics Content Standards

NS 1.0, 1.5 Explain different interpretations of fractions, for example, parts of a whole, parts of a set, and division of whole numbers by whole numbers; explain equivalents of fractions (see Standard 4.0).

NS 1.0, 1.7 Write the fraction represented by a drawing of parts of a figure; represent a given fraction by using drawings; and relate a fraction to a simple decimal on a number line.

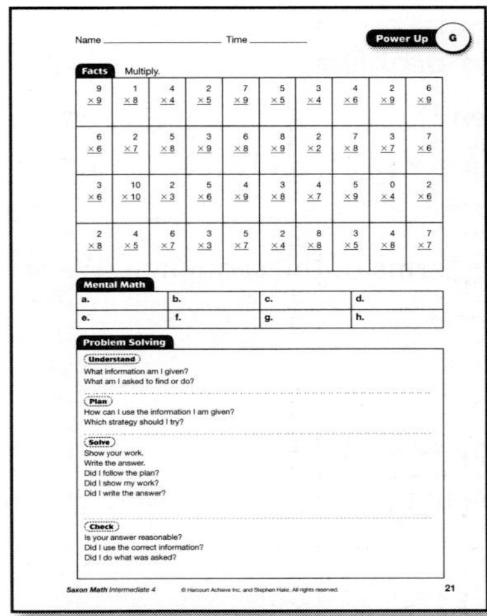
Name ______ Time ______ **Power Up G**

Facts Multiply.

9 × 9	1 × 8	4 × 4	2 × 5	7 × 9	5 × 5	3 × 4	4 × 6	2 × 9	6 × 9
6 × 6	2 × 7	5 × 8	3 × 9	6 × 8	8 × 9	2 × 2	7 × 8	3 × 7	7 × 6
3 × 6	10 × 10	2 × 3	5 × 6	4 × 9	3 × 8	4 × 7	5 × 9	0 × 4	2 × 6
2 × 8	4 × 5	6 × 7	3 × 3	5 × 7	2 × 4	8 × 8	3 × 5	4 × 8	7 × 7

Mental Math

a.	b.	c.	d.
e.	f.	g.	h.

Problem Solving

Understand
What information am I given?
What am I asked to find or do?

Plan
How can I use the information I am given?
Which strategy should I try?

Solve
Show your work.
Write the answer.
Did I follow the plan?
Did I show my work?
Did I write the answer?

Check
Is your answer reasonable?
Did I use the correct information?
Did I do what was asked?

Saxon Math Intermediate 4 21

Power Up G Worksheet

Universal Access

Reaching All Special Needs Students

Special Education Students	At-Risk Students	English Learners	Advanced Learners
• Inclusion (TM) • Adaptations for Saxon Math	• Error Alert (TM) • Reteaching Masters • Refresher Lessons for California Standards	• English Learners (TM) • Developing Academic Language (TM) • English Learner Handbook	• Extend the Example (TM) • Extend the Problem (TM) • Online Activities

TM=Teacher's Manual

Developing Academic Language

Maintained
difference
fraction
improper fraction
mixed number

English Learner
deck

Problem Solving Discussion

Problem

Find the next five terms in this sequence. Then describe the sequence in words.

$$\frac{1}{2}, \frac{2}{4}, \frac{3}{6}, \frac{4}{8}, \_\_, \_\_, \_\_, \_\_, \_\_, \ldots$$

Focus Strategy  **Find/Extend a Pattern**

Understand *Understand the problem.*

"What information are we given?"

The first four terms in a sequence are $\frac{1}{2}$, $\frac{2}{4}$, $\frac{3}{6}$, and $\frac{4}{8}$.

"What are we asked to do?"

We are asked to find the next five terms of the sequence. We are also asked to describe the sequence in words.

Plan *Make a plan.*

"What problem-solving strategy will we use?"

We will *find the pattern* to the sequence and then *extend the pattern*.

Solve *Carry out the plan.*

"What pattern do you notice in the numerators of the first four terms?"

They are consecutive counting numbers.

"What pattern do you notice in the denominators of the first four terms?"

Each of the denominators is double the numerator of the fraction.

"What are the next five terms in the sequence?"

$\frac{5}{10}, \frac{6}{12}, \frac{7}{14}, \frac{8}{16}, \frac{9}{18}$

Check *Look back.*

"Are our answers reasonable?"

We know that our answers are reasonable, because each fraction we wrote has a denominator that is double the fraction's numerator.

"What fraction is each term equal to? How can we describe the sequence in words?"

Each term is equivalent to the fraction $\frac{1}{2}$. The numerators count up by 1 from left to right, and each denominator is double the numerator of the fraction.

LESSON 112

• Simplifying Fraction Answers

California Mathematics Content Standards

NS 1.0, 1.5 Explain different interpretations of fractions, for example, parts of a whole, parts of a set, and division of whole numbers by whole numbers; explain equivalents of fractions (see Standard 4.0).

NS 1.0, 1.7 Write the fraction represented by a drawing of parts of a figure; represent a given fraction by using drawings; and relate a fraction to a simple decimal on a number line.

facts Power Up G

mental math Find each fraction of 60 in problems **a–c.**

a. **Fractional Part:** $\frac{1}{4}$ of 60 15

b. **Fractional Part:** $\frac{2}{4}$ of 60 30

c. **Fractional Part:** $\frac{3}{4}$ of 60 45

d. **Number Sense:** 30×12 360

e. **Money:** Taima had $10.00. Then she spent $5.63 on a journal. How much money does she have left? $4.37

f. **Estimation:** Eight bottles of laundry detergent cost $40.32. Round that amount to the nearest dollar and then divide by 8 to estimate the cost per bottle. 5 bottles

g. **Calculation:** $\frac{1}{2}$ of 24, ÷ 6, square the number, + 8, × 2 24

h. **Simplify:** $m^2 - 36$ when $m = 6$ 0

problem solving Choose an appropriate problem-solving strategy to solve this problem. Find the next five terms in this sequence. Then describe the sequence in words.

$$\frac{1}{2}, \frac{2}{4}, \frac{3}{6}, \frac{4}{8}, \_\_\_, \_\_\_, \_\_\_, \_\_\_, \_\_\_, \ldots$$

$\frac{5}{10}, \frac{6}{12}, \frac{7}{14}, \frac{8}{16}, \frac{9}{18}$; Each term is equivalent to $\frac{1}{2}$. The numerators increase by 1 from left to right, and the denominators increase by 2.

We often write answers to math problems in the simplest form possible. If an answer contains a fraction, there are two procedures that we usually follow.

1. We write improper fractions as mixed numbers (or whole numbers).
2. We reduce fractions when possible.

Facts Multiply.

9 × 9 = 81	1 × 8 = 8	4 × 4 = 16	2 × 5 = 10	7 × 9 = 63	5 × 5 = 25	3 × 4 = 12	4 × 6 = 24	2 × 9 = 18	6 × 9 = 54
6 × 6 = 36	2 × 7 = 14	5 × 8 = 40	3 × 9 = 27	6 × 8 = 48	8 × 9 = 72	2 × 2 = 4	7 × 8 = 56	3 × 7 = 21	7 × 6 = 42
3 × 6 = 18	10 × 10 = 100	2 × 3 = 6	5 × 6 = 30	4 × 9 = 36	3 × 8 = 24	4 × 7 = 28	5 × 9 = 45	0 × 4 = 0	2 × 6 = 12
2 × 8 = 16	4 × 5 = 20	6 × 7 = 42	3 × 3 = 9	5 × 7 = 35	2 × 4 = 8	8 × 8 = 64	3 × 5 = 15	4 × 8 = 32	7 × 7 = 49

Power Up

Facts

Distribute **Power Up G** to students. See answers below.

Count Aloud

Before students begin the Mental Math exercises, do these counting exercises as a class.

Count up and down by eights from 24 to 88.

Mental Math

Encourage students to share different ways to mentally compute these exercises. Strategies for exercises are listed below.

a. Find $\frac{1}{2}$ of $\frac{1}{2}$ of 60

$\frac{1}{2}$ of 60 = 30; $\frac{1}{2}$ of 30 = 15

Decompose 60

(40 + 20) ÷ 4 = (40 ÷ 4) + (20 ÷ 4); 10 + 5 = 15

d. Decompose 12

30 × (10 + 2) = 300 + 60 = 360

Double 30 and Halve 12

30 × 2 = 60; 12 ÷ 2 = 6; 60 × 6 = 360

Problem Solving

Refer to **Problem-Solving Strategy Discussion,** p. 737B.

New Concept

Instruction

In this lesson, students learn that we sometimes must simplify answers that are fractions, improper fractions, or mixed numbers.

(continued)

New Concept (Continued)

Example 1
Error Alert

Remind students that a fraction is improper if its numerator is greater than or equal to its denominator.

Example 2
Active Learning

Ask students to sketch or draw a picture to show that $\frac{2}{4}$ and $\frac{1}{2}$ are equivalent fractions.

Example 3
Explanation

As you discuss the solution, remind students that we can add the fraction parts of the mixed numbers because the denominators of the fractions are the same. After discussing the solution, ask:

"Why is $\frac{3}{3}$ equal to 1? Include the word 'division' in your answer." Sample: A fraction bar represents division, and $3 \div 3 = 1$.

Example 4
Instruction

On the board or overhead, demonstrate the division of 7 by 5 to show that $\frac{7}{5} = 1\frac{2}{5}$.

Example 5
Extend the Example

After you discuss the solution, challenge your advanced learners to answer this question.

"Subtraction is used to solve this problem. How could subtraction be used to check the answer?" Subtract $5\frac{2}{8}$ from $6\frac{5}{8}$ and compare the result to $1\frac{3}{8}$.

(continued)

Example 1

Thinking Skills
Justify
Explain why $\frac{4}{3} = 1\frac{1}{3}$.

Sample: $\frac{4}{3} = \frac{3}{3} + \frac{1}{3}$, and $1\frac{1}{3} = 1 + \frac{1}{3}$.

Add: $\frac{2}{3} + \frac{2}{3}$

We add the fractions and get the sum $\frac{4}{3}$. Notice that $\frac{4}{3}$ is an improper fraction. We take the extra step of changing $\frac{4}{3}$ to the mixed number $\mathbf{1\frac{1}{3}}$.

$\frac{2}{3} + \frac{2}{3} = \frac{4}{3}$

$\frac{4}{3} = 1\frac{1}{3}$

Example 2

Subtract: $\frac{3}{4} - \frac{1}{4}$

We subtract and get the difference $\frac{2}{4}$. Notice that $\frac{2}{4}$ can be reduced. We take the extra step of reducing $\frac{2}{4}$ to $\frac{1}{2}$.

$\frac{3}{4} - \frac{1}{4} = \frac{2}{4}$

$\frac{2}{4} = \frac{1}{2}$

Example 3

Nicholas exercises each day by walking. The route he walks each morning is $3\frac{1}{3}$ miles long, and the route he walks each evening is $4\frac{2}{3}$ miles long. Altogether, how many miles does Nicholas walk each day?

We add the mixed numbers and get the sum $7\frac{3}{3}$. Notice that $\frac{3}{3}$ is an improper fraction equal to 1. So $7\frac{3}{3} = 7 + 1$, which is 8. Nicholas walks **8 miles** altogether.

$3\frac{1}{3} + 4\frac{2}{3} = 7\frac{3}{3}$

$7\frac{3}{3} = 8$

Example 4

Add: $5\frac{3}{5} + 6\frac{4}{5}$

We add the mixed numbers and get $11\frac{7}{5}$. Notice that $\frac{7}{5}$ is an improper fraction that can be changed to $1\frac{2}{5}$. So $11\frac{7}{5}$ equals $11 + 1\frac{2}{5}$, which is $\mathbf{12\frac{2}{5}}$.

$5\frac{3}{5} + 6\frac{4}{5} = 11\frac{7}{5}$

$11\frac{7}{5} = 12\frac{2}{5}$

Example 5

Thinking Skills
Represent
Draw a picture to show that $\frac{2}{8} = \frac{1}{4}$.

Sample:

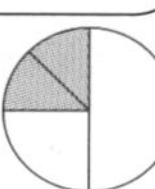

A piece of fabric $1\frac{3}{8}$ yards in length was cut from a bolt of fabric that measured $6\frac{5}{8}$ yards long. How long is the piece of fabric left on the bolt?

We subtract and get $5\frac{2}{8}$. Notice that $\frac{2}{8}$ can be reduced, so we reduce $\frac{2}{8}$ to $\frac{1}{4}$ and get $5\frac{1}{4}$. The length of the fabric is $\mathbf{5\frac{1}{4}}$ **yards.**

$6\frac{5}{8} - 1\frac{3}{8} = 5\frac{2}{8}$

$5\frac{2}{8} = 5\frac{1}{4}$

Math Background

A statement that two fractions are equal is called a *proportion.* Here are some proportions:

$$\frac{3}{4} = \frac{15}{20} \qquad \frac{2}{6} = \frac{8}{24} \qquad \frac{2}{3} = \frac{t}{15} \qquad \frac{2}{3} = \frac{6}{n}$$

In the last two proportions, there is an unknown. Students learn one method of solving such proportions in the lesson. Another method involves *cross-multiplying.* For this method, we use the following fact: If $\frac{a}{b} = \frac{c}{d}$, then $a \times d = b \times c$. (In other words, the top of the first fraction times the bottom of the second equals the bottom of the first fraction times the top of the second.) So, in the third proportion above, we know that $2 \times 15 = 3t$. When simplifying, we get $30 = 3t$, so $t = 10$. In the last proportion above, $2n = 3 \times 6$. After multiplying, we get $2n = 18$, so $n = 9$.

Lesson Practice Simplify the answer to each sum or difference:

a. $\frac{4}{5} + \frac{4}{5}$ $1\frac{3}{5}$ b. $\frac{5}{6} - \frac{1}{6}$ $\frac{2}{3}$ c. $3\frac{2}{3} + 1\frac{2}{3}$ $5\frac{1}{3}$

d. $5\frac{1}{4} + 6\frac{3}{4}$ 12 e. $7\frac{7}{8} - 1\frac{1}{8}$ $6\frac{3}{4}$ f. $5\frac{3}{5} + 1\frac{3}{5}$ $7\frac{1}{5}$

g. $4\frac{3}{10} - 3\frac{1}{10}$ $1\frac{1}{5}$ h. $\frac{3}{4} + \frac{3}{4}$ $1\frac{1}{2}$ i. $\frac{5}{8} - \frac{1}{8}$ $\frac{1}{2}$

Written Practice

Distributed and Integrated

►*1. (21, Inv. 5) **Interpret** Use the information in the graph to answer parts **a–c**.

High Temperatures for the Week

Temperature: 50°F, 60°F, 70°F; Day of the Week: S M T W T F S

a. On which day was the temperature the highest? Wednesday

b. What was the high temperature on Tuesday? About 54°F

c. From Monday to Wednesday, the temperature went up how many degrees? 15°F

2. (66, 88, 101) Use a formula for parts **a** and **b**.

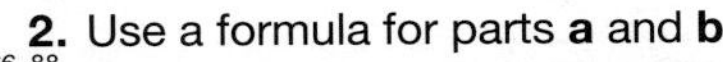

a. What is the perimeter of this rectangle? 78 m

b. What is the area of the rectangle? 360 m^2

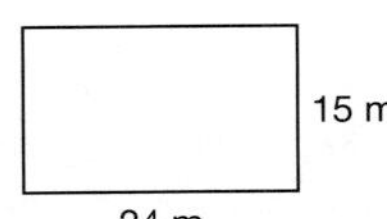

15 m

24 m

►*3. (63) **Analyze** Simplify each expression. Remember to use the order of operations.

a. $3 \times 5 + (12 \div 6)$ 17
b. $15 \div 3 - (3 + 2)$ 0
c. $14 + (8 - 2) \times 5$ 44
d. $6 \times (20 - 12) - 5$ 43

*4. (74, 106) **Represent** What fractional part of the months of the year begins with J? Reduce the fraction if necessary. $\frac{3}{12} = \frac{1}{4}$

5. (110, Inv. 11) There are 52 cards in a deck. Four of the cards are aces. What is the probability of drawing an ace from a full deck of cards? $\frac{1}{13}$

New Concept *(Continued)*

Lesson Practice

Guided Practice

Use these problems as guided practice to check the students' understanding of today's concept.

Problems a–f

Before students complete any arithmetic, ask:

"How do we know when a fraction cannot be reduced?" Sample: A fraction cannot be reduced when 1 is the only number that can divide both the numerator and the denominator.

Problem d

Error Alert

The sum of the fractions is $\frac{4}{4}$. Make sure students understand that $\frac{4}{4}$ is equal to 1, and should be added to the sum of the whole numbers $(5 + 6 + 1 = 12)$.

Closure

The questions below help assess the concepts taught in this lesson.

Write "$\frac{3}{4} + \frac{3}{4}$" and "$7\frac{5}{9} - 1\frac{2}{9}$" on the board or overhead. Then say:

"Find each sum or difference. Make sure your answers are in simplest form" $1\frac{1}{2}$; $6\frac{1}{3}$

After the arithmetic has been completed, ask:

"Did you need to reduce the sum or the difference to simplest form? Explain why or why not." Yes, both the sum and the difference needed to be reduced; sample: A factor that can divide both 6 and 4 $\left(\frac{3}{4} + \frac{3}{4} = \frac{6}{4}\right)$ is 2, and a factor that can divide both 3 and 9 $\left(7\frac{5}{9} - 1\frac{2}{9} = 6\frac{3}{9}\right)$ is 3.

English Learners

Explain that the word **deck** has several meanings but when someone mentions "a deck of cards" it means a pack of playing cards.

Ask students if they have ever played or seen someone else play with a **deck** of cards. Ask:

"How many cards does a deck of cards normally have?" 52

Inclusion

Use this strategy if the student displays:

- Difficulty with Large Group Instruction.
- Difficulty with Abstract Processing.

Simplifying Fraction Answers (Pairs)

Material: fraction manipulatives

- Write $\frac{3}{5} + \frac{3}{5}$ on the board. Have students work in pairs and use the fifths fraction circles to solve this problem. Ask, ***"How many parts?"*** 6 ***"How many parts are in one whole?"*** 5
- Write $= \frac{6}{5}$ on the board. Tell students to rearrange the fraction parts to make as many whole circles as possible. Ask, ***"How many whole circles are made?"*** 1 ***"What fraction is left over?"*** $\frac{1}{5}$
- Read, ***"Jane walked her dog $2\frac{1}{4}$ miles on Monday and $1\frac{1}{4}$ miles on Tuesday. How many miles did she walk?"*** $3\frac{1}{2}$

Written Practice

Math Conversations

Independent Practice and Discussions to Increase Understanding

Problem 1 **Interpret**

Extend the Problem

Ask students to write a problem that can be solved using data from the graph, and write the answer to the problem on a separate sheet of paper. Then have pairs of students exchange, solve the problems, and compare answers.

(continued)

Written Practice *(Continued)*

Math Conversations *(cont.)*

Problem 3 Analyze

"When do we follow the order of operations?" Whenever more than one operation is present in an expression or equation

"State the order of operations." Complete the operation(s) inside parentheses first. Multiply and divide from left to right. Add and subtract from left to right.

Problem 7

"How do we know when a fraction can be reduced?" Sample: when the numerator and the denominator can be divided by the same number that is greater than 1

Problem 8 Evaluate

Extend the Problem

Challenge your advanced learners with this question:

"Does this line intersect the vertical axis of the coordinate plane above the origin, at the origin, or below the origin? Explain how you know." Above the origin; sample: If we substitute 0 for x, we find that $y = 1$, so the line intersects the y-axis at (0, 1), which is above the origin.

Problem 9 Represent

Suggest that students insert commas in the number before they try to write it using words.

Extend the Problem

Write "27,386,415 rounds to 27,390,000" on the board or overhead. Then ask:

"What place was 27,386,415 rounded to if it changed to 27,390,000 after being rounded?" The ten-thousands place

Problems 12–14

Remind students to write their answers in simplest form.

Problem 22

Before students complete the arithmetic, point out that dividing a number by 2 is the same as finding $\frac{1}{2}$ of the number, and then encourage them to use mental math to find the quotient.

(continued)

6. **Classify** Name each shape: (96)

a.  cylinder b. 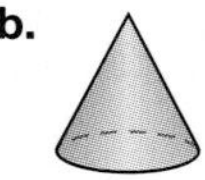 cone c. 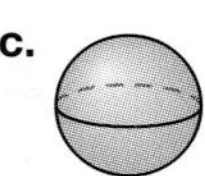 sphere

▶ *7. Write the reduced form of each fraction: (106)

a. $\frac{6}{8}$ $\frac{3}{4}$ b. $\frac{4}{9}$ $\frac{4}{9}$ c. $\frac{4}{16}$ $\frac{1}{4}$

▶ *8. **Evaluate** This table represents the equation $y = 3x + 1$ and shows the values of y when x is 4. What is y when x is 5? 16 (64, 93)

x	y
3	10
4	13
5	?

▶ *9. **Represent** Use words to write the number 27386415. twenty-seven million, three hundred eighty-six thousand, four hundred fifteen (49)

10. **Represent** Point W stands for what number on this number line? Point W is at 1. (Inv. 2)

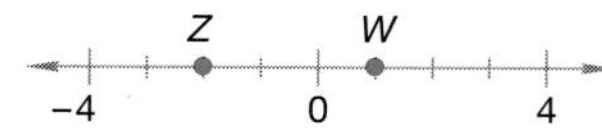

11. **Represent** Draw two parallel segments that are one inch long and one inch apart. Then make a quadrilateral by drawing two more parallel segments. What type of quadrilateral did you draw? See student work; a parallelogram (possibly a square) (90)

▶ *12. $4\frac{4}{5} + 3\frac{3}{5}$ $8\frac{2}{5}$ (112) ▶ *13. $5\frac{1}{6} + 1\frac{2}{6}$ $6\frac{1}{2}$ (112) ▶ *14. $7\frac{3}{4} + \frac{1}{4}$ 8 (112)

*15. $6\overline{)508}$ 84 R 4 (72) *16. $4\overline{)3018}$ 754 R 2 (79) 17. $5\frac{3}{8} + 5\frac{1}{8}$ $10\frac{1}{2}$ (112)

*18. 25×408 10,200 (111) 19. 702×36 25,272 (107) 20. 147×54 7938 (107)

21. $8\overline{)5766}$ 720 R 6 (83) ▶ *22. $2\overline{)440}$ 220 (83)

23. $4.75 + 16.14 + 10.9$ 31.79 (45) 24. $18.4 - (4.32 - 2.6)$ 16.68 (9, 45)

*25. **Estimate** In the year 2000 the population of the state of California was 33,871,648. Round that number to the nearest million. 34,000,000 (104)

740 ***Saxon Math*** *Intermediate 4*

▶*26. (104) **Estimate** Round 297,576,320 to the nearest hundred million. 300,000,000

27. (Inv. 6, 95) On Jahzara's first nine games she earned these scores:

90, 95, 80, 85, 100, 95, 75, 95, 90

Use this information to answer parts **a** and **b.**

a. What is the median and range of Jahzara's scores? median, 90; range, 25

b. What is the mode of Jahzara's scores? 95

28. (43, Inv. 8) Write these numbers in order from least to greatest: $5.02, 5\frac{11}{100}, 5.67, 5\frac{83}{100}$

$5\frac{11}{100}$ 5.67 5.02 $5\frac{83}{100}$

29. (54) Maranie wanted to divide 57 buttons into 9 groups. How many groups will Maranie have? Will there be any buttons left over? 6 groups; 3 left over

▶*30. (96, 108, 109) **a.** **Explain** Which prism has more vertices? Explain why? The hexagonal prism has 2 more vertices than the pentagonal prism; A hexagon has 6 vertices and a pentagon has 5 vertices; Each prism has 2 congruent bases; $2 \times 5 = 10$, $2 \times 6 = 12$, $12 - 10 = 2$

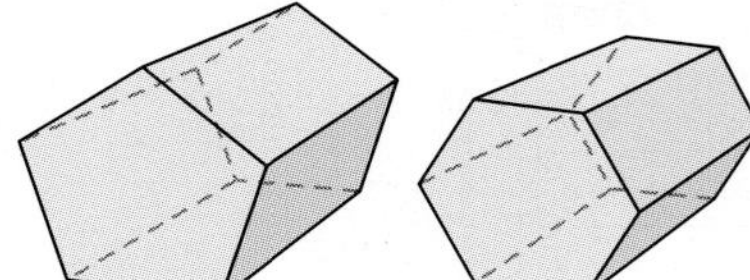

b. **Justify** A pyramid can have a base that is any polygon. How many vertices does a pentagonal pyramid have? 6; 5 on the base and 1 at the apex

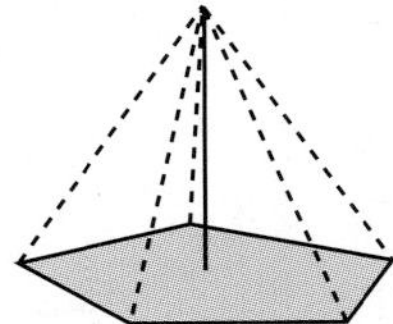

Looking Forward

Finding equivalent fractions with a specified denominator prepares students for:

- **Lesson 113,** multiplying denominators to find a common denominator.

Written Practice *(Continued)*

Math Conversations *(cont.)*

Problem 26 Estimate

"Which digit in the number is in the hundred millions place?" The first digit (2)

Problem 30a Explain

If students have difficulty identifying the number of vertices each prism has, point out that the vertices of each base are congruent, or identical. Then explain that students should focus their attention on one base of each prism—the number of vertices altogether for each prism will be double the number of vertices each base has.

Some students may find it helpful to trace one base of each prism and then mark each vertex on the tracings.

Errors and Misconceptions

Problem 1

Make sure students recognize that the first T at the bottom of the graph stands for Tuesday and the second T stands for Thursday.

Problem 26

When rounding to a given place value, students must make sure that the answer they give is representative of that place value. Point out that saying numbers aloud can be used to help check the reasonableness of an answer that involves rounding. For example, explain that the word hundred should be spoken if a number is to be rounded to the nearest hundred, and the correct answer should be able to be read as "one hundred" or "two hundred" or "three hundred," and so on.

Problem 27

Make sure students recall that numbers must be arranged in order before the median can be identified, and that the numbers may be ordered from least to greatest or from greatest to least.

Planning & Preparation

• Renaming Fractions and Common Denominators

Objectives

- Find a fraction with a specified denominator that is equivalent to a given fraction.
- Rename fractions whose denominators are not equal by using a common denominator of the fractions.
- Multiply denominators to find a common denominator.

Prerequisite Skills

- Finding equivalent fractions.
- Identifying factors of a given number.

Materials

Instructional Masters

- Power Up I Worksheet

Manipulative Kit

- Rulers
- Overhead fraction circles, color tiles*

Teacher-provided materials

- Construction paper, fraction bars*

**optional*

California Mathematics Content Standards

NS 1.0, 1.5 Explain different interpretations of fractions, for example, parts of a whole, parts of a set, and division of whole numbers by whole numbers; explain equivalents of fractions (see Standard 4.0).

MR 2.0, 2.4 Express the solution clearly and logically by using the appropriate mathematical notation and terms and clear language; support solutions with evidence in both verbal and symbolic work.

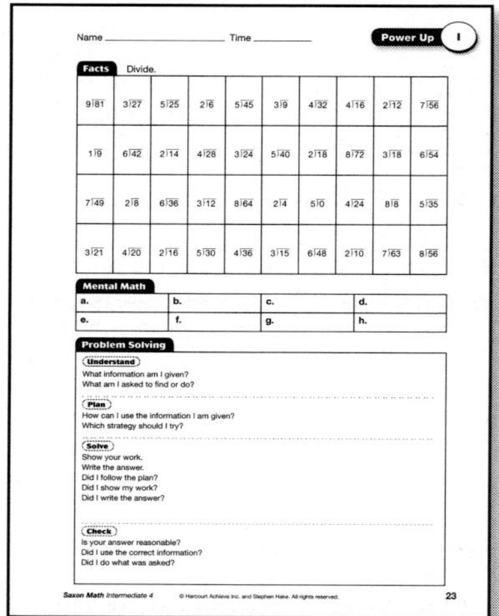

Name ______________ Time ________ **Power Up I**

Facts Divide.

$9\overline{)81}$	$3\overline{)27}$	$5\overline{)25}$	$2\overline{)6}$	$5\overline{)45}$	$3\overline{)9}$	$4\overline{)32}$	$4\overline{)16}$	$2\overline{)12}$	$7\overline{)56}$
$1\overline{)9}$	$6\overline{)42}$	$2\overline{)14}$	$4\overline{)28}$	$3\overline{)24}$	$5\overline{)40}$	$2\overline{)18}$	$8\overline{)72}$	$3\overline{)18}$	$6\overline{)54}$
$7\overline{)49}$	$2\overline{)8}$	$6\overline{)36}$	$3\overline{)12}$	$8\overline{)64}$	$2\overline{)4}$	$5\overline{)0}$	$4\overline{)24}$	$8\overline{)8}$	$5\overline{)35}$
$3\overline{)21}$	$4\overline{)20}$	$2\overline{)16}$	$5\overline{)30}$	$4\overline{)36}$	$3\overline{)15}$	$6\overline{)48}$	$2\overline{)10}$	$7\overline{)63}$	$8\overline{)56}$

Mental Math

a.	b.	c.	d.
e.	f.	g.	h.

Problem Solving

Understand
What information am I given?
What am I asked to find or do?

Plan
How can I use the information I am given?
Which strategy should I try?

Solve
Show your work.
Write the answer.
Did I follow the plan?
Did I show my work?
Did I write the answer?

Check
Is your answer reasonable?
Did I use the correct information?
Did I do what was asked?

Saxon Math Intermediate 4 © Harcourt Achieve Inc. and Stephen Hake. All rights reserved. 23

Power Up I Worksheet

Universal Access

Reaching All Special Needs Students

Special Education Students	At-Risk Students	English Learners	Advanced Learners
• Inclusion (TM) • Adaptations for Saxon Math	• Alternative Approach (TM) • Error Alert (TM) • Reteaching Masters • Refresher Lessons for California Standards	• English Learners (TM) • Developing Academic Language (TM) • English Learner Handbook	• Extend the Example (TM) • Extend the Problem (TM) • Early Finisher (SE) • Online Activities

TM=Teacher's Manual
SE=Student Edition

Developing Academic Language

New	Maintained	English Learner
least common denominator	denominator equivalent fraction	hint

Problem Solving Discussion

Problem

The numbers 1, 8, and 27 begin the sequence below. (Notice that $1 = 1^3$, $8 = 2^3$, and $27 = 3^3$.) Find the next three numbers in the sequence.

1, 8, 27, __, __, __, ...

Focus Strategy

Find/Extend a Pattern

Understand *Understand the problem.*

"What information are we given?"

The first three terms of a sequence are 1, 8, and 27.

The first three terms are the cubes of the counting numbers 1, 2, and 3.

"How do we calculate 1 cubed, 2 cubed, and 3 cubed?"

$1 \times 1 \times 1 = 1$

$2 \times 2 \times 2 = 8$

$3 \times 3 \times 3 = 27$

"What are we asked to do?"

We are asked to find the next three terms in the sequence.

"Would anyone like to give an estimate for how large the next three terms in this sequence will be?"

Discuss student responses.

Plan *Make a plan.*

"What problem-solving strategy will we use?"

We will *extend the pattern.*

Solve *Carry out the plan.*

"How will we calculate the next three terms?"

We will cube the numbers 4, 5, and 6:

$4^3 = 4 \times 4 \times 4 = 64$

$5^3 = 5 \times 5 \times 5 = 125$

$6^3 = 6 \times 6 \times 6 = 216$

"What are the next three terms of the sequence?"

64, 125, and 216

Check *Look back.*

"Did we complete the task that was assigned?"

Yes. We found that the next three terms of the sequence are 64, 125, and 216.

"Are our answers reasonable?"

We know that our answers are reasonable because we continued the sequence of the cubes of the counting numbers. In the problem, we were given the cubes of 1, 2, and 3. The numbers 64, 125, and 216 are the cubes of 4, 5, and 6.

"Do the results match your expectations?"

Students might be surprised by how rapidly cubed numbers increase in size.

Facts
Distribute **Power Up I** to students. See answers below.

Count Aloud
Before students begin the Mental Math exercises, do these counting exercises as a class.

Count up and down by threes from 3 to 36.

Mental Math
Encourage students to share different ways to mentally compute these exercises. Strategies for exercises are listed below.

a. Add $\frac{1}{2}$ of 6 and $\frac{1}{2}$ of 1

$\frac{1}{2}$ of $6 = 3$; $\frac{1}{2}$ of $1 = \frac{1}{2}$; $3 + \frac{1}{2} = 3\frac{1}{2}$

b. Add $\frac{1}{2}$ of 10 and $\frac{1}{2}$ of 1

$\frac{1}{2}$ of $10 = 5$; $\frac{1}{2}$ of $1 = \frac{1}{2}$; $5 + \frac{1}{2} = 5\frac{1}{2}$

c. Add $\frac{1}{2}$ of 20 and $\frac{1}{2}$ of 1

$\frac{1}{2}$ of $20 = 10$; $\frac{1}{2}$ of $1 = \frac{1}{2}$; $10 + \frac{1}{2} = 10\frac{1}{2}$

d. Add $\frac{1}{2}$ of 32 and $\frac{1}{2}$ of 1

$\frac{1}{2}$ of $32 = 16$; $\frac{1}{2}$ of $1 = \frac{1}{2}$; $16 + \frac{1}{2} = 16\frac{1}{2}$

Problem Solving
Refer to **Problem-Solving Strategy Discussion,** p. 742B.

California Mathematics Content Standards

NS 1.0, 1.5 Explain different interpretations of fractions, for example, parts of a whole, parts of a set, and division of whole numbers by whole numbers; explain equivalents of fractions (see Standard 4.0).

MR 2.0, 2.4 Express the solution clearly and logically by using the appropriate mathematical notation and terms and clear language; support solutions with evidence in both verbal and symbolic work.

• Renaming Fractions and Common Denominators

facts Power Up I

mental math An odd number can be written as an even number plus 1. For example, 9 is 8 + 1. So half of 9 is half of 8 plus half of 1, which is $4 + \frac{1}{2}$, or $4\frac{1}{2}$. Use this strategy to find half of each odd number in problems **a–d.**

a. **Fractional Part:** 7 $3\frac{1}{2}$

b. **Fractional Part:** 11 $5\frac{1}{2}$

c. **Fractional Part:** 21 $10\frac{1}{2}$

d. **Fractional Part:** 33 $16\frac{1}{2}$

e. **Probability:** If the chance of rain is $\frac{3}{10}$, what is the chance that it will not rain? $\frac{7}{10}$

f. **Estimation:** Uzuri's mother filled the car with gasoline, which cost \$33.43. Then her mother bought snacks for \$4.48. Estimate the total cost. \$37 or \$38

g. **Calculation:** $\frac{1}{2}$ of 100, − 1, $\sqrt{\ }$, + 2, $\sqrt{\ }$, + 1, $\sqrt{\ }$ 2

h. **Simplify:** $n^2 + 1$ when $n = 1$ 2

problem solving Choose an appropriate problem-solving strategy to solve this problem. The numbers 1, 8, and 27 begin the sequence below. (Notice that $1 = 1^3$, $8 = 2^3$, and $27 = 3^3$.) Find the next three numbers in the sequence.

1, 8, 27, 64, 125, 216, …

Facts Divide.

9 9)81	9 3)27	5 5)25	3 2)6	9 5)45	3 3)9	8 4)32	4 4)16	6 2)12	8 7)56
9 1)9	7 6)42	7 2)14	7 4)28	8 3)24	8 5)40	9 2)18	9 8)72	6 3)18	9 6)54
7 7)49	4 2)8	6 6)36	4 3)12	8 8)64	2 2)4	0 5)0	6 4)24	1 8)8	7 5)35
7 3)21	5 4)20	8 2)16	6 5)30	9 4)36	5 3)15	8 6)48	5 2)10	9 7)63	7 8)56

New Concept

Remember that when we multiply a fraction by a fraction name for 1, the result is an equivalent fraction. For example, if we multiply $\frac{1}{2}$ by $\frac{2}{2}$, we get $\frac{2}{4}$. The fractions $\frac{1}{2}$ and $\frac{2}{4}$ are equivalent fractions because they have the same value.

$$\frac{1}{2} \times \frac{2}{2} = \frac{2}{4}$$

Sometimes we must choose a particular multiplier that is equal to 1.

Example 1

Thinking Skills

Discuss

How can we check the answer?

Sample: Divide the numerator and the denominator of the product by 3; $\frac{3 \div 3}{12 \div 3} = \frac{1}{4}$

Find the equivalent fraction for $\frac{1}{4}$ whose denominator is 12.

To change 4 to 12, we must multiply by 3. So we multiply $\frac{1}{4}$ by $\frac{3}{3}$.

$$\frac{1}{4} \times \frac{3}{3} = \frac{3}{12}$$

The fraction $\frac{1}{4}$ is equivalent to $\mathbf{\frac{3}{12}}$.

Example 2

Thinking Skills

Verify

How can we check the answer?

Sample: Divide the numerator and the denominator of the product by 5; $\frac{10 \div 5}{15 \div 5} = \frac{2}{3}$

Complete the equivalent fraction: $\frac{2}{3} = \frac{?}{15}$

The denominator changed from 3 to 15. Since the denominator was multiplied by 5, the correct multiplier is $\frac{5}{5}$.

$$\frac{2}{3} \times \frac{5}{5} = \frac{10}{15}$$

Thus, the missing numerator of the equivalent fraction is **10.**

Two or more fractions have **common denominators** if their denominators are equal.

$\frac{3}{8}$ $\frac{5}{8}$	$\frac{3}{8}$ $\frac{5}{9}$
These two fractions have common denominators.	These two fractions do *not* have common denominators.

We will use common denominators to rename fractions whose denominators are not equal.

New Concept

Instruction

In this lesson, students will learn to rename fractions. Renaming fractions is a prerequisite skill for adding and subtracting fractions that have different denominators—renaming the fractions produces a common denominator.

Remind students that another name for *equivalent* fractions is *equal* fractions.

Active Learning

Ask students to sketch or draw a picture to show that $\frac{3}{6}$ and $\frac{6}{12}$ are equivalent fractions (or you can use overhead fraction manipulatives to demonstrate this fact).

Example 1

Error Alert

After students answer the **Discuss** question, remind them that because multiplication was used to find the answers, division is used to check because multiplication and division are inverse operations—one operation undoes the other.

Example 2

Extend the Example

Explain that $\frac{2}{3} = \frac{?}{15}$ is an example of a proportion, and the missing number in a proportion can be located anywhere in the proportion. Then write "$\frac{3}{4} = \frac{15}{n}$" on the board or overhead and challenge your advanced learners to name the value for n that results in a fraction that is equivalent to $\frac{3}{4}$, and explain their answer. $n = 20$; sample: To change the numerator 3 to 15, we multiply by 3 by 5, so we multiply the denominator 4 by 5.

(continued)

New Concept (Continued)

Lesson Practice

Guided Practice

Use these problems as guided practice to check the students' understanding of today's concept.

Problem c
Extend the Problem

Write the proportion $\frac{?}{3} = \frac{8}{12}$ on the board or overhead and challenge your students to name the missing number, and explain how they know. 2; sample: $12 \div 4 = 3$, so I need to divide 8 by 4, and $8 \div 4 = 2$.

Problems a–c
Error Alert

Before students write the number that completes each equivalent fraction, ask:

"What number will you multiply the numerator by to find the missing number?" **a:** 3; **b:** 3; **c:** 2

Make sure students understand that the relationship of the two denominators is used to name the number each numerator is multiplied by.

Closure The questions below help assess the concepts taught in this lesson.

"Explain how multiplication is used to find an equivalent fraction. Give an example to support your answer." Multiply the given fraction by a fraction that is equivalent to 1, such as $\frac{2}{2}$, $\frac{3}{3}$, $\frac{4}{4}$, and so on; sample: $\frac{1}{2} \times \frac{5}{5} = \frac{5}{10}$

"Why doesn't multiplying a fraction by a fraction such as $\frac{2}{2}$ or $\frac{3}{3}$ change the value of the fraction?" $\frac{2}{2}$ and $\frac{3}{3}$ are equivalent to 1, and multiplying a number by 1 does not change the value of the number.

Example 3

Rename $\frac{2}{3}$ and $\frac{3}{4}$ so that they have a common denominator of 12.

To rename a fraction, we multiply it by a fraction name for 1. To change the denominator of $\frac{2}{3}$ to 12, we multiply $\frac{2}{3}$ by $\frac{4}{4}$. To change the denominator of $\frac{3}{4}$ to 12, we multiply $\frac{3}{4}$ by $\frac{3}{3}$.

$$\frac{2}{3} \times \frac{4}{4} = \frac{8}{12} \qquad \frac{3}{4} \times \frac{3}{3} = \frac{9}{12}$$

$$\frac{2}{3} = \mathbf{\frac{8}{12}} \qquad \frac{3}{4} = \mathbf{\frac{9}{12}}$$

Example 4

Math Language

One way to find a *common denominator* is to multiply the denominators.

$3 \times 4 = 12$

When we multiply two numbers, each number is a factor of the product.

Rename $\frac{1}{2}$ and $\frac{1}{3}$ so that they have a common denominator.

This time we need to find a common denominator before we can rename the fractions. The denominators are 2 and 3. The product of 2 and 3 is 6, so 6 is a common denominator.

To get denominators of 6, we multiply $\frac{1}{2}$ by $\frac{3}{3}$, and we multiply $\frac{1}{3}$ by $\frac{2}{2}$.

$$\frac{1}{2} \times \frac{3}{3} = \frac{3}{6} \qquad \frac{1}{3} \times \frac{2}{2} = \frac{2}{6}$$

$$\frac{1}{2} = \mathbf{\frac{3}{6}} \qquad \frac{1}{3} = \mathbf{\frac{2}{6}}$$

Lesson Practice

Complete each equivalent fraction:

a. $\frac{1}{4} = \frac{?}{12}$ 3 **b.** $\frac{2}{3} = \frac{?}{9}$ 6 **c.** $\frac{1}{4} = \frac{?}{8}$ 2

d. Rename $\frac{1}{2}$ and $\frac{1}{5}$ so that they have a common denominator of 10. $\frac{5}{10}$, $\frac{2}{10}$

e. Rename $\frac{1}{2}$ and $\frac{5}{6}$ so that they have a common denominator of 12. $\frac{6}{12}$, $\frac{10}{12}$

Rename each of these fractions with a denominator of 12.

f. $\frac{2}{3}$ $\frac{8}{12}$ **g.** $\frac{3}{4}$ $\frac{9}{12}$ **h.** $\frac{1}{6}$ $\frac{2}{12}$

Written Practice *Distributed and Integrated*

1. (Inv. 3, 88) Zuna used 1-foot-square floor tiles to cover the floor of a room 15 feet long and 12 feet wide. How many floor tiles did she use? 180 floor tiles

744 Saxon Math Intermediate 4

Math Background

Any composite number can be "broken down" into a product of prime numbers. For example, we can break 60 into a product of primes as follows: $60 = 10 \times 6 = 2 \times 5 \times 2 \times 3$.

This idea can be used to find the least common denominator for two fractions. Below we find the least common denominator of $\frac{7}{12}$ and $\frac{11}{20}$.

Steps	Example
1. Write each denominator as a product of prime numbers.	$12 = 2 \times 2 \times 3$ $20 = 2 \times 2 \times 5$
2. Find the shortest string of factors that includes all the factors of both numbers.	$2 \times 2 \times 3 \times 5$ is the shortest string that inclues both $2 \times 2 \times 3$ and $2 \times 2 \times 5$
3. The product of the string from Step 2 is the least common denominator.	The least common denominator is $2 \times 2 \times 3 \times 5 = 60$

744 Saxon Math Intermediate 4

2. (20, 45, 81) **a.** What is the perimeter of this triangle? 5.3 cm

1.2 cm, 1.9 cm, 2.2 cm

b. Is this triangle equilateral, isosceles, or scalene? scalene

▶ ***3.** (94) **Represent** Elsa found that $\frac{3}{8}$ of the 32 pencils in the room had no erasers. How many pencils had no erasers? Draw a picture to illustrate the problem. 12 pencils

3. 32 pencils

$\frac{3}{8}$ had no erasers.	4 pencils
	4 pencils
	4 pencils
$\frac{5}{8}$ had erasers.	4 pencils
	4 pencils
	4 pencils
	4 pencils
	4 pencils

▶ ***4.** (91) **Estimate** Estimate the product of 75 × 75. Explain your reasoning. 80 × 80 = 6400 rounded to the nearest ten

***5.** (103) Complete each equivalent fraction:

a. $\frac{3}{5} = \frac{?}{10}$ 6 **b.** $\frac{2}{3} = \frac{?}{9}$ 6 **c.** $\frac{1}{4} = \frac{?}{8}$ 2

***6.** (113) Write these fractions with a common denominator by multiplying the denominators. Which fraction is greater? $\frac{24}{30} < \frac{25}{30}$ so, $\frac{4}{5} < \frac{5}{6}$

$\frac{4}{5}$ and $\frac{5}{6}$

7. (28, 51, 101) Fausta bought 2 DVDs priced at $21.95 each and 2 CDs priced at $14.99 each. The tax was $4.62. What was the total cost of the items? Explain how you found your answer. $78.50; sample: I added the price of 2 DVDs and 2 CDs and their tax.

8. (60) Roger drove 285 miles in 5 hours. What was his average speed in miles per hour? 57 miles per hour

▶ **9.** (98, 103) **Multiple Choice** Which of these fractions is *not* equivalent to $\frac{1}{2}$? D

A $\frac{4}{8}$ **B** $\frac{11}{22}$ **C** $\frac{15}{30}$ **D** $\frac{12}{25}$

▶ ***10.** (106) Write the reduced form of each fraction:

a. $\frac{8}{10}$ $\frac{4}{5}$ **b.** $\frac{6}{15}$ $\frac{2}{5}$ **c.** $\frac{8}{16}$ $\frac{1}{2}$

▶ ***11.** (104) **Represent** Use words to write the number 123415720 then round it to the nearest hundred thousand. one hundred twenty-three million, four hundred fifteen thousand, seven hundred twenty; 123,400,000

12. (45) 8.3 + 4.72 + 0.6 + 12.1 25.72

13. (9, 45) 17.42 − (6.7 − 1.23) 11.95

▶ ***14.** (112) $3\frac{3}{8} + 3\frac{3}{8}$ $6\frac{3}{4}$

▶ ***15.** (112) $4\frac{1}{6} + 2\frac{1}{6}$ $6\frac{1}{3}$

▶ ***16.** (112) $1\frac{1}{6} + \frac{1}{6}$ $1\frac{1}{3}$

Inclusion

Use this strategy if the student displays:

- Difficulty with Abstract Processing.
- Poor Retention.

Renaming Fractions and Common Denominators (Small Group)

Materials: construction paper, scissors

- Write $\frac{1}{2}$ on the board and have students fold the construction paper to make a model of $\frac{1}{2}$. Then write $\frac{2}{4}$ on the board. Ask, ***"How can we change halves into fourths?"*** Folding in half again.
- Have students refold and then fold the paper in half again to create fourths. Ask, ***"$\frac{1}{2}$ is equal to how many fourths?"*** $\frac{2}{4}$
- Write $\frac{1}{2} = \frac{2}{4}$ on the board. Tell students to look at the numerators and denominators and ask, ***"What was the numerator and denominator in the original fraction multiplied by?"*** 2
- Write $\frac{1}{2}$ and $\frac{1}{3}$ on the board. Ask students to think of a number that both 2 and 3 are factors of. Ask, ***"What is a common multiple of 2 and 3?"*** 6

Write $\frac{1}{2} = \frac{?}{6}$ and $\frac{1}{3} = \frac{?}{6}$ on the board. Have students solve.

Written Practice

Math Conversations

Independent Practice and Discussions to Increase Understanding

Problem 3 Represent

Manipulative Use

Some students may find it helpful to model the problem. Distribute 32 tiles or cubes to those students.

Problem 4 Estimate

Extend the Problem

Challenge those students who estimated by rounding each factor of 75 to 80 to demonstrate or explain how to make an estimate that is closer to the exact product. Sample: Rounding both factors of 75 × 75 to 80 will create an estimate that is farther from the exact product than rounding one factor down to 70 and rounding the other factor up to 80; 70 × 80 = 5600

Problem 9 Multiple Choice

Test-Taking Strategy

Remind students that some test questions can be answered using only mental math, and then ask them to state a generalization about the numerator and the denominator of any fraction that is equivalent to $\frac{1}{2}$. The numerator will be half the denominator, or the denominator will be double the numerator.

Encourage students to use the generalization to help choose the correct answer using only mental math.

Problem 10

"What operation is used to reduce a fraction?" division

Problem 11 Represent

Some students will find it helpful to place commas, and then read the number, before writing the word name.

Problems 14–19

Before students complete any arithmetic, ask:

"How do we know when a fraction can be reduced?" Sample: when the numerator and the denominator can be divided by the same number that is greater than 1

The answers for problems **14, 16, 17,** and **19** will need to be reduced to simplest form.

(continued)

Written Practice *(Continued)*

Math Conversations *(cont.)*

Problem 29 **Predict**

Make sure all of your students know that there are 52 cards in a deck of cards.

Problem 30 **Represent**

Manipulative Use

Students will need a ruler to draw and divide the rectangle. On each side of the rectangle, students should place tick marks at intervals of 1 cm. Connecting the tick marks will divide the rectangle into square centimeters.

Errors and Misconceptions

Problems 14–19

Some students will find it helpful to write the problems vertically.

Problem 23

Have students who write the answer as $590 note that the answer is missing a decimal point. Point out that because the divisor of the division is a whole number, a decimal point can be placed in the quotient before any steps of the division are completed. In other words, placing the decimal point first will help prevent forgetting to place it later.

Early Finishers

Before solving the problem, invite volunteers to describe different strategies for estimating the area. Sample: Count whole squares and half squares.

▶ * **17.** (112) $5\frac{5}{6} - 1\frac{1}{6}$ $4\frac{2}{3}$

▶ * **18.** (100) $\frac{2}{8} - \frac{1}{8}$ $\frac{1}{8}$

▶ * **19.** (112) $1\frac{4}{6} - \frac{1}{6}$ $1\frac{1}{2}$

* **20.** (88) 87×16 1392

* **21.** (107) 49×340 16,660

* **22.** (107) 504×30 15,120

23. (83) $35.40 ÷ 6 $5.90

24. (79) $8\overline{)5784}$ 723

25. (83) $7\overline{)2385}$ 340 R 5

26. (83) $3\overline{)312}$ 104

* **27.** (72) $8\overline{)450}$ 56 R 2

* **28.** (75) $5\overline{)450}$ 90

▶ **29.** (110, Inv. 11) **Predict** What is the probability of drawing a heart from a full deck of cards? (*Hint:* There are 13 hearts in a deck.) $\frac{1}{4}$

▶ * **30.** (18, 19, 42) **Represent** Draw a rectangle that is 5 cm long and 2 cm wide, and divide the rectangle into square centimeters. Then shade $\frac{3}{10}$ of the rectangle.

5 cm

2 cm

Real-World Connection

Estimate the area of the pentagon. Each small square represents one square inch. About 18 sq. in

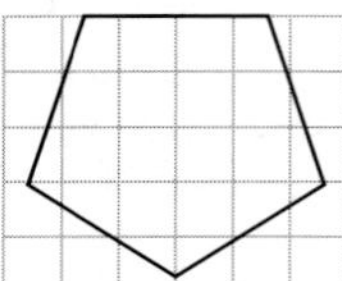

English Learners

Explain that the word **hint** means a helpful suggestion or clue.

Sometimes people give clues to help speed up or make easier the process of solving something.

Ask:

"If you are playing guess a number and you are thinking of 52, what could be a hint you can reveal to others?"

Sample: it is a 2 digit number, it is an even number, the sum of both digits is 7

Looking Forward

Common Denominators will be further developed in ***Saxon Math*** *Intermediate 5.*

Planning & Preparation

• Perimeter and Area of Complex Figures

Objectives

- Determine the perimeter of a complex figure.
- Determine the area of a figure by breaking it into rectangles.
- Use the perimeter and area formulas.

Prerequisite Skills

- Using the formula $A = l \times w$ to find the area of a rectangle.
- Classifying polygons by the number of sides.

Materials

Instructional Masters

- Power Up H Worksheet
- Lesson Activity 8*

Manipulative Kit

- Rulers, Relational GeoSolids*

Teacher-provided materials

- String, grid paper*

**optional*

California Mathematics Content Standards

NS 1.0, 1.4 Decide when a rounded solution is called for and explain why such a solution may be appropriate.

AF 1.0, 1.4 Use and interpret formulas (e.g., area = length × width or $A = lw$) to answer questions about quantities and their relationships.

MG 1.0, 1.1 Measure the area of rectangular shapes by using appropriate units, such as square centimeter (cm^2), square meter (m^2), square kilometer (km^2), square inch (in^2), square yard (yd^2), or square mile (mi^2).

MG 1.0, 1.4 Understand and use formulas to solve problems involving perimeters and areas of rectangles and squares. Use those formulas to find the areas of more complex figures by dividing the figures into basic shapes.

SDAP 2.0, 2.2 Express outcomes of experimental probability situations verbally and numerically (e.g., 3 out of 4; 3 /4).

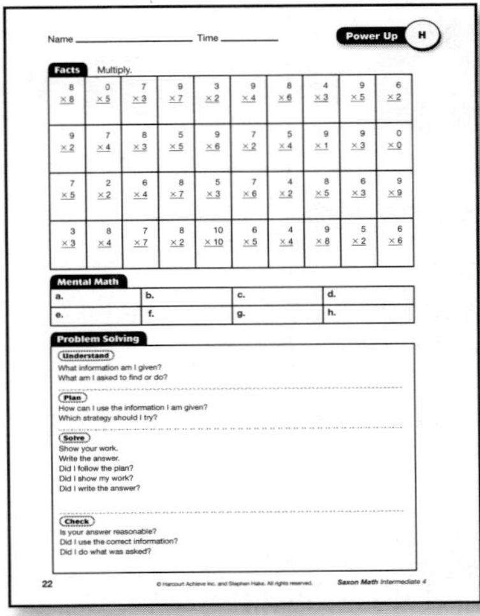
Name ____________ Time ________ **Power Up H**

Facts Multiply.

8 × 8	0 × 5	7 × 3	9 × 7	3 × 2	9 × 4	8 × 6	4 × 3	9 × 5	6 × 2
9 × 2	7 × 4	8 × 3	5 × 5	9 × 6	7 × 2	5 × 4	9 × 1	9 × 3	0 × 0
7 × 5	2 × 2	6 × 4	8 × 7	5 × 3	7 × 6	4 × 2	8 × 5	6 × 3	9 × 9
3 × 3	8 × 4	7 × 7	8 × 2	10 × 10	6 × 5	4 × 4	9 × 8	5 × 2	6 × 6

Mental Math

a.	b.	c.	d.
e.	f.	g.	h.

Problem Solving

Understand
What information am I given?
What am I asked to find or do?

Plan
How can I use the information I am given?
Which strategy should I try?

Solve
Show your work.
Write the answer.
Did I follow the plan?
Did I show my work?
Did I write the answer?

Check
Is your answer reasonable?
Did I use the correct information?
Did I do what was asked?

22 © Harcourt Achieve Inc. and Stephen Hake. All rights reserved. *Saxon Math Intermediate 4*

Power Up H Worksheet

Universal Access

Reaching All Special Needs Students

Special Education Students	At-Risk Students	English Learners	Advanced Learners
• Inclusion (TM) • Adaptations for Saxon Math	• Alternative Approach (TM) • Error Alert (TM) • Reteaching Masters • Refresher Lessons for California Standards	• English Learners (TM) • Developing Academic Language (TM) • English Learner Handbook	• Extend the Example (TM) • Extend the Problem (TM) • Online Activities

TM=Teacher's Manual

Developing Academic Language

Maintained	English Learner
area	blueprint
formula	
perimeter	

Problem Solving Discussion

Problem

A spinner has 5 sectors. If the spinner is spun once, what is the probability of the arrow stopping in sector A? sector B? sector E?

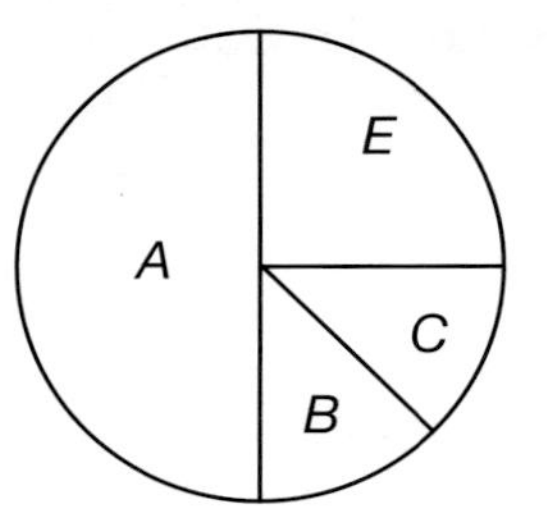

Focus Strategy

Use Logical Reasoning

Understand *Understand the problem.*

"What information are we given?"

We are shown a picture of the spinner.

"What are we asked to do?"

We are asked to find the probability of the arrow stopping on sectors A, B, and E.

Plan *Make a plan.*

"What problem-solving strategy can we use?"

We can *use logical reasoning* to find the probability of each event.

Solve *Carry out the plan.*

"Let's start with sector A. We can see that it is the largest of the sectors. What fraction of the whole spinner does sector A represent?"

$\frac{1}{2}$

"What could we say about the probability of the arrow stopping in sector A?"

We can expect the arrow to stop in sector A $\frac{1}{2}$ of the total number of times the spinner is spun.

"How can we find the probability of sector E?"

We can see that sector E is $\frac{1}{4}$ of the whole spinner. So, the probability of the arrow stopping on sector E is $\frac{1}{4}$.

"What is the probability of sector B?"

Sector B is $\frac{1}{8}$ of the whole spinner. The probability of the arrow stopping on sector B is $\frac{1}{8}$.

Check *Look back.*

"Is our answer reasonable? How can we check our answer?"

We can determine that our answer is reasonable by adding the probability of each sector together.

$$\frac{1}{2} + \frac{1}{4} + \frac{1}{8} + \frac{1}{8} = 1$$

LESSON 114

• Perimeter and Area of Complex Figures

California Mathematics Content Standards

AF 1.0, 1.4 Use and interpret formulas (e.g., area = length × width or $A = lw$) to answer questions about quantities and their relationships.

MG 1.0, 1.1 Measure the area of rectangular shapes by using appropriate units, such as square centimeter (cm^2), square meter (m^2), square kilometer (km^2), square inch (in^2), square yard (yd^2), or square mile (mi^2).

MG 1.0, 1.4 Understand and use formulas to solve problems involving perimeters and areas of rectangles and squares. Use those formulas to find the areas of more complex figures by dividing the figures into basic shapes.

Power Up

facts Power Up H

mental math

a. **Fractional Part:** $\frac{1}{4}$ of 24 6

b. **Fractional Part:** $\frac{1}{2}$ of 24 12

c. **Fractional Part:** $\frac{3}{4}$ of 24 18

d. **Number Sense:** 20 × 250 5000

e. **Measurement:** The half-gallon container is half full. How many quarts of liquid are in the container? 1 qt

f. **Estimation:** Each square folding table is 122 cm on each side. Estimate the total length of 4 folding tables if they are lined up in a row. 480 cm

g. **Calculation:** $6^2 - 6$, + 20, ÷ 2, − 1, ÷ 2 12

h. **Simplify:** $z^2 - 1$ when $z = 1$ 0

problem solving

A spinner has 4 sectors. If the spinner is spun once, what is the probability of the arrow stopping in sector *A*? sector *B*? sector *E*? $\frac{1}{2}$; $\frac{1}{8}$; $\frac{1}{4}$

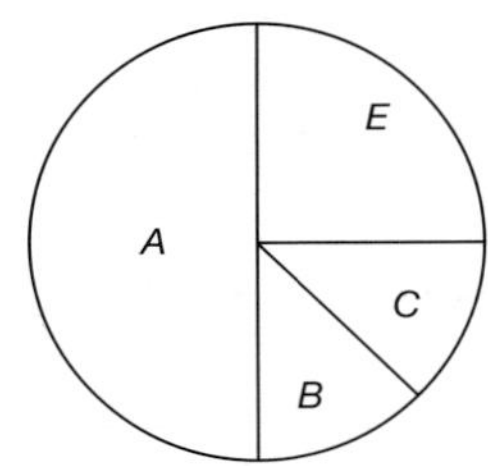

Facts Multiply.

8 × 8 = 64	0 × 5 = 0	7 × 3 = 21	9 × 7 = 63	3 × 2 = 6	9 × 4 = 36	8 × 6 = 48	4 × 3 = 12	9 × 5 = 45	6 × 2 = 12
9 × 2 = 18	7 × 4 = 28	8 × 3 = 24	5 × 5 = 25	9 × 6 = 54	7 × 2 = 14	5 × 4 = 20	9 × 1 = 9	9 × 3 = 27	0 × 0 = 0
7 × 5 = 35	2 × 2 = 4	6 × 4 = 24	8 × 7 = 56	5 × 3 = 15	7 × 6 = 42	4 × 2 = 8	8 × 5 = 40	6 × 3 = 18	9 × 9 = 81
3 × 3 = 9	8 × 4 = 32	7 × 7 = 49	8 × 2 = 16	10 × 10 = 100	6 × 5 = 30	4 × 4 = 16	9 × 8 = 72	5 × 2 = 10	6 × 6 = 36

Power Up

Facts

Distribute **Power Up H** to students. See answers below.

Count Aloud

Before students begin the Mental Math exercises, do these counting exercises as a class.

Count up and down by fives from 15 to 95.

Mental Math

Encourage students to share different ways to mentally compute these exercises. Strategies for exercises are listed below.

a. Divide by 4

$\frac{1}{4}$ of 24 = 24 ÷ 4 = 6

Find $\frac{1}{2}$ of $\frac{1}{2}$ of 24

$\frac{1}{2}$ of 24 = 12; $\frac{1}{2}$ of 12 = 6

d. Double 10 × 250

10 × 250 = 2500; 2500 × 2 = 5000

Attach Two Zeros to 2 × 25

2 × 25 = 50; 20 × 250 = 5000

Problem Solving

Refer to **Problem-Solving Strategy Discussion,** p. 747B.

New Concept

Observation

Display the *Geometric Formulas* poster as you complete this lesson.

Active Learning

For each formula in the table, ask students to explain what each letter represents.

A = area; l = length; w = width; P = perimeter; s = side

(continued)

New Concept *(Continued)*

Example

Math Language

Explain that figures such as the figure in this example are often called *complex* figures.

Error Alert

As you discuss how the figure can be divided into two parts to find its area, some students may assume that there is only one way to divide the figure. Point out that there is often more than one way to divide a complex figure, and lead students to conclude that whenever more than one way is possible, one way can be used to solve the problem, and a different way can be used to check the answer.

Extend the Example

To provide extra practice with this concept and to confirm the area calculation, divide the figure as shown below and ask advanced learners to find the area of each part, and then add those areas to find the area of the entire figure. area $= 600 \text{ ft}^2 + 800 \text{ ft}^2 = 1400 \text{ ft}^2$

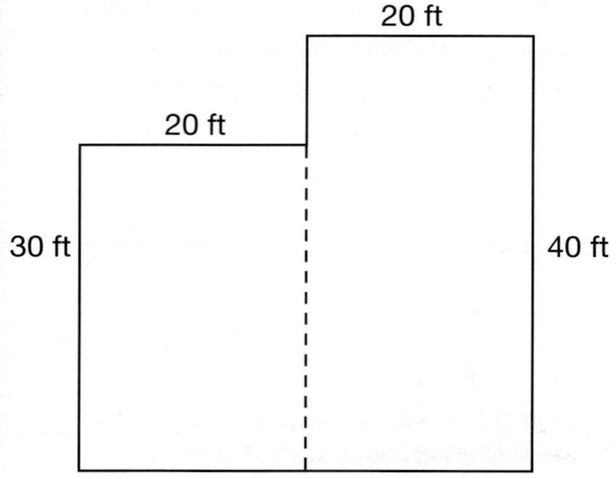

Drawing software may be useful for students to use to determine the area of complex figures. They may design their own figure by combining rectangles and squares, then find total area.

(continued)

New Concept

Recall that we find the area of a rectangle by multiplying its length by its width.

Area = length × width

This expression is a formula for finding the area of any rectangle. Usually formulas are written so that a letter represents each measure.

Below we list several common formulas. In these formulas, P stands for perimeter, and s represents the side length of a square.

Some Common Formulas

Area of a rectangle	$A = lw$
Perimeter of a rectangle	$P = 2(l + w)$ $P = 2l + 2w$
Area of a square	$A = s^2$
Perimeter of a square	$P = 4s$

Some figures are combinations of rectangles. In this example we see that the floor area of the house can be found by dividing the figure into rectangles and then adding the areas of the rectangles.

Example

Thinking Skills

Justify

Why can't we use the perimeter formula for this figure?

The perimeter formula is for rectangles and squares.

The diagram shows the blueprint of a one-story house.

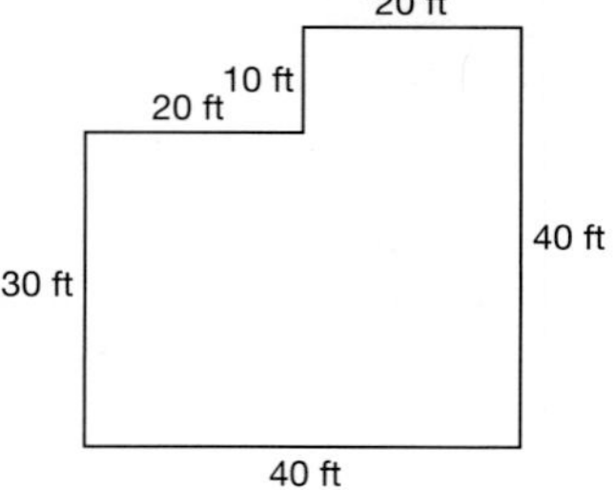

a. What is the perimeter of the house?

b. What is the floor area of the house?

a. The perimeter of the house is the distance around the house. We add the lengths of the six sides.

$$30 + 40 + 40 + 20 + 10 + 20 = 160$$

Adding the lengths of the sides, we find that the perimeter of the house is **160 ft.**

b. To find the floor area we first divide the figure into two rectangles. We show one way to do this.

English Learners

Explain that a **blueprint** is a drawing made by the person who designs a building. It explains how to construct the building.

Blueprints are traditionally reproduced on a blue background.

Ask students to share the terms for those who design and construct buildings. Sample: architect, engineer, plumber, carpenter, and electrician

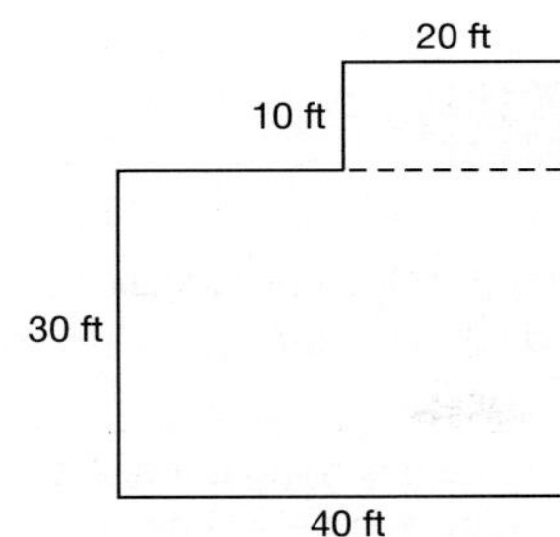

> **Thinking Skills**
>
> **Verify**
>
> What formula did we use to find the area? $A = lw$

We have divided the figure with dashes, and we have labeled the length and width of both rectangles. Now we find the area of each rectangle.

$$\begin{aligned} \text{Small rectangle} &= 200 \text{ ft}^2 \\ + \text{ Large rectangle} &= 1200 \text{ ft}^2 \\ \hline \text{Total Area of Figure} &= 1400 \text{ ft}^2 \end{aligned}$$

Adding the areas of the two rectangles, we find that the total floor area is **1400 sq. ft.**

Classify What is the name of the polygon in this example? hexagon

Lesson Practice

Find the perimeter and area of each figure.

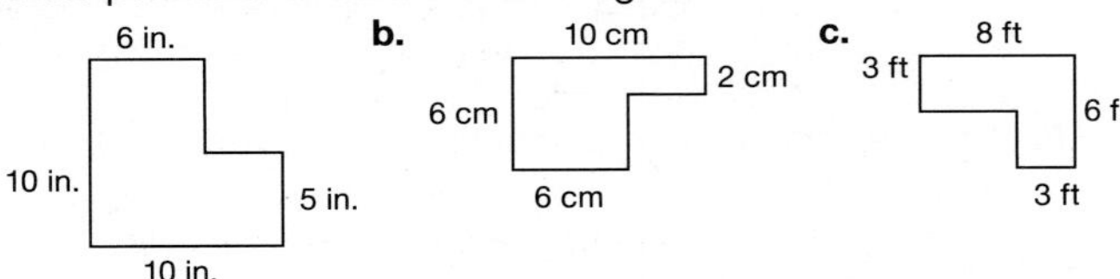

a. $P = 40$ in.; $A = 80$ sq in.

b. $P = 32$ cm; $A = 44$ sq cm

c. $P = 28$ ft; $A = 33$ sq ft

The figure at right shows the boundary of a garden. Refer to the figure to answer questions **d** and **e**.

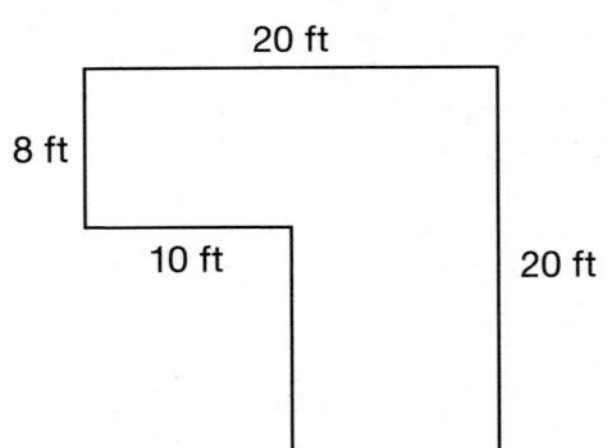

d. How many feet of wire fence are needed to enclose the garden along its boundary? 80 ft

e. What is the area of the garden? 280 sq ft

Math Background

"If I know the perimeter of a rectangle, can I figure out its area?" No. Two or more rectangles may have a perimeter of 20 units, but their areas are not necessarily the same.

"If I know the perimeter of a square, can I figure out its area?" Yes. Divide the perimeter by four and multiply the quotient by itself.

Inclusion

Use this strategy if the student displays:

- Difficulty with Large Group Instruction.
- Slow Learning Rate.

Perimeter and Area of Complex Figures (Individual)

Materials: string, ruler,

- Have students draw a closed polygon on their paper. The polygon can be any shape and have any number of sides. Have students use string to measure the perimeter of the shape.
- Students should measure the perimeter's length on the string using a ruler. Ask, ***"What do you measure to find a shape's perimeter?"*** The distance around the shape
- Have students create another shape and exchange papers with a partner.

New Concept *(Continued)*

Lesson Practice

Guided Practice

Use these problems as guided practice to check the students' understanding of today's concept.

Problem d
Extend the Problem

Ask your students:

"If wire fencing costs $5.19 per foot, how much would it cost to enclose the garden?" $415.20

Problem e
Error Alert

Before students solve the problem, make sure they recognize that they must divide the figure into two parts and then find the sum of the areas of those parts.

To check their answer, ask students to divide the figure a different way and then to find the area a second time. (One way to divide the figure is into 10×20 and 10×8 parts; another way is to divide it into 8×20 and 12×10 parts)

Also watch for opportunities to remind students that measures of area are given in square units.

Closure

The questions below help assess the concepts taught in this lesson.

Write the formulas $P = 2l + 2w$ and $A = s^2$ on the board or overhead. Then say:

"Explain how the formula $P = 2l + 2w$ is used to find the perimeter of a rectangle." Sample: Substitute the length of the rectangle for l and substitute the width of the rectangle for w. Multiply l by 2 and multiply w by 2, and then add the products.

"Explain how the formula $A = s^2$ is used to find the area of a square." Sample: Substitute the length of a side of the square for s. Then solve for A by multiplying the length times itself.

Written Practice

Math Conversations

Independent Practice and Discussions to Increase Understanding

Problem 7 (Predict)

Extend the Problem

"What is the probability of the spinner stopping on a prime number? Explain your answer." $\frac{1}{2}$; 2, 3, and 5 are prime numbers, 4 and 6 are composite numbers, and 1 is neither prime nor composite.

Problem 8 (Estimate)

"What place value are we to round this number to?" hundred thousands

"What consecutive multiples of $100,000 is this number between?" $200,000 and $300,000

"How do we decide which number—$200,000 or $300,000—is the correct answer?" Sample: Since $298,900 is greater than $250,000 (the amount halfway between $200,000 and $300,000), it rounds to $300,000.

Problem 9 (Classify)

Manipulative Use

Some students may benefit from examining the rectangular prism and the pyramid (using Relational GeoSolids) as they solve this problem.

(continued)

Written Practice

Distributed and Integrated

1. (73) The Lorenzos drank 11 gallons of milk each month. How many quarts of milk did they drink each month? 44 quarts

2. (94) Sixty people are in the marching band. If one fourth of them play trumpet, how many do not play trumpet? Draw a picture to illustrate the problem. 45 people

2. 60 people

$\frac{1}{4}$ play trumpet.	15 people
$\frac{3}{4}$ do not play trumpet.	15 people
	15 people
	15 people

3. (66) **a.** What is the area of this square? 100 mm^2

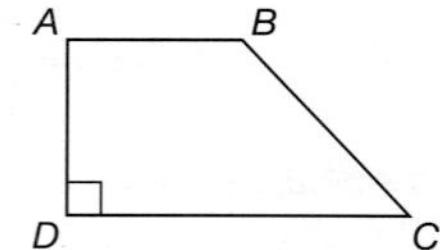

b. What is the perimeter of the square? 40 mm

4. (93) (Analyze) Esteban is 8 inches taller than Trevin. Trevin is 5 inches taller than Jan. Esteban is 61 inches tall. How many inches tall is Jan? 48 in.

5. (17, 33) Which line segments in figure *ABCD* appear to be parallel? $\overline{AB}$ (or $\overline{BA}$) and $\overline{DC}$ (or $\overline{CD}$)

***6.** (113) Rename each fraction so that the denominator is 20.

a. $\frac{1}{2}$ $\frac{10}{20}$ **b.** $\frac{3}{4}$ $\frac{15}{20}$ **c.** $\frac{3}{5}$ $\frac{12}{20}$

► **7.** (106, 110, Inv. 11) (Predict) If the arrow is spun, what is the probability that it will stop on a number greater than 4? $\frac{1}{3}$

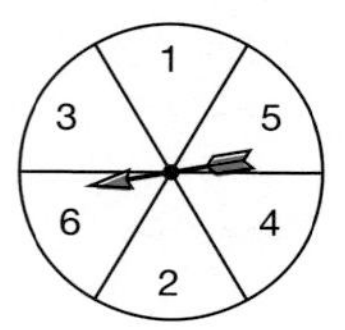

► ***8.** (48) (Estimate) The asking price for the new house was $298,900. Round that amount of money to the nearest hundred thousand dollars. $300,000

► **9.** (96, 109) (Classify) Name each of the following shapes. Then list the number of vertices, edges, and faces for each figure.

a.  Pyramid; 5 vertices, 8 edges, 5 faces

b. Rectangular solid; 8 vertices, 12 edges, 6 faces

Alternative Approach: Using Manipulatives

Have students use graph paper to draw rectangles with different dimensions but the same perimeter.

Ask students which numbers worked the best when drawing rectangles with different dimensions but the same perimeter. Ask if any students used fractions or decimals in their drawings.

Have students share their answers and reasoning.

*10. (106) Write the reduced form of each fraction:

a. $\frac{9}{15}$ $\frac{3}{5}$ b. $\frac{10}{12}$ $\frac{5}{6}$ c. $\frac{12}{16}$ $\frac{3}{4}$

11. (104) **Represent** Use digits to write one hundred nineteen million, two hundred forty-seven thousand, nine hundred eighty-four. 119,247,984

12. (9, 45) $14.94 - (8.6 - 4.7)$ 11.04

13. (9, 45) $6.8 - (1.37 + 2.2)$ 3.23

▶*14. (112) $3\frac{2}{5} + 1\frac{4}{5}$ $5\frac{1}{5}$

▶*15. (98, 100) $\frac{5}{8} + \frac{3}{8}$ 1

▶*16. (112) $3\frac{2}{6} + 1\frac{1}{6}$ $4\frac{1}{2}$

▶*17. (112) $5\frac{9}{10} - 1\frac{4}{10}$ $4\frac{1}{2}$

▶*18. (112) $\frac{5}{8} - \frac{3}{8}$ $\frac{1}{4}$

▶*19. (98, 100) $1 - \frac{1}{6}$ $\frac{5}{6}$

*20. (107) 38×217 8246

*21. (107) 173×60 10,380

*22. (85) 90×500 45,000

23. (83) $7\overline{)2942}$ 420 R 2

24. (75) $5\overline{)453}$ 90 R 3

*25. (79) $2\overline{)453}$ 226 R 1

▶*26. (33, 100, 112) **Connect** Segment *AC* is $3\frac{1}{2}$ inches long. Segment *AB* is $1\frac{1}{2}$ inches long. How long is segment *BC*? 2 in.

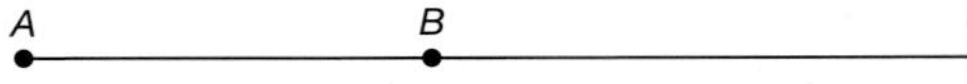

▶*27. (48) **Estimate** Fewer people live in Wyoming than in any other state. According to the 2000 U.S. census, 493,782 people lived in Wyoming. Round this number of people to the nearest hundred thousand. 500,000 people

*28. (113) **Connect** Rewrite $\frac{3}{4}$ and $\frac{5}{6}$ with a common denominator of 24.
$\frac{3}{4} = \frac{18}{24}$ and $\frac{5}{6} = \frac{20}{24}$

*29. (63) **Multiple Choice** If $s - 75 = t - 75$, which of the following is true? Why? C; Equals subtracted from equals are equal.

A $s > t$ **B** $s < t$ **C** $s = t$ **D** $s + 100 = t - 100$

Written Practice *(Continued)*

Math Conversations *(cont.)*

Problems 14–18

Before students complete any arithmetic, ask:

"How do we know when a fraction can be reduced?" Sample: when the numerator and the denominator can be divided by the same number that is greater than 1

Each sum or difference for these problems will need to be reduced to simplest form.

Problem 19

Make sure students understand that 1 is rewritten as $\frac{6}{6}$ to complete the subtraction.

Problem 26 Connect

Make sure students use arithmetic, and not a ruler, to find the length of segment *BC*.

Problem 27 Estimate

Extend the Problem

"In simplest form, what fraction of 1 million is 500,000?" $\frac{1}{2}$

(continued)

Written Practice *(Continued)*

Math Conversations *(cont.)*

Problem 30b Analyze

To check their answer, ask students to divide the figure a different way and find the area a second time.

Errors and Misconceptions

Problem 4

Some students may find it helpful if you suggest that this problem can be solved by first using Esteban's height to find Trevin's height, and then using Trevin's height to find Jan's height. (Trevin's height is 53 inches and Jan's height is 48 inches.)

Problem 10c

It is not correct for students to assume that using division once always reduces a fraction to simplest form. Have students note that the fraction $\frac{12}{16}$ will not be in simplest form if each term of the fraction is divided by 2. Although 2 is a factor of both terms, make sure students understand that the fraction is not in simplest form because 2 is not the greatest common factor (GCF) of 12 and 16.

Help students generalize from your explanation that dividing both terms of a fraction by the GCF of those terms will result in a fraction in simplest form. The use of any common factor other than the greatest common factor will result in a fraction that is not in simplest form.

***30.** (114) Analyze Workers are replacing a section of broken sidewalk. Before pouring the concrete, the workers build a frame along the perimeter.

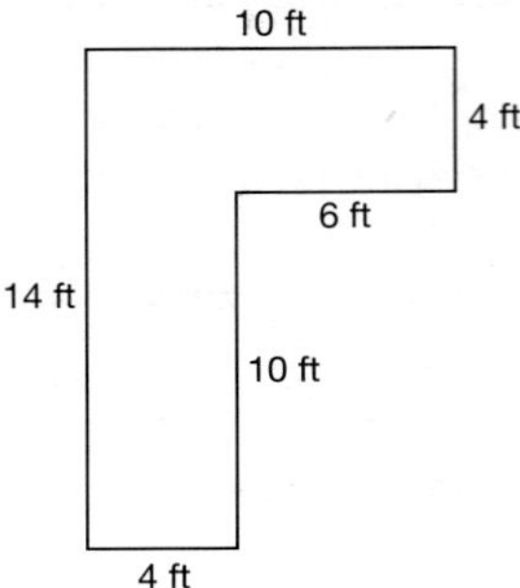

a. What is the perimeter of the replaced sidewalk? 48 ft

▸ **b.** What is the area of the replaced sidewalk? 80 sq. ft

752 ***Saxon Math*** *Intermediate 4*

Looking Forward

Perimeter and area of complex figures will be further developed in ***Saxon Math*** *Intermediate 5.*

Cumulative Assessments and Test-Day Activity

Assessments

Distribute **Power-Up Test 22** and **Cumulative Test 22** to each student. Have students complete the **Power-Up Test** first. Allow 10 minutes. Then have students work on the **Cumulative Test.**

Test-Day Activity

The remaining class time can be spent on **Test-Day Activity 11.** Students can begin the task in class or complete it during another class period.

ENGLISH/SPANISH MATH GLOSSARY

GLOSSARY

A

acute angle (17)
An angle whose measure is more than 0° and less than 90°.

right angle — obtuse angle

acute angle — not **acute angles**

*An **acute angle** is smaller than both a right angle and an obtuse angle.*

ángulo agudo Ángulo que mide más de 0° y menos de 90°.
*Un **ángulo agudo** es menor que un ángulo recto y que un ángulo obtuso.*

acute triangle (81)
A triangle whose largest angle measures less than 90°.

right triangle — obtuse triangle

acute triangle — not **acute triangles**

triángulo acutángulo Triángulo cuyo ángulo mayor mide más que 0° y menos que 90°.

addend (4)
Any one of the added numbers in an addition problem.

$2 + 3 = 5$ *The **addends** in this problem are 2 and 3.*

sumando Cualquiera de los números en un problema de suma.
$2 + 3 = 5$ *Los **sumandos** en este problema son el 2 y el 3.*

addition (12)
An operation that combines two or more numbers to find a total number.

$7 + 6 = 13$ *We use **addition** to combine 7 and 6.*

suma Una operación que combina dos o mas números para encontrar un número total.
$7 + 6 = 13$ *Usamos la **suma** para combinar el 7 y el 6.*

a.m. (13)
The period of time from midnight to just before noon.

*I get up at 7 **a.m.**, which is 7 o'clock in the morning.*

a.m. Período de tiempo desde la medianoche hasta justo antes del mediodía.
*Me levanto a las 7 **a.m.**, lo cual es las 7 en punto de la mañana.*

angle (17)
The opening that is formed when two lines, line segments, or rays intersect.

*These line segments form an **angle**.*

ángulo Abertura que se forma cuando se intersecan dos rectas, segmentos de recta o rayos.
*Estos segmentos de recta forman un **ángulo**.*

apex (96)
The vertex (pointed end) of a cone or top of a pyramid.

ápice El vértice (punta) de un cono.

approximation (maintained)
See **estimate**.

aproximación Ver **estimar**.

area (Inv. 3)
The number of square units needed to cover a surface.

5 in. — 2 in.

*The **area** of this rectangle is 10 square inches.*

área El número de unidades cuadradas que se necesita para cubrir una superficie.
*El **área** de este rectángulo es de 10 pulgadas cuadradas.*

array (Inv. 3)
A rectangular arrangement of numbers or symbols in columns and rows.

XXX
XXX
XXX
XXX

*This is a 3-by-4 **array** of X's. It has 3 columns and 4 rows.*

matriz Un arreglo rectangular de números o símbolos en columnas y filas.
*Esta es una **matriz** de X de 3 por 4. Tiene 3 columnas y 4 filas.*

Associative Property of Addition (26)
The grouping of addends does not affect their sum. In symbolic form, $a + (b + c) = (a + b) + c$. Unlike addition, subtraction is not associative.

$(8 + 4) + 2 = 8 + (4 + 2)$ — $(8 - 4) - 2 \neq 8 - (4 - 2)$

*Addition is **associative**.* — *Subtraction is not **associative**.*

propiedad asociativa de la suma La agrupación de los sumandos no altera la suma. En forma simbólica, $a + (b + c) = (a + b) + c$. A diferencia de la suma, la resta no es asociativa.
$(8 + 4) + 2 = 8 + (4 + 2)$ — $(8 - 4) - 2 \neq 8 - (4 - 2)$
*La suma es **asociativa**.* — *La resta no es **asociativa**.*

Associative Property of Multiplication (26)
The grouping of factors does not affect their product. In symbolic form, $a \times (b \times c) = (a \times b) \times c$. Unlike multiplication, division is not associative.

$(8 \times 4) \times 2 = 8 \times (4 \times 2)$ — $(8 \div 4) \div 2 \neq 8 \div (4 \div 2)$

*Multiplication is **associative**.* — *Division is not **associative**.*

propiedad asociativa de la multiplicación La agrupación de los factores no altera el producto. En forma simbólica, $a \times (b \times c) = (a \times b) \times c$. A diferencia de la multiplicación, la división no es asociativa.
$(8 \times 4) \times 2 = 8 \times (4 \times 2)$ — $(8 \div 4) \div 2 \neq 8 \div (4 \div 2)$
*La multiplicación es **asociativa**.* — *La división no es **asociativa**.*

GLOSSARY

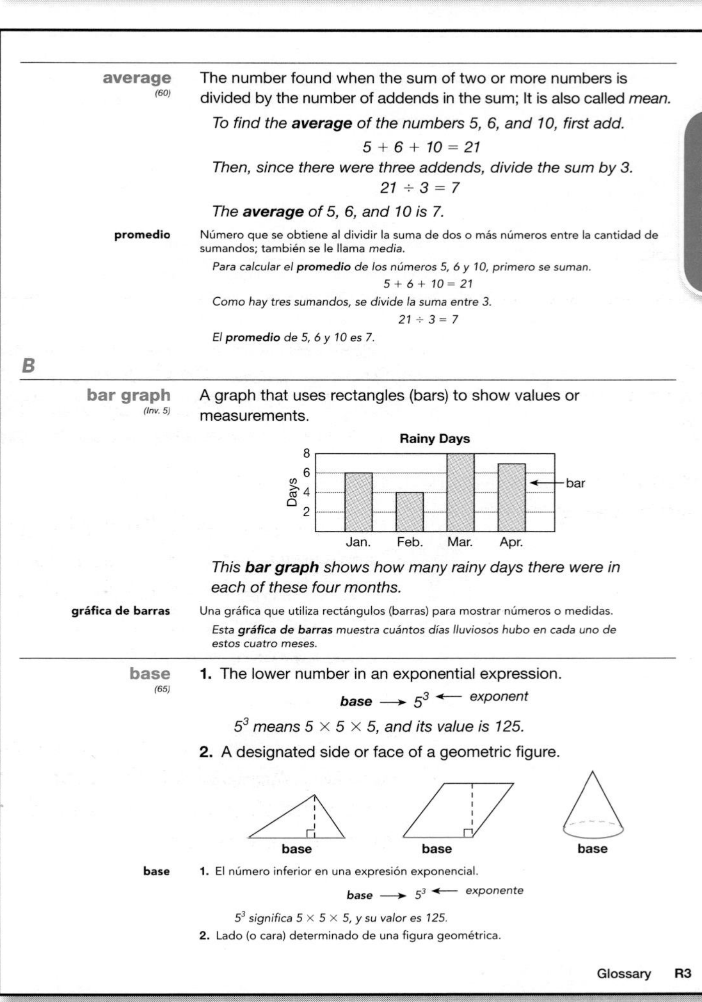

average (60)
The number found when the sum of two or more numbers is divided by the number of addends in the sum; It is also called *mean*.

*To find the **average** of the numbers 5, 6, and 10, first add.*
$5 + 6 + 10 = 21$
Then, since there were three addends, divide the sum by 3.
$21 \div 3 = 7$
*The **average** of 5, 6, and 10 is 7.*

promedio Número que se obtiene al dividir la suma de dos o más números entre la cantidad de sumandos; también se le llama *media*.
*Para calcular el **promedio** de los números 5, 6 y 10, primero se suman.*
$5 + 6 + 10 = 21$
Como hay tres sumandos, se divide la suma entre 3.
$21 \div 3 = 7$
*El **promedio** de 5, 6 y 10 es 7.*

B

bar graph (Inv. 5)
A graph that uses rectangles (bars) to show values or measurements.

*This **bar graph** shows how many rainy days there were in each of these four months.*

gráfica de barras Una gráfica que utiliza rectángulos (barras) para mostrar números o medidas.
*Esta **gráfica de barras** muestra cuántos días lluviosos hubo en cada uno de estos cuatro meses.*

base (65)
1. The lower number in an exponential expression.

base ⟶ 5^3 ⟵ exponent

5^3 means $5 \times 5 \times 5$, and its value is 125.

2. A designated side or face of a geometric figure.

base — base — base

base
1. El número inferior en una expresión exponencial.

base ⟶ 5^3 ⟵ exponente

5^3 significa $5 \times 5 \times 5$, y su valor es 125.

2. Lado (o cara) determinado de una figura geométrica.

base-ten system (2)
A place-value system in which each place value is 10 times larger than the place value to its right.

*The decimal system is a **base-ten system.***

sistema base diez Un sistema de valor posicional en el cual cada valor posicional es 10 veces mayor que el valor posicional que está a su derecha.
*El sistema decimal es un **sistema base diez**.*

bias (Inv. 6)
Favoring one choice over another in a survey.

"Which do you prefer with lunch: cool, sweet lemonade or milk that has been out of the refrigerator for an hour?"
*Words like "cool" and "sweet" **bias** this survey question to favor the choice of lemonade.*

sesgo Dar preferencia a una opción más que a otras en una encuesta.
*"¿Qué prefieres tomar en tu almuerzo: una limonada dulce y fresca o leche que ha estado una hora fuera del refrigerador?" Palabras como "dulce" y "fresca" introducen **sesgo** en esta pregunta de encuesta para favorecer a la opción de limonada.*

borrowing (maintained)
See **regrouping.**

tomar prestado Ver **reagrupar.**

C

calendar (maintained)
A chart that shows the days of the week and their dates.

SEPTEMBER 2007						
S	M	T	W	T	F	S
						1
2	3	4	5	6	7	8
9	10	11	12	13	14	15
16	17	18	19	20	21	22
23	24	25	26	27	28	29
30						

calendar

calendario Una tabla que muestra los días de la semana y sus fechas.

capacity (73)
The amount of liquid a container can hold.

*Cups, gallons, and liters are units of **capacity.***

capacidad Cantidad de liquido que puede contener un recipiente.
*Tazas, galones y litros son medidas de **capacidad**.*

cardinal numbers (maintained)
The counting numbers 1, 2, 3, 4, ...

números cardinales Los números de conteo 1, 2, 3, 4, ...

Celsius (21)
A scale used on some thermometers to measure temperature.

*On the **Celsius** scale, water freezes at 0°C and boils at 100°C.*

Celsius Escala que se usa en algunos termómetros para medir la temperatura.

*En la escala **Celsius**, el agua se congela a 0°C y hierve a 100°C.*

GLOSSARY

center (18)
The point inside a circle from which all points on the circle are equally distant.

2 in.
A

*The **center** of circle A is 2 inches from every point on the circle.*

centro Punto interior de un círculo o esfera, que equidista de cualquier punto del círculo o de la esfera.

*El **centro** del círculo A está a 2 pulgadas de cualquier punto del círculo.*

centimeter (42)
One hundredth of a meter.

*The width of your little finger is about one **centimeter.***

centímetro Una centésima de un metro.

*El ancho de tu dedo meñique mide aproximadamente un **centímetro.***

century (maintained)
A period of one hundred years.

*The years 2001–2100 make up one **century.***

siglo Un período de cien años.

*Los años 2001–2100 forman un **siglo.***

certain (110)
We say that an event is *certain* when the event's probability is 1. This means the event will definitely occur.

seguro Decimos que un suceso es ***seguro*** cuando la probabilidad del suceso es 1. Esto significa que el suceso ocurrirá definitivamente.

chance (Inv. 11)
A way of expressing the likelihood of an event; It is the probability of an event expressed as a percent.

*The **chance** of rain is 20%. It is not likely to rain.*

*There is a 90% **chance** of snow. It is likely to snow.*

posibilidad Modo de expresar la probabilidad de ocurrencia de un suceso; la probabilidad de un suceso expresada como porcentaje.

*La **posibilidad** de lluvia es del 20%. Es poco probable que llueva.*

*Hay un 90% de **posibilidad** de nieve. Es muy probable que nieve.*

chronological order (maintained)
The order of dates or times when listed from earliest to latest.

1951, 1962, 1969, 1973, 1981, 2001

*These years are listed in **chronological order.** They are listed from earliest to latest.*

orden cronológico El orden de fechas o tiempos cuando se enlistan del más temprano al más tardío.

1952, 1962, 1969, 1973, 1981, 2001

*Estos años están listados en **orden cronológico.** Están listados del más temprano al más tardío.*

circle (18)
A closed, curved shape in which all points on the shape are the same distance from its center.

circle

círculo Una forma cerrada curva en la cual todos los puntos en la figura están a la misma distancia de su centro.

circle graph (Inv. 5)
A graph made of a circle divided into sectors. Also called *pie chart* or *pie graph.*

Shoe Colors of Students

Brown 4
Red 2
Blue 4
Black 6

*This **circle graph** displays data on students' shoe color.*

gráfica circular Una gráfica que consiste de un círculo dividido en sectores. También llamada *diagrama circular.*

*Esta **gráfica circular** representa los datos de los colores de los zapatos de los estudiantes.*

circumference (maintained)
The distance around a circle; The perimeter of a circle.

A

*If the distance from point A around to point A is 3 inches, then the **circumference** of the circle is 3 inches.*

circunferencia La distancia alrededor de un círculo; el perímetro de un círculo.

*Si la distancia desde el punto A alrededor del círculo hasta el punto A es 3 pulgadas, entonces la **circunferencia** del círculo mide 3 pulgadas.*

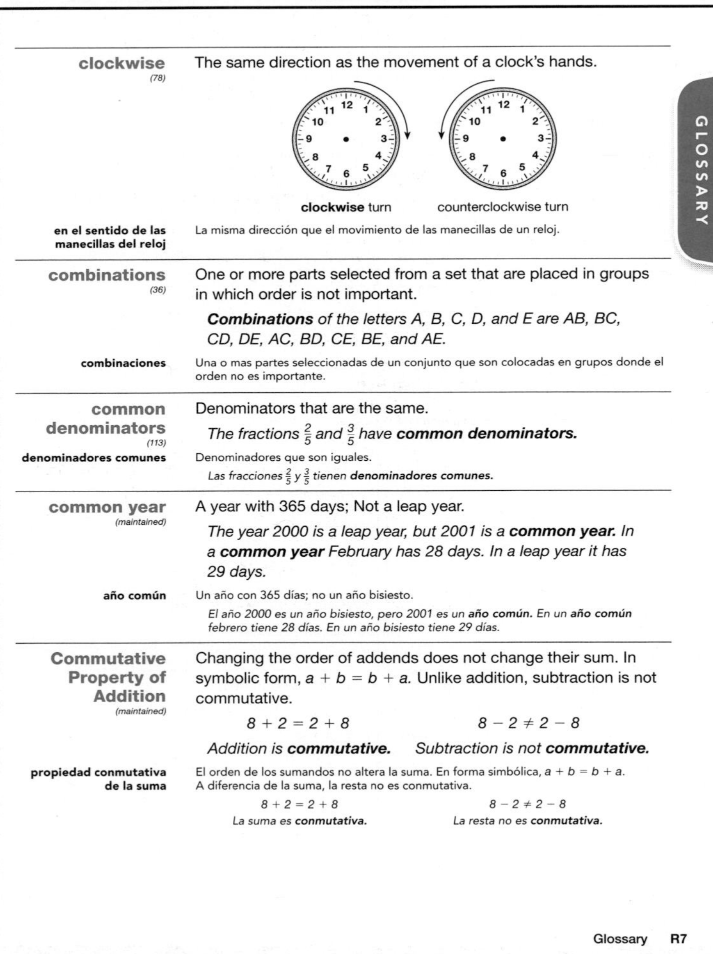

clockwise (78)
The same direction as the movement of a clock's hands.

en el sentido de las manecillas del reloj La misma dirección que el movimiento de las manecillas de un reloj.

GLOSSARY

combinations (36)
One or more parts selected from a set that are placed in groups in which order is not important.

***Combinations** of the letters A, B, C, D, and E are AB, BC, CD, DE, AC, BD, CE, BE, and AE.*

combinaciones Una o mas partes seleccionadas de un conjunto que son colocadas en grupos donde el orden no es importante.

common denominators (113)
Denominators that are the same.

*The fractions $\frac{2}{5}$ and $\frac{3}{5}$ have **common denominators.***

denominadores comunes Denominadores que son iguales.

*Las fracciones $\frac{2}{5}$ y $\frac{3}{5}$ tienen **denominadores comunes.***

common year (maintained)
A year with 365 days; Not a leap year.

*The year 2000 is a leap year, but 2001 is a **common year.** In a **common year** February has 28 days. In a leap year it has 29 days.*

año común Un año con 365 días; no un año bisiesto.

*El año 2000 es un año bisiesto, pero 2001 es un **año común.** En un **año común** febrero tiene 28 días. En un año bisiesto tiene 29 días.*

Commutative Property of Addition (maintained)
Changing the order of addends does not change their sum. In symbolic form, $a + b = b + a$. Unlike addition, subtraction is not commutative.

$8 + 2 = 2 + 8$ $8 - 2 \neq 2 - 8$

*Addition is **commutative.*** *Subtraction is not **commutative.***

propiedad conmutativa de la suma El orden de los sumandos no altera la suma. En forma simbólica, $a + b = b + a$. A diferencia de la suma, la resta no es conmutativa.

$8 + 2 = 2 + 8$ $8 - 2 \neq 2 - 8$

*La suma es **conmutativa.*** *La resta no es **conmutativa.***

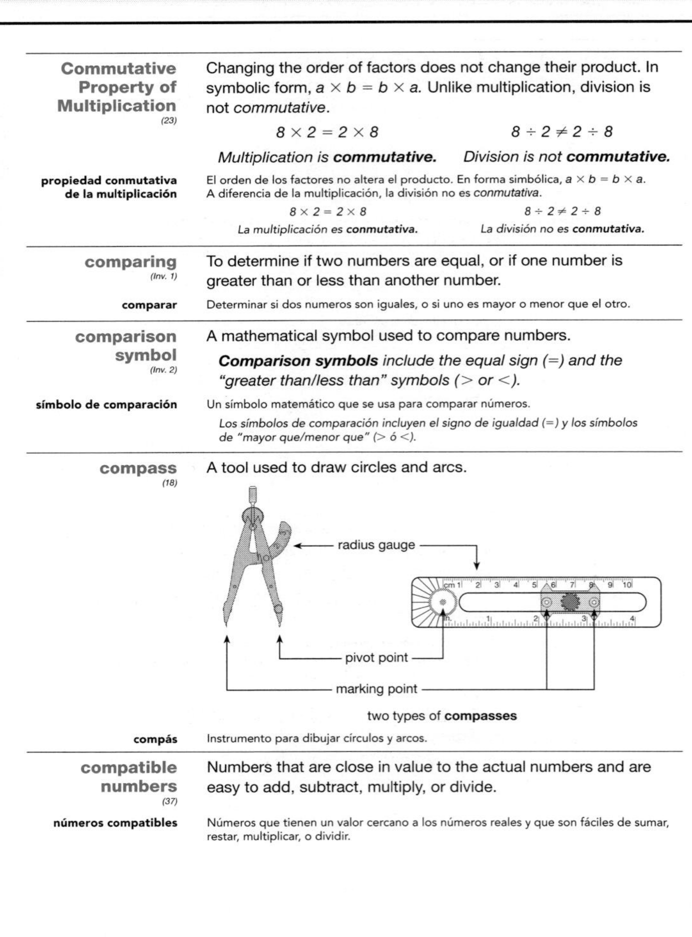

Commutative Property of Multiplication (23)
Changing the order of factors does not change their product. In symbolic form, $a \times b = b \times a$. Unlike multiplication, division is not *commutative.*

$8 \times 2 = 2 \times 8$ $8 \div 2 \neq 2 \div 8$

*Multiplication is **commutative.*** *Division is not **commutative.***

propiedad conmutativa de la multiplicación El orden de los factores no altera el producto. En forma simbólica, $a \times b = b \times a$. A diferencia de la multiplicación, la división no es *conmutativa.*

$8 \times 2 = 2 \times 8$ $8 \div 2 \neq 2 \div 8$

*La multiplicación es **conmutativa.*** *La división no es **conmutativa.***

comparing (Inv. 1)
To determine if two numbers are equal, or if one number is greater than or less than another number.

comparar Determinar si dos numeros son iguales, o si uno es mayor o menor que el otro.

comparison symbol (Inv. 2)
A mathematical symbol used to compare numbers.

***Comparison symbols** include the equal sign (=) and the "greater than/less than" symbols (> or <).*

símbolo de comparación Un símbolo matemático que se usa para comparar números.

Los símbolos de comparación incluyen el signo de igualdad (=) y los símbolos de "mayor que/menor que" (> ó <).

compass (18)
A tool used to draw circles and arcs.

two types of **compasses**

compás Instrumento para dibujar círculos y arcos.

compatible numbers (37)
Numbers that are close in value to the actual numbers and are easy to add, subtract, multiply, or divide.

números compatibles Números que tienen un valor cercano a los números reales y que son fáciles de sumar, restar, multiplicar, o dividir.

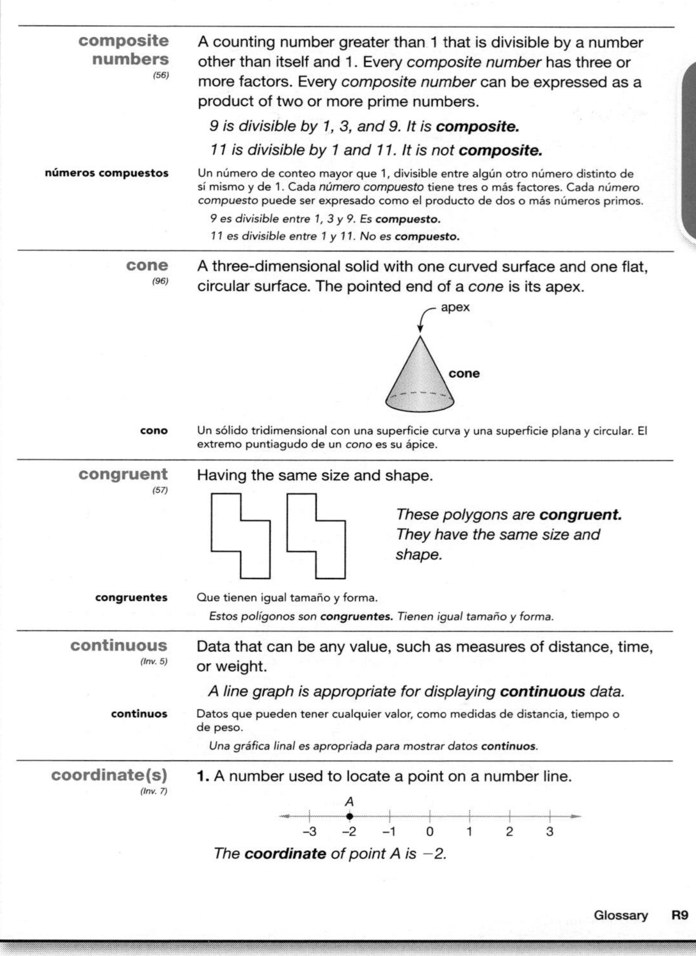

composite numbers (56)
A counting number greater than 1 that is divisible by a number other than itself and 1. Every *composite number* has three or more factors. Every *composite number* can be expressed as a product of two or more prime numbers.

*9 is divisible by 1, 3, and 9. It is **composite.***

*11 is divisible by 1 and 11. It is not **composite.***

números compuestos
Un número de conteo mayor que 1, divisible entre algún otro número distinto de sí mismo y de 1. Cada *número compuesto* tiene tres o más factores. Cada *número compuesto* puede ser expresado como el producto de dos o más números primos.

*9 es divisible entre 1, 3 y 9. Es **compuesto.***

*11 es divisible entre 1 y 11. No es **compuesto.***

cone (96)
A three-dimensional solid with one curved surface and one flat, circular surface. The pointed end of a *cone* is its apex.

cono
Un sólido tridimensional con una superficie curva y una superficie plana y circular. El extremo puntiagudo de un *cono* es su ápice.

congruent (57)
Having the same size and shape.

*These polygons are **congruent.** They have the same size and shape.*

congruentes
Que tienen igual tamaño y forma.

*Estos polígonos son **congruentes.** Tienen igual tamaño y forma.*

continuous (Inv. 5)
Data that can be any value, such as measures of distance, time, or weight.

*A line graph is appropriate for displaying **continuous** data.*

continuos
Datos que pueden tener cualquier valor, como medidas de distancia, tiempo o de peso.

*Una gráfica lineal es apropriada para mostrar datos **continuos.***

coordinate(s) (Inv. 7)
1. A number used to locate a point on a number line.

*The **coordinate** of point A is −2.*

Glossary R9

2. A pair of numbers used to locate a point on a *coordinate* plane.

*The **coordinates** of point B are (2, 3). The **x-coordinate** is listed first, and the **y-coordinate** is listed second.*

coordenada(s)
1. Número que se utiliza para ubicar un punto sobre una recta numérica.

*La **coordenada** del punto A es −2.*

2. Par ordenado de números que se utiliza para ubicar un punto sobre un plano coordenado.

*Las **coordenadas** del punto B son (2, 3). La **coordenada x** se escribe primero, seguida de la **coordenada y**.*

coordinate plane (Inv. 7)
A grid on which any point can be identified by its distances from the *x*- and *y*-axes.

plano coordenado
Una cuadrícula en la cual cualquier punto puede ser identificado por sus distancias de los ejes *x* y *y*.

counter-clockwise (78)
The direction opposite of the movement of a clock's hands.

counterclockwise turn   clockwise turn

en sentido contrario a las manecillas del reloj
La dirección opuesta al movimiento de las manecillas de un reloj.

R10 *Saxon Math Intermediate 4*

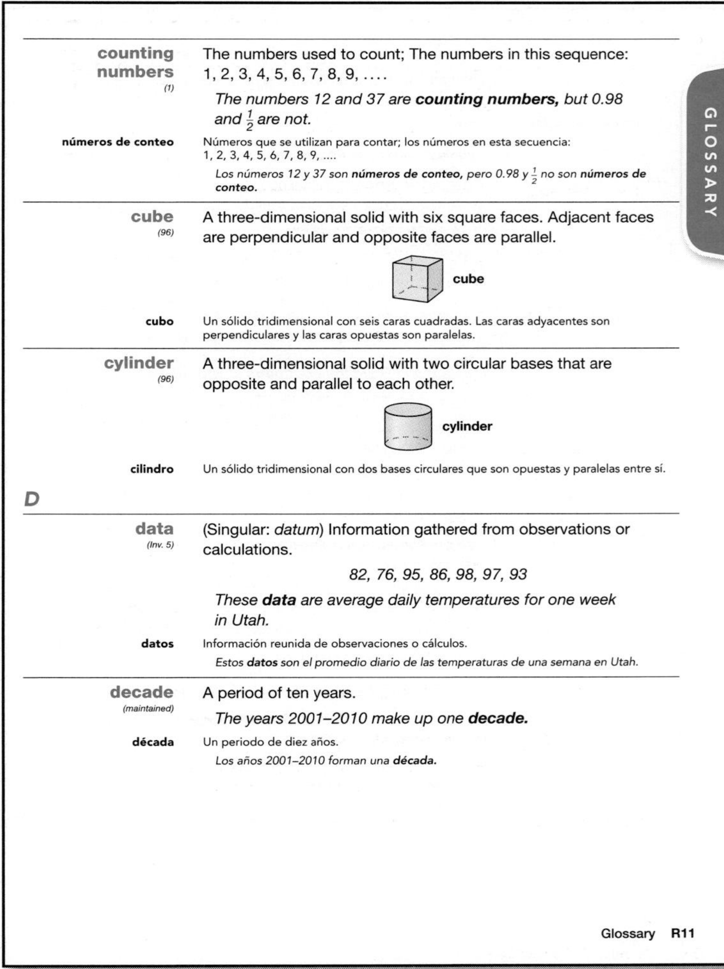

counting numbers (1)
The numbers used to count; The numbers in this sequence: 1, 2, 3, 4, 5, 6, 7, 8, 9, ...

*The numbers 12 and 37 are **counting numbers,** but 0.98 and $\frac{1}{2}$ are not.*

números de conteo
Números que se utilizan para contar; los números en esta secuencia: 1, 2, 3, 4, 5, 6, 7, 8, 9, ...

*Los números 12 y 37 son **números de conteo,** pero 0.98 y $\frac{1}{2}$ no son **números de conteo.***

cube (96)
A three-dimensional solid with six square faces. Adjacent faces are perpendicular and opposite faces are parallel.

cubo
Un sólido tridimensional con seis caras cuadradas. Las caras adyacentes son perpendiculares y las caras opuestas son paralelas.

cylinder (96)
A three-dimensional solid with two circular bases that are opposite and parallel to each other.

cilindro
Un sólido tridimensional con dos bases circulares que son opuestas y paralelas entre sí.

D

data (Inv. 5)
(Singular: *datum*) Information gathered from observations or calculations.

82, 76, 95, 86, 98, 97, 93

*These **data** are average daily temperatures for one week in Utah.*

datos
Información reunida de observaciones o cálculos.

*Estos **datos** son el promedio diario de las temperaturas de una semana en Utah.*

decade (maintained)
A period of ten years.

*The years 2001–2010 make up one **decade.***

década
Un periodo de diez años.

*Los años 2001–2010 forman una **década.***

Glossary R11

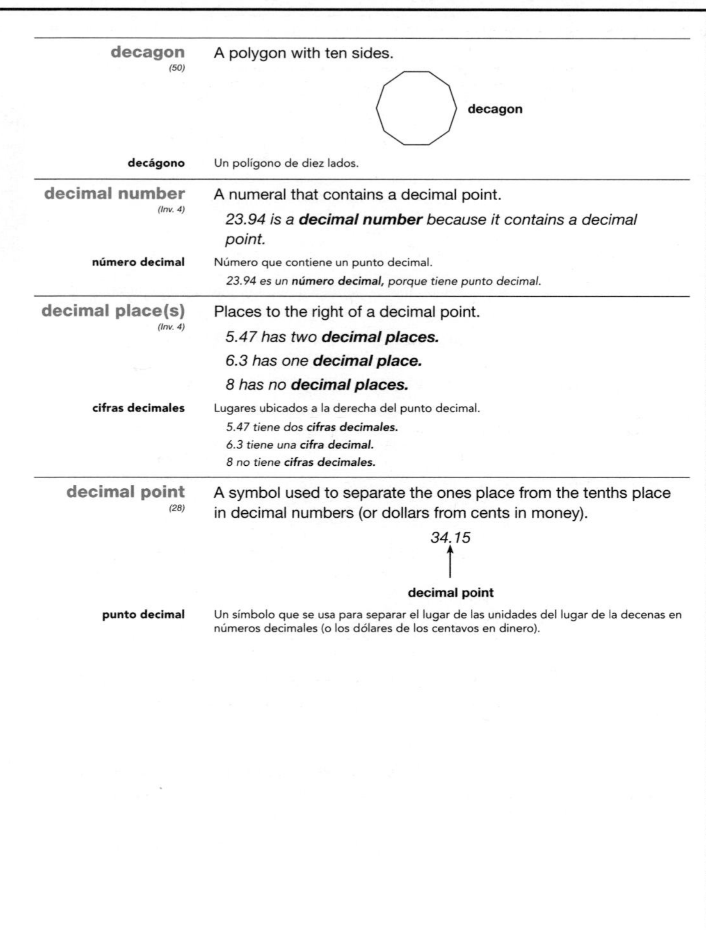

decagon (50)
A polygon with ten sides.

decágono
Un polígono de diez lados.

decimal number (Inv. 4)
A numeral that contains a decimal point.

*23.94 is a **decimal number** because it contains a decimal point.*

número decimal
Número que contiene un punto decimal.

*23.94 es un **número decimal,** porque tiene punto decimal.*

decimal place(s) (Inv. 4)
Places to the right of a decimal point.

*5.47 has two **decimal places.***

*6.3 has one **decimal place.***

*8 has no **decimal places.***

cifras decimales
Lugares ubicados a la derecha del punto decimal.

*5.47 tiene dos **cifras decimales.***

*6.3 tiene una **cifra decimal.***

*8 no tiene **cifras decimales.***

decimal point (28)
A symbol used to separate the ones place from the tenths place in decimal numbers (or dollars from cents in money).

punto decimal
Un símbolo que se usa para separar el lugar de las unidades del lugar de la decenas en números decimales (o los dólares de los centavos en dinero).

R12 *Saxon Math Intermediate 4*

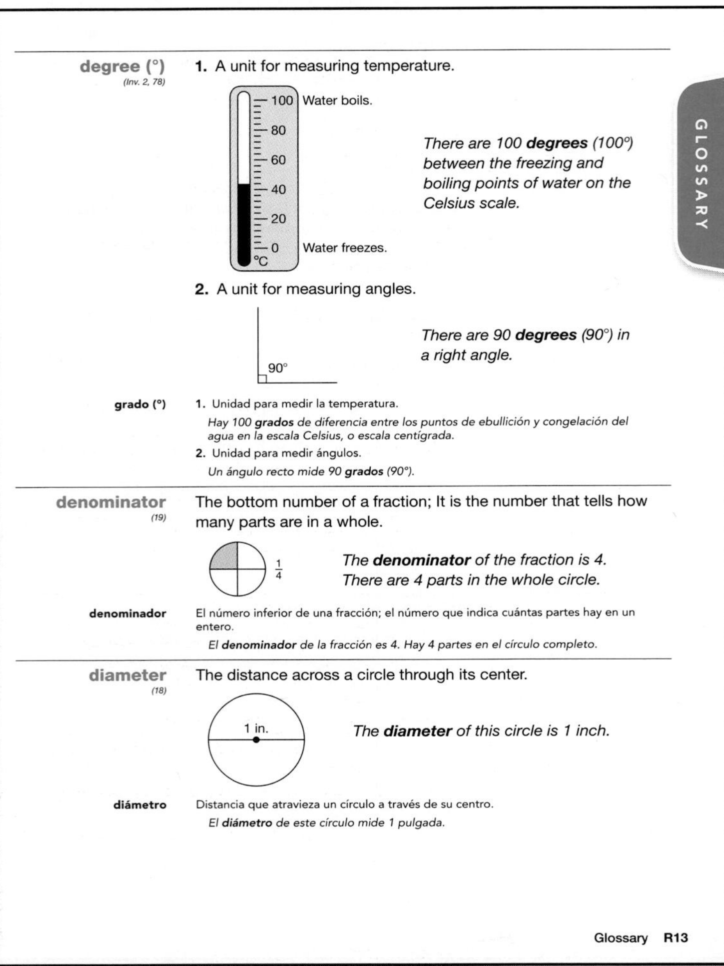

degree (°) (Inv. 2, 78)
1. A unit for measuring temperature.

*There are 100 **degrees** (100°) between the freezing and boiling points of water on the Celsius scale.*

2. A unit for measuring angles.

*There are 90 **degrees** (90°) in a right angle.*

grado (°)
1. Unidad para medir la temperatura.
*Hay 100 **grados** de diferencia entre los puntos de ebullición y congelación del agua en la escala Celsius, o escala centígrada.*
2. Unidad para medir ángulos.
*Un ángulo recto mide 90 **grados** (90°).*

denominator (19)
The bottom number of a fraction; It is the number that tells how many parts are in a whole.

$\frac{1}{4}$ *The **denominator** of the fraction is 4. There are 4 parts in the whole circle.*

denominador
El número inferior de una fracción; el número que indica cuántas partes hay en un entero.
*El **denominador** de la fracción es 4. Hay 4 partes en el círculo completo.*

diameter (18)
The distance across a circle through its center.

*The **diameter** of this circle is 1 inch.*

diámetro
Distancia que atravieza un círculo a través de su centro.
*El **diámetro** de este círculo mide 1 pulgada.*

GLOSSARY

Glossary R13

difference (maintained)
The result of subtraction.
*12 − 8 = 4 The **difference** in this problem is 4.*

diferencia
Resultado de una resta.
*12 − 8 = 4 La **diferencia** en este problema es 4.*

digit (1)
Any of the symbols used to write numbers:
0, 1, 2, 3, 4, 5, 6, 7, 8, 9.
*The last **digit** in the number 2587 is 7.*

dígito
Cualquiera de los símbolos que se utilizan para escribir números:
0, 1, 2, 3, 4, 5, 6, 7, 8, 9.
*El último **dígito** del número 2587 es 7.*

digital form (13)
When referring to clock time, *digital form* is a way to write time that uses a colon and a.m. or p.m.
*11:30 a.m. is **digital form.***

forma digital
Cuando nos referimos al tiempo marcado por un reloj, la *forma digital* es una manera de escribir tiempo que usa dos puntos y a.m. o p.m.
*11:30 a.m. está en **forma digital.***

Distributive Property (102)
A number times the sum of two addends is equal to the sum of that same number times each individual addend.

$$a \times (b + c) = (a \times b) + (a \times c)$$
$$8 \times (2 + 3) = (8 \times 2) + (8 \times 3)$$
$$8 \times 5 = 16 + 24$$
$$40 = 40$$

*Multiplication is **distributive** over addition.*

propiedad distributiva
Un número multiplicado por la suma de dos sumandos es igual a la suma de los productos de ese número por cada uno de los sumandos.

$$a \times (b + c) = (a \times b) + (a \times c)$$
$$8 \times (2 + 3) = (8 \times 2) + (8 \times 3)$$
$$8 \times 5 = 16 + 24$$
$$40 = 40$$

*La multiplicación es **distributiva** con respecto a la suma.*

dividend (54)
A number that is divided.

$12 \div 3 = 4$ $\quad 3\overline{)12}$ (quotient 4) $\quad \frac{12}{3} = 4$ *The **dividend** is 12 in each of these problems.*

dividendo
Número que se divide.

$12 \div 3 = 4$ $\quad 3\overline{)12}$ (quotient 4) $\quad \frac{12}{3} = 4$ *El **dividendo** es 12 en cada una de estas operaciones.*

R14 *Saxon Math Intermediate 4*

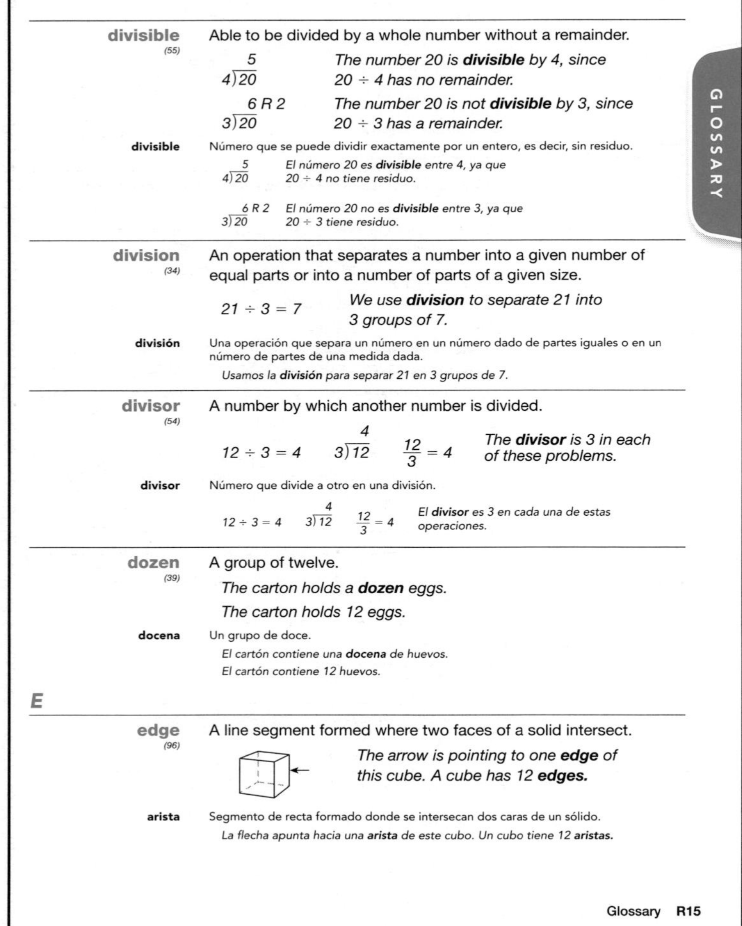

divisible (55)
Able to be divided by a whole number without a remainder.

$4\overline{)20}$ (quotient 5) *The number 20 is **divisible** by 4, since 20 ÷ 4 has no remainder.*

$3\overline{)20}$ (quotient 6 R 2) *The number 20 is not **divisible** by 3, since 20 ÷ 3 has a remainder.*

divisible
Número que se puede dividir exactamente por un entero, es decir, sin residuo.

$4\overline{)20}$ (5) *El número 20 es **divisible** entre 4, ya que 20 ÷ 4 no tiene residuo.*

$3\overline{)20}$ (6 R 2) *El número 20 no es **divisible** entre 3, ya que 20 ÷ 3 tiene residuo.*

division (34)
An operation that separates a number into a given number of equal parts or into a number of parts of a given size.

$21 \div 3 = 7$ *We use **division** to separate 21 into 3 groups of 7.*

división
Una operación que separa un número en un número dado de partes iguales o en un número de partes de una medida dada.
*Usamos la **división** para separar 21 en 3 grupos de 7.*

divisor (54)
A number by which another number is divided.

$12 \div 3 = 4$ $\quad 3\overline{)12}$ (quotient 4) $\quad \frac{12}{3} = 4$ *The **divisor** is 3 in each of these problems.*

divisor
Número que divide a otro en una división.

$12 \div 3 = 4$ $\quad 3\overline{)12}$ (quotient 4) $\quad \frac{12}{3} = 4$ *El **divisor** es 3 en cada una de estas operaciones.*

dozen (39)
A group of twelve.
*The carton holds a **dozen** eggs.*
The carton holds 12 eggs.

docena
Un grupo de doce.
*El cartón contiene una **docena** de huevos.*
El cartón contiene 12 huevos.

E

edge (96)
A line segment formed where two faces of a solid intersect.

*The arrow is pointing to one **edge** of this cube. A cube has 12 **edges.***

arista
Segmento de recta formado donde se intersecan dos caras de un sólido.
*La flecha apunta hacia una **arista** de este cubo. Un cubo tiene 12 **aristas.***

GLOSSARY

Glossary R15

elapsed time (13)
The difference between a starting time and an ending time.
*The race started at 6:30 p.m. and finished at 9:12 p.m. The **elapsed time** of the race was 2 hours 42 minutes.*

tiempo transcurrido
La diferencia entre el tiempo de comienzo y tiempo final.
*La carrera comenzó a las 6:30 p.m. y terminó a las 9:12 p.m . El **tiempo transcurrido** de la carrera fue de 2 horas 42 minutes.*

elevation (9)
A measure of distance above sea level.
*At it's peak, Mount Whitney in California has an **elevation** of 14,494 ft above sea level.*

elevación
Una medida de distancia arriba del nivel del mar.
En su cima, Mount Whitney en California está 14,494 pies arriba del nivel del mar.

endpoint(s) (17)
The point(s) at which a line segment ends.

A ——— B

*Points A and B are the **endpoints** of line segment AB.*

punto(s) extremo(s)
Punto(s) donde termina un segmento de recta.
*Los puntos A y B son los **puntos extremos** del segmento AB.*

equal to (Inv. 2)
Has the same value as.
*12 inches are **equal to** 1 foot.*

es igual a
Con el mismo valor.
*12 pulgadas **es igual a** 1 pie.*

equation (4)
A number sentence that uses an equal sign (=) to show that two quantities are equal.

$x = 3$ $\quad 3 + 7 = 10$ — **equations**
$4 + 1$ $\quad x < 7$ — not **equations**

ecuación
Enunciado que usa el símbolo "=" para indicar que dos cantidades son iguales.

$x = 3$ $\quad 3 + 7 = 10$ — son **ecuaciones**
$4 + 1$ $\quad x < 7$ — no son **ecuaciones**

equiangular (81)
A figure with angles of the same measurement.
*An equilateral triangle is also **equiangular** because its angles each measure 60°.*

equiangular
Una figura con ángulos de la misma medida.
*Un triángulo equilátero es también **equiangular** porque sus tres ángulos miden 60°.*

R16 *Saxon Math Intermediate 4*

equilateral triangle (18)

A triangle in which all sides are the same length and all angles are the same measure.

*This is an **equilateral triangle.** All of its sides are the same length. All of its angles are the same measure.*

triángulo equilátero Triángulo que tiene todos sus lados de la misma longitud.

*Éste es un **triángulo equilátero.** Sus tres lados tienen la misma longitud. Todos sus ángulos miden los mismo.*

---

equivalent fractions (103)

Different fractions that name the same amount.

$\frac{1}{2}$ = $\frac{2}{4}$

*$\frac{1}{2}$ and $\frac{2}{4}$ are **equivalent fractions.***

fracciones equivalentes Fracciones diferentes que representan la misma cantidad.

*$\frac{1}{2}$ y $\frac{2}{4}$ son **fracciones equivalentes.***

---

estimate (22)

To find an approximate value.

*I **estimate** that the sum of 203 and 304 is about 500.*

estimar Encontrar un valor aproximado.

*Puedo **estimar** que la suma de 199 más 205 es aproximadamente 400.*

---

evaluate (9)

To find the value of an expression.

*To **evaluate** a + b for a = 7 and b = 13, we replace a with 7 and b with 13:*

$$7 + 13 = 20$$

evaluar Calcular el valor de una expresión.

*Para **evaluar** a + b, con a = 7 y b = 13, se reemplaza a por 7 y b por 13:*

$$7 + 13 = 20$$

---

even numbers (1)

Numbers that can be divided by 2 without a remainder; the numbers in this sequence: 0, 2, 4, 6, 8, 10, ...

***Even numbers** have 0, 2, 4, 6, or 8 in the ones place.*

números pares Números que se pueden dividir entre 2 sin residuo; los números en esta secuencia: 0, 2, 4, 6, 8, 10, ...

*Los **números pares** terminan en 0, 2, 4, 6, u 8 en el lugar de las unidades.*

---

exchanging (maintained)

See **regrouping.**

cambiar *Ver* ***reagrupar.***

---

expanded form (5)

A way of writing a number that shows the value of each digit.

*The **expanded form** of 234 is 200 + 30 + 4.*

forma desarrollada Una manera de escribir un número mostrando el valor de cada dígito.

*La **forma desarrollada** de 234 es 200 + 30 + 4.*

---

exponent (65)

The upper number in an exponential expression; it shows how many times the base is to be used as a factor.

base ⟶ 5^3 ⟵ exponent

5^3 means 5 × 5 × 5, and its value is 125.

exponente El número superior en una expresión exponencial; muestra cuántas veces debe usarse la base como factor.

base ⟶ 5^3 ⟵ exponente

5^3 significa 5 × 5 × 5, y su valor es 125.

---

exponential expression (65)

An expression that indicates that the base is to be used as a factor the number of times shown by the exponent.

$$4^3 = 4 \times 4 \times 4 = 64$$

*The **exponential expression** 4^3 uses 4 as a factor 3 times. Its value is 64.*

expresión exponencial Expresión que indica que la base debe usarse como factor el número de veces que indica el exponente.

$$4^3 = 4 \times 4 \times 4 = 64$$

*La **expresión exponencial** 4^3 se calcula usando 3 veces el 4 como factor. Su valor es 64.*

---

expression (9)

A number, a letter, or a combination of both. *Expressions* do not include comparison symbols, such as an equal sign.

*3n is an **expression** that can also be written as 3 × n.*

expresión Un número, una letra o una combinación de los dos. Las *expresiones* no incluyen símbolos de comparación, como el signo de igual.

*3n es una **expresión** que también puede ser escrita como 3 × n.*

F

face (96)

A flat surface of a geometric solid.

*The arrow is pointing to one **face** of the cube. A cube has six **faces.***

cara Superficie plana de un cuerpo geométrico.

*La flecha apunta a una **cara** del cubo. Un cubo tiene seis **caras.***

---

fact family (maintained)

A group of three numbers related by addition and subtraction or by multiplication and division.

*The numbers 3, 4, and 7 are a **fact family.** They make these four facts:*

3 + 4 = 7   4 + 3 = 7   7 − 3 = 4   7 − 4 = 3

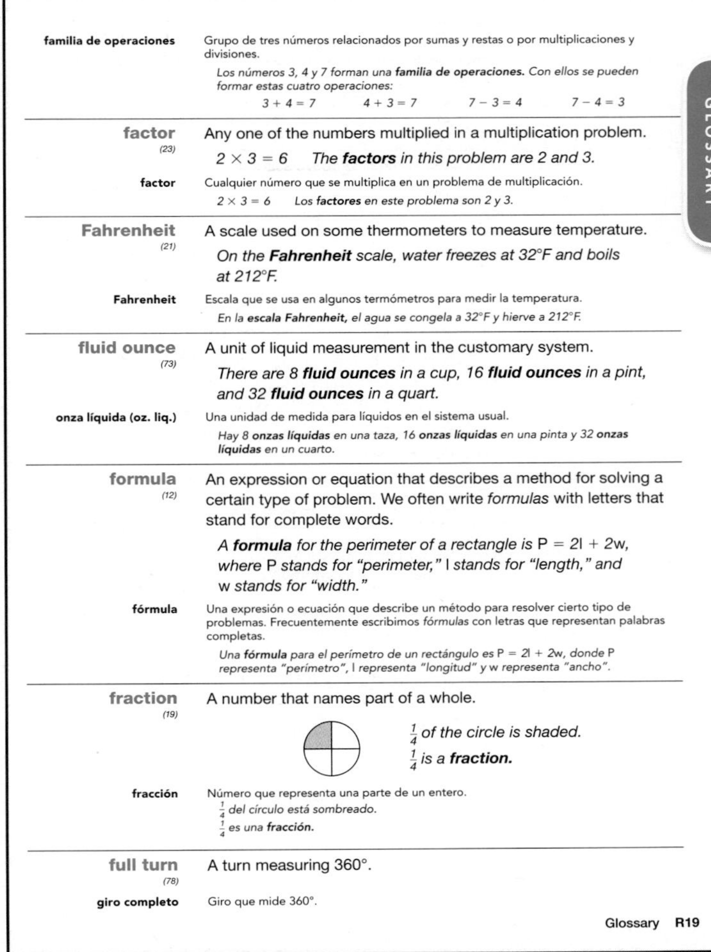

familia de operaciones Grupo de tres números relacionados por sumas y restas o por multiplicaciones y divisiones.

*Los números 3, 4 y 7 forman una **familia de operaciones.** Con ellos se pueden formar estas cuatro operaciones:*

3 + 4 = 7   4 + 3 = 7   7 − 3 = 4   7 − 4 = 3

---

factor (23)

Any one of the numbers multiplied in a multiplication problem.

*2 × 3 = 6   The **factors** in this problem are 2 and 3.*

factor Cualquier número que se multiplica en un problema de multiplicación.

*2 × 3 = 6   Los **factores** en este problema son 2 y 3.*

Fahrenheit (21)

A scale used on some thermometers to measure temperature.

*On the **Fahrenheit** scale, water freezes at 32°F and boils at 212°F.*

Fahrenheit Escala que se usa en algunos termómetros para medir la temperatura.

*En la **escala Fahrenheit,** el agua se congela a 32°F y hierve a 212°F.*

---

fluid ounce (73)

A unit of liquid measurement in the customary system.

*There are 8 **fluid ounces** in a cup, 16 **fluid ounces** in a pint, and 32 **fluid ounces** in a quart.*

onza líquida (oz. liq.) Una unidad de medida para líquidos en el sistema usual.

*Hay 8 **onzas líquidas** en una taza, 16 **onzas líquidas** en una pinta y 32 **onzas líquidas** en un cuarto.*

---

formula (12)

An expression or equation that describes a method for solving a certain type of problem. We often write *formulas* with letters that stand for complete words.

*A **formula** for the perimeter of a rectangle is P = 2l + 2w, where P stands for "perimeter," l stands for "length," and w stands for "width."*

fórmula Una expresión o ecuación que describe un método para resolver cierto tipo de problemas. Frecuentemente escribimos *fórmulas* con letras que representan palabras completas.

*Una **fórmula** para el perímetro de un rectángulo es P = 2l + 2w, donde P representa "perímetro", l representa "longitud" y w representa "ancho".*

---

fraction (19)

A number that names part of a whole.

$\frac{1}{4}$ of the circle is shaded.
*$\frac{1}{4}$ is a **fraction.***

fracción Número que representa una parte de un entero.

$\frac{1}{4}$ del círculo está sombreado.
*$\frac{1}{4}$ es una **fracción.***

---

full turn (78)

A turn measuring 360°.

giro completo Giro que mide 360°.

Glossary R19

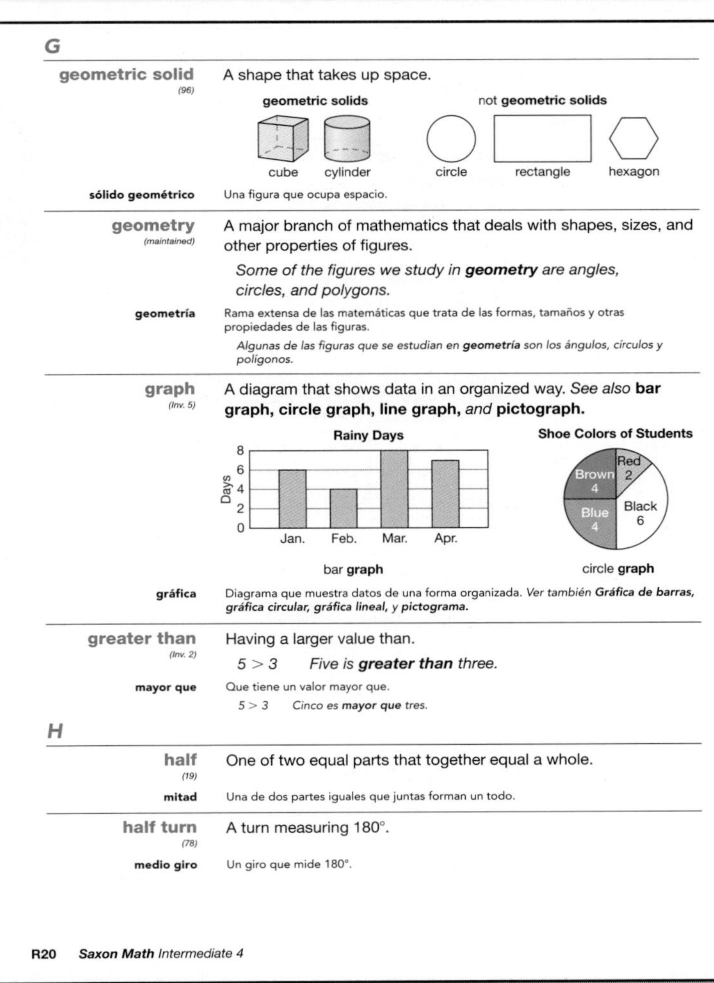

G

geometric solid (96)

A shape that takes up space.

sólido geométrico Una figura que ocupa espacio.

---

geometry (maintained)

A major branch of mathematics that deals with shapes, sizes, and other properties of figures.

*Some of the figures we study in **geometry** are angles, circles, and polygons.*

geometría Rama extensa de las matemáticas que trata de las formas, tamaños y otras propiedades de las figuras.

*Algunas de las figuras que se estudian en **geometría** son los ángulos, círculos y polígonos.*

---

graph (Inv. 5)

A diagram that shows data in an organized way. *See also* **bar graph, circle graph, line graph,** *and* **pictograph.**

bar **graph**   circle **graph**

gráfica Diagrama que muestra datos de una forma organizada. *Ver también* ***Gráfica de barras, gráfica circular, gráfica lineal,*** *y* ***pictograma.***

---

greater than (Inv. 2)

Having a larger value than.

*5 > 3   Five is **greater than** three.*

mayor que Que tiene un valor mayor que.

*5 > 3   Cinco es **mayor que** tres.*

H

half (19)

One of two equal parts that together equal a whole.

mitad Una de dos partes iguales que juntas forman un todo.

---

half turn (78)

A turn measuring 180°.

medio giro Un giro que mide 180°.

R20 Saxon Math Intermediate 4

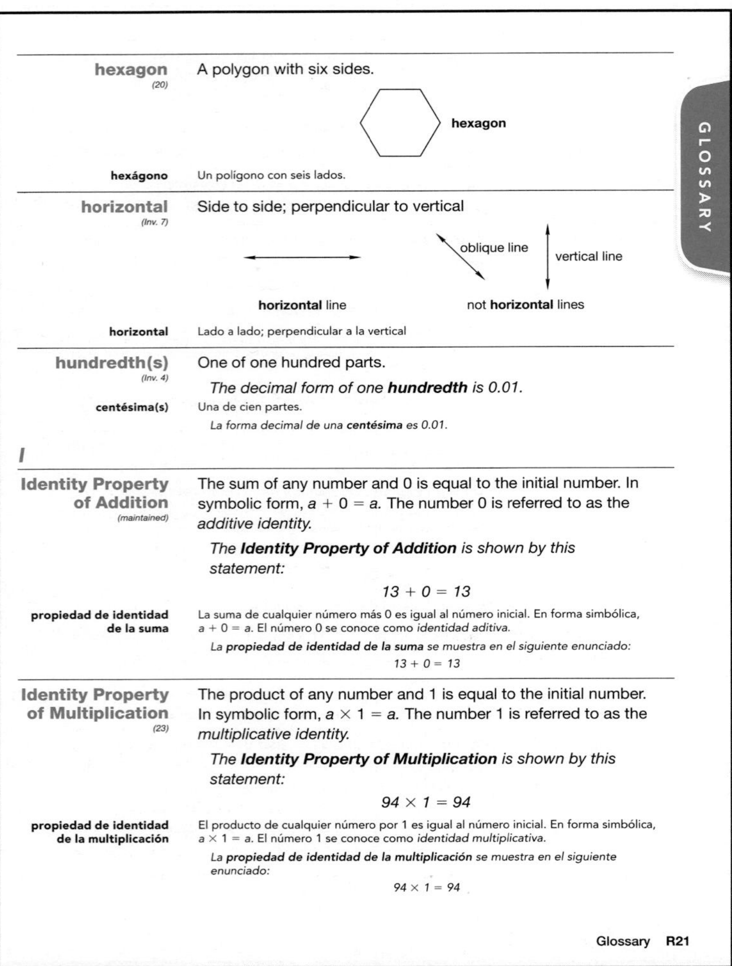

hexagon (20) A polygon with six sides.

hexagon

hexágono Un polígono con seis lados.

horizontal (Inv. 7) Side to side; perpendicular to vertical

horizontal line — not **horizontal** lines (oblique line, vertical line)

horizontal Lado a lado; perpendicular a la vertical

hundredth(s) (Inv. 4) One of one hundred parts.

*The decimal form of one **hundredth** is 0.01.*

centésima(s) Una de cien partes.

*La forma decimal de una **centésima** es 0.01.*

I

Identity Property of Addition (maintained) The sum of any number and 0 is equal to the initial number. In symbolic form, $a + 0 = a$. The number 0 is referred to as the *additive identity.*

*The **Identity Property of Addition** is shown by this statement:*

$$13 + 0 = 13$$

propiedad de identidad de la suma La suma de cualquier número más 0 es igual al número inicial. En forma simbólica, $a + 0 = a$. El número 0 se conoce como *identidad aditiva.*

*La **propiedad de identidad de la suma** se muestra en el siguiente enunciado:*

$$13 + 0 = 13$$

Identity Property of Multiplication (23) The product of any number and 1 is equal to the initial number. In symbolic form, $a \times 1 = a$. The number 1 is referred to as the *multiplicative identity.*

*The **Identity Property of Multiplication** is shown by this statement:*

$$94 \times 1 = 94$$

propiedad de identidad de la multiplicación El producto de cualquier número por 1 es igual al número inicial. En forma simbólica, $a \times 1 = a$. El número 1 se conoce como *identidad multiplicativa.*

*La **propiedad de identidad de la multiplicación** se muestra en el siguiente enunciado:*

$$94 \times 1 = 94$$

Glossary R21

GLOSSARY

improper fraction (89) A fraction with a numerator greater than or equal to the denominator.

$\frac{4}{3}$ $\frac{2}{2}$ *These fractions are **improper fractions.***

fracción impropia Fracción con el numerador igual o mayor que el denominador.

$\frac{4}{3}$ $\frac{2}{2}$ *Estas fracciones son **fracciones impropias.***

intersect (17) To share a common point or points.

*These two lines **intersect.** They share the common point M.*

intersecar Compartir uno o varios puntos en común.

*Estas dos rectas se **intersecan.** Tienen el punto común M.*

intersecting lines (17) Lines that cross.

intersecting lines

líneas que se cruzan o intersecan Líneas que se cruzan.

inverse operation(s) (8) An operation that "undoes" another.

*Subtraction is the **inverse operation** of addition.*

operaciones inversas Una operación que cancela a otra.

*La resta es la **operación inversa** de la suma.*

isosceles triangle (81) A triangle with at least two sides of equal length and two angles of equal measure.

*Two of the sides of this **isosceles triangle** have equal lengths. Two of the angles have equal measures.*

triángulo isósceles Triángulo que tiene por lo menos dos lados de igual longitud y dos lados de igual medida.

*Dos de los lados de este **triángulo isósceles** tienen igual longitud. Dos de los ángulos tienen medidas iguales.*

R22 *Saxon Math* Intermediate 4

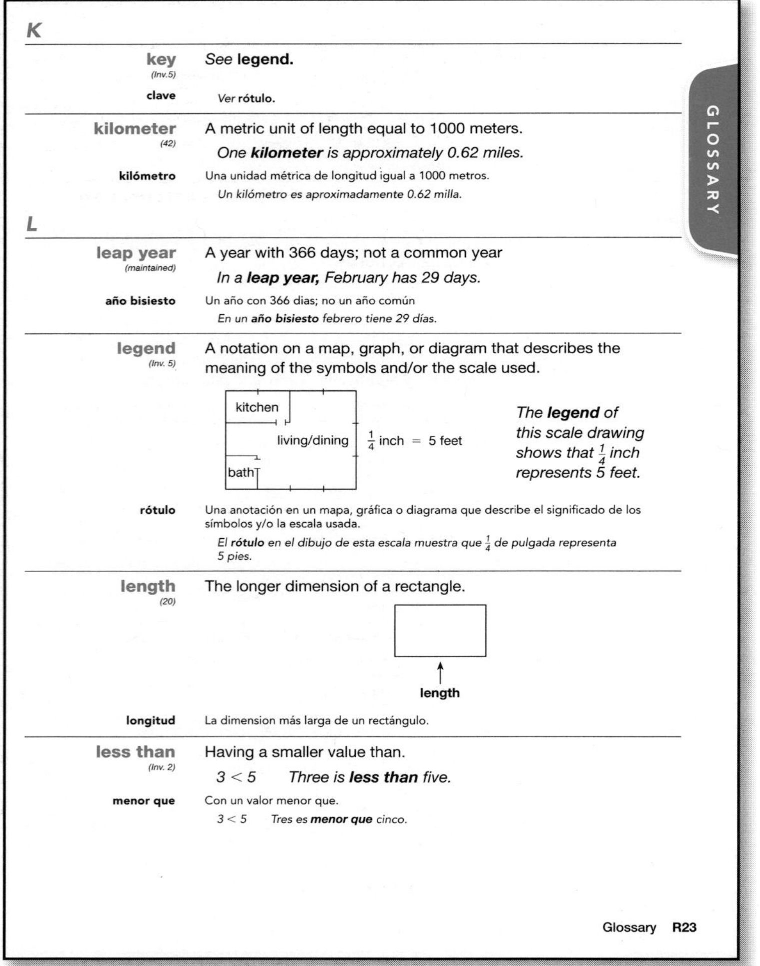

K

key (Inv. 5) *See* **legend.**

clave *Ver* **rótulo.**

kilometer (42) A metric unit of length equal to 1000 meters.

*One **kilometer** is approximately 0.62 miles.*

kilómetro Una unidad métrica de longitud igual a 1000 metros.

Un kilómetro es aproximadamente 0.62 milla.

L

leap year (maintained) A year with 366 days; not a common year

*In a **leap year,** February has 29 days.*

año bisiesto Un año con 366 días; no un año común

*En un **año bisiesto** febrero tiene 29 días.*

legend (Inv. 5) A notation on a map, graph, or diagram that describes the meaning of the symbols and/or the scale used.

*The **legend** of this scale drawing shows that $\frac{1}{4}$ inch represents 5 feet.*

rótulo Una anotación en un mapa, gráfica o diagrama que describe el significado de los símbolos y/o la escala usada.

*El **rótulo** en el dibujo de esta escala muestra que $\frac{1}{4}$ de pulgada representa 5 pies.*

length (20) The longer dimension of a rectangle.

length

longitud La dimension más larga de un rectángulo.

less than (Inv. 2) Having a smaller value than.

$3 < 5$ *Three is **less than** five.*

menor que Con un valor menor que.

$3 < 5$ *Tres es **menor que** cinco.*

Glossary R23

GLOSSARY

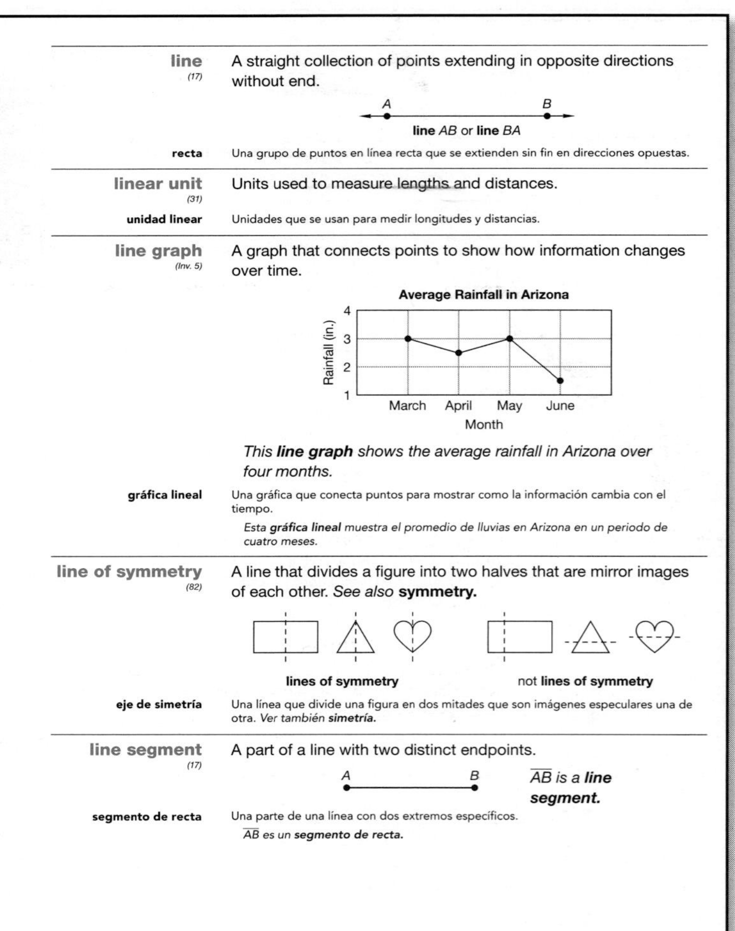

line (17) A straight collection of points extending in opposite directions without end.

line *AB* or **line** *BA*

recta Una grupo de puntos en línea recta que se extienden sin fin en direcciones opuestas.

linear unit (31) Units used to measure lengths and distances.

unidad linear Unidades que se usan para medir longitudes y distancias.

line graph (Inv. 5) A graph that connects points to show how information changes over time.

*This **line graph** shows the average rainfall in Arizona over four months.*

gráfica lineal Una gráfica que conecta puntos para mostrar como la información cambia con el tiempo.

*Esta **gráfica lineal** muestra el promedio de lluvias en Arizona en un periodo de cuatro meses.*

line of symmetry (82) A line that divides a figure into two halves that are mirror images of each other. *See also* **symmetry.**

lines of symmetry — not **lines of symmetry**

eje de simetría Una línea que divide una figura en dos mitades que son imágenes especulares una de otra. *Ver también* ***simetría.***

line segment (17) A part of a line with two distinct endpoints.

*$\overline{AB}$ is a **line segment.***

segmento de recta Una parte de una línea con dos extremos específicos.

*$\overline{AB}$ es un **segmento de recta.***

R24 *Saxon Math* Intermediate 4

liter (73) A metric unit of capacity or volume.

*A **liter** is a little more than a quart.*

litro Una unidad métrica de capacidad o volumen.

*Un **litro** es un poco más que un cuarto.*

lowest terms (106) A fraction is in *lowest terms* if it cannot be reduced.

*In **lowest terms,** the fraction $\frac{8}{20}$ is $\frac{2}{5}$.*

mínima expresión Una fracción está en su mínima expresión si no se puede reducir.

*En su **mínima expresión** la fracción $\frac{8}{20}$ es $\frac{2}{5}$.*

M

mass (80) The amount of matter an object contains. A kilogram is a metric unit of *mass*.

*The **mass** of a bowling ball would be the same on the moon as on Earth, even though the weight of the bowling ball would be different.*

masa La cantidad de materia que contiene un objeto. Un kilogramo es una unidad métrica de *masa*.

*La **masa** de una bola de boliche sería la misma en la Luna que en la Tierra. Aunque el peso de la bola de boliche sería diferente.*

median (Inv. 6) The middle number (or the average of the two central numbers) of a list of data when the numbers are arranged in order from least to the greatest.

1, 1, 2, 4, 5, 7, 9, 15, 24, 36, 44

*In this list of data, 7 is the **median.***

mediana Número de en medio (o el promedio de los dos números centrales) en una lista de datos, cuando los números se ordenan de menor a mayor.

1, 1, 2, 4, 5, 7, 9, 15, 24, 36, 44

*En esta lista de datos, 7 es la **mediana.***

meter (42) The basic unit of length in the metric system.

*A **meter** is equal to 100 centimeters, and it is slightly longer than 1 yard.*

*Many classrooms are about 10 **meters** long and 10 **meters** wide.*

metro La unidad básica de longitud en el sistema métrico

*Un **metro** es igual a 100 centímetros y es un poco más largo que una yarda.*

*Muchos salones de clase son de alrededor de 10 **metros** de largo y 10 **metros** de ancho.*

metric system (42) An international system of measurement in which units are related by a power of ten. Its also called the *International System of Measurement.*

*Centimeters and kilograms are units in the **metric system.***

sistema métrico Un sistema internacional de medidas en donde las unidades se relacionan con una potencia de diez. También llamado el *Sistema internacional.*

*Los centímetros y los kilogramos son unidades del **sistema métrico.***

midnight (13) 12:00 a.m.

***Midnight** is one hour after 11 p.m.*

medianoche 12:00 a.m.

*La **medianoche** es una hora después de las 11 p.m.*

millimeter (42) A metric unit of length.

*There are 1000 **millimeters** in 1 meter and 10 **millimeters** in 1 centimeter.*

milímetro Una unidad métrica de longitud.

*Hay 1000 **milímetros** en 1 metro y 10 **milímetros** en 1 centímetro.*

mixed number (32) A number expressed as a whole number plus a fraction.

*The **mixed number** $5\frac{3}{4}$ means "five and three fourths."*

número mixto Un número expresado como un número entero más una fracción.

*El **número mixto** $5\frac{3}{4}$ significa "cinco y tres cuartos."*

mode (Inv. 6) The number or numbers that appear most often in a list of data.

5, 12, 32, 5, 16, 5, 7, 12

*In this list of data, the number 5 is the **mode**.*

moda Número o números que aparecen con más frecuencia en una lista de datos.

5, 12, 32, 5, 16, 5, 7, 12

*En esta lista de datos, el número 5 es la **moda.***

multiple (22) A product of a counting number and another number.

*The **multiples** of 3 include 3, 6, 9, and 12.*

múltiplo Producto de un número de conteo y otro número

*Los **múltiplos** de 3 incluyen 3, 6, 9 y 12.*

multiplication (23) An operation that uses a number as an addend a specified number of times.

*$7 \times 3 = 21$ — We can use **multiplication** to*
$7 + 7 + 7 = 21$ — use 7 as an addend 3 times.

multiplicación Una operación que usa un número como sumando un número específico de veces.

*$7 \times 3 = 21$ — Podemos usar la **multiplicación** para usar*
$7 + 7 + 7 = 21$ — el 7 como sumando 3 veces.

multiplication table (23) A table used to find the product of two numbers. The product of two numbers is found at the intersection of the row and the column for the two numbers.

tabla de multiplicación Una tabla que se usa para encontrar el producto de dos números. El producto de dos números se encuentra en la intersección de la fila y la columna para los dos números.

N

negative numbers (Inv. 2) Numbers less than zero.

*-15 and -2.86 are **negative numbers.***

*19 and 0.74 are not **negative numbers.***

números negativos Los números menores que cero.

*-15 y -2.86 son **números negativos.***

*19 y 0.74 no son **números negativos.***

net (97) An arrangement of edge-joined polygons that can be folded to become the faces of the geometric solid.

red Un arreglo de polígonos unidos por el borde que pueden ser doblados para convertirse en las caras de un sólido geométrico.

noon (13) 12:00 p.m.

***Noon** is one hour after 11 a.m.*

mediodía 12:00 p.m.

***Mediodía** es una hora después de las 11 a.m.*

number line (Inv. 2) A line for representing and graphing numbers. Each point on the line corresponds to a number.

−2 −1 0 1 2 3 4 5 **number line**

recta numérica Recta para representar y graficar números. Cada punto de la recta corresponde a un número.

number sentence (maintained) A complete sentence that uses numbers and symbols instead of words. *See also* **equation.**

*The **number sentence** $4 + 5 = 9$ means "four plus five equals nine."*

enunciado numérico Un enunciado completo que usa números y símbolos en lugar de palabras. *Ver también* **ecuación.**

*El **enunciado numérico** $4 + 5 = 9$ significa "cuatro más cinco es igual a nueve".*

numerator (19) The top number of a fraction; The number that tells how many parts of a whole are counted.

$\frac{1}{4}$ *The **numerator** of the fraction is 1. One part of the whole circle is shaded.*

numerador El término superior de una fracción. El número que nos dice cuantas partes de un entero se cuentan.

*El **numerador** de la fracción es 1.*

Una parte del círculo completo esta sombreada.

O

obtuse angle (17) An angle whose measure is more than 90° and less than 180°.

obtuse angle — right angle, acute angle: not **obtuse angles**

*An **obtuse angle** is larger than both a right angle and an acute angle.*

ángulo obtuso Ángulo que mide más de 90° y menos de 180°.

*Un **ángulo obtuso** es más grande que un ángulo recto y que un ángulo agudo.*

obtuse triangle (81) A triangle whose largest angle measures more than 90° and less than 180°.

obtuse triangle — acute triangle, right triangle: not **obtuse triangles**

triángulo obtusángulo Triángulo cuyo ángulo mayor mide más que 90° y menos que 180°.

octagon (20) A polygon with eight sides.

octagon

octágono Un polígono con ocho lados.

odd numbers (1) Numbers that have a remainder of 1 when divided by 2; The numbers in this sequence: 1, 3, 5, 7, 9, 11, ...

***Odd numbers** have 1, 3, 5, 7, or 9 in the ones place.*

números impares Números que cuando se dividen entre 2 tienen residuo de 1; los números en esta secuencia: 1, 3, 5, 7, 9, 11....

*Los **números impares** tienen 1, 3, 5, 7, ó 9 en el lugar de las unidades.*

order of operations (9) The set of rules for the order in which to solve math problems.

*Following the **order of operations,** we multiply and divide within an expression before we add and subtract.*

orden de operaciones El conjunto de reglas del orden para resolver problemas matemáticos.

*Siguiendo el **orden de operaciones** multiplicamos y dividimos dentro de la expresión antes de sumar y restar.*

ordinal numbers (maintained) Numbers that describe position or order.

*"First," "second," and "third" are **ordinal numbers.***

números ordinales Números que describen posición u orden.

*"Primero", "segundo" y "tercero" son **números ordinales.***

origin (Inv. 7) (1) The location of the number 0 on a number line.

-3 -2 -1 0 1 2 3

origin on a number line

(2) The point (0, 0) on a coordinate plane.

origin on a coordinate plane

origen (1) La ubicación del número 0 en una recta numérica.
(2) El punto (0, 0) en un plano coordenado.

ounce (80) A unit of weight in the customary system. It is also a measure of capacity. *See also* **fluid ounce.**

*Sixteen **ounces** equals a pound. Sixteen **fluid ounces** equals a pint.*

onza Una unidad de peso en el sistema usual. También es una medida de capacidad. *Ver también* **onza líquida.**

*Dieciseis **onzas** es igual a una libra. Dieciseis **onzas líquidas** es igual a una pinta.*

outcome (110) The end result of a probability experiment.

resultado El resultado final de un experimento de probabilidad.

Glossary R29

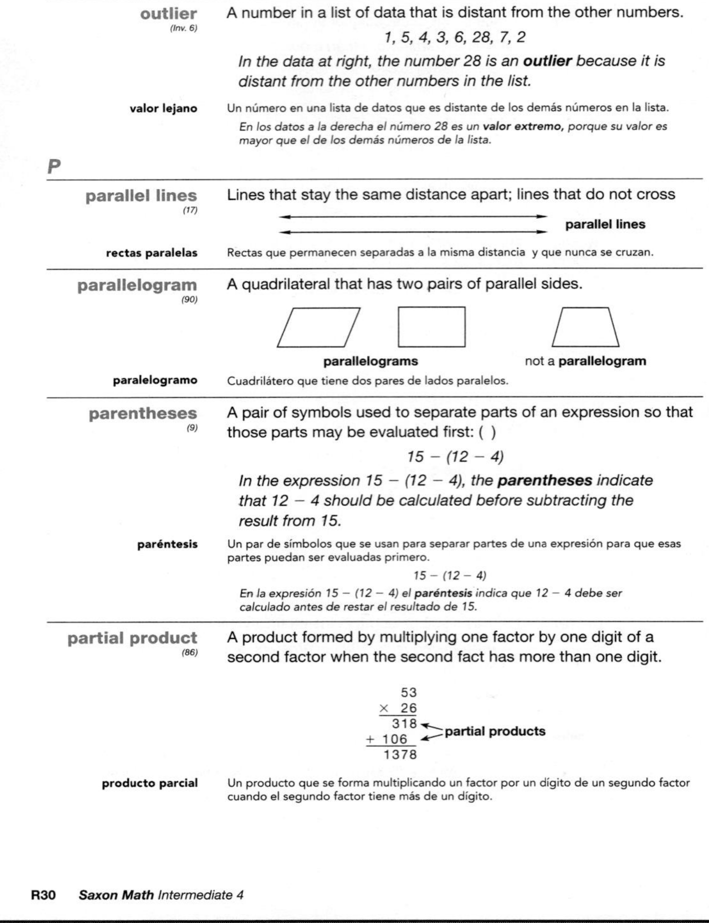

outlier (Inv. 6) A number in a list of data that is distant from the other numbers.

1, 5, 4, 3, 6, 28, 7, 2

*In the data at right, the number 28 is an **outlier** because it is distant from the other numbers in the list.*

valor lejano Un número en una lista de datos que es distante de los demás números en la lista.

*En los datos a la derecha el número 28 es un **valor extremo,** porque su valor es mayor que el de los demás números de la lista.*

P

parallel lines (17) Lines that stay the same distance apart; lines that do not cross

parallel lines

rectas paralelas Rectas que permanecen separadas a la misma distancia y que nunca se cruzan.

parallelogram (90) A quadrilateral that has two pairs of parallel sides.

parallelograms not a **parallelogram**

paralelogramo Cuadrilátero que tiene dos pares de lados paralelos.

parentheses (9) A pair of symbols used to separate parts of an expression so that those parts may be evaluated first: ( )

15 − (12 − 4)

*In the expression 15 − (12 − 4), the **parentheses** indicate that 12 − 4 should be calculated before subtracting the result from 15.*

paréntesis Un par de símbolos que se usan para separar partes de una expresión para que esas partes puedan ser evaluadas primero.

15 − (12 − 4)

*En la expresión 15 − (12 − 4) el **paréntesis** indica que 12 − 4 debe ser calculado antes de restar el resultado de 15.*

partial product (86) A product formed by multiplying one factor by one digit of a second factor when the second fact has more than one digit.

```
   53
 × 26
  318  ← partial products
+ 106  ←
 1378
```

producto parcial Un producto que se forma multiplicando un factor por un dígito de un segundo factor cuando el segundo factor tiene más de un dígito.

R30 *Saxon Math* Intermediate 4

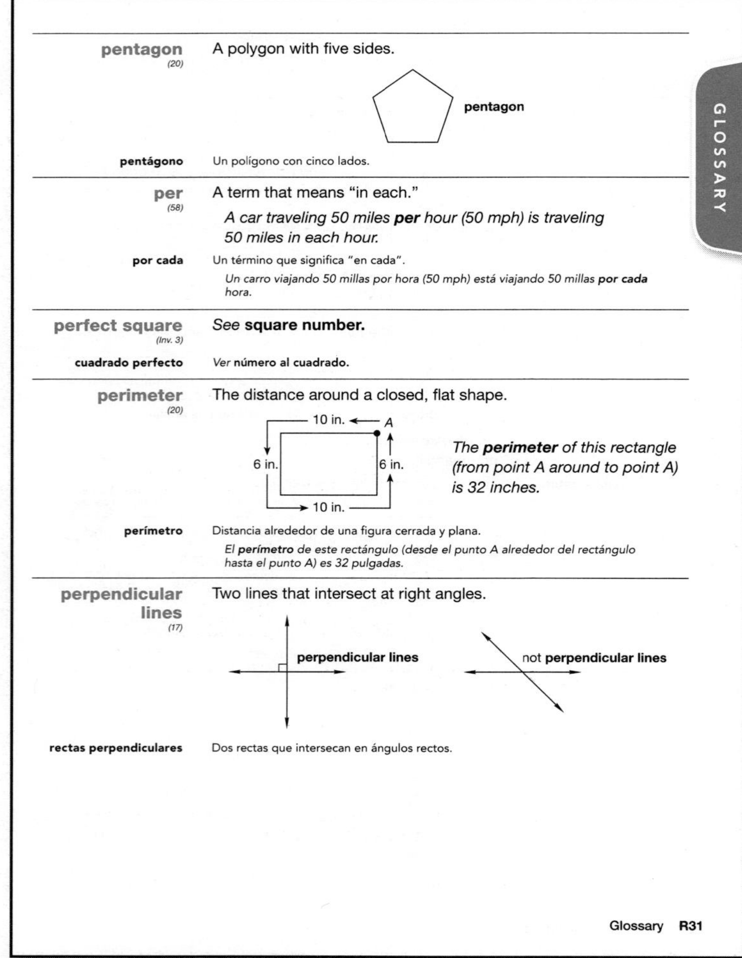

pentagon (20) A polygon with five sides.

pentagon

pentágono Un polígono con cinco lados.

per (58) A term that means "in each."

*A car traveling 50 miles **per** hour (50 mph) is traveling 50 miles in each hour.*

por cada Un término que significa "en cada".

*Un carro viajando 50 millas por hora (50 mph) está viajando 50 millas **por cada** hora.*

perfect square (Inv. 3) *See* **square number.**

cuadrado perfecto *Ver* **número al cuadrado.**

perimeter (20) The distance around a closed, flat shape.

10 in. A 6 in. 6 in. 10 in.

*The **perimeter** of this rectangle (from point A around to point A) is 32 inches.*

perímetro Distancia alrededor de una figura cerrada y plana.

*El **perímetro** de este rectángulo (desde el punto A alrededor del rectángulo hasta el punto A) es 32 pulgadas.*

perpendicular lines (17) Two lines that intersect at right angles.

perpendicular lines not **perpendicular lines**

rectas perpendiculares Dos rectas que intersecan en ángulos rectos.

Glossary R31

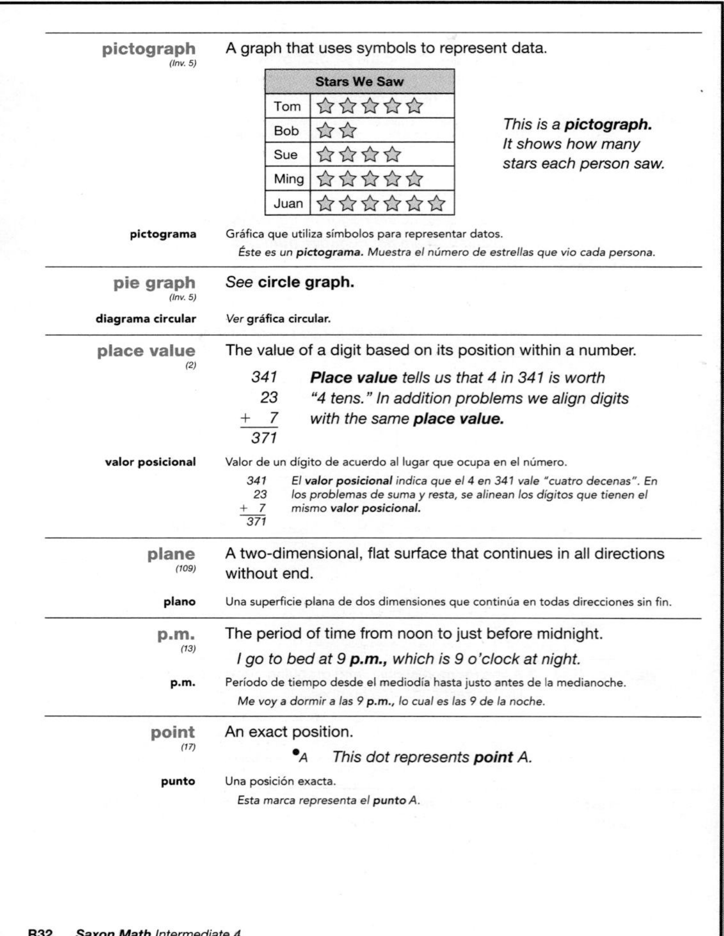

pictograph (Inv. 5) A graph that uses symbols to represent data.

Stars We Saw	
Tom	☆☆☆☆☆
Bob	☆☆
Sue	☆☆☆☆
Ming	☆☆☆☆☆
Juan	☆☆☆☆☆☆

*This is a **pictograph.** It shows how many stars each person saw.*

pictograma Gráfica que utiliza símbolos para representar datos.

*Éste es un **pictograma.** Muestra el número de estrellas que vio cada persona.*

pie graph (Inv. 5) *See* **circle graph.**

diagrama circular *Ver* **gráfica circular.**

place value (2) The value of a digit based on its position within a number.

```
 341
  23
+  7
 371
```

Place value** tells us that 4 in 341 is worth "4 tens." In addition problems we align digits with the same **place value.

valor posicional Valor de un dígito de acuerdo al lugar que ocupa en el número.

*El **valor posicional** indica que el 4 en 341 vale "cuatro decenas". En los problemas de suma y resta, se alinean los dígitos que tienen el mismo **valor posicional.***

plane (109) A two-dimensional, flat surface that continues in all directions without end.

plano Una superficie plana de dos dimensiones que continúa en todas direcciones sin fin.

p.m. (13) The period of time from noon to just before midnight.

*I go to bed at 9 **p.m.,** which is 9 o'clock at night.*

p.m. Período de tiempo desde el mediodía hasta justo antes de la medianoche.

*Me voy a dormir a las 9 **p.m.,** lo cual es las 9 de la noche.*

point (17) An exact position.

•*A* *This dot represents **point** A.*

punto Una posición exacta.

*Esta marca representa el **punto** A.*

R32 *Saxon Math* Intermediate 4

polygon (20) A closed, flat shape with straight sides.

polygons — not polygons

polígono Figura cerrada y plana que tiene lados rectos.

population (Inv. 6) A group of people about whom information is gathered during a survey.

*A soft drink company wanted to know the favorite beverage of people in Indiana. The **population** they gathered information about was the people of Indiana.*

población Un grupo de gente de la cual se obtiene información durante una encuesta.

*Una compañía de sodas quería saber cuál es la bebida favorita de la gente en Indiana. La **población** de la cual recolectaron información fue la gente de Indiana.*

positive numbers (Inv. 2) Numbers greater than zero.

*0.25 and 157 are **positive numbers.***

*−40 and 0 are not **positive numbers.***

números positivos Números mayores que cero.

*0.25 y 157 son **números positivos.***

*−40 y 0 no son **números positivos.***

pound (80) A customary measurement of weight.

*One **pound** is 16 ounces.*

libra Una medida usual de peso.

*Una **libra** es igual a 16 onzas.*

prime number (55) A counting number greater than 1 whose only two factors are the number 1 and itself.

*7 is a **prime number.** Its only factors are 1 and 7.*

*10 is not a **prime number.** Its factors are 1, 2, 5, and 10.*

número primo Número de contes mayor que 1, cuyos dos únicos factores son el 1 y el propio número.

*7 es un **número primo.** Sus únicos factores son 1 y 7.*

*10 no es un **número primo.** Sus factores son 1, 2, 5 y 10.*

prism (108) *See* **geometric solid.**

prisma *Ver* **sólido geométrico.**

probability (110) A way of describing the likelihood of an event; the ratio of favorable outcomes to all possible outcomes

*The **probability** of the spinner landing on C is $\frac{1}{4}$.*

probabilidad Manera de describir la ocurrencia de un suceso; la razón de resultados favorables a todos los resultados posibles.

*La **probabilidad** de obtener 3 al lanzar un cubo estándar de números es $\frac{1}{6}$.*

product (23) The result of multiplication.

*$5 \times 3 = 15$ The **product** of 5 and 3 is 15.*

producto Resultado de una multiplicación.

*$5 \times 3 = 15$ El **producto** de 5 por 3 es 15.*

proper fraction (89) A fraction whose denominator is greater than its numerator.

*$\frac{3}{4}$ is a **proper fraction.***

*$\frac{4}{3}$ is not a **proper fraction.***

fracción propia Una fracción cuyo denominador es mayor que el numerador.

*$\frac{3}{4}$ es una **fracción propia.***

*$\frac{4}{3}$ no es una **fracción propia.***

Property of Zero for Multiplication (23) Zero times any number is zero. In symbolic form, $0 \times a = 0$.

*The **Property of Zero for Multiplication** tells us that $89 \times 0 = 0$.*

propiedad del cero en la multiplicación Cero multiplicado por cualquier número es cero. En forma simbólica, $0 \times a = 0$.

*La **propiedad del cero en la multiplicación** dice que $89 \times 0 = 0$.*

pyramid (96, 109) A three-dimensional solid with a polygon as its base and triangular faces that meet at the apex.

pyramid

pirámide Figura geométrica de tres dimensiones, con un polígono en su base y caras triangulares que se encuentran en un vértice.

Q

quadrilateral (20) Any four-sided polygon.

*Each of these polygons has 4 sides. They are all **quadrilaterals.***

cuadrilátero Cualquier polígono de cuatro lados.

*Cada uno de estos polígonos tiene 4 lados. Todos son **cuadriláteros.***

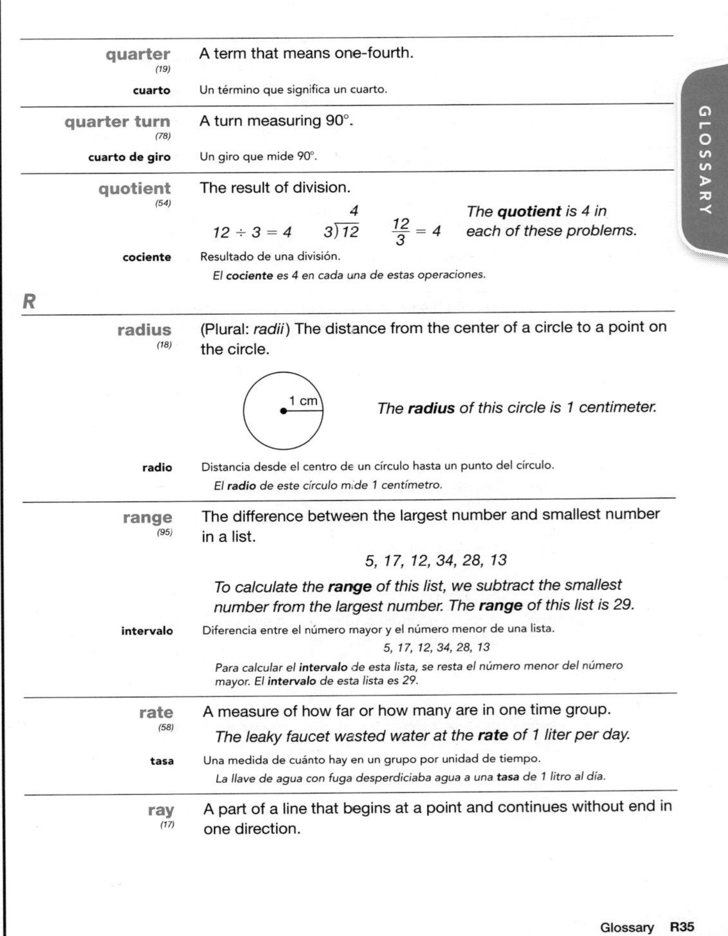

quarter (19) A term that means one-fourth.

cuarto Un término que significa un cuarto.

quarter turn (78) A turn measuring 90°.

cuarto de giro Un giro que mide 90°.

quotient (54) The result of division.

$12 \div 3 = 4$ $3\overline{)12}$ with 4 $\frac{12}{3} = 4$ *The **quotient** is 4 in each of these problems.*

cociente Resultado de una división.

*El **cociente** es 4 en cada una de estas operaciones.*

R

radius (18) (Plural: *radii*) The distance from the center of a circle to a point on the circle.

*The **radius** of this circle is 1 centimeter.*

radio Distancia desde el centro de un círculo hasta un punto del círculo.

*El **radio** de este círculo mide 1 centímetro.*

range (95) The difference between the largest number and smallest number in a list.

5, 17, 12, 34, 28, 13

*To calculate the **range** of this list, we subtract the smallest number from the largest number. The **range** of this list is 29.*

intervalo Diferencia entre el número mayor y el número menor de una lista.

5, 17, 12, 34, 28, 13

*Para calcular el **intervalo** de esta lista, se resta el número menor del número mayor. El **intervalo** de esta lista es 29.*

rate (58) A measure of how far or how many are in one time group.

*The leaky faucet wasted water at the **rate** of 1 liter per day.*

tasa Una medida de cuánto hay en un grupo por unidad de tiempo.

*La llave de agua con fuga desperdiciaba agua a una **tasa** de 1 litro al día.*

ray (17) A part of a line that begins at a point and continues without end in one direction.

Glossary R35

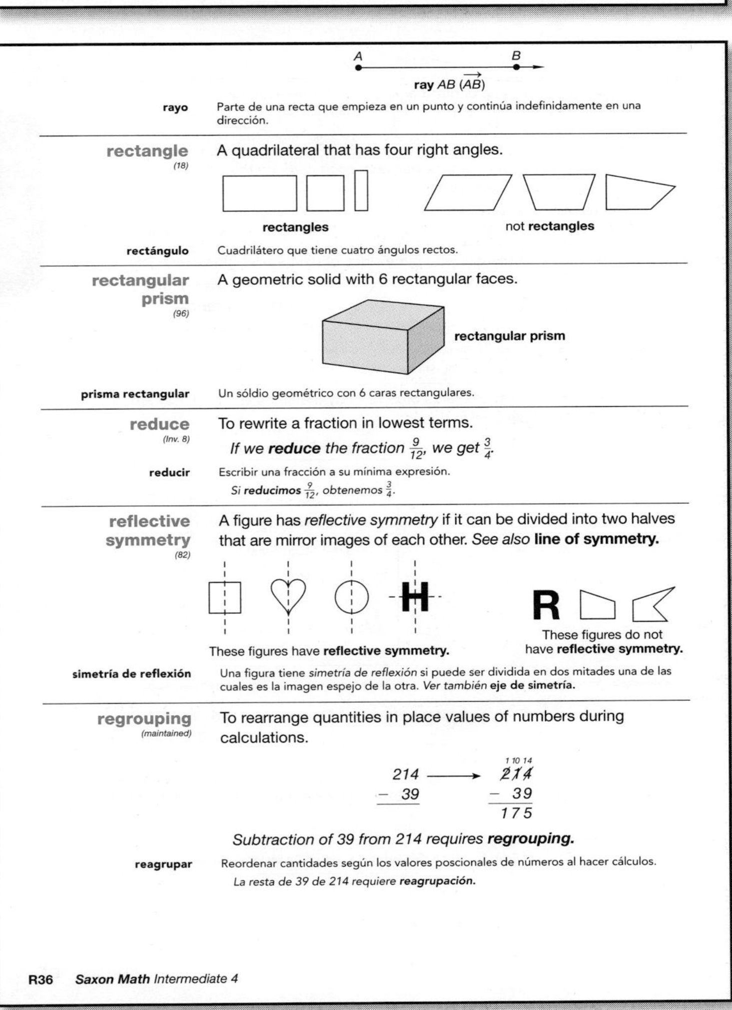

ray AB ($\overrightarrow{AB}$)

rayo Parte de una recta que empieza en un punto y continúa indefinidamente en una dirección.

rectangle (18) A quadrilateral that has four right angles.

rectangles — not rectangles

rectángulo Cuadrilátero que tiene cuatro ángulos rectos.

rectangular prism (96) A geometric solid with 6 rectangular faces.

rectangular prism

prisma rectangular Un sólido geométrico con 6 caras rectangulares.

reduce (Inv. 8) To rewrite a fraction in lowest terms.

*If we **reduce** the fraction $\frac{9}{12}$, we get $\frac{3}{4}$.*

reducir Escribir una fracción a su mínima expresión.

*Si **reducimos** $\frac{9}{12}$, obtenemos $\frac{3}{4}$.*

reflective symmetry (82) A figure has *reflective symmetry* if it can be divided into two halves that are mirror images of each other. *See also* **line of symmetry.**

These figures have **reflective symmetry.** — These figures do not have **reflective symmetry.**

simetría de reflexión Una figura tiene *simetría de reflexión* si puede ser dividida en dos mitades una de las cuales es la imagen espejo de la otra. *Ver también* **eje de simetría.**

regrouping (maintained) To rearrange quantities in place values of numbers during calculations.

$214 - 39 \rightarrow 175$

*Subtraction of 39 from 214 requires **regrouping.***

reagrupar Reordenar cantidades según los valores posicionales de números al hacer cálculos.

*La resta de 39 de 214 requiere **reagrupación.***

R36 *Saxon Math* Intermediate 4

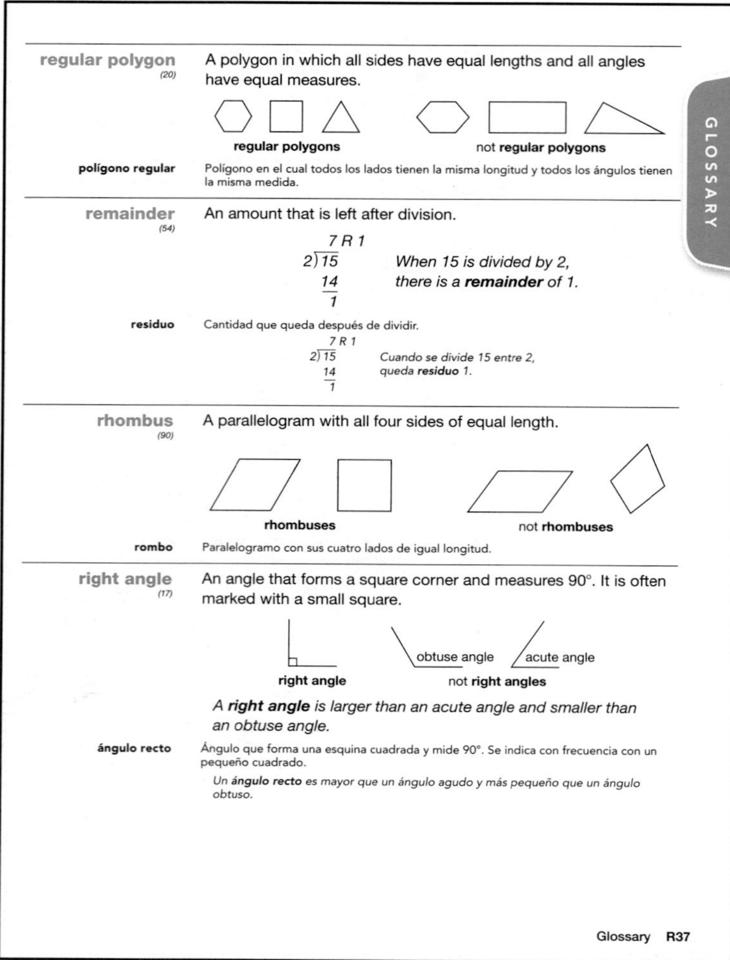

regular polygon (20) A polygon in which all sides have equal lengths and all angles have equal measures.

polígono regular Polígono en el cual todos los lados tienen la misma longitud y todos los ángulos tienen la misma medida.

remainder (54) An amount that is left after division.

$$\begin{array}{r} 7\ R\ 1 \\ 2\overline{)15} \\ \underline{14} \\ 1 \end{array}$$

When 15 is divided by 2, there is a ***remainder*** *of 1.*

residuo Cantidad que queda después de dividir.

$$\begin{array}{r} 7\ R\ 1 \\ 2\overline{)15} \\ \underline{14} \\ 1 \end{array}$$

Cuando se divide 15 entre 2, queda ***residuo*** *1.*

rhombus (90) A parallelogram with all four sides of equal length.

rombo Paralelogramo con sus cuatro lados de igual longitud.

right angle (17) An angle that forms a square corner and measures 90°. It is often marked with a small square.

A ***right angle*** *is larger than an acute angle and smaller than an obtuse angle.*

ángulo recto Ángulo que forma una esquina cuadrada y mide 90°. Se indica con frecuencia con un pequeño cuadrado.

Un ***ángulo recto*** *es mayor que un ángulo agudo y más pequeño que un ángulo obtuso.*

Glossary R37

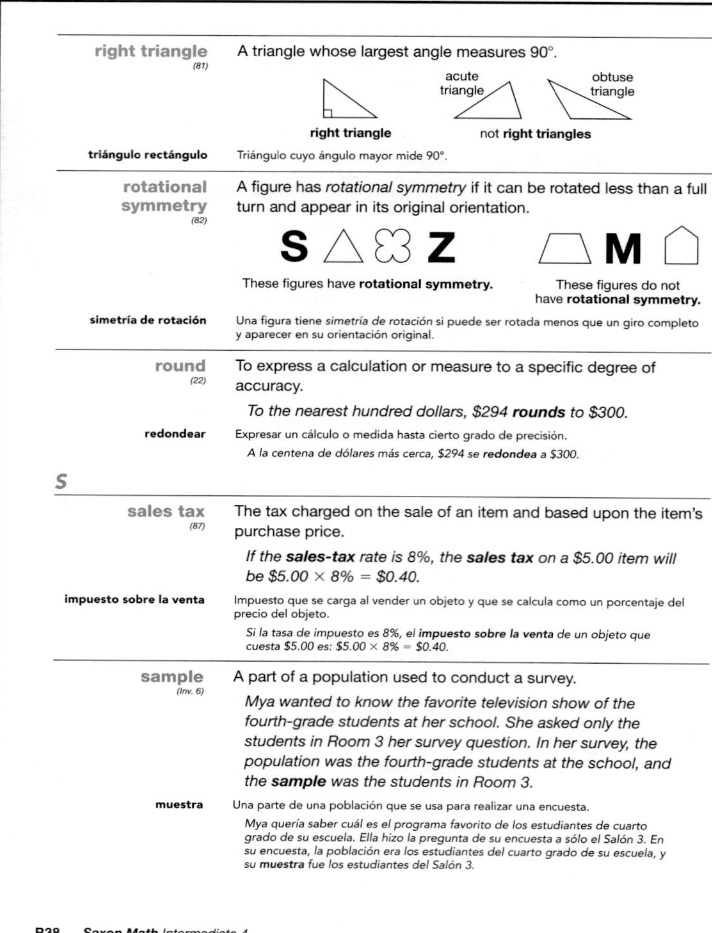

right triangle (81) A triangle whose largest angle measures 90°.

triángulo rectángulo Triángulo cuyo ángulo mayor mide 90°.

rotational symmetry (82) A figure has *rotational symmetry* if it can be rotated less than a full turn and appear in its original orientation.

simetría de rotación Una figura tiene *simetría de rotación* si puede ser rotada menos que un giro completo y aparecer en su orientación original.

round (22) To express a calculation or measure to a specific degree of accuracy.

To the nearest hundred dollars, $294 ***rounds*** *to $300.*

redondear Expresar un cálculo o medida hasta cierto grado de precisión.

A la centena de dólares más cerca, $294 se ***redondea*** *a $300.*

S

sales tax (87) The tax charged on the sale of an item and based upon the item's purchase price.

If the ***sales-tax*** *rate is 8%, the* ***sales tax*** *on a $5.00 item will be $5.00 × 8% = $0.40.*

impuesto sobre la venta Impuesto que se carga al vender un objeto y que se calcula como un porcentaje del precio del objeto.

Si la tasa de impuesto es 8%, el ***impuesto sobre la venta*** *de un objeto que cuesta $5.00 es: $5.00 × 8% = $0.40.*

sample (Inv. 6) A part of a population used to conduct a survey.

Mya wanted to know the favorite television show of the fourth-grade students at her school. She asked only the students in Room 3 her survey question. In her survey, the population was the fourth-grade students at the school, and the ***sample*** *was the students in Room 3.*

muestra Una parte de una población que se usa para realizar una encuesta.

Mya quería saber cuál es el programa favorito de los estudiantes de cuarto grado de su escuela. Ella hizo la pregunta de su encuesta a sólo el Salón 3. En su encuesta, la población era los estudiantes del cuarto grado de su escuela, y su ***muestra*** *fue los estudiantes del Salón 3.*

R38 *Saxon Math Intermediate 4*

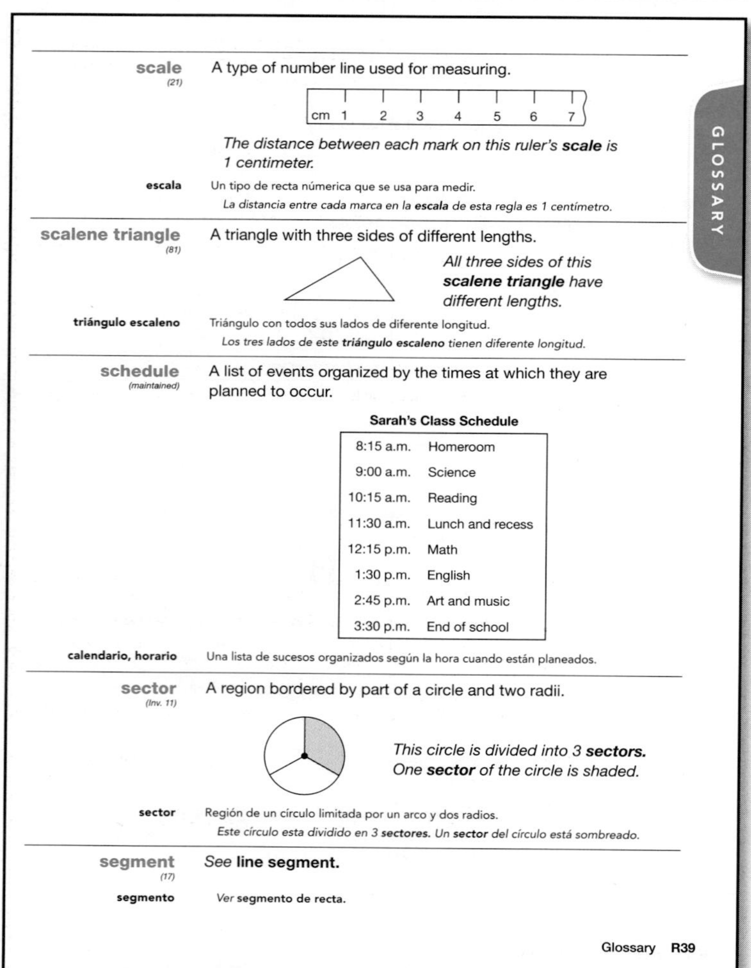

scale (21) A type of number line used for measuring.

The distance between each mark on this ruler's ***scale*** *is 1 centimeter.*

escala Un tipo de recta númerica que se usa para medir.

La distancia entre cada marca en la ***escala*** *de esta regla es 1 centímetro.*

scalene triangle (81) A triangle with three sides of different lengths.

All three sides of this ***scalene triangle*** *have different lengths.*

triángulo escaleno Triángulo con todos sus lados de diferente longitud.

Los tres lados de este ***triángulo escaleno*** *tienen diferente longitud.*

schedule (maintained) A list of events organized by the times at which they are planned to occur.

Sarah's Class Schedule

8:15 a.m.	Homeroom
9:00 a.m.	Science
10:15 a.m.	Reading
11:30 a.m.	Lunch and recess
12:15 p.m.	Math
1:30 p.m.	English
2:45 p.m.	Art and music
3:30 p.m.	End of school

calendario, horario Una lista de sucesos organizados según la hora cuando están planeados.

sector (Inv. 11) A region bordered by part of a circle and two radii.

This circle is divided into 3 ***sectors.*** *One* ***sector*** *of the circle is shaded.*

sector Región de un círculo limitada por un arco y dos radios.

Este círculo esta dividido en 3 ***sectores.*** *Un* ***sector*** *del círculo está sombreado.*

segment (17) *See* **line segment.**

segmento *Ver* **segmento de recta.**

Glossary R39

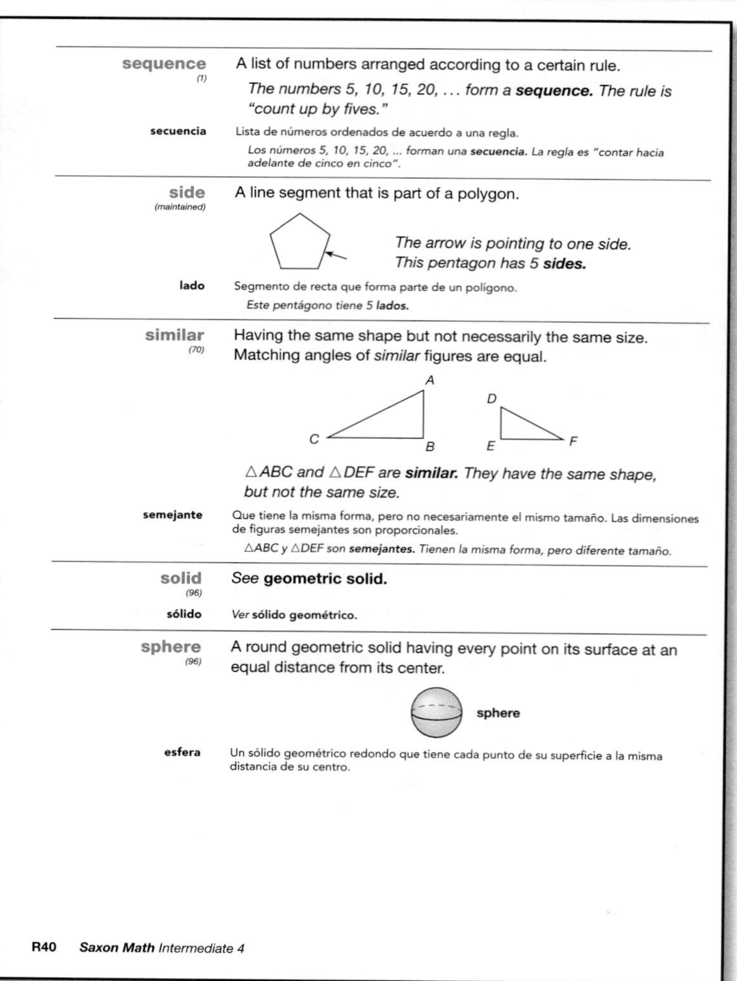

sequence (1) A list of numbers arranged according to a certain rule.

The numbers 5, 10, 15, 20, . . . form a ***sequence.*** *The rule is "count up by fives."*

secuencia Lista de números ordenados de acuerdo a una regla.

Los números 5, 10, 15, 20, ... forman una ***secuencia.*** *La regla es "contar hacia adelante de cinco en cinco".*

side (maintained) A line segment that is part of a polygon.

The arrow is pointing to one side. This pentagon has 5 ***sides.***

lado Segmento de recta que forma parte de un polígono.

Este pentágono tiene 5 ***lados.***

similar (70) Having the same shape but not necessarily the same size. Matching angles of *similar* figures are equal.

△ABC and △DEF are ***similar.*** *They have the same shape, but not the same size.*

semejante Que tiene la misma forma, pero no necesariamente el mismo tamaño. Las dimensiones de figuras semejantes son proporcionales.

△ABC y △DEF son ***semejantes.*** *Tienen la misma forma, pero diferente tamaño.*

solid (96) *See* **geometric solid.**

sólido *Ver* **sólido geométrico.**

sphere (96) A round geometric solid having every point on its surface at an equal distance from its center.

esfera Un sólido geométrico redondo que tiene cada punto de su superficie a la misma distancia de su centro.

R40 *Saxon Math Intermediate 4*

square (18)
1. A rectangle with all four sides of equal length.

12 mm / 12 mm / 12 mm / 12 mm — *All four sides of this **square** are 12 millimeters long.*

2. The product of a number and itself.

*The **square** of 4 is 16.*

cuadrado
1. Un rectángulo con sus cuatro lados de igual longitud.
*Los cuatro lados de este **cuadrado** miden 12 milímetros.*
2. El producto de un número por sí mismo.
*El **cuadrado** de 4 es 16.*

square centimeter (Inv. 3)
A measure of area equal to that of a square with 1-centimeter sides.

1 cm / 1 cm — **square centimeter**

centímetro cuadrado Medida de un área igual a la de un cuadrado con lados de 1 centímetro.

square foot (Inv. 3)
A unit of area equal to a square with 1-foot sides.

pie cuadrado Unidad de área igual a un cuadrado con lados que miden un pie de longitud.

square inch (Inv. 3)
A measure of area equal to that of a square with 1-inch sides.

1 in. / 1 in. — **square inch**

pulgada cuadrada Medida de un área igual a la de un cuadrado con lados de 1 pulgada.

square number (25)
The product when a whole number is multiplied by itself.

*The number 9 is a **square number** because $9 = 3^2$.*

número al cuadrado El producto de un número entero multiplicado por sí mismo.
*El número 9 es un **número al cuadrado** porque $9 = 3^2$.*

square root (Inv. 3)
One of two equal factors of a number. The symbol for the principal, or positive, *square root* of a number is $\sqrt{\ }$.

*A **square root** of 49 is 7 because $7 \times 7 = 49$.*

raíz cuadrada Uno de dos factores iguales de un número. El símbolo de la *raíz cuadrada* de un número es $\sqrt{\ }$, y se le llama *radical.*
*La **raíz cuadrada** de 49 es 7, porque $7 \times 7 = 49$.*

Glossary R41

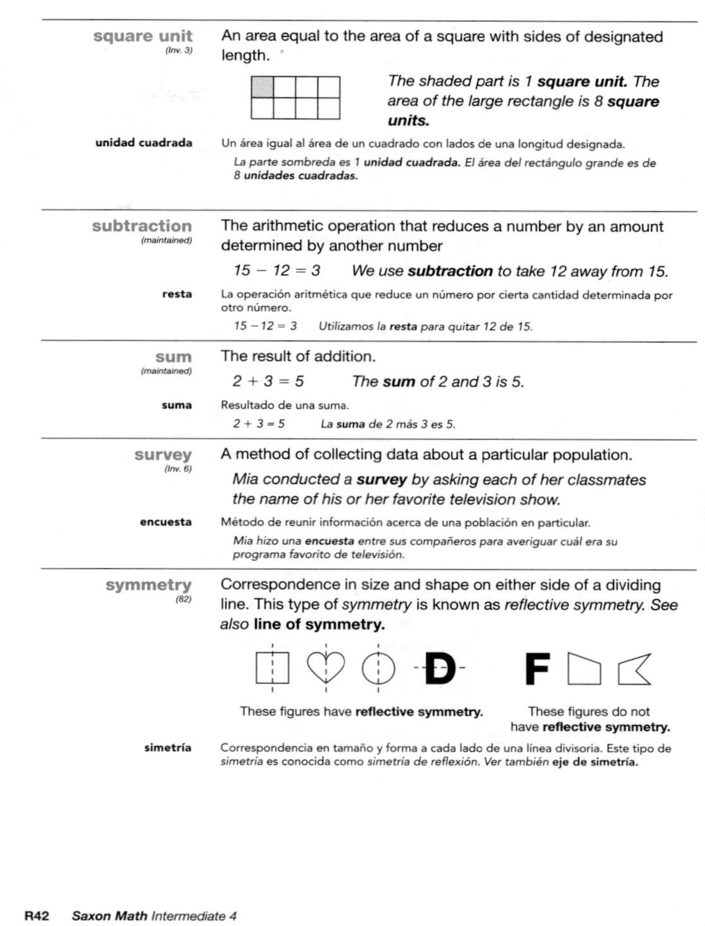

square unit (Inv. 3)
An area equal to the area of a square with sides of designated length.

*The shaded part is 1 **square unit.** The area of the large rectangle is 8 **square units.***

unidad cuadrada Un área igual al área de un cuadrado con lados de una longitud designada.
*La parte sombreda es 1 **unidad cuadrada.** El área del rectángulo grande es de 8 **unidades cuadradas.***

subtraction (maintained)
The arithmetic operation that reduces a number by an amount determined by another number

$15 - 12 = 3$ *We use **subtraction** to take 12 away from 15.*

resta La operación aritmética que reduce un número por cierta cantidad determinada por otro número.
$15 - 12 = 3$ *Utilizamos la **resta** para quitar 12 de 15.*

sum (maintained)
The result of addition.

$2 + 3 = 5$ *The **sum** of 2 and 3 is 5.*

suma Resultado de una suma.
$2 + 3 = 5$ *La **suma** de 2 más 3 es 5.*

survey (Inv. 6)
A method of collecting data about a particular population.

*Mia conducted a **survey** by asking each of her classmates the name of his or her favorite television show.*

encuesta Método de reunir información acerca de una población en particular.
*Mia hizo una **encuesta** entre sus compañeros para averiguar cuál era su programa favorito de televisión.*

symmetry (82)
Correspondence in size and shape on either side of a dividing line. This type of *symmetry* is known as *reflective symmetry. See also* **line of symmetry.**

These figures have **reflective symmetry.** These figures do not have **reflective symmetry.**

simetría Correspondencia en tamaño y forma a cada lado de una línea divisoria. Este tipo de *simetría* es conocida como *simetría de reflexión. Ver también* **eje de simetría.**

R42 *Saxon Math Intermediate 4*

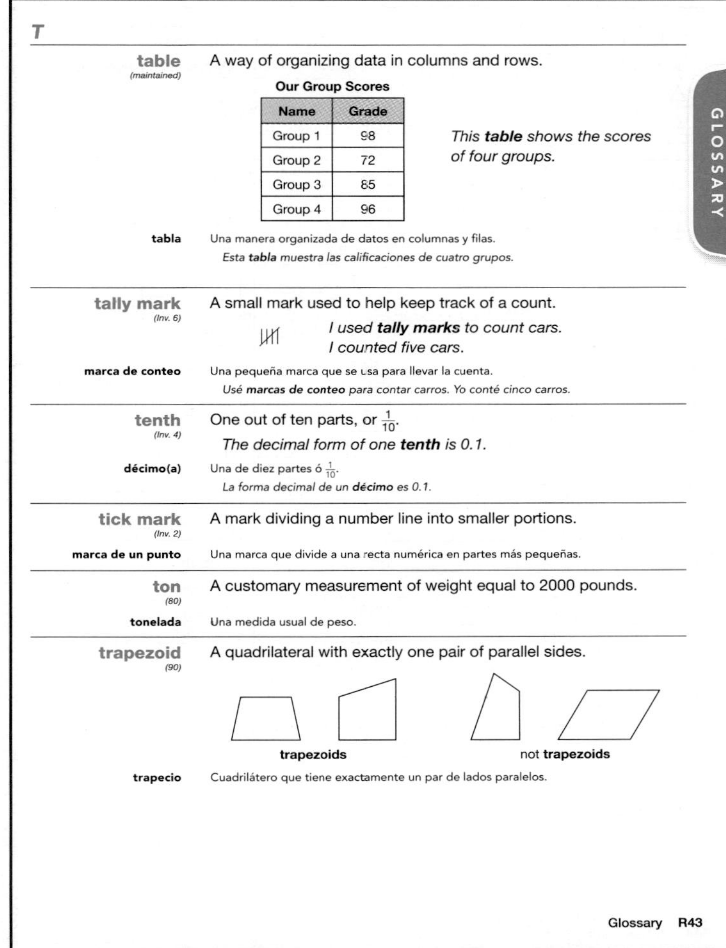

T

table (maintained)
A way of organizing data in columns and rows.

Our Group Scores

Name	Grade
Group 1	98
Group 2	72
Group 3	85
Group 4	96

*This **table** shows the scores of four groups.*

tabla Una manera organizada de datos en columnas y filas.
*Esta **tabla** muestra las calificaciones de cuatro grupos.*

tally mark (Inv. 6)
A small mark used to help keep track of a count.

*I used **tally marks** to count cars. I counted five cars.*

marca de conteo Una pequeña marca que se usa para llevar la cuenta.
*Usé **marcas de conteo** para contar carros. Yo conté cinco carros.*

tenth (Inv. 4)
One out of ten parts, or $\frac{1}{10}$.

*The decimal form of one **tenth** is 0.1.*

décimo(a) Una de diez partes ó $\frac{1}{10}$.
*La forma decimal de un **décimo** es 0.1.*

tick mark (Inv. 2)
A mark dividing a number line into smaller portions.

marca de un punto Una marca que divide a una recta numérica en partes más pequeñas.

ton (80)
A customary measurement of weight equal to 2000 pounds.

tonelada Una medida usual de peso.

trapezoid (90)
A quadrilateral with exactly one pair of parallel sides.

trapezoids not **trapezoids**

trapecio Cuadrilátero que tiene exactamente un par de lados paralelos.

Glossary R43

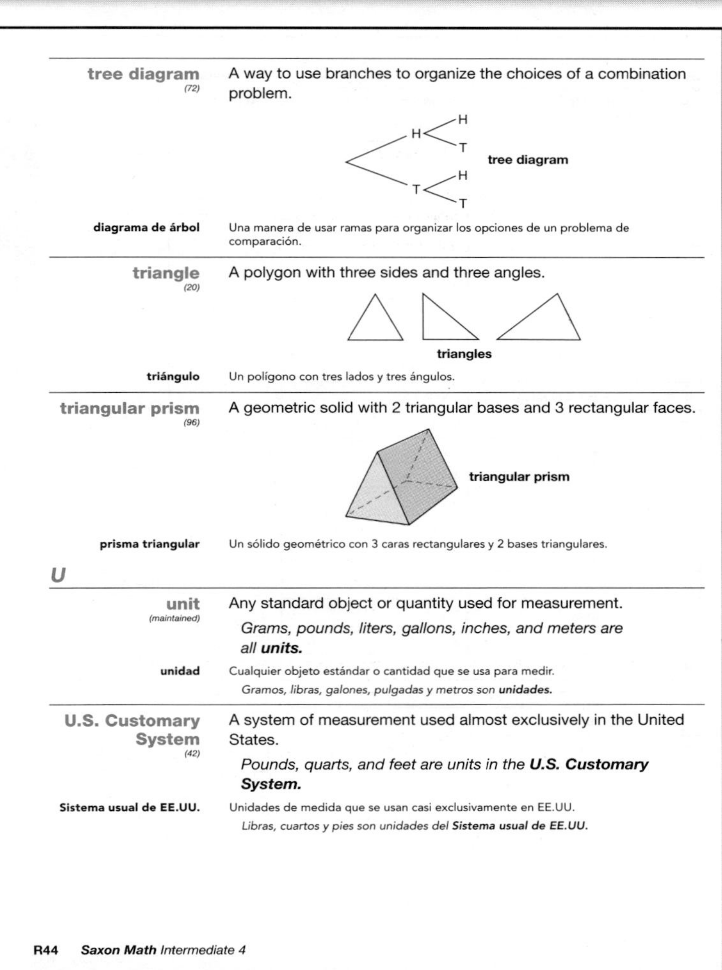

tree diagram (72)
A way to use branches to organize the choices of a combination problem.

tree diagram

diagrama de árbol Una manera de usar ramas para organizar los opciones de un problema de comparación.

triangle (20)
A polygon with three sides and three angles.

triangles

triángulo Un polígono con tres lados y tres ángulos.

triangular prism (96)
A geometric solid with 2 triangular bases and 3 rectangular faces.

triangular prism

prisma triangular Un sólido geométrico con 3 caras rectangulares y 2 bases triangulares.

U

unit (maintained)
Any standard object or quantity used for measurement.

*Grams, pounds, liters, gallons, inches, and meters are all **units.***

unidad Cualquier objeto estándar o cantidad que se usa para medir.
*Gramos, libras, galones, pulgadas y metros son **unidades.***

U.S. Customary System (42)
A system of measurement used almost exclusively in the United States.

*Pounds, quarts, and feet are units in the **U.S. Customary System.***

Sistema usual de EE.UU. Unidades de medida que se usan casi exclusivamente en EE.UU.
*Libras, cuartos y pies son unidades del **Sistema usual de EE.UU.***

R44 *Saxon Math Intermediate 4*

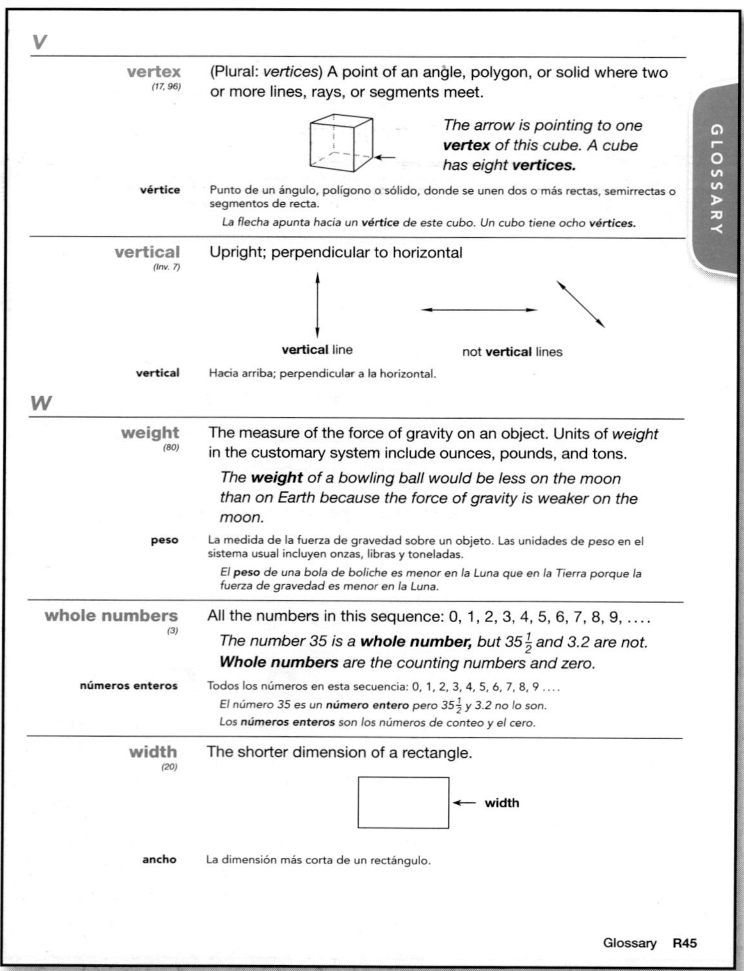

V

vertex (17, 96) (Plural: *vertices*) A point of an angle, polygon, or solid where two or more lines, rays, or segments meet.

*The arrow is pointing to one **vertex** of this cube. A cube has eight **vertices.***

vértice Punto de un ángulo, polígono o sólido, donde se unen dos o más rectas, semirrectas o segmentos de recta.

*La flecha apunta hacia un **vértice** de este cubo. Un cubo tiene ocho **vértices.***

vertical (Inv. 7) Upright; perpendicular to horizontal

vertical Hacia arriba; perpendicular a la horizontal.

W

weight (80) The measure of the force of gravity on an object. Units of *weight* in the customary system include ounces, pounds, and tons.

*The **weight** of a bowling ball would be less on the moon than on Earth because the force of gravity is weaker on the moon.*

peso La medida de la fuerza de gravedad sobre un objeto. Las unidades de peso en el sistema usual incluyen onzas, libras y toneladas.

*El **peso** de una bola de boliche es menor en la Luna que en la Tierra porque la fuerza de gravedad es menor en la Luna.*

whole numbers (3) All the numbers in this sequence: 0, 1, 2, 3, 4, 5, 6, 7, 8, 9, ...

*The number 35 is a **whole number,** but 35$\frac{1}{2}$ and 3.2 are not. **Whole numbers** are the counting numbers and zero.*

números enteros Todos los números en esta secuencia: 0, 1, 2, 3, 4, 5, 6, 7, 8, 9 ....

*El número 35 es un **número entero** pero 35$\frac{1}{2}$ y 3.2 no lo son. Los **números enteros** son los números de conteo y el cero.*

width (20) The shorter dimension of a rectangle.

ancho La dimensión más corta de un rectángulo.

GLOSSARY

Glossary R45

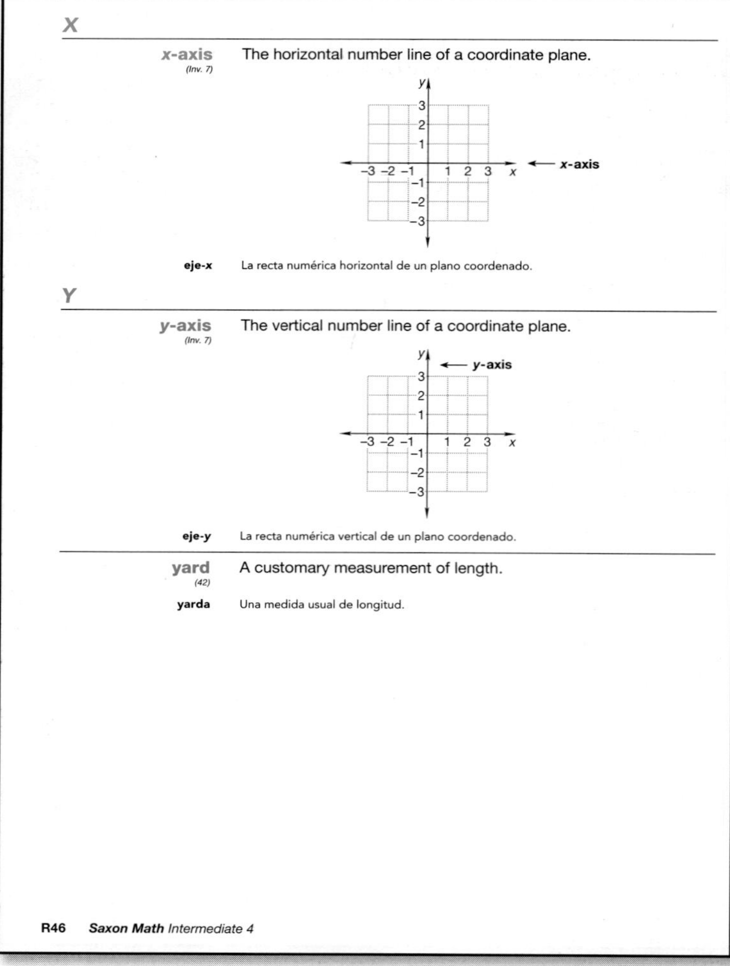

X

x-axis (Inv. 7) The horizontal number line of a coordinate plane.

eje-x La recta numérica horizontal de un plano coordenado.

Y

y-axis (Inv. 7) The vertical number line of a coordinate plane.

eje-y La recta numérica vertical de un plano coordenado.

yard (42) A customary measurement of length.

yarda Una medida usual de longitud.

R46 *Saxon Math* Intermediate 4

Symbols

Symbol	Meaning	Example
△	Triangle	△*ABC*
∠	Angle	∠ABC
→	Ray	$\overrightarrow{AB}$
↔	Line	$\overleftrightarrow{AB}$
—	Line segment	$\overline{AB}$
⊥	Perpendicular to	AB ⊥ BC
||	Parallel to	AB || BC
<	Less than	2 < 3
>	Greater than	3 > 2
=	Equal to	2 = 2
°F	Degrees Fahrenheit	100°F
°C	Degrees Celsius	32°C
∟	Right angle (90° angle)	⊡
...	And so on	1, 2, 3, ...
×	Multiply	9 × 3
·	Multiply	3 · 3 = 9
÷	Divide	9 ÷ 3
+	Add	9 + 3
−	Subtract	9 − 3
⟌	Divided into	3⟌9
R or r	Remainder	3 R 2
x^2	"x" squared (times itself)	$3^2 = 3 \times 3 = 9$
x^3	"x" cubed	$3^3 = 3 \times 3 \times 3 = 27$
√	Square root	$\sqrt{9} = 3$ because $3 \times 3 = 9$.

Abbreviations

Abbreviation	Meaning
ft	Foot
in.	Inch
yd	Yard
mi	Mile
m	Meter
cm	Centimeter
mm	Millimeter
km	Kilometer
L	Liter
ml or mL	Milliliter
lb	Pound
oz	Ounce
kg	Kilogram
g	Gram
mg	Milligram
qt	Quart
pt	Pint
c	Cup
gal	Gallon

Formulas

Purpose	Formula
Perimeter of a rectangle	$P = 2l + 2w$
Perimeter of a square	$P = 4s$
Area of a square	$A = s^2$
Area of a rectangle	$A = l \cdot w$
Volume of a cube	$V = s^3$
Volume of a rectangular prism	$V = l \cdot w \cdot h$

GLOSSARY

Glossary R47

Símbolos/Signos

Símbolo/Signo	Significa	Ejemplo
△	Triángulo	△*ABC*
∠	Ángulo	∠ABC
→	Rayo	$\overrightarrow{AB}$
↔	Recta	$\overleftrightarrow{AB}$
—	Segmento de recta	$\overline{AB}$
⊥	Perpendicular a	AB ⊥ BC
||	Paralelo a	AB || BC
<	Menor que	2 < 3
>	Mayor que	3 > 2
=	Igual a	2 = 2
°F	Grados Fahrenheit	100°F
°C	Grados Celsius	32°C
∟	Ángulo recto (ángulo de 90°)	⊡
...	Y más, etcétera	1, 2, 3, ...
×	Multiplica	9 × 3
·	Multiplica	3 · 3 = 9
÷	Divide	9 ÷ 3
+	Suma	9 + 3
−	Resta	9 − 3
⟌	Dividido entre	3⟌9
R or r	Residuo	3 R 2
x^2	"x" al cuadrado (por sí mismo)	$3^2 = 3 \times 3 = 9$
x^3	"x" al cubo	$3^3 = 3 \times 3 \times 3 = 27$
√	Raíz cuadrada	$\sqrt{9} = 3$ por que $3 \times 3 = 9$.

Abreviaturas

Abreviatura	Significa
pie	pie
pulg	pulgada
yd	yarda
mi	milla
m	metro
cm	centímetro
mm	milímetro
km	kilómetro
L	litro
mL	mililitro
lb	libra
oz	onza
kg	kilogramo
g	gramo
mg	miligramo
ct	cuarto
pt	pinta
tz	taza
gal	galón

Fórmulas

Propósito	Fórmula
Perímetro de un rectángulo	$P = 2L + 2a$
Perímetro de un cuadrado	$P = 4l$
Área de un cuadrado	$A = l^2$
Área de un rectángulo	$A = L \cdot a$
Volumen de un cubo	$V = l^3$
Volumen de un prisma rectangular	$V = L \cdot a \cdot h$

R48 *Saxon Math* Intermediate 4

A

Abbreviations. *See also* **Symbols and signs**
a.m., 74
Celsius (°C), 136
centimeter (cm), 282–283
cup (c), 488
Fahrenheit (°F), 136
fluid ounce (fl oz), 488
foot (ft), 283
gallon (gal), 488
grams (g), 533
inch (in.), 283
kilograms (kg), 533
kilometer (km), 283
liter (L), 489
meter (m), 283
mile (mi), 283
millimeter (mm), 282–283
ounce (oz), 532
pint (pt), 488
p.m., 74
pound (lb), 532
quart (qt), 488
yard (yd), 283

Act it out, 5

Act it out. *See also* **Problem-solving discussion**

Activities
arrays to find factors, 371–372
collecting data, 629
comparing fractions, 382–383
congruence and rotations, 521
constructing prisms, 640–641
degrees and rotations, 518–519
different areas, 206
different perimeters, 124–125
displaying information on graphs, 338–340
drawing a circle, 111
drawing number lines, 130
estimating perimeter and area, 202
finding perimeter and area, 202
finding time, 76
fraction manipulatives, 537–538
geometric solids in the real world, 635–636
graphing pay rates, 666
improper fractions and mixed numbers, 588
measuring temperature, 137
mixed numbers and improper fractions, 588
models of pyramids, 716–717
multiplication table to divide, 227
perimeter and area, 202
probability experiments, 728–730
quadrilaterals and symmetry, 596
quadrilaterals in the classroom, 596
real-world segments and angles, 104
reflections and lines of symmetry, 549–550
relating fractions and decimals, 538–539
rotations and congruence, 521
rotations and degrees, 518–519
similarity and congruence, 464
symmetry and quadrilaterals, 596
writing word problems, 61

Acute angles, 103–105

Acute triangles, 542–543

Addends, missing, 23–24

Addition
algorithm, 36–37
Associative Property of, 36, 168
checking answers by, 84
columns of numbers, 63–64
Commutative Property of, 36
of decimals, 299–301
of fractions, 738
of fractions with common denominators, 660–661
inverse operations, 42–43, 54, 84, 183
of large numbers, 344–345
mixed numbers, 661
of money amounts, 32–33, 344–345
regrouping, 32–33, 63–65
repeated, 258
"some plus some more" formula, 68–70
of three-digit numbers, 31–33
word problems, 69

Advanced Learners. *See* **Enrichment**

Algorithms
addition, 36–37
division, 485–486
multiplication, 150–153
subtraction, 58

a.m., 74

Angles
acute, 103–105
defined, 103
obtuse, 103–105
in parallelograms, 594
in quadrilaterals, 595
right, 103–105

Approximation. *See* **Estimation**

Area
activities, 202
of complex figures, 748–749
models, 198–204, 371–372
and perimeter, 206–208
of rectangles, 442–444, 649

Arithmetic answers, estimation, 410–412

Arithmetic operations. *See* **Addition**; **Division**; **Multiplication**; **Subtraction**

Arrays, 198, 371–372

Assessment. *See* **Benchmark Assessment**; **Cumulative Assessment**; **Power-Up Tests**

Associative Property
of Addition, 168
of Multiplication, 168–169

B

Bar graphs
defined, 335
display data using, 336
making, 339, 507–508

Base, 437. *See also* **Exponents**

Base-ten system, 271

Bases of geometric solids, 710, 712

Benchmark Assessment, 7E, 63E, 135E, 205E, 275E, 343E, 409E, 473E, 541E, 603E, 669E, 732E

C

Calculation (mental math), 233, 239, 247, 253, 259, 265, 275, 281, 287, 293, 299, 305, 311, 318, 323, 329, 343, 349, 355, 361, 369, 376, 381, 387, 393, 399, 409, 417, 423, 431, 436, 441, 447, 451, 457, 463, 473, 479, 487, 493, 499, 505, 513, 517, 525, 531, 541, 547, 555, 561, 567, 572, 577, 581, 586, 593, 603, 609, 615, 622, 627, 633, 639, 646, 653, 659, 669, 674, 681, 689, 695, 700, 705, 710, 715, 721, 732, 737, 742, 747

Calculators, 350, 607

Capacity, 487–489

Celsius (°C), 136

Center, 111

Centimeter (cm), 282

Cents and dollars, 181–184. *See also* **Money**

Chance. *See* **Probability**

Checking answers. *See* **Inverse operations**

Circle graphs
defined, 335
display data using, 338
making, 340

Circles
activity, 111
concepts of, 111
as plane figures, 716

Classification
of geometric solids, 634–636
of polygons, 123
of quadrilaterals, 594–596
of triangles, 542–543

Clockwise, 518–520

Columns of numbers, 63–64

Combining, word problems about, 59, 67–70. *See also* **Addition**

References in color indicate content exclusive to the Teacher's Manual.

Commas, 174, 324
Common denominators. *See also* **Denominators**
addition and subtraction of fractions, 660–661
renaming, 743–744
Common factors. *See* **Factors**
Communication
discuss, 20, 23, 33, 37, 48, 54, 77, 143, 144, 150, 242, 248, 289, 294, 320, 350, 351, 407, 408, 425, 443, 465, 471, 472, 494, 507, 514, 519, 534, 589, 601, 602, 604, 611, 617, 624, 628, 629, 641, 655, 661, 733
explain, 16, 22, 30, 34, 55, 57, 66, 72, 88, 106, 114, 119, 120, 125, 126, 139, 146, 159, 160, 179, 185, 186, 190, 191, 209, 221, 237, 243, 245, 250, 251, 257, 261, 262, 263, 290, 297, 303, 308, 315, 316, 328, 334, 335, 336, 337, 338, 353, 358, 360, 365, 373, 378, 385, 395, 402, 405, 408, 411, 418, 426, 427, 428, 429, 433, 440, 445, 456, 462, 466, 467, 470, 483, 484, 486, 491, 492, 496, 509, 515, 522, 535, 544, 566, 569, 571, 583, 597, 598, 600, 607, 613, 614, 620, 625, 637, 643, 656, 658, 663, 668, 672, 676, 680, 691, 692, 697, 704, 713, 726, 727, 728, 734, 741
formulate, 10, 15, 22, 25, 28, 44, 50, 55, 59, 60, 61, 65, 70, 71, 78, 84, 86, 93, 98, 99, 105, 108, 112, 114, 117, 119, 125, 138, 140, 141, 145, 148, 153, 158, 160, 164, 170, 172, 177, 184, 190, 195, 209, 216, 228, 238, 243, 250, 257, 261, 263, 264, 268, 270, 277, 280, 285, 290, 296, 301, 314, 316, 320, 326, 347, 353, 357, 360, 365, 373, 378, 389, 390, 396, 401, 404, 405, 426, 433, 434, 435, 462, 492, 508, 522, 530, 564, 569, 589, 637, 655, 666, 668, 672, 676, 677, 686, 691
Communication
discuss, 406, 471, 472, 602
explain, 66, 72, 106, 114, 119, 139, 169, 190, 250, 251, 257, 263, 297, 334, 335, 336, 338, 360, 373, 405, 412, 427, 440, 470, 483, 509, 515, 522, 535, 566, 569, 597, 601, 613, 620, 637, 643, 663, 672, 704, 712, 719, 728, 741
formulate, 10, 16, 29, 44, 50, 55, 70, 78, 84, 86, 92, 93, 98, 105, 106, 112, 118, 125, 138, 153, 158, 160, 165, 170, 172, 177, 185, 209, 229, 238, 250, 261, 268, 285, 291, 296, 302, 314, 321, 327, 357, 360, 366, 373, 389, 390, 396, 401, 404, 405, 434, 435, 462, 509, 564, 569, 637, 668, 672
Commutative Property
of Addition, 36
of Multiplication, 152
Comparing
decimals, 276
equivalent decimals, 295
estimates, 410
fractions, 189, 648
hundred thousands, 175
number lines for, 132
numbers in millions, 313, 325
and ordering fractions, 382–384
temperatures, 136–137
by using place value, 20
word problems about, 61, 96–98
words to write comparisons, 133
Compasses, 111
Compatible numbers, 249, 501. *See also* **Estimation**
Complex figures, 748–749
Composite numbers, 377–378
Cones, 716
Congruence
of geometric figures, 383, 463–465
of prisms, 711–712
rotations and, 521
Connections, 27, 28, 90, 124, 136, 157, 162, 168, 193, 214, 226, 248, 266, 306, 324, 338, 350, 369, 394, 411, 432, 458, 463, 474, 594, 601, 611, 617, 647, 666, 682, 716. *See also* **Math and Other Subjects**; **Math-to-Math Connections**; **Real-World Connections**
Content highlights. *See* **Section overviews**
Content trace. *See* **Section overviews**
Coordinates
locating on a graph, 468–472
subtracting, 598–602
Coordinate plane, 468–472
Counterclockwise, 518–520
Counting numbers, 8
Cubed numbers, 437–438
Cubes, 716
Cumulative Assessment, 7D, 57, 63D, 94, 127, 135D, 166, 197, 205D, 238, 270, 275D, 304, 334, 343D, 375, 403, 409D, 440, 467, 473D, 504, 536, 541D, 571, 599, 603D, 632, 664, 669D, 699, 726, 732D, 752
Cup (c), 488
Customized Assessments, 7E, 63E, 135E, 205E, 275E, 343E, 409E, 473E, 541E, 603E, 669E, 732E

D

Data. *See also* **Graphs**
collecting with surveys, 404–408
displaying using graphs, 335–342
line plots and, 407
median, 407, 627–628
mode, 406, 628–629
range, 628
Decagons, 331
Decimal numbers. *See* **Decimals**
Decimal points
aligning, 299–301
"and" in reading or writing, 273–274
and cent signs, 181–184
in decimal division, 527
money and, 183
place values, 276–277
Decimals
comparing and ordering, 611–612
equivalent, 294–295, 418
place value, 276–277
relating to fractions, 271–274
Degrees, 518–520
Denominators. *See also* **Common denominators**
defined, 115
reducing fractions, 700–702
Developing Academic Language, 7G, 13A, 17A, 23A, 27A, 31A, 37A, 41A, 46A, 53A, 59B, 63G, 67A, 73A, 81A, 89A, 95A, 101A, 109A, 115A, 121A, 128B, 135G, 141A, 149A, 156A, 161A, 167A, 173A, 180A, 187A, 193A, 198B, 205G, 213A, 219A, 225A, 233A, 239A, 247A, 253A, 259A, 265A, 271B, 275G, 281A, 287A, 293A, 299A, 305A, 311A, 318A, 323A, 329A, 335B, 343G, 349A, 355A, 361A, 369A, 376A, 381A, 387A, 393A, 399A, 404B, 409G, 417A, 423A, 431A, 436A, 441A, 447A, 451A, 457A, 463A, 468B, 473G, 479A, 487A, 493A, 499A, 505A, 513A, 517A, 525A, 531A, 537B, 541G, 547A, 555A, 561A, 567A, 572A, 577A, 581A, 586A, 593A, 600B, 603G, 609A, 615A, 622A, 627A, 633A, 639A, 646A, 653A, 659A, 665B, 669G, 674A, 681A, 689A, 695A, 700A, 705A, 710A, 715A, 721A, 727B, 732G, 737A, 742A, 747A. *See also* **Math Language**
Diagrams. *See* **Draw a Picture or Diagram; Graphs**
Diameter, 111
Difference. *See also* **Subtraction**
finding for three-digit numbers, 54–55
larger-smaller, 83, 96–98
Digits
defined, 9
writing whole numbers, 18–19
Discuss. *See* **Communication**
Distance. *See* **Length**
Distributive Property, 674–675
Division
algorithm, 483–484
and multiplication answers, estimating, 604–605
answers ending with zeros, 500–501
fraction representation of, 120
multiplication as inverse of, 226, 234–235
with three-digit answers, 526–527, 556–557
with two-digit answers, 452–454, 457–460, 481

word problems, 356–357, 452–454, 457–459, 481–482, 501, 527
by zero, 232

Dollars. *See also* **Money**
and cents, 181–184
fractions of, 188–190
rounding to nearest, 306–307

Double bar graphs, 507–508

Draw a picture or diagram, 5

Draw a Picture or Diagram. *See also* **Problem-solving discussion**

Drawing, to compare fractions, 383. *See also* **Graphs**

E

Early Finishers. *See* **Enrichment**

Edges, 635

Elapsed-time, 74–77

Elevens, facts, 194

Endpoints
as coordinates on a graph, 600
of segments, 102

English learners, 10, 14, 20, 24, 27, 33, 40, 43, 48, 54, 62, 65, 68, 75, 84, 93, 97, 104, 122, 118, 112, 131, 136, 143, 150, 159, 163, 170, 174, 182, 188, 194, 200, 206, 214, 221, 226, 234, 242, 249, 254, 261, 267, 271, 276, 282, 288, 294, 301, 307, 312, 320, 325, 331, 337, 344, 350, 357, 363, 374, 377, 384, 389, 395, 401, 405, 410, 419, 425, 434, 439, 448, 453, 458, 464, 468, 475, 480, 488, 494, 501, 506, 514, 518, 528, 532, 538, 542, 548, 557, 563, 570, 573, 578, 583, 588, 597, 601, 605, 614, 619, 624, 628, 636, 640, 647, 654, 662, 665, 670, 675, 682, 691, 696, 702, 706, 713, 716, 722, 728, 735, 739, 746, 748

Enrichment
Early Finishers, 52, 80, 108, 148, 212, 231, 246, 264, 270, 280, 304, 348, 386, 392, 416, 467, 478, 498, 512, 554, 608, 673, 679, 720, 746
Investigations, 59–62, 128–134, 198–204, 271–274, 335–342, 404–408, 468–472, 537–540, 600–602, 665–668, 727–731

Enrichment
Connections, 27, 28, 338, 601, 666
Extend the Problem, 11, 16, 20, 21, 22, 24, 25, 28, 34, 39, 40, 44, 45, 50, 51, 56, 66, 71, 78, 79, 85, 94, 99, 100, 106, 107, 113,118, 126, 127, 132, 139, 140, 146, 154, 158, 159, 160, 165, 166, 171, 172, 177, 178, 185, 191, 192, 195, 196, 198, 199, 209, 210, 211, 216, 217, 218, 222, 223, 224, 229, 237, 238, 244, 246, 250, 257, 262, 263, 268, 270, 272, 273, 274, 278, 279, 285, 291, 302, 303, 309, 310, 314, 315, 316, 321, 322, 327, 333, 335, 336, 337, 338, 346, 347, 352, 353, 358, 359, 360, 366, 367, 373, 374, 380, 384, 386, 390, 397, 398, 402, 405, 406, 407, 413, 415, 422, 423, 427, 428, 433, 434, 435, 439, 440, 444, 446, 450, 455, 456, 460, 461, 465, 466, 472, 477, 481, 483, 484, 490, 496, 497, 499, 502, 509, 510, 516, 522, 524, 528, 535, 543, 544, 546, 551, 558, 559, 560, 563, 564, 566, 571, 575, 576, 578, 579, 580, 584, 590, 596, 597, 599, 601, 602, 606, 607, 612, 614, 619, 625, 637, 643, 644, 649, 651, 658, 662, 668, 686, 692, 693, 698, 702, 708, 709, 714, 719, 724, 726, 728, 731, 734, 739, 744, 745, 749, 750

Equal groups
division, 452
rate word problems formula, 388–389
word problems about, 60–61

Equations. *See also* **Representation**
graphing, 470–472
solving graphing relationships of, 665–668
two-step, 432–433, 616–618

Equations. *See also* **Focus strategies**

Equilateral triangles, 110, 542–543

Equivalent decimals
concepts of, 294–295
rounding to nearest tenth, 418

Equivalent fractions
concepts of, 682–684
finding common denominators, 688
fraction manipulatives, 537–539

Errors and misconceptions, 12, 16, 22, 26, 28, 35, 40, 45, 52, 57, 66, 72, 80, 86, 94, 107, 114, 119, 127, 140, 148, 155, 160, 166, 172, 179, 186, 192, 197, 212, 218, 224, 230, 238, 246, 252, 257, 264, 270, 280, 286, 292, 299, 304, 310, 316, 322, 328, 334, 348, 354, 360, 368, 375, 380, 386, 392, 398, 403, 416, 422, 428, 435, 440, 446, 450, 456, 462, 467, 478, 484, 498, 504, 512, 516, 524, 530, 536, 546, 554, 560, 566, 571, 576, 580, 585, 592, 599, 608, 614, 621, 626, 632, 638, 645, 652, 658, 664, 673, 679, 687, 694, 699, 704, 709, 714, 720, 726, 736, 741, 746, 752

Estimation
area and perimeter, 202, 649
arithmetic answers, 410–412
mental math, 135, 141, 149, 156, 161, 167, 173, 180, 193, 205, 213, 219, 225, 233, 239, 247, 253, 259, 265, 275, 281, 287, 293, 299, 305, 311, 318, 323, 329, 349, 355, 361, 369, 376, 381, 387, 393, 399, 409, 417, 423, 431, 436, 441, 447, 451, 457, 463, 473, 479, 487, 493, 499, 505, 513, 517, 525, 531, 541, 547, 555, 561, 567, 572, 577, 581, 586, 593, 603, 609, 615, 622, 627, 633, 639, 646, 653, 659, 669, 674, 681, 689, 695, 700, 705, 710, 715, 721, 732, 737, 742, 747
multiplication and division answers, 604–605

Even number sequences, 9

Expanded form
multiplication method, 258
numbers through ten-thousands, 175
two-digit numbers, 680
of whole numbers, 27–28

Experimental probability, 727–731

Explain. *See* **Writing about mathematics**

Exponents, 437–438

Expressions
defined, 47
evaluating, 48–49
writing, 427–428

Extend the Example, 8, 9, 14, 20, 24, 27, 32, 38, 42, 48, 54, 61, 64, 75, 83, 92, 98, 104, 111, 117, 123, 131, 133, 137, 144, 150, 157, 163, 168, 175, 183, 188, 194, 207, 215, 221, 227, 228, 235, 241, 249, 255, 261, 267, 276, 277, 283, 289, 294, 301, 306, 313, 320, 325, 331, 345, 351, 357, 363, 370, 377, 382, 383, 388, 389, 394, 400, 405, 411, 418, 424–425, 432, 437–438, 442, 448, 454, 459, 464, 474, 481, 489, 495, 501, 507, 514, 519, 521, 526, 532, 542, 549, 557, 562, 568, 573, 578, 582, 587-588, 594–595, 604, 611, 617, 623, 628, 634, 648, 661, 671, 675, 683, 690, 696, 701, 706, 712, 722, 733, 738, 743, 748

Extend the problem. *See* **Enrichment**

F

Faces, 633–634, 711

Fact families, 232

Factoring whole numbers, 371–373, 695–696

Factors. *See also* **Prime factorization**
defined, 152
and multiples, 369–373
missing, 220
of prime numbers, 377
writing, 157

Fahrenheit (°F), 136

Figures. *See* **Geometric figures**

Find/Extend a pattern, 5

Find/Extend a pattern. *See also* **Problem-solving discussion**

Fives, facts, 157

Fluid ounces (fl oz), 487–488

Focus skill. *See* **Make Generalizations**

Focus strategies
Act It Out or Make a Model, 7–8
Draw a Picture, 46–48, 239–240
Find/Extend a Pattern, 41–42, 141–142
Guess and Check, 89–90
Make a Diagram, 479–480
Make a Table, 17–18
Make an Organized List, 239–240, 305–306

INDEX

Focus strategies, *continued*
Make it Simpler, 121–122, 659–660
Use a Model, 265–266
Use Logical Reasoning, 73–74
Work Backwards, 381–382
Write a Number Sentence or Equation, 180–181

Focus strategies
Act It Out or Make a Model, 7H, 13B, 31B, 37B, 67B 265B, 499B, 581B, 674B
Draw a Picture or Diagram, 46B, 53B, 135H, 161B, 173B, 239B, 247B, 259B, 275H, 281B, 293B, 311B, 387B, 431B, 479B, 505B, 513B, 541H, 547B, 555B, 567B, 572B, 586B, 603H, 633B
Find/Extend a Pattern, 41B, 63H, 67B, 141B, 156B, 161B, 193B, 205H, 219B, 233B, 275H, 293B, 299B, 311B, 323B, 329B, 343H, 369B, 399B, 417B, 609B, 622B, 695B, 710B, 737B, 742B
Guess and Check, 89B, 95B, 115B, 167B 376B, 393B, 531B, 577B, 732H
Make an Organized List, 156B, 239B, 305B, 355B, 409H, 441B, 561B, 572B, 633B, 646B, 715B
Make it Simpler, 121B, 187B, 318B, 431B, 447B, 499B, 581B, 593B, 639B, 653B, 689B, 721B
Make or Use a Table, Chart, or Graph, 17B, 23B, 27B, 213B, 225B, 361B, 393B, 399B, 463B, 487B, 525B
Use Logical Reasoning, 73B, 81B, 101B, 109B, 115B, 149B, 167B, 253B, 281B, 318B, 343H, 369B, 423B, 436B, 451B, 463B, 493B, 517B, 531B, 615B, 639B, 674B, 700B, 705B, 747B
Work Backwards, 381B, 451B, 473H, 493B, 653B, 747B
Write a Number Sentence or Equation, 180B, 187B, 205H, 219B, 253B, 349B, 417B, 457B, 473H, 487B, 513B, 517B, 555B, 577B, 593B, 627B, 669H, 681B, 689B, 700B, 705B, 721B, 732H

Foot (ft), 283

Formulas
for area, 442–444, 670, 748
for complex figures, 748
conversion, units of measure, 670
defined, 68
for perimeter, 443, 670, 748
rates, 400, 670–671

Formulate a problem. *See* **Communication**

Four-digit whole numbers, 174

Four-step problem-solving process, 1–8, 17–18, 41–42, 46–47, 73–74, 89–90, 97, 121–122, 141–142, 180–181, 239–240, 265–266, 305–306, 381–382, 479–480, 659–660

Four-step problem-solving process, 7H, 13B, 17B, 23B, 27B, 31B, 37B, 41B, 46B, 53B, 63H, 67B, 73B, 81B, 89B, 95B, 101B, 109B, 115B, 121B,135H, 141B, 149B, 156B, 161B, 167B, 173B, 180B, 187B, 193B, 205H, 213B, 219B, 225B, 233B, 239B, 245B, 253B, 259B, 265B, 275H, 281B, 287B, 293B, 299B, 305B, 311B, 318B, 323B, 329B, 341H, 349B, 355B, 361B, 369B, 376B, 381B, 387B, 393B, 399B, 409H, 417B, 423B, 431B, 436B, 441B, 447B, 451B, 457B, 463B, 473H, 479B, 487B, 493B, 499B, 505B, 513B, 517B, 525B, 531B, 541H, 547B, 555B, 561B, 567B, 572B, 577B, 581B, 586B, 593B, 603H, 609B, 615B, 622B, 627B, 633B, 639B, 646B, 653B, 659B, 669H, 674B, 681B, 689B, 695B, 700B, 705B, 710B, 715B, 721B, 732H, 737B, 742B, 747B

Fractional Part (mental math), 361, 399, 409, 417, 447, 457, 473, 517, 525, 577, 581, 586, 653, 700, 705, 710, 715, 721, 732, 737, 742, 747

Fractions. *See also* **Denominators**; **Mixed numbers**; **Numerators**
addition of, 538, 660–661, 738
comparing, 536
comparing and ordering, 382–384, 610–612
defined, 115
and dollars, 188–190
equal to one-half and one, 647–648
equivalent, 537–539, 682–683, 688
finding common denominators, 743–744
of a group, 514, 622–624
improper, 587–588
mental math, 409, 447
mixed numbers, 214–216, 738
names, 116
ordering, 537–538
reducing, 538, 700–702
relating to decimals, 271–274
remaining, 448
renaming, 494, 744
representing, 115–117
simplifying, 737–739
subtraction of, 538–539, 660–661, 738
two-step problems with, 622–624

G

Gallon (gal), 488–489

Geometric figures
bases of, 710, 712
circles, 111, 716
congruence in, 383, 463–465
perimeter, 122–125, 202, 206–208, 649, 747–748
plane figures, 716
polygons, 122–123, 330–331, 548
prisms, 639–641, 710–712
pyramids, 716–717
quadrilaterals, 123, 330–331, 593–596
rectangles, 110, 122–123, 207–208, 284, 442–444, 464, 548, 594, 649
similarity in, 463–465
solids, 634–636, 716
squares, 110, 443, 549, 594, 716
triangles, 110, 123–124, 220, 330–331, 465, 542–543, 716

Geometry (mental math), 141, 149, 161, 173, 205, 219, 247, 259, 275, 417, 423, 441, 451, 547, 633, 659, 674, 710

Grams (g), 533

Graphs. *See also* **Number lines**
and analyzing relationships, 665–668
bar, 335–336, 339, 507–508
circle, 335, 338, 340
on the coordinate plane, 468–472
displaying data using, 335–342
of equations, 470–472
line, 335, 337, 339–340, 471
line plots, 407
pictographs, 335–336

Greater than (>)
number lines, 132–133
word problems about comparing, 96–98

Grouping property. *See* **Associative Property**; **Parentheses**

Guess-and-check, 5

Guess and Check. *See also* **Problem-solving discussion**

H

Half, 116

Half-line, 102

Halfway, 267

Hexagonal prisms, 711

Hexagons, 123, 330

Higher order thinking skills. *See* **Thinking skills**

Hundred millions
reading and writing, 324–326
rounding, 689–691

Hundred thousands
rounding, 319, 690
writing numbers through, 174–176

Hundreds
in multiplication, 562–563
or tens, rounding to nearest, 142–145
and tens, multiplying multiples, 248–249
writing numbers, 18–20

Hundredths
place value, 271
and tenths on a number line, 288–290

I

Identity Property of Multiplication, 152

Impossible events, 721

Improper fractions
changing to whole or mixed numbers, 653–656
and mixed numbers, 587–589

Inch (in.), 281–284

Inclusion, 8, 14, 21, 25, 28, 34, 39, 42, 47, 55, 60, 65, 70, 76, 83, 90, 97, 104, 111, 117, 124, 130, 137, 144, 152, 157, 162, 169, 176, 182, 189, 195, 201, 207, 215, 222, 228, 236, 241, 248, 255, 260, 266, 273, 277, 285, 289, 296, 302, 306, 313, 321, 324, 332, 338, 346, 351, 358, 364, 371, 379, 385, 390, 396, 402, 406, 411, 420, 426, 433, 437, 444, 449, 454, 460, 466, 469, 476, 482, 490, 497, 503, 508, 514, 518, 527, 534, 537, 544, 549, 558, 564, 569, 575, 579, 584, 589, 595, 600, 604, 611, 617, 625, 630, 637, 642, 648, 656, 663, 666, 672, 676, 684, 692, 698, 703, 708, 713, 717, 724, 729, 734, 739, 745, 749

Information
- finding to solve problems, 506–508
- removing unnecessary, 506–508

Intersecting lines, 103

Inverse operations
- addition and subtraction, 42–43, 54, 183
- division and multiplication, 226, 234–235

Investigations. *See also* **Enrichment**
- analyzing relationships, 600–602
- area models, 198–204
- collecting data with surveys, 404–408
- coordinate graphing, 466–470
- displaying data using graphs, 335–342
- equivalent fractions with manipulatives, 537–540
- coordinate graphing, 665–668
- numbers lines, 128–134
- probability experiments, 727–731
- relating fractions and decimals, 271–274
- writing word problems, 59–62

Isosceles triangles, 542–543, 548

K

Key, 335

Kilograms (kg), 533

Kilometer (km), 283

L

Language, math. *See* **Developing Academic Language**; **Math Language**; **Reading Math**

Large numbers
- addition of, 344
- multiplication of, 394–395
- reading and writing numbers in millions, 312–314
- rounding, 318–320
- subtraction of, 350–351

Legends, 335

Length. *See also* **Perimeter**
- defined, 122
- measurement, 281–284
- rounding, 308

Less than (<)
- number lines, 132–133
- word problems about comparing, 96

Lesson highlights. *See* **Section overviews**

Lesson planner. *See* **Section overviews**

Likely events, 722

Line graphs
- defined, 335, 471
- display data using, 337
- making, 339–340

Line of symmetry, 548–549

Line plots, 407

Line segments. *See also* **Segments**
- defined, 102
- naming, 220–221

Linear units, 206

Lines, 220. *See also* **Number lines**; **Segments**

Liter (L), 488–489

Logical reasoning. *See* **Use Logical Reasoning**

Looking Forward, 6, 12, 16, 22, 26, 30, 35, 40, 45, 52, 57, 62, 66, 72, 80, 86, 94, 100, 108, 114, 119, 127, 134, 140, 148, 155, 160, 166, 172, 179, 186, 192, 197, 204, 212, 218, 224, 231, 238, 246, 252, 257, 264, 270, 274, 280, 286, 292, 298, 304, 310, 316, 322, 328, 334, 342, 348, 354, 360, 368, 375, 380, 386, 392, 398, 403, 408, 416, 422, 428, 435, 440, 446, 450, 456, 462, 467, 478, 484, 492, 498, 504, 512, 516, 524, 530, 536, 540, 546, 554, 560, 566, 571, 576, 580, 585, 592, 599, 608, 614, 621, 626, 632, 638, 645, 652, 658, 664, 668, 673, 679, 687, 694, 699, 704, 709, 714, 720, 726, 731, 736, 741, 746, 752

M

Make an Organized List, 5

Make an Organized List. *See also* **Problem-solving discussion**

Make Generalizations, 121–122

Make it Simpler, 5

Make it Simpler. *See also* **Problem-solving discussion**

Make or Use a Table, Chart, or Graph, 5

Make or Use a Table, Chart, or Graph. *See also* **Problem-solving discussion**

Manipulative Use. *See also* **Representation**
- Alternative Approach, 9, 15, 29, 33, 43, 48, 61, 69, 82, 91, 123, 142, 153, 175, 194, 235, 283, 295, 307, 312, 320, 326, 331, 336, 345, 389, 412, 418, 427, 445, 455, 461, 465, 477, 491, 496, 500, 507, 515, 538, 545, 550, 556, 562, 570, 576, 578, 585, 594, 606, 610, 623, 629, 634, 642, 647, 661, 677, 693, 697, 702, 711, 725, 750
- Inclusion, 426, 433, 449, 454, 466, 469, 482, 490, 503, 508, 527, 534, 537, 544, 549, 558, 564, 584, 589, 595, 604, 617, 648, 663, 739
- Math Conversations, 172, 216, 434, 539, 545, 559, 570, 606, 621, 626, 631, 638, 644, 645, 657, 662, 672, 677, 687, 692, 707, 745, 746, 750
- New Concepts, 19, 32, 69, 74, 76, 104, 111, 116, 136, 182, 188, 200, 254, 283, 338, 362, 363, 382, 464, 521, 548, 549, 588, 596, 635, 636, 640, 644, 647, 654, 657, 682, 684, 689, 692, 717

Mass vs. weight, 532–534

Math and Other Subjects
- Math and History, 140, 177, 190, 327, 333, 346, 358, 375, 569, 579, 619, 657
- Math and Geography, 30, 56, 72, 86, 99, 100, 112, 119, 166, 172, 175, 197, 209, 211, 212, 224, 238, 250, 257, 264, 268, 298, 303, 312, 346, 348, 353, 366, 554, 563, 589, 624, 630, 658, 678, 707, 735, 740, 751
- Math and Science, 44, 62, 65, 148, 177, 211, 228, 231, 261, 264, 292, 298, 309, 366563, 599, 623, 624, 664, 719
- Math and Sports, 39, 65, 80, 84, 95, 138, 139, 164, 172, 190, 211, 218, 246, 283, 304, 309, 356, 360, 400, 543, 558, 564, 571, 58, 590, 591, 599, 605, 613, 619, 637, 638, 662, 684, 685, 686, 691, 692, 698, 707, 713, 741

Math Background, 1, 9, 24, 32, 38, 49, 56, 59, 64, 74, 92, 96, 102, 112, 116, 128, 136, 142, 151, 158, 168, 176, 190, 195, 198, 206, 216, 227, 234, 242, 250, 254, 262, 272, 278, 284, 288, 294, 314, 319, 325, 330, 337, 352, 356, 362, 378, 383, 394, 400, 407, 411, 418, 425, 432, 438, 442, 452, 459, 464, 474, 481, 489, 495, 515, 518, 526, 533, 539, 543, 559, 563, 568, 574, 582, 587, 605, 618, 623, 628, 635, 641, 649, 655, 660, 667, 670, 675, 683, 690, 697, 701, 707, 712, 716, 723, 728, 738, 744, 749

Math Content Highlights. *See* **Section Overviews**

Math Language, 14, 24, 42, 47, 48, 110, 111, 116, 142, 150, 168, 206, 226, 283, 313, 370, 388, 488, 506, 587, 640, 682, 695, 716, 744

Math Language, 42, 48, 75, 110, 122, 150, 151, 220, 254, 330, 331, 364, 370, 452, 453, 487, 689, 700, 748. *See also* **Developing Academic Language**

Math Process Highlights. *See* **Section Overviews**

Math-to-Math Connections. *See also* **Connections**; **Real-World Connections**
- Fractions and Algebra, 573, 655, 661, 724, 743, 744

INDEX

Math-to-Math Connections, *continued*
Fractions and Measurement, 610, 650, 654, 667
Measurement and Geometry, 122–125, 626, 666

Measurement. *See also* **Units of measure**
of area, 198–204
of length, 281–284
linear, 206
mental math, 141, 149, 156, 161, 173, 180, 187, 193, 205, 213, 219, 225, 233, 239, 247, 259, 265, 275, 281, 287, 293, 299, 305, 323, 329, 343, 349, 369, 381, 387, 393, 417, 431, 457, 463, 493, 499, 505, 513, 517, 531, 541, 577, 581, 586, 615, 622, 627, 695, 747
metric system, 283, 488
perimeter, 122–125, 202, 206–208, 284, 649, 748–749
of temperature, 135–138
of turns, 518–521

Measures of central tendency. *See* **Median**; **Mode**; **Range**

Median, 407, 627–628

Memory group, 193–194

Mental Math. *See* **Calculation**; **Estimation**; **Fractional Part**; **Geometry**; **Measurement; Money**; **Number Sense**; **Percent**; **Powers and roots**; **Probability**; **Review**; **Simplify**; **Time**

Meter (m), 283

Metric system, 283, 488, 533. *See also* **Units of measure**

Mile (mi), 283

Milliliter (mL), 488

Millimeter (mm), 282–283

Millions
reading and writing, 312–313
rounding, 319, 690

Mirror image, 548–549. *See also* **Symmetry**

Missing numbers. *See also* **Unknown numbers**
addends, 42–43
inverse operations, 42
in subtraction, 37–39, 42

Mixed numbers. *See also* **Improper fractions**
addition of, 661, 738
changing improper fractions to, 654
defined, 661
and fractions, 213–214
and improper fractions, 587–589
subtraction of, 661, 738

Mode, 406, 628–629

Models, area, 198–204. *See also* **Representation**

Money
addition of, 32–33, 344–345
in division, 527
estimation of amount, 411–412
finding information to solve problems, 506–507
formulas, 670
mental math, 67, 73, 81, 89, 95, 101, 109, 115, 121, 135, 141, 149, 156, 161, 167, 173, 180, 187, 193, 213, 233, 239, 253, 259, 265, 275, 281, 287, 293, 299, 305, 318, 323, 329, 349, 355, 361, 369, 376, 381, 387, 393, 399, 409, 417, 423, 431, 436, 441, 451, 463, 473, 479, 487, 499, 505, 513, 517, 541, 555, 567, 572, 586, 593, 603, 609, 627, 633, 639, 646, 653, 659, 669, 674, 681, 695, 700, 715, 721, 737
mixed numbers for, 182
multiplication of, 395, 475, 706
place value shown with, 13–14
rounding, 143, 307, 317, 345, 418–419
subtraction of, 83
word problems, 69–70
writing amounts of, 182

Multiples
of 10, 473–475
of 10 and 100, 248–249, 568–569
of 10, 11, and 12, 194
and factors, 369–372

Multiplication. *See also* **Exponents**
by 10, 100, and 1000, 562–563
algorithm, 258
Associative Property of, 168–169
checking answers, 459
Commutative Property of, 152
concept of, 150–152
defined, 150
Distributive Property of, 674–675
and division answers, estimating, 604–605
division as inverse of, 226–228, 234–235
expanded form, 258
facts, 151, 157, 162–164, 193–194
facts for 0's, 1's, 2's, and 5's, 157
facts for 9's and squares, 162–164
Identity Property of, 152
of large numbers, 394–395
memory group, 193
by multiples of ten, 473–475
multiples of 10's, 11's, and 12's, 194
multiples of 10's and 100's, 248–249
multiplication algorithm, 258
relation to division, 225–228
repeated addition, 258
sign, 150
of three-digit numbers, 732–733
of three-digit numbers by two-digit numbers, 705–706
of two-digit numbers, 253–255, 572–573, 680
of two two-digit numbers, 572–574, 581–583
using tens and ones, 258
word problems, 260–261, 475

Multiplication table
concept of, 151
using to divide, 227

N

Naming. *See* **Renaming**; **Classification**

Negative numbers, 130

Nets, 640, 642, 717

Nines, in multiplication, 162

Nonprime numbers. *See* **Composite numbers**

Notation. *See* **Expanded form**

Number lines. *See also* **Graphs**
decimals on, 611
fractions on, 610–611
rounding with, 266, 307
tenths and hundredths, 288–290
tick marks on, 128
two-step word problems, 617
using, 128–133

Number Sense (mental math), 7, 13, 17, 23, 27, 31, 37, 41, 46, 53, 63, 67, 73, 81, 89, 95, 101, 109, 115, 121, 135, 141, 149, 156, 161, 167, 173, 180, 187, 193, 205, 213, 219, 225, 233, 239, 247, 253, 281, 287, 293, 305, 311, 318, 323, 329, 343, 349, 376, 381, 387, 393, 409, 417, 423, 431, 436, 441, 447, 451, 457, 463, 473, 479, 487, 493, 499, 505, 513, 517, 525, 531, 541, 547, 555, 561, 567, 572, 577, 581, 586, 593, 603, 609, 615, 622, 627, 633, 639, 646, 653, 659, 669, 674, 681, 689, 695, 700, 705, 710, 721, 732, 737, 747

Number sentences. *See* **Equations**

Number systems, 174

Numbers. *See also* **Decimals**; **Mixed numbers**; **Whole numbers**
composite, 377
counting, 8
even, 9
large, reading and writing, 312–314
missing, 37–38, 43
negative, 130
odd, 9
positive, 130
prime, 376–377

Numerators. *See also* **Fractions**
defined, 115
reducing fractions, 701–702

O

Obtuse angles, 103–105

Obtuse triangles, 542

Octagonal prisms, 711

Octagons, 123, 331

Odd number sequences, 9

Online resources, Real-world investigations, 302, 408, 549

Online resources. *See also* **Section overviews**
Real-world investigations, 302, 408, 549

One
fractions equal to, 647
in multiplication, 157

Operations. *See* **Inverse operations**; **Order of Operations**

Order of Operations
concept of, 47–49, 241–243, 424–426
parentheses in, 167
writing expressions with, 241–243

Ordered pairs
coordinates of points, 470
defined, 468
graphing, 667

Ordering numbers
and comparing fractions, 382–383
decimal numbers, 277, 611
equivalent decimals, 295
fractions, 610–612
hundred thousands, 175
numbers in millions, 313, 324–326
by using place-value alignment, 20

Origin, 468

Ounce (oz), 532

Outcomes, 721–723

P

Parallel lines, 102

Parallelograms, as quadrilaterals, 594

Parentheses
Associative Property and, 167–170
in coordinates, 468
in order of operations, 47
simplifying with, 424–426

Pentagonal prisms, 711

Pentagons, 123, 330–331

Percent (mental math), 343, 349, 393

Perfect squares, 203

Performance Tasks, 57, 127, 197, 270, 334, 403, 465, 534, 591, 664, 726

Perimeter
activities about, 202, 206
and area, 206–208
of complex figures, 748–749
concepts of, 122–125
of rectangles, 123, 206–208, 284, 649

Perpendicular lines
angles, 103
line segments, 220–221

Pictographs, 335–336, 338–339

Pie charts. *See* **Circle graphs**

Pie graphs. *See* **Circle graphs**

Pint (pt), 488–489

Place value
commas and, 174
decimals, 276–277
demonstrated with money, 13–15
subtracting across zeros, 87–88
in whole numbers, 689–691

Plane figures, 716

p.m., 74

Polygons. *See also* specific polygons by name
classifying, 123
concepts of, 330–332
lines of symmetry, 548
perimeter of, 122

Population, 404

Positive numbers, 130

Pounds (lb), 532–533, 617

Power-Up. *See* **Mental Math** (Power-Up); **Problem-Solving problems** (Power-Up)

Power-Up discussion. *See* **Problem-solving discussion**

Power-Up Tests, 57, 94, 127, 166, 197, 238, 270, 304, 334, 375, 403, 440, 504, 571, 632, 699, 752

Powers and roots (mental math), 281, 287, 293, 305, 343, 399, 436, 441, 473, 493, 531, 581, 681. *See also* **Exponents**

Powers of ten. *See* **Exponents**

Prime factorization, 696. *See also* **Factors**

Prime numbers
concepts, 376–378
defined, 695
factors of, 696

Prisms. *See also* **Rectangular prisms**
bases of, 710–712
concepts of, 710–712
congruence of, 711–712
constructing, 639–641, 640–642
hexagonal, 711
octagonal, 711
pentagonal, 711
rectangular, 641, 711
trapezoidal, 711
triangular, 642, 711

Probability
experiments, 727–731
mental math, 732, 742
simple, 721–723

Problem solving, four-step process
Act It Out or Make a Model, 7–8
defined, 1–6
Draw a Picture, 46–47, 239–240
Find/Extend a Pattern, 41–42, 141–142
Guess and Check, 89–90
Make a Diagram, 479–480
Make a Table, 17–18
Make an Organized List, 239–240, 305–306
Make it Simpler, 121–122, 659–660
Use a Model, 265–266
Use Logical Reasoning, 73–74
Work Backwards, 381–382
Write a Number Sentence or Equation, 180–181

Problem solving, four-step process, 1A

Problem-solving discussion
Act It Out or Make a Model, 7H, 13B, 31B, 37B, 265B, 499B, 581B, 674B
Draw a Picture or Diagram, 46B, 53B, 135H, 161B, 173B, 239B, 247B, 259B, 275H, 281B, 293B, 311B, 387B, 431B, 479B, 505B, 513B, 541H, 547B, 555B, 567B, 572B, 586B, 633B
Find/Extend a Pattern, 41B, 63H, 67B, 141B, 156B, 161B, 193B, 205H, 219B, 233B, 275H, 293B, 299B, 311B, 323B, 329B, 343H, 369B, 399B, 417B, 609B, 622B, 695B, 710B, 737B, 742B
Guess and Check, 89B, 95B, 115B, 376B, 393B, 531B, 577B, 732H
Make an Organized list, 156B, 239B, 305B, 355B, 409H, 441B, 561B, 572B, 633B, 646B, 659B, 715B
Make it Simpler, 121B, 187B, 318B, 431B, 447B, 499B, 581B, 593B, 639B, 653B, 689B, 721B
Make or Use a Table, Chart, or Graph, 17B, 23B, 27B, 213B, 225B, 361B, 393B, 399B, 463B, 487B, 525B
Use Logical Reasoning, 73B, 81B, 101B, 109B, 115B, 149B, 167B, 253B, 281B, 318B, 343H, 369B, 423B, 436B, 451B, 463B, 493B, 517B, 531B, 615B, 639B, 674B, 700B, 705B, 747B
Work Backwards, 381B, 451B, 473H, 493B, 653B, 747B
Write a Number Sentence or Equation, 180B, 187B, 205H, 219B, 253B, 349B, 417B, 457B, 473H, 487B, 513B, 517B, 555B, 577B, 593B, 627B, 669H, 681B, 689B, 700B, 705B, 721B, 732H

Products. *See also* **Multiplication**
defined, 152
estimation of, 410
writing, 157

Properties. *See* specific property by name

Property of Zero for Multiplication, 152

Proportions. *See* **Rates**

Pyramids, 331, 716–717

Q

Quadrilaterals
classifying, 123, 593–596
parallelograms as, 594
as polygons, 330–331
rectangles *See* **Rectangles**
squares *See* **Squares**

Quart (qt), 488–489

Quarter, 116

R

Radius (radii), 111

Range, 628

Rate
with a given total, 400–401
word problems, 388–389, 400–401

Rays, 102–105

Reading
large numbers, commas in, 174
and writing numbers in hundred millions, 324–326
and writing numbers in millions, 312–314

INDEX

Reading Math, 8, 18, 69, 74, 82, 90, 96, 174, 234, 248, 260, 300, 356, 388, 400, 432, 443, 452, 489, 494, 506, 616, 675

Reading math, 103, 142, 174, 437, 443

Real-World Connections, 74, 130, 135, 143, 199, 206, 212, 231, 246, 260, 264, 270, 271, 280, 304, 306, 312, 348, 375, 386, 388, 392, 404, 405, 518, 535, 548, 687, 708, 725, 735. *See also* **Connections**; **Math-to-Math Connections**

Real-world investigations, 302, 408, 549

Rectangles
- area of, 207, 442–444, 649
- concept of, 110
- congruence and similarity, 464
- lines of symmetry, 548
- as parallelograms, 594
- perimeter of, 123, 206–208, 284, 649

Rectangular prisms, 641, 711

Reducing fractions
- concepts, 700–702
- manipulatives for, 538

Regrouping
- adding columns of numbers, 63–64
- adding three-digit numbers, 32–33
- subtracting across zeros, 82–84
- subtracting three-digit numbers, 53–54

Regular polygons, 330–331

Relationships
- analyzing, 600–602
- graphing, 665–668
- inverse operations. *See* **Inverse operations**

Remainders
- concept of, 362–365
- defined, 362
- of fractions, 447–448
- two-digit answers with, 480–482
- in word problems, 577–578

Renaming. *See also* **Naming**
- common denominators, 743–744
- fractions, 494, 743–744

Representation
- model, 124, 125, 127, 158, 159, 172, 206, 216, 254, 263, 269, 286, 315, 341, 371, 380, 382, 389, 420, 421, 440, 464, 469, 471, 472, 516, 518, 521, 530, 537, 545, 585, 595, 601, 643, 647, 648, 654, 668, 672, 677, 717, 718, 730
- represent, 10, 15, 19, 20, 21, 23, 24, 26, 28, 29, 30, 33, 34, 35, 39, 40, 44, 45, 50, 55, 65, 72, 75, 78, 79, 84, 93, 107, 110, 111, 113, 114, 117, 118, 119, 124, 125, 126, 131, 132, 133, 139, 140, 145, 146, 147, 153, 154, 158, 160, 165, 166, 170, 176, 177, 178, 179, 184, 185, 186, 190, 191, 192, 195, 196, 198, 199, 200, 202, 206, 208, 209, 215, 216, 217, 222, 223, 230, 231, 236, 237, 243, 244, 245, 250, 251, 255, 256, 262, 268, 269, 278, 285, 291, 295, 296, 297, 298, 302, 303, 304, 309, 314, 315, 316, 321, 322, 326, 327, 328, 332, 336, 339, 340, 341, 345, 347, 351, 352, 359, 360, 365, 371, 374, 380, 384, 385, 396, 401, 402, 403, 405, 406, 413, 414, 415, 420, 421, 426, 427, 435, 439, 444, 446, 448, 460, 461, 465, 476, 477, 482, 483, 502, 509, 510, 516, 521, 522, 523, 524, 528, 529, 535, 536, 542, 544, 545, 546, 549, 552, 553, 558, 559, 564, 565, 570, 574, 575, 576, 579, 584, 591, 598, 602, 607, 612, 613, 618, 619, 621, 624, 625, 626, 630, 632, 637, 643, 644, 648, 650, 656, 657, 662, 663, 665, 671, 676, 685, 692, 694, 698, 699, 704, 707, 714, 718, 724, 730, 731, 734, 736, 739, 740, 745, 746, 751

Representation. *See also* **Manipulative Use**
- model, 159, 172, 217, 263, 269, 286, 331, 420, 421, 469, 471, 472, 537, 538, 545, 601, 602, 672, 677, 717, 718, 730
- represent, 15, 16, 20, 26, 28, 29, 34, 39, 50, 55, 72, 78, 79, 84, 107, 117, 126, 131, 132, 133, 139, 145, 146, 153, 154, 159, 177, 178, 185, 191, 195, 196, 199, 209, 210, 215, 216, 217, 222, 229, 237, 244, 250, 257, 262, 269, 278, 285, 291, 295, 297, 298, 302, 309, 314, 321, 322, 327, 331, 346, 347, 352, 359, 365, 383, 385, 390, 402, 406, 415, 427, 435, 439, 440, 445, 446, 450, 460, 466, 477, 483, 524, 529, 535, 536, 545, 553, 559, 570, 575, 579, 591, 602, 607, 612, 613, 619, 621, 624, 626, 630, 631, 643, 644, 650, 656, 662, 665, 672, 685, 694, 707, 734, 740, 745, 746

Review (mental math), 37, 41, 95

Rhombus, 594

Right angles, 103–105

Right triangles, 542–543

Roots. *See* **Square roots**

Rotational symmetry, 550

Rounding. *See also* **Estimation**
- large numbers, 319–320
- money, 143, 307, 317
- to nearest ten or hundred, 142–145
- to nearest tenth, 418–419, 534
- to nearest thousand, 266–267
- to nearest whole number, 306–308, 648
- whole numbers through hundred millions, 689–691

Rules. *See* **Order of Operations**

S

Sample, 404

Scale, 135

Scalene triangles, 542

Section overviews
- Content trace, 7F, 63F, 135F, 205F, 275F, 343F, 409F, 473F, 541F, 603F, 669F, 732F
- Math content highlights, 7B, 63B, 135B, 205B, 275B, 343B, 409B, 473B, 541B, 603B, 669B, 732B
- Math process highlights, 7B, 63B, 135B, 205B, 275B, 343B, 409B, 473B, 541B, 603B, 669B, 732B
- Lesson planner, 7A, 63A, 135A, 205A, 275A, 341A, 409A, 473A, 541A, 603A, 669A, 732A
- Technology, 7C, 63C, 135C, 205C, 275C, 343C, 409C, 473C, 541C, 603C, 669C, 732C

Segments, 102–105, 220–221. *See also* **Lines**

Separating, word problems about, 60, 90–93. *See also* **Subtraction**

Sequences, 8–10

Sets, fractions of, 514

Shapes, complex. *See* **Complex figures**

Sides
- geometric solids, 634–636
- polygons, 123
- of quadrilaterals, 595
- triangles, 542–543

Signs. *See* **Symbols and signs**

Similar figures, 463–465

Simplify
- exponents, 437–438
- fractions, 737–739
- mental math, 603, 609, 615, 622, 627, 633, 639, 646, 653, 659, 669, 674, 681, 689, 695, 700, 705, 710, 715, 721, 732, 737, 742, 747
- order of operations for, 47–49, 424–426

Solids, geometric, 633–636, 716

Solving equations. *See* **Equations**

"Some plus some more" formula, 68–70

"Some went away" formula, 90–92

Square centimeters (cm^2), 200

Square corners, 103, 110

Square feet (ft^2), 201

Square inches (in^2), 200

Square roots
- of perfect squares, 203
- and powers (mental math) 281, 287, 293, 305, 343, 399, 436, 441, 473, 493, 531, 581, 681
- symbol for, 203

Square units, 206

Squared numbers
in multiplication, 163
perfect squares, 203, 443

Squares
area of, 443
concept of, 110
lines of symmetry, 549
as parallelograms, 594
as plane figures, 716

Statistical operations. *See also* **Data**
median, 407, 627–628
mode, 406, 628–629
range, 628

Subtraction. *See also* **Difference**
across zeros, 82–84, 87–88
Commutative Property of, 58
of decimals, 299–301
of fractions, 738
of fractions with common denominators, 660–662
inverse operations, 42–43, 54, 84, 183
of large numbers, 350–351
missing numbers in, 37–39
of mixed numbers, 661
of money, 350
"some went away" formula, 90–92
of three-digit numbers, 54–55
word problems, 70

Sums, estimation of, 410. *See also* **Addition**

Surface area. *See* **Area**

Surveys, data collection, 404–408

Symbols and signs. *See also* **Abbreviations**
cent sign (¢), 181
comparison (<, >, =), 132
decimal point (.), 181
degree (°), 136
for division (÷), 234
letters to represent unknowns (*n*), 24
multiplication (×), 150, 235, 432
negative numbers (–), 130
parentheses (), 168
perpendicular to (⊥), 103, 220
square (n^2), 198–202
square root (√), 203

Symmetry, 548–551

T

Teacher Tip, 10, 18, 34, 38, 44, 54, 75, 96, 110, 118, 137, 146, 153, 164, 174, 198, 208, 214, 229, 235, 250, 267, 276, 300, 308, 314, 319, 330, 372, 377, 422, 427, 478, 484, 496, 502, 509, 521, 529, 535, 539, 546, 551, 606, 616, 655, 665, 671, 693, 696, 706

Technology. *See also* **Section overviews**
331, 375, 465, 532, 542, 600, 642, 690, 716, 748

Temperature, 135–138

Ten thousands, rounding, 320

Tens
facts, 194
in multiplication, 562–563
multiplying multiples of, 248–249
multiplying by multiples of, 473–475
rounding to nearest, 142–145

Tenths
and hundredths on a number line, 288–290
place value, 271
rounding to nearest, 418, 534

Test-Day Activity, 94, 166, 238, 304, 375, 440, 504, 571, 632, 699, 752

Test-Taking Strategy, 11, 16, 22, 26, 30, 34, 40, 45, 51, 56, 66, 72, 79, 85, 100, 106, 107, 113, 127, 140, 147, 155, 158, 160, 165, 172, 186, 196, 211, 223, 230, 252, 257, 263, 269, 272, 279, 286, 292, 298, 304, 310, 316, 321, 328, 334, 354, 360, 373, 379, 385, 392, 402, 403, 413, 421, 446, 450, 466, 483, 490, 496, 511, 515, 529, 530, 559, 565, 571, 585, 625, 664, 672, 679, 686, 709, 714, 718, 724, 728, 736, 745

Thermometers. *See* **Temperature**

Thinking skills
analyze, 28, 110, 151, 214, 350, 568, 723
conclude, 64, 152, 542
connect, 14, 82, 102, 128, 234, 301, 356, 364, 410
discuss, 23, 33, 37, 54, 144, 150, 242, 248, 289, 294, 320, 350, 351, 407, 408, 410, 452, 458, 514, 526, 548, 556, 562, 701, 743
estimate, 605
evaluate, 573
generalize, 157, 162, 276, 288, 394, 395, 562, 706
justify, 32, 527, 582, 706, 738, 748
model, 206, 216, 254, 263, 269, 286, 315, 341, 371, 380, 382, 389, 595
represent, 738 *See also* **Representation**; **Represent**
summarize, 143
verify, 32, 116, 188, 215, 226, 254, 330, 389, 411, 452, 458, 481, 500, 514, 556, 568, 594, 616, 623, 683, 743, 749

Thousands
in multiplication, 562–563
rounding to nearest, 266–267

Three-digit numbers
adding, 31–33
division answers as, 526–527, 556–558
multiplication, 732–734
multiplied by two-digit numbers, 705–706
subtracting, 53–55

Tick marks on number lines, 128

Time (mental math), 141, 149, 156, 161, 180, 187, 193, 205, 213, 219, 225, 239, 259, 265, 275, 299, 311, 329, 349, 361, 369, 376, 381, 387, 399, 417, 431, 451, 479, 487, 517, 555, 567, 572, 577, 581, 586, 615, 669, 674, 681, 689, 705, 715. *See also* **Elapsed-time**

Tons, 532–534

Trapezoidal prisms, 711

Trapezoids, 594

Triangles
classifying, 542–543
concept of, 110
congruence and similarity, 463–465
equilateral, 110
obtuse, 542
perimeter of, 123–124
perpendicular segments, 220
as plane figures, 716
as polygons, 330–331
similarity and congruence of, 465

Triangular prisms, 642, 711

Turns, measuring, 518–521

Twelves, facts, 194

Two-digit numbers
division of, 451–454, 457–460, 480–482
multiplied by three-digit numbers, 705–706
multiplying, 572–574, 680
multiplying two, 581–583
with remainder, 481–482

Two-step equations, 432

Two-step problems
fraction of a group, 622–624
word problems, 616–618

Twos, facts, 157

U

Unit multipliers. *See* **Conversion**

Units of measure. *See also* **Measurement**
capacity, 487–489
metric system, 283, 488, 533
U.S. Customary System, 283, 487, 532

Unknown numbers, 48–49. *See also* **Missing numbers**

Unlikely events, 721–723

U.S. Customary System, 283, 487–488, 532. *See also* **Units of measure**

Use Logical Reasoning, 5

Use Logical Reasoning. *See also* **Problem-solving discussion**

V

Vertex (vertices)
of angles, 103
of solids, 635

Vocabulary. *See* **Developing Academic Language; Math language**

INDEX

W

Weight *vs.* mass, 532–534

Whole numbers
- changing improper fractions to, 653–656
- factoring, 695–697
- fractions to nearest, 648
- names of, 18
- rounding, 306–308, 317, 648, 689–691
- through hundred millions, 689–691
- through hundred thousands, 174–176
- writing, 18–20, 174–176

Width, 122

Word problems
- about combining, 68–70
- about comparing, 96–98
- about division, 356–357, 452–454, 457–459, 481–482, 501, 527
- about fractions of a group, 494–495
- about multiplication, 260–261, 475
- about rates, 388–389, 400–401
- about separating, 90–93
- involving decimals, 307–308
- with remainders, 577–578
- two-step, 616–618
- writing, 59–62

Work Backwards, 5

Work Backwards. *See also* **Problem-solving discussion**

Write a Number Sentence or Equation, 5

Write a number sentence or equation. *See also* **Problem-solving discussion**

Writing about mathematics
- explain, 16, 22, 30, 34, 55, 57, 66, 72, 88, 106, 114, 119, 120, 125, 126, 139, 146, 159, 160, 179, 185, 186, 190, 191, 209, 221, 237, 243, 245, 250, 251, 257, 261, 262, 263, 290, 297, 303, 308, 315, 316, 328, 334, 335, 336, 337, 338, 353, 358, 360, 365, 373, 378, 385, 395, 402, 405, 407, 412, 418, 426, 427, 428, 429, 433, 440, 445, 456, 462, 466, 467, 470, 483, 484, 486, 492, 496, 509, 515, 522, 535, 544, 566, 569, 571, 583, 597, 598, 600, 607, 613, 614, 620, 625, 637, 643, 656, 658, 663, 668, 672, 676, 680, 691, 692, 697, 704, 713, 726, 727, 728, 734, 741
- exponents, 438
- expressions, 429–430
- large numbers, 312–313
- numbers through 999, 18–20
- numbers through hundred thousands, 174–176
- and problem-solving, 6
- and reading numbers in millions, 312–314
- word problems, 59–61

X

***x*-axis**
- coordinate on, 600
- defined, 468

×-symbol for multiplication. *See* **Symbols and signs**

Y

***y*-axis**
- coordinate on, 600
- defined, 468

Yard (yd), 283

Z

Zero
- dividing by, 232
- division answers, 500–501, 556–557
- in multiplication, 157, 248–249, 473–475, 568–569
- as placeholder, 573
- subtracting across, 82–84, 87–88